World Dictionary

of Foreign Expressions

Expressions

A Resource for Readers and Writers

World Dictionary
of **Foreign**
Expressions

A Resource for Readers and Writers

by **Gabriel G. Adeleye**
with **Kofi Acquah-Dadzie**
edited by **Thomas J. Sienkewicz**
with **James T. McDonough, Jr.**

Bolchazy-Carducci Publishers, Inc. ✦ Wauconda, Illinois, USA

General Editor
Laurie Haight

Contributing Editors
Aaron E. Baker
Georgia Irby-Massie
Allan Kershaw

Typesetting and Cover Design
Charlene Hernandez

Bolchazy-Carducci Publishers, Inc.

1000 Brown Street, Unit 101
Wauconda, Illinois 60084 USA

http://www.bolchazy.com

Printed in the United States of America
by Maple-Vail Book Manufacturing Group
1999

Hardbound, ISBN 0-86516-422-3
Paperback, ISBN 0-86516-423-1

Library of Congress Cataloging-in-Publication Data

Adeleye, Gabriel, 1940-
    World dictionary of foreign expressions : a resource for readers and writers / by
Gabriel G. Adeleye with Kofi Acquah-Dadzie ; edited by Thomas J. Sienkewicz and
James T. McDonough
        p.   cm.
    Includes bibliographical references.
    ISBN 0-86516-422-3 (alk. paper)
    ISBN 0-86516-423-1 (pbk. : alk. paper)
    1. English language--Foreign words and phrases--Dictionaries. I. Acquah-Dadzie,
Kofi, 1939- II. Sienkewicz, Thomas J. III. McDonough, James T. IV. Title.
    PE1582.A3 A34 1999
    422'.4'03--dc21
                                            98-40788
                                           CIP

Acknowledgments

From Aihe, D. O., and P. A. Oluyede. *Cases and Materials on Constitutional Law in Nigeria*. Ibadan, Nigeria: University Press Limited and Oxford: Oxford University Press, 1979. Reprinted by permission of Oxford University Press.

From Asante, S. K. B. *Property Law and Social Goals in Ghana, 1844–1966*. Accra: Ghana Universities Press, 1975. Reprinted by permission of Ghana Universities Press.

From *Greek Religion* by Walter Burkert. Copyright © 1985 by Basil Blackwell and the President and Fellows of Harvard College. Reprinted by permission of Harvard University Press.

From Eysenck, H. J. *Psychology Is About People*. (Allen Lane, The Penguin Press, 1972) copyright (c) H. J. Eysenck, 1972 (pp. 10, 26, 63, 67, 69, 69–70). Reproduced by Penguin Books Ltd. Reprinted by permission of Penguin Books Ltd.

From *The Economist*. The Economist Newspaper Group, Inc. (c) 1987. Reprinted with permission.

From the Catholic News Service. August 18, 1997. Reprinted with permission.

From Freedland, M. R. *The Contract of Employment*. Oxford: Oxford University Press, 1976. Reprinted by permission of Oxford University Press.

From Grant, Michael. *Nero*. New York: Dorset Press, 1970. Reprinted by permission of Weidenfeld & Nicolson, Orion Publishing Group.

From *The Guardian*. Reprinted by permission of Guardian Newspapers Limited.

From Hart, H. L. A. *Punishment and Responsibility*. Oxford: Oxford University Press, 1978. Reprinted by permission of Oxford University Press.

Jaeger, Werner. *Paideia: The Ideals of Greek Culture*. Translated by Gilbert Highet. Oxford: Oxford University Press, 1970. Reprinted by permission of Blackwell Publishers Ltd.

From Laistner, M. L. W. *Greater Roman Historians*. Copyright (c) 1947 Regents of the University of California, (c) renewed 1975 Harry Caplan.

To our parents

David and *Victoria Adeleye*

and

Kwesi Acquah and *Mary Adwubi Twumasi*

Contents

Acknowledgments v

Dedication vii

Table of Contents ix

Authors' Acknowledgments xi

Foreword xiii

Author's Preface xv

Editor's Preface xvii

Guide to the Entries xxi

Table of Abbreviations xxiii

Bibliography xxv

Words and Expressions 1

Authors' Acknowledgments

The completion of work brings a peculiar, almost inexplicable, feeling. It is a mélange of several elements which include pleasure, self-satisfaction, excitement, and exhilaration, even if the achievement should be barely minimal. We would like to share this inexplicable feeling with a number of personae who in one way or the other, consciously or unconsciously, contributed to the completion of the work.

First, we need to express our profound gratitude to our immediate families—Ruth, Vicky, Bisi, Dupe, and Alex (in the case of G. A.) and Ama and Kwesi (in the case of K. A.) for their confidence in us and cooperation. Secondly, we must express our gratitude to two colleagues, Dr. K. Opoku Agyeman and Dr. Tijjani El-Miskin, the former for vetting some materials in French, the latter for going through some materials in Italian, Spanish, and Arabic. We need also to thank Mr. Boateng, former Acting Head of the Department of Business Studies, University of Maiduguri, for placing at our disposal his excellent library of magazines and newspapers. We are also immensely grateful to the entire staff of the faculty of the Law Library at the University of Maiduguri for placing at our disposal all the law books from which we extracted the Latin expressions. We must also thank a number of publishers for generously permitting us to use extracts from their publications.

Moreover, we must express our profound gratitude to the United States Information Agency, The Center for International Exchange of Scholars (Washington), Monmouth College (Ill.), and the University of Arkansas (Fayetteville) for G. A.'s opportunity to work in the United States for eighteen months, which contributed immensely to the completion of the work. Furthermore, G. A. is very grateful to the Computer Center of Monmouth College for scanning the two manuscripts and to the Department of Education Technology (University of Arkansas, Fayetteville) especially Mr. Bart Cohen, for his exceptional altruism, generosity, and patience in typesetting, combining, and preparing the manuscripts. Finally, G. A. needs to say a big thank you to his good friend, Mr. Alfred Kojo Anderson, for coming in at the right time to bring the typesetting and the printing to a successful end.

Foreword

This is a very useful book. The English of lawyers, physicians, academics, journalists, and others is replete with foreign phrases, many of them traps for the unwary. For example, how many intelligent people (for that matter, how many intelligent lawyers?) think *bona fides* is plural? Or that there is such a thing as a *causus belli*? Even if one has studied Latin and smiles at errors like these, no one can possibly master every language from which English draws proverbial wisdom and *bons mots*; therefore, even the multilingual can profit from *World Dictionary of Foreign Expressions: A Resource for Readers and Writers*.

When confronted with a puzzling piece of Latin or of Law French, a lawyer usually turns to *Black's Law Dictionary*. But the *World Dictionary of Foreign Expressions* contains many legal phrases not found in Black's, in addition to a wealth of nonlegal material. In fact, this book is more comprehensive than any other dictionary of foreign phrases with which I am acquainted: the compilations of Carroll, Guinagh, Jones, Mawson, Phythian, and Tuleja are skimpy by comparison.

World Dictionary of Foreign Expressions offers more, however, than just abundant material. The authors not only identify the language from which the phrase is drawn and give a polished translation. They also provide a literal, word-for-word explication of each phrase, which lets the reader know as exactly as possible what the phrase means and facilitates memorization. Moreover, many entries provide quotations from recent scholarship or journalism to give the reader an idea of how the phrases are and should be used. The format is uncomplicated and easy on the eyes.

Busy professionals who need accurate information quickly will get exactly what they require from *World Dictionary of Foreign Expressions*. Leisurely word-lovers will be instructed and entertained. In short: this is a marvelous reference tool.

Aaron E. Baker, Ph.D., J.D.

Author's Preface

The idea of writing this book was conceived by my co-author, Mr. Kofi Acquah-Dadzie. In his long career in the legal profession—as student, legal officer of a bank, attorney, magistrate, and teacher of law—he has been observing the difficulties encountered by many students, teachers, and practitioners of law who have little or no knowledge of Latin. Latin is so inextricably intertwined with the legal profession that there is hardly a textbook of law which is not generously flavored with Latin expressions. To help alleviate the problems of lawyers who have negligible knowledge of Latin, my co-author conceived the idea of writing a dictionary of Latin legal expressions and enlisted my assistance.

The work began with a collection of both Latin maxims and expressions—individual words, phrases, and clauses—which have been incorporated into the English language and have become, so to speak, a distinguishing feature of the diction of educated people. These expressions include *de jure, de facto, ex cathedra, ad infinitum, ab initio, ante quem,* and *sine qua non.* We also included abbreviations and popular quotations.

We then considered how to present the translations in such a way that readers might derive maximum benefit from the work. It seemed to us that mere translations of expressions would only scratch the surface of the problem. We deemed it necessary, therefore, to help readers to understand how the translations or meanings are obtained. Accordingly, we decided to present both literal and polished or conventional translations. To facilitate the process of understanding the literal translations, we put down the meanings of individual words of an expression and indicated with numbers the sequence of their appearance in each translation. In this way the reader becomes an active participant in the process, is not reduced to the status of a mere receptor of our translations or views, and can even construct alternative versions. In short, the translations are presented in such a way that a reader may either read all sections of an entry or, if making a quick reference, read only the polished translation. Moreover, to enhance the usefulness of the work, we deemed it necessary to give examples of usage of many expressions by either constructing sentences ourselves or quoting from authorities. Furthermore, in many cases we show the parts of speech of expressions as well as the plural and singular forms of nouns.

We completed the work, to which we gave the title, *A Dictionary of Latin Expressions for Lawyers and Men of Letters,* in 1986. As we awaited acceptance of the work for publication, I became more and more convinced of the need for another work covering not only expressions from other foreign languages which have been incorporated into the English language but also Latin expressions which had escaped our attention. Other foreign languages which attracted my attention include French, German, Classical Greek, as well as neologisms derived therefrom, Italian, Spanish, Portuguese, Russian, Arabic, Hebrew, Japanese, Chinese, Persian, Turkish, and Hindi. The work, to which I gave the title *An English Dictionary of Foreign Expressions for Lawyers, Scholars, Journalists, Etc.,* follows the same format as the previous work and each entry shows, in addition, the language of provenance or derivation. The work was completed in 1989.

Our efforts to get the two manuscripts published suffered various setbacks. Eventually we accepted the suggestion of a publisher to merge the two works. Hence the birth of this book.

It goes without saying that foreign expressions which have been incorporated into the English language serve a useful purpose in enhancing the profundity, richness, and quality of scripts. Such expressions are used for various reasons. First, there may not be suitable equivalent expressions in English. Second, a writer may wish to avoid the use of an English expression which seems obscene or indecent. Third, there may be the need to portray and capture the true local associations and color of foreign institutions. Besides, some expressions are used in certain contexts and their replacement with English translations would detract from their charm, forcefulness, or succinctness. Furthermore, some are technical terms used in certain professions. Finally, such expressions are the hallmark of scholars of diverse and solid educational background.

Though foreign expressions serve a useful purpose, they can be not only a nuisance but also a cause of considerable embarrassment. For a reader who does not know their meanings, such words and phrases can interrupt the continuity of comprehension, undermine the reader's self-confidence, and, as it were, embarrassingly expose some lacunae in his/her educational background. Nor are scholars who presume to be au fait with the use of such expressions spared embarrassment. Thus it is not unusual to find in respectable books, newspapers, and magazines foreign expressions used incorrectly. The following is a random selection of such errors:

1. "this **criteria**" instead of "these **criteria**"
2. "It is for . . . his lawyer to do **allocutor**" instead of "It is for . . . his lawyer to do **allocutus**"
3. " . . . drawn from all the **stratas** of our society" instead of " . . . drawn from all the **strata** of our society"
4. " . . . a writ of **habeus corpus**" instead of " . . . a writ of **habeas corpus**"
5. " . . . are professors **emeritus**" instead of " . . . are professors **emeriti**"
6. "**autrevois** convict" instead of "**autrefois** convict"
7. "**fieri faci**" instead of "**fieri facias**" or "**fieri feci**"
8. "**per res judicata**" instead of "**per res judicatas**"
9. "**ad nuseum**" instead of "**ad nauseam**"
10. "**suo moto**" instead of "**suo motu**"
11. "**in pari delectio**" instead of "**in pari delicto**"
12. "**inter vives**" instead of "**inter vivos**"
13. "**nonemo dat quod non habet**" instead of "**nemo dat quod non habet**"
14. "**abinitio**" instead of "**ab initio**"
15. "**ex faciae curiae**" instead of "**ex facie curiae**"
16. "**Res ipsa locutur**" instead of "**Res ipsa loquitur**"
17. "**in durante ville**" instead of "**in durante vita**"

This work cuts across the boundaries of disciplines. The legal practitioner, to be sure, is generously provided for, but there is hardly a practitioner of any discipline—historian, journalist, theologian, linguist, medical practitioner, natural scientist, psychologist, political scientist, sociologist, archaeologist, anthropologist, etc.—who will not find something of interest in the work. Above all, the book is written for those who have little or no knowledge of Latin and other foreign languages and want to get reasonably good comprehension of what they read in newspapers, magazines, journals, and books. If such readers should find the book useful, we shall be immensely gratified.

Fayetteville, Arkansas, 1993

G. A.

Editor's Preface

I first met Gabriel Adeleye in 1980 while he was a Fulbright-Hays Visiting Lecturer at Howard University in Washington, D.C. We maintained a trans-atlantic correspondence for many years until I was privileged to have Gabriel as a colleague for a second time in 1992 when he came to Monmouth College in Monmouth, Illinois, again as a Fulbright scholar. Over the years I have come to know other members of his family, especially his wife Ruth, and his daughters Victoria and Eugenia, both of whom are alumnae of Monmouth College. It was a great loss when Gabriel died suddenly in 1994, shortly after his return to Nigeria following his second Fulbright sojourn in the United States.

Gabriel spoke often of this dictionary and worked studiously on it in his final years. I was honored that his widow entrusted the unfinished manuscript to my care after his death and I am very pleased that others will now be able to benefit from the meticulous scholarship that this book represents.

Most of my editorial efforts have centered on standardizing the format of entries and on preparing the manuscript for American users. For this reason, I have taken the liberty of replacing British spellings with American ones ("honor" for "honour," for example). I have also attempted to neutralize gender wherever possible, by replacing "he" with "one," "man" with "person," etc. Most of the content of the entries remains as Gabriel wrote it, although I have added a considerable number of new entries and explanations. While Gabriel collected or wrote most of the usage citations which appear in individual entries, a few of these are mine. The strong African focus of this material represents the particular charm and value of this dictionary.

As Gabriel explains in his preface, this dictionary was originally intended to assist scholars and professionals in understanding foreign-language words and expressions which they might find in their reading. The emphasis is on legal, philosophical, historical, and literary material. While some scientific words are included, especially a number of phobias, readers are advised to consult specialized dictionaries like *Taber's Medical Dictionary* (Philadelphia: F. A. Davis, 1997) for vocabulary in the health care professions. Nor will the reader find the vocabulary of scientific taxonomy here. Also excluded is the foreign vocabulary which has enriched English language references to flora and fauna in words like **tomato** (Nahuatl), **rhinoceros** (Greek), **aardvark** (Afrikans), and **dachshund** (German). Foreign words for foods and drink like **saki** (Japanese) and clothing like **sari** (Hindi) are also not included here unless they have other significance, especially religious, like **yarmulke** (Yiddish).

As editor, I am responsible for all the citations for the signs of the zodiac, for many of the mottoes of U.S. states, and for rhetorical devices. In order to enhance the international flavor of this dictionary, I have also substantially increased the number of citations from Hebrew, Hindi, Japanese, and Yiddish. I trust that users will find these useful additions and not mere intrusions.

It was Gabriel's decision to provide both English and foreign language plurals for entries only when both are used in English. So the English-formed plurals **administrators** and **aegises** appear in the entry but not the Latin **administratores** or **aigideis** which would never be used in an English context. When both foreign-language and English-formed plurals appear, the foreign-language plural usually appears first, so "**anathemata** or **anathemas**." I have, however, added to the etymology information which Gabriel often did not supply, such as more literal transliteration of Greek words like **aion** for "aeon."

I have resisted the impulse to spell Latin legal phrases with more classical orthography. Instead, I have retained the spelling commonly used in quotation but indicated in the word-by-word translation where such spelling deviates from classical practice. So I leave **solemniter** in **omnia praesumuntur solemniter esse acta** but write **sol(l)emniter** in the bracketed translation section. So, too, the classical **ob(o)edentia** is spelled **obedentia** in **obedentia est legis essentia**.

Users of this dictionary may, at times, note the absence of an occasional foreign word or phrase. Such lacunae are inevitable in an opus of this scope. Linguists would call the entries in this dictionary loan words or phrases. This means, technically, that the entries should appear in English essentially as they appear in the original language. While allowance must be made for alphabetic transliteration, as in the case of Greek and Russian, and for minor variations in orthography which result from pronunciation (English **pug** for Hindi **pag**), words which have been significantly altered morphologically (English **oblique** from Latin **obliquus**) are derivatives rather than loan words and do not appear in this dictionary. Other loan words, like **major**, **minor**, **restaurant**, and **trombone**, have been so thoroughly anglicized that they are included here only for the sake of illustration.

Since the emphasis in this dictionary is on written rather than spoken materials, no pronunciation guides for foreign words and phrases are provided. Most of the words in this dictionary have a wide variety of pronunciations, depending upon the context in which they are used and users' familiarity with the source language. While we could have in many cases indicated the foreign language pronunciation that some readers might consider to be the "correct" one, we felt strongly that other pronunciations have legitimacy.

The strongest example of this is the case of Latin, where the choice of a "correct" pronunciation is highly problematic. Classicists do not agree upon how Latin was pronounced when originally spoken, and many other pronunciations have arisen and found acceptance after Latin ceased to be a spoken language and instead became the language of the Catholic church and the legal, medical, and scientific professions. We therefore did not feel that it was legitimate to choose, say, the "Classical" pronunciation over the "Restored Classical," or either of those over any of the multiple Continental/Ecclesiastical pronunciations or any of the variety of legal pronunciations (e.g. American, British, Indian). Another factor to consider is that the more a word or phrase is used in English, the more Anglicized the pronunciation becomes. Two examples will suffice: English speakers have Anglicized the pronunciation of Wanderlust so that the w is pronounced as in English, while the German pronunciation would be "van·der·loost" (with the "oo" as in book). Similarly, hors d'oeuvre (singular) and hors d'oeuvres (plural) would be pronounced the same in French; in English, the final s is pronounced in the plural form. Using the native rather than the Anglicized pronunciation in either of these cases would be considered inappropriate in many settings. The question then becomes, which pronunciation should be offered, the German or French pronunciation, or the Anglicized one? Since any pronunciation we chose would be wrong in some circles, we chose to assume that the user should make the decision. Users desiring guidance on the correct pronunciation of languages in their countries of origin should consult an appropriate foreign language dictionary. The use of macrons over foreign language vowels is intended only to serve as an orthographic rather than pronunciation guide, especially in the case of transliterated Greek words like **apostrophē**.

Gabriel intended this book to be called *An English Dictionary of Foreign Expressions for Lawyers, Journalists, Scholars, Etc.* The publisher has wisely, I think, renamed it *World Dictionary of Foreign Expressions: A Resource for Readers and Writers.* I would like to express my gratitude here to Lou Bolchazy, Marie Bolchazy, Laurie Haight, Charlene Hernandez, and others at Bolchazy-Carducci Publishers who have made this dream of Gabriel Adeleye a reality. I also wish to thank the Monmouth College Faculty Development Committee for its financial support of this project. Frances Stauffer and Michele Pasley (MC '01) offered patient and valuable assistance in seeking permissions to reproduce copyrighted material. Bill Urban was of help several times when it mattered most, and Aaron Baker and Anne W. Sienkewicz devoted many hours of effort to proofreading the manuscript in its various transformations. I am particularly grateful to my co-editor, James T. McDonough, Jr., who spared the authors and me many embarrassing gaffes. Any that remain are my own.

I have learned much from my modest efforts to edit such an impressive tome and trust that those who open this book will find much of value inside. Vade mecum.

Monmouth College
Monmouth, Illinois
January, 1999
T. J. S.

Guide to the Entries

Each entry is organized in the following way:

1. The foreign word or phrase in bold.
2. The part of speech, abbreviated in italics. Gender is also indicated here, where appropriate.
3. The plural and alternative gender forms of the foreign word in bold. Anglicized plurals are also provided here, where appropriate.
4. The following information is provided within hard brackets:
   a. Language of origin indicated in abbreviated form.
   b. Translation of individual words or word elements. Numbers in parentheses indicate the order in which the words are translated into English.
   c. A literal, word-for-word English translation of the entire word or phrase.
5. A usage label, such as Law, Mecidine, etc., indicated in italics.
6. A fuller, more polished translation of the foreign word or phrase.
7. Phrases and sentences in italics illustrating the use of the word or phrase in English. Many of these examples are cited from periodicals and books listed in the bibliography. References to these materials is by author or journal title followed by year of publication and page number.
8. If the word or phrase is used in English in a different part of speech, this is indicated by a dash followed by the part of speech, abbreviated in italics, and an appropriate definition.
9. In many entries "see also" and "cf." direct the reader to similar words or phrases in other parts of the dictionary.

A Table of Abbreviations appears on pages xxiii–xxiv.

Table of Abbreviations

abbr.	abbreviation
adj.	adjective
adv.	adverb
Afr.	Afrikaans
Arab.	Arabic
Aram.	Aramaic
attrib.	attributive
cf. **confer** (L.)	compare
Chin.	Chinese
constr.	construction
Dan.	Danish
e.g. **exempli gratia** (L.)	for example
Eng.	English
et al. **et alii** or **aliae** or **alia** (L.) .	and others
etc. **et cetera** (L.)	and the rest, and so on
fem.	female, feminine
Fr.	French
Ger.	German
Gk.	Greek
Haw.	Hawaiian
Heb.	Hebrew
i.e. **id est** (L.)	that is
int.	international
interj.	interjection
intr.	intransitive
Ir.	Irish
It.	Italian
Japan.	Japanese
L.	Latin
masc.	male, masculine
Med.	medieval
n.	noun
neut. **neuter** (L.)	neither masculine nor feminine
Neo-Gk.	neo-Greek
Neo-L.	neo-Latin
Norw.	Norwegian
Obs. Fr.	obsolete French
Obs. It.	obsolete Italian

Pers.	Persian
pl.	plural
Port.	Portuguese
pref.	prefix
prep.	preposition
pron.	pronoun
q.v. **quod vide** (L.)	which see
Russ.	Russian
Skt.	Sanskrit
sing.	singular
Sp.	Spanish
suf.	suffix
Swed.	Swedish
tr.	transitive
Turk.	Turkish
U.S.A.	United States of America
v.	verb
var.	variant
Yid.	Yiddish

Bibliography

Adewoye, O. A. 1977. *The Judicial System in Southern Nigeria (1854–1954)*. London: Longman.

Aihe, D. O., and P. A. Oluyede. 1979. *Cases and Materials on Constitutional Law in Nigeria*. Ibadan, Nigeria: University Press Limited and Oxford: Oxford University Press.

The American Heritage College Dictionary. 1993. 3rd ed. Boston: Houghton Mifflin.

American Heritage Dictionary of the English Language. 1976. 2nd ed. Edited by William Morris. Boston: Houghton Mifflin.

Asante, S. K. B. 1975. *Property Law and Social Goals in Ghana, 1844–1966*. Accra: Ghana Universities Press.

Baker, Daniel B. 1992. *Power Quotes: 4,000 Trenchant Soundbites on Leadership & Liberty, Treason & Triumph, Sacrifice and Scandal, Risk & Rebellion, Weakness & War, and Other Affaires Politiques*. Detroit: Visible Ink.

Bartlett, John. 1980. *Familiar Quotations*. 15th ed. Boston: Little, Brown.

Bentsi-Enchill, K. 1964. *Ghana Land Law*. London: Sweet & Maxwell.

Betteridge, Harold T. 1962. *The New Cassell's German Dictionary*. New York: Funk & Wagnalls.

Black, H. C. 1979. *Black's Law Dictionary*. 5th ed. St. Paul, Minn.: West Publishing Co.

Bliss, A. J. 1980. *A Dictionary of Foreign Words and Phrases in Current English*. London: Routledge and Kegan Paul.

Branyon, Richard A. 1997. *Latin Phrases & Quotations*. Rev. ed. New York: Hippocrene Books, 1997.

Buckland, W. W., and P. Stein. 1966. *A Textbook of Roman Law: From Augustus to Justinian*. Cambridge: Cambridge University Press.

Burke, J. 1976. *Osborn's Concise Law Dictionary*. London: Sweet & Maxwell.

———. 1977. *Jowitt's Dictionary of English Law*. London: Sweet & Maxwell.

Burkert, Walter. 1985. *Greek Religion*. Cambridge, Mass.: Harvard University Press.

Cary, M. A. 1970. *A History of Rome*. London: Macmillan.

Cary, M. A., et al., ed. 1968. *The Oxford Classical Dictionary*, Oxford University Press, London, 1968.

Colinvaux, R. 1979. *The Law of Insurance*. London: Sweet & Maxwell.

Cretney, S. M. 1976. *Principles of Family Law*. London: Sweet & Maxwell.

Crystal, David. 1994. *The Cambridge Biographical Encyclopedia*. Cambridge and New York: Cambridge University Press.

Curzon, L. B. 1979. *Jurisprudence*. Plymouth, England: Pitman Publishing (formerly Macdonald & Evans).

Dauzat, Albert. 1938. *Dictionnaire Étymologique de la langue française*. Paris: Larousse.

Dubois, M., et al., ed. 1981. *Dictionnaire Français Anglais*. Paris: Larousse.

Ehrlich, Eugene. 1985/1987. *Amo, Amas, Amat and More*. New York: Harper & Row.

————. 1995. *Veni vidi vici: Conquer your enemies, impress your friends with everyday Latin*. New York: HarperCollins.

————. 1997. *Les Bons Mots: How to Amaze Tout le Monde with Everyday French*. New York: Henry Holt.

Eysenck, H. J. 1982. *Psychology Is About People*. Middlesex, England: Penguin Books.

Ezejiofor, G., C. O. Okonkwo, and C. U. Ilegbune. 1982. *Nigerian Business Law*. London: Sweet & Maxwell.

Flexner, Stuart Berg. 1987. *The Random House Dictionary of the English Language*. 2nd ed. New York: Random House.

Freedland, M. R. 1976. *The Contract of Employment*. Oxford: Oxford University Press.

Girard, Denis, et al., ed. 1965. *The New Cassell's French Dictionary*. New York: Funk & Wagnalls.

Glare, P. G. W., ed. 1982. *Oxford Latin Dictionary*. Oxford: Clarendon Press.

Gove, P. B., et al., ed. 1966. *Webster's Third New International Dictionary*. Chicago: G. & C. Merriam.

Grant, Michael. 1970. *Nero*. New York: Dorset Press.

Graveson, R. H. 1974 *Conflict of Laws: Private International Law*. London: Sweet and Maxwell.

Guterman, Norbert. 1966. *The Anchor Book of Latin Quotations with English Translations*. New York: Doubleday, Anchor.

Halliwell, Leslie. 1997a. *Halliwell's Film & Video Guide*. Edited by John Walker. New York: HarperCollins.

————. 1997b. *Halliwell's Filmgoer's Companion*. 12th ed. Edited by John Walker, New York: HarperCollins.

Hanbury, H. G. 1962. *Modern Equity: The Principles of Equity*. London: Sweet and Maxwell.

HarperCollins German Dictionary: German-English, English-German. 1990. London: Collins. New York: Harper & Row.

Hart, H. L. A. 1978. *Punishment and Responsibility*. Oxford: Oxford University Press.

Jaeger, Werner. 1970. *Paideia: The Ideals of Greek Culture*. Translated by Gilbert Highet. Oxford: Oxford University Press.

James, W. R. 1982. *Modern Land Law of Nigeria*. Ile-Ife, Nigeria: Obafemi Awolowo University Press Limited (Formerly University of Ife Press).

Jeffares, A. Norman, and Martin Gray. 1995/1997. *A Dictionary of Quotations*. New York: HarperCollins.

Jolowicz, H. F. 1965. *Historical Introduction to the Study of Roman Law*. Cambridge: Cambridge University Press.

Laistner, M. L. W. 1966. *The Greater Roman Historians*. Berkeley and Los Angeles: University of California Press.

Langan, St. J., and D. G. Lawrence. 1976. *Civil Procedure*. London: Sweet & Maxwell.

Lesky, A. 1966. *A History of Greek Literature*. Translated by J. Willis and C. de Heer. New York: Methuen & Co.

Lewis, C. T. 1962. *A Latin Dictionary for Schools*, London: Oxford University Press.

Lewis, J. R. 1976. *Law for the Construction Industry*. London: Macmillan.

Liddell, H. G., and R. Scott. 1966. *A Greek-English Lexicon*. 9th ed. Revised and augmented by Sir Henry S. Jones et al. London: Oxford University Press.

Lloyd, Norman. 1968. *The Golden Encyclopedia of Music*. Racine, Wisc.: Golden Press.

Macrone, Michael. 1991. *It's Greek to Me!: Brush up Your Classics*. New York: HarperCollins, Cader Books.

Major, W. T. 1978. *The Law of Contract.* Plymouth: Pitman Publishing (formerly Macdonald & Evans).

Mansion, J. E. 1980. *Harrap's New Standard French and English Dictionary.* London: Harrap.

Megarry, Sir Robert E. 1955. *Miscellany-at-Law: A Diversion for Lawyers and Others.* London: Sweet & Maxwell.

————. 1973. *A Second Miscellany-at-Law: A Further Diversion for Lawyers and Others.* London: Sweet and Maxwell.

Megrah, M., and F. Ryder. 1972. *Byles on Bills of Exchange.* London: Sweet & Maxwell.

Messinger, H., and W. Rudenberg. 1969. *Langenscheidt Concise German Dictionary.* Berlin and Munich: Langenscheidt.

Morford, Mark P. O., and Robert J. Lenardon. 1999. *Classical Mythology.* 6th ed. New York: Longman.

Morris, J. H. C. 1973. *Dicey and Morris on the Conflict of Laws.* London: Sweet & Maxwell.

Morwood, James. 1998. *A Dictionary of Latin Words and Phrases.* Oxford: Oxford University Press.

Newmark, Maxim. 1950. *Dictionary of Foreign Words and Phrases.* New York: Barnes & Noble.

Newton, C. R. 1983. *General Principles of Law.* London: Sweet & Maxwell.

Nwabueze, B. O. 1982. *A Constitutional History of Nigeria.* New York: Longman.

Olawoyin, G. A. 1977. *Status and Duties of Company Directors.* Ile-Ife, Nigeria: Obafemi Awolowo University Press Limited (formerly University of Ife Press).

The Oxford Dictionary of Quotations. 1955. 2nd ed. London: Oxford University Press.

The Oxford Dictionary of Quotations. 1979. 3rd ed. London: Oxford University Press.

Parry, Sir David. 1961. *The Law of Succession.* London: Sweet & Maxwell.

Paxton, J., ed. 1975. *Everyman's Dictionary of Abbreviations.* London: J. M. Dent and Sons.

Quinn, Arthur. 1982. *Figures of Speech: 60 Ways to Turn a Phrase.* Salt Lake City: Gibbs M. Smith, Inc.

Randel, Don Michael. 1978. *Harvard Concise Dictionary of Music.* Cambridge, Mass.: Harvard University Press.

Rees, Nigel. 1997. *Cassell Companion to Quotations.* London: Cassell.

Robinson, C. E. 1974. *A History of Rome.* London: Methuen & Co.

Rogers, W. H. V. 1975. *Winfield and Jolowicz on Tort.* London: Sweet & Maxwell.

Sine nomine. 1915. *Latin for Lawyers.* London: Sweet and Maxwell.

Speake, Jennifer, ed. 1997. *Oxford Dictionary of Foreign Words and Phrases.* Oxford: Oxford University Press.

Stone, Jon R. 1996. *Latin for the Illiterati.* New York and London: Routledge.

Suret-Canale, J. 1971. *French Colonialism in Tropical Africa 1900–1945.* Translated by T. Gottheiner. London: C. Hurst & Co.

Taylor, Elizabeth A. 1988. *Dorland's Illustrated Medical Dictionary.* 27th ed. Philadelphia: W. B. Sauders Co.

Thomas, Clayton L., ed. 1977. *Taber's Cyclopedic Medical Dictionary.* 18th ed. Philadelphia: F. A. Davis Co.

Traupman, John Charles. 1995. *The Bantam New College Latin & English Dictionary.* Rev. ed. New York: Mass Market Paperbacks.

Van Roey, Jacques, Sylviane Granger, and Helen Swallow. 1991/1993. *Dictionary of faux amis.* 2nd ed. Paris: Duculot.

Vernoff, Edward, and Rima Shore. 1987. *The International Dictionary of 20th Century Biography*. New York: New American Library.

Warner, Carolyn. 1992. *Treasury of Women's Quotations*. Englewood Cliffs, New Jersey: Prentice-Hall.

Weir, T. A. 1974. *Casebook on Tort*. London: Sweet & Maxwell.

Magazines and Newspapers

Catholic News Service, Washington, D.C.

The Economist, The Economist Newspaper Ltd, London.

The Guardian, Guardian Newspapers, Oshodi, Lagos.

New African, IC Magazines, London.

Newsweek International, Newsweek, New York.

South, South Publications, London.

Sunday Tribune, African Newspapers of Nigeria, Ibadan.

Time International, Time Inc., New York.

West Africa, West Africa Publishing Co., London.

World Dictionary
$_{of}$ **Foreign**
Expressions

A Resource for Readers and Writers

A

A.A.C. *abbr.* for **anno ante Christum** (q.v.).

A.A.C.N. *abbr.* for **anno ante Christum natum** (q.v.).

a aver et tener [Obs. Fr. **a** to (1); **aver** to have (2); **et** and (3); **tener** to hold (4): to have and to hold.] *Law.* To keep in one's possession. Used in former times for the conveyance or the transfer of property.

A.B. *abbr.* for **Artium Baccalaureus** (q.v.).

ab absurdo *adj./adv.* [L. **ab** from, by (1); **absurdo** the absurd (2): from the absurd.] From absurdity. Based on absurdity. *Logic.* Used to describe an assertion rendered false by its absurdity. *She attempted to prove her point by resorting to an ab absurdo argument.*

ab abusu ad usum non valet consequentia. [L. **ab** from, by (2); **abusu** an abuse (3); **ad** to, at, for, according to (4); **usum** use (5); **non** not (6); **valet** is valid (7); **consequentia** consequence (1): A consequence from abuse to use is not valid.] An inference of the use of a thing from its abuse is invalid.

a baculo *adj./adv.* [L. **a** from, by (1); **baculo** rod (2): by the rod.] Relying on the stick. *Logic.* Applicable to an argument which, far from appealing to reason, appeals to force. *The a baculo argument was unsuccessful.*

ab aeterno *adv.* [L. **ab** from, by (1); **aeterno** everlasting, eternal (2): from everlasting.] From time immemorial. From a time in the past which supposedly has no beginning. *This has been the custom in the village ab aeterno and so the people are unlikely to abolish it.*

abandon *n., pl.* **abandons** [Fr. carelessness, neglect.] 1. Giving oneself to natural impulses. Freedom from inhibition or constraint. Absence of restraint. *Though misfortune is unpleasant, when it does come, one should face it with fortitude and not succumb to it with abandon.* 2. Carefree freedom, usually with no regard whatsoever for possible consequences. Exuberance. *The indignation of the rioters was so intense that they destroyed property, both public and private, with abandon.*

ab ante *adv.* [L. **ab** from, by (1); **ante** before (2): from before.] In advance. *Sam's suggestion that the terms of the proposed reconciliation be consented to ab ante was rejected by Adam.*

ab antiquo *adv.* [L. **ab** from, by (1); **antiquo** ancient (2): from the ancient.] From old times. From ancient times. *The custom of exchanging gifts among merchants has been in existence ab antiquo.*

à bas *interj.* [Fr. **à** to, toward, in, by, with, until (1); **bas** low, below (2): toward below.] Down with! *À bas all tyrants and despots!*

ab assuetis non fit injuria. [L. **ab** from, by (1); **assuetis** accustomed, familiar (things) (2); **non** not (4); **fit** is made, done (5); **injuria** injury, wrong (3): From accustomed things injury is not done.] *Law.* No legal injury arises from a situation to which one has long been accustomed.

abattoir *n., pl.* **abattoirs** [Fr. slaughterhouse.] 1. A place where goats, sheep, cattle, and other animals are killed and their flesh processed. 2. The site of the slaying of a large number of living things. *The street seemed like an abattoir after the terrorist attack.*

a bene placito *adv.* [L. **a** from, by (1); **bene** well (3); **placito** one pleased (2): by one well pleased.] At will. At one's pleasure.

ab extra *adv.* [L. **ab** from, by (1); **extra** outside of, beyond (2): from outside of.] From without. Not coming from the mind.

à bientôt *interj.* [Fr. **à** to, toward, in, by, with, until (1); **bientôt** soon, shortly, before long (2): until soon or before long.] So long! Bye-bye! See you again soon! Cf. **adieu**; **adiós**; **aloha**; **au revoir**; **auf Wiedersehen**; **ciao**; **hasta la vista**; **hasta luego**; **sayonara**; and **vale**.

ab imo pectore *adv.* [L. **ab** from, by (1); **imo** the deepest, the bottom (2); **pectore** chest, heart (3): from the deepest heart.] With deepest affection. From the bottom of one's heart. *I would like to thank you ab imo pectore.*

ab inconvenienti *adj./adv.* [L. **ab** from, by (1); **inconvenienti** unsuitable, inconvenient (thing) (2): from an inconvenient thing.] From/based on unsuitability, inconvenience, or hardship. An argument ab inconvenienti is based on the difficulties, disastrous consequences, or inconvenience involved in pursuing a line of reasoning. *No legal system could fail to take cognizance of the argument ab inconvenienti in order to avoid a result that might involve a total destruction of society* (Nwabueze 1982:176). See **argumentum ab inconvenienti**, etc.

ab incunabulis *adv.* [L. **ab** from, by (1); **incunabilis** baby clothes, cradle (2): from the cradle.] From the beginning. From infancy. Cf. **incunabulum**.

ab initio *adv.* [L. **ab** from, by (1); **initio** beginning (2): from the beginning.] From the inception or outset. *The investigator is assuming ab initio that the suspect is guilty. Since the court has no jurisdiction, the judgment is void ab initio.* Cf. **ex post facto** and **postea**.

ab initio mundi *adv.* [L. **ab** from, by (1); **initio** beginning (2); **mundi** of world (3): from the beginning of the world.] From the very beginning. *This has been the situation ab initio mundi.*

ab intestato *adv.* [L. **ab** from, by (1); **intestato** intestate (2): from intestate.] From an intestate, from someone who dies with no legal will. a) *There are laws governing acquisition of property ab intestato.* b) *[A heres is the] universal successor of a deceased person in virtue of his rights under the jus civile. He might be appointed by will or take ab intestato* (Burke 1976:163). Cf. **ex testamento**.

ab intra *adv.* [L. **ab** from, by (1); **intra** within (2): from within.] From inside. *The confusion which disrupted the court proceedings started ab intra.*

ab invito *adv./adj.* [L. **ab** from, by (1); **invito** unwilling (2): by an unwilling.] By an unwilling person/ party. *The transfer of property was made ab invito.*

ab irato *adv./adj.* [L. **ab** from, by (1); **irato** angry (2): by an angry.] By a person who is angry. *Law.* Used to describe a will or gift made under the influence of anger or hatred, and detrimental to the interests of relatives.

à bon droit *adv.* [Fr. **à** to, toward, in, by, with, until (1); **bon** good (2); **droit** right (3): with good right.] With good reason. Rightly. Legitimately. Justly.

ab origine *adv.* [L. **ab** from, by (1); **origine** beginning, commencement (2): from the beginning.] From the beginning or creation of the world. *It can be said with a reasonable degree of justification that human nature has hardly changed ab origine.*

aborigine *n.* [from L. **ab origine**, based upon a folk etymology for the unknown ancestors of the Romans believed to have lived on the Apennines.] The indigenous inhabitants of a place, particularly those natives who lived there before the arrival of conquering invaders, colonizers, or settlers. *The Aborigines of Australia, like those of Africa, have black skin pigmentation.*

ab ovo *adv.* [L. **ab** from, by (1); **ovo** egg (2): from the egg.] From the beginning. *The audience found it difficult to understand the lecture, since the speaker discussed the issues haphazardly instead of treating the topic ab ovo.* Cf. **ab ovo usque ad mala**.

ab ovo usque ad mala Horace (65–8 B.C.). *Satires* I,3,6–7. [L. **ab** from, by (1); **ovo** egg (2); **usque** all the way (3); **ad** to, at, for, according to (4); **mala** apples (5): from the egg all the way to the apples.] From soup to nuts. From the beginning to the end. All the way through. Cf. **ab ovo**.

à bras ouverts *adv.* [Fr. **à** to, toward, in, by, with, until (1); **bras** hands, arms (3); **ouverts** open, free (2): with open arms.] Gladly. Heartily. *When the prodigal son returned home, his father welcomed him à bras ouverts.*

absens haeres non erit [L. **absens** absent, an absent person (1); **haeres** heir (4); **non** not (2); **erit** (3): An absent person will not be heir.] *Law.* Someone who is not present is unlikely to inherit. An absent person is not likely to be named as an heir.

absentem laedit cum ebrio qui litigat. [L. **absentem** absent (person) (6); **laedit** injures, harms (5); **cum** with, together (3); **ebrio** drunken (person) (4); **qui** who (1); **litigat** disputes, quarrels, goes to law (2): Who goes to law with a drunken person harms an absent person.] *Law.* Someone who brings legal action against a person who is drunk injures a person who is not present.

absente reo *abbr.* **abs. re.** *adv.* [L. **absente** (with) being absent (2); **reo** (with) accused, defendant (1): with the accused being absent.] *Law.* In the absence of the accused/defendant. The defendant/accused being absent.

absentia ejus qui reipublicae causa abest neque ei neque alii damnosa esse debet. [L. **absentia** absence (1); **ejus** of him (2); **qui** who (3); **rei publicae** of the public affair, the state (6); **causa** for the sake (5); **abest** is absent (4); **neque** neither (10); **ei** to him (11); **neque** nor (12); **alii** to another (13); **damnosa** injurious (9); **esse** to be (8); **debet** ought, should (7): The absence of him who is absent for the sake of the state should be injurious neither to him nor to another.] *Law.* A person's absence on a national assignment should not have an adverse effect on his case or on that of another.

absit *n.* [L. Let him/her be absent.] Permission for absence, especially from school.

absit omen *interj.* [L. **absit** may it be away, absent (2); **omen** omen (1): May the omen be absent.] May it not happen! God forbid! *The entire family is expecting Mr. Stone today and, if he does not come, absit omen, ignominy will be inevitable.*

absolutum dominium *n.* [L. **absolutum** absolute (1); **dominium** ownership, rule, dominion (2): absolute power.] Absolute power or sovereignty. *The leader of the junta claimed that they removed the President because he was aiming at absolutum dominium.*

abs. re. *abbr.* for **absente reo** (q.v.).

abstractum *n., pl.* **abstracta** [L. abstract, diverted or excluded thing.] Something which is abstract. An abstract entity (e.g., a class name, a universal, etc.). Cf. **concretum.**

abundans cautela non nocet. [L. **abundans** abundant, excessive (1); **cautela** caution, precaution (2); **non** not (3); **nocet** does harm, hurt, injure (4): Excessive precaution does not hurt.] Abundant/excessive caution does not do harm. One cannot be too careful.

ab urbe condita *abbr.* **A.U.C.** *adv.* [L. **ab** from, by (1); **urbe** city (2); **condita** having been founded (3): from the city having been founded.] From the founding of the city of Rome, i.e., 753 B.C. Used for chronology. *Ancient Romans dated events ab urbe condita, from the traditional date of the foundation of Rome.* See **anno urbis conditae** and **post urbem conditam.** —*Ab urbe condita From the Founding of the City,* the title of a history of Rome by Livy (59 B.C.–17 A.D.).

abus de confiance *n.* [Fr. **abus** abuse, misuse (1); **de** of (2); **confiance** confidence, trust (3): abuse of confidence.] *Law.* Abuse/breach of confidence. Abuse/breach of trust. Embezzlement. Fraudulent misuse, i.e., of goods, funds, documents, contracts, etc., given for a specific purpose. Cf. **détournement.**

abusus non tollit usum [L. **abusus** abuse, ill-use (1); **non** not (2); **tollit** takes away (3); **usum** use (4): Abuse does not take away use.] *Law.* Misuse does not, in itself, justify denial of use.

ab utili *adv.* [L. **ab** from, by (1); **utili** the useful (2): from the useful.] *Logic.* Based on usefulness. From utility.

A.C. *abbr.* for 1. **Anno Christi** (q.v.). 2. **Ante Christum** (q.v.).

academia *n.* [L. from Gk. **akadēmia.**] 1. The Greek grove where Plato taught his students. 2. University. Academic environment. Academic life, pursuit, interests, etc. *Academia thrives best when there is no or little governmental interference.*

a caelo *adv./adj.* [L. **a** from (1); **caelo** sky, heaven (2): from the sky.] From heaven.

a caelo ad centrum *var.* of **a caelo usque ad centrum** (q.v.).

a caelo usque ad centrum *adv./adj.* [L. **a** from (1); **caelo** sky, heaven (2); **usque** (3) all the way; **ad** to, at, for, according to (4); **centrum** center (5): from the sky all the way to the center.] From heaven all the way to the center of the earth. *In former times it was maintained that ownership of landed property extends a caelo usque ad centrum, but this doctrine is obsolete, as evidenced by the flight of airplanes.*

a capite ad calcem [L. **a** from, away (1); **capite** head (2); **ad** to, at, for, according to (3); **calcem** heal, foot (4): from head to heal.] From head to toe. All the way through. Cf. **ab ovo usque ad mala.**

a cappella or **a capella** *adv.* [It. **a** at, in the manner of (1); **cappella** chapel (2): at chapel.] *Music.* In a style characterized by the absence of instrumental or orchestral accompaniment. *He passed a group singing a cappella, letting some high sweet harmonies drift up into the metropolitan air (Time Int. 1981). —adj.* Characterized by, or specializing in, music unaccompanied by instruments or orchestra.

accelerando *adj./adv.* [It. accelerating.] *Music.* Increasing the tempo little by little.

accessio cedit principali. [L. **accessio** increase, addition (1); **cedit** yields, accrues (2); **principali** to principal (3): An increase accrues to the principal.] *Law.* An accessory thing belongs to the owner of the principal thing.

accessorium non ducit sed sequitur suum principale. [L. **accessorium** accessory (thing) (1); **non** not (2); **ducit** leads (3); **sed** but (4); **sequitur** follows (5); **suum** its own (6); **principale** principal (thing) (7): An accessory does not lead but follows its own principal.] *Law.* An accessory thing does not lead but follows its principal. See **accessorium non trahit principale; accessorius sequitur** etc.; **derivativa potestas** etc.; **quae accessionum** etc.; **res accessoria sequitur** etc.; **sublato fundamento** etc.; **sublato principali** etc.; **terra transit** etc.; and **ubi non est principalis** etc.

accessorium non trahit principale. [L. **accessorium** accessory (1); **non** not (2); **trahit** drags (3); **principale** principal (4): An accessory thing does not drag a principal thing.] *Law.* An accessory does not take along with it a principal; e.g., the release of a surety does not necessarily imply the release of a principal, though the release of the latter implies the release of the former. See **accessorium non ducit** etc.

accessorius sequitur naturam sui principalis. [L. **accessorius** accessory (1); **sequitur** follows (2); **naturam** nature (3); **sui** of its own, one's own, his/her own (4); **principalis** (of) principal (5): An accessory follows the nature of its own principal.] *Law.* An accessory to a crime cannot be guilty of a crime higher than that of his/her principal. See **accessorium non ducit** etc.

accidia *n.* [L. from Gk. **akēdia** carelessness, indifference.] **Acedia** (q.v.).

accipere quid ut justitiam facias non est tam accipere quam extorquere. [L. **accipere** to accept (1); **quid** something (2); **ut** in order that (3); **justitiam** justice (5); **facias** you may do (4); **non** not (7); **est** is (6); **tam** so much (8); **accipere** to accept (9); **quam** as (10); **extorquere** to extort (11): To accept something in order that you may do justice is not so much to accept as to extort.] *Law.* Accepting something in order to do justice is extortion rather than acceptance.

accolade *n., pl.* **accolades** [F. embrace, bracket, hug.] 1. A manner of greeting, especially one which involves embracing and kissing a person on both cheeks. *Her father drew her near and gave her the accolade.* 2. A ceremony marking the bestowal or conferment of knighthood which consists of embracing, kissing, or tapping the shoulder with the flat of a sword. 3. Mark of recognition or acknowledgment. Award. Approval. Praise. a) *Michel's Paris restaurant . . . won two stars, while his father Joseph's sumptuous La Bonne Auberge . . . was awarded three, the highest accolade* (*Newsweek Int.* March 31, 1980:11). b) *Through hard work, dedication and altruism he won the accolade of his colleagues.* Cf. **kudos**.

accouchement *n., pl.* **accouchements** [Fr. delivery, labor.] Confinement. Childbirth. Labor. Parturition. A woman's giving birth to a child. *Law.* It is a very important evidence for proving parentage, if given by an eyewitness such as a medical practitioner or a midwife.

accoutrement or **accouterment** *n.* [Fr. equipment.] Accessories. Supplementary pieces of clothing or equipment, such as gloves and hat for someone in business or a canteen and compass for a soldier. Usually used in the plural. —**accoutrements** or **accouterments** Superficial rather than real items of identification. *He displayed only the accoutrements of intelligence.*

accusare nemo se debet nisi coram Deo. [L. **accusare** to accuse (3); **nemo** no one, nobody (1); **se** himself (4); **debet** ought, should (2); **nisi** unless, except (5); **coram** before, in the presence of (6); **Deo** God (7): No one should accuse himself/herself except before God.] *Law.* An accused person is entitled to make a plea of not guilty. Also, a witness is not obliged to give a response or submit a document which will incriminate himself/herself. See **nemo tenetur armare** etc.; **nemo tenetur edere** etc.; **nemo tenetur prodere seipsum**; and **nemo tenetur seipsum accusare**.

accusator post rationabile tempus non est audiendus nisi se bene de omissione excusaverit. [L. **accusator** accuser (1); **post** after (5); **rationabile** reasonable (6); **tempus** time (7); **non** not (3); **est** is (2); **audiendus** to be heard (4); **nisi** unless, except (8); **se** himself (10); **bene** well (11); **de** of, from, about, for (12); **omissione** delay, omission (13); **excusaverit** he will have excused (9): An accuser is not to be heard after a reasonable time unless he will have excused himself well about the delay.] *Law.* After a reasonable length of time, an accuser should not be given a hearing unless he/she can satisfactorily explain the delay.

acedia *n.* [Gk. **akēdia**: **a-** no (1); **kedos** care (2): no care, carelessness, indifference.] Spiritual indifference and apathy. See **accidia**.

acephalia *n.* [L. from Gk. **akephalos**: **a-** no (1); **kephalē** head (2): no head, headless, without head.] *Medicine.* Headlessness. Applicable to a fetus.

acephalus *n., pl.* **acephali** [L. from Gk. **akephalos**: **a-** no (1); **kephalē** head (2): no head, headless, without head.] *Medicine.* A fetus with no head. Cf. **amelus** and **amorphus**.

ac etiam [L. **ac** and (1); **etiam** also (2): and also.] *English Law.* Formerly used for the introduction of a clause which states the actual cause of a legal action when a fictitious cause had previously been alleged for the purpose of establishing jurisdiction.

à chacun son goût [Fr. **à** to, toward, in, by, with, until (1); **chacun** each, each one (2); **son** his/her (3); **goût** taste, liking (4): to each one his/her taste.] Each one or everyone to his/her taste/liking. "One man's meat is another man's poison." See **chacun à son goût**; **de gustibus non** etc.; **homo mensura**; **homo mensura omnium**; and **panton chrematon** etc.

Achilles or **Achilleus** or **Akhilleus** *n.* [Gk. **Akhilleus**.] *Greek Mythology.* Son of Peleus and Thetis, Achilles was a very brave warrior who participated in the Greek expedition against Troy, quarreled over a captive girl with Agamemnon, commander-in-chief of the Greeks, and withdrew from battle, thus making it possible for the Trojan prince, Hector, to perform heroic deeds. Achilles was eventually placated and returned to the battlefield to kill Hector. According to one legend, the only part of his body which was vulnerable was his heel, which was held by his mother when she plunged him into the River Styx to secure his invulnerability. —**Achilles' heel** One's vulnerable or weak point. a) *Jeko is a man of indisputable incorruptibility and probity but, even so, he has his Achilles' heel: an inability to resist the allurements of the fair sex.* b) *The southern flank of NATO has long been regarded as the Achilles' heel of the alliance, largely because of the unresolved Cyprus dispute between Turkey and Greece* (*Newsweek Int.* Feb. 8, 1982:18). c) *The Achilles' heel of this was that various other local events might have taken place on that other day, so that Michael O'Flaherty's funeral, which had taken place on the Monday, might emerge as part of the tale of events which, occurring in fact on the Monday, were being sworn to Tuesday* (Megarry 1973:86).

acme *n., pl.* **acmes** [Gk. **akmē** highest point of anything, culmination.] The culminating point of anything. Zenith. Highest stage of a thing's development. Peak. Point of perfection. Apex. *The very year which marked the acme of the power of the kingdom happened to be a turning point in its fortunes.* See **apogée**.

A.C.N. *abbr.* for **Ante Christum natum** (q.v.).

a coelo *var.* of **a caelo** (q.v.).

a coelo ad centrum *var.* of **a caelo ad centrum** (q.v.).

a coelo usque ad centrum *var.* of **a caelo usque ad centrum** (q.v.).

a communi observantia non est recedendum. [L. **a** from (1); **communi** common (2); **observantia** observance (3); **non** not (5); **est** it is (4); **recedendum** to be departed, withdrawn (6): From common observance it is not to be departed.] There should be no departure from common observance.

a contrario *adv.* [L. **a** from, by (1); **contrario** the contrary (2): from the contrary.] From, by, or based on contraries or opposite points of view. Cf. **au contraire**.

a contrario sensu *adv.* [L. **a** from, by (1); **contrario** contrary, opposite (2); **sensu** sense (3): from the contrary sense.] On the other hand. *The statement of the accused person is ambiguous, for it could exonerate him or, a contrario sensu, incriminate him.*

acromania *n.* [Neo-Gk. from Gk. **akromanēs** on the verge of madness.] *Medicine.* Violent madness which is usually incurable.

acrophobia *n.* [Neo-Gk. from Gk. **akro(n)** height, peak (2); **phob(os)** fear (1): fear of height.] Abnormal or excessive fear of being at a very high point, e.g., on the roof of a high building.

a cruce salus [L. **a** from, away (1); **cruce** cross (2); **salus** safety, salvation (3): from the cross, salvation.] *Christianity.* Salvation comes from the Cross. Cf. **nullu salus extra ecclesiam**.

acta *pl. n.* [L. things done, deeds.] Official acts. Transactions. Recorded proceedings. *The secretary informed the delegates that the acta of the conference would be published soon.*

acta est fabula Suetonius. *Augustus* XCIX,1. [L. **acta** done (3); **est** is, has been (2); **fabula** story, play (1): The play has been done.] The play is finished. According to Suetonius, these were some of the last words of the emperor Augustus. Cf. **La commedia** etc. and **La farce** etc.

acta exteriora indicant interiora secreta. [L. **acta** acts, deeds, actions (2); **exteriora** outward, external (1); **indicant** show, disclose, indicate (3); **interiora** inner, interior, deeper (4); **secreta** secrets, hidden things (5): Outward actions show inner secrets.] A person's actions indicate hidden intentions. For this reason, sometimes the law permits an inference of a person's former intention from subsequent acts.

acta jure gestionis *n., sing.* **actum jure gestionis** [L. **acta** acts, deeds (1); **jure** by right, law (2); **gestionis** of managing, doing (3): acts by right of managing.] Acts by right of business or commerce. Cf. **acta jure imperii**.

acta jure imperii *n., sing.* **actum jure imperii** [L. **acta** deeds, acts (1); **jure** by right, law (2); **imperii** of sovereignty, authority (3): acts by right of sovereignty.] Acts by right of government. Cf. **acta jure gestionis**.

acte authentique *n., pl.* **actes authentiques** [Fr. **acte** deed, act (2); **authentique** legal, authentic (1): authentic or legal deed.] *French Law.* A deed executed in accordance with some laid down formalities and in the presence of a duly authorized official such as a mayor, notary, or huissier.

acte de francisation *n., pl.* **actes de francisation** [Fr. **acte** certificate, document (1); **de** of (2); **francisation** registration as a French ship (3): document of registration as a French ship.] *French Law.* Certificate of registration as a French ship.

acte d'héritier *n., pl.* **actes d' héritier** [Fr. **acte** action, deed (1); **d'** of (2); **héritier** heir, inheritor (3): act of heir.] *French Law.* Act of inheritance. An action, whether explicit or implicit, on the part of an heir which indicates his intention to accept the inheritance.

acte gratuit *n., pl.* **actes gratuits** [Fr. **acte** action, deed (2); **gratuit** gratuitous, uncalled for (1): a gratuitous act.] An act which is uncalled for. An impulsive act. An act with no rational motive.

actio *n., pl.* **actiones** [L. action, deed, legal suit.] *Law.* A legal action. A right of action. A suit at law.

actio bonae fidei *n., pl.* **actiones bonae fidei** [L. **actio** action, deed, legal suit (1); **bonae** of /for good (2); **fidei** (of/for) faith (3): legal suit for good faith.] *Roman Law.* A legal action in which the trial judge is given considerable discretion to take into consideration all aspects of good faith, equity, and conscience. Cf. **actio stricti juris**.

actio calumniae *n., pl.* **actiones calumniae** [L. **actio** action, deed, legal suit (1); **calumniae** of/for trickery, misrepresentation, malicious prosecution (2): a legal suit for misrepresentation.] *Law.* An action against misrepresentation or malicious prosecution.

actio civilis *n., pl.* **actiones civiles** [L. **actio** action, deed, legal suit (2); **civilis** civil (1): a civil action.] *Law.* A civil suit. *An actio civilis was commenced against the driver for causing damage to property.* Cf. **actio criminalis**.

actio communi dividundo *n., pl.* **actiones communi dividundo** [L. **actio** action, deed, legal suit (1); **communi** for common (thing) (2); **dividundo** (for) to be divided (3): legal suit for a common thing to be divided.] *Roman Law.* A legal action for securing division of property owned jointly. Similar to modern judicial process for partition.

actio confessoria *n., pl.* **actiones confessoriae** [L. **actio** action, deed, legal suit (2); **confessoria** confessing, acknowledging (1): acknowledging legal suit.] *Roman Law.* A legal action for establishing one's right to a thing, such as usufruct or servitude. See **vindicatio servitutis** and **vindicatio ususfructus**. Cf. **actio negatoria**.

actio criminalis *n., pl.* **actiones criminales** [L. **actio** action, deed, legal suit (2); **criminalis** criminal (1): criminal act.] *Law.* A criminal suit. *Unlawful harm to another can invite an actio criminalis.* Cf. **actio civilis**.

actio de dolo malo *n.pl.* **actiones de dolo malo** [L. **actio** action, deed, legal suit (1); **de** of, from, about, for (2); **dolo** fraud, deceit (4); **malo** bad, criminal (3): legal suit for criminal fraud.] *Law.* A legal action for criminal fraud. A legal suit brought by a person defrauded against the individual who committed fraud and this individual's heirs. See **dolus malus**.

actio doli *n., pl.* **actiones doli** [L. **actio** action, deed, legal suit (1); **doli** of /for fraud, deceit (2): legal suit for fraud.] *Roman Law.* A legal action for fraud or deceit. It may, for instance, be brought when a party to a contract interfered with it, thus frustrating the efforts of the other party to perform it.

actio empti *n., pl.* **actiones empti** [L. **actio** action, deed, legal suit (1); **empti** of/for purchase (2): legal suit for purchase.] *Law.* A legal action for purchase or for contract of purchase, i.e., a suit to force a seller to fulfill his obligations or compensate the buyer. Cf. **actio venditi**.

actio ex contractu *pl. n.* **actiones ex contractu** [L. **actio** action, deed, legal suit (1); **ex** from, arising from (2); **contractu** drawing together, shrinking, contract, agreement (3): a legal suit arising from a contract.] *Law.* A legal action based on a contract.

actio ex delicto *n., pl.* **actiones ex delicto** [L. **actio** action, deed, legal suit (1); **ex** from, arising from (2); **delicto** offense, wrong (3): legal suit arising from offense.] *Law.* Action of tort. A legal action arising from misconduct or malfeasance. *The actio ex delicto instituted against the police officer by Mr. Edet in connection with his arrest and detention was dismissed on the ground that the act was legally justified.*

actio ex stipulatu *n., pl.* **actiones ex stipulatu** [L. **actio** action, deed, legal suit (1); **ex** from, arising from (2); **stipulatu** agreement (3): a legal action arising from an agreement.] *Law.* A suit for enforcing a stipulation. *The heavy damages awarded against the defendant resulted from actio ex stipulatu.*

actio familiae erciscundae *var.* of **actio familiae herciscundae** (q.v.).

actio familiae herciscundae or **actio familiae erciscundae** *n., pl.* **actiones familiae herciscundae** or **actiones familiae erciscundae** [L. **actio** action, deed, legal suit (1); **familiae** of /for estate, family property (2); **herciscundae** (of/for) to be divided (3): legal suit for family property to be divided.] *Roman Law.* A legal action for dividing family property or an inheritance among the members of the family or heirs, respectively.

actio finium regundorum or **finium regundorum actio** *n., pl.* **actiones finium regundorum** or **finium regundorum actiones** [L. **actio** action, deed, legal suit (1); **finium** of /for boundaries (2); **regundorum** (of) to be determined (3): legal suit for boundaries to be determined.] *Law.* A legal action for the determination of boundaries. Action for redefining or regulating boundaries, i.e., settling boundary disputes. *The owner of the adjoining land is contemplating bringing an actio finium regundorum.*

actio furti *n., pl.* **actiones furti** [L. **actio** action, deed, legal suit (1); **furti** of /for theft (2): legal suit for theft.] *Law.* A legal action arising from theft. *The accused person was imprisoned when he pleaded guilty to the actio furti brought against him.*

actio in factum *n., pl.* **actiones in factum** [L. **actio** action, deed, legal suit (1); **in** against (2); **factum** deed, act, fact (3): legal suit against a deed.] *Law.* A legal action adapted for the needs of a specific case.

actio injuriarum *n., pl.* **actiones injuriarum** [L. **actio** action, deed, legal suit (1); **injuriarum** of /for injuries, wrongs, trespasses (2): legal suit for wrongs.] *Law.* A legal action respecting wanton interference with the right of another person.

actio in jus *n., pl.* **actiones in jus** [L. **actio** action, deed, legal suit (1); **in** against (2); **jus** right, law (3): legal suit against right.] *Law.* A legal action against a right or principle based on a recognized law.

actio in personam *n., pl.* **actiones in personam** [L. **actio** action, deed, legal suit (1); **in** against (2); **personam** person (3): legal suit against a person.] *Law.* A legal action arising from a personal liability. *Non-payment of a debt can provide the subject-matter of an actio in personam.* Cf. **actio in rem**.

actio in rem *n., pl.* **actiones in rem** [L. **actio** action, deed, legal suit (1); **in** against (2); **rem** matter, thing, property, business, affair (3): legal suit against a thing.] A legal action to recover a thing in the possession of another. Action to enforce a right. *Whereas an actio in personam is for the enforcement of a right against an individual violating that right, an actio in rem is for a right to a thing, which right is enforceable against the whole world.* See **in rem**; **in rem actio** etc.; **jus in re** and **jus in rem**. Cf. **actio in personam**; **in personam**; **jus ad rem**; **jus in personam**; and **personalis actio**.

actio negativa *n., pl.* **actiones negativae** See **actio negatoria**.

actio negatoria *n., pl.* **actiones negatoriae** [L. **actio** action, deed, legal suit (2); **negatoria** denying (1): denying legal suit.] *Roman Law.* A legal action denying a right to something, such as usufruct or servitude. Cf. **actio confessoria**.

actio negotiorum gestorum *n., pl.* **actiones negotiorum gestorum** [L. **actio** action, deed, legal suit (1); **negotiorum** of/for businesses (2); **gestorum** (of/for) done (3): legal suit for businesses done.] *Roman Law.* Legal action for claiming remuneration for work done. It could include claiming funeral expenses from a husband for burying his wife.

actio non datur non damnificato. [L. **actio** action, deed, legal suit (1); **non** not (2); **datur** is given (3) **non** not (4); **damnificato** to an injured, wronged (person) (5): A legal suit is not given to an unwronged person.] *Law.* A legal action is not given to a person who is not wronged/injured; i.e., the injury suffered should be deemed actionable; otherwise the doctrine of damnum sine injuria becomes applicable. See **damnum absque injuria**; **damnum sine injuria**; **damnum sine injuria esse potest**; **injuria absque damno**; and **non omne damnum** etc. Cf. **lex**

semper dabit remedium; ubi jus ibi remedium; and ubicunque est injuria etc.

actio non facit reum, nisi mens sit rea. [L. actio action, deed, legal suit (1); non not (2); facit makes (3); reum guilty (4); nisi unless (5); mens mind, intention (6); sit be, is (7); rea guilty (8): A deed does not make guilty unless the intention be guilty.] Law. An action does not make a person guilty unless the intention be evil/criminal. See actus non facit etc.

actio noxalis or noxalis actio n., pl. actiones noxales or noxales actiones [L. actio action, deed, legal suit (1); noxalis relating to damage (2): legal suit relating to damage.] Roman Civil Law. A legal action arising from damage or injury caused by somebody's slave or animal to the person or property of another. The owner could either pay for the damage or hand over the slave or animal to the complainant.

actio personalis n., pl. actiones personales [L. actio action, deed, legal suit (2); personalis personal (1): a personal legal suit.] Civil and Common Law. A personal legal action. An action in personam (q.v.), i.e., an action against a person.

actio personalis moritur cum persona. [L. actio action, deed, legal suit (2); personalis personal (1); moritur dies (3); cum with (4); persona person (5): A personal legal suit dies with the person.] The right to pursue a personal legal action dies with the person. Law. The maxim was originally applicable to many forms of action, but it has been modified and is no longer applicable to a number of actions; e.g., actions based on contract or misappropriation of property. It is, however, still applicable to actions such as false imprisonment, slander, or libel.

actio pro socio n., pl. actiones pro socio [L. actio action, deed, legal suit (1); pro for, as (2); socio partner, associate (3): legal suit as partner.] Roman Law. A legal action brought in the capacity of a partner. Action brought by a partner against the remaining members of a partnership.

actio rei uxoricae n., pl. actiones rei uxoricae [L. actio action, deed, legal suit (1); rei (of/for) property (2); uxoricae of /for wife (3): legal suit for the property of the wife.] Law. A legal action which asserts the property of the wife.

actio rerum amotarum n., pl. actiones rerum amotarum [L. actio action, deed, legal suit (1); rerum of /for matters, things, property (2); amotarum (of/for) removed (3): legal suit for things removed.] Law. A legal action for things removed. In cases of divorce, an action instituted by a husband against the wife for removing property in anticipation of divorce, or vice versa.

actio stricti juris n., pl. actiones stricti juris [L. actio action, deed, legal suit (1); stricti of /for tight, strict (2); juris of/for right, law (3): legal suit of strict law.] Roman Law. A legal action in which the judge is to make a decision in accordance with strict legal rules without reference to considerations of equity. See jus strictum. Cf. actio bonae fidei.

actio venditi n., pl. actiones venditi [L. actio action, deed, legal suit (1); venditi of /for sale (2): legal suit for sale.] Law. A legal action for sale or contract of sale, i.e., an action to force the purchaser to fulfill his obligations. Cf. actio empti.

actore non probante reus absolvitur. [L. actore with prosecutor, plaintiff, complainant (1); non not (2); probante (with) proving (3); reus accused, defendant (4); absolvitur is acquitted, discharged (5): With the plaintiff not proving, the defendant is acquitted.] Law. If the prosecutor/plaintiff fails to prove his case, the accused/defendant is acquitted. See actori incumbit etc.

actori incumbit onus probandi. [L. actori plaintiff, prosecutor (4); incumbit weighs upon, oppresses (3); onus burden (1); probandi of proving (2): The burden of proving weighs upon the plaintiff.] Law. The burden of proof lies on the plaintiff or prosecutor. See actore non probante etc.; affirmanti, non etc.; affirmantis est probare; ei incumbit probatio etc.; ei qui affirmat etc.; factum negantis etc.; in re dubia etc.; per rerum naturam etc.; probandi necessitas etc.; semper necessitas etc.; and semper praesumitur etc.

actor qui contra regulam quid adduxit non est audiendus. [L. actor plaintiff, prosecutor (1); qui who (2); contra against, opposite (5); regulam rule (6); quid something, anything (4); adduxit has adduced (3); non not (8); est is (7); audiendus to be heard (9): A plaintiff who has adduced something against the rule is not to be heard.] Law. A prosecutor/ plaintiff who challenges a rule must not be given a hearing.

actor sequitur forum rei. [L. actor plaintiff (1); sequitur follows (2); forum court (3); rei of the matter, thing, property, business, affair (4): The plaintiff follows the court of the thing.] Law. The plaintiff goes to the court which has jurisdiction over the disputed object.

actum fide abbr. a.f. adj. [L. actum done, having been done (1); fide in faith (2): done in faith.] Done in good faith.

actus n., pl. actus [L. a driving, a setting in motion, an act.] 1. An act or action. Something done. 2. Roman Law. A right of way, specifically the right to drive animals or a carriage over another's landed property.

actus curiae n. [L. actus act, deed (1); curiae of court (2): an act of court.] An act of the court, i.e., an act such as delay caused by the court. As a general rule, neither party in a suit can be inconvenienced or prejudiced by an actus curiae.

actus curiae neminem gravabit. [L. actus act, deed (1); curiae of court (2); neminem no one, nobody (4); gravabit will oppress, inconvenience (3): An act of the court will inconvenience no one.] Law. Nobody should suffer from an act of the court. An act of the court should prejudice nobody. See **actus legis**; **actus legis nemini facit injuriam**; **actus legis nemini est damnosus**; **executio juris** etc.; **lex nemini facit injuriam**; and **lex nemini operatur iniquum**.

actus Dei *n.* [L. **actus** act, deed (1); **Dei** of God (2): an act of God.] *Law.* An extraordinary natural act of violence such as an earthquake, flood, or storm, which can be neither predicted nor prevented. *The nonperformance of an obligation attributable to actus Dei is excusable.* See **actus Dei nemini est damnosus**.

actus Dei nemini est damnosus. [L. **actus** act, deed (1); **Dei** of God (2); **nemini** to nobody, no one (5); **est** is (3); **damnosus** injurious (4): An act of God is injurious to no one.] *Law.* No one should suffer in consequence of an act of God. See **actus Dei**; **actus Dei nemini facit injuriam**; **actus Dei nemini nocet**; **vis divina**; and **vis major**.

actus Dei nemini facit injuriam. [L. **actus** act, deed (1); **Dei** of God (2); **nemini** to nobody, no one (5); **facit** does, makes (3); **injuriam** injury (4): An act of God does injury to nobody.] *Law.* Nobody's case should be prejudiced by an act of God. See **actus Dei nemini est damnosus**.

actus Dei nemini nocet. [L. **actus** act, deed (1); **Dei** of God (2); **nemini** to nobody, no one (4); **nocet** does harm, hurts, injures (3): An act of God does harm to nobody.] *Law.* Nobody should suffer legally from an act of God. See **actus Dei nemini est damnosus**.

actus legis *n.* [L. **actus** act, deed (1); **legis** of law (2): act of law.] An act of law, i.e., a change in a person's legal status; e.g., an inability to fulfill an obligation which is solely attributable to the operation of law or an act backed by judicial authority. See **actus curiae neminem gravabit**.

actus legis nemini est damnosus. [L. **actus** act, deed (1); **legis** of law (2); **nemini** to no one, nobody (5); **est** is (3); **damnosus** injurious, hurtful (4): Act of law is hurtful to nobody.] *Law.* An act of law is injurious or does injury to nobody; i.e., if one is unable to fulfill an obligation and the inability is caused by the operation of law or supported by judicial authority, then one should suffer no legal harm. See **actus curiae neminem gravabit**.

actus legis nemini facit injuriam. [L. **actus** act, deed (1); **legis** of law (2); **nemini** to no one (5); **facit** does (3); **injuriam** injury (4): An act of law does injury to no one.] See **actus curiae neminem gravabit**.

actus legitimi non recipiunt modum. [L. **actus** acts, deeds (2); **legitimi** legal (1); **non** not (3); **recipiunt** admit, welcome (4); **modum** limit, restriction (5): Legal acts do not admit restriction.] Legal acts are not subject to limitation.

actus me invito factus non est meus actus. [L. **actus** act, deed (1); **me** with me (3); **invito** (with being) unwilling (4); **factus** done (2); **non** not (6); **est** is (5); **meus** my (7); **actus** act (8): An act done with

me being unwilling is not my act.] *Law.* An act of mine which is contrary to my will is not my act. See **nihil consensui tam** etc. and **non videtur consensum** etc.

actus non facit reum nisi mens sit rea. [L. **actus** act, deed (1); **non** not (2); **facit** makes (3); **reum** answerable, guilty (4); **nisi** unless (5); **mens** mind, intention (6); **sit** be, is (7); **rea** answerable, guilty (8): An act does not make one guilty unless the intention be guilty.] *Law.* An act by itself does not make a person guilty, unless done with evil intent. See **actio non facit** etc.; **affectus punitur** etc.; **animus ad se** etc.; **in atrocioribus** etc.; **in criminalibus sufficit** etc.; **in criminalibus, voluntas** etc.; **in maleficiis** etc.; **non est reus** etc.; **omne actum** etc.; **tolle voluntatem** etc.; **voluntas et propositum** etc.; **voluntas in delictis** etc.; and **voluntas reputatur** etc. Cf. **les lois** etc. and **officit conatus** etc.

actus reus *n.* [L. **actus** act, deed (1); **reus** guilty, answerable for (2): a deed or an act answerable for or guilty.] A wrongful deed. *Actus reus must be combined with mens rea before a person can be said to be criminally liable.*

acumen *n., pl.* **acumina** [L. a point, acuteness, sharpness, keenness.] Acuteness of the mind. Sharpness of judgment. Keen perception or discernment. Ability to comprehend or understand clearly. Shrewdness, especially in practical affairs. a) *mental acumen;* b) *critical acumen;* c) *intellectual acumen;* d) *commercial acumen;* e) *Financial acumen was only one of Lee's talents* (*Time Int.* 1982).

A.D. *abbr.* for **Anno Domini** (q.v.).

A.D. or **a.d.** *abbr.* for **ante diem** (q.v.).

ad absurdum *adv.* [L. **ad** to, at, for, according to (1); **absurdum** absurd or silly (thing) (2): to an absurd or silly thing.] *Logic.* To the point of silliness or absurdity. a) *As a precaution against the abuse of omens by obstructive magistrates—a practice which Caesar's colleague Bibulus had recently carried ad absurdum* . . . (Cary 1970:390); b) . . . *the democratic principle was bound to develop ad absurdum whenever the democratic state . . . really became the domination of the masses* (Jaeger 1970:290).

ad abundantiorem cautelam *adv.* [L. **ad** to, at, for, according to (1); **abundantiorem** fuller, more abundant (2); **cautelam** caution (3): for more abundant caution.] For greater caution. By way of being more cautious. See **ad cautelam ex superabundanti**; **ad majorem cautelam**; **ex abundanti cautela**; **in majorem cautelam**; **ob majorem cautelam**; **per majorem cautelam**; and **pro majori cautela**.

adagio *adv./adj.* [It. **ad** at (1); **agio** ease (2): at ease.] *Music.* In an easy manner or tempo. —*n., pl.* **adagios** 1. *Music.* A section or piece of music played in an easy manner, faster than a **largo** (q.v.). 2. *Ballet.* That portion of a **pas de deux** (q.v.) which requires great control and skill in movement.

ad aliud examen *adj.* [L. **ad** to, at, for, according to (1); **aliud** another (2); **examen** examination, consideration (3): for another consideration.] *Law.* For another court or tribunal. Belonging to another court, tribunal, or jurisdiction.

ad alium diem *adv.* [L. **ad** to, at, for, according to (1); **alium** another (2); **diem** day (3): to another day.] To another day. *Consideration of the rest of the matter was deferred ad alium diem.*

ad arbitrium *adv.* [L. **ad** to, at, for according to (1); **arbitrium** will, pleasure (2): according to pleasure.] At will. *The decision of the judge to remand the accused person in custody was taken ad arbitrium.*

ad astra per ardua [L. **ad** to, at, for, according to (1); **astra** stars (2); **per** through (3); **ardua** steep things, difficult things (4): to the stars through difficult things.] To the stars through difficulties. Cf. **ad astra per aspera**.

ad astra per aspera [L. **ad** to, at, for, according to (1); **astra** stars (2); **per** through (3); **aspera** rough things, dangers (4): to the stars through dangers.] To the stars through dangers. Motto of the State of Kansas. Cf. **ad astra per ardua**.

A.D.C. or **ADC** or **a.d.c.** *abbr.* for **aide-de-camp** (q.v.).

Ad Caesarem Senem de Re Publica Oratio [L. **ad** to, at, for, according to (2); **Caesarem** Caesar (3); **senem** old man (4); of, from, about, for (5); **re** matter, thing, property, business, affair (7); **publica** public (6); **oratio** speech, oration (1): speech to Caesar (as) an old man about the public affair.] *Speech to Caesar as an Old Man Concerning the Republic*, a work by the Roman historian Sallust (86–35 B.C.).

ad captandum vulgus or **ad captandum** *adj./adv.* [L. **ad** to, for (1); **captandum** to be allured, to be enticed (3); **vulgus** crowd (2): for the crowd to be enticed.] *Logic.* Designed to please the crowd. *An argument ad captandum vulgus is an argument in which the speaker principally aims at arousing emotions.* See **argumentum ad captandum**.

ad captum vulgi *adj.* [L. **ad** for, to (1); **captum** comprehension, capacity (2); **vulgi** of crowd (3): for the comprehension of the crowd.] To be understood by anybody with ordinary intelligence.

ad cautelam ex superabundanti *adv.* [L. **ad** to, for (1); **cautelam** caution (2); **ex** from, out of (3); **superabundanti** superabundant (thing) (4): for caution out of a superabundant thing.] For greater caution. By way of being more cautious. See **ad abundantiorem cautelam**.

ad certum diem *adv.* [L. **ad** to, for (1); **certum** fixed, definite (2); **diem** day (3): for a fixed day.] For a set date. *In view of the impending transfer of the judge, hearing of the murder case was set ad certum diem.*

ad colligenda bona *adj.* [L. **ad** to, for (1); **colligenda** to be collected (3); **bona** the goods (2): for the goods to be collected.] *Law.* In order to collect the goods. To collect the goods. *An administrator ad colligenda bona is one who has been permitted to collect the property of a deceased person, particularly perishable goods, when the normal administration cannot be approved immediately.*

ad colligendum *adj.* [L. **ad** to, at, for, according to (1); **colligendum** collecting (2): for collecting.] *Law.* For the purpose of collecting. Used for describing trustees and administrators.

ad crumenam *adj.* [L. **ad** to, at, for, according to (1); **crumenam** money-bag, purse (2): for the money-bag.] *Logic.* To the purse. Applicable to an argument designed to appeal to the audience's preoccupation with monetary matters. See **argumentum ad crumenam**.

add. *abbr.* for **addenda** See **addendum**.

addendum *n., pl.* **addenda** [L. that which must be added.] A thing that is to be added or is added. An addition. An appendix. *He submitted a fifteen-page addendum to his original petition.*

ad defendendum *adv.* [L. **ad** to, at, for, according to (1); **defendendum** defending (2): for defending.] To defend.

ad diem *adv.* [L. **ad** to, at, for, according to (1); **diem** day (2): at the day.] At the appointed day. *The meeting will certainly take place ad diem.*

ad ea quae frequentius accidunt jura adaptantur. [L. **ad** to, for (3); **ea** those (things) (4); **quae** which (5); **frequentius** rather often (7); **accidunt** happen, occur (6); **jura** rights, laws (1); **adaptantur** are adapted (2): Laws are adapted to cases which occur rather often.] Laws are adapted to usual rather than unusal circumstances.

ad effectum *abbr.* **ad effect.** [L. **ad** to, at, for, according to (1); **effectum** effect (2): to effect.] To the effect. To the end. Until effective.

ad effectum sequentem [L. **ad** to, at, for, according to (1); **effectum** effect (3); **sequentem** following (2): to the following effect.] To the following end.

adeste, fideles / laeti triumphantes / venite, venite in Bethlehem. [L. **adeste** be present (1); **fideles** faithful (2); **laeti** joyful, happy (3); **triumphantes** triumphant, victorious (4); **venite** come (5); **venite** come (6); **in** into, to, against, for (7); **Bethlehem** Bethlehem (8): Be present, O faithful, / joyful, triumphant (ones). / Come, come to Bethlehem.] O come, all ye faithful, / joyful and triumphant. / O come ye, O come ye, to Bethlehem. A Christmas carol.

ad eund. *abbr.* for **ad eundem gradum** (q.v.).

ad eundem gradum or **ad eundem** *adj./adv.* [L. **ad** to, at, for, according to (1); **eundem** the same (2); **gradum** rank (3): to the same degree or class.] Used particularly for the granting of an honorary degree by a university to a person who actually studied elsewhere.

à deux *adj.* [Fr. **à** to, toward, in, by, with, until (1); **deux** two (2): by two.] For only two persons. Done intimately or privately between two persons. Applicable to meals, discussions, meetings, etc. a) *Oblivious to the presence of others, the lovers devoted the whole* *evening to conversation à deux.* b) *John and Mary settled their differences during a quiet dinner à deux.* —*adv.* Intimately or privately among only two persons. *John and Mary had a nice evening, dining and dancing à deux.* Cf. **à trois.**

ad extremum *adv.* [L. **ad** to, at, for, according to (1); **extremum** the last, extreme (2): to the last.] To the very end. *In the court, counsel for the accused dragged the same argument ad extremum.* Cf. **in extremis.**

ad filum aquae *adv.* [L. **ad** to, at, for, according to (1); **filum** thread (2); **aquae** of water (3): to the thread of the water.] *Law.* To the middle or central line of the stream. When the boundary between the lands of land-owners is formed by a non-tidal stream or river, it is presumed that the boundary is an imaginary line along the center of the stream or river. See **ad medium filum aquae; filum aquae; usque ad filum aquae;** and **usque ad medium filum aquae.** Cf. **ad filum viae; ad medium filum viae; filum viae;** and **usque ad filum viae.**

ad filum viae *adv.* [L. **ad** to, at, for, according to (1); **filum** thread (2); **viae** of way, road (3): to the thread of the way.] *Law.* To the middle of the way/road. To the central line of the way/road. When the boundary between the lands of land-owners is formed by a road, it is presumed that the boundary is an imaginary line along the center of the road, subject, of course, to the rights of the local authorities and the public. Cf. **ad filum aquae.**

ad finem *abbr.* **ad fin.** or **a. f.** *adv.* [L. **ad** to, at, for, according to (1); **finem** end (2): to the end.] Used in bibliographical citations to indicate that the reader should continue from a point to the end of a section.

ad fundandam jurisdictionem *adv.* [L. **ad** to, at, for, according to (1); **fundandam** to be founded (3); **jurisdictionem** jurisdiction (2): for the jurisdiction to be founded.] In order to establish the basis of jurisdiction. *Counsel for the plaintiff advanced a preliminary point ad fundandam jurisdictionem.*

ad Graecas Kalendas [L. **ad** to, at, for, according to (2); **Graecas** Greek (3); **Kalendas** Calends (4): on the Greek Calends.] Never. *It will come to pass ad Graecas Kalendas.* Cf. **ad Graecas Kalendas soluturos.**

ad Graecas Kalendas soluturos Augustus Caesar (63 B.C.–14 A.D.). [L. **ad** to, at, for, according to (2); **Graecas** Greek (3); **Kalendas** Calends (4); **soluturos** those about to pay (1): those about to pay on the Greek Calends.] They will pay their debts on the Greek Calends; i.e., they will never pay their debts, since in the Greek calendar there was no Calends, the first day of the Roman month and the traditional day for making debt payments.

ad h. l. *abbr.* for **ad hunc locum** (q.v.).

ad hoc *adv.* [L. **ad** to, at, for, according to (1); **hoc** this (2): for this.] For this particular purpose. For this

particular occasion. *At the meeting a special number of investigators were appointed ad hoc to consider the matter.* —*adj.* Made, appointed, established, constituted for, or dealing with, a particular purpose. *He urged the need to adopt a well considered policy rather than ad hoc plans.*

ad hominem *adj.* [L. **ad** to, at, for, according to (1); **hominem** person (2): to the person.] *Logic.* Designed to arouse emotions, or directed against a person. An ad hominem argument is an argument in which the speaker attacks his opponent's character and concentrates on exploiting the audience's prejudices instead of dwelling on issues or his opponent's contentions. *No doubt, the role of the courts in the application of law in the settlement of disputes would be seriously whittled down if ad hominem legislation were to be made the general practice* (Nwabueze 1982:212). See **argumentum ad hominem.**

ad hunc locum *abbr.* **ad h. l.** or **a. h. l.** *adv.* [L. **ad** to, at, for, according to (1); **hunc** this (2); **locum** place (3): at this place.] On this passage.

ad idem *adj./adv.* [L. **ad** to, at, for, according to (1); **idem** the same (2): to the same.] Of the same mind. Agreed. In agreement. The expression is used with reference to the making of contracts. a) *The two sides were not ad idem; so the negotiation failed.* b) *The court held that the parties were never ad idem as to the subject matter of the proposed sale, and that the contract was therefore void* (Ezejiofor et al. 1982:54). See **assensio mentium; consensus ad idem;** and **idem.**

adieu *interj.* [Fr. **à** to, toward, in, by, with, until (1); **Dieu** God: with God.] I entrust you to God. Go with God. Goodbye! Farewell! *Adieu, James!* —*n., pl.* **adieux** or **adieus** 1. Farewell. Leave-taking. a) *The memorable but painful ceremony was climaxed by an emotional scene in which the final-year students made their adieus.* b) *. . . he bade adieu to film-making to work with video in 1972* (*Newsweek Int.* Nov. 12, 1979: 59). 2. *Law.* Used for final and complete dismissal from court. See **à bientôt.** Cf. **adiós.**

ad impossibilia *adv.* [L. **ad** to, at, for, according to (1); **impossibilia** impossible (things) (2): to impossible things.] To the impossible. *Generally, children should be encouraged to work hard, but they should not be urged on ad impossibilia.*

ad infinitum *adv./adj.* [L. **ad** to, at, for, according to (1); **infinitum** the infinite (2): to the infinite.] Without end. Endlessly. Indefinitely. a) *The speaker kept talking ad infinitum.* b) *Theoretically, the consequences of any conduct may be endless, but no defendant is responsible ad infinitum for all the consequences of his wrongful conduct . . .* (Rogers 1975:88). Cf. **in infinitum.**

ad initium *abbr.* **ad init.** *adv.* [L. **ad** to, at, for, according to (1); **initium** beginning (2): at the beginning.] At the beginning, from the start.

ad inquirendum *n.* [L. **ad** to, at, for, according to (1); **inquirendum** inquiring (2): for inquiring.] For investigation or inquiry. *Law.* A writ ordering that inquiry be conducted into a matter. Cf. **ad melius inquirendum**.

ad interim *abbr.* **A. I.** or **a. i.** or **ad int.** *adv.* [L. **ad** to, at, for, according to (1); **interim** meanwhile, in the meantime (2): for the meanwhile.] Provisionally. Temporarily. In the meantime. *The committee served ad interim.* —*adj.* Temporary. Effective, pending a permanent arrangement. *An ad interim committee was appointed.*

adiós or **adios** *interj.* [Sp. **adiós** from **a** to, toward, in, by, with, until (1); **Diós** God (2): with God.] I entrust you to God. Go with God. Goodbye! Farewell! See **à bientot**. Cf. **adieu**.

aditus *n., pl.* **aditus** or **adituses** [L. entrance, passage.] Entry.

ad lib. *abbr.* for **ad libitum** (q.v.).

ad libitum *abbr.* **ad lib.** *adv.* [L. **ad** to, at, for, according to (1); **libitum** pleasure (2): at pleasure.] In accordance with a person's wishes. As much as one pleases or desires. —*adj.* Done, said, devised, etc. spontaneously. *An ad lib. discussion.* —*n., pl.* **ad libs** Things done, said, devised, etc. spontaneously. *The ad libs in the comedy routine were hilarious.* —*v.* To act spontaneously. *He ad libbed the response.*

ad limina [L. **ad** to, at, for, according to (1); **limina** thresholds (2): to the thresholds.] 1. *Christianity.* A pilgrimage to the tombs of St. Peter and St. Paul in Rome. 2. *Christianity.* A trip to Rome by a bishop to provide the Pope with a report on conditions in his diocese. 3. A trip to company headquarters or a report or appeal to the board of directors, president, or some high authority in an organization. *The district manager's appeal ad limina led to a policy change by the board of directors.*

ad litem *adj./adv.* [L. **ad** to, at, for, according to (1); **litem** suit, action (2): for the suit.] *Law.* For the legal suit. *A guardian ad litem is usually appointed to act for a minor who is sued.* See **administrator ad litem**.

ad litem decidendam *adv.* [L. **ad** to, at, for, according to (1); **litem** suit, action (2); **decidendam** to be decided, to be determined (3): for the suit to be determined.] *Law.* For the determination of the legal suit.

ad litis decisionem *adv.* [L. **ad** to, at, for, according to (1); **litis** of suit, action (3); **decisionem** determination, settlement (2): for determination of the suit.] *Law.* For the settlement/determination of the legal suit.

ad litis ordinationem *adv.* [L. **ad** to, at, for, according to (1); **litis** of suit, action (3); **ordinationem** arrangement, disposition (2): for the arrangement of the suit.] *Law.* For the disposition of the legal suit.

ad locum *abbr.* **ad loc.** [L. **ad** to, at, for, according to (1); **locum** place (2): to the place.] At the place. Used to indicate location in a book.

ad majorem cautelam *adv.* [L. **ad** to, at, for, according to (1); **majorem** greater (2); **cautelam** caution,

security (3): for greater caution.] For greater caution or security. See **ad abundantiorem cautelam**.

ad majorem Dei gloriam *abbr.* **A.M.D.G.** [L. **ad** to, at, for, according to (1); **majorem** greater (2); **Dei** of God (4); **gloriam** glory (3): for the greater glory of God.] For the greater glory of God. Motto of the Society of Jesus (the Jesuits).

ad majorem patriae gloriam *adv.* [L. **ad** to, at, for, according to (1); **majorem** greater (2); **patriae** of fatherland, native land (4); **gloriam** glory (3): for the greater glory of the fatherland.] For the greater glory of the country. *Victory . . . had once glorified only the family of the winner; but now, as the whole citizen community felt itself to be one family, victory served ad majorem patriae gloriam* (Jaeger 1970:108).

ad manum *adj.* [L. **ad** to, at, for, according to (1); **manum** hand (2): at hand.] Handy. Ready to be used.

ad manum mortuam *adv.* [L. **ad** to, at, for, according to (1); **manum** hand (3); **mortuam** dead (2): to a dead hand.] In mortmain.

ad medium filum aquae [L. **ad** to, at, for, according to (1); **medium** middle (2); **filum** thread (3); **aquae** of water (4): to the middle thread of the water.] *Law.* To the middle line of the stream. Applicable to ownership of the soil of a river's bed when a running stream separates lands owned by two persons. Each owner owns the soil up to the middle of the stream. See **ad filum aquae**.

ad medium filum viae [L. **ad** to, at, for, according to (1); **medium** middle (2); **filum** thread (3); **viae** of way, road, path (4): to the middle thread of the way.] To the middle of the road. Cf. **ad filum aquae**.

ad melius inquirendum *n.* [L. **ad** to, at, for, according to (1); **melius** better (3); **inquirendum** examining, investigating (2): for examining better.] For better investigation or inquiry. *Law.* A writ asking a coroner to conduct an inquest again. Cf. **ad inquirendum**.

administrator or *fem.* **administratrix** *n., pl.* **administrators** or *fem.* **administratrices** The Latin masc. pl. **administratores** is not common in English. [L. manager, conductor.] 1. *Law.* A person legally appointed by a court to manage the estate of a deceased person. 2. A person engaged in administrative work as a) a person empowered to govern a colony; b) an official who directs the affairs of an institution, a business organization, a government agency, etc.; c) a priest authorized to manage temporarily the affairs of a church.

administrator ad colligendum bona defuncti *n.* [L. **administrator** manager, conductor (1); **ad** to, at, for, according to (2); **colligendum** collecting (5); **bona** goods, property (3); **defuncti** of the deceased (4): manager for collecting the goods of the deceased.] *Law.* One who supervises the collection of the property of a deceased person. *Between the burial and the final obsequies, a period of two to three weeks* *normally elapses. The head of the appropriate extended family acts as a sort of administrator ad colligendum bona defuncti who supervises the proper custody and preservation of the goods of the deceased until a successor is appointed duly authorised to administer them* (Bentsi-Enchill 1964:164).

administrator ad litem *n.* [L. **administrator** manager, conductor (1); **ad** to, at, for, according to (2); **litem** action, suit (3): manager for the action.] *Law.* One who supervises a legal suit. Applicable to one appointed a special administrator to represent an estate in an action because either there is no executor or the executor is incapable of acting. See **ad litem.**

administrator pendente lite *n.* [L. **administrator** manager, conductor (1); **pendente** (with) pending (3); **lite** with suit (2): manager with a suit pending.] *Law.* An administrator appointed to manage the estate of a decedent temporarily when a suit on intestacy has not been determined.

administratrix *fem.* of **administrator** (q.v.).

ad misericordiam *adj./adv.* [L. **ad** to, at, for, according to (1); **misericordiam** pity, compassion, mercy (2): for pity.] Applicable to an argument or a plea for mercy. *The defense attorney's arguments ad misericordiam had no effect whatsoever on the judge.*

Admodum Reverendus or **Reverendus Admodum** *abbr.* **Adm. Rev.** *adj.* [L. **admodum** very, exceedingly (1); **reverendus** reverend (2): very reverend.] Very Reverend. Title applied to a member of the clergy.

ad nauseam *adv.* [L. **ad** to, at, for, according to (1); **nauseam** disgust, seasickness (2): to disgust.] To the point of sickness. In a disgusting/sickening manner. *He kept harping on one aspect of the matter ad nauseam.*

ad non executa *adv.* [L. **ad** to, at, for, according to (1); **non** not (2); **ex(s)ecuta** (things) executed (3): for the things not executed.] *Law.* For the things which have not been executed by an executor. *The Administrator of Estates was appointed ad non executa in regard to the estate of the deceased.*

ad officium justiciariorum spectat, unicuique coram eis placitanti justitiam exhibere. [L. to, at, for, according to (2); **officium** duty (3); **justi(t)iariorum** of justices (4); **spectat** it pertains, relates (1); **unicuique** to each individual, everyone (7); **coram** before, in the presence of (9); **eis** them (10); **placitanti** pleading (8); **justitiam** justice (6); **exhibere** to deliver, administer (5): It pertains to the duty of justices to deliver justice to everyone pleading before them.] *Law.* It is the duty of justices to deliver justice to every individual who pleads before them. See **justitia nemini** etc.

ad omnia tempora *adv.* [L. **ad** to, at, for, according to (1); **omnia** all (2); **tempora** times (3): at all times.] For all times. Always. *Judicial precedents are established to assist the courts ad omnia tempora.*

Adonis *n.* [Gk.] 1. *Greek and Roman Mythology.* A youth so handsome that he captured the love of Aphrodite (Venus), goddess of love. *Very few women can resist Ademola's sex appeal. He has the face of Adonis and the strength of Hercules.* 2. A very handsome young man. *Mustapha, the Adonis of the campus, is pursued by beautiful young ladies to such an extent that he hardly gets time for his studies.*

adoptio *n.* [L. adoption.] *Law.* Legal process in which a child transfers his legal rights and duties from his natural parents to adoptive parents. Adoption in England is entirely the creature of statute. No provision for it was made until 1926. *English law thus differs sharply from civil law systems which, inheriting the Roman concepts of adoptio and adrogatio, recognise legal transfers from one family group to another* (Cretney 1976:383). See **adrogatio.**

ad personam *adj./adv.* [L. **ad** to, at, for, according to (1); **personam** person (2): to the person.] *Logic.* **Ad hominem** (q.v.). Designed to excite emotions and appealing to personal prejudices and sentiments, instead of concentrating on issues. Applicable to an argument.

ad pios usus *adv.* [L. **ad** to, at, for, according to (1); **pios** religious (2); **usus** uses, benefits (3): for religious uses.] For religious purposes. For charitable or pious purposes. Applicable to donations, bequests, etc. *The Deacon donated the sum of $500,000 ad pios usus.*

ad prosequendam *adv., short form* for **ad litem prosequendam** [L. **ad** to, at, for, according to (1); **litem** suit, case (2); **prosequendam** to be prosecuted (3): for a suit to be prosecuted.] *Law.* In order to prosecute a suit. To prosecute. *It was such a crucial case that the Attorney General himself appeared in court with a team ad prosequendam.*

ad punctum temporis *adv.* [L. **ad** to, at, for, according to (1); **punctum** point (2); **temporis** of time (3): at the point of time.] At an instant. At a moment. At the smallest portion of time.

ad quaestionem facti non respondent judices; ad quaestionem juris non respondent juratores. [L. **ad** to, at, for, according to (4); **quaestionem** question (5); **facti** of fact, deed (6); **non** not (2); **respondent** answer (3); **judices** judges (1); **ad** to, at, for, according to (10); **quaestionem** question (11); **juris** of right, law (12); **non** not (8); **respondent** answer, respond (9); **juratores** jurors (7): Judges do not respond to a question of fact; jurors do not respond to a question of law.] *Law.* Judges do not answer to a question of fact; jurors do not answer to a question of law; i.e., jurors decide questions of fact, while judges decide questions of law. See **ad quaestiones legis** etc.; **de jure judices** etc.; **juratores sunt judices facti**; and **quemadmodum ad quaestionem** etc. Cf. **veritas habenda** etc.

ad quaestiones legis judices, et non juratores, respondent. [L. **ad** to, at, for, according to (3); **quaestiones** questions (4); **legis** of law (5); **judices** judges (1); **et** and (6); **non** not (7); **juratores** jurors (8); **respondent** answer, respond (2): Judges respond to questions of law, and not jurors.] *Law.* Judges, not jurors, decide questions of law. See **ad quaestionem facti** etc.

ad quem *adj./adv.* [L. **ad** to, at, for, according to (1); **quem** whom, which (2): to which.] To which date or time. Cf. **dies a quo.**

ad referendum *adv.* [L. **ad** to, at, for, according to (1); **referendum** referring (2): for referring.] For further consideration. *The docket was sent back to the Attorney General ad referendum.*

ad rem *adv./adj.* [L. **ad** to, at, for, according to (1); **rem** matter, thing, property, business, affair (2): to the thing.] To the point. Without digression. To the purpose. Relevant to the matter being discussed. —*adv. His shallow-mindedness is suggested by his inability to speak ad rem.* —*adj. It is a very convincing ad rem argument.*

adrogatio *n.* [L. adrogation.] *Civil Law.* The adoption of a person who is under age (*impubes*), i.e., a boy who is less than fourteen years old and a girl under twelve years of age. See **adoptio.**

adroit *adj.* [Fr. from à to, toward, in, by, with, until (1); **droit** right (2): toward the right.] Right-handed. Skillful. Clever.

ads. *abbr.* for **ad sectam** (q.v.).

adscriptus glebae *n., pl.* **adscripti glebae** [L. **adscriptus** added, assigned (1); **glebae** to land (2): assigned to the land.] An ancient Roman slave attached to, cultivating, and to be transferred with, the land.

ad sectam *abbr.* **ads.** [L. **ad** to, at, for, according to (1); **sectam** side, party (2): at the side.] *Law.* At the suit of. Used in the title of a case when the defendant's name appears first (e. g., Smith **ads.** Jones, instead of Smith v. Jones).

adstante febre *abbr.* **adst. feb.** [L. **adstante** (with) being at hand, existing (2); **febre** with fever (1): with fever being at hand.] *Medicine.* When there is fever.

ad summam *adv.* [L. **ad** to, at, for, according to (1); **summam** the top, summit (2): at the top.] On the whole. Generally. In short. In a word. In conclusion. *He submitted, ad summam, that he would not defend the action.*

ad terminum annorum *adv.* [L. **ad** to, at, for, according to (1); **terminum** term, end (2); **annorum** of years (3): for a term of years.] For a specific number of years. *A lease is usually granted ad terminum annorum.*

adulterinus *n., pl.* **adulterini** [L. false, not genuine person.] An adulterine person. A person born to parents who are not legally married to each other. *Section 1 of the Legitimacy Act 1959 applies only to legitimation of the issue of adulterous unions. Its subsection (2), therefore . . . deals with adulterini* (Graveson 1974:373).

ad unum omnes *n.* [L. **ad** to, at, for, according to (2); **unum** one (person) (3); **omnes** all (1): all to one person.] Everyone.

ad us. ext. *abbr.* for **ad usum externum** (q.v.).

ad usum externum *abbr.* **ad us. ext.** *adj.* [L. **ad** for, to (1); **usum** use (3); **externum** external, outward (2): for external use.] *Medicine.* For external application. Not to be taken internally.

ad val. *abbr.* for **ad valorem** (q.v.).

ad valorem *abbr.* **adv.** or **ad val.** *adj.* [L. **ad** to, at, for, according to (1); **valorem** strength (2): according to strength.] According to, based on, or in proportion to the value. Used with respect to taxation (1) of goods on the basis of the value declared in the invoice and (2) of property on the basis of the assessed value. *The purchase tax on cars is usually ad valorem.*

adventitia bona *pl. n.* [L. **adventi(c)ia** accidental (1); **bona** goods (2): accidental goods.] *Roman Law.* Applicable to goods which one acquires by one's own exertions, as distinct from goods obtained by inheritance.

adventitia dos *n., pl.* **adventitiae dotes** [L. **adventi(c)ia** foreign, accidental (1); **dos** dowry (2): foreign dowry.] *Roman Law.* Dowry which is not derived from the property of the wife's father or paternal grandfather, but from any other source such as the estate of the wife herself or of the wife's mother. See **dos.**

ad ventrem inspiciendum [L. **ad** to, at, for, according to (1); **ventrem** belly, womb (2); **inspiciendum** to be inspected, to be examined (3): for a womb to be inspected.] For examining a womb. A writ summoning a jury of experienced elderly women to determine a pregnancy.

ad verbum *adj./adv.* [L. **ad** to, at, for, according to (1); **verbum** word (2): to a word.] Verbatim. Word for word.

ad verecundiam *adj./adv.* [L. **ad** to, at, for, according to (1); **verecundiam** modesty, bashfulness (2): for modesty.] Applicable to an argument for the sake of modesty.

ad vitam *adj./adv.* [L. **ad** to, at, for, according to (1); **vitam** life (2): for life.] For the duration of one's life. *The privileges were conferred on her ad vitam.* Cf. **autre vie.**

ad vitam aut culpam *adj./adv.* [L. **ad** to, at, for, according to (1); **vitam** life (2); **aut** or (3); **culpam** blame, fault (4): for life or fault.] For life or until terminated on account of misconduct. Originally used to qualify a feudal tenure and, subsequently, tenure of office. *Dictators who assume the title of "President for life" could at least be gracious enough to make it "President ad vitam aut culpam."*

ad vivum *adj.* [L. **ad** to, at, for, according to (1); **vivum** alive, living (person) (2): according to a living person.] *Painting.* Lifelike. Based on a living model.

advocatus Dei *n., pl.* **advocati Dei** [L. **advocatus** advocate, pleader (1); **Dei** of God (2): advocate of God.] God's advocate. Specifically, an official of the Roman Catholic Church entrusted with the duty of refuting arguments brought by the **advocatus diaboli** (q.v.) against the canonization or beatification of a person. Cf. **promotor fidei**.

advocatus diaboli *n., pl.* **advocati diaboli** [L. **advocatus** advocate, pleader (1); **diaboli** of devil (2): advocate of the devil.] 1. The devil's advocate. A person who looks for faults. 2. *Roman Catholic Church.* The advocate who argues against the canonization or beatification of a person. See **promotor fidei**. Cf. **advocatus Dei**.

ad voluntatem [L. **ad** to, at, for, according to (1); **voluntatem** will, consent (2): at will.] At the consent.

ad voluntatem domini *adv.* [L. **ad** to, at, for, according to (1); **voluntatem** will, consent (2); **domini** of lord, master (3): at the will of the master.] At the will or consent of the lord, master, or owner.

adytum (L.) or **adyton** (Gk.) *n., pl.* **adyta** [L. from Gk. **aduton**: **a-** no, not (1); **duō** enter (2): not to be entered.] 1. The innermost recess of a temple, sanctuary, or shrine which was accessible only to priests, and from which oracles were pronounced. 2. A private chamber. A place of retreat. An inner sanctum. A holy place. *It is nice to have an adytum, where one can retire and enjoy solitude, far away from the insanity of the crowd.* See **sanctum** and **sanctum sanctorum**.

A.E.D. *abbr.* for **Artium Elegantium Doctor** (q.v.).

aedificare in tuo proprio solo non licet quod alteri noceat. [L. **aedificare** to build erect (3); **in** on, in (4); **tuo** your (5); **proprio** own (6); **solo** soil, land, ground (7); **non** not (1); **licet** it is allowed, lawful (2); **quod** (that) which, what (8); **alteri** to another (10); **noceat** would do harm, hurt, injure (9): It is not lawful to build on your own land what would do harm to another.] *Law.* It is unlawful for a landowner to erect on his/her land a structure which infringes on the rights of others. See **sic utere tuo** etc.

aedificatum solo solo cedit. [L. **aedificatum** that which has been built (1); **solo** on ground, land (2); **solo** to ground, land (4); **cedit** accrues (3): That which has been built on the land accrues to the land.] *Law.* Any building erected on the land belongs to the land. See **quicquid plantatur** etc.

aedificia solo cedunt. [L. **aedificia** buildings, structures (1); **solo** to the land, soil (3); **cedunt** accrue (2): Buildings accrue to the land.] *Law.* Buildings belong to the owner of the land. See **quicquid plantatur** etc.

aegis or **aigis** *n., pl.* **aegises** or **aigises** [Gk. **aigis**.] 1. The goatskin shield of the god Zeus (Jupiter) usually used by his divine daughter Athena (Minerva). 2. Protection. Patronage. Sponsorship. Auspices. Shield. Favorable circumstances. *Some criminals perpetrate atrocities under the unholy aegis of highly placed members of the community.* 3. Leadership. Direction. Control. Guidance. *Optimists have been hoping that under the aegis of the President the economy will improve.*

aegrotat *n., pl.* **aegrotats** [L. He is sick.] 1. A medical certificate indicating that a student cannot attend lectures or perform any duty because of sickness. 2. A degree awarded to a candidate by a university when the student fails to take examinations for medical reasons.

aemulatio vicini *n., pl.* **aemulationes vicinorum** [L. **aemulatio** rivalry, competition (1); **vicini** of neighbor (2): rivalry of neighbor.] *Civil and Scots Law.* Exercising a legal right with the sole intention of annoying or harming another person.

aenigma *var.* of **enigma** (q.v.).

aeon or **eon** *n., pl.* **aeons** or **eons** [Gk. **aion** age, generation, long space of time.] Age. A very long span of time. a) *Mr Mensah waited for what seemed like an aeon before the good news of the birth of a baby boy was brought to him.* b) *He still remembers that day eons ago when he first met her.*

aequam servare mentem Horace (65–8 B.C.). *Odes* II,3,1–2. [L. **aequam** even, level (2); **servare** to keep, preserve (1); **mentem** mind (3): to keep an even mind.] To be level-headed. To remain undisturbed. *Life can be very tempestuous but, whatever happens, one should stick to the golden rule of aequam servare mentem.*

aequior est dispositio legis quam hominis. [L. **aequior** more equitable, fairer (4); **est** is (3); **dispositio** disposition, arrangement (1); **quam** than (5); **hominis** of person, human being (6): Disposition of law is fairer than (disposition) of a person.] *Law.* The disposition of the law is more equitable than that made by an individual person.

aequitas *n.* [L. equity, fairness, humanity.] *Civil Law.* Equity. Justice which conforms to natural law or right. See **aequum et bonum**; **aequum et bonum est lex legum**; **ex aequitate**; **ex aequo et bono**; and **secundum aequum et bonum**. Cf. **apex juris**; **ex rigore juris**; **strictum jus** and **summum jus**.

aequitas est correctio justae legis qua parte deficit quod generatim lata est. [L. **aequitas** equity (1); **est** is (2); **correctio** improvement, correction (3); **justae** of just (4); **legis** (of) law (5); **qua** in which (6); **parte** (in) part (7); **deficit** it is wanting, deficient, falls short (8); **quod** because (9); **generatim** generally, in general (11); **lata est** it was passed (10): Equity is a correction of just law in which part it is wanting because it was passed generally.] *Law.* Equity serves the purpose of correcting deficiencies in a law which, though just, becomes deficient in a particular situation, since it was passed to cover a general situation. See **aequitas est correctio legis** etc.

aequitas est correctio legis generaliter latae, qua parte deficit. [L. **aequitas** equity (1); **est** is (2); **correctio** correction (3); **legis** of law (4); **generaliter** generally (6); **latae** (of) passed (5); **qua** in which (7); **parte** (in) part (8); **deficit** it is wanting, deficient, falls short (9): Equity is a correction of the law passed generally in which part it is wanting.] *Law.* Equity serves the purpose of correcting deficiencies in a law passed to cover a general situation. See **aequitas est correctio justae legis** etc.

aequitas est perfecta quaedam ratio quae jus scriptum interpretatur et emendat; nulla scriptura comprehensa, sed sola ratione consistens. [L. **aequitas** equity, fairness (1); **est** is (2); **perfecta** perfect, excellent (3); **quaedam** a certain, a kind of, so to speak (5); **ratio** reason (4); **quae** which (6); **jus** right, law (11); **scriptum** written (10); **interpretatur** interprets (7); **et** and (8); **emendat** emends, corrects (9); **nulla** in no (13); **scriptura** (in) writing (14); **comprehensa** comprehended, perceived (12); **sed** but (15); **sola** alone (18); **ratione** (with) reason (17); **consistens** consisting in, consistent with (16): Fairness is a perfect reason, so to speak, which interprets and emends the written law; perceived in no writing but consistent with reason alone.] *Law.* Equity is a perfect kind of reason which interprets and corrects written law; it is comprehended by no writing but consists in reason alone.

aequitas non facit jus sed juri auxiliatur. [L. **aequitas** equity, fairness (1); **non** not (2); **facit** makes (3); **jus** law (4); **sed** but (5); **juri** right, law (7); **auxiliatur** assists (6): Fairness does not make law, but assists law.] *Law.* Equity does not make law, but it aids the law.

aequitas numquam contravenit leges. [L. **aequitas** equity, fairness (1); **numquam** never (2); **contravenit** contravenes, opposes (3); **leges** laws (4): Fairness never opposes laws.] *Law.* Equity never contravenes or counteracts the laws; i.e., equity supplements the law by, for instance, giving full relief in cases where the law merely gives relief partially.

aequitas sequitur legem. or **equitas sequitur legem.** [L. **aequitas** equity, fairness (1); **sequitur** follows (2); **legem** law (3): Fairness follows law.] *Law.* Equity follows the law. Applicable to interpretation of statutes and the construction of legal instruments. Cf. **lex aliquando** etc.

aequo animo *adv.* [L. **aequo** (with) fair, impartial (1); **animo** with mind (2): with fair mind.] With an equable mind. With equanimity. *He arbitrated the dispute between his wife and a neighbor aequo animo and adjudged his wife blameworthy.*

aequum et bonum *n.* [L. **aequum** the equitable (thing) (1); **et** and (2); **bonum** the good (thing) (3): The equitable and the good thing.] Equity. Fairness. See **aequitas.**

aequum et bonum est lex legum. [L. **aequum** the equitable (thing) (1); **et** and (2); **bonum** the good (thing)

(3); **est** is (4); **lex** law (5); **legum** of laws (6): The equitable and the good thing is the law of laws.] Equity, i.e., what is equitable and good, is the law of laws. See **aequitas.**

Aesculapius *n.* [L. from Gk. **Asklēpios.**] 1. *Greek and Roman Mythology.* Mortal son of the god Apollo by the unfaithful Koronis. The father of medicine. 2. A medical practitioner. A physician.

aetatis suae [L. **aetatis** (of) age (2); **suae** (of) one's own, his/her (1): of one's own age.] At the age of. Used to indicate the age of the deceased on tombstones or the age of the subject on artwork. Cf. **anno aetatis suae.**

a.f. *abbr.* for 1. **actum fide** (q.v.). 2. **ad finem** (q.v.).

affaire *n., pl.* **affaires** [Fr. affair, matter, scandal.] 1. A love affair or **affaire d'amour** (q.v.). *Ever since the traumatic end of her engagement to William, Comfort has been flitting from one affaire to another.* 2. A scandalous matter. An affair, episode, or matter which arouses general dispute, anxiety, speculation, etc. Usually used with names of persons. a) *the Ali affaire*; b) *the Jones affaire*; c) *the Ajadu affaire*; d) *the Monica Lewinsky affaire.* See **l'affaire.**

affaire d'amour *n., pl.* **affaires d'amour** [Fr. **affaire** affair, matter (1); **d'** of (2); **amour** love (3): a matter of love.] A love affair. A romantic attachment of a man to a woman or vice versa, which is usually of a short duration. An immoral sexual relationship. Cf. **affaire de coeur.**

affaire de coeur *n., pl.* **affaires de coeur** [Fr. **affaire** affair, matter (1); **de** of (2); **coeur** heart, soul (3): affair of heart.] A romantic affair or a love affair, usually of a short duration. **Affaire d'amour** (q.v.).

affaire d'honneur *n., pl.* **affaires d'honneur** [Fr. **affaire** affair, matter (1); **d'** of (2); **honneur** honor (3): matter or affair of honor.] A matter which involves honor. A duel. *An affaire d'honneur led to the premature death of Alexander Hamilton (1757–1804) at the hands of Aaron Burr (1756–1836).*

affectus punitur licet non sequatur effectus. [L. **affectus** disposition (1); **punitur** is punished (2); **licet** even if, although (3); **non** not (5); **sequatur** may follow (6); **effectus** result, accomplishment (4): The disposition is punished even if the result may not follow.] *Law.* The intention is punished, even if the desired result is not accomplished. See **actus non facit** etc.

afficionado *var.* of **aficionado** (q.v.).

affidavit *n., pl.* **affidavits** [L. He has made an oath. He has pledged his faith.] A written statement, signed and sworn to by the deponent in the presence of an authorized officer, such as a commissioner for oaths or magistrate. It usually shows the name and address of the deponent as well as the statement. *The President provided evidence in the case by means of affidavit.*

affirmanti, non neganti, incumbit probatio. [L. **affirmanti** (on, to) the one affirming, asserting (3); **non** not (4); **neganti** (on, to) the one denying (5);

incumbit weighs upon, oppresses (2); **probatio** proof (1): Proof weighs on the one affirming, not on the one denying.] The burden of proof lies on the one who affirms, not on the one who denies; i.e., it is incumbent upon a person who makes an allegation to prove it by adducing relevant evidence. See **actori incumbit** etc.

affirmantis est probare. [L. **affirmantis** of the one asserting, affirming (2); **est** it is (1); **probare** to prove (3): It is of the one asserting to prove.] It is the obligation of the one who makes an assertion to prove it. See **actori incumbit** etc.

affirmatio unius exclusio est alterius. [L. **affirmatio** affirmation (1); **unius** of one (2); **exclusio** exclusion (4); **est** is (3); **alterius** of the other (5): Affirmation of one is exclusion of the other.] *Law.* The affirmation of the one is or implies the exclusion of the other. See **designatio unius** etc.

afflatus *n., pl.* **afflatus** or **afflatuses** [L. from **ad** to, at, for, according to (2) and **flatus** blowing, breathing (1): blowing to.] Inspiration. Strength, knowledge, or power supernaturally imparted. Divine impulse or revelation. *He rarely contributes to discussions but, whenever he does, his contribution seems to be fired by an inexplicable afflatus.* See **inflatus**.

aficionado or **afficionado** or *fem.* **aficionada** or **afficionada** *n., pl.* **aficionados** or **afficionados** or *fem.* **aficionadas** or **afficionadas** [Sp. amateur.] 1. An enthusiastic admirer of bullfighting. 2. A fan. An enthusiastic admirer, supporter, follower, or champion. a) *Michael Jackson aficionados.* b) *Diana Ross aficionadas.* c) *Felix Liberty aficionados.* d) *Though the soccer match was scheduled to begin at 4.00 p.m., afficionados of the sport started entering the stadium as early as 10:00 a.m.* e) *For the aficionados, disco fever is far more than a Saturday night phenomenon* (*Newsweek Int.* Jan. 1, 1979:56).

à fond *adv.* [Fr. **à** to, toward, in, by, with, until (1); **fond** bottom (2): to bottom.] To the bottom. Thoroughly. Through and through. To the utmost. Up to the hilt. Exhaustively. a) *The lecturer knows his field à fond.* b) *He is such a dedicated leader that his followers support him à fond.*

a fortiori *adv.* [L. **a** from, by (1); **fortiori** the stronger (2): from the stronger.] Much more. With a stronger or greater reason. All the more certainly. *If a man is prejudiced, a fortiori, his mental vision is limited. —adj.* More certain or conclusive. a) *a fortiori proof.* b) *a fortiori argument.* See **a multo fortiori**.

Afrique Occidentale Française *abbr.* **A.O.F.** *n.* [Fr. **Afrique** Africa (3); **Occidentale** West (2); **Française** French (1): French West Africa.] The French colonies in West Africa or the areas of Africa once under French colonial control.

agape *n., pl.* **agapae** or **agapai** or **agapes** [Gk. **agapē** love, love of God for man, love feast.] 1. Love feast or common feast of fellowship observed by the early

Christians. It included prayers, songs, readings from the Scripture, and donations for the poor. 2. Genuine fraternal love among Christians. 3. Spontaneous and altruistic love, which considers neither the benefit to be derived nor the merit of the one loved. 4. God's love for man. See **caritas**.

agapemone *n., pl.* **agapemones** [Neo-Gk. from Gk. **agapē** love (1); **monē** station (2): love-station.] An institution or place where free love is practiced. Derived from the name given to a settlement founded c.1849 at Spaxton in England which was notorious for immorality or the practice of free love. *Stella brought infamy to the respectable Drobu clan by converting the mansion inherited from her father into an agapemone.*

agenda *n., pl.* **agendas** (**Agenda** is plural in Latin but is often used as a singular in English.) [L. things that must be done.] A list of matters to be discussed or things to be done, especially at a meeting. Program. Memorandum book. *Before each meeting the secretary despatches copies of the agenda to members.*

agenesia *n.* [Gk. **a-** no, not (1); **genesis** creation, beginning (2): no creation.] *Medicine.* Inability to reproduce, whether in man or woman. See **impotentia generandi.** Cf. **anaphrodisia**.

agent de change *n., pl.* **agents de change** [Fr. **agent** agent (1); **de** of (2); **change** exchange (3): agent of exchange.] 1. A stockbroker. An exchange broker. A licensed broker who, in some European countries, especially in France, is a member of the board constituting the official **bourse** (q.v.). 2. A dealer in the exchange of currency.

agentes et consentientes pari poena plectentur. [L. **agentes** acting (1); **et** and (2); **consentientes** consenting, agreeing (3); **pari** with/by equal (5); **poena** (with/by) punishment (6); **plectentur** shall be punished (4): Acting and consenting shall be punished with equal punishment.] *Law.* Acting and consenting parties suffer the same penalty. See **qui non improbat, approbat**.

agent provocateur *n., pl.* **agents provocateurs** [Fr. **agent** agent (2); **provocateur** provocative; provoking (1): provocative or provoking agent.] A spy. An undercover man. A secret agent. A professional or hired agitator. A person employed to infiltrate an organization or to associate with suspected persons and, by pretending to be sympathetic, to collect evidence against them or to incite them to illegal action which would result in their arrest and punishment. a) *One characteristic feature of the reign of tyrants is the covert appointment of agents provocateurs who, pretending to be friends, collect incriminating information from unwary citizens and report to the authorities.* b) *. . . overeager investigators can become agents provocateurs inciting crimes that otherwise would not have been committed* (*Newsweek Int.* Feb. 18, 1980:26).

aggiornamento *n., pl.* **aggiornamentos** [It. updating.] The bringing up to date or modernization of an institution or an organization, especially applied to the Roman Catholic Church during the Second Vatican Council (1962–1965).

agitprop *short form* of **otdel agitatsii i propagandy** *n.* [Russ. **(otdel)** agency (3); **agit(atsii)** agitation (1); **(i)** and (2); **prop(agandy)** propaganda (3): agitation and propaganda agency.] 1. Political propaganda. Communist propaganda in particular. 2. The government agency which disseminates such propaganda.

agnomen *n., pl.* **agnomina** [L. from **ad** to, at, for, according to (2) and **nomen** name (1): a name for, an additional name.] 1. An addition to the three normal names of a Roman, e.g., *Africanus* in *Publius Cornelius Scipio Africanus.* 2. An epithet. A nickname. *Margaret Thatcher's agnomen was the Iron Lady.* Cf. **nomen.**

agnosia *n.* [Gk. **a-** no, not (1); **gnosis** knowledge (2): no knowledge, ignorance, lack of acquaintance.] *Medicine.* Inability, either complete or partial, to recognize things through the senses of sight, hearing, or touching. It is usually caused by brain damage.

Agnus Dei *n.* [L. **agnus** lamb (1); **Dei** of God (2): lamb of God.] 1. Lamb of God. A reference to Jesus as the sacrificial Pascal lamb and the first words of a prayer for mercy and peace in many Christian liturgies. 2. A musical composition based upon this prayer.

agora *n., pl.* **agorae** or **agoras** [Gk. assembly, a place of assembly, a marketplace.] 1. An ancient Greek marketplace. 2. A place of assembly. A place where people meet for social or political functions. *The World Wide Web is quickly becoming an electronic agora.*

agoraphobia *n.* [Neo-Gk. from Gk. **agora** market-place (2); **phob(os)** fear (1): fear of the market-place.] *Psychology.* Abnormal fear of being in, or crossing, open places or spaces. Cf. **claustrophobia.**

agrapha *pl. n.* (*sing.* **agraphon**) [Gk. **a-** no, not (1); **grapha** written, things written (2): not written, unwritten things.] Sayings of Jesus Christ which are not recorded in the canonical gospels but can be found in other Christian writings. Cf. **apocrypha.**

a gratia *adj./adv.* [L. **a** by, from (1); **gratia** grace (2): by grace.] Not by right. *The tenant occupies the house a gratia.*

A.H. *abbr.* for 1. **Anno Hebraico** (q.v.). 2. **Anno Hegirae** (q.v.).

a.h.l. *abbr.* for **ad hunc locum** (q.v.).

A.H.S. *abbr.* for **Anno humanae salutis** (q.v.).

à huis clos *adv./adj.* [Fr. **à** to, toward, in, by, with, until (1); **huis** door (3); **clos** closed (2): in a closed door.] Behind a closed door. Secretly. **In camera** (q.v.). Cf. **Huis Clos.**

A.I. *abbr.* for **anno inventionis** (q.v.).

A.I. or **a.i.** *abbr.* for **ad interim** (q.v.).

aid-de-camp *var.* of **aide-de-camp** (q.v.).

aide *abbr.* for **aide-de-camp** (q.v.).

aide-de-camp or **aid-de-camp** *abbr.* **A.D.C.** or **ADC** or **a.d.c.** or **aide** *n., pl.* **aides-de-camp** or **aids-de-camp** or **aides** [Fr. **aide** aide, assistant (1); **de** of (2); **camp** camp (3): assistant of the camp.] 1. A military or naval officer who serves as a superior 'officer's assistant or attendant. *Mrs. Fobo resents the constant intrusion upon the privacy of her family by her husband's aide-de-camp, Captain Sawu.* 2. A person who serves as the confidential assistant of a higher officer, such as a President, Prime Minister, Minister, or diplomat. *Each morning . . . he . . . sits down to a working breakfast with his aides . . .* (*Newsweek Int.* June 11, 1979:10).

aide-mémoire *n., pl.* **aide-mémoires** [Fr. **aide** aide, assistant (2); **mémoire** memory (1): memory aid.] 1. Something which aids the memory. A mnemonic device. An aid or help to the memory. 2. An outline or summary of significant aspects of a proposal or diplomatic communication. A memorandum. *All that seems to exist is an aide-memoire prepared by Crocker which has been seen and approved, but not even initialled, by Pretoria and Angola* (*New African* 1984). Cf. **memoria technica.**

Aide-toi, le Ciel t'aidera. Jean de la Fontaine (1621–1695). [Fr. **aide** help (1); **toi** yourself (2); **le** the (3); **Ciel** heaven; sky (4); **t'** you (6); **aidera** will help, aid (5): Help yourself; heaven will help you.] Heaven helps those who help themselves. Cf. **audentis fortuna juvat; fortis fortuna adjuvat;** and **On dit que** etc.

aikido *n.* [Japan. **ai** mutual (1); **ki** spirit (2); **do** art (3): mutual spirit art.] A Japanese form of self defense which takes advantage of an opponent's strength and body weight.

ailurophobia *n.* [Neo-Gk. from Gk. **ailuro(s)** cat (2); **phob(os)** fear (1): fear of cats.] *Psychology.* Inordinate fear of cats.

a justitia (quasi a quodam fonte) omnia jura emanant. [L. **a** from, by (1); **justitia** justice (2); **quasi** as if, as though (3); **a** from (4); **quodam** a certain (5); **fonte** fountain, spring (6); **omnia** all (7); **jura** rights, laws (8); **emanant** proceed, emanate, flow out (9): From justice, as though from a fountain, all rights flow.] All rights emanate from justice as from a spring or fountain.

A.L. *abbr.* for **anno lucis** (q.v.).

à la or **a la** *short form* of **à la mode de** (q.v.). [Fr. **à** to, toward, in, by, with, until (1); **la** the (2): in the (manner of).] After the manner of. Following the style of. In accordance with the fashion of. In the fashion of. As done by. a) *The chef prepares dishes in a variety of national styles, including à la chinoise, à la polonaise, à la russe, and à la florentine.* b) *She wore a suit à la Chanel and her hair à la Marie Antoinette.* c) *The computers were programmed to produce music à la Mozart and art à la Picasso.* d) *. . . it appears* the fireworks are "generating more light than heat" à la Chinweizu (The Guardian 1986). Cf. **à la française**.

à la carte abbr. **a.l.c.** adj./adv. [Fr. **à** to, toward, in, by, with, until (1); **la** the (2); **carte** card, bill, menu (3): by the menu.] By the card. By or from the bill of fare. Applicable to a meal ordered dish by dish or course by course, each of which is priced separately. a) *Terry and Sarah went to a restaurant where they celebrated her birthday with an à la carte dinner.* b) *They dined à la carte.*

à la française adj./adv., short form of **à la mode française** [Fr. **à** to, toward, in, by, with, until (1); **la** the (2); **mode** way, manner (4); **française** French (3): in the French way.] In the French manner, style, or fashion. After the French fashion or manner. a) *She prepared the sauce à la française.* b) *Leopold Senghor [1906–] . . . had indeed always said that there should be a commonwealth à la française . . . (West Africa 1986).*

alameda n., pl. **alamedas** [Sp. **álameda** a grove of poplar trees.] A boulevard or park, especially one which is tree-shaded.

alamo n., pl. **alamos** [Sp. **álamo** a poplar tree.] A popular or cottonwood tree, common in the southwestern U.S.A. **—the Alamo** A religious building constructed at a mission in San Antonio, Texas, after 1744. The site of a major battle in the war for Texas independence in 1836.**—Los Alamos** pl. An area north of Santa Fe, New Mexico, where the first atomic bombs were created during World War II.

à la mode adj. [Fr. **à** to, toward, in, by, with, until (1); **la** the (2); **mode** fashion (3): in the fashion.] Fashionable. In fashion. In vogue. Chic. Stylish. *He is a dashing young man who always wears à la mode French suits.* **—adv.** 1. According to, or in accordance with, the latest fashion, conventions,or ideas. 2. *American.* With ice cream. *Pie à la mode.*

à la mode de [Fr. **à** to, toward, in, by, with, until (1); **la** the (2); **mode** way, manner (3); **de** of (4): in the manner of.] After the manner of. Following the style of. In accordance with the fashion of. In the fashion of. As done by. *They are cousins à la mode de Bretagne; i.e., they are distant or "kissing" cousins.*

À la Recherche du temps perdu [Fr. **à** to, toward, in, by, with, until (1); **la** the (2) **recherche** search, research (3); **du** of the (4); **temps** time, weather (5); **perdu** lost, passed (6): in the search of the time lost.] *Remembrance of Things Past*, the collected novels of Marcel Proust (1871–1922). Cf. **fugit irreparibile tempus** and **temps perdu**.

à la rigueur adv. [Fr. **à** to, toward, in, by, with, until (1); **la** the (2); **rigueur** harshness, strictness (3): with the strictness.] With full application of the rules. Strictly by the rules.

à la sauce hollandaise adv. [Fr. **à** to, toward, in, by, with, until (1); **la** the (2); **sauce** sauce (4); **hollandaise** Dutch (3): with the Dutch sauce.] In the Dutch way or manner. *In 1982 . . . Holland elected the first government of Mr. Ruud Lubbers [1939–], who set out to give the country a dose of Thatcherism à la sauce hollandaise (The Economist 1987).*

a latere adj./adv. [L. **a** from (1); **latere** side (2): from the side.] *Law.* 1. Collateral. Collaterally. Descended from a common ancestor, but not on the same line. (Applicable to inheritance.) 2. Incidental. Casual. Incidentally. Casually. Not following the legitimate or regular course. (Applicable to a proceeding or process.) 3. Representing with full powers. Plenipotentiary. **—legate a latere** a very high-ranking confidential legate in the Roman Catholic Church who is sent by the Pope on a particular mission. Cf. **de latere**.

albino n., pl. **albinos** [Port. white.] A human being or an animal which does not have natural pigment, the skin and hair being whitish, the eyes pink.

a.l.c. abbr. for **à la carte** (q.v.).

alea jacta est. Julius Caesar (100–44 B.C.). [L. **alea** a die in a dice game (1); **jacta** thrown, cast (3); **est** is, has been (2): The die has been cast.] The die is cast. See **alea jacta esto**, **jacta alea est**, and **Rubicon**.

alea jacta esto. Julius Caesar (100–44 B.C.). [L. **alea** a die in a dice game (1); **jacta** thrown, cast (3); **est** let he/she/it be (2): Let the die be cast.] The die is cast. Quoted by Suetonius (born c. 69 A.D.) at I, 32.

al fine adv. [It. **al** to the (1); **fine** end (2): to the end.] *Music.* To the end of the piece. Cf. **da capo**.

alfresco or **al fresco** adj. [It. in the open.] Done in **fresco** (q.v.). 1. A painting made outdoors. 2. Open-air. Outdoor. Done or performed in the open air or outdoors. a) *We traveled to Lagos yesterday to watch an alfresco dramatic performance.* b) *After a tiring session, we retired for an alfresco lunch.* **—adv.** 1. In the fresco style. 2. In the open air. a) *People are clamoring for the performance of the drama alfresco.* b) *We found the tourists as they were having lunch alfresco.*

algesia n. [Neo-Gk. from Gk. **algeō** feel pain: sense of pain.] Sensitivity to pain.

algolagnia n. [Neo-Gk. from Gk. **algo(s)** pain (1); **lagneia** coition, sexual intercourse (2): painful sexual intercourse.] *Psychology.* Deriving sexual pleasure from experiencing pain (i.e., masochism) or from treating one's partner cruelly (i.e., sadism).

algophilia n. [Neo-Gk. from Gk. **algo(s)** pain (2); **philia** fondness (1): fondness of pain.] *Psychology.* Abnormal pleasure in the pain suffered by either oneself or another person.

algophobia n. [Neo-Gk. from Gk. **algo(s)** pain (2); **phob(os)** fear (1): fear of pain.] Abnormal or excessive fear of pain.

alias short form of **alias dictus** adv. [L. **alias** at another time, at other times, some other time (1); **dictus** called (2): at other times called.] Otherwise called or known as. The word is usually used in legal proceedings to establish a connection between the various names which a person bears. *Adamu, alias Tough Guy. —n., pl.* **aliases** A false or assumed name. *The notorious criminal, who has been using many aliases, was arrested yesterday.*

alibi *adv.* [L. elsewhere, in/at another place.] Elsewhere. In/at another place. *The accused person secured his acquittal principally by proving himself alibi. —n., pl.* **alibis** 1. The plea that at the time the crime was committed one was not at the place of commission but elsewhere. *The accused person pleaded alibi when the charge was read and explained to him.* 2. An excuse. *This is the usual alibi which lecturers make for their failure to publish articles.*

alieni generis *adj.* [L. **alieni** of another, another's (1); **generis** of kind, class, group (2): of another kind or class.] Of another sort.

alieni juris *adj.* [L. **alieni** of another (2); **juris** of right, law (1): of the law of another.] *Law.* Subject to, or under, the authority of another person. Controlled by another person. Used with reference to those who are not legally qualified to act on their own behalf (e.g., minors). Cf. **sui juris.**

À l'impossible nul n'est tenu. [Fr. **à** to, toward, in, by, with, until (1); **l'** the (2); **impossible** impossible (3); **nul . . . n'** no one, nobody (4); **est** is (5); **tenu** held (6): To the impossible no one is held.] *Law.* No one is under any obligation to do the impossible. See **impotentia excusat legem.**

alio intuitu *adv.* [L. **alio** with another, different (1); **intuitu** (with) intuition, consideration (2): with a different consideration.] With a motive different from the ostensible one. With a different object or view.

aliquando bonus dormitat Homerus. Horace (65–8 B.C.). *Ars Poetica* 359. [L. **aliquando** sometimes, occasionally (1); **bonus** good (2); **dormitat** sleeps, nods (4); **Homerus** Homer (3): Sometimes good Homer sleeps.] Occasionally even the good Homer nods. Even the best sometimes err.

aliquis non debet esse judex in propria causa quia non potest esse judex et pars. [L. **aliquis** anyone, someone (1); **non** not (3); **debet** ought, should (2); **esse** to be (4); **judex** judge (5); **in** in, on (6); **propria** one's own personal (7); **causa** cause, case, reason (8); **quia** because (9); **non** not (11); **potest** he/she can, is able (10); **esse** to be (12); **judex** judge (13); **et** and (14); **pars** party (15): Someone should not be judge in one's own cause because he/she cannot be judge and party.] *Law.* One should not be a judge in his/her own cause, because one cannot be judge and party at the same time. See **nemo debet esse** etc.

aliquot *adj.* [L. some, several.] 1. Contained a definite number of times in some other quantity. *Three is an aliquot part of twenty seven.* 2. Fractional. *Each of the co-heirs received an aliquot part of the inheritance.*

aliud est celare, aliud tacere. [L. **aliud** one (thing) (2); **est** it is (1); **celare** to hide, conceal (3); **aliud** another (thing) (4); **tacere** to be silent (5): It is one thing to conceal, another thing to be silent.] *Law.* Concealment and silence are two different things. Concealment is one thing, silence another. See **unum est tacere** etc.

aliud est possidere, aliud esse in possessione. [L. **aliud** one (thing) (3); **est** it is (2); **possidere** to possess (1); **aliud** another (thing) (7); **esse** to be (4); **in** in, on (5); **possessione** possession (6): To possess is one thing, to be in possession another.] *Law.* Possession is one thing, being in possession another.

aliunde *adv./adj.* [L. from another source, from elsewhere.] From elsewhere. From another person or place. a) *The witness who produced the document was requested by the court to explain the contents by evidence aliunde.* b) *The party propounding a will is bound to call one of the attesting witnesses, if available, to prove execution, even if evidence of due execution is forthcoming aliunde* (Parry 1961:67).

aliyah *n., pl.* **aliyot** or **aliyoth** or **aliyahs** [Heb. 'alīya ascent.] 1. Ascending the platform in a Jewish synagogue in order to say a blessings at a reading of the Torah. 2. Jewish immigration to Israel.

Alki or **Al-ki** [Chinook by and by.] By and by. Hope for the future. The Motto of the State of Washington.

Allahu akbar [Ar. **Allahu** God (1); **akbar** great (2): God (is) great.] God is great. *When the chartered Air France 747 jetliner appeared in the pink haze of Teheran's morning sky, the rhythmic chant of "Allahu akbar" . . . spread from the airport throughout the city* (*Newsweek Int.* Feb. 12, 1979:8).

allegans contraria non est audiendus. [L. **allegans** one alleging (1); **contraria** conflicting (things) (2); **non** not (4); **est** is (3); **audiendus** to be heard (5): One alleging conflicting things is not to be heard.] *Law.* A person who makes conflicting allegations must not be heard. Applicable to a witness who during cross-examination contradicts himself/herself or blows "hot and cold."

allegans suam turpitudinem non est audiendus. [L. **allegans** one alleging (1); **suam** his/her own (2); **turpitudinem** base act, infamy, turpitude (3); **non** not (5); **est** is (4); **audiendus** to be heard, must be heard (6): Someone alleging his own base act must not be heard.] *Law.* A person who alleges his/her own turpitude is not to be heard; i.e., a person may testify to his/her own infamy, but not as a basis for a claim or right.

allegari non debuit quod probatum non relevat. [L. **allegari** to be alleged (7); **non** not (6); **debuit** should, ought to have been (5); **quod** (that) which, what (1); **probatum** having been proved (2); **non** not (3); **relevat** relieves, alleviates (4): That which, having been proved, does not alleviate, should not have been alleged.] *Law.* An allegation, which, when proved, is irrelevant, should not have been made.

allegata et probata *pl. n.* [L. **allegata** alleged (things) (1); **et** and (2); **probata** proved (things) (3): alleged and proved things.] *Law.* Allegations and proofs, i.e., of a party to a suit. See **secundum allegata et probata.**

allegatio contra factum non est admittenda. [L. **allegatio** allegation (1); **contra** against, opposite (2); **factum** deed, act, fact (3); **non** not (5); **est** is (4); **admittenda** to be admitted, must be admitted (6): An allegation against a deed/fact is not to be admitted.] *Law.* An allegation which is contrary to a deed/fact is inadmissible. A rule of evidence excluding all false statements.

allegro *abbr.* **allo** *adj.* [It. glad, merry.] *Music.* Brisk. Lively. —*adv.* In a lively and brisk manner or time. In quick time. —*n.* A piece, passage, dance, or ballet step performed in a lively and brisk manner.

alleluia *interj.* [Gk. **allēlouia** from Heb. **hallellû** praise (1); **Yāh** God (2): Praise God.] **Hallelujah** (q.v.). —*n., pl.* **alleluias.** A cry of "Praise God."

allemande *fem. n., pl.* **allemandes** [Fr. German.] 1. A 16th-century dance "in the German style" in 2/2 time or the music written to accompany such a dance. 2. A 19th-century dance in 3/4 time. 3. A step in square or contradance where dancers advance through the groups by taking the hand of first one and then another partner.

allo. *abbr.* for **allegro** (q.v.).

allocatur *n., pl.* **allocaturs** [L. It is allowed.] *Law.* In former times, a writ or order granting or allowing a request, such as an appeal or assessment of damages.

allocutus *n.* [L. he having spoken, the speaker.] The right given to a convicted person as to what he/she has to say before judgment is passed on him/her. Allocution. *When it was time for allocutus, the convict informed the judge that he had nothing to say.*

allonge *n., pl.* **allonges** [Fr. extension piece.] A slip of paper affixed to a promissory note, bill of exchange, or any such document to facilitate more endorsements.

alma mater *n., pl.* **almae matres** or **alma maters** [L. **alma** fostering, nourishing (1); **mater** mother (2): nourishing or fostering mother.] A school, college, or university where one was educated and from which one graduated. a) *According to records at her alma mater, Smith College, the First Lady's celebration was two years overdue* (*Newsweek Int.* July 18, 1983:15). b) *. . . he came to Ibadan to deliver a lecture early this year at his alma mater the University of Ibadan* (*Sunday Tribune* 1986).

almemar *n.* [Heb. **'almēmār** pulpit.] **Bema** (q.v.).

alogia *n.* [Neo-Gk. from Gk. **a-** no, not; **logos** word, speech: no speech, speechlessness.] *Medicine.* Inability to speak, particularly when it is the result of a brain lesion.

aloha *interj.* [Hawaiian love, affection.] Greetings! Goodbye! Farewell! Usual form of greeting in Hawaii.

alpha *n., pl.* **alphas** [Gk.] 1. The first letter of the Greek alphabet which is the equivalent of "A" or "a." 2. The first in an order or sequence. The beginning. *I am*

the Alpha and the Omega (Revelations 1:8). Cf. **omega.**

Also sprach Zarathustra [Ger. **also** thus (1); **sprach** spoke (2); **Zarathustra** Zarathustra (3): thus spoke Zarathustra.] *Thus Spoke Zarathustra,* a four volume treatise (1883) about the **Übermensch** (q.v.) or superman by Friedrich Nietzsche (1844–1900). 2. A 1896 tone poem by Richard Strauss (1864–1949) based upon Nietzsche's work.

alt. dieb. *abbr.* for **alternis diebus** (q.v.).

alter ego *n., pl.* **alter egos** [L. **alter** another, the second (1); **ego** I (2): another I, a second I.] 1. Second self. A trusted friend. *Adebayo is Musa's alter ego.* 2. A confidential representative. *Law.* The doctrine of alter ego holds the individual member or members of a corporation responsible, and not the corporation, for any unlawful act done in the name of the corporation, but in reality to promote his/her or their own private interests. a) *. . . if a company wanted to appoint an agent, its members, regarded as the alter ego of the company, could rightly make the appointment* (Olawoyin 1977:18). b) *If the servant does not act bona fide, presumably he is liable on the ground that he has ceased to be his employer's alter ego* (Rogers 1975:452).

alternatim *adv.* [L. one after another.] In alternation. 1. *Music.* A composition, especially ecclesiastical, in which there is an alternation of choirs, of musical styles, or of voice and instrumentation. 2. Any alternation of style or form. *The writer used prose and poetry alternatim.*

alternativa petitio non est audienda. [L. **alternativa** a different, alternative (1); **petitio** petition, claim (2); **non** not (4); **est** is (3); **audienda** to be heard (5): A different claim is not to be heard.] *Law.* An alternative petition/claim must not to be heard.

alternis diebus *abbr.* **alt. dieb.** [L. **alternis** on alternate (1); **diebus** (on) days (2): on alternate days.] *Medicine.* Every other day. See **diebus alternis.**

alternis horis *abbr.* **alt. hor.** [L. **alternis** in alternate (1); **horis** (in) hours (2): in alternate hours.] *Medicine.* Every two hours. Every other hour. *The drugs prescribed by the medical practitioner are to be taken alternis horis.*

alternis noctibus *abbr.* **alt. noc.** [L. **alternis** on alternate (1); **noctibus** (on) nights (2): on alternate nights.] *Medicine.* Every other night.

alt. hor. *abbr.* for **alternis horis** (q.v.).

alt. noc. *abbr.* for **alternis noctibus** (q.v.).

alto *n., pl.* **altos** [It. high, tall.] *Music.* 1. The lower female singing voice. 2. The highest voice of a boy or man. 3. A person who sings or an instrument which plays such a part.

alumnus or *fem.* **alumna** *n., pl.* **alumni** or *fem.* **alumnae** [L. foster son/daughter, ward, pupil, disciple.] 1. A graduate of a particular school, college, institution, or university. *A meeting of the alumni of the*

University of Ghana, Legon, will be held on Friday.
2. A former member, employee, contributor, or in-
mate. *Woodstock alumni were eager to participate
in an anniversary experience.*

A luta continua. [Port. **a** the (1); **luta** struggle (2);
continua continues (3): The struggle continues.] A
political and military slogan in Portuguese colonies
in Africa.

A luta do povo e justa. [Port. **a** the (1); **luta** struggle
(2); **do** of the (3); **povo** people (4); **e** is (5); **justa** just
(6): The struggle of the people is just.] A political
and military slogan in Portuguese colonies in Africa.
Cf. **O povo** etc.

A.M. *abbr.* for 1. **Anno mundi** (q.v.). 2. **Annus
mirabilis** (q.v.). 3. **Artium Magister** (q.v.). 4. **Ave
Maria** (q.v.).

A.M. or **a.m.** *abbr.* for **ante meridiem** (q.v.).

ama et fac quod vis. [L. **ama** love (1); **et** and (2); **fac**
do, make (3); **quod** that which, what (4); **vis** you
want, wish (5): Love, and do what you want.] Love
and do whatever you wish. A variation of **dilige et
quod vis fac** (q.v.).

amantium irae amoris integratio est. Terence (c.185–
159 B.C.). *Andria* 555. [L. **amantium** of those loving
(2); **irae** angers, indignations (1); **amoris** of love (5);
integratio renewing, restoring (4); **est** is (3). The
angers of those loving is renewing of love.] Quarrels
among lovers tend to renew or strengthen their love.

amateur *n., pl.* **amateurs** [Fr. lover, fancier.] 1. A person
who is devoted to, fond of, or an admirer of something.
*Amateurs of the proscribed magazine were overjoyed
when it reappeared on the newsstand.* 2. A person
who engages in a pursuit, study, etc. as a pastime
and not a profession. *The celebrated archaeologist
could not conceal his excitement when an amateur
brought a skull and some objects found at the bank
of a river.* 3. A person who engages in sports, plays
a game, or performs as a musician, artist, etc. for pleasure and not for financial remuneration. *To boost
competition the Tour also allowed amateurs to race
for the first time this year.* (*Newsweek Int.* July 25,
1983:49). 4. A person who engages in any activity
superficially or without due experience or competence. *A glance at the painting clearly shows that it
is the work of an amateur.* —*adj.* Of, characteristic
of, relating to, or having the position of, an amateur
or a nonprofessional person. a) *Amateur wrestling*;
b) *amateur boxers*; c) *amateur athletes*; d) *amateur
actors*; e) . . . *in Japanese homes, bars and night clubs
where amateur singers are not the least bit shy about
picking up a microphone to belt out a song . . .*
(*Newsweek Int.* July 11, 1983:3). Cf. **dilettante** 2.

a maximis ad minima [L. **a** from, by (1); **maximis**
greatest (things) (2); **ad** to, at, for, according to (3);
minima smallest, least (things) (4): from the greatest
to the least.] From the most important to the least
important. All-inclusive.

Amazon *n., pl.* **Amazons** [Gk. **Amazōn.**] *Greek and
Roman Mythology.* A member of a mythological race
of female warriors who were believed to live on the
borders of the then known world and who frequently
engaged in wars with the Greeks. —**amazon** 1. A
female soldier or warrior. 2. A tall, vigorous, manly
woman. A **virago** (q.v.).

ambiance or **ambience** *n.* [Fr. atmosphere.] Environment. Circumstances. Surroundings. Cf. **ambiente**.

ambidexter *n., pl.* **ambidexters** [L. from **ambi** on both
sides (2) and **dexter** right, skillful (1): skillful with
both (hands).] A lawyer (or jury) who takes remuneration (or bribes) from both parties. *In 1673 it was
established that one Simon Mason, an attorney, "had
been an ambidexter, viz. after he was retained by
one side he was retained on the other side; . . ."*
(Megarry 1973:49).

ambiente *n., pl.* **ambientes** [It. and Sp. atmosphere,
environment.] Surroundings. Circumstances. **Milieu**
(q.v.). *Children should be brought up in a good social
ambiente.* Cf. **ambiance**.

**ambigua responsio contra proferentem est
accipienda.** [L. **ambigua** ambiguous (1); **responsio**
response, answer (2); **contra** against, opposite (5);
proferentem the one uttering (6); **est** is (3);
accipienda to be accepted (4): An ambiguous response is to be accepted against the one uttering it.]
Law. An ambiguous response must be interpreted to
the detriment of the respondent. Cf. **quaelibet
concessio** etc.

ambiguitas contra stipulatorem est. [L. **ambiguitas**
ambiguity (1); **contra** against, opposite (3); **stipulatorem**
one making stipulation (4); **est** is (2): Ambiguity is
against the one making the stipulation.] *Law.* Ambiguity
is interpreted to the disadvantage of the party that makes
the stipulation. See **quaelibet concessio** etc.

**ambiguum pactum contra venditorem inter-
pretandum est.** [L. **ambiguum** ambiguous (1);
pactum agreement, contract (2); **contra** against,
opposite (5); **venditorem** seller, vendor (6);
interpretandum to be interpreted (4); **est** is (3): An
ambiguous contract is to be interpreted against the
seller.] *Law.* An ambiguous contract must be interpreted to the detriment of the seller. Cf. **quaelibet
concessio** etc.

**ambiguum placitum interpretari debet contra
proferentem.** [L. **ambiguum** ambiguous (1);
placitum plea, pleading (2); **interpretari** to be interpreted (4); **debet** ought, should (3); **contra** against,
opposite (5); **proferentem** the one uttering (6): An
ambiguous plea should be interpreted against the one
uttering it.] *Law.* An ambiguous plea should be interpreted to the detriment of the party making it.
Cf. **quaelibet concessio** etc.

ambrosia *n.* [Gk. from **a-** no, not (1); **brotos** mortal,
human (2): not mortal.] 1. *Greek and Roman Mythology.* The elixir of life used as food by the gods. Also,

the perfume used by the gods. 2. Something with a very pleasant taste or scent. *The bride was very charming; she must have sprayed her clothes with the best ambrosia on earth.*

ambulatoria est voluntas defuncti usque ad vitae supremum exitum. [L. **ambulatoria** ambulatory (4); **est** is (3); **voluntas** will (1); **defuncti** of the deceased (2); **usque** as far as (5); **ad** to, at, for, according to (6); **vitae** of life (9); **supremum** last (7); **exitum** end, termination (8): The will of the deceased is ambulatory as far as to the last end of life.] A person's will is capable of alteration until the last point of life. See **Legatum morte** etc.

am. cur. *abbr.* for **amicus curiae** (q.v.).

A.M.D.G. *abbr.* for **ad majorem Dei gloriam** (q.v.).

âme damnée *n., pl.* **âmes damnées** [Fr. **âme** soul, spirit (2); **damnée** damned, condemned (1): a condemned or damned soul.] A person who willingly and devotedly serves as another's slave, stooge, instrument, or tool. *Blado is a principled man who, in a world of sycophants and praise singers, has resolutely refused to be the âme damnée of the powers that be.*

amelus *n., pl.* **ameli** [L. from Gk. **a-** without (1) and **melos** limb (2): without limb.] *Medicine.* A fetus which has no limbs. Cf. **acephalus** and **amorphus**.

amende honorable *n., pl.* **amendes honorables** [Fr. **amende** amends, apology (2); **honorable** honorable, respectable (1): honorable apology or amends.] Full acknowledgment of, and apology for, an error, offense or insult.

amen *interj.* [Hebrew. **'āmēn** truly, verily. So be it.] The end of a prayer or a sign of approval. *Forever and ever. Amen.* —*n., pl.* **amens** A statement of assent or approval. *At the end of the speech enthusiastic amens resounded throughout the hall.*

amens *n.* [L. mindless, insane, frantic.] A person who is completely insane. A mentally deficient person. An idiot. See **amentia** Cf. **demens.**

a mensa et thoro *adj.* [L. **a** from (1); **mensa** table (2); **et** and (3); **t(h)oro** bed (4): from table and bed.] *Law.* From bed and board. From board and bed. Used with reference to a kind of divorce or separation in which the couple, though remaining husband and wife, cannot cohabit. Cruelty was one of the grounds for such divorce or separation.

amens amans *n., pl.* **amentes amantes** or **amantes amentes** Plautus (c.50–184 B.C.). *Mercator* 81. [L. **amens** mindless, insane, mad (1); **amans** lover (2): insane lover.] Anyone in love is insane.

amentia *n.* [L. **ab** from, away from, out of (1); **mens** mind (2): out of mind, senselessness, want of reason, insanity.] Insanity. Mental deficiency. Idiocy. Inadequate development of the intellect. See **amens, anoesia, anoia,** and **demens.**

à merci *adv.* [Fr. **à** to, toward, in, by, with, until (1); **merci** mercy, pity, discretion (2): at mercy.] Mercilessly.

At discretion. *The triumvirs exercised unlimited rights of conscription and taxed the Roman empire à merci* (Cary 1970:430).

amicus curiae *abbr.* **am. cur.** *n., pl.* **amici curiae** [L. **amicus** friend (1); **curiae** of court (2): friend of court.] *Law.* A friend of the court. 1. *General.* A bystander who makes a suggestion or statement on a legal matter to assist the court. 2. *Specific.* A person (or government) who files a brief or argues orally before an appellate court on behalf of a party with interest in a pending case which, generally, concerns matters of wide public interest.

amicus medicorum *n., pl.* **amici medicorum** [L. **amicus** friend (1); **medicorum** of physicians, medical practitioners (2): a friend of physicians.] Physicians' friend. *Thanks to the efficacy of modern medicine, gout, which used to be opprobrium medicorum, mainly because doctors could not treat it, has become amicus medicorum.* Cf. **opprobrium medicorum.**

amicus usque ad aras *n.* [L. **amicus** friend (1); **usque** all the way (2); **ad** to, at, for, according to (3); **aras** altars (4): a friend all the way to the altars.] A friend in all matters but religion.

amnesia *n.* [Neo-Gk. from Gk. **a-** no, not (1); **mnēmē** memory (2): no memory, forgetfulness.] *Medicine* and *Law.* Loss of memory which could be the result of injury to the brain, fatigue, hysteria, epilepsy, or illness, or could be caused by **anesthesia** (q.v.). Amnesia generally involves loss of memory of personal identity. There are three kinds. First, the patient, usually an aged person, easily forgets new impressions. Second, the patient cannot recall previous experiences. Third, the patient can remember only some periods of his/her life. Generally, amnesia does not render a person incapable of standing trial.

amor nummi *n.* [L. **amor** love (1); **nummi** coin, cash (2): love of coin.] Love of money.

amor omnia vincit [L. **amor** love (1); **omnia** all (things), everything (3); **vincit** conquers (2): Love conquers all things.] Love is stronger than everything else. Cf. **labor vincit omnia.**

amor patriae *n.* [L. **amor** love (1); **patriae** country, fatherland (2): love of country.] Love of one's own country.

amorphus *n., pl.* **amorphi** or **amorphuses** [L. from Gk. **amorphos**: **a-** no (1) and **morphē** shape (2): no shape, shapeless, without form.] *Medicine.* A fetus which has no heart, head or limbs. Cf. **acephalus** and **amelus.**

amor sceleratus habendi Ovid (43 B.C.–17 A.D.). *Metamorphoses* I,131. [L. **amor** love (2); **sceleratus** wicked, hated (1); **habendi** of having, of possessing (3): wicked love of having.] The accursed desire for acquisitions.

amor vincit omnia. Cf. **amor omnia vincit.**

amour *n., pl.* **amours** [Fr. love, affection, passion.] 1. Courtship. 2. Love affair, especially one which is illicit. *After wading through a series of amours, Semo* settled down and is now a respectable husband and father. 3. Sexual love. Love-making. *Film-making has desecrated the sanctity of amour.* 4. A lover. A person who is loved. A mistress. *When will Bart put an end to his habit of changing amours?*

amourette *n., pl.* **amourettes** [Fr. a little love affair, a passing love affair.] 1. An ephemeral or transient love affair. 2. A woman who is engaged in an ephemeral or transient love affair.

amour propre *n.* [Fr. **amour propre** self-love.] Self-esteem. Self-respect. Self-pride. Vanity. Egotism. Pride. Desire for admiration. a) *In a second swipe at Soviet amour-propre Carter encouraged speculation that the U.S. might boycott the Summer Olympics in Moscow* (*Newsweek Int.* Jan. 21, 1980:7). b) *The chief's amour propre was severely wounded when most of his subjects refused to acknowledge what he regarded as a great achievement.*

amparo *n., pl.* **amparos** [Sp. protection, refuge.] *Spanish Law.* A certificate issued, as protection, to a person claiming land, pending the surveying of the land and the actual vesting of the full title.

a multo fortiori *adj./adv.* [L. **a** from (1); **multo** much, far (2); **fortiori** stronger (3): from much the stronger.] With a much stronger reason. Much more certainly. Much more certain/conclusive. A more emphatic form of **a fortiori** (q.v.).

anabasis *n., pl.* **anabases** [Gk. **ana** up, back (2); **basis** going (1): a going up, an expedition up from the coast.] Marching up. An advance by a military force. —**Anabasis** *The March Upcountry,* an eye-witness account by Xenophon (c.430–c.355 B.C.) of the journey upcountry, i.e., back to the sea, by a group of Greek mercenaries stranded in the heart of the Persian empire after their employer Cyrus was killed at the battle of Cunaxa in 401.

anacoluthon *n., pl.* **anacolutha** or **anacoluthons** [Gk. **an-** no, not (1); **akolouthon** following (2); not following, inconsistent.] *Rhetoric.* An inconsistency in sentence grammar caused by a sudden change of construction from one phrase to the next; e.g., "All of us face troubles in the distant future—the intervening time is advantageous."

anacrisis *n., pl.* **anacrises** [Gk. **ana** up, back (2); **krisis** judgment (1): judgment back, examination or inquiry, particularly prior examination of parties to a suit.] *Civil Law.* Investigation of truth in which torture is usually applied.

anaemia *var.* of **anemia** (q.v.).

anaesthesia *British var.* of **anesthesia** (q.v.).

anagenesis *n., pl.* **anageneses** [Gk. **ana** up, back (2); **genesis** birth (1): birth back, regeneration.] Regeneration or reproduction (e.g., of tissue).

analecta *pl. n.* [Gk. selections.] A collection of literary extracts, i.e., pieces chosen from a single literary work or from several different works. An anthology.

analgesia *n.* [Neo-Gk. from Gk. **an-** no, not (1); **alg(os)** pain (2): no pain, insensibility, want of feeling.] Insensitivity to pain at a time when a person retains his/her consciousness.

analysandum *n., pl.* **analysanda** [L. that which must be analyzed.] Something to be analyzed. Something to be defined.

analysans *n., pl.* **analysans** [L. analyzing.] Something which serves the purpose of analyzing or defining.

analysis *n., pl.* **analyses** [Gk. **analusis** releasing, dissolving.] Resolution or solution of a problem. Breaking up or separating a whole thing into its constituent parts as well as commenting on and assessing or judging it. A thorough, detailed, or comprehensive study of something that is complex. a) *They did not subject the diaries to enough informed historical analysis* (*Newsweek Int.* May 16, 1983:16). b) Devil on the Cross *is a striking piece of writing which combines simplicity of story and theme with an extreme richness of texture and depth of analysis* (Nicholas Owen in *West Africa* 1982).

anamnesis *n., pl.* **anamneseis** or **anamneses** [Gk. **anamnēsis: ana** up, back, again (2); **mnēmē** remembering (1): remembering back, calling to mind, reminiscence.] 1. Reminiscence. Recalling to mind a previous experience. 2. *Medicine.* Information on a patient's background used for analysis of his/her condition.

anaphora *n., pl.* **anaphorae** or **anaphoras** [Gk. **ana** up, back, again (2); **phora** coming, rising (1): coming up, repetition.] *Rhetoric.* Using the same word or phrase at the beginning of a series of phrases or sentences; e.g., "Thou shalt not . . ." in the Ten Commandments or "Blessed are they who . . ." in the Beatitudes. Cf. **epistrophe**.

anaphrodisia *n.* [Gk. **an-** no, not (1); **Aphrodisia** belonging to Aphrodite (2): not belonging to Aphrodite, insensibility to love, inability to inspire love.] *Medicine.* Inability to engage in sexual intercourse, whether of a man or a woman. See **dyspareunia** and **impotentia coeundi**. Cf. **agenesia**.

anastrophe *n., pl.* **anastrophae** or **anastrophes** [Gk. **anastrophē: ana** up, back, again (2); **strophē** turning (1): turning back.] *Rhetoric.* A reversal of normal word order; e.g., "A song I sing."

anathema *n., pl.* **anathemata** or **anathemas** [Gk. **anathēma: ana** up, back, again (2); **thēma** something placed (1): something placed up, anything dedicated, an accursed person or thing.] 1. *Christianity.* A punishment, imposed by the authorities of a church, which bans the culprit from all intercourse with the church and its members. A person cursed by a church. 2. Denouncing something as accursed. Curse. Imprecation. 3. A person or something intensely hated, disliked, abhorred or detested. *. . . those northern businessmen for whom populism is anathema* (*The Economist* 1987).

anathema sit [Gk. **anathēma** accursed (2); L. **sit** let him/her/it be (1): Let him/her/it be accursed.] *Christianity*. Let this person or this belief be damned. A forumula used by ecclesiastical authorities to exclude a person from the church community. Cf. **anathema**.

ancienne cuisine *n*. [Fr. **ancienne** ancient, old, former (1); **cuisine** cooking, cookery (2): ancient or old cooking.] The old or outdated style of cooking. *To celebrate . . . the restaurant's 400th birthday . . . a star-studded cast of diners sits down for five memorable meals of ancienne cuisine* (*Newsweek Int*. Oct. 18, 1982:1). See **cuisine**.

ancien régime *n., pl.* **anciens régimes** [Fr. **ancien** ancient, old, former (1); **régime** system, government (2): old government.] 1. The old or ancient system of government, i.e., before a particular significant period. Specifically, in France, the socio-political system which preceded the Revolution of 1789. a) *And in Spain, the vulnerable fledgling democracy is seeking a popular mandate at a time when it is threatened . . . by entrenched partisans of Franco's ancien régime* (*Newsweek Int*. Feb. 19, 1979:37). b) *Recruitment was carried out partly on a volunteer basis, but mainly by conscription. As in France under the ancien régime lots were drawn* (Suret-Canale 1971:337). 2. An obsolete system or mode.

ancilla *n., pl.* **ancillae** [L. a maidservant, handmaid.] 1. Accessory. Something which is an adjunct, particularly, to something big. 2. Helper. Something which assists in achieving or understanding something complicated or difficult. *Knowledge of a people's language is an indispensable ancilla to meaningful research on their culture, history, etc.*

ancipitis usus *adj*. [L. **ancipitis** of twofold, double (1); **usus** (of) use (2): of twofold or double use.] *International Law*. Applicable to something (e.g., coal) which can be used for civil or military purposes.

andante *adj./adv*. [It. walking.] *Music*. In a walking tempo. At a slow pace. —*n., pl.* **andantes** A section of a composition played at a slow pace.

androgynus *n., pl.* **androgyni** [L. from Gk. **androgunos**: **andr(os)** male, man (1); **gunē** woman (2): manwoman.] A hermaphrodite. An androgyne. An effeminate man. Cf. **virago**.

andromania *n*. [Neo-Gk. from Gk. **andr(os)** male, man (2); **mania** fondness, enthusiasm for (1): fondness for males.] Excessive desire by a woman for sexual activity and pleasure. See **aphrodisia, erotomania, nymphomania,** and **uteromania**. Cf. **androphobia** and **satyriasis**.

androphobia *n*. [Neo-Gk. from Gk. **andr(os)** male, man (2); **phob(os)** fear (1): fear of males.] Excessive fear of males, especially a woman's dread of sexual relationship with a man. Cf. **andromania**.

androphonomania *n*. [Neo-Gk. from Gk. **andr(os)** male, man (1); **phono(s)** slaying (2); **mania** madness (3): male-slaying madness.] *Law*. Homicidal madness or insanity.

anemia or **anaemia** *n*. [Gk. from **an-** no, not (1); **(h)aim(a)** blood (2): no blood, want or lack of blood.] 1. *Medicine*. Lack of adequate blood. 2. Absence or want of vitality. Emptiness, debility, or lifelessness. *The erudite professor complained that academia was dying slowly from the peculiar disease of intellectual anemia.*

anesthesia or **anaesthesia** (British) *n., pl.* **anesthesias** or **anaesthesias** [Gk. **anaisthēsia**: **an-** no, not (1); **aisthēsis** feeling (2): no feeling, unconsciousness, insensibility to pleasure or pain.] 1. Loss of feeling as a result of some abnormality or some injury to the nervous system. 2. *Medicine*. Loss of feeling and, sometimes, consciousness induced by drugs so that the patient would not experience pain, especially during surgery.

Angelus *n*. [L. angel from Gk. **aggelos** messenger.] *Christianity*. 1. The first word of a prayer celebrating the annunciation and traditionally recited three times a day, at 6 A.M., at noon, and at 6 P.M. 2. The prayer itself. 3. The bell rung to remind the faithful to recite this prayer.

angina pectoris *n*. [L. **angina** strangling (1); **pectoris** of breast, chest (2): strangling of the chest.] *Medicine*. A heart disease, characterized by spasm or sharp pain in the chest and apprehension of imminent death. *The drugs offer their greatest promise in the treatment of the crushing, disabling chest pains of angina pectoris* (*Newsweek Int*. March 30, 1981:44).

Anglomania *n*. [Neo-L. and Gk. from L. **Angl(us)** English (2); Gk. **mania** enthusiasm (1): enthusiasm for English.] Excessive desire for, fondness for, or attachment to, English things, practices, customs and institutions on the part of a non-English person. *Some citizens of countries which are former British colonies are so carried away by their Anglomania that they travel often to Britain for shopping, medical attention, etc.* See **Anglophilia** and **Francophilia**. Cf. **Anglophobia, Francophobia, Gallophobia** and **Germanophobia**.

Anglophilia *n*. [Neo-L. and Gk. from L. **Angl(us)** English (2); Gk. **philia** fondness, liking for (1): fondness or liking for English.] Excessive fondness, liking, or admiration for England as well as English things, practices, customs, institutions, etc., on the part of a non-English person. See **Anglomania**.

Anglophobia *n*. [Neo-L. and Gk. from L. **Angl(us)** English (2); Gk. **phob(os)** fear, dread (1): fear or dread of English.] Excessive fear or hatred of England as well as English things, practices, customs, institutions, etc. on the part of a non-English person. Cf. **Anglomania**.

Angst or **angst** *n., pl.* **Ängste** or **angsts** [Ger. **Angst** fear, dread, anguish.] A feeling of anxiety. *Lack of* *paternal attention and the conspicuous hostility of their stepmother have combined to set up for the miserable children an angst.*

anguis in herba *n.* [L. **anguis** snake, serpent (1); **in** in, on (2); **herba** grass (3): snake in the grass.] A drawback or defect. An unsuspected danger. See **latet anguis in herba**.

angulus terrarum *n.* [L. **angulus** corner, angle (1); **terrarum** of the world, lands (2): corner of the world.] A corner or angle in the world, i.e., a place where one feels most comfortable or at ease. *Every Friday evening the Jacksons depart from the city for their angulus terrarum, a village about twenty miles away.*

anhedonia *n.* [Gk. **an-** no, not (1); **hēdonē** pleasure (2): no pleasure, lack of pleasure.] Inability to experience pleasure or happiness. Insensitivity to pleasure or happiness. *Peter's anhedonia is such that his relatives and friends hesitate to invite him to parties.*

anima *n., pl.* **animae** or **animas** [L. soul, person, life, a living being.] 1. The animal soul, i.e., the soul which man shares with all animals. 2. *Psychology.* The inward personality or true inner self of an individual.

anima mundi *n.* [L. **anima** mind, soul (1); **mundi** of the world (2): mind of the world.] World soul. An organizing principle or power of the universe. Cf. **atman**.

anima vagula *n.* [L. **anima** soul, mind, spirit (2); **vagula** small wandering (1): a small wandering soul.] My little wandering soul! Attributed to the Roman emperor Hadrian as his dying words.

animo cancellandi *adv.* [L. **animo** with mind, intention (1); **cancellandi** of/for destroying, canceling (2): with a mind for destroying.] *Law.* With the intention of destroying or canceling a will. *For, in an affair at Pisa, where for some time their quarters were, the lady appears to have torn it* [i.e., the will] *piecemeal animo (as lawyers say) cancellandi* (L. J. Knight Bruce quoted in Megarry 1955:114). See **animus cancellandi**.

animo et corpore or **corpore et animo** *adv.* [L. **animo** with/by mind (1); **et** and (2); **corpore** with/by body (3): with mind and body.] *Law.* By the mind and by the body. By physical act and intention. Deliberately and physically. Used of an offense committed both by intent and by physical act. *When a person commits an offense animo et corpore, he cannot escape criminal liability.* See **animo et facto**; **animus et factum**; and **facto et animo**.

animo et facto *adv.* [L. **animo** in/with mind (1); **et** and (2); **facto** in/with deed, act, fact (3): in mind and deed.] *Law.* By design and deed. *Investigations revealed that the crime was committed animo et facto.* See **animo et corpore**.

animo felonico *adv.* [L. **animo** (with) intention (2); **felonico** with felonious (1): with felonious intention.]

Law. With criminal intent. *Although the suspect denies the offense, it is clear that he acted animo felonico and actually caused harm to the complainant.*

animo furandi *adv.* [L. **animo** with mind, intention (1); **furandi** of/for stealing (2): with a mind for stealing.] *Law.* With the intention of stealing. With intent to steal. *The accused person clearly entered the premises animo furandi.* See **animus furandi**.

animo lucrandi *adv.* [L. **animo** with mind, intention (1); **lucrandi** of/for gaining, making profit (2): with a mind for making profit.] With the intention of gaining or making profit. With intent to gain or make profit. *It goes without saying that a trader engages in business animo lucrandi, but equity demands that whatever profit is made should be reasonable.* See **animus lucrandi**.

animo manendi *adv.* [L. **animo** with mind, intention (1); **manendi** of/for remaining (2): with a mind for remaining.] With the intention of remaining. With intent to remain. See **animus morandi**.

animo morandi *adv.* [L. **animo** with mind, intention (1); **morandi** of/for staying, remaining (2): with a mind for staying.] With the intention of staying/remaining. With intent to stay/remain. *After a sojourn of thirty years in the U.S.A. he has returned home animo morandi.* See **animus morandi**.

animo revertendi. *adv.* [L. **animo** with mind, intention (1); **revertendi** of/for returning (2): with mind for returning.] With the intention of returning. With intent to return. *He went to Lagos yesterday animo revertendi.* Cf. **animus non revertendi**.

animo revocandi *adv.* [L. **animo** with mind, intention (1); **revocandi** of/for summoning again, recovering, revoking (2): with a mind for summoning again.] With the intention of summoning again/recovering/revoking. With intent to summon again/recover/revoke. See **animus revocandi**. Cf. **sine animo revocandi**.

animo testandi *adv.* [L. **animo** with mind, intention (1); **testandi** of/for making a will, testifying (2): with a mind for making a will.] *Law.* With the intention of making a will or testifying. With intent to make a will or testify. *For a will to be valid, the testator must have made it animo testandi.* See **animus testandi**.

animus *n., pl.* **animi** or **animuses** [L. mind, intention.] 1. Mind. Spirit. Feeling. Objective. *His animus was not to murder the deceased but to defend himself.* 2. Animosity. Ill will. Grudge. Malice. Hostility, usually latent but deeply-rooted. *The principal's attitude clearly shows that he bears animus against the teacher.* 3. *Psychology.* The inner male drive, especially in a female.

animus ad se omne jus ducit. [L. **animus** mind, intention (1); **ad** to, at, for, according to (5); **se** itself (6); **omne** all (3); **jus** right, law (4); **ducit** leads (2): Intention leads all law to itself.] The law pays particular attention to the intention. See **actus non facit** etc.

animus cancellandi *n.* [L. **animus** mind, intention (1); **cancellandi** of/for canceling (2): a mind for canceling.] *Law.* Intention of canceling or destroying a will. Intent to cancel or destroy a will. Cf. **animo cancellandi**.

animus capiendi *n.* [L. **animus** mind, intention (1); **capiendi** of/for capturing, seizing (2): a mind for seizing.] Intention of taking or capturing. Intent to take or capture.

animus dedicandi *n.* [L. **animus** mind, intention (1); **dedicandi** of/for dedicating, consecrating (2): a mind for dedicating.] *Law.* Intention of dedicating, consecrating, or donating. Intent to dedicate, consecrate, or donate. Applicable to land used for highway.

animus defamandi *n.* [L. **animus** mind, intention (1); **defamandi** of/for defaming (2): mind for defaming.] *Law.* Intention of defaming. Intent to defame. *The false statement he made about his friend indicates that he had animus defamandi.*

animus deferendi *n.* [L. **animus** mind, intention (1); **deferendi** of/for postponing, delaying (2): a mind for postponing.] *Law.* Intention of securing postponement. Intent to secure postponement. Cf. **animus differendi**.

animus derelinquendi *n.* [L. **animus** mind, intention (1); **derelinquendi** of/for abandoning, deserting (2): a mind for abandoning.] *Law.* Intention of deserting or abandoning. Intent to desert or abandon. *A husband who willingly absents himself from his matrimonial home for a very long time clearly has animus derelinquendi.* Cf. **animus deserendi**.

animus deserendi *n.* [L. **animus** mind, intention (1); **deserendi** of/for abandoning, deserting (2): a mind for abandoning.] *Law.* Intention of deserting. Intent to desert. Applicable, especially, to desertion of a husband or wife. Cf. **animus derelinquendi**.

animus differendi *n.* [L. **animus** mind, intention (1); **differendi** of/for postponing, delaying (2): a mind for postponing.] *Law.* Intention of delaying or securing postponement. Cf. **animus deferendi**.

animus donandi *n.* [L. **animus** mind, intention (1); **donandi** of/for giving (2): a mind for giving.] *Law.* Intention of giving. Intent to give. *A gift is not valid if the donor has no animus donandi.*

animus et factum *n.* [L. **animus** mind, intention (1); **et** and (2); **factum** deed, act, fact (3): the mind and the deed.] *Law.* The intention and the act. Intention combined with the act. *If one wants to change his domicile, there must be animus et factum before the exercise could be considered to be legally completed.* See **animo et corpore**.

animus furandi or furandi animus *n.* [L. **animus** mind, intention (1); **furandi** of/for stealing, pilfering (2): a mind for stealing.] *Law.* Intention of stealing. Intent to steal. *The concealment of the money in his socks clearly suggests that Bob had animus furandi.* See **animo furandi**.

animus hominis est anima scripti. [L. **animus** mind, intention (1); **hominis** of a human, person (2); **est** is (3); **anima** soul (4); **scripti** of what is written (5): The intention of a person is the soul of what is written.] *Law.* A party's intention is the soul of the instrument; i.e., the intention of the person who executes an instrument is the basis of its validity.

animus irritandi *n.* [L. **animus** mind, intention (1); **irritandi** of/for irritating. provoking (2): a mind for irritating.] *Law.* Intention of irritating or provoking. Intention of causing irritation or provocation. *It was only an animus irritandi, which, happening to be exercised upon a genus irritabile, produced unexpected violence of resentment* (Ben Jonson in Megarry 1973:340). See **genus irritabile**.

animus lucrandi *n.* [L. **animus** mind, intention (1); **lucrandi** of/for gaining, making profit (2): a mind for making profit.] *Law.* Intention of making profit or gaining. Intent to make profit or gain. *He had animus lucrandi and this accounts for his full participation in the carriage of the goods.* See **animo lucrandi**.

animus manendi *n.* [L. **animus** mind, intention (1); **manendi** of/for remaining (2): a mind for remaining.] *Law.* Intention of remaining. Intent to remain; i.e., intent to establish domicile or permanent residence. See **animus morandi**.

animus morandi *n.* [L. **animus** mind, intention (1); **morandi** of/for delaying, remaining (2): a mind for delaying.] *Law.* Intention of remaining or delaying. Intent to remain or delay; i.e., intention to establish domicile or permanent residence. See **animo manendi**; **animo morandi**; **animus manendi**; and **animus residendi**.

animus non revertendi *n.* [L. **animus** mind, intention (1); **non** not (2); **revertendi** of/for returning (3): a mind for not returning.] *Law.* Intention of not returning. Intent not to return. Applicable to the loss of animals such as homing pigeons which usually go out and return home. See **sine animo revertendi**. Cf. **animo revertendi** and **animus revertendi**.

animus possidendi *n.* [L. **animus** mind, intention (1); **possidendi** of/for possessing (2): a mind for possessing.] *Law.* Intention of possessing. Intent to possess. *Any person claiming ownership of property must have animus possidendi.*

animus quo *n.* [L. **animus** mind, intention (1); **quo** with which (2): mind with which.] *Law.* The intention with which. The intent with which.

animus recipiendi *n.* [L. **animus** mind, intention (1); **recipiendi** of/for receiving (2): mind for receiving.] *Law.* Intention of receiving. Intent to receive. *In the bribery case, the prosecution proved that the accused had animus recipiendi and did receive the bribe from the applicant.*

animus recuperandi *n.* [L. **animus** mind, intention (1); **recuperandi** of/for recovering (2): mind for recovering.]

Law. Intention of recovering. Intent to recover. *The plaintiff brought the action after informing the squatters about his animus recuperandi.*

animus residendi *n*. [L. **animus** mind, intention (1); **residendi** of/for residing, abiding (2): mind for residing.] *Law*. Intention of residing in a country. Intent to reside in a country. *A person's state of mind may be relevant to the issue [whether] he is present in a country as a traveler or as an inhabitant; but, subject to this point, residence may be established without any mental element. There is no requirement of animus residendi* (Morris 1973:96). See **animus morandi**.

animus restituendi *n*. [L. **animus** mind, intention (1); **restituendi** of/for restoring (2): mind for restoring.] *Law*. Intention of restoring. Intent to restore.

animus revertendi *n*. [L. **animus** mind, intention (1); **revertendi** of/for returning (2): mind for returning.] *Law*. Intention of returning. Intent to return. Applicable, especially, to domesticated animals which have the habit of going out and returning home. Cf. **animus non revertendi**.

animus revocandi *n*. [L. **animus** mind, intention (1); **revocandi** of/for recalling, revoking (2): mind for recalling.] *Law*. Intention of recalling or revoking. Intent to revoke, i.e., a will. *After the execution of the will, the testator had animus revocandi and he invited his lawyer to prepare another.* See **animo revocandi**. Cf. **sine animo revocandi**.

animus signandi *n*. [L. **animus** mind, intention (1); **signandi** of/for affixing a seal to (2): mind for affixing a seal to.] *Law*. The intention to sign an instrument.

animus testandi *n*. [L. **animus** mind, intention (1); **testandi** of/for making a will, testifying (2): mind for making a will.] *Law*. Intention of making a will or testifying. Intent to make a will or testify. *It is very unfortunate that he died intestate, for he declared his animus testandi only three days before the incident.* See **animo testandi**.

animus vicino nocendi *n*. [L. **animus** mind, intention (1); **vicino** neighbor (3); **nocendi** of/for doing harm, hurting, injuring (2): mind for harming a neighbor.] *Law*. Intention of harming a neighbor. Intent to hurt a neighbor. *The English law . . . presents us with no scientific analysis of the degree to which the intent to harm or, in the language of the civil law, the animus vicino nocendi, may enter into or affect the conception of a personal wrong . . .* (Weir 1974:479).

année terrible *n., pl.* **années terribles** [Fr. **année** year (2); **terrible** terrible, dreadful (1): terrible year.] A dreadful year. *It will take a long time before many Nigerians forget the années terribles which came in the wake of the fall of the First Republic.* Cf. **annus terribilis**.

an nescis, mi fili, quantilla prudentia regitur orbis? Swedish Count Oxenstiern (1583–1654). [L. **an** or (1); **nescis** do you not know (2); **mi** my (3); **fili** son (4); **quantilla** with how little/small (5); **prudentia** (with) sagacity, intelligence (6); **regitur** is ruled, governed (8); **orbis** world (7): Do you not know, my son, with how little intelligence the world is ruled?] Do you not know, my son, with what little sagacity (or wisdom) the world is governed?

annexe *n., pl.* **annexes** [Fr. building attached to or adjoining a larger one.] 1. Annex. Outlying building. *The man seems to have an annexe in the State House . . . (The Guardian* 1986). 2. A rider; i.e., to a bill. Schedule; i.e., to an act. 3. Appendix. Supplement; i.e., to a report or book. *With 320 articles and nine annexes, the draft treaty for an international "Law of the Sea" is a bewilderingly complex document . . . (Newsweek Int.* March 23, 1981:22).

anni nubiles *pl. n*. [L. **anni** years (2); **nubiles** marriageable (1): marriageable years.] The age of marriage, i.e., of a woman. *Ordinarily, a woman who has not reached anni nubiles must obtain the consent of her parents before contracting marriage.*

anno aetatis suae *adv*. [L. **anno** in the year (1); **aetatis** (of) age (3); **suae** (of) one's own, his/her (2): in the year of one's own age.] At the age of. Used to indicate the age of the deceased on tombstones or the age of the subject on artwork. Cf. **aetatis suae**.

anno ante Christum *abbr*. **A.A.C.** *adv*. [L. **anno** in the year (1); **ante** before (2); **Christum** Christ (3): in the year before Christ.] In the year before the birth of Jesus Christ. B.C. See **anno ante Christum natum**, **ante Christum**, and **ante Christum natum**. Cf. **anno Christi** and **anno post Christum natum**.

anno ante Christum natum *abbr*. **A.A.C.N.** *adv*. [L. **anno** in the year (1); **ante** before (2); **Christum** Christ (3); **natum** having been born (4): in the year before Christ having been born.] In the year before Jesus Christ's birth. B.C. See **anno ante Christum**.

anno Christi *abbr*. **A.C.** *adv*. [L. **anno** in the year (1); **Christi** of Christ (2): in the year of Christ.] In the year of the birth of Jesus Christ. A.D. Cf. **anno ante Christum**.

anno Domini *abbr*. **A.D.** *adv*. [L. **anno** in the year (1); **Domini** of Lord (2): in the year of the Lord.] In the year of the birth of the Lord (Jesus Christ), as opposed to B. C. or Before Christ. Christian chronology, which is based on the date of the birth of Christ. —*n*. The approach or advance of old age. *Anno Domini has a way of instilling sobriety and sanity in even the most reckless man.*

anno Hebraico *abbr*. **A.H.** *adv*. [L. **anno** in year (2); **Hebraico** in Hebrew (1): in the Hebrew year.] In the Jewish year, calculated from the year of creation, 3761 B.C.

anno Hegirae *abbr*. **A.H.** *adv*. [L. **anno** in the year (1); **Hegirae** from Ar. **Hijrah** migration (2): in the year of the migration.] In the year of the Hegira. Muslim chronology which is based on the Hijrah, the migration of the prophet Mohammed and his followers from Mecca to Medina, in A.D. 622. See **Hegira**.

anno humanae salutis *abbr.* **A.H.S.** *adv.* [L. **anno** in year (1); **humanae** of human (2); **salutis** (of) safety, salvation (3): in the year of human salvation.] In the year of the salvation of humankind (by Jesus Christ).

anno inventionis *abbr.* **A.I.** *adv.* [L. **anno** in year (1); **inventionis** of invention, discovery (2): in the year of discovery.] In the year of the invention or discovery.

anno lucis *abbr.* **A.L.** *adv.* [L. **anno** in the year (1); **lucis** of light (2): in the year of light.] In the year of light or creation. Chronology used by many Freemasons who take 4,000 B. C. as the year of the creation of the world, roughly following the Book of Genesis. By their chronological computation, therefore, A.D. 1989 should be anno lucis 5989. Cf. **anno mundi** and **anno orbis conditi**.

anno mundi *abbr.* **A.M.** *adv.* [L. **anno** in the year (1); **mundi** of the world (2): in the year of the world.] Chronology based on the date the world is supposed to have been created, e.g., 4,004 B.C. Cf. **anno lucis** and **anno orbis conditi**.

anno orbis conditi *abbr.* **A.O.C.** *adv.* [L. **anno** in the year (1); **orbis** of the world (2); **conditi** (of) having been founded, founded (3): in the year of the world having been founded.] In the year of the creation (or foundation) of the world. In the year of the creation. Cf. **anno lucis** and **anno mundi**.

anno post Christum natum *abbr.* **A.P.C.** *adv.* [L. **anno** in the year (l); **post** after (2); **Christum** Christ (3); **natum** having been born (4): in the year after Christ having been born.] In the year after Christ's birth. **A.D.** (q.v.). Cf. **anno ante Christum**.

anno regni *abbr.* **A.R.** *adv.* [L. **anno** in the year (1); **regni** of reign (2): in the year of the reign.] Generally followed by the name of the king or queen and the number of years of the reign; e.g., *anno regni 6*, i.e., in the 6th year of the reign. See **anno regni reginae** and **anno regni regis**.

anno regni reginae *abbr.* **A.R.R.** *adv.* [L. **anno** in the year (1); **regni** of the reign (2); **reginae** of the queen (3): in the year of the reign of the queen.] See **anno regni**.

anno regni regis *abbr.* **A.R.R.** *adv.* [L. **anno** in the year (1); **regni** of the reign (2); **regis** of the king (3): in the year of the reign of the king.] See **anno regni**.

anno salutis *abbr.* **A.S.** *adv.* [L. **anno** in the year (1); **salutis** of safety, deliverance (2): in the year of safety.] In the year of redemption or salvation.

anno urbis conditae *abbr.* **A.U.C.** *adv.* [L. **anno** in the year (l); **urbis** of the city (2); **conditae** (of) having been founded (3): in the year of the city having been founded.] In the year of the foundation (or founding) of the city; i.e., 753 B.C., the traditional date of the foundation of Rome. See **ab urbe condita** and **post urbem conditam**.

annuit coeptis [L. **annuit** he/she signifies approval, approves (1); **coeptis** things begun, undertakings (2): He approves undertakings.] He (i.e., God) approves our undertakings. Motto on the reverse of the great seal of the United States of America, reproduced on the back of the one-dollar bill. This phrase is based on Vergil's *Georgics* I, 40.

annus horribilis *n.* [L. **annus** year (2); **horribilis** horrible (1): horrible year.] A disastrous year. A year of great trial and tribulation. *Because of all her family difficulties the queen described 1992 as an annus horribilis.* Cf. **année terrible**.

annus inceptus pro completo habetur. [L. **annus** year (1); **inceptus** begun (2); **pro** as (4); **completo** completed (5); **habetur** is had, held, regarded (3): A year begun is held as completed.] *Law.* A year begun is considered completed. Cf. **dies inceptus** etc.

annus luctus *n.* [L. **annus** year (1); **luctus** of grief, mourning (2): year of mourning.] *Roman Law.* A widow should not remarry during the year of mourning. This was to obviate the possibility of the birth of a child with disputed parentage. The practice is observed with variations in some African societies.

annus mirabilis *abbr.* **A.M.** *n., pl.* **anni mirabiles** [L. **annus** year (2); **mirabilis** wonderful, extraordinary (1): wonderful year.] A particularly notable year. a) *For the U.S.A., an annus mirabilis is 1776.* b) *Nigeria's annus mirabilis is 1960, while Ghana's is 1957.* c) *For Britain, 1666, the year of the great fire in London as well as of the defeat of the Dutch fleet, is regarded as an annus mirabilis.* d) *As we celebrate our annus mirabilis year by year, our leaders should endeavor to justify the significance of the occasion by improving the quality of life in the country.*

annuus reditus *n.* [L. **annuus** yearly (1); **reditus** revenue, income, return (2): yearly revenue.] A yearly revenue, income, or return. A yearly rent.

anoesia *n.* [Gk. **a-** no, not (1); **noēsis** understanding (2): no understanding, want of understanding.] Idiocy. Mental deficiency. See **amentia** and **anoia**.

anoia *n.* [Gk. **a-** no, not (1); **nous** mind (2): no mind, want of understanding, folly.] Deficiency of the mind, especially idiocy. See **amentia** and **anoesia**.

anomia *n.* [Gk. **a-** no, not (1); **nom(os)** law (2): no law, lawlessness, lawless conduct, anomy.] 1. A situation or state in which no laws or norms are observed. A societal situation in which accepted standards of belief, behavior, conduct, etc. have been undermined or weakened. 2. A state of normlessness in an individual, principally manifested by anxiety, isolation from society, and disorientation.

anomie *n., pl.* **anomies** [Fr. from Gk. **anomia** lawlessness.] Anomy. **Anomia** (q.v.). *Both the police and the underworld are the involuntary victims of the glaring contradictions in the unfolding Nigerian sociocultural anomie* (*The Guardian* 1986).

anorexia *n.* [Gk. **an-** no, not (1); **orexis** appetite (2): no appetite, want of desire or appetite.] *Medicine.* Prolonged loss of appetite. *And the British released convicted bomber Dolours Price . . . because she was "in imminent danger of sudden collapse and death" from anorexia* (*Newsweek Int.* May 4, 1981:9).

anorexia nervosa *n.* [Neo-Gk./L. from Gk. **anorexia** want of appetite (2); L. **nervosa** nervous (l): nervous want of appetite.] *Medicine.* Morbid loss of appetite due to psychological reasons, and usually accompanied by emaciation of the body. *Growing despondent, she began to show signs of anorexia nervosa, and her weight plunged from 137 pounds to 87 pounds in three months* (*Newsweek Int.* July 11, 1983:11).

Anschluss *n., pl.* **Anschlüsse** or **Anschlusses** [Ger. **Anschluß**: **an** in, close to (2); **Schluß** close, end (1): close in, connection, political union.] An alliance or union. A political or economic union of one country with another. Used especially of the German-Austrian union of 1938. *The Senegal-Gambia Anschluss, called Senegambia, seems to be a union of two unequal parties.*

an sich *adj.* [Ger. **an** in (1); **sich** itself (2): in itself.] Potentially. In its essential or true nature. Cf. **Ding an sich**.

ante *prep.* [L. before.] Used for chronology (e.g., *ante 1960*). —*adv.* Mentioned previously. Above. Supra. Used for bibliographical reference. —*pref.* Prior. Prior to. Preceding. Earlier than. In front of. a) *ante-natal*. b) *ante-bellum*.

ante-bellum *adj.* [L. **ante** before (1); **bellum** war (2): before the war.] 1. Existing or occurring before the war. *Nigeria should learn a lesson from the civil war and take steps to rectify the socio-economic and political ills of the ante-bellum period, which continue to plague the nation.* 2. *American.* Pre-Civil War. *Alabama refurbished the entire exterior of its ante-bellum capitol in Montgomery in 1981 for roughly $3 million* (*Time Int.* 1982). Cf. **post-bellum**.

Ante Christum *abbr.* **A.C.** *adv.* [L. **ante** before (1); **Christum** Christ (2): before Christ.] (In the year) before Christ. B.C. See **anno ante Christum**.

Ante Christum natum *abbr.* **A.C.N.** *adv.* [L. **ante** before (1); **Christum** Christ (2); **natum** having been born (3): before Christ having been born.] Before the birth of Christ. B.C. See **anno ante Christum**.

ante diem *abbr.* **A.D.** or **a.d.** *adj./adv.* [L. **ante** before (1); **diem** day (2): before the day.] Before the day appointed. Early. *The loan payments were completed ante diem.*

ante litem motam *adv.* [L. **ante** before (1); **litem** suit (2); **motam** having been moved, set in motion (3): before a suit having been set in motion.] Before litigation was in contemplation. Before the controversy arose. a) *There is ample evidence that the parties lived under the same roof ante litem motam.* b) *Declarations by deceased relatives made ante litem motam are admissible to prove matters of family pedigree or legitimacy* (Burke 1976:28). Cf. **post litem motam**.

ante meridiem *abbr.* **A.M.** or **a.m.** *adj.* [L. **ante** before (1); **meridiem** noon, midday (2): before noon.] Before noon. In the morning. *It was agreed that the parties should meet at nine o'clock ante meridiem.* Cf. **post meridiem**.

ante mortem *adj.* [L. **ante** before (1); **mortem** death (2): before death.] Occurring before death. a) *an ante mortem diagnosis*; b) *ante mortem interest.* Cf. **post mortem**.

ante natus or **ante-natus** *n., pl.* **ante nati** or **ante-nati** [L. **ante** before (2); **natus** born (1): born before.] 1. A person born before a momentous event and whose legal status is affected by that event. 2. *Britain.* A person born before the union with Scotland. 3. *U.S.A.* A person born before the signing of the Declaration of Independence. 4. A person born before the marriage of the parents. Cf. **post natus**.

ante-partum *adj.* [L. **ante** before (1); **partum** birth, delivery (2): before birth.] Preceding childbirth. Pertaining to the period before the birth of a child. *The baby's sickness is probably attributable to ante-partum infection.*

ante rem *adv./adj.* [L. **ante** before (1); **rem** matter, thing, property, business, affairs (2): before the thing.] *Philosophy.* Existing before something else, especially a general or universal concept existing before a particular one. Cf. **post rem**.

anti *pref.* [Gk. opposite, over against.] 1. Opposing, disputing or challenging the claims of. *Antichrist.* 2. Opposite to. a) *anticlimax*; b) *antigravity*. 3. Hostile or opposed to in sentiment, opinion, sympathy, act, etc. a) *antiapartheid*; b) *anti-communist*; c) *antisocial*; d) *anti-democratic*. 4. Fighting against. Attacking. a) *antiballistic*; b) *antiaircraft*; c) *antibacterial*. —*adj.* Against or opposed to, especially a proposal, motion, policy, etc. *During the debate the anti side was very vociferous.* —*n., pl.* **antis** A person who is opposed or in opposition to something. *The matter generated considerable emotional controversy, as the pros and antis seemed ready to resort to physical violence.*

antichresis *n., pl.* **antichreses** [Gk. **antichrēsis**: **anti** against, opposite (1); **chrēsis** use, employment (2): opposite use, substitution of usufruct for interest.] *Law.* A kind of mortgage contract whereby the debtor pledges his/her property, and the creditor takes the income from the mortgaged property in lieu of interest on the debt. In French law, the debtor could claim the excess, if the income exceeded the interest.

antiphrasis *n., pl.* **antiphrases** [Gk. **anti** against, opposite (2); **phrasis** saying, speaking (1): saying the opposite.] *Rhetoric.* Using a word, either ironically or humorously, in a connotation contrary to the usual connotation; e. g., "a mountain 100 ft. high."

antithesis *n., pl.* **antitheses** [Gk. **anti** against, opposite (2); **thesis** putting, placing (1): putting opposite.] 1. Opposition. Counter-proposition. Substitution of the contradictory. 2. Contrary. Direct opposite. *Only the most gullible and naive person would expect a regime which came to power through means that are the very antithesis of democracy to be always preoccupied with legal niceties* (*The Guardian* 1987). 3. *Rhetoric.* Balanced contrast of ideas, concepts, etc., which are directly opposite to each other; e.g., "The regime, which promised democracy, has instituted a reign of terror" and "We want deeds, not words."

antonomasia *n., pl.* **antonomasias** [Gk. **anti** against, opposite (2); **onoma** name (1): name opposite, the use of an epithet, patronymic or appellation for a proper name, and vice versa.] *Rhetoric.* 1. Using another designation in place of one which is common or normal; e.g., "Chief executive" for the "President" or "Vice-Chancellor." 2. Using an epithet or an official title instead of a proper name; e.g., "his honor" instead of "Judge Anas." 3. Using a characteristic proper name for a member of a class or group of people; e.g., "a Methuselah" for "a very old man." 4. Forming a verb or a common noun from a proper name; e.g., "The government has Shugabaed a prominent lecturer."

A.O.C. *abbr.* for **anno orbis conditi** (q.v.).

A.O.F. *abbr.* for **Afrique Occidentale Française** (q.v.).

à outrance or **à l'outrance** *adv.* [Fr. **à** to, toward, in, by, with, until (1); **outrance** excess (2): to excess.] To the bitter end. In an exaggerated manner. To the utmost. To the death. To a finish. Unsparingly. Unremittingly. Unmercifully. *He is an evil-minded man who persecutes his rivals à outrance.* Cf. **guerre à outrance** and **outrance**.

apanage or **appanage** *n., pl.* **apanages** or **appanages** [Fr. attribute, prerogative, lot, portion.] 1. Property, allowance, revenue, office, etc., given to a prince or a member of the royal family for his/her support. 2. Something which naturally or necessarily accompanies something else. *John's main defect is lack of good character, the apanage of good upbringing.* 3. A territory which is a principality or a dependency.

à part entière *adv.* [Fr. **à** to, toward, in, by, with, until (1); **part** part (3); **entière** entire, whole (2): by the entire part.] Entirely. Wholly. Completely. Fully. In all respects. *The French schoolchild or elector . . . was given to believe that the policy of direct administration was aimed at gradually raising the blacks of Africa to the condition of the French à part entière* (Suret-Canale 1971:83).

apartheid *n.* [Afr. apartness, separateness, separation, segregation.] Racial separation or segregation, particularly the system of political, social and economic segregation and discrimination between Europeans and non-Europeans practiced by the government of the Union of South Africa. *Nadine Gordimer, 58, has won international acclaim for her sharp-edged portrayals of South African life under apartheid* (*Newsweek Int.* Nov. 8, 1982:56). —*adj.* Of, relating to, characteristic of apartheid. a) *In recent and separate elections the coloured and Indian communities . . . have confirmed their rejection of the apartheid system* (*South* 1984). b) *Critics of Pretoria's apartheid policies charge that the government's indifference to blacks' education perpetuates their second-class status* (*Newsweek Int.* Nov. 24, 1980:22).

apatheia *n.* [Gk. **a-** no, not (1); **path(os)** feeling (2): no feeling.] Freedom from emotion. Freedom from excitement.

A.P.C.N. *abbr.* for **anno post Christum natum** (q.v.).

aperçu *n., pl.* **aperçus** [Fr. glimpse, idea, brief account, statement.] 1. A glimpse. An intuitive insight or understanding. An immediate impression. *From the outside, celebrity means receiving invitations to all the best parties, swapping aperçus with the noterati . . .* (*Time Int.* 1980). 2. An outline. A summary. A brief sketch or survey. *She reduced her doctoral dissertation of 300 pages to an aperçu of four pages.*

apex *n., pl.* **apices** or **apexes** [L. extreme end or point, summit, top, a projecting point, the highest ornament.] 1. Top. Summit. Peak. *The apex of Mt. Everest.* 2. Tip. *The apex of the tongue.* 3. The culmination; climax. *He reached the apex of his career in 1982 when he was appointed Chief Justice.* 4. *Mining Law.* The edge of a vein of mineral.

apex juris *n.* [L. **apex** summit, extreme point (1); **juris** of right, law (2): summit or extreme point of law.] Extreme application of a rule of law; i.e., a stricter application of a rule of law than that of summum jus. Cf. **aequitas**.

aphasia *n.* [Gk. **a-** no (1); **phasis** speaking (2): no speaking, speechlessness.] 1. Inability to speak caused by perplexity or fear. 2. *Medicine.* A disease of the brain which involves the loss of the power to speak articulately. It may take the form of inability to vocalize words and to write words as one desires (*motor aphasia*) or inability to understand language, whether written or spoken (*sensory aphasia*). Cf. **aphonia**.

aphonia *n.* [Gk. **aphōnia**: **a-** no (1); **phōn(ē)** sounding, voicing (2): no sounding.] Speechlessness. *Medicine.* Inability to speak articulately as a result of defects in the vocal organs. When partial, the patient is able to whisper. Cf. **aphasia**.

aphrodisia *n.* [Gk. belonging to Aphrodite (Venus), the goddess of love, sexual pleasures.] Violent sexual desire. See **andromania**.

apices juris non sunt jura. [L. **apices** extreme points (1); **juris** of right, law (2); **non** not (4); **sunt** are (3); **jura** rights, laws (5): Extreme points of law are not laws.] Extremes of law (or mere subtleties of law) are bad rules of law.

apices litigandi *n.* [L. **apices** extreme points (1); **litigandi** of that which must be disputed, of litigation (2): extreme points of litigation.] Subtle or very fine points of litigation.

aplomb *n., pl.* **aplombs** [Fr. **a** to, toward (1); **plomb** lead, lead-weight (2): toward lead; i.e., nerve, self-possession.] Self-possession. Self-confidence. Self-assurance. Poise. Assurance of manner. a) *Throughout the interview he spoke and conducted himself with remarkable aplomb.* b) *With a deft combination of diplomatic finesse and public relations aplomb, he has managed to focus the camera on himself* (Newsweek Int. Aug. 9, 1982:11).

apocrypha *pl. n.*, sometimes used as *sing.* [Gk. **apo** from, away (2); **krupt(ō)** hide, conceal (1): things hidden away or concealed.] 1. Statements, sayings, or writings whose authorship or authenticity is doubtful. *Among the apocrypha attributed to the author is a collection of risqué poems.* 2. *Christianity.* Books of Holy Scripture whose authorship and authenticity were considered doubtful by the Jews and are, therefore, not included in the canon; e.g., the Book of Tobit. Cf. **agrapha.**

apodosis *n., pl.* **apodoses** [Gk. **apo** from, away (2); **dosis** giving (1): giving away.] *Rhetoric.* Clause answering to the protasis. The main clause or conclusion of a conditional sentence; e. g., "I would have bought a pair of shoes [if my father had given me the money]." Cf. **hypothesis** 3 and **protasis** 3.

apogée or **apogee** *n., pl.* **apogées** or **apogees** [Fr. from Gk. **apo** from, away (1); **gē** earth (2): from the earth.] 1. Climax. Apex. Zenith. Culmination. Peak. The highest point. See **acme.** 2. *Astronomy.* The position in the orbit of the moon or any planet when it is farthest from the center of the earth.

apologia *n., pl.* **apologiae** or **apologias** [Gk. **apo** from, away (2); **log(os)** word, speech (1): a speech away, a defense speech.] A defense. A written or oral defense of a person's deeds or views. *This speech is not an apologia, but a clear and unequivocal statement of facts.* Cf. **apologia pro vita sua.**

apologia pro vita sua *n.* [L. **apologia** apology, defense (1); **pro** for, on behalf of, in accordance with, as (2); **vita** life (4); **sua** one's own (3): a defense for one's own life.] A formal defense, either written or oral, of one's life and principles, such as those of Socrates and John Henry Newman.

aposiopesis *n., pl.* **aposiopeses** [Gk. becoming silent.] *Rhetoric.* A figure whereby, for emphasis, because of modesty, or for some other reason, the writer or speaker breaks off the sentence abruptly; e,g, "His conduct was, . . . but need I say it?"

a posse ad esse [L. **a** from, by (1); **posse** to be able, possibility (2); **ad** to, at, for, according to (3); **esse** to be, being (4): from possibility to being.] From possibility to reality.

a posteriori *adj.* [L. **a** from (1); **posteriori** the latter, later (2): from the latter/later.] *Logic.* Empirical.

Inductive. Deriving propositions from the observation of facts. Relating to arguments based on observation. Deriving cause from effect. Relating to inductive reasoning. *He attempted to prove his point by resorting to an a posteriori demonstration.* —*adv.* By argument based on deriving cause from effect. Inductively. Empirically. Cf. **a priori.**

apostoli *pl. n.* [L. from Gk. **apostoloi** those sent away, messengers.] *Civil Law.* Apostles, i.e., dimissory letters from an inferior to a superior court, granted to a party who makes an appeal.

apostrophe *n., pl.* **apostrophes** [Gk. **apostrophē**: **apo** from, away (2); **strophē** turning (1): a turning away.] *Rhetoric.* Direct address of an absent person, an animal, or an inanimate object; e.g., "O death, where is thy sting?"

apotheosis *n., pl.* **apotheoses** [Gk. **apotheōsis**: **apo** from, away (2); **theōsis** making a god (1): making a god from.] Deification. Raising or elevating a human being to the status of a god. A person's or thing's ascension from mundane existence to celestial glory. *The apotheosis of Alexander the Great.* 2. The highest form or development of a thing. The quintessential form. A glorified ideal. A perfect form. a) *All communist regimes . . . cling to power by relying on variations of the coercive methods and totalitarian precepts that have attained their apotheosis in the U.S.S.R.* (Time Int. 1982). b) *For years the chief staple of Broadway has been British imports; in "Nickleby" that trend reaches its apotheosis* (Newsweek Int. Oct. 12, 1981:57).

app. *abbr.* for 1. **apparatus** 2. **appendix** (q.v.).

appanage *var.* of **apanage** (q.v.).

apparat *n., pl.* **apparats** [Russ. from L. **apparatus** (q.v.).] A bureaucracy or political machine, especially that of the U.S.S.R. *. . . the White House Military Office, one of the most powerful and least known apparats of the modern Presidency* (Newsweek Int. May 26, 1980:29).

apparatchik *n., pl.* **apparatchiki** or **apparatchiks** [Russ. agent of the **apparat.**] A Soviet bureaucrat. A secret agent of the Communists.

apparatus *abbr.* **app.** *n., pl.* **apparatus** or **apparatuses** [L. preparation, equipment, tools, instruments.] 1. A set of instruments, tools, machines, etc. designed to be used for a particular purpose (e.g., research). 2. A group of physical organs that unite to serve a specific purpose. 3. A combination of processes which ensure the functioning of an organization such as a government or a political party. *China's security apparatus has finally begun to recover from the organizational turmoil it suffered during the Cultural Revolution* (Newsweek Int. July 25, 1983:23).

apparatus belli *n., pl.* **apparatus belli** [L. **apparatus** equipment (1); **belli** of/for war (2): equipment for war.] The tools of war.

apparatus criticus *n., pl.* **apparatus critici** [L. **apparatus** equipment (2); **criticus** critical (1): critical equipment.] Variant readings added to a main text to show its treatment in manuscripts, earlier editions, etc. *The professor showed the students how to take advantage of the apparatus criticus in order to establish the text more firmly.*

appendix *abbr.* **app.** or **appx.** or **apx.** *n., pl.* **appendices** or **appendixes** [L. addition, continuation, supplement.] 1. Something added or appended to something else. An appendage. 2. Material, such as the tables or bibliography added to a book, particularly after the text. 3. Tube at the bottom of a balloon which is used for inflating or deflating it. 4. *Medicine.* A supplementary part or appendage of a bodily organ, particularly the vermiform appendix, i.e., an appendage of the large intestine which resembles a worm in shape.

appetitus societalis *n.* [L. **appetitus** eager desire, passion (1); **societalis** for/of association; community, fellowship (2): eager desire for fellowship.] Passion or eager desire for association/fellowship. *Grotius believed that man was distinguished from the animals by his appetitus societalis, a "domestic instinct" which led him to desire "peaceful organised society . . . with those of his own kind"* (Curzon 1979:64).

applicatio est vita regulae. [L. **applicatio** application (1); **est** is (2); **vita** life (3); **regulae** of rule (4): Application is the life of a rule.] A rule has meaning in the ways it is applied to particular situations and cases.

appliqué *n., pl.* **appliqués** [Fr. applied, fastened, attached.] A technique in needlework or woodwork, in which pieces cut from one material are attached on the surface of another material. —*v.* To use such a technique, especially for decorative purposes.

appoggiatura *n., pl.* **appoggiaturas** [It. leaning on.] *Music.* A note which leans on or is supported by another note, usually just above or below it.

apports en nature *pl. n., sing.* **apport en nature** [Fr. **apports** contributions (1); **en** in (2); **nature** kind, nature (3): contributions in kind.] *French Law.* A partner's contributions to the partnership apart from cash; these include securities, stock, and personal expertise.

appx. *abbr.* for **appendix** (q.v.).

après *prep.* [Fr. after.] Following. After. *Après Thoeni, Italy's skiers, homegrown and foreign, doubled . . .* (*Newsweek Int.* Feb. 19, 1979:56). —**après-ski.** A clothing style in winter holiday lodges. That which one wears after a day of skiing.

après moi le déluge [Fr. **après** after (1); **moi** me (2); **le** the (3); **déluge** deluge, flood (4): After me the deluge.] After me comes the flood, the disaster. Cf. **après nous**, etc.

après nous le déluge Mme de Pompadour (1721–1764). [Fr. **après** after (1); **nous** us (2); **le** the (3); **déluge** deluge, flood (4): After us the deluge.] After we are gone, there will come disaster. Cf. **après moi**, etc.

a priori *adj.* [L. **a** from (1); **priori** the previous, former (2): from the former.] *Logic.* Deriving effect from cause. From the cause to the effect. Relating to deductive reasoning. Based on assumption. Presumptive. *Proof a priori consists in demonstrating the necessary agreement of anything with a rational or social nature* (quoted by Curzon 1979:64). —*adv.* By argument based on deriving effect from cause, or on assumption. Presumptively. Deductively. Intuitively. —*n., pl.* **a prioris** Something such as a belief, conception, doctrine, or proposition which is a priori. Cf. **a posteriori**.

à propos or **apropos** *adj.* [Fr. **à** to, toward, in, by, with, until (1); **propos** purpose, matter, subject (2): to the purpose or matter.] Pertinent. Relevant. *If you do not have à propos comments, it would be wise for you to keep quiet.* —*adv.* 1. Pertinently. Just in time. In good time. To the purpose or point. *It is not clear whether or not it is a mere coincidence, but his father always arrives à propos whenever he is impecunious.* 2. Incidentally. By the way. *À propos, have you heard the good news?* —*prep.* Concerning. With respect to. In connection with. Regarding. *He said that he had no comment to make à propos the matter.*

apx. *abbr.* for **appendix** (q.v.).

aqua cedit solo. [L. **aqua** water (1); **cedit** accrues (2); **solo** to land, ground (3): Water accrues to the land.] *Law.* Water goes with the land; i.e., when land is sold, the water on it is included in the transaction.

aqua currit et debet currere, ut currere solebat. [L. **aqua** water (1); **currit** runs (2); **et** and (3); **debet** ought (4); **currere** to run (5) **ut** as (6); **currere** to run (8); **solebat** it was accustomed (7): Water runs and should run as it was accustomed to run.] *Law.* Water flows and should flow as it has flowed in the past; i.e., if a running stream is common property, its course should not be diverted.

aqua destillata *n., pl.* **aquae destillatae** [L. **aqua** water (2); **destillata** distilled, trickled (1): distilled water.] Purified water.

aqua et igne interdictus *adj.* [L. **aqua** water (2); **et** and (3); **igne** fire (4); **interdictus** forbidden (1): forbidden water and fire.] An ancient formula for banishment by denying the individual the basic elements of communal life, i.e., shared sources of water and fire.

aqua fortis or **aquafortis** *n.* [L. **aqua** water (2); **fortis** strong (1): strong water.] Nitric acid.

aqua pura *n., pl.* **aquae purae** [L. **aqua** water (2); **pura** pure, clean, unstained (1): clean water.] Pure water.

aqua regia *n., pl.* **aquae regiae** [L. **aqua** water (2); **regia** royal, kingly (1): royal water.] A liquid produced by mixing nitric acid and hydrochloric acid, and used for dissolving gold, platinum, etc.

aquarium *n., pl.* **aquaria** or **aquariums** [L. water carrier.] 1. A container, usually with glass sides, or an artificial pond in which living fishes or other aquatic animals are kept and displayed. 2. A building where aquatic items are kept and displayed.

Aquarius *n.* [L. the water carrier.] 1. *Astronomy.* A constellation located just below the equator near Pisces and Aquila. 2. *Astrology.* The eleventh sign of the zodiac dominant from January 20 through February 18. 3. A person born when this constellation is dominant.

aqua vitae *n.* [L. **aqua** water (1); **vitae** of life (2): water of life.] 1. Alcohol, particularly one distilled from the vine. 2. Strong alcoholic drink such as brandy or whisky. Cf. **eau de vie.**

Aquila *n.* [L. eagle.] A constellation near Aquarius and Pisces.

a quo *adj.* [L. **a** from (1); **quo** which (2): from which.] *Law.* Used to indicate a court or judge from which/ whom a case is removed. a) *the court a quo*; b) *the judge a quo.* See **dies a quo.**

A.R. *abbr.* for **anno regni** (q.v.).

arabesque *n., pl.* **arabesques** [Fr. Arabian, in the manner of an Arab.] 1. *Ballet.* A position in which the dancer extends one foot behind and balances on the other. 2. *Music.* A very short, capricious piece, usually written for the piano. 3. A complicated or complex pattern or design.

arbiter *n., pl.* **arbitri** or **arbiters** [L. judge, arbitrator, umpire, mediator.] 1. A judge or arbitrator appointed by parties or a court on behalf of the parties to decide a dispute between them. 2. A person or an agency entrusted with absolute power to determine or judge a dispute. *This consortium of American Universities is accustomed to a situation where their Supreme Court is the final arbiter of law in the land* (*The Guardian* 1986). 3. A person who exercises complete control over something. *His father is virtually a tyrant; he is the sole and unchallenged arbiter of the fortunes of everybody in the family.*

arbiter bibendi *n., pl.* **arbitri bibendi** [L. **arbiter** judge (1); **bibendi** of drinking (2): judge of drinking.] Master of ceremonies.

arbiter elegantiarum or **arbiter elegantiae** *n., pl.* **arbitri elegantiarum** or **arbitri elegantiae** [L. **arbiter** judge (1); **elegantiarum** of tastes, refinements, elegance (2): judge of tastes.] A judge or supreme authority in matters of taste and social behavior. a) *Gaius Petronius, attendant at the court of the Roman emperor Nero and author of the* Satyricon, *set the standards by which all subsequent arbiter elegantiarum must be judged.* b) *Mr. Applegate has become a leading arbiter elegantiae, and there is hardly a socialite in the city who has not consulted him on one thing or the other.*

arboretum *n., pl.* **arboreta** or **arboretums** [L. a place of trees.] A garden where rare trees and shrubs are cultivated and displayed or used for research and other educational purposes.

Arcadia [Gk. **Arkadia.**] 1. The central, mountainous region of the Peloponnesus noted especially for the rearing of sheep and goats. 2. Any place representing the peace and simplicity of pastoral life. Rustic tranquillity. Cf. **et in Arcadia ego.**

arcana imperii *pl. n.* [L. **arcana** secrets, mysteries (1); **imperii** of empire, sovereignty (2): secrets of empire/sovereignty.] State secrets. *Some civil servants frustrate journalists by putting even ordinary information in the category of arcana imperii.*

arcanum *n., pl.* **arcana** [L. a secret, mystery.] A secret. Confidential knowledge. Mysterious information which should not be divulged to the uninitiated. *Most African traditional medical practitioners regard their art as an arcanum.*

arcanum arcanorum *n.* [L. **arcanum** secret (1); **arcanorum** of secrets (2): secret of secrets.] The ultimate secret which, supposedly, is the foundation on which alchemy, astrology, and magic are built.

arc de triomphe *n., pl.* **arcs de triomphe** [Fr. **arc** arch (1); **de** of (2); **triomphe** triumph (3): arch of triumph.] Triumphal arch.

Architecturae Magister *abbr.* **Ar.M.** *n.* [L. **architecturae** of architecture (2); **magister** master (1): Master of Architecture.] A predoctoral graduate degree in architecture.

arcta et salva custodia *adv.* [L. **arcta** in close (1); **et** and (2); **salva** (in) safe (3); **custodia** (in) custody, imprisonment (4): in close and safe custody.] The type of custody for people arrested on a **capias ad satisfaciendum** (q.v.). See **in arcta** etc.

arena *n., pl.* **arenas** [L. **harena** sand, sandy place, sandy ground used for entertainment.] 1. *Ancient Rome.* The area in the middle of the amphitheater used for gladiatorial shows and other forms of entertainment. 2. The area in the middle of an enclosed place which is used for entertainment. 3. A building containing an area or areas used for entertainment. 4. A field of interest or activity. Scene of contest, struggle or competition. a) *When it comes to astuteness in the political arena, Simon is second to none.* b) *It* [i.e., the U.N.] *has become nothing more than an arena for politicking* (*Newsweek Int.* Nov. 3, 1980:10).

à rendre *adj.* [Fr. **à** to, toward, in, by, with, until (1); **rendre** to yield, render (2): to yield or render.] What is to be paid or rendered. *Law.* Used to describe "profits," and these cover services and rents.

Areopagus *n., pl.* **Areopaguses** [L. from Gk. **Areiopagos: Areo(s)** of Ares (2); **pagos** rock, hill (1): the hill of Ares.] 1. -The hill of the god Ares in Athens. 2. The council which met on this hill was originally Athens' principal and most influential governmental body, but was ultimately reduced to the status of a court for the trial of homicides. 3. A tribunal or group of persons whose decisions are authoritative.

arete *n.* [Gk. **aretē** excellence.] Excellence. Virtue.

argentum Dei *n., pl.* **argenta Dei** [L. **argentum** silver (2); **Dei** God's, of God (1): God's silver.] *Law.* God's penny. God's money; i.e., a small sum of money given as a token of good faith during or after the conclusion of a bargain. See **denarius Dei** and **denier à Dieu**. Cf. **pot-de-vin**.

argot *n., pl.* **argots** [Fr. slang, jargon.] 1. A special language, jargon, vocabulary, etc. used by a particular group of criminals or a particular social class or group. a) *the argot of armed robbers*; b) *the argot of Nigerian students*; c) *the argot of wrestling*. 2. Slang.

arguendi causa *adv.* [L. **arguendi** of arguing (2); **causa** for the sake, by reason (1): for the sake of arguing.] For argument's sake. For the sake of argument. a) *If I concede a point arguendi causa, it by no means signifies that it is the truth.* b) *Whilst granting arguendi causa that a communication which went no further would, in general, not, in the absence of circumstances giving a particular significance, amount to a threat or intimidation, I am unable to understand why it may not be an inducement* (Weir 1974:528).

arguendo *adv./adj.* [L. by arguing.] In the course of arguing or in the argument. a) *It often happens, arguendo, that a judge refers to some hypothetical cases.* b) *Mr. Justice Cave is reported as having said 'Chiswick is not the same place as London', to which Counsel answered 'It is the same postal district'. Mr. Justice Cave therefore said that that was very different. These remarks were arguendo and obiter* (Megrah and Ryder 1972:139).

argumentum ab auctoritate est fortissimum in lege. [L. **argumentum** argument, reasoning, inference (1); **ab** from, by (2); **auctoritate** authority (3); **est** is (4); **fortissimum** strongest (5); **in** in, on (6); **lege** law (7): Reasoning from authority is the strongest in law.] An argument supported by authority carries the greatest weight in law. See **argumentum ab auctoritate plurimum** etc.

argumentum ab auctoritate plurimum valet in lege. [L. **argumentum** argument, reasoning, inference (1); **ab** from, by (2); **auctoritate** authority (3); **plurimum** most, especially (4); **valet** is valid, prevails (5); **in** in, on (6); **lege** law (7): Reasoning from authority is most valid in law.] An argument supported by authority carries the greatest weight in law. See **argumentum ab auctoritate est** etc.

argumentum ab impossibili plurimum valet in lege. [L. **argumentum** argument, reasoning, inference (1); **ab** from, by (2); **impossibili** impossible (3); **plurimum** most, especially (4); **valet** is valid, prevails (5); **in** in, on (6); **lege** law (7): Reasoning from the impossible is most valid in law.] An argument based on an impossibility carries the greatest weight in law. See **impotentia excusat legem.**

argumentum ab impossibili valet in lege. [L. **argumentum** argument, reasoning, inference (1); **ab** from, by (2); **impossibili** the impossible (3); **valet**

prevails (4); **in** in, on (5); **lege** law (6): Reasoning from the impossible prevails in law.] An argument based on impossibility carries weight in law. See **impotentia excusat legem.**

argumentum ab inconvenienti est validum in lege; quia lex non permittit aliquod inconveniens. [L. **argumentum** argument, reasoning, inference (1); **ab** from, by (2); **inconvenienti** the inconvenient (3); **est** is (4); **validum** strong, valid (5); **in** in, on (6); **lege** law (7); **quia** because (8); **lex** law (9); **non** not (11); **permittit** permits, allows (10); **aliquod** any (12); **inconveniens** inconvenient (thing) (13): Reasoning from the inconvenient is valid in law because the law does not permit any inconvenient thing.] An argument based on inconvenience is valid in law because the law does not sanction any inconvenience. See **ab inconvenienti.**

argumentum ad captandum *n., pl.* **argumenta ad captandum** [L. **argumentum** argument, reasoning, inference (1); **ad** to, at, for, according to (2); **captandum** alluring, enticing (3): reasoning for alluring.] *Logic.* Argument designed to please the crowd. *Many successful politicians are adept at the use of argumenta ad captandum.* See **ad captandum vulgus.**

argumentum ad crumenam *n., pl.* **argumenta ad crumenam** [L. **argumentum** argument, reasoning, inference (1); **ad** to, at, for, according to (2); **crumenam** money-bag, purse (3): reasoning to the purse.] *Logic.* Argument designed to exploit the audience's preoccupation with financial considerations. *By making good use of argumentum ad crumenam, the Leader of the Opposition discredited the Ruling Party and paved the way for the fall of the government.* See **ad crumenam.**

argumentum ad hominem *n., pl.* **argumenta ad hominem** [L. **argumentum** argument, reasoning, inference (1); **ad** to, at, for, according to (2); **hominem** person, human being (3): reasoning to the person.] *Logic.* An argument designed to appeal to emotions rather than to reason. *Unprincipled and narrowminded people tend to resort to argumentum ad hominem.* See **ad hominem.**

argumentum ad ignorantiam *n., pl.* **argumenta ad ignorantiam** [L. **argumentum** argument (1); **ad** to, at, for, according to (2); **ignorantiam** ignorance (3): argument to ignorance.] An argument based upon ignorance; that is, one which attacks the logic and intelligence of one's opponent.

argumentum ad verecundiam *n., pl.* **argumenta ad verecundiam** [L. **argumentum** argument (1); **ad** to, at, for, according to (2); **verecundiam** decency (3): argument to decency.] An argument based upon decency or propriety.

argumentum a silentio *n., pl.* **argumenta a silentio** [L. **argumentum** argument, reasoning, inference (1);

a from, by (2); **silentio** silence (3): reasoning from silence.] **Argumentum ex silentio** (q.v.).

argumentum a simili valet in lege. [L. **argumentum** argument, reasoning, inference (1); **a** from (2); **simili** the like (3); **valet** is valid (4); **in** in, on (5); **lege** law (6): Reasoning from the like is valid in law.] An argument based on analogy is valid in law.

argumentum ex silentio *n., pl.* **argumenta ex silentio** [L. **argumentum** argument, reasoning, inference (l); **ex** from, arising from (2); **silentio** silence (3): reasoning from silence.] *Logic.* An argument based on the failure of an authority, writer, source, etc. to mention or refer to something.

Argus *n., pl.* **Arguses** [L. from Gk. **Argos** shiny, bright.] 1. *Greek and Roman Mythology.* A guard who could keep watch constantly with his many pairs of eyes, some of which could sleep while the rest stayed awake. 2. A person who is very watchful. A vigilant watchman. —**Argus-eyed** Vigilant. Sharp-sighted. Observant. *Though the criminal was operating under the cover of darkness, the Argus-eyed constable saw and arrested him.*

aria *n., pl.* **arias** [It. air, melody.] *Music.* 1. A solo sung with instrumental accompaniment, especially in an opera. 2. A melody.

Aries *n.* [L. ram.] 1. *Astronomy.* A ram-shaped constellation located near Pisces and Taurus. 2. *Astrology.* The first sign of the zodiac dominant from March 21 through April 19. 3. A person born when this constellation is dominant.

arioso *adv./adj.* [It. like an aria.] *Music.* In the manner of an aria. —*n., pl.* **ariosos** 1. A speaking style halfway between recitative and sung. Used especially in opera. 2. A composition for a vocal soloist in this style.

Ar.M. *abbr.* for **Architecturae Magister** (q.v.).

armada *n., pl.* **armadas** [Sp. navy.] 1. A large number of boats or ships. 2. A large fleet of warships, especially the Spanish Armada. *Britain's armada steamed slowly toward the Falkland Islands last week.* (*Newsweek Int.* April 26, 1982:53). 3. A large number of mobile things, especially vehicles. *The protesters arrived in an armada of cars, buses, and trucks.*

arma in armatos sumere jura sinunt. [L. **arma** arms, weapons (4); **in** against (5); **armatos** armed men (6); **sumere** to take up (3); **jura** rights, laws (1); **sinunt** allow, permit (2): The laws allow to take up arms against armed men.] It is lawful to take up arms against armed men.

aroma *n., pl.* **aromas** [Gk. **arōma** aromatic herb or spice.] 1. Smell or odor. 2. Fragrance. A marked pleasant odor or smell. *She came to the party wearing a perfume whose aroma won for her the admiration of many guests.* 3. Flavor. A peculiar, typical, or distinctive charm, quality, characteristic, atmosphere, etc. a) *As we entered the dark room, we could feel the unmistakable aroma of danger.* b) *There is*

indeed an aroma of the great days of the ancien régime about Touba (D. B. Cruise O'Brien in *West Africa* 1982).

arpeggio *n., pl.* **arpeggios** [It. like a harp.] *Music.* Singing or playing the notes in a chord in the manner of a harp, i.e., in quick succession rather than at the same time.

A.R.R. *abbr.* for 1. **anno regni reginae** (q.v.). 2. **anno regni regis** (q.v.).

arrière-pensée *n., pl.* **arrière-pensées** [Fr. **arrière** back, after (1); **pensées** thoughts (2): after thoughts.] Mental reservation. An undisclosed thought. An undisclosed intention. Hidden or ulterior motive. Prejudice. *He came to give testimony in the celebrated trial of the President without the slightest arrière-pensée.*

arrivé *adj.* [Fr. having arrived.] Successful. Having achieved success. Having risen rapidly to a position of fame, power, etc. —*n., pl.* **arrivés** A person who has arrived, has achieved success or has risen rapidly to a position of fame, power, etc. *The village's annual festival is an occasion when many arrivés come home and flaunt their new positions.*

arriviste *n., pl.* **arrivistes** [Fr. go-getter, timeserver, climber, unscrupulous person.] Upstart. A person who attempts to achieve success or acquire wealth by whatever means. A "get-rich-quick" person. a) *The national bias against business careers is an odd mélange, combining elements of the landed gentry's contempt for bourgeois arrivistes with socialist loathing for the "bosses"* (*Newsweek Int.* April 19, 1982:52). b) *The difficult times have given birth to a number of arrivistes who, though successful, lack the self-confidence of the old aristocrats.*

arrondissement *abbr.* **arron.** *n., pl.* **arrondissements** [Fr. roundness, district.] 1. The chief administrative subdivision of a French department. 2. A municipal ward or administrative district of a large French city. a) *He was living in Paris, 14 Marx-Dormoy Street in the 18th arrondissement* (*New African* 1978). b) *If each of the city's twenty arrondissements had its own mayor, they argued, neighborhood services could be improved.* (*Newsweek Int.* July 19, 1982:16).

Ars Amatoria *n.* [L. **ars** art, skill (2); **amatoria** loving, amorous (1): loving art.] *The Art of Love*, a poem by Ovid (43 B.C.–17 A.D.).

ars est celare artem. [L. **ars** art (2); **est** it is (1); **celare** to hide (3); **artem** art (4): It is art to hide art.] Genuine or true art conceals art; i.e., the best art is the most natural. Cf. **C'est une grande** etc.

ars gratia artis [L. **ars** art (1); **gratia** for the sake (2); **artis** of art (3): art for the sake of art.] Art for art's sake. Art done only for the purposes of esthetics (as opposed to financial gain, politics, religion, etc.). The motto of Louis B. Mayer, a founder of Metro-Goldwyn-Mayer (MGM) Studios. See **l'art pour l'art.**

ars longa vita brevis. [L. **ars** art (1); **longa** long (2); **vita** life (3); **brevis** short, brief (4): Art long, life short.] Art is long, life is short; i.e., art endures long beyond the span of an individual artist's life.

Ars Poetica *n.* [L. **ars** art, skill (2); **poetica** poetic (1): poetic art.] *The Art of Poetry*, a poem on poetry by Horace (65–8 B.C.).

Artium Baccalaureus *abbr.* **A.B.** *n.* [L. **artium** of arts (2); **baccalaureus** bachelor (1): Bachelor of Arts.] Cf. **Baccalaureus Artium.**

Artium Elegantium Doctor *abbr.* **A.E.D.** *n.* [L. **artium** (of) arts (3); **elegantium** of nice, fine, tasteful (2); **doctor** teacher (1): teacher of tasteful arts.] Doctor of Fine Arts. A terminal graduate degree in the fine arts.

Artium Magister *abbr.* **A.M.** *n.* [L. **artium** of arts (2); **magister** master (1): Master of Arts.] See **Magister Artium.**

art nouveau *n.* [Fr. **art** art (2); **nouveau** new (1): new art.] *Art.* An ornamental style popular in late 19th-century France and Britain.

a rubro ad nigrum [L. **a** from (1); **rubro** red (2); **ad** to, at, for, according to (3); **nigrum** black (4): from red to black.] *Law.* From the title to the main body. Deducing the meaning of a statute from the title. In ancient times, the title of a statute was written in red, the statute itself in black letters.

aruspex *var.* of **haruspex** (q.v.).

A.S. *abbr.* for **anno salutis** (q.v.).

à savoir *adv.* [Fr. **à** to, toward, in, by, with, until (1); **savoir** know (2): to know.] To wit. Namely. That is to say. **Videlicet** (q.v.).

asiento or **assiento** *n., pl.* **asientos** or **assientos** [Sp. agreement, contract, treaty.] *History.* A contract between Spain and another country or company for the supply of slaves for her American dominions.

asphyxia *n., pl.* **asphyxias** [Gk. **a-** no, (1); **sphuxi(s)** heartbeat, pulse (2): no heartbeat, stoppage of pulse.] *Medicine.* Suffocation.

assensio mentium *n.* [L. **assensio** agreement (1); **mentium** of minds (2): agreement of minds.] *Law.* Mutual consent or assent. *Assensio mentium is the most essential ingredient of a contract.* See **ad idem.**

assets entre main *n.* [Obs. Fr. **assets** possessions, belongings (1); **entre** between, within, in (2); **main** hand (3): possessions in hand.] *Law.* Assets in hand. Assets available to an executor or administrator for payment of debts.

assignatus utitur jure auctoris. [L. **assignatus** the assignee (1); **utitur** uses, enjoys (2); **jure** right, law (3); **auctoris** of assignor, principal (4): The assignee uses the right of assignor.] *Law.* The assignee enjoys the right of the assignor; i.e., when property is assigned, it carries with it to the assignee all the rights that the assignor had in it. See **qui in jus** etc.

assoluta *short form* of **prima ballerina assoluta** (q.v.).

asthenia *n.* [Gk. **astheneia**: **a-** no, without (1); **sthen(os)** strength (2): no strength.] *Medicine.* Weakness. Want of strength. Debility. Loss of strength.

asylum *n., pl.* **asylums** [L. from Gk. **asulon**: **a-** no, not, without (1); **sulon** seizure, right of seizure (2): no right of seizure, a place of refuge, a sanctuary.] 1. In antiquity a place of refuge, usually a temple, where criminals and debtors went for protection and from which it was sacrilegious to remove them forcibly. 2. *International Law.* A place of refuge for belligerents in neutral territory. 3. Shelter for the persecuted or those fearing persecution. *She fled to Britain for political asylum.* 4. An institution for protecting and helping the destitute, insane, afflicted, and unfortunate. *An asylum for the mentally disturbed.*

asyndeton *n., pl.* **asyndeta** or **asyndetons** [Gk. **asundeton**: **a-** no, not, without (1); **sun** with, together (3); **deton** that may be bound (2): that may not be bound together.] An unconnected thing. Thing without conjunctions. *Rhetoric.* A style in which conjunctions are omitted; e.g., "He came, he complained, he was ignored." Cf. **polysyndeton.**

ataraxia *n., pl.* **ataraxias** [Gk. **a-** no, not, without (1); **tarakhē** disturbance (2): no disturbance.] Impassiveness. Calmness. State of being unperturbed. Calmness and freedom from emotional disturbance. Mental detachment.

ataxia *n., pl.* **ataxias** [Gk. **a-** no, not, without (1); **taxi(s)** order (2): no order.] Disorder. Confusion. Indiscipline. *The country's political and socio-economic ataxia is such that only a genius can solve the problems.*

Ate *n.* [Gk. **Atē** goddess of infatuation and reckless ambition.] Delusion or spiritual blindness which prompts a person to commit the sin of **hubris** (q.v.), resulting in his/her downfall.

atelier *n., pl.* **ateliers** [Fr. studio, workshop.] The studio or workshop, especially of an artist.

a tergo *adv.* [L. **a** from (1); **tergo** the back, rear (2): from the back.] From the rear. From behind. *He slipped and would have fallen down, had he not been helped a tergo by his partner.* See **vis a tergo.**

à terme *adv.* [Fr. **à** to, toward, in, by, with, until (1); **terme** term (2): for term.] *Law.* For a term. For the term. For an/the appointed time.

à terme de sa vie *adv.* [Obs. Fr. **à** to, toward, in, by, with, until (1); **terme** term (2); **de** of (3); **sa** his/her (4); **vie** life (5): for the term of his/her life.] *Law.* For the rest of his/her life. For life. Cf. **autre vie.**

à terme que passé est *adv.* [Obs. Fr. **à** to, toward, in, by, with, until (1); **terme** term (2); **que** which (3); **passé** passed (5); **est** is, has (4): for a term which has passed.] *Law.* For a term which has expired.

athenaeum *n., pl.* **athenaea** or **athenaeums** [L. from Gk. **athēnaion**.] 1. Temple of Athena. 2. An institute at Rome established by the emperor Hadrian and used by orators as well as other men of letters for recitations and lectures. 3. A club or association of scientists and writers. 4. A library or reading-room. A place where books, journals, periodicals, magazines, newspapers, etc. are kept to be used by readers, researchers, etc. *The Boston Athenaeum.* 5. A periodical of literature and belles-lettres.

atman *n., pl.* **atmans** [Skt. **ātman** breath, spirit.] *Hinduism.* The human soul or consciousness. —**Atman** The world soul. Cf. **anima mundi.**

à tort *adv.* [Fr. **à** to, toward, in, by, with, until (1); **tort** wrong, fault, injustice (2): with fault.] Wrongfully. Unjustly. Wrongly.

à tort et à travers *adv.* [Fr. **à** to, toward, in, by, with, until (1); **tort** wrong, fault, injustice (2); **et** and (3); **à** with (4); **travers** fault, defect (5): with wrong and with fault.] Thoughtlessly. Recklessly. At random. With no consideration or discretion. Without rhyme or reason. Heedlessly. Indiscriminately.

à tort ou à droit *adv.* [Fr. **à** to, toward, in, by, with, until (1); **tort** wrong (2); **ou** or (3); **à** to, toward, in, by, with, until (4); **droit** right, law (5): with wrong or with right.] Justly or wrongly. Rightly or wrongly. With good or bad reason.

atrium *n., pl.* **atria** or **atriums** [L. central court.] 1. The hall, forecourt or principal room of an ancient Roman house. 2. A hall, ordinarily square in shape, of a modern house or building, which is usually used as a sitting room or for entertainment. *It was the hotel's weekly tea dance, and in the glass-walled, four-story atrium . . . the Steve Miller Band was playing songs from the swing era (Newsweek Int.* July 27, 1981:33). 3. *Medicine.* A body cavity or compartment, such as in the heart.

à trois *adj.* [Fr. **à** to, toward, in, by, with, until (1); **trois** three (2): for three.] Designed for three persons. Shared by three persons or individuals. Applicable to meals, discussions, meetings, etc. *The conjugal dispute between Bayo and Toyin was settled in the course of a discussion à trois at Gbadebo's apartment.* See **ménage à trois** Cf. **à deux.**

attaché *n., pl.* **attachés** [Fr. attached.] A person, particularly an expert, attached to his country's embassy or high commission. a) *commercial attaché;* b) *military attaché;* c) *press attaché;* d) *naval attaché.*

aubain *n., pl.* **aubains** [Fr. alien, foreigner.] *French Law.* A resident alien who in former times was subject to the **droit d'aubaine** (q.v.).

auberge *n., pl.* **auberges** [Fr. shelter, camp, inn.] A public house or tavern.

A.U.C. *abbr.* for 1. **ab urbe condita** (q.v.). 2. **anno urbis conditae** (q.v.).

au contraire *adv.* [Fr. **au** to the, toward the, in the, by the, with the, until the (1); **contraire** contrary, opposite (2): to the contrary.] On the contrary. *"I am not miserable," confided the beggar. "Au contraire, by the end of a day I earn more than most of my benefactors."* Cf. **a contrario.**

au courant *adj.* [Fr. **au** to the, toward the, in the, by the, with the, until the (1); **courant** current, stream, run (2): in the current.] Fully informed. Well-informed. Well posted. Up-to-date. Acquainted.

Fully familiar. Abreast. Cognizant or aware. Conversant. In touch. In the know. *One of the major functions of the mass media is to keep people au courant with developments in the country, in particular, and the world, in general.* See **au fait** 2.

auctoritate sua *adv.* [L. **auctoritate** (by/on) authority (2); **sua** by his/her own (1): by his/her own authority.] On his/her own authority. Done without being authorized by anybody else; i.e., done without authorization.

aucupia verborum sunt judice indigna. [L. **aucupia** catchings at (1); **verborum** of words (2); **sunt** are (3); **judice** judge (5); **indigna** unworthy (4): Catchings at words are unworthy of a judge.] *Law.* Verbal quibbles (or quibblings) are below the dignity of a judge.

audaces fortuna iuvat. [L. **audaces** daring, bold (3); **fortuna** fortune (1); **iuvat** helps, aids (2): Fortune helps the daring.] Fortune aids the bold.

audentis fortuna juvat. Vergil (70–19 B.C.). *Aeneid* X,284. [L. **audentis** daring (persons) (3); **fortuna** fortune, luck, chance (1); **juvat** helps, aids (2): Luck helps daring persons.] Fortune helps the daring. Cf. **Aide-toi** etc., **fortis fortuna adjuvat** and **On dit que** etc.

audi partem alteram. Augustine of Hippo (354-430 A.D.). *De Duabus Animabus* XIV,2. [L. **audi** hear, listen to (1); **partem** side, part (3); **alteram** other (2): Listen to the other side.] *Law.* Both sides should be heard. Generally, nobody should be condemned or punished without being given the opportunity to be heard. See **audiatur et** etc.; **nemo inauditus** etc.; **parte inaudita**; and **qui aliquid statuerit** etc.

audiatur et altera pars. [L. **audiatur** let it be heard, listened to (4); **et** also (3); **altera** the other (1); **pars** part, side (2): Let the other side also be heard.] *Law.* Both sides of a legal suit or case should be heard. See **audi partem alteram.**

audita querela *n.* [L. **audita** heard, having been heard (2); **querela** complaint, accusation (1): complaint having been heard.] An obsolete common law writ which formed the initial process in a suit that a judgment defendant brings, seeking relief against the results of the judgment by reason of some subsequent development, if the defendant did not have the opportunity to raise the issues. *The ancient remedy at common law of a writ audita querela was abolished in 1875 but analogous relief may be founded on the remarks of Lord Bramwell in* Nouvion v. Freeman, *"that the court may give relief . . . where the defendant would have got relief upon audita querela"* (Graveson 1974:627–628).

auditor *n., pl.* **auditors** [L. listener, hearer, pupil, scholar.] 1. A person who is part of an audience. 2. A disciple or pupil. 3. A student in a university who audits a course, i. e. who is not taking it for credit. 4. A person who gives a judicial hearing (e.g., in some European countries, an assessor to a court-martial).

5. A person who audits, i.e., examines and verifies, financial accounts.

auditorium *n., pl.* **auditoria** or **auditoriums** [L. a place for listeners, for an audience.] 1. The part of a theater set aside for the audience and spectators. 2. A large building, hall, or room used for lectures, film shows, dramatic performances, recitals, concerts, etc. a) *The performance—the French premiere—took place . . . in an auditorium resembling a gymnasium* (*Time Int.* 1981). b) *The press centre, a brand-new six-story building, includes a large auditorium for press conferences.* (*Newsweek Int.* July 14, 1980:54).

au fait *adj.* [Fr. **au** to the, toward the, in the, by the, with the, until the (1); **fait** act, point (2): to the point.] 1. Capable. Very competent. *The company wants to employ a person who is au fait in the management of offices.* 2. Well-informed. Acquainted. Familiar. Fully conversant. Instructed. a) *A supposedly educated person who is not au fait with current affairs is no better than an illiterate.* b) *Most of those who speak this lingua are very much au fait with the proper way of speaking English* (Thomas Cooke in *West Africa* 1985). 3. Proper. Socially acceptable. *He is a very weird man who does not care whether his behavior is au fait or not.* See **au courant**.

Aufgabe *n., pl.* **Aufgaben** [Ger. **auf** up, to (2); **Gabe** gift, that which is given (1): that which is given out, given to be done, task, assignment.] An exercise. A task assigned as a test or an experiment.

Aufklärung *n.* [Ger. **auf** up, to (2); **Klärung** clearing, lighting (1): clearing-up, enlightenment.] The Enlightenment or the Age of Reason, i.e., a philosophic movement in the 18th century, which put emphasis on reliance on reason, individualism, the questioning of traditional values and doctrines, the adoption of the empirical method in scientific research, etc. Cf. **Sturm und Drang** 2.

au fond *adv.* [Fr. **au** to the, toward the, in the, by the, with the, until the (1); **fond** bottom (2): to the bottom.] At heart. To the bottom. At bottom. Deep down. At root. Essentially. Basically. Fundamentally. In reality. In the main. All things considered. On the whole. a) *Stephen's neighbors shun his company, not knowing that he is au fond a very nice man.* b) *Prime Minister Asquith once remarked, "Clemmie, of whom I am quite fond, is au fond a thundering bore!"* (*Newsweek Int.* Dec. 3, 1979:58).

auf Wiedersehen *interj.* [Ger. **auf** on, at, upon, until (1); **wieder** again (3): **sehen** to see, seeing (2): until seeing again.] Until we meet again! Goodbye! Farewell! See **à bientôt**.

au naturel *adj.* [Fr. **au** to the, toward the, in the, by the, with the, until the (1); **naturel** natural, naturalness (2): in the natural.] 1. In the natural state. Nude. Naked. *The lovers had a lot of fun, swimming au naturel.* 2. Done, performed, accomplished, etc. in a natural manner, condition or style. Natural. *James is a very pleasant man, and one of his assets is his au naturel behavior.* 3. Cooked with no dressing. Uncooked. Unseasoned. *They enjoyed eating the fresh tomatoes au naturel.*

au pair *n.* [Fr. **au** to the, toward the, in the, by the, with the, until the (1); **pair** equal, even (2): on the equal.] 1. An arrangement whereby people exchange services without making monetary payments as, for instance, a person renders some domestic service and receives, in return, free board and lodging, or "A" teaches "B" Yoruba, while the latter teaches the former Hausa in return. 2. A person who renders such service and receives, in return, free board and lodging. *Green is an au pair, a live-in "family helper" in Paris* (*Newsweek Int.* April 14, 1980:47). —*adj.* Relating to, of, characteristic of, such an arrangement. *Most agencies that place au pair maids have recently begun accepting men* (*Newsweek Int.* April 14, 1980:47).

au pied de la lettre *adv.* [Fr. **au** to the, toward the, in the, by the, with the, until the (1); **pied** foot, base (2); **de** of (3); **la** the (4); **lettre** letter (5): to the foot of the letter.] Literally. To the letter. *The sentence, if taken au pied de la lettre, does not make sense.* Cf. **litteratim**.

aura *n., pl.* **aurae** or **auras** [Gk. and L. breeze, fresh air.] A subtle, inexplicable force, stimulus or matter which supposedly emanates from and, like an atmosphere, surrounds, a person, or thing. Aspect. Distinctive appearance, quality, impression or character. a) *aura of unreality;* b) *aura of success;* c) *aura of danger;* d) *aura of magnetism;* e) *Serge Semenenko . . . whose flair as an arranger of controversial rescue loans gave his career an aura of drama and mystery . . .* (*Time Int.* 1980).

aurea mediocritas *n.* [L. **aurea** golden (1); **mediocritas** mean, moderation (2): golden mean.] The golden mean. The safe or wise path between extremes. Moderation. *The old man always admonishes his children to follow the safe path by observing aurea mediocritas.* Cf. **juste-milieu; meden agan; medio tutissimus ibis; quicquid in excessu** etc.; and **via media**.

au revoir *interj.* [Fr. **au** to the, toward the, in the, by the, with the, until the (1); **revoir** seeing again (2): to the seeing again.] Until we meet again! Goodbye for now (or for the present.)! Farewell! So long! See **à bientôt**.

auslander *n., pl.* **auslanders** [Ger. **Ausländer: aus** from, away from (1); **Land** land (2): (one) away from the land.] Foreigner. Outsider.

auspex *n., pl.* **auspices** [L. from **av(is)** bird (1); **-spex** one who inspects (2): one who inspects birds, diviner, augur.] 1. An ancient Roman religious official who interpreted signs and omens, especially the flight of birds, in order to predict events. 2. Any prophet, soothsayer, seer. Cf. **haruspex**.

Aussage *n.* [Ger. **aus** out, from (2); **Sage** saying (1): a saying out or from, statement.] Declaration. Assertion. Used in the expression *Aussage test*, a procedure to determine the reliability of a witness which the examiner asks the respondent to describe something familiar to the former.

aut amat aut odit mulier: nihil est tertium. [L. **aut** either (1); **amat** loves (3); **aut** or (4); **odit** hates (5); **mulier** woman (2); **nihil** nothing (6); **est** is, has been (7); **tertium** third (thing) (8): Either a woman loves or hates; nothing is a third thing.] A woman either loves or hates; there is no third choice.

aut Caesar aut nullus [L. **aut** either (1); **Caesar** Caesar (2); **aut** or (3); **nullus** neither, not any, not at all: either Caesar or not at all.] Caesar or nothing. The motto of Caesare Borgia (1475 or 1476–1507).

auter droit *n.* [Obs. Fr. **auter** another, other (1); **droit** right (2): another right.] *Law.* The right of another. *Being vested in him* [i.e., executor or administrator] *in auter droit, it will not merge in any estate or interest vested in him, in his own right;* . . . (Parry 1961:211). See **autre droit**.

Autobahn or **autobahn** *n., pl.* **Autobahnen** or **autobahns** [Ger. **Auto** automobile, car (1); **Bahn** way, road, path (2): car-path.] Expressway. Superhighway. a) *Congested cities and autobahns have created a need for the kind of comfort European cars lack* (*Time Int.* 1979). b) *Japanese models ranked as five of the top six most reliable cars on West German autobahns* (*Newsweek Int.* Oct 27, 1980:55). Cf. **autoroute** and **autostrada**.

autochthon *n., pl.* **autochthons** or **autochthones** [Gk. **auto(s)** self (1); **chthon** land (2): self-land. Sprung from the land itself.] Aborigine. An original inhabitant of a place, region or country. An indigen. Something such as a plant or animal that is indigenous.

auto-da-fé *n., pl.* **autos-da-fé** [Port. from L. **auto** act, deed (1); **da** of the (2); **fé** faith, belief (3): act of the faith.] Pronouncement of judgment by the Inquisition upon a heretic and the execution of the sentence, especially by public burning carried out by secular authorities.

automaton *n., pl.* **automata** or **automatons** [Gk. self-acting.] Acting of one's own will. A robot. A contrivance which seems to be imitating the actions of men and animals. A relatively self-moving mechanism. A creature, especially a human being, which acts automatically, mechanically, or involuntarily and does not seem to apply intelligence. *He is a tyrant of the worst kind who hates independent, rational action and apparently wants all citizens to behave like automata.*

autophobia *n.* [Neo-Gk. from Gk. **auto(s)** self (2); **phob(os)** fear (1): fear of self.] *Psychology.* Pathological fear of loneliness.

autoroute *n., pl.* **autoroutes** [Fr. **auto** automobile, car (1); **route** path, way, road (2): car path.] Expressway.

Superhighway. Freeway. *Already trucks are restricted to certain hours on the autoroutes . . .* (*Newsweek Int.* Aug. 15, 1983:16). Cf. **Autobahn** and **autostrada**.

autostrada *n., pl.* **autostradas** [It. **auto** automobile, car (1); **strada** path, way, road (2): car path.] Highway. Expressway. Cf. **Autobahn** and **autoroute**.

autre droit *n.* [Fr. **autre** another, other (1); **droit** right (2): another right.] *Law.* Another's right. The right of another. Applicable to a person who acts in right of another; e.g., a trustee for the **cestui que trust** (q.v.). See **auter droit**; **en autre droit**; **in autre droit**; and **in jure alterius**.

autrefois *adv.* [Fr. **autre** another, other (1); **fois** time, period (2): another time.] Formerly. In former times. Of old.] *Law.* Formerly. In the past. Before. At another time. Used to qualify "acquit" and "convict." —**autrefois acquit** *n.* Formerly acquitted. Plea of an accused that he had previously been tried for the same offense and acquitted. —**autrefois convict** *n.* Formerly convicted. Plea of an accused that he had previously been tried for the same offense and convicted. The connotation in either case is that the matter is a res judicata and so cannot be revived. See **res judicata**.

Autres temps, autres moeurs. [Fr. **autres** other (1); **temps** times, periods (2); **autres** other (3); **moeurs** customs, manners (4): Other times, other manners.] Each age has its manners or customs. Cf. **tempora mutantur, et nos** etc. and **tempora mutantur; nos et** etc.

autre vie *n.* [Fr. **autre** other, another (1); **vie** life (2): another life.] *Law.* The life of another. Another's life. Used to qualify tenancy of an estate. See **per autre vie**; **pur autre vie**; and **pur terme d'autre vie**. Cf. **ad vitam**; **à terme de sa vie**; and **de sa vie**.

av. *abbr.* for **avocat** (q.v.).

A.V. or **a.v.** *abbr.* for **ad valorem** (q.v.).

À vaincre sans péril, on triomphe sans gloire. Pierre Corneille (1606–1684). *Le Cid* II,2. [Fr. **à** to, toward, in, by, with, until (1); **vaincre** conquer, vanquish (2); **sans** without (3); **péril** danger, hazard (4); **on** one, man (5); **triomphe** triumphs, conquers (6); **sans** without (7); **gloire** glory, pride (8): In conquering without danger, one triumphs without glory.] Victory without peril is a triumph without glory.

aval *n., pl.* **avals** [Fr. backing, guarantee, endorsement.] *French and Canadian Law.* Subscribing a signature at the bottom of a bill of exchange or a promissory note to guarantee its acceptance at maturity.

avalanche *n., pl.* **avalanches** [Fr. a large snowfall down a mountainside.] 1. A large mass of ice, earth, snow, debris, or rock falling from the mountainside or precipice. 2. A large, overwhelming flood, shower, or mass of something. a) *. . . sifting through an avalanche of applications . . .* (*The Guardian* 1986). b) *[The] commission chairman . . . was dumbfounded by the fact that an avalanche of memoranda had come from*

Nigeria's western half (Tunde Agbabiaka in *West Africa* 1986).

avant-garde *n., pl.* **avant-gardes** [Fr. **avant** in front, before (2); **garde** guard, corps (1): the guard in front, vanguard, advanced guard.] 1. People who create or apply original ideas, techniques, etc. in any field, especially the arts. Pioneers. People in the forefront of a movement or ahead of their times. 2. A group of people such as writers, artists, or scholars who adopt an unorthodox approach. . . . *the show would be worth seeing, if only for the glimpse it gives of an endangered species, the Soviet avant-garde* (*Newsweek Int.* Nov. 28, 1983:58). —*adj.* Characteristic of, relating to, of, the avant-garde. a) *Avant-garde artist;* b) *avant-garde composer;* c) *avant-garde film maker;* d) *avant-garde magazine;* e) . . . *the avant-garde troupe that shocked audiences in the late '60s with its taunts and onstage nudity is blossoming in Paris* (*Newsweek Int.* Aug. 2, 1982:41).

ave *interj.* [L. hail.] Hello. —*n., pl.* **aves** 1. A greeting. 2. *Christianity.* The Hail Mary, a prayer to Mary the Mother of Jesus. Cf. **Ave Maria**; **ciao**; and **salve**.

ave atque vale Catullus (c.84–c.54 B.C.). *Carmina* CI,10. [L. **ave** hail (1); **atque** and (2); **vale** farewell (3): hail and farewell.] Hello and goodby.

Ave, Caesar, morituri te salutant. [L. **ave** hail (1) **Caesar** Caesar (2); **morituri** (those) about to die (3); **te** you (5); **salutant** they salute (4): Hail, Caesar, those about to die salute you.] Greetings, Caesar. Those who are about to die greet you. Greeting of Roman gladiators as they entered the amphitheater.

Ave Maria [L. **ave** hail (1); **Maria** Mary (2): Hail, Mary.] *Christianity.* The first words of a prayer to Mary the Mother of Jesus. —*n.* 1. The prayer itself. 2. A musical composition based upon this prayer; e.g. "Ave Maria" by Franz Schubert (1791–1828).

a verbis ad verbera [L. **a** from, by (1); **verbis** words (2); **ad** to, at, for, according to (3); **verbera** rods, whips, floggings (4): from words to whips.] From a battle of words to a battle of blows. *The encounter between the rivals in love swiftly moved a verbis ad verbera.*

a verbis legis non est recedendum. [L. **a** from (1); **verbis** words (2); **legis** of law, statute (3); **non** no, not (5); **est** it is (4); **recedendum** to be departed (6): From the words of statute it is not to be departed.] *Law.* There should be no departure from the words of a statute; i.e., a statute/law should be observed to the letter.

a vinculo matrimonii *adj.* [L. **a** from (1) **vinculo** bond (2); **matrimonii** of marriage (3): from the bond of marriage.] *Law.* From the bonds of matrimony or wedlock. Used with reference to complete divorce. a) *Divorce a vinculo matrimonii.* b) *He was granted a decree a vinculo.*

avocat *abbr.* **av.** *n., pl.* **avocats** [Fr. lawyer.] Lawyer. Attorney. Counsel. Advocate. *After a mere two hours of wrangling among the avocats, however, the judge threw the case out on technical grounds* (*Newsweek Int.* Dec. 17, 1979:21).

axioma medium *n., pl.* **axiomata media** [L. **axioma** from Gk. **axiōma** something worthy, honorable, fitting (2); **medium** middle, midway (1): something midway fitting.] *Philosophy.* A rule or principle which is midway between simple, empirical laws and natural laws.

ayah *n., pl.* **ayahs** [Hindi āyā from Port. **aia** from Latin **avia**: grandmother.] An Indian woman who serves as a maid or nurse.

ayatollah *n.* [Pers. from Ar. **'āyatullāh**: **'āyah** a verse of the Koran, miracle (1); **allāh** God (2): miracle of God.] *Islam.* 1. A male Shiite leader who gains political status from his religious standing and virtue. 2. An honorific title for someone in this position.

B

b. *abbr.* for **bis** (q.v.).

B.A. *abbr.* for **Baccalaureus Artium** (q.v.).

babu or **baboo** *n., pl.* **babus** or **baboos** [Hindi **bābū** father.] 1. A title of courtesy used for males in Hindi-speaking areas. Mister. 2. A Hindi-speaking clerk who understands English. 3. A derogatory term for a Hindi-speaker who has learned some English. See **Herr**; **Monsieur**; **san**; **Senhor**; **Señor**; and **Signor**.

babushka *n., pl.* **babushkas** [Russ. little woman, grandmother, head scarf.] A woman's head scarf tied under the chin.

baccalauréat *n.* [Fr. high school diploma.] Baccalaureate. *The lycées at Dakar and Saint Louis were, in practice, only open to the sons of French or assimilated officials . . . whose parents could afford to pay their fees up to the baccalauréat level* (Suret-Canale 1971:388). Cf. **lycée**.

Baccalaureus Artium *abbr.* **B.A.** *n.* [L. **baccalaureus** bachelor (1); **artium** of arts (2): Bachelor of Arts.] An undergraduate degree in the liberal arts. Cf. **Artium Baccalaureus**.

Baccalaureus Chirurgiae *abbr.* **B.Ch.** or **B.Chir.** *n.* [L. **baccalaureus** bachelor (1); **chirurgiae** of surgery (2): Bachelor of Surgery.] A undergraduate degree in medicine with a specialization in surgery. Cf. **Chirurgiae Baccalaureus**.

Baccalaureus Chirurgiae Dentalis *abbr.* **B.Ch.D.** *n.* [L. **baccalaureus** bachelor (1); **chirurgiae** (of) surgery (3); **dentalis** of teeth, dental (2): Bachelor of Dental Surgery.] An undergraduate degree for completion of a dental curriculum.

Baccalaureus Utriusque Juris *abbr.* **B.U.J.** *n.* [L. **baccalaureus** bachelor (1); **utriusque** of each of two (2); **juris** (of) right, law (3): bachelor of each of two laws.] Bachelor of both Canon and Civil Law. An undergraduate degree in both canon and civil law.

Bacchae *pl. n.* [Gk. female followers of Bacchus.] *The Bacchants*, a tragedy by Euripides (c.480–407/6

B.C.), produced in Athens posthumously (c.406 B.C.) about the conflict between Dionysus (Bacchus), the god of wine, and his cousin Pentheus, king of Thebes.

bacchanalia *n., pl.* **bacchanalias** [L. things connected with Bacchus.] 1. *Greek and Roman Mythology.* Feast of Bacchus, the god of wine. Revelries celebrated in honor of Bacchus. 2. Orgy. A feast in which alcoholic drinks flow freely. A bacchanalian festival.

Bacchus *n.* [L. Greek and Roman god of wine.] *Greek and Roman Mythology.* The deity Dionysus, god of wine, ecstatic religious celebration, fertility, and nature. *Intoxicated and inebriated, after taking an excessive dose of the gift of Bacchus, he started misbehaving.*

badinage *n.* [Fr. joking.] Joking, usually playful but sometimes critical. Flirtatious conversation.

bagatelle *n., pl.* **bagatelles** [Fr. trifle.] 1. Something trivial or unimportant. *John rebuked Veronica for treating a serious matter as though it were a mere bagatelle.* 2. A short musical composition or poem with a light tone. 3. A game similar to pool or billiards, played on a rectangular table with sticks and balls.

bahuvrihi *n.* [Skt. **bahu** much (1); **vrīhi** rice (2): much rice, wealthy.] 1. *Ancient India.* A social class identified by their possession of much rice. 2. A member of this social class. —**bahuvrihi compound** *Linguistics.* A compound word consisting of adjectival and nominal parts in which a possession or characteristic feature is used to identify and name the owner; e.g., "hard-hat" for a construction worker or "four-eyes" for someone who wears eyeglasses.

baksheesh *n., pl.* **baksheesh** [Pers. bakhshish present.] A small gift, tip, or gratuity in the Near East.

balalaika *n., pl.* **balalaikas** [Russ. stringed musical instument.] A three-stringed musical instrument with a triangular soundbox.

ballerina *n., pl.* **ballerinas** or **ballerine** [It. a female ballet dancer.] A female ballet dancer, especially one who plays the leading role. *The 14-year-old ballerina* *from New York City put on three strong performances and, to her astonishment, won the gold medal in the junior division.* (*Newsweek Int.* Aug. 15, 1983:27).

ballet blanc *n., pl.* **ballets blancs** [Fr. **ballet** ballet (2); **blanc** white (1): white ballet.] A form of classical dance or ballet in which the female dancers wear white clothing.

ballet bouffe *n., pl.* **ballets bouffes** [Fr. **ballet** ballet (2); **bouffe** comic (1): comic ballet.] A form of classical dance or ballet with a humorous or comic tone.

ballet d'action *n., pl.* **ballets d'action** [Fr. **ballet** ballet (1); **d'** of (2); **action** plot, action (3): ballet of action or plot.] A form of classical dance or ballet which has a plot or tells a story.

ballon d'essai *n., pl.* **ballons d'essai** [Fr. **ballon** balloon (1); **d'** of (2); **essai** trial, test (3): balloon of trial.] Trial balloon. Pilot balloon. A feeler. A project designed to test public opinion. *The project was canceled when it became clear that reaction to the ballon d'essai was unfavorable.*

bambino *n., pl.* **bambini** or **bambinos** [It. infant or child.] 1. Baby. Child. Infant. 2. An image or picture of the infant Jesus.

banc *n.* [Fr. bench, seat, bar, dock.] *Law.* The bench used by the judge of a court. The permanent or regular site of a court. The seat of judgment. The full court. See **banc le common pleas, banc le roy,** and **en banc.**

banc le common pleas *n.* [Obs. Fr. **banc** bench (1); **le** the (2); **common** common (3); **pleas** pleas (4): bench of common pleas.] The court of common pleas. Cf. **banc le roy.**

banc le roy *n.* [Obs. Fr. **banc** bench (1); **le** the (2); **roy** king (3): bench of the king.] The king's bench or court. Cf. **banc le common pleas.**

banzai *interj.* [Japan. from Chin. ten thousand years.] May you live ten thousand years. Used as a battle cry or patriotic shout.

barathrum *n., pl.* **barathra** [L. an abyss, gulf, pit, chasm.] An abyss. Hell. A bottomless pit. *Prisons are supposed to be correctional centers, but some of them are such filthy places that life there is like life in a barathrum.*

barcarole or **barcarolle** *n., pl.* **barcaroles** or **barcarolles** [Fr. from It. **barcaruolca** boatman's song.] *Music.* 1. The song of a Venetian gondolier with a rowing rhythm. 2. Any musical composition which uses the rhythms of a gondolier's song.

bar mitzvah or **bar mizvah** *n., pl.* **bar mitzvahs** or **bar mizvahs** [Heb. **bar mishwa**: **bar** son (1); **mishwa** command (2): son of command.] *Judaism.* 1. The ceremony at which a thirteen-year-old Jewish boy comes of age and takes responsiblity for his own religious and ethical obligations. 2. A boy recognized at such a ceremony. —*v.* To conduct such a ceremony. Cf. **bat mitzvah.**

baroque *adj.* [Fr. odd, quaint, whimsical.] *European Art and Architecture.* Pertaining to the exaggerated or grotesque style of the seventeenth and eighteenth centuries. *The asking price for a baroque castle can run into the millions* (*Newsweek Int.* July 26, 1982:25).

barrage *n., pl.* **barrages** [Fr. bar, dam, barrier.] 1. A barrier of uninterrupted artillery, mortar, or machine-gun fire. A barrier or concentration of mines or other weapons. *Behind a barrage of 122-mm artillery fire, the invaders took over the town of Massaka . . .* (*Newsweek Int.* March 12, 1979:21). 2. A sustained discharge, flow, shower, or outpour of something. a) *a barrage of words*; b) *a barrage of instructions*; c) *a barrage of protests*; d) *No sooner had the magazine hit the stands than a barrage of absolute denials shot across international borders* (*Newsweek Int.* April 2, 1979:28). 3. An artificial dam built in a river to store water for diversion into canals for either irrigation or navigation. — *v. tr.* To attack with a shower or flow of something. To deliver a shower or flow of something. *She barraged him with questions on everything from working women to Vietnam* (*Newsweek Int.* March 5, 1979:14).

barrio *n., pl.* **barrios** [Sp. an open space.] 1. A neighborhood or district in a Spanish-speaking city. 2. A Spanish-speaking neighborhood, district, or community in a U.S. city.

bas bleu *n., pl.* **bas bleus** [Fr. **bas** stocking (2); **bleu** blue (1): blue stocking.] A female pedant. A learned or scholarly woman. A woman who has, or pretends to have, interest in literary and intellectual activities. *Africa now has many bas bleus who compete favorably with their male counterparts.*

bas relief *n., pl.* **bas reliefs** [Fr. **bas** low (1); **relief** relief (2): low relief.] *Art.* Figures sculptured not in the round but only to a small depth on a flat background. Cf. **mezzo relievo** and **relievo.**

basso *n., pl.* **bassos** [It. low.] *Music.* A bass or low-range voice or singer, especially in opera.

basso buffo *n., pl.* **bassos buffos** [It. **basso** low, bass (2); **buffo** comic, buffoon (1): comic bass.] *Music.* A bass who sings a comic role, especially in opera.

basso cantante *n., pl.* **bassos cantantes** [It. **basso** low, bass (2); **cantante** singing (1): singing bass.] *Music.* A high-range bass voice or singer.

basso continuo *n., pl.* **bassos continuos** [It. **basso** low, bass (2); **continuo** continuous (1): continuous bass.] *Music.* Figured bass or thoroughbass. A musical accompaniment for **continuo** (q.v.) or bass voice, in which chords are indicated by a numerical shorthand and the accompanist is expected to improvise. Used especially in the baroque period (1600-1750).

basso ostinato *n., pl.* **bassos ostinatos** [It. **basso** low, bass (2); **ostinato** obstinate, persistent (1): obstinate bass.] *Music.* A melodic line or passage, usually bass, which is repeated and varied in a composition. Cf. **ostinato.**

basso profundo *n., pl.* **bassos profundos** [It. **basso** low, bass (2); **profundo** profound, deep (1): deep bass.] *Music.* A deep bass or low-range voice or singer.

Basta! *interj.* [It. enough.] That's enough!

bathos *n.* [Gk. depth.] 1. Bottom. Nadir. The lowest point. *When a person who holds a very responsible position descends to such a bathos of puerility and irrationality, then there is, indeed, cause for alarm.* 2. *Rhetoric.* Unexpected change from the sublime or elevated to the commonplace or ridiculous. 3. Anticlimax. Ridiculous descent from a high to a low position. Humiliation. *His career will undoubtedly provide useful material for a study in bathos, the fall of the mighty.* 4. Excessive pathos or sentimentality. *The novel has an admirable plot and it could have been an outstanding piece of work, were it not for the author's penchant for bathos.*

bat mitzvah or **bat mizvah** *n., pl.* **bat mitzvahs** or **bat mizvahs** [Heb. **bat mishwa**: **bat** daughter (1); **mishwa** command (2): daughter of command.] *Judaism.* 1. The ceremony at which a Jewish girl between the ages of twelve and fourteen comes of age and takes responsiblity for her own religious and ethical obligations. 2. A girl recognized at such a ceremony. —*v.* To conduct such a ceremony. Cf. **bar mitzvah.**

baton *n., pl.* **batons** [Fr. stick.] A short stick used by a musical conductor, a band drum major, or a sports relay team.

Baton Rouge *n.* [Fr. **baton** stick (2); **rouge** red (1): red stick.] The red stick. The capital of Louisiana.

b.c.b.g. *abbr.* for **bon chic, bon genre** (q.v.). *That's very b.c.b.g.!*

B.Ch. *abbr.* for **Baccalaureus Chirurgiae** (q.v.).

B.Ch.D. *abbr.* for **Baccalaureus Chirurgiae Dentalis** (q.v.).

B.Chir. *abbr.* for **Baccalaureus Chirurgiae** (q.v.).

beatae memoriae *abbr.* **B.M.** *adj.* [L. **beatae** of blessed, happy (1); **memoriae** (of) memory (2): of blessed memory.] Deceased.

beatus or *fem.* **beata** *n., pl.* **beati** or *fem.* **beatae** [L. blessed person.] *Roman Catholicism.* A beatified person.

beau *n., pl.* **beaux** or **beaus** [Fr. lovely, beautiful, fair, handsome, good-looking.] 1. Dandy. A man who pays excessive attention to his clothing, etiquette, and looks. 2. A man who escorts, goes out frequently with, or pays considerable attention to, a woman. 3. A man who is in love with a woman. A lover. *Sharon and her beau intend to announce their engagement by the end of the month.*

beau geste *n., pl.* **beaux gestes** or **beau gestes** [Fr. **beau** lovely, beautiful, fair, handsome, good-looking (1); **geste** gesture, action, deed, exploit (2): beautiful gesture.] A noble or courteous gesture or deed.

beau idéal or **beau ideal** *n., pl.* **beaux idéals** or **beau ideals** [Fr. **beau** lovely, beautiful, fair, handsome, good-looking (1); **idéal** ideal (2): beautiful ideal.] 1. A concept of perfect beauty. 2. *Art.* The Neoclassical concept of abstract perfection. 3. A perfect model or type.

beau monde *n., pl.* **beaux mondes** [Fr. **beau** lovely, beautiful, fair, handsome, good-looking (1); **monde** world, society (2): beautiful world or society.] Fashionable society, set, or world. The world of fashion and high society. The best society. The smart set. *Last week the beau monde of Houston and Austin turned out at $1,000-a-crack fund-raisers to aid the troubled Glen candidacy* (*Newsweek Int.* Jan 2, 1984:14). See **haut monde** and **tout le haut monde.**

beaux arts *pl. n.* [Fr. **beaux** lovely, beautiful, fair, handsome, good-looking (1); **arts** arts (2): beautiful arts.] The fine arts, including painting, sculpture, and music. *Her love of the beaux arts permeated everything she did.*

beaux yeux *pl. n.* [Fr. **beaux** lovely, beautiful, fair, handsome, good-looking (1); **yeux** eyes (2): beautiful eyes.] The charm, beauty, and attraction which inspires love, fascination, faithfulness, and devotion. *Philip is undoubtedly a patriot, a man who entered politics not for personal aggrandizement but for the beaux yeux of his country.*

behemoth *n., pl.* **behemoths** [Heb. **behēmot** beasts.] An object of enormous size and strength. *The social welfare behemoth was of major concern to the voters.*

bel canto *n.* [It. **bel** beautiful, pretty (1); **canto** song (2): beautiful song.] *Music.* A form of traditional Italian vocal music, especially singing opera, which emphasizes a refined and beautiful tone and careful technique. *The works of Rossini and Donizetti are perennial favorites of Italian bel canto.*

bel esprit *n., pl.* **beaux esprits** [Fr. **bel** beautiful, fine (1); **esprit** spirit, mind (2): fine mind.] A wit. A witty person. A person who is quick in perceiving and expressing amusing points of view, especially one who is very skilled in banter. A highly intelligent person. *Hardly any intelligent person meets Mr. Cross, a bel esprit, without being impressed.*

belle *n., pl.* **belles** [Fr. a beautiful woman or girl.] A charming, beautiful, popular, and attractive girl or woman. The most beautiful woman or girl of a group or locality. A beauty. *It was a great party, attended by many pretty ladies, but Alice was easily the belle of the ball.*

belle dame *n., pl.* **belles dames** [Fr. **belle** beautiful, fine-looking (1); **dame** woman, lady (2): beautiful woman.] Beautiful, fair, or fine-looking lady. *Catullus . . . obtained admission to high society at Rome and burnt his wings in the flame of a boyish passion for the belle dame Clodia* (Cary 1970:464).

belle époque *n.* [Fr. **belle** fine, lovely (1); **époque** epoch, age (2): lovely age.] Fine age. —*adj.* Characteristic of, relating to, showing qualities of **La Belle Époque** (q.v.). *Maxim's, the belle époque restaurant on the Rue Royale in Paris* (*Newsweek Int.* Feb. 28, 1983:3).

belles-lettres *pl. n.* [Fr. **belles** fine, beautiful (1); **lettres** letters, literature (2): beautiful literature.] Fine literature.

Sophisticated and serious literature, such as works on literary criticism or philosophy, studied more for aesthetic value than for practical purposes. *The medical student saw little value in the study of belles-lettres.*

Bellum Gallicum *n.* [L. **bellum** war (2); **Gallicum** (1): the Gallic war.] *The Gallic War*, a commentary on his conquest of France (58–51 B.C.) by Julius Caesar (100–44 B.C.).

bema *n.* [Gk. **bēma** step, platform.] 1. *Judaism.* The platform used for services in a synagogue. 2. *Orthodox Christianity.* The sanctuary. The place where the altar is located. Cf. **almemar.**

Benedictus *adj.* [L. from **bene** well (1); **dictus** spoken (2): well spoken, blessed.] The first word of a Latin hymn based either on Matthew 21:9 ("Blessed is he who comes in the name of the Lord.") or Luke 1:68 ("Blessed be the Lord God of Israel."). —*n.* A prayer based upon one of these sources.

bene esse *n.* [L. **bene** well (2); **esse** to be (1): to be well.] Well-being. Prosperity. A good, luxurious, or comfortable life. Cf. **bien-être** and **esse.**

bénéfice *n., pl.* **bénéfices** [Fr. benefit, advantage, privilege, profit.] *French Law.* A privilege, advantage, or benefit derived from the law rather than from agreement concluded by parties.

bénéfice de discussion *n.* [Fr. **bénéfice** benefit, advantage (1); **de** of (2); **discussion** discussion, deliberation (3): advantage of discussion.] *Law.* Benefit of deliberation or discussion. **Beneficium discussionis** (q.v.).

bénéfice de division *n.* [Fr. **bénéfice** benefit, advantage (1); **de** of (2); **division** division, separation (3): advantage of separation.] *Law.* Benefit of division. **Beneficium divisionis** (q.v.).

bénéfice d'inventaire *n.* [Fr. **bénéfice** benefit, advantage (1); **d'** of (2); **inventaire** inventory, stocktaking (3): advantage of stocktaking.] *Law.* Benefit of inventory. **Beneficium inventarii** (q.v.).

beneficium *n., pl.* **beneficia** [L. a favor, benefit, kindness, power, honor.] *Roman and Civil Law.* Right, benefit, favor, privilege.

beneficium abstinendi *n.* [L. **beneficium** privilege, right (1); **abstinendi** of abstaining, refraining (2): the privilege of abstaining.] *Roman Law.* The power/privilege of refusing. The power granted an heir to decline the inheritance. See **potestas abstinendi.** Cf. **tempus deliberandi.**

beneficium cedendarum actionum *n.* [L. **beneficium** privilege, right (1); **cedendarum** (of) to be yielded, yielding (3); **actionum** of suits, actions (2): privilege of actions/suits to be yielded.] *Roman and Civil Law.* Right of yielding actions/suits. The right of a surety, before the payment of his principal's debt, to insist that the creditor hand over to him the actions against the debtor or any co-surety.

beneficium competentiae *n.* [L. **beneficium** privilege, right (1); **competentiae** of competency (2): privilege

of competency.] *Roman and Civil Law.* 1. The right of a judgment debtor to pay to his creditors as much as will leave him enough to live a decent life. 2. The privilege, enjoyed by those under gratuitous obligations, to retain enough for their livelihood in the event of indigence.

beneficium discussionis *n.* [L. **beneficium** privilege, right (1); **discussionis** of discussion (2): right of discussion.] *Roman, Civil, and Scots Law.* The right of a surety to insist that the creditor sue the principal debtor first and exhaust every facility before suing him.

beneficium divisionis *n.* [L. **beneficium** privilege, right (1); **divisionis** of division (2): right of division.] *Roman and Scots Law.* The right of a surety who is sued by the creditor to insist that the other co-sureties also be sued or that he/she pay only his/her proportionate share of the debt.

beneficium inopi bis dat, qui dat celeriter. Publilius Syrus (c.85–43 B.C.). *Sententiae* 6. [L. **beneficium** benefit, favor (2); **inopi** poor, needy, destitute (3); **bis** twice, doubly (4); **dat** he gives (1); **qui** who (5); **dat** he gives (6); **celeriter** quickly (7): He gives a benefit to a poor person twice who gives quickly.] A person who gives quickly to the destitute gives him/her a double benefit. See **bis dat** etc. and **qui cito** etc. Cf. **minus solvit** etc. and **qui serius** etc.

beneficium inventarii *n.* [L. **beneficium** privilege, right (1); **inventarii** of inventory (2): privilege of inventory.] *Roman and Civil Law.* The privilege of an heir to have an inventory of the testator's property made within the required time, and to be liable for debts, charges, and legacies only to the value of the inheritance as indicated in the inventory.

beneficium invito non datur. [L. **beneficium** privilege, right (1); **invito** to unwilling (person) (4); **non** not (2); **datur** is given (3): a privilege is not given to an unwilling person.] A privilege is not granted against the wishes of the recipient. See **invito beneficium** etc.

beneficium non datur nisi officii causa. [L. **beneficium** privilege, benefit (1); **non** not (2); **datur** is given (3); **nisi** except, unless (4); **officii** of duty; office (6); **causa** for the sake of, on account of (5): Benefit is not given except on account of duty.] Remuneration is only awarded for duties which have been performed.

beneficium ordinis *n.* [L. **beneficium** privilege, right (1); **ordinis** of rank, order (2): privilege of rank.] The privilege of order. **Beneficium discussionis** (q.v.).

beneficium separationis *n.* [L. **beneficium** privilege, right (1); **separationis** of separation (2): privilege of separation.] *Roman and Civil Law.* The right to have the estate of a deceased person separated from that of the heir so that the former could be proceeded against in favor of the creditor.

bene quiescat. *abbr.* **B.Q.** [L. **bene** well (2); **quiescat** may he/she rest, repose (1): May he/she rest (or repose) well.] May he/she rest in peace.

benigne faciendae sunt interpretationes chartarum, ut res magis valeat quam pereat; et quae libet concessio fortissime contra donatorem interpretanda est. [L. **benigne** liberally (5); **faciendae** to be made (4); **sunt** are (3); **interpretationes** interpretations (1); **chartarum** of writings, deeds (2); **ut** in order that (6); **res** thing, matter, property, business, affair (7); **magis** rather, more (9); **valeat** may prevail (8); **quam** than (10); **pereat** may perish (11); **et** and (12); **quae libet** any, all, every (13); **concessio** grant (14); **fortissime** most/ very strongly (17); **contra** against, opposite (18); **donatorem** donor, grantor (19); **interpretanda** to be interpreted (16); **est** is (15): Interpretations of deeds are to be made liberally in order that the matter may prevail rather than perish; and every grant is to be interpreted most strongly against the grantor.] *Law.* Deeds must be interpreted liberally in order that their purpose may stand rather than fail; and every grant must be interpreted most strongly against the grantor. See **quaelibet concessio** etc.

benignius leges interpretandae sunt quo voluntas earum conservetur. [L. **benignius** more liberally (4); **leges** laws (1); **interpretandae** to be interpreted (3); **sunt** are (2); **quo** by which, in order that (5); **voluntas** purpose, aim (7); **earum** their, of them (6); **conservetur** may be preserved (8): Laws are to be interpreted more liberally in order that their aim may be preserved.] Laws must be interpreted more liberally in order that their purpose may be preserved.

ben trovato or *fem.* **ben trovata** *adj.* [It. **ben** well (1); **trovato** found (2): well found.] Appropriate, though untrue. Ingeniously fabricated, devised or invented. *There are many stories about the hero's exploits, most of them ben trovato.* —*n., pl.* **ben trovati** A happy or ingenious fabrication, device or invention. Cf. **Se non é vero** etc.

berceuse *n., pl.* **berceuses** [Fr. a woman who rocks a cradle, a cradle song.] 1. A lullaby. 2. *Music.* A composition which comforts like a lullaby.

bête noire *n., pl.* **bêtes noires** [Fr. **bête** animal, beast (2); **noire** black, dark (1): black beast.] A bugbear. An enemy. A pet aversion. Somebody or something which is intensely hated, feared, and scrupulously avoided. *The Cameroonian press . . . says the measures are the only alternative to the IMF which is "the bête noire of the Third World" (West Africa* 1987). Cf. **bête rouge**.

bête rouge *n., pl.* **bête rouges** [Fr. **bête** animal, beast (2); **rouge** red, purple (1): red/purple beast.] Source of embarrassment, provocation, annoyance, or aversion. Applicable, particularly, to Russia or the Russians. . . . *a "wrong signal" to the Soviets so long as they remain a danger to Poland and the bête rouge of American foreign policy (Newsweek Int.,* May 4, 1981:19). Cf. **bête noire**.

bethel *n., pl.* **bethels** [Heb. **bêt 'el**: **bêt** house (1); **'el** God (2): house of God.] 1. A holy place or religious shrine, especially a chapel for sailors. 2. *British.* A meeting place for Non-conformists, especially Baptists and Methodists.

bêtise *n., pl.* **bêtises** [Fr. stupidity, foolishness, absurdity, piece of folly.] 1. Stupidity. Folly. Absurdity. Ignorance. Tactlessness. 2. An act of stupidity. An act of folly. *He is so notorious for his bêtises that his colleagues pay no more attention to them.*

beziehungsweise *abbr.* **bzw.** *adv.* [Ger. **Beziehung** a connection, relation (2); **weise** by way of (1): by way of a connection or relation.] Respectively.

b.f. *abbr.* for **bonum factum** (q.v.).

bibliomania *n.* [Neo-Gk. from Gk. **biblio(n)** book (1); **mania** enthusiasm, passion (2): book passion.] Excessive preoccupation with collecting, acquiring, and owning books. *Bibliomania is an expensive abnormality.*

bibliotheca *n., pl.* **bibliothecas** or **bibliothecae** [L. from Gk. **biblio(n)** book (1); **thēkē** case (2): book case.] 1. A collection of books. A library. 2. A catalog of books. A list of books. Cf. **bibliotheque**.

bibliotheque *n., pl.* **bibliotheques** [Fr. **bibliothèque** from Gk. **biblio(n)** book (1); **thēkē** case, place for (1): bookcase.] A library. Cf. **bibliotheca**.

B.I.D. or **b.i.d.** *abbr.* for **bis in die** (q.v.).

bidonville *n., pl.* **bidonvilles** [Fr. **bidon** a gas can, oil drum (1); **ville** town, city (2): an oil-drum town, shanty-town.] Suburbs consisting of buildings made of boxes, wood, or other improvised material. *Nomads and peasants uprooted from the Senegal River valley have flocked to the towns, swelling the bidonvilles . . . (New African* 1978).

bienes comunes *pl. n.* [Sp. **bienes** property (2); **comunes** common (1): common property.] *Spanish Law.* Things like rain, water, air, and sea, which are not the exclusive property of any individual, but are to be used by everybody. See **bienes publicos**; **cosas comunes**; and **juris publici**.

bienes publicos *pl. n.* [Sp. **bienes** property (2); **publicos** public (1): public property.] *Spanish Law.* Things such as shores, public roads, rivers, and harbors which belong to the entire nation and can be used by every citizen or inhabitant of the territory. See **bienes comunes**.

bien-être *n., pl.* **bien-êtres** [Fr. **bien** well (1); **être** to be, being (2): well-being.] Well-being. Prosperity. —*pl.* Material goods. Comforts. Cf. **bene esse**.

biennium *n., pl.* **biennia** or **bienniums** [L. **bi(s)** twice (1); **ann(us)** year (2): two years.] A period of two years. Cf. **decennium, quadrennium, quinquennium,** and **triennium**.

biens immeubles *pl. n.* [Fr. **biens** belongings, goods, property (2); **immeubles** immovable, real (1): immovable belongings.] *French Law.* Immovable property. Real estate. See **immeubles**. Cf. **biens meubles**.

biens meubles *pl. n.* [Fr. **biens** belongings, goods, property (2); **meubles** movable (1): movable belongings.] *French Law.* Movable property. Movables. Personal estate. See **meubles**, **mobilia**, and **res mobiles**. Cf. **biens immeubles** and **immeubles**.

bienvenida *n.* [Sp. **bien** well (1); **venida** come (2): welcome.] Greetings. . . . *the bienvenida for Maria . . . (Newsweek Int.* Dec. 19, 1983:3). Cf. **bienvenue**.

bienvenue *n.* [Fr. **bien** well (1); **venue** come (2): welcome.] Greetings. Cf. **bienvenida**.

Bildungsroman *n., pl.* **Bildungsromans** [Ger. **Bildung** education (1); **Roman** novel (2): education novel.] A novel about a young person's coming of age and quest for personal identity; e.g., Charles Dickens' *David Copperfield.*

billet-doux *n., pl.* **billets-doux** [Fr. **billet** note (2); **doux** sweet (1): sweet note.] A love letter.

bimbo *n.* [It. baby.] *Slang.* An offensive term for young woman who is very beautiful but not very smart.

bis *abbr.* **b** *adv.* [L. twice, on two occasions.] 1. *Music.* Again. Used either to direct that a passage should be repeated or in requesting an encore. 2. Twice. Used, especially, in an address or an account, to indicate that something appears twice.

bis dat qui cito dat. Publilius Syrus (c.85–43 B.C.). [L. **bis** twice (5); **dat** he gives (4); **qui** (one) who (1); **cito** quickly; speedily (3); **dat** gives (2): One who gives quickly gives twice.] A person who gives quickly gives twice. See **beneficium inopi** etc.

bis in die *abbr.* **B.I.D.** or **b.i.d.** *adv.* [L. **bis** twice (1); **in** in, on (2); **die** day (3): twice in a day.] *Medicine.* Two times a day. Twice daily.

bis peccare in bello non licet. [L. **bis** twice, two times (4); **peccare** to sin (3); **in** in, on; (4); **bello** war (5); **non** not (1); **licet** it is permitted (2): It is not permitted to sin twice in war.] One does not have the luxury of making a second error in war.

bis pueri senes [L. **bis** twice, for a second time (3); **pueri** boys (2); **senes** old men (1): Old men are boys for a second time.] Old men relive their youth. Cf. **senex bis puer**.

bis vivit qui bene vivit. [L. **bis** twice, for a second time (2); **vivit** he lives (1); **qui** who (3); **bene** (5); **vivit** lives (4): He lives twice who lives well.] A person who lives life well lives two lives.

bitte schön *adv.* [Ger. **bitte** please (2); **schön** pretty (1): pretty please.] Please. Cf. **bitte sehr; per favore; por favor; prego**; and **s'il vous plaît**.

bitte sehr *adv.* [Ger. **bitte** please (2); **sehr** very, much (1): very please.] Please. Cf. **per favore; por favor; prego**; and **s'il vous plaît**.

bizarre *adj.* [Fr. from Sp. **bizarro** brave.] Odd. Weird. Strange. Grotesque. Peculiar. Whimsical. Extraordinary. Fantastic. Outlandish. *Nobody was interested in culture . . . except as a curiosity and something bizarre* (Suret-Canale 1971:369).

blagueur *n., pl.* **blagueurs** [Fr. joker.] One who tells tall tales.

blasé or *fem.* **blasée** *adj.* [Fr. satiated, indifferent, tired.] Satiated. Bored. Apathetic. Uninterested. Showing no signs of deriving pleasure or enjoyment from something. *He is a difficult father, who is always blasé about his son's achievements.*

blitz *short form* of **blitzkrieg** (q.v.) *n., pl.* **blitzes** [Ger. **Blitz** lightning.] 1. An intensive full-scale aerial attack. An air raid. 2. An intensive, fast, and full-scale war, characterized by surprise attack and close coordination between air and ground forces. *Soviet forces continued their blitz through eastern Afghanistan, rolling over any insurgents in their path (Newsweek Int.* March 24, 1980). 3. A quick, intensive or overwhelming campaign, military or nonmilitary. a) *advertisement blitz*; b) *campaign blitz*; c) *communication blitz*; d) *media blitz*; e) *promotional blitz*; f) *propaganda blitz*. —*adj.* Of, characteristic of, to be expected in, being the consequence of a blitz. *The operations were conducted by a general who believes in blitz, not Fabian, tactics.* —*v. tr.* 1. To launch a rapid, vigorous, or violent attack against. a) *On the first day of the war, our men blitzed the capital town of the enemy so continuously that it was almost captured.* b) *Kennedy's current strategy is to blitz the state, keeping his flame aglow (Newsweek Int.* Nov. 26, 1979:39). 2. To destroy or damage through a rapid, vigorous, violent attack. *The capital town of the enemy was blitzed on the very first day of the war.* 3. To push or stampede. *The dictatorial chairman blitzed the committee into accepting the recommendations.*

blitzkrieg *short form* of **blitz** *n., pl.* **blitzkriegs** [Ger. **Blitzkrieg**: **Blitz** lightning (1); **Krieg** war (2): lightning war.] See **blitz** *n.* . . . *I want to be more careful. . . . But those guys want to make a blitzkrieg (Time Int.* 1982). Cf. **sitzkrieg**.

bloc *n., pl.* **blocs** [Fr. block, lump, coalition.] 1. A temporary coalition of parties in the legislative assembly of a country, usually for support of the government. 2. A union or combination of persons, groups, or countries which have common interests or objectives. a) *anti-war bloc*; b) *Asian bloc*; c) *East bloc*; d) *Soviet bloc.*

Blut und Eisen *n.* Otto von Bismarck (1815–1898). [Ger. **Blut** blood (1); **und** and (2); **Eisen** iron (3): blood and iron.] Military power used for the achievement of a definite purpose. See **Eisen und Blut**.

b.m. *abbr.* for 1. **beatae memoriae** (q.v.). 2. **bonae memoriae** (q.v.).

bona *pl. n.* [L. goods, property.] 1. *Roman Law.* Applicable to all kinds of property, but specifically to real estate. 2. *Civil Law.* Applicable to personal and real property. 3. *Common Law.* Applicable to movables.

bona adventitia *pl. n.* [L. **bona** goods, property (2); **adventi(c)ia** foreign, accidental (1): accidental goods.] *Roman Law*. All the property which a person acquires through his own efforts, as distinct from property received from the father. A son can keep such property as his own, though his father can enjoy its usufruct. See **peculium adventitium**. Cf. **bona materna**.

bona confiscata *pl. n*. [L. **bona** goods (2); **confiscata** confiscated (1): confiscated goods.] Goods forfeited to the national treasury. Cf. **bona forisfacta**.

bonae fidei *adj*. [L. **bonae** of good (1); **fidei** (of) faith (2): of good faith.] *Civil Law*. In good faith. *Bonae fidei contracts*.

bonae fidei emptor *n*. [L. **bonae** of good (2); **fidei** (of) faith (3); **emptor** purchaser (1): a purchaser of good faith.] *Law*. A purchaser in good faith; i.e., a purchaser who sincerely believes that the vendor has the right to sell property or that the article does not belong to another person.

bonae fidei possessor *n*. [L. **bonae** of good (2); **fidei** (of) faith (3); **possessor** holder, possessor (1): holder of good faith.] *Law*. A possessor in good faith; i.e., a person who sincerely believes that he/she has a better right to a possession than anybody else. **Bona fide possessor** (q.v.).

bonae fidei possessor in id tantum quod ad se pervenerit tenetur. [L. **bonae** of good (2); **fidei** of faith (3); **possessor** holder, possessor (1); **in** into, to, against, for (5); **id** that (7); **tantum** only (6); **quod** which (8); **ad** to, at, for, according to (10); **se** himself (11); **pervenerit** will have come (9); **tenetur** is held, liable (4): A possessor of good faith is held for only that which will have come to himself.] *Law*. A possessor in good faith is liable only for that which he himself has got.

bonae memoriae *abbr*. **b.m.** *adj*. [L. **bonae** of good, happy (1); **memoriae** (of) memory (2): of happy memory.] Pleasantly remembered.

bona fide *adv*. [L. **bona** with good (1); **fide** (with) faith, trust (2): with good faith.] In good faith. Honestly. Sincerely. With sincerity. *If the servant does not act bona fide, presumably he is liable . . .* (Rogers 1975:452). —*adj*. 1. Made without deceit or fraud. *Bona fide agreement*. 2. Legally valid. Legitimate. a) *Illegal aliens were deported to their bona fide countries*. b) *The goods found in my house are my bona fide property*. 3. Sincere. Honest. *A bona fide upholder of the principles of egalitarianism*. Cf. **dolus malus**.

bona fide possessor *n*. [L. **bona** in good (2); **fide** (in) faith (3); **possessor** holder, possessor (1): a holder with good faith.] *Law*. A possessor in good faith; i.e., a person who owns property which he/she can transfer and is ignorant of any defect in his/her right of possession. **bonae fidei possessor** (q.v.). Cf. **possessor mala fide**.

bona fides *n*. [L. **bona** good (1); **fides** faith (2): good faith.] Sincerity. Honest or sincere intention. Lack of deceit. *Due to his unquestionable bona fides, his claim to the "lost and found" article was granted*. Cf. **dolus malus**.

bona fides exigit ut quod convenit fiat. [L. **bona** good (1); **fides** faith (2); **exigit** demands, requires (3); **ut** that (4); **quod** (that) which, what (5); **convenit** is agreed on, settled (6); **fiat** may be done, happen (7): Good faith requires that what is agreed upon happen.] *Law*. Good faith demands that what is agreed on be done.

bona fides non patitur ut bis idem exigatur. [L. **bona** good (1); **fides** faith (2); **non** not (3); **patitur** allows, permits (4); **ut** that (5); **bis** twice (8); **idem** the same (thing) (6); **exigatur** be demanded, exacted (7): Good faith does not allow that the same thing be exacted twice.] *Law*. Good faith does not permit that payment be demanded on the same thing twice. Cf. **jus non patitur** etc.

bona forisfacta *pl. n*. [L. **bona** goods, property, possessions (1); **forisfacta** that have been made public (2): Goods which have been made public.] Forfeited property. Cf. **bona confiscata**.

bona fugitivorum *pl. n*. [L. **bona** goods, property, possessions (1); **fugitivorum** of fugitives, deserters (2): goods of fugitives.] *Law*. Property belonging to fugitives.

bona gratia *adv*. [L. **bona** by good (1); **gratia** (by) grace, harmony (2): by good grace/harmony.] By mutual agreement/consent. Voluntarily. *Roman Law*. Applicable to a kind of divorce in which the parties separated either without giving any reason or by mutual agreement.

bona immobilia *pl. n*. [L. **bona** goods, property, possessions (2); **immobilia** immovable (1): immovable goods/property.] Land. Immovables. Cf. **bona mobilia**.

bona materna *pl. n*. [L. **bona** goods, property, possessions (2); **materna** of the mother (2): goods of the mother.] *Roman Law*. The goods which a dependent son, i.e., one who is subject to his father's power, acquires from his mother. Cf. **bona adventitia** and **peculium adventitium**.

bona mobilia *pl. n*. [L. **bona** goods, property, possessions (2); **mobilia** movable (1): movable goods/property.] Movables. Possessions which can move or be moved from place to place. Cf. **bona immobilia**.

bona notabilia *pl. n*. [L. **bona** goods, property, possessions (2); **notabilia** noteworthy, remarkable (1): noteworthy goods.] *Law*. Noteworthy or notable property. Goods of a decedent which are valuable enough to be accounted for. Goods which are worthy of notice.

bonanza *n., pl.* **bonanzas** [Sp. fair weather, prosperity, success.] 1. A mass of ore rich in gold and silver. A mine with such rich ore. The product of such a mine. A very prosperous gold mine or oil well. *The company's* team of explorers found a bonanza estimated to be worth billions of dollars. 2. An enterprise which unexpectedly turns out to be very profitable. 3. A very large amount of money. a) Fred is one of the beneficiaries who put the back-pay bonanza to good use. b) The real bonanza . . . will come from the estimated $70 million that will be earned by the sale of tour T-shirts, posters, programs, buttons . . . (Newsweek Int. March 5, 1984:49). —adj. Characterized by or producing great wealth. Sam's wealth is mostly derived from the bonanza contract he obtained from the government.

bona paraphernalia pl. n. [L. **bona** goods, property, possessions (2); **paraphernalia** paraphernal, alongside the dowry (1): paraphernal goods, property alongside the dowry.] Civil Law. The goods of a wife other than those which form part of the dowry (e.g., jewels, clothes, etc.). Cf. **conquêts**. See also **paraphernalia**.

bona peritura pl. n. [L. **bona** goods, property, possessions (1); **peritura** about to perish, going to perish (2): goods going to perish, that will perish.] Law. Perishable property or goods. The court had to expedite the trial in view of the fact that the subject matters of dispute were bona peritura.

bon appétit interj. [Fr. **bon** good (1); **appétit** appetite (2): good appetite.] Happy dining! Cf. **buon appetito**.

bona vacantia or **vacantia bona** pl. n. [L. **bona** goods, property, possessions (2); **vacantia** vacant, unoccupied, empty (1): vacant/unoccupied goods.] Civil Law. Goods which have no apparent owner or claimant (e.g., shipwrecks). Goods whose legitimate owners are unknown or cannot be determined. Goods of an intestate who has no next of kin. An inheritance which no competent man has accepted or claimed. The court held that land alienated absolutely will escheat to the grantor in the event of it becoming bona vacantia through the death of the grantee without a successor (James 1982:149).

bon chic, bon genre abbr. **b.c.b.g.** n. [Fr. **bon** good (1); **chic** stylish (2); **bon** good (3); **genre** type, kind (4): good style, good type.] Someone or something stylish and in good social standing. Cf. **chic**.

bonhomie n. [Fr. **bon** good (1); **homme** man, person (2): good nature, amiableness, easy temper.] Good-natured friendliness. Warm spontaneous geniality. Sincere atmosphere or air of good cheer. Pleasantness of manner. Joviality. His bonhomie is so infectious that wherever he goes everybody becomes cheerful.

boni judicis est judicium sine dilatione mandare executioni. [L. **boni** of good (2); **judicis** (of) judge (3); **est** it is (1); **judicium** judgment (5); **sine** without (7); **dilatione** delay (8); **mandare** to assign, entrust (4); **ex(s)ecutioni** to execution (6): It is of a good judge to entrust judgment to execution without delay.] Law. It is the mark of a good judge to see to the execution of judgment without delay.

boni judicis est lites dirimere. [L. **boni** of good (2); **judicis** (of) judge (3); **est** it is (1); **lites** litigations, suits (5); **dirimere** to frustrate, prevent (4): It is of a good judge to frustrate litigations.] It is the mark of a good judge to prevent litigations.

bon mot n., pl. **bons mots** or **bon mots** [Fr. **bon** good (1); **mot** word (2): good word.] Witticism. A clever, witty saying or remark. Wisecrack. The bon mots flowed . . . at the . . . dinner in Beverly Hills, honoring . . . Alfred Hitchcock (Time Int. 1979). Cf. **mot**.

Bonne Année! interj. [Fr. **bonne** good (1); **année** year (2): good year.] Happy New Year!

bonorum emptio n. [L. **bonorum** of goods, property (2); **emptio** purchase (1): purchase of goods.] Civil Law. The purchase of an insolvent debtor's estate, the purchaser being under obligation to settle the liabilities and debts up to a portion agreed upon during the purchase. Cf. **bonorum venditio** and **distractio bonorum**.

bonorum venditio n. [L. **bonorum** of goods, property (2); **venditio** sale (1): sale of goods.] Sale of property. Cf. **bonorum emptio**.

bonsai n. [Japan. from **bon** pot, basin (1); **sai** to plant (2): a pot to plant, a potted plant.] 1. The art of dwarfing ornamental trees and growing them in small containers. 2. An artificially-dwarfed ornamental tree grown in a small container.

bon ton n., pl. **bons tons** [Fr. **bon** good (1); **ton** form, manners, breeding (2): good form, manners, or breeding.] Good taste. Stylishness. The fashionable thing. The proper thing. Every age has its bon ton and thus it comes about that a bon ton which has been rejected by one generation is, surprisingly, adopted by a subsequent generation.

bonum factum abbr. **b.f.** n. [L. **bonum** good (1); **factum** deed, act, fact (2): good deed.] An approved act.

bonum necessarium extra terminos necessitatis non est bonum. [L. **bonum** good (thing) (2); **necessarium** necessary (1); **extra** outside of, beyond (6); **terminos** bounds, limits (7); **necessitatis** of compulsion, urgency, necessity (8); **non** not (4); **est** is (3); **bonum** good (5): A necessary good thing is not good outside of the limits of compulsion.] Law. A good measure born of necessity ceases to be good when it leaves the limits of necessity.

bonum publicum abbr. **b.p.** n. [L. **bonum** good (thing) (2); **publicum** public (1): public good thing.] The public good. Government exists primarily for bonum publicum.

bonus n., pl. **bonuses** [L. good.] 1. Something given or received beyond what is ordinarily expected. Mrs. Adelabu gave each of her children a bonus of $10.00 pocket money for their good conduct. 2. Money given in addition to the regular salary to reward meritorious service or as an inducement. At the end-of-year party, the Managing Director gave each employee a bonus *of $200.* 3. A subsidy given by government to an industry. *The government pays the firm a bonus of $400,000 per annum to keep it in operation.* 4. Money which, apart from interest or royalties, is paid for a loan, for the grant of a charter to a company, or for the lease or transfer of property such as oil lands. 5. A sum which is paid to a professional athlete by a team in addition to the salary. *Samuel is the only bonus player of the team.*

bonus judex secundum aequum et bonum judicat, et aequitatem stricto juri praefert. [L. **bonus** good (1); **judex** judge (2); **secundum** according to (4); **aequum** the fair (5); **et** and (6); **bonum** the good (7); **judicat** judges, decides (3); **et** and (8); **aequitatem** equity (10); **stricto** to strict (11); **juri** (to) right, law (12); **praefert** prefers (9): A good judge judges according to the fair and the good, and prefers equity to strict law.] *Law.* A good judge passes judgment in accordance with equity, and prefers equity to strict law.

bonus paterfamilias *n.* [L. **bonus** good (1); **paterfamilias** father of the family (2): a good father of the family.] *Roman Law.* A good head of the family. *[In Roman law the usufructuary] owed a duty to conduct himself as a bonus paterfamilias in the care of the res* (Asante 1975:8).

bon vivant *n., pl.* **bons vivants** or **bon vivants** [Fr. **bon** good (1); **vivant** living (person) (2): good living person.] A jolly fellow. A person who enjoys the pleasures of life. A person who likes good living. An epicure. An easygoing person. A person with sophisticated tastes, especially in drinks and food. A gourmet. a) *A bon vivant who dressed exquisitely, chainsmoked elegantly, kept a wife, a mistress, a secretary/lover and a stable full of expensive automobiles . . .* (*Newsweek Int.* Jan. 31, 1983:48). b) *He was . . . a charming, multilingual bon vivant who always found time for foreign visitors, especially journalists* (*Time Int.* 1982). Cf. **bon viveur** and **boulevardier.**

bon viveur *n., pl.* **bons viveurs** or **bon viveurs** [Fr. **bon** good (1); **viveur** fast/free liver (2): a good fast/free liver.] A person who lives a high and fast life. A person who is socially active. A person who frequents sophisticated places of resort, such as theaters, dancing halls, or clubs. Cf. **bon vivant** and **boulevardier.**

bon voyage *n.* [Fr. **bon** good (1); **voyage** journey (2): good journey.] A happy, good, or pleasant journey. *Rose and Elizabeth went to the airport to wish Timothy a bon voyage. —interj.* Have a good trip. *"Bon voyage," Anita said tearfully.*

bordello *n., pl.* **bordellos** [It. a brothel.] A house where prostitutes ply their trade. *Hookers from all around France arrived in Paris last week to protest legislation that would get them off the street and into municipally controlled bordellos* (*Newsweek Int.* Feb. 5, 1979:15). Cf. **lupanar.**

bordereau *n., pl.* **bordereaux** [Fr. memorandum, account, docket.] 1. A detailed memorandum. 2. *Insurance.* A summary or description of transactions between an agent and a company, or one prepared by a former underwriter for the benefit of a reinsurer.

borné or *fem.* **bornée** *adj.* [Fr. limited, restricted.] Limited in outlook, intelligence, depth of perception, variety of interests, scope, etc. Narrow-minded. Provincial. Parochial. a) *a bornée girl*; b) *a borné official.*

boudoir *n., pl.* **boudoirs** [Fr. a sulking room, a woman's private chamber.] A room which a lady can use as her private bedroom, as dressing room, and as a place to entertain her friends. *In public, Mrs. Bods behaves as though her husband is her lord, but in the privacy of her boudoir, roles are reversed. —adj.* Of, characteristic of, relating to, used in, a boudoir. *A boudoir lamp.*

boulevardier *n., pl.* **boulevardiers** [Fr. frequenter of the boulevards.] Man-about-town. Man with sophisticated taste in fashion. **Bon vivant** (q.v.). Cf. **bon viveur.**

bouleversement *n., pl.* **bouleversements** [Fr. an overturning.] Complete confusion, disruption. *She underwent a bouleversement in her feelings when she saw her husband with another woman.*

boulimia *var.* of **bulimia** (q.v.).

bouquiniste *n., pl.* **bouquinistes** [Fr. a person who sells second-hand books.] A used-book merchant, especially in a small street stall. *They made a habit of frequenting the bouquinistes along the Seine every Sunday afternoon.*

bourgeois or *fem.* **bourgeoise** *adj., pl.* **bourgeois** or *fem.* **bourgeoises** [Fr. *adj.* middle-class, common, plain; *n.,* citizen, civilian, commoner, townsman.] 1. Characteristic of the middle classes or the townsman. 2. Belonging to, characteristic of, the classes which engage in trade and own property. *. . . it now confronts such bourgeois problems as sagging exports, runaway labor costs and middle-class malaise . . .* (*Newsweek Int.* Nov. 12, 1979:35). 3. *Pejorative.* Tending to be preoccupied with selfish materialism, accumulation of wealth and property as well as respectable position in society. Exhibiting mediocre views and tastes. Narrow-minded. *The gaudy decor of the room revealed the bourgeois tastes of its inhabitants.* 4. *Politics.* Capitalistic. Preoccupied with commerce and industry. *According to Marxist theory, the interests of the proletariat are in constant conflict with bourgeois concerns. —n.* 1. An inhabitant of a bourg. 2. A member of the middle classes. A businessman. A person who derives his/her wealth from trade and industry. A capitalist. A person whose socio-political views are dominated by the interests of private property ownership. 3. A philistine. A narrow-minded person. A person preoccupied with materialism and showing negligible interest in intellectual values. *He is such a bourgeois that he cares little about art beyond its resale value.* See **bourgeoisie; grande bourgeoisie; haute bourgeoisie; petit bourgeois;** and **petite bourgeoisie.**

bourgeoisie *n.* [Fr. the social class of the bourgeois.] The middle classes. A society dominated by the middle classes. See **bourgeois.**

bourrée *n., pl.* **bourrées** [Fr. stuffed, crammed, packed, packed sticks, a dance.] 1. A traditional French dance of the Auvergne believed to have originated in dances around piles of fagots. 2. Music played for this dance. 3. *Ballet.* A dance step also called **pas de bourrée** (q.v.).

bourse *n., pl.* **bourses** [Fr. purse, stock exchange, money market, scholarship, grant.] 1. Market. An exchange. A stock exchange. A place where merchants, brokers, and bankers meet for business transactions. *In just one session of trading last week, shares on the Paris Bourse dropped more than 2 per cent, . . . (Newsweek Int.* May 11, 1981:12). 2. A scholarship or grant to pursue academic activities.

boustrophedon *n.* [Gk. **boustrophēdon: bous** ox (1); **strophēdon** turning (2): ox-turning.] Writing the way a field is plowed by an ox, i.e., from left to right then right to left, etc.

boutique *n., pl.* **boutiques** [Fr. shop, stall, booth.] A small shop, particularly one which specializes in fashionable clothes and accessories for ladies.

b.p. *abbr.* for **bonum publicum** (q.v.).

b.q. *abbr.* for **bene quiescat** (q.v.).

brava *fem.* for **bravo** (q.v.).

bravo or *fem.* **brava** *adj., pl.* **bravi** or **bravos** or *fem.* **brave** [It. courageous, excellent.] (You are) excellent! —*interj.* Excellent! Well done! a) *Bravo to Richard Schickel for his incisive review of* Star Trek . . . (*Time Int.* 1980). b) *Bravo for a job well done* . . . (*The Guardian* 1986). c) *The opera house was filled with shouts of "Brava" after the soprano finished her aria.* —*n.* 1. Shout of approval, commendation, approbation or sanction. *The outstanding performance was greeted with wild bravos.* 2. Villain. Assassin. Thug. Cutthroat. —*v. tr.* To show approval, approbation, or admiration by shouting bravo. *The entire audience, with no exception, bravoed the performance.*

bravura *n., pl.* **bravuras** [It. bravery.] 1. Exhibition of brilliance or daring. *He slips with stunning bravura in and out of the parts of the egomaniacal Richard III, the self-pitying Lear and, stripped nearly naked, Timon of Athens (Newsweek Int.* May 30, 1983:64). 2. *Music.* A piece or passage which demands considerable spirit and skill on the part of the performer. —*attr.* Performing or behaving in a brilliant, daring, or spirited manner.

brevet *n., pl.* **brevets** [Fr. certificate, patent, commission.] 1. *French Law.* A document from a government, giving a private individual a title, privilege, benefit, or dignity. 2. *Military.* A commission which gives an officer promotion to a higher rank, though he/she does not receive the corresponding salary or authority.

brevet d'invention *n.* [Fr. **brevet** patent, license (1); **d'** of (2); **invention** discovery, invention (3): a patent for a discovery.] Patent for an invention. Letters patent.

bric-à-brac *n., pl.* **bric-à-bracs** [Fr. curios, bits and pieces, odds and ends.] Curios. A miscellaneous collection of small decorative articles, art objects, antiques, etc., which have sentimental value. *The townhouse was filled with a life-long accumulation of antiques and bric-à-brac.*

brigatista *n., pl.* **brigatisti** [It. a member of a brigade.] A member of the Red Brigade. *The authorities also stumbled upon a possible link with the abduction by brigatisti of U.S. Brigadier General James Dozier . . . (Time Int.* 1982).

brochure *n., pl.* **brochures** [Fr. booklet, pamphlet.] A small book or pamphlet.

brontophobia *n.* [Neo-Gk. from Gk. **bronto(s)** thunder (2); **phob(os)** fear (1): fear of thunder.] *Psychology.* Excessive fear of thunder.

brouhaha *n., pl.* **brouhahas** [Fr. uproar, din, commotion, hubbub.] 1. Hubbub. A confused mixture of sounds, particularly voices. 2. Hullabaloo. Furor. Uproar. Fuss. Unwarranted excitement, publicity, or attention. . . . *a legal brouhaha over the film's worldwide distribution rights delayed the première for four months (Newsweek Int.* March 12, 1979:57).

brutum fulmen *n., pl.* **bruta fulmina** [L. **brutum** heavy, inert, irrational (1); **fulmen** thunderbolt (2): a heavy thunderbolt.] An empty threat or noise. a) *Since the court has no jurisdiction, the quit order issued against the tenant is no more than a brutum fulmen.* b) *One of the reasons for applying the lex situs is that any adjudication which was contrary to what the lex situs had decided or would decide would be in most cases a brutum fulmen, since in the last resort the land can only be dealt with in a manner permitted by the lex situs* (Morris 1973:61).

buffet *n., pl.* **buffets** [Fr. sideboard, refreshment room, refreshment table.] 1. A counter where refreshments are sold, as in a railway station, a train, a hotel, or theater. 2. A meal, usually a light refreshment, served informally on a sideboard to guests who stand or sit casually and eat. a) *a buffet luncheon;* b) *a buffet supper.*

B.U.J. *abbr.* for **Baccalaureus Utriusque Juris** (q.v.).

bulimia or **boulimia** *n., pl.* **bulimias** or **boulimias** [Gk. being ox-hungry.] *Medicine.* Abnormal hunger. Abnormal craving for food. A disease characterized by binge-eating followed by purging. See **polyphagia.**

Bundesbank *n.* [Ger. **Bund** association, federation (1); **Bank** bank (2): federation bank.] The federal bank of the Federal Republic of Germany. *The Bundesbank is holding interest rates high to protect the Deutschmark (Newsweek Int.* Dec. 15, 1980:47).

Bundeskanzleramt *n.* [Ger. **Bund** association, federation (1); **Kanzleramt** office of chancellor (2): federation office of chancellor.] Office of the Federal Chancellor, i.e., of Germany. *And he still feels the glow of admiration when meeting with foreign statesmen, either in his drab modernistic Bundeskanzleramt or abroad* (*Newsweek Int.* April 26, 1982:35).

Bundesstaat *n., pl.* **Bundesstaaten** or **Bundesstaats** [Ger. **Bund** association, federation (1); **Staat** state (2): federation state.] A federated state. A federation.

Bundestag *n., pl.* **Bundestage** or **Bundestags** [Ger. **Bund** association, federation (1); **Tag** meeting, diet, assembly (2): federation assembly.] Federal Diet. Lower House. Lower House of Parliament, specifically in the Federal Republic of Germany. . . . *the Bundestag approved a measure designed to encourage some of the 4.5 million foreign workers in the country to return home* (*Newsweek Int.* Dec.12, 1983:14).

Bundeswehr *n.* [Ger. **Bund** association, federation (1); **wehr** defense (2): federation defense.] Defense forces of the Federal Republic of Germany established in 1954/5 by the Treaty of Paris. *With 500,000 troops, the Bundeswehr is by far the largest single military force in Western Europe* (*Newsweek Int.* Nov 17, 1980:36).

buon appetito *interj.* [It. **buon** good (1); **appetito** appetite (2): good appetite.] Happy dining! Cf. **bon appétit**.

bureau *n., pl.* **bureaux** or **bureaus** [Fr. desk, writing table, office, department, committee, board.] 1. A writing desk which has drawers. 2. A low chest of drawers, fitted with a mirror, usually used in a bedroom. 3. A unit of the administrative or executive division of a government. a) *State research bureau*; b) *planning bureau*; c) *weather bureau*; d) *The Federal Bureau of Investigation* (F.B.I.); e) *Bureau of Labor Statistics*; f) *Bureau of Land Management*. 4. A business agency which coordinates activities and serves as the center for making contacts and exchanging information, inter alia. 5. A branch of a news media or wirecommunication organization in an important city. *Times Bonn Bureau*.

bureau de change *n., pl.* **bureaux de change** [Fr. **bureau** office (1); **de** of (2); **change** change, exchange (3): office of change.] Foreign exchange office. Office of the money-changer. Office of currency exchange.

burlesque *n., pl.* **burlesques** [Fr. comic.] 1. A dramatic performance or written work which uses a tone inappropriate to the subject matter to create ridicule or humor. So a serious topic is presented humorously or a light subject is presented seriously. 2. A distorted or absurd imitation. A mockery. 3. A motley theatrical performance combining ribald humor, striptease, song, and dance. —*v.* To mock, to imitate in a distorted, humorous manner. —*adj.* 1. Mocking. Distorted. Humorous. 2. Pertaining to a motley theatrical performance combining ribald humor, striptease, song, and dance. a) *a burlesque dancer*; b) *a burlesque theater*.

bzw. *abbr.* for **beziehungsweise** (q.v.).

C

c. *abbr.* for 1. **circa** (q.v.). 2. **circiter** (q.v.). 3. **circum** (q.v.).

ca. *abbr.* for **circa** (q.v.).

C.A. *abbr.* for 1. **chargé d'affaires** (q.v.). 2. **corps d'armée** [Fr. **corps** body (1); **d'** of (2); **armée** army (3): body of the army.] Army Corps.

cabala or **cabbala** or **kabala** or **kabbala** *n.* [Heb. **qabbāla** tradition, doctrine.] 1. *Judaism.* Mystical teachings based upon rabbinical tradition and esoteric interpretation of scripture. 2. Any collection of secret teachings.

caballero *n., pl.* **caballeros** [Sp. horse groom.] 1. A Spanish knight or gentleman. 2. A skilled horseman.

cabana *n., pl.* **cabanas** [Sp. **cabaña** hut.] A beachhouse or shelter.

cabaret *n., pl.* **cabarets** [Fr. restaurant, tavern, nightclub, pub, wineshop.] 1. A shop which sells wine and liquor. 2. A restaurant which, in addition to its normal services, provides entertainment in the form of music and dancing. 3. The floor show provided at such a restaurant.

cabotinage *n., pl.* **cabotinages** [Fr. third-rate acting, barn-storming, self-advertisement.] Playing to the gallery. Exaggerated or extravagant acting with the deliberate intention of attracting the attention of the audience.

cache *n., pl.* **caches** [Fr. hiding-place.] 1. A hiding place where explorers, campers, etc. store provisions and tools. A place for storage. 2. Something concealed or preserved in a hiding place. *... they found a cache of firearms and ammunition, bomb-making equipment* ... (*Newsweek Int.* Nov. 2, 1981:39). 3. A place where a group of insects hibernate. 4. A group of insects hibernating in the same hiding place. 5. *Computer Science.* An area of the central processing unit of a computer used for temporary storage and quick retrieval of data.

cache-cache *n.* [Fr. **cache** hiding-place.] Hide-and-seek. Peekaboo. *The flirtatious young couple played cache-cache with their eyes from opposite sides of the room.*

cache-pot *n., pl.* **cache-pots** [Fr. **cache** hiding place (2); **pot** pot, vessel (1): a pot hiding place.] A container for a flower pot.

cachet *n., pl.* **cachets** [Fr. seal, mark, stamp.] 1. A stamp, seal, or sign indicating official sanction or approval. *The much-rumored project has now received the cachet of the board of directors.* 2. Prestige. Reputation. Recognition. Mark of excellence. A distinct quality or feature which confers prestige, respect, or honor. *Kinski now has international cachet as a serious actress* ... (*Newsweek Int.,* Feb. 23, 1981:53).

c.-à-d. *abbr.* for **c'est-à-dire** (q.v.).

cachexia *n.* [Gk. **kakhexia: kak(os)** bad, evil (1); **hexis** condition, state (2): bad condition.] A debilitating loss of weight and muscle tone as a result of prolonged disease.

cadastre or **cadaster** *n., pl.* **cadastres** or **cadastrers** [Fr. land survey, register.] A register of land ownership for tax purposes.

cadaver *n., pl.* **cadavers** [L. a dead body, a corpse.] Dead human body.

cadeau *n., pl.* **cadeaux** [Fr. gift, present.] A gift. A present.

cadenza *n., pl.* **cadenzas** [It. falling.] 1. A showy interpolation by a vocal soloist. 2. An elaborate solo section intended to demonstrate the virtuosity of an instrumental performer in a concerto.

cadet *n., pl.* **cadets** [Fr. younger, junior, youngest, young fellow.] 1. Younger brother, son or division of a family. Youngest son. A person belonging to a younger division of a family. 2. A person undergoing training in the armed forces to become a commissioned officer. 3. A junior person who is undergoing training in an occupation or business.

cadit quaestio. [L. **cadit** falls (2); **quaestio** inquiry, question (1): The inquiry/question falls.] There is no more room for argument. The discussion comes to an end. *If the tribunal recommended that the question should not be so referred, then cadit quaestio* (Nwabueze 1982:114).

cadre *n., pl.* **cadres** [Fr. framework, skeleton, nucleus, manager, executive.] 1. Framework. Skeletal organization. 2. A nucleus of trained members of an organization who have the capacity of becoming leaders and training others in the field. A small group of important people. . . . *as cadres of qualified scientists have been built up, more advanced training has been undertaken at selected institutions* (Peter Collins in *West Africa* 1985).

caduceus *n., pl.* **caducei** [L. from Gk. **karukeion** herald's staff.] 1. A herald's staff, especially the one carried by Hermes, the Greek messenger god. This staff is topped by a circle and a half circle. 2. Hermes' staff with wings and entwined serpents added. Associated with medicine and physicians.

cael. *abbr.* for **caelavit** (q.v.).

caelavit *abbr.* **cael.** [L. He/she engraved it.] Engraved by. Used to indicate the author of an engraving. Cf. **delineavit; fecit; invenit; invenit et delineavit; pinxit**; and **sculpsit**.

Caesar *n., pl.* **Caesars** [L. a Roman gens or tribe name.] 1. Gaius Julius Caesar (100–44 B.C.), the famous general and statesman of Rome, who was assassinated on the Ides of March, 44 B.C. 2. A Roman emperor. 3. An emperor, dictator, despot, or autocrat. *The country's Caesar is becoming more irresponsible than the notorious Nero.* 4. A temporal or earthly ruler. *Christians, in due compliance with the instructions of Jesus, pay allegiance to both God and Caesar.* Cf. **czar** and **Kaiser**.

Caesar non supra grammaticos [L. **Caesar** Caesar (1); **non** (2); **supra** above (3); **grammaticos** grammarians (4): Caesar (is) not over the grammarians.] The power of a Caesar, i.e., a political ruler, does not include power over grammar. Political power has its limits.

caesura *n., pl.* **caesurae** or **caesuras** [L. a cutting.] 1. Any break or interruption, but especially a pause in a line of verse or a breathing point in a musical melody. 2. *Greek and Latin Poetry.* A word which ends in the middle of a metrical foot.

caetera desunt. *var.* of **cetera desunt** (q.v.).

caeteris paribus *var.* of **ceteris paribus** (q.v.).

caeteris tacentibus *var.* of **ceteris tacentibus** (q.v.).

caeterorum *var.* of **ceterorum** (q.v.).

café or **cafe** *n., pl.* **cafés** or **cafes** [Fr. coffee, coffee house, coffee shop.] 1. Coffee. 2. A room where coffee and light refreshments are served. Coffee house. Coffee shop. 3. A restaurant. A barroom. A saloon . . . *the seedy cafés can offer only coffee and the occasional beer* (*Newsweek Int.* July 7, 1980:12).

café au lait *n., pl.* **cafés au lait** [Fr. **café** coffee (1); **au** to the, toward the, in the, by the, with the, until the (2); **lait** milk (3): coffee with the milk.] Coffee with

milk, especially hot milk. White coffee. . . . *crowds lined up for steaming cups of café au lait* . . . . (*Newsweek Int.* May 18, 1981:52). Cf. **café noir**.

café noir *n., pl.* **cafés noirs** [Fr. **café** coffee (2); **noir** black (1): black coffee.] Coffee without cream or milk. Cf. **café au lait**.

Ça ira. [Fr. **ça** it (1); **ira** will go (2): It will go.] It will happen without doubt. 1. The first words of a French revolutionary song. 2. Any song or slogan urging revolutionary violence.

caldera *n., pl.* **calderas** [Sp. caldron.] A large volcanic crater.

Calliope *n.* [Gk. **Kalliopē: kalli-** beautiful (1); **op(s)** voice (2): beautiful voice.] *Greek Mythology.* She of the beautiful voice. The muse of epic poetry. —**calliope** *n., pl.* **calliopes** *Music.* A steam-operated pipe organ used especially at circuses, parades, and merry-go-rounds. Often transported on wagons.

calumniandi animo *adv.* [L. **calumniandi** of accusing falsely, slandering (2); **animo** with intention (1): with the intention of accusing falsely.] *Law.* With the intention of slandering. With intent to slander. With a malicious design. *It cannot be disputed that he made the statement against his friend calumniandi animo.*

cam. *abbr.* for **camouflage** (q.v.).

camaraderie *n., pl.* **camaraderies** [Fr. comradeship.] Good fellowship. Spirit of familiarity, friendship, mutual cooperation, trust, loyalty and goodwill which exists among comrades. . . . *in the disco and game rooms, the village comes alive with the sort of international camaraderie that is supposed to make the hassles of the Olympics worthwhile* (*Newsweek Int.* Feb. 25, 1980:46-47).

camarilla *n., pl.* **camarillas** [Sp. small or little room.] Clique. Cabal. A group of scheming advisers who usually surround a potentate. *The new boss is surrounded by a camarilla comprising people who are primarily interested in obtaining undeserved promotions and settling old scores.*

camera *n., pl.* **camerae** [L. room, chamber.] A judge's chamber. Cf. **in camera**. —*pl.* **cameras** 1. A piece of equipment used for taking photographs. 2. A piece of equipment used for transmitting television images. 3. **Camera obscura** (q.v.).

camera lucida *n., pl.* **camerae lucidae** or **camera lucidas** [L. **camera** room, chamber (2); **lucida** light (1): light room.] A piece of equipment which uses a prism to project an image on a flat surface for the purpose of tracing.

camera obscura *n., pl.* **camerae obscurae** or **camera obscuras** [L. **camera** room, chamber (2); **obscura** dark (1): dark room.] A darkened enclosure through which an image is projected through a small opening onto the back of the enclosure.

Camorra *n.* [It. a shirt, a secret organization.] A clandestine organization founded in Naples in the early

19th-century for the purpose of blackmail and extortion. —**camorra** *pl.* **camorras** Any clandestine criminal organization. Cf. **dacoit**; **mafia**; **petit truand**; and **yakuza**.

camouflage *abbr.* **cam.** *n., pl.* **camouflages** [Fr. disguise, makeup.] 1. *Military.* Disguising an object so that the enemy may not discover what it is, its nature, and its position. 2. Using disguise to conceal something. 3. A disguise. Conduct, behavior, or device which aims at deception or concealing something. False pretense. —*v. tr.* To disguise or conceal. *They camouflaged their guilt behind a mask of bravura.*

campanile *n., pl.* **campaniles** [It. belltower.] A tall building with bells, especially one adjacent to a church.

campesino *n., pl.* **campesinos** [Sp. a field worker.] A Latin-American rustic, farm laborer, or farmer. *Tens of thousands of campesinos who once streamed from farms to Mexico City to find $200-a-month construction jobs are staying home this year* (*Newsweek Int.* Oct. 18, 1982:46).

campus *n., pl.* **campi** or **campuses** [L. field, plain.] 1. The site of a university, college or school. *Ben is traveling to his home-town today, but hopes to return to campus next week.* 2. A school, college or division of a university which has almost every necessary facility and can operate independently, but is linked to, and administered by, a university. *The University of Jos was formerly a campus of the University of Ibadan.* 3. The world of academia. The university as a social and educational entity. *Politicians seem to expect too much from the campus and, if they had their own way, universities would become technical schools.*

canaille *n., pl.* **canailles** [Fr. rabble, mob, riffraff, populace.] The general populace. The masses. The proletariat. *There can be no meaningful political stability until the problems of the urban canaille have received the necessary attention.* See **demos** 2; **hoi polloi**; **sans-culottes**; and **vulgus**. Cf. **la crème de la crème**.

canard *n., pl.* **canards** [Fr. duck, deceiving story.] 1. An intentionally false story. *The police report published in the newspaper was merely a canard intended to deceive the perpetrators of the crime.* 2. A wing-like stabilizer attached to the fuselage of some aircraft.

Cancer *n.* [L. crab.] 1. *Astronomy.* A crab-shaped constellation located near Gemini and Leo. 2. *Astrology.* The fourth sign of the zodiac dominant from June 22 through July 22. 3. A person born under this constellation. —**cancer** 1. An abnormal, malignant growth of cells. 2. The disease caused by such abnormal growth. 3. A spreading evil. *The cancer of drug abuse.*

cantabit vacuus coram latrone viator. Juvenal (c.60–117 A.D.). *Satires* X,22. [L. **cantabit** will sing (3); **vacuus** empty, devoid (1); **coram** in the presence of, in the face of (4); **latrone** highwayman, robber, brigand (5); **viator** traveler (2): An empty traveler will sing in the presence of a brigand.] A traveler who has no money will sing when confronted by a brigand.

cantata *n., pl.* **cantatas** [It. sung.] *Music.* A composition, originally religious in context, for both voice and instruments in various combinations of solos, choruses, and recitatives.

cantatrice *n., pl.* **cantatrices** or **cantatrici** [It. and Fr. a female singer.] A woman or girl who is a professional singer, especially an operatic singer.

cantor *n., pl.* **cantors** [L. singer.] One who leads the congregation of a church or synagogue in singing. *. . . cantors with splendid voices are still in demand for the High Holidays, and some are hired for the weekend by wealthy congregations* (*Newsweek Int.* June 1, 1981:41).

cantus firmus *n., pl.* **canti firmi** [L. **cantus** song (2); **firmus** fixed, set (1): fixed song.] *Music.* The melody around which other, i.e. counter, melodies are worked, especially in medieval religious chant.

capax doli *adj.* [L. **capax** capable (1); **doli** of willful wrong (2): capable of willful wrong.] *Law.* Capable of committing a crime. Intelligent enough to be held criminally liable. *At the age of eighteen, a person is deemed to be capax doli.*

capax negotii *adj.* [L. **capax** fit for, capable of (1); **negotii** (of) business (2): capable of business.] Capable of transacting business. Competent to transact business. *An infant is not deemed to be capax negotii.*

Capelle *var.* of **Kapelle** (q.v.).

Capellmeister *var.* of **Kapellmeister** (q.v.).

capias *n., pl.* **capiases** [L. You may take. You should seize.] *Law.* That you take. A legal writ which empowers the officer to arrest the one who is named in it or to seize his/her goods. See **fieri facias**.

capias ad audiendum judicium *n.* [L. **capias** you may/should seize (1); **ad** to, at, for, according to (2) **audiendum** to be heard (4); **judicium** judgment (3): You should seize for judgment to be heard.] You should seize for the hearing of judgment. *Law.* A writ ordering that an accused in a case of misdemeanor be brought to hear judgment.

capias ad respondendum *abbr.* **ca. resp.** *n.* [L. **capias** you may/should seize (1); **ad** to, at, for, according to (2); **respondendum** answering (3): You should seize for answering.] *Law.* A writ, usually used for commencing action, which orders that an accused person be arrested, kept in custody, and brought to court on a specified day to answer the complaint of the plaintiff.

capias ad satisfaciendum *abbr.* **ca. sa.** *n.* [L. **capias** you should/may seize (1); **ad** to, at, for, according to (2); **satisfaciendum** satisfying (3): You should seize for satisfying.] *Law.* A writ ordering that a party be arrested, kept in custody, and brought to court on a specified day to make satisfaction for debt or damages.

Capischi? *v.* [It. Do you understand?] *Slang.* It is clear? Do you get the point?

capitatim *adj.* [L. by/of the head.] So much per head. By the head. Applicable to taxes or levies calculated per head. *A capitatim tax.*

capite minutus or **capite deminutus** *n.* [L. **capite** by head (2); **minutus** diminished, reduced (1): diminished by the head.] One who has lost status. *Civil Law.* A person who has lost some civil rights, such as citizenship, freedom, or membership in a family. A person who has suffered capitis diminutio. See **capitis diminutio.**

capitis diminutio or **capitis deminutio** *n.* [L. **capitis** of head, life (2); **diminutio** forfeiture, loss (1): loss/forfeiture of life/head.] Loss of civil rights. *Roman Law.* A citizen's loss of legal status which may include loss of freedom, membership in a family, and, even, citizenship. See **capite minutus; capitis diminutio maxima; capitis diminutio media; capitis diminutio minima;** and **diminutio.**

capitis diminutio maxima or **capitis deminutio maxima** *n.* [L. **capitis** of head, life (3); **diminutio** loss (2); **maxima** greatest (1): the greatest loss of head/life.] *Roman Law.* The highest form of loss of civil rights; i.e., losing freedom and becoming a slave. See **capitis diminutio.**

capitis diminutio media or **capitis deminutio media** *n.* [L. **capitis** of head, life (3); **diminutio** loss (2); **media** middle, moderate (1): moderate loss of head/life.] *Roman Law.* A moderate loss of status; i.e., losing citizenship and family rights but retaining personal freedom. See **capitis diminutio.**

capitis diminutio minima or **capitis deminutio minima** *n.* [L. **capitis** of head, life (3); **diminutio** loss (2); **minima** least, lowest (1): the least/lowest loss of head/life.] *Roman Law.* The least loss of status, i.e., losing membership in a family, but retaining personal freedom and citizenship. See **capitis diminutio.**

capriccio *n., pl.* **capriccios** [It. whimsical.] 1. *Music.* A lively instrumental composition written in a free-flowing style. 2. A joke. A trick. 3. A sudden change in intention or thought. A whim. Cf. **capriccioso** and **caprice.**

capriccioso *adj./adv.* [It. whimsical.] *Music.* In a whimsical style. Cf. **capriccio** and **caprice.**

caprice *n., pl.* **caprices** [Fr. from It. **capriccio** whimsical.] 1. *Music.* A **capriccio** (q.v.). 2. A sudden change in intention or thought. A whim. *Their decision to attend the concert was a caprice which they regretted.*

Capricornus *n.* [L. from **capr(i)** goat (1); **cornu** horn (2): goat horn.] 1. *Astronomy.* Capricorn. A goat-shaped constellation located near Aquarius and Sagittarius. 2. *Astrology.* The tenth sign of the zodiac, dominant from December 22 through January 19. 3. A person born under this constellation.

caput *n., pl.* **capita** [L. head, life.] 1. The three fundamental rights, namely freedom, citizenship and family rights. 2. The head of a person. 3. Personality.

caput mortuum *n., pl.* **capita mortua** [L. **caput** head (2); **mortuum** dead (1): dead head.] Worthless residue. The residue after something had been distilled.

carabiniere *n., pl.* **carabinieri** [It. a soldier armed with a musket.] A member of Italy's national police force. *Legions of carabinieri pressed on with the manhunt but most of their tips and leads took them up blind alleys* (*Newsweek Int.* Jan. 11, 1982:15).

carcer ad homines custodiendos, non ad puniendos, dari debet. [L. **carcer** prison (1); **ad** to, at, for, according to (4); **homines** humans, people (5); **custodiendos** to be kept (6); **non** not (7); **ad** to, at, for, according to (8); **puniendos** to be punished (9); **dari** to be applied, devoted (3); **debet** ought, should (2): A prison ought to be devoted to people to be kept, not to people to be punished.] *Law.* Imprisonment should serve the purpose of keeping individuals away from society, not that of punishing them.

cardialgia *n., pl.* **cardialgias** [Neo-Gk. from **kardi(a)** (1); **alg(os)** pain, suffering (2): heart pain.] *Medicine.* Heartburn. Cardiac pain. Pain in the heart.

cardiophobia *n., pl.* **cardiophobias** [Neo-Gk. from Gk. **kardi(a)** heart (2); **phob(os)** fear (1): fear of heart.] *Medicine.* Morbid, abnormal, or excessive fear of heart disease.

ca. resp. *abbr.* for **capias ad respondendum** (q.v.).

cargo *n., pl.* **cargoes** or **cargos** [Sp. charge, load, burden, responsibility.] The freight, load, or goods conveyed by a ship, vehicle, or airplane. Usually applicable to only the goods. Animals and persons are not included.

carillon *n., pl.* **carillons** [Fr. bells.] *Music.* 1. A set of bells arranged chromatically so that tunes can be played from a keyboard or electronically. 2. A composition for such bells.

carillonneur *n., pl.* **carillonneurs** [Fr. bell player.] Someone who plays a **carillon** (q.v.).

carissima *adj.* [It. dearest.] A term of affection.

caritas *n.* [L. love, regard, esteem.] *Christianity.* Charity. Christian love. A human's special love for God and a human's love for others for the sake of God. A human's love for others as brothers and sisters, since all persons are the sons and daughters of God. God's love for mankind. See **agape.**

carmen *n., pl.* **carmina** [L. a song, poem, verse, prophecy, or incantation.] A song or poem. —**Carmen** A first name for either a man or a woman. —**Carmina** a collection of poems, especially those by Catullus (c.84–c.54 B.C.).

carousel or **carrousel** *n., pl.* **carousels** or **carrousels** [Fr. a knight's tournament.] 1. A merry-go-round. 2. A piece of equipment which carries articles around in a circle, especially luggage in an airport.

carpe diem. Horace (65–8 B.C.). *Odes* I,2,8. [L. **carpe** take, snatch, seize (1); **diem** day (2): Seize the day.]

Seize the opportunity. Make use of the day. —*n., pl.* **carpe diems** Enjoying the pleasures of the day with no regard for the future. *Their carpe diems were transformed into dies iraes as a result of the stock market crash.* Cf. **dum loquimur** etc.

carptim *adv.* [L. in pieces, in different places, at different times.] Piecemeal. Selectively. In parts. *One school of thought believes that historiography cannot be completely objective, since most historians write carptim.*

carte blanche *n., pl.* **cartes blanches** [Fr. **carte** chart, card (2); **blanche** white, blank, clean (1): a white or blank card.] 1. A document signed and given to the other party for him/her to fill in whatever he/she may deem fit. 2. Free hand. Unrestricted delegated authority. Full power of discretion. Unlimited freedom of action. Full power to act for the best. Unlimited authority. a) *The order was only a carte blanche for the thugs and bullies to have their own revenge on the Ghanaians who had been considered threats to their own existence* (John Mensah in *West Africa* 1983). b) *. . . he gave me carte blanche . . . to take the necessary measures against certain "leopards," among them Litho and his businesses* (*New African* 1983). c) *John Pistone, director of the U.S. bishops' Secretariat for the Diaconate and himself a deacon, said the rules changes should not be viewed "as a carte blanche" for widowed deacons to remarry and stay in active ministry* (Jerry Filteau in *Catholic News Service*, August 24, 1997:2).

carte d'entrée *n., pl.* **cartes d'entrée** [Fr. **carte** card (1); **d'** of (2); **entrée** entry, admission (3): card of entry or admission.] Ticket. Card for admission. Admission ticket or card. Cf. **entrée**.

carte de visite *abbr.* **c.d.v.** *n., pl.* **cartes de visite** [Fr. **carte** card (1); **de** of (2); **visite** visit, call (3): card of visit.] Calling card.

carte d'identité *n., pl.* **cartes d'identité** [Fr. **carte** card (1); **d'** of (2); **identité** identity (3): card of identity.] Identity card. ID card. ID.

cartel *n., pl.* **cartels** [Fr. coalition, combine, trust.] 1. A letter of challenge, as for a duel. 2. An agreement between belligerent powers respecting prisoners, deserters, intercommunications, etc. 3. A voluntary combination of independent enterprises engaged in the production and distribution of similar commodities, aimed at limiting competition by controlling production, pricing, and sales. The enterprises could also cooperate by standardizing products and exchanging knowledge, patents, trademarks, etc. . . . *the U.S. government . . . is to be found among those urging OPEC to behave like a cartel* (O. Ugochukwu in *West Africa* 1986). Cf. **zaibatsu**.

Carthago delenda est. See **delenda est Carthago**.

ca. sa. *abbr.* for **capias ad satisfaciendum** (q.v.).

Casanova *n., pl.* **Casanovas** [It.] 1. Giacomo Girolamo Casanova, an Italian adventurer (1725–1798) whose work *Histoire de ma vie (Story of My Life)*, won for him the notorious reputation of a philanderer. 2. A male lover who is not only promiscuous but also unscrupulous. *His reputation as a Casanova preceded him and his arrival was not welcome in her eyes.*

Casbah or **casbah** *n., pl.* **Casbahs** or **casbahs** [Fr. from Ar. **qasbah** fortress.] A castle in North Africa.

cas de conscience *n.* [Fr. **cas** case, matter (1); **de** of (2); **conscience** principles, conscience (3): a case of principles.] A matter of conscience or morality. Cf. **crise de conscience**.

cas fortuit *n.* [Fr. **cas** circumstance, matter (2); **fortuit** accidental, fortuitous (1): an accidental circumstance.] *Insurance Law.* An unavoidable accident. An accidental or fortuitous event. An act of God. See **casus fortuitus**.

casino *n., pl.* **casinos** [It. a little or small house.] A building where public entertainment is provided, the principal item of amusement being gambling.

Cassandra *n., pl.* **Cassandras** [Gk. **Kassandra**.] 1. *Mythology.* The beautiful daughter of Priam, king of Troy, who was destined never to be believed even when accurately predicting misfortunes like the birth of Paris (whose amorous escapade led to the Trojan war) and the consequences of accepting the gift of the wooden horse. 2. A prophet or prophetess of misfortune, doom, or disaster. a) *Recent developments clearly show that Emily is a veritable Cassandra.* b) *. . . the trend has become sufficiently clear to indicate that the Cassandras might have been wrong after all . . .* (*Newsweek Int.* March 26, 1979:21).

castrato *n., pl.* **castrati** [It. an emasculated or castrated man or boy.] *Music.* A singer castrated at an early age to preserve his soprano voice. *. . . in the nineteenth century . . . castrati finally disappeared from Europe's stages . . .* (*Newsweek Int.* March 8, 1982:56).

casus belli *n., pl.* **casus belli** [L. **casus** occasion, event, case (1); **belli** of war (2): occasion of war.] Excuse, grounds, or cause for war. An event or action which justifies the declaration of war. *Britain and France regarded Hitler's invasion of Poland as a casus belli.*

casus foederis *n., pl.* **casus foederis** [L. **casus** occasion, event, case (1); **foederis** of treaty (2): occasion of the treaty.] A case which is, or is considered to be, governed by the provisions of an agreement or treaty. *The movement of citizens of ECOWAS countries from one to another is a casus foederis.*

casus fortuitus *n., pl.* **casus fortuiti** [L. **casus** occasion, event, case (2); **fortuitus** accidental (1): accidental event.] *Law.* An accidental event. An inevitable accident. A fortuitous event or occurence. Something such as a loss which happens in spite of every precaution taken. See **cas fortuit**.

casus fortuitus non est sperandus, et nemo tenetur divinare. [L. **casus** occasion, event, accident, case (2); **fortuitus** accidental (1); **non** not (4); **est** is (3);

sperandus to be expected, looked for (5); **et** and (6); **nemo** no one (7); **tenetur** is obligated, bound (8); **divinare** to foresee, predict (9): An accidental event is not to be expected and no one is obligated to foresee it.] *Law.* An accidental event is an unexpected event and no one is obligated to foresee it. The maxim, though generally valid, is not applicable to cases where the liability is the consequence of a party's act. See **impotentia excusat legem.**

casus major *n., pl.* **casus majores** [L. **casus** occasion, event, accident, case (2); **major** major (1): a major event.] *Law.* An extraordinary accident or casualty.

casus non praestatur. [L. **casus** occasion, event, accident, case (1); **non** not (2); **praestatur** is vouched for (3): An accident is not vouched for.] *Law.* Nobody should be held responsible for an accidental occurrence; i.e., a party to a contract cannot be held responsible for accidental non-fulfilment of the contract.

casus omissus *n., pl.* **casus omissi** [L. **casus** occasion, event, accident, case (2); **omissus** left, out, omitted (1): an omitted event.] *Law.* An omitted case. Used with reference to a case which no statute has made provisions for and is thus governed by common law. Also applicable to a circumstance for which a treaty has made no provision. See **casus omissus et oblivioni** etc.

casus omissus et oblivioni datus dispositioni communis juris relinquitur. [L. **casus** occasion, event, accident, case (1); **omissus** left out, omitted (2); **et** and (3); **oblivioni** to forgetfulness, oblivion (5); **datus** given (4); **dispositioni** to disposition (7); **communis** of common (8); **juris** (of) right, law (9); **relinquitur** is left (6): A case omitted and given to oblivion is left to the disposition of common law.] *Law.* A case not covered by statute and consigned to oblivion should be decided according to common law. See **casus omissus.**

catabasis *var.* of **katabasis** (q.v.).

catachresis *n., pl.* **catachreses** [Gk. **katachrēsis: kata** down, from, complete (1); **chrēsis** a use (2): complete use, excessive use, misuse of language.] *Rhetoric.* Misuse or misapplication of words or figures of speech; e.g., "blind legs or arms."

catalogue raisonné *n., pl.* **catalogues raisonnés** [Fr. **catalogue** list (2); **raisonné** controlled, reasoned, measured (1): measured list.] A list of items, such as artwork and books, collected in a single volume along with commentary and detailed description, especially for a show or public exhibition.

catalysis *n., pl.* **catalyses** [Gk. **kata** down, from, complete (1); **lusis** loosening, destruction (2): complete loosening, dissolution, dismissal, termination, settlement of dispute.] *Science.* 1. The process whereby a substance accelerates or facilitates a chemical reaction without being affected. 2. The process or situation whereby an agent or force provokes an action or reaction between a number of forces or persons without being affected.

catastrophe *n., pl.* **catastrophes** [Gk. **katastrophē: kata** down, from, complete (2); **strophē** turning (1): turning down, dénouement, ruin, undoing, end, conclusion.] 1. The climax of the unraveling of the plot in a drama or a novel. **Dénouement** (q.v.). 2. A disaster. A sudden occurrence that brings considerable agony or suffering. A very serious calamity. . . . *a chronic balance of payments deficit, famine and refugee problems, renewed insurgency in the south and acute social unrest have brought the country to the brink of catastrophe* (South 1985).

catechesis *n., pl.* **catecheses** [Gk. **katēchēsis: kata** down, from, complete (2); **ēche(ō)** to sound (1): sound from, verbal instruction.] Basic oral instruction in a subject, especially in Christianity.

catharsis *n., pl.* **catharses** [Gk. **katharsis** purification, cleansing from guilt or defilement.] 1. *Medicine.* Purgation. Emptying of the bowels as by the use of a purgative. 2. Purgation, release, or purification of one's emotions, especially through drama or voluntarily recounting one's deep feelings to another person. Any purgation or purification which effects release from tension or produces spiritual rejuvenation. . . . *I needed to write something; something that would serve, perhaps, as a catharsis to help relieve me of the burden of now terrible memories* (The Guardian 1986).

cathedra *n., pl.* **cathedras** [L. from Gk. **kat(a)** down, from, complete (2); **(h)edra** chair, stool (1): a seat down, chair, stool.] The official throne or chair of a bishop or the Pope. See **ex cathedra.**

cathedraticum *n., pl.* **cathedratica** [L. **cathedra** chair, stool (2); **-aticum** thing related to, (1): thing related to the chair.] *Roman Catholic Church.* A sum of money paid annually by a parish for the sustenance of the bishop.

catholicon *n., pl.* **catholica** or **catholicons** [Gk. **katholikos** from **kat(a)** down, from, complete (2); **(h)ol(os)** whole (1): completely whole, entire, general, universal.] Panacea. Cure-all. A remedy for every problem. *Though this drug is for a specific malady, it is being advertised as a catholicon.*

caudillo *n., pl.* **caudillos** [Sp. small or little head.] *Spain and Latin-America.* A leader or captain of military troops, usually guerrilla forces. A political leader, boss, or ruler with troops loyal to him personally. *In 1928 Alvaro Obregon, who had emerged from the civil war as Mexico's strongest caudillo, was murdered . . .* (The Economist 1987). See **el Caudillo.** Cf. **duce; Führer** and **Il Duce.**

causa calumniae *adv.* [L. **causa** for the sake (1); **calumniae** of misrepresentation, false accusation (2): for the sake of misrepresentation.] For the sake of misrepresentation, false accusation, or blackmail.

causa causans *n.* [L. **causa** cause, case, reason (1); **causans** alleging as a cause, making a pretext (2): cause making a pretext.] Cause alleging a reason. The immediate cause. The precipitating cause. The last factor in a chain of causes. a) *The harm inflicted on the victim's head was the causa causans of his death.* b) *In* Payne v. Railway Executive *(1952) I.K.B. 26, Bradburn's case was followed and applied to the plaintiff's pension from the Royal Navy. . . . The causa causans of the receipt by the plaintiff of his disability pension was his service in the Royal Navy; the injury was but the causa sine qua non* (Weir 1974:542). See **causa proxima; causa proxima non** etc.; **causa sine qua non;** and **in jure, non remota** etc. Cf. **causa remota.**

causa data et non secuta *n.* [L. **causa** cause, case, reason (1); **data** given (2); **et** and (3); **non** not (4); **secuta** having followed (5): cause given and not having followed.] *Law.* An action for claiming something, if the condition on which it was given was not satisfied.

causa frigiditatis naturalis *adv.* [L. **causa** by reason, because (1); **frigiditatis** (of) frigidity, coldness, sterility (3); **naturalis** of natural (2): because of frigidity.] *Law* and *Medicine.* By reason of natural frigidity/coldness. Because of natural sterility. *Thus in one case in 1560, or 1561, after a sentence of divorce causa frigiditatis naturalis had been pronounced, both husband and wife married other persons and later had children* (Megarry 1955:121).

causa justa *n., pl.* **causae justae** [L. **causa** cause, case, reason (2); **justa** just (1): a just cause.] *Law.* A true/just cause, ground, or motive. *The judge ruled that the suit was based on causa justa and asked counsel for plaintiff to proceed with presentation of the case.*

causa matrimonialis *n., pl.* **causae matrimoniales** [L. **causa** cause, case, reason (2); **matrimonialis** matrimonial, of/for marriage (1): reason for marriage.] *Law.* Matrimonial cause. *A causa matrimonialis is always a delicate matter, particularly where the couple have children.*

causa mortis *abbr.* **C.M.** or **c.m.** *var.* of **mortis causa** (q.v.).

causa mortis donatio or **donatio mortis causa** *n., pl.* **causa mortis donationes** or **donationes mortis causa** [L. **causa** on account of, by reason (2); **mortis** of death (3); **donatio** gift, donation (1): a gift by reason of, or on account of, death.] *Law.* A donation or gift made in anticipation of death. A gift of personal goods made by a sick person in anticipation, fear, or contemplation of death. Such a gift becomes the absolute property of the donee on the death of the donor. On the other hand, the donor may get back the gift, if he/she recovers from the sickness, or the donee dies before him/her, or if for any reason the donor decides to withdraw the gift.

causa movens *n.* [L. **causa** cause, case, reason (2); **movens** moving (1): moving cause or reason.] *Law.* The reason which prompts one to institute legal action.

causa proxima *n., pl.* **causae proximae** [L. **causa** cause, case, reason (2); **proxima** nearest, next (1):

the nearest cause.] *Law.* The proximate, immediate, primary, or efficient cause; i.e., a cause directly responsible for an occurrence. See **causa causans.**

causa proxima non remota spectatur. [L. **causa** cause, case, reason (4); **proxima** immediate, nearest (1); **non** not (2); **remota** remote (3); **spectatur** is looked at, considered (5): The nearest, not the remote, cause is looked at.] *Law.* The immediate, not the remote, cause is considered; i.e., the immediate cause carries more weight than the remote. See **causa causans.**

causa rei *n., pl.* **causae rei** [L. **causa** cause, case, reason (1); **rei** of matter, thing, property, business, affair (2): cause of a thing.] *Civil Law.* Fruits of a thing. All the things which would have been derived from property, if it had not been unlawfully taken away from the rightful owner.

causa remota *n., pl.* **causae remotae** [L. **causa** cause, case, reason (2); **remota** remote (1): a remote cause.] A cause which is not immediate or proximate. A cause which is not directly responsible for an occurrence. Cf. **causa causans.**

causa sine qua non *n., pl.* **causae sine quibus non** [L. **causa** cause, case, reason (1); **sine** without (2); **qua** which (3); **non** not (4): cause without which not.] A cause without which the occurrence would not have taken place. A but-for cause. The immediate or proximate cause. *The barrel in the middle of the road was the causa sine qua non of the motor accident.* See **causa causans.**

causa testamentaria *n., pl.* **causae testamentariae** [L. **causa** cause, case, reason (2); **testamentaria** testamentary, relating to wills (1): a case relating to wills.] *Law.* A testamentary case. *In a causa testamentaria, the courts usually attempt to ascertain whether or not the testator was sanae mentis et bonae memoriae.*

causa turpis *n., pl.* **causae turpes** [L. **causa** cause, case, reason (2); **turpis** base, disgraceful (1): a base cause.] *Law.* A disgraceful cause or consideration. *No valid agreement can be founded on causa turpis.* See **ex turpi causa** etc.

causa vaga et incerta non est causa rationabilis. [L. **causa** cause, case, reason (4); **vaga** vague (1); **et** and (2); **incerta** uncertain (3) **non** not (6); **est** is (5); **causa** cause, case, reason (8); **rationabilis** reasonable (7): A vague and uncertain cause is not a reasonable cause.] *Law.* A cause which is vague and uncertain is not considered to be a reasonable cause; it is worthless.

cause célèbre *n., pl.* **causes célèbres** [Fr. **cause** cause, case, reason (2); **célèbre** famous (1): a famous case.] 1. *Law.* A famous or celebrated case, trial, or lawsuit. A case which arouses considerable public interest. A case famous because of the parties involved or the sensational and interesting nature of the revelations. *But when the presiding judge finally handed down the verdict last week, even Spanish liberals and feminists who had made the trial a national cause célèbre* *were stunned and smiling* (*Newsweek Int.* April 5, 1982:13). 2. An episode, affair or incident so notorious that it attracts attention. *One recent incident quickly became a cause célèbre* (*Newsweek Int.* April 20, 1981:18).

cause illicite *n., pl.* **causes illicites** [Fr. **cause** cause, consideration (2); **illicite** unlawful, illicit (1): an unlawful cause.] *French Law.* Unlawful, base, illicit, or scandalous cause or consideration. **Turpis causa** (q.v.).

causerie *n., pl.* **causeries** [Fr. chat, gossip.] 1. An informal conversation, particularly about intellectual matters. *They spent the evening in causerie and never dealt with the business at hand.* 2. A short piece written in such a conversational manner.

cautio *n., pl.* **cautiones** [L. precaution, security, bond, bail, surety.] *Roman, Scots, and Civil Law.* An agreement of guarantee or indemnity, such as 1. A written assurance which serves as evidence of money received, or acknowledges a promise made. 2. An agreement by one providing a pledge or security. 3. An agreement, usually imposed by a judge, which requires one to guarantee to protect another from harm or loss likely to be caused by either the one or a person for whom the one is responsible.

cautio pro expensis *n., pl.* **cautiones pro expensis** [L. **cautio** precaution, security, bond, bail, surety (1); **pro** for (2); **expensis** costs, expenses (3): security for expenses.] *Law.* Warranty for costs or expenses. *Usually a defendant in a suit has to provide cautio pro expensis whenever he/she intends to travel out of the jurisdiction.*

cautio usufructuaria *n., pl.* **cautiones usufructuariae** [L. **cautio** precaution, security, bond, bail, surety (1); **usufructuaria** for/of usufruct (2): security for usufruct.] *Roman Law.* Warranty given by a life tenant, or a tenant enjoying usufruct of an estate, to keep it in good condition.

cav. *abbr.* for **caveat** (q.v.).

C.A.V. *abbr.* for **curia advisari vult** (q.v.).

Cavallieria Rusticana *n.* [It. **cavallieria** cavalry, chivalry (2); **rusticana** rustic, country (1): rustic chivalry.] "Rustic Chivalry," an 1888 opera by Pietro Mascagni (1863–1945).

Ça va sans dire. [Fr. **ça** that (1); **va** goes (2); **sans** without (3); **dire** to say, saying (4): That goes without saying.] It goes without saying. It stands to reason. It is too obvious to say.

caveat *abbr.* **cav.** *n., pl.* **caveats** [L. Let him be careful. Let him beware.] Generally, a warning to be careful. 1. Caution. A warning against certain things. *In his address, the evangelist gave a caveat against certain practices.* 2. A notice given to a court or an official by an interested party against the performance of an act until the said party had been given a hearing. a) *Miss Vera Okafor has entered a caveat in a High Court to halt the probating of her late father's will.* b) *Mr. Sam Oke has entered a caveat against the*

marriage of Mr. Adaku to Miss Cecilia Audu. 3. Used in books to warn readers about other interpretations.

caveat actor [L. **caveat** let him/her beware/be careful (2); **actor** doer, actor, agent (1): Let the doer beware.] *Law.* A person acts at his/her own peril.

caveat emptor *abbr.* **C.E.** or **c.e.** [L. **caveat** let him/her beware/be careful (2); **emptor** buyer (1): Let the buyer beware.] *Law.* Buyer beware. A warning principle observed in purchases, particularly auctions, whereby it is the buyer who must ensure that he/she gets his/her money's worth for what he/she buys in both quality and quantity. Generally, unless there is fraud in the transaction, a purchaser has no remedy against the vendor for defective goods which are not covered by warranty. *The principle of caveat emptor applies outside contracts of sale* (per Lord Atkin in *Bell v. Lever Brothers Ltd.*, 1932 A.C. 161). See **caveat emptor, qui** etc. and **simplex commendatio** etc. Cf. **caveat venditor**.

caveat emptor, qui ignorare non debuit quod jus alienum emit. [L. **caveat** let him beware (2); **emptor** purchaser, buyer (1); **qui** who (3); **ignorare** to be ignorant, not to know (6); **non** not (5); **debuit** should, ought to have been (4); **quod** which, what, that (7); **jus** right, law (9); **alienum** of another (10); **emit** he/she buys (8): Let the purchaser be careful, who should not have been ignorant that he/she is buying another's right.] *Law.* Let the purchaser be careful, for he/she is presumed to be not unaware that what he/she is buying belongs to another. For instance, in the case of purchase of land, the purchaser is expected to inspect the land and the title deeds. See **caveat emptor**.

caveat venditor [L. **caveat** let him/her beware/be careful (2); **venditor** seller (1): Let the seller beware.] Seller beware. A warning principle of the civil law which is applicable to goods which are to be produced, to executory sales or to sales in which the purchaser does not have the opportunity to inspect the goods. Cf. **caveat emptor**.

caveat viator [L. **caveat** let him/her beware (2); **viator** wayfarer, traveler (1): Let the traveler beware.] *Law.* Traveler beware. Warning to travelers on the highway to avoid defects on the way by using due care and attention.

cave canem [L. **cave** beware of, be careful of (1); **canem** dog (2): Beware of the dog.] 1. Watch out for the dog. 2. A warning sign at houses where there are vicious dogs. *They foolishly ignored the cave canem as they approached the front door of the house.*

C.C. *abbr.* for **cepi corpus** (q.v.).

C.C. & C. *abbr.* for **cepi corpus et committitur** (q.v.).

C.D. *abbr.* for **corps diplomatique** (q.v.).

C. de G. *abbr.* for **Croix de Guerre** (q.v.).

Cdt. *abbr.* for **Commandant** (q.v.).

c.d.v. *abbr.* for **carte de visite** (q.v.).

C.E. or **c.e.** *abbr.* for **caveat emptor** (q.v.).

cedant arma togae. Cicero (106–43 B.C.). *De Officiis* I,22,82. [L. **cedant** let . . . yield, give place (1); **arma**

weapons, arms (2); **togae** to toga, citizen's cloak (3): Let arms yield to the citizen's cloak.] Let wars yield to peace. Let military government make room for (or give place to) civil government.

censor morum *n.* [L. **censor** censor, critic, severe judge (1); **morum** of morals (2): censor or critic of morals.] Severe judge of morals. *Agnes has practically assumed the role of censor morum and makes herself a nuisance by criticizing whatever her friends do.*

census *n., pl.* **censuses** [L. a registering of citizens and property.] 1. *Ancient Rome.* Counting of the male citizens and evaluation of property conducted regularly every fifth year. 2. Official counting of the population of a country, state, nation, city, district, or any political unit, usually accompanied by compilation of vital statistics of socio-economic significance. See **lustrum.**

cepi corpus *abbr.* **C.C.** *n.* [L. **cepi** I have taken (1); **corpus** body (2): I have taken the body.] *Law.* I have the defendant. Return to a writ of capias when the defendant has been arrested.

cepi corpus et committitur *abbr.* **C.C.&C.** *n.* [L. **cepi** I have taken (1); **corpus** body (2); **et** and (3); **committitur** he/she is committed (4): I have taken the body and he/she is committed.] *Law.* I have arrested the defendant and he/she is being held in prison. Return to a writ of capias when the defendant/accused has been arrested and placed in prison.

Cerberus *n., pl.* **Cerberi** or **Cerberuses** [L. from Gk. **Kerberos** name of a three-headed watchdog, meaning "Spot."] 1. *Greek and Roman Mythology.* A three-headed dog which guarded the entrance to Hades or the Lower World and was temporarily dragged out of its abode by Heracles (Hercules). 2. A gate keeper, watchdog, or custodian. *Her parents stood at the door like Cerberuses in order to keep the young man out of the house.* —**a sop to Cerberus** A bribe or concession to conciliate a person who is likely to be troublesome.

cercle *n., pl.* **cercles** [Fr. circle, sphere.] *History.* An administrative subdivision of a French colony.

cerebellum *n., pl.* **cerebella** or **cerebellums** [L. little or small brain.] The rear lower portion of the brain which coordinates the muscles, maintains equilibrium of the body, and is believed to contribute immensely toward mental ability. *I may not tax the old cerebellum much. But I don't need to* (*Newsweek Int.* June 20, 1983:44).

cerebrum *n., pl.* **cerebra** or **cerebrums** [L. the brain.] The anterior and upper part of the brain which controls functions such as memory, intellectual ability, sensation, movement, and speech.

certiorari *n., pl.* **certioraris** [L. to be shown, to be made more certain, to be informed of.] A writ from a superior to an inferior court, directing the latter to produce the records of a case for the sake of determining whether or not there were irregularities. *Whereas prohibition*

would lie where an administrative tribunal has not yet reached a decision, certiorari is the proper remedy for actions already completed (Aihe and Oluyede 1974:167).

certum est quod certum reddi potest. [L. **certum** sure, certain (6); **est** is (5); **quod** (that) which (1); **certum** sure, certain (4); **reddi** to be rendered (3); **potest** can, is able (2): That which is able to be rendered sure is sure.] *Law.* That which can be rendered certain is certain. *Apparent vagueness may be cured . . . . by application of the maxim certum est quod certum reddi potest . . .* (Newton 1983:227). See **id certum est** etc., both the shorter and fuller forms.

cessante causa, cessat effectus. [L. **cessante** (with) ceasing (2); **causa** with cause, case, reason (1); **cessat** ceases (4); **effectus** result, effect (3): with the cause ceasing, the result ceases.] *Law.* When a cause ceases, the result/effect ceases. See **sublata causa** etc. and **ubi aliquid impeditur** etc.

cessante ratione legis, cessat et ipsa lex. [L. **cessante** (with) ceasing (3); **ratione** with reason (1); **legis** of law (2); **cessat** ceases (7); **et** also (6); **ipsa** itself (5); **lex** law (4): With the reason of a law ceasing, the law itself also ceases.] *Law.* When the reason for a law ceases, the law itself also ceases. Thus, the protection enjoyed by an ambassador, by a member of parliament, or by a judge performing judicial duties, respectively, lapses when the officials are no longer performing the functions for which the protection was given. Similarly, the protection enjoyed by the property-owner lapses when the property no longer belongs to him/her. See **lex plus laudatur** etc.

cessante statu primitivo, cessat derivativus. [L. **cessante** (with) ceasing (3); **statu** with condition, estate (2); **primitivo** with primitive, original (1); **cessat** ceases (5); **derivativus** the derived (4): With the primitive estate ceasing, the derived ceases.] *Law.* When the original estate ceases, whatever is derived from it also ceases.

cesset executio *n.* [L. **cesset** let it cease, stay (2); **ex(s)ecutio** execution (1): Let execution cease/stay.] *Law.* An order for a stay of execution.

cesset processus *n.* [L. **cesset** let it cease, stay (2); **processus** process (1): Let process stay/cease.] *Law.* A formal order for stay of proceedings. Record of a stay of proceedings.

cessio *n., pl.* **cessios** [L. surrendering, giving up.] *Civil Law.* A cession, an act of ceding or surrendering.

cessio bonorum *n.* [L. **cessio** cession, surrender (1); **bonorum** of goods, property (2): surrender of goods.] *Roman and Civil Law.* Surrender of property; e.g., by debtor to creditor. Voluntary bankruptcy. A process whereby the debtor could voluntarily surrender his property to his creditors. Though it does not discharge the debtor from liability for his debts, it obviates more serious penalties, such as arrest and imprisonment.

cessio in jure *var.* of **in jure cessio** (q.v.).

cession des biens *n.* [Fr. **cession** transfer, surrender, assignment (1); **des** of the (2); **biens** goods, belongings (3): transfer of belongings.] *French Law.* Transfer, surrender, or assignment of goods. **Cessio bonorum** (q.v.). The surrender of goods by an insolvent debtor to his creditors.

c'est-à-dire *abbr.* **c.à-d.** *adv.* [Fr. **c'** it, that (1); **est** is (2); **à** to, toward, in, by, with, until (3); **dire** to say (4): that is to say.] In other words. Namely. **Id est** (q.v.).

C'est double plaisir de tromper le trompeur. Jean de la Fontaine (1621–1695). *Fables* II,15. [Fr. **c'** it (1); **est** is (2); **double** double, twofold (3); **plaisir** pleasure, enjoyment (4); **de** of, in (5); **tromper** to deceive, cheat, trick (6); **le** the (7); **trompeur** deceiver, cheat (8): It is a double pleasure to cheat the cheat.] Cheating the cheat (or tricking the trickster) is doubly pleasant.

C'est la guerre. [Fr. **c'** it, that (1); **est** is (2); **la** the (3); **guerre** war (4): That is war.] That is what usually happens in war.

C'est la vie. [Fr. **c'** it, that (1); **est** is (2); **la** the (3); **vie** life (4): That is life.] That is what usually happens in real life. *The first shall be the last and the simpleton shall be preferred to the genius. C'est la vie.*

C'est le crime qui fait la honte, et non pas l'échafaud. [Fr. **c'** it (1); **est** is (2); **le** the (3); **crime** crime (4); **qui** which, that (5); **fait** makes, causes (6); **la** the (7); **honte** shame, disgrace (8); **et** and (9); **non pas** not (10); **l'** the (11); **échafaud** scaffold, gallows (12): It is the crime which causes disgrace, and not the gallows.] *Law.* It is the crime, not the punishment, which causes disgrace. See **ex delicto non** etc. and **Le crime fait** etc.

cestui que *adj.* [Obs. Fr. **cestui** he (1); **que** for whom (2): he for whom.] A person for whom/whose/who. Used to qualify *trust, use* and *vie* (lifetime, life). —**cestui que trust** [A person for whom the trust.] *Law.* A person for whom the trust is held. A beneficiary of trust. A person who has the equitable or beneficial interest in an estate, and accordingly enjoys the rent and profits from it, although the legal title to the estate is vested in a trustee. —**cestui que use** [A person for whom use of something is held.] *Law.* A person for whose use property is held by another. He accordingly enjoys the benefits and profits from the property, although the possession of, and legal title to, the property are vested in the other person. —**cestui que vie** [a person for whose life-time.] *Law.* A person on whose life a contract of insurance is made. A person whose life is coterminous with the duration of an estate, gift, trust, or a contract of insurance.

C'est une grande habileté que de savoir cacher son habileté. François, Duc de La Rochefoucauld (1613–1680). *Maximes* 245. [Fr. **c'** it (1); **est** is (2); **une** a (3); **grande** great, high (4); **habileté** cleverness, skill (5); **que** that (6); **de** of (7); **savoir** to know, knowing, to know how, knowing how (8); **cacher** to hide,

conceal (9); **son** one's (10); **habileté** cleverness, skill (11): It is a great cleverness that of knowing how to hide one's cleverness.] Knowing how to conceal one's cleverness is a great cleverness. Cf. **ars est** etc.

Cet animal est très méchant. Quand on l'attaque il se défend. [Fr. **cet** this (1); **animal** living thing, animal (2); **est** is (3); **très** very (4); **méchant** naughty, mean, bad (5); **quand** when, whenever (6); **on** one (7); **l'** it (9); **attaque** attacks, assaults (8); **il** it (10); **se** itself (12); **défend** defends, protects (11): This animal is very mean; when one attacks it, it defends itself.] This animal is so vicious that, when attacked, it defends itself. A self-evident and ironic truth applicable to an animal or person which defends itself under attack.

cetera desunt. [L. **cetera** the rest, the other things (1); **desunt** are missing (2): The other things are missing.] The rest is missing. Used to indicate that the remaining portions of a manuscript cannot be found. Cf. **desunt cetera** and **desunt nonnulla**.

cetera quis nescit? Ovid (43 B.C.–17 A.D.). *Amores* V,25. [L. **cetera** the rest, remaining (3); **quis** who (1); **nescit** does not know (2): Who does not know the rest?] Need I say the rest?

ceteris paribus or **caeteris paribus** *abbr.* **cet. par.** *adv.* [L. **ceteris** with the rest (1); **paribus** (with being) equal (2): with the rest being equal.] Other things being equal/the same. If all other factors remain unchanged. All other things being equal. *Ceteris paribus, it is better to live in one's own country than in a foreign country.*

ceteris tacentibus or **caeteris tacentibus** *adv.* [L. **ceteris** with the rest (1); **tacentibus** (with) being silent (2): with the rest being silent.] The others saying nothing. The other judges expressing no opinion.

ceterorum or **caeterorum** *adj.* [L. of the rest.] *Law.* A type of administration granted when a previously granted limited administration has proved to be inadequate.

cet. par. *abbr.* for **ceteris paribus** (q.v.).

cf. *abbr.* for **confer** (q.v.).

chachka or **tchotchke** or **tsatske** *n.* [Yid. **tshatshke** from Polish **czaczka** a showy trinket.] A piece of gaudy jewelry or ornament.

chaconne *n., pl.* **chaconnes** [Fr. from Sp. **chacona** a dance.] *Music.* 1. A slow dance marked by a repetitious bass melodic line, usually in triple meter, popular in the 18th century. 2. Music for such a dance or based upon the melodic bass line associated with this type of dance.

Chacun à son goût. [Fr. **chacun** each, each one (1); **à** to, toward, in, by, with, until (2); **son** his (3); **goût** taste, liking (4): Each one to his taste.] Everyone to his/her taste. Each one and his/her own taste. See **À chacun son goût**.

chagrin *n., pl.* **chagrins** [Fr. grief, vexation, sorrow, annoyance, worry.] Annoyance or mental distress caused by disappointment, wounded pride, humiliation, or awareness of mistake or failure. *Grace flew to London to visit her brother but found, to her chagrin, that he had left for Singapore.* —*v.* To cause someone to feel a sense of sorrow or regret. Cf. **La Peau de Chagrin.**

chagrin d'amour *n., pl.* **chagrins d'amour** [Fr. **chagrin** grief, worry (1); **d'** of (2); **amour** love (3): grief of love.] Distress caused by an unpleasant love-affair. Unhappy love-affair. Heartbreak. *Theresa is yet to recover from her chagrin d'amour.*

chanoyu *n.* [Japan. from **cha** tea (1); **no** 's (2); **yu** hot water (3): tea's hot water.] The Japanese tea ceremony. A ritual for the preparation and serving of tea.

chanson de geste *n., pl.* **chansons de geste** [Fr. **chanson** song (1); **de** of, by, from (2); **geste** gesture, action, deed, exploit (3): song of exploit.] 1. A medieval epic poem about the exploits of a chivalrous hero. *The Chanson de Roland.* 2. Any tale of valor and heroic deeds.

chantage *n., pl.* **chantages** [Fr. blackmail, blackmailing, extortion by threats.] Blackmail. Extortion through threatening to reveal scandalous information.

chanteur or *fem.* **chanteuse** *n., pl.* **chanteurs** or *fem.* **chanteuses** [Fr. a singer.] A singer or vocalist, especially one who sings ballads. *. . . the Belgian chanteur of solitude and love* (*Newsweek Int.* Jan.1, 1979:68).

Chanukah See **Hanukkah.**

chaos *n.* [Gk. **khaos** the first state of the universe, infinite darkness, any vast chasm or gulf.] 1. The confused, disordered condition of the primeval universe before orderly and distinct objects were formed. 2. A state of complete confusion in which there is no order or organization, nor can any rational prediction be made. *. . . despite subtle designs by foreign elements to cause chaos, the OATUU centre still holds* (*West Africa* 1986). Cf. **cosmos.**

chaperon or **chaperone** *n., pl.* **chaperons** or **chaperones** [Fr. hood or hooded cape, elderly or responsible person accompanying a young girl.] 1. A person, usually a matron, who accompanies one or several girls or unmarried women in public or to a social function such as a dance or party to protect them or ensure propriety. *Mrs. Smart served as chaperon to the girls who attended the dance.* 2. A person assigned the responsibility of ensuring propriety. —*v. tr.* To escort, guide, serve as an attendant or **chaperon.** See **duenna.**

charade *n., pl.* **charades** [Fr. riddle.] 1. A guessing game which uses gestures and actions as clues for words and phrases. 2. A farce. A parody.

chargé *abbr.* for **chargé d'affaires** (q.v.).

chargé d'affaires or **chargé des affaires** *abbr.* **c.a.** or **chargé** *n., pl.* **chargés d'affaires** or **chargés des affaires** [Fr. **chargé** charged (1); **d'** with (2); **affaires** affairs (3): charged with affairs.] Envoy or diplomatic agent. A member of the diplomatic corps of inferior rank who handles diplomatic affairs in the absence of the ambassador. A member of the diplomatic corps with a rank lower than that of an ambassador who directs the affairs of his country's embassy. a) *This led to the summoning by President Eyadema of Victor Djisan, Ghana's chargé d'affaires in Togo* (*West Africa* 1986). b) *Now a case has come to light involving the Burundi chargé d'affaires in Nairobi . . .* (*New African* 1980).

charis *n.* [Gk. **kharis** charm, grace.] Elegance. Style. Sophistication. *In spite of his renunciation of the politics of his native city, Plato remained an Athenian at heart. The charis of his dialogues is only imaginable in these surroundings . . .* (Lesky 1966:547).

charisma *n., pl.* **charismata** or **charismas** [Gk. **kharisma** grace, favor.] 1. Talent or spiritual gift bestowed as a divine favor or grace, which among early Christians was believed to be manifested in the ability to prophesy, to heal, or to speak in tongues. 2. A special talent inherent in some persons, especially leaders, whereby they can command enthusiastic popular support and, as though by magnetism, lead people without any opposition, complaints, or murmurings. a) *The pontiff was counting on his personal charisma to entice some central Americans back to the Roman Catholic Church from Protestant fundamentalist sects* (*Newsweek Int.* March 14, 1983:25). b) *In contrast to Walesa, the balding, stern-faced general projected no charisma* (*Time Int.* 1982). c) *Apart from his youth, good looks and crowd-pulling charisma, Sankara belonged to that almost extinct species in Africa, leaders genuinely committed to raising the quality of life of their people* (*The Guardian*, 1987).

Charybdis *n., pl.* **Charybdises** [Gk. **Kharubdis.**] 1. A mythological whirlpool off the northeastern coast of Sicily, opposite the monster Scylla. Charybdis supposedly sucked in and vomited water thrice a day. Sailors who tried to escape Scylla were lost to Charybdis and those escaping Charybdis fell victim to Scylla. 2. A serious danger. A devastating peril. *Faced with a choice between the Charybdis of an I.M.F. loan and the Scylla of operating SFEM, Nigeria's military government opted for the latter.* Cf. **Scylla.**

chasseur de têtes *n., pl.* **chasseurs de têtes** [Fr. **chasseur** hunter, huntsman (1); **de** of (2); **têtes** heads, brains (3): hunter of brains or heads.] A recruiting or placement agency or firm which specializes in the search for high-ranking experts in various fields. A head-hunter. *. . . while there were only a handful of European chasseurs de têtes a few years ago, there are now over 170 established firms with a combined income of over $100 million annually* (*Newsweek Int.* July 14, 1980:45).

cha(s)sid See **hasid.**

chassis *n., pl.* **chassis** [Fr. **châssis** frame.] The frame of an automobile, airplane, radio, TV, etc., upon which the body and the working parts are mounted. *. . . in dusty rural communities, potholes batter chassis and jangle motorists' nerves* (*Newsweek Int.* Aug. 2, 1982:22).

château *n., pl.* **châteaux** or **châteaus** [Fr. castle, palace, mansion, country-residence.] 1. A French feudal fortress or castle. 2. A French mansion or large country-house.

châtelaine *n., pl.* **châtelaines** [Fr. lady of the manor; landowner's wife.] 1. Mistress of a household, especially of a large household, château, castle, or large country house. 2. A woman's chain, worn at the waist, to which is attached a bunch of keys, trinkets, scissors, purse, etc.

chauffeur or *fem.* **chauffeuse** *n., pl.* **chauffeurs** or *fem.* **chauffeuses** [Fr. a driver.] A person employed by another to operate a motor vehicle for the transportation of the employer, other persons or goods. —*v. tr.* and *intr.* To drive. To operate a motor vehicle in the capacity of an employed driver. *Every day Mr. Treus is required to chauffeur the children to school before attending to other duties.*

chazan or **hazzan** or **chazzen** *n.* [Late Heb. **hazzān** cantor, singer.] *Judaism.* A cantor at a synagogue.

Ch.B. *abbr.* for **Chirurgiae Baccalaureus** (q.v.).

chef *n., pl.* **chefs** [Fr. head, chief, leader, founder.] 1. A chief, chieftain or leader of a group of people. 2. *short form* for **chef de cuisine** (q.v.).

chef d'agence *n., pl.* **chefs d'agence** [Fr. **chef** head, chief, leader, founder (1); **d'** of (2); **agence** agency, office, bureau (3): chief or head of the agency.] Chief official of the agency. Chief clerk. Executive officer. Office manager. *If the chef d'agence at Yaounde had simply looked at the ticket, he would have realised that the return date was incorrect* (Vincent Che in *West Africa* 1986).

chef de cabinet *n., pl.* **chefs de cabinet** [Fr. **chef** head, chief, leader, founder (1); **de** of (2); **cabinet** cabinet, office, ministry (3): chief of office or ministry.] In France, the principal or chief private secretary of a minister or prefect. a) *. . . he was . . . chef de cabinet of the minister for the colonies, Lebrun . . .* (Suret-Canale 1971:137). b) *. . . Yves Chalier [the chef de cabinet of the previous minister Christian Nucci] who fled the country . . .* (Kaye Whiteman in *West Africa* 1986).

chef de canton *n., pl.* **chefs de canton** [Fr. **chef** head, chief, leader, founder (1); **de** of (2); **canton** canton, district, region (3): chief of the district.] Canton chief. Cantonal chief. *History.* The second in the hierarchy of chiefs in French colonial tropical Africa.

chef d'école *n., pl.* **chefs d'école** [Fr. **chef** head, chief, leader, founder (1); **d'** of (2); **école** school, sect (3): founder or chief of school.] Leader or founder of a school; i.e., of musicians, philosophers, writers, artists, etc. An artist whose work is imitated.

chef de cuisine *short form* **chef** *n., pl.* **chefs de cuisine** [Fr. **chef** head, chief, leader, founder (1); **de** of (2);

cuisine kitchen, cooking (3): head of the kitchen.] Cook. A male cook. Head cook. A cook who is the head of the kitchen staff in an establishment such as a hotel or restaurant and, among other duties, orders foodstuffs, plans the menu, and directs the cooks. See **cuisinier**.

chef de subdivision *n., pl.* **chefs de subdivision** [Fr. **chef** head, chief, leader, founder (1); **de** of (2); **subdivision** subdivision (3): leader of a subdivision.] *History.* Chief of a subdivision. Chief executive of a subdivision of a circle in French colonial tropical Africa.

chef de village *n., pl.* **chefs de village** [Fr. **chef** head, chief, leader, founder (1); **de** of (2); **village** village (3): chief of the village.] Village chief. *History.* The third or lowest in the hierarchy of chiefs in French colonial tropical Africa.

chef d'oeuvre *n., pl.* **chefs d'oeuvre** [Fr. **chef** head, chief, leader, founder (1); **d'** of (2); **oeuvre** work (3): chief (piece) of work.] Masterpiece; i.e., in art, literature, etc.

chef d'orchestre *n., pl.* **chefs d'orchestre** [Fr. **chef** head, chief, leader, founder (1); **d'** of (2); **orchestre** orchestra (3): chief of orchestra.] *Music.* Leader or conductor of an orchestra. Bandmaster.

chef supérieur de province *n., pl.* **chefs supérieurs de province** [Fr. **chef** head, chief, leader, founder (2); **supérieur** superior, higher (1); **de** of (3); **province** province (4): superior chief of province.] Superior or paramount chief in a province. *History.* The first or highest in the hierarchy of chiefs in French colonial tropical Africa.

chemise de nuit *n., pl.* **chemises de nuit** [Fr. **chemise** shirt (1); **de** of (2); **nuit** night (3): shirt of night.] A man's nightshirt. A woman's nightdress or nightgown.

Cherchez la femme. Joseph Fouché (1763–1820). [Fr. **cherchez** look for, search for, find (1); **la** the (2); **femme** woman (3): Find the woman.] 1. Look for the woman; i.e., behind (or at the bottom of) everything there must be a woman. 2. Look for the hidden causes.

cher maître *n.* [Fr. **cher** dear (1); **maître** master, teacher (2): dear master.] Beloved master or teacher. Usually used as a form of address to a person who is an acknowledged expert, model, or master in a profession, or a person from whom one has learned a lot. It may also be used ironically.

cherub *n.* [Heb. **kerûb** supernatural creature.] 1. A heavenly winged creature. 2. An angel depicted as a small, chubby child. 3. A term of endearment for a young child.

Che sarà sarà. [It. **che** what (1); **sarà** will be (2); **sarà** will be (3): What will be will be.] Whatever we do, things will happen the way they will happen. Expressive of the view of predestination.

cheval de bataille *n., pl.* **chevals de bataille** [Fr. **cheval** horse (1); **de** of (2); **bataille** battle (3): horse of battle, warhorse.] A favorite argument or subject. Stock argument, subject or answer. An overworked argument or subject. *Please do not attempt to use that old cheval de bataille again!*

chevalier *n.* [Obs. Fr. horseman.] 1. A knight. 2. A chivalrous person. 3. *France.* A member of the nobility of the lowest rank.

chez *prep.* [Fr. with, among, at the house of, at the home of.] In the home/house of. At the home/house of. At the business establishment of. a) *Things are so bad chez Fishpaw that the family dog commits suicide* (*Newsweek Int.* June 1, 1981:59). b) *The Neizers came for dinner yesterday chez nous* (i.e., at our residence). c) *The famous writer is to have lunch chez Hanson tomorrow.*

chiaroscuro *n., pl.* **chiaroscuros** [It. from **chiaro** clear, bright (1); **oscuro** obscure, dark (2): bright dark.] *Art.* The use of dark and light in painting.

chiasmus *n., pl.* **chiasmi** [L. from Gk. **khiasmos** placing crosswise or in the form of the capital letter Chi, X-shaped.] *Rhetoric.* 1. A figure of speech which involves inverting the order of the sequence of elements or ideas in the latter of two juxtaposed and parallel clauses or phrases. 2. An instance of this figure of speech; e.g., "Initially a friend but an enemy eventually."

chic *n.* [Fr. style, elegance.] Style. Sophistication. Charm. Elegance. Fashion. Vogue. —*adj.* Fashionable. Stylish. Having elegance, charm or sophistication. In vogue. *The couple had fun at a chic new nightclub.* Cf. **bon chic**; **bon genre**; and **chichi**.

chicane *n., pl.* **chicanes** [Fr. chicanery, deception, quibbling.] Deception through using legalistic subterfuge. Pettifoggery. Swindling. Using tricks. Scheming. Quibble. —*v.* To trick or deceive.

chichi *pl. n.* [Fr. pretentious manners.] Exaggerated manners. —*adj.* Overly stylish. Consciously **chic** (q.v.).

Chimera or **Chimaera** *n., pl.* **Chimeras** or **Chimaeras** [L. from Gk. **Khimaira.**] 1. *Greek and Roman Mythology.* A fire-breathing she-monster, usually represented as triple-bodied, having a lion's head, goat's body and a snake's tail. 2. An imaginary monster like the original chimera. Something horrible or frightening. A fantastic fabrication made up of incongruous parts. *. . . such secrecy suggests to some that those who know but keep silent have something to hide, surely some chimera* (*West Africa* 1982). 3. A mental illusion. An impossible fancy or idea. A utopia. A dream or an objective which cannot be achieved. A figment of one's fertile imagination. *The stock-in-trade of some politicians is promises which turn out to be chimeras.*

Chi-Rho *n., pl.* **Chi-Rhos** [Gk. the letter chi (X) and the letter rho (P).] The first two letters of the Christ in Greek. Used as a monogram for the name.

chirographum apud debitorem repertum praesumitur solutum. [L. **chirographum** writing,

document (1); **apud** with, in the possession of (3); **debitorem** debtor (4); **repertum** found (2); **praesumitur** is presumed (5); **solutum** paid (6): A document found in the possession of the debtor is presumed paid.] *Law.* When an acknowledgment of debt is found in the debtor's possession, it is presumed that the debt has been paid.

chirographum non extans praesumitur solutum. [L. **chirographum** writing, document (1); **non** not (2); **extans** existing, being found (3); **praesumitur** it is presumed (4); **solutum** paid (5): A document not existing is presumed paid.] *Law.* When there is no evidence, it is presumed that the debt has been paid.

Chirurgiae Baccalaureus *abbr.* **Ch.B.** *n.* [L. **chirurgiae** of surgery (2); **baccalaureus** bachelor (1): Bachelor of Surgery.] An undergraduate degree in surgery. Cf. **Baccalaureus Chirurgiae.**

Chirurgiae Magister *abbr.* **Ch.M.** *n.* [L. **chirurgiae** of surgery (2); **magister** master (1): Master of Surgery.] A predoctoral graduate degree in surgery. Cf. **Magister Chirurgiae.**

Ch.M. *abbr.* for **Chirurgiae Magister** (q.v.).

Choephoroi *pl. n.* [Gk. **Khoēphoroi: khoē** libation (1); **phoroi** female bearers (2): female libation bearers.] *The Libation Bearers,* the second play of Aeschylus' (525/4–456/5 B.C.) trilogy *Oresteia,* produced in 458 B.C. This tragedy deals with the murder of Clytemnestra by her son Orestes. Cf. **Eumenides.**

chop *n.* [Hindi **chāp** seal.] 1. An official stamp, seal, or permit in southeast Asia. 2. A mark of quality on merchandise. *First chop.*

chose *n., pl.* **choses** [Fr. a thing, object, case, matter, affair.] A thing. A part of personal property. —**chose in action** *Law.* A right to a personal property, such as debts, damages arising from contract, stocks, a personal chattel, or shares, not actually in one's possession but recoverable through legal proceedings. Also the subject of a chose in action such as a note or bond. *A policy certainly must be transferred for though a chose in action cannot in law be assigned, yet in equity it may; . . .* (J. Ashhurst in *Delaney v. Stoddart* [1785], quoted by Colinvaux 1979:165). —**chose in possession** *Law.* A personal thing which is actually in one's possession. *Thus taxes which have been paid are a chose in possession, but taxes which are yet to be paid are a chose in action.*

chose jugée *n., pl.* **choses jugées** [Fr. **chose** a thing, object, case, matter, affair (1); **jugée** judged (2): a thing judged.] A matter which has been settled conclusively and is thus not worth discussing. **Res judicata** (q.v.).

chronique scandaleuse *n., pl.* **chroniques scandaleuses** [Fr. **chronique** report, history, news (2); **scandaleuse** scandalous, disgraceful (1): scandalous report.] A report, account, memoir, history, or biography which puts undue emphasis on scandalous details or gossip. *One may . . . commend him for his apparent neglect of those chroniques scandaleuses that drag their sordid and wearisome length through the pages of later writers* (Laistner 1966:798).

chutzpah *n.* [Yid. **khutspe** nerve, daring.] Effrontery. Boldness.

ciao *interj.* [It. from **ciau** a shortened dialect form of **schiavo** slave: (I am your) slave. At your service. Hello! Greetings! Goodbye!] Hi! An informal greeting. Cf. **à bientôt.**

ciborium *n., pl,* **ciboria** or **ciboriums** [L. from Gk. **ciborion** drinking cup.] *Christianity.* 1. A covered cup used to store consecrated hosts or Eucharistic wafers. 2. A fixed covering over an altar.

cicerone *n., pl.* **ciceroni** or **cicerones** [It. derived from Cicero (106–43 B.C.), the famous Roman orator, on account of the talkativeness of guides.] A guide who leads tourists or sightseers to places of interest and explains antiquities or interesting objects. Cf. **valet de place.**

ci-devant *adv.* [Fr. **ci** here (1); **devant** before (2): here before, previously, formerly.] *Rhetoric.* At a former or previous place. *On this point consult point 3 ci-devant in the outline. —adj.* Late. Ex-. One-time. Former. **Quondam** (q.v.). Heretofore. a) *A ci-devant senator;* b) *a ci-devant President,* c) *a ci-devant director. —n., pl.* **ci-devants** A person or thing which belongs to the past. A has-been. A retired person. A person who no longer exercises power or wields influence. *The divorcée nudged her friend as her ci-devant passed by.*

cinematheque *n., pl.* **cinematheques** [Fr. **cinémathèque: cinéma** film, cinema (2); **-thèque** place for (1): place for cinema.] A movie theater. Cf. **bibliothèque.**

cinéma vérité *n.* [Fr. cinema-truthfulness.] Realism in the making of films. *France did away with big studios when the new wave and cinéma vérité arrived . . .* (*Newsweek Int.* Oct. 11, 1982:53).

cinerarium *n.* [L. from **cinis** ashes.] A place to keep the ashes of a cremated person.

cinquecento *n.* [It. **cinque** five (1); **cento** hundred (2): the five hundreds.] The 1500s. The 16th century. Used especially in reference to Italian history, literature, and art. Cf. **quatrocento; seicento;** and **trecento.**

circa *abbr.* **c.** or **ca.** or **cir.** *prep.* [L. about, nearly, almost.] About. Around. Approximately. Used for dates and numerals when the exact number is unknown. a) *Mrs. Buraimoh was born circa 1943.* b) *Circa 700,000 persons attended the rally.*

circiter *abbr.* **c.** *prep.* [L. about, near.] Approximately. Around. **Circa** (q.v.).

circuitus est evitandus. [L. **circuitus** circling, circuitry (1); **est** is (2); **evitandus** to be avoided; shunned (3): Circling is to be avoided.] *Law.* Circling must be avoided. Circular arguments must not be used.

circuitus est evitandus; et boni judicis est lites dirimere, ne lis ex lite oriatur. [L. **circuitus** circling, circuitry (1); **est** is (2); **evitandus** to be avoided (3); **et** and (4); **boni** of good (6); **judicis** (of) judge (7); **est** it is (5); **lites** suits, litigations (9); **dirimere** to bring to end (8); **ne** in order that not, lest (10); **lis** suit, litigation (11); **ex** out of (13); **lite** suit, litigation (14); **oriatur** may arise (12): Circling is to be avoided; and it is of a good judge to bring suits to an end lest suit arise out of suit.] *Law.* Circling must be avoided; and it is the duty of a good judge to terminate suits in order that one litigation may not give birth to another. See **infinitum in** etc.

circulus in definiendo *n.* [L. **circulus** circle (1); **in** in, on (2); **definiendo** defining (3): circle in defining.] *Logic.* A vicious circle in the process of definition. Cf. **circulus inextricabilis** and **circulus in probando.**

circulus inextricabilis *n.* [L. **circulus** circle (2); **inextricabilis** inextricable, that cannot be unraveled (1): inextricable circle.] *Logic.* An insoluble problem. A solution which brings one back to "square one." Vicious circle. *Defining law is a classical example of circulus inextricabilis for, as in the case of the egg and the hen, law cannot be defined without reference to law courts.* Cf. **circulus in definiendo** and **circulus in probando.**

circulus in probando *n.* [L. **circulus** circle (1); **in** in, on (2); **probando** proving, to be proved (3): circle in proving.] *Logic.* Fallacious argumentation in which what is to be proved is assumed or taken for granted. *Instead of proving the point, he resorted to circulus in probando and was practically begging the question.* Cf. **circulus in definiendo** and **circulus inextricabilis.**

circum *abbr.* **c.** *prep.* [L. around, surrounding.] All around, about. Approximately.

circus *n., pl.* **circuses** [L. a circular line, circle.] l. *Ancient Rome.* A round, oval, or oblong place encircled by seats, used for public games such as athletic games, horsemanship, exhibition of wild beasts, or gladiatorial shows. The *Circus Maximus,* for instance, could accommodate c.100,000 spectators. 2. A spectacular traveling show, usually given in a large tent and including performances by acrobats, clowns, gymnasts, wild beasts, fire-eaters, etc. The company, i.e., persons and animals, giving such a show. *The children are excited because the circus is coming to town.* 3. A lively entertainment or activity which is comparable to a circus. *The political debate deteriorated until it became little more than a circus of accusation and counter-accusation.* 4. *British.* An open circular area where several streets meet. *London's Piccadilly Circus.*

cire perdue *n.* [Fr. **cire** wax (2); **perdue** lost, destroyed (1): lost wax.] A method of metal, especially bronze, casting which consists of using wax to make a model, casting it with clay, forming a mold, heating and melting out the wax, and then replacing it with metal.

citatio ad reassumendam causam *n.* [L. **citatio** summons, citation (1); **ad** to, at, for, according to (2); **reassumendam** to be taken up, revived (4); **causam** cause, case, reason (3): summons for the case to be taken up/revived.] Summons for taking up or reviving a case. *Civil Law.* A process whereby, if a party dies before the determination of a case, the plaintiff could proceed against the heir of the defendant or the plaintiff's heir could proceed against the defendant. The process is similar to bill of revivor.

cithara *n., pl.* **citharas** [L. from Gk. **kithara** a lyra, a stringed musical instrument.] A multi-stringed musical instrument similar to a modern guitar. Cf. **zither**.

civilis actio *n., pl.* **civiles actiones** [L. **civilis** civil (1); **actio** action, deed, legal suit (2): a civil legal suit.] *Law.* Any legal process dealing with the rights of private individuals as opposed to criminal, military, ecclesiastical, or foreign actions.

civilis et politica *adj.* [L. **civilis** civil (1); **et** and (2); **politica** political (3): civil and political.] That which is concerned with citizens and the political community rather than that which is natural and internal. *With such a conscience as is only naturalis et interna, this court has nothing to do; the conscience by which I am to proceed is merely civilis et politica, and tied to certain measures . . .* (per Lord Nottingham L.C., *Cook v. Fountain* (1676) 3 Swans. 585 at 600, quoted by Megarry 1955:140). Cf. **interna**.

civiliter mortuus *adj.* [L. **civiliter** civilly (1); **mortuus** dead (2): civilly dead.] Having lost civil rights. Dead as far as the law is concerned. The punishment inflicted on people convicted of serious crimes in certain places, including some states of the U.S.A. It involves forfeiture of all privileges and rights.

civis Romanus sum. Cicero (106–43 B.C.). *Against Verres* II,5,162. Also Acts 22:25–29. [L. **civis** citizen (3); **Romanus** Roman (2); **sum** I am (1): I am a Roman citizen.] I am a citizen of Rome.

civitas *n., pl.* **civitates** [L. the state, citizenship.] 1. Citizenship. Responsible citizenship. Membership in the community. *His labors have been to build in Singaporeans a sense of civitas . . . (Time Int.* 1982). 2. State. City-state. Community of citizens.

civitas Dei *n.* Augustine of Hippo (354-430 A.D.). [L. **civitas** state (1); **Dei** of God (2): state of God.] The city of God. Heaven. **Civitas Dei** The title of a theological treatise by Augustine.

clairvoyance *n., pl.* **clairvoyances** [Fr. clear-sightedness, perspicacity, vision.] Ability to see, discern, or perceive objects or matters which ordinarily are beyond human sight, discernment or perception. Clearness of sight or insight.

clairvoyant or *fem.* **clairvoyante** *n., pl.* **clairvoyants** or *fem.* **clairvoyantes** [Fr. clear-sighted, perspicacious, shrewd.] A person who can see matters which ordinarily cannot be seen. —*adj.* Having the talent of a clairvoyant. Clear-sighted. Perceptive. Discerning. See **voyant**.

clam *adv.* [L. stealthily.] *Civil Law.* By stealth. Secretly. Covertly.

claque *n., pl.* **claques** [Fr. applauders.] 1. People or a group hired to applaud during a show musical, theatrical, etc. *The claque almost ruined the show with their inexplicable and constant applause.* 2. A group of self-seeking followers or supporters who are always ready to sing the praises of their "master" or leader. *The claque of obsequious friends, who used to accompany him wherever he went, have disappeared unceremoniously.*

claqueur *n., pl.* **claqueurs** [Fr. hired applauder or clapper.] A person who belongs to a claque. A person who is employed to applaud.

claustrophobia *n.* [Neo-L. and Gk. from L. **claustr(um)** lock, bolt (2); Gk. **phob(os)** fear (1): fear of lock or bolt.] *Psychology.* Abnormal fear of being in a confined or closed place, such as a cave, small room, elevator or academic discipline. *African writers often complain of being trapped in a ghetto labeled African literature, . . . It is a position that can lead to a peculiar sense of claustrophobia . . .* (Robert Fraser in *West Africa* 1982). Cf. **agoraphobia**.

clausulae inconsuetae semper inducunt suspicionem. [L. **clausulae** closings, clauses, sentences (2); **inconsuetae** unusual (1); **semper** always (3); **inducunt** excite, arouse (4); **suspicionem** suspicion (5): Unusual clauses always arouse suspicion.] *Law.* Unusual sentences or parts of sentences in legal instruments always induce suspicion; i.e., they warrant careful examination. Cf. **dona clandestina** etc.

clausula quae abrogationem excludit ab initio non valet. [L. **clausula** closing, clause, sentence (1); **quae** which (2); **abrogationem** repeal (4); **excludit** prevents, excludes (3); **ab** from, by (7); **initio** beginning (8); **non** not (5); **valet** is valid (6): A clause which forbids its repeal is not valid from the beginning.] *Law.* A sentence in a legal instrument which excludes repeal of the instrument is invalid from the very beginning.

clausula rebus sic stantibus [L. **clausula** closing, clause, sentence (1); **rebus** with matters, things, property, business, affairs (2); **sic** thus, so (4); **stantibus** (with) standing (3): a clause with things standing thus.] *Law.* A clause affirming the validity of a contract as long as the situation remains unchanged. An implicit or explicit clause signifying that a contract remains valid if the circumstances under which it was concluded remain unchanged, but subject to modification if they change. Applicable, for instance, to situations where there is inflation or depreciation of currency.

clausum fregit [L. **clausum** enclosure, inclosed parcel of land (2); **fregit** he broke (1): He broke the enclosure.] *Old Legal Pleading.* He broke the close. Technical expression used in some actions of trespass. The expression is still preserved in **quare clausum fregit** (q.v.). See **de clauso fracto.**

cleptomania *var.* of **kleptomania** (q.v.).

cliché *n., pl.* **clichés** [Fr. stereotype, a hackneyed, worn-out, or stock expression.] 1. A stereotyped phrase, expression, or idea. 2. *Arts.* A hackneyed or overworked theme, idea, situation, or plot. *She amply substantiates the old cliché about the deadliness of the female of the species* (*Newsweek Int.* Nov. 12, 1979:9). —*adj.* Hackneyed. Stereotyped. Worn-out. *She produced a paper devoid of originality and mainly concerned with obvious and cliché matters.*

clientèle or **clientele** *n., pl.* **clientèles** or **clienteles** [Fr. patronage, customers.] A body of clients, patrons, or customers. a) *The success of Sheikh Hamallah deprived the traditional marabouts of their clientele and their income* . . . (Suret-Canale 1971:435-436). b) *Luciano* . . . *often spends weeks or months deciding which storefront will attract the most desirable clientele.* (*Newsweek Int.* Aug. 22, 1983:39).

clique *n., pl.* **cliques** [Fr. gang, clan, set.] A small exclusive group of persons bound together by some common interests, views, or objectives. a) *Government does not exist for itself, nor for the clique around the centre of power, but for the entire society* (*Sunday Tribune* 1986). b) *The group that seized the Holy Mosque was a clique of deviants who had misinterpreted Islam* (*Newsweek Int.* March 3, 1980:23).

cloture *n., pl.* **clotures** [Fr. clôture end, closure, termination, adjournment.] A procedure whereby debate, especially unreasonable debate, in a legislative body is brought to an end by taking the vote or adopting some other permissible method.

C.M. or **c.m.** *abbr.* for **causa mortis** (q.v.).

cocotte *n., pl.* **cocottes** [Fr. hen, darling.] A prostitute, harlot, or tart. A woman of easy virtue. A loose girl or woman. Cf. **femme libre; meretrix;** and **succuba.**

codex *n., pl.* **codices** [L. tree trunk, tablet.] 1. A medieval manuscript. 2. A collection of laws or rules. 3. A collection of pharmaceutical formulas and information.

cogitationis poenam nemo patitur. [L. **cogitationis** of thought, imagination (4); **poenam** punishment (3); **nemo** no one (1); **patitur** suffers (2): No one suffers punishment of thought.] *Law.* A person is not punished for his/her thoughts.

cogito *n.* [L. I think, I ponder.] *Philosophy.* The principle that the fact that a person thinks is an indication of his existence. See **cogito, ergo sum.**

cogito, ergo sum. René Descartes (1596–1650). *Discours de la Méthode.* [L. **cogito** I think, ponder (1); **ergo** therefore, consequently (2); **sum** I am, exist, live (3): I think; therefore, I am.] I know I exist because I know I think. See **cogito.**

cognomen *n., pl.* **cognomina** or **cognomens** [L. surname, family name.] 1. *Roman Law.* A family name. *Cato is the cognomen in the name Marcus Porcius Cato.* 2. A surname or a family name. *In Nigeria,*

Adetunji is the cognomen in the name, James Gbadebo Adetunji. Cf. **nomen.**

cognoscente *n., pl.* **cognoscenti** [Obs. It. for **conoscente** a knower, a knowledgeable person.] One who claims to, or does, have expert knowledge in fashion or the fine arts. A **connoisseur** (q.v.).

cognovit actionem or **cognovit** *n.* [L. **cognovit** he has acknowledged, recognized (1); **actionem** action (2): He has acknowledged/recognized the action.] *Law.* He has confessed the action. A written confession by defendant of the accusation against him. The defendant thus avoids paying for the costs of the trial.

coheredes una persona censentur, propter unitatem juris quod habent. [L. **coheredes** coheirs (1); **una** one (3); **persona** person (4); **censentur** are thought, held, (2); **propter** on account of (5); **unitatem** unity (6); **juris** of right, law (7); **quod** which (8); **habent** they have, hold, regard (9): Coheirs are thought one person on account of the unity of right which they have.] *Law.* Coheirs are considered one person on account of the unity of right which they have.

coiffeur or *fem.* **coiffeuse** *n., pl.* **coiffeurs** or *fem.* **coiffeuses** [Fr. hairdresser.] Hair-stylist.

coiffure *n., pl.* **coiffures** [Fr. hairstyle.] A way of styling or arranging the hair. . . . *the fetchingly simple coiffure of the blue-blooded lass* . . . (*Newsweek Int.* March 23, 1981:46).

coitus *n.* [L. joining, union, coming together, coition, copulation, sexual intercourse.] The act of inserting the penis into the vagina. Sexual intercourse. *Extraverts start having coitus earlier* [i.e., than introverts] . . . (Eysenck 1982:69). See **pareunia.**

coitus coram testibus *n.* [L. **coitus** joining, union, coming together, coition, copulation, sexual intercourse (1); **coram** before, in the presence of (2); **testibus** witnesses (3): sexual intercourse before witnesses.] *Antiquity.* A procedure for disproving a charge of impotency. See **le congrès.**

coitus interruptus *n., pl.* **coitus interrupti** [L. **coitus** joining, union, coming together, coition, copulation, sexual intercourse; (2); **interruptus** interrupted (1): interrupted sexual intercourse.] *Law.* Deliberate interruption of sexual intercourse to prevent the semen's ejaculation into the vagina and to avoid pregnancy. It is tantamount to cruelty if done against the wife's will, and could be adequate ground for separation or divorce. Cf. **coitus reservatus.**

coitus reservatus *n., pl.* **coitus reservati** [L. **coitus** joining, union, coming together, coition, copulation, sexual intercourse (2); **reservatus** reserved, kept back (1): reserved sexual intercourse.] **Coitus interruptus** (q.v.).

cojones *pl. n.* [Sp. from **cojón** testicle.] *Slang.* Testicles. Balls. Guts. Bravery.

collage *n., pl.* **collages** [Fr. pasting, gluing, sticking, gumming.] *Art.* A picture made of fragments of papers, photographs, and other materials glued to a cardboard, canvas, etc. Such a style of portraiture.

collatio bonorum *n., pl.* **collationes bonorum** [L. **collatio** bringing together, collation, contribution (1); **bonorum** of goods, property (2): contribution of goods.] 1. *Civil or Scots Law.* The obligation of an heir or legatee to return to the testator's or ancestor's estate the gifts received from the latter during his/her lifetime to ensure equitable distribution of the inheritance. 2. The practice of contributing advances from the father into a hotchpot, or a blending of property belonging to a group of individuals, in order to ensure equitable distribution of the common fund after the father's death.

collectanea *pl. n.* [L. collected things.] Literary items, such as notes, passages, or quotations, collected from a number of sources.

collegium *n., pl.* **collegia** or **collegiums** [L. a joining together, a collection of professional colleagues, a guild.] 1. Association, board, society, corporation, guild, company, or college. 2. *Roman and Civil Law.* An association formed by individuals of the same rank, class, or station to promote a business or an enterprise.

col legno *adv.* [It. **col** with the (1); **legno** wood (2): with the wood.] *Music.* Playing a violin or other stringed instrument with the back of the bow rather than with the cord.

colloquium *n., pl.* **colloquia** or **colloquiums** [L. a speaking together, conversation, discourse.] 1. Conversation. 2. Conference, particularly a seminar in which a number of lecturers take turns in leading. 3. *Legal Pleading.* The part of a lawsuit accusing someone of slander in which the plaintiff avers that the defendant uttered the slanderous words about him/her or the matter in question at a particular time.

colon *n., pl.* **colons** [Fr. colonist, farmer, planter, settler.] A farmer, settler, or owner of a plantation in a French colony.

coloratura *n.* [It. colored.] *Music.* The elaborate use of trills and scales in vocal performance especially to demonstrate the skill of the singer.

colore officii *adv.* [L. **colore** with color, appearance (1); **officii** of duty, office (2): with the color of office.] By color of office. Illegally under the mask of official authority. *The police constable, acting colore officii, arrested and detained his personal enemy.* See **ex colore officii**.

colossus *n., pl.* **colossi** or **colossuses** [L. from Gk. **kolossos** gigantic statue.] 1. A gigantic or huge statue. *Emma Lazarus called the Statue of Liberty the "New Colossus."* 2. A person, nation, corporation, body, or something of such size, power, brilliance, scope, extent, strength, etc. as to dominate or impress others. *In a continent whose political landscape is littered with ruthless and less-than-mediocre despots, he stood out like a colossus* (*The Guardian* 1987).

coma *n., pl.* **comas** [Gk. **kōma** deep sleep, lethargic state.] 1. *Medicine.* A condition of deep unconsciousness caused by injury, disease, or poison. *The old man lay in a coma for over six months before he was officially pronounced dead.* 2. A state of physical or mental lethargy or sluggishness. Torpor. *Unless a great leader emerges to arouse the nation from the prevalent coma, it will be impossible to save it from imminent catastrophe.*

Comdt. *abbr.* for **Commandant** (q.v.).

comédienne *n., pl.* **comédiennes** [Fr. an actress in comedy.] A comic actress or, by extension, any actress. Cf. **tragédienne**.

comitas *n.* [L. friendliness, courtesy, civility.] Courteousness. Affability. Comity. A favor granted to another country or nation not as a right but purely as an indulgence.

comitas gentium *n.* [L. **comitas** friendliness, courtesy, civility (1); **gentium** of nations, peoples (2): friendliness of nations.] Comity of nations. See **comitas inter gentes**.

comitas inter communitates *n.* [L. **comitas** friendliness, courtesy, civility (1); **inter** among, between (2); **communitates** communities (3): friendliness between communities.] Comity between, or of, communities.

comitas inter gentes *n.* [L. **comitas** friendliness, courtesy, civility (1); **inter** between, among (2); **gentes** nations (3): friendliness between nations.] *International Law.* Comity between nations. Informal courtesy among nations whereby a nation even within its territory respects the laws and judicial decisions of another nation and gives due consideration to persons from other nations. *Peace in the world depends largely on comitas inter gentes.* See **comitas gentium**.

comitatus *n., pl.* **comitatus** or **comitatuses** [L. an escort, a train, retinue, band.] 1. The retinue of a king, chieftain, prince, or high official. 2. County. County court. Cf. **posse comitatus**.

comitia calata *pl. n.* [L. **comitia** assembly (2); **calata** summoned, called together (1): summoned assembly.] *Ancient Rome.* The assembled people. Cf. **comitia centuriata** and **comitia curiata**.

comitia centuriata *pl. n.* [L. **comitia** assembly (2); **centuriata** centuriate (1): centuriate assembly.] *Ancient Rome.* A legislative, judicial, and electoral body of the Roman people, the comitia centuriata was essentially a military body, originally organized in centuries or groups of one hundred citizens. Its decisions generally reflected the wishes of the well-to-do. Cf. **comitia calata** and **comitia curiata**.

comitia curiata *pl. n.* [L. **comitia** assembly (2); **curiata** curiate (1): curiate assembly.] *Ancient Rome.* A legislative, judicial, and electoral body of the Roman people. Voting was done by associations (curiae). The body played a prominent role during the monarchy, but it subsequently declined in importance. Cf. **comitia calata** and **comitia centuriata**.

Commandant *abbr.* **Cdt.** or **Comdt.** *n., pl.* **Commandants** [Fr. commander.] Commanding officer or commander, i.e., of a military unit or of a place.

commandant de cercle *n., pl.* **commandants de cercle** [Fr. **commandant** commanding or chief officer (1); **de** of (2); **cercle** circle (3): commanding officer of a circle.] *History.* Chief executive of a circle, i.e., a territorial unit of French colonial tropical Africa.

commanditaire *n., pl.* **commanditaires** [Fr. sleeping, limited, or silent partner.] *French Law.* A silent, dormant or limited partner in a **commandite** (q.v.).

commandite *n., pl.* **commandites** [Fr. limited partnership, capital invested by dormant partners.] 1. *French Law.* A partnership in which some members provide money, while others provide labor and expertise instead of money. 2. *Civil Law.* A partnership in which one party (one person or more) is jointly and severally liable, while the other party (one person or more) is a dormant partner, providing capital stock or fund and being liable merely to the extent of the capital or fund provided. See **commanditaire** and **société en commandite.** Cf. **société anonyme.**

commando *n., pl.* **commandos** [Afr. from Dutch. **kommando** a military unit.] 1. A special military unit designed to make quick raids against the enemy. 2. A member of such a military unit.

commedia dell'arte *n.* [It. **commedia** comedy (1); **dell'** of the (2); **arte** art (3): comedy of the art.] A type of theatrical performance characterized by slapstick comedy, stock characters, and improvisation and popular in 16th–18th century Italy.

comme il faut *adv./adj.* [Fr. **comme** like, as (1); **il** it (2); **faut** is necessary (3): as it is necessary.] As necessary. As fashion dictates. *Marie's parents were glad to find her young men well behaved and entirely comme il faut.*

commenda *n., pl.* **commendas** [L. trust, something entrusted.] 1. *Middle Ages.* A kind of trust in which one gives to another person goods for a particular purpose; e.g., to be sold abroad. 2. *French Law.* Delivery of a benefice to another person, whether a cleric or layman, who does not have legal title, to hold in custody and manage until a person with legal title is appointed. Cf. **in commendam.**

commendatio *n., pl.* **commendationes** or **commendatios** [L. recommendation, commendation.] Direction. Suggestion. *Augustus further retained or resumed the right . . . of presenting candidates for magistracies by direct nomination or by commendatio . . .* (Cary 1970:477).

commercia belli *pl. n., sing.* **commercium belli** [L. **commercia** intercourses, communications (1); **belli** of war (2): communications of war.] Contracts or agreements between nations that are at war. The agreements on peaceful relations cover such areas as capitulation, armistice, truce, safeguards, passports, safe conduct, and cartels.

commercium *n., pl.* **commercia** [L. articles bought and sold, objects of trade.] *Civil Law.* Trade. Commerce. Commercial intercourse or transaction. Business or mercantile intercourse.

commercium jure gentium commune esse debet, et non in monopolium et privatum paucorum quaestum convertendum. [L. **commercium** commerce, trade (1); **jure** by right, law (2); **gentium** of nations (3); **commune** common (6); **esse** to be (5); **debet** ought, should (4); **et** and (7); **non** not (8); **in** into, to, against, for (10); **monopolium** monopoly, cartel (11); **et** and (12) **privatum** personal, private (13); **paucorum** of few (15); **quaestum** profit, gain, advantage (14); **convertendum** to be converted, turned (9): Commerce by the law of nations ought to be common and not to be turned into a monopoly and personal profit of few.] Commerce, according to international law, should be common and should not be converted into a monopoly for the private gain of a few persons.

commissar *n., pl.* **commissars** [Russ. **komissar** from Ger. **Kommissar** from Med. L. **commissarius** agent, deputy.] 1. A Communist Party official in charge of indoctrination and maintenance of party loyalty. 2. A person who tries to control public sentiment and opinion. a) *a commissar of etiquette;* b) *a commissar of fashion.*

committitur *n.* [L. He/she is committed.] *Law.* An order or minute indicating that the person whose name is set down is committed to the sheriff's custody.

commodans *n., pl.* **commodantes** [L. lending, granting, supplying.] *Roman Law.* A person who lends something to another to be used temporarily and gratis, and to be returned in kind. See **commodatarius** and **commodatum.**

commodatarius *n., pl.* **commodatarii** [L. recipient of a loan.] *Roman Law.* A person who receives something which is loaned to be used temporarily and gratis, and to be returned in kind. See **commodans** and **commodatum.**

commodati actio *n., pl.* **commodati actiones** [L. **commodati** of/for loan, something loaned (2); **actio** action, deed, legal suit (1): legal suit for a loan.] *Civil Law.* A legal action for the recovery of something loaned and not returned in kind. Cf. **prêt à usage.**

commodatum *n., pl.* **commodata** [L. that which is loaned.] *Roman Law.* A loan. The gratuitous lending of something to be used temporarily and returned in kind. See **commodans** and **commodatarius.**

commodum *n., pl.* **commoda** [L. convenience, advantage, profit, gain.] Advantage. Profit. Gain. *Generally, a person who enjoys the commodum of a thing must bear its onus.* Cf. **onus.**

commodum ex injuria non oritur. [L. **commodum** convenience, advantage, profit, gain (1); **ex** out of, from (4); **injuria** wrong, injury (5); **non** not (2);

oritur arises (3): Advantage does not arise from wrong.] *Law.* Advantage should not be derived from injustice or wrong-doing. See **ex turpi causa** etc.

commodum ex injuria sua nemo habere debet. [L. **commodum** convenience, advantage, profit, gain (4); **ex** from (5); **injuria** wrong, injury, injustice (7); **sua** his/her own (6) **nemo** no one (1); **habere** to have, hold, regard (3); **debet** ought, should (2): No one ought to have an advantage from his/her own wrong.] *Law.* No one should gain from an injustice he/she has perpetrated. See **ex turpi causa** etc.

commorientes *pl. n.* [L. those dying together.] Partners in death. A number of persons who die at the same time as a result of the same disaster.

commune *n., pl.* **communes** [Fr. parish, smallest territorial district administered by a mayor.] 1. A small administrative unit with a council and mayor in some European countries. 2. A revolutionary governmental body as, for instance, the committee of the French people in the revolution of 1793 and that of 1871. 3. A small community in which people have close ties, observing common interests and owning property in common. *A would-be messiah . . . ordered his . . . followers to drink from a tub of poison at the cult's commune in Guyana and more than 900 of them died* (*Newsweek Int.* Jan. 1, 1979:15).

commune bonum *n.* [L. **commune** common (1); **bonum** good (thing) (2): the common good.] That which is good for the community at large rather than for an individual alone.

communiqué *n., pl.* **communiqués** [Fr. official pronouncement, press release.] Official or brief formal announcement, communication, or report, usually issued to the press. *. . . the National Union of Ghana Students (NUGS) in its communiqué at its just-ended congress described the four arrested people . . .* (Crideon Yaoui in *West Africa* 1986).

communis opinio *n.* [L. **communis** common, general, universal (1); **opinio** opinion (2): common opinion.] Common, general, or popular opinion. *No responsible government will treat communis opinio with levity.* Cf. **vox populi**.

communis stipes *n.* [L. **communis** common (1); **stipes** stock (2): common stock.] A common ancestor. *The two families are bound together by communis stipes.*

compare *n., pl.* **compares** [It. godfather, old friend, accomplice, crony.] An old friend or acquaintance. Someone from the same town or region. An accomplice in crime.

compendium *n., pl.* **compendia** or **compendiums** [L. weighed together, profit, gain, shortcut.] 1. A succinct summary, abstract, or abridgment of a larger work. 2. A work which treats briefly important aspects of an entire field or subject. A brief and comprehensive account. *Biobaku's chapter is a good compendium on Egba history* (Kemi Rotimi in *West Africa* 1986).

3. A catalog or inventory. *It is an outrageous compendium of nonstop jokes and puns, both good and bad . . .* (*Newsweek Int.* July 19, 1982:51). Cf. **epitome**.

compère *n., pl.* **compères** [Fr. godfather, fellow sponsor, announcer.] *Chiefly British.* Master of ceremonies during an entertainment, such as a dance, party, or contest. —*v. intr.* To serve as a master of ceremonies. —*v., tr.* To direct, manage or conduct.

compos mentis *adj.* [L. **compos** master of, possessing (1); **mentis** of mind (2): master of mind.] *Law.* Sane in mind. Of sound mind. A person who is compos mentis is one who is deemed to be of sound mind, understanding, and memory, and thus capable of transacting legal business. *One of the prerequisites of a valid will is that the testator must be compos mentis.* See **sanae mentis et bonae memoriae.** Cf. **dum non fit compos mentis; non compos mentis;** and **non sanae mentis.**

compos sui *adj.* [L. **compos** master of, possessing (1); **sui** of himself/herself, oneself (2): master of himself/herself.] Able to use one's limbs. Able to move about. *His excuse that he could not appear in court on account of physical debility was rejected because he was found to be compos sui.*

comprador or **compradore** *n., pl.* **compradors** or **compradores** [Port. buyer.] An agent of foreign political or business concerns in a colony or former colony. *The economies of many Third World countries have been ruined by compradors who, appearing under the guise of patriots, secure high governmental positions.* —*adj.* Of, characteristic of, relating to, a comprador. *. . . a comprador class of officers and men who are pale imitations of their former masters rather than real thinkers . . .* (Lindsay Barrett in *West Africa* 1986).

con *abbr.* for **contra** *prep.* [L. against, opposite.] Against. Contrary to. In contradiction or opposition to. *Arguments con the proposal carried the day.* —*adv.* Against. On the opposite or negative side. *Instead of examining both sides of the issue, he argued con all the time.* —*adj.* Taking or urging the negative or opposite side. *The con arguments seem to be very cogent.* —*n., pl.* **cons** Evidence or argument contrary to a point of view, position or statement. The opposition. The negative or contrary. *To get a balanced view of a question, one needs to consider the pros and cons.* Cf. **pro.**

con amore *adv.* [It. **con** with (1); **amore** love (2): with love.] With love, enthusiasm, devotion, delight, eagerness, or zest. *With the demise of his brother, he brought his nephews and nieces to his household and took care of them con amore.*

conatus quid sit, non definitur in jure. [L. **conatus** attempt, effort, endeavor (2); **quid** what (1); **sit** is, may be (3); **non** not (4); **definitur** is defined, established (5); **in** in, on (6); **jure** right, law (7): What an attempt is, is not defined in law.] The meaning of the word "attempt" is not defined in law.

con brio *adv.* [It. **con** with (1); **brio** vigor (2): with vigor.] Energetically. Vigorously. a) *The reforms have been criticized con brio.* b) . . . *celebrating his 75th birthday by frugging con brio* . . . (*Newsweek Int.* Oct. 16, 1978:55).

con buena fe *adv.* [Sp. **con** with (1); **buena** good (2); **fe** faith (3): with good faith.] *Spanish Law.* With good faith. In good faith.

conceptus *n., pl.* **concepti** or **conceptuses** [L. one conceived.] A fetus. A concept. A product, result, or consequence of conception.

concertino *n., pl.* **concertini** or **concertinos** [It. a little concert.] 1. A small or short concerto. 2. The instrument group which plays solo in a concerto grosso.

concerto *abbr.* **cto.** *n., pl.* **concerti** or **concertos** [It. concert.] *Music.* A composition for one or more solo voices or instruments, accompanied by an organ or orchestra. *The most engaging works of the evening, however, were two concertos* (*Newsweek Int.* March 3, 1980:44B).

concerto grosso *n., pl.* **concerti grossi** [It. **concerto** concert (2); **grosso** large (1): large concert.] *Music.* A composition, usually in three movements, in which a solo instrument group is accompanied by an orchestra.

concessionaire or **concessionnaire** *n., pl.* **concessionaires** or **concessionnaires** [Fr. concessionary, grantee, license holder.] A person or organization that has been given exclusive right to operate a booth for selling refreshments at a center of entertainment, to sell a particular type of commodity or provide a particular type of service at a particular place, or to sell food or refreshments at a factory, school, university, hospital, or any other institution.

concessio versus concedentem latam interpretationem habere debet. [L. **concessio** grant (1); **versus** against (6); **concedentem** the one granting (7); **latam** broad, wide (4); **interpretationem** interpretation (5); **habere** to have, hold, regard (3); **debet** ought, should (2): A grant ought to have a broad interpretation against the one granting.] *Law.* A grant should be given a broad interpretation and this should be applied against the one making the grant. See **quaelibet concessio** etc.

concierge *n., pl.* **concierges** [Fr. porter, janitor, or doorkeeper.] 1. An attendant, usually stationed at the main door of a building, whose duties include handling mail and overseeing the entrance and exit of people. 2. One who has the responsibility of providing assistance to guests and residents of a hotel or apartment building.

conciliabule *n., pl.* **conciliabules** [Fr. secret meeting, assembly, or deliberation.] A secret meeting, especially one held by malcontents, rebels, or conspirators plotting against government or a religious authority.

concilium *n., pl.* **concilia** [L. a council, plan.] An assembly for deliberation.

concordat *n., pl.* **concordats** [L. He/she is in harmony or agreement.] 1. An agreement, covenant, or compact respecting something. . . . *such a concordat* . . . *has to be the basis of any concerted approach to Africa's present crisis* (*West Africa* 1982). 2. An agreement between a government and a religious body on ecclesiastical affairs, as well as other matters of mutual interest; e.g., Mussolini's Concordat with the Vatican. 3. *French Law.* A compromise concluded between a bankrupt and his/her creditors whereby the former agrees to pay a portion of his/her debts within an appointed time, while the latter in turn agree to relinquish the rest of their claims, if the former keeps his/her word.

concordia discors Horace (65–8 B.C.). *Epistles* I,12,19. [L. **concordia** harmony, concord (2); **discors** discordant, inharmonious (1): discordant harmony.] Harmony in discord. Agreement in disagreement. Discordant harmony. Applicable, particularly, to achieving artistic harmony by juxtaposing elements which are seemingly incompatible.

concordia ordinum *n.* [L. **concordia** concord, agreement (1); **ordinum** of the orders, classes (2): agreement of the classes.] Concord among the political classes. A political principle first articulated by Cicero (106–43 B.C.).

concours *n., pl.* **concours** [Fr. competition.] Contest.

concours d'élégance *n.* [Fr. **concours** contest (1); **d'** of (2); **élégance** elegance, stylishness (3): contest of elegance.] A contest held at the end of an automobile rally in which the judges consider not speed but the appearance and outfitting of the competing cars.

concretum *n., pl.* **concreta** [L. solid, thick, hard, or concrete thing.] Something which is solid, concrete, particular, or actual. Cf. **abstractum**.

concurso *n.* [Sp. contest.] *Civil Law.* A proceeding whereby various creditors may establish their shares in the estate of an insolvent debtor. Cf. **juicio de concurso de acreedores**.

condicio praecedens adimpleri debet priusquam sequatur effectus. [L. **condicio** condition (2); **praecedens** preceding (1); **adimpleri** to be fulfilled, satisfied (4); **debet** ought, should (3); **priusquam** before (5); **sequatur** should follow (7); **effectus** effect, result (6): A preceding condition should be fulfilled before the effect should follow.] *Law.* A preceding condition should be satisfied before the effect can follow; e.g., a contract with a preceding condition cannot be binding until the condition has been satisfied.

condicio (or **conditio**) **sine qua non** *n., pl.* **condiciones** (or **conditiones**) **sine quibus non** [L. **condicio** condition (1); **sine** without (2); **qua** which (3); **non** not (4): condition without which not.] An indispensable condition. An absolutely unavoidable condition. A condition which must be satisfied by all means. a) *The upholdment of the people's human rights . . . is a conditio sine qua non on which any administration* *whether civilian or . . . military comes to power* (*The Guardian* 1987). b) *Is it inevitable or a conditio sine qua non for recovery that we must cut down in those areas where we have made major advances during the post-independence era . . . ?* (*West Africa* 1987).

condictio *n., pl.* **condictiones** [L. making a formal claim.] *Roman Law.* Action against a person to claim money or specific things, or for restoration of something.

condictio ex causa furtiva *n., pl.* **condictiones ex causa furtiva** [L. **condictio** making a formal claim (1); **ex** arising from (2); **causa** cause, case, reason (3); **furtiva** stolen, pilfered, of theft (4): making a formal claim arising from a case of theft.] *Roman Law.* A formal action to claim a stolen article from a thief or his heir. See **condictio furtiva** and **condictio rei furtivae.**

condictio ex lege *n., pl.* **condictiones ex lege** [L. **condictio** making a formal claim (1); **ex** arising from, according to (2); **lege** law (3): making a formal claim arising from law.] *Roman Law.* An action to enforce a right granted by law for which no remedy has been provided by law.

condictio furtiva *n., pl.* **condictiones furtivae** [L. **condictio** making a formal claim (1); **furtiva** of theft (2): making a formal action of theft.] A formal legal action for the recovery of a stolen object from a thief or his heirs. See **condictio ex causa furtiva** and **condictio rei furtivae.**

condictio indebiti *n., pl.* **condictiones indebiti** [L. **condictio** making a formal claim (1); **indebiti** of something not owed (2): making a formal claim of something not owed.] *Roman Law.* A formal action for the recovery of something mistakenly paid or given to the defendant.

condictio rei furtivae *n., pl.* **condictiones rei furtivae** [L. **condictio** making a formal claim (1); **rei** (of/for) thing (3); **furtivae** of stolen, pilfered (2): making a formal claim for a stolen thing.] **Condictio ex causa furtiva** (q.v.). **Condictio furtiva** (q.v.).

condictio triticaria *n., pl.* **condictiones triticariae** [L. **condictio** formal claim (1); **triticaria** of wheat (2): a formal claim of wheat.] *Roman Law.* An action for recovering fungible property, such as wheat, in the same amount and quality that the plaintiff had loaned to the defendant.

conditio sine qua non *var.* of **condicio sine qua non** (q.v.).

condo *short form* for **condominium** (q.v.).

condominium *short form* **condo** *n., pl.* **condominia** or **condominiums** [L. joint ownership.] 1. *Roman Law.* A sort of tenancy in common in which people have undivided shares in the property and can dispose of their shares. 2. A large estate in a residential, commercial, or industrial area owned jointly and severally by many persons. Each of the owners has his/her own individual unit apartment, store, or office, and at the same time has the right to use the common facilities of the estate . . . *a condominium buyer owns his apartment outright and has joint title with the other condo owners to the land surrounding his building* (*Time Int.* 1979). 3. The sovereignty of a number of states over a politically subject territory. A territory ruled by a number of states. *The Sudan was previously an Anglo/Egyptian condominium.*

condottiere or **condottiero** *n., pl.* **condottieri** [It. leader of a group of mercenary soldiers.] A mercenary soldier. A freelance. . . . *since the Triumvirate had now expired, he became in the eyes of the law a mere condottiere in the employ of the enemy queen* (Cary 1970:444).

conduit *n., pl.* **conduits** [Fr. pipe, duct, channel, tube, passage, culvert.] 1. A pipe or channel through which water or other liquids pass or are conveyed. 2. A tube or pipe which protects or insulates electric wires or cables. 3. A means for the distribution or conveyance of something such as money, support, or aid. *The United States says Mexico is a big supplier of marijuana and heroin to the American market, and the principal conduit for South American cocaine* (*The Economist* 1987).

confer *abbr.* **cf.** [L. compare.] Compare with. Used to draw readers' attention to a similar, contrasting, contradictory, or explanatory view or statement in the work or elsewhere.

conferencier *n., pl.* **conferenciers** [Fr. **conférencier** lecturer.] 1. A lecturer. A person who delivers a speech or an address. 2. A conferee. A person who participates in a diplomatic conference.

confessio facta in judicio omni probatione major est. [L. **confessio** confession (1); **facta** having been made (2); **in** in, on (3); **judicio** court (4); **omni** than every (7); **probatione** proof (8); **major** greater (6); **est** is (5): A confession having been made in court is greater than every proof.] *Law.* A confession made in court is the best proof.

confessio fidei *n., pl.* **confessiones fidei** [L. **confessio** confession (1); **fidei** of faith (2): confession of faith.] Open declaration of commitment to a cause.

confetti *pl. n.* [It. from **confetto** candy.] Tiny pieces or strips of paper, usually in a variety of colors, which are tossed and scattered as part of a celebration or festivity.

confirmare est id firmum facere quod prius infirmum fuit. [L. **confirmare** to confirm (1); **est** is (2); **id** that (5); **firmum** strong (4); **facere** to make (3); **quod** which (6); **prius** formerly, previously (8); **infirmum** weak (9); **fuit** was (7): To confirm is to make strong that which was previously weak.] *Law.* Confirmation makes valid what was previously invalid. See **confirmare est id quod** etc.

confirmare est id quod prius infirmum fuit firmare. [L. **confirmare** to confirm (1); **est** is (2); **id** that (4); **quod** which (5); **prius** formerly, previously (7);

infirmum weak (8); **fuit** was (6); **firmare** to strengthen (3): To confirm is to strengthen that which was formerly weak.] *Law.* Confirming strengthens that which was previously weak. See **confirmare est id firmum** etc.

confirmare nemo potest priusquam jus ei acciderit. [L. **confirmare** to confirm (3); **nemo** no one (1); **potest** can, is able (2); **priusquam** before (5); **jus** right, law (4); **ei** to him (7); **acciderit** it will have reached, come (6): No one can confirm a right before it will have come to him.] *Law.* No one can confirm a right which does not belong to him/her.

confirmatio est nulla ubi donum praecedens est invalidum. [L. **confirmatio** confirmation (3); **est** there is (1); **nulla** no (2); **ubi** where (4); **donum** gift (6); **praecedens** preceding (5); **est** is (7); **invalidum** invalid (8): There is no confirmation where the preceding gift is invalid.] *Law.* Where a preceding gift is invalid it cannot be confirmed.

confiserie *n., pl.* **confiseries** [Fr. a confectionery, confectioner's shop, candy store.] 1. A shop where sweets are sold. 2. The sweets themselves.

confitens reus *n., pl.* **confitentes rei** [L. **confitens** confessing (1); **reus** accused person (2): a confessing accused person.] *Law.* An accused person who admits being guilty.

confiteor *v.* [L. I confess.] I confess my sins. The first word of a Christian prayer of contrition. —*n.* 1. A Christian act of contrition beginning with the phrase "I confess." The prayer itself. 2. Any admission of guilt.

confrater *n., pl.* **confraters** or **confratres** [L. brother.] 1. A member of a brotherhood or confraternity, i.e., an association of men, or of men and women, formed for religious or charitable activities, or to promote their profession. 2. An associate of a monastery who enjoys some benefits and privileges but is exempted from some responsibilities. Cf. **confrère**.

confrère *n., pl.* **confrères** [Fr. brother, colleague, fellow member.] Fellow. Comrade. Applicable to members of a society, religious brotherhood, profession or academic discipline. *The physician would not agree to the operation before consulting with his confrères.* Cf. **confrater**.

confrérie *n., pl.* **confréries** [Fr. confraternity, brotherhood, sisterhood.] An association of persons who share a common interest.

confusio bonorum *n.* [L. **confusio** confusion (1); **bonorum** of goods (2): confusion of goods.] *Common Law.* The intermixing of goods, whether liquid or solid, belonging to various owners, to such an extent that the individual shares cannot be identified.

congé *n., pl.* **congés** [Fr. leave, dismissal, discharge, permission, farewell, notice to leave or quit, clearance.] 1. Formal permission given by a person in authority to somebody to depart. *After a marathon meeting with the President, the Minister could not disguise his excitement on being given his congé.* 2. Dismissal from, or notice to quit, a service. *Veronica's involvement in the scandal was the principal cause of her congé.* 3. A ceremonious bow as a mark of respect or an indication that one is taking leave. 4. Farewell. Taking leave. *At the end of the party, all the guests made their congés.* 5. Clearance given to a vessel.

congé définitif *n.* [Fr. **congé** leave, dismissal, discharge, permission, farewell, notice to leave or quit, clearance (2); **définitif** final, definitive (1): final dismissal.] Final departure or leave-taking.

congé d'élire or **congé d'eslire** or **congé délire** *n.* [Fr. **congé** leave, dismissal, discharge, permission, farewell, notice to leave or quit, clearance; (1); **d'** of, to (2); **élire** to appoint, choose, elect (3): permission to elect.] Permission to elect or appoint a nominated or recommended candidate. *Augustus further retained or resumed the right . . . of presenting candidates for magistracies by direct nomination or by commendatio either of which procedures would leave the Popular Assembly with a mere congé d'élire* (Cary 1970:477).

congé d'emparler *n.* [Fr. **congé** leave, dismissal, discharge, permission, farewell, notice to leave or quit, clearance; (1); **d'** of, to (2); **emparler** to imparl, to talk together (3): leave to imparl.] *Law.* Permission of imparlance or time for either party in a legal action to respond to the pleading of the other party. Permission, formerly given to the defendant, before pleading, to confer with the plaintiff and reach an amicable settlement. See **licentia loquendi**.

congeries *n., pl.* **congeries** [L. a heap, mass, pile.] A collection, heap, or mass of things, individuals, ideas, etc. A cluster or agglomeration. *Inundated with a congeries of suggestions, he could not make up his mind on what course of action to adopt.*

conjectio causae *n.* [L. **conjectio** conjecture, interpretation (1); **causae** of cause, case, reason (2): A conjecture/interpretation of the case.] *Civil Law.* A brief statement of the case by an advocate at the beginning of the trial.

conjunctio corporum *n.* [L. **conjunctio** union, uniting (1); **corporum** of bodies (2): union of bodies.] Bodily union or physical contact.

conjunctio mariti et feminae est de jure naturae. [L. **conjunctio** union (1); **mariti** of husband (2); **et** and (3); **feminae** of wife, woman (4); **est** is (5); **de** of, from, about (6); **jure** right, law (7); **naturae** of nature (8): The union of husband and wife is from the law of nature.] *Law.* The union of husband and wife is a matter of natural law. See **maris et feminae** etc.

connoissement *n.* [Obs. Fr. for **connaissement** bill of lading, invoice, shipping-bill.] *French Law.* Bill of lading. An instrument, signed by the management of a ship, showing the goods in the ship, the party who sent the various goods, the party who would be the recipient, and an undertaking to convey the goods.

See **conocimiento de embarque; poliza de carga-mento;** and **polizza di carico.**

connoisseur *n., pl.* **connoisseurs** [Obs. Fr. for **connaisseur** good judge.] 1. A person who is an authority on, an expert in, understands thoroughly, and is fully qualified to judge critically, a subject, especially in the field of fine arts. *. . . the connois-seurs most likely to buy Chinese art . . . (Newsweek Int.* Aug. 2, 1982:44). 2. A judge or critic who shows good and discriminating taste and profound appre-ciation. *. . . a connoisseur of the rarest wines . . . (The Guardian* 1986).

connubium or **conubium** *n., pl.* **connubia** or **conubia** [L. marriage.] *Roman and Civil Law.* Wedlock. Right of intermarriage.

conocimiento *short form* for **conocimiento de embarque** (q.v.).

conocimiento de embarque *short form* **conocimiento** *n.* [Sp. **conocimiento** knowledge (1); **de** of (2); **embarque** shipment, goods (3): knowledge of goods.] Bill of lading. See **connoissement.**

conquêts *pl. n.* [Fr. property which husband and wife have acquired conjointly or individually.] *French Law.* Property acquired by husband and wife, whether individually or jointly, during the marriage. Such property is a joint acquisition and each party is entitled to half of it. Cf. **bona; dote; maritagium; paraphernalia** 1; **parapherna; paraphernalia** 1; **régime dotal;** and **société d'acquêts.**

conquistador *n., pl.* **conquistadors** or **conquistadores** [Sp. conqueror.] *History.* A person who participated in the Spanish conquest of the Americas in the 16th century.

conseil de famille *n.* [Fr. **conseil** council (1); **de** of (2); **famille** family (3): council of family.] Family coun-cil. Board of guardians. *French Law.* This council has to sanction certain acts; e.g., a guardian's accep-tance or rejection of an inheritance or a gift inter vivos for the minor.

Conseil d'État *n.* [Fr. **conseil** council (1); **d'** of (2); **état** state (3): council of state.] Privy Council. *France.* A judicial council established as far back as 1302, which gives advice or decides on national matters referred to it by Parliament, the Cabinet, the king, and now the President of the Republic.

conseil judiciaire *n., pl.* **conseils judiciaires** [Fr. **conseil** counselor, counsel (2); **judiciaire** judicial (1): judicial counsel.] A guardian or administrator ap-pointed on the order of the court. *French Law.* A conseil judiciaire may be appointed to administer the property of a prodigal, i.e., a young spendthrift. See **curator prodigi.**

consensu *adv.* [L. by agreement or concord.] Through a contract. By, from, or by reason of, a contractual obligation. *A liability could arise consensu.*

consensu omnium *adv.* [L. **consensu** by/with agreement (1); **omnium** of all, everyone (2): by the agreement

of everyone.] With the consent of all. *It was decided consensu omnium that the new policy would take effect immediately.*

consensus *n., pl.* **consensuses** [L. agreement, unanimity, accord.] Unanimity. Accord. General agreement. Collective opinion. Verdict of the majority. a) *. . . it is not possible to achieve meaningful consensus on matters that involve risks (The Guardian* 1986). b) *There was considerable debate but the meeting came to an end with no consensus being reached.*

consensus ad idem *n.* [L. **consensus** agreement (1); **ad** to, at, for, according to (2); **idem** the same (3): agreement to the same.] Agreement as to the same thing. A harmony of minds. *Parties to a contract must, inter alia, have reached a consensus ad idem for it to be valid.* See **ad idem.**

consensus facit legem. [L. **consensus** agreement, unanimity (1); **facit** makes (2); **legem** law (3): Agree-ment makes the law.] *Law.* The agreement of parties to a contract serves as the law of the contract. See **contractus legem** etc.; **conventio et modus** etc.; **le contrat fait** etc.; and **pacta dant** etc. Cf. **conventio privatorum** etc.

consensus non concubitus facit matrimonium; et consentire non possunt ante annos nubiles. [L. **consensus** consent (1); **non** not (2); **concubitus** concubinage, cohabitation (3); **facit** makes (4); **matri-monium** marriage (5); **et** and (6); **consentire** to consent (9); **non** not (8); **possunt** they can, are able (7); **ante** before (10); **annos** years (12); **nubiles** marriageable (11): Consent, not cohabitation, makes marriage, and they cannot consent before marriageable years.] *Law.* Consent, not cohabitation, constitutes marriage, and a couple cannot consent before the marriageable age. *Thus the church reconciled the two views: that of the early church that consummation was necessary to form a marriage; that, derived from Roman law, that consensus non concubitus facit matrimonium* (Cretney 1976:7). See **nuptias non concubitus** etc.

consensus tollit errorem. [L. **consensus** consent, agreement (1); **tollit** removes (2); **errorem** mistake, error (3): Consent removes error.] *Law.* Agreement elimi-nates mistake. The doctrine of waiver, which is widely applied in pleading and judicial proceedings, depends on this maxim. See **qui non improbat, approbat.**

consentiente domino *adv.* [L. **consentiente** (with) agreeing (2); **domino** with master, lord, owner (1): with the master agreeing.] With the consent of the master, lord, or owner.

consentientes et agentes pari poena plectentur. [L. **consentientes** those consenting, agreeing (1); **et** and (2); **agentes** those doing (3); **pari** with equal (5); **poena** (with) punishment (6); **plectentur** shall be punished (4): Those agreeing and those doing shall be punished with equal punishment.] *Law.* Wrong-doers and those who connive with them suffer the same punishment. See **qui non improbat, approbat.**

consilia multorum quaeruntur in magnis. [L. consilia counsels (1); multorum of many (2); quaeruntur are sought (3); in in, on (4); magnis great things (5): The counsels of many are sought in great things.] The advice of many persons is sought when considering important matters.

consortium n., pl. consortia or consortiums [L. fellowship, society, participation.] 1. Fellowship, partnership, association, society, or club. 2. Law. Marital fellowship or conjugal association of man and woman with the attendant right to each other's affection, company, cooperation and assistance. *Damages can be sought for the loss of consortium caused by death or injury through negligence on the part of a third party.* 3. A cooperative association of organizations or institutions. *The Associated Colleges of the Midwest is a consortium of thirteen small liberal arts colleges.* 4. An international banking or business group or agreement, especially for operating an industry in, or giving financial aid to, a country or a number of countries. a) *. . . a consortium of banks have been financing its operations* (Ibrahim Adam in *West Africa* 1986). b) *. . . the Brazilian Government guaranteed a $180 million line of credit to help the consortium of 23 banks, insurance companies and industrial groups pay off Jari's creditors* (*Newsweek Int.* Feb. 8, 1982:40).

consortium et servitium n. [L. consortium company, fellowship (1); et and (2); servitium service, servitude (3): company and service.] *Law*. Companionship and help. *A husband has a right to the consortium et servitium of his wife; i.e., to her society and service* (Burke 1976:89).

constitutiones tempore posteriores potiores sunt his quae ipsas praecesserunt. [L. constitutiones laws (1); tempore in time (3); posteriores later (2); potiores better, preferable (5); sunt are (4); his than these (6); quae which (7); ipsas them, themselves, the very ones (9); praecesserunt preceded (8): Laws later in time are better than these which preceded them.] Later laws supersede preceding ones. See lex posterior etc.

constitutum n., pl. constituta [L. agreement, compact.] *Roman Law*. An informal agreement whereby one undertakes to fulfill his/her or another's obligation on an appointed day and at a particular place.

constitutum possessorium n., pl. constituta possessiorum [L. constitutum agreement (1); possessorium of possessors (2): an agreement of the possessors.] *Roman Law*. An informal agreement in which the legal possessor of personal or real property declares his/her intention to remain in control, while the legal possession is transferred to another.

constructio ad sensum [L. constructio construction, structure (1); ad to, at, for, according to (2); sensum sense (3): construction according to sense.] *Rhetoric*. The use of words according to sense and meaning rather than grammatical rule.

consuetudo curiae n., pl. consuetudines curiae [L. consuetudo custom, usage, tradition (1); curiae of court (2): custom of the court.] The custom of a court. The practice of a court.

consuetudo est altera lex. [L. consuetudo custom, usage, tradition (1); est is (2); altera another, a second (3); lex law (4): Custom is a second law.] Custom is another source of law. Cf. optima legum etc.

consuetudo est optimus interpres legum. [L. consuetudo custom, usage, tradition (1); est is (2); optimus best (3); interpres interpreter (4); legum of laws (5): Custom is the best interpreter of the laws.] Habit, custom, or common usage offers the best explanation of the law. See optima legum etc.

consuetudo et communis assuetudo vincit legem non scriptam, si sit specialis; et interpretatur legem scriptam, si lex sit generalis. [L. consuetudo custom, usage, tradition (1); et and (2); communis common (3); assuetudo usage, habit (4); vincit overcomes (5); legem law (6); non not (7); scriptam written (8); si if (9); sit it be (10); specialis special (11); et and (12); interpretatur interprets (13); legem law (15); scriptam written (14); si if (16); lex law (17); sit be, is (18); generalis general (19): Custom and common usage overcome the unwritten law, if it be special, and interpret the written law, if it be general.] Habit and common practice supercede special unwritten laws but explain general written laws.

consuetudo, licet sit magnae auctoritatis, numquam tamen praejudicat manifestae veritati. [L. consuetudo custom, usage, tradition (1); licet even if, though (2); sit it be (3); magnae of great (4); auctoritatis (of) authority (5); numquam never (7); tamen nevertheless, yet (6); praejudicat prejudices (8); manifestae evident, manifest (9); veritati truth (10): Custom, even if it be of great authority, yet never prejudices evident truth.] Even if a custom should be of great authority, it should never interfere with manifest truth.

consuetudo loci conservanda est. [L. consuetudo custom, usage, tradition (1); loci of place (2); conservanda to be observed (4); est is (3): The custom of a place is to be observed.] *Law*. The common custom of a place must be observed.

consuetudo mercatorum n. [L. consuetudo custom, usage, tradition (1); mercatorum of merchants (2): custom of merchants.] Customary practice among merchants. Cf. jus mercatorum and lex mercatoria.

consuetudo neque injuria oriri neque tolli potest. [L. consuetudo custom, usage, tradition (1); neque neither (3); injuria from/by injury (7); oriri to arise (4); neque nor (5); tolli to be removed, taken away (6); potest can, is able (2): Custom can neither arise from nor be removed by injury.] *Law*. Habit or general practice can neither be established by injury nor taken away by it.

consuetudo semel reprobata non potest amplius induci. [L. consuetudo custom, usage, tradition (1);

semel once (2); **reprobata** rejected (3); **non** not (5); **potest** can, is able (4); **amplius** longer, any more (6); **induci** to be introduced (7): A custom, once rejected, can no longer be introduced.] Once abandoned, a custom loses its validity.

consuetudo volentes ducit, lex nolentes trahit. [L. **consuetudo** custom, usage, tradition (1); **volentes** the willing (3); **ducit** leads (2); **lex** law (4); **nolentes** the unwilling (6); **trahit** drags (5): Custom leads the willing, law drags the unwilling.] Custom leads people in accordance with their will, while law drags them against their will.

consummatum est. [L. **consummatum** completed, consummated (2); **est** it is, has been (1): It has been completed.] It is finished. It is consummated. The last words of Jesus on the cross at John 19:30. Used in reference to the completion of any major task.

contadino *n., pl.* **contadini** or **contadinos** [It. country person.] A peasant or an inhabitant of a rural area, especially in Italy.

contagion *n., pl.* **contagions** [Fr. infection, contagiousness.] 1. The spreading or transmission of disease through direct contact or indirect means. 2. An infectious disease. *The Ministry of Health has so far failed to diagnose the contagion which has already claimed sixty lives.* 3. Something such as a virus which serves as an agent for producing or spreading disease. 4. An infectious, dangerous, or corrupting influence or quality. *Drug addiction among the youth, a terrible contagion, should be extirpated.* 5. The spreading or transmission of ideas, influence, emotion, doctrine, false rumors, etc. *A contagion of wild ecstasy swept through the fanatics.* 6. Ideas, influence, emotion, etc., which spread. *This was the period when national pride became a contagion* . . . (Thomas Cooke in *West Africa* 1985). Cf. **contagium.**

contagium *n., pl.* **contagia** [L. touching, contact, infection, taint, pollution.] *Medicine.* A living organism or virus which can cause a communicable disease. Cf. **contagion** 3.

conte *n., pl.* **contes** [Fr. story, tale, short story.] A short story, particularly one that treats adventure or folk tale subjects. A narrative which, though shorter than a conventional novel, is longer than the usual short story.

contemporanea expositio *n.* [L. **contemporanea** contemporaneous (1); **expositio** explanation, exposition (2): contemporaneous explanation or exposition.] An explanation based upon the time when a law, custom, or other matter originated and the circumstances under which it occurred. *In the absence of contemporanea expositio much is left to supposition and inferences from judicial pronouncements and the works of anthropologists* (James 1982:177).

contemporanea expositio est optima et fortissima in lege. [L. **contemporanea** contemporaneous (1);

expositio exposition, explanation (2); **est** is (3); **optima** best (4); **et** and (5); **fortissima** strongest (6); **in** in, on (7); **lege** law (8): A contemporaneous explanation is the best and the strongest in law.] *Law.* In interpreting a statute, great authority should be attached to the interpretation given to it by judges or jurists who lived about the time or not long after the time when it was made.

conteur *n., pl.* **conteurs** [Fr. a story-teller.] A person who recites, narrates, or writes short stories.

continuo *n., pl.* **continuos** [It. **continuo** continuous.] *Music.* The base part in **basso continuo** (q.v.).

continuum *n., pl.* **continua** or **continuums** [L. a continuous, uninterrupted, unbroken, or connecting (thing).] 1. A continuous whole. A continuity. Something which is absolutely continuous or the same, and whose parts cannot be distinguished except by making reference to something else; e.g., duration or time whose parts can be distinguished only by reference to number or such expressions as before/after and now/then. 2. Something with a discernible common factor in the midst of confusing uncertain variations. *There are certain personality traits common to all (or at least most) psychotics, and these can be discovered in 'normal' people as well; . . . there is a continuum from the most normal person to the psychotic* (Eysenck 1982:67).

contra bonos mores *abbr.* **contr. bon. mor.** *adj./adv.* [L. **contra** against, opposite (1); **bonos** good (2); **mores** morals, behavior, conduct (3): against good morals.] Contrary to the norms of decent conduct. *Three residents of the village were summoned to appear before the traditional court to explain their conduct in acting contra bonos mores.*

contra bonos mores et decorum *adj./adv.* [L. **contra** against, opposite (1); **bonos** good (2); **mores** morals, behavior, conduct (3); **et** and (4); **decorum** propriety (5): against good morals and propriety.] Contrary to good character and manners. *The official was censured and suspended for acting contra bonos mores et decorum.*

contra bonum morem *adj./adv.* [L. **contra** against, opposite (1); **bonum** good (2); **morem** custom (3): against good custom.] Contrary to good custom.

contractus bonae fidei *n., pl.* **contractus bonae fidei** [L. **contractus** drawing together, shrinking, contract, agreement (1); **bonae** of good (2); **fidei** (of) faith (3): contract of good faith.] *Roman Law.* A contract whose enforcement, when made the subject of litigation, required that the judge should not merely apply the strict law but should also examine the circumstances under which the contract was made and take into consideration equity and matters of good faith.

contractus contra bonos mores *n.* [L. **contractus** drawing together, shrinking, contract, agreement (1); **contra** against, opposite (2); **bonos** good (3); **mores**

morals (4): contract against good morals.] *Law.* An immoral contract. A contract based upon actions which are not decent and fair. As a rule, such contracts are unenforceable and void. See **ex turpi causa** etc.

contractus est quasi actus contra actum. [L. **contractus** drawing together, shrinking, contract, agreement (1); **est** is (2); **quasi** as it were, so to speak (3); **actus** act (4); **contra** against, opposite (5); **actum** act (6): A contract is, so to speak, an act against an act.] *Law.* An agreement between partners is an action performed to prevent another action.

contractus ex turpi causa *n.* [L. **contractus** drawing together, shrinking, contract, agreement (1); **ex** arising from (2); **turpi** base, disgraceful (3); **causa** cause, case, reason (4): contract arising from a base cause.] *Law.* A contract founded on a vile or morally reprehensible cause. Like a contractus contra bonos mores, this type of contract is unenforceable and void. See **ex turpi causa** etc.

contractus ex turpi causa, vel contra bonos mores, nullus est. [L. **contractus** drawing together, shrinking, contract, agreement (1); **ex** arising from (2); **turpi** base, disgraceful (3); **causa** cause, case, reason (4); **vel** or (5); **contra** against, opposite (6); **bonos** good (7); **mores** morals (8); **nullus** worthless, null (10); **est** is (9): A contract arising from a base cause or against good morals is worthless.] *Law.* A contract founded on an evil, disreputable, or immoral cause is null and void. See **ex turpi causa** etc.

contractus fiduciae *n.* [L. **contractus** drawing together, shrinking, contract, agreement (1); **fiduciae** of trust, confidence (2): contract of trust.] *Roman and Civil Law.* A contract in which one person sells something, usually by a formal ceremony of mancipation, to another with the understanding that the purchaser will sell the thing back to the original owner when certain conditions have been fulfilled.

contractus legem ex conventione accipiunt. [L. **contractus** drawings together, shrinkings, contracts, agreements (1); **legem** law (3); **ex** from (4); **conventione** agreement (5); **accipiunt** receive (2): Contracts receive law from agreement.] *Law.* Contracts derive the force of law from the agreement of the parties. See **consensus facit legem.**

contradance See **contredanse.**

contra formam statuti *adv.* [L. **contra** against, opposite (1); **formam** form (2); **statuti** of statute (3): against the form of a statute.] *Criminal Law.* Used to end an indictment which deals with an offense forbidden by statute.

contra jus belli *adj./adv.* [L. **contra** against, opposite (1); **jus** right, law (2); **belli** of war (3): against the law of war.] Against the law governing wars.

contra jus commune *adj./adv.* [L. **contra** against, opposite (1); **jus** right, law (3); **commune** common (2): against common law.] In defiance of the rule of common law. Contrary to the common law. Against the common law.

contra legem terrae *adj./adv.* [L. **contra** against, opposite (1); **legem** law (2); **terrae** of land (3): against the law of the land.] Contrary to the law of the country or civic authority. *It is contra legem terrae to misappropriate public funds.*

contra libertatem matrimonii *adv.* [L. **contra** against, opposite (1); **libertatem** freedom (2); **matrimonii** of marriage (3): against the freedom of marriage.] Contrary to the right of an individual to marry and to have a family.

contra mundum *adj./adv.* [L. **contra** against, opposite (1); **mundum** world, universe (2): against the world.] Contrary to every general opinion. *James has an obnoxious habit of defending views which are contra mundum.*

contra negantem principia non est disputandum. [L. **contra** against, opposite (4); **negantem** one denying (5); **principia** principles, elements (6); **non** not (2); **est** it is (1); **disputandum** to be disputed (3): It is not to be disputed against one denying principles.] There is no point in arguing with a person who denies fundamental principles. Cf. **principiorum non** etc.

contra pacem *adj./adv.* [L. **contra** against, opposite (1); **pacem** peace (2): against the peace.] *Law.* Against the interest of public order and tranquility. The expression is used in the prosecution of cases of trespass with the connotation that the alleged offense was tantamount to a breach of peace.

contrapposto *n.* [It. from **contra** against, opposite (2); **posto** set, placed (1): set opposite.] *Art.* The depiction of a human figure with the lower body turned in a different direction from the upper body.

contra proferentem *adj./adv.* [L. **contra** against, opposite (1); **proferentem** one putting forth, proffering or proposing (2): against the one proposing.] *Law.* Against or to the disadvantage of the one who makes a proposal or puts something forth. Cf. **ambiguitas contra stipulatorem est.**

contra proferentes *adj./adv.* [L. **contra** against, opposite (1); **proferentes** those putting forth, proffering or proposing (2): against those proposing.] *Law.* Against or to the disadvantage of those who propose something. Generally, when a written document is ambiguous, it is interpreted to the disadvantage of the one or those who chose the language of the document. *But a clause is only to be construed contra proferentes in cases of real ambiguity* (Colinvaux 1979:35). See **ambiguitas contra stipulatorem est.**

contra rerum naturam *adj./adv.* [L. **contra** against, opposite (1); **rerum** of matters, things, property, business, affairs (3); **naturam** nature (2): against the nature of things.] Contrary to the natural order. Impossible. *It is contra rerum naturam for a girl to be older than her grandmother.*

contraria contrariis curantur [L. **contraria** contrary, opposite (things) (1); **contrariis** by contrary, opposite (things) (3); **curantur** are cured (2): Opposite things are cured by opposites.] Opposites heal opposites.

contrarium *n., pl.* **contraria** [L. that which is opposite, contrary, reverse.] 1. One of two opposing objects. 2. *Logic.* One of two contrary statements.

contra spoliatorem omnia praesumuntur. [L. **contra** against, opposite (3); **spoliatorem** spoiler, robber, plunderer (4); **omnia** everything, all things (1); **praesumuntur** are presumed (2): All things are presumed against the robber.] *Law.* Every circumstance or disadvantage is presumed against a person who seizes property unlawfully or violently from someone else.

contrat *n., pl.* **contrats** [Fr. contract, agreement, deed.] *French Law.* A legal agreement, contract, or compact.

contrat aléatoire *n., pl.* **contrats aléatoires** [Fr. **contrat** contract, agreement, deed (2); **aléatoire** aleatory, problematical, uncertain, risky, chancy (1): a problematical agreement.] *French Law.* An aleatory contract. A contract whose performance depends on contingencies or uncertain events.

contrat à titre onéreux *n., pl.* **contrats à titre onéreux** [Fr. **contrat** contract, agreement, deed (1); **à** to, toward, in, by, with, until (2); **titre** title, claim (4); **onéreux** burdensome (3): contract for burdensome claim.] *French Law.* Contract for valuable consideration; i.e., a contract in which each party is under obligation to perform some duty to the other or is subject to certain liabilities or payments.

contrat commutatif *n., pl.* **contrats commutatifs** [Fr. **contrat** contract, agreement, deed (2); **commutatif** commutative, interchangeable (1): an interchangeable agreement.] *French Law.* A commutative contract. A contract in which "A" does for "B" the equivalent of what "B" did for "A."

contrat synallagmatique *n., pl.* **contrats synallagmatiques** [Fr. **contrat** contract, agreement, deed (2); **synallagmatique** bilateral (1): a bilateral agreement.] *French Law.* A bilateral contract, i.e., a contract in which the parties are bound to do to each other what is proper and just.

contra veritatem lex numquam aliquid permittit. [L. **contra** against, opposite (5); **veritatem** truth (6); **lex** law (1); **numquam** never (2); **aliquid** anything (4); **permittit** allows, permits (3): The law never allows anything against truth.] The law never allows anything which is contrary to truth.

contr. bon. mor. *abbr.* for **contra bonos mores** (q.v.).

contrectatio rei alienae, animo furandi, est furtum. [L. **contrectatio** touching (1); **rei** of matter, thing, property, business, affair (2); **alienae** of another (person) (3); **animo** with intention (4); **furandi** of stealing (5); **est** is (6); **furtum** theft (7): The touching of a thing of another person with the intention of stealing is theft.] *Law.* The touching of the property of another person with intent to steal is theft. See **furtum est** etc.

contredanse or **contredance** or **contradance** or **contradanse** *n., pl.* **contredanses** or **contredances** or **contradances** or **contradanses** [Fr. from **contre** against, opposite (2); **danse** dance (1): dance opposite.] 1. A folk dance in which partners dance opposite each other in two lines. 2. Music for such a dance.

contrefaçon *n., pl.* **contrefaçons** [Fr. from **contre** against, opposite (1); **façon** fashion, manner (2): against fashion, counterfeit, forgery, fraudulently copying or imitating.] *French Law.* 1. The illegal act of printing or seeing to the printing of a book without securing the permission of the one who holds the copyright. Infringement of copyright or patent. 2. A counterfeit copy. A forgery.

contretemps *n., pl.* **contretemps** [Fr. from **contre** against, opposite (1); **temps** time, weather (2): against time, mishap, delay.] 1. An unexpected event which disrupts the routine. 2. An unfortunate event. An inconvenience. 3. *Music.* A note which is played against the beat. A syncopated note.

conubium *var.* of **connubium** (q.v.).

conventio et modus vincunt legem. [L. **conventio** compact, contract (1); **et** and (2); **modus** harmony, agreement (3); **vincunt** overcome (4); **legem** law (5): Contract and agreement overcome/supersede the law.] Agreements made by parties to a contract, conditions attached to a grant, and covenants respecting lease and conveyance are binding on the parties and thus overrule the law. There are, however, exceptions to the rule. The rule is not applicable where a contract violates the express provisions of a law, is contrary to public interest, policy, morality, etc, or is injurious to the interests of third parties. See **consensus facit legem.**

conventio privatorum non potest publico juri derogare. [L. **conventio** agreement (1); **privatorum** of private (persons) (2); **non** not (4); **potest** can (3); **publico** public (6); **juri** right, law (7); **derogare** to detract from, diminish (5): The agreement of private persons cannot detract from public right.] *Law.* Private individuals cannot make an agreement which renders the law inapplicable and detracts from the public right. See **jus publicum privatorum** etc.; **pacta privata** etc.; **pacta quae contra** etc.; and **privatorum conventio** etc. Cf. **consensus facit legem.**

Conviviorum Saturnaliorum Libri Septem [L. **conviviorum** feast, banquet, entertainment (4); **Saturnaliorum** Saturnalian (3); **libri** books (2); **septem** seven (1): seven books of Saturnalian entertainment.] *Seven Books of Saturnalian Entertainment,* a dialogue on a wide range of topics by the grammarian Macrobius (late 4th/early 5th century A.D.). More commonly called **Saturnalia** (q.v.).

coolie or **cooley** *n., pl.* **coolies** [Hindi kulī.] A derogatory term for an unskilled Asian worker.

coopérant *n., pl.* **coopérants** [Fr. a cooperator, one who works together.] A young person who is doing military service abroad, serving as a cultural or technical adviser in the Service de la Coopération, a program similar to the American Peace Corps. . . . *apart from the abiding French influence in terms of language, coopérants and commercial interests, a number of other foreign powers have become embroiled in the multifarious conflicts in Chad . . .* (*West Africa* 1982).

coprolalia *n., pl.* **coprolalias** [Neo-Gk. from Gk. **kopro(s)** excrement (1); **lalia** talk (2): excrement-talk, foul language.] 1. Obsession with the use of obscene language. 2. The use of obscene language to achieve sexual satisfaction.

coquette *n., pl.* **coquettes** [Fr. a flirt.] A woman or girl who, though not in love, tries to attract the attention of men.

coram judice *adv./adj.* [L. **coram** before, in the presence of (1); **judice** judge (2): before a judge.] In the presence of a judge who has jurisdiction. A legal suit is not valid if it does not take place coram judice, i.e., before a judge who has jurisdiction to hear the case. *The altercation between the plaintiff and the defendant took place coram judice.* Cf. **coram non judice**.

coram nobis *adv.* [L. **coram** before (1); **nobis** us (2): before us.] In our presence. —*n.* A writ of error or review based on alleged errors of fact, and addressed to the very court which tried the case. —*adj.* Based on, or relating to, such a writ. See **error coram nobis**. Cf. **coram vobis**.

coram non judice *adv./adj.* [L. **coram** before, in the presence of (1); **non** not (2); **judice** judge (3): before one not a judge.] Before one who is not a judge. The expression is used with reference to a judge who either is not competent or has no jurisdiction. Cf. **coram judice**.

coram paribus *adv./adj.* [L. **coram** before, in the presence of (1); **paribus** equals (2): before equals.] Before one's peers. *A man's real ability is assessed by his performance coram paribus.*

coram populo *adv./adj.* [L. **coram** before, in the presence of (1); **populo** people (2): before the people.] In public. Publicly. Openly. *He was so overwhelmed by the multitude of his misfortunes that he shed tears coram populo.*

coram rege *adj./adv.* [L. **coram** before, in the presence of (1); **rege** king (2): in the presence of the king.] Before the king. *After the other two courts had split away, judicial functions continued to be exercised by the Curia Regis in a court called coram rege . . .* (Newton 1983:12).

coram vobis *adv.* [L. **coram** before, in the presence of (1); **vobis** you (2): before you, in your presence.] *n.* A writ of error or review based on alleged errors of fact, and directed by the court of review to the court which originally tried the case. —*adj.* Based on,

relating to such a writ. See **error coram vobis**. Cf. **coram nobis**.

corban *n.* [Heb. **qurbān** sacrifice, gift, offering.] *Judaism.* A Jewish sacrifice formerly made at the Temple in Jerusalem.

cordon *n., pl.* **cordons** [Fr. **cordon** ribbon, cordon, band, rope.] 1. A guard stationed around the perimeter of an area to enclose or protect it. a) *a military cordon*; b) *a naval cordon*. 2. An ornamental ribbon, cord, or insignia worn especially for honorific purposes. 3. *Botany.* A fruit tree pruned in such a way that it needs support to stand. 4. *Architecture.* An ornamental molding or band which runs horizontally across the façade of a building. A stringcourse. —*v.* to form a line or a guard in order to control access to and from an area. *The police cordoned off the scene of the crime.*

cordon bleu *n., pl.* **cordons bleus** [Fr. **cordon** ribbon, cordon, band, rope (2); **bleu** blue (1): blue ribbon or cordon.] 1. Decorative blue ribbon, especially one worn by members of the Order of the Holy Ghost. A person entitled to wear the blue ribbon. 2. A person of eminent authority, distinction or rank, particularly a first-rate cook.

cordon rouge *n., pl.* **cordons rouges** [Fr. **cordon** ribbon, cordon, band, rope (2); **rouge** red (1): red ribbon.] 1. Decorative red sash, particularly one worn by members of the **Légion d'Honneur** (q.v.). A person entitled to wear the red sash. 2. A person of authority, distinction or rank second only to that of the cordon bleu, especially a second-ranking cook.

cordon sanitaire *n., pl.* **cordon sanitaires** or **cordons sanitaires** [Fr. **cordon** ribbon, cordon, band, rope (2); **sanitaire** sanitary, medical (1): sanitary rope.] 1. Quarantine line. A line or chain of quarantine officials stationed round an infected area to ensure that the disease does not spread. 2. A chain of nations formed as a buffer or protection alongside or around a nation which is considered to be dangerous either militarily or ideologically. a) *. . . South African forces promptly invaded southern Angola, wiping out nationalist guerrilla bases along the border with Namibia and turning over a cordon sanitaire to the pro-Western Angolan rebels of Jonas Savimbi* (*Newsweek Int.* Nov. 9, 1981:15). b) *Napata, if it had not proved so weak, would have been precisely the kind of buffer-state which the Romans liked to maintain as a cordon sanitaire* (Grant 1970:113).

cornucopia *n., pl.* **cornucopias** [L. **cornu** horn (1) and **copia** plenty, supply (2): horn of plenty.] 1. *Greek and Roman Mythology.* The horn of the sea-goat Amalthea which had the magical power of producing whatever its possessor wanted. 2. *Art Design and Architecture.* A decorative goat's horn, depicted as overflowing with grain, fruit, and flowers, which serves as a symbol of abundance. 3. Abundant supply. Something which provides an overabundance of things that one desires. . . . *the Haitian sees a cornucopia of dishes to be washed, hospital floors to be mopped* (*Newsweek Int.* July 7, 1980:31).

corpore et animo *adv.* [L. **corpore** by body (1); **et** and (2); **animo** by mind (3): by the body and the mind.] By physical act and intention. Physically and deliberately. Used of an offense committed both by physical act and by intent.

corps *n., pl.* **corps** [Fr. body, corporation, staff, main part, company.] 1. A subdivision or unit of the military establishment. A tactical unit which usually comprises two or more divisions and other arms of the military establishment. a) *special military corps*; b) *the United States Marine Corps*; c) *a select corps of trained fighters.* 2. A body of persons who are associated in one way or the other. A body of persons engaged in the same occupation or activity. a) *the diplomatic corps*; b) *the press corps*; c) *senior officer corps.*

corps de ballet *n., pl.* **corps de ballet** [Fr. **corps** body, corporation, staff, main part, company (1); **de** of (2); **ballet** ballet (3): company of the ballet.] The dancers, chorus, or ensemble of a ballet company, excluding the principal members and soloists. a) *The corps de ballet is astonishing in its precision, its split-second timing, its anticipation of the beat more like a flight of birds than a flock of girls.* (*Newsweek Int.* June 30, 1980:48). b) *. . . young members of Mr. Béjart's corps de ballet . . . are among the best paid in the field* (*The Economist*, 1987).

corps d'élite *n., pl.* **corps d'élite** [Fr. **corps** body, corporation, staff, main part, company (1); **d'** of (2); **élite** choice, select few (3): a body of select few.] 1. A body of picked or selected soldiers. Crack unit or regiment. 2. A body of the best, the elect, or selected few in any group or category. *The school sent for the competition eight students, its corps d'elite.*

corps diplomatique *abbr.* **C.D.** *n.* [Fr. **corps** body, corporation, staff, main part, company (2); **diplomatique** diplomatic, of diplomats (1): diplomatic body.] *International Law.* The entire body of diplomats, ministers, ambassadors, and attachés accredited to a government. —*adj.* Of, belonging to, relating to, characteristic of, a diplomatic body. *He also produced his corps diplomatique identity card, in spite of which the policeman ordered him to accompany him to the police station* (*New African* 1978).

corpus *n., pl.* **corpora** [L. body, corpse, person, substance, matter, mass, structure.] 1. The body of a human being or an animal, whether alive or dead. 2. The main part, mass or aggregate of an organ, a structure, men, laws, things, etc. a) *the corpus of the civil law*; b) *the corpus of the canon law.* 3. The main body, capital or the principal sum of a fund, estate, or trust, as distinct from the interest or income. 4. The essence or physical substance of something, as distinct from an intellectual concept. *James and Deborah*

have been feuding for years, the corpus of the controversy being landed property bequeathed by their father. 5. *Law.* A substantial or concrete fact, as distinct from the doubtful and ambiguous. A fact indicating that a crime has actually been committed, such as the body of a murdered person (corpus delicti). 6. *Law.* A real act indicating power over something, as distinct from intention to exercise the power. 7. The totality or the entire sum of scholarly work on a particular subject or of a particular type or by an author or a group of authors. a) *the Achebe corpus*; b) *the Soyinka corpus*; c) *The distinguished scholar's recent work is likely to occupy a prominent place in the corpus of Nigerian literature.* 8. A collection of evidence, recorded utterances, or knowledge. *He searched in vain through the entire corpus of material without finding a clue.*

Corpus Christi *n., pl.* **Corpus Christis** [L. **corpus** body, corpse, person, substance, matter, mass, structure (1); **Christi** of Christ (2): body of Christ.] 1. *Roman Catholic Church.* A feast traditionally celebrated in honor of the Eucharist or the Blessed Sacrament on the Thursday following Trinity Sunday. 2. A city in Texas.

corpus delicti *n., pl.* **corpora delicti** [L. **corpus** body, corpse, person, substance, matter, mass, structure (1); **delicti** of crime, offense (2): the body of the crime/ offense.] *Law.* 1. The facts of an offense. The totality of the various facts, ingredients, etc. which indicate that a crime has been committed. 2. The physical object on which a crime has been committed; e.g., the body of an assassinated person, the remains of the demolished house, etc.

corpus in corpore *n.* [L. **corpus** body, corpse, person, substance, matter, mass, structure (1); **in** in, on (2); **corpore** body (3): a body in a body.] A body within a body. An organization within an organization. A state within a state.

corpus juris *n., pl.* **corpora juris** [L. **corpus** body, corpse, person, substance, matter, mass, structure (1); **juris** of right, law (2): the body of law.] A comprehensive or complete collection of a country's laws, such as corpus juris civilis (the body of the civil law) and corpus juris canonici (the body of the canon law).

corpus politicum mysticum *n.* [L. **corpus** body, corpse, person, substance, matter, mass, structure (3); **politicum** political, civil (2); **mysticum** mystical, mystic (1): a mystical political body.] The state as a mystical political group or organization, developed by Francisco Suárez (1548–1617), a Spanish Jesuit, philosopher, and theologian.

corpus vile *n., pl.* **corpora vilia** [L. **corpus** body, corpse, person, substance, matter, mass, structure (2); **vile** cheap, worthless (1): worthless body.] Something which is deemed to be of such negligible value that one can conveniently use it for experiment without worrying about damage or loss. *The irresponsible* *mechanic worked on the car as though it were a corpus vile.*

corral *n., pl.* **corrals** [Sp. enclosure.] 1. A fenced area for containing livestock, especially horses and cattle. 2. The circular camp created by wagons grouped for purposes of self-defense. —*v.* 1. To enclose livestock in a fenced area. 2. To organize wagons in a defensive circle. 3. To force into a situation. *He corralled me into purchasing two tickets to his charity affair.*

corrida *n., pl.* **corridas** [Sp. running.] Bullfight. Bullfighting. . . . *the two legendary Spanish bullfighters . . . stepped back into the ring for a charity corrida . . . (Newsweek Int.* April 28, 1980: 31).

corrigendum *n., pl.* **corrigenda** [L. that which must be corrected.] Correction of errors, especially in a printed work. *It is an up-to-date book with a corrigendum which includes even minor errors.* Cf. **erratum.**

corvée *n., pl.* **corvées** [Fr. fatigue, duty, statute-labor, a piece of drudgery, unpleasant task.] 1. Labor which a vassal must give to his lord in a feudal society. 2. Labor, whether unpaid or partly paid for, exacted instead of taxes for the construction or repair of roads, canals, bridges, etc. 3. A drudgery. An unpleasant, burdensome and inevitable task. A laborious and compulsory task.

cosa juzgada *n.* [Sp. **cosa** thing (1); **juzgada** judged (2): a thing judged.] A matter adjudged. A case adjudged or determined. See **res judicata.**

Cosa Nostra *n.* [It. **cosa** thing (2); **nostra** our (1): our thing, our organization.] The American equivalent of the **mafia** (q.v.).

cosas comunes *pl. n.* [Sp. **cosas** things (2); **comunes** common (1): common things.] *Spanish Law.* Things which belong to, and may be used by, all persons, and cannot be appropriated as an individual's personal property. They include running water, air, and the sea. Res communes. See **bienes comunes.**

coshar or **cosher** See **kosher.**

Così fan tutte [It. **così** in this way (3); **fan** do, act (2); **tutte** all (women) (1): All women act in this way.] *They All Act That Way,* the title of a 1790 opera by Wolfgang Amadeus Mozart (1756–1791).

cosmonaut *n., pl.* **cosmonauts** [Russ. **kosmonaut** from Gk. **kosmo(s)** order, universe, world (1); **naut(el)** sailor (2): universe sailor.] A Russian space traveler. An astronaut.

cosmopolis *n., pl.* **cosmopolises** [Gk. **kosmopolis** from **kosm(os)** order, universe, world (1) and **polis** city, state (2): world-state.] 1. A city where persons of many nationalities live. A city which enjoys international importance. 2. A world-community of citizens bound by moral or legal principles. Cf. **Weltstadt.**

cosmos *n., pl.* **cosmoses** or **cosmos** [Gk. **kosmos** order, universe, world.] Order. Harmony. The universe conceived of as a harmonious and orderly whole. . . . *heaven and earth and generally all parts*

of the cosmos are seen in relations which pass influences from one to the other (Lesky 1966:680). Cf. **chaos.**

coterie *n., pl.* **coteries** [Fr. clique, circle, set.] A **clique** (q.v.). An association or exclusive group of persons who have common interests, objectives and tastes. . . . *a coterie of protagonists whose ultimate aim, it now clearly appears, is to narrow the base of education in the state* (*Sunday Tribune* 1986).

couchant *adj.* [Fr. lying down for the night, sleeping.] 1. *Law.* Lying down. Spending the night. Applicable to trespassing animals. 2. *Heraldry.* Of animals lying down with the head raised. See **levant** and **levant et couchant.**

couchette *n., pl.* **couchettes** [Fr. little bed.] 1. A sleeping compartment for four to six passengers on a European passenger train. 2. A bed in one of these compartments.

coup *short form* for **coup d'état** (q.v.).

coup *n., pl.* **coups** [Fr. blow, stroke, knock, hit.] 1. A hit or stroke in a game. 2. A very successful stroke, plan, trick, action, device, etc. *Hassan has been credited with a diplomatic coup which has put Algeria in its place, dealt a death blow to Polisario . . . (South* 1984).

coup de force *n., pl.* **coups de force** [Fr. **coup** blow, stroke, knock, hit (2); **de** of (2); **force** force, power (3): a stroke of force.] Coup d'état (q.v.).

coup de grâce *n., pl.* **coups de grâce** [Fr. **coup** blow, stroke, knock, hit (l); **de** of (2); **grâce** favor, mercy (3): stroke of favor or mercy.] 1. A death blow. A fatal blow or shot given mercifully to bring to an end the suffering of a seriously wounded person or animal. A merciful finishing blow or shot. *Without warning, a gunman shot Zemour twice in the back and then applied the coup de grâce: a bullet in the face* (*Newsweek Int.* Aug. 15, 1983:17). 2. A decisive blow or shot. A finishing blow or stroke. An act, incident, or event which decisively ends something. . . . *their private game plan aimed at a knockout in four punches: a Carter victory in Iowa, a respectable run in the Northeast, a sweep in the south in March and a coup de grâce in Illinois* (*Newsweek Int.* Feb. 4, 1980:36).

coup de main *n., pl.* **coups de main** [Fr. **coup** blow, stroke, knock, hit (1); **de** of (2); **main** hand (3): stroke of hand.] A surprise attack. A sudden forceful attack. A vigorous attack. A foray. A raid. An unexpected vigorous or forceful development. a) . . . *in an attempt to carry the fortress by a coup de main his troops got out of hand and were hurled back with considerable loss* (Cary 1970:386). b) *The Senate's coup de main began when . . . Moynihan unveiled a blistering resolution to condemn Reagan's "breach of faith" with millions of American workers now approaching retirement* (*Newsweek Int.* June 1, 1981:26).

coup de maître *n., pl.* **coups de maître** [Fr. **coup** blow, stroke, knock, hit (1); **de** of (2); **maître** master (3):

stroke of master.] A masterstroke. A masterly stroke. An action or performance befitting a master.

coup d'état or **coup d'etat** *short form* **coup** *n., pl.* **coups d'état** or **coups d'etat** [Fr. **coup** blow, stroke, knock, hit (1); **d'** of (2); **état** state, condition (3): stroke of state.] 1. The use of force to overthrow a government or to remove the personnel of a government. *Efforts to raise food prices have led to coups d'etat in the past two years in Guinea-Bissau, Upper Volta and Liberia* (*Newsweek Int.* July 19, 1982:24). 2. A violent and unexpected move to reformulate governmental policy. A revolution. See **Machtübernahme** and **putsch**.

coup de théâtre or **coup de theatre** *n., pl.* **coups de théâtre** or **coups de theatre** [Fr. **coup** blow, stroke, knock, hit (1); **de** of (2); **théâtre** theater, drama (3): stroke of theater.] 1. A sudden and thrilling turn in a drama. 2. A sudden, unexpected, sensational, and striking development. An unexpected sensational action. *From 1980 onwards Chad has been the central drama at every summit, and in 1981 President Mitterand's first such meeting coincided with the coup de théâtre of the Libyan withdrawal of its troops* (*West Africa* 1985). 3. An action which aims at achieving dramatic effect. *The demonstrators marched to the embassy of the offending nation, carrying placards, singing and dancing, and in a symbolic act, a coup de théâtre, burnt replicas of its flag.*

coup d'oeil *n., pl.* **coups d'oeil** [Fr. **coup** blow, stroke, knock, hit (1); **d'** of (2); **oeil** eye (3): a stroke of eye.] A quick glance or survey.

coupé or **coupe** *n., pl.* **coupés** or **coupes** [Fr. cut.] 1. An enclosed four-wheeled carriage with two seats inside and one outside. 2. A two-door automobile with a roof.

couplet *n., pl.* **couplets** [Fr. a pair.] 1. Two lines of verse joined by rhyme and meter. 2. A pair. Two similar items grouped together.

courante *n., pl.* **courantes** [Fr. running.] *Music.* 1. A type of dance popular in France from 1550 to 1750 and characterized by leaping and running of the dancers. 2. A movement in a suite or partita with a complicated rhythm based upon the traditional dance.

couture *n., pl.* **coutures** [Fr. needlework, sewing.] Dressmaking, especially the business of designing, sewing, and distributing fashionable clothing for women. *Yves Saint Laurent toasted his twentieth anniversary as the king of couture last week . . .* (*Newsweek Int.* Feb 8, 1982:50). See **haute couture**.

couturier or *fem.* **couturière** *n., pl.* **couturiers** or *fem.* **couturières** [Fr. ladies' tailor, dressmaker, seamstress.] Dressmaker. A person or establishment that designs and sews fashionable dresses. . . . *James Galanos, the California couturier who gave his celebrated client the $10,000-plus one-shoulder inaugural ball gown . . .* (*Newsweek Int.* Feb. 1, 1982:39).

cr. *abbr.* for **crescendo** (q.v.).

C.R. *abbr.* for **Curia Regis** (q.v.).

crassa ignorantia *n.* [L. **crassa** thick, fat, stupid (1); **ignorantia** ignorance (2): thick ignorance.] Complete ignorance. *The judge rebuked the counsel for crassa ignorantia of the law.*

crassa negligentia *n.* [L. **crassa** thick, fat, stupid (1); **negligentia** negligence (2): thick negligence.] Complete negligence or neglect. *The accused person was sentenced to ten years' imprisonment for crassa negligentia in the motor accident which claimed several lives.* Cf. **nimia negligentia**.

crèche *n., pl.* **crèches** [Fr. day nursery, manger, crib.] 1. A day nursery. A hospital for foundlings. . . . *she set up a health clinic and also a crèche for the black children of the township* (Paul Egbunike in *West Africa* 1986). 2. A representation of the crib of the infant Jesus at the stable in Bethlehem as he was surrounded by Joseph, Mary, shepherds, magi, and animals. Cf. **santon**.

Credo *v.* [L. I believe.] I believe. *Christianity.* The first word of either of the two basic Christian professions of faith, the "Apostles' Creed" or the "Nicene Creed." —*n.* 1. The name of either of these creeds. 2. One of these Christian creeds put in a choral setting. —**credo** *n., pl.* **credos** Any creed, tenet, or doctrine. A statement of beliefs or principles. A system which serves as a guide to what one must do. a) . . . *Libé has fallen victim to its own egalitarian credo* (*Newsweek Int.* March 9, 1981:53). b) . . . *we joined Yakubu . . . in his credo that money was no problem but how to spend it* (*The Guardian*, 1986).

credo in unum Deum. [L. **credo** I believe (1); **in** in (2); **unum** one (3); **Deum** God (4): I believe in one God.] The first words of the Nicene Creed, a basic statement of Christian faith promulgated at the Council of Nicaea in A.D. 325.

crematorium *n., pl.* **crematoria** or **crematoriums** [Neo-L. a place for burning, a crematory.] A furnace used for cremation. A building in which such a furnace is located.

crème de la crème *n.* [Fr. **crème** cream (1); **de** of (2); **la** the (3); **crème** cream (4): cream of the cream.] Best of the best. Most eminent, the flower, the cream, or the select few among the elite. a) *It was a memorable party, attended by the crème de la crème of the Lagos society.* b) *We have here in Abuja the crème de la crème of the African and non-African intellectual and academic community . . .* (Adebayo Adedeji in *West Africa* 1987). See **la crème de la crème**.

crescendo *abbr.* **cr.** or **cres.** or **cresc.** [It. growing.] *Music.* Gradually increasing in volume, loudness or force. —*n., pl.* **crescendi** or **crescendos** 1. An increase in volume, loudness, or force, particularly in the playing or singing of music. A passage performed with such increase. 2. A gradual increase in volume, loudness, force, or intensity. Movement, progress, or advance towards a climax. a) *Delegations of Cubans* *and SWAPO militants march past and earn a warm crescendo of applause,* . . . (*West Africa* 1985). b) *Kubrick builds this two-hour-and-twenty-minute crescendo of terror with a mastery that is itself more than a bit demonic* (*Newsweek Int.* June 2, 1980:52). 3. The peak or climax of such increase in volume, loudness, force, intensity, or progressive movement.

crescente malitia crescere debet et poena. [L. **crescente** (with) increasing (2); **malitia** (with) evildoing, roguery (1); **crescere** to increase (6); **debet** ought, should (5); **et** also (4); **poena** punishment (3): with evildoing increasing, punishment also ought to increase.] *Law.* As evildoing increases, the penalty also ought to increase. See **ex frequenti** etc. and **multiplicata transgressione** etc.

crescit eundo. Lucretius (c.94–c.55 B.C.). *De Rerum Natura* VI,341. [L. **crescit** he/she/it grows (1); **eundo** by going (2): It grows by going.] It grows as it goes. Motto of the State of New Mexico.

cretin *n., pl.* **cretins** [Fr. **crétin** idiot, fool, half-wit, moron.] A person suffering from congenital thyroid deficiency. A mentally deficient person. An idiot or moron.

cri de coeur *n., pl.* **cris de coeur** [Fr. **cri** cry, shout (1); **de** of (2); **coeur** heart, soul (3): cry of heart.] A passionate complaint, utterance, or appeal. A profound utterance of anguish. Spontaneous expression of a person's passionate desire. a) *No man is so heartless that he cannot be touched by a cri de coeur.* b) *In a cri de coeur against the gloom, Giersch at one point asked his colleagues on the board for reasons for optimism* (*Time Int.* 1981).

cri du coeur *n., pl.* **cris du coeur** [Fr. **cri** cry, shout (1); **du** of the (2); **coeur** heart, soul (3): cry of the heart.] **Cri de coeur** (q.v.).

crimen extraordinarium *n., pl.* **crimina extraordinaria** [L. **crimen** crime, offense, accusation (2); **extraordinarium** uncommon, extraordinary (1): extraordinary crime.] *Roman Law.* A crime considered extraordinary in that no punishment had been fixed for it by written law and the judge was required to use his discretion in determining an appropriate punishment.

crimen falsi or **falsi crimen** *n.* [L. **crimen** crime, offense, accusation (1); **falsi** of falsehood, fraud, deceit (2): crime of falsehood.] 1. Crime of falsifying, falsification, or forgery. 2. *Roman Law.* The crime of falsifying includes all crimes committed by deceit and fraud. 3. *Modern Civil Law.* A crime of falsehood, including forgery, perjury, and similar offenses.

crimen furti *n.* [L. **crimen** crime, offense, accusation (1); **furti** of theft, robbery (2): accusation of theft.] *Law.* The offense/charge of theft. *In crimen furti the prosecution must prove, inter alia, asportation.* Cf. **crimen roberiae.**

crimen incendii *n.* [L. **crimen** crime, offense, accusation (1); **incendii** of burning (2): crime of burning.]

Law. Arson. The malicious and intentional destruction of property by burning.

crimen laesae majestatis *n.* [L. **crimen** crime, offense, accusation (1); **laesae** of injured (2); **majestatis** (of) majesty (3): crime of injured majesty.] *Law.* Treason. *Two politicians were accused of crimen laesae majestatis, an offense which is capital.* See **laesa majestas** and **lèse majesté.**

crimen laesae majestatis omnia alia crimina excedit quoad poenam. [L. **crimen** crime, offense, accusation (1); **laesae** of injured (2); **majestatis** (of) majesty (3); **omnia** all (5); **alia** other (6); **crimina** crimes (7); **excedit** exceeds (4); **quoad** as far as (8); **poenam** punishment (9): The crime of injured majesty exceeds all other crimes as far as punishment is concerned.] *Law.* The crime of treason attracts the heaviest penalty.

crimen raptus *n.* [L. **crimen** crime, offense, accusation (1); **raptus** of rape, abduction (2): the crime of rape.] *Law.* The crime of rape or abduction. *The prosecution in crimen raptus has to prove, in particular, penetration by the accused and the lack of consent on the part of the victim.*

crimen roberiae *n.* [L. **crimen** crime, offense, accusation (1); **roberiae** of robbery, theft (2): crime of robbery.] *Law.* The crime of robbery or theft. Cf. **crimen furti.**

crimen trahit personam. [L. **crimen** crime, offense, accusation (1); **trahit** drags (2); **personam** person (3): The crime drags the person.] *Law.* A criminal must be brought to trial at the court which has jurisdiction over the place where the crime was committed.

crime passionnel *n., pl.* **crimes passionnels** [Fr. **crime** crime (2); **passionnel** passion-related (1): passion-related crime.] A sexually motivated crime. Love tragedy. Crime of passion. A crime prompted by jealousy. A crime committed when passion is at its peak; e.g., murder of a wife or husband for adultery. *His family contends that he was the victim of a crime passionnel,* . . . (*Newsweek Int.* Aug. 15, 1983:17).

crimina morte extinguuntur. [L. **crimina** crimes, offenses, accusations (1); **morte** by death (3); **extinguuntur** are extinguished (2): Crimes are extinguished by death.] *Law.* Crimes die with the criminal; i.e., a criminal case ends with the death of the accused and cannot be inherited. See **in restitutionem** etc.

crimine ab uno / disce omnes Vergil (70–19 B.C.). *Aeneid* II,65–66. [L. **crimine** crime (3); **ab** from, away (1); **uno** one (person) (2); **disce** learn about (4); **omnes** all, everyone (5): From one crime / learn about all.] From one crime learn about all Greeks. A reference to the Greeks' use of the Trojan horse to deceive the Trojans.

crise de coeur *n., pl.* **crises de coeur** [Fr. **crise** crisis (1); **de** of (2); **coeur** heart, soul (3): crisis of heart.] Emotional or sentimental crisis. A very disturbing love affair.

crise de conscience *n., pl.* **crises de conscience** [Fr. **crise** crisis (1); **de** of (2); **conscience** conscience (3): crisis of conscience.] A mental crisis in which one feels remorse for one's acts, conduct, etc. *After a decade of vicious struggle for power and unscrupulous conduct, Albert underwent a crise de conscience and turned a new leaf.* Cf. **cas de conscience.**

crise de nerfs or crise des nerfs *n., pl.* **crises de nerfs** or **crises des nerfs** [Fr. **crise** crisis (1); **de(s)** of (the) (2); **nerfs** nerves (3): crisis of (the) nerves.] A point of high nervous tension. A nervous attack.

crisis *n., pl.* **crises** or **crisises** [Gk. **krisis** moment of decision, judgment, dispute, a turning point of a disease, a sudden change for better or worse.] 1. A crucial, decisive, or critical point in the course of affairs. A turning point or the moment of decision. Social, psychological or political instability, difficulty, or turbulence which demands transformation of the status quo. a) *diplomatic crisis;* b) *economic crisis;* c) *financial crisis;* d) *political crisis;* e) *We had traversed a constitutional crisis without catastrophe.* (*Time Int.* 1982); f) *Both the GNPP and PRP were children of crisis* (*New African* 1983). 2. A decisive moment in the course of the action of a drama. 3. *Medicine.* a) The turning point in a severe disease, whether for better or worse, but usually for the better. b) A sudden violent attack of pain. . . . *a large number of cases of severe sickle cell crises in Africa are due to malaria* (Allison Perry in *West Africa* 1985).

criterion *abbr.* **crit.** *n., pl.* **criteria** or **criterions** [Gk. **kriterion** standard, a means for judging.] 1. A characteristic trait, feature, or mark. 2. A yardstick. A standard for judgment, decision, or comparison. a) *In a situation where the criteria for advancement are bastardized, it may be dignifying to live in respectable obscurity.* b) *My negative attitude towards Nigerian lawyers arises out of a conviction that, measured by any criterion, they have fallen far short of societal expectations* (*The Guardian* 1987).

criterium *n., pl.* **criteria** [L. from Gk. **kriterion.**] Criterion (q.v.).

critique *n., pl.* **critiques** [Fr. criticism, review, censure, piece of criticism.] 1. Criticism. An act of criticizing. . . . *the only serious critique of the regime has come from the Union of Cameroonian Peoples* (Mark Doyle in *West Africa* 1985). 2. A critical review, essay, examination, or assessment of a thing, such as a literary or artistic work. *Ronay remains unruffled by critiques of his critique* (*Newsweek Int.* Nov., 26, 1979:52).

Croesus. *n., pl.* **Croesuses** or **Croesi** [L. from Gk. **Kroisos.**] 1. The last king of Lydia, who ruled from c.560 to 546 B.C. He was defeated and overthrown by the Persian king, Cyrus. Croesus was a man of fantastic wealth and was famous for his generous donations to Greek temples, especially the oracle of Apollo at Delphi. 2. A very wealthy man. A multi-millionaire or billionaire. *Some Croesuses do not utilize their wealth to promote philanthropic causes, but gloat over it and act arrogantly, hardly ever bearing in mind that they will one day leave everything behind.*

croix de guerre *abbr.* **c. de g.** *n., pl.* **croix de guerre** [Fr. **croix** cross (1); **de** of (2); **guerre** war (3): cross of war.] War cross. Military Cross. *France.* A military decoration which was introduced in 1915. *Numerous croix de guerre were distributed, even to officers who had prudently taken cover in cellars during the bombardment* (Suret-Canale 1971:470).

crux *n., pl.* **cruces** or **cruxes** [L. cross.] 1. A problem. A difficulty. 2. The heart of the matter. The major point of difficulty. *The crux of the problem.*

cto. *abbr.* for **concerto** (q.v.).

cucullus non facit monachum. [L. **cucullus** hood (1); **non** not (2); **facit** makes (3); **monachum** monk (4): The hood does not make a monk.] Clothes do not make the man. Wearing a habit does not make a person a monk. One cannot acquire an inner quality by merely putting on the outward appearance. *The guest speaker asserted that the mere acquisition of a university degree does not make one an educated person, adding that cucullus non facit monachum.*

cui. *abbr.* for **cuisine** (q.v.).

cui bono *n.* Cicero (106–43 B.C.). *Pro Roscio* 56. [L. **cui** to/for whom (1); **bono** for good, advantage (2): to whom for an advantage.] *Law.* For/to whose good or advantage. The principle that a person who stands to gain from something is most likely to do it. Thus, where there are two or more suspects and the culprit is not clearly identified, a cui bono method of investigation could be very helpful.

cuicunque aliquis quid concedit concedere videtur et id sine quo res ipsa esse non potuit. [L. **cuicunque** to whomsoever, whomever (1); **aliquis** anybody, anyone (2); **quid** something (4); **concedit** grants (3); **concedere** to grant (6); **videtur** he/she seems (5); **et** also (8); **id** that (7); **sine** without (9); **quo** which (10); **res** matter, thing, property, business, affair (11); **ipsa** itself (12); **esse** to be, exist (15); **non** not (14); **potuit** could, was able (13): To whomsoever anyone grants something, he/she seems to grant that also without which the thing itself could not exist.] *Law.* A person who grants something to another is deemed to grant that also without which what is granted is of no use; e.g., if "A" grants to "B" the right to fish in his ("A"'s) pond, "B" is implicitly granted the right to come to the bank of the pond to fish. See **quae cohaerent** etc.; **quando lex aliquid** etc.; **qui concedit aliquid concedere** etc.; **qui concedit aliquid concedit** etc.; **parte quacumque** etc.; and **ubi aliquid concedit** etc.

cui licet quod majus non debet quod minus est non licere. [L. **cui** (he) to whom (1); **licet** is allowed, permitted (4); **quod** (that) which, what (2); **majus** greater, bigger (3); **non** not (6); **debet** ought, should

(5); **quod** (that) which, what (9); **minus** less, smaller (11); **est** is (10); **non** not (7); **licere** to be allowed, permitted (8): He to whom that which is bigger is allowed should not be not allowed that which is smaller.] *Law.* A person who is empowered to do what is more important should have the power to do what is less important. See **majus continet minus.**

cuis. *abbr.* for **cuisine** (q.v.).

cuisine *abbr.* **cui.** or **cuis.** *n., pl.* **cuisines** [Fr. kitchen, cooking, cookery, food.] Style of cooking or preparing food. Food. Meal. a) *Most African foods have a distinctive taste and, wherever Africans go, they never forget the distinctive African cuisine.* b) *The restaurant is famous for its variety of cuisine, including oriental, continental, and African.* See **ancienne cuisine; grande cuisine; haute cuisine;** and **nouvelle cuisine.**

cuisinier or *fem.* **cuisinière** *n., pl.* **cuisiniers** or *fem.* **cuisinières** [Fr. cook.] One who prepares food. See **chef de cuisine.**

cujus est commodum ejus debet esse incommodum. [L. **cujus** of whom (1); **est** there is (2); **commodum** advantage, profit (3); **ejus** of him (4); **debet** there ought, should (5); **esse** to be (6); **incommodum** disadvantage, loss (7): Of whom there is the advantage, of him there ought to be the disadvantage.] *Law.* Whoever enjoys the advantage of a facility should also bear its disadvantage. See **qui sentit commodum** etc.

cujus est solum ejus est usque ad caelum et ad inferos. [L. **cujus** of whom (1); **est** is (2); **solum** soil, ground (3); **ejus** of him (4); **est** it is (5); **usque** as far as (6); **ad** to, at, for, according to (7); **caelum** sky, heaven (8); **et** and (9); **ad** to, at, for, according to (10); **inferos** the inhabitants of the underworld (11): Of whom is the soil, of him it is as far as to the sky and to the inhabitants of the underworld.] *Law.* The owner of the soil owns what is above and what is beneath it. A landowner owns everything on the land, i.e., buildings, trees, water, etc. and the space above it to an indefinite extent. Similarly, he owns everything below it down to the center of the earth; e.g., minerals, oil, and ore. See **usque ad caelum.**

cujus regio, ejus religio. [L. **cujus** of whom (1); **regio** region, district (2); **ejus** of him/her (3); **religio** religion (4): Of whom the region, of him/her the religion.] The one who rules the region dictates the religion there. A principle adopted at the Diet of Augsburg in 1555.

cul-de-sac *n., pl.* **culs-de-sac** or **cul-de-sacs** [Fr. **cul** end (1); **de** of (2); **sac** bag, sack (3): end of bag or sack.] 1. Dead end. Blind alley. A street with no exit at the other end. *The attempt of the armed robbers to escape came to an abrupt end when they drove into a cul-de-sac.* 2. A point beyond which one cannot advance any more. a) *The research which began on a promising note ended in a cul-de-sac.* b) *Allen has set his film in a resort hotel and cast himself as a film maker . . . who finds himself in a creative*

cul-de-sac (Time Int. 1980). c) *The retreat, which began when the Israelis discovered they had advanced up a cul-de-sac, proved equally divisive (South* 1985). Cf. **impasse.**

culpa *n., pl.* **culpae** [L. fault, error, blame, guilt, failure.] *Roman and Civil Law.* Actionable negligence, neglect, or fault. Though there are various degrees, the basic meaning is failure to exercise the requisite care or attention under the circumstances. See **culpa lata; culpa levis; culpa levis in abstracto; culpa levis in concreto; culpa levissima; culpa magna; crassa negligentia; negligentia; negligentia semper habet** etc.; and **nimia negligentia.**

culpa caret qui scit sed prohibere non potest. [L. **culpa** fault, error, blame, guilt, failure (8); **caret** he is free from (7); **qui** (he) who (1); **scit** knows (2); **sed** but (3); **prohibere** to prevent (6); **non** not (5); **potest** can, is able (4): He who knows but cannot prevent is free from blame.] *Law.* A person who knows what is wrong but cannot prevent it is free from blame. Cf. **qui non improbat, approbat.**

culpa est immiscere se rei ad se non pertinenti. [L. **culpa** fault, error, blame, guilt, failure (2); **est** it is (1); **immiscere** to join, mix, blend with (2); **se** oneself (3); **rei** matter, thing, property, business, affair (4); **ad** to, at, for, according to (7); **se** oneself (8); **non** not (5); **pertinenti** concerning, pertaining (6): It is a fault to join oneself with a matter not pertaining to oneself.] *Law.* It is blameworthy to meddle with matters which do not concern one.

culpa lata or **lata culpa** *n.* [L. **culpa** fault, error, blame, guilt, failure (2); **lata** wide, extensive (1): wide fault.] *Roman and Civil Law.* Gross negligence. Failure to exercise the care expected of even an inattentive person. Indifference. The absence of even the least care. See **culpa.**

culpa lata dolo aequiparatur. [L. **culpa** fault, error, blame, guilt, failure (2); **lata** broad, extensive (1); **dolo** wrong, malice (4); **aequiparatur** equals, rivals (3): Extensive fault equals a wrong.] *Law.* Gross negligence is equivalent to malice.

culpa levis or **levis culpa** *n.* [L. **culpa** fault, error, blame, guilt, failure (2); **levis** slight (1): slight fault.] Ordinary negligence. *Roman and Civil Law.* Failure to exercise the care expected of a diligent and prudent person. See **culpa.**

culpa levis in abstracto *n.* [L. **culpa** fault, error, blame, guilt, failure (2); **levis** slight (1); **in** in, on (3); **abstracto** the abstract (4): slight fault in the abstract.] *Roman and Civil Law.* Failure to exercise a very high level of care expected of a prudent person. See **culpa.**

culpa levis in concreto *n.* [L. **culpa** fault, error, blame, guilt, failure (2); **levis** slight (1) **in** in, on (3); **concreto** concrete (4): slight fault in the concrete.] *Roman and Civil Law.* Failure to exercise in another's interest the care which one would exercise in one's personal affairs. See **culpa.**

culpa levissima or **levissima culpa** *n.* [L. **culpa** fault, error, blame, guilt, failure (2); **levissima** slightest (1): slightest negligence/fault.] *Roman and Civil Law.* Failure to exercise the care expected of an extraordinarily diligent and prudent person. See **culpa.**

culpa magna or **magna culpa** *n.* [L. **culpa** fault, error, blame, guilt, failure (2); **magna** great (1): great negligence/fault.] Gross negligence/fault. **Culpa lata** (q.v.). See **culpa.**

culpa teneat suos auctores. [L. **culpa** fault, error, blame, guilt, failure (1); **teneat** should hold (2); **suos** its (3); **auctores** authors, doers (4): Crime should hold its authors.] *Law.* A wrongdoer should be held responsible for only his/her wrong. See **nemo ex alterius** etc.

culpa tenet suos auctores. [L. **culpa** fault, error, blame, guilt, failure (1); **tenet** holds (2); **suos** its (3); **auctores** authors (4): Crime holds its authors.] *Law.* A wrongdoer is held responsible for only his/her wrong. See **nemo ex alterius** etc.

cum *prep.* [L. with, together with, in the company of, along with.] Together with. Accompanied by. *The house serves as the residence-cum-office of the managing director of the company.*

cum adsunt testimonia rerum, quid opus est verbis? [L. **cum** when (1); **adsunt** are present (4); **testimonia** evidences (2); **rerum** of matters, things, property, business, affairs (3); **quid** what (5); **opus** need (6); **est** is there (7); **verbis** for words (8): When evidences of things are present, what need is there for words?] *Law.* What is the need for words, when proofs of facts are available? Cf. **in claris** etc.

cum confitente sponte mitius est agendum. [L. **cum** with, together with, in the company of, along with (4); **confitente** one confessing (5); **sponte** voluntarily, spontaneously (6); **mitius** more mildly, rather mildly (3); **est** it is, there is (1); **agendum** to be treated/dealt, treating, dealing (2): There is dealing more mildly with one confessing spontaneously.] *Law.* A person who confesses spontaneously is dealt with more leniently.

cum copula *adj./adv.* [L. **cum** with, together with, in the company of, along with (1); **copula** connection, bond (2): with connection/bond.] With copulation. Used of a marriage which has been consummated by sexual intercourse.

cum de lucro duorum quaeritur, melior est causa possidentis. [L. **cum** when (1); **de** of, from, about, for (3); **lucro** gain, profit (4); **duorum** of two (5); **quaeritur** it is asked, investigation is made (2); **melior** better (9); **est** is (8); **causa** cause, case, reason (6); **possidentis** of the one possessing (7): When it is asked about the gain of two, the cause of the one possessing is better.] *Law.* When investigation is made about the gain of two persons, the person who possesses the disputed object has a better case. See **in aequali jure melior** etc.

cum duo inter se pugnantia reperiuntur in testamento ultimum ratum est. [L. **cum** when (1); **duo** two (2); **inter** among (4); **se** themselves (5); **pugnantia** fighting things (3); **reperiuntur** are found (6); **in** in, on (7); **testamento** will (8); **ultimum** last (thing) (9); **ratum** approved, valid (11); **est** is (10): When two things fighting among themselves are found in a will, the last thing is valid.] *Law.* When two contradictory clauses are found in a will, the last clause is given preference. This maxim is subject to the general principle that the intention of the testator should first, as far as possible, be ascertained. See **si duo in testamento** etc. and **testamenta cum duo** etc.

cum grano salis *adv.* [L. **cum** with, together with, in the company of, along with (1); **grano** grain (2); **salis** of salt (3): with a grain of salt.] With some allowance for exaggeration. With some caution. Taking into consideration the possibility of exaggeration. *The defense counsel submitted in his address that, in view of a number of inconsistencies discovered during cross examination, the evidence of the witness must be taken cum grano salis.*

cum laude *adj./adv.* [L. **cum** with, together with, in the company of, along with (1); **laude** praise (2): with praise.] With honor/distinction. The expression is used to indicate meritorious performance in college. *John was a bright student and he graduated cum laude.* See **magna cum laude** and **summa cum laude.**

cum onere *adj./adv.* [L. **cum** with, together with, in the company of, along with (1); **onere** burden (2): with the burden.] *Law.* Together with the incumbrance. An estate cum onere is one which has a burden, incumbrance, or charge attached to it.

cum par delictum est duorum, semper oneratur petitor et melior habetur possessoris causa. [L. **cum** when (1); **par** equal (3); **delictum** fault (4); **est** there is (2); **duorum** of two (5); **semper** always (7); **oneratur** is burdened, overwhelmed (8); **petitor** plaintiff, claimant (6); **et** and (9); **melior** better (13); **habetur** is had, held, regarded (12); **possessoris** of possessor (11); **causa** cause, case, reason (10): When there is equal fault of two, the plaintiff is always burdened and the cause of the possessor is regarded better.] *Law.* When both parties are equally at fault, the plaintiff always loses his case and the cause of the person in possession of the property is deemed better. See **in aequali jure melior** etc.

cum privilegio *adv.* [L. **cum** with, together with, in the company of, along with (1); **privilegio** privilege, special enactment (2): with privilege.] With license. With permission. Used especially in a book to show that the publication is duly authorized.

cum tacent clamant Cicero (106–43 B.C.). *In Catilinam* I,21. [L. **cum** while, when (1); **tacent** they are silent (2); **clamant** they shout (3): While they are silent, they shout.] Their silence is a loud cry.

cum testamento annexo *abbr.* **C.T.A.** or **c.t.a.** *adj.* [L. **cum** with, together with, in the company of, along with (1); **testamento** will (2); **annexo** annexed, attached (3): with the will annexed.] *Law.* With the will attached. An administrator cum testamento annexo is appointed when the testator appoints no executor, or the executors appointed do not act, or the will is incomplete. *For if he* [i.e., the executor] *dies before proving, or if he "renounces probate," i.e., refuses to act, then the court appoints in his place an administrator cum testamento annexo, just as it does in a case where there is a will, but no executor named in it* (Hanbury 1962:452).

cum testamento annexo de bonis non *adj.* [L. **cum** with, together with, in the company of, along with (1); **testamento** will (2); **annexo** annexed (3); **de** of, from, about, for (4); **bonis** goods (5); **non** not (6): with the will annexed about the goods not.] *Law.* With the will annexed about the goods not already administered. Applicable to an administrator appointed in case of **cum testamento annexo** (q.v.), when the executor dies. *But if he (i.e., the executor) dies after probate, then, unless he was one of several joint executors, in which case the office goes to the others by jus accrescendi, he is succeeded by his own executor, or if he has none, an administrator cum testamento annexo de bonis non must be appointed* (Hanbury 1962:452). See **de bonis non administratis**.

cunnilingus *n., pl.* **cunnilinguses** [L. licking of the vulva.] Sexual activity which involves stimulating the sexual organ of the female with the tongue or lips. *Cunnilingus and fellatio are more frequent among extraverts than among introverts . . .* (Eysenck 1982:69–70). Cf. **fellatio**.

cunnus *n., pl.* **cunni** [L. the external sexual or genital organs of a female.] The vulva. The female **pudenda**. (q.v.).

cur. *abbr.* for **curia** (q.v.).

cur. adv. vult *abbr.* for **curia advisari vult** (q.v.).

curateur *n., pl.* **curateurs** [Fr. curator, trustee, administrator, guardian.] *French Law.* A person entrusted with the duty of administering the affairs and property of an independent minor.

curator *n., pl.* **curatores** or **curators** [L. guardian or trustee.] 1. *Roman Law.* A person appointed to manage the affairs of a person who is legally not competent to do so; e.g., a spendthrift, a lunatic, or a person who, though past the age of puberty, is a minor. 2. A person appointed by the court to take charge of, and care for, property. 3. The administrator of a museum, document collection, hospital, or other public institution.

curator ad hoc *n., pl.* **curatores ad hoc** or **curators ad hoc** [L. **curator** guardian, trustee (1); **ad** to, at, for, according to (2); **hoc** this (3): guardian/trustee for this.] *Law.* A guardian appointed to take care of a specific matter.

curator ad litem *n., pl.* **curatores ad litem** or **curators ad litem** [L. **curator** guardian, trustee (1); **ad** to, at, for, according to (2); **litem** suit (3): guardian for the suit.] *Law.* A guardian appointed for an action or a suit.

curator bonis *n., pl.* **curatores bonis** or **curators bonis** [L. **curator** guardian, trustee (1); **bonis** for goods, property (2): a guardian/trustee for goods.] *Civil and Scots Law.* A guardian responsible for the custody of the property/goods of a person who is incompetent or a minor.

curator bonorum distrahendorum *n., pl.* **curatores bonorum distrahendorum** or **curators bonorum distrahendorum** [L. **curator** guardian, trustee (1); **bonorum** of goods (2); **distrahendorum** (of) to be divided (3): guardian of goods to be divided.] *Civil Law.* A curator assigned the duty of selling the property of a debtor and sharing the proceeds among the creditors.

curator prodigi *n.* [L. **curator** guardian (1); **prodigi** of a wasteful, lavish person (2): guardian of wasteful person.] *Roman Law.* An administrator assigned the responsibility of administering the property of a spendthrift, i.e., a person who has wasted his own property or property inherited from an intestate. Cf. **conseil judiciare**; **prodigi interdictio**; and **prodigue**.

curia *abbr.* **cur.** *n., pl.* **curiae** [L. court, association, senate-house, meeting-place of the senate, the senate.] 1. *Roman Law.* A political division upon which the **comitia curiata** (q.v.) was based. Each of the three tribes was divided into ten curiae; there were thus thirty curiae. 2. *Medieval Europe.* A court of justice, usually held at the sovereign's palace. 3. *Roman Catholic Church.* The full body of all the administrative units, tribunals, etc., which help the Pope in the administration and government of the church. *As executor of reform within the Roman Curia under Paul VI, . . . Benelli established himself as an able administrator . . .* (Newsweek Int. Oct. 16, 1978:58).

curia advisari vult. *abbr.* **c.a.v.** or **cur. adv. vult** [L. **curia** court (1); **advisari** to be advised.(3); **vult** wishes (2): The court wishes to be advised.] *Law.* The court wants to be advised. Commonly used in the reports where the court suspends its judgment to consider certain points of law, especially new ones.

Curia Regis *abbr.* **C.R.** *n.* [L. **curia** court, council (2); **regis** king's (1): King's Council or Court.] *Medieval Europe.* A small council, England's chief court, which comprised the great officers of state who not only resided at, but also served as officers of, the palace. *In the thirteenth century it became the practice of aggrieved subjects to send petitions to the Curia Regis* (Newton 1983:16).

curiosa *pl. n.* [L. careful, thoughtful, or curious things.] Rarities. Rare things. Curiosities. Curious things.

Books which are rare or strange such as pornographic or erotic books. Cf. **erotica; esoterica**; and **facetiae**.

curiosa felicitas *n.* Petronius (died 66 B.C.). *Satyricon* 118. [L. **curiosa** careful, thoughtful, curious (1); **felicitas** felicity, happiness (2): careful felicity.] A beautiful literary style which is the product of thoughtful and careful choice of expressions.

currente calamo *adv.* [L. **currente** with running (1); **calamo** (with) pen (2): with running pen.] Offhand. Without careful consideration. Without any profound reflection. *Please feel free to vet this script thoroughly, since it was written currente calamo.*

curriculum *n., pl.* **curricula** or **curriculums** [L. course, race course, career.] 1. The totality of courses which an educational institution or any of its departments offers. *The senate of the university has set up a committee entrusted with the duty of enlarging its curriculum.* 2. All the planned activities of an educational institution. 3. A schedule of work.

curriculum vitae *abbr.* **c.v.** *n., pl.* **curricula vitae** [L. **curriculum** course, race course, career (1); **vitae** of life (2): course of life.] A brief account of a person's life. A brief statement of one's career, including biographical data, which an applicant attaches to his application for employment. **Résumé** (q.v.).

currit quatuor pedibus. or **quatuor pedibus currit.** [L. **currit** it runs (1); **quat(t)uor** four (2); **pedibus** on feet (3): It runs on four feet.] It runs on all fours. The metaphor "running on all fours" means that two things are exactly the same in all circumstances and aspects. Used in law and logic to show, inter alia, that a quotation is applicable wholly and exactly. Cf. **nullum simile est idem nisi quatuor pedipus currit** and **nullum simile quatuor pedibus currit.**

currit tempus contra desides et sui juris contemptores. [L. **currit** runs (2); **tempus** time (1); **contra** against, opposite (3); **desides** indolent, idle persons (4); **et** and (5); **sui** of their own (7); **juris** (of) right, law (8); **contemptores** those who despise or disregard (6): Time runs against indolent persons and those who despise their own right.] *Law.* Time runs against the indolent and those who disregard their rights.

cursillo *n., pl.* **cursillos** [Sp. a little course.] *Roman Catholicism.* A brief but often intensive period of study, especially in religious education. Such programs originated in Spain and have spread throughout the Catholic world.

cursus curiae est lex curiae. [L. **cursus** course, way (1); **curiae** of court (2); **est** is (3); **lex** law (4); **curiae** of court (5): The course of the court is the law of the court.] *Law.* The practice of the court is the court's law. Thus, if a proceeding does not conform with the practice of the court or is not held within the time prescribed by the court, it may be deemed irregular and set aside.

cursus honorum *n., pl.* **cursus honorum** [L. **cursus** course (1); **honorum** of honors, offices (2): course of offices.] 1. *Ancient Rome.* The sequence of public offices held by Roman politicians at certain minimum ages, beginning with the office of aedile and culminating in that of consul. 2. A typical career path. *The ambitious salesperson quickly rose through the cursus honorum of the company until she became a member of the board of directors.*

custodia legis *adv.* [L. **custodia** in the custody (1); **legis** of law (2): in the custody of the law.] In legal custody. Applicable to property kept by the court under the writ of replevin until the case is determined.

custome serra prise stricte. [Obs. Fr. **custome** custom (1); **serra** will be (2); **prise** valued (3); **stricte** strictly (4): Custom will be valued strictly.] Custom should be given a strict interpretation.

custos morum *n., pl.* **custodes morum** [L. **custos** guardian (1); **morum** of morals (2): guardian of morals.] A protector of public morality. Applicable to a body entrusted with the duty of ensuring compliance with a community's rules on morality. *But, as R. v. Newland (1953) would seem to indicate, the claim of the court to be the custos morum of its community has not been consistently made, . . .* (Adewoye 1977:93–94).

custos pacis *n., pl.* **custodes pacis** [L. **custos** guardian (1); **pacis** of peace (2): guardian of the peace.] A protector of the public peace.

c.v. *abbr.* for **curriculum vitae** (q.v.).

cy-pres or **cyprès** or **cypres** *adj.* [Obs. Fr. as near as possible.] As close as possible. *Law.* Used to qualify a doctrine, i.e., *cypres doctrine.* This is a doctrine whereby, if it would be illegal or impossible to apply the literal interpretation of an instrument, the court should resort to equity and adopt an interpretation which is as close as possible to the intention of the instrument. This doctrine is particularly applicable to wills and donations for charitable purposes. *But where there was a gift of the whole residue for a defined charitable purpose, the surplus not required for such purpose was held applicable cyprès although there was not indicated any charitable intention in the wider sense* (Parry 1961:83).

czar or **tsar** *n., pl.* **czars** or **tsars** [Russ. tsar from L. Caesar emperor.] 1. The male emperor of Russia. 2. An autocrat. *A banking czar.* 3. *U.S.A.* An individual with widespread authority and power. *A drug czar.* Cf. **Caesar** and **Kaiser.**

D

d. *abbr.* for **denarius** (q.v.).

da capo *abbr.* **D.C.** or **d.c.** *adv./adj.* [It. **da** from the (1); **capo** head, top (2): from the head.] *Music.* From the top. From the beginning. To be repeated from the beginning. Used in directions. —*n., pl.* **da capos** *Music.* Part of a piece which is to be, or must be, repeated. Cf. **al fine.**

dacha or **datcha** *n., pl.* **dachas** or **datchas** [Russ. gift, land, country house.] A country house or villa in Russia. *Gradually, Krushchev began speaking out on political issues to the inner circle of friends and relatives at his dacha . . .* (*Newsweek Int.* Jan. 1, 1979:27).

dacoit or **dakoit** *n.* [Hindi **dakait.**] An member of a gang of armed robbers of India and Burma. Originally these gangs lived in the hills. The term has been generalized to apply to any armed gang. Cf. **Camorra; mafia; petit truand;** and **yakuza.**

daimyo or **daimio** *n., pl.* **daimyo** or **daimyos** or **daimio** or **daimios** [Japan. **dai** great (1); **myō** name (2): great name.] A feudal lord of ancient Japan.

dal segno *abbr.* **D.S.** *adv.* [It. **dal** from the (1); **segno** sign (2): from the sign.] *Music.* From the sign. Used to indicate the point at which a repeat begins.

damnatio memoriae *n., pl.* **damnatios memoriae** [L. **damnatio** condemnation, obliteration (1); **memoriae** of memory (2): condemnation of memory.] An official attempt to remove the name and memory of an individual from all public monuments. *The damnatio memoriae of Stalin's reign was swift and thorough throughout the Soviet Union.*

damnosa hereditas or **damnosa haereditas** or **hereditas damnosa** or **haereditas damnosa** *var.* of **hereditas damnosa** (q.v.).

damnum *n., pl.* **damna** [L. damage, injury, loss.] *Law.* Damage to, or loss of, something which belongs to a person, such as character or property, through negligence, fraud, or even accident. It may, or may not, involve violation of legal rights.

damnum absque injuria *n.* [L. **damnum** damage, injury, loss (1); **absque** away from, without (2); **injuria** injury; wrong, injustice (3): loss/damage without injury/wrong.] *Law.* Loss/harm without injury to a legal right. Applicable to a loss which does not involve a violation of legal rights and so does not require action against the offender. See **actio non datur** etc.

damnum emergens *n.* [L. **damnum** damage, injury, loss (2); **emergens** rising, emerging (1): rising/emerging damage.] *Law.* Actual/real damage, as distinct from expected damage. *The loss may be in the nature of a damnum emergens not merely a lucrum cessans.* (Hanbury 1962:522). Cf. **damnum infectum** and **lucrum cessans.**

damnum fatale *n.* [L. **damnum** damage, injury, loss (2); **fatale** fated, destined (1): destined damage.] *Law.* Damage which is the result of inevitable accident or actus Dei, such as lightning, shipwreck, or earthquake. *A party to a contract cannot bear a loss arising out of damnum fatale.*

damnum infectum *n.* [L. **damnum** damage, injury, loss (2); **infectum** undone, unaccomplished (1): unaccomplished damage.] *Roman Law.* Damage/loss expected or threatened, but not yet inflicted. See **lucrum cessans.** Cf. **damnum emergens.**

damnum rei amissae *n.* [L. **damnum** damage, injury, loss (1); **rei** of matter, thing, property, business, affair (2); **amissae** (of) lost (3): damage of the thing lost.] *Civil Law.* A loss emanating from a payment made as a result of an error of law.

damnum sentit dominus. [L. **damnum** damage, injury, loss (3); **sentit** feels, suffers (2); **dominus** lord, owner (1): The owner suffers the loss.] *Law.* When goods are contracted for sale and they are destroyed accidentally, the party who is currently the owner suffers the loss, unless there is an agreement to the contrary. See **periculum rei** etc.

damnum sine injuria *n.* [L. **damnum** damage, injury, loss (1); **sine** without (2); **injuria** injury (3): damage without injury.] *Law.* Damage without legal injury. A damage/harm for which the law provides no remedy. See **actio non datur** etc.

damnum sine injuria esse potest. [L. **damnum** damage, injury, loss (1); **sine** without (4); **injuria** injury/wrong, injustice (5); **esse** to be (2); **potest** there can, it is possible (2): Damage can be without injury.] *Law.* There can be damage without injury. In such cases there can be no action, for there is no jus (right) and the maxim **ubi jus ibi remedium** (q.v.) is not applicable. See **actio non datur** etc.

Damocles *n.* [Gk. **Damoklēs.**] 1. A courtier of Dionysius I, tyrant of Syracuse in Sicily who lived from c.430 to 367 B.C. Because Damocles excessively praised his happiness, the tyrant invited him to a sumptuous banquet and symbolically demonstrated the insecurity of a tyrant's happiness by suspending over Damocles' head a sword hanging by a single hair. —**sword of Damocles** An imminent danger, catastrophe, or disaster, especially at a time of prosperity. A disaster which may happen any time. a) . . . *with the possibility of another terrorist attack hanging over the world like a sword of Damocles* . . . (Benjamin Yaw Owusu in *West Africa* 1986); b) *No sword of Damocles will be hanging over our heads* (*Time Int.* 1982).

dans ce meilleur des mondes possibles Voltaire (1694–1778). *Candide* 23. [Fr. **dans** in (1); **ce** this (2); **meilleur** best (3); **des** of the (4); **mondes** worlds (6); **possibles** possible (5): the best of the possible worlds.] The best of all possible worlds. Cf. **Tout est pour le mieux** etc.

Dans ce pays-ci il est bon de tuer de temps en temps un amiral pour encourager les autres. Voltaire (1694–1778). *Candide*, 23. [Fr. **dans** in (1); **ce** this (2); **pays** country, land (3); **-ci** here (4); **il** it (5); **est** is (6); **bon** good (7); **de** to (8); **tuer** kill (9); **de** from (12); **temps** time, weather (13); **en** in, to (14); **temps** time, weather (15); **un** an (10); **amiral** admiral (11); **pour** to, in order to (16); **encourager** encourage (17); **les** the (18); **autres** others (19): In this country here it is good to kill an admiral from time to time in order to encourage the others.] In this nation [i.e., England], it is wise policy to execute an admiral occasionally in order to encourage the other admirals to perform their duties satisfactorily.

danse d'école *n., pl.* **danses d'école** [Fr. **danse** dance (1); **d'** of (2); **école** school (3): dance of school.] Classical or traditional ballet. Ballet in which traditional rules are strictly observed.

danse du ventre *n., pl.* **danses du ventre** [Fr. **danse** dance (1); **du** of the (2); **ventre** belly, abdomen (3): dance of the belly.] Belly dance.

danse macabre *n., pl.* **danses macabres** [Fr. **danse** dance (2); **macabre** macabre, gruesome, ghastly (1): macabre dance.] 1. The dance of death. A dance of the Middle Ages in which a skeleton, which represents death, leads to the grave a procession of skeletons or

living people. 2. Something as horrifying as a danse macabre. *The spider performed a dance macabre around the butterfly.*

dans et retinens, nihil dat. [L. **dans** giving (1); **et** and (2); **retinens** retaining (3); **nihil** nothing (5); **dat** one gives (4): Giving and retaining, one gives nothing.] *Law.* A person who gives something and yet retains possession gives nothing.

danseur or *fem.* **danseuse** *n., pl.* **danseurs** or *fem.* **danseuses** [Fr. dancer.] A ballet dancer.

danseur noble *n., pl.* **danseurs nobles** [Fr. **danseur** dancer (2); **noble** noble, lofty (1): noble dancer.] A male dancer who serves as a ballerina's partner.

Das Kapital *n.* [Ger. **das** the (1); **Kapital** capital, stock, funds (2): the capital.] *Capital,* an economic treatise in three volumes (1867, 1885, 1895) by Karl Marx (1818–1883).

Das Lied von der Erde *n.* [Ger. **das** the (1); **Lied** song (2); **von** of (3); **der** the (4); **Erde** earth (5): the song of the earth.] "The Song of the Earth," a symphonic song by Gustav Mahler (1860–1911).

Das Rheingold *n.* [Ger. **das** the (1); **Rhein** Rhine (2); **Gold** gold (3): the Rhine gold.] "The Rhine Gold," the first opera (1854) in the Ring tetralogy by Richard Wagner (1813–1883). Cf. **Der Ring des Nibelungen.**

data et accepta *pl. n.* [L. **data** (things) given (1); **et** and (2); **accepta** (things) accepted, received (3): things given and received.] Expenses and income.

dation *n., pl.* **dations** [Fr. giving, conferring.] *Civil Law.* The legal act of conferring or giving something. Dation differs from a donation for, whereas the latter implies that the donor is acting with generosity, dation implies that the gift is given under an obligation.

datum *n., pl.* **data** or **datums** The use of **data** as a singular, while common, is often considered to be substandard. [L. that which is given, something given.] A fact or principle which is granted, assumed, or admitted. Something which serves as the basis of an argument, inference, or discussion. a) *The lecturer made sweeping generalizations based on grossly inadequate data.* b) *Adequate data are not yet available.*

dauphin *n.* [Fr.] The oldest male heir of the king of France. The next in line of succession to the throne. Cf. **infante.**

dauphine *n.* [Fr.] The wife of the **dauphin** (q.v.). Cf. **infanta.**

D.B. *abbr.* for **Divinitatis Baccalaureus** (q.v.).

D.C. or **d.c.** *abbr.* for **da capo** (q.v.).

d.d. in d. *abbr.* for **de die in diem** (q.v.).

de aequitate *adv./adj.* [L. of, from, about, for (1); **aequitate** equity (2): from equity.] According to equity. According to the principles of equity. By equity. In equity. De aequitate may be used in opposition to **de jure** (q.v.) to draw a distinction between the principles of equity and the strict application of the law.

de aetate probanda *n.* [L. **de** of, from, about, for (1); **aetate** age (2); **probanda** to be proved (3): for an age to be proved.] *Law.* An ancient writ issued to summon a jury for the purpose of determining the age of a tenant-in-chief when there was doubt.

De amicitia *n.* [L. **de** of, from, about, for (1); **amicitia** friendship (2): about friendship.] *On Friendship*, a philosophical dialogue by Cicero (106–43 B.C.).

de annuo reditu *n.* [L. **de** of, from, about, for (1); **annuo** yearly, annual (2); **reditu** return, rent, income, revenue (3): for annual rent.] *Law.* A writ for the recovery of an annuity whether in money or in goods.

debacle *n., pl.* **debacles** [Fr. **débâcle** breaking-up, breakdown, collapse, ruin, rout, downfall.] 1. Stampede, rout, panic or violent dispersion, i.e., of an army or mob. *The battle ended with the debacle of the enemy.* 2. A complete failure. Collapse. A sudden disgraceful end. Downfall. An unexpected breakdown. . . . *I did not see how the Democrats could recover from their electoral debacle* . . . (*Time Int.* 1982). 3. A sudden breaking of ice in a river. The rush of water and ice which is the result of the breaking.

de bene esse *abbr.* **d.b.e.** *adv./adj.* [L. **de** of, from, about, for (1); **bene** well (3); **esse** to be, being (2): of being well, of well-being.] *Law.* Provisionally. Conditionally. The expression is used with reference to various things done provisionally. For instance, an examination de bene esse is one in which evidence is taken from somebody who is seriously ill, or too old, or about to travel before the trial, and out of court because he/she may not be available at the time of trial. The evidence is used, if the situation persists, but if the person can appear in court at the time of the trial, the evidence is taken in the normal manner. See **del bien estre.**

debet esse finis litium. [L. **debet** there ought, should (1); **esse** to be (2); **finis** end (3); **litium** of suits, litigations (4): There ought to be an end of litigations.] *Law.* Litigation should not go on ad infinitum; i.e., it should not continue indefinitely. See **infinitum in** etc.

debet sua cuique domus esse perfugium tutissimum. [L. **debet** ought, should (4); **sua** one's own (2); **cuique** to each one (1); **domus** house, residence (3); **esse** to be (5); **perfugium** refuge, shelter (7); **tutissimum** safest (6): To each one, one's own house should be the safest refuge.] Each person's house should be his/her safest refuge; i.e., a person's home is his/her castle. See **domus sua** etc.

de bien et de mal [Fr. **de** of (1); **bien** good (2); **et** and (3); **de** of (4); **mal** evil (5): of good and evil.] For good and evil. *Law of Former Times.* Used by an accused person to indicate total submission to the verdict of a jury. See **de bono et malo.**

debile fundamentum fallit opus. [L. **debile** weak, infirm (1); **fundamentum** foundation, basis (2); **fallit** makes slip, disappoints, betrays (3); **opus** work, structure (4): A weak foundation makes slip the structure.] *Law.* A weak foundation puts the entire structure in jeopardy. Thus when a will is not

properly attested in accordance with the provisions of statute, it is void. Also, when the cause of an action collapses, the action itself necessarily collapses.

debita sequuntur personam debitoris. [L. **debita** debts (1); **sequuntur** follow (2); **personam** person (3); **debitoris** of debtor (4): Debts follow the person of the debtor.] *Law.* Debts follow the debtor; i. e. a debt must be repaid wherever the debtor is found. Cf. **debitum et contractus** etc.

debitor non praesumitur donare. [L. **debitor** debtor (1); **non** not (2); **praesumitur** is presumed (3); **donare** to make a donation (4): A debtor is not presumed to make a donation.] *Law.* Whatever a debtor gives to his creditor, it is presumed to be given in satisfaction of his obligation or debt.

debitorum pactionibus creditorum petitio nec tolli nec minui potest. [L. **debitorum** of debtors (9); **pactionibus** by agreements, pacts (8); **creditorum** of creditors (2); **petitio** claim, suit (1); **nec** neither (4); **tolli** to be removed (5); **nec** nor (6); **minui** to be diminished, lessened (7); **potest** can, is able (3): The claim of creditors can neither be removed nor diminished by agreements of debtors.] *Law.* Agreements among debtors have no effect whatsoever on the claims/rights of creditors. See **res inter alios acta alteri** etc.

debitum et contractus sunt nullius loci. [L. **debitum** debt (1); **et** and (2); **contractus** drawing together, shrinking, contract, agreement (3); **sunt** are (4); **nullius** of no (5); **loci** (of) place (6): Debt and agreement are of no place.] *Law.* Debt and contract have no specific locality; i.e., they belong to no specific jurisdiction. Cf. **debita sequuntur** etc.

de bonis asportatis *n.* [L. **de** of, from, about, for (1); **bonis** goods (2); **asportatis** that have been carried away, removed (3): of goods that have been carried away.] *Law.* For goods removed. For removing goods. An action of trespass for the recovery of monetary damages from a person who has unlawfully damaged or removed property.

de bonis non *short form* of **de bonis non administratis** (q.v.).

de bonis non administratis *adj.* [L. **de** of, from, about, for (1); **bonis** goods (2); **non** not (3); **administratis** administered (4): of goods not administered.] *Law.* About the goods of a decedent not yet administered. Applicable to a letter of administration to an administrator who succeeds one who has not completely settled the estate. *A niece of the testatrix subsequently obtained a grant of administration de bonis non* . . . (Hanbury 1962:461). See **cum testamento annexo** etc.

de bonis propriis *adj.* [L. **de** of, from, about, for (1); **bonis** goods, property (3); **propriis** one's own, own (2): from one's own property/goods.] *Law.* From one's own pocket. Used with reference to a judgment against an executor, especially in a case of **devastavit** (q.v.) which must be satisfied from his/her own financial resources.

de bonis testatoris *adj.* [L. **de** of, from, about, for (1); **bonis** property, goods (2); **testatoris** of testator (3): about the property of the testator.] *Law.* Of the goods of the testator. Applicable to a judgment which awards execution against a testator's property. *For the rule is that the presence of assets is conclusively presumed from a judgment de bonis testatoris being recovered against the representative* (Hanbury 1962:505).

débonnaire also **debonair, debonaire, debonnaire** *adj.* [Fr. good-natured, easy-going.] Affable. Genial. Kindly. Gracious. Gentle. Carefree. *Anne has fallen in love with a débonnaire man whom she met only a couple of weeks ago.*

de bono et malo [L. **de** of, from, about, for (1); **bono** good (2); **et** and (3); **malo** evil (4): of good and evil.] For good and evil. See **de bien et de mal.**

débris or **debris** *n., pl.* **débris** or **debris** [Fr. fragments, remains, wreckage, ruins.] The remains or fragments of something which was previously whole but has been destroyed. Ruins. Wreckage. Rubbish. a) *A rescue team searches for survivors in the debris of the hotel disaster . . . (Newsweek Int.* Jan 4, 1982:43). b) *Below the topsoil of China lies the accumulated debris of 4,000 years of civilization (The Economist* 1987).

début or **debut** *n., pl.* **débuts** or **debuts** [Fr. beginning, start, first appearance, first production.] 1. First public appearance of an artist such as a singer, actor, or dancer. a) *Tony's band had a successful début at the Federal Hotel yesterday.* b) *. . . last week . . . Dimitris Sgouros, a 12-year-old Greek pianist from Piraeus, prepared to make his American debut in Carnegie Hall (Newsweek Int.* April 26, 1982:49). 2. Formal introduction to society. A woman's or girl's first appearance at adult social functions.— *v. intr.* To make a debut or first appearance. *. . . disc brakes and radial tires debuted on European cars long before they were introduced in the U.S. (Newsweek Int.* June 4, 1979:37). —*v. tr.* To introduce or present for the first time to the public. *The band will debut its first record album next week.*

debutant *fem.* **debutante** *n., pl.* **debutants** or *fem.* **debutantes** [Fr. **débutant(e)** a beginner, novice.] A person who is making his/her debut. A performer or an artist who is making his/her first public appearance. *"Solo-Solo," who was a debutant in the music industry only last year, is already a celebrity. —Fem.* A lady who is introduced for the first time to adult or high society. a) *Stop treading timorously like a reluctant debutante, . . . (The Economist* 1987). b) *We attended a festival at our village last week and witnessed a very impressive parade of debutantes.*

decemvir *n., pl.* **decemviri** or **decemvirs** [L. **decem** ten (1); **vir** man (2): ten man, one of a body of ten.] A member of a body, group, council, association, commission, or ruling body of ten. Cf. **duovir; duumvir; quattuorvir; quindecemvir; quinquevir; septemvir;** and **triumvir.**

decennium *n., pl.* **decennia** or **decenniums** [L. a period of ten years.] A decade. Cf. **biennium.**

deceptis non decipientibus jura subveniunt. [L. **deceptis** to the deceived (3); **non** not (4); **decipientibus** to the deceiving (5); **jura** rights, laws (1); **subveniunt** give help to (2): Laws give help to the deceived, not to the deceiving.] *Law.* The laws come to the aid of those who are deceived, not those who deceive.

decessit sine prole. *abbr.* **D.S.P.** or **d.s.p.** [L. **decessit** he/she departed, died (1); **sine** without (2); **prole** offspring, issue (3): He/she died without offspring or issue.] He/she died without children. Usually used in family trees or genealogical tables. Cf. **obiit sine prole.**

decessit sine prole legitima. *abbr.* **D.S.P.L.** or **d.s.p.l.** [L. **decessit** he/she died (1); **sine** without (2); **prole** offspring, issue (4); **legitima** legitimate (3): He/she died without legitimate issue.] He/she died without legitimate children. Cf. **obiit sine prole.** See also **sine legitima prole** and **sine prole legitima.**

decessit sine prole mascula. *abbr.* **D.S.P.M.** or **d.s.p.m.** [L. **decessit** he/she died (1); **sine** without (2); **prole** offspring, issue (4); **mascula** male (3): He/ she died without male issue.] He/she died without male children. Usually used in genealogical tables. Cf. **obiit sine prole.** See also **sine prole mascula** and **sine mascula prole.**

decessit sine prole mascula superstite. *abbr.* **D.S.P.M.S.** or **d.s.p.m.s.** [L. **decessit** he/she died (1); **sine** without (2); **prole** offspring, issue (5); **mascula** male (4); **superstite** surviving (3): He/ she died without surviving male issue.] He/she died without living male children. Cf. **obiit sine prole.**

decessit sine prole superstite. *abbr.* **D.S.P.S.** or **d.s.p.s.** [L. **decessit** he/she died (1); **sine** without (2); **prole** offspring, issue (4); **superstite** surviving (3): He/she died without surviving issue.] He/she died without living children. Cf. **obiit sine prole.** See also **sine prole superstite.**

decessit sine prole virili. *abbr.* **D.S.P.V.** or **d.s.p.v.** [L. **decessit** he/she died (1); **sine** without (2); **prole** offspring, issue (4); **virili** male (3): He/she died without male issue.] He/she died without male children. Usually used in genealogical tables. Cf. **obiit sine prole.**

déclassé or *fem.* **déclassée** *adj.* [Fr. degraded, ostracized, taken out of one's class.] 1. Having lost, been reduced, or lowered in, rank, class, or social standing. *Ben's uncle, the arrogant businessman, is now déclassé to such an extent that he dines at cheap restaurants.* 2. Of low or inferior status. *In these days of harsh economic realities riding in a Volkswagon Beetle is no longer deemed to be déclassé. —n., pl.* **déclassés** or *fem.* **déclassées** A person who is déclassé or has lost his social standing. *When Peter was at the* *peak of his career, he had many friends but, now that he is a déclassé, everybody shuns his company.*

de clauso fracto *adj.* [L. **de** of, from, about, for (1); **clauso** enclosed area, enclosure (3); **fracto** broken (2): of broken enclosed area.] *Law.* Of broken enclosure. Of breach of enclosure. Used in old legal pleading for action against a person who trespasses on real property. See **clausum fregit**.

décolletage *n., pl.* **décolletages** [Fr. low-cut neck, uncovering the shoulders and neck, low dress.] A woman's dress which leaves the shoulders and neck exposed. A woman's dress which has a low-cut neckline. . . . *Judy . . . settled instead for some discreetly snipped décolletage on the front of the jacket and a more provocative peek on the derrière side* (*Newsweek Int.* March 12, 1979:57).

décolleté *adj.* [Fr. low-necked, low-cut.] 1. *Fashion.* Leaving the shoulders and neck bare or exposed. *. . . the young designers of her décolleté dress . . . were picked to do her wedding gown* (*Newsweek Int.* March 23, 1981:47). 2. Wearing a dress with a low-cut neckline or one which leaves the shoulders and neck exposed. *His attention was attracted by a woman who entered the room décolleté.*

de consilio curiae *adv.* [L. **de** of, from, about, for (1); **consilio** advise (2); **curiae** of court (3): from the advice of the court.] *Law.* By the advice of the court. By the court's direction. *The petitioner in the divorce case surrendered the children to the respondent de consilio curiae.*

décor or **decor** *n., pl.* **décors** or **decors** [Fr. decoration, scene, setting.] Decoration or ornament. Scenery, furnishings, fittings, or anything which enhances the general appearance of a room, office, theater, public building, or mansion.

De corona *n.* [L. **de** of, from, about, for (1); **corona** crown (2): about the crown.] *On the Crown* the Latin title of a speech (330 B.C.) by the Athenian orator Demosthenes (384–322 B.C.) in which he defends his long-term policies towards the kingdom of Macedonia.

decorum *n., pl.* **decorums** [L. seemliness, propriety.] 1. Propriety. Good taste and behavior. Correct conduct and manners. *Jeremiah usually does things with the proper decorum.* 2. Orderliness. The quality of being proper, orderly or decorous. *Hardly anybody transacts business with that company without being impressed by its decorum.* 3. Usually pl. Convention. What polite society requires. *The people are ordinarily very friendly, but they become very hostile when foreigners trample upon their customary decorums.*

découpage or **decoupage** *n., pl.* **découpages** or **decoupages** [Fr. cutting or carving out.] *Art.* Decoration with cutouts, especially of paper or cloth.

decretum *n., pl.* **decreta** [L. decree, resolution.] An ordinance or decision.

de cujus *adj.* [L. **de** of, from, about, for (1); **cujus** of whom, whose (2): whose.] *Law.* From whose. Used with reference to the person by whom, through whom, from whom, or under whom a claim is made by another person.

de cursu *adj.* [L. **de** of, from, about, for (1); **cursu** course (2): from course.] From normal practice. Used to describe usual and formal proceedings and writs, as distinguished from those that are incidental, summary, etc. *Proceedings de cursu.*

de debito *n.* [L. **de** of, from, about, for (1); **debito** debt (2): about debt.] *Law.* A writ of debt.

de deceptione *n.* [L. **de** of, from, about, for (1); **deceptione** deceit (2): about deceit.] *Law.* A writ of deceit. A writ against a person who acted in another's name to the latter's detriment.

de derrière *adv.* [Fr. **de** of, from, about, for (1); **derrière** back, behind (2): from the back.] From behind. At the back. Behind. *This time she was posed modestly de derrière hawking the pedestrian virtues of a billboard-rental firm* (*Newsweek Int.* Sept. 21, 1981:33).

de die in diem *abbr.* **d.d. in d.** or **de d. in d.** *adv.* [L. **de** from, of (1); **die** day (2); **in** into, to, against, for (3); **diem** day (4): from day to day.] Daily. a) *In view of the limited period of time within which to submit its report, the committee had to meet de die in diem.* b) *If I wrongfully place something on your land and leave it there, that is not simply a single act of trespass, but is a continuing trespass giving rise to a fresh cause of action de die in diem* (Rogers 1975:553).

dedimus or **dedimus potestatem** *n.* [L. **dedimus** we have given (1); **potestatem** power (2): We have given power.] 1. *Britain.* A writ empowering private persons to perform some of the functions of a judge, such as administering oaths of office and examining witnesses. 2. *U.S.A.* A legal authorization to take testimony.

de d. in d. *abbr.* for **de die in diem** (q.v.).

de dolo malo *adj.* [L. **de** of, from, about, for (1); **dolo** deceit (3); **malo** bad (2): about bad deceit.] Of fraud. Based on fraud. See **dolus malus**.

de excommunicato capiendo or *fem.* **de excommunicata capienda** *n.* [L. **de** of, from, about, for (1); **excommunicato** excommunicated (person) (2); **capiendo** to be seized (3): for an excommunicated (person) to be seized.] *Obsolete. Church Law.* A writ authorizing the arrest and detention of an excommunicated person until he has been pardoned by the church.

de executione judicii *n.* [L. **de** of, from, about, for (1); **ex(s)ecutione** execution (2); **judicii** of judgment (3): about the execution of judgment.] *Law.* A writ ordering the execution of judgment.

de facto *adv.* [L. **de** of, from, about, for (1); **facto** deed, act, fact (2): from the deed/act.] In fact. Actually. As a matter of fact, though not of law. In reality. —*adj.* Exercising powers or privileges in practice but not by legally sanctioned right. *Bukar is the de jure head of department but, since he has other engagements, his work in the department is done by Smith, the de facto head of department.* Cf. **de jure.**

Defensor Fidei *abbr.* **D.F.** *n., pl.* **Defensores Fidei** [L. **defensor** defender (1); **fidei** of faith, honesty (2): Defender of the faith.] Though not of exclusive use, a title conferred on Henry VIII (1491–1547) of England by Pope Leo X (1475–1521) for writing the *Assertio Septem Sacramentorum* ("The Assertion of the Seven Sacraments") to criticize the doctrines of Martin Luther (1483–1546). Cf. **Fidei Defensor.**

de fide *adj.* [L. **de** of, from, about, for (1); **fide** faith, honesty (2): from faith.] As a matter of faith. Regarded as a compulsory article of faith. *Do you want us to accept this view as proved or de fide?*

de fide et officio judicis non recipitur quaestio; sed de scientia sive error sit juris sive facti. [L. **de** of, from, about, for (1); **fide** fidelity, honesty (2); **et** and (3); **officio** sense of duty, conscience (4); **judicis** of judge (5); **non** not (7); **recipitur** is welcomed (8); **quaestio** question (6); **sed** but (9); **de** of, from, about, for (10); **scientia** knowledge (11); **sive** whether (12); **error** error, mistake (13); **sit** be, is (14); **juris** of right, law (15); **sive** or (16); **facti** of fact (17): About the honesty and sense of duty of a judge a question is not welcomed, but about his knowledge, whether the mistake be of law or of fact.] *Law.* No question will be entertained about a judge's honesty and sense of duty, but a question is entertained about his knowledge as to whether there is an error of law or of fact. No action is entertained against a judge for an act done in the performance of his judicial duties as long as it falls within his sphere of jurisdiction. If, however, he commits an error, it may be rectified in an appellate court.

défilade *n., pl.* **défilades** [Fr. a marching in single file.] 1. An 18th-century military maneuver in which troops march in single file in order to avoid enfilade, i.e., the sweeping gunfire of the enemy. 2. A procession in single file. *The spectacle of 200 horsemen charging and stopping in a thundering défilade has to be seen to be appreciated* (Lindsay Barrett in *West Africa* 1986).

De finibus bonorum et malorum *n.* [L. **de** of, from, about, for (1); **finibus** ends (2); **bonorum** of good (things) (3); **et** and (4); **malorum** bad (things) (5): about the ends of good things and bad things.] *On the Ends of Good and Bad*, a philosophical treatise by Cicero (106–43 B.C.).

defunctus sine prole *adj.* [L. **defunctus** dead (1); **sine** without (2); **prole** offspring, children (3): dead without offspring.] Dead, leaving no issue. May be used in family trees. *The plaintiff proved convincingly*

not only that the testator could not be considered as *defunctus sine prole* but also that the plaintiff was the legitimate son of the testator. See **mortuus sine prole** and **sine prole.**

de gratia *adv./adj.* [L. **de** of, from, about, for (1); **gratia** favor (2): from favor.] By favor. Of grace/favor. May be used in opposition to de jure to draw a distinction between what is enjoyed by favor and what is enjoyed by legal rights. *He enjoys an influential position de gratia and not de jure.* Cf. **de jure.**

de gustibus non est disputandum. Usually written in the shorter form **de gustibus** [L. **de** of, from, about, for (1); **gustibus** tastes (2); **non** not (4); **est** it is (3); **disputandum** to be disputed, controverted (5): Concerning tastes, it is not to be disputed.] There is no point in questioning another person's taste. *I do not understand why he should fall in love with her, but de gustibus.* See **à chacun son goût.**

de haut en bas also **du haut en bas** *adv.* [Fr. **de** from, of (1); **haut** high, top (2); **en** to, into (3); **bas** low, bottom (4): from top to bottom.] From head to toe. In a condescending manner. With an air of superiority. Haughtily. Arrogantly. Contemptuously. *He quit his job because his boss consistently talked to him de haut en bas.*

dehors *prep.* [Fr. outside, without, out of.] *Law.* Out of. Unconnected with. Foreign to. Alien to. Applicable to records, agreements, wills, etc. *The plaintiff's lawyers would permit nothing dehors agreement to be used as evidence.*

de identitate nominis *n.* [**de** of, from, about, for (1); **identitate** identity (2); **nominis** of name (3): about identity of name.] A writ which lay for a person arrested and imprisoned as a result of mistaken identity where one bears the same name as the actual culprit.

Dei gratia *abbr.* **D.G.** *adv.* [L. **Dei** of God (2); **gratia** by grace (1): by the grace of God.] By divine favor. Used almost exclusively by kings and queens, and signifying that monarchy is a divine right.

Dei judicium *n.* [L. **Dei** of God (2); **judicium** judgment (1): the judgment of God.] *Saxon Law.* Trial by ordeal.

de incremento *adj.* [L. **de** of, from, about, for (1); **incremento** increase (2): about increase.] *Law.* Of increase. In addition. Additional. Applicable to costs in civil actions determined by the court in addition to the normal costs assessed by the jury.

de inofficioso testamento *adj.* [L. **de** of, from, about, for (1); **inofficioso** undutiful (2); **testamento** will (3): concerning an undutiful will.] *Law.* Used in connection with a form of action which aims at setting aside a will that ignores the natural rights of children, widow, widower, or other immediate relatives. See **donatio inofficiosa.**

de integro *adv.* [L. **de** of, from, about, for (1); **integro** fresh, entire, whole (2): from fresh.] Anew. A second time. Afresh. Once more. *The children of the deceased have decided to share his estate de integro, taking into consideration each beneficiary's age.* See **de novo** and **ex integro**.

de jactura evitanda *adv.* [L. **de** of, from, about, for (1); **jactura** loss, damage (2); **evitanda** to be avoided (2): for loss to be avoided.] *Law.* Applicable to a defendant in the same way as **de lucro captando** (q.v.) is applicable to the plaintiff.

déjà vu *n.* [Fr. **déjà** already, previously (1); **vu** seen (2): already seen.] 1. *Art.* Work lacking originality or repeating hackneyed themes, ideas, formulae, etc. *But the wild choreography and the Fellinian excesses projected a depressing sense of déjà vu* (*Newsweek Int.* June 2, 1980:51). 2. *Psychology.* The illusion of remembering or having previously experienced something which one is now experiencing for the first time. *He felt an eerie sense of déjà vu as he entered the home of his new acquaintance.* See **paramnesia** 2.

dejecta *pl. n.* [L. things expelled, ejected, or dislodged.] Excrement. Stool. Droppings. Cf. **egesta** and **excreta**.

de jure *adv.* [L. **de** of, from, about, for (1); **jure** right, law (2): from right.] By a rightful title. By right. As a matter of law. —*adj.* Legitimate. Recognized by law. Exercising the powers of, functioning as, enjoying the privileges of, legally, legitimately or as a matter of law. *In the absence of Mr. Cross, the de jure governor, Mr. Reece is serving as the governor.* The expression is used with reference to a position, benefit, power, etc. enjoyed by legal right. Cf. **de aequitate**; **de gratia**; and **ex gratia**.

de jure judices de facto juratores respondent. [L. **de** of, from, about, for (3); **jure** right, law (4); **judices** judges (1); **de** about (6); **facto** deed, act, fact (7); **juratores** jurors (5); **respondent** respond, answer (2): Judges answer about law, jurors about fact.] *Law.* Judges decide questions of law, jurors questions of fact. See **ad quaestionem facti** etc.

de jure stricto *adv./adj.* [L. **de** of, from, about, for (1); **jure** right, law (2); **stricto** strict (2): from strict law.] In strict law. *If the case had been decided de jure stricto, the defendant would have had to pay heavy damages.*

del. *abbr.* for **delineavit** (q.v.).

de latere *adv./adj.* [L. **de** of, from, about, for (1); **latere** side (2): from the side.] Collaterally. On the side. Cf. **a latere**.

delator *n., pl.* **delatores** or **delators** [L. an informer, accuser.] A professional informer. A denouncer. *Suspicious, incompetent, power-obsessed and intolerant rulers tend to rely inordinately on the services of obnoxious delators.*

del bien estre *adv.* [Obs. Fr. **del** of (1); **bien** well (3); **estre** to be, being (2): of being well.] *Former English Legal Practice.* Conditionally. See **de bene esse**.

del credere *adj.* [It. **del** of the (1); **credere** to believe, believing (2): of believing.] Of belief. *Law.* Concerning a transaction in which an agent or merchant, for a higher commission, guarantees payment to the principal by a third party who purchases goods on credit. The expression is used to describe the agent, merchant, or commission involved in such a transaction.

delectus personae *n.* [L. **delectus** choice (1); **personae** of person (2): choice of a person.] The right of partners in a firm or corporation to impose restrictions on admission and to admit those whom they consider satisfactory.

delegata potestas non potest delegari. [L. **delegata** delegated (1); **potestas** power (2); **non** not (4); **potest** can, is able (3); **delegari** to be delegated (5): A delegated power cannot be delegated.] *Law.* A deputy cannot appoint his own deputy, particularly when the position involves the exercise of discretion. See **delegatus delegare** etc.; **delegatus non** etc.; and **vicarius non** etc.

delegatus delegare non potest. [L. **delegatus** delegate (1); **delegare** to delegate (4); **non** not (3); **potest** can, is able (2): A delegate cannot delegate.] An agent cannot delegate his duties to another agent or, for that matter, a person who has been assigned a delegated function cannot delegate it to another person except by express authorization. *It is a general rule that if a power is conferred on a person which involves the exercise of discretion, the donee cannot assign or delegate to another the execution of the trust or confidence so reposed in him. Delegatus delegare non potest . . .* (Parry 1961:233). See **delegata potestas** etc.

delegatus non potest delegare. See **delegatus delegare non potest.** *The maxim delegatus non potest delegare applies in respect to the power of allotment given to directors* (Olawoyin 1977:114). See **delegata potestas** etc.

De legibus *n.* [L. **de** of, from, about, for (1); **legibus** laws (2): about the laws.] *On the Laws*, a philosophical dialogue and political treatise by Cicero (106–43 B.C.).

delenda est Carthago. Cato the Elder (234–149 B.C.). [L. **delenda** to be destroyed (3); **est** is (2); **Carthago** Carthage (1): Carthage is to be destroyed.] Carthage must be destroyed.

deliberandum est diu quod statuendum est semel. [L. **deliberandum** to be deliberated (6); **est** is (5); **diu** long, a long time (7); **quod** (that) which, what (1); **statuendum** to be decided, determined (3); **est** is (2); **semel** once, once and for all (4): That which is to be decided once and for all is to be deliberated upon for long.] A decision which is to be made once and for all demands long deliberation.

delicatessen *n., pl.* **delicatessens** [Ger. **Delikatessen**: **Delikat** delicacy (2); **essen** to eat (1): to eat a delicacy.] A shop where prepared foods, especially fancy meats, cheeses, and salads, are sold.

delicatus debitor est odiosus in lege. [L. **delicatus** luxurious, voluptuous (1); **debitor** debtor (2); **est** is (3);

odiosus hateful, odious (4); **in** in, on (5); **lege** law (6): A luxurious debtor is hateful/odious in law.] The law feels ill will toward a debtor who lives luxuriously.

delicta majorum immeritus lues. [L. **delicta** offenses, transgressions (3); **majorum** of ancestors (4); **immeritus** undeserving, undeserved (2); **lues** you will atone for, expiate (1): You will, though undeserving, atone for the offenses of your ancestors.] Innocent heirs will pay for the offenses of their ancestors.

delineavit *abbr.* **del.** [L. He/she drew it.] Used to indicate the author of a painting or drawing. Cf. **caelavit.**

delirium *n., pl.* **deliria** or **deliriums** [L. craziness, madness, silliness.] 1. *Medicine.* A temporary mental disturbance characterized by excitement, restlessness, confusion, incoherence, disorientation, hallucinations, and delusions. Though usually caused by high fever or toxemia, it may also occur during mental illness. 2. Wild, frenzied enthusiasm or excitement.

delirium tremens *abbr.* **d.t.** *n.* [L. **delirium** craziness, madness, silliness (2); **tremens** shaking, trembling (1): trembling madness.] *Medicine.* Madness due to alcohol. Delirium tremens is a violent madness caused by prolonged and excessive use of alcoholic drinks. Its principal characteristics are restlessness, dreadful hallucination, sweating, shaking body and confused mentality. *. . . and where a person suffering from delirium tremens tore up his will and on his recovery said that he was mad to do it, there was held to be no revocation* (Parry 1961:28).

de lucro captando *adv.* [L. **de** of, from, about, for (1); **lucro** gain, advantage (2); **captando** to be seized (3): for gain to be seized.] *Law.* For gaining advantage. Applicable to a plaintiff just as **de jactura evitanda** (q.v.). is applicable to a defendant.

de luxe or **deluxe** *adj.* [Fr. **de** from, of (1); **luxe** luxury (2): of luxury.] First-class. Choice. Sumptuous. Very luxurious. Very elegant. Of superior or very high quality. *Our wealthy neighbor has ten cars, all of them de luxe.* —*adv.* Luxuriously. In a luxurious manner. Sumptuously. *We had a pleasant vacation, traveling, lodging and dining de luxe.* See **luxe.**

de majori et minori non variant jura. [L. **de** of, from, about, for (1); **majori** greater (2); **et** and (3); **minori** less, smaller (4); **non** not (7); **variant** vary, differ (6); **jura** rights, laws (5): About the greater and the less laws do not vary.] *Law.* Laws make no distinction between the greater and the less offense.

démarche *n., pl.* **démarches** [Fr. step, proceeding, overture, representation.] 1. Proceeding. Course of action. Maneuver. *We need to embark upon a démarche which will yield the desired results.* 2. A diplomatic move. A diplomatic maneuver. 3. A representation of views, ideas, or demands, whether formal or informal, to a public functionary. *Members of the union made a démarche to the management about conditions of service.*

de materia in exitu *adj.* [L. **de** of, from, about, for (1); **materia** matter, subject (2); **in** in, on (3); **exitu** departure, outcome, issue (4): about the matter in issue.] Concerning the matter at hand.

de medietate linguae *adj.* [L. **de** of, from, about, for (1); **medietate** the middle, midst (2); **linguae** of language (3): from the middle of language.] *Law.* Of a jury half of whom are aliens, while the other half are citizens. Applicable to an arrangement in English law before 1870 whereby an alien or a foreign trader could be tried before such a jury.

de melioribus damnis *adj.* [L. **de** of, from, about, for (1); **melioribus** better (2); **damnis** damages (3): for/ of the better damages.] *Law.* Applicable to an action involving a joint tort where the damages against the defendants have been assessed separately and the plaintiff chooses which of the defendants against whom to take judgment.

demens *n.* [L. out of one's senses, foolish, distracted.] A person who is out of his senses or has lost his mind. Cf. **amens, amentia,** and **dementia.**

démenti *n., pl.* **démentis** [Fr. contradiction, refutation, denial.] A formal or official statement denying the veracity of a report. *The Ministry of Information issued a démenti on the incident reported by the newspaper, but people still preferred the newspaper's version to the Ministry's.*

dementia *n., pl.* **dementiae** or **dementias** [L. madness, insanity, senselessness.] Mental disorder. A form of mental disorder marked by considerable decline in the patient's former intellectual ability and from which there cannot be full recovery. a) *His erratic behavior is not unlike that of a person who is suffering from dementia.* b) *Sir Matthew Hale thought that dementia was one of several other forms of incapacity which might exempt a person from criminal liability, but which ordinarily do not excuse him from civil liability . . .* (Rogers 1975:609).

dementia affectata *n.* [L. **dementia** madness, insanity, senselessness (2); **affectata** affected, feigned (1): affected/feigned madness.] Pretended insanity.

dementia praecox or **dementia precox** *n., pl.* **dementiae praecoces** or **dementiae precoces** [L. **dementia** madness, insanity, senselessness (2); **praecox** premature (1): premature madness.] *Medicine.* **Schizophrenia** (q.v.). Adolescent insanity. The term covers a wide variety of mental disturbances that occur at a relatively early age.

demi-mondain or **demi mondain** *adj.* [Fr. **demi** half, partial (1); **mondain** social (2): half social.] Belonging to the outskirts of society. Characteristic of the **demi-monde** (q.v.).

demi-mondaine or **demi mondaine** *n., pl.* **demi-mondaines** or **demi mondaines** [Fr. **demi** half, partial (1); **mondaine** socialite (2): half socialite, a woman on the fringe of society.] A woman who belongs to the **demi-monde** (q.v.). A woman of questionable reputation. See **hetaera.**

demi-monde or **demi monde** *n., pl.* **demi-mondes** or **demi mondes** [Fr. **demi** half, partial (1); **monde** world, society (2): half world, dissolute society, outskirts of society.] 1. Class of women on the edge of respectable society who are not prostitutes but who are supported financially by wealthy lovers. 2. People, such as professionals, who are engaged in dubious, improper, unprofessional or illegal activities. See **hetaera.**

de minimis *adj.* [L. **de** of, from, about, for (1); **minimis** very little (things) (2): about very little things.] Trivial. Minute. Trifling. Insignificant. Unimportant. Minimal. Tiny. Microscopic. *The electoral commissioners, for example, often said that a particular challenge by PAN was de minimis; . . .* (*The Economist* 1987).

de minimis non curat lex. [L. **de** of, from, about, for (4); **minimis** very little (things) (5); **non** not (2); **curat** cares (3); **lex** law (1): The law does not care about very little things.] The law pays no attention to trifles.

demi-saison *adj.* [Fr. **demi** half (1); **saison** season (2): half season.] Pertaining to the period of time between one social season and another. *Demi-saison fashion.*

démodé *adj.* [Fr. outmoded.] Old-fashioned. Out of date. Outdated. Outmoded. Obsolete. a) *Fashions have a way of moving in cycles, and a fashion which is démodé today may well be the fashion of a subsequent age.* b) *The publishers took a long time to release the book and, by the time it came out, it had become démodé.* Cf. **dépassé.**

demoiselle *n., pl.* **demoiselles** or **desmoiselles** [Fr. an unmarried woman.] A young lady. An unmarried lady. A damsel. A spinster.

de morte hominis nulla est cunctatio longa. [L. **de** of, from, about, for (1); **morte** death (2); **hominis** of person, human being (3); **nulla** no (4); **est** is (6); **cunctatio** delay (5); **longa** long (7): About the death of person no delay is long.] Where there is a question of life or death, no delay is too long. See **in favorem vitae** etc.; **interest reipublicae quod** etc.; and **La ley favour** etc.

de mortuis nil nisi bonum. [L. **de** of, from, about, for (1); **mortuis** dead (persons) (2); **nil** nothing (3); **nisi** except, unless (4); **bonum** good (5): About dead persons, nothing except good.] Say nothing but what is good about the dead.

demos *n., pl.* **demoi** [Gk. **dēmos** district, sovereign people, common people, democracy, popular assembly.] 1. *Ancient Greece.* The people of a state, particularly a democratic state. *The demos of ancient Athens wielded power both in theory and in practice.* 2. The populace. The masses. The common people. *Democracy, though commendable, can easily deteriorate into the tyranny of the demos.* 3. The entire people of a nation. See **canaille.**

de nada [Sp. **da** of (1); **nada** nothing (2): of nothing.] It was nothing. You're welcome. Cf. **de rien** and **prego.**

denarius *n., pl.* **denarii** [L. coin.] *Ancient Rome.* 1. A silver coin. 2. The denarius aureus, a gold coin worth 25 silver denarii. —*abbr.* **d.** *Great Britain. Obsolete.* A penny. E.g., one penny = 1 d. Cf. **dinaro** and **shekel.**

denarius Dei *n.* [L. **denarius** coin (1); **Dei** of God (2): God's coin.] A penny or small sum of money given as a token or other pledge, particularly after the conclusion of a bargain or contract of purchase. See **argentum Dei.**

De natura deorum *n.* [L. **de** of, from, about, for (1); **natura** nature (2); **deorum** of the gods (3): about the nature of the gods.] *On the Nature of the Gods*, a theological treatise by Cicero (106–43 B.C.).

denier à Dieu *n., pl.* **deniers à Dieu** [Fr. **denier** penny (1); **à** to, toward, in, by, with, until (2); **Dieu** God (3): a penny to God.] God's penny. Pledge money. Deposit on transaction. **denarius Dei.** See **argentum Dei.**

de non apparentibus, et non existentibus, eadem est ratio. [L. **de** of, from, about, for (1); **non** not (2); **apparentibus** appearing (things) (3); **et** and (4); **non** not (5); **existentibus** existing (things) (6); **eadem** the same (9); **est** is (3); **ratio** principle, consideration (7): About things not appearing and about things not existing, the principle is the same.] *Law.* The rule in legal proceedings about things not apparent and things not existing is the same; i.e., documents, deeds, etc. which cannot be produced in court are regarded as nonexistent. See **idem est non esse** etc. and **quod non apparet** etc.

de non sane memorie *adj.* [Obs. Fr. **de** of (1); **non** not (2); **sane** sound (3); **memorie** memory (4): of not sound memory.] Of unsound memory. **Non compos mentis** (q.v.).

de nos jours *adj.* [Fr. **de** of, by, from (1); **nos** our (2); **jours** days (3): of our days.] Belonging to our time. Contemporary. *The fashion de nos jours is much more practical than it was years ago.*

dénouement or **denouement** *n., pl.* **dénouements** or **denouements** [Fr. an untying or unraveling; a solution, issue, end, outcome, unraveling of plot of play.] 1. The final solution or unraveling of the complexities of the plot of a play or other literary work. *There is also the victorious struggle, used here as the dénouement, of the strong man with the demon of death, . . .* (Lesky 1966:36). 2. The final outcome of a complicated situation or a series of events. *The complicated and sordid affair reached its dénouement when the evil machinations of the overambitious official were exposed.*

de nouveau *adv.* [Fr. **de** of, by, from (1); **nouveau** new (2): from new.] Anew. Again. **De novo** (q.v.).

de novo *adv.* [L. **de** of, from, about, for (1); **novo** new (2): from new.] Anew. A second time. Afresh. Over again. *The case was tried de novo on the orders of the Chief Justice.* See **de integro** and **ex integro.**

Dentariae Medicinae Doctor *abbr.* **D.M.D.** *n.* [L. **dentariae** of Dental (2); **medicinae** (of) medicine

(3); **doctor** teacher (1): teacher of dental medicine.] Doctor of Dental Medicine. A terminal graduate degree in dentistry.

Deo adjuvante *adv.*[L. **Deo** with God (1); **adjuvante** helping (2): with God helping.] With the help of God. Cf. **Deo favente**; **Deo volente**; and **Domino volente**.

de odio et atia *n.* [L. **de** of, from, about, for (1); **odio** hatred (2); **et** and (3); **atia** ill will, malice (4): of hatred and ill will.] *Law.* A writ authorizing the sheriff to find out whether a suspect imprisoned for murder was imprisoned on the basis of reasonable suspicion or merely on account of hatred and ill will. If the first alternative could not be supported, a second writ is issued admitting the suspect to bail. Cf. **propter odium et atiam**.

Deo favente *adv.* [L. **Deo** with God (1); **favente** supporting, showing favor (2): with God supporting.] With the favor of God. Cf. **Deo adjuvante**; **Deo volente**; and **Domino volente**.

De officiis *n.* [L. **de** of, from, about, for (1); **officiis** offices, duties, tasks (2): about duties.] *On Duty*, a philosophical dialogue by Cicero (106–43 B.C.).

Deo gratias *abbr.* **D.G.** *interj.* [L. **Deo** to God (2); **gratias** thanks (1): Thanks to God.] Thanks to God.

Deo optimo maximo *abbr.* **D.O.M.** [L. **Deo** to God (1); **optimo** (to) best (2); **maximo** (to) greatest (3): To God, best, greatest.] To God, the best and the greatest. A dedicatory inscription on some works of art.

Deo volente *abbr.* **D.V.** *adv.* [L. **Deo** with God (1); **volente** (with) being willing (2): with God being willing.] God willing. If God permits. With the permission, approval, or sanction of God. *I intend to visit my brother tomorrow, Deo volente.* Cf. **Deo adjuvante**; **Deo favente**; and **Domino volente**.

dépassé *adj.* [Fr. passed, exceeded, surpassed.] Past. Outdated. Obsolete. Outmoded. Out-of-date. a) *In these brash and brutal 1980s, the idea of a meditation room for officials to go and brood about peace, somehow seems dépassé, . . . (West Africa* 1985). b) *The publishers took a long time to release the book and, by the time it came out, the data had become dépassé.* Cf. **démodé**.

dépaysé *fem.* **dépaysée** *adj.* [Fr. strange, out of one's element.] Placed in a strange environment. Not being in one's element or at home. Displaced. *In a society where there is excessive emphasis on ethnicity, one usually feels dépaysé when one leaves his/her locality and resides elsewhere.*

depositum *n., pl.* **deposita** or **depositums** [L. a deposit, trust, bailment.] 1. *Roman and Civil Law.* A bailment of goods to be kept gratis for the bailor's use, the bailee or depositary deriving no benefit from it. 2. Deposit. Something, such as money, put at a place for safekeeping or as a pledge. 3. A depository or place of deposit.

depositum miserabile *n., pl.* **deposita miserabilia** [L. **depositum** deposit (2); **miserabile** miserable (1): miserable deposit.] Necessary deposit. See **depositum necessarium**.

depositum necessarium *n., pl.* **deposita necessaria** [L. **depositum** deposit (2); **necessarium** necessary (1): necessary deposit.] Property deposited with, or entrusted to, another person when there is an unexpected emergency or a disaster such as fire, flood, or earthquake. See **depositum miserabile**.

depot *n., pl.* **depots** [Fr. dépôt deposit, storeroom, storehouse, warehouse, depository.] 1. *Law.* A deposit. Something deposited either voluntarily or under compulsion. 2. *Law.* Something deposited in accordance with the agreement of the parties, or because of a pending litigation, or in compliance with the order of a court. 3. A place where things are stored and distributed. A warehouse. 4. A place where military, para-military, and naval equipment or supplies are received, stored, classified, maintained, and forwarded. 5. A place where military or police recruits are trained. 6. A railroad or bus station.

de profundis *n.* [**de** of, from, about (1); **profundis** the depths (2): from the depths.] Out of the depths. 1. The first words of Psalm 130. 2. An especially profound and sorrowful expression of misery or despondency. *His statement after his condemnation to death was an unforgettable de profundis which aroused immense sympathy among the audience.*

déraciné *adj., pl.* **déracinés** [Fr. uprooted.] Displaced. Removed from the normal place or position. —*n.* Someone who has been displaced from his/her home, country, occupation, or social position. *The déracinés gathered together daily to commiserate with each other.*

de rationabili parte bonorum *n.* [L. **de** of, from, about, for (1); **rationabili** reasonable (2); **parte** part, portion (3); **bonorum** of the goods, property (4): about a reasonable portion of the goods/property.] *Law.* A writ which lay for the children and widow against the executors of the deceased person's will to recover a third or a reasonable portion of the estate after the debts had been settled. *. . . a special common law writ called 'de rationabili parte bonorum' by which wife and children could enforce recovery of their shares* (Bentsi-Enchill 1964:204).

de règle *adj./adv.* [Fr. **de** of, by (1); **règle** order, rule (2): of/by rule, order or law.] According to rule or order. Required or dictated by convention, rule or law. Customary.

De re publica *n.* [L. **de** of, from, about, for (1); **re** matter, thing, business, affair (3); **publica** public (2): about the public affair, about the republic.] *On the Republic*, a philosophical dialogue and political treatise by Cicero (106–43 B.C.) in which Scipio Aemilianus, Laelius, and other Romans of the 2nd century B.C. discuss the ideal state. The book survives only in part, including the **Somnium Scipionis** (q.v.).

de rerum natura Lucretius (c.94–c.55 B.C.). [L. **de** of, from, about, for (1); **rerum** of matters, things, property, business, affairs (3); **natura** nature (2): about the nature of things.] Concerning the nature of things. —**De rerum natura** *On the Nature of Things*, the title of Lucretius' philosophical epic poem on epicurean philosophy and the atomic theory of Democritus.

Der Fliegende Holländer *n.* [Ger. **der** the (1); **fliegende** flying (2); **Holländer** Hollander, Dutchman (3): the flying Dutchman.] "The Flying Dutchman," an 1841 opera by Richard Wagner (1813–1883).

Der Freischütz *n.* [Ger. **der** the (1); **frei** free (2); **Schütz** shooter (3): the free shooter.] "The Free Shooter," the first German romantic opera (1821) by Carl Maria von Weber (1786–1826). The plot is based upon a suitor contest in the form of a shooting match in which the suitor sells his soul for some magic bullets.

de rien *adv.* [Fr. **de** of (1); **rien** nothing (2): of nothing.] It was nothing. You're welcome. Cf. **da nada** and **prego**.

de rigueur *adj.* [Fr. **de** of, in (1); **rigueur** strictness, severity (2): in strictness.] Obligatory. Indispensable. Proper. Compulsory. Required by the dictates of custom, etiquette, or fashion. *For that one night, suits and ties are de rigueur even for IBM's most honored researchers* (*Newsweek Int.* Jan 10, 1983:39).

derivativa potestas non potest esse major primitiva. [L. **derivativa** derived (1); **potestas** power (2); **non** not (4); **potest** can, is able (3); **esse** to be (5); **major** greater, bigger (6); **primitiva** than primitive, original (7): Derived power cannot be greater than the original/principal power.] *Law.* An authority which is derived cannot be greater than the authority from which it is derived. See **accessorium non ducit** etc.

dernier cri *n.* [Fr. **dernier** last, latest (1); **cri** cry, shout (2): the latest cry.] The latest fashion, style, or thing. The newest fashion. The rage. The last word. The most authoritative thing. *Joe and Mary are a dashing couple and they are always the first to wear the dernier cri in town.*

dernier ressort *n.* [Fr. **dernier** last, latest (1); **ressort** resort, line (2): last resort.] Last expedient. Final recourse. *After countless futile complaints, Irene took to legal redress as her dernier ressort.*

derrière or **derriere** *n., pl.* **derrières** or **derrieres** [Fr. behind, posterior.] The posterior. The behind. The buttocks. *She slipped on the ice and fell on her derrière.*

Der Ring des Nibelungen *n.* [Ger. **der** the (1); **Ring** ring (2); **des** of the (3); **Nibelungen** Nibelungs (4): the ring of the Nibelung.] 1. The ring of the **Nibelung** (q.v.). A magic ring taken from a wealthy dwarf by the Norse hero Siegfried. 2. An operatic tetralogy by Richard Wagner (1813–1883). Cf. **Das Rhinegold**; **Die Walküre**; and **Nibelungenlied**.

Der Schauspieldirecktor *n.* [Ger. **der** the **Schauspiel** play (2); **Direcktor** director (3): the play director.] "The Play Director." "The Impresario." A one-act satirical opera for which Wolfgang Amadeus Mozart (1756–1791) wrote the music.

desaparecido *n., pl.* **desaparecidos** [Sp. disappeared, vanished, or missing person.] *Argentina.* Thousands of men, women, and children who vanished during the military regime's war against leftist "subversionists" in the 1970s. *. . . right-wing officers arrested six prominent human-rights activists and detained 68 relatives of desaparecidos* (*Newsweek Int.* March 30, 1981:23).

de sa vie *adj.* [Fr. **de** of (1); **sa** his/her, one's own (2); **vie** life, lifetime (3): of one's own lifetime.] *Law.* For one's own lifetime. During one's lifetime. Applicable to tenancy of an estate. Cf. **autre vie**.

descriptio personae *n.* [L. **descriptio** description (1); **personae** of person (2): description of the person.] *Law.* Matter which merely describes the persons of the parties and has no effect on a legal document's validity. Cf. **designatio personae**.

deshabille or **dishabille** *n.* [Fr. **déshabillé** undressed.] 1. A state of partial undress. *The police burst into the room to encounter a very distressed couple in extreme deshabille.* 2. Casual dress. *The princess greeted her visitors in simple deshabille.*

desideratum *abbr.* **desid.** *n., pl.* **desiderata** [L. that which is desired.] Something desired as essential or necessary. Something aimed at or sought for. *Peace of mind is a desideratum for anybody who wants to live a happy and successful life.*

desiderium *n., pl.* **desideria** [L. desire, longing.] An ardent longing or desire. Used especially with reference to feeling of grief for something that is lost.

designatio personae *n.* [L. **designatio** designation, specification (1); **personae** of person (2): designation of the person.] *Law.* Matter which not only designates the persons of the parties to a legal document but also is essential to its validity. Cf. **descriptio personae**.

designatio unius est exclusio alterius, et expressum facit cessare tacitum. [L. **designatio** specification (1); **unius** of one (2); **est** is (3); **exclusio** exclusion (4); **alterius** of another, the other (5); **et** and (6); **expressum** the expressed (7); **facit** makes (8); **cessare** to cease (10); **tacitum** the unmentioned, implied (9): The specification of one is the exclusion of the other, and the expressed makes the implied to cease.] *Law.* When one is specified/appointed, the other is excluded, and what is expressed supersedes what is implied. See **affirmatio unius** etc.; **enumeratio unius** etc.; **expressio unius est** etc.; **expressio unius personae** etc.; **expressum facit** etc.; **inclusio unius** etc.; and **posito uno** etc.

de similibus idem est judicandum. [L. **de** of, from, about, for (1); **similibus** like, similar (things) (2); **idem** the same (5); **est** it is (3); **judicandum** to be judged, decided (4): About like things, it is to be judged the same.] *Law.* The judgment in similar cases must be the same. See **de similibus idem est judicium.**

de similibus idem est judicium [L. **de** of, from, about, for (1); **similibus** like, similar (things) (2); **idem** the same (5); **est** is (4); **judicium** judgment (3): About like things, the judgment is the same.] *Law.* The judgment in similar cases is the same. See **de similibus idem est judicandum; eadem est ratio** etc.; **in consimili casu, consimile** etc.; **ubi eadem ratio, ibi idem jus**; and **ubi eadem ratio, ibi eadem lex** etc.

de son tort *adj.* [Fr. **de** of (1); **son** his/her, one's own (2); **tort** wrong, fault (3): of one's own wrong.] Wrongful. Unlawful. Illegitimate. *Law.* Used to describe an executor, administrator or trustee who assumed the position wrongfully or without lawful authority. *If, when there is no lawful representative, one who is neither executor nor administrator, intermeddles with the goods of the deceased, or does any act which is characteristic of the office of executor, he thereby makes himself liable as an executor de son tort* (Parry 1961:296).

desunt cetera. or **desunt caetera.** [L. **desunt** are missing (2); **cetera** the rest, the other things (1): The rest are missing.] **cetera desunt** (q.v.).

desunt nonnulla. [L. **desunt** are missing (2); **nonnulla** not-none, some, several (things) (1): Some things are missing.] Some portions are missing. Used to indicate that substantial portions of a manuscript cannot be found. Cf. **cetera desunt** and **desunt cetera.**

de tempore in tempus *adv.* [L. **de** of, from, about, for (1); **tempore** time (2); **in** into, to, against, for (3); **tempus** time (4): from time to time.] Occasionally. Cf. **de temps en temps.**

de temps en temps *adv.* [Fr. **de** from (1); **temps** time, weather (2); **en** in, to (3); **temps** time, weather (4): from time to time.] Occasionally. Now and then. Cf. **de tempore in tempus.**

détente *n., pl.* **détentes** [Fr. relaxation, slackening, improvement, easing.] Relaxation, easing or slackening of strained political relations between countries. a) *East-West détente.* b) *Until now, the most difficult single obstacle to Sino-Soviet détente has been the Kremlin's unwillingness to take the first step in breaking the deadlock* (*Newsweek Int.* Aug. 2, 1982:33).

detour *n., pl.* **detours** [Fr. **détour** turning away, indirect route.] 1. A roundabout route, especially a temporary alternate to a main road or path. 2. A temporary departure from a main or usual course of action. —*v.* To turn aside from a main route or course of action.

détournement *n.* [Fr. diversion, misappropriation, embezzlement, fraudulent misuse.] *Law.* Misappropriation of a master's property by a servant. Abuse of confidence or trust, i.e., fraudulent misuse of goods, money, documents, etc. given for a specific purpose. Cf. **abus de confiance.**

détournement de pouvoir *n.* [Fr. **détournement** diversion (1); **de** of (2); **pouvoir** power, authority (3): diversion of power.] Abuse of power. Using power, conferred for one purpose, to achieve a different goal. *The official behaves as though the institution is his patrimony and, by a flagrant détournement de pouvoir, he uses its resources for his selfish ends.*

de toutes pièces *adv.* [Fr. **de** from (1); **toutes** all (2); **pièces** parts, pieces (3): from all parts.] Completely. Wholly. Entirely. At all points. Fully. *Credit must be given to Bonsu for conceiving the idea de toutes pièces.*

de trop *adj.* [Fr. **de** of (1); **trop** too much (2): of too much.] Too much. Too many. Unwanted. In excess. Superfluous. Unwelcome. *Wearing a woollen three-piece suit at Maiduguri in April is simply de trop.*

de una parte *adj./adv.* [L. **de** of, from, about, for (1); **una** one (2); **parte** part, side (3): from one part/side.] *Law.* From one party. Applicable to a deed where the grant or obligation is unilateral. *Anda signed and executed a deed de una parte today.* See **ex parte.**

deus ex machina or *fem.* **dea ex machina** *n., pl.* **dei ex machina** or *fem.* **deae ex machina** [L. **deus** God (1); **ex** out of (2); **machina** machine (3): a god out of a machine.] 1. *Greek Tragedy.* A contrivance introduced extraneously to solve the complexities of a play. 2. A person/thing which appears to solve a seemingly insoluble problem. *In her testimony, Mrs. Obi described her husband as an indolent man who makes no effort to solve the problems of the family, and apparently looks for a deus ex machina.*

Deus vobiscum [L. **Deus** God (1); **vobis** you (3); **cum** with, together (2): God with you (pl.).] May God be with you. Cf. **Dominus vobiscum.**

Deus vult [L. **Deus** God (1); **vult** wishes (2): God wishes.] God wishes it. This phrase, shouted out to Pope Urban II at the Council of Clermont in 1095, became the slogan of the First Crusade.

Deutschland über alles *n.* [Ger. **Deutschland** Germany (1); **über** over, above (2); **alles** everything (3): Germany over everything.] The title of German national anthem until the end of the Second World War.

devastavit *n., pl.* **devastavits** [L. He has laid waste. He has devastated.] *Law.* 1. An administrator's or executor's wasting of the goods, or mismanagement of the estate, of the decedent, for which the administrator or executor can be sued by creditors and legatees. *A devastavit is a mismanagement of the estate in misapplying its assets* (Hanbury 1962:506). 2. A writ for seeking remedy for such wastage.

de ventre inspiciendo *n.* [L. **de** of, from, about, for (1); **ventre** womb, belly (2); **inspiciendo** to be inspected/examined (3): for a womb to be inspected.] *Law.* Writ to ascertain whether or not a woman is pregnant.

de verbo in verbum *adv./adj.* [L. **de** of, from, about, for (1); **verbo** word (2); **in** into, to, against, for (3); **verbum** word (4): from word to word.] Word for word.

The witness quoted the statement of the accused person de verbo in verbum. See **verbatim et litteratim**.

dewan *n.* [Hindi **dīvān** from Pers. a bundle of sheets of paper, an account book, a roster, an assembly.] A government official in India. Cf. **divan**.

d'expression française *adj.* [Fr. **d'** of (1); **expression** expression, utterance (3); **française** French (2): of French expression.] Francophone. French-speaking. *... let us start with the literature on West Africa d'expression française written in English* (Y.Y. in *West Africa* 1982).

D.F. *abbr.* for **Defensor Fidei** (q.v.).

D.G. *abbr.* for 1. **Dei gratia** (q.v.). 2. **Deo gratias** (q.v.).

dharma *n.* [Skt. statute, law.] 1. *Hinduism and Buddhism.* The ordering principle of the universe and the code of individual conduct based upon this principle. 2. *Hinduism.* The obligations of an individual based upon caste, custom, and law. 3. *Buddhism.* The collective teachings of Buddha.

dharna *n.* [Hindi **dharnā**.] A fast carried out at the door of a debtor or wrong-doer in order to obtain justice.

diacope *n., pl.* **diacopae** or **diacopes** [Gk. **diakopē**: **dia** through, across, completely (2); **kopē** cutting (1): cutting through.] *Rhetoric.* A form of **epizeuxis** (q.v.) or word repetition in which the repeated words are separated by another word; e.g., "I shall say it again and again and again: Your boys are not going to be sent into any foreign wars" (Franklin Delano Roosevelt in 1940).

diaeresis or **dieresis** *n., pl.* **diaereses** or **diereses** [Gk. **diaiersis**: **dia** through, across, completely (2); **(h)airesis** taking (1): taking apart, dividing.] *Linguistics.* Resolution of a diphthong. 2. The diacritic sign; i.e., two periods [¨] put over a vowel as an indication that it is to be pronounced separately; e.g., naïve.

diagnosis *n., pl.* **diagnoses** [Gk. **diagnōsis**: **dia** through, across, completely (2); **gnōsis** knowing (1): knowing through, knowing completely, knowing apart, power of discernment, means of discerning or distinguishing.] 1. *Medicine.* Examining symptoms or signs to recognize a disease and determine its nature. The decision itself. *... the diagnosis of the disease indicated that it was either yellow fever or infectious hepatitis* (*Sunday Tribune*, 1986). 2. An analysis or investigation to determine the nature or cause of a situation, condition, event, problem, difficulty, or phenomenon. *The novel presents the moving drama of an adolescent youth, the story of whose near destruction underscores the author's perceptive diagnosis of a social illness plaguing his society* (*West Africa* 1987).

diaspora *n., pl.* **diasporas** [Gk. **dia** through, across, in different directions, completely (2); **spora** sowing, scattering (1): sowing in different directions, dispersion.] 1. Jews living outside Palestine after the Babylonian captivity. Jews living outside Palestine or modern Israel, or anywhere in the so-called Gentile

world. 2. The dispersion, scattering or spread of people of one nationality, race, faith, etc. into other countries. *Ghanaians in the diaspora are in many respects very different from the nationals of other African countries* (Thomas Cooke in *West Africa* 1985). 3. People of one country, continent, faith, etc. dispersed or scattered into other countries, continents, etc. *The Ghanaian diaspora in Britain has features which distinguish it from other African diasporas.*

dictamen *n., pl.* **dictamina** [Late L. that which is said, a saying, decree.] Pronouncement. Rule. Dictate. *The world is full of many worthless men who do not act according to the dictamen of reason or conscience, but are mere puppets manipulated by unscrupulous potentates.*

dictator or *fem.* **dictatrix** *n., pl.* **dictators** or *fem.* **dictatrices** [L. one who says repeatedly or orders.] 1. *Ancient Rome.* A chief magistrate nominated by a consul after a proposal by the Senate during times of emergency and invested with absolute power and authority. The dictator had to abdicate office after six months or as soon as the emergency which necessitated his appointment had come to an end. 2. A person, leader, or ruler who wields power autocratically, absolutely, authoritatively, ruthlessly, oppressively, or brutally.

dictum *n., pl.* **dicta** [L. word, saying.] 1. Saying. Statement. A formal or authoritative pronouncement. *The dictum, "Man is the measure of all things," has almost the same meaning as the dictum, "Beauty is in the eyes of the beholder."* 2. *Law.* An opinion expressed by a judge on a point which may not necessarily arise from or be related to a case in question.

dictum de omni et nullo [L. **dictum** maxim, saying (1); **de** of, from, about, for (2); **omni** everything (3); **et** and (4); **nullo** nothing (5): maxim about everything and nothing.] *Logic.* An axiom or rule which maintains that any affirmation or denial about a class is applicable to every individual member of the class.

diebus alternis *abbr.* **dieb. alt.** [L. **diebus** (on) days (2); **alternis** on alternate (1): on alternate days.] Every other day. See **alternis diebus**.

Die Entführung aus dem Serail *n.* [Ger. **die** the (1); **Entführung** abduction (2); **aus** from (3); **dem** the (4); **Serail** seraglio, harem (5): the abduction from the seraglio.] "Abduction from the Seraglio," a comic opera (1782) by Wolfgang Amadeus Mozart (1756–1791), his first in German. Cf. **seraglio**.

Die Frau ohne Schatten *n.* [Ger. **die** the (1); **Frau** woman (2); **ohne** without (3); **Schatten** a shadow, figure (4): the woman without a shadow.] "The Woman without a Shadow," an opera by Richard Strauss (1864–1949).

die goldene medina *n.* [Yid. **die** the (1); **goldene** golden (2); **medina** state (3): the golden Medina.] The golden state or place of refuge, like the city of Medina in Saudi

Arabia which served as the refuge for the prophet Muhammad. . . . *most Soviet Jewish émigrés regard the U.S. as die goldene medina . . . (Time Int.* 1982).

Die Jungfrau von Orleans *n.* [Ger. **die** the (1); **Jungfrau** maid, young woman, girl (2); **von** of, from (3); **Orleans** Orleans (4): the maid of Orleans.] "The Maid of Orleans," a play about Joan of Arc by Friedrich von Schiller (1759–1805).

Die Meistersinger von Nürnberg *pl. n.* [Ger. **die** the (1); **Meistersinger** mastersingers (2); **von** of, from (3); **Nürnberg** Nurenburg (4): the mastersingers of Nurenburg.] "The Mastersingers of Nurenburg," a 1867 opera by Richard Wagner (1813–1883).

Die Politik ist keine exakte Wissenschaft. Otto von Bismarck (1815–1898). [Ger. **die** the (1); **Politik** politics (2); **ist** is (3); **keine** not an (4); **exakte** exact, precise (5); **Wissenschaft** knowledge, science, scholarship (6): The politics is not an exact science.] Politics is not an exact science.

Die Religion ist das Opium des Volkes. Karl Marx (1818–1883). [Ger. **die** the (1); **Religion** religion (2); **ist** is (3); **das** the (4); **Opium** opium (5); **des** of the (6); **Volkes** people (7): Religion is the opium of the people.] Religion serves as a narcotic for the masses or common people.

dies ad quem *n.* [L. **dies** day (1); **ad** to, at, for, according to (2); **quem** which (3): the day to which.] *Civil Law.* The day of the conclusion of a transaction; e.g., interest on a loan. Cf. **dies a quo.**

dies a quo *n.* [L. **dies** day (1); **a** from (2); **quo** which (3): the day from which.] *Civil Law.* The day of the commencement of a transaction; e.g., interest on a loan. See **a quo; terminus a quo;** and **terminus post quem.** Cf. **ad quem; dies ad quem; terminus ad quem;** and **terminus ante quem.**

dies Dominicus *n.* [L. **dies** day (1); **dominicus** of the lord (2): the day of the Lord.] The Lord's day, i.e., Sunday.

dies Dominicus non est juridicus. [L. **dies** day (1); **dominicus** of the lord (2); **non** not (4); **est** is (3); **juridicus** of justice (5): The day of the Lord is not a day of justice.] Sunday is not a court day. Sunday is not a day for legal proceedings.

dies inceptus pro completo habetur. [L. **dies** day (1); **inceptus** begun (2); **pro** as (4); **completo** completed (5); **habetur** is had, held, regarded (3): A day begun is regarded as a day completed.] A partial day is counted like a full day in a legal contract or agreement. Cf. **annus inceptus** etc.

dies irae *n.* [L. **dies** day (1); **irae** of wrath, anger (2): day of wrath or anger.] 1. The Last Day. The Day of Judgment. 2. The first words and the name of a 13th-century Latin hymn about the Last Judgment traditionally sung at a funeral Mass. 3. Any day of wrath or judgment. *The spendthrift dreaded the dies irae when his notes came due.*

dies non *n.* [L. **dies** day (1); **non** not (2): a day not.] A day on which business is not conducted.

Die Tat ist alles, nicht der Ruhm. Johann Wolfgang von Goethe (1749–1832). *Faust* II. [Ger. **die** the (1); **Tat** act, deed (2); **ist** is (3); **alles** all, everything (4); **nicht** not (5); **der** the (6); **Ruhm** glory, fame (7): The deed is everything, not the fame.] The deed is everything, the glory nothing.

Dieu et mon droit [Fr. **Dieu** God (1); **et** and (2); **mon** my (3); **droit** right, law (4): God and my right.] Motto on the royal arms of England. It was first adopted by Richard I.

Dieu me pardonnera. C'est son métier. Heinrich Heine (1797–1856). [**Dieu** God (1); **me** me (3); **pardonnera** will forgive, pardon (2); **c'** it (4); **est** is (5); **son** his (6); **métier** trade, profession (7): God will pardon me. It is His trade.] It is God's job to forgive me.

Dieu son acte [Obs. Fr. **Dieu** God (1); **son** his (2); **acte** act, deed (3): God, His act.] *Archaic Law.* An act of God. **Actus Dei** (q.v.).

Die Walküre *pl. n.* [Ger. **die** the (1); **Walküre** Valkuries (2): the Valkuries.] "The Valkuries," the first opera (1854) in the Ring tetralogy by Richard Wagner (1813–1883). Cf. **Das Rhinegold; Der Ring des Nibelungen;** and **Nibelungenlied.**

Die Zauberflöte *n.* [Ger. **die** the (1); **Zauber** magic (2); **flöte** flute (3): the magic flute.] "The Magic Flute," a 1791 German opera by Wolfgang Amadeus Mozart (1756–1791).

differentia *n., pl.* **differentiae** [L. difference, diversity, distinction.] 1. A mark or characteristic which distinguishes one thing from another, especially one species from others or another in the same genus. 2. A feature, characteristic, factor, etc., which distinguishes one individual, condition, state, group, or class from another. *Man is essentially an animal, but there are some differentiae which distinguish him from the lower animals.*

difficile est longum subito deponere amorem. Catullus (87–54 B.C.). *Carmina* LXXVI,13. [L. **difficile** difficult (2); **est** it is (1); **longum** long, long-continued (5); **subito** suddenly (3); **deponere** to put/lay aside, get rid of (4); **amorem** love (6): It is difficult suddenly to lay aside long-continued love.] It is hard for someone to put aside a long-standing love on short notice.

difficilior lectio *n., pl.* **difficiliores lectiones** [L. **difficilior** more difficult (1); **lectio** reading (2): more difficult reading.] The more difficult reading. A principle of manuscript editing which assumes that the harder reading is more likely than an easier reading to be closer to original text. Cf. **varia lectio.**

difficilius est invenire quam vincere. Julius Caesar (101–44 B.C.). [L. **difficilius** more difficult (2); **est** it is (1); **invenire** to find out, discover (3); **quam** than (4); **vincere** to overcome, subdue (5): It is more difficult to find out (or discover) than to subdue.] It is harder to find a way than to conquer. *I may say in this case, difficilius est invenire quam vincere, as Caesar said when he and his Army ran about the Alps to find out a way* (per Treby C. J. in Monnington v. Davis [1695] Fort. 224 at 227 quoted by Megarry 1955:158).

diktat *n., pl.* **diktats** [Ger. **Diktat** dictation, an order, command, imposition.] A settlement, treaty, etc., imposed by a victorious power on a defeated enemy. **Fiat** (q.v.). *"The Soviet Union is a great power which has never allowed and will never allow anyone to speak to it in the language of blackmail and diktat,"* Tass snapped (*Newsweek Int.* Jan. 11, 1982:8).

dilationes in lege sunt odiosae. [L. **dilationes** delays, postponements (1); **in** in, on (2); **lege** law (3); **sunt** are (4); **odiosae** hateful, vexatious, unpleasant (5): Delays in law are hateful.] *Law.* Adjournments/delays in legal proceedings are vexatious. See **infinitum in** etc.

dilemma *n., pl.* **dilemmas** [Gk. **di** twice, in two (1); **lēmma** premise, proposition (2): a proposition in two, an ambiguous proposition.] 1. An argument or debate in which an opponent is offered a choice between two alternatives, neither of which is favorable. 2. A situation in which one has to choose between two alternatives, neither of which is pleasant, satisfactory, appealing, or desirable. a) *Rifaat demonstrates the dilemma of woman, the tragedy of being without a man and the disaster of being with one* (Dr. C.O. Ogunyemi in *West Africa* 1985). b) *But to the country's 270 Olympic hopefuls . . . the dilemma was real enough; to boycott the Moscow Games or go for the gold* (*Newsweek Int.* June 30, 1980:46). 3. A perplexing or difficult problem. A problem for which there is no apparent satisfactory solution.

dilettante *n., pl.* **dilettantes** or **dilettanti** [It. one delighting in, a lover.] 1. A person who loves or admires the arts. A connoisseur. 2. A person who pursues, cultivates or shows interest in art, literature, or a branch of knowledge just for amusement or superficially, and does not make it his/her profession. *Sometimes Mr. Marti forgets that he is merely a dilettante and attempts to compete with professional artists.* Cf. **amateur.**

dilexi justitiam et odi iniquitatem, propterea morior in exilio. Gregory VII (c.1020–1085). [L. **dilexi** I have loved, valued (1); **justitiam** justice (2); **et** and (3); **odi** I hate, dislike (4); **iniquitatem** injustice, unfairness (5); **propterea** therefore, for that reason (6); **morior** I die (7); **in** in, on (8); **exilio** exile (9): I have loved justice and I hate injustice; for this reason I die in exile.] I die away from my homeland because I have cherished what is just and hated what is unjust.

dilige et quod vis fac. Augustine of Hippo (354–430). *In Joann.* VII,8. [L. **dilige** love, esteem (1); **et** and

(2); **quod** that which (4); **vis** you wish (5); **fac** do, make (3): Love and do that which you wish.] Love and do whatever you want. Cf. **ama et fac quod vis.**

dimidium facti qui coepit habet. Horace (65–8 B.C.). *Epistles* II,2,40. [L. **dimidium** half (4); **facti** of the deed (5); **qui** (he) who (1); **coepit** has begun (2); **habet** has, holds, regards (3): He who has begun has half of the deed.] He who begins a project has completed half of it. Well begun is half done.

diminutio *n.* [L. decrease, lessening, abatement, loss, forfeiture.] A taking away. Loss or deprivation. See **capitis diminutio.**

dinaro *n., pl.* **dinaros** [Sp. from L. **denarius** coin.] Money. Cf. **denarius** and **shekel.**

Ding an sich *n., pl.* **Dinge an sich** [Ger. **Ding** thing, matter (1); **an** in (2); **sich** itself, themselves (3): a thing in itself.] *Philosophy.* Metaphysical reality. The ultimate reality underlying, or as distinguished from, what can be seen in, or perceived about, an object. See **noumenon.** Cf. **an sich** and **phenomenon.**

dinghy *n., pl.* **dinghies** [Hindi **dīngī** a small boat.] Any small boat, especially a rowboat or inflatable raft.

dipsomania *n.* [Neo-Gk. from Gk. **dips(a)** thirst (2); **mania** insanity (1): insanity of thirst.] *Medicine.* Alcoholism. Abnormal desire for intoxication either through liquor or drugs. See **potomania.**

dirigisme *n., pl.* **dirigismes** [Fr. planning, planned economy, controlled finance.] Economic planning. Planned economy. Planning and control of the economy by the state. *Initially the government adopted a policy of laissez-faire but, when the economy slumped dreadfully, it resorted to dirigisme.*

dirigo [L. I direct.] I lead. Motto of the State of Maine.

dis aliter visum. Vergil (70–19 B.C.). *Aeneid* II,428. [L. **dis** to the gods (3); **aliter** otherwise, differently (2); **visum** having seemed (1): having seemed otherwise to the gods.] God thought (or decided) otherwise. It was not so fated. *Femi planned to proceed for postgraduate studies in engineering, but Dis aliter visum.*

Discours de la Méthode. [Fr. **discours** discourse (1); **de** from, of (2); **la** the (3); **méthode** method (4): the discourse of the method.] *Discourse on Method,* a mathematical and philosophical treatise (1637) by René Descartes (1596–1650). See **cogito ergo sum.**

dishabille *var.* of **deshabille** (q.v.).

disjecta membra *pl. n.* **disjecta** [L. scattered, dispersed (1); **membra** limbs, members (2): scattered limbs or members.] Fragments of a passage, quotation, work, etc. Disjointed or scattered fragments. *The work has not survived in its entirety; what we have are disjecta membra.*

dissentiente *adj.* [L. dissenting, disagreeing.] *Law.* Used to qualify the name of a judge or the names of judges to indicate a dissenting opinion. *Thus in Gregory v. Cattle the headnote shows that the decision was reached by a court consisting of "Charles J. and Hallet*

J. (haesitante), Stable J. dissentiente" (Megarry 1955:310). Cf. **dubitante**; **haesitante**; **nemine contradicente**; **nemine dissentiente**; and **una voce**.

distingué or *fem.* **distinguée** *adj., pl.* **distingués** or *fem.* **distinguées** [Fr. distinguished.] Eminent. Elegant. Imposing. Illustrious.

distractio bonorum *n.* [L. **distractio** dividing, separating (1); **bonorum** of goods (2): a dividing/separating of goods.] *Law.* The retail sale of portions of an insolvent estate to realize enough to satisfy the claims of creditors. Cf. **bonorum emptio**.

distractio pignoris *n.* [L. **distractio** dividing, separating (1); **pignoris** of pledge, security (2): a dividing/separating of pledge.] *Law.* The sale by the creditor of a thing pledged to satisfy his/her claim, if the debtor failed to repay the loan.

distrait or *fem.* **distraite** *adj., pl.* **distraits** or *fem.* **distraites** [Fr. distracted.] Unfocused. Distracted. Absent-minded.

dit *adj.* [Fr. called.] Also known as. Used to indicate a second or alternative name, as *Jean Baptiste Poquelin dit Molière* (1622–1673).

ditat Deus. [L. **ditat** makes rich, enriches (2); **Deus** God (1): God makes rich.] God enriches. Motto of the State of Arizona.

ditto *abbr.* **do.** *n., pl.* **dittos** [It. having been said.] 1. Something or the same thing mentioned above or previously. Used to avoid repetition of a word or words. *He placed a bed in Sale's room; ditto in Aliyu's room.* 2. An exact or approximate copy. *The pleasure of having children is to have a child who is one's ditto.* 3. Marks (″) used to show that the information above should be repeated. —*v. tr.* To a repeat statement, deed, action, etc. *Edwin's successor is absolutely devoid of originality and initiative; he keeps dittoing his predecessor's letters, memoranda, circulars, ideas, etc.* —*v. intr.* To repeat a statement, deed, action, etc. —*adv.* In the same way or manner. Likewise. As previously, aforesaid, or before. *Cognizant of the fact that the electorate was impressed by his previous performance, the politician promised to act ditto.*

diva *n., pl.* **divas** [It. goddess.] The leading, or distinguished, female singer in an opera or concert group. *Diva Beverly Sills stepped into her final dramatic role at the Met last week as Norina . . .* (*Newsweek Int.* Dec. 18, 1978:25). See **prima donna** 1.

divan *n., pl.* **divans** [Pers. **dīvān** a bundle of sheets of paper, an account book, a roster, an assembly.] 1. A couch without a back, often lined with pillows. 2. *Arabia and Ancient Persia.* A collection of literary writings by a single author. 3. An early Islamic census. 4. *Turkey.* A government council or the hall in which it is held. 5. *Moslem Countries.* A department or office of the government. 6. A room with one open side facing a garden, vista, etc. 7. A smoking room or a cigar shop. Cf. **dewan**.

diverso intuitu *adv.* [L. **diverso** with different, contrary (1); **intuitu** (with) view, contemplation (2): with different view or contemplation.] According to a different point of view, perspective, or opinion. *Almost every member of the committee opined that the project should be abandoned, but the chairman, diverso intuitu, disagreed and imposed his decision on the rest.*

divertimento *n., pl.* **divertimentos** [It. diversion.] 1. An entertainment or amusement. 2. *Music.* An instrumental composition which is light in tone and intended primarily for entertainment. See **divertissement**.

divertissement *n., pl.* **divertissements** [Fr. amusement, recreation, relaxation, entertainment, diversion.] 1. An activity which gives pleasure or amusement. *. . . a deliciously accelerating divertissement on the theme of role-playing, sexual and otherwise* (*Newsweek Int.* March 29, 1982:49). 2. *Music.* A **divertimento** (q.v.). 3. *Music.* An operatic interlude which can consist of instrumental compositions, dance, etc. 4. *Music.* A selection of operatic pieces performed as a single composition.

divide et impera *n.* [L. **divide** divide (1); **et** and (2); **impera** rule (3): Divide and rule.] Divide and conquer. The practice, policy, etc. of imposing authority, order, or imperial rule by encouraging disunity among subjects or subordinates. *From time immemorial imperialists have been using to good effect the obnoxious tactics of divide et impera.*

Divinitatis Baccalaureus *abbr.* **D.B.** *n.* [L. **divinitatis** of divinity (2); **baccalaureus** bachelor (1): Bachelor of Divinity.] An undergraduate degree in theological studies.

divisum imperium *n.* [L. **divisum** divided (1); **imperium** command, authority (2): divided command/authority.] *Law.* Divided jurisdiction, i.e., the handling of the same subject by courts of common law and equity.

divorcé *fem.* **divorcée** *n., pl.* **divorcés** or *fem.* **divorcées** [Fr. divorced.] A divorced person.

dixi *v.* [L. I have spoken.] I am finished speaking. Used to mark closure to a speech or to end discussion on a matter. Cf. **dixit**.

dixit *v.* [L. He has spoken.] He has finished speaking. Thus he spoke.

D.Litt. *abbr.* for **Doctor Litterarum** (q.v.).

D.M.D. *abbr.* for **Dentariae Medicinae Doctor** (q.v.).

do. *abbr.* for **ditto** (q.v.).

docendo discimus [L. **docendo** by teaching (2); **discimus** we learn (1): We learn by teaching.] Teachers learn from the act of teaching.

Doctor Honoris Causa *abbr.* **Dr. h.c.** *n.* [L. **doctor** teacher (1); **honoris** of honor (3); **causa** for the sake (2): teacher for the sake of honor.] Doctor for the sake of honor. Honorary doctor. A person awarded an honorary doctoral degree. Cf. **honoris causa**.

Doctor Litterarum *abbr.* **D.Litt.** *n.* [L. **doctor** teacher (1); **litterarum** of letters, literature (2): teacher of letters.] Doctor of Letters. A terminal graduate degree in literature.

Doctor Oeconomiae *abbr.* **D.Oec.** *n.* [L. **doctor** teacher (1); **oeconomiae** of economics (2): teacher of economics.] Doctor of Economics. A terminal graduate degree in economics.

doctrinaire *n., pl.* **doctrinaires** [Fr. pedantic, illiberal, doctrinary, doctrinarian.] 1. A member of a French political party (1815–1830), which held neither an ultra-royalist nor a revolutionary position, but sought a government combining both monarchy and a parliamentary system. 2. A person who attempts to apply a doctrine or theory, especially one that is political, without considering the practical implications. —*adj.* Dogmatic. Theoretical. Of, relating to, pertaining to, or characteristic of, a doctrinaire. Obstinately committed to a theory or doctrine without any consideration whatsoever of its practical implications. a) *As a true-blue conservative, he had been widely expected to select a rigidly doctrinaire jurist in order to stamp his own political ideology on the court* (*Time Int.* 1981). b) *Today, the adoption of a more pragmatic and less doctrinaire approach to issues is quite fashionable* (*The Guardian*, 1987).

D.Oec. *abbr.* for **Doctor Oeconomiae** (q.v.).

dogma *n., pl.* **dogmata** or **dogmas** [Gk. opinion, belief, notion, decision, judgment, decree.] 1. An established or authoritative opinion or tenet. . . . *the Soviets allowed the Poles to violate the communist dogma that party civilians must always control the military* . . . (*Time Int.* 1982). 2. Doctrine formally proclaimed or stated by a school of philosophers, artists, theologians, etc. *Pope Pius XII* [Eugenio Pacelli, 1876–1958, Pope: 1939–1958.] *invoked the doctrine of papal infallibility* . . . *to proclaim as Catholic dogma the bodily assumption of the Virgin Mary into heaven* (*Newsweek Int.* May 18, 1981:52). 3. A vehement or pompous expression of a baseless opinion, put forth as an authoritative tenet. . . . *both Marx and Engels mistrusted the use of the word "Marxism" because they sensed in it the odour of dogma* . . . ('Niyi Alabi in *West Africa* 1983).

dojo *n.* [Japan. **dōjō.**] A school for learning Japanese arts of self-defense.

dolce far niente *n., pl.* **dolce far nientes** [It. **dolce** sweet (1); **far** to do (2); **niente** nothing (3): sweet to do nothing.] Sweet idleness. Pleasant relaxation in careless laziness. *When one has accomplished a great feat, one may justifiably take some time off and enjoy dolce far niente.*

dolce stil nuovo *n.* [It. **dolce** sweet, pleasant (1); **stil** style (3); **nuovo** new (2): sweet new style.] The new, sweet style used by Dantie Alighieri (1265–1321) in his poetry including **La Vita Nuova** (q.v.). Emphasized sincere feelings over elaborate form.

dolce vita *n.* [It. **dolce** sweet, pleasant (1); **vita** life (2): sweet life.] A life of affluence, luxury and sensual pleasures. . . . *Energy Minister Yitzhak Modai denounced Aridor for creating an economic dolce vita in Israel* (*Newsweek Int.* Aug. 22, 1983:23). See **la dolce vita.**

doli capax *adj.* [L. **doli** of malice, guile, fraud (2); **capax** capable (1): capable of fraud.] *Law.* Capable of crime/guilt. Applicable to a person who by age, intelligence, and mental capacity is sufficiently mature to be legally responsible for his/her wrongful acts. Cf. **doli incapax.**

doli incapax *adj.* [L. **doli** of malice, guile, fraud (2); **incapax**; incapable (1): incapable of fraud/malice.] *Law.* Incapable of crime/guilt. Applicable to a person who by reason of age, intelligence, and mental capacity is considered to be not sufficiently mature to be legally responsible for his/her wrongful acts. Cf. **doli capax.**

dolo malo pactum se non servabit. [L. **dolo** (with) fraud (3); **malo** with evil, bad (2); **pactum** pact, agreement (1); **se** itself (6); **non** not (4); **servabit** will preserve, maintain (5): A pact made with evil fraud will not maintain itself.] *Law.* An agreement made with fraud will not stand. See **ex turpi causa** etc.

dolosus versatur in generalibus. [L. **dolosus** deceitful (person) (1); **versatur** is engaged, occupies himself (2); **in** in, on (3); **generalibus** general (things) (4): A deceitful person occupies himself in general things.] A deceitful person uses general terms. Cf. **fraus latet** etc. and **in generalibus latet error.**

dolus *n.* [L. guile, deceit, deception, trickery, fraud.] *Roman, Civil, and Scots Law.* 1. Guile. Deceit. Deceitfulness. Fraud. A contrivance to deceive another. An act or omission designed to deceive the other party or betray the confidence reposed in one. 2. Deception. Fraud. Willful misconduct. Criminal intent. *Unlike culpa, which is merely negligence and for which one may not be liable if it produces damage, one is always liable for dolus which produces damage.*

dolus auctoris non nocet successori. [L. **dolus** fraud, deceit, guile (1); **auctoris** of father, progenitor (2); **non** not (3); **nocet** hurts (4); **successori** successor (5): The fraud of a father does not hurt the successor.] A successor should not be answerable for an ancestor's fraud. See **in restitutionem** etc.

dolus bonus *n.* [L. **dolus** fraud, deceit, guile (2); **bonus** good (1): good deceit.] Cunning, dexterity, or sagacity in transactions or bargaining which is not actionable, punishable, or which may not constitute ground for rescinding the transaction arising from it. Cf. **dolus malus.**

dolus et fraus nemini patrocinentur. [L. **dolus** fraud, deceit, guile (1); **et** and (2); **fraus** fraud (3); **nemini** no one, nobody (5); **patrocinentur** should protect, support (4): Deceit and fraud should protect no one.] No one should derive an advantage/benefit from deceit and fraud. See **ex turpi causa** etc.

dolus malus *n.* [L. **dolus** fraud, guile, deceit (2); **malus** bad, criminal (1): bad deceit.] *Law.* Fraud.

Misrepresentation or fraud which is actionable or may constitute ground for rescinding a transaction arising from it. See **actio de dolo malo; de dolo malo; exceptio doli mali; ex dolo malo; mala fide;** and **mala fides.** Cf. **bona fide, bona fides,** and **dolus bonus.**

D.O.M. *abbr.* for **Deo optimo maximo** (q.v.) and for **Domino optimo maximo** (q.v.).

domani *adv.* [It. tomorrow.] Tomorrow. Sometime future. **Mañana** (q.v.).

domicilium *n.* [L. habitation, abode, home, dwelling-place.] A person's permanent home, sometimes as distinct from his place of residence. See **domicilium habitationis.**

domicilium habitationis *n.* [L. **domicilium** home, abode (1); **habitationis** of dwelling, habitation (2): home of habitation.] A permanent place of abode. See **domicilium.**

domina *n., pl.* **dominae** [L. mistress, lady.] A woman of rank. A wife. Cf. **dominus.**

domina litis *n., pl.* **dominae litis** [L. **domina** mistress (1); **litis** of suit (2): mistress of the suit.] A female client in a lawsuit. Cf. **dominus litis.**

dominatrix *fem. n., pl.* **dominatrices** [L. she who dominates.] 1. An overbearing woman. 2. A dominating female partner in a sadomasochistic sexual relationship.

dominium *n., pl.* **dominia** or **dominiums** [L. ownership, rule, dominion.] 1. *Roman Law.* Paramount ownership. Eminent domain. Absolute ownership of property (corporeal), including the right to use the property, derive profit from it and to dispose of it, subject, of course, to the state's power. *The dominium of Roman law was unique and indivisible; ownership of land was exclusively vested in the dominus, and the interest which another person had in such land was no more than a servitude* (Asante 1975:63). 2. Sovereignty. Political power. Suzerainty. Lordship. Dominion.

dominium directum *n.* [L. **dominium** ownership, rule, dominion (2); **directum** direct (1): direct ownership.] *Law.* The general ownership of property by a person who holds the title. See **dominus directus.** Cf. **dominium utile.**

dominium directum et utile *n.* [L. **dominium** ownership, rule, dominion (4); **directum** direct (1); **et** and (2); **utile** useful (3): direct and useful ownership.] *Law.* Absolute ownership, including exclusive use.

dominium maris *n.* [L. **dominium** ownership, rule, dominion (1); **maris** of sea (2): sovereignty of the sea.] Mastery over the sea.

dominium maris Balthici *n.* [L. **dominium** ownership, rule, dominion (1); **maris** (of) sea (3); **Balthici** of Baltic (2): sovereignty of the Baltic sea.] Mastery over the Baltic Sea.

dominium non potest esse in pendenti. [L. **dominium** ownership, rule, dominion (1); **non** not (3); **potest** can, is able (2); **esse** to be (4); **in** in, on (5); **pendenti**

hanging, being suspended (6): Ownership cannot be in hanging.] Ownership cannot be held in suspense/abeyance.

dominium plenum or **plenum dominium** *n.* [L. **dominium** ownership, rule, dominion (2); **plenum** full (1): full ownership.] Absolute ownership, including exclusive use. **Dominium directum et utile** (q.v.).

dominium utile *n.* [L. **dominium** ownership, rule, dominion (2); **utile** useful, serviceable (1): serviceable ownership.] *Roman and Feudal Law.* Usufruct or the right of a person, such as a vassal tenant, who uses property but does not have title to it. Cf. **dominium directum.**

Domino optimo maximo *abbr.* **D.O.M.** [L. **Domino** to Lord (1); **optimo** (to) best (2); **maximo** (to) greatest (3): To the Lord, best, greatest.] To the Lord, the best and the greatest. Motto of the Benedictine religious order; **D.O.M.** appears on labels of Benedictine liqueur because it was originally made by Benedictine monks.

domino volente *adv.* [L. **domino** with the lord (1); **volente** (with) being willing (2): with the lord being willing.] With the consent/permission of the lord, owner, or master. Cf. **Deo volente.**

dominus *n., pl.* **domini** [L. master, lord.] 1. Owner of property, as distinct from user. *The dominium of Roman law was unique and indivisible; ownership of land was exclusively vested in the dominus, . . .* (Asante 1975:63). 2. A principal, as distinct from an agent. 3. *Feudal Law.* A lord, a knight, or a gentleman who is the lord of a manor. 4. *Civil Law.* A husband. Cf. **domina.**

dominus directus *n., pl.* **domini directi** [L. **dominus** lord, master (2); **directus** direct (1): direct master.] Direct owner. The person who has direct ownership of property. See **dominium directum.**

Dominus illuminatio mea [L. **Dominus** Lord (1); **illuminatio** light (3); **mea** my (2): Lord my light.] The Lord is my light. Motto of Oxford University.

dominus litis *n., pl.* **domini litis** [L. **dominus** master (1); **litis** of suit (2): master of the suit.] Male client in a lawsuit. Cf. **domina litis.**

Dominus vobiscum [L. **Dominus** Lord (1); **vobis** you (3); **cum** with, together (2): The Lord with you (pl.).] May the Lord be with you. The response is **et cum spiritu tuo** (q.v.).

domitae naturae *adj.* [L. **domitae** of tamed (1); **naturae** (of) nature (2): of tamed nature.] Domesticated. Applicable to domestic animals, as distinguished from those **ferae naturae,** i.e., wild animals.

domitae naturae animalia *pl. n.* [L. **domitae** of tamed, domesticated (2); **naturae** (of) nature (3); **animalia** animals (1): animals of domesticated/tamed nature.] Domesticated animals. Animals of tame disposition. See **mansuetae naturae.** Cf. **ferae naturae** and **ferae bestiae.**

Domus Procerum *abbr.* **Dom. Proc.** or **D.P.** *n.* [L. **domus** house (1); **procerum** of leading men, nobles (2): House of Nobles.] The House of Lords. *All that remains is a collection of decisions which, however sound in substance, can hardly in their manner be a subject for pride in dom. proc.* (Megarry 1973:60).

domus sua cuique est tutissimum refugium. [L. **domus** house, residence, abode (3); **sua** one's own, his/her own (2); **cuique** to each one (1); **est** is (4); **tutissimum** safest (5); **refugium** refuge, place of refuge (6): To each one his/her own abode is the safest place of refuge.] *Law*. A person's residence is his safest place of refuge; i.e., a person's house is his/her castle. Hence, if a thief enters a person's house and he/she kills the thief in defense of himself/herself, family, and property, he/she has not committed a felony. See **debet sua cuique** etc.; **domus tutissimum** etc.; **nemo de domo** etc.; and **quodcunque aliquis** etc.

domus tutissimum cuique refugium atque receptaculum. [L. **domus** house, residence, dwelling-place (2); **tutissimum** safest (3); **cuique** to each one (1); **refugium** place of refuge (4); **atque** and (5); **receptaculum** place of shelter/retreat (6): To each one the dwelling-place is the safest place of refuge and retreat.] *Law*. A person's residence is his/her safest place of refuge and retreat. See **domus sua** etc.

dona clandestina sunt semper suspiciosa. [L. **dona** gifts (2); **clandestina** secret, concealed, clandestine (1); **sunt** are (3); **semper** always (4); **suspiciosa** suspicious (5): Concealed gifts are always suspicious.] Clandestine gifts always arouse suspicion. Cf. **clausulae inconsuetae** etc.

donandi animo *adv.* [L. **donandi** of giving a present (2); **animo** with intention (1): with the intention of giving a present or gift.] As a gift. *"A" is not obliged to pay for the bicycle since "B," his friend, gave it to him donandi animo.*

donari videtur, quod, nullo jure cogente, conceditur. [L. **donari** to be given as a gift (7); **videtur** it seems (6); **quod** (that) which (1); **nullo** with no (3); **jure** (with) right, law (4); **cogente** (with) compelling (5); **conceditur** is given, granted (2): That which is given with no law compelling seems to be given as a gift.] *Law*. A gift is apparently something which is given under no legal compulsion.

donatio *n., pl.* **donationes** [L. a gift, donation.] A gift or donation. The transfer of the title and possession of property from one person to another without payment for it or any other consideration.

donatio ante nuptias *n., pl.* **donationes ante nuptias** [L. **donatio** donation, gift (1); **ante** before (2); **nuptias** marriage (3): a gift before marriage.] A premarital gift. *The building which is the subject matter of dispute was a donatio ante nuptias.* Cf. **donatio propter nuptias.**

donatio condicionalis *n., pl.* **donationes condicionales** [L. **donatio** gift, donation (2); **condicionalis** conditional (1): a conditional gift.] A gift with conditions/ strings attached to it. See **donatio sub modo.**

donatio inofficiosa *n., pl.* **donationes inofficiosae** [L. **donatio** gift, donation (2); **inofficiosa** undutiful, inofficious (1): undutiful gift.] A gift of such magnitude as to adversely affect the entitlement of the natural heirs. See **de inofficioso testamento**; **inofficiocidad**; **querela inofficiosi testamenti**; and **testamentum inofficiosum.**

donatio inter vivos *n., pl.* **donationes inter vivos** [L. **donatio** gift, donation (1); **inter** among (2); **vivos** the living (3): a gift among the living.] *Law*. A gift between living persons. A voluntary gift from one person to another. In civil law, the gift is executed and becomes irrevocable when it is accepted by the donee, but in common law, there should be actual delivery of the gift before it becomes valid.

donatio mera or **donatio pura** *n., pl.* **donationes merae** or **donationes purae** [L. **donatio** gift, donation (2); **mera** (or **pura**) pure, genuine (1): pure gift.] A charitable gift. A generous gift with no strings attached and under no compulsion. A species of **donatio inter vivos** (q.v.).

donatio mortis causa *n., pl.* **donationes mortis causa** [L. **donatio** gift (1); **mortis** (of) death (3); **causa** on account of (2): gift on account of death.] *Law*. A deathbed gift. A gift made in expectation of immediate death. The donor retains the right of revoking the gift which only becomes permanent upon the death of the donor.

donatio non praesumitur. [L. **donatio** gift, donation (1); **non** not (3); **praesumitur** is presumed (2): A gift is not presumed.] *Law*. A gift should not be taken for granted; i.e., the intention to give a gift must be explicit.

donatio perficitur possessione accipientis. [L. **donatio** gift, donation (1); **perficitur** is effected, perfected (2); **possessione** by possession (3); **accipientis** of the one receiving (4): A gift is effected by the possession of the one receiving.] The process of making a gift is not complete until the right of possession is transferred to the recipient. See **donator numquam** etc.

donatio propter nuptias *n., pl.* **donationes propter nuptias** [L. **donatio** gift, donation (1); **propter** because of, on account of (2); **nuptias** marriage (3): gift on account of marriage.] *Roman Law*. A gift made on account of marriage. It is similar to **donatio ante nuptias** (q.v.), but whereas the latter was given before marriage, **donatio propter nuptias**, introduced by an ordinance of Justinian, was given after marriage. It was given by the bridegroom to the bride, and was usually used to defray the expenses of the marriage.

donatio pura See **donatio mera.**

donatio relata *n., pl.* **donationes relatae** [L. **donatio** gift, donation (2); **relata** returned, recompensed (1): a returned or recompensed gift.] A gift made in gratitude/ return for services previously rendered. See **donatio remuneratoria.**

donatio remuneratoria *n., pl.* **donationes remuneratoriae** [L. **donatio** gift, donation (1); **remuneratoria** of recompense, of remuneration (2): gift of recompense.] A gift made in appreciation of previous services rendered (e.g., pension). See **donatio relata.**

donatio stricta et coarctura *n., pl.* **donationes strictae et coarcturae** [L. **donatio** gift, donation (1); **stricta** tight (2); **et** and (3); **coarctura** about to confine (4): a gift tight and about to confine.] A restricted gift; e.g., estate in tail.

donatio sub modo or **donatio modalis** *n., pl.* **donationes sub modo** or **donationes modales** [L. **donatio** gift, donation (1); **sub** under (2); **modo** restriction (3): a gift/donation under restriction.] A gift made for some special purpose or on condition that the recipient should put it to a particular use; e. g. an endowment fund for hospitals, scholarships, or colleges. See **donatio condicionalis.**

donator numquam desinit possidere antequam donatorius incipiat possidere. [L. **donator** donor, giver (1); **numquam** never (2); **desinit** ceases (3); **possidere** to possess (4); **antequam** before, until (5); **donatorius** donee, recipient (6); **incipiat** begins (7); **possidere** to possess (8): A donor never ceases to possess until the recipient begins to possess.] *Law.* A donor continues to possess until the right of possession is transferred to the recipient. See **donatio perficitur** etc.

donec probetur in contrarium [L. **donec** until, as long as (1); **probetur** it be (or it is) proved (2); **in** into, to, against, for (3); **contrarium** the contrary (4): until it be proved to the contrary.] Until the opposite is determined.

doppelgänger or **doppelganger** *n., pl.* **doppelgängers** or **doppelgangers** [Ger. **Doppelgänger**: **doppel** double (1); **Gänger** goer (2): double goer.] A person's spectral double.

dormit aliquando lex, moritur numquam. [L. **dormit** sleeps (2); **aliquando** sometimes, now and then (3); **lex** law (1); **moritur** dies (5); **numquam** never (4): A law sleeps sometimes, but it never dies.] Cf. **dormiunt aliquando** etc.

dormiunt aliquando leges, numquam moriuntur. [L. **dormiunt** sleep (2); **aliquando** sometimes, now and then (3); **leges** laws (1); **numquam** never (4); **moriuntur** die (5): The laws sleep sometimes, they never die.] The laws may sleep now and then, but they never die; e.g., contractual obligations may be suspended in times of war, but the contract would still be binding. Cf. **dormit aliquando** etc.

dos *n., pl.* **dotes** [L. dowry, marriage portion.] *Roman Law.* A dowry. A wife's marriage portion. The property

brought by the wife or contributed by somebody on behalf of the wife to the husband to help in the maintenance of the family. Originally, it became the husband's absolute property, but by the time of Justinian, it had to be returned to the donor when the marriage ended through either death or divorce. See **adventitia dos**; **profectitia dos**; and **receptitia dos.**

dos moi pou sto kai kino ten gen. Archimedes (c. 287– 212 B.C.). [Gk. **dōs** give (1); **moi** to me (2); **pou** where (3); **stō** I am to stand (4); **kai** and (5); **kinō** I shall move (6); **tēn** the (7); **gēn** earth (8): Give me where I am to stand and I shall move the earth.] Give me a place to stand and I shall move the earth (with a lever). Cf. **pou sto.**

dos rationabilis *n., pl.* **dotes rationabiles** [L. **dos** dowry (2); **rationabilis** reasonable (1): a reasonable dowry.] *English Law.* A reasonable portion of the husband's estate, about one third, to which a widow is entitled.

dossier *n., pl.* **dossiers** [Fr. chairback, record, file, documents, papers.] A file. A collection of documents, reports, relevant data, records, etc., respecting a subject, usually a person's life or activities, which is being investigated or studied. *The administration of the university is compiling dossiers on lecturers suspected of holding radical views.*

dote *n.* [Sp. dowry.] *Spanish Law.* Dowry. A wife's marriage portion. The property which is the wife's contribution to the marriage, particularly for defraying the expenses of the marriage. Cf. **conquêts.**

double entendre *n., pl.* **doubles entendres** or **double entendres** [Fr. **double** double, twofold (1); **entendre** to mean, meaning (2): double meaning.] 1. An ambiguous expression. An expression which may be interpreted in several ways. *Our friend in his characteristic manner kept on using language pregnant with double entendres.* 2. An expression which has two meanings, one of which is usually indecent or risqué. *It was a gathering of people of diverse background, and the comic displayed his well-known versatility by telling jokes full of double entendres.*

douceur *n., pl.* **douceurs** [Fr. sweetness, softness, charm.] A present or favor. An inducement. A conciliatory gesture or gift. A gratuity. *Two days after hurting his wife's feelings, Bob took her out, as a douceur, for dinner at a prestigious restaurant.* Cf. **pourboire.**

douceur de vivre *n.* [Fr. **douceur** sweetness, softness (1); **de** of (2); **vivre** living, to live (3): sweetness of living.] Pleasure or sweetness of life. Pleasant living. Enjoyment of the pleasures of life. *Hard work is the most reliable route to douceur de vivre.*

do ut des *n.* [L. **do** I give (1); **ut** in order that (2); **des** you may give (3): I give in order that you may give.] *Roman Law.* A commutative (or quid pro quo) type of contract in which something is given by one party to be reciprocated by the other party. See **quid pro quo.**

do ut facias *n.* [L. **do** I give (1); **ut** in order that (2); **facias** you may do (3): I give in order that you may do.] *Roman Law.* A commutative (or quid pro quo) type of contract in which one party gives something to be reciprocated by the other party's doing or performing a service. See **quid pro quo.**

doyen *fem.* **doyenne** *n., pl.* **doyens** or *fem.* **doyennes** [Fr. dean, senior, oldest member.] Dean. Senior or oldest member of a group or body, such as the diplomatic corps. A person tacitly acknowledged as the spokesperson of a group. A person who by reason of long experience has acquired authority in a field. a) *Hayek at 85 is still the doyen of monetarists . . .* (*Newsweek Int.* March 3, 1980:36). b) *Zik of Africa, doyen of Nigerian journalism, was recently named recipient of the John Kwegyir Aggrey Award* (*The Guardian* 1986).

D.P. *abbr.* for **Domus Procerum** (q.v.)

drama *n., pl.* **dramas** [Gk. deed, act, play, action represented on the stage.] 1. A play. A composition, whether in prose or verse, portraying life, character, passion, or a moral, to be performed on stage by actors. *. . . Phrynichus also made contemporary history the material of his dramas* (Lesky: 1966:230). 2. A situation, an event, or series of events with conflicting forces not unlike those in a play. *In a country with a solid democratic tradition, a government's fall is not necessarily a moment of high drama . . .* (*Newsweek Int.* Feb. 16, 1981:8).

dramatis personae *pl. n.* [L. **dramatis** of drama (2); **personae** characters (1): characters of a drama.] 1. The characters in a drama, poem, or novel. 2. The people participating in a real event or a number of events. *When the protracted dispute was referred to the head of the clan, he advised the dramatis personae to exercise restraint.*

Drang nach Osten *n.* [Ger. **Drang** drive (1); **nach** to (2); **Osten** east (3): a drive to the east.] 1. Germany's policy of expansion towards eastern Europe. 2. Any policy of expansion towards the East.

dressage *n.* [Fr. straightening, erecting, dressing, preparing, training.] Training a horse to obey a series of a rider's slight body movements in order to execute complex maneuvers. Cf. **passage.**

Dr. h.c. *abbr.* for **Doctor Honoris Causa** (q.v.).

droit *n.* [Fr. law, right.] *French Law.* 1. Right. Equity. Justice. Law in the abstract. 2. A right, power or privilege. 3. The entire body of law.

droit common *n.* [Obs. Fr. **droit** law, right (2); **common** common (1): the common law.] English or Anglo-Saxon, as opposed to Roman, law. Law based upon custom and practice rather than legislation. Cf. **droit coutumier** and **lex communis.**

droit coutumier *n.* [Fr. **droit** law, right (2); **coutumier** customary, common (1): customary law.] *French*

Law. Common law. Unwritten law. Cf. **droit common** and **lex communis.**

droit d'accession *n.* [Fr. **droit** law, right (1); **d'** of (2); **accession** accession, addition (3): right of accession.] *French Law.* Property obtained by changing the form or species of another's property. Through the mode of transforming the property of another by changing its material into another species. **Specificatio** (q.v.).

droit d'accroissement *n.* [Fr. **droit** law, right (1); **d'** of (2); **accroissement** increase, growth, accretion (3): right of increase.] *French Law.* Right of accretion. The right of an heir or a legatee, in the event of the refusal or inability of a co-heir or co-legatee to accept his/her share, to take such share in addition to his/hers.

droit d'aubaine *n.* [Fr. **droit** law, right (1); **d'** of (2); **aubaine** escheat, windfall (3): right of windfall.] *French Law.* Right of escheat. The right, formerly enjoyed by the state of France but abolished in 1819, of confiscating all the property of a deceased alien, both movable and immovable. See **aubain.** Cf. **jus albanagii.**

droit de déshérence *n.* [Fr. **droit** law, right (1); **de** of (2); **déshérence** disinheritance, escheat (3): right of disinheritance.] *French Law.* Right of escheat or disinheritance. A prerogative right which the French state may exercise when a person is convicted of a felony. Cf. **mort civile** and **mortuus civiliter.**

droit de détraction *n.* [Fr. **droit** law, right (1); **de** of (2); **détraction** detraction, depreciation (3): right of detraction.] *French Law.* Right of detraction; i.e., tax levied on property obtained by inheritance or testamentary disposition, when it is being removed from one country or state to another.

droit de naufrage *n.* [Fr. **droit** law, right (1); **de** of (2); **naufrage** shipwreck, wreck (3): right of shipwreck.] *Law.* A right, now abolished, enjoyed by the lord or king who owned the coast, of seizing the wreckage, when a boat was wrecked, and either killing or enslaving the crew.

droit de suite *n.* [Fr. **droit** law, right (1); **de** of (2); **suite** continuation, pursuit (3): right of continuation or pursuit.] *Law.* 1. The right of a creditor to press his/her claim even if the property of the debtor has been taken over by some other persons. 2. A lord's right to pursue a serf.

droit droit *n.* [Fr. right right, a double right.] *Law.* The right of both possession and property. Originally, in some legal systems, the two rights were distinct and their concurrence in one person meant a complete title to property. See **plurimum juris** and **plurimum possessionis.**

droit du seigneur or **droit de seigneur** *n.* [Fr. **droit** law, right (1); **du** of the (2); **seigneur** lord (3): right of the lord.] *Jus primae noctis* (q.v.). A right which supposedly empowered a feudal lord to have sexual intercourse with the bride of a vassal on the wedding night.

droit écrit *n*. [Fr. **droit** law, right (2); **écrit** written (1): written law.] *French Law*. Statute law. The corpus of the civil law. Cf. **jus scriptum**.

droit maritime *n*. [Fr. **droit** law, right (2); **maritime** maritime, naval (1): maritime law.] Navigation laws.

droit naturel *n*. [F. **droit** law, right (2); **naturel** natural (1): natural law.] 1. The law of nature. 2. Natural right. 3. *Political Philosophy*. A person's natural right to a decent means of sustenance.

D.S. *abbr*. for **dal segno** (q.v.).

D.S.P. or **d.s.p.** *abbr*. for **decessit sine prole** (q.v.).

D.S.P.L. or **d.s.p.l.** *abbr*. for **decessit sine prole legitima** (q.v.).

D.S.P.M. or **d.s.p.m.** *abbr*. for **decessit sine prole mascula** (q.v.).

D.S.P.M.S. or **d.s.p.m.s.** *abbr*. for **decessit sine prole mascula superstite** (q.v.).

D.S.P.S. or **d.s.p.s.** *abbr*. for **decessit sine prole superstite** (q.v.).

D.S.P.V. or **d.s.p.v.** *abbr*. for **decessit sine prole virili** (q.v.).

d.t. *abbr*. for **delirium tremens** (q.v.).

duas uxores eodem tempore habere non licet. [L. **duas** two (4); **uxores** wives (5); **eodem** at the same (6); **tempore** (at) time (7); **habere** to have, hold, regard (3); **non** not (1); **licet** it is lawful, allowed (2): It is unlawful to have two wives at the same time.] A rule applicable in European and western countries, but not applicable to some societies, particularly in Africa.

dubitante *adj*. [L. with (him/her) doubting.] *Law*. Questioning the decision. Affixed to a judge's name to show that he/she doubted the decision reached. *Despite objections to the admissibility of such authority, Bramwell and Buggallay L. JJ (Thesigger L. J. dubitante) held that it was receivable* (Megarry 1955:356). Cf. **dissentiente**.

dubitatur [L. It is doubted.] *Law*. Used in reports to signify that there is some doubt about a point.

duce or Duce *n*. [It. leader.] Leader of a group. Dictator. Title adopted by Benito Mussolini. . . . *the neofascist Italian Social Movement . . . whose leaders have wanted the Duce's 66-year-old son, Vittorio, . . . to join them in the Italian Parliament* (*Newsweek Int.* Aug. 1, 1983:21). See **Il Duce**. Cf. **caudillo**; **El Caudillo**; and **Führer**.

duces tecum *short form* of **subpoena duces tecum** (q.v.).

Du contrat social *n*. [Fr. **du** of/on the (1); **contrat** contract, agreement (3); **social** social (2): on the social contract.] *On the Social Contract*, a 1762 political and philosophical treatise by Jean-Jacques Rousseau (1712–1778).

duenna *n., pl.* **duennas** [Sp. **dueña** governess.] A woman, usually elderly or married, who accompanies a girl or an unmarried woman to a social function to ensure propriety. See **chaperon**.

du haut en bas *adv*. [Fr. **du** from the (1); **haut** high, top (2); **en** to, into (3); **bas** low, bottom (4): from the top to bottom.] **De haut en bas** (q.v.).

dulce domum *n*. [L. **dulce** a sweet (thing) (1); **domum** home (2): A sweet (thing) is home.] Home, sweet home.

dulce est desipere in loco. Horace (65–8 B.C.). *Odes* IV,12,28. [L. **dulce** sweet (2); **est** it is (1); **desipere** to be foolish, silly (3); **in** in, on (4); **loco** place (5): It is sweet to be foolish in place.] It is sweet to be frivolous at the right time and place. For a fuller form of the quotation, see **misce stultitiam** etc.

dulce et decorum est pro patria mori. Horace (65–8 B.C.). *Odes* III,2,13. [L. **dulce** sweet (2); **et** and (3); **decorum** fitting, proper (4); **est** it is (1); **pro** for, on behalf of (6); **patria** fatherland, country (7); **mori** to die (5): It is sweet and fitting to die for one's fatherland (or country).] Dying for one's country is both proper and pleasant.

duma *n., pl.* **dumas** [Russ.] 1. An official council or public assembly in czarist Russia before 1905. 2. The lower house of the post-communist Russian parliament. —**Duma** The national parliament of Russia from 1905 to 1917.

dum anima est, spes est. Cicero (106–43 B.C.). *Letters to Atticus* IX,10. [L. **dum** as long as, while, provided that (1); **anima** soul, person, life, a living being (3); **est** there is (2); **spes** hope (5); **est** there is (4): While there is life, there is hope.] As long as someone remains alive, there is some hope for the future. Cf. **dum spiro, spero** and **modo liceat vivere** etc.

dum bene se gesserit *adv*. [L. **dum** as long as, while, provided that (1); **bene** well (3); **se gesserit** he/she will have behaved (2): as long as he/she will have behaved well.] During good conduct. Used with reference to an appointment whose tenure is determined not by the pleasure of the authorities but by the death or misconduct of the appointee. Cf. **durante beneplacito** and **quamdiu se** etc.

dum casta *adv*. [L. **dum** while, provided that (1); **casta** chaste (2): while chaste.] Used with reference to the status of a woman who is a virgin, divorced, or a widow as a condition for acceptance of a legacy or payment of alimony. Variations of the expression are 1. **dum casta vixerit** While she lives chaste. 2. **dum sola** While single or unmarried. 3. **dum sola fuerit** As long as she is single/unmarried. 4. **dum sola et casta vixerit** As long as she lives single and chaste. 5. **dum vidua** While a widow. *The court made an order to the effect that alimony should continue to be paid dum casta vixerit.* See **durante casta viduitate**; **durante viduitate**; and **durante virginitate**.

dum fervet opus *adv*. [L. **dum** while (1); **fervet** glows, rages (3); **opus** work (2): while the work glows/rages.] At the peak (or in the heat) of the action. *He caused considerable indignation by disrupting the proceedings dum fervet opus.*

dum fuit infra aetatem *adv.* [L. **dum** while (1); **fuit** he/she was (2); **infra** below (3); **aetatem** age (4): while he/she was below age.] *English Law.* While under age. Applicable to an old writ in which an adult attempts to regain ownership of property which was alienated in infancy.

dum loquimur, fugerit invida aetas; carpe diem, quam minimum credula postero. Horace (65–8 B.C.). *Odes* IV, 11, 7–8. [L. **dum** while (1); **loquimur** we speak, talk (2); **fugerit** will have fled (5); **invida** envious (3); **aetas** time, age (4); **carpe** pluck, seize (6); **diem** day (7); **quam minimum** as little as possible (9); **credula** trusting, confiding in (8); **postero** future (day) (10): While we speak, envious time will have fled; seize the day, trusting as little as possible in a future day.] As we speak, jealous time will have fled; so pluck the fruits of the present day and trust as little as possible in the future. Cf. **carpe diem.**

dummkopf *n., pl.* **dummkopfs** [Ger. **dumm** stupid, dumb (1); **Kopf** head (2): dumb head.] *Slang.* An idiot. A stupid person.

dum non fit compos mentis *adv./adj.* [L. **dum** while (1); **non** not (3); **fit** he/she is made, becomes (2); **compos** master of, possessing (4); **mentis** of mind (5): while he/she does not become the master of his/her mind.] While he/she is not of sound mind. *Old English Law.* A writ to be used by the heirs of a person who lost title to land while non compos mentis for its recovery. Cf. **compos mentis** and the references cited therein.

dum spiro, spero. [L. **dum** while (1); **spiro** I breathe (2); **spero** I hope (3): While I breathe, I hope.] While there is life, there is hope. As long as I live, all is not lost. Motto of the State of South Carolina. Cf. **dum anima est, spes est.**

dum vivimus, vivamus. [L. **dum** while (1); **vivimus** we live (2); **vivamus** let us live (3): While we live, let us live.] While we are alive, let us enjoy life. Based upon Catullus (c.84–54 B.C.). *Carmina* V,1–6.

duo *n., pl.* **duos** [L. and It. two.] A duet. A piece of music designed for two instruments or singers. A pair. A body or group of two persons or things. . . . *two other terrorist duos announced that they too had made love behind the bars* (*Time Int.* 1983).

duomo *n., pl.* **duomos** [It. dome, cathedral.] A cathedral in Italy.

duo non possunt in solido unam rem possidere. [L. **duo** two (persons) (1); **non** not (3); **possunt** can, are able (2); **in** in, on (7); **solido** the whole, the entire (8); **unam** one (5); **rem** matter, thing, property, business, affair (6); **possidere** to possess (4): Two persons cannot possess one thing in the entirety.] *Law.* Ownership of a whole cannot be shared; right of ownership must be divided into portions. See **duorum in solidum** etc.

duorum in solidum dominium vel possessio esse non potest. [L. **duorum** of two (persons) (7); **in** into, to,

against, for (8); **solidum** the whole, the entire (9); **dominium** ownership, rule, dominion (4); **vel** or (5); **possessio** possession (6); **esse** to be (3); **non** not (2); **potest** there can, it is possible (1): There cannot be ownership or possession of two persons for the whole.] *Law.* Two persons cannot own or possess a thing in the entirety. See **duo non possunt** etc.

duovir *n., pl.* **duoviri** [L. **duo** two (1); **vir** man (2): two men, one of a body of two men.] **Duumvir** (q.v.). Cf. **decemvir.**

duplex *adj.* [L. twofold, double, complex.] Twofold. Double. Consisting of, or having, two parts. a) *a duplex tool.* b) *a duplex apartment.* —*n., pl.* **duplexes** Something twofold or double. A double apartment. A house of two self-sufficient units for two families. Cf. **triplex.**

durance vile *n.* [Obs. Fr. **durance** endurance, constraint, confinement (2); **vile** harsh (1): harsh confinement.] Imprisonment. *He spent twenty years in durance vile.*

durante absentia *adv.* [L. **durante** (with) continuing, lasting, persevering (2); **absentia** with absence (1): with the absence continuing/persevering.] *Law.* During absence. Usually used with reference to the administration of a deceased person's estate which is granted during the inordinate absence of the executor. *The Probate Division now exercised the jurisdiction of the ecclesiastical court to make grants durante absentia* (Parry 1961:179).

durante beneplacito *adv.* [L. **durante** (with) continuing, lasting (2); **beneplacito** with pleasure, discretion (1): with the pleasure/discretion continuing.] During the pleasure of the king. At the discretion of the king. Used in relation to tenure of an office, which depends on the discretion of the employer, particularly a king; e.g., the tenure of office of English judges in former times. Cf. **dum bene** etc. and **quamdiu se** etc.

durante casta viduitate *adv.* [L. **durante** (with) continuing, lasting (3); **casta** with chaste (1); **viduitate** (with) widowhood (2): with chaste widowhood continuing.] During chaste widowhood. See **dum casta.**

durante furore *adv.* [L. **durante** (with) continuing, lasting (1); **furore** with insanity, madness, fury (2): with continuing fury.] During a period of violent insanity. *The defense counsel submitted that his client cannot be held answerable for an incident which occurred durante furore.*

durante minore aetate *adv.* [L. **durante** (with) continuing, lasting, persevering (3); **minore** with minor (1); **aetate** (with) age (2): with minor age continuing/persevering.] During minor age. While one is a minor or while they are minors. *A grant of administration durante minore aetate usually contains the limitation "until he shall attain the age of twenty-one," or until one of them shall attain the age of twenty-one* (Parry 1961:185).

durante viduitate *adv.* [L. **durante** (with) continuing, lasting (2); **viduitate** with widowhood, bereavement

(1): with widowhood continuing.] During widowhood. See **dum casta**.

durante virginitate *adv.* [L. **durante** (with) continuing, lasting (2); **virginitate** with virginity (1): with virginity continuing.] During virginity; i.e., as long as she has not had sexual intercourse. See **dum casta**.

durante vita *adv.* [L. **durante** (with) continuing, lasting, persevering (2); **vita** with life (1): with life continuing.] During life. As long as he/she is alive. *A person may make a gift of his properties to any person he wishes durante vita.*

Du sublime au ridicule il n'y a qu'un pas. Napoleon I (1769–1821). [Fr. **du** from the (1); **sublime** sublime, exalted (2); **au** to the, toward the, in the, by the, with the, until the (3); **ridicule** ridiculous, ludicrous (4); **il . . . y a** there is (5); **n' . . . qu'** only (6); **un** one (7); **pas** step (8): From the sublime to the ridiculous there is only one step.] There is but one step from the sublime to the ridiculous.

duumvir *n., pl.* **duumviri** or **duumvirs** [L. **duum** of two (1); **vir** man (2): of two men.] 1. *Ancient Rome.* A member of a board of two officials, magistrates, etc. appointed to perform a specific function; e.g., to serve as judges of a criminal court, to guard the Sibylline books, or to build a temple. 2. A member of a body, group, board, council, association, commission, or ruling body of two men. Cf. **decemvir**.

D.V. *abbr.* for **Deo volente** (q.v.).

dybbuk *n., pl.* **dybbukkim** or **dybbuks** [Heb. **dibbūq** ghost.] *Judaism.* The restless soul of a dead person which wanders around and takes possession of a living person.

dynamis *n.* [Gk. **dunamis** ability, power.] Potentiality. Capability.

dysacousia or **dysacousis** *n.* [Neo-Gk. from Gk. **dus**-bad, hard, unlucky (1); **akousis** hearing (2): bad or unlucky hearing.] *Medicine.* A state or condition in which sounds are confused and hearing is impaired, sometimes painfully.

Dyscolus *n.* [Gk. **Duskolos: dus** bad, hard, unlucky (1); **kulos** juice (2): bad juice.] *Old Cantankerous*, the only surviving play of Menander (344/3 B.C.–292/1 B.C.). The title refers to the grouchy old man around whom the plot revolves.

dyspareunia *n.* [Neo-Gk. from Gk. **duspareunos: dus**-bad, hard, unlucky (1); **par(a)** alongside (2); **eunē** bed, marriage bed (3): unlucky alongside the bed, ill-mated.] *Medicine.* Difficult or painful sexual intercourse. See **anaphrodisia**.

dysphagia *n.* [Neo-Gk. from Gk. **dus**- hard, difficult, unlucky (1); **phag(ein)** eating (2): hard or difficult eating.] *Medicine.* Difficulty in eating or swallowing.

dysphasia *n.* [Neo-Gk. from Gk. **dus**- hard, difficult, unlucky (1); **phasi(s)** expression, utterance (2): difficult expression or utterance.] *Medicine.* Inability to speak or understand language, being the result of impairment of the brain.

dysphrasia *n.* [Neo-Gk. from Gk. **dus**- hard, difficult, unlucky (1); **phrasi(s)** speech, expression (2): hard speech.] Inability to speak well, being the result of a lesion in the brain.

dystokia or **dystocia** *n., pl.* **dystokias** or **dystocias** [Gk. **dustokia: dus**- hard, difficult, unlucky (1); **tok(os)** child-birth (2): difficult childbirth, suffering in childbirth.] *Medicine.* Painful, slow, or difficult childbirth. Cf. **eutocia** and **oxytocia**.

E

eadem est ratio, eadem est lex. [L. **eadem** the same (1); **est** is (2); **ratio** reason (3); **eadem** the same (4); **est** is (5); **lex** law (6): The same is the reason, the same is the law.] *Law.* Where the reason is the same, the same law is applicable.

eadem sunt quorum unum potest substitui alteri salva veritate. Gottfried Wilhelm Leibniz (1646–1716). [L. **eadem** the same things (2); **sunt** they are, have been (1); **quorum** of which, them (4); **unum** one (3); **potest** can, is able to (5); **substitui** to be substituted (6); **alteri** for the other (of two) (7); **salva** (with being) safe, unharmed (9); **veritate** with truth (8): They are the same things (if) one of them can be substituted for the other with the truth safe.] Two expressions are deemed to be synonymous if one can be substituted for the other with no effect upon the validity of either expression. Cf. **salva veritate.**

ea intentione *adv.* [L. **ea** with that (1); **intentione** (with) intention (2): with that intention.] With that purpose. *Dan decided to murder Abel. Therefore, ea intentione, he proceeded to Abel's residence with a pistol and shot him dead.*

ea quae, commendandi causa, in venditionibus dicuntur, si palam appareant, venditorem non obligant. [L. **ea** those (things) (1); **quae** which (2); **commendandi** of commending (7); **causa** for the sake (6); **in** in, on (4); **venditionibus** sales (5); **dicuntur** are said (3); **si** if (8); **palam** plainly, openly (10); **appareant** they appear, they are visible (9); **venditorem** seller, vendor (13); **non** not (12); **obligant** bind, make liable (11): Those things which are said in sales for the sake of commending, if they appear plainly, do not bind the vendor.] *Law.* Those things which are said during sales for commendation do not bind the vendor, if they are plainly visible.

eau de cologne *n., pl.* **eaux de cologne** [Fr. **eau-de-cologne: eau** water (1); **de** of (2); **cologne** Cologne (3): water of Cologne.] A perfume composed of alcohol and scented oils.

eau de vie *n., pl.* **eaux de vie** [Fr. **eau** water (1); **de** of (2); **vie** life (3): water of life.] Brandy. Cf. **aqua vita.**

E.C. or **e.c.** *abbr.* for **exempli causa** (q.v.).

ecce homo *abbr.* **ecc. hom.** John 19:5. [L. **ecce** See! Behold! (1); **homo** person, human being (2): See! The person.] "Behold the man." Pontius Pilate addresses these words to the crowd in reference to Jesus, scourged and crowned with thorns. —*n. Art.* A picture or representation showing Jesus Christ wearing the crown of thorns and a purple robe.

ecclesia *n., pl.* **ecclesiae** [Gk. **ekklēsia** assembly.] 1. *Ancient Greece.* An assembly of citizens of a city-state. Such a body usually performed legislative functions, considering proposals or bills prepared by the council. 2. *Christianity.* A Church. The entire body of Christians forming a spiritual society. A group of Christians who worship together.

ecclesia non moritur. [L. **ecclēsia** church (1); **non** not (2); **moritur** dies (3): The Church does not die.] *Christianity.* The church does not fail or pass away.

Ecclesiazusai *pl. n.* [Gr. **Ekklēsiazusai** assembly women.] *The Assemblywomen,* a 392 B.C. comedy by Aristophanes (448?–?380 B.C.) in which the women of Athens take over the **ecclesia** (q.v.) and run the city.

échelon or **echelon** *n., pl.* **échelons** or **echelons** [Fr. rung, level, grade, step, stage.] 1. An arrangement of troops, airplanes, ships, etc. in the form of a series of steps. 2. One of a series of grades or levels of command, responsibility, leadership, or authority in an organization. A group of persons occupying a particular level or grade of responsibility in an organization. a) *The upper echelons of the military are solidly behind the Shah . . .* (*Newsweek Int.* Jan. 1, 1979:20). b) *It was felt that the nature of media work made women journalists content to stay out of the top echelons of the profession . . .* (*West Africa* 1985).

echolalia *n.* [Neo-Gk. from Gk. **ēchō** echo (1); **lalia** talk, chat (2): echo-talk.] *Medicine.* A kind of insanity which takes the form of constantly repeating what others say.

éclat *n., pl.* **éclats** [Fr. splinter, burst, flash, brightness, brilliancy, pomp, splendor, glamor, display.] 1. Splendor. Brilliance. Brilliant or dazzling effect. Brilliant success. *Due to excessive party patronage through which buffoons, quacks and political charlatans wrangle themselves into positions of authority and responsibility, the Federal and many state executives have been lacking in éclat* (Dr. Tunde Adeniran in *West Africa* 1982). 2. Show of pomp. Display of pageantry. Publicity. Ostentatious display. *Akanbi marked his return home from his sojourn in Britain with great éclat, driving a friend's deluxe car.*

école *n., pl.* **écoles** [Fr. school.] A school or group, especially of writers, artists, scholars, etc.

École des Femmes *n.* [Fr. **école** school (1); **des** of the (2); **femmes** women (3): school of the women.] *School for Women*, a 1662 comedy by Molière (1622–1673).

e contra *adv.* [L. **e** from, out of (1); **contra** against, opposite (2): from opposite.] On the contrary. See **e converso**.

e converso *adv.* [L. **e** from, out of (1); **converso** converse, contrary (2): from the converse.] Conversely. On the contrary. *The prosecutor advised the witness to give testimony against the accused but, e converso, he testified in his favor.* See **e contra**.

edictum *n., pl.* **edicta** [L. spoken forth, edict, ordinance, proclamation, manifesto.] Originally, in ancient Rome, a proclamation issued by the praetor on assumption of office, showing the rules which he would follow during his term of office. During the imperial era the Emperor, by virtue of his position as an extraordinary magistrate, issued edicta and his edicts carried the force of law.

editio princeps *abbr.* **E.P.** or **e.p.** *n., pl.* **editiones principes** [L. **editio** edition, statement (2); **princeps** first, original, foremost (1): first edition.] The first printed version of a book previously available only in manuscript form.

e.g. *abbr.* for 1. **ejusdem generis** (q.v.). 2. **exempli gratia** (q.v.).

egesta *pl. n.* [L. things discharged or removed.] Excretions. Excrement. Cf. **dejecta** and **excreta**.

ego *n., pl.* **egos** [L. "I."] 1. Self-respect. Self-esteem. *The student's ego was shattered by his poor performance in the examination.* 2. Arrogance. Boastfulness. a) *Tunji's greatness is enhanced by his self-effacement and the absence of even a spark of ego in him.* b) *The head of the institution expects every member of staff to flatter him and massage his ego.* 3. *Psychology.* The conscious part of one's personality which harmonizes the demands of the id, the superego and the reality of the world. 4. Used in the drawing of genealogical tables for representing the person whose genealogy is being traced.

eheu fugaces Horace (65–8 B.C.). *Odes* II,14,1. [L. **eheu** alas (1); **fugaces** fleeing (2): alas fleeing.] Alas for the fleeing years.

eidolon *n., pl.* **eidola** or **eidolons** [Gk. **eidōlon** phantom, image, idea.] 1. A bodiless form or image. A phantom. *Now that we are awake, we may discard the eidolons of our former sleep and face reality.* 2. An ideal figure or model. *A father should try as much as possible to educate his children, but he should refrain from creating in his mind an eidolon which the children should imitate in all details.*

ei incumbit probatio, qui dicit, non qui negat; cum per rerum naturam factum negantis probatio nulla sit. [L. **ei** (to) him (3); **incumbit** weighs upon, burdens (2); **probatio** proof (1); **qui** who (4); **dicit** asserts, affirms (5); **non** not (6); **qui** (him) who (7); **negat** denies (8); **cum** since (9); **per** through, by (10); **rerum** of matters, things, property, business, affairs (12); **naturam** nature (11); **factum** deed, act, fact (17); **negantis** of the one denying (16); **probatio** proof (15); **nulla** no (14); **sit** there is (13): Proof weighs upon him who asserts, not on him who denies, since, by the nature of things, there is no proof of the one denying fact.] The burden of proof lies on one who makes an assertion, not on one who denies it, since, by the nature of things, a person who denies a fact has no means of proof. See **actori incumbit** etc.

Eine kleine Nachtmusik *n.* [Ger. **eine** a, an (1); **kleine** little (2); **Nacht** night (3); **Musik** music (4): a little night music.] "A Little Night Music," a musical composition for strings by Wolfgang Amadeus Mozart (1756–1791).

Ein' feste Burg ist unser Gott / ein' gute Wehr und Waffen. Martin Luther (1483–1546). [Ger. **ein'** a, an (1); **feste** solid, firm, strong, mighty (2); **Burg** fortress, stronghold, castle (3); **ist** is (4); **unser** our (5); **Gott** God (6); **ein'** a (7); **gute** good (8); **Wehr** defense, arms, armament (9); **und** and (10); **Waffen** weapon (11): A strong citadel is our God / A good armament and weapon.] A mighty fortress is our God / A bulwark never failing. The first lines of a Lutheran hymn.

Ein Heldenleben *n.* [Ger. **ein** a, an (1); **Helden** hero's (2); **Leben** life (3): a hero's life.] "A Hero's Life," a tone poem (1899) by Richard Strauss (1864–1949) in which the composer portrays himself as a hero.

Ein unnütz Leben ist ein früher Tod. Johann Wolfgang von Goethe (1749–1832). *Iphigenie auf Tauris* I,2,2. [Ger. **ein** a, an (1); **unnütz** useless, unprofitable (2); **Leben** life, existence (3); **ist** is (4); **ein** a, an (5); **früher** early, premature, untimely (6); **Tod** death (7): A useless life is an early death.] A wasted life is equivalent to dying young.

ei qui affirmat, non ei qui negat, incumbit probatio. [L. **ei** him (3); **qui** who (4); **affirmat** affirms (5); **non** not (6); **ei** one, him/her (7); **qui** who (8); **negat** denies (9); **incumbit** weighs upon, burdens (2); **probatio**

proof (1): Proof weighs upon one who affirms, not on one who denies.] The burden of proof lies on the person who affirms a fact, not on the one who denies it. See **actori incumbit** etc.

eisdem modis dissolvitur obligatio quae nascitur ex contractu, vel quasi, quibus contrahitur. [L. **eisdem** in the same (9); **modis** (in) ways (10); **dissolvitur** is dissolved (8); **obligatio** obligation (1); **quae** which (2); **nascitur** proceeds, arises (3); **ex** from (4); **contractu** drawing together, shrinking, contract, agreement (5); **vel** or (6); **quasi** a sort of, quasi (7); **quibus** in which (11); **contrahitur** it is contracted (12): An obligation which proceeds from a contract or a quasi, is dissolved in the same ways in which it is contracted.] *Law.* An obligation which originates from a contract or a quasi contract is dissolved in the same way that it was contracted. See **eodem modo quo quid constituitur dissolvitur.**

Eisen und Blut See **Blut und Eisen.**

ejaculatio praecox *n., pl.* **ejaculationes praecoces** [L. **ejaculatio** ejaculation (2); **praecox** premature (1): premature ejaculation.] Premature ejaculation during sexual intercourse.

ejusdem generis *abbr.* **e.g.** *adj.* [L. **ejusdem** of the same (1); **generis** (of) kind, class (2): of the same kind, class, character, or nature.] *Law.* The expression is generally used for limiting the application of a general term to a specific kind or group of things. *The goods sent by the manufacturer are not ejusdem generis as those mentioned in the contract.*

ejus est interpretari cujus est condere. [L. **ejus** of him (2); **est** it is (1); **interpretari** to interpret (3); **cujus** of whom (4); **est** it is (5); **condere** to make, establish (6): It is of him to interpret of whom it is to make.] It is the duty of the lawmaker to interpret the law (a maxim of the civil law no longer applicable).

ejus nulla culpa est cui parere necesse sit. [L. **ejus** of him (1); **nulla** no (7); **culpa** fault, error, blame, guilt, failure (8); **est** there is (6); **cui** to whom (2); **parere** to obey (5); **necesse** necessary (4); **sit** it should be, is (3): Of him to whom it is necessary to obey, there is no blame.] *Law.* A person who is bound to obey an order cannot be held responsible for an act; e.g., an executioner who executes a criminal or a police officer who, in the process of performing his duty, kills a suspect who resists arrest. See **qui jussu** etc.

élan *n., pl.* **élans** [Fr. spring, spirit, dash, outburst, impetus.] Enthusiasm. Zest. Vivacity. Ardor. Spirit. Dash. *Whatever Joe decides to do, he does it with considerable élan.*

El Caudillo *n.* [Sp. **el** the (1); **caudillo** leader (2): the leader, particularly one who has soldiers' personal loyalty.] Title, equivalent to **Il Duce** (q.v.). and **Führer** (q.v.), given to Generalissimo Franco. *Pro-Franco military men, disgruntled at losing the sweeping power they held under El Caudillo, have responded to the violence with increasing criticism*

of government "softness". . . (*Newsweek Int.* Jan 22, 1979:11). See **caudillo.**

Eldorado or **El Dorado** *n., pl.* **Los Dorados** or **Losdorados** or **El Dorados** [Sp. **el** the (1); **dorado** golden (place) (2): the golden place.] 1. The name given to a fantastically rich place which European explorers of the 16th century hoped to discover in South America. 2. A golden opportunity. A fabulously rich place. A place which offers fantastic opportunities for wealth and comfortable life. a) *In much of the Third World, the United States is viewed as a virtual El Dorado* (*Newsweek Int.* Sept. 28, 1981:51). b) *During the 1970s Nigeria, thanks to the oil boom, became a veritable Eldorado, and attracted foreigners from almost every corner of the world.*

electa una via, non datur recursus ad alteram. [L. **electa** (with) having been chosen (3); **una** with one (1); **via** (with) way (2); **non** not (7); **datur** is given (8); **recursus** retreat, return (4); **ad** to, at, for, according to (5); **alteram** the other (6): With one way having been chosen, return to the other is not given.] When one of two options has been chosen, it is not permissible to fall back on the other. See **electio semel** etc.

electiones fiant rite et libere sine interruptione aliqua. [L. **electiones** selections, elections (1); **fiant** should be made, conducted (2); **rite** duly, properly (3); **et** and (4); **libere** freely (5); **sine** without (6); **interruptione** interruption, interference (8); **aliqua** any (7): Elections should be conducted properly and freely without any interruption.] The conduct of elections should be proper, free, and without interference.

electio semel facta non patitur regressum. [L. **electio** election, choice (1); **semel** once (2); **facta** having been made (3); **non** not (4); **patitur** allows, permits (5); **regressum** return, retreat (6): A choice having once been made does not permit a retreat.] *Law.* Once a formal decision has been made to pursue a legal action and the process has started, the decision cannot be recalled. See **electa una** etc.

Electra complex See **Oedipus.**

elegantiae arbiter *n., pl.* **elegantiae arbitri.** Tacitus (c.55 –c.117 A.D.). *Annales* XVI,18. See **arbiter elegantiarum.**

elegit *n., pl.* **elegits** [L. He/she has chosen.] *English Law.* A judicial writ of execution, now obsolete, whereby a defendant's goods and/or lands could be delivered on account of debt to the plaintiff until the debt was paid off through the rents and profits, or the debtor's interest expired. Cf. **fieri facias.**

Elementa *pl. n.* [L. elements.] *The Elements,* the Latin title of the Greek *Stoicheia,* in which Euclid (fl. 3rd century B.C.) outlines his mathematical principles.

elenchus or **elenchos** *n., pl.* **elenchi** [L. **elenchus** from Gk. **elenchos** cross-examination, testing, scrutiny with the aim of refuting a point or some points.] *Logic.* Refutation of a proposition by syllogism or the deductive method. *Socrates, with his well-known method of elenchos, subjected almost every aspect of life to inquiry.*

élite or **elite** *n., pl.* **élites** or **elites** [Fr. choice, pick, flower, select few.] The flower, cream, choice part, aristocracy, or the superior part. A select few. A group in the society regarded as superior. A small group of citizens who exert influence or wield power. A special unit of highly trained soldiers. The specific meaning of the word depends upon its context, as shown in the following examples. a) *academic élite*; b) *African élite*; c) *bourgeois élite*; d) *business élite*; e) *educated élite*; f) *intellectual élite*; g) *ruling élite*; h) *Western educated élite.* —*adj.* Select, superior, choice, or picked. a) *élite cavalry regiment*; b) *élite Special Air Service*; c) . . . *the 14,000-man "Brunette" armored division, an élite corps* . . . (*Newsweek Int.* Dec 20, 1982:10).

Elle flotte, elle hésite; en un mot, elle est femme. Jean Racine (1636–1699). [Fr. **elle** she (1); **flotte** wavers, fluctuates (2); **elle** she (3); **hésite** hesitates, falters (4); **en** in (5); **un** a (6); **mot** word (7); **elle** she (8); **est** is (9); **femme** woman (10): She wavers, she hesitates; in a word, she is woman.] Because she wavers and hesitates she is a female. Cf. **varium et mutabile** etc.

ellipsis *n., pl.* **ellipses** [Gk. **elleipsis** defect, omission of a letter.] *Rhetoric.* 1. Marks which indicate an omission of words, phrases, or clauses in a written passage; e.g., a series of periods. 2. An abrupt transition from one topic to another, with no regard whatsoever for logical sequence. *Frequent use of ellipsis in his speech made his argument difficult to follow.*

El Niño [Sp. **el** the (1); **niño** child, boy (2): the child, the Christ child.] A periodic warming of Pacific waters off the coast of South America with significant climatic effects over much of the Pacific Ocean and the Americas. This warming process usually begins at Christmastime.

el presidente *n.* [Sp. **el** the (1); **presidente** president, chairman (2): the president.] The chief executive of the state. *Mexican courts cannot override laws decreed by el presidente,* . . . (*Newsweek Int.* July 5, 1982:40).

Elysium *n., pl.* **Elysiums** or **Elysia** [L.] 1. *Greek and Roman Mythology.* A blessed place where happy souls, particularly the souls of some favored heroes, went to live after death. 2. Paradise. A place, state, or abode of exceptional happiness. *The policemen found the accused at his residence in unmistakable Elysium as he entertained a number of guests.* Cf. **Hades**; **Tartarus**; and **Valhalla**.

embargo *n., pl.* **embargoes** [Sp. attachment, legal seizure, arrest.] 1. A governmental order forbidding ships to enter or depart from ports in the country. 2. Governmental prohibition of commercial activities either partially or completely. *Libya has hinted that it might stop oil shipments because of an American*

embargo *on sales of military aircraft to the Arab state* (*Newsweek Int.* June 25, 1979:37). 3. Prohibition, stoppage, or restraint. *The government has passed a decree imposing an embargo on promotion of public officials.* —*v. tr.* To prohibit movement of ships or commercial activities. . . . *the U.S. decision to embargo grain sales to the Soviet Union* . . . (*Newsweek Int.* Jan. 28, 1980:45).

embarras de choix *n.* [Fr. **embarras** embarrassment, difficulty (1); **de** of (2); **choix** choice (3): embarrassment of choice.] Too much to choose from. Difficulty in selecting or choosing from too many attractive alternatives. See **embarras de richesse**.

embarras de richesse *n.* [Fr. **embarras** embarrassment, difficulty (1); **de** of (2); **richesse** wealth, riches (3): an embarrassment of wealth.] A rich supply or abundance of details, materials, etc. which presents difficulties in choosing from among attractive alternatives. *This embarras de richesse presented serious problems of selection, organisation and presentation which I cannot pretend wholly to have solved* (Megarry 1973:ix). See **embarras de choix**.

embouchure *n., pl.* **embouchures** [Fr. mouth.] *Music.* 1. The position of the mouth and lips of a musician playing a wind instrument. 2. A mouthpiece.

embroglio *var.* of **imbroglio** (q.v.).

e mera gratia *adv.* [L. **e** out of, from (1); **mera** pure, mere (2); **gratia** favor, kindness (3): from mere/pure favor.] Purely out of kindness. *His request was granted not from any other consideration but e mera gratia.*

emeritus or *fem.* **emerita** *adj., pl.* **emeriti** or *fem.* **emeritae** [L. well-deserved, having finished work or service.] Retired but holding, as honorary title, his/her last position during service. Retired after gaining recognition. a) *emeritus professor*; b) *Professor Emeritus of Medicine*; c) *emerita professor*; d) *Professor Emerita of Philosophy;* e) *emeritus general.* —*n.* A person retired from service but retaining, as honorary title, his/her last position. *The eminent professor of surgery joined the ranks of the emeriti last year.* See **professor emeritus**.

emesis *n., pl.* **emeses** [Gk. vomiting.] *Medicine.* Act of vomiting. See **hyperemesis** and **hyperemesis gravidarum**.

émigré or **emigré** or **emigre** or *fem.* **émigrée** *n., pl.* **émigrés** or **emigrés** or **emigres** or *fem.* **émigrées** [Fr. one who has emigrated or left the country.] A person who leaves his country for political or other reasons. a) *Soviet émigré*; b) *Nicaraguan émigré*; c) *Polish émigré*; d) *Recently, one train from Moscow carried 48 Jewish émigrés (Time Int.* 1982); e) *Our embassies and high commissions must be reorganised to undertake effective mobilisation of Ghanaian émigrés wherever they are* . . . (K. Kuma in *West Africa* 1981).

éminence grise *n., pl.* **éminences grises** [Fr. **éminence** eminence, prominence (2); **grise** grey, dull (1): grey eminence.] 1. The nickname of Père Joseph, a monk and diplomat of France who was the confidential agent of the statesman, Cardinal Richelieu. 2. A confidential agent who unobtrusively and unofficially wields power. The power behind the ruler or the throne. a) . . . *Egon Bahr, the éminence grise of Schmidt's Social Democratic Party* . . . (*Newsweek Int.* Aug. 9, 1982:16). b) *It is widely believed that the wives of many rulers serve as éminences grises and are the real authors of some crucial decisions.*

eminentissimo or *fem.* **eminentissima** *n., pl.* **eminentissimi** or **eminentissimos** or *fem.* **eminentisime** [It. most prominent, eminent.] A very prominent person. A person of very high position in society.

emir *n., pl.* **emirs** [Fr. **émir** from Ar. **'amīr** commander.] A ruler in Near Eastern countries.

emissio *n., pl.* **emissiones** [L. sending forth.] Ejaculation. *There were three canonical conditions for virility: erectio, introductio and emissio* . . . (Eysenck 1982:63). Cf. **erectio** and **introductio**.

emphyteusis *n., pl.* **emphyteuses** [Gk. **enphuteusis:** **en** in (2); **phuteusis** planting (1): planting in, implanting, hereditary leasehold of property.] *Roman and Civil Law.* 1. A contract by which landed property was leased to a person forever or for a long period of time, subject, inter alia, to the payment of an annual rent and the improvement of the property by cultivation, building, etc. The lessee could give the property to another person or bequeath it to his/her heirs, provided that the terms of the contract were observed. 2. The right or tenure of such inheritable and alienable leasehold. See **emphyteuta, jure emphyteutico, jus emphyteuticarium,** and **jus emphyteuticum.**

emphyteuta *n., pl.* **emphyteutae** [Late L. from Gk. **emphuteutēs: en** in (2); **phyteutēs** one who is planted (1): one who is planted in, one who has been planted or settled.] *Civil Law.* A tenant who enjoys a perpetual or long lease. A tenant or lessee under **emphyteusis** (q.v.).

emporium *n., pl.* **emporia** or **emporiums** [L. from Gk. **emporion** a place of trade, market, mart, market-town.] A commercial center. A reasonably big center of business. A marketplace. A store selling a large variety of merchandise. *The small shop, which Mrs. Brown established ten years ago, has become an emporium, attracting customers from every part of the state.*

emptio bonorum or **bonorum emptio** *n.* [L. **emptio** purchase (1); **bonorum** of goods, property (2): purchase of goods.] *Civil Law.* Public sale of a debtor's property for the creditor's benefit. The purchaser acquires all the debtor's property and assets, and is required to settle liabilities and debts in accordance with a formula agreed upon during the transaction.

emptio et venditio or **emptio-venditio** *n.* [L. **emptio** purchase, buying (l); **et** and (2); **venditio** selling (3):

buying and selling.] *Roman Law.* A contract between two parties whereby one party buys something to be sold by the other at a fixed price.

enallage *n., pl.* **enallagae** or **enallages** [Gk. **enallagē** change, interchange.] *Rhetoric.* A change in grammar for effect or emphasis; e.g., "We was robbed!" For more examples, see Quinn 1982.

en autre droit *adv.* [Fr. **en** in, on, at (1); **autre** other (2); **droit** right (3): in other right.] *Law.* In the right of another person. See **autre droit.**

en banc *adv./adj.* [Fr. **en** in, on, at (1); **banc** bench (2): in bench.] *Law.* In full court. At a session of the court with all the judges sitting. At a court sitting with full authority. Applicable to a session of court where all the members, rather than a judge, panel, or the normally required quorum, participate and decide. This usually happens when a Court of Appeal is handling an important case. *The verdict of a court en banc.* See **in banc.**

en bloc *adv.* [Fr. **en** in, on, at (1); **bloc** block, lump (2): in a block.] All together. As a body. As a whole. As a unit. Wholesale. In a mass. In a lump. In one piece. *Henceforth Augustus' prerogative was voted en bloc to each new emperor without any restrictions of time* (Cary 1970:531). See **en gros** and **en masse.**

enceinte *adj.* [Fr. pregnant.] With child. Pregnant. *Thanks to modern fertility drugs, Mrs. Hack is now enceinte.*

enceinte *n., pl.* **enceintes** [Fr. belted in, walled in.] 1. Wall. Fence. Enclosure. 2. *Military.* Fortification surrounding a town or castle. Town or castle surrounded by fortification.

en clair *adv.* [Fr. **en** in, on, at (1); **clair** clear, plain (2): in clear or plain.] In plain clear language. Unambiguously. Clearly. Not in code. —*adj.* Clear. Plain. Unambiguous. Applicable, particularly, to diplomatic communications despatched by telegraph. *He tried to no purpose to explain why he misunderstood the message which was en clair.*

enclave *n., pl.* **enclaves** [Fr. enclosure, enclosed piece of land.] 1. Territory or district of one country completely surrounded by foreign territory. 2. Unique, distinct, or homogeneous district, area, or region in a country, city, etc. a) . . . *South Africa's Group Areas Act, a rigidly enforced pillar of apartheid that divides the country's residential areas into racial enclaves: white, colored, black and Indian* (*Newsweek Int.* April 19, 1982:35). b) *Ilorin . . . is an enclave of Yoruba-speaking people still under Dan Fodio's emirate* (*The Guardian* 1986).

encomienda *n., pl.* **encomiendas** [Sp. commission, concession, assignment, holding.] *Spanish Law.* A grant of both land and the native inhabitants which in former times the Crown made to Spanish colonists in Spain's overseas possessions.

encomium *n., pl.* **encomia** or **encomiums** [L. from Gk. **enkomion** laudatory ode, panegyric, eulogy.] A speech of praise. Panegyric. Eulogy. *He is such a dedicated, patriotic, conscientious, selfless, and talented statesman that no amount of encomium will do adequate justice to him.*

encore *n., pl.* **encores** [Fr. again, once more, anew.] 1. A request, usually in the form of shouting "Encore!" and clapping by the audience, for the reappearance of a performer or the repetition of an act. *The audience enjoyed the musical show to such an extent that they kept interrupting the show with shouts of encore.* 2. Reappearance of a performer or repetition of a performance on the request of the audience. *... the 32-year-old Briton romped through the first of eight concerts and returned for three tumultuous encores ... (Newsweek Int. June 4, 1979:19). —v. tr.* To request, usually by shouting "Encore!" and clapping, the reappearance of a performer or the repetition of a performance. *It was such a melodious song that it was encored several times.*

en échelon *adv./adj.* [**en** in, on, at (1); **échelon** step rung (2): in step.] In the form of a series of steps. In stepped formation.

en famille *adj./adv.* [Fr. **en** in, on, at (1); **famille** family (2): in family.] 1. At home. Exclusively with one's family. Treated as one belonging to the family. Among or with one's family. As a family. 2. As if in a family. Informally. *A reliable source has hinted that, in spite of the uncompromising attitude of the Administration, the President and some prominent aides worry en famille about the regime's loss of popularity.*

enfant chéri or *fem.* **enfant chérie** *n., pl.* **enfants chéris** or *fem.* **enfants chéries** [Fr. **enfant** child (2); **chéri** dear, beloved (1): dear child.] A pampered or spoiled child. A very dear child. Cf. **enfant gâté.**

enfant de miracle *n., pl.* **enfants de miracle** [Fr. **enfant** child (1); **de** of (2); **miracle** miracle, wonder (3): child of miracle.] A child whose birth, though a source of joy, was entirely unexpected. Applicable to a child born to elderly parents.

enfant gâté *n., pl.* **enfants gâtés** [Fr. **enfant** child (2); **gâté** pampered, spoilt (1): a pampered child.] A child who is spoiled. Cf. **enfant chéri.**

enfant terrible *n., pl.* **enfants terribles** [Fr. **enfant** child (2); **terrible** terrible, dreadful (1): terrible child.] 1. An unruly child. A problem child. Little terror. A child who causes embarrassment by making unpleasant or indiscreet remarks, or by uncontrollable conduct. *The Johnsons feel very uneasy whenever they visit friends, accompanied by their daughter Jane, an enfant terrible.* 2. A person who embarrasses his/her party, friends, allies, associates, etc., or who compromises his/her cause, by acts of indiscretion. A person or new member of a group who, by his/her conduct or opinions, embarrasses or annoys his/her colleagues, who hold orthodox, conventional, or conservative views. a) *The former enfant terrible of French*

composers, who combines a brilliant mathematical mind with an expert musical ear, Boulez ... (Time Int. 1981); b) ... he was elected to Parliament, where he quickly established himself as a witty and outspoken back-bencher, the enfant terrible of the Labor Party (Newsweek Int. Nov. 24, 1980:14).*

en fête *adj.* [Fr. **en** in, on, at (1); **fête** festival, feast (2): in festival.] Wearing festal dress. In a festive mood. In a holiday spirit or mood.

en garde [Fr. **en** in, on, at (1); **garde** guard (2): on guard.] On the alert. Watch out!

en gros *adv.* [Fr. **en** in, on, at (1); **gros** bulk, mass (2): in bulk.] By wholesale. On the whole. In a lump. In the main. See **en bloc** and **en masse.**

enigma or **aenigma** *n., pl.* **enigmata** or **aenigmata** or **enigmas** or **aenigmas** [Gk. **ainigma** riddle.] 1. A riddle. Something such as a statement, remark, speech or writing which is obscure or puzzling. *Any comment made by Zorro is usually an enigma and, to understand it, you need to be alert, ingenious, and very intelligent.* 2. Mystery. An inexplicable situation, incident, event, circumstance, or occurrence. A problem which is difficult to solve. *This brilliant work has solved many problems which have hitherto been enigmas.* 3. A person who is not easy to understand. A person who is inscrutable. A person who is a bundle of inconsistencies. a) *He spent most of his life in obscurity; he was an enigma even to many of the theological students who presumably knew him best (Time Int. 1980).* b) *Adio has been Shehu's friend for over ten years, but he is such an enigma that the latter knows very little about him.*

en masse *adv.* [Fr. **en** in, on, at (1); **masse** bulk, mass (2): in bulk.] In a mass. In a body. In great numbers. As one body. At wholesale. All together. As a whole. Collectively. In full force. In a lump. a) *... African countries supported the effort of the Palestinians en masse and broke diplomatic relations with Israel ... (Kole Omotoso in West Africa 1986).* b) *We are therefore calling on all Nigerians aged 18 and above to come en masse to vote in local government elections ... on 12th December, 1987 (The Guardian 1987).* See **en bloc** and **en gros.**

en ménage *adv.* [Fr. **en** in, on, at (1); **ménage** household, married couple (2): in a household.] As a married couple. Like husband and wife. Implying that they are actually not married. *The two students live together en ménage.*

en mort mayne *adv.* [Obs. Fr. **en** in, on, at (1); **mort** dead (2); **mayne** hand (3): in dead hand.] In mortmain. In permanent ownership. Cf. **in mortua manu** and **manus mortua.**

ennui *n., pl.* **ennuis** [Fr. boredom, tediousness, wearisomeness, tedium.] 1. Boredom. Weariness emanating from lack of interest. Discontent. Dissatisfaction. *It has been a very uneventful retirement, mostly characterized by ennui.* 2. Anything which causes boredom or weariness.

enosis *n.* [Mod. Gk. **henōsis** union.] Union, especially the unification of the island of Cyprus with the nation of Greece.

en passant *abbr.* **e.p.** *adv.* [Fr. **en** in, on, at (1); **passant** passing (2): in passing.] Incidentally. By the way. Cursorily. *In his speech he referred, en passant, to the uncooperative attitude of some members of staff.*

en pension *adv./adj.* [Fr. **en** in, on, at (1); **pension** board and lodging (2): in board and lodging.] Paying or charged a fixed amount for board and lodging. Residing as a boarder. *Since she was given a meager traveling allowance, she planned to live en pension at one of the inexpensive boardinghouses of New York.*

en plein air *adv.* [Fr. **en** in, on, at (1); **plein** full, complete (2); **air** air (3): in full air.] In the open air. Cf. **al fresco**.

en poste *adv.* [Fr. **en** in, on, at (1); **poste** post, appointment (2): at post.] In office. *. . . the country's triad of financial advisers . . . remain en poste under the new regime . . . (West Africa* 1984).

en prince *adv.* [Fr. **en** in, on, at, in the manner of (1); **prince** prince (2): in the manner of a prince.] In princely fashion. Lavishly. *The Cromwells entertained the 100 guests at the party en prince.*

en principe *adv.* [Fr. **en** in, on, at (1); **principe** principle (2): in principle.] As a matter of principle. On principle. As a principle. As a rule. Theoretically. In theory. *The two parties accepted the proposals en principe and agreed to meet subsequently for detailed discussions.*

enragé *n., pl.* **enragés** [Fr. *adj.* mad, crazy, enthusiastic or *n.* one who is mad, a fan.] A fan. An enthusiastic supporter or follower. A fanatic. An enthusiast. *Only among the enragés of the CPP was he to find a responsive cord and the stimulus which he clearly needed for his brand of politics* (Dr. M. Anafu in *West Africa* 1983).

en rapport *adj.* [Fr. **en** in, on, at (1); **rapport** connection, contact (2): in connection or contact.] In harmony. In a condition of mutual understanding, sympathy, or relationship. *For a leader to be successful, he must be en rapport with his followers.*

en route *abbr.* **e.r.** *adj./adv.* [Fr. **en** in, on, at (1); **route** road, course, route (2): on the road.] Along the way. In the course of a journey or voyage. On the way. On one's way. While being transported. a) *. . . U.S. peacemaker Philip Habib arrived in Jerusalem en route to Damascus and Amman . . . (Newsweek Int.* March 15, 1982:24); b) *I also spotted Senator Onyeabor Obi, en route from an international conference on the legal profession* (*The Guardian* 1986). Cf. **en voyage** and **in itinere**.

ensemble *n., pl.* **ensembles** [Fr. together, at the same time, whole, set, unit, unity, harmony.] 1. The whole. Something regarded as a whole. Music of several parts which make one whole. *The music in the first scene of act three . . . includes three grandiose ensembles,*

all of which use musical material from the opera's prologue (*Newsweek Int.* March 12, 1979:59). 2. A complete costume made up of several items which are harmonious. *Armani displayed fifteen leather outfits, among them a culotte-and-shirt ensemble in neon jade, purple and mint green . . . (Newsweek Int.* Oct. 19, 1981:56). 2. A number of separate furnishings which harmonize and form one group. 3. A group of people who act together to achieve a particular objective; e.g., a group of musicians, a group of dancers, etc. *Twelve string instrumentalists calling themselves City of London Sinfonia arrive for two special concerts. . . . Works in the repertoire of the ensemble include Mozart's* Eine Kleine Nacht-musik . . . (*The Guardian* 1986).

ense petit placidam sub libertate quietem. [L. **ense** (by, with) a sword (1); **petit** he/she looks for, seeks (2); **placidam** pleasing, pleasant (3); **sub** under, beneath (5); **libertate** liberty, freedom (6); **quietem** quiet, tranquillity (4): With a sword he/she looks for pleasing tranquillity under freedom.] By the sword he/she seeks pleasant quiet under liberty. Motto of the State of Massachusetts.

en-soi *adv.* [Fr. **en** in (1); **soi** oneself, himself, herself, itself, themselves (2): in itself.] Being in itself as opposed to **pour-soi** (q.v.), as developed by Jean-Paul Sartre (1905–1980) in **L'Être et le néant** (q.v.). Cf. **eo ipso**.

en suite *adv./adj.* [Fr. **en** in, on, at (1); **suite** succession, series, continuation (2): in succession.] 1. In a succession. In a series. 2. One leading to, or opening into, another. Applicable to rooms. *The family lives in a magnificent house of seven rooms, each equipped with a bathroom en suite.* 3. Arranged in a harmonious set. *After a day of hard work, Tunji always goes home to relax in his favorite chair with a footstool en suite.*

entente *n., pl.* **ententes** [Fr. arrangement, understanding.] 1. A friendly understanding. An agreement. 2. An understanding or agreement, less formal and binding than an alliance, among friendly nations to pursue a common foreign policy. *Black African nations have railed against Reagan's entente with Pretoria* (*Newsweek Int.* Nov. 9, 1981:16). 3. Nations that are parties to such an agreement. *The four nations turned out to be strange bedfellows and so constituted a weak entente.*

entente cordiale *n.* [Fr. **entente** agreement, understanding (2); **cordiale** cordial, hearty (1): hearty agreement.] A cordial or friendly understanding, especially between two nations on matters of foreign policy. *With the establishment of an entente cordiale between the two nations, peace has been restored to the border.*

entourage *n., pl.* **entourages** [Fr. circle of friends, following, advisers, surroundings, environment.] 1. A building's surroundings. *It is not easy to decide which is more beautiful, the mansion or its entourage.* 2. An important person's retinue, attendants, followers, or associates. *The paramount chief arrived at the meeting with an entourage of twenty subchiefs.*

entr'acte *n., pl.* **entr'actes** [Fr. **entracte** from entre between, among (1); acte act, action, deed (2): between acts, an intermission.] 1. An interval or interlude between two acts of a play, opera, etc. *Before starting on the narrative of the great Persian expedition . . . , as a kind of entr'acte between that and the Ionian revolt, Herodotus relates various hostile undertakings against Greek cities . . .* (Lesky 1966:313). 2. A dance, a musical piece, etc., performed during such interval.

entrada *abbr.* **etr.** *n., pl.* **entradas** [Sp. entrance, entry, admission.] A journey or expedition into a territory which has not been explored.

entrant *n., pl.* **entrants** [Fr. incomer, one entering.] A person who enters a competition, school, college, profession, etc. a) *The principal of the school warned old students not to maltreat new entrants.* b) *Among the entrants was a team from Colombia, expert in mountain racing . . .* (*Newsweek Int.* July 25, 1983:49).

entrée or **entree** *n., pl.* **entrées** or **entrees** [Fr. entry, entrance, admittance, admission, access.] 1. Entrance. *The girl's conspicuous entrée into the hall attracted comments from almost everybody.* 2. Right, privilege or permission to enter or to be admitted. Qualification for entrance or admission. *My father insists that no one should enter his bedroom without obtaining entrée.* 3. *France.* A dish served between the principal courses of a dinner. 4. *U.S.A.* The main dish of a dinner. Cf. **carte d'entrée.**

entre nous *adv.* [Fr. **entre** between (1); **nous** us, ourselves (2): between us.] Between ourselves. Between you and me. In confidence. *Desmond committed an unpardonable breach of trust when he disclosed to Margaret what I had told him entre nous.*

entrepôt *n., pl.* **entrepôts** [Fr. a warehouse, storehouse, emporium.] 1. A warehouse where goods are deposited. A storehouse. An intermediary place where imported or exported goods are collected and distributed. *As the first port of call for ships coming from Europe, . . . Dakar was naturally destined to play the role of entrepôt between Europe and subsequent ports of call* (Suret-Canale 1971:194). 2. *France.* A place where temporarily imported goods are kept to be re-exported subsequently without payment of duty.

entrepreneur or *fem.* **entrepreneuse** *n., pl.* **entrepreneurs** or *fem.* **entrepreneuses** [Fr. contractor.] 1. A person who, at his/her own financial risk, establishes, organizes, and manages a business enterprise. *Many entrepreneurs, who often devote themselves to business at the expense of family, watch from retirement or the grave as the bequests they cared about almost collapse or pass into other hands* (*Newsweek Int.* Dec. 12, 1983:45). 2. A promoter, organizer, manager, and practitioner of an activity or enterprise. 3. A person who serves as an intermediary or middleman.

enumeratio unius est exclusio alterius. [L. **enumeratio** enumeration (1); **unius** of one (2); **est** is (3); **exclusio** exclusion (4); **alterius** of the other (5): The enumeration of one is the exclusion of the other.] *Law.* A principle whereby if one thing or a number of things in a group are enumerated, the others in the group are deemed to have been excluded. See **designatio unius** etc.

en ventre sa mère *adj.* [Obs. Fr. **en** in, on, at (1); **ventre** belly, stomach (2); **sa** one's (3); **mère** mother (4): in the belly of one's mother.] *Law.* In the form of a fetus. Unborn. In utero. In some cases a child en ventre sa mère, i.e., an unborn child, is regarded as a child in being and thus entitled to benefits such as taking a legacy or having a guardian. *A child en ventre sa mère, who is in due course born, is included in a gift to children as if he were actually born . . .* (Parry 1961:128). See **fetus**; **in ventre sa mere**; and **qui in utero** etc.

environs *pl. n.* [Fr. the area, the vicinity.] The surroundings. Environment. The area immediately surrounding a city, monument, or event.

envoûtement *n., pl.* **envoûtements** [Fr. spell, magic, charm, bewitchment.] Magic which involves the use of a person's image, picture, or likeness to harm him/her by influencing his/her fate.

en voyage *adv.* [Fr. **en** in, on, at (1); **voyage** journey, voyage (2): on a journey.] While on a voyage or journey. While traveling. Cf. **en route** and **in itinere.**

E.O. or **e.o.** *abbr.* for **ex officio** (q.v.).

eodem ligamine quo ligatum est dissolvitur. [L. **eodem** by the same (2); **ligamine** (by) band (3); **quo** by which (4); **ligatum est** it was bound together (5); **dissolvitur** it is dissolved, annulled (1): It is dissolved by the same band by which it was bound together.] *Law.* A contract is dissolved by the same means by which it was made. See **eodem modo quo quid constituitur dissolvitur.**

eodem modo quo quid constituitur dissolvitur. [L. **eodem** by/in the same (3); **modo** (by) way (4); **quo** in which (5); **quid** something (1); **constituitur** it is made, established (6); **dissolvitur** it is dissolved (2): Something is dissolved in the same way in which it is made.] *Law.* A thing is dissolved in the same way that it is made. See **eisdem modis dissolvitur** etc.; **eodem ligamine** etc.; **eodem modo quo quid constituitur, eodem** etc.; **jura eodem modo** etc.; **naturale est** etc.; **nihil est magis** etc.; **nihil tam conveniens** etc.; **nihil tam naturale** etc.; **nudi consensus** etc.; **omnia quae jure** etc.; **quo ligatur** etc.; **quo modo quid** etc.; **solvitur eo ligamine** etc.; **unumquodque dissolvitur** etc.; **unumquodque eodem modo** etc.; and **verborum obligatio** etc.

eodem modo quo quid constituitur, eodem modo destruitur. [L. **eodem** by/in the same (1); **modo** (by/in) way (2); **quo** in which (3); **quid** something (4); **constituitur** is made, established (5); **eodem** in the same (6); **modo** (in) way (7); **destruitur** it is destroyed, torn down (8): In the same way in which something is made, in the same way it is destroyed.] A thing is destroyed in the same way in which it is made. See **eodem modo quo quid constituitur dissolvitur.**

eo intuitu *adv.* [L. **eo** with that (1); **intuitu** (with) consideration, view (2): with that view.] With that intent/object. *Adams had tried on a number of occasions to steal stencils from the secretary's office and, eo intuitu, he brought a large envelope to the office.*

eo ipso *adv.* [L. **eo** by him/it (1); **ipso** himself/itself (2): by it itself.] By the thing itself. Cf. **en-soi.**

eon *var.* of **aeon** (q.v.).

eo nomine *adv.* [L. **eo** by that (1); **nomine** (by) name (2): by that name.] In/under/by that name or appellation. *Investigations revealed that he is not known eo nomine.*

e.p. *abbr.* for **en passant** (q.v.).

E.P. or **e.p.** *abbr.* for **editio princeps** (q.v.).

epanalepsis *n., pl.* **epanalepses** [Gk. **ep(i)** at, on, after, in addition to (3); **ana** up, back, again (2); **lēpsis** taking hold, seizing, capturing (1): seizing again in addition to, resumption, repetition.] *Rhetoric.* Ending a sentence with the same word or words with which it began; e.g., **nil posse creari de nilo** (q.v.) or "Nothing to be able to be created out of nothing."

epanorthosis *n., pl.* **epanorthoses** [Gk. **epanorthōsis: ep(i)** at, on, after, in addition to (2): **anorthōsis** restoration (1): restoration on, setting right, correcting.] *Rhetoric.* Placing a word or phrase immediately after another for greater emphasis or clarification; e.g., "He hurt, indeed destroyed, her."

épater les bourgeois Alexandre Private d'Anglemont (died 1859). [Fr. **épater** to shock (1); **les** the (2); **bourgeois** bourgeois (3): to shock the bourgeois.] In order to startle established society. In order to be unconventional.

epexegesis *n., pl.* **epexegeses** [Gk. **epexēgēsis: ep(i)** at, on, after, in addition to (2); **exēgēsis** statement, narrative, explanation (1): narrative in addition to, detailed account, explanation.] *Rhetoric.* An expression which follows a word, phrase, clause or text, and qualifies or explains it; e.g., "The great Ghanaian pan-Africanist, Kwame Nkrumah."

ephemeron *n., pl.* **ephemera** [Gk. **ephēmeron: epi** at, on, after, in addition to (1); **hēmer(a)** day (2): (a thing) on a day.] 1. Something which is short-lived or intended to have a short life-span, such as an organization, office, or publication. 2. An insect which spends only a day in its adult or winged stage.

epigone *n., pl.* **epigones** [Ger. from Gk. **epigonos** successor, decadent, imitator.] A second-rate imitator. **Epigonos** (q.v.).

epigonos *n., pl.* **epigonoi** or **epigoni** [Gk. **epi** at, on, after, in addition to (2); **gonos** that which is born,

child (1): that which is born after, successor, descendant.] 1. *Greek Mythology.* One of the sons of the seven chiefs who attacked Thebes and fell in the process. The sons themselves subsequently attacked Thebes. 2. A follower who imitates the leader. A poor imitator of an eminent author, artist, musician, philosopher, etc. *The novel, the work of an epigonos, is replete with hackneyed themes and rarely rises beyond the ordinary.* See **epigone.**

epigramma *n., pl.* **epigrammata** [Gk. from **epi** at, on, after, in addition to (2); **gramma** thing written (1): thing written on.] 1. A tombstone inscription, often written in verse. 2. An epigram, i.e., a short poem usually consisting of an elegiac couplet or a small number of elegiac couplets. —**Epigramma** A collection of epigrams, especially those of Martial (c.A.D. 40–103/4).

epiphenomenon *n., pl.* **epiphenomena** or **epiphenomenons** [Gk. **epiphainomenon: epi** at, on, after, in addition to (2); **phainomenon** that which appears (1): that which appears on, something appearing on the surface.] 1. A secondary phenomenon, event, or development, which accompanies, and supposedly emanated from, the original phenomenon, event, or development. *A serious-minded person pursues his objective with tenacity of purpose and does not permit his attention to be distracted by epiphenomena.* 2. *Medicine.* A secondary disease or symptom which arises in the course of a disease. *The diagnosis of the disease was complicated by a number of epiphenomena which subsequently emerged.*

epistemophilia *n., pl.* **epistemophiliae** or **epistemophilias** [Neo-Gk. from Gk. **epistemē** knowledge (2); **philia** love (1): love of knowledge.] Inordinate pursuit of, or preoccupation with, knowledge.

epistrophe *n., pl.* **epistrophae** or **epistrophes** [Gk. **epi** at, on, after, in addition to (2); **strophē** turning (1): turning after.] *Rhetoric.* Using the same word or phrase at the end of a series of phrases or sentences. Cf. **anaphora.**

epistula *n., pl.* **epistulae** [L. letter.] A letter. An epistle. —**Epistulae** A collection of letters, especially those of Cicero (106–43 B.C.) and Seneca (c.4 B.C.–65 A.D.).

epit. *abbr.* for **epitome** (q.v.).

épître *n, pl.* **épitres** [Fr. from L. **epistula** letter.] A formal letter, especially one intended for publication. —**Épitres** A collection of formal letters, such as those of Jean Chapelain (1595–1674).

epithalamium (L.) or **epithalamion** (Gk.) *n., pl.* **epithalamia** or **epithalamiums** [Gk. **epi** at, on, after, in addition to (1); **thalamion** that which regards the chamber, especially the marriage chamber (2): that which regards at the marriage chamber, a bridal song sung at the marriage bed.] A nuptial poem, song, or ode honoring or praising a bridegroom or bride. See **prothalamium.**

epitome *abbr.* **epit.** *n., pl.* **epitomes** [Gk. **epitomē: epi** at, on, after, in addition to (2); **tomē** cutting (1): cutting at, a shortening, abridgment.] 1. Abstract. Summary. Abridgment. **Compendium** (q.v.). Brief statement. *The magazine carries weekly epitomes of great works.* Cf. **précis, résumé,** and **synopsis.** 2. Embodiment. Ideal. A person or thing which remarkably symbolizes a quality, character, trait, type, etc. a) *Dupe is the epitome of all the qualities that Musa desires in his ideal woman.* b) *Walter Matthau, the epitome of slob insouciance . . . (Time Int.* 1982). c) *Unsmiling and self-effacing, he seemed the epitome of the colorless bureaucrat (Newsweek Int.* Jan. 5, 1981:9).

epizeuxis *n., pl.* **epizeuxes** [Gk. **epi** at, on, after, in addition to (2); **zeuxis** yoking, joining (1): yoking in addition.] *Rhetoric.* Repeating the same word or phrase in quick succession for effect or emphasis; e,g, "What a joy, joy, joy it is to see you again!" Cf. **diacope.**

e pluribus unum [L. **e** out of, from (2); **pluribus** more, several (persons or things) (3); **unum** one (1): one out of several.] One out of many. Motto of the U.S.A. *. . . I see also the whole people of America, one nation formed of many people. E pluribus unum* (Pope John Paul II in *Newsweek Int.* Oct. 15, 1979:56).

epos *n.* [Gk. word, song.] 1. Epic poetry in general or an epic poem in particular. 2. The cultural inheritance of a society, especially as it is preserved in oral tradition.

equitas sequitur legem. See **aequitas sequitur legem.**

e.r. *abbr.* for **en route** (q.v.).

erectio *n.* [L. a straightening, elevating.] *Physiology.* Enlargement of a body part by blood (e.g., of the penis or the clitoris). Cf. **emissio** and **introductio.**

ergo *adv.* [L. therefore.] Consequently. Accordingly. Then. Hence. Sometimes used to lay emphasis on an illogical inference. a) *"Thou shalt not bear false witness against thy neighbour." Ergo, thou shalt bear false witness in his favour if required . . .* (Megarry 1973:86). b) *. . . he maintains that well-being is not a quality per se, but a form of equilibrium. Ergo, cancer is not a cause of unbalance but a consequence (Time Int.* 1982).

ergomania *n.* [Neo-Gk. from Gk. **ergo(n)** work (2); **mania** madness, enthusiasm (1): madness with work, enthusiasm for work.] *Psychology.* Mental disorder which takes the form of excessive enthusiasm for, or devotion to, work. Cf. **ergophobia.**

ergophobia *n.* [Neo-Gk. from Gk. **ergo(n)** work (2); **phob(os)** fear (1): fear of work.] *Psychology.* Excessive fear or dislike of work. Cf. **ergomania.**

Erinys *n., pl.* **Erinyes** [Gk. **Erinus** avenging deity, guilt, remorse, punishment visited upon the guilty.] 1. *Greek and Roman Mythology.* One of a group of avenging deities who punish murder and other offenses by tormenting the criminal. Avenging Fury. *As though tormented by the Erinyes, the suspect began to have nightmares.* 2. Guilty conscience. Remorse.

Eros *n.* [Gk. **Erōs** sexual love.] 1. The Greek god of falling in and out of love. Also known by the Latin name Cupid.

2. *Psychology.* The psychological drive for reproduction and sexual enjoyment. —**eros** *n., pl.* **erotes** *Art.* A naked and winged little boy carrying bow and arrows.

erotica *pl. n.* [Gk. **erōtika** things related to sexual love, erotic things.] Books and art which treat sexual love, especially in a sensuous manner. *Pornography is the product of woman-hatred, marked by cruelty or violence, and shouldn't be confused with erotica, which is rooted in the idea of free will and love* (Steinem in *Newsweek Int.* Nov. 5, 1979:30). Cf. **curiosa; esoterica;** and **facetiae.**

erotogenesis *n.* [Neo-Gk. from Gk. **erō(s)** love (2); **genesis** production, generation (1): production or generation of love.] Stimulation of sexual feeling.

erotomania *n.* [Gk. **erō(s)** love (1); **mania** madness (2): love madness, raving love.] Insanity which takes the form of excessive desire for sexual intercourse. See **andromania.**

errare humanum est. [L. **errare** to err, to make a mistake (2); **humanum** human (3); **est** is, has been (2): To err is human.] To make a mistake is human.

erratum *n., pl.* **errata** [L. that which has wandered, a fault, an error.] A mistake, usually a misstatement or misprint. *The book has in its appendix a corrigendum showing the errata and their corrections.* Cf. **corrigendum.**

error coram nobis *n.* [L. **error** mistake, error (1); **coram** before, in the presence of (2); **nobis** us (3): the error/mistake before us.] *Law.* A mistake in the proceedings before us. A writ, brought directly to the court which pronounced judgment, for review or modification on account of an error of fact which renders the validity of the proceedings questionable. See **coram nobis.** Cf. **error coram vobis.**

error coram vobis *n.* [L. **error** mistake, error (1); **coram** before, in the presence of (2); **vobis** you (3): the error/mistake before you.] *Law.* A mistake in the proceedings before you. A writ for review or modification, based on alleged error of fact, issued from an appellate court to the court which pronounced judgment. See **coram vobis.** Cf. **error coram nobis.**

errores ad sua principia referre, est refellere. [L. **errores** errors, mistakes (2); **ad** to, at, for, according to (3); **sua** their (4); **principia** origins, beginnings (5); **referre** to refer (1); **est** is (6); **refellere** to refute, rebut, expose (7): To refer errors to their origins is to refute them.] The best way of exposing an error is to trace it back to its origin.

error in vacuo *n.* [L. **error** error, mistake (1); **in** in, on (2); **vacuo** void, vacuum (3): error in the void.] *Law.* A harmless error, i.e., an error in legal proceedings which has no adverse effect. The judge may be criticized, but it would be no ground for retrial of the case.

error nominis *n.* [L. **error** error, mistake (1); **nominis** of name (2): mistake of name.] *Law.* A mistake respecting a name. *Error nominis on a certificate can* *cause the holder a great deal of embarrassment.* Cf. **error personae.**

error nominis numquam nocet, si de identitate rei constat. [L. **error** error, mistake (1); **nominis** of name (2); **numquam** never (3); **nocet** does harm, hurts, injures (4); **si** if (5); **de** of, from, about, for (7); **identitate** identity (8); **rei** of the matter, thing, property, business, affair (9); **constat** it is agreed, known, established (6): Error of name never does harm, if it is established about the identity of the thing.] *Law.* A mistake respecting a name is never harmful, if the identity of the thing is established. See **falsa demonstratio non nocet.**

error personae *n.* [L. **error** error, mistake (1); **personae** of person (2): error/mistake of person.] *Law.* A mistake respecting the identity of a person. Cf. **error nominis.**

error qui non resistitur, approbatur. [L. **error** error, mistake (1); **qui** which (2); **non** not (3); **resistitur** is resisted, opposed (4); **approbatur** is approved (5): An error which is not resisted is approved.] *Law.* An error which is not resisted is deemed to have been approved. Thus, a person who knowingly makes it possible for another to commit fraud is equally culpable. Also, if property is being sold at auction and a person who has title to it knowingly fails to raise any objection, he/she forfeits his/her title to it. See **qui non improbat, approbat.**

ersatz *n.* [Ger. **Ersatz** substitute.] 1. A substitute. Something artificial used in place of a natural product. 2. A substitute which, though superficially similar to the original product, is inferior or spurious. —*adj.* Substitute. Fake. Imitation. Inferior. Spurious. Not genuine. Counterfeit. a) *The old woman advised her granddaughter to avoid a particular market, which is notorious for the sale of ersatz products.* b) *The council is dominated by hypocritical and obsequious members who save valuable time on ersatz issues.*

eruv *n., pl.* **eruvim** [Heb.] 1. The specifically-defined area where Orthodox Jews can spend the Sabbath. 2. Any area or zone to which specific activities are restricted.

erythrophobia *n.* [Neo-Gk. from Gk. **eruthro(s)** red (2); **phob(os)** fear (1): fear of red.] *Psychology.* 1. Abnormal fear or dislike of the color red. 2. Abnormal fear of blushing.

escapade *n., pl.* **escapades** [Fr. adventure, prank, freak.] A foolish adventure. A daring exploit. A wild prank. A mischievous act. An adventure involving unorthodox, immoral, or mischievous conduct. *Daniel's amorous escapades have won for him the animosity of husbands, boyfriends, and maltreated women.*

esoterica *pl. n.* [Gk. **esōterika** inner things.] 1. Esoteric, mysterious or secret items. Things meant for a select few or the initiated. 2. Pornography. Cf. **curiosa;** **erotica;** and **facetiae.**

esplanade *n., pl.* **esplanades** [Fr. a flat, level space.] 1. The open area on top of a wall in a medieval castle or the open space between the castle and its adjacent town. 2. A broad, open area in a city, especially a river walk or road.

esprit *n., pl.* **esprits** [Fr. mind, spirit, wit, intellect.] Lively wit. Cleverness. Liveliness. Vivacity. *During holidays Mother, with her unique esprit, entertains us and makes the days pass like a flash of lightning.*

esprit de corps *n.* [Fr. **esprit** spirit (1); **de** of (2); **corps** body (3): spirit of body.] Selfless, enthusiastic, and unflinching devotion and loyalty to one's group, association, or society and its traditions, objectives, and interests. Fraternity. Public spirit. Team spirit. a) *Both of us were therefore attracted to each other as characteristic of the military ethos of esprit de corps* (*Sunday Tribune* 1986). b) *For no body of men were ever more strongly united by mutual loyalty and esprit de corps than the governing caste of Rome* (Robinson 1974:106). Cf. **Gemeinschaftsgefühl.**

esprit de l'escalier *n., pl.* **esprits de l'escalier** Denis Diderot (1713–1784). [Fr. **esprit** mind, spirit, wit, intellect (1); **de** of (2); **l'** the (3); **escalier** stair, staircase (4): wit of the stair.] Staircase wit. The witty response which one conceives when it is too late, i.e., when descending the stairs from a salon or room where the original remark was made.

esse *n.* [L. to be, to exist.] *Philosophy.* Existence. Mere existence. Essence. Essential nature. Cf. **bene esse.**

esse quam videri [L. **esse** being, to be (1); **quam** rather than (2); **videri** seeming, to seem (3): being rather than seeming.] To be rather than to seem. To be in reality instead of merely seeming to be. Motto of the State of North Carolina.

est aliquid quod non oportet etiam si licet; quicquid vero non licet certe non oportet. [L. **est** there is (1); **aliquid** something (2); **quod** which (3); **non** not (4); **oportet** is proper, becoming (5); **etiam** even (6); **si** if (7); **licet** it is lawful, permitted (8); **quicquid** whatever, whatsoever (10); **vero** but in fact, however (9); **non** not (11); **licet** it is lawful, permitted (12); **certe** certainly (13); **non** not (14); **oportet** is proper, becoming (15): There is something which is not proper even if it is lawful; however, whatever is not lawful is certainly not proper.] *Law.* Something may be improper even though lawful, but whatever is unlawful is certainly improper. Cf. **multa non vetat** etc. and **non omne quod** etc.

esto perpetua. [L. **esto** be, let him/her/it be (1); **perpetua** *fem.* eternal, perpetual (2): Let her be eternal.] Let it last forever. Motto of the State of Idaho.

et al. *abbr.* for l. **et alibi** (q.v.). 1. **et alibi** (q.v.). 2. **et alii** (q.v.).

et alibi *abbr.* **et al.** *adv.* [L. **et** and (1); **alibi** elsewhere (2): and elsewhere.] And in other places. Used in bibliographical references to indicate that something can be found elsewhere in the book, work, article, etc.

et alii *pl. n.* or *fem.* **et aliae** or *neut.,* **et alia** *abbr.* **et al.,** *masc. sing.* **et alius** *fem.* **et alia** or *neut.* **et aliud** [L. **et** and (1); **alii** others (2): and others.] And others (e.g., people, authors, places, things). a) *Okoro et alii*; b) *Ngozi et aliae.*

étatisme *n., pl.* **étatismes** [Fr. belief in the state.] A political doctrine affirming state control of all aspects of economic and social life. State control. State socialism. State management. Etatism. Statism.

et cetera *abbr.* **etc.** [L. **et** and (1); **cetera** others, the rest (2): and others.] And the rest. And so on. And so forth. *The police are probing allegations of bribery, embezzlement, corruption, robbery, et cetera in the ministry.* —*n.* **etcetera** A number or list of persons or things. *A short etcetera of people to be invited for the ceremony has already been compiled.* —*pl.* **etceteras** Additional or other things. Extras. Sundries. *Emily took for the excursion a suitcase full of clothing, cosmetics, provisions, and etceteras.*

et cum spiritu tuo [L. **et** and (1); **cum** with, together with, in the company of, along with (2); **spiritu** spirit (4); **tuo** (3): and with your spirit.] And with you. The response to **dominus vobiscum** (q.v.).

e tenebris lux [L. **e** out of, from, directly after, away from (2); **tenebris** darkness, gloom (3); **lux** light (1): light out of darkness.] Light in a dark place. 1. A reference to God's creation of light from darkness in Genesis 1:4. 2. The moment of intellectual or spiritual enlightenment after a period of dark confusion or despair. *The students struggled with the difficult text for a long time and only a few of them found e tenebris lux.*

ethos *n.* [Gk. custom, usage, character, disposition.] The character, spirit, values, ideals, standards, beliefs, customs, and practices of an institution, people, community, region, age, or epoch. *The reforms are doomed to failure mainly because the ethos of the people was not taken into consideration.*

et id genus omne [L. **et** and (1); **id** that (3); **genus** kind (4); **omne** all (2): and all that kind.] And everything of the sort.

et in Arcadia ego. [L. **et** and, even (1); **in** in, on (3); **Arcadia** Arcadia (4); **ego** I (2): And I in Arcadia.] Even I am in Arcadia. A tombstone inscription in which "I" can represent the deceased, the tomb, or a personification of Death and Arcadia represents the tranquillity and contentment of the countryside. Often associated with the paintings of N. Poussin and J. Reynolds. Cf. **Arcadia.**

etiquette *n., pl.* **etiquettes** [Fr. **étiquette** ceremony, formality.] 1. Behavior required by rule or custom. Conventional behavior, propriety, or decorum required by good education, the norms of society, or regulations. a) *social etiquette*; b) *table etiquette*. 2. Code of ethics binding on professionals. a) *professional etiquette*; b) *medical etiquette*; c) *athletic etiquette*; d) *journalistic etiquette.*

etr. *abbr.* for **entrada** (q.v.).

et semel emissum volat irrevocabile verbum. Horace (65–8 B.C.). *Epistles* XVIII,71. [L. **et** and (1); **semel**

once (3); **emissum** uttered, having been uttered (4); **volat** flies, spreads quickly (5); **irrevocabile** irrevocable, unalterable (6); **verbum** word (2): And a word, once having been uttered, flies, irrevocable.] Once a word has been uttered, it spreads rapidly, never to be recalled.

et sequens *abbr.* **et seq.** [L. **et** and (1); **sequens** the following one (2): and the following one.] See **et sequentes.**

et sequentes *masc.* and *fem. pl.* of **et sequens** or *neut. pl.* **et sequentia** *abbr.* **et seq** or **et seqq** or **et sqq.** [L. **et** and (1); **sequentes** following ones (2): and the following ones.] And those following. And the following. Used for references in book; e.g., "See p. 6 et seq." means "See p. 6 and the following pages."

et sic ulterius *adv.* [L. **et** and (1); **sic** so, thus (2); **ulterius** farther (3): and thus farther.] And so on.

et tu? *interj.* [L. **et** and, too, also, even (2); **tu** you (1): You too!] You also! An exclamatory expression of surprise, shock, disbelief, disappointment, etc. *Et tu, David Stockman?* (*Newsweek Int.* Nov. 23, 1981:36). See **et tu, Brute?**

et tu, Brute? *interj.* Julius Caesar. (100–44 B.C.). [L. **et** and, too, also, even (2); **tu** you (1); **Brute** Brutus (3): You too, Brutus!] You also, Brutus! 1. A Latin translation of **kai su teknon** (q.v.), the Greek words uttered by Julius Caesar on the Ides of March (March 15), 44 B.C., when he saw Brutus among the assassins. 2. A reproach to a friend or trusted person who has conspired with others against one. Exclamatory expression of surprise, shock, etc. *When Phil noticed that the bullet had been fired by Amos, he shouted "Amos! Et tu, Brute?" and fell dead.* Cf. **et tu?**

étude or **etude** *n., pl.* **études** or **etudes** [Fr. study.] *Music.* 1. A composition used to develop the performer's technique. 2. A composition performed to demonstrate the performer's technique and for aesthetic reasons.

étui *n., pl.* **étuis** [Fr. case.] A small box, usually decorated and used for storing needles and other artifacts.

et uxor *abbr.* **et ux.** [L. **et** and (1); **uxor** wife (2): and wife.] And wife. *Law.* Used to include a wife along with her husband. *Mr. Benson et ux.*

etymon *n., pl.* **etyma** or **etymons** [Gk. **etumon** a true, real thing.] *Linguistics.* The primitive or original form of a word. A foreign word from which a particular word is derived.

euge *interj.* [Gk. Well done!] Bravo! (q.v.). —*n., pl.* **euges** An expression of approval for a commendable act. *His performance drew loud euges from the audience.*

Eumenides *pl. n.* [Gk. gracious goddesses.] *The Eumenides,* the third play in the *Oresteia* (458 B.C.) by Aeschylus (525/4–456/5 B.C.). In this play Orestes is placed on trial for the murder of his mother and the **Erinyes** (q.v.) are transformed from avenging deities into gracious ones. Cf. **Choephoroi.**

eundo, morando, et redeundo [L. **eundo** in going (1); **morando** in remaining, staying (2); **et** and (3);

redeundo in returning (4): in going, remaining and returning.] *Law.* While going, remaining there, and returning. Applicable to benefits or privileges enjoyed by witnesses, legislators, etc. They include payment of expenses and freedom from arrest, and they cover the entire period, starting from their departure for the place where they are to perform their duties and ending with their return home.

eunomia *n.* [Gk. from **eu-** good, well (1); **nomos** law, order (2): good order.] A situation in which a society has good laws which are well administered.

euphoria *n.* [Gk. endurance, contentment, well-being.] An extraordinary feeling of well-being and excitement, sometimes appropriate, but sometimes baseless or at variance with reality, and sometimes resulting from mental disorder, liquor, or drugs. a) *The film takes place in a day and a night, moving from the euphoria of mother and daughter reuniting to a shattering outbreak of recrimination . . . (Newsweek Int. Oct. 16, 1978:42).* b) *Mentally, marijuana produces euphoria, a sense of relaxed well-being and a slowed perception of the passage of time (Newsweek Int. Jan. 14, 1980:46).*

eureka *interj.* [Gk. **heurēka** I have found it.] I have discovered [it.]. I have found [it.]. I have found [the solution for the problem.]. 1. An expression uttered by Archimedes of Syracuse (287–212 B.C.), when, in an attempt to determine whether or not a crown was made of pure gold, he stepped into a bathtub and discovered the principle of specific gravity. 2. An exclamatory expression of excitement, triumph, happiness, etc. on making a discovery. *"The average guy sitting in a lab makes a discovery, shouts, 'Eureka,' and then asks, 'What do I do?'" says Peter Laing . . . (Newsweek Int. Aug. 15, 1983:36).* Motto of the State of California. —*n., pl.* **eurekas** The discovery itself. *Vaccination is just one of many eurekas which have changed the world.* —*adj.* Excited and happy in the moment of discovery. *The eureka feeling.*

eutelegenesis *n.* [Neo-Gk. from Gk. **eutelē(s)** cheap, easy (1); **genesis** production, generation (2): easy production or generation.] *Medicine.* In vitro fertilization and embryo transfer. Artificial insemination. Reproduction through the test-tube process. *Eutelegenesis has brought relief to women previously thought barren.*

euthanasia *n., pl.* **euthanasias** [Gk. **eu** good, well (1); **thana(tos)** death (2): a good death.] *Medicine.* A painless or easy death. A means of effecting an easy death. The practice or act of causing, without pain, the death of a person who is suffering from a painful or incurable disease. a) *The medical practitioner refused, on moral and religious grounds, to end the patient's life by euthanasia.* b) *If we don't find a way to cure dementia, we are going to have to start thinking very seriously about euthanasia (Newsweek Int. Jan 23, 1984:32).*

eutocia *n., pl.* **eutocias** [Gk. **eutokia: eu** good, well (1); **tok(os)** childbirth (2): good childbirth.] *Medi-*

cine. Normal or easy childbirth. See **oxytocia.** Cf. **dystokia.**

evangelium *n.* [L. from Gk. **euangelion** good news.] The gospel.

eventus varios res nova semper habet. [L. **eventus** consequences, results (6); **varios** diverse, various (5); **res** matter, thing, property, business, affair (2); **nova** new (1); **semper** always (3); **habet** has, holds, regards (4): A new thing always has various results.] An innovation always brings various consequences.

évolué *n., pl.* **évolués** [Fr. developed, advanced.] *French Colonial Tropical Africa.* An enlightened, cultured, or broad-minded native (or subject) elite. *The economic up-swing of 1925, which put an end to a political movement among the évolués that had come into existence in Libreville . . . (Suret-Canale 1971:438).* —*adj.* Of, belonging to, characteristic of, enlightened native (or subject) elite. *. . . évolué elements moved among the people and helped to give direction to the uprising . . . (Suret-Canale 1971:428).* Cf. **notable évolué.**

ex *prep.* [L. out of, from, directly after, away from.] 1. From. Out of. Directly from. *The company sent the goods ex its factory.* 2. Without. Free from. Devoid of. a) Used of shares, rights, or interest to indicate that there is no specific value. *The newspaper carries an advertisement of shares ex rights.* b) Used of goods to indicate that the purchaser is to bear the expenses of transportation from the specified place. *The ex factory price of the car is $10,000.* —*pref.* Former. Previous. a) *ex-president;* b) *ex-minister;* c) *ex-wife;* d) *ex-convict;* e) *ex-coach.* —*n., pl.* **exes** A person who previously held a specific position, post, or place, especially a former husband, boyfriend, wife, or girlfriend. *Glen was extremely indignant when he heard that Sam, his bosom friend, was involved in a serious amorous relationship with his ex, Sue.*

ex abundanti cautela *adv.* [L. **ex** out of, from, directly after, away from (1); **abundanti** overflowing, abundant (2); **cautela** caution (3): from abundant caution.] From excess of caution. a) *The moneylender demanded two sureties for the loan ex abundanti cautela.* b) *I will add four observations ex abundanti cautela* (Hart 1978:50). See **ad abundantiorem cautelam.**

exacta *n.* [Sp. from **quiniela** game of chance (2); **exacta** exact (1): exact game of chance.] A type of bet in which one must predict exactly the first- and second-place winners in a race or competition. Cf. **perfecta.**

ex adverso *adj.* [L. **ex** out of, from, directly after, away from (1); **adverso** the opposite direction (2): from the opposite direction.] On/from the other side. *After counsel for plaintiff had concluded his case, counsel ex adverso was asked to proceed.*

ex aequitate *adv.* [L. **ex** out of, from, directly after, away from (1); **aequitate** equity, fairness (2): out of fairness.] According to equity. In equity. *The mortgagor* *of any kind of property is allowed to redeem it from the mortgageè ex aequitate.* See **aequitas.**

ex aequo et bono *adv.* [L. **ex** out of, from, directly after, away from (1); **aequo** the fair (2); **et** and (3); **bono** the good (4): from the fair and the good.] In justice and good faith. On the merits of the case. In accordance with equity and conscience. Usually used in international law when a case arising from agreement of the principals is to be settled on the basis of reason and equity rather than specific legal points. See **aequitas.**

ex Africa semper aliquid novi. Pliny the Elder (A.D.23–79). *Historia Naturalis* II,8,42. [L. **ex** out of, from, directly after, away from (1); **Africa** Africa (2); **semper** always (3); **aliquid** something (4); **novi** (of) new (5): From Africa always something new.] Out of Africa there is always something new. Africa is always producing something new.

ex altera parte *adj.* [L. **ex** out of, from, directly after, away from (1); **altera** the other (2); **parte** part (3): from the other part.] Of the other part.

examen *n., pl.* **examens** [Fr. from L. examination, investigation, trial.] A trial. An examination. Inquiry. Investigation. Critical study. *Persons in responsible positions are urged to have a periodic examen of conscience to reassure themselves of the fairness and efficacy of their acts.*

examen computi *n.* [L. **examen** trial (1); **computi** of account, computation, reckoning (2): trial of computation.] The balancing of an account.

ex animo *adv.* [L. **ex** out of, from, directly after, away from (1); **animo** heart, mind (2): from the heart.] Deeply. In earnest. Sincerely. Wholeheartedly. With no reservation.

ex ante *adj.* [L. **ex** out of, from, directly after, away from (1); **ante** before (2): from before.] Subjective. Based on, or derived from, assumption. Based on estimates. a) *By the time the building was completed, the actual cost exceeded the ex ante cost by $100,000.* b) *On assumption of office Mark found that his ex ante expectations did not conform with the reality.* Cf. **ex post.**

ex antecedentibus et consequentibus fit optima interpretatio. [L. **ex** out of, from, directly after, away from (4); **antecedentibus** the preceding, foregoing (things) (5); **et** and (6); **consequentibus** the consequent, the following (things) (7); **fit** is made (3); **optima** best (1); **interpretatio** interpretation (2): The best interpretation is made from the preceding and consequent (things).] A passage is best understood by considering what precedes and what follows it. See **ex praecedentibus** etc.

ex arbitrio judicis *adv.* [L. **ex** out of, from, directly after, away from (1); **arbitrio** pleasure, will (2); **judicis** of judge (3): from the pleasure of the judge.] At the judge's discretion. *Bail may be granted to an accused person ex arbitrio judicis.*

ex assensu curiae *adv.* [L. **ex** out of, from, directly after, away from (1); **assensu** assent, agreement, approval (2); **curiae** of court (3): from the approval of the court.] With the consent of the court. *The surety was discharged ex assensu curiae.*

ex assensu patris *adv.* [L. **ex** out of, from, directly after, away from (1); **assensu** assent, agreement, approval (2); **patris** of father (3): from the approval of the father.] With the consent of the father. Applicable to a kind of dower, specifically a parcel of land from the estate of the father-in-law given to the wife with his express consent.

ex assensu suo *adv.* [L. **ex** out of, from, directly after, away from (1); **assensu** assent, agreement, approval (3); **suo** his/her own (2): from his/her own assent.] With his/her consent.

ex cathedra *adv./adj.* [L. **ex** out of, from, directly after, away from (1); **cathedra** chair, seat, stool (2): from the chair.] With official authority. By virtue of one's office. Authoritatively. Authoritative. The expression apparently derives its connotation from the authority with which a professor or Pope speaks from his chair. a) *The official was speaking ex cathedra;* b) *an ex cathedra statement;* c) *He declared ex cathedra what was the Benin native law and custom relevant to the case he was trying* (Adewoye 1977:87).

excelsior *adj.* [L. higher.] Ever upward. Motto of the State of New York. —**Excelsior** Title of a poem by Henry Wadsworth Longfellow (1807–1882).

exceptio *n., pl.* **exceptiones** [L. exception.] *Civil Law.* Pleading. An exception or objection. For instance, a defendant, while admitting that the truth of a plaintiff's cause of action adduces additional facts in response.

exceptio doli mali *n.* [L. **exceptio** exception, restriction, limitation (1); **doli** (of) deceit (3); **mali** of bad, criminal (2): exception of bad deceit.] An exception of fraud. See **dolus malus.**

exceptio firmat regulam in contrarium. [L. **exceptio** exception, restriction, limitation (1); **firmat** proves (2); **regulam** rule (3); **in** to, into (4); **contrarium** the contrary (5): An exception proves the rule to the contrary.] An exception proves the contrary rule. Cf. **exceptio probat regulam.**

exceptio metus *n.* [L. **exceptio** exception, restriction, limitation (1); **metus** of fear (2): exception of fear.] Plea of compulsion/fear. Plea of duress.

exceptio probat regulam. [L. **exceptio** exception, restriction, limitation (1); **probat** proves (2); **regulam** rule (3): The exception proves the rule.] An exception is the proof of the rule or regulation. Cf. **exceptio firmat** etc.

exceptio probat regulam de rebus non exceptis. [L. **exceptio** exception, restriction, limitation (1); **probat** proves (2); **regulam** rule (3); **de** of, from, about, for (4); **rebus** matters, things, property, business, affairs

(5); **non** not (6); **exceptis** excepted (7): The exception proves the rule about matters not excepted.] An exception proves the rule except in situations which have been excluded.

exceptio quae firmat legem, exponit legem. [L. **exceptio** exception, restriction, limitation (1); **quae** which (2); **firmat** proves (3); **legem** law (4); **exponit** explains, teaches (5); **legem** law (6): An exception which proves the law explains it.] An exception which affirms the law also teaches it.

exceptio quoque regulam declarat. [l. **exceptio** exception, restriction, limitation (1); **quoque** also (2); **regulam** rule (4); **declarat** discloses, shows, proves (3): An exception also proves the rule.] An exception reveals the rule.

exceptio rei judicatae n. [L. **exceptio** exception, restriction, limitation (1); **rei** of a matter, thing, property, business, affair (2); **judicatae** (of) tried, decided (3): an exception of the thing decided.] *Law.* An exception of a matter already determined. A plea that the subject-matter of a legal action had been decided in a former action.

exceptio temporis n. [L. **exceptio** exception, restriction, limitation (1); **temporis** of time (2): exception of time.] *Law.* A plea that the time permissible for bringing legal action has expired.

exceptis excipiendis adv. [L. **exceptis** (with) having been taken out, excepted (2); **excipiendis** with the things that must be taken out (1): with the things that must be taken out having been taken out.] When all necessary exceptions have been made. *The government has promulgated a decree on traveling outside the country, exceptis excipiendis.* Cf. **mutatis mutandis.**

excerpta pl. n. [L. things selected, chosen, extracted or picked out.] Excerpts, clippings, selections, little bits or fragments of a work or writing. *The writer quoted excerpta from a standard work to support his views.*

exciseuse n., pl. **exciseuses** [Fr. excisor.] One who circumcises females. *The professional exciseuse escaped prosecution by fleeing to Mali, but the dead girl's parents now face trial on charges of criminal negligence* (*Newsweek Int.* Nov. 1, 1982:48).

ex colore officii adv. [L. **ex** out of, from, directly after, away from (1); **colore** color, appearance (2); **officii** of office, duty (3): from/out of color of office.] By color of office. Under pretense of office. (Acting) illegally under the mask of office. *The principal of the school, ex colore officii, ordered the students to embark on a big agricultural project, which ultimately became his property.* See **colore officii.**

ex comitate adv. [L. **ex** out of, from, directly after, away from (1); **comitate** friendliness, courtesy, civility (2): from courtesy.] Out of courtesy. *Thus, Lord Brougham in* Warrender v. Warrender *said "The courts of England can hardly be said to act from courtesy ex comitate but ex debito justitiae"* (Graveson 1974:619).

ex comitate et jure gentium adv. [L. **ex** out of, from, directly after, away from (1); **comitate** friendliness, courtesy, civility (2); **et** and (3); **jure** right, law (4); **gentium** of nations (5): from courtesy and the law of nations.] On the bases of international comity and law. *"The general rule," affirmed Lord Mansfield in 1760, "established ex comitate et jure gentium, is that the place where the contract is made, and not where the action is brought, is to be considered in expounding and enforcing the contract . . ."* (*Robinson v. Bland* [1760.] 2 Burr. 1077. Quoted by Graveson 1974:414). Cf. **comitas gentium** and **jus gentium.**

ex comparatione scriptorum adv./adj. [L. **ex** out of, from, directly after, away from (1); **comparatione** comparison (2); **scriptorum** of writings (3): from comparison of writings.] From comparison of handwritings. *Arguing on the basis of evidence obtained ex comparatione scriptorum, the judge concluded that the accused was not the one who defrauded the bank and ordered that he be acquitted and discharged.*

ex concessis adv. [L. **ex** out of, from, directly after, away from (1); **concessis** (things) conceded, agreed upon, granted (2): from things conceded or granted.] From what has already been conceded.

ex consulto adv. [L. **ex** out of, from, directly after, away from (1); **consulto** consultation, deliberation, resolution (2): from consultation or deliberation.] With consultation or deliberation. Deliberately. *The evidence adduced so far clearly shows that she acted ex consulto.* Cf. **ex industria.**

ex contractu adv./adj. [L. **ex** out of, from, directly after, away from (1); **contractu** drawing together, shrinking, contract, agreement (2): from contract.] Arising from a contract. Based upon a contract. *The answer . . . seems to be that a minor cannot be sued if the cause of action against him arises substantially ex contractu or if to allow the action would be to enforce the contract indirectly, but if the wrong is independent of the contract, then the minor may be sued even though but for the contract he would have had no opportunity of committing the tort* (Graveson 1974:601).

excreta pl. n. [L. things sifted out, separated or kept away.] Feces, sweat, urine, and other body waste. *. . . sentences range from 10 years to 60 years, with half of each sentence slated to be served carrying excreta (human) . . .* (*West Africa* 1982). Cf. **dejecta** and **egesta.**

ex curia adv./adj. [L. **ex** out of, from, directly after, away from (1); **curia** court (2): out of court.] Away from court.

excursus n., pl. **excursus** or **excursuses** [L. excursion, running out.] A digression. An incidental discussion. *An interesting aspect of the historical work of Herodotus, the pater historiae, is the excursus in which he tells stories.*

excusat aut extenuat delictum in capitalibus quod non operatur idem in civilibus. [L. **excusat** it excuses (1); **aut** or (2); **extenuat** diminishes (3); **delictum** wrong (4); **in** in, on (5); **capitalibus** capital (cases) (6); **quod** which (7); **non** not (8); **operatur** works (9); **idem** the same (10); **in** in, on (11); **civilibus** civil (cases) (12): It excuses or diminishes a wrong in capital cases which does not work the same in civil cases.] *Law.* A consideration which excuses or extenuates a wrongful act in criminal cases may not have the same effect in civil proceedings.

ex debito justitiae *adv./adj.* [L. **ex** out of, from, directly after, away from (1); **debito** debt (2); **justitiae** of justice (3): from a debt of justice.] *Law.* As a debt of justice. As a matter of right or a legal obligation. *. . . a judgment obtained in default of appearance against the company could not be set aside ex debito justitiae, but only on the company's filing an affidavit to show that it had a defence on the merits* (Langan and Lawrence 1976:24).

ex decreto *adv./adj.* [L. **ex** out of, from, directly after, away from (1); **decreto** decree, resolution (2): from decree.] According to edict or official pronouncement. *Ex decreto all senior officials had to swear a new oath of allegiance to the new government.*

ex delicto *adv./adj.* [L. **ex** out of, from, directly after, away from (1); **delicto** crime, fault, delict (2): from a crime.] Arising from a crime, tort, or fault. As a result or consequence of a crime. From a wrongful act. *Any injury ex delicto may be remedied by way of compensation.*

ex delicto non ex supplicio emergit infamia. [L. **ex** out of, from, directly after, away from (3); **delicto** wrong (4); **non** not (5); **ex** out of, from, directly after, away from (6); **supplicio** punishment (7); **emergit** arises, emerges (2); **infamia** disgrace, infamy (1): Disgrace arises from the wrong, not from the punishment.] *Law.* It is the wrongful act, not the punishment, that brings disgrace. See **C'est le crime** etc. and **Le crime fait** etc.

ex directo *adv.* [L. **ex** out of, from, directly after, away from (1); **directo** the direct, precise (2): from the direct.] Directly. Immediately. *In matters affecting the liberty of a citizen, it is imperative that the courts act ex directo.*

ex diuturnitate temporis *adv.* [L. **ex** out of, from, directly after, away from (1); **diuturnitate** length, long duration (2); **temporis** of time (3): from long duration of time.] From length of time. After some time. From lapse of time. *The defendant's evidence revealed that the plaintiff had abandoned his interest in the land ex diuturnitate temporis.* Cf. **ex diuturno tempore.**

ex diuturnitate temporis, omnia praesumuntur solemniter esse acta. [L. **ex** out of, from, directly after, away from (1); **diuturnitate** length, long duration (2); **temporis** of time (3); **omnia** all (things) (4); **praesumuntur** are presumed (5); **solemniter**

solemnly, duly (7); **esse acta** to have been done (6): After long duration of time, all things are presumed to have been done duly.] *Law.* After lapse of time, it is presumed that all things were done in the proper way. Thus the law will presume in favor of the legality of a marriage, if it was celebrated many years ago. Similarly, it will presume in favor of the honesty of a transaction, if it was concluded many years ago. Cf. **omnia praesumuntur legitime** etc. and **omnia praesumuntur rite** etc.

ex diuturno tempore *adv.* [L. **ex** out of, from, directly after, away from (1); **diuturno** lengthy, long (2); **tempore** time (3): from lengthy time.] From length of time. *The defendant derived his title to the land ex diuturno tempore.* Cf. **ex diuturnitate temporis.**

ex diversis causis *adv.* [L. **ex** out of, from, directly after, away from (1); **diversis** different, diverse, conflicting, opposite (2); **causis** causes (3): from different/diverse causes.] For different reasons.

ex dolo malo *adv./adj.* [L. **ex** out of, from, directly after, away from (1); **dolo** fraud, deceit (3); **malo** bad, criminal (2): out of bad deceit.] *Law.* From fraud. *No advantages may be derived ex dolo malo.* See **dolus malus.**

ex dolo malo non oritur actio. [L. **ex** out of, from, directly after, away from (4); **dolo** fraud (6); **malo** bad (5); **non** not (2); **oritur** arises (3); **actio** action, deed, legal suit (1): A legal suit does not arise from bad fraud.] *Law.* A legal action based on fraud is not entertained. A court of law does not entertain an action to enforce an illegal contract or one based on immoral consideration. See **ex turpi causa** etc.

exeat *n., pl.* **exeats** [L. Let him/her go out.] 1. A 16th-century stage direction equivalent to **exit** (q.v.). 2. A document permitting an individual's temporary absence, particularly, from school or college. *It is an infringement of a regulation of the university to travel outside the campus without obtaining an exeat.* 3. Letter of excardination, i.e., transferring a cleric from one diocese to another.

exeant *n., pl.* **exeants** [L. Let them go out.] 1. A 16th-century stage direction equivalent to **exeunt** (q.v.). 2. A document permitting two or more individuals to be temporarily absent, particularly, from school or college. 3. Letter of excardination, i.e., transferring two or more clerics from one diocese to another.

executio bonorum *n.* [L. **ex(s)ecutio** execution (1); **bonorum** of goods, property (2): execution of goods.] *Old English Law.* The administration and management of goods or property.

executio est executio juris secundum judicium. [L. **ex(s)ecutio** execution (1); **est** is (2); **ex(s)ecutio** execution (3); **juris** of right, law (4); **secundum** according to (5); **judicium** judgment (6): Execution is execution of law according to judgment.] *Law.* Execution is the execution of a law in accordance with a judgment. See **executio est finis** etc.

executio est finis et fructus legis. [L. ex(s)ecutio execution (1); est is (2); finis end (3); et and (4); fructus fruit, product (5); legis of law (6): Execution is the end and the fruit of law.] Law. Execution is the goal and product of the law. See executio est executio etc.

executio juris non habet injuriam. [L. ex(s)ecutio execution, administration (1); juris of right, law (2); non not (3); habet has, holds, regards (4); injuriam injury (5): Execution of the law does not have injury.] Law. Administration of the law is not harmful. See actus curiae neminem gravabit.

executione facienda n. [L. ex(s)ecutione with execution (1); facienda to be done (2): with an execution to be done.] Law. A writ authorizing the execution of a judgment.

executione judicii n. [L. ex(s)ecutione with execution (1); judicii of judgment (2): with execution of judgment.] Law. A writ to a judge of a lower court ordering him to execute a judgment or account for the delay in the execution.

exegesis n., pl. exegeses [Gk. exēgēsis narrative, explanation, interpretation.] Explanation, exposition, or critical interpretation of a written work, especially a text of Holy Scripture. a) His carefully thought out piece is a modern exegesis of an established and immutable truth (Time Int. 1983). b) There was much contradictory exegesis as to whether Carter was speaking from real confidence or only from pique at Kennedy's presidential teasing . . . (Newsweek Int. June 25, 1979:32).

exegi monumentum aere perennius. Horace (65–8 B.C.). Odes III,30,1. [L. exegi I have brought forth (1); monumentum monument, public work (2); aere than bronze (4); perennius more lasting (3): I have brought forth a monument more lasting than bronze.] I have finished a work more durable than bronze. For a shorter form of the quotation, see monumentum etc.

exempla illustrant, non restringunt, legem. [L. exempla examples (1); illustrant elucidate, illustrate (2); non not (3); restringunt restrain (4); legem law (5): Examples elucidate, not restrain, the law.] Law. Examples clarify rather than confine the law.

exemplar n., pl. exemplars [L. model, pattern, example, transcript.] An ideal model or example. A standard specimen. A copy of a text. Archimedes of Syracuse (c.287–212 B.C.) is a classic exemplar of the eccentric scholar. Cf. exemplum.

exempli causa abbr. E.C. or e.c. adv. [L. exempli of example (2); causa for the sake (1): for the sake of example.] For example. For instance. A variant of exempli gratia (q.v.).

exempli gratia abbr. e.g., ex. g. or ex. gr. adv. [L. exempli of example (2); gratia for the sake (1): for the sake of example.] For example. For instance. Cf. exempli causa.

exemplum n., pl. exempla [L. sample, specimen, model, example, lesson, warning.] 1. A short story told or written for the purpose of a moral or in support of an argument. His Evagoras . . . and his constant use of exempla from the heroic and the strictly historical ages of Greece are all significant (Laistner 1966:3–4). 2. A model. An example. Amadu is an exemplum of traditional morality. 3. Civil Law. Copy. An authorized copy. Cf. exemplar.

ex empto adv./adj. [L. ex out of, from, directly after, away from (1); empto purchase, contract of purchase (2): arising from purchase.] Out of purchase. As a result of purchase. Founded on purchase. He derived his title to the chain of buildings ex empto.

ex eodem negotio adv./adj. [L. ex out of, from, directly after, away from (1); eodem the same (2); negotio business, affair (3): out of the same business/affair.] From the same affair. The arrest and prosecution of the two foreigners arose ex eodem negotio.

exeunt v. intr. [L. They go out.] They go off the stage. They go out. Used as a direction in dramatic performances to signify that some, or all, of the actors leave the stage.

exeunt omnes v. intr. [L. exeunt they leave, go out (2); omnes all (1): They all go out.] They all leave the stage. Used as a direction in dramatic performances to signify that all the actors leave the stage.

ex eventu adj./adv. [L. ex out of, from, directly after, away from (1); eventu event, occurrence (2): after the occurrence or the event.] With the benefit of hindsight. He necessarily fared badly by such a judgment passed ex eventu . . . (Lesky 1966:606). Cf. vaticinatio ex eventu.

ex facie adv. [L. ex out of, from, directly after, away from (1); facie face (2): from the face.] Apparently. In the light of what is apparent. . . . a contract which is ex facie lawful will be treated as illegal if both parties knew of the illegal purpose (Major 1978:146).

ex facto adv./adj. [L. ex out of, from, directly after, away from (1); facto deed, act, fact (2): from the deed.] From a fact. In consequence of a fact. Actually. Used sometimes as a synonym of de facto (q.v.). Cf. de jure. See ex post facto.

ex facto illicito non oritur actio. [L. ex out of, from, directly after, away from (1); facto deed, act, fact (3); illicito illicit, illegal (2); non not (5); oritur arises (6); actio action, deed, legal suit (4): From an illegal deed a legal suit does not arise.] Law. A legal action based on an illegal act is not entertained. See ex turpi causa etc.

ex facto jus oritur. [L. ex out of, from, directly after, away from (3); facto deed, act, fact (4); jus right, law (1); oritur arises, originates (2): The law originates from the deed.] A rule of law exists in theory until it takes a concrete form when an act is done to which it is applicable.

ex fictione juris adv. [L. ex out of, from, directly after, away from (1); fictione fiction (2); juris of right, law (3): from a fiction of law.] By a fiction of law. By a legal fiction.

ex frequenti delicto augetur poena. [L. ex out of, from, directly after, away from (3); frequenti frequent, numerous (4); delicto wrongdoing, crime (5); augetur is increased (2); poena punishment (1): Punishment is increased from frequent crime.] *Law.* As crimes increase, punishment correspondingly increases. See crescente malitia etc. and multiplicata transgressione etc.

ex fumo dare lucem [L. ex out of, from, directly after, away from (3); fumo smoke (4); dare to give (1); lucem light (2): to give light out of smoke.] To clarify what is not clear. To explain the obscure. *It is the duty of those who have to expound a will, if they can, ex fumo dare lucem* (per Shadwell v.-C. in *De Beauvoir v. De Beauvoir* [1846] 15 L.J. Ch. 305 at 308. Quoted by Megarry 1955:160).

ex g. *abbr.* for exempli gratia (q.v.).

ex gr. *abbr.* for exempli gratia (q.v.).

ex gratia *adv./adj.* [L. ex out of, from, directly after, away from (1); gratia grace, favor (2): from favor.] From grace. As a favor. Gratuitous. Not as a legal obligation. a) *He is actually not entitled to pension payments, but he receives them ex gratia.* b) *In Edwards v. Skyways Ltd. (1964), it was held that an employee air pilot was entitled to enforce his employer's promise to make an ex gratia payment equivalent to the employer's contribution to a pension fund on the termination of his employment* (Major 1978:26). Cf. de jure.

ex hypothesi *adv.* [L. ex out of, from, directly after, away from (1); hypothesi hypothesis (2): from the hypothesis.] Hypothetically. Supposedly. *Since all human beings share the same genus and species, homo sapiens, they are, ex hypothesi, the same; in practice, however, there are differences among individual persons.*

exigi facias *n.* [L. exigi to be demanded (2); facias you should cause (1): You should cause to be demanded.] A writ of exigent. *Law of Former Times.* A writ issued to summon a person to appear in court or, in default, to be outlawed.

ex improviso *adv.* [L. ex out of, from, directly after, away from (1); improviso the unforeseen, unexpected (2): from the unexpected or unforeseen.] Unexpectedly. Suddenly. *The matter, which appeared moribund, was, ex improviso, revived by the complainant.*

ex industria *adv.* [L. ex out of, from, directly after, away from (1); industria diligence, assiduity (2): out of diligence.] Diligently. On purpose. Intentionally. *The evidence clearly shows that he planned and committed the act ex industria.* Cf. ex consulto.

ex integro *adv.* [L. ex out of, from, directly after, away from (1); integro fresh, new (2): from fresh/new.] Afresh. Anew. All over again. *The contractor did the work so poorly that he was ordered to do it ex integro.* See de integro and de novo.

exit *v. intr.* [L. He/she goes out.] 1. *Theater.* To leave the stage. *Exit Macbeth.* 2. To go out. To depart. To die. *The boy exited the room.* —*n., pl.* exits 1. An actor's departure from the stage. 2. Departure. Going out. Leaving the scene of an activity. Departure from life, i.e., death. *His exit from the room was accompanied by a great fanfare.* 3. Outlet. A way, road, or passage to be used when going out. A door to be used when leaving a building. *A fire exit.*

exitus *n., pl.* exitus [L. a going out, departure, outlet, end, conclusion, termination.] 1. Outcome. End. Result. Issue. Conclusion or end of pleadings. 2. A duty on exports. Rents and profits from tenements, land, etc. 3. Death, particularly as a result of a fatal disease. 4. Outlet for excretion.

ex jure naturae *adv./adj.* [L. ex out of, from, directly after, away from (1); jure right, law (2); naturae of nature (3): from the law of nature.] According to the rule of nature. *The offense of murder is forbidden ex jure naturae.* Cf. ex jure naturali.

ex jure naturali *adj./adv.* [L. ex out of, from, directly after, away from (1); jure right, law (3); naturali natural (2): from natural law.] According to natural law. *Human actions, ex jure naturali, must be in conformity with what is rational.* Cf. ex jure naturae.

ex justa causa *adv./adj.* [L. ex out of, from, directly after, away from (1); justa just (2); causa cause, case, reason (3): from a just cause.] From a lawful cause. *The plaintiff instituted the action ex justa causa.*

ex justitia *adv./adj.* [L. ex out of, from, directly after, away from (1); justitia justice, equity (2): from justice.] From a just/lawful cause. *The case against the defendant was dismissed by the court ex justitia.*

ex l. *abbr.* for ex libris (q.v.).

ex lege *adv./adj.* [L. ex out of, from, directly after, away from (1); lege law (2): from law.] According to the law. By the law. As a matter of law. *Ordinarily, every case which is brought to court is decided ex lege.* See ex legibus.

ex legibus *adv./adj.* [L. ex out of, from, directly after, away from (1); legibus laws (2): from laws.] According to the laws. By the laws. See ex lege.

ex libris *prep.* [L. ex out of, from, directly after, away from (1); libris books (2): from the books.] Belonging to the library of. One of the books of. Written on bookplates to indicate the owner of the book; i.e., *ex libris John Mensah* means John Mensah's book. —*n., pl.* ex libris Bookplate.

ex maleficio *adj./adv.* [L. ex out of, from, directly after, away from (1); maleficio offense, crime, wrongdoing (2): from wrongdoing.] Based on, or on account of, misconduct. *The permanent secretary was suspended ex maleficio.*

ex maleficio non oritur contractus. [L. ex out of, from, directly after, away from (4); maleficio evil deed, misdeed (5); non not (3); oritur arises (2); contractus drawing together, shrinking, contract, agreement (1): A contract does not arise from a misdeed.] *Law.* A contract based on a misdeed is invalid. See **ex turpi causa** etc.

ex malis moribus bonae leges natae sunt. [L. **ex** out of, from, directly after, away from (5); **malis** bad, evil (6); **moribus** morals, conduct, habit (7); **bonae** good (1); **leges** laws (2); **natae** born (4); **sunt** are, have been (3): Good laws have been born out of evil morals.] Good laws are promulgated to counteract misbehavior.

ex malitia *adv.* [L. **ex** out of, from, directly after, away from (1); **malitia** malice, ill will, spite (2): from/out of malice.] From malice. Maliciously. *The plaintiff is suing the defendant for publishing an article on him ex malitia.*

ex mero motu *adv.* [L. **ex** out of, from, directly after, away from (1); **mero** pure, genuine (2); **motu** emotion, impulse (3): out of pure/genuine impulse.] Of one's own free will. Of his/her own accord. Voluntarily. *The candidate of the People's Party stepped down from the Presidential race ex mero motu.* See **ex proprio motu; ex voluntate; motu proprio; sua sponte;** and **suo motu.**

ex mora *adv./adj.* [L. **ex** out of, from, directly after, away from (1); **mora** delay (2): from delay.] As a result of delay.

ex more *adv.* [L. **ex** out of, from, directly after, away from (1); **more** custom, habit (2): from custom.] By custom.

ex multitudine signorum colligitur identitas vera. [L. **ex** out of, from, directly after, away from (4); **multitudine** large number (5); **signorum** of signs, indications (6); **colligitur** is deduced, considered (3); **identitas** identity (2); **vera** true (1): True identity is deduced from a large number of signs.] True identity is established from a multiplicity of indications.

ex necessitate *adv.* [L. **ex** out of, from, directly after, away from (1); **necessitate** compulsion, urgency, necessity (2): from compulsion.] By force of necessity. *The minister, after a long deliberation, decided, ex necessitate, to tender his resignation from office.*

ex necessitate legis *adv./adj.* [L. **ex** out of, from, directly after, away from (1); **necessitate** compulsion, urgency, necessity (2); **legis** of law (3): from compulsion of law.] By necessity of law. *All professionals had to pay a special tax ex necessitate legis.*

ex necessitate rei *adv.* [L. **ex** out of, from, directly after, away from (1); **necessitate** compulsion, urgency, necessity (2); **rei** of the matter, thing, property, business, affair (3): from the compulsion of the thing.] Out of the urgency of the situation or the case. *When Funso's father received the unpleasant news of his son's imprisonment for failure to pay the fine, he immediately despatched an emissary with the requisite amount, ex necessitate rei.*

ex nihilo nihil fit. [L. **ex** out of, from, directly after, away from (3); **nihilo** nothing (4); **nihil** nothing (1); **fit** is made (2): Nothing is made out of nothing.] *Philosophy.* Nothing comes out of nothing.

ex nudo pacto non oritur actio. [L. **ex** out of, from, directly after, away from (1); **nudo** naked, bare (2); **pacto** pact, agreement (3); **non** not (5); **oritur** arises (6); **actio** action, deed, legal suit (4): From a naked agreement a legal suit does not arise.] *Law.* A bare pact cannot serve as ground for any legal action. A civil and common law maxim which maintains that a legal action cannot be grounded on a contract made without a formal or solemn promise. Cf. **ex turpi causa** etc.

exodus *abbr.* **exod.** *n., pl.* **exoduses** [L. from Gk. **exodos: ex** out of, from (2); **(h)odos** road, path (1): road out, going out.] 1. The departure of the Hebrew people from Egypt. 2. A mass emigration or departure. Emigration or departure of a large number of people. a) *... the exodus of teachers from the Universities ... (West Africa* 1981). b) *The exodus of both citizens and expatriates is mainly attributable to the country's worsening economy.* —**Exodus** The second book of the Bible describing the flight of the Hebrews from Egypt.

ex officio or **ex officiis** *abbr.* **ex off.** *adj./adv.* [L. **ex** out of, from, directly after, away from (1); **officio** office, duty, obligation, service (2): from the office.] By virtue of a person's office. By reason of a person's office or position. a) *The Military Governor ... must be appointed one of the trustees ex officio* (James 1982:39). b) *As the chief executive of the institution, he is required to serve, ex officio, as a member of all the boards of the institution.* c) *Paul's father is an ex officio member of the executive committee.*

exoneretur *n., pl.* **exonereturs** [L. Let him/her be relieved or discharged.] A note on a bailpiece acknowledging the discharge of a surety.

exordium *n., pl.* **exordia** or **exordiums** [L. introduction, preface.] The introductory part of a composition, speech, discourse, or document.

exoterica *pl. n.* [Gk. **exōterika** outer things.] Doctrines, discourses, or works meant for the layman, the uneducated or the general public. Exoteric, popular, or commonplace doctrines, works, etc. *Since his works are essentially exoterica, they lack the profundity of those of a specialist.*

exotica *pl. n.* [Gk. **exōtika** foreign or alien things.] Strange, mysterious or romantic things, items, features or information. *It is time we abandoned the dishonest (but lucrative) rubbish that a film cannot sell unless it is replete with bare-breasted damsels ... and mindless garbage of exotica straight from Tarzan's Africa* (Niyi Osundare in *West Africa* 1982).

ex pacto illicito non oritur actio. [L. **ex** out of, from, directly after, away from (1); **pacto** agreement, contract

(3); **illicito** illicit, illegal (2); **non** not (5); **oritur** arises (6); **actio** action, deed, legal suit (4): From an illegal contract a legal suit does not arise.] *Law.* A legal action does not proceed from an illegal contract or agreement. See **ex turpi causa** etc.

ex parte *adj./adv.* [L. **ex** out of, from, directly after, away from (1); **parte** side, part (2): from a part.] *Law.* By one party only. For one party only. From the point of view of only one side. Used in relation to such matters as commissions, injunctions, testimonies, and hearings in which the proceedings are conducted in the presence, or on the papers, of one party, while the other party is either absent or not served with notice. a) *The plaintiff filed a motion ex parte to set aside the default judgment.* b) *Instead of allowing free discussions to determine the best course of action, the chairman imposed his ex parte view on the committee.* See **de una parte.** Cf. **ex utraque parte** and **inter partes.**

ex parte materna *adv./adj.* [L. **ex** out of, from, directly after, away from (1); **parte** side, part (3); **materna** maternal, of the mother (2): from the maternal side.] On the maternal side. Of/on the side of the mother. *He traces his ancestry ex parte materna.* Cf. **ex parte paterna.**

ex parte paterna *adv./adj.* [L. **ex** out of, from, directly after, away from (1); **parte** part, side (3); **paterna** paternal, of the father (2): from the paternal side.] On the paternal side. Of/on the side of the father. *She is a woman of dual identity, being French ex parte materna and German ex parte paterna.* Cf. **ex parte materna.**

ex pede Herculem [L. **ex** out of, from, directly after, away from (1); **pede** foot (2); **Herculem** Hercules (1): From (his) the foot (we can measure) Hercules.] Hercules from his foot. To acquire information about the whole from a small part, just as the Greek mathematician Pythagoras tried to calculate the height of the hero Hercules from his foot.

expedit reipublicae ne sua re quis male utatur. [L. **expedit** it is expedient, advantageous (1); **rei publicae** to the public affair, the state (2); **ne** that not (3); **sua** his own (6); **re** matter, thing, property, business, affair (7); **quis** anyone (4); **male** wrongly, badly (8); **utatur** should use (5): It is expedient to the state that anyone should not use his property wrongly.] *Law.* It is a matter of concern to the state that no one should put his/her property to improper use. See **sic utere tuo** etc.

expedit reipublicae ut sit finis litium. [L. **expedit** it is expedient, advantageous (1); **rei publicae** to the public affair, the state (2); **ut** that (3); **sit** there should be (4); **finis** end (5); **litium** of suits (6): It is expedient to the state that there should be an end of suits.] *Law.* It is to the interest of the state that suits be brought to an end; i.e., that law suits not continue indefinitely. See **infinitum in** etc.

expende Hannibalem: quot libras in duce summo invenies? Juvenal (c.60-117 A.D.). *Satires* X,147.

[L. **expende** weigh, examine (1); **Hannibalem** Hannibal (2); **quot** how many (3); **libras** pounds (4); **in** in, on (6); **duce** leader, ruler (8); **summo** highest (7); **invenies** will you find (5): Weigh Hannibal: how many pounds will you find in the highest leader?] Weigh Hannibal? How much will the greatest leader weigh (when he is dead)? How important is fame and power after the person is dead?

expensae litis *pl. n.* [L. **expensae** expenses, payments (1); **litis** of suit (2): expenses of the suit.] Costs/expenses of a suit awarded to a winning party. *Expensae litis are mostly awarded on the final determination of the suit.*

experientia docet. [L. **experientia** experience (1); **docet** teaches (2): Experience teaches.] Experience is a veritable teacher. One learns from experience. Cf. **fabula docet.**

expilatio *n., pl.* **expilationes** [L. a pillaging, plundering.] *Civil Law.* Unlawful appropriation of goods after someone dies and before the heir(s) take possession. Technically, the offense is different from **furtum** (q.v.) (theft).

explanandum *n., pl.* **explananda** [L. thing to be explained, thing which must be explained.] *Philosophy.* A word or expression which needs to be explained. Cf. **explanans**; **explicandum**; **explicans**; and **explicatum.**

explanans *n., pl.* **explanantia** [L. explaining thing.] *Philosophy.* The meaning of a word or expression. See **explanandum.**

explicandum *n., pl.* **explicanda** [L. thing to be explained, thing which must be explained.] *Philosophy.* A word or expression which needs to be expounded or explicated. See **explanandum.**

explicans *n., pl.* **explicantia** [L. explaining thing.] *Philosophy.* The meaning of a word or expression. See **explanandum.**

explication de texte *n., pl.* **explications de texte** [Fr. **explication** explanation (1); **de** of (2); **texte** text (3): explanation of the text.] A textual analysis.

explicatum *n., pl.* **explicata** [L. that which has been explained.] *Philosophy.* The meaning of a word or expression. See **explanandum.**

exposé or **expose** *n., pl.* **exposés** or **exposes** [Fr. account, exposition, statement, explanation, report.] 1. A statement, recital, account, exposition or explanation of facts or beliefs. 2. Revelation or exposure of something discreditable about a person, institution, government, etc. a) *The shocking stories . . . include exposés of the shooting of Palestinian children by army patrols and brutal tear-gas attacks on Arab high schools* (Newsweek Int. Jan. 11, 1982:49). b) *an exposé of "the prevailing situation in Nigerian society"* (Chris Dunton in *West Africa* 1982). 3. *Diplomacy.* A written statement, explaining the reasons for a conduct or an act.

ex post *adj.* [L. **ex** out of, from, directly after, away from (1); **post** after (2): from after.] Objective. Factual.

Based on, or derived from, certain knowledge. *The investigator insisted that he was interested in ex post, not ex ante, information.* Cf. **ex ante.**

ex postfacto or **ex post facto** *adj.* [L. **ex** out of, from, directly after, away from (1); **postfacto** something done afterwards (2): from something done afterwards.] Retrospective. Retroactive. Done after the fact. a) *Many distinguished jurists condemn ex post facto laws.* b) *English law and judicial procedure conferred undoubted benefits on Nigerians . . . , but one should be wary of the danger of ex post facto rationalisation of British intentions* (Adewoye 1977:31). —*adv.* Retrospectively. Retroactively. *Lawmakers are advised to refrain from making laws ex post facto, for such laws seem unfair.* See **postea.** Cf. **ab initio.**

ex praecedentibus et consequentibus est optima interpretatio. [L. **ex** out of, from, directly after, away from (4); **praecedentibus** the preceding (things) (5); **et** and (6); **consequentibus** the consequent, following (things) (7); **est** is (3); **optima** best (1); **interpretatio** interpretation (2): The best interpretation is from the preceding things and the following things.] A passage is best understood by considering what precedes and what follows it. See **ex antecedentibus** etc.

expressa nocent, non expressa non nocent. [L. **expressa** expressed (things) (1); **nocent** do harm, hurt, injure (2); **non** not (3); **expressa** expressed (things) (4); **non** not (5); **nocent** harm (6): Expressed things do harm, not expressed things do not harm.] Things that are expressed harm; things which are not expressed do not harm; i.e., sometimes keeping silent may be more helpful than talking. See **expressa non prosunt** etc.

expressa non prosunt quae non expressa proderunt. [L. **expressa** expressed (things) (1); **non** not (2); **prosunt** are useful, beneficial (3); **quae** which (4); **non** not (5); **expressa** expressed (things) (6); **proderunt** will be useful, beneficial (7): Expressed things are not beneficial which not expressed will be beneficial.] There are certain things which are harmful when said, but will be beneficial when not said. See **expressa nocent** etc.

expressio eorum quae tacite insunt nihil operatur. [L. **expressio** expression (1); **eorum** of those (things) (2); **quae** which (3); **tacite** tacitly, silently (5); **insunt** are in, are implied (4); **nihil** nothing (7); **operatur** performs, achieves (6): The expression of those things which are tacitly implied achieves nothing.] It is superfluous expressly to mention those things which are implied; i.e., there is no point in mentioning what is implied. Cf. **non solent quae** etc. and **omissio eorum quae** etc.

expressio unius est exclusio alterius. [L. **expressio** expression (1); **unius** of one (2); **est** is (3); **exclusio** exclusion (4); **alterius** of the other (5): The expression of the one is the exclusion of the other.] *Law.* A principle whereby if one or more things of a group are specifically mentioned, the others are automatically excluded. See **designatio unius** etc.

expressio unius personae est exclusio alterius. [L. **expressio** expression (1); **unius** of one (2); **personae** (of) person (3); **est** is (4); **exclusio** exclusion (5); **alterius** of the other (6): The expression of one person is the exclusion of the other.] *Law.* The express mention of one person is the exclusion of another; i.e., when one person is specifically mentioned, it implies that a second person is excluded. See **designatio unius** etc.

expressis verbis *adv.* [L. **expressis** with express (1); **verbis** (with) words (2): with express words.] Expressly. Explicitly. Definitely. *No judge has yet dissented expressis verbis from Lord Atkin's statement of the principles that should guide a court in the absence of an express choice of proper law by the parties* (Graveson 1974:414).

expressum facit cessare tacitum. [L. **expressum** the expressed (1); **facit** makes (2); **cessare** to cease, stop (4); **tacitum** unmentioned, kept secret (3): The expressed makes the unmentioned to cease.] When something is expressed, it supersedes what is implied. See **designatio unius** etc.

ex professo *adv.* [L. **ex** out of, from, directly after, away from (1); **professo** confessed, avowed, professed (thing) (2): from the professed or avowed thing.] In accordance with one's avowal or claim. Professedly.

ex proprio motu *adv.* [L. **ex** out of, from, directly after, away from (1); **proprio** his/her/its/their, one's own (2); **motu** impulse (3): from one's own impulse.] Of a person's own accord. Spontaneously. *David donated blood ex proprio motu to save a life.* See **ex mero motu.**

ex proprio vigore *adv.* [L. **ex** out of, from, directly after, away from (1); **proprio** his/her/its/their, one's own (2); **vigore** force, vigor (3): from one's own force.] Of a person's own force or strength.

ex provisione mariti *adv.* [L. **ex** out of, from, directly after, away from (1); **provisione** provision, foresight (2); **mariti** of husband (3): from the provision of the husband.] From the husband's resources. *During his absence the wife maintained and cared for the children ex provisione mariti.*

ex relatione *abbr.* **ex rel.** *prep.* [L. **ex** out of, from, directly after, away from (1); **relatione** report, proposition, information (2): from the report/information.] Upon information/motion of. On relation of. *Law.* Applicable to proceedings instituted by the state, acting on information brought by an interested party. *State ex rel. Seidu v. Gambari.* —*adv./adj.* A case is described as reported ex relatione when the reporter was not present during the proceedings but derived his information from a person who was present.

ex rigore juris *adv.* [L. **ex** out of, from, directly after, away from (1); **rigore** stiffness, harshness (2); **juris**

of right, law (3): from the harshness of the law.] *Law.* In accordance with the strictness of the law. *If the case had been considered ex rigore juris, there can be no doubt that the accused would have been condemned to death.* Cf. **aequitas.**

ex se natus or *fem.* **ex se nata** *adj., pl.* **ex se nati** or *fem.* **ex se natae** [L. **ex** out of, from, directly after, away from (2); **se** himself/herself (3); **natus** born (1): born out of himself/herself, themselves.] Self-made. *Sam has every justification to be proud of his achievements, for he is ex se natus.*

exsequatur *n., pl.* **exsequaturs** [L. Let him/her perform, execute or enforce.] *International Law.* A written official authorization/recognition given to a consular officer by the government to which he is accredited.

ex silentio *adj./adv.* [L. **ex** out of, from, directly after, away from (1); **silentio** silence (2): from silence.] From the fact of the unavailability of evidence. *Ex silentio arguments stand on shaky foundations and can, like a house of cards, be easily demolished.* See **argumentum a silentio** and **argumentum ex silentio.**

ex statuto *adj./adv.* [L. **ex** out of, from, directly after, away from (1); **statuto** statute (2): from statute.] *Law.* According to the statute or law. *After listening to the arguments of both the prosecution and the defense, the judge declared his intention to decide the case ex statuto.*

ex tempore or **extempore** *adv.* [L. **ex** out of, from, directly after, away from (1); **tempore** time (2): from time.] Without reflection, preparation, or premeditation. Instantaneously. *He was interviewed ex tempore.* —*adj.* Extemporaneous. Instantaneous. Offhand. a) *He delivered an ex tempore judgment.* b) *He made ex tempore statements which, predictably, contained some half-truths.*

ex testamento *adv.* [**ex** out of, from, directly after, away from (1); **testamento** will (2): from a will.] *Law.* Under a will. In accordance with a will. *He claimed absolute title to the building ex testamento.* Cf. **ab intestato.**

extortio est crimen quando quis colore officii extorquet quod non est debitum, vel supra debitum, vel ante tempus quod est debitum. [L. **extortio** extortion (1); **est** is (2); **crimen** crime (3); **quando** when (4); **quis** one, anyone (5); **colore** by color (6); **officii** of office (7); **extorquet** extorts, obtains by force (8); **quod** (that) which, what (9); **non** not (11); **est** is (10); **debitum** owed, due (12); **vel** or (13); **supra** above (14); **debitum** owed, due (15); **vel** or (16); **ante** before (17); **tempus** time (18); **quod** which (19); **est** is (20); **debitum** owed, due (21): Extortion is the crime when one by color of office extorts what is not due, or above the due, or before the time which is due.] *Law.* The crime of extortion involves extorting, by color of office, what is not due or anything beyond what is due or obtaining it before the appropriate time.

ex tota materia emergat resolutio. [L. **ex** out of, from, directly after, away from (3); **tota** whole, entire (4); **materia** subject matter (5); **emergat** should arise (2); **resolutio** explanation, resolution (1): The explanation should arise from the entire subject matter.] *Law.* In explaining a statute, one should take into consideration all aspects of it.

extra *prep.* [L. outside of, beyond.] Outside of. Except. Besides. Beyond. Without. Apart from. —*adj.* Additional. Greater or more than the usual, ordinary, expected, regular, or necessary. *The children have started extra lessons in preparation for the forthcoming examination.* —*adv.* Uncommonly. Unusually. To a point, extent, or degree which is more than the ordinary, regular or usual. Especially. a) *The man was extra happy to hear the news.* b) *She is extra naïve.* c) *The boy usually wears extra-large clothes.* —*n., pl.* **extras** 1. A thing which is additional such as a fee, point, or worker. *The restaurant serves meals at $5.00 a plate, but there are extras for those who want delicacies.* 2. A thing which is superior in quality. —*pref.* Beyond. More than. Outside. a) *extra-ordinary*; b) *extraterritorial;* c) *extracurricular*; d) *extrasensory.*

extra commercium *adj.* [L. **extra** outside of, beyond (1); **commercium** commerce (2): outside of commerce.] *Law.* Cannot be acquired or owned privately. Applicable to such things as state-owned property, navigable waters, or air. *It may, of course, be objected that this proposal amounts to designating family property as extra commercium* (Asante 1975:260). See **extra patrimonium.** Cf. **in commercio** and **in patrimonio.**

extra dictione *adj.* [L. **extra** beyond (1); **dictione** wording, saying (2): beyond wording.] *Logic.* Beyond the wording. A logical fallacy which is not based upon the wording of the phrase. The opposite of **in dictione** (q.v.).

extra judicium *adj./adv.* [L. **extra** outside of, beyond (1); **judicium** court proceeding, trial (2): outside of court proceeding.] *Law.* Extrajudicial. Out of court. Not related to a case before a court. *The statement made by the judge, though significant, is essentially extra judicium.*

extra jus *adj./adv.* [L. **extra** outside of, beyond (1); **jus** right, law (2): beyond the law.] More than is required by the law. *The plaintiff's demand, though seemingly reasonable, is extra jus and, therefore, cannot be granted.* See **extra legem.**

extra legem *adj./adv.* [L. **extra** outside of, beyond (1); **legem** law (2): beyond the law.] Out of the law. Extralegal. Outside the scope of the protection offered by the law. See **extra jus.**

extra legem positus est civiliter mortuus. [L. **extra** outside of, beyond (2); **legem** law (3); **positus** having been placed (1); **est** is (4); **civiliter** citizen-like, in regard to citizenship (6); **mortuus** dead (5): Having been placed outside of the law, he is dead so far as citizenship is concerned.] *Law.* Whoever is placed outside the law is, as far as civil rights are concerned, dead. Applicable to outlawry.

extra muros *adj.* [L. **extra** outside of, beyond (1); **muros** walls (2): beyond the walls.] Outside the walls. Extramural. External. a) *The manager of the company notified the employees in a strongly-worded letter that it would not be responsible for their activities extra muros.* b) *The university has instituted the award of degrees extra muros.*

extraneus heres or **extraneus haeres** *n., pl.* **extranei heredes** or **extranei haeredes** [L. **extraneus** strange, external (1); **heres** heir (2): strange/external heir.] An heir from outside the family. In Roman law, one becomes such an heir only after formally accepting the inheritance. *Nobody can be compelled to act as trustee against his will . . . for if he meddles with the estate his conduct will almost certainly be construed as acceptance. Once he has accepted, it is no longer open to him to disclaim. His position furnishes an exact counterpart to that of the extraneus heres in Roman law* (Hanbury 1962:222).

extraordinaire *adj., pl.* **extraordinaires** [Fr. extraordinary, amazing, fantastic.] Unusual. Out of the ordinary. a) *a film extraordinaire*; b) *a chef extraodinaire.*

extra patrimonium *adj.* [L. **extra** outside of, beyond (1); **patrimonium** inheritance, patrimony (2): outside of inheritance.] *Law.* That which cannot be acquired or owned privately. Not subject to private acquisition or ownership. See **extra commercium.** Cf. **in commercio** and **in patrimonio.**

extra territorium *adv.* [L. **extra** outside of, beyond (1); **territorium** domain, district, territory (2): outside of the district.] Beyond or outside the territory. *The jurisdiction of the court was ousted because the offense was committed extra territorium.*

extra territorium jus dicenti impune non paretur. [L. **extra** outside of, beyond (3); **territorium** domain, district, territory (4); **jus** right, law (2); **dicenti** to the one pronouncing, delivering (1); **impune** with impunity, without punishment (7); **non** not (5); **paretur** there is obeying (6): To the one pronouncing law outside the district, there is no obeying with impunity.] *Law.* When a judge pronounces judgment on a matter outside his jurisdiction, his judgment is flouted with impunity. See **factum a judice** etc.; **judici officium** etc.; **judicium a non** etc.; **jus non habenti** etc. Cf. **qui jussu judicis** etc.

extravaganza *n., pl.* **extravaganzas** [It. extravagance, something extravagant.] 1. A literary, musical, or dramatic work or performance which is elaborate, marked by non-adherence to conventional form, and often has elements of parody or burlesque. 2. A spectacular show, entertainment, or activity which is bound to attract attention. a) *. . . Ronald Reagan's aides mounted a four-day $8 million extravaganza of balls, concerts and receptions . . . (Newsweek Int.* Feb. 2, 1981:35). b) *. . . Iran's new leaders last week staged their first diplomatic extravaganza: the welcoming to Tehran of Palestine Liberation Organization Leader Yasser Arafat (Time Int.* 1979). 3. Something, such as an ornament for clothing or a building, which is so bizarre or spectacular that it has to attract attention. *The city is well-known for its architectural extravaganzas.*

extra viam *adv.* [L. **extra** outside of, beyond (1); **viam** way (2): outside the way.] Outside the road. Used in common law pleading in matters of trespass to rebut a plea of right of way by indicating that the trespass was committed outside the legally permissible limit.

extra vires *adj./adv.* [L. **extra** outside, beyond (1); **vires** power (2): outside/beyond power.] *Law.* Beyond the scope of legal power or authority. See **ultra vires.** Cf. **intra vires.**

extremis probatis, praesumuntur media. [L. **extremis** with extreme (things) (1); **probatis** (with) having been proved (2); **praesumuntur** are presumed (4); **media** middle (things) (3): With extreme things having been proved, middle things are presumed.] When extreme points have been proved, intermediate points are presumed.

ex turpi causa non oritur actio. [L. **ex** out of, from, directly after, away from (1); **turpi** base, disgraceful (2); **causa** cause, case, reason (3); **non** not (5); **oritur** arises (6); **actio** action, deed, legal suit (4): From a base cause legal suit does not arise.] *Law.* A disgraceful matter or consideration cannot serve as the foundation of a legal action. See **causa turpis; commodum ex injuria non oritur; commodum ex injuria sua** etc.; **contractus contra bonos mores; contractus ex turpi causa; contractus ex turpi causa, vel** etc.; **dolo malo** etc.; **dolus et fraus** etc.; **ex dolo malo non** etc.; **ex facto illicito** etc.; **ex maleficio non** etc.; **ex pacto illicito** etc.; **ex turpi contractu** etc.; **fraus et dolus** etc.; **frustra legis auxilium** etc.; **injuria non excusat injuriam; injuria propria non** etc.; **jus ex injuria** etc.; **L'obligation sans cause** etc.; **merito beneficium** etc.; **nemo allegans** etc.; **nemo ex dolo suo** etc.; **nemo ex proprio** etc.; **nemo ex suo delicto** etc.; **non facias** etc.; **nullus commodum** etc.; **pacta quae turpem** etc.; **qui per fraudem** etc.; **quid turpi** etc.; **turpis causa** and **turpis contractus.** Cf. **ex nudo pacto** etc.; **nuda pactio** etc.; and **nudum pactum ex quo** etc.

ex turpi contractu actio non oritur. [L. **ex** out of, from, directly after, away from (4); **turpi** base, disgraceful (5); **contractu** drawing together, shrinking, contract, agreement (6); **actio** action, deed, legal suit (1); **non** not (2); **oritur** arises (3): A legal suit does not arise from a base contract.] *Law.* Legal action does not arise from an immoral/base contract or legal agreement. See **ex turpi causa** etc.

ex utraque parte *adv.* [L. **ex** out of, from, directly after, away from (1); **utraque** each of two (2); **parte** side (3): from each of two sides.] On both sides. *An objective assessment can be made by considering the matter ex utraque parte.* Cf. **ex parte**.

exuviae *pl. n.* [L. garments and skins which are stripped off.] Skin, shell, etc. of an animal, such as a snake, that has been shed or cast off.

ex visceribus *adv.* [L. **ex** out of, from, directly after, away from (1); **visceribus** bowels, entrails (2): from the bowels.] From the very essence of the matter.

ex visceribus testamenti *adv./adj.* [L. **ex** out of, from, directly after, away from (1); **visceribus** bowels, entrails (2); **testamenti** of will (3): from the bowels of the will.] *Law.* From, or based upon, the inherent purpose or intention of the will. *We are not . . . to draw the sources of our judgment from the mere language or construction of other wills differently compounded, but from the language and intention of the testator in the will before us, or as it is sometimes expressed, ex visceribus testamenti* (per Lord Ellenborough C.J. in *Doe d. Wright v. Jesson* [1816] 5 M and S: 95 at 97. Quoted by Megarry 1955:160).

ex visceribus verborum *adv.* [L. **ex** out of, from, directly after, away from (1); **visceribus** bowels, entrails (2); **verborum** of words (3): from the bowels of the words.] From the words themselves. From mere words. *It is easy to deduce, ex visceribus verborum,*

that the defendant published the article with malicious intent.

ex visitatione Dei *adv.* [L. **ex** out of, from, directly after, away from (1); **visitatione** dispensation, visitation (2); **Dei** of God (3): from the dispensation of God.] By the dispensation of God. On account of physical inability.

ex visu scriptionis *adv.* [L. **ex** out of, from, directly after, away from (1); **visu** sight (2); **scriptionis** of writing (3): from the sight of the writing.] After an examination of the handwriting. *The police in the forensic laboratory identified the writer of the letter ex visu scriptionis.*

ex vi termini *adv.* [L. **ex** out of, from, directly after, away from (1); **vi** force, strength (2); **termini** of end, limit, term (3): from the force of the term.] From the meaning of the term. From the intrinsic meaning of the term. *A conspiracy to injure involves ex vi termini an intention and agreement to injure, or more accurately, a common intention and agreement to injure* (Weir 1974:531).

ex voluntate *adv.* [L. **ex** out of, from, directly after, away from (1); **voluntate** will, choice, inclination (2): from will/choice.] Willingly. Voluntarily. Of his/her own accord. *The suspect wrote down the statement ex voluntate.* See **ex mero motu**.

ex voto *n., pl.* **ex votos** [L. **ex** out of, from, directly after, away from (1); **voto** prayer, promise, vow (2): from a vow.] An offering or gift made, especially to a god, in return for a favor granted. *The church walls were covered with ex votos.*

F

F. *abbr.* for 1. **fecit** (q.v.). 2. **fiat** (q.v.). 3. **formula** (q.v.). 4. **forte** (q.v.).

faber est suae quisque fortunae. Sallust (86–35 B.C.). *Ad Caesarem Senem de Re Publica Oratio* I,2. [L. **faber** maker, carpenter (3); **est** is (2); **suae** of his/her own (4); **quisque** each one (1); **fortunae** (of) fortune (5): Each one is the maker of his/her own fortune.] Each person is the architect of his/her own fate. See **faber fortunae suae**.

faber fortunae suae *n.* [L. **faber** maker, carpenter (1); **fortunae** (of) fortune (3); **suae** of his/her own (2): maker of his/her own fortune.] Architect of his/her own fate. *In a society where there are equal opportunities, each person may rightly be regarded as faber fortunae suae.* See **faber est** etc.

fabula docet *n.* [L. **fabula** story (1); **docet** teaches (2): Story teaches.] The principle or view that a story teaches a lesson or serves a didactic purpose. *The peculiarity of Thucydides' political philosophy . . . is that he preaches no general doctrine: there is no fabula docet in his work* (Jaeger 1970:390). Cf. **experientia docet**.

fac. *abbr.* for 1. **façade** (q.v.). 2. **facsimile** (q.v.).

façade or **facade** *n., pl.* **façades** or **facades** *abbr.* **fac.** [Fr. front, face, appearance.] 1. The front or prominent exterior face of a building. 2. A superficial (or false) aspect or appearance of a thing. Window-dressing. a) *The architect Adolf Loos, who wanted to strip the ornament from the facade of Viennese life . . .* (*Newsweek Int.* March 3, 1980:45). b) *The fragile facade of unity could crumble* (*Newsweek Int.* June 23, 1980:22).

facetiae *pl. n.* [L. wit, witty sayings, witticisms, humor.] 1. Witty sayings or writings. Humorous sayings or writings. Jokes. 2. Short humorous stories, which are often obscene. Books which treat sexual love. Cf. **curiosa**; **erotica**; and **esoterica**.

faciendum *n., pl.* **facienda** [L. that which must be done.] Something which has to be done. A necessary deed.

facile princeps *adj.* [L. **facile** easily (1); **princeps** first, foremost (2): easily first/foremost.] Easily preeminent. Indisputably the first or leader. *Laura, always facile princeps, established her superiority during the final examinations.*

facilis descensus Averni Vergil (70–19 B.C.). *Aeneid* VI,126. [L. **facilis** easy (3); **descensus** descent (1); **Averni** of Avernus, hell (2): the descent of Avernus (is) easy.] The descent to hell is easy. The return is more difficult.

facio ut des *n.* [L. **facio** I do (1); **ut** so that (2); **des** you may give (3): I do so that you may give.] *Civil Law.* A form of contract in which one party does something in order that the other may give something in return. See **quid pro quo**.

facio ut facias *n.* [L. **facio** I do (1); **ut** so that (2); **facias** you may do (3): I do so that you may do.] *Civil Law.* A form of contract in which one party does something in order that the other may do something in return. See **quid pro quo**.

façon de parler *n., pl.* **façons de parler** [Fr. **façon** manner, way (1); **de** of (2); **parler** to speak, speaking (3): way of speaking.] Manner, style, or way of speaking or speech. Form of speech. *The top schools normally set the standards in virtually everything from academic performance to sports and even more interestingly the students' façon de parler* (Thomas Cooke in *West Africa* 1985).

facs. *abbr.* for **facsimile** (q.v.).

facsimile or **fac simile** *abbr.* **fac.** or **facs.** *n., pl.* **facsimiles** or **fac similes** [L. **fac** do, make (1); **simile** similar (2): Make similar.] An exact reproduction or copy. A **replica** (q.v.). *"The notes of Lord Kenyon and of Sir J. Burrow on this point are in such perfect harmony, that the one may be considered a fac simile of the other"* (*Giles v. Grover* 1832, quoted by Megarry 1973:127). —*short form* **fax** *v.* To make or send a copy of a document or image via electronic

---

139

means, especially over telephone lines. —*n., pl.* **faxes** The copy made or produced by this process.

facta armorum *pl. n.* [L. **facta** deeds, acts, facts (1); **armorum** of arms (2): feats of arms.] Military exploits or achievements. *The facta armorum of Alexander the Great have won for him undying fame both in antiquity and among posterity.*

facta non verba [L. **facta** deeds, acts, facts (1); **non** not (2); **verba** words (3): deeds not words.] Actions, not words; i.e., what is needed is action not mere words. *He is a man of action whose guiding motto is facta non verba.* See **facta sunt** etc.

facta sunt potentiora verbis. [L. **facta** deeds, acts, facts (1); **sunt** are (2); **potentiora** more powerful, stronger (3); **verbis** than words (4): Deeds are stronger than words.] Deeds are more powerful than words; i.e., actions speak louder than words. See **facta non verba.**

factio testamenti or **testamenti factio** *n., pl.* **factiones testamenti** or **testamenti factiones** [L. **factio** making, preparing (1); **testamenti** of will (2): the making of a will.] *Civil Law.* The right or ability to make a will. *An infant is deficient in factio testamenti by reason of age.*

facto *adv.* [L. by deed, act, fact.] In fact. By the fact. By an act. See **ipso facto.**

facto et animo *adv.* [L. **facto** by deed, act, fact (1); **et** and (2); **animo** by intention (3): by deed and intention.] In fact and intention. By deed and design. *The evidence shows that the offense was committed facto et animo.* See **animo et corpore.**

factotum *n., pl.* **factotums** [Med. L. from L. **fac** do, make (1); **totum** the whole, all (2): Do all or the whole.] 1. An all-purpose servant. A person employed to do every kind of work. A person entrusted with diverse responsibilities. *The tenants tired of dealing with a factotum instead of with the landlord himself.* 2. *Printing.* A very big decorative capital letter.

factum *n., pl.* **facta** [L. deed, act, fact.] 1. *Civil Law.* A fact, a circumstance, an event, or a statement of facts in a case in a lawcourt. a) *The question of abandonment of land is one of factum and animus* (James 1982:214). b) *In questions involving the factum or the contents of a will, the declarations of the testator himself are admissible as evidence to show his state of mind at the time . . .* (Parry 1961:70). 2. *Old English Law.* An act and deed, especially one which is illegal. 3. *Old English Law.* A sealed instrument or a deed of conveyance. 4. *Testamentary Law.* The formal execution of a will.

factum a judice quod ad ejus officium non spectat non ratum est. [L. **factum** deed, act, fact (1); **a** by (2); **judice** judge (3); **quod** which (4); **ad** to, at, for, according to (7); **ejus** his/her (8); **officium** duty, office (9); **non** not (5); **spectat** relates, pertains (6); **non** not (11); **ratum** valid (12); **est** is (10): An act

by a judge which does not relate to his/her office is not valid.] An act by a judge which does not relate/ pertain to his/her jurisdiction is null and void. See **extra territorium jus** etc.

factum cuique suum, non adversario, nocere debet. [L. **factum** deed, act, fact (2); **cuique** to each one (5); **suum** one's own (1); **non** not (6); **adversario** to (the) opponent, adversary (7); **nocere** to do harm, hurt, injure (4); **debet** ought, should (3): One's own act should do harm to each one, not to the opponent.] *Law.* A party's own act should be harmful to himself/ herself, not to the opponent. See **factum unius** etc.

factum infectum fieri nequit. [L. **factum** deed, act, fact (1); **infectum** undone (4); **fieri** to become, be made (3); **nequit** cannot (2): An act cannot become undone.] What is done cannot be undone.

factum juridicum *n., pl.* **facta juridica** [L. **factum** deed, act, fact (2); **juridicum** juridical (1): juridical fact.] *Law.* A fact pertaining to the law; i.e., one of the factors which constitute an obligation.

factum negantis nulla probatio sit. [L. **factum** deed, act, fact (2); **negantis** of the one denying (1); **nulla** no (4); **probatio** proof (5); **sit** there should be (3): Of the one denying a fact, there should be no proof.] It is not obligatory for a person who denies a fact to prove it. See **actori incumbit** etc.

factum probandum *n., pl.* **facta probanda** [L. **factum** deed, act, fact (2); **probandum** that must be proved (1): a deed that must be proved.] A fact which requires proof. The fact in issue. Applicable in the law of evidence. Cf. **factum probans.**

factum probans *n., pl.* **facta probantia** [L. **factum** deed, act, fact (2); **probans** proving (1): a proving fact.] Circumstantial evidence. Evidentiary fact. Fact given in evidence to prove **factum probandum** (q.v.). Cf. **facta probanda.**

factum unius alteri nocere non debet. [L. **factum** deed, act, fact (1); **unius** of one (person) (2); **alteri** to the other (6); **nocere** to do harm, injure (5); **non** not (4); **debet** ought, should (3): The deed of one person ought not do harm to the other.] *Law.* One person's deed should not be harmful to another. See **factum cuique** etc.

facultas probationum non est angustanda. [L. **facultas** opportunity (1); **probationum** of proofs (2); **non** not (4); **est** is (3); **angustanda** to be narrowed, restricted (5): The opportunity of proofs is not to be narrowed.] *Law.* Opportunity for offering proof or testimony must not be restricted. See **nemo prohibetur** etc.

faenus nauticum *n.* [L. **faenus** interest (2); **nauticum** nautical, maritime (1): maritime interest.] *Roman Law.* Interest on maritime loans payable only when the ship with its cargo arrived safely at port.

fainéant or **faineant** *n., pl.* **fainéants** or **faineants** [Fr. idle, lazy, idler, lazy-bones, sluggard.] An irresponsible, lazy person. An idler. *With the appointment of a fainéant as head of the institution, things began to fall apart.* —*adj.* Indolent. Lazy. Idle. *A fainéant man has been appointed the new head of the institution.* Cf. **roi fainéant.**

fait accompli *n., pl.* **faits accomplis** [L. **fait** deed (2); **accompli** accomplished, completed (1): an accomplished deed.] An accomplished fact. A thing which is accomplished or done and, presumably, cannot be reversed. A definite situation. a) *Positions were being worked out in advance, and then presented to SWAPO as a fait accompli, . . .* (*West Africa* 1982). b) *Faced with a fait accompli, the Administration responded gracefully* (*Newsweek Int.* July 14, 1980:21).

falsa demonstratione legatum non perimitur. [L. **falsa** by false (4); **demonstratione** (by) description (5); **legatum** legacy, bequest (1); **non** not (2); **perimitur** is destroyed, prevented (3): A legacy is not prevented by false description.] False/erroneous description does not render a legacy null and void. See **falsa demonstratio non nocet.**

falsa demonstratio non nocet. [L. **falsa** false (1); **demonstratio** description (2); **non** not (3); **nocet** does harm, hurts, injures (4): False description does not harm.] *Law.* False/erroneous description does not hurt an instrument. Where there are both true and erroneous descriptions of a person or thing in a legal instrument and the true description sufficiently establishes the identity of the subject, the false description is rejected and the instrument is validated. See **error nominis numquam** etc., **falsa demonstratione** etc.; **falsa grammatica** etc.; **falsa orthographia** etc.; **grammatica falsa** etc.; **idem sonans; mala grammatica non** etc.; **nihil facit error** etc.; **nil facit error** etc.; **verba intentioni** etc.; and **veritas nominis** etc.

falsa grammatica non vitiat concessionem. [L. **falsa** false (1); **grammatica** grammar (2); **non** not (3); **vitiat** vitiates, taints (4); **concessionem** grant (5): False grammar does not vitiate a grant.] *Law.* Bad grammar does not impair a grant. See **falsa demonstratio non nocet.**

falsa orthographia non vitiat concessionem. [L. **falsa** false (1); **orthographia** spelling (2); **non** not (3); **vitiat** vitiates, taints (4) **concessionem** grant (5): False spelling does not vitiate a grant.] *Law.* Bad/erroneous spelling does not impair a grant. See **falsa demonstratio non nocet.**

falsetto *n., pl.* **falsettos** [It. a little false.] *Music.* 1. A male voice singing in a high range beyond that normally reached by a tenor. 2. One who sings in such a range.

falsi crimen See **crimen falsi.**

falsus in uno, falsus in omnibus. [L. **falsus** false (1); **in** in, on (2); **uno** one (3); **falsus** false (4); **in** in, on (5); **omnibus** all (6): False in one, false in all.] *Law.* False in one instance, false in all. A maxim on weight of evidence, which maintains that, if a witness deliberately tells lies in one detail, the jury could ignore the entire testimony. The maxim, however, does not exonerate the jury from the duty of weighing every detail of the testimony and accepting whatever is true.

familia *n., pl.* **familiae** [L. household, family.] The Roman family comprised the paterfamilias, his wife, his legitimate sons and their wives, adopted sons and their wives, unmarried daughters, grandchildren, and slaves. See **jus vitae necisque; materfamilias; paterfamilias; patria potestas; patria potestas in pietate** etc.; and **potestas.**

famille de robe *n., pl.* **familles de robe** [Fr. **famille** family (1); **de** of (2); **robe** gown, robe (3): family of the gown.] A family which includes a long line of lawyers and judges.

famosus libellus *n.* [L. **famosus** slanderous, scandalous, defamatory (1); **libellus** indictment, complaint, libel (2): a scandalous libel.] A libelous document or writing.

fana *n.* [Ar. annihilation.] *Islam.* The replacement of one's human identity, thoughts, and concerns with those of God.

fandango *n., pl.* **fandangoes** [Sp. (from uncertain source) song, dance.] 1. A brisk Spanish or South American dance. 2. Music for this dance. 3. Nonsensical, ridiculous or improper act, behavior, or speech. Tomfoolery, especially in public or serious affairs. *The chairman of the board urged members to stop their irrational fandangoes and approach the business with due seriousness.*

fantasia *n., pl.* **fantasias** [It. fantasy.] *Music.* 1. A composition in which fancy and free association dominate over formal structure. 2. A composition which incorporates a selection from other compositions. *Walt Disney's "Fantasia."* Cf. **fantasie.**

fantasie *n., pl.* **fantasies** [Fr. fantasy.] **Fantasia** (q.v.).

farce *n., pl.* **farces** [Fr. stuffing.] 1. A play in which plot and/or characters are exaggerated or stuffed like a roast chicken for comic effect. 2. A play or performance which is a joke or mockery. 3. A stuffing for a roasted fowl.

farceur or *fem.* **farceuse** *n., pl.* **farceurs** or *fem.* **farceuses** [Fr. practical joker, trickster, humorist, comic fellow.] 1. A practical joker. A funny person. A person who should not be taken seriously. 2. A person who is skilled in acting or writing farce.

farrago *n., pl.* **farragoes** [L. mixed fodder, mash, mixture.] Medley. Mixture. Hodgepodge. A confused, irrational, or incongruous assemblage. *His critics describe his speech as a farrago of distortions, misrepresentations, half-truths mixed with some truth.*

fasces *pl. n.* [L. bundles.] *Ancient Rome.* The axes bound with rods which accompanied magistrates as a symbol of their authority.

fas est et ab hoste doceri. Ovid (43 B.C.–17 A.D.). *Metamorphoses* IV,28. [L. **fas** lawful, proper (2); **est** it is (1); **et** even, also (4); **ab** from, by (5); **hoste** enemy (6); **doceri** to be taught (3): It is proper to be taught even by an enemy.] One can learn even from an enemy.

fata morgana *n.* [It. **fata** fairy (1); **Morgana** Morgan (2): Fairy Morgan, Morgan Le Fay.] 1. Sister of King Arthur associated with southern Italy by Norman settlers. 2. A mirage seen on the coasts of Sicily and Italy, or in the Straits of Messina. 3. Any mirage. A thing which is illusory or insubstantial. a) *The fata morgana of trouble-free friendship.* b) *The fata morgana of marriage with no problems.*

fatetur facinus qui judicium fugit. [L. **fatetur** confesses, acknowledges (4); **facinus** crime, misdeed (5); **qui** (one) who (1); **judicium** judgment, trial (3); **fugit** flees (2): One who flees a trial confesses the crime.] *Law.* A person who flees judicial trial practically admits guilt.

fatigue *n., pl.* **fatigues** [Fr. weariness, weakness, tiredness, hard work, heavy duty.] 1. Weariness, tiredness, or exhaustion caused by mental or physical exertion. *By the end of the strenuous exercise, most of the participants had dropped off from sheer fatigue.* 2. Labor. Toil. A duty or task which causes tiredness. 3. Punitive menial work assigned to a soldier. —*pl.* Uniform worn in the field or when a fatigue is given.... *they were still outfitted in U.S.-supplied camouflage fatigues* (*Newsweek Int.* Dec. 5, 1983:31).

fatti maschi, parole femmine. [It. **fatti** deeds, acts (1); **maschi** masculine, manly (2); **parole** words (3); **femmine** female, womanly (4): Masculine acts, female words.] Manly deeds, womanly words. Forceful deeds and soft words. Motto of the State of Maryland.

Fatwa or **fatwa** or **fatwah** or **fetwah** *n.* [Ar. legal instruction.] 1. *Islam.* A legal ruling by a **mufti** (q.v.). 2. Any formal condemnation.

fauna *n., pl.* **faunae** or **faunas** [L. goddess of the groves, associated with the fauns.] Animals. Animal life. All the animals peculiar to or found in a particular area, district, environment, or period. Cf. **flora**.

faute de mieux *adv.* [Fr. **faute** lack, want (1); **de** of (2); **mieux** better (3): want of better.] For want or lack of something better. In the absence of something better. *It is not a challenging position, but she accepted it faute de mieux.* —*adj.* Accepted, adopted, or used for want of something better. *He accepted a faute de mieux appointment and, predictably, is already disillusioned.*

faux *adj.* [Fr. false, artificial.] Not real. a) *faux furs*; b) *faux pearls*; c) *faux tears.*

faux amis *pl. n.* [Fr. **faux** false, insincere (1); **amis** friends (2): false friends.] *Linguistics.* Deceptive cognates. Words from two different languages which are identical or nearly identical in form but are different in meaning; e.g., use of Fr. *assister* "to be present" to mean "to help," based on meaning of Eng. *assist.*

faux pas *n., pl.* **faux pas** [Fr. **faux** false, wrong (1); **pas** step, pace (2): false step.] A blunder, mistake, slip or indiscretion in remark, action, etc., especially in a social or diplomatic context. *... all ... must now be bowing their proud heads in utter shame over what, in essence, is a blatant offence of protocol, an unforgiveable diplomatic faux pas* (Sampha Kamara in *West Africa* 1983). Cf. **gaffe**.

favorabiliores rei potius quam actores habentur. [L. **favorabiliores** more favored (3); **rei** defendants (1); **potius** rather, more (4); **quam** than (5); **actores** plaintiffs (6); **habentur** are had, held, regarded (2): Defendants are held more favored than plaintiffs.] *Law.* The condition of the defendant is considered to be better than that of the plaintiff. See **in aequali jure melior** etc.

fax *short form* of **facsimile** (q.v.).

F.C. *abbr.* for **fideicommissum** (q.v.).

F.D. *abbr.* for **Fidei defensor** (q.v.).

fec. abbr. for 1. **fecit** (q.v.). 2. **fecerunt** (q.v.).

fecerunt *abbr.* **fec.** or **ff.** [L. They made or did.] *pl.* of **fecit** (q.v.).

fecit *abbr.* **f.** or **fec.** [L. He/She made or did.] His/Her creation or work. Used on a work of art, painting, sculpture, etc. to indicate the one who executed or created it. Cf. **caelavit**.

fele absente, mures ludent. [L. **fele** with cat (1); **absente** (with) being absent, away (2); **mures** mice (3); **ludent** will play (4): With the cat being absent, the mice will play.] When the cat is away, the mice will play. *To support his thesis on the disadvantages of strict parenting, he quoted the dictum* Fele absente, mures ludent.

felicitaciones *n., sing.* **felicitación** [Sp. felicitations.] Congratulations. Best wishes. Many happy returns. *The Salvadoran leader appeared on television to announce that he had sent his personal felicitaciones to the White House* (*Time Int.* 1982).

felix culpa *n., pl.* **felices culpae** [L. **felix** lucky, happy (1); **culpa** fault, error, blame, guilt, failure (2): happy fault.] 1. *Christianity.* The fall of Adam and Eve. Their sin is a happy fault because it led to the salvation of humankind by Jesus Christ. 2. Any mistake or error which turns out to be fortuitous, helpful, or serendipitous. *The discovery of smallpox vaccine was due to Jenner's felix culpa.*

felix opportunitate *adj.* [L. **felix** fortunate, lucky (1); **opportunitate** with the opportunity, right time, convenience (2): lucky with the opportunity.] Fortunate at the right time.

felix ... opportunitate mortis *adj.* [L. **felix** fortunate, lucky (1); **opportunitate** with the opportunity, right time, convenience (2); **mortis** of death (3): lucky with the opportunity of death.] Fortunate to have died at the right time.

fellatio *n.* [L. sucking.] Sexual activity which involves stimulating the penis with the mouth. Cf. **cunnilingus**.

felo de se *n., pl.* **felones de se** or **felos de se** [Anglo-L. **felo** felon, evildoer, rogue (1); **de** about (2); **se** self (3): evildoer about self.] 1. Killer of self. Suicide. 2. A person who deliberately kills himself/herself or dies from the consequences of his/her commission of an illegal act.

felonia implicatur in qualibet proditione. [L. **felonia** felony, crime (4); **implicatur** is involved, implied (5), **in** in, on (1); **qualibet** any one, all, every (2); **proditione** treason, treachery (3): in every treason, a felony is involved.] *Law.* A crime is implied in every act of treason.

feme covert *n., pl.* **femes covert** or **femmes couvertes** [Obs. Fr. **feme** woman, wife (2); **covert** covered (1): covered woman.] *Law.* A married woman protected by her husband. In former times, a feme covert suffered some liabilities. For instance, her property was under her husband's control. Cf. **feme sole**.

feme sole *n., pl.* **femes sole** [Obs. Fr. **feme** woman, wife (2); **sole** single, sole (1): a single woman.] *Law.* 1. A spinster, an unmarried woman, a widow, a divorcée or woman legally separated from her husband. 2. A married woman who uses the status of an unmarried woman, i.e., whose property is not under the control of her husband. Cf. **feme covert**.

femme or **feme** *n., pl.* **femmes** or **femes** [Fr. woman, wife.] A woman.

femme de chambre *n., pl.* **femmes de chambre** [Fr. **femme** woman, wife (1); **de** of, from, about, for (2); **chambre** room, chamber (3): woman of the chamber.] A chamber maid.

femme du monde *n., pl.* **femmes du monde** [Fr. **femme** woman, wife (1); **du** of the (2); **monde** world, society (3): woman of the world.] A lady. Society woman. A worldly woman. A sophisticated woman. A woman of good upbringing or training. Cf. **gens du monde** and **homme du monde**.

femme du peuple *n., pl.* **femmes du peuple** [Fr. **femme** woman, wife (l); **du** of the (2); **peuple** people, working classes (3): woman of the people.] A woman of humble origins. A lady whose manners suggest a humble background. A woman of the working class. Cf. **homme du peuple**.

femme fatale *n., pl.* **femmes fatales** [Fr. **femme** woman, wife (2); **fatale** fatal (1): a fatal woman.] 1. A dangerous woman. *With such male-chauvinistic aides and uncompromising policies, it is no wonder that many women see Thatcher as the femme fatale for British feminism* (*Newsweek Int.* March 10, 1980:9). 2. A flirt. A woman who attracts men in an inexplicable and mysterious manner. *Andy lost his sobriety the moment he met the femme fatale and is yet to recover it.* 3. A seductress who entices men into embarrassing or dangerous situations. A woman who seduces men through the use of her charm and then proceeds to exploit them. *"Poor Mummy . . . she*

was a true femme fatale. She killed with a touch." (*Time Int.*, 1982). Cf. **jeune fille fatale**.

femme libre *n., pl.* **femmes libres** [Fr. **femme** woman, wife (2); **libre** free, unattached (1): a free woman.] An unattached woman. A woman of loose morals. Cf **cocotte**; **meretrix**; and **succuba**.

femme savante *n., pl.* **femmes savantes** [Fr. **femme** woman (2); **savante** learned, scholarly (1): a learned woman.] A learned, knowledgeable or erudite woman. A blue-stocking. Cf. **bas bleu** and **Les femmes savantes**.

Fe que no duda es fe muerta. [Sp. **fe** faith, trust (1); **que** which, that (2); **no** not (3); **duda** doubts, hesitates, questions (4); **es** is (5); **fe** faith, trust (7); **muerta** dead, killed (6): Faith which does not doubt is dead faith.] A faith which does not question is a faith with no life. Based upon Miguel de Unamuno's (1864–1937) **La vida es duda** etc. (q.v.). Cf. **La foi consiste** etc.

ferae bestiae *pl. n.* [L. **ferae** wild, untamed (1); **bestiae** beasts (2): wild beasts.] Wild, untamed animals. Cf. **domitae naturae animalia**.

ferae naturae *adj.* [L. **ferae** of wild, untamed (1); **naturae** (of) nature (2): of wild nature.] *Law.* Undomesticated. Untamed. Used to describe such wild animals as foxes which cannot be claimed to be anybody's absolute property, though a person can exercise qualified property rights over them by, for instance, capturing them or owning the land where they are found. *At common law the keeper of an animal was strictly liable, independently of negligence, for damage done by the animal if (a) the animal was ferae naturae* [i.e., belonged to a dangerous species] *or (b) the animal was mansuetae naturae* [i.e., did not belong to a dangerous species] *and he knew of its vicious characteristics* (Rogers 1975:394). Cf. **domitae naturae animalia**.

fere libenter homines id quod volunt credunt. Julius Caesar (100–44 B.C.). *De Bello Gallico* III,18. [L. **fere** usually, generally (1); **libenter** willingly (3); **homines** people, human beings (2); **id** that (5); **quod** which (6); **volunt** they wish, want (7); **credunt** they believe (4): Usually people willingly believe that which they want.] By their own choice human beings usually believe what they want. Cf. **populus vult decipi** and **quod enim mavult** etc.

fermata *n., pl.* **fermatas** [It. stopped, held.] 1. *Music.* A notation which indicates that a note (or rest) should be held beyond the time indicated by the tempo. 2. *Italy.* A public transportation stop.

fest *n., pl.* **fests** [Ger. **Fest** celebration, feast.] A commemoration or celebration. Cf. **fête** and **festa**.

festa *n., pl.* **feste** or **festas** [It. festival.] A celebration or holiday to mark the feast day of a patron saint. Cf. **fête** and **fiesta**.

festina lente. Augustus (63 B.C.–14 A.D.). Cited in Suetonius (born c. 69 A.D.) in II,23. [L. **festina** make haste (1); **lente** slowly, leisurely (2): Make haste slowly.] With deliberate speed. *He* [i.e., Justice F.A. van der Meulen] *added what might have been an important canon of his judicial belief: "Festina lente must undoubtedly be the watchword when applying (British) institutions to peoples such as those in Nigeria"* . . . (Adewoye 1977:256).

festinatio justitiae est noverca infortunii. [L. **festinatio** hastening (1); **justitiae** of justice (2); **est** is (3); **noverca** stepmother (4); **infortunii** of calamity, misfortune (5): Hastening of justice is the stepmother of calamity.] Hasty justice is the stepmother of calamity. Haste fosters misfortune in attempted justice.

Festschrift *n., pl.* **Festschriften** or **Festschrifts** [Ger. **Fest** festival (1); **Schrift** writing (2): festival writing.] Commemorative publication. Publication in honor of somebody. A work of various contributions by students, lecturers, professors, colleagues, and admirers in honor of a scholar, particularly on a special occasion.

Festspielhaus *n.* [Ger. **Fest** festival (1); **Spiel** play (2); **Haus** house (3): festival playhouse.] The opera house built specifically for the performance of the operas of Richard Wagner (1813–1883) in Bayreuth, Germany.

fête or **fete** *n., pl.* **fêtes** or **fetes** [Fr. festival, celebration.] 1. The feast day of a saint. 2. A festival, feast, or festivity. Merry-making. A festive party. a) *Almost everybody . . . sneered in private at the Shah's Ozymandian megalomania, symbolized by a $100 million fete he staged at Persepolis in 1971 . . . (Time Int.* 1980). b) *. . . Stewart Mott threw a $25,000 fete to celebrate his l0th anniversary as a Washingtonian* (*Newsweek Int.* July 25, 1983:29). 3. A lavish outdoor entertainment. —*v.* To entertain. To celebrate. *They feted the couple on the occasion of their 50th wedding anniversary.* Cf. **festa** and **fiesta**.

fête de la musique *n., pl.* **fêtes de la musique** [F. **fête** festival, feast, entertainment (1); **de** of (2); **la** the (3); **musique** music (4): festival of the music.] Musical festival, show, or entertainment. *It was the second fête de la musique, and the merrymaking last week was bigger and better than last year's* (*Newsweek Int.,* July 4, 1983: 45).

fetus or **foetus** *n., pl.* **fetuses** or **foetuses** [L. a bringing forth, offspring.] *Medicine.* An unborn vertebrate which has passed through the early stages of development in the womb, especially an unborn child which is at least three-months old. A fully or reasonably developed embryo. *The operation . . . could lead to an abortion for both fetuses . . .* (*Newsweek Int.* June 29, 1981:54). See **en ventre sa mère**.

ff. *abbr.* for 1. **fecerunt** (q.v.). 2. **fragmenta** (q.v.)

fiancé or *fem.* **fiancée** *n., pl.* **fiancés** or *fem.* **fiancées** [Fr. betrothed, engaged.] A person to whom one is engaged to be married.

fiasco *n., pl.* **fiascoes** or **fiascos** [It. bottle.] A flop. An ignominious, complete or ridiculous failure, especially

in the case of an ambitious or grandiose project. a) *The much publicized venture ended in a fiasco.* b) *The result has been another resounding fiasco . . .* (*New African* 1979). c) *Reagan's team believes that détente was a fiasco that succeeded only in lulling the West into a false sense of security, while Moscow conducted an unprecedented military buildup* (*Newsweek Int.* April 20, 1981:23). d) *. . . there was much talk of the fiasco which befell the EEC foreign ministers on a similar dialogue-promoting venture last August* (*West Africa* 1985).

fiat *abbr.* **f.** or **ft.** *n., pl.* **fiats** [L. Let it be done.] Official endorsement. Permission. Command. Authoritative decision/sanction. Arbitrary edict. Summary pronouncement, whether judicial or executive. a) *The very debatable and controversial question was settled by the fiat of the chairman of the committee.* b) *The Attorney General gave his fiat for a suit to be instituted against the government.*

fiat justitia et ruant caeli. William Watson (c.1559–1603). [L. **fiat** let it be done (2); **justitia** justice (1); **et** and, even, also (3); **ruant** let them tumble down, fall down (5); **caeli** the heavens (4): Let justice be done and let the heavens fall down.] *Law.* Let justice be done, even though the heavens should fall.

fiat justitia, ruat caelum. [L. **fiat** let it be done (2); **justitia** justice (1); **ruat** let it tumble down, fall down (4); **caelum** sky, heaven (3): Let justice be done; let heaven fall down.] *Law.* Let justice be done, even if the heavens should tumble down (or even though the heavens should fall).

fiat lux. Genesis 1:3. [L. **fiat** let there become, be (1); **lux** light (2): Let there be light.] The words with which God creates light.

fiat opportunitas, ruat caelum. [L. **fiat** let it be done (2); **opportunitas** convenience, right time, opportunity, suitableness (1); **ruat** let it tumble down, fall down (4); **caelum** sky, heaven (3): Let convenience be done; let heaven fall down.] *Law.* Let what is convenient or suitable be done even if the sky should fall as a consequence.

fiat quod prius fieri consuevit. [L. **fiat** let it be done (1); **quod** (that) which, what (2); **prius** previously, formerly (5); **fieri** to be done (4); **consuevit** is accustomed (3): Let it be done which is accustomed to be done previously.] Let what is usually done be done.

fiat voluntas tua [L. **fiat** be done (3); **voluntas** will (2); **tua** (1): Your will be done.] Let your will be done. 1. *Christianity.* A phrase from the **Pater Noster** (q.v.) or Lord's Prayer which Jesus taught his disciples at Matthew 6:9–11. 2. An acknowledgment of someone else's power or authority.

fiche *n., pl.* **fiches** [Fr. a small slip of paper or record.] A document on a small piece of paper or other material, especially a **microfiche** (q.v.).

fideicommissum *abbr.* **F.C.** *n., pl.* **fideicommissa** [L. That which has been bequeathed in/to trust.] 1. A kind of trust involving a gift of property to a person. 2. *Roman Property Law.* A gift made either in anticipation of death or by will which the donee is required under specified conditions to give to a third person.

Fidei Defensor *abbr.* **F.D.** or **Fid. def.** *n., pl.* **Fidei Defensores** See **Defensor Fidei.**

fides servanda est. [L. **Fides** faith, confidence (1); **servanda** to be preserved, observed (3); **est** is (2): Faith is to be preserved/observed.] *Law.* Faith must be preserved or observed; i.e., an agent should see to it that the confidence reposed in him is not betrayed.

fides servanda est; simplicitas juris gentium praevaleat. [L. **fides** faith, confidence (1); **servanda** to be preserved, observed (3); **est** is (2); **simplicitas** simplicity (4); **juris** of right, law (5); **gentium** of nations (6); **praevaleat** should prevail (7): Faith is to be preserved; the simplicity of the law of nations should prevail.] *Law.* Faith must be preserved; the simplicity of international law should prevail. Applicable to bills of exchange.

fiducia *n.* [L. trust.] Confidence. **Contractus fiduciae** (q.v.).

fidus Achates *n.* Vergil (70–19 B.C.). *Aeneid* VI,158 et al. [L. **fidus** faithful (1); **Achates** Achates (2): faithful Achates.] 1. Aeneas' faithful friend in Vergil's *Aeneid.* 2. A true friend. *From all indications, Peter is David's fidus Achates.*

fieri facias *abbr.* **fi. fa.** *n.* [L. **fieri** to be done, to happen (2); **facias** you may cause (1): you may cause to happen.] *Law.* You may/should cause it to be done. A writ ordering the sheriff or any officer to levy the goods and chattels of the judgment debtor and pay the required sum to the judgment creditor. See **capias; elegit; fieri feci; levari facias; nulla bona;** and **venditioni exponas.**

fieri facias de bonis propriis *n.* [L. **fieri** to be done, to happen (2); **facias** you should cause (1); **de** of, from, about, for (3); **bonis** goods, property (5); **propriis** one's own, his/her/their own (4): You should cause to be done about one's own goods.] *Law.* A writ ordering the sheriff to seize the property of the executor for the satisfaction of the testator's debts if, after the issue of a writ **fieri facias de bonis testatoris,** a return is made that there are no leviable goods (**nulla bona**) or that the executor has mismanaged the estate (**devastavit**). Cf. **fieri facias de bonis testatoris; saisie-exécution;** and **saisie-immobilière.**

fieri facias de bonis testatoris *n.* [L. **fieri** to be done, to happen (2); **facias** you should cause (1); **de** of, from, about, for (3); **bonis** goods, property (4); **testatoris** of testator (5): You should cause to be done about the testator's property.] *Law.* A writ issued ordinarily against an executor sued for a debt incurred by the testator. See **fieri facias de bonis propriis.**

fieri feci *n.* [L. **fieri** to be done, to happen (2); **feci** I have caused (1): I have caused to be done.] *Law.* The return made by a sheriff or any competent officer to

a **fieri facias** (q.v.). when he/she has recovered either the whole or some of the required amount.

fiesta *n., pl.* **fiestas** [Sp. entertainment, festival, party, public holiday, church feast.] A festival, feast, or public holiday. A festival celebrated to mark the feast day of a saint. A religious festival. a) *. . . the stylish architectural confines of the National Theatre . . . will play host for four days to a literary fiesta reminiscent of the FESTAC '77 colloquium . . .* (*The Guardian* 1986). b) *Members of the church are making hectic preparations for next Sunday's fiesta.* Cf. **festa** and **fête.**

fiesta nacional *n.* [Sp. **fiesta** entertainment, festival (2); **nacional** national (1): national entertainment.] National pastime. *In fact, most Spaniards don't even consider bullfighting to be the fiesta nacional any more* (*Newsweek Int.* Nov. 27, 1978:5).

fi. fa. *abbr.* for **fieri facias** (q.v.).

fil d'Ariane *n.* [Fr. **fil** thread (1); **d'** of (2); **Ariane** Ariadne (3): thread of Ariadne.] 1. *Greek Mythology.* The thread which Ariadne, daughter of Minos, the king of Crete, gave to the Athenian hero Theseus to enable him to escape from the labyrinth in Crete after he killed the Minotaur. 2. A clue or key to any perplexity, problem, or inextricable situation. *The committee has reached a cul-de-sac and is yet to find the fil d'Ariane for unraveling the complexities of the problem.*

filioque *n.* [L. **filio** to/for the son (2); **que** and (1): and to the son.] 1. And in the son. A phrase from the Christian creed accepted by the western churches but not the eastern churches. 2. Any point leading to a significant rupture between two people or two groups. *Their disagreement about the election became a filioque which they never resolved.*

filius familias or **filiusfamilias** *n., pl.* **filii familiae** or **filii familiarum** [L. son of the family.] *Roman Law.* A son who is under the power of the paterfamilias or who has not been emancipated. *In its early stages there was little freedom for women and for the filius familias, and almost none for the slave* (Curzon 1979:165). Cf. **paterfamilias.**

filius nullius See **nullius filius.**

filius populi *n., pl.* **filii populi** [L. **filius** son (1); **populi** of people (2): A son of the people.] A bastard. An illegitimate son. See **nullius filius.**

filius terrae or **terrae filius** *n., pl.* **filii terrae** or **terrae filii** [L. **filius** son (1); **terrae** of earth, land (2): son of earth/land.] A person of humble/undistinguished birth.

film noir *n., pl.* **films noirs** [Fr. **film** film (2); **noir** black, gloomy, dismal (1): a gloomy film.] A film which has a tragic theme and a pessimistic tone. *—attrib.* Of, characteristic of, relating to, having features of a film noir. *With a superb cast at their disposal, they've taken a somewhat preposterous film noir plot and enriched it with quirky, meaty characterizations to produce a nervous comedy . . .* (*Newsweek Int.* March 16, 1981:51). See **pièce noire.**

fils *adj*. [Fr. son.] Junior. Preceded by a name. Used to distinguish a son from a father, particularly when the two bear the same name. *Dumas, fils*. Cf. **père**.

filum aquae *n., pl.* **fila aquarum** [L. **filum** thread (1); **aquae** of water (2): thread of water.] *Law*. Thread of a stream. An imaginary division of a river between two landowners. See **ad filum aquae**.

filum viae *n., pl.* **fila viarum** [L. **filum** thread (1); **viae** of road (2): the thread of the road.] *Law*. The middle line of a road; i.e., the boundary between the landowners on either side of the road. Cf. **ad filum aquae**.

finale *n., pl.* **finales** [It. final, last.] The end of something, especially the closing scene or part of a public performance. a) *His brother, Maurice, . . . joined Gregory on-stage during the finale of his last show in an explosion of fancy footwork* (*Newsweek Int.* Jan 18, 1982:23). b) *He had hoped that he might yet succeed in freeing the Americans and give his presidency something of an upbeat finale* (*Time Int.* 1981).

fin de guerre *adj.* [F. **fin** end (1); **de** of (2); **guerre** war (3): end of war.] Of, characteristic of, relating to, the era at the end of a war.

fin de régime *n.* [Fr. **fin** end (1); **de** of (2); **régime** government (3): end of a government.] The end or fall of a government or an administration. *The economic malaise is also a symptom of political unease, accentuated by a feeling of fin de regime . . .* (*West Africa* 1982).

fin de saison *n.* [Fr. **fin** end (1); **de** of (2); **saison** season (3): end of season.] The end of the social season. —*adj.* Characterized by the end of the social season. *The fin de saison conversation of the summer residents focused upon winterizing cabins and traveling hardships.*

fin-de-siècle or **fin de siecle** *adj.* [Fr. **fin** end (1); **de** of (2); **siècle** century, age (3): end of century.] 1. Relating to the end of a century or of an era, especially the 19th century. 2. Characterized by, similar to, or relating to, the artistic and literary style of the end of the 19th century. Decadent. *With inordinate emphasis on aestheticism and escapism . . . pictures of French subjects, including the extraordinary "Soir Bleu," which is redolent of fin de siecle ennui* (*Newsweek Int.* March 2, 1981:43).

fine *n.* [It. boundary, limit, end.] The end, especially the end of a piece of music or the end of a film. Cf. **finis**.

finesse *n.* [Fr. delicacy, perception, keenness.] 1. Delicacy and skill in the completion of a task, especially a work of art, performance, dispute, or negotiation. 2. A trick or stratagem in a game of chance, dispute, or negotiation in which one concedes an advantage in order to gain another one. —*v.* To use delicacy, skill, or trickery in the completion of a task or to win a game of chance.

finis *n., pl.* **finises** [L. boundary, limit, end, fine.] Conclusion. A fine. *Malam Bukar made it clear that the finis of his case with Malam Musa was yet to be seen,*

since he intended to appeal to the Supreme Court. Cf. **fine**.

finis coronat opus. [L. **finis** boundary, limit, end, fine (1); **coronat** crowns (2); **opus** work, labor (3): The end crowns the work.] The end is the climax of the work. This expression has several connotations, including: 1. A work is no real work until it has been completed. 2. Finishing touches make a work complete. 3. One is neither successful nor a failure until he/she has reached the end of life.

finis finem litibus imponit. [L. **finis** boundary, limit, end, fine (1); **finem** boundary, limit, end (3); **litibus** to litigations (4); **imponit** imposes (2): A fine imposes an end to litigations.] *Law*. A fine puts an end to litigations.

finis unius diei est principium alterius. [L. **finis** boundary, limit, end, fine (1); **unius** of one (2); **diei** (of) day (3); **est** is (4); **principium** beginning, commencement (5); **alterius** of another (6): The end of one day is the commencement of another.] The end of one day marks the beginning of the next day.

Finita la commedia. [It. **finita** finished (3); **la** the (1); **commedia** comedy (2): The comedy is finished.] The comedy has come to an end. The farce is over. A variation of **La commedia è finita** (q.v.). See **La farce est jouée**.

finium regundorum actio See **actio finium regundorum**.

firmior et potentior est operatio legis quam dispositio hominis. [L. **firmior** firmer, stronger (4); **et** and (5); **potentior** more powerful, mightier (6); **est** is (3); **operatio** operation (1); **legis** of law (2); **quam** than (7); **dispositio** arrangement, disposition (8); **hominis** of a person, a human being (9): The operation of the law is firmer and mightier than the disposition of a person.] The application of law or legal process takes precedence over the actions of individuals. Thus, if a husband agrees to pay the wife's debt, this arrangement does not prevent the creditor from bringing action against the wife. See **fortior et potentior** etc. Cf. **fortior est custodia** etc.

fiscus *n., pl.* **fisci** [L. a wicker basket, money bag, purse, state treasury.] The emperor's private purse. The imperial treasury. Originally, in Rome, the private treasury of the emperor, but ultimately the state treasury.

fl. *abbr.* for **floruit** (q.v.).

flagrans crimen *n.* [**flagrans** burning, blazing (1); **crimen** crime (2): blazing crime.] *Law*. A fresh crime. A recent crime. A crime in the very process of being committed. *The police have just uncovered a flagrans crimen.*

flagrante bello *adv.* [L. **flagrante** (with) burning, blazing (2); **bello** with war (1): with the war blazing.] As the war was being fought or was going on. In the heat of the war. *The platoon commander deserted his unit flagrante bello.* Cf. **in flagrante bello**.

flagrante delicto *adj./adv.* [L. **flagrante** (with) burning, blazing (2); **delicto** with crime (1): with the crime blazing.] In the very act of committing a crime. Immediately after the crime. Red-handed. *Though the thief was apprehended flagrante delicto, he pleaded innocent.* Cf. **in flagrante delicto.**

fleur-de-lis or **fleur-de-lys** *n., pl.* **fleurs-de-lis** or **fleurs-de-lys** [Fr. **fleur** flower (1); **de** of (2); **lis** lily (3): flower of lily, lily flower.] 1. Iris. 2. A formalized iris with three petals which appeared on the emblem of the French kings and which has continued, from time to time, to symbolize France and the French people.

fleur du mal *n., pl.* **fleurs du mal** [Fr. **fleur** flower (1); **du** of the (2); **mal** evil, harm (3): flower of the evil.] A literary or artistic work which is scandalous, derived from *Les Fleurs du mal*, decadent poetry composed by the French poet Charles Baudelaire (1821–1867). —*attrib.* Of, characteristic of, relating to, having features of fleurs du mal. *The problem is not just the shocking, fleurs du mal content though that would scare off any Hollywood producer . . .* (*Newsweek Int.* May 9, 1983:54).

flor. *abbr.* for **floruit** (q.v.).

flora *n., pl.* **florae** or **floras** [L. **Flora** goddess of flowers.] 1. Plants. Plant life. All the plants peculiar to, or that are to be found in, a particular area, district, situation or period. 2. A list or catalog of the plants in an area or time period. Cf. **fauna.**

floruit *abbr.* **fl.** or **flor.** *n., pl.* **floruits** [L. He/she/it flourished.] A period which marks the peak of the development of something: a person, a movement, etc. Used to indicate the period when a writer, artist, etc. was active, if the dates of birth and death are not known. *Eusebius puts his floruit in 467, which fits quite well* (Lesky 1966:202).

flotilla *n., pl.* **flotillas** [Sp. A small fleet.] 1. A fleet of small boats or warships. A small fleet. . . . *when a fierce storm with near hurricane-force winds lashed the straits . . . a major disaster threatened the main body of the flotilla* (*Time Int.* 1980). 2. A group of things, persons, airplanes, etc. which resembles a fleet of boats or ships.

flumina et portus publica sunt, ideoque jus piscandi omnibus commune est. [L. **flumina** rivers (1); **et** and (2); **portus** harbors, ports (3); **publica** public (5); **sunt** are (4); **ideoque** and for that reason, and therefore (6); **jus** right, law (7); **piscandi** of fishing (8); **omnibus** to all (11); **commune** common (10); **est** is (9): Rivers and harbors are public, and, for that reason, the right of fishing is common to all.] *Law.* Rivers and harbors are public property and, therefore, fishing rights in such places belong to everybody.

folie à deux *n., pl.* **folies à deux** [Fr. **folie** madness, insanity, folly (1); **à** to, toward, in, by, with, until (2); **deux** two (3): madness by two.] The having or holding of the same delusional, false, or misleading ideas by two closely associated persons, usually the consequence of transference from one to the other. *What astonishes here is Seabrook's ability both to present the full horror of this complex folie à deux of "frozen, terrified dependency" and to examine what led his mother to it* (*Newsweek Int.* April 7, 1980:54).

folie de doute or **folie du doute** *n., pl.* **folies de doute** or **folies du doute** [Fr. **folie** madness, insanity, folly (1); **de** of (2); **doute** doubt, uncertainty (3): madness of doubt or uncertainty.] *Psychology.* A pathological inability to reach decisions, particularly one in which a person cannot decide between simple options or one is not sure of having done some simple or ordinary things.

folie de grandeur *n., pl.* **folies de grandeur** [Fr. **folie** madness, insanity, folly (1); **de** of (2); **grandeur** greatness, magnitude (3): folly of greatness.] *Psychology.* Delusion of grandeur. An illusion, delusion, or false belief that one is great or one is a very important person. A mania for acquiring magnificent or colossal objects. See **megalomania.**

folio recto *abbr.* **F.R.** or **f.r.** or **recto** *n.* [L. **folio** with leaf, page (1); **recto** (being) straight (2): with leaf or page being straight.] 1. The front of a leaf, i.e., of a manuscript. The side of a leaf that should be the first to be read. 2. The page on the right (i.e., of a book). The page which usually carries an odd number. 3. The front cover (i.e., of a book). The front of a book's jacket. Cf. **folio verso.**

folio verso *abbr.* **F.V.** or **f.v.** or **verso** *n.* [L. **folio** with leaf, page (1); **verso** (with) having been turned (2): with leaf or page having been turned.] 1. The side of a sheet or leaf (i.e., of a manuscript) that is the second to be read. 2. The left-hand page (i.e., of a book). The page of a book that usually carries an even number. 3. The back cover (i.e., of a book). The back of a book's jacket. Cf. **folio recto.**

fons et origo *n.* [L. **fons** source, fountain, well (1); **et** and (2); **origo** origin (3): source and origin.] Original source. Foundation. a) *The deteriorating national economy is generally assumed to be the fons et origo of the prevalent immorality.* b) *Government should ensure that nothing is done to undermine the claim of the Supreme Court to be fons et origo of justice.*

for. *abbr.* for **forte** (q.v.).

force de frappe *n., pl.* **forces de frappe** [L. **force** force, power (1); **de** of (2); **frappe** striking, impression (3): force of striking.] Strike force. A striking force, especially nuclear striking force. a) *Last year French President Valéry Giscard d'Estaing announced that France was planning to develop its own neutron bomb to add to its force de frappe* (*Newsweek Int.* Feb. 16, 1981:13). b) *France's pique is understandable enough, since its technocrats count on their electronics and telecommunications industries to become a sort of industrial force de frappe* (*Newsweek Int.* Oct. 11, 1982:36).

force majeure *n.* [Fr. **force** force, power (2); **majeure** major, superior (1): superior force.] 1. Absolute necessity. Overpowering circumstances. Absolute compulsion. Irresistible force or power. **Vis major** (q.v.). *No sane person attempts to argue with or resist force majeure.* 2. *Law.* Applicable to a clause inserted in contracts (e.g., those of insurance and construction), for the protection of the parties, if circumstances which are unanticipated, unavoidable or beyond the control of the parties frustrate the performance of the contract.

format *n., pl.* **formats** [Fr. size and shape, form and size.] 1. The size and shape of a book or publication. 2. The general style or makeup of a book, newspaper, magazine, publication, etc. . . . *Lapham has proposed changing the format of the magazine to include a mixture of original writing and articles reprinted from magazines and newspapers* . . . (*Newsweek Int.* July 11, 1983:5). 3. The general plan, pattern, procedure, or arrangement of an organization, project, entertainment, etc. *The new head of the institution reorganized its administration, introducing new formats for almost everything.*

formula *abbr.* **f.** *n., pl.* **formulae** or **formulas** [L. a form, rule, prescription, regulation, principle.] 1. Set or fixed words used regularly, especially in a ceremony and, in common-law practice, in judicial proceedings. 2. A formal statement expressing a principle and serving as the basis for discussions, negotiations, etc. a) *The opposing parties took a long time to agree on a formula for settling their differences.* b) *Jordan and the PLO have renewed the search for a formula for lasting peace in the Middle East . . .* (*South*, 1985). 3. A prescription or recipe showing how something is done, especially how food or medicine is prepared. a) *Umaru received the formula for the medicine from a neighbor.* b) *. . . Hollywood has found a formula to win back foreign audiences it was losing to television* (*Newsweek Int.* Sept. 28, 1981:48). 4. A mixture of milk or other substitute used for feeding babies. *Feshbach also says that Soviet babies are often placed in daycare centres and fed inferior formulas, making them vulnerable to influenza and other epidemic diseases* (*Newsweek Int.* Jan. 28, 1981:7). 5. A symbol expressing a rule, a general fact, a mathematical principle, or the constituents of a chemical substance.

forsan et haec olim meminisse juvabit. Vergil (70–19 B.C.). *Aeneid* I,203. [L. **forsan** perhaps (1); **et** and, even (3); **haec** these (things) (4); **olim** one day (5); **meminisse** to remember, recollect (2); **juvabit** it will delight, be delightful, be pleasing (1): Perhaps it will delight to remember even these things one day.] Someday it will be pleasing to remember even these woes. Cf. **haec olim meminisse juvabit.**

forte *abbr.* **f.** or **for.** [It. from L. strong.] *adv./adj.* In a strong manner. Loud. —*n., pl.* **fortes** 1. *Music.* A loud musical passage. Cf. **piano.** 2. A person's strong point. A field in which a person is very outstanding. *John probably has many weaknesses, but there can be no doubt that courtesy is his forte.*

fortior est custodia legis quam hominis. [L. **fortior** stronger (4); **est** is (3); **custodia** protection, custody (1); **legis** of law (2); **quam** than (5); **hominis** of a person, human being (6): The protection of the law is stronger than a human being's.] The protection provided by the law is stronger than that provided by a human being. Cf. **firmior et** etc. and **fortior et potentior** etc.

fortior et potentior est dispositio legis quam hominis. [L. **fortior** stronger (4); **et** and (5); **potentior** more efficacious, powerful (6); **est** is (3); **dispositio** disposition, arrangement (1); **legis** of law (2); **quam** than (7); **hominis** of a person, human being (8): The disposition of the law is stronger and more powerful than a human being's.] The disposition of the law is stronger and more efficacious than that of a person; i.e., the law can set aside an individual's will or expressed desire. See **firmior et** etc. Cf. **fortior est custodia** etc.

fortis fortuna adjuvat. Terence (c.185–159 B.C.). *Phormio*,203. [L. **fortis** brave, valiant, strong (persons) (3); **fortuna** fortune (1); **adjuvat** helps (2): Fortune helps the brave.] Luck helps those who are brave. Cf. **Aide-toi** etc.; **audentis fortuna juvat;** and **On dit que** etc.

fortissimo *abbr.* **ff** *adv./adj.* [It. very loud or strong.] Very loud. Very loudly. Used as a musical direction. —*n., pl.* **fortissimi** or **fortissimos** *Music.* A passage sung, played, or recited very loudly. A very loud sound, passage, or tone. Cf. **pianissimo.**

forum *n., pl.* **fora** or **forums** [L. an open space, marketplace, public place, court.] 1. *Ancient Rome.* The marketplace, comprising an open space surrounded by shops and public buildings and serving as center of business transactions and judicial proceedings. 2. A court or tribunal. a) *The judge ruled that the court was not the proper forum for cases of a political nature.* b) *The forum will decide whether English law or customary law is to be applied.* 3. A public place of meeting for open discussions. *This square has served as the city's forum for ages.* 4. A journal or newspaper for open discussions. *The management of the newspaper declared their intention to make it a forum in which national issues will be discussed.*

forum actus *n.* [L. **forum** forum, court, tribunal (1); **actus** of the act, action (2): forum of the act.] *Law.* The forum or court of the action; i.e., the court which exercises jurisdiction over the place where the act in question was done.

forum competens *n.* [L. **forum** forum, court, tribunal (2); **competens** competent (1): competent court.] *Law.* A court which has jurisdiction to determine a matter. Cf. **forum non competens.**

forum conscientiae *n.* [L. **forum** forum, court, tribunal (1); **conscientiae** of conscience (2): the forum of conscience.] The court of conscience or moral sense. a) *The Court of Chancery was established as a forum conscientiae.* b) *Aisha decided not to sue Ali but to refer the matter to forum conscientiae.* See **in foro conscientiae.**

forum contractus *n.* [L. **forum** forum, court, tribunal (1); **contractus** of drawing together, shrinking, contract, agreement (2): the forum of contract.] *Law.* The court of the contract. The court which exercises jurisdiction over the place where the contract was made. *The defense counsel argued that the court was not competent to try the case, since it was not the forum contractus.*

forum conveniens *n.* [L. **forum** forum, court, tribunal (2); **conveniens** suitable (1): suitable forum.] *Law.* Suitable court. The jurisdiction, district, or state most suitable for the trial of a cause, taking into consideration the interests of the litigants and the public. *The Kano court is the forum conveniens to handle the action for wrongful dismissal, since the cause of action arose there.* Cf. **forum non conveniens.**

forum domicilii *n.* [L. **forum** forum, court, tribunal (1); **domicilii** of domicile (2): the court of domicile.] *Law.* The court of the domicile or residence; i.e., of the area where the defendant resides. *The divorce suit can appropriately be heard and determined at the forum domicilii of the couple.*

forum non competens *n.* [L. **forum** forum, court, tribunal (3); **non** not (1); **competens** competent (2): a not competent court.] *Law.* A court which does not have jurisdiction to determine a matter. *The magistrate's court was adjudged a forum non competens to try a case of culpable homicide.* Cf. **forum competens.**

forum non conveniens *n.* [L. **forum** court (3); **non** not (1); **conveniens** suitable (2): a not suitable court.] *Law.* An unsuitable court. A doctrine whereby a court of law, though having full jurisdiction over a case before it, decides not to consider the case on its merits on the ground that the interest of justice would be better served if the case were tried in a different district. In exercising such discretionary power, the court takes into consideration the interests of the parties, accessibility of the court, facilities for compelling unwilling witnesses to appear, inter alia. a) *The High Court at Jos was considered a forum non conveniens since one of the parties objected to the trial there on the ground that the transaction took place at Enugu.* b) *The House of Lords has affirmed that the doctrine of forum non conveniens is one of Scottish but not of British law (Graveson 1974:150).* Cf. **forum conveniens.**

forum originis *n.* [L. **forum** forum, court, tribunal (1); **originis** of origin (2): the court of origin.] *Law.* The court of one's place of birth. *For the sake of convenience,*

the Chief Justice directed that the case respecting the child's paternity should be tried at the forum originis of the plaintiff.

forum rei *n.* [L. **forum** forum, court, tribunal (1); **rei** of matter, thing, property, business, affair (2): court of the thing.] *Law.* The court of the place where the disputed thing is situated.

forum rei gestae *n.* [L. **forum** forum, court, tribunal (1); **rei** of the matter, thing, property, business, affair (2); **gestae** of done, transacted, accomplished (3): the court of the thing done.] *Law.* The court of the place where an act was done. Ordinarily, most cases are brought, first, before the forum rei gestae and then, should the need arise, are transferred to other courts.

forum rei sitae *n.* [L. **forum** forum, court, tribunal (1); **rei** of the matter, thing, property, business, affair (2); **sitae** (of) situated (3): the court of the property situated.] *Law.* The court which has jurisdiction over the place where the property is situated. *Judicially, it is advantageous to try cases in the forum rei sitae.*

foyer *n.* [Fr. home, social center.] 1. The lobby or entrance hall of a large building, especially a hotel. 2. The vestibule of a home. 3. A shelter or hostel. *Many West African residents in Paris live in foyers.*

fracas *n., pl.* **fracas** or **fracases** [Fr. uproar, tumult, din, clash.] A noisy fight or quarrel. A brawl. *What started as a minor dispute between two spectators degenerated into a fracas in which a large number of people exchanged blows freely.*

fractionem diei non recipit lex. [L. **fractionem** fraction, portion (4); **diei** of day (5); **non** not (2); **recipit** receives, accepts, allows (3); **lex** law (1): The law does not accept a portion of a day.] The law does not recognize any units of time smaller than twenty-four hours.

fragmenta *abbr.* **ff.** *pl. n.* [L. fragments.] Fragments, especially of a literary work.

France d'Outre-mer *n.* [Fr. **France** France (1); **d'** of (2); **Outre-mer** overseas (3): France of overseas.] Overseas France. *Nevertheless, the pretense that colonial policy led to the formation of a "France d'Outre-mer" was carefully cultivated* (Suret-Canale 1971:83).

France noire *n.* [Fr. **France** France (2); **noire** black, negro (1): Black France.] Black Frenchmen. Frenchmen of Negro ancestry, i.e., from Africa or the West Indies. *The events of the next five months will tell whether France noire has succeeded in stemming the tide of racism* (B. Diarra in *West Africa* 1985).

Francophilia *n.* [Neo-L. and Gk. from Late L. **Franc(us)** French (2); Gk. **philia** fondness, liking for (1): fondness or liking for French things.] A fondness, liking, or admiration for France as well as French things, practices, customs, institutions, etc. Cf. **Anglomania.**

Francophobia *n.* [Neo-L. and Gk. from L. **Franc(us)** French (2); Gk. **phob(os)** fear, dread (1): fear or dread of French things.] Fear or hatred of France as well as French things, practices, customs, institutions, etc. Cf. **Anglomania**.

Franglais *n.* [Fr. from **français** French (1); **anglais** English (2): French-English.] A blend of French and English, such as "le weekend" or "le pullover."

frater *n., pl.* **fratres** or **fraters** [L. brother.] 1. Brother. 2. A member of a religious order (e.g., the Benedictine order). 3. A member of a fraternity.

Frau *n., pl.* **Frauen** [Ger. woman, female.] 1. A wife. A housewife. 2. Mrs. Prefixed to the name of a married German woman as a title of courtesy. Cf. **Fräulein; hausfrau; Madame; Mademoiselle; Senhora; Senhorita; Señora; Señorita; Signora;** and **Signorina**.

Fräulein *abbr.* **Frl.** *n., pl.* **Fräulein** [Ger. unmarried woman or lady.] 1. A young unmarried woman, especially of Germany. 2. A German governess. 3. Miss. Prefixed to the name of an unmarried German girl or woman as a title of courtesy. Cf. **Frau; Madame; Mademoiselle; Senhora; Senhorita; Señora; Señorita; Signora;** and **Signorina**.

fraus est celare fraudem. [L. **fraus** fraud (2); **est** it is (1); **celare** to hide, conceal (3); **fraudem** fraud (4): It is fraud to conceal fraud.] *Law.* Concealment of deceit is a deceitful act. See **qui non improbat, approbat**.

fraus est odiosa et non praesumenda. [L. **fraus** fraud (1); **est** is (2); **odiosa** hateful, odious (3); **et** and (4); **non** not (5); **praesumenda** to be presumed (6): Fraud is hateful and not to be presumed.] *Law.* Deceit is odious and must not be presumed.

fraus et dolus nemini patrocinari debent. [L. **fraus** fraud (1); **et** and (2); **dolus** deceit (3); **nemini** to no one, nobody (6); **patrocinari** to give protection, support (5); **debent** ought, should (4): Fraud and deceit ought to give protection to no one.] *Law.* No one should derive an advantage from fraud and deceit. See **ex turpi causa** etc.

fraus et jus numquam cohabitant. [L. **fraus** fraud (1); **et** and (2); **jus** right, law (3); **numquam** never (4); **cohabitant** live together, cohabit (5): Fraud and law never cohabit.] *Law.* Law cannot exist with deliberate trickery or deceit. See **jus est norma** etc. and **jus et fraus** etc.

fraus latet in generalibus. [L. **fraus** fraud (1); **latet** is concealed, lies hidden (2); **in** in, on (3); **generalibus** general (things) (4): Fraud is concealed in general things.] *Law.* Deceit is concealed in general expressions. Cf. **dolosus versatur** etc. and **in generalibus latet error**.

Frère Jacques or **Frere Jacques** *n.* [Fr. **frère** brother, monk (1); **Jacques** Jacques, John (2): brother John.] A traditional French song also popular in English translation.

fresco *n., pl.* **frescos** or **frescoes** [It. fresh, cool.] *Art.* 1. Method of painting on damp or wet plaster. 2. A painting done in this way. Cf. **alfresco**.

frisson *n., pl.* **frissons** [Fr. shudder, shiver, chill, thrill.] An instant of extreme excitement or emotion marked especially by a shudder. a) *A frisson of fear seized her when she opened her door and found a man sitting in the living room.* b) *Knowing that Fonda has had well-publicized battles with her father adds an extra frisson to their tug of war* (*Newsweek Int.* Nov. 30, 1981:57).

Frl. *abbr.* for **Fräulein** (q.v.).

fronde *n.* [Fr. catapult, sling.] 1. La Fronde, a mid-17th-century uprising of aristocracy and bourgeoisie against Regent Anne of Austria and her son King Louis XIV. 2. Political opposition, usually one that is violent and/or quixotic. 3. A group of malcontents.

frondeur *n., pl.* **frondeurs** [Fr. slinger, critic, fault-finder, rebel.] A dissident. A rebel. A quixotic critic of the authorities. A malcontent, usually in a political context.

fructus pendentes pars fundi videntur. [L. **fructus** fruits (2); **pendentes** hanging (1); **pars** part (4); **fundi** of land, farm (5); **videntur** are seen, regarded as (3): Hanging fruits are seen as part of the land.] *Law.* Hanging fruits are considered to be part of the land; i.e., the fruit is the property of the owner of the land.

frui *adv.* [L. to enjoy.] *Civil Law.* For enjoyment, as opposed to **uti** (q.v.), i.e., for necessary use.

frustra agit qui judicium prosequi nequit cum effectu. [L. **frustra** in vain, to no purpose (8); **agit** acts, sues, prosecutes (7); **qui** (he) who (1); **judicium** judgment (4); **prosequi** to follow up (3); **nequit** cannot, is not able (2); **cum** with (5); **effectu** effect, result (6): He who cannot follow up the judgment with effect, sues to no purpose.] *Law.* It is futile to bring a suit, if the judgment cannot be executed effectively.

frustra est potentia quae numquam venit in actum. [L. **frustra** in vain, to no purpose (1); **est** is (2); **potentia** power (3); **quae** which (4); **numquam** never (5); **venit** comes (6); **in** into, to, against, for (7); **actum** act, action (8): In vain is the power which never comes into act.] *Law.* Power which is never exercised is futile.

frustra legis auxilium quaerit qui in legem committit. [L. **frustra** in vain, to no purpose (1); **legis** of law (8); **auxilium** help, aid (7); **quaerit** seeks, look for (6); **qui** (one) who (2); **in** into, to, against, for (4); **legem** law (5); **committit** commits, perpetrates (3): In vain does one who commits against the law look for the help of the law.] Someone who commits an offense against the law looks in vain for the aid of the law. See **ex turpi causa** etc.

frustra petis quod mox es restiturus. [L. **frustra** in vain, to no purpose (1); **petis** you ask for, sue for (2); **quod** (that) which (3); **mox** soon (6); **es** you are (4); **restiturus** about to restore (5): To no purpose do you ask for that which you are about to restore soon.] *Law.* It is futile to ask/sue for something which one will soon restore. Cf. **frustra petis quod statim** etc. and **non videtur quisquam** etc.

frustra petis quod statim alteri reddere cogeris. [L. **frustra** in vain, to no purpose (1); **petis** you ask for, sue for (2); **quod** (that) which (3); **statim** immediately (7); **alteri** to another (6); **reddere** to return, restore (5); **cogeris** you will be compelled (4): In vain do you ask for that which you will be compelled to restore to another immediately.] *Law.* It is futile to ask/sue for something which one will be compelled to restore to another immediately. Cf. **frustra petis quod mox** etc. and **non videtur quisquam** etc.

frustra probatur quod probatum non relevat. [L. **frustra** in vain, to no purpose (1); **probatur** is proved (2); **quod** (that) which (3); **probatum** having been proved (4); **non** not (5); **relevat** avails, alleviates (6): In vain is proved that which having been proved does not avail.] It is futile to prove a point which, when proved, is of no avail.

ft. *abbr.* for **fiat** (q.v.).

fucus *n.* [L. red dye, face paint, pretense.] Pretense. Disguise. Dissimulation. Deceit. Facade. *He presented his case with apparent honesty, but the discerning eyes of the judge could see through the fucuses of his hypocrisy.*

fuerunt *v.* [L. They have been.] They were. They are dead.

fugit irreparibile tempus Vergil (70–19 B.C.). *Georgics* III,285. [L. **fugit** flees (3); **irreparibile** irretrievable (1); **tempus** time (2): irretrievable time flees.] Time flies irretrievably. Once it is gone, time cannot be recalled. Cf. **À la Recherche du temps perdu** and **temps perdu.**

fugue *n., pl.* **fugues** [Fr. flight.] *Music.* A contrapuntal composition in which two or more voices offer variations in a musical theme.

Führer or **Fuhrer** or **Fuehrer** *n., pl.* **Führers** or **Fuhrers** or **Fuehrers** [Ger. leader, chief, head, commander.] A person occupying an authoritative position. A leader of a group, especially a tyrant, dictator, or despot. Applicable, especially, to Adolf Hitler. *Hitler had scorned Owens and his black teammates as "America's black auxiliaries." And Jesse had made a mockery of the Führer's words and the Aryan "master race" philosophy (Newsweek Int.* April 14, 1980:53). See **caudillo.**

Führerprinzip *n.* [Ger. **Führer** leader, commander (1); **Prinzip** principle (2): leader principle, principle of leadership.] Principle of authoritarian or totalitarian leadership. Doctrine or theory emphasizing the desirability and efficiency of dictatorship. *The choice of General Tufa, an advocate of Führerprinzip, as leader of the junta clearly suggests that the new regime intends to be dictatorial.*

fuit *v.* [L. He/she has been.] He/she was. He/she is dead.

fulcrum *n., pl.* **fulcra** or **fulcrums** [L. bedpost, foot of a couch.] 1. The point around which a lever turns.

2. Support. Prop. Something which serves as the leverage/support for an action, decision, etc. *Journalists should be careful and objective in their presentation of facts, for whatever they write serves as the fulcrum of readers' judgment.*

functus officio *adj.* [L. **functus** having performed (1); **officio** duty, office (2): having performed the duty/office.] With no more official authority. No longer holding public appointment. Of no further effect. Used with reference to an officer who has left his office, or a power, agency, or an instrument which has served its purpose and is of no more effect. *The president lost his re-election campaign and became functus officio.*

fungibiles res or **res fungibiles** *n., sing.* **fungibilis res** or **res fungibilis** [L. **fungibiles** fungible, substitutable or **res** matters, things, property, business, affairs (2): substitutable things.] *Civil Law.* Fungible things; i.e., things which are such that they can be replaced in equal quality and quantity (e.g., oil, bags of grain, etc.). Cf. **res non fungibiles.**

furandi animo *adv.* [L. **furandi** of stealing (2); **animo** with the intention (1): with the intention of stealing.] *Roman Law.* With intent to steal. *To prove theft (furtum), it must be established that the accused person touched the object furandi animo.*

furandi animus See **animus furandi.**

furiosis nulla voluntas est. [L. **furiosis** to insane, mad (persons) (1); **nulla** no (3); **voluntas** will, free-will (4); **est** there is (2): To insane persons there is no free-will.] *Law.* Insane individuals have no free-will. A insane person cannot be tried for his/her offenses, since he/she cannot distinguish between good and bad. Cf. **insanus est qui** etc.

furioso *n., pl.* **furiosos** [It. violent, furious.] A fanatic. A man who is insane or furious. —*adj./adv.* Vigorous. Forceful. Vigorously. Forcefully. *As the piece develops, a furioso section for the ensemble is followed by electronic responses from the soloists until the entire orchestra begins to fragment, a violin jutting out here, a trombone blasting there (Time Int.* 1981).

furiosus absentis loco est. [L. **furiosus** insane, mad (person) (1); **absentis** of absent (person) (4); **loco** in place (3); **est** is (2): An insane person is in the place of an absent person.] An insane person is like a person who is absent. Cf. **insanus est qui** etc.

furiosus solo furore punitur. [L. **furiosus** insane, mad (person) (1); **solo** (by) only, alone (4); **furore** by insanity, madness, fury (3); **punitur** is punished (2): An insane person is punished by madness alone.] *Law.* An insane person's sole punishment is insanity; i.e., he/she cannot be punished according to the law. Cf. **insanus est qui** etc.

furiosus stipulari non potest nec aliquid negotium agere quia non intelligit quod agit. [L. **furiosus** insane, mad (person) (1); **stipulari** to covenant, bargain (4); **non** not (3); **potest** can, is able (2); **nec** nor, and not (5); **aliquid** any, some (7); **negotium** business (8); **agere** to do, transact (6); **quia** because (9); **non** not (10); **intelligit** he/she understands (11); **quod** (that) which, what (12); **agit** he/she does, is doing (13): An insane person cannot bargain or transact any business because he/she does not understand what he/she is doing.] *Law.* A insane person cannot enter into a contractual obligation or a business transaction because he/she is unable to understand what he/she is doing. Cf. **insanus est qui** etc.

furor contrahi matrimonium non sinit quia consensu opus est. [L. **furor** insanity, madness, rage (1); **contrahi** to be contracted (5); **matrimonium** marriage (4); **non** not (2); **sinit** allows (3); **quia** because (6); **consensu** of consent (9); **opus** need (8); **est** there is (7): Insanity does not allow marriage to be contracted because there is need of consent.] *Law.* Insanity disqualifies one from contracting marriage because consent is required. See **insanus est qui** etc.

furore *n., pl.* **furores** [It. rage, wrath.] General excitement or commotion. A controversy. General uproar or disturbance. a) *The political furore within the PRP in the state started early in 1980 . . .* (Olu Akinyeye in *West Africa* 1982). b) *The furore generated by the Chief Engineer's scandalous conduct led to a chain of events which culminated in the termination of his appointment.*

furor loquendi *n.* [L. **furor** insanity, madness, rage (1); **loquendi** of speaking (2): madness for speaking.] A rage or passion for speaking. *The audience lost interest as the speakers argued among themselves in a furor loquendi.*

furor scribendi *n.* [L. **furor** insanity, madness, rage (1); **scribendi** of writing (2): madness for writing.] A rage/passion for writing. *His novel was the result of a four-month furor scribendi.*

furtum *n., pl.* **furta** [L. theft.] *Roman and Civil Law.* Unauthorized profit-making from, or misappropriation of, the property of another.

furtum conceptum *n., pl.* **furta concepta** [L. **furtum** theft (1); **conceptum** taken in, received (2): theft taken in or received.] *Civil Law.* Theft discovered by searching somebody's premises. In such a case actio concepti lies against the occupant of the house.

furtum est contrectatio rei alienae fraudulenta, cum animo furandi, invito illo domino cujus res illa fuerat. [L. **furtum** theft (1); **est** is (2); **contrectatio** touching (4); **rei** of matter, thing, property, business, affair (5); **alienae** of another (6); **fraudulenta** fraudulent, deceitful (3); **cum** with (7); **animo** intention (8); **furandi** of stealing (9); **invito** (with being) unwilling (12) **illo** with that (10); **domino** (with) owner (11); **cujus** of whom, whose (13); **res** matter, thing, property, business, affair (14); **illa** that (15); **fuerat** had been (16): Theft is the fraudulent touching of the property of another with the intention of stealing, with that owner being unwilling whose property that had been.] *Law.* Theft is the fraudulent touching of another's property with intent to steal, against the will of the person who was the owner of that property. See **contrectatio rei** etc.

furtum manifestum *n., pl.* **furta manifesta** [L. **furtum** theft (2); **manifestum** open, manifest (1): open theft.] An act of open or manifest stealing. A theft in which the thief is apprehended in the very act of commission.

furtum oblatum *n., pl.* **furta oblata** [L. **furtum** theft (1); **oblatum** offered (2): theft offered.] *Civil Law.* An act of theft offered. Applicable to the discovery of stolen property brought to a person's house with the clear intention that it shall be found there and is, in fact, found there. The occupant of the house may bring actio oblati against the person who brought the stolen property to the house.

furtum usus *n., pl.* **furta usus** [L. **furtum** theft (1); **usus** of use (2): theft of use.] Trespass involving temporary deprivation of movable property.

fusillade *n., pl.* **fusillades** [Fr. firing, shooting, volley of musketry.] 1. A volley. Simultaneous, rapid, and continuous shooting by many guns. *Two of the general's aides and a driver also died in the fusillade* (*Newsweek Int.* June 4, 1979:9). 2. Firing squad. *As a condemned armed robber, he will certainly die by the fusillade.* 3. Any kind of vigorous outburst. A sustained flow of criticism. *The fusillade which greeted the government's decision is a clear indication of people's rejection of the new policy.* —*v.* To inflict a rapid discharge of gunfire.

F.V. or **f.v.** *abbr.* for **folio verso** (q.v.).

G

gaffe *n., pl.* gaffes [Fr. blunder.] 1. A diplomatic or social blunder. An indiscreet remark or act. *It is incredible that such a meticulous official could have committed such a gaffe.* 2. A mistake or error.

gaga *adj.* [Fr. silly, crazy.] Foolish. Crazy. Insane.

gala *n., pl.* galas [It. merrymaking, pleasure.] A festival. A festive occasion. Entertainment given to mark a special event or occasion. *At a gala last week in honor of the Joffrey Ballet's inaugural season as Los Angeles's first resident dance company, . . .* (*Newsweek Int.* May 16, 1983:25). —*adj.* Festive. Done with ceremony and pomp. a) *It was a gala occasion and everybody wore suitably gala clothes.* b.) *He plans to . . . add glamour to the Rue Royale restaurant by staging gala evenings* (*Newsweek Int.* May 18, 1981:39).

Gallia est omnis divisa in partes tres. Julius Caesar (100–44 B.C.). *Bellum Gallicum* I,1,1. [L. Gallia Gaul, France (2); est is, has been (3); omnis all (1); divisa divided (4); in into, to, against, for (5); tres three (6): All Gaul is divided into three parts.] All of Gaul is divided into three parts. The first words of Caesar's Bellum Gallicum (q.v.).

gallio *n.* [L. from L. Junius Gallio.] 1. The Roman proconsul of Achaea c. A.D. 52. who dismissed Jewish charges against the apostle Paul. Moreover, when a mob beat up Sosthenes, the Jewish priest in charge of the synagogue, he ignored the incident (Acts 18:12–17). 2. An indifferent, careless and irresponsible person, particularly an official.

Gallophobia *n.* [Neo-L. and Gk. from L. Gall(us) a Gaul, Gallic, French person, French (2); Gk. phob(os) fear, dread (1): fear or dread of a Gaul.] Fear of the French people and things French. Francophobia (q.v.). Cf. Anglomania.

garçon *n., pl.* garçons [Fr. boy, waiter.] A waiter.

Gastarbeiter *n., pl.* Gastarbeiter [Ger. Gast guest, visiter, stranger (1); Arbeiter worker (2): guest worker.] Foreign worker. Immigrant worker. *The new chancellor will also try to stem the swelling influx of Gastarbeiter . . .* (*Newsweek Int.* Oct. 11, 1982:9).

Gasthaus *n., pl.* Gasthaüser [Ger. Gast guest (1); Haus house (2): guesthouse.] An inn.

gastronome *n., pl.* gastronomes [Fr. from Gk. gast(ē)r stomach (1); nom(os) law (2): stomach law.] An epicure. A person who likes good living. A person who is an expert judge of good food and wine. See gourmand and gourmet.

gâteau or gateau *n., pl.* gâteaux or gateaux [Fr. cake.] 1. A shaped mass of baked dough or batter, especially one which is rich and fancy. 2. Something enjoyable and easy. *She has played Phaedra to Hedda Gabler, so portraying Colette and aging from 16 to 81 ought to be a piece of gâteau.* (*Newsweek Int.* Feb. 22, 1982:39).

gauche *adj.* [Fr. left, clumsy, awkward, uncouth.] 1. Socially clumsy or awkward. Devoid of social graces. Tactless. a) *The lady was embarrassed by the gauche conduct of her escort.* b) *The speaker eulogized the old woman saying, inter alia, that in her long life she had never said or done anything gauche.* 2. Crude. Unpolished. Applicable to style, techniques, etc. *Sometimes a good story can be vitiated by a reporter's gauche narrative style.*

gaucherie *n., pl.* gaucheries [Fr. left-handedness, clumsiness, awkwardness, blunder.] A clumsy, tactless, awkward, or unpolished action, behavior, social act or literary style. *His gaucheries are such that no associate is willing to invite him to social functions.*

gaudeamus igitur / juvenes dum sumus. / post jucundam juventutem, / post molestam senectutem, / nos habebit humus. [L. gaudeamus let us rejoice, be glad (1); igitur therefore, then (2); juvenes young, youthful (5); dum while (3); sumus we are (4); post after (6); jucundam pleasant, delightful (7); juventutem youth, age of youth (8); post after (9); molestam troublesome, irksome (10); senectutem old age (11); **nos** us (14); **habebit** will have, hold, regard (13); **humus** earth (12): Let us therefore rejoice / while we are young; / after pleasant youth, / after irksome old age, / earth will have us.] Song of medieval German students about the joyful pleasures of youth and inevitability of death after a troublesome old age.

gaudium certaminis *n., pl.* **gaudia certaminis** [L. **gaudium** joy, delight (1); **certaminis** of contest, competition (2): joy of contest or competition.] The pleasure of the competition. The enjoyment or pleasure derived from a good argument or debate. *The essence of taking part in a contest is not victory but gaudium certaminis.*

gavotte *n., pl.* **gavottes** [Fr. a person from Gap in the French Alps.] *Music.* 1. A peasant dance from the French Alps which is characterized by jumps or leaps in a 4-beat meter and which became popular at the French court in the 16th and 17th centuries. 2. Music for such a dance or in the style of such a dance.

gazette *n., pl.* **gazettes** [Fr. newspaper.] A newspaper, journal, or periodical.

Gedankenexperiment *n.* [Ger. **Gedanke** thought (1); **Experiment** experiment, trial, test (2): thought experiment, experiment of thought.] A scientific test which involves formulating a hypothesis only in thought. *If we should conduct the Gedankenexperiment of imagining a world peopled exclusively by fools, what would be the status of the leading person?*

Gedanken sind zollfrei. Friedrich von Schiller (1759–1805). [Ger. **Gedanken** thoughts (1); **sind** are (2); **zollfrei** duty-free, toll-free (3): Thoughts are duty-free.] Thought is free. Ideas are not taxable. Ideas cross national borders.

gegenschein *n.* [Ger. **Gegenschein: gegen** against (2); **Schein** light, shine (1): light against.] *Astronomy.* A glow in the sky opposite the location of the sun.

geisha *n., pl.* **geisha** or **geishas** [Japan. **gei** art (1); **sha** person (2): an art person.] A Japanese woman who entertains men at professioinal and social gatherings with conversation, song, and dance.

Geisteswissenschaften *pl. n.* [Ger. **Geistes** of the spirit, mind, intellect (2); **Wissenschaften** knowledges, sciences, scholarships (1): sciences of the mind.] The humanities. See **humanitas**.

Gemeinschaft *n., pl.* **Gemeinschaften** [Ger. community, partnership, union, association.] 1. A social relationship in which people are bound by strong mutual bonds of fellowship and kinship. 2. A community in which people observe such relationship. Cf. **Gesellschaft**.

Gemeinschaftsgefühl *n., pl.* **Gemeinschaftsgefühle** [Ger. **Gemeinschaft** community, partnership, union, association (1); **Gefühl** feelings (2): community feelings.] Fellow feeling. The feeling of belonging to a group or an association. The feeling of having a common heritage or purpose. Community spirit. Cf. **esprit de corps**.

Gemini *n.* [L. twins.] 1. *Astronomy.* A constellation which is shaped like human twins and which includes the stars Castor and Pollux, named after the twin brothers of Greek and Roman mythology. 2. *Astrology.* The third sign of the zodiac dominant from May 21 through June 21. 3. A person born under this sign.

gemütlich *adj.* [Ger. pleasant, cosy, comfortable, informal.] Sociable. Genial. Jovial. Good natured. Friendly.

gemütlichkeit *n.* [Ger. **Gemütlichkeit** pleasantness.] Sociability. Geniality. Joviality. Good nature. Friendliness. *But all the gemütlichkeit could not conceal the fact that the United States and its allies were sharply at odds over a peace strategy for the Middle East . . . (Newsweek Int.* June 30, 1980:8).

gendarme *abbr.* **gend.** *n., pl.* **gendarmes** [Fr. guard, soldier, police officer, constable.] A rural French police officer. A police officer in continental Europe. A police officer in a Francophone country. An armed police officer. A soldier assigned police duty. *Gendarmes should in the execution of their duties use only the minimum force to arrest a suspect* (Michael N. Ndansi in *West Africa* 1981).

gendarmerie *n., pl.* **gendarmeries** [Fr. constabulary.] A body of police officers. A body of armed police officers. A body of soldiers assigned police duties. a) *Senegalese soldiers thus became the gendarmerie of the French empire* (Suret-Canale 1971:337). b) *A former head of the gendarmerie, he took over effective command of the southern dominated Chad army . . . (New African* 1980).

generale dictum generaliter est intelligendum. [L. **generale** general (1); **dictum** saying (2); **generaliter** generally (5); **est** is (3); **intelligendum** to be understood (4): A general saying is to be understood generally.] A general saying must be interpreted in a general, rather than a specific, sense. See **generale dictum generaliter est interpretandum; generalia verba** etc.; **generalis regula** etc.; **quando charta continet** etc.; **quando lex est specialis** etc.; **quando verba statuti** etc.; **statutum generaliter est** etc. and **ubi lex est** etc.

generale dictum generaliter est interpretandum. [L. **generale** general (1); **dictum** saying (2); **generaliter** generally (5); **est** is (3); **interpretandum** to be interpreted (4): A general saying is to be interpreted generally.] See **generale dictum generaliter est intelligendum.**

generalia specialibus non derogant. [L. **generalia** general (things) (1); **specialibus** special (things) (4); **non** not (2); **derogant** derogate/detract from (3): General things do not detract from special ones.] General statements do not diminish specific ones. See **quando lex est specialis** etc.

generalia verba sunt generaliter intelligenda. [L. **generalia** general (1); **verba** words (2); **sunt** are (3); **generaliter** generally (5); **intelligenda** to be understood (4): General words are to be understood generally.] General words must be understood in a general sense. See **generale dictum generaliter est intelligendum.**

generalis regula generaliter est intelligenda. [L. **generalis** general (1); **regula** rule (2); **generaliter** generally (5); **est** is (3); **intelligenda** to be understood (4): A general rule is to be understood generally.] A general rule must be interpreted in a general, rather than a specific, way. See **generale dictum generaliter est intelligendum.**

generalissimo *n., pl.* **generalissimos** [It. chief general.] Commander-in-chief. The supreme commander of the armed forces, i.e., combined military, air, and naval forces. . . . *under the command of their chosen generalissimo they would fight with a grim tenacity* . . . (Robinson 1974:29). Cf. **supremo.**

genesis *n., pl.* **geneses** [Gk. origin, source, manner of birth, production, coming into being, creation.] The beginning, origin, or starting point of a thing. The coming into being of a thing. The process of origin. a) *the genesis of a problem*; b) *The genesis of a malady*; c) *the genesis of an idea*; d) *. . . post-colonial political confusion and violence in African politics have their genesis in the dissent and disarray arising from colonial manipulation of classes and groups within the indigenous community before independence* (Lindsay Barrett in *West Africa* 1986). —**Genesis** The first book of the Old Testament, which deals with the creation of the world.

genetrix *n., pl.* **genetrices** [L. female producer, she who bears.] Mother.

genitalia *pl. n.* [L. genitals.] Reproductive organs, particularly the external ones. a) *Children do not know the anatomical terms, of course, but when given dolls with genitalia, they can point out what happened* (*Time Int.*1983). b) *Psychoanalyst Erik Erikson contended that the nature of human genitalia influences the way males and females think* (*Newsweek Int.* June 1, 1981:49).

genius *n., pl.* **genii** or **geniuses** [L. guardian spirit, taste, inclination, talent.] The guiding spirit or tutelary deity of a person or place. *She always attributes her achievements to the aid of her genius.* 2. A person or spirit which has a good or bad influence on another's character, conduct, behavior, etc. *Serwa's career was progressing with remarkable success when she came under the influence of Akosua, her evil genius, and then a drastic decline set in.* 3. Natural ability, aptitude, fitness, or talent. Remarkable natural intellectual and creative ability. a) *Ibrahim has a genius for making everybody comfortable in his company.* b) *She's shown a genius for designing stage sets and costumes*

. . . (*Newsweek Int.* July 14, 1980:35). 4. A person who is exceptionally endowed with natural intellectual and creative ability. A person whose intelligence quotient (I.Q.) is very high, i.e., over 140. *Kwabena is such a genius that whatever he undertakes is accomplished with immense success.* 5. A strong bent, disposition, penchant, inclination, flair, tendency, etc. *The negotiations were proceeding smoothly when Tolabi, with his genius for saying the wrong thing, ruined everything.*

genius domus *n., pl.* **genii domus** [L. **genius** guardian spirit, taste, talent, inclination (1); **domus** of home, house (2): guardian spirit of a house.] Protective spirit of a home or house. A spirit which influences the minds of the residents of a house.

genius loci *n., pl.* **genii loci** [L. **genius** tutelary deity (1); **loci** of place (2): the tutelary deity of a place.] 1. The tutelary spirit or guardian deity of a particular place. 2. The associations, spirit, atmosphere, etc. which influence the minds of residents of, or visitors to, a place. *The sons and daughters of the village owe their prosperity to the genius loci.*

genre *n., pl.* **genres** [Fr. kind, sort, type, species, style.] 1. Category. Kind. Type. Species. *The meals, though seemingly different, belong to the same genre.* 2. Category, kind, style, or type of artistic or literary work. a) *Though the two musical groups specialize in different genres, they share one quality, namely emphasis on drums.* b) *The Fan has one element that its competitors in the horror genre lack—chic* (*Newsweek Int.* June 1, 1981:59). c) *But all these differences cannot obscure the fact that the* Iliad *and the* Odyssey *belong to the same genre* (Lesky 1966:42). 3. A group of artistic works sharing a common style, content, etc. Literary, artistic, theatrical, and musical compositions of the same category. a) *the science fiction genre*; b) *the short-story genre*; c) *The conversation piece was a popular artistic genre in the eighteenth century*; d) *Tragedy and comedy are the two major dramatic genres of ancient Greece*; e) *The madrigal was a musical genre popular in sixteenth-century Italy.* 4. *Painting.* Painting style in which scenes of everyday life are portrayed realistically. *The artist's three works in genre were in stark contrast to her other compositions.* —*attrib.* Realistic. Everyday. *Genre-painting.*

genro *n., pl.* **genros** [Japan **genrō.**] One of the elder male advisors of the emperor in Japan.

gens du monde *n.* [Fr. **gens** people, folks (1); **du** of the (2); **monde** world (3): people of the world.] Society people. Socialites. Fashionable people or society. Cf. **femme du monde** and **homme du monde.**

genus *n., pl.* **genera** [L. kind, class, sort, race.] 1. A group, kind or class having a common characteristic or common characteristics. 2. A group of things, plants, animals, etc. which are closely related. A group which can have subgroups (species) and can also be absorbed into another group. *History is a genus and has sub-groups or species which include economic history, political history, military history, modern history, history of science, and history of language.*

genus irritabile *n., pl.* **genera irritabilia** [L. **genus** kind, class, sort, race, (2); **irritabile** excitable, irritable (1): an irritable kind.] An irritable or excitable kind or type. See **animus irritandi**.

Germanophobia *n.* [Neo-L. and Gk. from L. **German(us)** German (2); Gk. **phob(os)** fear, dread (1): fear or dread of German.] Excessive fear or hatred of Germany as well as German things, practices, customs, institutions, etc. Cf. **Anglophobia**.

gerontophilia *n.* [Neo-Gk. from Gk. **geron** old man (2); **philia** fondness, liking (1): fondness or liking for old people.] Preference for sexual relationship with elderly persons.

Ges. *abbr.* for **Gesellschaft** (q.v.).

Gesamtkunstwerk *n., pl.* **Gesamtkunstwerke** [Ger. **gesamt** whole (1); **Kunst** art (3); **Werk** work (2): whole work of art.] *Art.* A complete work of art. A comprehensive artistic work. An artistic work whose accomplishment requires all, or many of, the various art forms. . . . *a successful attempt to capture the quintessence of the traditional African theatre, an art of mixed arts, a communal gesamtkunstwerk of dance, music, poetry, mime and narrative* (*West Africa* 1983).

Gesellschaft *abbr.* **Ges.** *n., pl.* **Gesellschaften** or **Gesellschafts** [Ger. society.] l. A social relationship in which people are bound by impersonal relationships. 2. A community in which people observe such relationships. Cf. **Gemeinschaft**.

gestalt or **Gestalt** *n.* [Ger. **Gestalt** shape.] The combination of various biological, psychological, physical, and other elements which create a whole larger than the sum of its parts.

Gestapo *short form* of **Geheime Staatspolizei** *n., pl.* **Gestapos** [Ger. **ge(heime)** secret (1); **Sta(ats)** of the state (3); **Po(lizei)** police (2): secret police of the state.] 1. Germany's secret state police during the period of the Nazis. 2. A secret police organization which adopts terrorist and underhand tactics, and usually operates against persons suspected to be engaged in subversive, seditious or treasonable activities. —*attrib.* Of, characteristic of, relating to, the Gestapo and its activities. *The Civil Rights Organization has sent a letter of protest to the President, condemning the Gestapo tactics of the nation's law enforcement agencies.*

gestio pro herede or **gestio pro haerede** *n.* [L. **gestio** doing, behavior (1); **pro** as, just as (2); **herede** heir (3): behavior as heir.] *Roman, Civil, and Scots Law.* Behavior as heir, such as collecting rents from the estate of the decedent, which shows intention to accept the inheritance and thus makes one liable for an ancestor's debts.

ghat or **ghaut** *n.* [Hindi **ghāt**.] 1. A stairway leading down into a river. 2. A mountain pass.

ghetto *n., pl.* **ghettos** or **ghettoes** [It. Jewish quarter.] 1. *Med. Italy.* A Jewish quarter in Italy. A quarter of a city almost exclusively inhabited by Jews. 2. A quarter of a city or a district almost exclusively inhabited by a racially underprivileged group, or a group considered inferior by reason of religion, race, culture, color, etc. a) "*. . . he goes back to the ghetto where he has no rights and remains a Bantu and must carry that document of oppression . . .*" (Winnie Mandela quoted in *West Africa* 1986). b) *. . . in a predominantly immigrant ghetto south of Le Havre . . . a French textile worker . . . ordered a group of people in the street below to stop making so much noise* (*Newsweek Int.* July 25, 1983:18). 3. A slum. A heavily populated area, usually in a city, with dilapidated buildings, unsanitary environment, and very poor residents.

gigantesque *adj.* [Fr. gigantic.] Huge. Colossal. Of enormous size. *The gigantesque book carries a correspondingly gigantesque price tag.*

gigolo *n., pl.* **gigolos** [Fr. ladies' man, fancy man.] 1. A man who is by profession the dancing partner of a woman. 2. A young man who escorts a woman, usually an elderly woman, for remuneration. 3. A man who is a prostitute for female customers.

gigue *n., pl.* **gigues** [Fr. from English jig.] *Music.* 1. A fast-paced traditional peasant dance. 2. Music written for this dance or in the style of this dance, such as the first movement of *Images*, an orchestral composition by Claude Debussy (1862–1918).

glasnost *n.* [Russ. **glasnost'** public information.] The policy of the Soviet government to encourage frank and open discussion of social problems.

Gleichschaltung *n., pl.* **Gleichschaltungen** [Ger. **gleich** equal, even (1); **Schaltung** connection (2): equal connection, political coordination or unification.] Political, social, or cultural uniformity or standardization of life through forcible repression of thought, expression, and action as well as liquidation of political opponents. *The country's experiment in Gleichschaltung is fiercely resisted by a very vocal intelligentsia and is doomed to failure.*

glissade *n., pl.* **glissades** [Fr. a slide.] 1. *Ballet.* A sliding step. 2. A slide used to descend an ice- or snow-covered slope. —*v. Ballet.* To use a sliding step.

glissando *n., pl.* **glissandi** [It. sliding.] *Music.* Playing a sequence of notes or a scale in a rapid, sliding fashion.

glockenspiel *n., pl.* **glockenspiels** [Ger. **Glocken** bells (2); **Spiel** play (1): play of bells.] *Music.* A percussion instrument similar to a xylophone with steel bars of varying length which are struck by hand-held hammers.

gloria in excelsis Deo. Luke 2:14. [L. **gloria** glory (1); **in** in, on (3); **excelsis** highest (4); **Deo** to God (2): Glory to God in the highest.] 1. The first words of a

Christian prayer also known as the "Gloria." 2. A musical composition based on this prayer.

Gloria Patri *abbr.* **G.P.** *interj.* [L. **gloria** glory (1); **Patri** to father (2): glory to the Father.] 1. Glory to God the Father. The first words of a Christian prayer also known as the doxology. 2. The doxology itself.

glossolalia *n., pl.* **glossolalias** [Neo-Gk. from Gk. **gloss(a)** tongue (1); **lalia** talk, chat (2): Tongue-talk. Talking with the tongue.] Gift of tongues. The unintelligible language used by members of Pentacostal churches when they believe they are receiving the Holy Ghost.

gnome *n., pl.* **gnomae** or **gnomes** [Gk. **gnomē** thought, judgment, opinion, maxim.] Maxim. Aphorism. Adage. Proverb. A brief saying expressing a general truth, a fundamental principle, or rule of behavior. *Olu's grandfather deems a speech incomplete if it is not ended with an impressive gnome.*

gnosis *n.* [Gk. knowledge.] *Theology.* An innate knowledge of God and the spiritual world, especially that to which the Gnostics aspired.

gnothi seauton. [Gk. **gnothi** know (1); **seauton** yourself, thyself (2): Know yourself.] Know yourself; i.e., know your capabilities and limitations. See **Il connait** etc.; **illi mors** etc. and **nosce te ipsum.**

golem *n.* [Heb. **gōlem** lump, clod, fool.] *Judaism.* A human being created artificially and given life by supernatural power.

Götterdämmerung *n., pl.* **Götterdämmerungen** [Ger. **Götter** of the gods (2); **Dämmerung** twilight (1): twilight of the gods.] 1. The end of the world. The death of the Norse gods. 2. An 1874 opera by Richard Wagner (1813–1883). —**Götterdämmerung** or **götterdämmerung** Disintegration and collapse of an order, political, social, economic, etc. that is usually accompanied by disastrous confusion, violence, and turbulence. a) *In early 1945 Nazis began to realize that their götterdämmerung was fast approaching.* b) *The sunny and cheerful exception to the prevalent theme of electronic Götterdämmerung, and one of the few games so far that women play in large numbers, is Bally's Pac Man (Time Int.1982).* —*attrib.* Of, characteristic of, relating to, the end of the world or an order.

Gott sei dank. [Ger. **Gott** God (1); **sei** be (2); **dank** thanked (3): God be thanked.] Thank God.

gourmand or *fem.* **gourmande** *n., pl.* **gourmands** or *fem.* **gourmandes** [Fr. greedy, gluttonous, gormandizer.] A glutton. A person who eats ravenously. A person who is too fond of choice or good food. —*adj.* Gluttonous. Ravenous. See **gastronome** and **gourmet.**

gourmandise *n., pl.* **gourmandises** [Fr. greediness, gluttony.] 1. Greediness, gluttony. 2. Indulgence in good eating. Fondness of choice food and drinks. Cf. **gastronome, gourmet,** and **gourmand.**

gourmet *n., pl.* **gourmets** [Fr. an epicure, gourmet.] A discriminating judge of good food and drink. See **connoisseur** 2, **gastronome,** and **gourmand.**

goy *n., pl.* **goyim** or **goys** [Yid. from Heb. nation, gentile, non-Jew.] A derogatory term for a non-Jewish person. See **shegetz** and **shiksa.**

gracias *n., pl.* [Sp. thanks.] Thank you. Cf. **grazie** and **merci.**

gradatim *adv.* [L. by steps.] By degrees. Step by step. Gradually. *Nemesis pursues its prey gradatim until it catches up with it.*

Graecum est; non potest legi. [L. **Graecum** Greek (thing) (2); **est** is, has been (1); **non** not (3); **potest** is able, can (4); **legi** to be read (5): The thing is Greek; it is not able to be read.] The writing is Greek; it cannot be read. Possibly the source for William Shakespeare's "It's Greek to me."

graffito *n., pl.* **graffiti** [It. a little scratch.] Writing, words, sketch, figure, cartoon, drawing, message, or portrait inscribed on a wall, rock, or art object. a) *To please the generals, a Turkish civilian scrubs political graffiti off a wall in Istanbul (Time Int.* 1980). b) *. . . in a community that is deeply hostile to criticisms . . . graffiti provide one of the major opportunities for communicating opinions about the society and the university to a larger audience (Sunday Tribune* 1986).

grammatica falsa non vitiat chartam. [L. **grammatica** grammar (1); **falsa** false (1); **non** not (3); **vitiat** invalidates (4); **chartam** paper, writing (5): False grammar does not invalidate a paper.] *Law.* Bad grammar does not make a deed invalid; i.e., the validity of a legal document cannot be contested on the grounds that its grammar is incorrect. See **falsa demonstratio non nocet.**

grammatici certant et adhuc sub judice lis est. Horace (65–8 B.C.) *Ars Poetica* 78. [L. **grammatici** grammarians, philologists (1); **certant** contend, compete (2); **et** and (3); **adhuc** still (6); **sub** before, under (7); **judice** judge (8); **lis** suit, dispute (4); **est** is (5): Grammarians contend and the dispute is still before the judge.] Scholars argue and the controversy continues unresolved.

grand cru *n., pl.* **grands crus** [Fr. **grand** great, noble, high, grand (1); **cru** wine, vintage (2): great vintage.] High-class wine. Wine from a famous vineyard. *The grands crus wines, especially those grown on the Côte d'Or . . . can be sampled along with lesser vintages at wine caves or the many charming restaurants along the road (Time Int.* 1979).

grande bourgeoisie *n.* [Fr. **grande** great, noble, high, grand (1); **bourgeoisie** middle class (2): high middle class.] Upper middle class. . . . *the abnormal proportion of overpaid sinecures which . . . were a means for the French grande bourgeoisie to find employment for part of their superfluous numbers.* (Suret-Canale 1971:348). See **bourgeois.**

grande cuisine *n.* [Fr. grande great, noble, high, grand (1); cuisine cooking, cookery (2): grand cooking.] Great, fashionable, or luxurious cooking or meal. Old style of cooking which aims at preparing rich, savory, and calorific meals. *The nouvelle style started as a less fattening, innovative alternative to cholesterol-happy grande cuisine (Newsweek Int.* Dec. 7, 1981:46). See cuisine.

grande dame *n.* [Fr. grande great, noble, high, grand (1); dame lady (2): noble lady.] A grand, great, or noble woman. A lady of high or noble birth. A lady, ordinarily elderly, who is high-ranking, has dignified bearing, and enjoys high social prestige. . . . *the grand dame of American chroreography will team up with the Joffrey Ballet in a PBS television special, . . . (Newsweek Int.* Jan 28, 1980:51). b) *Adeoti's aunt, a grande dame, supports her engagement to Bolaji, and this is likely to eliminate the opposition of some members of the family.*

grande lacune *n., pl.* grandes lacunes [Fr. grande great, noble, high, grand (1); lacune gap, omission, deficiency (2): great gap.] A big gap, omission, oversight, or deficiency. *This type of cooperation is essentially political and does not involve joint projects. This is the grande lacune in Africa . . .* (Howard Schissel in *West Africa* 1982).

grand jeté *n., pl.* grands jetés [Fr. grand great, noble, high, grand (1); jeté step (2): a great step.] 1. A big step, leap, or jump. *After that, it may be just a grand jeté to stardom for the talented Healy . . . (Newsweek Int.* Aug. 15, 1983:27). 2. *Ballet.* A sharp leap accompanied by a high kick.

grand luxe *n.* [Fr. grand great, noble, high, grand (1); luxe luxury (2): great luxury.] The peak of luxury. The highest form or degree of luxury.

grand mal *n.* [Fr. grand great, noble, high, grand (1); mal sickness, disease (2): great disease.] *Medicine.* Epilepsy, particularly a violent one with convulsive spasms. Cf. petit mal.

grand marabout *n., pl.* grands marabouts [Fr. grand great, noble, high, grand (1); Ar. marabout Muslim religious leader (2): great Muslim religious leader.] A politically or socially influential Muslim leader. Cf. marabout.

Grand Prix *n., pl.* Grands Prix [Fr. grand great, noble, high, grand (1); prix (2): big prize.] 1. Championship race. An international car race over a long distance, most of the route being winding. *Argentine Grand Prix.* 2. Any prestigious international contest as in boat racing, tennis, etc. a) *. . . allowing track clubs to accept cash prizes for their members at the "amateur" Grand Prix series . . . (Newsweek Int.* July 11, 1983:42). b) *Lendl, 21, netted his seventh straight Grand Prix win by taking the Volvo Masters tournament from Vitas Gerulaitis, 27, at Madison Square Garden . . . (Newsweek Int.* Feb. 1, 1982:21).

grand projet *n., pl.* grands projets [Fr. grand great, noble, high, grand (1); projet project, scheme, plan (2): big project.] A grand plan. An ambitious scheme. *. . . although economic prospects are grim in the short run, "they look much better in the long run, as many of the grands projets may eventually become operational"* (M.D. in *West Africa* 1983).

grand seigneur *n., pl.* grands seigneurs [Fr. grand great, noble, high, grand (1); seigneur lord, nobleman (2): a great lord.] 1. A great lord. A great nobleman. 2. A man of aristocratic and dignified bearing. *The Managing Director of ZATIS, a grand seigneur, was one of the dignitaries who attended the fund-raising ceremony.*

grand siècle *n., pl.* grands siècles [Fr. grand great, noble, high, grand (1); siècle age, century (2): the great age.] The great century. The good old days. The seventeenth century. Especially, the lifespan of Louis XIV (1638–1715). *But, as in the grand siècle, these deficiencies were made up for by an abundance of domestic servants* (Suret-Canale 1971:320).

gran rifiuto *n.* [It. gran great (1); rifiuto refusal (2): great refusal.] Refusal, decline, or rejection of high position, honor, reward, etc. *Sylvester disclosed in confidence to his close friend that his gran rifiuto was prompted by his conviction that he could not perform effectively in an administration headed by a mediocrity.* Cf. il gran rifiuto.

gratis *adv./adj.* [L. for thanks.] For only a "thank-you." Without charge, reward, consideration, or recompense. Done, given or received gratuitously. Free. a) *The speaker distributed pamphlets among the audience gratis.* b) *The lawyer prepared the documents for the client gratis.*

gratis dictum *n., pl.* gratis dicta [L. gratis for thanks; (2); dictum saying, something said (1): saying without reward.] A voluntary assertion. A mere assertion. A statement which one is not legally obliged to make.

gravamen *n., pl.* gravamina or gravamens [Med. L. accusation.] Grievance. Formal complaint. The gist, basis, or burden of a grievance, complaint, charge, etc. *The gravamen of the offense rests on the stabbing of the victim without provocation.*

gravida *n., pl.* gravidas or gravidae [L. pregnant, with child.] *Medicine.* A pregnant woman. Usually qualified with a number to show the number of pregnancies the woman has had. Cf. multigravida; nulligravida; primigravida; secundigravida; and unigravida.

gravitas *n.* [L. seriousness.] A sense of gravity and dignity.

grazie *pl. n.* [It. thanks.] Thank you. *The visit of Alessandro Pertini . . . to Washington gave President Reagan the chance to say grazie in person (Newsweek Int.* April 5, 1982:19).

Grenzbegriff *n.* [Ger. Grenz boundary (1); Begriff concept (2): boundary concept.] *Philosophy.* An idea or concept in the philosophy of Emmanuel Kant (1724–1804) which illustrates the restriction of human sense perception.

griffonage *n., pl.* **griffonages** [Fr. **griffonnage** scrawl, scribble.] An illegible script or writing. A careless or crude handwriting.

gringo *n., pl.* **gringos** [Sp. foreign.] *Latin America.* A foreigner, especially a white North American or English person. Usually used with derogatory connotation. *You need something from the gringo—just leave it to me. I know how to deal with them (Newsweek Int.* April 14, 1980:21). —*adj.* White North American or English. *Now, it is not just the IMF but a bunch of gringo bankers who can decide how the economy will be run (South* 1984).

grisette *n., pl.* **grisettes** [Fr. coquettish working-girl or shopgirl.] 1. A working-class French girl. 2. A girl or woman, who has a decent job and also engages in prostitution. *One of the secretaries, apparently a grisette, always comes to work visibly tired.*

grosse aventure *n.* [Fr. **grosse** big (1); **aventure** chance, venture (2): big chance or venture.] *French Maritime Law.* A contract of bottomry; i.e., a contract in which a ship is used as security for a loan. In such a contract the lender assumes the risk of losing his/her investment if the ship is lost.

grotesque *adj.* [Fr. from It. **grottesco** from **grotta** cave: of a cave or grotto.] Distorted. Bizarre. *The badly broken bone jutted out through the skin of his arm at a grotesque angle.* —*n.* 1. Something distorted or bizarre. 2. An artistic style which combines natural and bizarre forms or shapes.

grotesquerie or **grotesquery** *n.* [Fr.] 1. Something distorted or bizarre. 2. A distortion.

Grundgedanke *n., pl.* **Grundgedanken** [Ger. **Grund** ground, foundation (1); **Gedanke** thought (2): foundational thought.] Fundamental idea. Basic or fundamental conception.

gubernator or *fem.* **gubernatrix** *n., pl.* **gubernators** or *fem.* **gubernatrices** [L. helmsman, steersman, leader.] A director. A ruler. A governor.

guerre à outrance *n., pl.* **guerres à outrance** [Fr. **guerre** war (1); **à** to, toward, in, by, with, until (2); **outrance** excess (3): war to excess.] Total, full-scale or all-out war. *In this age of nuclear warfare, all sane men sincerely pray that there should be no conflict which would precipitate a guerre à outrance.* Cf. **à outrance** and **outrance**.

guerrilla *n., pl.* **guerrillas** [Sp. little war.] 1. A person who participates in irregular warfare. A person belonging to an independent predatory group or band which operates during war. A member of a group of men who move in small bands, engaged in irregular warfare. *Early this month, guerrillas used limpet mines*

to blow up storage tanks at a heavily guarded plant in Sasolburg . . . (Newsweek Int. June 30, 1980:24). 2. A soldier belonging to a military unit which operates behind the lines of the enemy. —*attrib.* Of, relating to, characteristic of, typical of, guerrillas. *To rout Kurdish guerrilla forces, the army and air force have bombed the provincial capital of Sanandaj . . . (Time Int.*1980).

guillotine *n., pl.* **guillotines** [Fr. a beheading device named after Joseph Ignace Guillotin (1738–1814).] 1. A device employing a falling sharp blade used to behead the condemned. 2. A paper cutter or similar device which operates like the beheading machine. —*v.* To behead by means of a guillotine.

Gulag or **gulag** *n., pl.* **Gulags** or **gulags** *short form* of **Glavnoe upravlenie ispravitel'no-trudovykh lagerei** [Russ. **g(lavnoe)** chief (1); **u(pravlenie)** management, administration, government (2); **(ispravitel'no-)** (of) correctional (3); **(trudovykh)** (of) labor (4); **lag(erei)** of camps (5): Chief Administration of Correctional Labor Camps.] 1. The system of slave-labor camps in the Soviet Union. 2. A forced labor camp, especially one for political insurgents and protestors.

guru *n., pl.* **gurus** [Hindi **gurū** venerable, weighty.] 1. *Hinduism.* A personal instructor, teacher, or guide in spiritual or religious matters. *The President's free-spending wife . . . once flew to India for a personal meeting with her guru . . . (Newsweek Int.* Feb. 19, 1979:15). 2. *Sikhism.* One of the ten principal religious leaders generally recognized by the Sikhs, starting from Nanak (1469-1539) and ending with Gobind Singh (1666-1708). 3. One who serves as a personal guide, teacher or authority in basic intellectual and spiritual affairs. a) *Professor Alec Nove, a guru among analysts of communist economies . . . (The Economist* 1987). b) *His iconoclastic theories about language and writing have supplanted the structuralist movement of the 1950s and made him something of a guru to avant-garde academics . . . (Newsweek Int.* May 11, 1981:46).

gusto *n.* [It. pleasure, taste, delight, will, whim.] Profound appreciation. Enthusiastic, intense, or keen enjoyment or delight. a) *. . . the diminutive Teng is a larger-than-life rustic whose earthy charm does not quite conceal the power he wields, or the gusto with which he wields it (Newsweek Int.* Feb. 5, 1979:22). b) *Shortly another anniversary will be upon us. . . . We must not celebrate it with gusto* (Harrison E. Tucker in *West Africa* 1986).

gymnasium *n., pl.* **gymnasia** or **gymnasiums** [L. from Gk. **gumnasion** a place to exercise naked.] 1. An indoor sports facility. 2. *Germany.* A college preparatory high school.

H

habanera *n., pl.* **habaneras** [Sp. **habañera** Havanan.] *Music.* 1. A slow dance which originated in Havana, Cuba, and became popular in Spain c.1850. 2. Music for this dance or in the style of this dance.

hab. corp. *abbr.* for **habeas corpus** (q.v.).

habeas corpus *abbr.* **hab. corp.** or **H.C.** *n.* [L. **habeas** you may/should have, hold, regard (1); **corpus** body (2): You may hold the body.] *Law.* You are permitted to hold the body. The individual may be kept in custody. The preface to several common law writs which aim at bringing before a judge or a court a person, usually in custody. Ordinarily, the privilege is not to be suspended except during periods of great national or public danger such as war.

habeas corpus ad deliberandum et recipiendum *n.* [L. **habeas** you may/should have, hold, regard (1); **corpus** body (2); **ad** to, at, for, according to (3); **deliberandum** deliberating (4); **et** and (5); **recipiendum** receiving (6): You may hold the body for deliberating and receiving.] *Law.* A writ issued to transfer an accused from one jurisdiction to another where the offense took place. Cf. **habeas corpus ad prosequendum**.

habeas corpus ad faciendum et recipiendum *n.* [L. **habeas** you may/should have, hold, regard (1); **corpus** body (2); **ad** to, at, for, according to (3); **faciendum** doing (4); **et** and (5); **recipiendum** receiving (6): You may hold the body for doing and receiving.] *Civil Law.* A writ issued by a superior court ordering a lower court to produce a defendant and the cause of his/her detention. Also called **habeas corpus cum causa** (q.v.).

habeas corpus ad prosequendum *n.* [L. **habeas** you may/should have, hold, regard (1); **corpus** body (2); **ad** to, at, for, according to (3); **prosequendum** prosecuting (4): You may hold the body for prosecuting.] *Law.* A writ requiring the transfer of a prisoner from one jurisdiction to another, where the offense was committed, for trial. Cf. **habeas corpus ad deliberandum et recipiendum**.

habeas corpus ad respondendum *n.* [L. **habeas** you may/should have, hold, regard (1); **corpus** body (2); **ad** to, at, for, according to (3); **respondendum** answering (4): You may hold the body for answering.] *Civil Law.* A writ to transfer a defendant from the custody of one court to another to respond to a suit.

habeas corpus ad satisfaciendum *n.* [L. **habeas** you may/should have, hold, regard (1); **corpus** body (2); **ad** to, at, for, according to (3); **satisfaciendum** satisfying (4): You may hold the body for satisfying.] *English Legal Practice.* A writ in which a plaintiff summons a prisoner to a superior court for the process of executing a judgment delivered in a lower court.

habeas corpus ad subjiciendum *n.* [L. **habeas** you may/should have, hold, regard (1); **corpus** body (2); **ad** to, at, for, according to (3); **subjiciendum** submitting (4): You may hold the body for submitting.] *Law.* A writ requiring inquiry into the legality of the imprisonment or detention of a person.

habeas corpus ad testificandum *n.* [L. **habeas** you may/should have, hold, regard (1); **corpus** body (2); **ad** to, at, for, according to (3); **testificandum** testifying (4): You may hold the body for testifying.] *Law.* A writ requiring the presence of a prisoner in court to testify.

habeas corpus cum causa *n.* [L. **habeas** you may/should have, hold, regard (1); **corpus** body (2); **cum** with (3); **causa** cause, case, reason (4): You may hold the body with cause.] **habeas corpus ad faciendum et recipiendum** (q.v.).

habemus optimum testem, confitentem reum. [L. **habemus** we have, hold, regard (1); **optimum** best (2); **testem** witness (3); **confitentem** confessing (4); **reum** defendant, accused (5): We hold the best witness, a confessing defendant.] *Law.* We have in the confessing accused person the best witness; i.e., when an accused person pleads guilty, there is no need for further inquiry.

habemus Papam [L. **habemus** we have (1); **Papam** pope (2): We have a pope.] We have a new pope.

The words used to announce the election of a new pope. Also used to announce the selection of a new official, colleague, etc.

habendum *n., pl.* **habendums** [L. to be had, held, regarded.] *Law.* The part of a deed which in former times defined an estate, showing the extent of ownership and sometimes the kind of tenancy, but which is now infrequent or merely formal.

habendum et tenendum [L. **habendum** to be had, held, regarded (1); **et** and (2); **tenendum** to be held (3): to be had and to be held.] *Law.* To have and to hold. Used formerly in instruments for conveying the title of land from one person to another.

habere facias possessionem *n.* [L. **habere** to have, hold, regard (2); **facias** you may/should make, do cause, ensure (1); **possessionem** possession (3): You may cause to have possession.] *Law.* The writ to be used in case of eviction by a successful party for the purpose of regaining actual possession of property which the other party still occupies.

habere facias visum *n.* [L. **habere** to have, hold, regard (2); **facias** you may/should cause, ensure (1); **visum** view (3): You may cause to have a view.] *Law.* A writ directed to a holder of lands or holdings to permit the sheriff to have a view.

habitant or **habitan** *n., pl.* **habitants** or **habitans** [Fr. inhabitant.] *Quebec* and *Louisiana*. A farmer of French-Canadian descent.

habitat *n., pl.* **habitats** [L. He/she/it inhabits or dwells.] 1. The natural dwelling-place, region, environment, site, etc. where a species of animals or plants lives, grows, and thrives. 2. The usual home, environment, resort, etc. of a people or something. *Though Black people can be found in almost every part of the world, their habitat is Africa.*

habitué *n., pl.* **habitués** [Fr. regular attendant, visitor or customer, frequenter or haunter.] A person who goes frequently to a place or type of place. a) *The plane is full of Nigerian habitués of London.* b) *Habitués of the restaurant have decided to boycott the place because of deteriorating services.*

habitué de la maision *n., pl.* **habitués de la maision** [Fr. **habitué** frequenter, regular customer (1); **de** of (2); **la** the (3); **maision** house (4): frequenter of the house.] Regular guest at a house. Friend of the family. Regular customer at a restaurant, an establishment etc.

hac voce *abbr.* **H.V** or **h.v.** *adv.* [L. **hac** with this (1); **voce** word, voice (2): with this word.] Under this word. Bibliographical reference entries in dictionaries and works which are arranged alphabetically. See **hoc verbo** and **sub voce**.

hacienda *n., pl.* **haciendas** [Sp.] 1. A large farm or plantation, especially in the Spanish colonies of the Americas. 2. The big house where the owner of such an estate lives.

hac lege [L. **hac** with this (1); **lege** law (2): with this law.] Under this stipulation or regulation.

Hades *n.* [Gk. **Haidēs** the god of the underworld, the underworld.] 1. *Greek Mythology.* a) The god of the lower world. b) The abode of the dead. The netherworld. 2. Hell. *If you are not satisfied, you can go to Hades.* Cf. **Elysium**; **Tartarus**; and **Valhalla**.

Hadith or **Hadit** *n., pl.* **Hadithat** or **Hadiths** or **Hadits** [Ar. **hadīt** tradition, report.] *Islam.* A record of the pronouncements and traditional customs of the prophet Mohammed and the Companions, which is an appendix to the Koran. Cf. **Sunna**.

hadj *var.* of **hajj** (q.v.).

haec olim meminisse juvabit. Cf. **forsan et haec olim meminisse juvabit**.

haeredes proximi *var.* of **heredes proximi** (q.v.).

haeredes remotiores *var.* of **heredes remotiores** (q.v.).

haereditas *var.* of **hereditas** (q.v.).

haereditas ab intestato *var.* of **hereditas ab intestato** (q.v.).

haereditas damnosa *var.* of **hereditas damnosa** (q.v.).

haereditas jacens *var.* of **hereditas jacens** (q.v.).

haereditas legitima *var.* of **hereditas legitima** (q.v.).

haereditas luctuosa *var.* of **hereditas luctuosa** (q.v.).

haereditas testamentaria *var.* of **hereditas testamentaria** (q.v.).

haeres *var.* of **heres** (q.v.).

haeres ab intestato *var.* of **heres ab intestato** (q.v.).

haeres factus *var.* of **heres factus** (q.v.).

haeres institutus *var.* of **heres institutus** (q.v.).

haeres legitimus *var.* of **heres legitimus** (q.v.).

haeres natus *var.* of **heres natus** (q.v.).

haeres necessarius *var.* of **heres necessarius** (q.v.).

haeres suus *var.* of **heres suus** (q.v.).

haesitante *adj.* [L. with him/her hesitating or being stuck.] *Law.* Used to qualify the name of a judge or the names of judges to indicate a hesitating opinion. Cf. **dissentiente**.

hafiz *n.* [Pers. from Ar. **hāfiz** one who memorizes, guards.] 1. A person who has memorized the Koran. 2. An honorific title for such a person.

Haggadah or **Haggada** *n., pl.* **Haggadoth** [Heb. **haggāda** a narrative, telling.] *Judaism.* 1. The body of traditional Jewish literature in general, and the non-legal portion of the Talmud in particular. 2. The story of the Hebrew exodus from Egypt as told in the Book of Exodus and as read at the Passover Seder. Cf. **Halakah**.

haiku *n., pl.* **haiku** or **haikus** [Japan. **hai** amusement, entertainment (1); **ku** sentence (2): an amusement sentence.] An unrhymed poem, often written about nature or the seasons, in a formal sequence of five-, seven-, and five-syllable lines. Cf. **hokku**.

hajj or **hadj** or **haj** *n., pl.* **hajjes** or **hadjes** or **hajes** [Ar. pilgrimage.] The pilgrimage to **Mecca** (q.v.) which Muslims who can afford it are required to undertake as a religious duty at least once in their lifetime.

hakim *n., pl.* **hakims** [Ar. **hākim** wise, wise man.] A physician (usually male) in a Muslim country.

hakim or **hakeem** *n., pl.* **hakims** or **hakeems** [Ar. **hakīm** ruler.] A male ruler or judge in a Muslim country.

Halakah or **Halacha** *n.* [Heb. **halāka** rule, tradition.] *Judaism.* The legal portion of Talmudic literature. An interpretation of the laws of scripture. Cf. **Haggadah.**

halal *n.* [Ar. **halāl** a lawful thing.] Meat slaughtered according to Muslim holy law or **shari'a** (q.v.). —*adj.* 1. Pertaining to meat slaughtered in this way. 2. Allowed by Muslim holy law.

halcyon *n, pl.* **halcyons** [L. **alcyōn** or **halcyōn** from Gk. **halkuōn** kingfisher.] 1. A kingfisher. 2. *Greek and Roman Mythology.* A mythical bird which had the ability to calm the sea where it made its nest. —*adj.* Calm. Peaceful. *Halcyon days.*

hallazgo or **hallazco** *n.* [Sp. discovery, reward for finding.] *Spanish Law.* Discovering, coming into possession of, and becoming the owner of, something which is ownerless, such as **bona vacantia** (q.v.). Cf. **terra manens** etc.

hallel *n.* [Heb. **hallēl** song of praise.] *Judaism.* A chant based upon Psalms 113 through 118 used on special Holy Days.

hallelujah *interj.* [Heb. **halleluyāh: hallelu** praise (1); **Yāh** God (2): Praise God.] Praise God! A shout of praise or joy. —*n., pl.* **hallelujahs** A cry of "Praise God." *The hallelujahs echoed through the congregation as the dynamic preacher spoke.* Cf. **alleluia.**

hamartia *n., pl.* **harmartias** [Gk. a missed shot, a mistake or error, a sin.] A fatal flaw or error, especially a sin, which causes the downfall of a character in a drama or literary work.

Hanukkah or **Hanukah** or **Chanukah** *n.* [Heb. **hanukka** dedication.] *Judaism.* An eight-day festival celebrating the rededication of the Jewish Temple in Jerusalem after the victory of the Maccabees in 165 B.C.

haole *n., pl.* **haoles** [Haw. foreigner.] A Hawaiian resident who is not a native, especially a white non-resident.

hapax *n., pl.* **hapaxes.** Short form of **hapax legomenon** (q.v.).

hapax legomenon *n., pl.* **hapax legomena** [Gk. **hapax** once, once only (2); **legomenon** being said (1): being said once only.] A word or expression which appears only once in a document, book, or the records of a language.

haphtarah or **haftarah** or **haftorah** *n., pl.* **haphtaroth** or **haphtoroth** or **haphtorot** or **haphtoros** [Heb. **haptāra** conclusion, dismissal.] *Judaism.* A reading from the prophets which follows each lesson of the Torah read in synagogue on the Sabbath.

hara-kiri or **hari-kari** *n., pl.* **hara-kiris** or **hari-karis** [Japan. **hara** abdomen, belly (1); **kiri** to cut (2): belly cutting.] 1. Suicide through the process of cutting the belly which Japanese samurai either practiced voluntarily to obviate disgrace or had to undergo as punishment imposed by the feudal court in lieu of the normal death penalty. **Seppuku** (q.v.). 2. Suicide. *The Japanese business community reacted with anger at the LDP's political hara-kiri (Newsweek Int.* May 26, 1980:33).

harem *n., pl.* **harems** [Turk. from Ar. **harim** a sacred, forbidden place.] 1. A section of a building set aside for female members of a Muslim household. 2. A collective term for these women. 3. A group of women serving the sexual pleasure of one male. Cf. **seraglio.**

haruspex or **aruspex** *n., pl.* **haruspices** or **aruspices** [L. soothsayer, diviner.] 1. A soothsayer or diviner, particularly a person who predicts events by examining natural phenomena. 2. A prophet or prognosticator. *It was a very unanticipated event; indeed, it baffled the community's leading haruspices.* Cf. **auspex.**

hashish or **hasheesh** *n., short form* **hash** [Ar. **hasīs** hemp, grass.] A refined extract of the female cannabis plant which is inhaled or chewed to stimulate a state of euphoria. Cf. **marijuana.**

hasid or **Has(s)id** or **cha(s)sid** or **Chas(s)id** *n., pl.* **hasidim** or **Has(s)idim** or **chas(s)idim** or **Chas(s)idim** [Heb. **hasīd** pious.] *Judaism.* An Hasidic Jew. A follower of the teachings and way of life of Israel Baal Shem Tov, an 18th-century religious leader and mystic who taught that a life dedicated to God should be joyous.

hasta la vista *interj.* [Sp. **hasta** until (1); **la** the (2); **vista** sight (3): until the sight.] See you again! Until we meet again! Farewell! See **à bientôt.**

hasta luego *interj.* [Sp. **hasta** until (1); **luego** next, then (2): until then.] So long! Goodbye! See **à bientôt.**

Hauptfeind *n.* [Ger. **Haupt** head, chief (1); **Feind** enemy (2): chief enemy.] 1. Satan. 2. Chief, principal, or main enemy.

hausfrau *n., pl.* **hausfrauen** or **hausfraus** [Ger. **Hausfrau: Haus** house, home (1); **Frau** woman, wife: housewife.] Mistress or lady of the household. *. . . matronly and dignified offstage, every inch the well-dressed Hausfrau . . . (Newsweek Int.* Oct. 26, 1981:53).

haustus *n., pl.* **haustus** [L. a drawing, drinking.] *Roman and Civil Law.* The right to draw water from a well or spring on another's property as well as the attendant right to go to and from the well or spring.

haut or *fem.* **haute** *adj.* [Fr. high, eminent.] Honorable. Fashionable. High-class. a) *. . . the White House acknowledgment that Nancy accepted an unspecified number of haute frocks during 1981 without paying for them has become a lively controversy (Newsweek Int.* Feb. 1, 1982:39). b) *The cuisine is not haute, but it is plentiful and fresh, based largely on fish and pork (Time Int.*1979). Cf. **haute couture** and **haute cuisine.**

haute bourgeoisie *n.* [Fr. **haute** high, eminent (1); **bourgeoisie** middle class (2): high middle class.] Upper middle class. Professional class. See **bourgeois.**

haute couture n. [Fr. **haute** high, eminent (1); **couture** dressmaking, sewing (2): high dressmaking or sewing.] 1. High-style, high-class, or fashionable dressmaking or dress-designing. The art of dress-designing or designing women's high fashions. Fashionable clothes or dresses. *But in haute couture, Yves Saint Laurent, Pierre Cardin and almost two dozen others showed the verve that has long kept high fashion indisputably French* (*Newsweek Int.* Jan. 2, 1984:58). 2. Leading establishments engaged in creating high fashions for women. Cf. **haut** and **couture**.

haute cuisine n. [Fr. **haute** high, aristocratic, eminent, noble (1); **cuisine** cooking, food (2): high cooking or food.] High-class or fashionable cooking. Luxurious or high-class meals. . . . *a business class that has grown plump on fine wine and haute cuisine . . .* (*Newsweek Int.* Nov. 30, 1981:18). —*attrib.* Of, relating to, characteristic of, high-class cookery or meals. *The crew dined on an haute cuisine space menu of crab soup, paté de foie gras and lobster pilaf* (*Newsweek Int.* July 5, 1982:31). See **cuisine**.

haute noblesse n. [Fr. **haute** high, eminent (1); **noblesse** nobility (2): high nobility.] Upper noble class. *A bourgeois by origin, he had a better understanding than Caesar, the scion of the haute noblesse, of the problems of ways and means . . .* (Cary 1970:511).

haute politique n. [Fr. **haute** high, eminent (1); **politique** politics, policy (2): high politics.] Negotiations conducted by high-ranking officials. Political intrigue which is beyond the comprehension of ordinary citizens.

hauteur n., pl. **hauteurs** [Fr. haughtiness, arrogance.] Condescending attitude or manner. a) *She lives nowadays in secluded hauteur in Paris' Montparnasse, revealing herself only in her memoirs* (*Time Int.* 1979). b) *He is certainly very intelligent and capable, but his hauteur has won for him the animosity of his colleagues and subordinates.*

haut monde n. [Fr. **haut** high, eminent (1); **monde** world (2): high world.] High society. The elite of the society. Fashionable society. The best circles. *Refusing to accept the moral or sartorial dictates of the haut monde, she lived and dressed as she pleased* (*Newsweek Int.* Jan. 25, 1982:56). See **beau monde** and **tout le haut monde**.

hazzan See **chazan**.

H.C. *abbr.* for 1. **habeas corpus** (q.v.). 2. **hors concours** (q.v.).

H.C. or **h.c.** *abbr.* for **honoris causa** (q.v.).

H.D. *abbr.* for **Humanitatum Doctor** (q.v.).

Heauton Timorumenos n. [Gk. **heauton** self (1); **timorumenos** being tormented (2): being self tormented.] *The Self-Tormentor*, a Latin comedy by Terence (died 159 B.C.).

hebephrenia n. [Neo-Gk. from Gk. **hēbē** youth (2); **phrēn** diaphragm, midriff, mind (1): mind of youth.] *Medicine*. A type of schizophrenia which is characterized by hallucinations, silliness, delusions, and puerile behavior.

hegemon n., pl. **hegemons** [Gk. leader, guide, commander, chief.] A person or state which enjoys hegemony or political leadership. *In contemporary international politics, there can be little or no doubt that there is one acknowledged hegemon, namely the U.S.A.*

Hegira or **Hejira** n. [L. from Ar. **hijrah** migration.] 1. The migration of the prophet Mohammed from Mecca to Medina in A.D. 622. 2. The Muslim era as reckoned from this date. See **Anno Hegirae**. —**hegira** or **hejira** pl. **hegiras** or **hejiras** Departure, flight, journey, or trip from a dangerous or unpleasant place to a safe or pleasant place. Exodus. Emigration. *The attractions of the cities vis-à-vis the hardships of the rural areas are the main reason for the prevalent hegira from the villages to the urban areas in many developing countries.*

hélas interj. [Fr. alas.] Alas.

helix n., pl. **helices** [Gk. spiral.] A spiral-shaped object.

hematemesis n., pl. **hematemeses** [Neo-Gk. from Gk. **haima** of blood (2); **emesis** vomiting (1): vomiting of blood.] *Medicine*. Vomiting blood.

hemiplegia n., pl. **hemiplegias** [Gk. **hēmiplēgia**: **hemi** half (1); **plēg(ē)** blow (2): half blow.] *Medicine*. Paralysis which affects only one side of the body or a part of it and is frequently the result of injury to the opposite side of the brain. See **paralysis**.

hendiadys n. [L. from Gk. **hen** one (1); **dia** through, across (2); **du(o)** two (3): one through two.] One by means of two. *Rhetoric*. The joining of two nouns to express an idea more commonly represented by means of a noun and an adjective; e.g., "by arms and force" instead of "by armed force."

Hercules n., pl. **Herculeses** [L. equivalent of Gk. **Hēraklēs**: **Hēra** Hera (2); **kle(o)s** glory (1): glory of Hera.] 1. *Greek. and Roman Mythology*. A hero famous for his extraordinary strength and courage who successfully completed twelve almost impossible assignments or labors, including the slaying of the **Hydra** (q.v.) and the dragging of **Cerberus** (q.v.), from **Hades** (q.v.). 2. A man of extraordinary physical strength. a) *Daley Thompson, the smooth muscled black Hercules, will probably go down in sporting history as the best, most complete decathlon star ever* (*New African* 1983). b) *Fancying himself a Hercules, Kobina attempted to carry a big bag of rice and in the process sprained his back.*

Hercules Furens n. [L. **Hercules** Hercules (2); **furens** mad (1): mad Hercules.] 1. *The Mad Hercules*, the Latin title of a Greek play (414 B.C.) by the Athenian tragedian Euripides (died c.408 B.C.) in which the hero Heracles goes mad and kills his wife and children. 2. A Latin play by Seneca the Younger (c. 4 B.C.–65A.D.), based upon the Euripiden tragedy.

heredad n., pl. **heredads** [Sp. inheritance.] *Spanish Law*. 1. An inheritance. 2. Cultivated land.

heredad yacente *n.* [Sp. **heredad** inheritance (2); **yacente** recumbent, lying (1): lying inheritance.] A vacant succession. An inheritance upon which the heir has not entered. **hereditas jacens** (q.v.).

heredero *n., pl.* **herederos** [Sp. heir.] *Spanish Law.* An heir. **Heres** (q.v.).

heredes proximi or **haeredes proximi** *n., sing.* **heres proximus** or **haeres proximus** [L. **heredes** heirs (2); **proximi** next, nearest (1): nearest heirs.] Next or nearest heirs. A deceased person's children or descendants, as opposed to **heredes remotiores** (q.v.).

heredes remotiores or **haeredes remotiores** *n., sing.* **heres remotior** or **haeres remotior** [L. **heredes** heirs (2); **remotiores** more distant, remote (1): more distant heirs.] More remote heirs, i.e., kinsmen apart from children or descendants, as opposed to **heredes proximi** (q.v.).

hereditas or **haereditas** *n., pl.* **hereditates** or **haereditates** [L. state of being an heir, inheritance.] *Roman and Civil Law.* Inheritance. Succession. Succession to the rights and liabilities of a deceased person, whether he/she died testate or intestate.

hereditas ab intestato or **haereditas ab intestato** *n., pl.* **hereditates ab intestato** or **haereditates ab intestato** [L. **hereditas** inheritance (1); **ab** from, by (2); **intestato** intestate (3): inheritance from intestate.] Inheritance from someone who died without making a will. Cf. **heres ab intestato** and **successio ab intestato**.

hereditas damnosa *n.* [L. **hereditas** inheritance (2); **damnosa** ruinous, detrimental (1): ruinous inheritance.] 1. Insolvent inheritance. Burdensome inheritance. *Roman Law.* An inheritance from one who died insolvent and whose debts the heir must discharge. An inheritance, which is so burdened with debt as to be a liability rather than an asset. 2. Generally, a burdensome or unrewarding inheritance.

hereditas est successio in universum jus quod defunctus habuerit. [L. **hereditas** inheritance (1); **est** is (2); **successio** succession (3); **in** into, to, against, for (4); **universum** whole, entire, collective (5); **jus** right, law (6); **quod** which (7); **defunctus** the deceased (8); **habuerit** had, held, regarded (9): Inheritance is succession into the entire right which the deceased had.] *Law.* Inheritance is succession to every right which the deceased possessed. Cf. **hereditas nihil** etc.

hereditas jacens or **haereditas jacens** *n., pl.* **hereditates jacentes** or **haereditates jacentes** [L. **hereditas** inheritance (2); **jacens** lying, inactive (1): inactive/lying inheritance.] Vacant succession. An inheritance upon which the heir has not entered. *In order that there shall be nothing like the Roman hereditas jacens, it is provided . . . that until that Division* [i.e., Probate, Divorce and Admiralty] *makes an appointment, the property shall vest in its President* (Hanbury 1962:455). Cf. **testamentum destitutum**.

hereditas legitima or **haereditas legitima** *n., pl.* **hereditates legitimae** or **haereditates legitimae** [L. **hereditas** inheritance, succession (2); **legitima** lawful, legitimate (1): lawful inheritance.] An inheritance obtained through the operation of the law and not by the will of the deceased. See **heres legitimus** etc.

hereditas luctuosa or **haereditas luctuosa** *n., pl.* **hereditates luctuosae** or **haereditates luctuosae** [L. **hereditas** inheritance, succession (2); **luctuosa** mournful, sad, sorrowful (1): mournful inheritance/succession.] A sad inheritance/succession; e.g., a parent inheriting a son's or daughter's estate. See **tristis successio**.

hereditas nihil aliud est quam successio in universum jus quod defunctus habuerit. [L. **hereditas** inheritance (1); **nihil** nothing (3); **aliud** other (4;) **est** is (2); **quam** than (5); **successio** succession (6); **in** into, to, against, for (7); **universum** whole, entire (8); **jus** right, law (9); **quod** which (10); **defunctus** the dead (person) (11); **habuerit** had, held, regarded (12): Inheritance is nothing other than succession into the entire right which the dead person had.] *Law.* Inheritance is nothing else than succession to all the rights of the deceased. Cf. **hereditas est successio** etc.

hereditas testamentaria or **haereditas testamentaria** *n., pl.* **hereditates testamentariae** or **haereditates testamentariae** [L. **hereditas** inheritance, succession (2); **testamentaria** testamentary (1): testamentary inheritance.] Inheritance by means of a will. Cf. **heres factus**.

heres or **haeres** *n., pl.* **heredes** or **haeredes** [L. heir, successor.] Successor of a deceased person.

heres ab intestato or **haeres ab intestato** *n., pl.* **heredes ab intestato** or **haeredes ab intestato** [L. **heres** heir, successor (1); **ab** from, by (2); **intestato** intestate (3): heir from the intestate.] Heir or successor of someone who dies without a will. Cf. **hereditas ab intestato** and **successio ab intestato**.

heres est eadem persona cum antecessore. [L. **heres** heir, successor (1); **est** is (2); **eadem** the same (3); **persona** person (4); **cum** with (5); **antecessore** predecessor, antecedent (6): An heir is the same person with the predecessor.] *Law.* An heir is the same person as his/her predecessor; i.e., an heir inherits all the rights and obligations of the deceased.

heres factus or **haeres factus** *n., pl.* **heredes facti** or **haeredes facti** [L. **heres** heir, successor (2); **factus** made, having been made (1): (one) having been made heir.] *Civil Law.* A person appointed heir by will. A testamentary heir. Cf. **hereditas testamentaria**.

heres institutus or **haeres institutus** *n., pl.* **heredes instituti** or **haeredes instituti** [L. **heres** heir, successor (2); **institutus** appointed, designated (1): appointed heir.] A person appointed heir through the will of the deceased. Testamentary heir.

heres legitimus or **haeres legitimus** *n., pl.* **heredes legitimi** or **haeredes legitimi** [L. **heres** heir, successor (2); **legitimus** lawful, legitimate (1): lawful heir.] A person who becomes heir by virtue of his/her birth to parents who were lawfully wedded. See **heres legitimus est** etc.

heres legitimus est quem nuptiae demonstrant. [L. **heres** heir, successor (2); **legitimus** lawful, legitimate (1); **est** is (3); **quem** (the one) whom (4); **nuptiae** marriage (5); **demonstrant** point(s) out (6): The legitimate heir is the one whom marriage points out.] *Law.* The legal heirs are those born to parents lawfully wedded. See **hereditas legitima.** Cf. **pater is est quem** etc.

heres natus or **haeres natus** *n., pl.* **heredes nati** or **haeredes nati** [L. **heres** heir, successor (2); **natus** born (1): born heir.] *Civil Law.* A person born heir, as opposed to a person made heir by other means.

heres necessarius or **haeres necessarius** *n., pl.* **heredes necessarii** or **haeredes necessarii** [L. **heres** heir, successor (2); **necessarius** necessary, of necessity (1): necessary heir.] *Roman Law.* Heir of necessity. A slave appointed heir by his master and who automatically becomes free and heir on his master's death. Cf. **heres suus.**

heres suus or **haeres suus** *n., pl.* **heredes sui** or **haeredes sui** [L. **heres** heir, successor (2); **suus** one's own, his/her own (1): one's own heir.] *Roman Law.* A son who on the death of the father becomes **sui juris** (q.v.) and inherits the decedent's property either by will or by intestacy. The word "suus" distinguishes him from a slave. Cf. **heres necessarius.**

Herr *n., pl.* **Herren** [Ger. lord, master, Mr.] 1. A title of courtesy used for males in German-speaking countries. See **babu; Monsieur; san; Senhor; Señor;** and **Signor.**

Herrenvolk *n., pl.* **Herrenvölker** or **Herrenvolks** [Ger. **Herr** lord, master, Mr. (1); **Volk** people, race (2): master race.] A people who believe that they are a superior race and must, therefore, rule inferior peoples. *White South Africans, like Hitler's Germans, seem to regard themselves as a Herrenvolk.*

hetaera or **hetaira** *n., pl.* **hetaerae** or **hetaeras** or **hetairai** or **hetairas** [Gk. **hetaira** a female companion or comrade, a courtesan.] A woman paid for sexual services. See **demimondaine** and **demimonde.**

heterozetesis *n., pl.* **heterozeteses** [Neo-Gk. from Gk. **hetero(s)** another, different (2); **zētēsis** seeking, search, inquiry, investigation (1): inquiry or investigation of another or different thing.] *Logic.* A fallacy in which one supposes that one is settling the point at issue when one is actually preoccupied with a different question altogether. **Ignoratio elenchi** (q.v.).

heureka *var.* of **eureka** (q.v.).

Heureux qui comme Ulysse a fait un beau voyage. Joachim Du Bellay (1522–1560). *Les Regrets* 31. [Fr. **heureux** happy (1); **qui** (he) who (2); **comme** like (3); **Ulysse** Ulysses (4); **a** has (5); **fait** made (6); **un** a (7); **beau** lovely, beautiful, fair, handsome, good-looking (8); **voyage** voyage, trip (9): Happy he who, like Ulysses, has made a beautiful voyage.] Happy the traveler, like Ulysses, who has made a successful voyage and returned home.

hexahemeron or **hexaemeron** *n., pl.* **hexahemerons** or **hexaemerons** [Gk. **hex** six (1); **hēmer(a)** day (2): six days, a space or period of six days.] The six days of the creation of the universe, as in the Bible's Genesis.

HH.D. *abbr.* for **Humanitatum Doctor** (q.v.).

H.I. *abbr.* for **hic jacet** (q.v.).

hiatus *n., pl.* **hiatuses** [L. aperture, cleft, opening.] 1. A gap. An aperture. A break in something. A space in which something is missing. A lacuna. *To be sure, the institution has regulations, but there is a wide hiatus between theory and practice.* 2. A lapse, break, or interruption in continuity or time. *Academic departments of the university have been asked to introduce programs to fill the long hiatus between the end of one session and the beginning of another.* 3. *Linguistics.* The occurrence, pronunciation, or juxtaposition of two vowels, which are not a diphthong, with no consonant separating them; e.g., "sofa arm."

hic et nunc [L. **hic** here (1); **et** and (2); **nunc** now (3): here and now.] Immediately.

hic et ubique *adv.* [L. **hic** here (1); **et** and (2); **ubique** everywhere (3): here and everywhere.] Here and everywhere. —*n.* A person who is always wandering about aimlessly or for insignificant purposes.

hic iacet *abbr.* **H.I.** *var.* of **hic jacet** (q.v.).

hic iacet sepultus *abbr.* **H.I.S.** *var.* of **hic jacet sepultus** (q.v.).

hic jacet *abbr.* **H.J.** *n., pl.* **hic jacets** [L. **hic** here (1); **jacet** he/she lies, lies at rest (2): Here he/she lies.] Here lies. Epitaph. Inscription on tombstone.

hic jacet sepultus *abbr.* **H.J.S.** [L. **hic** here (1); **jacet** he lies (2); **sepultus** buried (3): Here he lies buried.] Here lies buried.

hic requiescit in pace. *abbr.* **H.R.I.P.** [L. **hic** here (1); **requiescit** he/she rests, reposes (2); **in** in, on (3); **pace** peace (4): Here he/she rests in peace.] Here rests in peace.

hic sepultus *abbr.* **H.S.** [L. **hic** here (1); **sepultus** buried, interred (2): Here buried.] Here is buried.

hic sepultus est. *abbr.* **H.S.E.** [L. **hic** here (1); **sepultus** buried (3); **est** is (2): Here is buried.] Here is or lies buried.

hic situs *abbr.* **H.S.** [L. **hic** here (1); **situs** laid up, deposited, situated (2): Here deposited.] Here is buried.

hic situs est. *abbr.* **H.S.E.** [L. **hic** here (1); **situs** laid up, deposited, situated (3); **est** is (2): Here is deposited.] Here is or lies buried.

Hier stehe ich. Ich kann nicht anders. Gott helfe mir. Amen. Martin Luther (1483–1546) at the Diet of

Worms (1521). [Ger. **hier** here (1); **stehe** stand (3); **ich** I (2); **Ich** I (4); **kann** can, am able (5); **nicht** nothing (6); **anders** different (7); **Gott** God (8); **helfe** help (9); **mir** me (10); **Amen** Amen (11): Here I stand. I can nothing different. God help me. Amen.] Here I stand. I can do nothing else. God help me. Amen.

hinc illae lacrimae Terence (c.185–159 B.C.). *Andria* 126. [L. **hinc** hence (1); **illae** those (2); **lacrimae** tears (3): hence those tears.] That is the cause of those woes or troubles. Cf. **lacrimae rerum** and **sunt lacrimae rerum**.

hiragana *n.* [Japan. **hira** ordinary, plain (1); **kana** character (2): ordinary character.] A Japanese script used for informal writing. Cf. **kana**; **kanji**; and **katakana**.

H.I.S. *abbr.* for **hic iacet sepultus** (q.v.).

Histoire Amoureuse des Gaules *n.* [Fr. **histoire** history (2); **amoureuse** amorous (1); **des** of the (3); **Gaules** Gauls, French (4): amorous history of the Gauls.] *Amorous History of the Gauls*, a collection of lightly veiled contemporary profiles, often scandalous, by Bussy-Rabutin (1618–1693).

Historia Naturalis *n.* [L. **historia** history (2); **naturalis** natural (1): natural history.] *Natural History*, an encyclopedia of natural phenomena by Pliny the Elder (23–79 A.D.).

historia vitae magistra [L. **historia** history (1); **vitae** of life (3); **magistra** school-mistress, instructress (2): history, school-mistress of life.] History serves a didactic purpose. History, the guide to life. History, giver of instructions on life. *The brief sentences in which Thucydides outlines this last purpose of his writing should not be taken as a simple application of the tag* historia vitae magistra *(Lesky 1966:474).* See **magistra vitae**.

H.J. *abbr.* for **hic jacet** (q.v.).

H.J.S. *abbr.* for **hic jacet sepultus** (q.v.).

H.M.P. *abbr.* for **hoc monumentum posuit** (q.v.).

Hochkonjunktur *n.* [Ger. **hoch** high (1); **Konjunktur** conjuncture, joining together, trend, business cycle (2): high business cycle.] Boom. Prosperity. A period of considerable commercial boom or prosperity, particularly during the height of the holiday season when there is an influx of tourists.

hoc intuitu *adv.* [L. **hoc** with this (1); **intuitu** (with) consideration, contemplation (2): with this consideration.] With this expectation.

hoc monumentum posuit *abbr.* **H.M.P.** [L. **hoc** this (2); **monumentum** monument, memorial (3); **posuit** he/she set up, erected, built (1): He/she built this monument.] He/she erected this monument.

hoc titulo *abbr.* **H.T.** or **h.t.** *adv.* [L. **hoc** with this (1); **titulo** (with) title (2): with this title.] Under this title. In this title. Used in bibliographical references.

hoc verbo *abbr.* **H.V.** or **h.v.** *adv.* [L. **hoc** with this (1); **verbo** (with) word (2): with this word.] Under this word. Bibliographical reference to entries in dictionaries and works arranged alphabetically. See **hac voce**.

hoi polloi *pl. n.* [Gr. **hoi** the (1); **polloi** many (2): the many.] The common people. The ordinary people. The masses. The multitude. The throng. The populace. The rabble. Although "hoi" means "the," the expression sometimes uses the English definite article. a) *. . . la crème de la crème contributed $500 each to the Met to dine. . . . Then 1,500 of the hoi polloi, at $100 a head, stormed the place to dance to Lester Lanin's orchestra . . . (Newsweek Int.* Dec. 20, 1982:18). b) *The success of his political career is attributable to the fact that, though a member of the aristocracy, he knows how to relate to hoi polloi.* See **canaille**.

hokku *n., pl.* **hokku** [Japan. **hok** first, opening (1); **ku** stanza (2): first stanza.] A **haiku** (q.v.).

homicidium *n.* [L. the killing of a person, homicide.] *Law.* The taking away of the life of another.

homicidium ex casu *n.* [L. **homicidium** homicide (1); **ex** arising from, out of, by reason of (2); **casu** accident, occurrence (3): homicide arising from accident.] *Law.* Accidental homicide. *Police investigations revealed that what was suspected to be murder was in reality homicidium ex casu.*

homicidium ex justitia *n.* [L. **homicidium** homicide (1); **ex** arising from, out of, by reason of (2); **justitia** justice (3): homicide by reason of justice.] *Law.* Homicide in the process of administering justice or executing the sentence of a court of law. *Hanging of a prisoner after a conviction for murder is a good example of homicidium ex justitia.* See **qui jussu** etc.

homicidium ex necessitate *n.* [L. **homicidium** homicide (1); **ex** arising from, out of, by reason of (2); **necessitate** compulsion, urgency, necessity (3): homicide by reason of compulsion.] *Law.* Homicide prompted by unavoidable necessity. *Defense counsel pleaded that his client committed homicidium ex necessitate, for the armed robber's trespass to his residence compelled him to protect his life, family and property.*

homicidium ex voluntate *n.* [L. **homicidium** homicide (1); **ex** arising from, out of, by reason of (2); **voluntate** free will, inclination (3): homicide out of free will.] *Law.* Willful/voluntary homicide; i.e., homicide committed deliberately and thus culpable.

homicidium per infortunium *n.* [L. **homicidium** homicide (1); **per** by, through (2); **infortunium** misfortune, calamity (3): homicide through misfortune.] *Law.* Homicide by misadventure. A species of excusable homicide, as when a person accidentally causes the death of another in the process of performing a lawful act. See **per infortunium**.

homicidium se defendendo *n.* [L. **homicidium** homicide (1); **se** one's self (3); **defendendo** by defending (2): homicide by defending one's self.] *Law.* Homicide committed in the process of self-defense. A kind of excusable homicide, as when a person is suddenly attacked and has no other probable way of escaping from attack. See **se defendendo** and **vim vi** etc.

hominum causa jus constitutum est. [L. **hominum** of humans, people (5); **causa** for the sake (4); **jus** right, law (1); **constitutum** established (3); **est** is, has been (2): Law has been established for the sake of humans.] Laws exist for the benefit of humankind.

homme d'affaires *n., pl.* **hommes d'affaires** [Fr. **homme** person, human being, man, a male (1); **d'** of (2); **affaires** business, affairs (3): a man of affairs.] A business man.

homme de coeur *n., pl.* **hommes de coeur** [Fr. **homme** person, human being, a man, a male (1); **de** of (2); **coeur** heart, feelings (3): a man of heart.] A noble heart. A great-hearted man. A man of feeling. A sensitive man. A man of keen sensibility. A generous man. See **homme sensible**.

homme de lettres *n., pl.* **hommes de lettres** [Fr. **homme** person, human being, a man, a male (1); **de** of (2); **lettres** letters, literature (3): a man of letters.] A literary man. A man engaged in literary activities.

homme d'esprit *n., pl.* **hommes d'esprit** [Fr. **homme** person, human being, a man, a male (1); **d'** of (2); **esprit** wit (3): a man of wit.] A wit. A witty man. A man with a nice wit or sense of humor. A man of brilliant repartee.

homme du monde *n., pl.* **hommes du monde** [Fr. **homme** person, human being, a man, a male (1); **du** of the (2); **monde** world (3): a man of the world.] Society man. A man of high society. Man-about-town. A gentleman. A man of good training or upbringing. Cf. **femme du monde** and **gens du monde**.

homme du peuple *n., pl.* **hommes du peuple** [Fr. **homme** person, human being, a man, a male (1); **du** of the (2); **peuple** people (3): a man of the people.] A man of humble origins. A man whose manners suggest a humble background. A man of working-class background. Cf. **femme du peuple**.

homme sensible *n., pl.* **hommes sensibles** [Fr. **homme** person, human being, a man, a male (2); **sensible** sensitive, impressionable (1): a sensitive man.] A sensitive or impressionable man. A man of keen sensibility. A man of feeling. See **homme de coeur**.

homo *n.* [L. a person, human being, human.] The human race. The genus of human beings.

homo aequalis *n.* [L. **homo** person, human being, human (2); **aequalis** equal (1): an equal person.] An egalitarian. A member of an egalitarian society, i.e., a society which observes equality. Cf. **homo hierarchicus**.

homo alieni juris *n.* [L. **homo** person, human being, human (1); **alieni** of another (3); **juris** of right, law (2): a person of the law of another.] *Law.* A person under the control of another; e.g., a child who is under his/her father's authority and, legally, cannot manage his/her own affairs. Cf. **sui juris**.

homo economicus *var.* of **homo oeconomicus** (q.v.).

homoeoteleuton *var.* of **homoioteleuton** (q.v.).

homo erectus *n.* [L. **homo** person, human being, human (2); **erectus** erect, upright (1): erect or upright human.] *Anthropology.* A human being at the stage of evolution when an erect posture was assumed.

homo faber *n.* [L. **homo** person, human being, human (1); **faber** maker (2): human maker.] *Anthropology.* The human manufacturer of tools. A human being at the stage in the process of evolution when tools could be made. Cf. **faber est suae** etc. and **faber fortunae suae**.

homo habilis *n.* [L. **homo** person, human being, human (2); **habilis** fit, apt (1): fit or apt human.] *Anthropology.* A capable or able human. A human who has ability. A human being at the stage of evolution when tools and crude shelters were made and used.

homo hierarchicus *n.* [L. **homo** person, human being, human (2); **hierarchicus** hierarchical (1): a hierarchical human.] *Anthropology.* A human being of a society characterized by hierarchy or inequality. Cf. **homo aequalis**.

homoioteleuton or **homoeoteleuton** *n., pl.* **homoioteleutons** or **homoioteleuta** or **homoeoteleutons** or **homoeoteleuta** [Gk. **homoi(os)** same, like (1); **teleut(ē)** ending (2): the same ending, the like ending of several clauses or verses.] *Rhetoric.* The appearance in a document or book of two or more words, clauses, phrases, lines, verses, etc. with similar or the same endings. *The typist was asked to take note of the numerous homoioteleutons in the draft so as not to make typographical mistakes.* Cf. **saut de même au même**.

homoiousion *n.* [Gk. **homoi(os)** like, similar (1); **ousi(a)** substance (2): similar substance.] *Christianity.* A theological doctrine which maintains that Christ and God or the Son and the Father are of similar, though not necessarily of the same, substance. A doctrine which was rejected as heretical by the Council of Nicaea in 325. Cf. **homoousion**.

homo legalis *n., pl.* **homines legales** [L. **homo** person, human being, human (2); **legalis** legal, lawful (1): a legal human.] *Law.* A legal person. A lawful human being. A person who is legally recognized as a member of the community or as a citizen. A person who is not infamous, nor outlawed nor excommunicated. Cf. **probus et legalis homo**.

homologoumena or **homologumena** *pl. n.* [Gk. **homo(s)** same (1); **logoumena** things being said (2): same things being said, things having agreed upon or granted.] *Christianity.* Books of the New Testament which from very early times have been recognized as authoritative and biblical.

homo ludens *n.* [L. **homo** person, human being (2); **ludens** playing (1): playing human being.] A definition of a human being as a creature which plays and jokes.

homo mensura omnium [L. **homo** person, human being, human (1); **mensura** measure (2); **omnium** of all (3): the human (is) measure of all.] Human beings as the measure of all things. A human being is the measure of all things. A doctrine originally expounded by the Greek philosopher Protagoras (c. 481–411 B.C.), who said "A human is the measure of all things, of things that are, that they are, and of things that are not, that they are not." The doctrine denies absolute values, standards, and knowledge, and holds that everything is relative to human judgment. See **à chacun son goût**.

homo oeconomicus *n*. [L. **homo** person, human being, human (1); **oeconomicus** of domestic economy (2): a person of domestic economy.] A person connected with the society of market or monetary economy.

homoousion *n*. [Gk. **homo(s)** same (1); **ousi(a)** substance (2): same substance.] *Christianity*. A theological doctrine which maintains that Christ and God or the Son and the Father are of the same substance. This is the orthodox doctrine as opposed to the condemned doctrine of **homoiousion** (q.v.).

homo sapiens *n*. [L. **homo** person, human being, human (1); **sapiens** being wise (2): a human being wise.] A wise human being. Modern-day human beings in relation to the process of evolution. Human beings think reflectively and have large, complex brains. Some scholars regard homo sapiens as the immediate predecessor of the modern human, which they prefer to designate as homo sapiens sapiens.

homo sui juris *n*. [L. **homo** person, human being, human (1); **sui** of one's own, his/her own (2); **juris** (of) right, law (3): a human of one's own law.] *Law*. A person under his/her own control; i.e., one who enjoys full civil and social rights, who is not under the authority of another person, and who can manage his/her own affairs. See **sui juris**.

homo sum; humani nil a me alienum puto. Terence (c.185–159 B.C.). *Heauton Timorumenos* I,1,25. [L. **homo** person, human being, human (2); **sum** I am (1); **humani** of human (5); **nil** nothing (4); **a** from (7); **me** me (8); **alienum** alien, foreign (6); **puto** I consider, regard (3): I am a human being; I regard nothing of human foreign from me.] I am a human being; I consider nothing human as alien to me.

homunculus *n., pl.* **homunculi** [L. a small person, human being.] A human being in miniature. A dwarf. A midget.

honcho *n., pl.* **honchos** [Japan. **han** squad (1); **chō** chief, leader (2): squad chief.] Leader. The person in charge. Used in slang. *The head honcho.*

Hon(n)i soit qui mal y pense. [Fr. **honni** shamed, dishonored (1); **soit** be (2); **qui** (one) who (3); **mal** bad, evil (5); **y** there, of it (6); **pense** thinks (4): Shamed be one who thinks bad of it.] Shame be to him/her who thinks evil of it. Motto of the Order of the Garter.

honorarium *n., pl.* **honoraria** or **honorariums** [L. that which is honorary, that which is for the sake of honor.] An honorary reward or payment, usually given as remuneration for a service which ordinarily attracts no monetary reward. a) *After his retirement from service, he supplemented his meager retirement*

benefits with honoraria from speeches. b) *A barrister intending to practise [in England.] must spend twelve months as a pupil. His fees are an honorarium, and no action lies to recover them . . .* (Burke 1976:47).

honores mutant mores. [L. **honores** posts, offices (1); **mutant** change (2); **mores** manners, habits (3): Posts change habits.] High position tends to change a person's character (or attitude).

honoris causa *abbr.* **H.C.** or **h.c.** *adv./adj.* [L. **honoris** of honor (2); **causa** for the sake (1): for the sake of honor.] As a token of honor/respect. Applicable to a college or university degree conferred on a person who has not actually fulfilled the normal requirements, as an honor for meritorious public service. *Several politicians who ostentatiously display their doctoral titles were conferred with the titles honoris causa rather than for actual academic accomplishments.*

honoris respectum *adv./adj.* [L. **honoris** of honor (2); **respectum** in respect, consideration (1): in respect of honor.] By reason of honor. By reason of privilege. Used as a reason for disqualification from serving on a jury. For instance, a Member of Congress who is empanelled for jury service may challenge himself/ herself on the ground of privilege.

hora *n*. [Heb. from Gk. **choros** circular dance.] A circular folk dance of Israel and Romania.

horologium *n., pl.* **horologia** [L. from Gk. **hōr(a)** hour, season (1) and **log(os)** word, speech (2): hour speech, something that speaks the hour, a clock.] Timepiece. An instrument used to tell time.

horresco referens. Vergil (70–19 B.C.). *Aeneid* II,204. [L. **horresco** I shudder, am terrified (1); **referens** reporting, recounting (2): I shudder recounting.] I shudder to recount, relate or report. *The encounter with the highwayman horresco referens was dreadful.*

horribile dictu *interj*. [L. **horribile** horrible, terrible (1); **dictu** in the saying (2): horrible in the saying.] A terrible thing to say. *The armed robbers entered the house, stole almost everything there and, horribile dictu, decapitated all the residents.*

horror vacui *n*. [L. **horror** horror, dread (1); **vacui** of empty space (2): horror of empty space.] A horror or dread of empty space, particularly in art.

hors catalogue *adj*. [Fr. **hors** out of, outside (1); **catalogue** catalog, price list (2): outside the catalog.] Not listed or included in the catalog or price list.

hors concours *abbr.* **H.C.** *adv*. [Fr. **hors** out of, outside (1); **concours** competition, contest (2): outside, or out of, competition.] In the mode, style, manner, or fashion of a person or thing which cannot compete. *Citizens of the ostracized country who registered for the athletic contests were shunned and treated hors concours.* —*adj*. 1. Disqualified. Not allowed to compete. Excluded from competition. Not for competition. *Joe cannot play for his club this year, for he is twenty years of age and thus hors concours.* 2. Supreme. Unrivaled. Unequaled. Peerless. Matchless. Without rival or equal. *There is no point in comparing Moses with his colleagues, for he is clearly hors concours.*

hors de combat *adj./adv.* [Fr. **hors** out of, outside (1); **de** of (2); **combat** action, combat, fight (3): out of combat, action, or fight.] Disabled. In a weak or disabled condition. Knocked down. *Philip used to be a formidable politician but, now that he is a septuagenarian, he has declared himself hors de combat and counsels young politicians.*

hors d'oeuvre *n., pl.* **hors d'oeuvres** or **hors d'oeuvre** Usually used in the plural. [Fr. **hors** out of, outside (1); **d'** of (2); **oeuvre** work (3): outside of the work.] An assortment of appetizers. A tasty dish taken at the beginning of a meal for whetting the appetite.

hors série *adj.* [Fr. **hors** out of, outside (1); **série** series (2): outside of the series.] Excluded from the series. Not included in the series. Added subsequently. Specially made or manufactured. Used especially in reference to a special issue of a journal or periodical.

hortorium *n., pl.* **hortoria** or **hortoriums** [Neo-L. a place for produce.] An institution where specimens of vegetables, fruits, flowers, etc. are collected, nursed, preserved and studied.

hosanna or **hosannah** *interj.* [Gk. **hōsanna** from Heb. **hosa‘ nā’**: **hosa‘** save, deliver (2); **nā’** I pray, please (1): Please save.] Used to shout praise or worship of God. —*n.* A any loud cry of devotion and religious fervor.

hospice *n., pl.* **hospices** [Fr. poorhouse, hospital.] 1. An establishment, usually maintained by a religious order, which provides food and resting-place for travelers. 2. Lodging for students, destitutes, young workers, etc., usually provided by a religious order. 3. Hospital for patients on the verge of death.

hospitia curiae *n., sing.* **hospitium curiae** [L. **hospitia** inns (1); **curiae** of court (2): inns of court.] Inns of the court. Legal inns. *If one wishes to qualify for legal practice in England, one must apply to a hospitium curiae for admission.*

hospitium *n., pl.* **hospitia** [L. inn.] Lodging. Inn. Hostel. Hospice.

hostis humani generis *n.* [L. **hostis** enemy (1); **humani** of human (2); **generis** (of) race, kind (3): an enemy of the human race.] Enemy of the human race or of humankind. Applicable, especially, to a pirate. See **pirata est** etc.

hôtel de ville *n., pl.* **hôtels de ville** [Fr. **hôtel** mansion, hotel (1); **de** of (2); **ville** town, city (3): mansion of town or city.] City hall. Town hall. *When the Mayor of Marseilles . . . warmly welcomed the "hero of Dahomey" General Dodds . . . , there was no reaction from the Guesdists who were opposed to any official reception at the hôtel de ville . . .* (Suret-Canale 1971:124).

hôtel-Dieu *n., pl.* **hôtels-Dieu** [Fr. **hôtel** hotel (1); **Dieu** (of) God (2): hotel of God.] God's hotel. A hospital.

hôtelier or **hotelier** *n., pl.* **hôteliers** or **hoteliers** [Fr. a hotelkeeper.] Proprietor of a hotel. Manager of a hotel.

houp-la *interj.* [Fr. **houp** hey (1); **là** there (2): Hey, there!] Hey, look at that over there! Used in response to an unusual, sudden, or noteworthy event. —*n.* A hullabaloo. An unnecessary disturbance. *Let's stop all this houp-la and get back to work!*

houri or **huri** *n., pl.* **houris** or **huris** [Fr. from Pers. **hūri** nymph of paradise.] 1. *Islam.* One of the dark-eyed young and perfectly beautiful virgins who are believed by Muslims to live with the blessed ones in Paradise. 2. A very charming and beautiful young woman.

H.R.I.P. *abbr.* for **hic requiescit in pace** (q.v.).

H.S. *abbr.* for 1. **hic sepultus** (q.v.). 2. **hic situs** (q.v.).

H.S.E. *abbr.* for 1. **hic sepultus est** (q.v.). 2. **hic situs est** (q.v.).

H.T. or **h.t.** *abbr.* for **hoc titulo** (q.v.).

hubris or **hybris** *n.* [Gk. **hubris** wanton violence caused by insolence.] Wanton arrogance. Overweening pride. Arrogant pride. The kind of sin which begins with **ate** (q.v.), leading to the crossing of limits and culminating in the punishment of the culprit, his/her fall, overthrow or disgrace. a) *It is a common story; the forger is inevitably brought down by his own hubris, or so it appears* (*Newsweek Int.* May 16, 1983:15). b) *It is not mere hubris to argue that Homo Sapiens is special in some sense for each species is unique in its own way . . .* (*Newsweek Int.* March 29, 1982:44). Cf. **sophrosyne**.

Huis Clos *n.* [Fr. **huis** doors (2); **clos** closed (1): closed doors.] *No Exit,* a play by the French existentialist philosopher Jean-Paul Sartre (1905–1980).

hula *n., pl.* **hulas** [Haw.] A dance native to Polynesia and characterized by distinctive movements of the hips, arms, and hands.

humaniora *abbr.* **hum.** *pl. n.* [L. more humane things.] The humanities. See **humanitas**.

humanitas *n.* [L. human nature, humanity, civilization, cultivating.] Liberal education. Humanities. Study of the liberal arts. The attitude towards the problems of humanity as well as the morality inculcated by a study of the humanities. See **Geisteswissenschaften**; **humaniora**; and **litterae humaniores**.

Humanitatum Doctor *abbr.* **HH.D.** *n.* [L. **humanitatum** of Humanities (2); **doctor** teacher (1): teacher of humanities.] Doctor of Humanities. An academic degree, usually honorary, for outstanding work in the humanities.

humanum est errare [L. **humanum** a human (thing) (3); **est** is, has been (2); **errare** to err, to make a mistake (1): To make a mistake is a human thing.] To err is a human characteristic.

huri *n., pl.* **huris** See **houri**.

H.V. or **h.v.** *abbr.* for 1. **hoc voce** (q.v.). 2. **hoc verbo** (q.v.).

hybris *var.* of **hubris** (q.v.).

Hydra *n.* [Gk. **Hudra** water serpent.] *Greek and Roman Mythology.* A huge monster with many heads which was killed by Heracles (Hercules). The monster's central head was immortal and, when one of its heads was cut off, it was replaced by two, unless the wound was burned with hot iron. *The situation in Africa is like the multi-headed Hydra. As soon as we get one crisis under control, another pops up (Newsweek Int.* July 19, 1982:22). —**hydra** *pl.* **hydras** A complicated problem or obstacle which produces more difficulties as one solves or eliminates some aspects of the problem or obstacle. *The nation's economic problems, which initially seemed by no means intractable to most observers, are proving to be a hydra.*

hydrophobia *n.* [Neo-Gk. from **hud(o)r** water (2); **phob(os)** fear of (1): fear of water.] *Psychology.* 1. Morbid fear of water. 2. *Medicine.* Rabies.

hyp. *abbr.* for **hypothesis** (q.v.).

hypallage *n., pl.* **hypallages** [Gk. **hupallagē** interchange, exchange.] *Rhetoric.* A restructuring of standard word order; e.g., "The book closed he" instead of "He closed the book." Cf. **hyperbaton.**

hyperbaton *n., pl.* **hyperbatons** [Gk. **huper,** over, above, in excess (2): **bain(ō)** go, step (1): stepping over, overstepping.] *Rhetoric.* A violent change in the normal order of words for effect or emphasis; e.g., **quem Deus vult perdere, prius dementat** (q.v.) or "Whom God wants to destroy, He first makes mad." Cf. **hypallage.**

hyperbole *n., pl.* **hyperboles** [Gk. **huperbolē: huper** over, above, in excess (2); **bolē** throwing, shooting (1): shooting over, overshooting, over-strained phrase, excess.] An obvious exaggeration. Extravagant exaggeration, as in representing something as far bigger or smaller than it actually is, or depicting an impossibility as a reality. An extravagant or exaggerated statement; e.g., "She shed rivers of tears." *Even allowing for official hyperbole, the results have been impressive (Newsweek Int.* Oct. 19, 1981:45). Cf. **litotes** and **meiosis.**

hyperemesis *n.* [Neo-Gk. from Gk. **huperemeō: hyper** over, above, in excess (2); **emeō** I vomit (1): I vomit violently.] *Medicine.* Violent vomiting. Excessive vomiting. See **emesis** and **hyperemesis gravidarum.**

hyperemesis gravidarum *n.* [Neo-Gk **huperemesis** violent vomiting (1); L. **gravidarum** of pregnant women (2): violent vomiting of pregnant women.] *Medicine.* Pregnancy-related excessive vomiting. Excessive vomiting in the course of pregnancy which usually begins as an exaggerated form of morning sickness.

hyphaeresis *n., pl.* **hyphaereses** [Gk. **hupairesis: hup(o)** under, below, beneath (2); **(h)airesis** taking (1): a taking away from under, an omission.] *Linguistics.* The omission of a letter, sound, or syllable in a word; e.g., "di'mond" for "diamond."

hypochondria *n.* [Gk. **hupo** under, below, beneath (1); **chondr(os)** cartilage (2): under the cartilage, the abdomen, the soft parts of the body below the cartilage and above the navel.] *Medicine.* An intense state of mental and spiritual depression usually related to pathological anxiety about one's physical condition. In antiquity the abdomen was believed to be the seat of this mental condition. Cf. **malade imaginaire.**

hypodynamia *n., pl.* **hypodynamias** [Neo-Gk. from Gk. **hupo** under, below, beneath (1); **dynami(s)** power, ability (2): under-ability.] Decrease or reduction in power, strength, or ability.

hypostasis *n., pl.* **hypostases** [Gk. from **hupo** under, below (2); **stasis** standing (1): standing under, foundation.] 1. *Philosophy.* The foundation or underpinnings of reality. 2. *Theology.* One of the persons of the Trinity, and, especially, the combined divine and human person of Jesus Christ. 3. The settling of objects in a fluid. 4. An object which has settled in a fluid. Sediment.

hyposthenia *n.* [Neo-Gk. from Gk. **hupo** under, below, beneath (1); **sthen(os)** strength, might (2): under strength.] Physical weakness. Lack of strength.

hypoth. *abbr.* for **hypothesis** (q.v.).

hypothèque *n.* [Fr. mortgage.] *French Law.* Mortgage on real estate. Hypothecation. The right acquired by a creditor to sell real property, given to him as security, for the satisfaction of the debt, if the debtor should default.

hypothermia *n.* [Neo-Gk. from Gk. **hupothermos: hupo** under, below, beneath (1); **thermos** warm, hot (2): under hot, less than hot.] *Medicine.* Drop in the temperature of the body below the normal level. Sometimes induced by artificial means for the purpose of heart surgery. *If body temperature falls too low, there is a danger of death due to hypothermia (Newsweek Int.* Feb. 28, 1983:39).

hypotheses non fingo Isaac Newton (1642–1727). [L. **hypotheses** hypotheses, conjectures (3); **non** not (1); **fingo** I shape, mold (2): I do not shape hypotheses.] I do not make hypotheses.

hypothesis *abbr.* **hyp.** or **hypoth.** *n., pl.* **hypotheses** [Gk. **hupothesis: hupo** under, below, beneath (2): **thesis** placing (1): placing under, supposition, proposal, suggestion, subject proposed for discussion, the presupposition of an action, premise.] 1. A tentatively assumed proposition from which logical or empirical inferences may be drawn to test its validity or consistency with facts. a) *. . . we must acknowledge that the hypothesis is at present, though not improbable, based on insufficient evidence* (Jaeger 1970:193). b) *As long as excavations continue, our knowledge of prehistory is, at best, a working hypothesis to be constantly tested as archaeology unearths new evidence.* 2. An assumption or supposition made in the course, and for the sake, of argument. 3. *Rhetoric.*

The "if" clause, i.e., the antecedent clause in a conditional statement. See **protasis.** Cf. **apodosis.**

hysteron proteron *n.* [Gk. **husteron** later, latter (1); **proteron** former (2): latter former.] 1. *Rhetoric.* A figure of speech in which the natural, logical, or rational order is reversed; e.g., "They ate and cooked their meal very quickly." 2. *Logic.* A fallacy in which what should follow from what is proved is taken as the premise.

hysteropotmos *n., pl.* **hysteropotmoi** [Gk. **husteropotmos: husteron** later, latter (1); **potmos** fate, death (2): later fate, a person supposed dead who reappears alive.] A person who, after being presumed dead, surprisingly comes home after a long period of absence. A person who, after being presumed killed in battle, escapes from captivity and surprisingly returns home.

I

I. *abbr.* for 1. **imperator** (q.v.). 2. **imperatrix** (q.v.). 3. **imperium** (q.v.).

I.A. or **i.a.** *abbr.* for 1. **in absentia** (q.v.). 2. **inter alia** (q.v.).

iacet hic *abbr.* **I.H.** or **i.h.** See **hic iacet**.

ibidem *abbr.* **Ibid.** or **Ib.** *adv.* [L. in the same place.] In the same place. In the same book, article, or work. On the same page or pages. Used in footnotes to avoid repeating source data such as author, title, and other information indicated in an immediately preceding footnote.

I.C. *abbr.* for **Jesus Christus** (q.v.).

Ich kann nicht anders. Martin Luther (1483–1546) at Diet of Worms (1521). [Ger. **Ich** I (1); **kann** can (2); **nicht** no, not (3); **anders** other (4): I can no other.] I cannot do anything else. I have no other viable option or alternative. My hands are tied. See **Hier stehe ich** etc.

ichor *n.* [Gk. **ichōr** immortal blood.] *Greek and Roman Mythology.* The blood of the immortal gods.

icon *n., pl.* **icons** [Gk. **eikōn** likeness, image, representation, semblance.] 1. An image. A symbol. A representation. A sacred image. *Her yellow ribbon headband had become a hostage icon, and cultural officer Kathryn Koob wore it proudly when she stepped off the plane . . .* (*Newsweek Int.* Feb. 2, 1981:23). 2. An idol. Something which is given uncritical devotion.

ictus *abbr.* for **jurisconsultus** (q.v.).

id. *abbr.* for **idem** (q.v.).

id *n., pl.* **ids** [L. it.] *Psychology.* An individual's primitive, inherited, unconscious, or instinctive impulses.

I.D.A. *abbr.* for **Immortalis Dei Auspicio** (q.v.).

id certum est quod certum reddi potest. [L. **id** that (1); **certum** certain, definite (3); **est** is (2); **quod** which (4); **certum** certain, definite (7); **reddi** to be made, rendered (6); **potest** can, is able (5).] *Law.* That is certain which can be made certain. For fuller form, see next maxim. See also **certum est quod** etc.

id certum est quod certum reddi potest, sed id magis certum est quod de semetipso est certum. [L. **id** that (1); **certum** certain, definite (3); **est** is (2); **quod** which (4); **certum** certain, definite (7); **reddi** to be made, rendered (6); **potest** can, is able (5); **sed** but (8); **id** that (9); **magis** more, rather (11); **certum** certain, definite (12); **est** is (10); **quod** which (13); **de** of, from, about, for (14); **semetipso** itself, its own self (15); **est** is (16); **certum** certain, definite (17): That is certain which can be made certain, but that is more certain which of itself is certain.] *Law.* What can be made certain is certain, but what is certain of itself is more certain. For shorter form, see preceding maxim. See also **certum est quod** etc.

idée fixe *n., pl.* **idées fixes** [Fr. **idée** idea, thought (2); **fixe** fixed (1): a fixed idea.] A set idea. An obsession. *Throughout May '68 that one notion was de Gaulle's idée fixe and it finally brought him down* (*Newsweek Int.* March 24, 1980:11).

idem *abbr.* **id.** *pron.* [L. the same (thing).] 1. Usually used in bibliographies so as not to mention the name of an author and title of a book when one reference to it immediately follows another. 2. *Law.* Used with the connotation of agreement. *The two parties could not enter into a binding contract because they were not at idem.* See **ad idem**.

idem agens et patiens esse non potest. [L. **idem** the same (person) (1); **agens** the one doing (5); **et** and (6); **patiens** the one suffering (7); **esse** to be (4); **non** not (3); **potest** can, is able (2): The same person cannot be the one doing and the one suffering.] The same person cannot perform two opposing functions; i.e., plaintiff and defendant, physician and patient, etc.

idem est facere, et non prohibere cum possis; et qui non prohibet, cum prohibere possit, in culpa est (aut jubet). [L. **idem** the same (8); **est** it is (7); **facere** to do (1); **et** and (2); **non** not (3); **prohibere** to prevent (4); **cum** when (5); **possis** you can, are able (6); **et** and (9); **qui** (he) who (10); **non** not (11); **prohibet**

prevents (12); **cum** when (13); **prohibere** to prevent (15); **possit** he can, is able (14); **in** in, on (17); **culpa** fault, error, blame, guilt, failure (18); **est** is (16); **aut** or (19); **jubet** orders, commands (20): "To do" and "not to prevent" when you can is the same thing; and he who does not prevent when he can prevent is in fault (or orders it).] *Law.* Committing an offense and not preventing it when one is in a position to prevent it are one and the same thing. A person who does not prevent an offense when he is in a position to do so is blameworthy (or does the same as a person who orders the offense). See **qui non improbat, approbat.**

idem est nihil dicere, et insufficienter dicere. [L. **idem** the same (7); **est** is (6); **nihil** nothing (2); **dicere** to say (1); **et** and (3); **insufficienter** insufficiently, inadequately (5); **dicere** to say (4): To say nothing and to say it insufficiently is the same.] *Law.* Saying nothing and saying it insufficiently are one and the same thing. Applicable to prisoner's plea.

idem est non esse, et non apparere. [L. **idem** the same (7); **est** it is (6); **non** not (1); **esse** to exist, be (2); **et** and (3); **non** not (4); **apparere** to appear (5): Not to exist and not to appear is the same.] *Law.* Not to exist and not to appear are one and the same thing; i.e., facts not appearing during proceedings are regarded as nonexistent. See **de non** etc. and **quod non apparet** etc.

idem est non probari et non esse; non deficit jus, sed probatio. [L. **idem** the same (7); **est** is (6); **non** not (1); **probari** to be proved (2); **et** and (3); **non** not (4); **esse** to be, exist (5); **non** not (9); **deficit** fails, is wanting (10); **jus** right, law (8); **sed** but (11); **probatio** proof (12): Not to be proved and not to exist is the same; the law does not fail, but proof.] *Law.* Something which is not proved and something which does not exist are one and the same thing. The fault is not with the law but with the proof.

idem est scire aut scire debere aut potuisse. [L. **idem** the same (3); **est** is (2); **scire** to know (1); **aut** either (4); **scire** to know (8); **debere** to be under obligation, be bound (5); **aut** or (6); **potuisse** to have been able (7): To know is the same as either to be under obligation or to have been able to know.] *Law.* Either being under obligation to know or being able to know is the same as knowing.

idem per idem *n.* [L. **idem** the same (1); **per** through (2); **idem** the same (3): the same through the same.] A kind of illustration which makes no real addition to the determination of the question under consideration.

idem quod *abbr.* **I.Q.** or **i.q.** *pron.* [L. **idem** the same (1); **quod** which, as (2): the same as.] The same as. Namely.

idem sonans *adj.* [L. **idem** the same (2); **sonans** sounding (1): sounding the same.] *Law.* Of the same sound. Applicable to a rule that the wrong spelling of a material word but with the same sound as the intended

word in a document by no means invalidates the instrument; e.g., Mohammed for Muhammad. —*v.* To sound the same. *When we let in direct evidence of intent on the question of who or what is meant by a proper name, I still stick to my old explanation that by the theory of speech the proper name means only one person or thing though it may idem sonans with another proper name . . .* (per J. Holmes, Holmes-Pollock Letters 1941 Vol. 1:90, quoted by Megarry 1955:264). Cf. **falsa demonstratio non nocet.**

idem velle atque idem nolle, ea demum firma amicitia est. Sallust (86–34 B.C.). *Catiline* 20. [L. **idem** the same (thing) (2); **velle** to wish, desire (1); **atque** and (3); **idem** the same (thing) (5); **nolle** not to wish, desire (4); **ea** that (6); **demum** indeed, certainly, in fact (7); **firma** true, lasting, enduring (9); **amicitia** friendship (10); **est** is (8): To desire the same thing and not to desire the same thing that, indeed, is true friendship.] Having the same desires and the same dislikes—that, indeed, is true friendship.

id est *abbr.* **i.e.** [L. **id** that (1); **est** is (2): that is.] That is to say.

id genus omne [L. **id** it, that (2); **genus** kind, class, sort, race, species (3); **omne** all (1): all that kind.] All that sort.

idioglossia *n., pl.* **idioglossias** [Neo-Gk. from Gk. **idio(s)** peculiar, personal, one's own (1); **gloss(a)** tongue, language (2): of peculiar or distinct language.] Such poor pronunciation of words that one seems to be using a language which is known to no one other than the speaker. Cf. **idiolalia.**

idiolalia *n., pl.* **idiolalias** [Neo-Gk. from Gk. **idio(s)** peculiar, personal, one's own (1); **lalia** talk, chat (2): peculiar talk.] **Idioglossia** (q.v.).

idiot savant *n., pl.* **idiots savants** or **idiot savants** [Fr. **idiot** idiot (2); **savant** learned, skillful (1): learned idiot.] A person who, generally, is mentally deficient but is inexplicably brilliant in one particular field.

I.D.N. *abbr.* for **in Dei nomine** (q.v.).

idoneus homo *n., pl.* **idonei homines** [L. **idoneus** suitable, capable, responsible (1); **homo** person, human being (2): a suitable/ responsible person.] *Civil and Common Law.* A solvent or responsible person. A lawful and upright person.

id possumus quod de jure possumus. [L. **id** that (2); **possumus** we can (1); **quod** which (3); **de** of, from, about, for (4); **jure** right, law (5); **possumus** we can (6): We can do that which from law we can do.] We are permitted to do that which we are lawfully permitted to do.

id quod erat demonstrandum *abbr.* **I.Q.E.D.** [L. **id** that (1); **quod** which (2); **erat** was (3); **demonstrandum** to be proved, established (4): that which was to be proved.] *Mathematics* and *Logic.* That which had to be proved.

id quod nostrum est sine facto nostro ad alium transferri non potest. [L. **id** that (1); **quod** which

(2); **nostrum** ours (4); **est** is (3); **sine** without (10); **facto** deed, act, fact (12); **nostro** our (11); **ad** to, at, for, according to (8); **alium** another (9); **transferri** to be transferred (7); **non** not (6); **potest** can, is able (5): That which is ours cannot be transferred to another without our action.] *Law.* What is ours cannot be transferred to another person without our action. See **quod meum est** etc.

id solum nostrum quod debitis deductis nostrum est. [L. **id** that (1); **solum** alone (2); **nostrum** ours (3); **quod** which (4); **debitis** with debts (7); **deductis** (with) having been deducted, subtracted (8); **nostrum** ours (6); **est** is (5): That alone is ours which is ours, with the debts having been deducted.] *Law.* What is solely ours is what is ours after debts have been deducted.

i.e. *abbr.* for **id est** (q.v.).

Iesus Christus *var.* of **Jesus Christus** (q.v.).

Iesus Hominum Salvator *abbr.* **I.H.S.** *var.* of **Jesus Hominum Salvator** (q.v.).

Iesus Mundi Salvator *abbr.* **I.M.S.** *var.* of **Jesus Mundi Salvator** (q.v.).

Iesus Salvator Mundi *abbr.* **I.S.M.** *var.* of **Jesus Salvator Mundi** (q.v.).

igloo *n., pl.* **igloos** [Inuit house.] A temporary Inuit dwelling, usually dome-shaped and made out of packed snow.

ign. *abbr.* for **ignotus** (q.v.).

ignis fatuus *n., pl.* **ignes fatui** [L. **ignis** fire (2); **fatuus** foolish, silly (1): foolish fire.] Will-of-the-wisp. 1. A phosphorescent light which appears sometimes in the night, usually in marshy places. 2. A deceptive ideal, purpose, goal or objective. Something that is deceptive or misleading. *Anybody who is looking for the ignis fatuus of a marriage without disagreements is obviously not ready for wedlock.*

ignoramus *n., pl.* **ignoramuses** [L. We are ignorant. We do not know.] 1. *Law.* An endorsement which in former times a grand jury wrote on a bill of indictment when it deemed the accusation groundless or the evidence inadequate to support the accusation. No bill. Not a true bill. 2. A very ignorant person. Dunce. *Though Mr. Smith is an ignoramus, he puts on the airs of a learned and erudite person.*

ignorantia eorum quae quis scire tenetur non excusat. [L. **ignorantia** ignorance (1); **eorum** of those (things) (2); **quae** which (3); **quis** one (4); **scire** to know (6); **tenetur** is bound, obligated (5); **non** not (7); **excusat** excuses (8): Ignorance of those things which one is bound to know does not excuse.] *Law.* Ignorance of what one must know is not an excuse.

ignorantia facti *n.* [L. **ignorantia** ignorance (1); **facti** of deed, act, fact (2): ignorance of fact.] *Law.* Ignorance of a material fact. See **regula est** etc.

ignorantia facti excusat. [L. **ignorantia** ignorance (1); **facti** of deed, act, fact (2); **excusat** excuses (3): Ignorance of the fact excuses.] *Law.* Contracts made and things done when one is ignorant of a material fact are invalid. See **regula est** etc.

ignorantia facti excusat; ignorantia juris non excusat. [L. **ignorantia** ignorance (1); **facti** of fact (2); **excusat** excuses (3); **ignorantia** ignorance (4); **juris** of right, law (5); **non** not (6); **excusat** excuses (7): Ignorance of fact excuses; ignorance of law does not excuse.] *Law.* Ignorance of fact is a good excuse, but ignorance of the law is no valid excuse. See **regula est** etc. Cf. **lex succurrit ignoranti.**

ignorantia judicis foret calamitas innocentis. [L. **ignorantia** ignorance (1); **judicis** of judge (2); **foret** would be (3); **calamitas** disaster, calamity (4); **innocentis** of the innocent (5): Ignorance of a judge would be a disaster of the innocent.] *Law.* Ignorance on the part of the judge would be a disaster for the innocent.

ignorantia juris haud excusat. [L. **ignorantia** ignorance (1); **juris** of right, law (2); **haud** not, by no means (3); **excusat** excuses (4): Ignorance of the law by no means excuses.] *Law.* Ignorance of the law is not a valid excuse. See **regula est** etc.

ignorantia juris neminem excusat. [L. **ignorantia** ignorance (1); **juris** of right, law (2); **neminem** no one, nobody (4); **excusat** excuses (3): Ignorance of the law excuses nobody.] *Law.* No one is excused from the law because of ignorance. See **regula est** etc.

ignorantia juris non excusat. [L. **ignorantia** ignorance (1); **juris** of right, law (2); **non** not (3); **excusat** excuses (4): Ignorance of the law does not excuse.] *Law.* Ignorance of the law is no excuse. See **regula est** etc.

ignorantia juris quod quisque scire tenetur non excusat. [L. **ignorantia** ignorance (1); **juris** of right, law (2); **quod** which (3); **quisque** each one (4); **scire** to know (6); **tenetur** is bound, under obligation (5); **non** not (7); **excusat** excuses (8): Ignorance of the law which each one is bound to know does not excuse.] *Law.* Ignorance of a/the law which everyone is bound to know is no valid excuse. See **regula est** etc.

ignorantia juris quod quisque tenetur scire, neminem excusat. [L. **ignorantia** ignorance (1); **juris** of right, law (2); **quod** which (3); **quisque** each one (4); **tenetur** is bound, under obligation (5); **scire** to know (6); **neminem** nobody, no one (8); **excusat** excuses (7): Ignorance of a/the law which everybody is bound to know excuses nobody.] *Law.* Ignorance of a law which everyone is bound to know does not excuse anyone. See **regula est** etc.

ignorantia juris sui non praejudicat juri. [L. **ignorantia** ignorance (1); **juris** (of) right, law (3); **sui** of one's (2); **non** not (5); **praejudicat** prejudices (4); **juri** right, law (6): Ignorance of one's right does not prejudice the right.] *Law.* Ignorance of one's right is not detrimental to the right.

ignorantia lectionis et linguae *n.* [L. **ignorantia** ignorance (1); **lectionis** of reading (2); **et** and (3); **linguae** of language (4): ignorance of reading and of language.] *Law.* Ignorance of written and spoken language.

ignorantia legis neminem excusat. [L. **ignorantia** ignorance (1); **legis** of law (2); **neminem** nobody, no one (4); **excusat** excuses (3): Ignorance of the law excuses no one.] *Law.* Ignorance of the law does not excuse anybody. See **regula est** etc.

ignorantia legis non excusat. [L. **ignorantia** ignorance (1); **legis** of law (2); **non** not (3); **excusat** excuses (4): Ignorance of the law does not excuse.] *Law.* Ignorance of the law is no excuse. See **regula est** etc.

ignorantia praesumitur ubi scientia non probatur. [L. **ignorantia** ignorance (1); **praesumitur** is presumed (2); **ubi** where, when (3); **scientia** knowledge (4); **non** not (5); **probatur** is proved (6): Ignorance is presumed when knowledge is not proved.] *Law.* Ignorance is presumed where there is no proof of knowledge.

ignorare legis est lata culpa. [L. **ignorare** to be ignorant (1); **legis** of law (2); **est** is (3); **lata** gross, serious (4); **culpa** fault, error, blame, guilt, failure (5): To be ignorant of the law is serious fault/neglect.] *Law.* Ignorance of the law is a serious fault. See **culpa lata.**

ignoratio elenchi *n.* [L. **ignoratio** ignorance (1); **elenchi** of proof (2): ignorance of proof.] 1. *Logic.* Ignorance of proof. A fallacy which involves supposing that by arguing to settle a different issue, one has settled the point at issue. 2. An argument which is irrelevant.

ignotum per ignotius *n.* [L. **ignotum** unknown, unfamiliar (thing) (1); **per** through (2); **ignotius** more unknown or unfamiliar (thing) (3): unknown thing through the more unknown thing.] The unknown through the more unknown. Attempting to explain what is unknown by making reference to what is even more unknown. *He is an incompetent teacher who usually confuses students by resorting to ignotum per ignotius.* Cf. **obscurum per obscurius.**

I.H. or **i.h.** *abbr.* for **iacet hic** (q.v.).

ihram *n.* [Ar. **'ihrām** prohibited.] *Islam.* 1. The state of personal preparation and self-denial, including sexual abstinence, during a pilgrimage. 2. The double piece of cotton clothing worn by such a pilgrim.

IHS *abbr. for* **Iesous** [Gk. **Iēsous** from Heb. **Jehosua** or **Joshua** God is salvation.] Jesus. The capital letter "H" represents the Greek capital letter eta.

ikebana *n.* [Japan. from **ikeru** to arrange (2); **hana** flower (1): flower arranging.] The Japanese art of floral arranging.

Il connaît l'univers et ne se connaît pas. Jean de la Fontaine (1621–1695). *Fables* 8. [Fr. **il** he (1); **connait** knows (2); **l'** the (3); **univers** world, universe (4); **et** and (5); **ne . . . pas** not (7); **se** himself (8); **connaît** knows (6): He knows the world and does

not know himself.] He knows the world but does not know himself. See **gnothi seauton.**

Il Duce *n.* [It. **il** the (1); **duce** leader (2): the leader.] The Dictator. Benito Mussolini's title. . . . *"Mussolini the Social Fascist," a full-length study that portrays Il Duce as a pioneering socialist (Newsweek Int.* Aug. 1, 1983:21). Cf. **Duce.**

Il faut cultiver notre jardin. Voltaire (1694–1778). *Candide* 30. [Fr. **il** it (1); **faut** is necessary (2); **cultiver** to farm, cultivate, till (3); **notre** our (4); **jardin** garden (5): It is necessary to till our garden.] We must till (or cultivate) our own garden; i.e., we must tend to our own affairs.

il gran rifiuto Dante Alighieri (1265–1321). *Inferno* III,60. [It. **il** the (1); **gran** great, large (2); **rifiuto** refusal, denial (3): the great refusal.] The great denial. Cf. **gran refiuto.**

illicitum collegium *n., pl.* **illicita collegia** [L. **illicitum** illegal, illicit (1); **collegium** corporation, association (2): an illegal corporation.] An organization operating illegally. *The illicitum collegium had no business complaining about the fraud committed by its accountant.*

illi mors gravis incubat / qui notus nimis omnibus / ignotus moritur sibi. Seneca "The Younger" (c.4 B.C.–65 A.D.). *Thyestes* 401–403. [L. **illi** that person (4); **mors** death (3); **gravis** heavy, burdensome (1); **incubat** lies upon, rests on (2); **qui** who (5); **notus** known (6); **nimis** too much, excessively (7); **omnibus** to all (8); **ignotus** unknown (10); **moritur** dies (9); **sibi** to himself/herself (11): Heavy lies death upon that person / who, known too much to all, / dies unknown to himself/herself.] Death lies heavily upon him/her who, though known too much to all others, dies unknown to himself/herself. See **gnothi seauton.**

illud quod alias licitum non est necessitas facit licitum; et necessitas inducit privilegium quoad jura privata. [L. **illud** that (1); **quod** which (2); **alias** at other times, otherwise (3); **licitum** permitted, lawful, allowed (6); **non** not (5); **est** is (4); **necessitas** necessity (7); **facit** makes (8); **licitum** permitted, lawful (9); **et** and (10); **necessitas** compulsion, urgency, necessity (11); **inducit** introduces (12); **privilegium** a special enactment, privilege (13); **quoad** as far as (14); **jura** rights, laws (16); **privata** private (15): That which at other times is not lawful compulsion makes lawful; and compulsion introduces a privilege as far as private rights.] *Law.* Necessity makes lawful what otherwise is unlawful; and necessity introduces a privilege as far as private rights are concerned. See **necessitas quod** etc.

illuminati *n., sing.* **illuminato** [It. the illuminated or lighted.] Those who are, or claim to be, exceptionally enlightened.

Il Maestro *n.* [It. **il** the (1); **maestro** master, great artist (2): the master.] The great artist. *His film-making* prowess has earned [Federico Fellini] *the sobriquet "Il Maestro"*... (*Newsweek Int.* March 12, 1979:57). See **maestro.**

Il ne faut pas être plus royaliste que le roi. [Fr. **il** it (1); **ne** . . . **pas** not (3); **faut** is necessary (2); **être** to be (4); **plus** more (5); **royaliste** royalist (6); **que** than (7); **le** the (6); **roi** king (9): It is necessary not to be more royalist than the king.] One should not be more royalist than the king. See **plus royaliste que** etc.

Il Papa *n.* [It. **il** the (1); **Papa** Pope (2): the Pope.] The Pope. The Supreme Pontiff of the Roman Catholic Church. *After declaring his joy at being back at the altar of St. Peter's, Il Papa exuberantly descended into the square to bless his flock* (*Newsweek Int.* Oct. 19, 1981:55).

Il Trovatore *n.* [It. **il** the (1); **trovatore** troubadour, strolling minstrel (2): the troubadour.] "The Troubadour," an 1853 opera by Giuseppe Verdi (1813–1901). Cf. **troubadour.**

imago *n., pl.* **imagines** or **imagoes** [L. image, conception, idea, copy, representation.] 1. A mature, adult, sexually developed insect. 2. *Psychology.* a) An idealized concept of a parent formed in infancy and retained in the unconscious mind during adulthood. b) An idealized conception of anybody, including oneself.

imam or **Imam** *n., pl.* **imams** or **Imams** [Ar. **imām** leader.] *Islam.* Any one of a number of religious, political, or intellectual leaders in an Islamic community.

imbroglio or **embroglio** *n., pl.* **imbroglios** or **embroglios** [It. mess, muddle.] 1. A pile of disorganized material. *He is an untidy official whose desk is always filled with an imbroglio of files, papers, letters, pamphlets and books.* 2. A state of affairs which is difficult, complicated, and confusing or one which causes embarassment, misunderstanding, or argument. *The Syrian ambassador in Britain, who was sent packing in the British-Syrian imbroglio* . . . (*The Guardian* 1986).

Imitatio Christi [L. **imitatio** imitation (1); **Christi** of Christ (2): imitation of Christ.] *Imitation of Christ*, a religious treatise by Thomas à Kempis (1380-1471).

immeubles *pl. n.* [Fr. immovable or fixed things.] *French Law.* **Res immobiles** (q.v.). **Bona immobilia** (q.v.). Property regarded as immovable. There are three kinds: things which by their very nature cannot be moved, such as landed property or real estate; things which by their purpose or destination are not to be removed from the property (e.g., agricultural implements and other things supplied by the landlord); and things which are annexed to something else and so cannot be detached or moved away (e.g., easements). Cf. **biens meubles.**

immobilia situm sequuntur. [L. **immobilia** immovable (things) (1); **situm** site, position, location (3); **sequuntur** follow (2): immovable things follow the location.] *Law.* Immovable things follow their

position/location; i.e., immovable things belong to the place where they are found.

Immortalis Dei Auspicio *abbr.* **I.D.A.** [L. **immortalis** of immortal (2); **Dei** (of) God (3); **Auspicio** by the guidance, will (1): by the will of immortal God.] By the guidance or will of immortal God.

imp. *abbr.* for **imperator** (q.v.) or **imprimatur** (q.v.).

impasse *n., pl.* **impasses** [Fr. blind alley, dilemma, deadlock.] 1. A blind alley. A dead end. 2. A deadlock. An apparently insoluble problem. A difficulty for which there is no easy solution or escape. a) *An independent state . . . is the one and only solution I will accept to the Palestinian impasse* (*Time Int.*1980). b) *By the time Daniel left the office of the Director, they had reached an impasse, as the latter seemed either unable or unwilling to correct a glaring mistake.* Cf. **cul-de-sac.**

impedimenta *pl. n.* [L. hindrances, impediments.] An obstacle to the completion of a task or journey. Traveling equipment. Luggage. *The tired traveler happily deposited all his impedimenta at the residence of his friend, giving instructions that his children would come to collect them.*

imperator *abbr.* **I.** or **imp.** *n., pl.* **imperators** [L. commander, general, emperor.] Emperor. Commander. General. Supreme leader.

imperatrix *abbr.* **I.** or **impx.** *n., pl.* **imperatrices** [L. female commander or general, empress.] Empress.

imperio rationis *adv.* [L. **imperio** with command, order (1); **rationis** of reason (2): with command of reason.] With the command of reason. Listening to the voice of reason. *Admittedly, the actions of men in authoritative positions are governed by regulations, but sometimes they must act with discretion and imperio rationis.*

imperitia culpae adnumeratur. [L. **imperitia** inexperience, ignorance (1); **culpae** blame, fault (3); **adnumeratur** is reckoned, counted with (2): Inexperience is counted with a fault.] Inexperience (or lack of skill) is considered to be a fault. *The rule imperitia culpae adnumeratur is just as true in English law as in Roman law* (Rogers 1975:62).

imperium *n., pl.* **imperia** or **imperiums** [L. supreme authority, command, empire.] 1. Absolute/supreme power, especially over a large area. Empire. The territory/area over which supreme power or regulatory control is exercised. *The British can never forget their glorious days when they exercised imperium over vast portions of the world.* 2. Regulatory control or powers. *After the suit, he relinquished every imperium over the disputed land.* 3. The right to command. The right of jurisdiction. Sovereignty. Executive power. *The Head of State exercises imperium over the entire country.* 4. *Roman Law.* Imperium also means the power to hear cases and deliver judgments.

imperium in imperio *n.* [L. **imperium** power, government, sovereignty (1); **in** in, on (2); **imperio**

power, government, sovereignty (3): power in power.] Government in government. Power within power. Sovereignty within sovereignty. *A state in a federal republic is, so to speak, an imperium in imperio.*

impetitio vasti *n.* [L. **impetitio** impeachment (1); **vasti** of waste (2): impeachment of waste.] *Law.* Impeachment for abuse, destruction, deterioration, mismanagement, alteration, etc. of estate, houses, land, garden, etc. by a tenant or a person rightfully in charge of the property.

impetus *n., pl.* **impetus** or **impetuses** [L. assault, attack.] 1. A driving force. *Security agents are trying to determine the impetus behind the organization whose clandestine activities are under investigation.* 2. Incentive. Encouragement. *The student's poor performance is attributable to lack of impetus to study.*

imponderabilia *pl. n.* [L. unweighable, imponderable things.] Imponderables. Issues, factors or considerations which cannot be weighed or evaluated. *The question hinged on various imponderabilia.*

impossibilium nulla obligatio est. [L. **impossibilium** of impossible (things) (4); **nulla** no (2); **obligatio** obligation (3); **est** there is (1): There is no obligation of impossible things.] *Law.* No one is obliged to do the impossible. See **impotentia excusat legem.**

impotentia coeundi *n.* [L. **impotentia** inability, weakness (1); **coeundi** of associating, combining (2): inability of associating.] *Medicine.* Inability to have sexual intercourse. Difficulty in having sexual intercourse. See **anaphrodisia.**

impotentia excusat legem. [L. **impotentia** helplessness, impossibility (1); **excusat** excuses (2); **legem** law (3): Helplessness excuses law.] *Law.* Impossibility of satisfying an obligation imposed by a law is a valid excuse. Where a party through no fault on his/her part cannot perform an obligation imposed by the law, he/she is generally excused by the law. See **À l'impossible** etc.; **argumentum ab impossibili plurimum** etc.; **argumentum ab impossibili valet** etc.; **casus fortuitus** etc.; **impossibilium nulla** etc.; **lex neminem cogit ad** etc.; **lex nil frustra jubet; lex non cogit** etc.; **lex non intendit** etc.; **lex non praecipit** etc.; **nemo tenetur ad impossibile;** and **quod vanum** etc.

impotentia generandi *n.* [L. **impotentia** inability, weakness (1); **generandi** of procreating, reproducing (2): inability for procreating.] *Medicine.* Inability to reproduce. Applicable to both men and women. See **agenesia.** Cf. **anaphrodisia.**

impresa *n., pl.* **impresas** [It. undertaking.] A family or personal standard or emblem, usually consisting of symbolic images and a motto.

impresario *n., pl.* **impresari** or **impresarios** [It. one who undertakes.] 1. Producer, manager, director or conductor. 2. A promoter. One who handles the business transactions of a performer, singer, musical

group, a concert company, an opera, etc. *Behind every great rock star stands a great impresario. Elvis had the Colonel, and the Beatles had Brian Epstein . . .* (*Newsweek Int.* June 22, 1981:51).

imprimatur *abbr.* **imp.** *n., pl.* **imprimaturs** [L. Let it be printed, marked, stamped.] 1. A license or permission granted by some countries and churches, and especially by the Roman Catholic Church, for printing or publishing a book. Approval of publication in countries where there is censorship. 2. A publisher's name and address as well as date of the book's publication often placed at the bottom of the title page. 3. Approval. Sanction. Mark of approval. a) *. . . the film's bold imprimatur of colonialism* (H.O. Ekwuazi in *West Africa* 1985). b) *And the project had the imprimatur of mighty* Time Inc. *. . .* (*Newsweek Int.* May 16, 1983:15).

imprimis *adv.* [L. with the first (things).] Among the first.

impromptu *adj.* [Fr. without preparation.] Done, arranged, formed, improvised, composed, spoken, etc. without previous preparation, on the spur of the moment, hastily, extemporaneously, offhand. a) *An impromptu meeting was convened to discuss the unexpected emergency.* b) *The President held an impromptu news conference.* —*adv.* Extemporaneously. On the spur of the moment. Without previous preparation, study, rehearsal, consideration, etc. *His brilliance, intelligence, and erudition are manifested by his ability to lecture impromptu on a wide range of topics.* —*n., pl.* **impromptus** 1. Something done, arranged, formed, said, composed, etc. without preparation, on the spur of the moment, extemporaneously, hastily, offhand. 2. *Music.* A short composition, especially for the piano, which is intended to give the impression of being an improvisation. *This humorous impromptu was misconstrued as a mark of perverseness.* —*v. tr.* To improvise. To do, arrange, form, say or compose on the spur of the moment.

impunitas semper ad deteriora invitat. [L. **impunitas** lack of punishment, impunity (1); **semper** always (2); **ad** to, at, for, according to (4); **deteriora** worse (things) (5); **invitat** invites (3): Lack of punishment always invites to worse things.] Impunity always serves as an invitation to commit worse crimes. See **interest reipublicae ne** etc.; **maleficia non debent** etc.; **minatur innocentibus** etc.; **spes impunitatis** etc.; and **ut poena** etc. Cf. **qui parcit nocentibus** etc.

impx. *abbr.* for **imperatrix** (q.v.).

I.M.S. *abbr.* for **Iesus Mundi Salvator** (q.v.).

in absentia *abbr.* **I.A.** or **i.a.** *adv.* [L. **in** in, on (1); **absentia** absence (2): in absence.] During absence. When/though absent. *The fugitive who was charged with the theft of a colossal sum of state funds was sentenced to fifteen years' imprisonment in absentia.*

in abstracto *adv.* [L. **in** in, on (1); **abstracto** the abstract (2): in the abstract.] From/in the abstract point of view. *The disputant insisted that the question could not be settled in abstracto.*

in actu *adv.* [L. **in** in, on (1); **actu** act, deed (2): in deed.] In reality. In application. *Theoretically, the concept is practical; in actu, I am less certain.*

in adversum *adj./adv.* [L. **in** in, to, against, for (1); **adversum** hostile, adverse (person) (2): against a hostile person.] Against an unwilling, hostile, or adverse person. Done without consent.

in aemulationem vicini or in emulationem vicini *adj./adv.* [L. **in** into, to, against, for (1); **aemulationem** rivalry, competition (2); **vicini** of neighbor (3): in rivalry of a neighbor.] *Law.* In dislike of a neighbor. In hatred of a neighbor. In envy of a neighbor. An act done in aemulationem vicini is one done with the sole purpose of hurting another person.

in aequali jure *adv.* [L. **in** in, on (1); **aequali** equal (2); **jure** right, law (3): in equal right.] In equal justice.

in aequali jure melior est conditio possidentis. [L. **in** in, on (1); **aequali** equal (2); **jure** right, law (3); **melior** better (7); **est** is (6); **conditio** condition (4); **possidentis** of the one possessing (5): In equal right the condition of the one possessing is better.] *Law.* In matters relating to equal right, the condition of the party in possession of the disputed object is better; i.e., possession by itself is adequate title and suffices against anybody who does not have a better title. Possession is nine tenths of the law. See **cum de lucro** etc.; **cum par delictum** etc.; **favorabiliores rei** etc.; **in pari causa possessor** etc.; **in pari delicto, potior est conditio possidentis**; **melior est conditio possidentis, ubi** etc.; **melior est conditio possidentis, et rei** etc.; **non possessori** etc.; **potior est conditio defendentis**; **potior est conditio possidentis**; and **quum de lucro** etc.

in aequali manu *adv.* [**in** in, on (1); **aequali** equal (2); **manu** hand (3): in equal hand.] *Law.* In the possession of an impartial party. *If parties to an instrument deposit it with a third person to be kept on certain conditions, the instrument is described as being held in aequali manu.*

in aeternum *adv.* [L. **in** into, to, against, for (1); **aeternum** perpetuity (2): into/for perpetuity.] For ever. *A bequest under a will is meant to benefit the donee in aeternum.*

in alieno solo *adv.* [L. **in** in, on (1); **alieno** of another, another's (2); **solo** ground, soil, land (3): in the land of another.] On another's land. *An unlawful activity in alieno solo may lead to a charge of trespass.*

in alio loco *adv.* [L. **in** in, on (1); **alio** another (2); **loco** place (3): in another place.] In a different location. *The court was informed by the prosecution that the accused person committed a similar offense in alio loco.*

in alta proditione nullus potest esse accessorius sed principalis solummodo. [L. **in** in, on (1); **alta** high (2); **proditione** treason (3); **nullus** no (one) (6); **potest** there can, is able (4); **esse** to be (5); **accessorius** accessory (7); **sed** but (8); **principalis** principal (10); **solummodo** only (9): In high treason no one can be accessory but only principal.] *Law.* In cases of high treason, there can be no accessory but only a principal.

in ambiguis orationibus maxime sententia spectanda est ejus qui eas protulisset. [L. **in** in, on (1); **ambiguis** ambiguous, doubtful (2); **orationibus** speeches, expressions (3); **maxime** especially, particularly (10); **sententia** purpose (4); **spectanda** to be considered (11); **est** is (9); **ejus** of him/her, the one (5); **qui** who (6); **eas** them (8); **protulisset** had published, uttered (7): In ambiguous expressions the purpose of the one who had uttered them is especially to be considered.] In ambiguous expressions we should consider, first and foremost, the purpose of the person who uttered them.

in ambiguo *adv.* [L. **in** in, on (1); **ambiguo** doubt, uncertainty (2): in doubt.] With misgivings. In uncertainty. *The prosecutor sought an adjournment in the case because he found himself in ambiguo.* See **in dubio**.

inamorato or *fem.* inamorata *n., pl.* inamoratos or *fem.* inamoratas [It. **innamorato** one inspired with love.] A lover. A person with whom one is in love. A person with whom one has an intimate affair. A sweetheart.

inane *adj.* [L. empty, void, worthless, useless.] 1. Insubstantial. Empty. *She disappeared into inane space.* 2. Silly. Insignificant. Empty. Shallow. Senseless. *Ben either made no contributions to the deliberations of the committee or made inane comments.*

inane nomen *n.* [L. **inane** empty, useless, worthless (1); **nomen** name (2): an empty name.] An empty, useless, or worthless name. An empty title. *On the surface, he is the head of the unit but, in reality, it is an inane nomen, for he has no power of initiative or discretion, being merely a puppet under remote control by unscrupulous potentates.*

in antis *n.* [L. **in** in, on (1); **antis** rows (2): in rows.] *Architecture.* A building style, popular in 19th-century England, in which a colonnade is created by extending the side walls out beyond the front wall.

in aperta luce *adv.* [L. **in** in, on (1); **aperta** open, clear, unclouded (2); **luce** light (3): in clear light.] In broad daylight. In the daytime. *The bank robbery took place in aperta luce.*

in arbitrium judicis *adv.* [L. **in** into, to, against, for (1); **arbitrium** judgment, decision, opinion (2); **judicis** of judge (3): to the judgment of the judge.] To the opinion of the judge. At the pleasure/discretion of the judge.

in arcta et salva custodia *adv.* [L. **in** in, on (1); **arcta** close, confined (2); **et** and (3); **salva** safe (4); **custodia** custody (5): in close and safe custody.] Under secure confinement and protection. *The judge ordered that the unruly accused person be placed in arcta et salva custodia.* See **arcta et** etc.

in articulo *adv.* [L. **in** in, on (1); **articulo** joint, moment, point of division (2): in the moment.] In a moment. Straightaway. Immediately. In the nick of time.

in articulo mortis *adv.* [L. **in** in, on (1); **articulo** joint, moment, point of division (2); **mortis** of death (3): in the moment of death.] At the point of death. a) *When visitors went to visit the chief, he appeared to be in articulo mortis.* b) *Musa's father distributed his properties, when he was in articulo mortis.* See **in extremis**.

in atrocioribus delictis punitur affectus licet non sequatur effectus. [L. **in** in, on (1); **atrocioribus** more serious, horrible, terrible (2); **delictis** crimes (3); **punitur** is punished (5); **affectus** disposition, intention (4); **licet** even if, although (6); **non** not (8); **sequatur** follows (9); **effectus** result, effect (7): In more horrible crimes the intention is punished even if the result does not follow.] *Law.* The intention to commit a more serious crime is punished even if the result does not follow. See **actus non facit** etc.

in autre droit *adv.* [Obs. Fr. **in** in, on (1); **autre** another (2); **droit** right (3): in another right.] *Law.* In another's right. In the right of another person. As a representative of another person. Applicable to executors, administrators, trustees, etc. See **autre droit**.

in banc *adv.* [Obs. Fr. **in** in, on (1); **banc** bench, court (2): in the bench.] On the bench. **En banc** (q.v.). *At Common law, serjeants had an exclusive right of audience in the Court of Common Pleas during term time, while sitting in banc* (Megarry 1973:23.).

in banco *adv.* [L. **in** in, on (1); **banco** bench (2): on the bench.] *Law.* While on the judicial bench.

in bonam partem *adv.* [L. **in** into, to, against, for (1); **bonam** good (2); **partem** side, part (3): into (or for) the good part.] In a favorable manner. To the advantage. *In case of ambiguity or doubt, the evidence should be interpreted in bonam partem of the accused.* See **in bona parte**. Cf. **in mala parte**.

in bona parte *adv.* [L. **in** in, on (1); **bona** good (2); **parte** side, part (3): in the good part.] **In bonam partem** (q.v.).

in bonis defuncti *adv.* [**in** in, on (1); **bonis** goods, property (2); **defuncti** of the deceased (3): in the property of the deceased.] Among the goods or belongings of the dead person. *In bonis defuncti were many things which were actually the property of various friends and relations.*

I.N.C. *abbr.* for **in nomine Christi** (q.v.).

in camera *adv./adj.* [L. **in** in, on (1); **camera** chamber (2): in chamber.] *Law.* In chambers. In private. A case is heard in camera when the judge either conducts the proceedings in his private room or gets the door of the court closed and allows only those connected with the case to remain. Cases are heard in camera to prevent publicity either in the public interest or if the nature of the proceedings demands it.

incapax copulandi *adj.* [L. **incapax** incapable (1); **copulandi** of coupling, uniting (2): incapable of coupling.] Incapable of having sexual intercourse.

incapax procreandi *adj.* [L. **incapax** incapable (1); **procreandi** of bringing forth, producing (2): incapable of producing.] Incapable of producing children. a) *According to the medical officer, Sam is incapax procreandi.* b) *The root cause of the perennial squabbles in the Blankson family is Mrs. Blankson's belief that her husband is incapax procreandi.*

in capita *adv./adj.* [L. **in** into, to, against, for (1); **capita** heads (2): to the heads.] By polls. Individually. *Distribution in capita is equal distribution among individuals.*

in capite *adj.* [L. **in** in, on (1); **capite** head (2): in head.] In chief. Applicable to feudal tenants who derive tenure directly from the Crown or the Lord.

in casu extremae necessitatis omnia sunt communia. [L. **in** in, on (1); **casu** case, event (2); **extremae** of extreme, utmost (3); **necessitatis** (of) compulsion, urgency, necessity (4); **omnia** all (things), everything (5); **sunt** are (6); **communia** common (7): In case of extreme compulsion all things are common.] *Law.* In the case of extreme necessity all things are common, i.e., public, property. In times of crisis/disaster a private property can become public property and used without liability for trespassing. For instance, in time of war a house may be pulled down, if the defense of the state so demands. Also, if a highway is impassable, a person may lawfully use adjoining land. See **jura publica** etc.; **Le salut** etc.; **lex citius** etc.; **lex necessitatis** etc.; **necessitas est** etc.; **necessitas publica** etc.; **privatum commodum** etc.; **privatum incommodum** etc.; **privilegium non valet** etc.; **salus populi** etc.; and **salus publica** etc. Cf. **nemo cogitur rem** etc.

In Catilinam *n.* [L. **in** into, against (1); **Catilinam** Catiline (2): against Catiline.] *Against Catiline,* a series of four speeches addressed by Cicero (106–43 B.C.) as consul to the Roman Senate about the conspiracy of Catiline to overthrow the government in 63 B.C.

incendium aere alieno non exuit debitorem. [L. **incendium** fire, conflagration (1); **aere** from bronze, money (6); **alieno** (from) another's, foreign (5); **non** not (2); **exuit** exempts, rescues (3); **debitorem** debtor (4): Fire does not exempt a debtor from another's money.] *Law.* Fire loss does not rescue a debtor from debt obligations.

incertae sedis *adj./adv.* [L. **incertae** of uncertain (1); **sedis** (of) abode, residence, habitation (2): of uncertain abode.] Residence unknown. In an uncertain situation/ position. Applicable to **taxa** (q.v.).

incerta persona *n., pl.* **incertae personae** [L. **incerta** uncertain, doubtful (1); **persona** person (2): uncertain person.] *Law.* A person who cannot be identified or ascertained. Applicable to a corporation, a juristic person, a posthumous heir, or a person whose identity cannot be established until after the will has been executed.

incerta pro nullis habentur. [L. **incerta** uncertain (things) (1); **pro** as, for (3); **nullis** no (things) (4); **habentur** are had, held, regarded (2): Uncertain things are regarded as no things.] Uncertain things, i.e., things which are not proved, are considered as nothing.

incipit *v.* [L. It begins.] Here begins. The traditional formula for beginning a new piece of writing in Latin or a vernacular language in the medieval period.

in civilibus ministerium excusat, in criminalibus non item. [L. **in** in, on (1); **civilibus** civil (things) (2); **ministerium** service, employment (3); **excusat** excuses (4); **in** in, on (5); **criminalibus** criminal (things) (6); **non** not (7); **item** likewise (8): In civil things employment excuses, in criminal things not likewise.] *Law.* In civil cases service is a valid excuse, but it is not so in criminal cases.

in claris non est locus conjecturis. [L. **in** in, on (1); **claris** clear, manifest (things) (2); **non** not (4); **est** there is (3); **locus** room, place (5); **conjecturis** for conjectures, guesses (6): In clear things there is not room for conjectures.] *Law.* When matters are clear, there is no room for conjectures. Cf. **cum adsunt** etc.

inclusio unius est exclusio alterius. [L. **inclusio** inclusion (1); **unius** of one (2); **est** is (3); **exclusio** exclusion (4); **alterius** of the other of two (5): Inclusion of one is the exclusion of the other of two.] *Law.* The inclusion of one person/thing implies the exclusion of the other. See **designatio unius** etc.

incognito or *fem.* **incognita** *adj.* [It. unknown.] Not identified. Unknown. Concealed or hidden under a fictitious name or false identity. *The corpse remained incognito for a long time. —n., pl.* **incognitos** or *fem.* **incognitas** 1. A person who appears, lives, travels, etc. with identity concealed. 2. The state or condition of such a person. —**incognita** *neut. pl. n.* Things or places which are uncertain or unknown. —*adv.* With one's name or identity concealed. Appearing, traveling, etc. under disguise or with a fictitious name. a) *The Prime Minister, traveling incognito, arrived at Kennedy International Airport yesterday and hurriedly took a taxi to an undisclosed destination.* b) *... the prince and the actress flew incognito to the Caribbean ...* (*Newsweek Int.* Oct. 18, 1982:23).

in commendam *adv.* [L. **in** into, to, against, for (1); **commendam** trust (2): into trust.] 1. In trust. Under the management or supervision of someone without legal title. Applicable to a benefice. 2. *Louisiana.* A limited partnership. Cf. **commenda.**

in commercio *adj.* [L. **in** in, on (1); **commercio** commerce (2): in commerce.] *Roman and Civil Law.* Able to be acquired or owned privately. Subject to private ownership. See **in patrimonio.** Cf. **extra commercium** and **extra patrimonium.**

incommunicado or **incomunicado** or *fem.* **incommunicada** or **incomunicada** *adv./adj.* [Sp. not in communication.] In a condition lacking means of communication. Being kept in solitary confinement. Not being allowed to communicate with unauthorized persons. a) *... the two women were ... then taken back to the Sihala police rest house outside Rawalpindi and kept incommunicado* (*Newsweek Int.* April 16, 1979:28). b) *The abuse of Namibians' most basic human rights where detainees are forcibly imprisoned; held incommunicado; denied the right to legal representation ...* (Nicholas R. Winterton in *West Africa* 1987).

in concreto *adv.* [L. **in** in, on (1); **concreto** concrete, solid (2): in concrete.] From a concrete point of view. Concretely. Cf. **in abstracto.**

in consimili casu *adv.* [L. **in** in, on (1); **consimili** very similar (2); **casu** event, occurrence (3): in a very similar event.] In a like case. *A precedent which was set in consimili casu was applied in this particular case.*

in consimili casu, consimile debet esse remedium. [L. **in** in, on (1); **consimili** very similar (2); **casu** event, case (3); **consimile** very similar (7); **debet** ought, should (5); **esse** to be (6); **remedium** remedy (4): In a very similar case the remedy ought to be very similar.] *Law.* In a like case the remedy ought to be entirely alike. See **de similibus idem est judicium.**

in consuetudinibus, non diuturnitas temporis sed soliditas rationis est consideranda. [L. **in** in, on (1); **consuetudinibus** customs (2); **non** not (3); **diuturnitas** long duration (4); **temporis** of time (5); **sed** but (6); **soliditas** solidness, solidity (7); **rationis** of reason (8); **est** is (9); **consideranda** to be considered (10): In customs, not long duration of time but solidness of reason is to be considered.] In deciding the validity of a custom, the solidity of its reason, not its antiquity, should be considered.

in contractibus, benigna; in testamentis, benignior; in restitutionibus, benignissima interpretatio facienda est. [L. **in** in, on (1); **contractibus** contracts (2); **benigna** liberal (3); **in** in, on (7); **testamentis** wills (8); **benignior** more liberal (9); **in** in, on (10); **restitutionibus** restorations, restitutions (11); **benignissima** most liberal (12); **interpretatio** interpretation (4); **facienda** to be made (6); **est** is (5): In contracts interpretation is to be made liberal; in wills more liberal; in restitutions most liberal.] *Law.* Contracts must be interpreted liberally, wills more liberally, and restitutions most liberally.

in contractibus tacite insunt quae sunt moris et consuetudinis. [L. **in** in, on (1); **contractibus**

contracts (2); **tacite** silently, tacitly (9); **insunt** are contained in (8); **quae** (things) which (3); **sunt** are (4); **moris** of custom, usage (5); **et** and (6); **consuetudinis** of custom, usage (7): In contracts things which are of custom and usage are silently contained.] *Law.* In contracts matters of usage and custom are implied (or are deemed to be incorporated).

in contumaciam *adv.* [L. **in** into, to, against, for (1); **contumaciam** stubbornness, obstinacy (2): into obstinacy.] In disobedience to, or contempt of, a court's summons or order. The expression is mostly used in ecclesiastical law with reference to a person who ignored a court's order or summons and was consequently convicted or condemned **in absentia**.

in corpore *adv.* [L. **in** in, on (1); **corpore** body (2): in body.] In substance.

in criminalibus, probationes debent esse luce clariores. [L. **in** in, on (1); **criminalibus** criminal (things) (2); **probationes** proofs (3); **debent** ought, should (4); **esse** to be (5); **luce** than light (7); **clariores** clearer (6): In criminal things proofs should be clearer than light.] *Law.* In criminal cases proofs should be clearer than light.

in criminalibus, sufficit generalis malitia intentionis cum facto paris gradus. [L. **in** in, on (1); **criminalibus** criminal (cases) (2); **sufficit** suffices (10); **generalis** general (3); **malitia** malice (4); **intentionis** of intention (5); **cum** with (6); **facto** deed, act, fact (7); **paris** of equal (8); **gradus** (of) degree (9): In criminal cases, a general malice of intention with an act of equal degree suffices (or is sufficient).] *Law.* In criminal cases, a malicious intent to cause general harm is sufficient, even if there was no intent to cause harm to the particular person harmed. See **actus non facit** etc.

in criminalibus, voluntas reputabitur pro facto. [L. **in** in, on (1); **criminalibus** criminal (cases) (2); **voluntas** will, desire (3); **reputabitur** will be regarded, reckoned (4); **pro** as, for (5); **facto** deed, act, fact (6): In criminal cases desire will be regarded as the act/deed.] *Law.* In criminal cases the intention to perform the act will be considered the act itself. The maxim needs to be qualified. The will cannot be taken for the act until something has been done in an attempt to put it into effect. See **actus non facit** etc.

incubus *n., pl.* **incubi** or **incubuses** [L. a person who lies upon.] 1. An evil spirit which is believed to lie upon people while asleep and, in the case of women, to have sexual intercourse with them. 2. Nightmare. A person/thing which, like a nightmare, oppresses people. *After the demise of his father when he was free from the incubus of parental control, he began to achieve spectacular success in all undertakings.*

incunabulum *n., pl.* **incunabula** [L. baby clothes, cradle.] 1. The early work of an author. 2. A book

published in the early days of printing, i.e., in the late 15th-century. 3. Anything in its earliest stages of development. Cf. **ab incunabulis**.

in curia *adv.* [L. **in** in, on (1); **curia** court (2): in court.] *Law.* In open court. a) *The judge demanded an apology from the counsel in curia.* b) *The convict insulted the judge in curia.*

in custodia legis *adv./adj.* [L. **in** in, on (1); **custodia** custody (2); **legis** of law (3): in the custody of the law.] *Law.* In legal custody. Applicable to deeds, documents, the subject-matter of disputes and exhibits kept by officials of the court.

I.N.D. *abbr.* for **in nomine Dei** (q.v.). Cf. **I.D.N.**

indecorum *n.* [L. that which is unbecoming or unseemly.] Something unbecoming or indecorous. Impropriety. *David regards Peter's conduct as an unforgivable indecorum.*

inde datae leges ne fortior omnia posset. [L. **inde** therefore (1); **datae** given (3); **leges** laws (2); **ne** in order that not (4); **fortior** stronger (person) (5); **omnia** all things, everything (7); **posset** might be able (6): Therefore laws were given in order that the stronger might not be able to do everything.] Therefore laws are promulgated in order that the stronger person may not do whatever he/she can and wishes.

in Dei nomine *abbr.* **I.D.N.** [L. **in** in, on (1); **Dei** of God (3); **nomine** name (2): in the name of God.] In God's name. Cf. **in nomine Dei**.

in delicto *adj./adv.* [L. **in** in, on (1); **delicto** fault, wrong, crime (2): in fault.] In the crime. *Alao informed the police of his own volition that Tola is a partner in delicto.* Cf. **in pari delicto**.

in deserto *adv./adj.* [L. **in** in, on (1); **deserto** solitary, lonely (2): in solitary.] In a solitary condition. By one's self. Alone.

index *n., pl.* **indices** or **indexes** [L. pointer finger, one who discloses, an informer, a spy, that which discloses.] 1. Something which points out or guides, especially an alphabetical list of items with page references found at the end of a publication. 2. *Mathematics.* A sign usually written as a superscript or a subscript and used to indicate the performance of a mathematical operation, such as an exponent. 3. *Roman Catholic Church* (formerly). A list of forbidden books and films. See **index expurgatorius** and **index librorum prohibitorum.** —*v.* 1. To point out or indicate. 2. To provide with an alphabetical list. *To index a book.*

index animi sermo. or **sermo index animi.** [L. **index** indicator, exponent (2); **animi** of mind, intention (3); **sermo** speech, language (1): Speech (is) an indicator of the mind.] Language is an indication of intention; i.e., the best guide to the meaning or intention of an instrument is its language. Also, speech shows what is in the mind. See **verba sunt** etc.

index expurgatorius *n., pl.* **indices expurgatorii** [L. **index** indicator, index, indication (2); **expurgatorius**

cleansing, purifying (1): cleansing or purifying index.] 1. A list of material (as in written works) that has been proscribed. 2. *Roman Catholic Church* (formerly). A list of books, initially published separately but subsequently published as part of the **Index Librorum Prohibitorum** (q.v.), which members of the church should not read, pending the deletion, alteration, or revision of the offending passages.

Index Librorum Prohibitorum *n., pl.* **indices librorum prohibitorum** [L. **index** indicator, index, indication (1); **librorum** (of) books (3); **prohibitorum** of prohibited, forbidden (2): index of forbidden or prohibited books.] 1. A list of books that have been proscribed or banned. 2. *Roman Catholic Church.* A list of books condemned by authority of the Church and, therefore, not to be read by members of the Church. *The name Index was chosen . . . "for what seemed like several good reasons; it was short; it recalled the Catholic Index Librorum Prohibitorum; . . ." (West Africa* 1981). Cf. **index expurgatorius.**

indicia *n., sing.* **indicium** [L. signs, marks, proofs, evidence, notices, indications.] 1. Evidence. Proof. *Press editorials, gossip, and informal conversation are generally regarded as indicia of people's attitude towards the government.* 2. Medicine. The symptoms of a disease or medical condition. *All the indicia of imminent death were present.*

in dictione *adj.* [L.**in** in, on (1); **dictione** wording, saying (2): in wording.] *Logic.* In the wording. A logical fallacy which is based upon the wording of the phrase. The opposite of **extra dictione** (q.v.).

indigénat *n.* [Fr. denizenship, the natives, indigenousness.] *French Colonial Administration.* Native status as distinct from French citizenship. Natives or subjects were under a different judicial system, which empowered officials to exact a summary penalty without going through formal judicial procedures. Cf. **indigenato.**

indigenato *n.* [Port. denizenship, the natives, indigenousness.] *Portuguese Colonial Administration.* Native status as distinguished from Portuguese citizenship. *Hitherto, under the indigenato system, Portuguese citizenship was conferred only on those who had reached a "certain degree of culture" (West Africa,* 1986). Cf. **indigénat.**

indigène or **indigene** *n., pl.* **indigènes** or **indigenes** [Fr. native.] Indigenous person, plant, or animal.

individuum *n., pl.* **individua** or **individuums** [L. atom, indivisible particle.] 1. An atom. An indivisible entity. 2. An individual entity, instance, or being, i.e., as distinct from a group.

indocilis pauperiem pati *adj., pl.* **indociles pauperiem pati** Horace (65–8 B.C.). *Odes* I,1,18. [L. **indocilis** untaught, untutored, untrained, unteachable (1); **pauperiem** poverty, limited means (3); **pati** to

endure, suffer (2): untutored to endure poverty.] Not taught how to endure poverty.

in dubiis, benigniora praeferenda sunt. [L. **in** in, on (1); **dubiis** doubtful (things) (2); **benigniora** more liberal (things) (3); **praeferenda** to be preferred (5); **sunt** are (4): In doubtful things more liberal things are to be preferred.] *Law.* In case of doubt, more liberal interpretations are preferable. See **in dubio, pars** etc.

in dubio *adj./adv.* [L. **in** in, on (1); **dubio** doubt (2): in doubt.] In case of uncertainty. *Since the court was in dubio, the accused was freed.* See **in ambiguo.**

in dubio, pars mitior est sequenda. [L. **in** in, on (1); **dubio** doubt (2); **pars** part (4); **mitior** milder (3); **est** is (5); **sequenda** to be followed (6): In doubt, the milder part is to be followed.] *Law.* In case of doubt the milder option must be followed. See **dubiis** etc.; **in dubio, sequendum** etc.; **in re dubia** etc.; **nobiliores et benigniores** etc.; **quisquis praesumitur** etc.; **semper in dubiis** etc.; **tutius erratur** etc.; and **tutius semper** etc.

in dubio, sequendum quod tutius est. [L. **in** in, on (1); **dubio** doubt (2); **sequendum** to be followed (6); **quod** (that) which (3); **tutius** safer (5); **est** is (4): In doubt, that which is safer is to be followed.] *Law.* In case of doubt we must adopt the safer course of action. See **in dubio, pars** etc.

induciae or **indutiae** *pl. n.* [L. suspension of hostilities, truce, armistice.] *International Law.* Suspension of hostilities. A truce. An agreement made during war to refrain from hostilities for some time.

induciae legales or **indutiae legales** or simply **induciae** or **indutiae** *pl. n.* [L. **induciae** truce (2); **legales** lawful, legal (1): legal or lawful truce.] *Roman, Civil, Scots, and English Law.* Permissible time during which (1) a party should appear to answer a citation or summons or (2) a party should prepare a case for trial.

in eadem causa *adv.* [L. **in** in, on (1); **eadem** the same (2); **causa** cause, case, reason (3): in the same case.] In the same state. *Instead of carrying out renovations on the buildings of the testator, the successor left them in eadem causa.*

inedita *pl. n.* [L. things not given forth.] Literary material which has not been published.

in emulationem vicini *var.* of **in aemulationem vicini** (q.v.).

in eodem negotio *adv.* [L. **in** in, on (1); **eodem** the same (2); **negotio** business, affair (3): in the same affair.] In the same matter or business.

in eo, quod plus sit, semper inest et minus. [L. **in** in, on (1); **eo** that (2); **quod** which (3); **plus** more, greater (5); **sit** is (4); **semper** always (7); **inest** there is in, is contained (6); **et** also (9); **minus** less (8): In that which is greater there is always contained the less also.] The less is always contained in the greater. See **majus continet minus.**

inertia *n., pl.* **inertiae** or **inertias** [L. inactivity, laziness, idleness.] 1. *Physics.* The characteristic of resting matter to stay at rest and of moving matter to move in a straight line until it meets a resisting force in the opposite direction. 2. Inertness. Inactivity. Sluggishness. Opposition to change. . . . *many marriages last from sheer inertia, for lack of any other option, or "for the sake of the children"* . . . (*Newsweek Int.* July 13, 1981:45). See **vis inertiae.**

in esse *adj./adv.* [L. **in** in, on (1); **esse** to be, being (2): in being.] Actually existing. In actual existence. Actually. In actual fact. *For a gift under a will to be valid, it must be given to a person in esse.* Cf. **in fieri** and **in posse.**

in excelsis *adv.* [L. **in** in, on (1); **excelsis** high, elevated, distinguished (things) (2): in high things.] In the highest, utmost, or supreme degree. Superlatively. *Okoro has, in excelsis, most of the qualities which are essential for success in life.*

in exitu *adv./adj.* [L. **in** in, on (1); **exitu** issue, event, result (2): in issue.] Of concern. In question. Under dispute.

in expeditione *adj./adv.* [L. **in** in, on (1); **expeditione** expedition, campaign (2): on an expedition.] During a campaign. While on military service.

in extenso *abbr.* **in ex.** *adv.* [L. **in** in, on (1); **extenso** length, the enlarged (2): in length.] At full length. From the beginning to the end. In its entirety. *At the moment I intend to touch on the matter in summary, but at the appropriate time I will treat it in extenso.*

in extremis *adv.* [L. **in** in, on (1); **extremis** extreme, utmost (things) (2): in extreme things.] In extremity. In desperate case. In extreme circumstances. At the point of death. *The old man postponed the drafting of his will until the last moment when he was in extremis.* See **in articulo mortis.** Cf. **ad extremum.**

inf. *abbr.* for **infra** (q.v.).

in facie curiae *adv.* [L. **in** in, on (1); **facie** face, presence (2); **curiae** of court (3): in the face of the court.] *Law.* In the presence of the court. Before the court. *The accused was denied bail for misbehaving in facie curiae.*

in facie ecclesiae *adv./adj.* [L. **in** in, on (1); **facie** face, presence (2); **ecclesiae** of assembly, church (3): in the face of the church.] In the presence of the church. Before the church. a) *In facie ecclesiae Carolyn expressed her disbelief in the teachings of the Bible.* b) *Under the canon law, adopted by the common law, marriage could be by (1) a public celebration of the marriage service in a church, known as a celebration in facie ecclesiae; (2) by a clandestine celebration anywhere conducted by one in priest's orders* (Burke 1976:214).

in faciendo *adv.* [L. **in** in, on (1); **faciendo** doing (2): in doing.] In the process of performing an act.

in facto *adv.* [L. **in** in, on (1); **facto** deed, act, fact (2): in deed.] In fact. In actuality.

infanta *n., pl.* **infantas** [Sp./Port. royal princess.] *Spain and Portugal.* Daughter of the king and queen. Also the wife of an **infante** (q.v.). Cf. **dauphine.**

infante *n., pl.* **infantes** [Sp./Port. royal prince.] *Spain and Portugal.* Son of the king and queen, though not the eldest. Cf. **dauphin** and **principe.**

in favorem vitae, libertatis, et innocentiae, omnia praesumuntur. [L. **in** into, to, against, for (3); **favorem** favor (4); **vitae** of life (5); **libertatis** of freedom (6); **et** and (7); **innocentiae** of innocence (8); **omnia** all (things) (1); **praesumuntur** are presumed (2): All things are presumed for the favor of life, freedom, and innocence.] *Law.* Every presumption is made in favor of life, freedom, and innocence. See **de morte hominis** etc.

inferno *n., pl.* **inferni** or **infernos** [It. hell.] 1. Hell. A place or situation where there is intolerable suffering, misery, or torment. 2. A place which resembles hell in its chaos, turbulence, darkness, lawlessness, etc. 3. Conflagration. Intolerable heat. a) *The smouldering embers of religious fanaticism . . . have leapt into an all-consuming inferno in the northeastern town of Gombe . . .* (*West Africa* 1985). b) *On a routine mission, a Marine Corps jet crashed on the deck of the U.S.S. Nimitz, turning the aircraft carrier into a floating inferno* (*Newsweek Int.* Jan. 4, 1982:31). —**Inferno** The title of the first part of **La Commedia Divina** (q.v.) of Dante Alighieri (1265–1321).

in fieri *adj.* [L. **in** in, on (1); **fieri** to become, becoming (2): in becoming.] In the process of being made.] In the process of development. Pending. *The establishment of a Legal Aid Council in the town is in fieri.* Cf. **in esse** and **in posse.**

in fine *adv.* [L. **in** in, on (1); **fine** end (2): in the end.] Finally. In sum.

infinitum in jure reprobatur. [L. **infinitum** the endless, unlimited (1); **in** in, on (2); **jure** right, law (3); **reprobatur** is condemned (4): The endless in law is condemned.] What is endless is reprehensible in law. Applicable to litigation. See **circuitus est evitandus; debet esse** etc.; **dilationes in lege** etc.; **expedit reipublicae ut** etc.; **interest reipublicae res judicatas** etc.; **interest reipublicae ut sit** etc.; **judicia sunt tanquam** etc.; **judicium semper** etc.; **lex dilationes** etc.; **lex reprobat moram; mora reprobatur** etc.; **nemo bis punitur** etc.; **nemo debet bis vexari pro** etc.; **nemo debet bis vexari si constet** etc.; **non bis in idem;** and **res judicata pro** etc.

in flagrante bello *adv.* [L. **in** in, on (1); **flagrante** burning, blazing (2); **bello** war (3): in blazing war.] As the war was being fought or was going on. In the heat of the war. Cf. **flagrante bello.**

in flagrante delicto *adj./adv.* [L. **in** in, on (1); **flagrante** burning, blazing (2); **delicto** crime (3): in blazing crime.] In the very act of committing a crime. Immediately after the crime. Red-handed. Cf. **flagrante delicto.**

inflatus *n., pl.* inflatus or inflatuses [L. a blowing in, inspiration.] Inspiration. **Afflatus** (q.v.).

in forma pauperis *adv./adj.* [L. **in** in, on (1); **forma** form, manner (2); **pauperis** of a pauper, poor (person) (3): in the manner of a pauper.] *Law.* In the manner, or with the status, of a pauper. As a poor person. Applicable to exemption from fees and costs of a legal suit on account of poverty. *Bosede was granted permission to file an appeal in forma pauperis.* See **pauper**. Cf. **non indiget**.

in foro conscientiae *adv.* [L. **in** in, on (1); **foro** forum, court (2); **conscientiae** of conscience (3): in the forum of conscience.] In the court or tribunal of conscience. Morally or privately, as opposed to legally. Viewed or viewing it from the moral, instead of the legal, context. *Mr. Adebayo made an extrajudicial contract with Mr. Popoola, although he was not unaware that it was binding only in foro conscientiae.* See **forum conscientiae**.

infra *abbr.* **inf.** *prep.* [L. below, under, within.] Below. Under. Beneath. Inferior to. —*adv.* Below. Underneath. Used in bibliographical references to direct the reader to something in a subsequent section of the book. See **post**. Cf. **supra**.

infra aetatem *adj.* [L. **infra** below, under, within (1); **aetatem** age (2): under age.] Below legal age. Not yet of age. Applicable to minors.

infra annos nubiles *adj./adv.* [L. **infra** below, under, within (1); **annos** years (3); **nubiles** marriageable (2): under marriageable years.] Below the age of marriage. *Aishatu was engaged when she was infra annos nubiles and the nuptial ceremony was held five years afterwards.*

infra annum *adv.* [L. **infra** below, under, within (1); **annum** year (2): under a year.] Within a year. In less than a year. *The court, ably and laudably, disposed of three hundred land cases infra annum.*

infra corpus civitatis *adv.* [L. **infra** below, under, within (1); **corpus** body (2); **civitatis** of country, state (3): within the body of the country.] Within the territorial limits of a country. *Aliens found infra corpus civitatis without valid immigration documents are usually arrested, detained, and deported.*

infra dignitatem *abbr.* **infra dig.** *adj.* [L. **infra** below, under, within (1); **dignitatem** dignity (2): beneath dignity.] Below dignity. Undignified. *It is infra dignitatem for counsel to fight in public.*

infra dignitatem curiae *adj.* [L. **infra** below, under, within (1); **dignitatem** dignity (2); **curiae** of court (3): below the dignity of the court.] Not worthy of the court's consideration or attention. *It is infra dignitatem curiae for it to offer an open advice to one of the parties in a dispute.*

infra furorem *adv.* [L. **infra** below, under, within (1); **furorem** madness, insanity (2): under insanity.] While insane. In a fit of insanity. *Benjamin killed his wife infra furorem.*

infra jurisdictionem *adj./adv.* [L. **infra** below, under, within (1); **jurisdictionem** jurisdiction (2): under jurisdiction.] Within the jurisdiction.

infra praesidia *adv./adj.* [L. **infra** below, under, within (1); **praesidia** guards, protection, garrison (2): under guards.] Completely under protection or control. In safe custody. Used in international law with respect to captured goods brought under the complete protection of the captors.

in fraudem creditorum *adv.* [L. **in** into, to, against, for (1); **fraudem** deceit, cheating (2); **creditorum** of creditors (3): for cheating of creditors.] *Law.* With intent to cheat (or defraud) creditors.

in fraudem legis *adv.* [**in** into, to, against, for (1); **fraudem** cheating, deceit, detriment (2); **legis** of law (3): for cheating of the law.] *Law.* For the detriment of the law. With intent to circumvent/evade the rules of law. *In fraudem legis learned counsel for the plaintiff quoted a provision from a repealed decree.*

in futuro *adv.* [L. **in** in, on (1); **futuro** the future (2): in the future.] At a future time. *As a result of the confusion which engulfed the installation of the chief, the government promulgated the Chieftaincy Decree to guide kingmakers in futuro.* Cf. **in praesenti**.

in generalibus latet error. [L. **in** in, on (3); **generalibus** general (things) (4); **latet** is concealed, lies hidden (2); **error** error, mistake (1): Error lies hidden in general things.] Error is concealed in general expressions. Cf. **dolosus versatur in generalibus** and **fraus latet** etc.

in genere *adv./adj.* [L. **in** in, on (1); **genere** kind, rank, class (2): in kind/class.] In quality. *The two television sets produced as exhibits agree in genere.* Cf. **in specie**.

ingenium *n., pl.* ingenia [L. mind, intellect.] Innate talent. Inborn ability.

ingénue *n., pl.* ingénues [Fr. ingenuous, simple, artless, guileless, innocent, unsophisticated.] 1. A naive, unsophisticated, innocent girl or young woman. *The Casanova's attempt to take advantage of the ingenue was aborted by the timely arrival of her friends.* 2. A character of that nature represented on the stage. 3. A naive, unsophisticated, innocent, simple, or inexperienced person. *The recommendation of Mr. Toks, an ingenue, for the position of Public Relations Officer of the firm was unanimously rejected by members of the Board of Directors.* —*adj.* Of, characteristic of, relating to an ingenue. Unsophisticated. **Naive** (q.v.). *Her ingenue comportment suggests that she is a new girl in town.*

in globo *adv.* [L. **in** in, on (1); **globo** globe, mass, body (2): in mass or body.] Completely. As a whole. Viewing it generally. Totally. **In toto** (q.v.). In its entirety.

in gremio *adv.* [L. **in** in, on (1); **gremio** bosom, lap, protection (2): in the lap or bosom.] In abeyance. See **in nubibus**.

in gremio legis *adv./adj.* [L. in in, on (1); gremio bosom, lap, protection (2); legis of law (3): in the bosom of the law.] Under the protection of the law. *In the constitution of every country, the fundamental human rights are in gremio legis.*

in hac parte *adv.* [L. in in, on (1); hac this (2); parte side (3): on this side.] In this behalf.

in heredes non solent transire actiones quae poenales ex maleficio sunt. [L. in into, to, against, for (10); heredes heirs (11); non not (7); solent are accustomed (8); transire to pass, cross over (9); actiones actions (1); quae which (2); poenales penal (4); ex arising from, out of (5); maleficio crime, evil deed (6); sunt are (3): Actions which are penal arising out of crime are not accustomed to pass to heirs.] *Law.* Criminal penal actions are usually not inherited by heirs. See in restitutionem etc.

in his quae de jure communi omnibus conceduntur, consuetudo alicujus patriae vel loci non est alleganda. [L. in in, on (1); his these (things) (2); quae which (3); de of, from, about, for (6); jure right, law (8); communi common (7); omnibus to all (5); conceduntur are granted (4); consuetudo custom, usage, tradition (9); alicujus of any (10); patriae (of) country (11); vel or (12); loci (of) place (13); non not (15); est is (14); alleganda to be alleged, adopted (16): In these things which are granted to all from common right, the custom of any country or place is not to be alleged.] *Law.* With respect to those rights which are universally granted to all persons, the custom of any country or place must not be used as an excuse for ignoring them.

in his verbis *adv.* [in in, on (1); his these (2); verbis words (3): in these words.] In these words. As follows. The expression is usually used to introduce quotations. *He addressed the audience in his verbis: "Distinguished ladies and gentlemen, I need not . . . ."*

in hoc signo vinces. [L. in in, on (1); hoc this (2); signo sign, standard (3); vinces you will conquer (4): In this sign you will conquer.] You will be victorious under this standard (the cross). Constantine is said to have seen these words in a vision, made the cross his military standard, and won the Battle of the Milvian Bridge (Oct. 28, 312 A.D.). Motto of the College of the Holy Cross.

in iisdem terminis *adv.* [L. in in, on (1); iisdem the same (2); terminis limits, boundaries (3): in the same limits.] In the same terms.

in infinitum *adv.* [L. in into, to, against, for (1); infinitum the endless, unceasing (2): into the endless/unceasing.] Indefinitely. Endlessly. Infinitely. Applicable to posts, positions or titles with perpetual succession. Cf. ad infinitum.

in initio *adv.* [L. in in, on (1); initio beginning (2): in the beginning.] At the beginning. *In the land suit, the plaintiff's devastating evidence, in initio, forced the defendant to seek an amicable settlement.*

in integrum *adv.* [L. in into, to, against, for (1); integrum the fresh, untainted, pure, whole (2): into the whole.] To the former condition. To the original state. *At the arbitration it was decided that the parties should be restored in integrum.*

in invidiam *adv.* [L. in into, to, against, for (1); invidiam prejudice, unpopularity (2): for unpopularity.] In order to arouse prejudice.

in invitum *adv.* [L. in into, to, against, for (1); invitum unwilling (person) (2): against an unwilling person.] Against a person's consent/will. Against a person who does not consent or assent. By force of law, regardless of consent. *A move for an amicable settlement made in invitum may not succeed.*

iniquissima pax est anteponenda justissimo bello. [L. iniquissima most unjust, unfair (1); pax peace (2); est is (3); anteponenda to be preferred, valued above (4); justissimo to most just, reasonable (5); bello (to) war (6): The most unjust peace is to be preferred to the most just war.] The most unjust peace is preferable to the most just war.

iniquum est aliquem rei suae esse judicem. [L. iniquum unfair, unjust (2); est it is (1); aliquem (that) one, anyone (3); rei (of) matter, affair (7); suae of his/her own (6); esse to be (4); judicem judge (5): It is unjust that one be a judge of his/her own affair.] *Law.* It is a travesty of justice for one to be a judge in his/her own cause. See nemo debet esse etc.

in itinere *adv./adj.* [L. in in, on (1); itinere way, journey (2): on the way.] On the way. During transportation. *The goods imported by United Company Ltd. were destroyed in itinere.* Cf. en route and en voyage.

in judicio non creditur nisi juratis. [L. in in, on (1); judicio judicial proceeding, legal process (2); non not (4); creditur belief is given (3); nisi except, unless (5); juratis to the sworn (6): In judicial proceeding belief is not given except to the sworn.] *Law.* In judicial proceedings, only those who have taken an oath are believed. See jurato creditur etc.

in jure *adv.* [L. in in, on (1); jure right, law (2): in law.] According to law. In right. In justice. In court. *The magistrate ruled that, in jure, the expatriate had the right to institute action against the Ministry of Education.*

in jure alterius *adv.* [L. in in, on (1); jure right, law (2); alterius of another (3): in the right of another.] *Law.* In another person's right. See autre droit.

in jure cessio *n.* [L. in in, on (2); jure right, law (3); cessio surrender, giving up (1): surrender in law.] *Law.* Handing over in a court of law. A legal procedure in ancient Rome whereby the defendant admits formally in the presence of the judge the validity of the plaintiff's claim to a disputed property and the judge accordingly sanctions the concession.

in jure, non remota causa sed proxima spectatur. [L. in in, on (1); jure right, law (2); non not (3);

remota remote (4); **causa** cause, case, reason (7); **sed** but (5); **proxima** proximate (6); **spectatur** is considered (8): In law not the remote, but the proximate, cause is considered.] *Law.* What is given legal consideration is the proximate, not the remote cause. In certain actions, such as those dealing with negligence, it is necessary to prove that the defendant's negligence was the proximate, not just the remote, cause of the harm or damage. See **causa causans.**

in jure omnis definitio periculosa est. [L. **in** in, on (1); **jure** right, law (2); **omnis** every (3); **definitio** definition (4); **periculosa** dangerous, hazardous (6); **est** is (5): In law every definition is dangerous.] *Law.* Every legal definition is hazardous. See **omnis definitio** etc.

in jure proprio *adv.* [L. **in** in, on (1); **jure** right, law (3); **proprio** one's own, individual (2): in one's own right.] *Law.* In the right belonging to one's self.

in jure uxoris *adv.* [L. **in** in, on (1); **jure** right, law (2); **uxoris** of wife (3): in the right of a wife.] *Law.* By the right of a wife. Applicable to a right, title, etc. which, though inherited by the wife, is exercised by the husband. Cf. **jure uxoris.**

injuria *n., pl.* **injuriae** [L. injury, wrong, insult.] Injustice. Invasion of the rights of another.

injuria absque damno *n.* [L. **injuria** injury, wrong (1); **absque** without, away from (2); **damno** damage (3): injury without damage.] *Law.* A legal injury which is not accompanied by damage. The expression is used with reference to the legal principle that a wrong which does not cause damage or loss is not actionable. Cf. **injuria sine damno.** See **actio non datur** etc.

injuria fit ei cui convicium dictum est, vel de eo factum carmen famosum. [L. **injuria** injury, wrong (1); **fit** is done (2); **ei** to him (3); **cui** to whom (4); **convicium** reproach, abuse, insult (5); **dictum est** has been said (6); **vel** or (7); **de** of, from, about, for (11); **eo** him (12); **factum (est)** has been made (10); **carmen** song, poem (9); **famosum** defamatory, slanderous (8): Injury is done to him to whom an insult has been said or a slanderous song has been made about him.] *Law.* A person about whom an insult has been uttered or a slanderous song composed has been injured.

injuria non excusat injuriam. [L. **injuria** injury, wrong (1); **non** not (2); **excusat** excuses (3); **injuriam** injury, wrong (4): A wrong does not excuse a wrong.] *Law.* Two wrongs do not make a right. See **ex turpi causa** etc.

injuria non praesumitur. [L. **injuria** injury, wrong (1); **non** not (2); **praesumitur** is presumed (3): Injury is not presumed.] *Law.* Wrong or harm is not taken for granted; i.e., it must be proven.

injuria propria non cadet in beneficium facientis. [L. **injuria** injury, wrong (2); **propria** one's own, individual (1); **non** not (3); **cadet** will fall (4); **in** into, to, against, for (5); **beneficium** favor, benefit (6); **facientis** of the one doing (7): One's own injury will not fall to the benefit of the one doing it.] *Law.* One should not derive a benefit from one's own injury (or wrongful act). See **ex turpi causa** etc.

injuria servi dominum pertingit. [L. **injuria** injury, wrong (1); **servi** of servant, slave (2); **dominum** master (4); **pertingit** reaches (3): The injury of a servant reaches the master.] *Law.* A master is liable for an injury caused by his servant. See **qui facit per alium** etc.

injuria sine damno *n.* [L. **injuria** injury, wrong (1); **sine** without (2); **damno** damage (3): injury without damage.] *Law.* A legal injury which is not accompanied by damage. Cf. **injuria absque damno.** See **actio non datur** etc.

in limine *abbr.* **in lim.** *adv./adj.* [L. **in** in, on (1); **limine** threshold (2): on the threshold.] At the very beginning or outset. At the preliminary stage. *Counsel's argument was dismissed in limine by the presiding judge because his propositions were not supported by legal authorities.*

in loc. *abbr.* for **in loco** (q.v.).

in loc. cit. *abbr.* for **in loco citato** (q.v.).

in loco *abbr.* **in loc.** *adv.* [L. **in** in, on (1); **loco** place (2): in place.] In place of. Instead of.

in loco citato *abbr.* **in loc. cit.** *adv.* [L. **in** in, on (1); **loco** place (2); **citato** cited, mentioned (3): in the place cited.] In the place mentioned.

in loco parentis *adv.* [L. **in** in, on (1); **loco** place, position (2); **parentis** of parent (3): in the place of a parent.] As a parent. Exercising parental influence, authority, and responsibility. *Mr. Akpan stands in loco parentis to his friend's son, Samuel Ajani.*

in loco tutoris *adv.* [L. **in** in, on (1); **loco** place (2); **tutoris** of guardian, tutor (3): in the place of a guardian.] As a guardian. *Dauda, who stands in loco tutoris towards Abudu, has disappointingly deserted him.*

in majorem cautelam [L. **in** into, to, against, for (1); **majorem** greater (2); **cautelam** caution (3): for greater caution.] For greater precaution. For greater security. See **ad abundantiorem cautelam.**

in majore summa continetur minor. [L. **in** in, on (1); **majore** greater (2); **summa** sum, substance (3); **continetur** is contained, comprised (4); **minor** less (5): In the greater sum is contained the lesser.] *Law.* The lesser sum is contained in the greater sum. When the totality of a debt has been settled, all the smaller items have been equally settled. See **majus continet minus.**

in malam partem *adv.* [L. **in** into, to, against, for (1); **malam** bad (2); **partem** part (3): into a bad part.] In a bad sense. Unfavorably.

in mala parte *adv.* [L. **in** in, on (1); **mala** bad (2); **parte** part, side (3): in the bad part.] Unfavorably. To the disadvantage. In a bad sense. **In malam partem** (q.v.). *In a case where a party makes an* ambiguous stipulation, the contract should be interpreted in malam partem of the said party. Cf. **in bonam partem** and **in bona parte.**

in maleficiis voluntas spectatur, non exitus. [L. **in** in, on (1); **maleficiis** offenses, crimes (2); **voluntas** intention (3); **spectatur** is considered (4); **non** not (5); **exitus** result (6): In crimes, the intention is considered, not the result.] In criminal cases what is considered is the intention, not the result. See **actus non facit** etc.

in maleficio, ratihabitio mandato comparatur. [L. **in** in, on (1); **maleficio** crime, evil deed (2); **ratihabitio** sanction, ratification (3); **mandato** to command, order (5); **comparatur** is compared (4): In crime, sanction is compared to order.] *Law.* In malfeasance, sanctioning the deed is tantamount to ordering it. Cf. **qui non improbat, approbat.**

in manibus curiae *adv.* [L. **in** in, on (1); **manibus** hands (2); **curiae** of court (3): in the hands of the court.] In the court's control. *The decision to grant or refuse bail rests in manibus curiae.*

in manu *adv./adj.* [L. **in** in, on (1); **manu** hand (2): in hand.] Red-handed; i.e., being apprehended with stolen goods or the smoking gun in one's possession. *Investigations in the celebrated case of robbery came to an end when Comfort was arrested with the stolen goods in manu.*

in medias res *adv.* [L. **in** into, to, against, for (1); **medias** middle, middle of (2); **res** matters, things, property, business, affairs (3): into the middle of things.] Into the heart of the matter. Starting in the middle of a story or narrative. *The speaker plunged in medias res, and it took the audience a long time to follow the thrust of the arguments.*

in memoriam *adv.* [L. **in** into, to, against, for (1); **memoriam** memory, remembrance (2): for memory.] In memory of. To the memory of. The expression is usually used on tributes to the dead.

in mercibus illicitis non sit commercium. [L. **in** in, on (1); **mercibus** goods, commodities (3); **illicitis** illicit, unlawful (2); **non** not (4); **sit** there should be (5); **commercium** trade, commerce (6): In illicit goods there should not be commerce.] *Law.* There should be no trade in illicit (or contraband) goods.

in mitiori sensu *adv.* [L. **in** in, on (1); **mitiori** milder (2); **sensu** sense (3): in a milder sense.] With a gentler interpretation. a) *Taking into consideration the ambiguities in the statute and the circumstantial nature of the evidence adduced, the judge interpreted the statute in mitiori sensu.* b) *And the words themselves shall be taken in mitiori sensu (James v. Rutlech* [1599] 4 Co. Rep. 176. Megarry: 1955:193).

in mora *adv./adj.* [L. **in** in, on (1); **mora** delay, procrastination (2): in delay.] *Law.* In default. Applicable to a debtor who failed to return the thing borrowed at the scheduled time. *Samata is now in mora for his inability to make payment on the stipulated date.*

in mortua manu *adv.* [L. **in** in, on (1); **mortua** dead (2); **manu** hand (3): in a dead hand.] *Law.* In mortmain. Applicable to property owned by religious bodies. Cf. **en mort mayne** and **manus mortua.**

in nomine Christi *abbr.* **I.N.C.** *adv.* [L. **in** in, on (1); **nomine** name (2); **Christi** of Christ (3): in the name of Christ.] *Christianity.* In Christ's name. In the name of Jesus Christ.

in nomine Dei *abbr.* **I.N.D.** *adv.* [L. **in** in, on (1); **nomine** name (2); **Dei** of God (3): in the name of God.] In God's name. Used as an introduction to wills and other legal documents. *In nomine Dei, let all that I wish for my heirs happen.* Cf. **in Dei nomine.**

in nomine Patri et Fili et Spiritus Sancti [L. **in** in, on (1); **nomine** name (2); **Patri** of the father (3); **et** and (4); **Fili** of the son (5); **et** and (6); **Spiritus** of the spirit, ghost (8); **Sancti** holy, sacred (7): In the name of the Father, and of the Son, and of the Holy Spirit.] *Christianity.* In the name of the Father, the Son, and the Holy Ghost. A prayer to the Divine Trinity.

in nomine Sanctae Trinitatis *abbr.* **I.N.S.T.** *adv.* [L. **in** in, on (1); **nomine** name (2); **sanctae** of holy (3); **trinitatis** (of) trinity (4): in the name of the Holy Trinity.] *Christianity.* In the name of the Holy Trinity, i.e., God the Father, God the Son, and God the Holy Spirit.

in novo casu, novum remedium apponendum est. [L. **in** in, on (1); **novo** new (2); **casu** case, event (3); **novum** new (4); **remedium** remedy (5); **apponendum** to be applied (7); **est** is (6): In a new case, a new remedy is to be applied.] A new remedy must be applied to a new case.

in nubibus *adv.* [L. **in** in, on (1); **nubibus** clouds (2): in the clouds.] In abeyance. In legal custody. Under the control of the law. a) *The distribution of the properties of the deceased has been in nubibus for a considerable period of time due to the absence of the head of the family.* b) *The usufruct . . . existed in nubibus . . .* (Asante 1975:9). See **in gremio.**

in nuce *adv.* [L. **in** in, on (1); **nuce** nut (2): in a nut.] In a nutshell. *In his opening remarks, he summarized the workers' demands in nuce.*

innuendo *n., pl.* **innuendos** [L. by nodding.] 1. A slight or indirect hint. 2. *Law.* The beginning of a charge of libel or slander in which the libelous or slanderous statement is explained.

in nullius bonis *adj.* [L. **in** in, on (1); **nullius** of no one, nobody (3); **bonis** goods, property (2): in the goods of nobody.] 1. *Law.* Nobody's goods. Belonging to nobody. 2. *Ancient Times.* Applicable to wreck and treasure-trove. See **nullius in bonis.**

in obscuris, inspici solere quod verisimilius est, aut quod plerumque fieri solet. [L. **in** in, on (1); **obscuris** obscure, unintelligible (things) (2); **inspici** to be considered, examined (4); **solere** to be accustomed (3); **quod** what, that which (5); **verisimilius** more probable, plausible (7); **est** is (6); **aut** or (8);

quod what, that which (9); **plerumque** generally, commonly (12); **fieri** to happen, be done (11); **solet** is accustomed (10): In obscure things to be accustomed to be considered what is more probable or what is accustomed to happen generally.] *Law.* In case of obscurity, it is the usual practice to consider what is more probable or what happens generally. Cf. **in dubio, pars** etc.

in odium spoliatoris omnia praesumuntur. [L. **in** into, to, against, for (3); **odium** hatred, enmity (4); **spoliatoris** of spoiler (5); **omnia** all (things), everything (1); **praesumuntur** are presumed (2): All things are presumed to the hatred of a spoiler.] *Law.* Every presumption is made to the disadvantage of a wrongdoer. See **omnia praesumuntur contra spoliatorem.**

inoficiocidad *n.* [Sp. absence of diligence.] *Spanish Law.* Any deed, such as a donation, testament, or dower, which is contrary to obligation, duty, natural affection, or piety. A deed which adversely affects the rights of heirs or creditors. Such a deed may be revoked or modified. See **donatio inofficiosa.**

in omnibus *adv.* [L. **in** in, on (1); **omnibus** all (things) (2): in all things.] In all. In everything. On all points. *The civil suit filed by the plaintiff is similar in omnibus to the one just decided.*

in omnibus quidem, maxime tamen in jure, aequitas spectanda sit. [L. **in** in, on (1); **omnibus** all (things) (2); **quidem** indeed (3); **maxime** especially, most particularly (5); **tamen** but, nevertheless (4); **in** in, on (6); **jure** right, law (7); **aequitas** equity (8); **spectanda** to be considered, regarded (10); **sit** should be (9): In all things, but especially in law, equity should be considered.] Fairness must be considered in everything but especially in regard to law.

inops consilii *adj.* [L. **inops** destitute, poor, indigent (1); **consilii** of advice, plan, judgment (2): destitute of advice.] Without advice. Without legal representation. *Law.* Applicable to a person who acts without legal counsel. *The accused chose to appear in court inops consilii and, not surprisingly, was found guilty.* See **in propria persona** and **pro se.**

in ovo *adv.* [L. **in** in, on (1); **ovo** egg (2): in the egg.] 1. In embryo. In the embryonic stage. *The nasty little boy seemed to be a bandit in ovo.* 2. At the beginning of a process. *In ovo, the problem seemed impossible, but with persistence they were able to find a solution.*

in pais or **in pays** *adv.* [Obs. Fr. **in** in, on (1); **pais** country (2): in the country.] *Law.* Without legal process. See **pais** 1.

in pari causa *adv.* [L. **in** in, on (1); **pari** equal, like (2); **causa** cause, case, reason (3): in an equal case.] In a case in which the parties have equal rights according to law.

in pari causa possessor potior haberi debet. [L. **in** in, on (1); **pari** equal (2); **causa** cause, case, reason (3); **possessor** the one in possession (4); **potior** better,

superior (7); **haberi** to be had, held, regarded (6); **debet** ought, should (5): In an equal case, the one in possession should be regarded as superior.] *Law.* In an equal case, the person in possession should be considered to have a better claim to the property. See **in aequali jure melior** etc.

in pari delicto *adv./adj.* [L. **in** in, on (1); **pari** equal, like (2); **delicto** fault, wrong (3): in equal wrong.] *Law.* Equally at fault. A person in pari delicto is also a **particeps criminis** (q.v.), but the latter is not always necessarily in pari delicto. Generally, where "A" has entered into a contract with "B" on account of intimidation, duress, compulsion, fraud, etc., "A" and "B" are deemed to be not in pari delicto, and the former may recover whatever he/she transferred or paid. Cf. **socius criminis.** See **in aequali jure melior** etc.

in pari delicto, potior est conditio defendentis. [L. **in** in, on (1); **pari** equal (2); **delicto** fault (3); **potior** better, preferable (4); **est** is (5); **conditio** condition (6); **defendentis** of the one defending (7): In equal fault better is the condition of the one defending.] *Law.* In a case where both parties are equally in fault, the condition of the defendant is better than that of the plaintiff. See **in aequali jure melior** etc.

in pari delicto, potior est conditio possidentis. [L. **in** in, on (1); **pari** equal, like (2); **delicto** fault (3); **potior** better, preferable (4); **est** is (5); **conditio** condition (6); **possidentis** of the one possessing (7): In equal fault better is the condition of the one possessing.] *Law.* In a case where both parties are equally in fault, the condition of the possessor is better than that of the opponent. See **in aequali jure melior** etc.

in pari materia *adv.* [L. **in** in, on (1); **pari** equal, like (2); **materia** matter, theme (3): in a like matter.] In an equal matter. In an analogous case. On the same matter/subject. *There is practically no precedent in pari materia with which this case can be compared.*

in parte sive in solido *adv.* [L. **in** in, on (1); **parte** part (2); **sive** or (3); **in** in, on (4); **solido** the whole, entire (5): in part or in the whole.] In part or as a whole. For a part or the whole. Cf. **in solido.**

in partibus infidelium *abbr.* **I.P.I.** *adv.* [L. **in** in, on (1); **partibus** parts, regions, districts (2); **infidelium** of the faithless, the unbelieving, the infidels (3): in the regions of the infidels/unbelievers.] 1. *Christianity.* In a non-Christian area. Applicable to a non-resident bishop of a diocese with a predominantly non-Christian population. 2. In the territory of (or among) ideologically hostile people. *His mission was rendered all the more herculean by the fact that he was propagating his doctrine in partibus infidelium.*

in parvo *adv.* [L. **in** in, on (1); **parvo** little (2): in little.] In miniature. In microcosm. *An observation of the working habits of officials in governmental institutions in any particular town shows, in parvo, the attitude of these officials in the entire country.*

in patrimonio *adj.* [L. **in** in, on (1); **patrimonio** inheritance (2): in the inheritance.] *Law*. Subject to private ownership. Can be acquired/owned privately. See **in commercio**. Cf. **extra commercium** and **extra patrimonium**.

in pays See **in pais**.

in pectore *adj.* [L. **in** in, on (1); **pectore** breast, heart (2): in the breast.] In secret. Secretly. *Though Peter is my friend, he keeps his plans in pectore and does not discuss them with me.* Cf. **in petto**.

in pendenti *adv.* [L. **in** in, on (1); **pendenti** the hanging (2): in the hanging.] In suspense/suspension. *In the absence of a successor, the distribution of the estate of the deceased was held in pendenti.*

in perpetuum *adv.* [L. **in** into, to, against, for (1); **perpetuum** perpetuity, all time (2): for perpetuity.] For ever. In perpetuity. *Executors of a will cannot hold the properties of the testator in perpetuum.*

in personam *adj./adv.* [L. **in** into, to, against, for (1); **personam** person (2): against the person.] *Law*. An action which is directed against a particular person and in which the court exercises power on the defendant alone. a) *Talatu instituted an action in personam against Diago in connection with a contract which the latter failed to complete.* b) *The only difference in this respect between a judgment in personam and a judgment in rem is that the former is conclusive only between the parties and their representatives, while the latter is conclusive against all the world* (Morris 1973:1019). Cf. **actio in rem**.

in petto *adj./adv.* [It. **in** in, on (1); **petto** breast, chest (2): in breast or chest.] Secretly. Privately. Without announcement or disclosure. Used especially for a Cardinal who is appointed by the Pope without being named in a meeting of the Church's governing body. Cf. **in pectore**.

in pios usus *adv.* [L. **in** into, to, against, for (1); **pios** religious, devout, loyal, dutiful (2); **usus** uses (3): for religious uses.] For religious purposes.

in plena vita *adv.* [L. **in** in, on (1); **plena** full (2); **vita** life (3): in full life.] In full life.

in pleno lumine *adv.* [**in** in, on (1); **pleno** full (2); **lumine** light (3): in full light.] In the light of day. In public. *The assassination of the Prime Minister took place in pleno lumine.*

in poenalibus causis benignius interpretandum est. [L. **in** in, on (1); **poenalibus** penal (2); **causis** causes, cases (3); **benignius** more liberally, favorably (6); **interpretandum** to be interpreted (5); **est** it is (4): In penal cases, it is to be interpreted more liberally.] *Law*. In penal cases, there is the need to make more liberal interpretation.

in pontificalibus *adj.* [L. **in** in, on (1); **pontificalibus** insignia or attire of a pontiff (2): in the insignia or attire of a pontiff.] In the vestments, insignia, or full attire of a bishop, cardinal, or pope. In one's official attire, insignia, or vestments. See **pontificalia**.

in posse *adj./adv.* [L. **in** in, on (1); **posse** to be able, being able (2): in being able.] In possibility. Not actually existing. Potentially. *A corporation in the process of being formed is a corporation in posse, while a corporation which is already formed is a corporation in esse.* See **in esse**; **in fieri**; and **posse**.

in potentia *adv.* [L. **in** in, on (1); **potentia** power, ability (2): in power.] In ability rather than fact. Potentially.

in potestate parentis *adj.* [L. **in** in, on (1); **potestate** power (2); **parentis** of parent (3): in the power of a parent.] *Law*. In the parent's control. Under the parent's supervision.

in pr. *abbr.* for **in principio** (q.v.).

in praesenti *adv.* [L. **in** in, on (1); **praesenti** the present (2): in the present.] At the moment. At the present time. *Capital punishment has been abolished in many countries in praesenti.* Cf. **in futuro**.

in praesentia majoris cessat potentia minoris. [L. **in** in, on (1); **praesentia** presence (2); **majoris** of greater, more (3); **cessat** ceases, stops (6); **potentia** power (4); **minoris** of lesser, smaller (5): In the presence of the greater, the power of the lesser ceases.] *Law*. The superior power overrides the inferior power; e.g., a superior court overrides the decision of an inferior court. The view of the majority overrides that of the minority. See **majus continet minus**.

in praesentia majoris potestatis, minor potestas cessat. [L. **in** in, on (1); **praesentia** presence (2); **majoris** of greater (3); **potestatis** (of) power (4); **minor** smaller (5); **potestas** power (6); **cessat** ceases, stops (7): In the presence of the greater power, the smaller power ceases.] *Law*. When a greater power is present, it absorbs the smaller power. A lesser authority is incorporated into a greater authority.

in pretio emptionis et venditionis, naturaliter licet contrahentibus se circumvenire. [L. **in** in, on (1); **pretio** price (2); **emptionis** of buying (3); **et** and (4); **venditionis** of selling (5); **naturaliter** naturally (7); **licet** it is permitted, allowed (6); **contrahentibus** to contracting (persons) (8); **se** themselves (10); **circumvenire** to outwit, cheat (9): In the price of buying and selling, it is permitted naturally to contracting persons to cheat themselves.] *Law*. In determining the price in a session of buying and selling, the contracting parties are naturally allowed to cheat themselves.

in primis *adv.* [L. **in** in, on (1); **primis** first (things) (2): in the first things.] In the first place. *In his presentation of the case, he argued, in primis, that . . . .*

in principio *abbr.* **in pr.** *adv.* Genesis I:1 and John I:1. [L. **in** in, on (1); **principio** origin, beginning, commencement (2): in origin.] In the beginning. At first. *In principio, all the workers agreed to pay the levy, but later on some of them decided against it.*

in propria causa nemo judex sit. [L. **in** in, on (1); **propria** one's own (2); **causa** cause, case, reason

(3); **nemo** no one (4); **judex** judge (6); **sit** should be (5): In one's own case no one should be judge.] *Law.* No one ought to be a judge in his/her own cause. See **nemo debet esse** etc.

in propria persona *adv.* [L. **in** in, on (1); **propria** one's own (2); **persona** person (3): in one's own person.] In one's own proper person. Without an attorney's assistance. Personally. *Despite the fact that Edwin appeared in propria persona, he was able to secure his acquittal.* See **inops consilii** and **pro se**.

in puris naturalibus *adj.* [L. **in** in, on (1); **puris** pure (2); **naturalibus** natural (3): in pure natural.] In a natural state. Completely naked. *The situation seemed quite complicated on the surface, but once some superficial difficulties were removed it was, in puris naturalibus, quite simple.*

inquisitor *n., pl.* **inquisitors** [L. searcher, examiner, inspector, investigator, collector of evidence.] 1. A person who questions or investigates. An official, such as a sheriff or coroner, whose functions involve inquiring or examining. 2. A person who is a member of an inquisition. An official of an investigating committee who asks questions harshly and completely ignores an individual's sensibilities, objections and rights. *Tumi resolutely shuns a political career, for he has a pathological fear of appearing one day before the official inquisitors of a military tribunal.*

in quo quis delinquit, in eo de jure est puniendus. [L. **in** in, on (1); **quo** what (2); **quis** any one (3); **delinquit** offends, does wrong (4); **in** in, on (5); **eo** that (6); **de** of, from, about, for (8) **jure** right, law (9); **est** he is (7); **puniendus** to be punished (10): In what any one offends, in that he is of right to be punished.] *Law.* A person should rightly be punished for the offense which he/she has committed; i.e., not for some other deed or action. See **nemo ex alterius** etc.

in re *prep.* [L. **in** in, on (1), **re** matter, thing, property, business, affair (2): in the thing/matter.] In the affair of. In the matter of. Concerning. In the case of. —*n. Law.* A judicial proceeding in which there is no opposing party but there is merely a matter to be decided, such as the estate of a bankrupt, a guardianship, or an application respecting a proposed highway.

in re aliena *adj./adv.* [L. **in** in, on (1); **re** matter, thing, property, business, affair (2); **aliena** of another (3): in the property of another.] In another's property. [In traditional property concepts] *the usufruct . . . was not a species of ownership; it consisted of perpetual rights of beneficial use in re aliena . . .* (Asante 1975:5).

in rebus *adv.* [L. **in** in, on (1); **rebus** matters, affairs (2): in matters.] *Law.* In the matters, affairs, or cases of. Followed by names of plaintiffs and defendants.

in rebus manifestis, errat qui auctoritates legum allegat; quia perspicua vera non sunt probanda. [L. **in** in, on (1); **rebus** matters (3); **manifestis** clear, evident (2); **errat** makes a mistake, errs (8); **qui** (he)

who (4); **auctoritates** authorities (6); **legum** of laws (7); **allegat** cites, quotes (5); **quia** because (9); **perspicua** manifest, clear (10); **vera** truths (11); **non** not (13); **sunt** are (12); **probanda** to be proved (14): In clear matters, he who cites authorities of laws makes a mistake because manifest truths are not to be proved.] *Law.* In clear cases, it is an error to cite legal authorities, because manifest truths need not be proved.

in re communi melior est conditio prohibentis. [L. **in** in, on (1); **re** matter, thing, property, business, affair (3); **communi** common (2); **melior** better (4); **est** is (5); **conditio** condition (6); **prohibentis** of one forbidding (7): In a common property, better is the condition of the one forbidding.] *Law.* In matters of joint ownership of property, the partner who exercises the right of veto has a better case. See **in re communi neminem** etc.; **in re communi potior** etc.; and **in re pari potiorem** etc.

in re communi neminem dominorum jure facere quicquam, invito altero, posse. [L. **in** in, on (2); **re** matter, thing, property, business, affairs (4); **communi** common (3); **neminem** none (5); **dominorum** of owners (6); **jure** by right, law (7); **facere** to do (8); **quicquam** anything (9); **invito** (with being) unwilling (11); **altero** with the other (10); **posse** to be able, (that) be able (1): that, in a common property, none of the owners by law is able to do anything, with the other being unwilling.] *Law.* In matters of joint ownership of property, none of the owners can rightly do anything against the will of the other. See **in re communi melior** etc.

in re communi potior est conditio prohibentis. [L. **in** in, on (1); **re** matter, thing, property, business, affair (3); **communi** common (2); **potior** better, preferable (4); **est** is (5); **conditio** condition (6); **prohibentis** of one forbidding (7): In a common property, preferable is the condition of the one forbidding.] *Law.* In matters of joint ownership of property, the partner who exercises the right of veto has a stronger case. See **in re communi melior** etc.

in re dubia, benigniorem interpretationem sequi, non minus justius est quam tutius. [L. **in** in, on (1); **re** matter, thing, property, business, affair (3); **dubia** doubtful (2); **benigniorem** more liberal, favorable (5); **interpretationem** interpretation (6); **sequi** to follow (4); **non** not (8); **minus** less (9); **justius** more just (10); **est** is (7); **quam** than (11); **tutius** safer (12): In a doubtful matter, to follow the more liberal interpretation is no less juster than (it is) safer.] *Law.* In case of doubt, following the more liberal interpretation is not only just but also safe. See **in dubio, pars** etc.

in re dubia magis inficiatio quam affirmatio intelligenda. [L. **in** in, on (1); **re** matter, thing, property, business, affair (3); **dubia** doubtful (2); **magis** rather, more (5); **inficiatio** negative, denial (4); **quam** than (6); **affirmatio** affirmative (7); **intelligenda** to be understood (8): In a doubtful thing, the negative rather than the affirmative is to be understood.] *Law.* In case of doubt, the negative is preferable to the affirmative. See **actori incumbit** etc.

in rem *adj.* [L. **in** into, to, against, for (1); **rem** matter, thing, property, business, affair (2): against a thing.] *Law.* Against a thing. Proceedings in rem are held in a court which has jurisdiction to determine right to, status of, or title to property and, though the judgment is binding on the whole world, the court may not necessarily have the power to enforce obedience on the parties affected. *Joe took an action in rem to recover his land from the squatters.* See **actio in rem.**

in rem actio est per quam rem nostram quae ab alio possidetur petimus, et semper adversus eum est qui rem possidet. [L. **in** into, to, against, for (2); **rem** matter, thing, property, business, affair (3); **actio** action, deed, legal suit (1); **est** is (4); **per** through, by (5); **quam** which (6); **rem** matter, thing, property, business, affair (9); **nostram** our (8); **quae** which (10); **ab** from, by (12); **alio** another (13); **possidetur** is possessed (11); **petimus** we demand, sue for, claim (7); **et** and (14); **semper** always (16); **adversus** against (17); **eum** the person (18); **est** it is (15); **qui** who (19); **rem** matter, thing, property, business, affair (21); **possidet** possesses (20): A legal suit against the thing is by which we seek our property which is possessed by another and (is) always against the person who possesses the property.] *Law.* A legal action against the thing is one by which we sue for our property which is possessed by another, and it is always directed against the one who possesses the property. See **actio in rem.**

in rem judicatam *adv.* [L. **in** into, to, against, for (1); **rem** matter, thing, property, business, affair (2); **judicatam** decided, concluded (3): into a matter decided.] *Law.* Into a matter conclusively settled. Into a judgment. *The contract which was the subject-matter of dispute between Banjo and Saka has passed in rem judicatam.* See **res judicata.**

in re pari potiorem causam esse prohibentis constat. [L. **in** in, on (l); **re** matter, thing, property, business, affair (3); **pari** equal (2); **potiorem** better, preferable (8); **causam** cause, case, reason (5); **esse** to be, (that) is (7); **prohibentis** of one forbidding, prohibiting (6); **constat** it is established, certain (4): In an equal thing it is established that the cause of the one forbidding is better.] *Law.* Where a thing is equally owned by several persons, it is established that the party who imposes his veto has a better case. Applicable to partnerships. See **in re communi melior** etc.

in re propria iniquum admodum est alicui licentiam tribuere sententiae. [L. **in** in, on (8); **re** matter, thing, property, business, affair (10); **propria** one's own (9); **iniquum** unfair, unjust (3); **admodum** absolutely (2); **est** it is (1); **alicui** to anyone (5); **licentiam** license, freedom (6); **tribuere** to give, assign (4);

sententiae of judgment (7): It is absolutely unjust to give anyone the freedom of judgment in one's own matter.] *Law.* It is an absolute travesty of justice to allow anyone to serve as a judge in his/her own cause. See **nemo debet esse** etc.

in rerum natura *adv./adj.* [L. **in** in, on (1); **rerum** of matters, things, property, business, affairs (3); **natura** nature (2): in the nature of things.] In the world of material things. In existence. Genuine. *The bailiff alleged that the plaintiff is fictitious or, in other words, not in rerum natura.*

in restitutionem, non in poenam heres succedit. [L. **in** into, to, against, for (3); **restitutionem** restoration (4); **non** not (5); **in** into, to, against, for (6); **poenam** penalty, punishment (7); **heres** heir, successor (1); **succedit** succeeds, inherits (2): An heir succeeds into restoration, not into punishment.] *Law.* An heir is liable to restore property unlawfully acquired by the ancestor but not to pay the penalty for an ancestor's criminal offense. See **crimina morte extinguuntur; dolus auctoris** etc.; **in heredes** etc.; **mors omnia solvit;** and **poena ex delicto** etc.

I.N.R.I. *abbr.* for **Jesus Nazarenus Rex Judaerum** (q.v.).

in s. *abbr.* for **in situ** (q.v.).

in saecula saeculorum *adv.* [L. **in** into, to, against, for (1); **saecula** ages, generations (2); **saeculorum** of ages, generations (3): to ages of ages.] For ever and ever. *The institution of marriage and the attendant procreation will continue to exist in saecula saeculorum.*

insanus est qui, abjecta ratione, omnia cum impetu et furore facit. [L. **insanus** mad, insane (2); **est** he/she is (1); **qui** who (3); **abjecta** (with) having been thrown away, cast aside (5); **ratione** with reason (4); **omnia** all (things) (7); **cum** with (8); **impetu** violence, force (9); **et** and (l0); **furore** rage, madness, fury (11); **facit** does (6): He/she is insane who, with reason having been thrown away, does all things with violence and fury.] A person who throws away reason and does everything with violence and fury is insane. Cf. **furiosis nulla** etc.; **furiosus absentis** etc.; **furiosus solo** etc.; and **furiosus stipulari** etc.

insculpsit *v.* [L. He/she sculpted.] He/she carved it. Used to indicate the creator of a piece of sculpture. Cf. **caelavit.**

in se *adv.* [L. **in** in, on (1); **se** one's self, him/her/itself, themselves (2): in itself.] In and of itself. By nature. Intrinsically.

in sha Allah or **inshallah** *interj.* [Ar. **in** if (1); **shā** wishes, wills (3); **Allāh** Allah, God (2): if Allah wills.] By the grace of Allah (or God). *There will, in sha Allah, be a meeting of the association today.* Cf. **Deo volente** and **laus Deo.**

insignia or **insigne** *n., pl.* **insignia** or **insignias** [L. mark, indication, sign, signal, badge, garb.] 1. A badge, emblem, symbol, or other distinguishing sign of authority, honor, dignity, or office. *A rival faction in the succession dispute has forcibly seized the insignia of the kingship.* 2. A characteristic, peculiar, or typical sign by which something is identified. Characteristics.

in simili materia *adv./adj.* [L. **in** in, on (1); **simili** similar, like (2); **materia** matter, subject-matter (3): in a similar matter.] Dealing with a similar matter. Dealing with a related subject.

in situ *abbr.* **in s.** *adv./adj.* [L. **in** in, on (1); **situ** position, site, situation (2): in position.] In its original or natural situation or position. Left untouched and undisturbed. a) *A developed land attracts heavier compensation than one left in situ.* b) *decomposition of rocks in situ.*

in solido *adv./adj.* [L. **in** in, on (1); **solido** solid, whole, entire (2): on the whole.] As a whole. Involving all. Joint and several. Jointly and severally. a) *The brothers are bound in solido by an agreement to pay the debt.* b) *The contract imposes on the entire family an in solido obligation.* Cf. **in parte** etc.

in solo alieno [L. **in** in, on (1); **solo** ground, land, soil (3); **alieno** another's (2): on another's land.] *Law.* On another's ground. On someone else's property. Cf. **in solo proprio.**

in solo proprio [L. **in** in, on (1); **solo** ground, land, soil (3); **proprio** one's own, individual (2): on one's own land.] *Law.* In one's own ground. On one's own property. Cf. **in solo alieno.**

insomnia *n., pl.* **insomnias** [L. sleeplessness.] *Medicine.* Sleeplessness. Inability to get the requisite amount of sleep over a period of time.

insouciance *n., pl.* **insouciances** [Fr. heedlessness, unconcern, carelessness.] Unconcern or indifference, especially to the impression which one creates. a) *Agnes always complains about Joel's insouciance over the clothes he wears.* b) *. . . the epitome of slob insouciance . . .* (*Time Int.* 1982).

in specie *adv./adj.* [L. **in** in, on (1); **specie** kind, appearance, resemblance, likeness (2): in likeness.] In kind. *James offered to lend Jonathan some commodities on condition that they would be returned in specie.* Cf. **in genere.**

inspeximus [L. We have inspected/examined.] We have inspected a document. *Law.* Used in charter or letters patent. *After the word inspeximus, the grantor recites verbatim and confirms the former grant and then adds other privileges, if need be.*

I.N.S.T. *abbr.* for **in nomine Sanctae Trinitatis** (q.v.).

instanter *adv.* [L. urgently, vehemently.] At once. Instantly. *Freddie ordered the intruder to leave his residence instanter.*

in statu nascendi *adv./adj.* [L. **in** in, on (1); **statu** condition, state, position (2); **nascendi** of being born (3): in the condition of being born.] In the nascent stage. In the course of being developed. *Though the manufacturing company is in statu nascendi, an advertisement has been placed in a national daily* newspaper asking prospective distributors to send applications with a deposit of $10,000 each.

in statu pupillari *adv./adj.* [L. **in** in, on (1); **statu** position, condition (2); **pupillari** of orphan, ward (3): in the position of an orphan or ward.] As a student, pupil or ward. Classified as a student or pupil. *Matriculation in the university qualifies one to be regarded in statu pupillari.*

in statu quo *adv.* [L. **in** in, on (1); **statu** state, condition (2); **quo** in which (3): in the state/condition in which.] In the former position. In the same state/condition. a) *By the decision of the appellate court in the ejection case, the applicant was left in statu quo.* b) [In civil cases.] *an interlocutory injunction may be granted at any time after the issue of the writ to maintain things in statu quo* (Burke 1976:178).

in stipulationibus cum quaeritur quid actum sit verba contra stipulatorem interpretanda sunt. [L. **in** in, on (1); **stipulationibus** agreements, stipulations (2); **cum** when (3); **quaeritur** it is asked, there is a question (4); **quid** what (5); **actum sit** has been done (6); **verba** words (7); **contra** against, opposite (10); **stipulatorem** one making the stipulation (11); **interpretanda** to be interpreted (9); **sunt** are (8): In agreements when there is a question as to what has been done, the words are to be interpreted against the one making the stipulation.] *Law.* In case of disputed stipulations, words must be interpreted against the one who made the stipulation; i.e., words of the stipulation should be interpreted against the one who made the stipulation, while words of the promise should be interpreted against the one who made the promise. See **quaelibet concessio** etc.

in stirpes *adv./adj.* [L. **in** into, to, against, for (1); **stirpes** descendants, family stocks (2): into family stocks.] *Law.* By stocks. By roots. By representation of branches of the decedent's descendants. Applicable to intestate inheritance and synonymous with per stirpes but distinguished from per capita (for each person).

institor *n., pl.* **institors** [L. factor, broker, hawker, peddler.] *Roman and Scots Civil Law.* An agent, such as a broker or manager of a business concern, whose transactions are binding on the principal.

Institutio Oratoria *n.* [L. **institutio** arrangement, instruction (2); **oratoria** oratorical (1): oratorical instruction.] *Oratorical Instruction*, a pedagogical treatise on oratory and rhetoric by Quintilian (c.35 A.D.–??).

int. *abbr.* for **interim** (q.v.).

intaglio *n., pl.* **intaglios** [It. engraving.] 1. The art of working lines, carvings, and designs into hard materials such as metal and stone. 2. An object worked in such a way.

integer *n., pl.* **integers** [L. untouched, entire, whole, complete.] 1. *Mathematics.* Any natural or whole number, such as 1, 2, 3, or 4, as distinguished from a fraction. 2. A whole. A complete or full entity. *For an organization to function successfully and meaningfully, its various parts should discard their individual aspirations and function as one body, an integer.*

integer vitae *adj.* [L. **integer** whole, complete, intact, virtuous (1); **vitae** of life (2): virtuous of life.] Living a virtuous life.

intégrant *adj.* [Fr. integral.] Constituent. Component. Inherent. *The chief accountant resents the deputy registrar's encroachment on an intégrant part of his powers.*

intellectus *n.* [L. discernment, perception, understanding.] Ability to understand and comprehend. The human intellect. *An adult, basically, is a person who has the requisite intellectus to understand his/her acts and their consequences.*

intelligentsia or **intelligentzia** *n., pl.* **intelligentsias** or **intelligentzias** [Russ. **intelligentsiya** the intellectuals.] Usually used as a collective sing. noun. 1. A class of highly educated and articulate persons who arrogate to themselves the right to participate in, and guide, national affairs. 2. A class of persons devoted to intellectual pursuits and engaged in mental rather than menial or manual work. *Along with so many other critics around the world, the French intelligentsia has detected an American crisis of faith . . .* (*Newsweek Int.* Feb. 23, 1981:50).

intentio inservire debet legibus, non leges intentioni. [L. **intentio** intention (1); **inservire** to be submissive (3); **debet** ought, should (2); **legibus** to laws (4); **non** not (5); **leges** laws (6); **intentioni** to intention (7): The intention ought to be submissive to the laws, not the laws to the intention.] The intention should conform to the laws and not vice versa. Applicable to the intention of the testator.

intentio mea imponit nomen operi meo. [L. **intentio** intention (2); **mea** my (1); **imponit** imposes (3); **nomen** name (4); **operi** (on) work, deed, action (6); **meo** on my (5): My intention imposes a name on my deed.] *Law.* My action derives its name from my intent. Cf. **actus non facit** etc.

inter absentes *adv./adj.* [L. **inter** among, between (1); **absentes** the absent (ones) (2): among the absent ones.] Among those not present. *The meeting had to be postponed thirty minutes, since prominent members of the association were inter absentes.* Cf. **inter praesentes.**

inter alia *abbr.* **I.A.**, **i.a.** or **int. al.** *adv.* [L. **inter** among, between (1); **alia** others, other (things) (2): among other things.] In addition to or together with other items or matters. *The new manager had to consider, inter alia, the problem of providing houses for the junior staff.*

inter alios *adv.* [L. **inter** among, between (1); **alios** some, other (people) (2): among other people.] 1. Among other persons. *Prominent guests at the reception were, inter alios, the Prime Minister, all*

Ministers, and most of the Permanent Secretaries. 2. *Law.* Between persons who are alien to the disputed matter. Cf. **inter ceteros.**

inter alios res gestas aliis non posse praejudicium facere saepe constitutum est. [L. **inter** between, among (5); **alios** some, other (persons) (6); **res** matters, things, property, business, affairs (3); **gestas** done (4); **aliis** to others (11); **non** not (8); **posse** to be able (7); **praejudicium** prejudice (10); **facere** to do, make (9); **saepe** often (2); **constitutum est** it has been established, decided that (1): It has often been established that things done among some persons cannot do prejudice to others.] *Law.* It has often been established that the acts of persons alien to a cause cannot prejudice it. See **res inter alios acta alteri** etc.

inter apices juris *adv.* [L. **inter** among, between (1); **apices** summits, highest ornaments (2); **juris** of right, law (3): among the highest ornaments of law.] *Law.* Among the extreme applications of law. Among the law's subtleties.

inter arma silent leges. See **silent enim leges inter arma.**

interbella or **interbellum** *adj.* [L. **inter** between (1); **bella** war(s) (2): between wars.] Happening, occurring or subsisting between wars, especially the period between the First and the Second World Wars. *Germans of the interbellum period deeply resented the terms of the treaty of Versailles and found no difficulty in supporting Hitler.*

inter ceteros *adv.* [L. **inter** among, between (1); **ceteros** the other (people) (2): among the other people.] Among the other persons. *The tribunal invited, inter ceteros, the former Minister of Finance.* Cf. **inter alios.**

inter conjuges *adj./adv.* [L. **inter** among, between (1); **conjuges** married persons (2): between married persons.] Between husband and wife. Between a married couple. *The courts usually handle matters inter conjuges with great care and concern.* See **inter virum et uxorem.**

interdictum *n., pl.* **interdicta** [L. prohibition.] Injunction. Interdict.

interest reipublicae ne maleficia remaneant impunita. [L. **interest** it interests, concerns, is expedient (1); **rei publicae** the public affair, the state (2); **ne** that not (3); **maleficia** crimes, evil deeds (4); **remaneant** should remain (5); **impunita** unpunished (6): It interests the state that crimes should not remain unpunished.] *Law.* It is a matter of interest/concern to the state that evil deeds should not go unpunished. See **impunitas semper** etc.

interest reipublicae ne sua quis male utatur. [L. **interest** it interests, concerns, is expedient (1); **rei publicae** the public affair, the state (2); **ne** that not (3); **sua** his/her own (6); **quis** any one (4); **male** badly, ruinously (7); **utatur** should use (5): It concerns the state that any one should not use his/her own ruinously.] *Law.* It is a matter of concern to the state that one should not put one's property to improper use. See **sic utere tuo** etc.

interest reipublicae quod homines conserventur. [L. **interest** it interests, concerns, is expedient (1); **rei publicae** the public affair, the state (2); **quod** that (3); **homines** human beings (4); **conserventur** be preserved (5): It concerns the state that human beings be preserved.] *Law.* It is a matter of concern to the state that human life be preserved. See **de morte hominis** etc.

interest reipublicae res judicatas non rescindi. [L. **interest** it interests, concerns, is expedient that (1); **rei publicae** the public affair, the state (2); **res** matters, things, property, business, affairs (3); **judicatas** decided, determined (4); **non** not (5); **rescindi** to be rescinded (6): It concerns the state that matters decided not be rescinded.] *Law.* It is a matter of concern to the state that judicial decisions not be revoked. See **infinitum in** etc.

interest reipublicae suprema hominum testamenta rata haberi. [L. **interest** it interests, concerns, is expedient (1); **rei publicae** the public affair, the state (2); **suprema** (that) last (3); **hominum** of human beings, persons (5); **testamenta** wills (4); **rata** valid, approved (7); **haberi** (to) be had, held, regarded (6): It concerns the state (that) last wills of human beings be regarded valid.] *Law.* It is a matter of interest/concern to the state that people's last wills be considered valid. See **in testamentis** etc.; **mens testatoris** etc.; **testatoris ultima** etc.; and **ultima voluntas** etc.

interest reipublicae ut carceres sint in tuto. [L. **interest** it interests, concerns, is expedient (1); **rei publicae** the public affair, the state (2); **ut** that (3); **carceres** prisons, jails (4); **sint** should be (5); **in** in, on (6); **tuto** safe, secure (condition) (7): It interests the state that prisons should be in secure condition.] *Law.* It is a matter of concern to the state that prisons be secure.

interest reipublicae ut quilibet re sua bene utatur. [L. **interest** it interests, concerns, is expedient (1); **rei publicae** the public affair, the state (2); **ut** that (3); **quilibet** anyone, all, everyone (4); **re** matter, thing, property, business, affair (7); **sua** his/her own (6); **bene** well, properly (8); **utatur** uses (5): It concerns the state that everyone uses his/her property well.] *Law.* It is in the state's interest that people use their property properly. See **sic utere tuo** etc.

interest reipublicae ut sit finis litium. [L. **interest** it interests, concerns, is expedient (1); **rei publicae** the public affair, the state (2); **ut** that (3); **sit** there should be (4); **finis** end (5); **litium** of lawsuits (6): It concerns the state that there should be an end of lawsuits.] *Law.* It is in the state's interest that a lawsuit not drag on forever. See **infinitum in** etc.

interim *abbr.* **int.** *n., pl.* **interims** [L. meanwhile, in the meantime.] The time intervening. Interval of time. *The*

interim between sessions of the conference was profitably utilized in exchanging pleasantries and making or renewing acquaintances. —*adv.* Meanwhile. *As he awaited his turn at the interview he, interim, kept musing upon the bright career awaiting him.* —*adj.* Temporary. Provisional. Happening, appointed, or made for the meantime. *The regime, which was heralded with fanfare and aroused great expectations, turned out to be a mere interim government.*

interim committitur *n.* [L. **interim** meanwhile, in the meantime (2); **committitur** he is committed (1): He is committed meanwhile.] *Law.* A court order committing a person to prison until the time when further action will be taken.

interiora secreta *pl. n.* [L. **interiora** inner, internal, more intimate (1); **secreta** secrets, mysteries (2): inner secrets.] Internal secrets. *The club has some interiora secreta which are not to be divulged to the uninitiated.*

intermedium *n., pl.* **intermedia** or **intermediums** [L. intermediate thing.] An intermediary. A medium. An agent. *The firm does not conduct business directly with the public, but through intermedia.*

intermezzo *n., pl.* **intermezzi** or **intermezzos** [It. intermediate thing.] 1. A musical or dramatic interlude between acts of a dramatic performance or opera. 2. A short independent piece in similar style. 3. A diversion, interlude, affair or episode. *She had insisted that her film career was finished, but now it turns out that the four years away from the camera were only an intermezzo* (*Newsweek Int.* July 6, 1981:19).

inter nos *adv.* [L. **inter** among, between (1); **nos** us (2): between us.] Between ourselves. *The courts will always enforce what we agree upon inter nos, unless the transaction is offensive to public policy, natural justice, equity, or good conscience.*

internuncio *n.* [It. internunzio a mediator, go-between, messenger.] 1. A go-between. A messenger operating between two parties. 2. A diplomatic representative of the Pope whose rank is lower than that of the nuncio. Cf. **internuntius.**

internuntius *n., pl.* **internuntii** [L. a mediator, go-between, messenger.] 1. **Internuncio** (q.v.). 2. A broker. A go-between. Cf. **internuncio.**

inter pares *adv./adj.* [L. **inter** among, between (1); **pares** equal (persons) (2): between equals.] Among equals. *At the morning's parade, the principal selected Kwame as a leader inter pares.* Cf. **parium judicium** and **per pares.**

inter partes *adv./adj.* [L. **inter** between, among (1); **partes** sides, parties (2): between parties.] Between the parties. *The court declared the agreement inter partes null and void on the ground that it was based on turpis causa.* Cf. **ex parte.**

inter praesentes *adv./adj.* [L. **inter** among, between (1); **praesentes** those present (2): among those present.] Among the parties present. *The Bar Association* *elected two members inter praesentes to represent it at the annual delegates' conference in New York.* Cf. **inter absentes.**

interpres legum *n., pl.* **interpretes legum** [L. **interpres** interpreter (1); **legum** of laws (2): interpreter of laws.] A person or thing which makes the law clear. *It is generally accepted that custom is the best interpres legum.*

interpretatio talis in ambiguis semper fienda est ut evitetur inconveniens et absurdum. [L. **interpretatio** interpretation (3); **talis** such (7); **in** in, on (1); **ambiguis** ambiguous (things) (2); **semper** always (5); **fienda** to be done (6); **est** is (4); **ut** that (8); **evitetur** be/is avoided (12); **inconveniens** inconvenient (9); **et** and (10); **absurdum** absurd (11): In ambiguous things, interpretation is always to be done such that the inconvenient and absurd is avoided.] Whenever there is ambiguity, interpretation should be made in such a way as to avoid an inconvenient and absurd solution.

interregnum *n., pl.* **interregna** or **interregnums** [L. an interval between two reigns.] The time between a monarch's death and the choice of a successor. A reign during a temporary vacancy or suspension of government. A period when the normal governmental activities are suspended. *Though only appointed acting President in an interregnum, he fancied himself the de jure President and took to arbitrary acts.*

interrex *n., pl.* **interreges** [L. a temporary king, viceroy, regent.] A provisional or temporary ruler. A person who wields supreme power during a transitional period. *The interrex, who was appointed after the coup d'état, has become the de jure Head of State.*

in terrorem *adv./adj.* [L. **in** into, to, against, for (1); **terrorem** terror (2): for terror.] For fright. By way of intimidation/threat. Applicable, among others, to a legacy given on condition that the legatee should not dispute certain aspects of the legacy. Also applicable to a condition which is a mere threat. *A clause fixing damages in the event of breach will not be implemented where it is in the nature of a penalty fixed in terrorem of the party in breach* (Freedland 1976:250-251).

inter se or **inter sese** *adv./adj.* [L. **inter** among, between (1); **se** or **sese** themselves (2): among themselves.] Among or between themselves. *The Senior Advocates held a meeting to discuss matters inter se.*

interstitium *n., pl.* **interstitia** or **interstitiums** [L. that which stands between.] The space in-between. An interstice.

inter virum et uxorem *adj./adv.* [L. **inter** among, between (1); **virum** man, husband (2); **et** and (3); **uxorem** wife (4): between husband and wife.] Between spouses. *Intervention in a dispute inter virum et uxorem is a delicate affair.* See **inter conjuges.**

inter vivos *adj./adv.* [L. **inter** among, between (1); **vivos** the living (2): between the living.] During life. From a living person to another. a) *A gift of a self-acquired property made inter vivos is valid in law.* b) *But if there is a sole survivor of family land, he is in the position of an individual landholder and can dispose of the land inter vivos or by will* (James 1982:51).

in testamentis plenius testatoris intentionem scrutamur. [L. **in** in, on (1); **testamentis** wills (2); **plenius** more fully (4); **testatoris** of testator (6); **intentionem** intention (5); **scrutamur** we carefully search (3): In wills we carefully search more fully for the intention of the testator.] *Law.* In wills we search scrupulously for the testator's intention. See **interest reipublicae suprema** etc.

intifada *n.* [Ar. **intifāda** shaking off.] A political and social movement by Palestinians to shake off the rule of Israel.

in totidem verbis *adv.* [L. **in** in, on (1); **totidem** just as many, just so many (2); **verbis** words (3): in just as many words.] In so many words. Word for word. In exactly the same words. *The lecturer penalized the student for using his handout in totidem verbis.* See **totidem verbis.**

in toto *adv.* [L. **in** in, on (1); **toto** the whole (2): on the whole.] As a whole. Totally. Completely. Entirely. Altogether. *I accept your suggestion in toto.*

in toto et pars continetur. [L. **in** in, on (1); **toto** whole (2); **et** also (5); **pars** part (3); **continetur** is contained, comprised (4): In the whole the part is also contained.] The whole contains the parts. See **majus continet minus.**

intra anni spatium *adv.* [L. **intra** within (1); **anni** of year (3); **spatium** interval, space (2): within the interval of a year.] Within a year.

in tractu temporis *adv.* [L. **in** in, on (1); **tractu** course, track (2); **temporis** of time (3): in the course of time.] Over a period of time. *The accountant confessed to the police that he had embezzled the colossal sum of money in tractu temporis.*

in traditionibus scriptorum, non quod dictum est, sed quod gestum est inspicitur. [L. **in** in, on (1); **traditionibus** deliveries (2); **scriptorum** of written (things) (3); **non** not (4); **quod** (that) which, what (5); **dictum** said (7); **est** is, has been (6); **sed** but (8); **quod** (that) which, what (9); **gestum** done (11); **est** is, has been (10); **inspicitur** is considered, investigated (12): In deliveries of written things, not what has been said, but what has been done, is considered.] *Law.* In the delivery of written documents, what is considered is not what has been said, but what is done; i.e., whatever is said in the process of delivery has no legal effect on the delivery. See **non quod dictum est** etc. Cf. **traditio loqui** etc.

intra fidem *adj.* [L. **intra** within (1); **fidem** belief, credence, faith (2): within belief.] Acceptable. Credible. *The evidence of the prosecution witness seems to be intra fidem.*

intra luctus tempus *adv.* [L. **intra** within (1); **luctus** of mourning (3); **tempus** time (2): within the time of mourning.] During the period of mourning. *The distribution of the properties of the deceased was held in abeyance intra luctus tempus.*

intra muros *adj.* [L. **intra** within (1); **muros** walls (2): within the walls.] Pertaining to the internal affairs or politics, i.e., of an organization, institution, etc. *The President asked her employees to be cautious about broadcasting intra muros matters.*

in transitu *abbr.* **in trans.** *adv.* [L. **in** in, on (1); **transitu** passage, transit (2): in passage.] During passage from one place to another. In transit. On the way. *If a buyer becomes insolvent before the goods arrive by sea, the seller has a remedy of stoppage in transitu before the ship docks at the port.*

intra parietes *adv.* [L. **intra** within (1); **parietes** walls (2): within walls.] Between walls. Out of court. In an amicable manner. *Though the dispute between Aikins and Hereford is undoubtedly a serious one, they opted to settle it intra parietes.*

intrapartum *adj.* [L. within birth or delivery.] *Medicine.* Happening to the mother during childbirth.

intra vires *adv./adj.* [L. **intra** within (1); **vires** power, strength (2): within the power.] Within the powers. Within the scope of authority. *It is intra vires of a court to try contempt committed in its face.* Cf. **extra vires** and **ultra vires**.

intra vitam *adv.* [L. **intra** within (1); **vitam** life (2): within life.] In the lifetime of the subject. During life. *The diagnosis which the doctor made intra vitam is at variance with the results of the postmortem examination.* —*adj.* **intravitam** Pertaining to a subject which is alive. *The post mortem examination does not support the doctor's intravitam diagnosis.*

intrigant or *fem.* **intrigante** *n., pl.* **intrigants** or *fem.* **intrigantes** [Fr. intriguer, schemer.] One who engages in secret plots or schemes. *The institution is full of intrigants whose stock-in-trade is abject servility and character assassination.*

intrigue *n., pl.* **intrigues** [Fr. scheme, plot, love affair.] 1. A clandestine, covert, or secret plot or plan. *The seat of power has been converted into a citadel of intrigues, where schemers ply their sordid trade.* 2. A secret or clandestine love affair, especially one in which a married woman is involved. —*v. intr.* 1. To plot or plan secretly. *Abraham alleged that Jose intrigued with Regina against him.* 2. To engage in a clandestine or secret love affair. —*v. tr.* 1. To acquire, make, or accomplish through clandestine plots. *The headmaster of the school is a man of negligible ability who intrigued his way into his position.* 2. To arouse the curiosity, interest, or desire of. *Adam brought some news which intrigued everybody in the room.*

introductio *n.* [L. leading in, introduction.] Insertion. Cf. **emissio** and **erectio**.

Introibo *v.* [L. I will go.] I will go. The first word of Psalm 43:4 with which the Tridentine Mass began. —*n.* The first prayer of the Mass.

Introit *n.* [L. He enters, he goes in.] *Christianity.* The beginning of a service, especially the first part of the Tridentine Catholic Mass.

intromissio *n.* [L. sending in, letting in, admitting.] 1. Meddling with the affairs of another. 2. Insertion, particularly of penis into vagina.

in usu *adv.* [L. **in** in, on (1): **usu** use (2): in use.] *Law.* In the process of being used.

in utero *adj./adv.* [L. **in** in, on (1); **utero** womb, uterus (2): in the womb/uterus.] *Medicine.* Before birth. In the womb. *The fact that the baby shows symptoms of a venereal disease suggests that the infection occurred in utero.*

inv. *abbr.* for **invenit** (q.v.).

in vacuo *adv.* [L. **in** in, on (1); **vacuo** vacuum, empty, void (2): in a vacuum.] In an empty space. Without context. a) *Laws are not made in vacuo, for their promulgation is prompted by some circumstances in the society and they are intended to achieve certain purposes.* b) *The Acting Attorney-General then proceeded to argue on his objection to the proceedings being brought in vacuo* (Aihe and Oluyede 1979:149).

inveniens libellum famosum et non corrumpens punitur. [L. **inveniens** (one) coming upon, finding (1); **libellum** writing (3); **famosum** defamatory, slanderous (2); **et** and (4); **non** not (5); **corrumpens** destroying, ruining (6); **punitur** is punished (7): One finding slanderous writing and not destroying (it) is punished.] *Law.* A person who finds but does not destroy a libelous publication is punished.

invenit *abbr.* **inv.** or **invt.** *v.* [L. He/she found, invented it.] He/she devised it. He/she discovered it. He/she designed it. Used to indicate the author of a design, invention, etc. Cf. **caelavit**.

invenit et delineavit *abbr.* **inv. et del.** [L. **invenit** he/she found, designed, invented (1); **et** and (2); **delineavit** he/she drew (3): He/she designed and drew it.] He/she is the designer and drawer. Cf. **caelavit**.

in ventre sa mere *adj.* [Obs. Fr. **in** in, on (1); **ventre** belly, stomach (2); **sa** one's (3); **mère** mother (4): in the belly of one's mother.] In the womb. **En ventre sa mère** (q.v.).

in verbo *abbr.* **I.V.** or **i.v.** *adv.* [L. **in** in, on (1); **verbo** word (2): in the word.] Under the word. Used for references to dictionaries and other works arranged alphabetically. See **in voce; quae vide; Q.V.; sub hac voce; sub hoc verbo; sub verbo;** and **sub voce**.

inv. et del. *abbr.* for **invenit et delineavit** (q.v.).

in via usucapiendi *adv.* [L. **in** in (1); **via** way, course (2); **usucapiendi** of acquiring ownership by use (3): in the course of acquiring ownership by use.] *Law.* In the course of acquiring ownership by use, prescription, or usucaption.

in vinculis *adv.* [L. in in, on (1); vinculis fetters, bonds, prison (2): in fetters.] 1. In custody. In chains. In prison. 2. *Figuratively.* In a condition close to servitude which is the result of acceptance of harsh terms. *Far from helping him to solve his problems, the loan which Keith received from the moneylender has put him in vinculis.*

in vino veritas [L. in in, on (2); vino wine (3); veritas truth (1): truth in wine.] There is truth in wine. Wine brings out the truth; i.e., under the influence of alcohol, a person's pent-up feelings and hidden thoughts, indeed, his/her true character, can be revealed. Cf. vulgoque veritas etc.

invita Minerva *adv.* [L. invita with unwilling (2); (with) Minerva (2): with an unwilling Minerva.] Without the sanction of Minerva, the Roman goddess of knowledge and the arts. Without the sanction of the gods. Without divine inspiration. Unwillingly.

invito beneficium non datur. [L. invito to the unwilling (person), against one's will (4); beneficium benefit, favor, honor (1) non not (2); datur is given (3): A benefit is not given to an unwilling person.] *Law.* A benefit is not given to a person against his/her will; i.e., when the law confers a privilege/benefit upon a person, he/she is free to decline it. See beneficium invito etc.

in vitro *adj./adv.* [L. in in, on (1); vitro glass (2): in glass.] *Medicine.* Outside the living body. In a test tube or any artificial device. *Thanks to the work of Drs. Patrick Steptoe and Robert Edwards, a potentially barren woman can now give birth to a child, even quadruplets, through the in vitro fertilization and embryo transfer process.*

in vivo *adj./adv.* [L. in in, on (1); vivo living (thing) (2): in a living thing.] Happening, observable, etc. in a plant's or animal's living body.

in voce *abbr.* I.V. or i.v. *adv.* [L. in in, on (1); voce word, voice (2): in the word.] Under the word. Used for references to dictionaries and other works arranged alphabetically. See in verbo and sub voce.

invt. *abbr.* for invenit (q.v.).

iota *n., pl.* iotas [Gk. the letter "i."] 1. The smallest letter of the Greek alphabet, i.e., "i." 2. The smallest possible quantity. A very small amount, degree, or quantity. a) *They can organize the affairs of the country as stupidly and selfishly as they desire without any iota of danger to the security of their jobs* (*The Guardian* 1987). b) *There is no iota of doubt in my mind that he is not qualified for his present position.*

I Pagliacci *pl. n.* [It. i the (1); pagliacci clowns, buffoons (2): the clowns.] "The Clowns," an 1892 opera by Ruggiero Leoncavallo (1858–1919).

I.P.I. or i.p.i. *abbr.* for in partibus infidelium (q.v.).

ipsae leges cupiunt ut jure regantur. [L. ipsae themselves (2); leges laws (1); cupiunt wish, desire (3); ut that (4); jure by right, law (6); regantur they be guided (5): The laws themselves desire that they be guided by right.] The laws themselves wish to be guided by what is right.

ipse dixit *n.* Cicero (106–43 B.C.). *De natura deorum* I,5,10. [L. ipse he himself (1); dixit said (2): He himself said.] A dictum (q.v.). A saying. An assertion based on authority, rather than proved. a) *Aristotle's ipse dixit that barbarians are natural slaves who should be treated like animals has almost unanimously been rejected by posterity.* b) *However, such a rule cannot justify the head in determining the tenancy on his mere ipse dixit that the land is required by the family* (James 1982:210).

ipsissima verba *pl. n.* [L. ipsissima the very, themselves (1); verba words (2): the very words.] The words themselves. The identical, precise, or exact words. *When she transcribes from the shorthand, he expects only his ipsissima verba* (*The Guardian* October 29, 1985:9).

ipsissimis verbis *adv.* [L. ipsissimis in the very, themselves (1); verbis (in) words (2): in the very words.] In the words themselves. In the same, identical, precise, or exact words.

ipso facto *adv.* [L. ipso (by) itself (2); facto by deed, act, fact (1): by the act/fact itself.] By the mere fact. By the very nature of the case. As a consequence of the mere fact/act. a) *He assumes that by my criticism of the young generation, ipso facto, I belong to the old school of thought.* b) *The official, who is resolutely opposed to irrational dictatorship, does not believe that the fact that an order has been issued means, ipso facto, that it has to be obeyed.* See facto.

ipso jure *adv.* [L. ipso (by) itself (2); jure by right, law (1): by law itself.] By operation of law. *The landlord forfeited one of his buildings ipso jure.*

I.Q. or i.q. *abbr.* for idem quod (q.v.).

I.Q.E.D. *abbr.* for id quod erat demonstrandum (q.v.).

ira furor brevis est. Horace (65–8 B.C.). *Epistles,* I,2,62. [L. ira anger (1); furor insanity, madness, rage (4); brevis brief, short (3); est is (2): Anger is a brief insanity.] Anger is a brief spell of madness.

irredenta *n., pl.* irredentas [It. unredeemed.] An area which historically, culturally, or ethnically is related to one country but is, de jure, incorporated into another. *European colonialism has created many irredentas in Africa.*

Islam *n.* [Ar. 'islām submission, resignation.] 1. The religious faith proclaimed by Mohammed and embraced by Muslims who, basically, submit themselves to the will of Allah by recognizing Allah as the only God and Mohammed's position as the instrument through whom the will of Allah was revealed. 2. The civilization or culture based on the Islamic religion. 3. The entire Muslim world. All Muslims. Cf. Muslim.

isogenesis *n.* [Neo-Gk. from Gk. **iso(s)** equal, like (1); **genesis** origin, source (2): equal or like origin.] Similarity or likeness in origin, source, or development.

issei *n., pl.* **issei** or **isseis** [Japan. from **is** first (1); **sei** generation (2): first generation.] A Japanese who has immigrated to the United States. A first-generation Japanese-American. Cf. **Nisei** and **Sansei**.

ita lex scripta est. [L. **ita** so (1); **lex** law (2); **scripta** written (4); **est** is, has been (3): So the law has been written.] That is what the law says.

ita te Deus adjuvet. [L. **ita** so (1); **te** you (4); **Deus** God (3); **adjuvet** let help (2): So let God help you.] So help you God.

ita utere tuo ut alienum non laedas. [L. **ita** in such a way (3); **utere** use (1); **tuo** yours (2); **ut** that (4); **alienum** another's (7); **non** not (5); **laedas** you hurt (6): Use yours in such a way that you not hurt another's.] *Law.* Use your property in such a way that you not harm your neighbor's. See **sic utere tuo** etc.

item *adv.* [L. in the same way.] Also. Used to mark each point in a list. —*n.* 1. A point in a list. A single object in a series or collection. 2. A brief notice in a journal or newspaper.

ite missa est [L. **ite** go (1); **missa** sent (3); **est** he/she/it is, has been (2): Go, she has been sent.] Go, the mass is ended. The conclusion of the Catholic liturgy.

iter *n., pl.* **itinera** or **iters** [L. journey, road, way, passage.] *Roman Law.* The right to pass over another's landed property either by horse or on foot.

izzat *n.* [Urdu 'izzat from Pers. 'izza glory.] Honor. **Kudos** (q.v.). Cf. **accolade** 3.

J

J. or **j.** *abbr.* for 1. **judex** (q.v.). 2. **jus** (q.v.).

j'accuse *n.* Émile Zola (1840–1902). [Fr. **j'** I (1); **accuse** accuse, charge (2): I accuse.] Accusation(s). Allegation(s). Charge(s). *The mayor also retaliated with his own j'accuse* (*Newsweek Int.*, Nov. 1, 1982:15).

jacens hereditas or **jacens haereditas** See **hereditas jacens**.

jacquerie *n.* [Fr. from **Jacques** James, a common male name like "John."] 1. "La Jacquerie" was an uprising of peasants against the French nobility in 1358. 2. Any revolt of peasants or the oppressed, especially a bloody one.

jacta alea est. Julius Caesar (100–44 B.C.). [L. **jacta** thrown, cast (3); **alea** die (1); **est** is, has been (2): The die has been thrown.] The die is cast. See **alea jacta esto**; **alea jacta est**; and **Rubicon**.

jacta est alea. See **jacta alea est.**

janitor *n., pl.* **janitors** [L. doorkeeper.] The building custodian responsible especially for cleaning, heating, etc.

januis clausis *adv.* [L. **januis** with doors (1); **clausis** (with) having been shut, closed (2): with doors having been shut or closed.] Secretly. In secret. Behind closed doors. In camera.

Janus *n.* [L. the god of entering and exiting, beginning and ending.] *Ancient Rome.* The guardian of doors, entrances, and gates and the god of beginnings and endings, Janus was represented as having two faces, one on the front of his head, the other at the back. The opening of the doors of his temple indicated that Rome was at war, while their closing indicated that Rome was at peace. *Laitin's argument is that each of these two schools of thought is like one or the other of the two faces of Janus— one looking into the past, the other into the future* (A.I. Asiwaju in *West Africa* 1987). —**Janus-faced** 1. Looking, viewing or gazing in two opposite directions. *The government was commended for presenting a Janus-faced budget, which takes due consideration of both the past and the future.* 2. Characterized by two contrasting features or aspects. —**Janus-like** Resembling Janus in that it looks, behaves, acts, etc. in contrasting or opposite ways. *Joan has been doing her best to understand Adam, but her efforts have been frustrated by the Janus-like nature of his behavior.*

J.B. *abbr.* for **Jurum Baccalaureus** (q.v.).

J.C. *abbr.* for **Jurisconsultus** (q.v.).

J.C.B. *abbr.* for 1. **Juris Canonici Baccalaureus** (q.v.). 2. **Juris Civilis Baccalaureus** (q.v.).

J.C.D. *abbr.* for 1. **Juris Canonici Doctor** (q.v.). 2. **Juris Civilis Doctor** (q.v.).

J.C.L. *abbr.* for 1. **Juris Canonici Licentiatus** (q.v.). 2. **Juris Civilis Licentiatus** (q.v.).

J.D. *abbr.* for 1. **Juris Doctor** (q.v.). 2. **Jurum Doctor** (q.v.).

Jeder nach seinen Fähigkeiten, jedem nach seinen Bedürfnissen. Karl Marx (1818–1883). [Ger. **Jeder** each (1); **nach** according to (2); **seinen** his (3); **Fähigkeiten** capabilities, abilities (4); **jedem** to each (5); **nach** according to (6); **seinen** his (7); **Bedürfnissen** needs, requirements (6): Each according to his abilities; to each according to his needs.] Each member of society should contribute according to his/her capabilities; society should give to each according to his/her needs. Cf. **suum cuique**.

jehad *var.* of **jihad** (q.v.).

je ne sais quoi or **je-ne-sais-quoi** *n.* [Fr. **je** I (1); **ne** not (3); **sais** know (2); **quoi** what, which (4): I know not what.] Something. Something or other. Something which is indefinable. A thing which defies adequate description or expression. *He has an air of je ne sais quoi about him.*

Jesus Christus *abbr.* **I.C.** *n.* [L. **Jesus** from Heb. **Jehosua** or **Joshua** God is salvation (1); L. **Christus** from Gk. **christos** anointed (2): Jesus Christ.] Jesus the Anointed.

Jesus Hominum Salvator *abbr.* **J.H.S.** *n.* [L. **Jesus** Jesus (1); **hominum** of human beings, people (3); **salvator** savior (2): Jesus, savior of human beings.] Jesus, Redeemer of Humankind.

Jesus Mundi Salvator *abbr.* **J.M.S.** *n.* [L. **Jesus** Jesus (l); **mundi** of world (3); **salvator** savior (2): Jesus, savior of the world.] Jesus, Redeemer of the World.

Jesus Nazarenus Rex Judaerum *abbr.* **I.N.R.I.** John 19:19. [L. **Jesus** Jesus (1); **Nazarenus** the Nazarene (2); **rex** king (3); **Judaerum** of the Jews (4): Jesus the Nazarene King of the Jews.] Jesus of Nazareth, King of the Jews. Words placed on the cross of Jesus by order of Pontius Pilate.

Jesus Salvator Mundi *abbr.* **J.S.M.** *var.* of **Jesus Mundi Salvator** (q.v.).

jeté *n., pl.* **jetés** [Fr. cast, flung, thrown, a step in a dance.] *Ballet.* A sharp leap during which the free leg is thrust outward. *To the rich sound of antiphonal brass, the dancers take to the air in jeté after jeté, in dazzling lifts, in fiery pas de deux . . .* (*Newsweek Int.* July 27, 1981:53).

jeu de mots *n., pl.* **jeux de mots** [Fr. **jeu** play, game (1); **de** of (2); **mots** words (3): play of words.] A play upon words. Pun.

jeu d'esprit *n., pl.* **jeux d'esprit** [Fr. **jeu** play, game (1); **d'** of (2); **esprit** mind, wit (3): game or play of mind.] Witticism. A piece of writing which displays wit or cleverness. *It is this kind of jeu d'esprit that makes his letters worth reading . . .* (*Newsweek Int.* March 23, 1981:49).

jeune fille fatale *n., pl.* **jeunes filles fatales** [Fr. **jeune** young (2); **fille** girl (3); **fatale** fatal (1): a fatal young girl.] 1. A dangerous girl or young woman. 2. A flirtatious girl. A girl or young woman who attracts men in an inexplicable and mysterious manner. 3. A young seductress who entices men into embarrassing or dangerous situations. A young woman who seduces men through the use of her charm and then proceeds to exploit them. Cf. **femme fatale.**

jeune premier *n., pl.* **jeunes premiers** [Fr. **jeune** young (man) (2); **premier** foremost (1): foremost young man.] An actor playing the juvenile lead, i.e., as the young hero. Cf. **jeune première.**

jeune première *n., pl.* **jeunes premières** [Fr. **jeune** young (woman) (2); **première** foremost (1): foremost young woman.] Leading young lady. An actress playing the juvenile lead, i.e., as the young heroine. Cf. **jeune premier.**

jeunesse dorée *n.* [Fr. **jeunesse** youth (2); **dorée** golden, gilded (1): gilded youth.] Wealthy and fashionable young people. *The jeunesse dorée in universities drive flashy cars and make their lecturers look like paupers.*

J.H.S. *abbr.* for **Jesus Hominum Salvator** (q.v.).

jihad or **jehad** *n., pl.* **jihads** or **jehads** [Ar. **jihād** struggle, contest.] *Islam.* 1. A struggle for personal, spiritual perfection. 2. A holy war waged by Muslims against those who have not embraced the Islamic faith. *It is doubtful that Sunnis would respond to a jihad proclaimed by a Shiite imam such as Khomeini* (*Newsweek Int.* Dec. 1, 1979:25). 3. A war, crusade or campaign undertaken in support of, or in opposition to, a doctrine, belief or principle.

jinriksha or **jinricksha** or **jinrikisha** *n.* [Japan. from **jin** person (1); **riki** strength, power (2); **sha** vehicle, carriage (3): person-power vehicle.] A small carriage with two-wheels and drawn by one or two people. A ricksha.

jiva *n., pl.* **jivas** [Skt. **jīva** soul.] *Hinduism and Janinism.* The soul or life-giving principle.

J.M.S. *abbr.* for **Jesus Mundi Salvator** (q.v.).

joie de vivre *n.* [Fr. **joie** enjoyment, delight (1); **de** of (2); **vivre** living (3): enjoyment of living.] Exhilaration. High spirits. Enthusiasm. Carefree or enthusiastic enjoyment of life. a) *Debts and a broken marriage tempered his joie de vivre . . .* (*Newsweek Int.* June 1, 1981:23). b) *John is a vivacious and charismatic man whose joie de vivre is truly infectious.*

jongleur *n., pl.* **jongleurs** [Fr. jester, entertainer.] *Medieval France and England.* A migrant entertainer who performed songs, recited poetry, etc.

jour en banc *n.* [Fr. **jour** day (1); **en** in (2); **banc** bench (3): a day in bench.] *Law.* A day in court; i.e., a day for appearance in court before a panel of judges, such as an appellate court. Cf. **jour en nisi prius** and **jour en pays.**

jour en nisi prius *n.* [Fr. **jour** day (1); Fr. **en** in (2); L. **nisi** unless (3); L. **prius** before (4): a day in unless before.] *Law.* A day for appearance before a court which tries factual issues. Such a court usually comprises a judge and a jury. See **jour en pays** and **nisi prius** Cf. **jour en banc.**

jour en pays *n.* [Fr. **jour** day (1); **en** in (2); **pays** the country (3): a day in the country.] A **jour en nisi prius** (q.v.) as opposed to a **jour en banc** (q.v.).

J.S.M. *abbr.* for **Jesus Salvator Mundi** (q.v.).

Jubilate Deo [L. **jubilate** rejoice, shout for joy (1); **Deo** God (2): Shout for joy to God.] 1. The first words of Psalm 100. 2. *Music.* A composition based upon this psalm. 3. Any joyous shout.

Judenhetze *n.* [Ger. **Juden** Jew (1); **Hetze** hunt, baiting (2): Jew-baiting.] Persecution of Jews. Anti-Semitism.

Judenrat *n., pl.* **Judenrats** [Ger. **Juden** Jew, Jewish (1); **Rat** council (2): Jewish council.] A committee for the Jewish community in an area under German control during the Second World War.

Judenrein *adj.* [Ger. **Juden** Jew, Jewish (1); **rein** pure, free (2): Jew free.] Without Jews. Used in Nazi Germany to refer to organizations and groups from which Jews had been removed.

judex *abbr.* **J.** or **j.** *n., pl.* **judices** *Roman Law.* [L. judge.] A private person entrusted with the duty of hearing and determining a case, and almost comparable to a modern arbitrator or referee appointed by a court. Judge.

judex ad quem *n.* [L. **judex** judge (1); **ad** to, at, for, according to (2); **quem** whom (3): a judge to whom.] *Law.* A judge of an appellate court. A judge to whom an appeal is made. Cf. **judex a quo**.

judex aequitatem semper spectare debet. [L. **judex** judge (1); **aequitatem** equity (5); **semper** always (3); **spectare** to look at, regard, consider (4); **debet** ought, should (2): A judge should always consider equity.] *Law.* A judge should always take equity into consideration.

judex ante oculos aequitatem semper habere debet. [L. **judex** judge (1); **ante** before (6); **oculos** eyes (7); **aequitatem** equity (5); **semper** always (3); **habere** to have, hold, regard (4); **debet** should, ought (2): A judge should always have equity before his eyes.] *Law.* A judge should always bear in mind the principles of equity.

judex a quo *n.* [L. **judex** judge (1); **a** from (2); **quo** whom (3): a judge from whom.] *Law.* A judge from whose court an appeal is made. Cf. **judex ad quem**.

judex bonus nihil ex arbitrio suo faciat, nec proposito domesticae voluntatis, sed juxta leges et jura pronuntiet. [L. **judex** judge (2); **bonus** good (1); **nihil** nothing (4); **ex** out of (5); **arbitrio** will, pleasure (7); **suo** his own (6); **faciat** may/should do (3); **nec** nor (8); **proposito** by proposal, design (9); **domesticae** of personal, one's own (10); **voluntatis** (of) wish, desire, choice (11); **sed** but (12); **juxta** in accordance with (14); **leges** laws (15); **et** and (16); **jura** rights, laws (17); **pronuntiet** should pronounce, decide (13): A good judge should do nothing out of his own will nor by the proposal of his own desire but should decide in accordance with the laws and rights.] *Law.* A good judge should set aside the dictates of his own will and desire, and pronounce judgment in accordance with the rules of law and justice. See **optima est lex** etc. Cf. **lex non exacte** etc.

judex damnatur ubi nocens absolvitur. Publilius Syrus (c.85–43 B.C.). *Sententiae* 247. [L. **judex** judge (1); **damnatur** is declared guilty, condemned (2); **ubi** when (3); **nocens** guilty, criminal (person) (4); **absolvitur** is set free, acquitted (5): A judge is declared guilty when a guilty person is set free.] *Law.* The judge is condemned when a criminal is acquitted.

judex debet judicare secundum allegata et probata. [L. **judex** judge (1) **debet** ought, should (2); **judicare** to judge, pass judgment (3); **secundum** in accordance with (4); **allegata** things alleged (5); **et** and (6); **probata** things proved (7): The judge ought to pass judgment in accordance with things alleged and things proved.] *Law.* A judge should pass judgment on the basis of the allegations and proofs. See **judicis est judicare** etc.

judex est lex loquens. [L. **judex** judge (1); **est** is (2); **lex** law (3); **loquens** speaking (4): The judge is the law speaking.] *Law.* A judge is the mouthpiece of the law.

judex habere debet duos sales: salem sapientiae, ne sit insipidus; et salem conscientiae ne sit diabolus. [L. **judex** judge (1); **habere** to have, hold, regard (3); **debet** ought, should (2); **duos** two (4); **sales** salts (5); **salem** salt (6); **sapientiae** of wisdom (7); **ne** in order that not, lest, so as not (8); **sit** he/she may be (9); **insipidus** insipid, tasteless (10); **et** and (11); **salem** salt (12); **conscientiae** of conscience (13); **ne** in order that not, so that not, so as not (14); **sit** he/she may be (15); **diabolus** diabolical, devilish, fiendish (16): A judge ought to have two salts: the salt of wisdom so that he/she may not be insipid; and the salt of conscience so that he/she may not be diabolical.] *Law.* A judge should have two kinds of salt: the salt of wisdom so as not to be unwise, and the salt of conscience so as not to be evil.

judex non potest esse testis in propria causa. [L. **judex** judge (1); **non** not (3); **potest** can, is able (2); **esse** to be (4); **testis** witness (5); **in** into, to, against, for (6); **propria** one's own, personal (7); **causa** cause, case, reason (8): A judge is not able to be a witness in a personal cause.] *Law.* A judge cannot bear witness in his/her own case. See **nemo debet esse** etc.

judex non potest injuriam sibi datam punire. [L. **judex** judge (1); **non** not (3); **potest** can, is able (2); **injuriam** injury, wrong (5); **sibi** to one's self, himself/herself (7); **datam** given (6); **punire** to punish (4): A judge cannot punish a wrong given to himself/herself.] *Law.* A judge cannot punish a wrong inflicted on himself/herself; i.e., a person cannot serve as a judge in a case affecting him/her personally. See **nemo debet esse** etc.

judex non reddit plus quam quod petens ipse requirit. [L. **judex** judge (1); **non** not (2); **reddit** gives back, restores, grants (3); **plus** more (4); **quam** than (5); **quod** what; (that) which (6); **petens** the person seeking or demanding, plaintiff (7); **ipse** himself/herself (8); **requirit** demands (9): A judge does not give back more than what the person seeking himself/herself demands.] *Law.* A judge does not grant more than that which is demanded by the plaintiff himself/herself. See **ne judex** etc.

judices non tenentur exprimere causam sententiae suae. [L. **judices** judges (1); **non** not (2); **tenentur** are bound, obligated (3); **exprimere** to express, articulate (4); **causam** cause, case, reason (5); **sententiae** (of) opinion, judgment, sentence (7); **suae** of their (6): Judges are not bound to express the reason for their opinion.] *Law.* Judges are not under obligation to explain the reason for their judgment.

judicia posteriora sunt in lege fortiora. [L. **judicia** judgments (2); **posteriora** later, latter (1); **sunt** are

(3); **in** in, on (5); **lege** law (6); **fortiora** stronger, more valid (4): Later judgments are stronger in law.] *Law.* Later (or more recent) judgments are more valid in law than earlier judgments. Cf. **judiciis posterioribus** etc.

judicia sunt tanquam juris dicta, et pro veritate accipiuntur. [L. **judicia** judgments (1); **sunt** are (2); **tanquam** as if, so to speak (3); **juris** of right, law (5); **dicta** sayings (4); **et** and (6); **pro** for, as (8); **veritate** truth (9); **accipiuntur** are accepted (7): Judgments are, so to speak, sayings of law and are accepted as truth.] *Law.* Judgments are, so to speak, pronouncements of the law and are considered to be true. See **infinitum in** etc. See also **judicium est quasi** etc.

judicia suum effectum habere debent. [L. **judicia** judgments (1); **suum** their own (4); **effectum** effect, result (5); **habere** to have, hold, regard (3); **debent** ought (2): Judgments ought to have their own effect.] *Law.* Judgments should be executed. Cf. **judicium non debet** etc.

judiciis posterioribus fides est adhibenda. [L. **judiciis** (to) judgments (5); **posterioribus** to later, latter (4); **fides** credence, credit (1); **est** is (2); **adhibenda** to be rendered, offered (3): Credence is to be rendered to later judgments.] *Law.* Later judgments must be given credence. Cf. **judicia posteriora** etc.

judici officium suum excedenti non paretur. [L. **judici** (to) a judge (3); **officium** duty, function, office (6); **suum** one's own, his/her own (5); **excedenti** exceeding, going beyond (4); **non** not, no (1); **paretur** it is obeyed/obedient, there is obeying/being obedient (2): There is no being obedient to the judge going beyond his/her function.] *Law.* The judgment of a judge who goes beyond his/her jurisdiction is not enforced i.e., is null and void. See **extra territorium jus** etc.

judicis est judicare secundum allegata et probata. [L. **judicis** of judge (2); **est** it is (1); **judicare** to judge, decide (3); **secundum** in accordance with (4); **allegata** things alleged (5); **et** and (6); **probata** things proved (7): It is of a judge to decide in accordance with things alleged and things proved.] *Law.* It is the duty of a judge to pronounce judgment in accordance with the allegations and proofs. See **judex debet judicare secundum** etc.

judicis est jus dicere non dare. [L. **judicis** of judge (2); **est** it is (1); **jus** right, law (4); **dicere** to declare, state (3); **non** not (5); **dare** to give (6): It is of a judge to declare right, not give it.] *Law.* It is the duty of a judge to declare or state, not create, the law.

judicium a non suo judice datum nullius est momenti. [L. **judicium** judgment (1); **a** by (3); **non** not (5); **suo** his/her/its own, appropriate (6); **judice** judge (4); **datum** given (2); **nullius** of no (8); **est** is (7); **momenti** (of) importance, weight (9): A judgment

given by a judge who is not appropriate is of no importance.] *Law.* A judgment delivered by a judge who has no jurisdiction over the case is null and void. See **extra territorium jus** etc.

judicium Dei *n.* [L. **judicium** judgment (1); **Dei** of God (2): judgment of God.] Trial by ordeal. It was believed in antiquity that the outcome of a trial by ordeal was an expression of the judgment of God.

judicium est quasi juris dictum. [L. **judicium** judgment (1); **est** is (2); **quasi** as it were, so to speak, as one might say (3); **juris** of right, law (5); **dictum** saying (4): Judgment is so to speak the saying of law.] *Law.* Judgment is, so to speak, an expression/saying of law. See **judicia sunt tanquam** etc.

judicium non debet esse illusorium; suum effectum habere debet. [L. **judicium** judgment (1); **non** not (3); **debet** ought, should (2); **esse** to be (4); **illusorium** illusory (5); **suum** its own (8); **effectum** effect (9); **habere** to have, hold, regard (7); **debet** ought, should (6): A judgment should not be illusory; it ought to have effect.] *Law.* A judgment should be true, not imaginary and it should have its effect; i.e., its decision should be carried out. Cf. **judicia suum** etc.

judicium parium *n.* [L. **judicium** judgment (1); **parium** of equal (persons) (2): judgment of equal persons.] *Former English Law.* Judgment of a person's peers. Trial by jury.

judicium redditur in invitum. [L. **judicium** judgment (1); **redditur** is given, delivered (2); **in** against, into (3); **invitum** unwilling (person) (4): Judgment is delivered against an unwilling person.] *Law.* Judgment is given against a person, whether he/she likes it or not.

judicium semper pro veritate accipitur. [L. **judicium** judgment (1); **semper** always (3); **pro** as, for (4); **veritate** truth (5); **accipitur** is accepted (2): Judgment is always accepted as the truth.] *Law.* A judgment is always considered to be true. See **infinitum in** etc.

judo *n.* [Japan. from **jū** soft (1); **dō** way (2): the soft way.] A form of Japanese wrestling used as sport and physical training and based upon the art of balance and leverage. Cf. **jujitsu.**

juge de paix *n., pl.* **juges de paix** [Fr. **juge** judge (1); **de** of (2); **paix** peace (3): judge of peace.] *French Law.* Justice (or judge) of the peace. A judge of low rank who not only serves as a police magistrate but also summarily decides minor controversies, especially those which hinge on matters of fact.

juge d'instruction *n., pl.* **juges d'instruction** [Fr. **juge** judge (1); **d'** of (2); **instruction** investigation (3): judge of investigation.] *French Law.* Examining magistrate. A magistrate for criminal cases who receives complaints, collects the evidence by interrogating parties and witnesses, investigates the case and formulates charges on the basis of the evidence. Though he does not determine guilt, his findings usually influence the proceedings in court. See **Untersuchungsrichter**.

Jugendstil *n.* [Ger. **Jugen** youth (1); **Stil** style (2): youth style.] The German equivalent of **art nouveau** (q.v.).

juggernaut *n.* [Hindi **jagannāth** from Skt. **jagat** moving, world (1); **nāthah** lord (2): moving lord, world lord.] 1.Title of the Hindi god Krishna. 2. A belief or organized group which demands absolute devotion. 3. An unavoidable, destructive power or force.

juicio de concurso de acreedores *n.* [Sp. **juicio** judgment (1); **de** of (2); **concurso** contest, assembly (3); **de** of (4); **acreedores** creditors (5): judgment of the contest of creditors.] *Spanish Law*. Where a debtor's estate is inadequate for settling the claims of his/her various creditors, a judgment directing that each creditor's claim should be considered in accordance with his rank and form. Cf. **concurso**.

jujitsu or **jujutsu** or **jiujitsu** or **jiujutsu** *n.* [Japan. **jūjitsu** from **jū** soft (1); **jitsu** arts (2): the soft arts.] A Chinese and Japanese art of self-defense based upon using a combination of special holds, throws, and blows against an attacker's own strength and body mass.

Julie ou la Nouvelle Héloïse *n.* [Fr. **Julie** Julie (1); **ou** or (2); **la** the (3); **nouvelle** new (4); **Héloïse** Heloise (5): Julie or the new Heloise.] *Julie or the New Heloise*, an epistolary novel (1761) by Jean-Jacques Rousseau (1712–1778).

Junior *abbr.* **Jr.** *adj.* [L. younger.] Younger in rank or age. Used as a title in a proper name to indicate the younger of two individuals with the same name, especially a son and his father. *John Fitzgerald Kennedy, Jr.* —*n.* **junior** *pl.* **juniors**. A third-year student in high school or college. Cf. **Senior**.

junta *n., pl.* **juntas** [Sp. council, board, assembly.] 1. A governmental consultative, deliberative, or legislative assembly, committee, or council. 2. A revolutionary, usually military, transitional government. a) *A fact-finding commission . . . paid a visit to Turkey to pose a few pointed questions to the five-member ruling junta* (*Time Int.*1982). b) *The Argentine military junta sounded a retreat to the barracks last week* (*Newsweek Int.* March 14, 1983:30). 3. A group of persons who have formed a close association for a common objective. *A number of lecturers have formed a scholarly junta to promote the publication of articles.*

Juppiter ex alto perjuria ridet amantum. Ovid (43 B.C.–17 A.D.). *Ars Amatoria* I,633. [L. **Juppiter** Jupiter (1); **ex** out of, from, away from (2); **alto** high (3); **perjuria** perjuries (5); **ridet** laughs at (4); **amantum** of those loving (6): Jupiter from high laughs at the perjuries of those loving.] From the heights of heaven Jupiter laughs at lovers' lies.

jura eodem modo destituuntur quo constituuntur. [L. **jura** rights, laws (1); **eodem** in the same (3); **modo** (in) way (4); **destituuntur** are abandoned,

abrogated (2); **quo** in which (5); **constituuntur** they are made, established (6): Laws are abandoned in the same way in which they are made.] *Law*. Laws are abolished in the same way in which they are established; i.e., the same procedure used to pass a law must be used to remove it. See **eodem modo quo quid constituitur dissolvitur**.

jura in personam *pl. n.* [L. **jura** rights, laws (1); **in** into, to, against, for (2); **personam** a person (3): rights against a person.] Rights against an individual. *The question whether equitable rights and interests are jura in rem or jura in personam is a question of more than purely academic importance . . .* (Hanbury 1962:444). Cf. **jura in rem**.

jura in re *pl. n.* [L. **jura** rights, laws (1); **in** in, on (2); **re** matter, thing, property, business, affair (3): rights in a thing.] Rights in a matter.

jura in rem *pl. n.* [L. **jura** rights, laws (1); **in** into, to, against, for (2); **rem** matter, thing, property, business, affair (3): rights against a thing.] Rights against something. *On the nature of equitable rights, Maitland was never tired of reiterating that, though they have come to look very like jura in rem, they can never gain a place in this category . . .* (Hanbury 1962:23). Cf. **jura in personam**.

jura majestatis *pl. n.* [L. **jura** rights, laws (1); **majestatis** of sovereignty, majesty (2): rights of sovereignty.] *Civil Law*. Rights of control or rule. Rights of majesty. Cf. **jura summi imperii**.

juramentum est indivisibile, et non est admittendum in parte verum et in parte falsum. [L. **juramentum** oath (1); **est** is (2); **indivisibile** indivisible (3); **et** and (4); **non** not (6); **est** is (5); **admittendum** to be received, admitted (7); **in** in, on (8); **parte** part (9); **verum** true (10); **et** and (11); **in** in, on (12); **parte** part (13); **falsum** false (14): An oath is indivisible and is not to be received in part true and in part false.] *Law*. An oath is indivisible and should not be regarded as partly true and partly false. Cf. **omne sacramentum** etc.

jura naturae sunt immutabilia. [L. **jura** rights, laws (1); **naturae** of nature (2); **sunt** are (3); **immutabilia** immutable, unchangeable, unalterable (4): The laws of nature are immutable.] The laws of nature cannot be changed.

jura novit curia. [L. **jura** rights, laws (3); **novit** knows, understands (2); **curia** court (1): The court knows the laws.] *Law*. It is the court which knows the laws.

jura publica anteferenda privatis. [L. **jura** rights, laws (2); **publica** public (1); **anteferenda** to be preferred, placed before (3); **privatis** private (ones) (4): Public rights are to be preferred to private ones.] *Law*. Public rights must take precedence over private ones. See **in casu extremae** etc.

jura sanguinis nullo jure civili dirimi possunt. [L. **jura** rights, laws (1); **sanguinis** of blood (2); **nullo**

by no (5); **jure** (by) right, law (7); **civili** (by) civil (6); **dirimi** to be destroyed, frustrated (4); **possunt** can, are able (3): Rights of blood can be destroyed by no civil law.] *Law.* Rights of kindred/blood cannot be destroyed by any civil law.

jura summi imperii *pl. n.* [L. **jura** rights, laws (1); **summi** of highest, topmost (2); **imperii** power, command (3): rights of the highest power.] Rights of sovereignty. Rights of absolute dominion. Cf. **jura majestatis.**

jurato creditur in judicio. [L. **jurato** to the sworn (4); **creditur** it is believed, belief is given (3); **in** in, on (1); **judicio** judgment (2): In judgment belief is given to the sworn.] *Law.* In delivering judgment, the person under oath is believed. See **in judicio** etc.

juratores sunt judices facti. [L. **juratores** jurors, juries (1); **sunt** are (2); **judices** judges (3); **facti** of fact, deed (4): Jurors are judges of fact.] *Law.* Jurors are judges of the fact or deed. See **ad quaestionem facti** etc.

Jur. D. *abbr.* for **Juris Doctor** (q.v.).

jure accrescendi *adv.* [L. **jure** by right, law (1); **accrescendi** of growing up, increasing, becoming greater (2): by right of increasing.] By the right of survivorship. *Tola became the sole beneficiary of the land jure accrescendi.* See **jus accrescendi.**

jure belli *adv.* [L. **jure** by right, law (1); **belli** of war (2): by the right of war.] By the law of war.

jure civili *adv.* [L. **jure** (by) law (2); **civili** by the civil law.] According to civil law.

jure dignitatis *adv.* [L. **jure** by right, law (1); **dignitatis** of dignity, distinction, eminence (2): by right of dignity.] By right of distinction. Because of honor. **Honoris causa** (q.v.). Applicable to an academic degree awarded to a person for distinguished services to the public.

jure divino *adv.* [L. **jure** (by) right, law (2); **divino** by divine (1): by divine right.] By right emanating from the law of God. *Kings generally believe that they hold their positions jure divino.*

jure domini *adv.* [L. **jure** by right, law (1); **domini** of master, owner, proprietor (2): by the right of the master.] By right of ownership. *The landlord, jure domini, notified the tenant to vacate the apartment within three months or be prepared to face the ignominy of ejection.*

jure emphyteutico *adv.* [L. **jure** (by) right, law (2); **emphyteutico** (by) emphyteutic, pertaining to an inheritable and alienable leasehold (1): by emphyteutic right.] *Law.* By right of inheritable and alienable lease-hold. By the right of emphyteusis. See **emphyteusis.**

jure gentium *adv.* [L. **jure** by right, law (1); **gentium** of nations (2): by law of nations.] By the law of nations. By international law. *A person who commits an offense regarded as a crime jure gentium may be* extradited, particularly if his country has a treaty with the country of refuge. See **jus gentium.**

jure humano *adv.* [L. **jure** by right, law (2); **humano** (by) human (1): by human law.] *Law.* By human law as opposed to natural or divine law.

jure mariti *adv.* [L. **jure** by right, law (1); **mariti** of husband (2): by right of a husband.] By the right of a husband. See **jus mariti.** Cf. **jure uxoris.**

jure naturae aequum est neminem cum alterius detrimento et injuria fieri locupletiorem. [L. **jure** by right, law (1); **naturae** of nature (2); **aequum** equitable, fair (4); **est** it is (3); **neminem** no one (5); **cum** with (8); **alterius** of another (12); **detrimento** loss, detriment (9); **et** and (10); **injuria** injury, harm (11); **fieri** to become, becomes (6); **locupletiorem** richer, wealthier (7): By the law of nature it is equitable (that) no one become richer with loss and injury of another.] *Law.* By the law of nature it is not equitable that a person should acquire wealth to the financial or physical loss of another. See **nemo debet ex** etc.

jure successionis *adv.* [L. **jure** by right, law (1); **successionis** of succession, inheritance (2): by right of succession.] According to the law of succession. *Johnson acquired the two buildings and five cars jure successionis.*

jure uxoris *adv.* [L. **jure** by right, law (1); **uxoris** of wife (2): by right of a wife.] By the right of a wife. Used, for instance, in common law, in a conveyance by a husband of the estate of his wife. Cf. **jure mariti.**

Juris Baccalaureus *abbr.* **J.B.** *n.* [L. **juris** (of) right, law (2); **baccalaureus** bachelor (1): Bachelor of Law.] An undergraduate degree in law.

Juris Canonici Baccalaureus *abbr.* **J.C.M.** *n.* [L. **juris** (of) right, law (3); **canonici** of canon (2); **baccalaureus** bachelor (1): Bachelor of Canon Law.] An undergraduate degree in canon law.

Juris Canonici Doctor *abbr.* **J.C.D.** *n.* [L. **juris** (of) right, law (3); **canonici** of canon (2); **doctor** teacher (1): teacher of canon law.] Doctor of Canon Law. A terminal graduate degree in canon law.

Juris Canonici Licentiatus *abbr.* **J.C.L.** *n.* [L. **juris** (of) right, law (3); **canonici** of canon (2); **licentiatus** licentiate (1): Licentiate in Canon Law.] An academic degree conferred by a university or seminary for completion of an advanced curriculum in canon law.

Juris Civilis Baccalaureus *abbr.* **J.C.B.** *n.* [L. **juris** (of) right, law (3); **civilis** of civil (2); **baccalaureus** bachelor (1): Bachelor of Civil Law.] An undergraduate degree in civil law.

Juris Civilis Doctor *abbr.* **J.C.D.** *n.* [L. **juris** (of) right, law (3); **civilis** of civil (2); **doctor** teacher (1): teacher of civil law.] Doctor of Civil Law. A terminal graduate degree in civil law.

Juris Civilis Licentiatus *abbr.* **J.C.L.** *n.* [L. **juris** (of) right, law (3); **civilis** of civil (2); **licentiatus** licentiate

(1): Licentiate in Civil Law.] An academic degree conferred by a European university for completion of an advanced curriculum in civil law.

jurisconsultus *abbr.* **i-ctus** or **J.C.** *n.* [L. skillful in the law, lawyer.] *Roman Law.* A person of remarkable legal knowledge who is consulted not only by advocates and magistrates but also by private individuals.

jurisdictionis fundandae causa *adv.* [L. **jurisdictionis** of jurisdiction (2); **fundandae** (of) to be established (3); **causa** for the sake (1): for the sake of jurisdiction to be established.] For the sake of establishing jurisdiction.

Juris Doctor *abbr.* **J.D.** or **Jur. D.** *n.* [L. **juris** of right, law (2); **doctor** teacher (1): teacher of law.] Doctor of Law. A terminal graduate degree in law.

juris effectus in executione consistit. [L. **juris** of right, law (2); **effectus** effect (1); **in** in, on (4); **ex(s)ecutione** execution (5); **consistit** consists in, depends upon (3): The effect of the law consists in execution.] The effect of the law depends upon its execution. The law draws its effectiveness from its enforcement.

juris et de jure *adj.* [L. **juris** of right, law (1); **et** and (2); **de** of, from, about, for (3); **jure** right, law (4): of law and of right.] *Law.* There are two kinds of presumption. Presumption juris et de jure is one whose rebuttal the law does not permit, being regarded as conclusive, while a presumption juris tantum is one which may be rebutted, if the evidence is available. See **praesumptio juris et de jure**. Cf. **juris tantum** and **praesumptio juris**.

juris ignorantia est cum jus nostrum ignoramus. [L. **juris** of right, law (3); **ignorantia** ignorance (2); **est** it is (1); **cum** when (4); **jus** right, law (7); **nostrum** our (6); **ignoramus** we are ignorant, do not know (5): It is ignorance of the law when we are ignorant of our right.] Ignorance of the law and ignorance of our rights are one and the same thing.

juris praecepta sunt haec: honeste vivere; alterum non laedere; suum cuique tribuere. [L. **juris** of right, law (4); **praecepta** precepts, rules (3); **sunt** are (2); **haec** these (1); **honeste** decently, properly (6); **vivere** to live (5); **alterum** another (9); **non** not (7); **laedere** to hurt (8); **suum** one's own, his/her own (12); **cuique** to each one (11); **tribuere** to give (10): These are rules of the law: to live decently; not to hurt another; to give to each one his/her own.] These are precepts of the law: living a decent life; refraining from harming another; and giving to each person his/her due.

juris publici or **publici juris** *adj.* [L. **juris** (of) right, law (2); **publici** of public, common (1): of public right.] *Law.* Of public use. Of common use. Applicable to such things as belong to the state and can be used by everybody; e.g., rivers, bridges, roads, harbors, etc. See **bienes comunes**.

juris tantum *adj.* [L. **juris** of right, law (1); **tantum** only, alone, merely (2): of law only.] *Law.* Of law alone. See **juris et de jure**.

Jurum Baccalaureus *abbr.* **J.B.** *n.* [L. **jurum** of rights, laws (2); **baccalaureus** bachelor (1): Bachelor of Laws.] An undergraduate degree in law.

Jurum Doctor *abbr.* **J.D.** *n.* [L. **jurum** of rights, laws (2); **doctor** teacher (1): teacher of laws.] Doctor of Laws. A terminal graduate degree in law.

jus *abbr.* **J.** or **j.** *n., pl.* **jura** [L. right, law.] *Roman Law.* 1. A court of justice. 2. That which is binding. Law. The law in the abstract or as an aggregate. A particular system of law; e.g., jus civile or the civil law. 3. A right. A legal right, power, authority, prerogative or permission. 4. Justice. Justness. 5. *Roman Law.* An action or proceeding before the praetor.

jus abstinendi *n.* [L. **jus** right, law (1); **abstinendi** of refraining, abstaining (2): right of abstaining or refraining.] *Roman Law.* The right of an heir to reject the inheritance if, for instance, it is overburdened with debt. Cf. **jus deliberandi**.

jus abutendi *n.* [L. **jus** right, law (1); **abutendi** of abusing, misusing (2): right of abusing.] The right to abuse. *Roman and Civil Law.* Absolute ownership, including the power to make full use of, alienate, and even destroy property. Cf. **jus utendi**.

jus accrescendi *n.* [L. **jus** right, law (1); **accrescendi** of growing up, increasing (2): right of increasing.] *Roman and Civil Law.* The right of survivorship. The right of accrual. A right relating to joint ownership, whereby on the death of a party, the remaining party automatically acquires the rights, property, liabilities, etc. of the deceased. a) *The doctrine of jus accrescendi is one of the main characteristics of a joint tenancy.* b) *But if he/she,* [i.e., the executor] *dies after probate, then, unless he was one of several joint executors, in which case the office goes to the others by jus accrescendi, ...* (Hanbury 1962:452). See **jure accrescendi**.

jus actus *n.* [L. **jus** right, law (1); **actus** of driving, way (2): right of driving or way.] *Roman Law.* The right of driving, i.e., the right to use a carriage, or drive cattle, through a place.

jus ad rem *n.* [L. **jus** right, law (1); **ad** to, at, for, according to (2); **rem** matter, thing, property, business, affair (3): right to a thing.] *Civil and Canon Law.* Right to acquire a particular property by reason of another person's legal obligation. *In contrast to jus in re, which is a complete right to a thing, jus ad rem is an incomplete right to a thing or a right without possession.* Cf **actio in rem**.

jus albanagii *n.* [Late L. **jus** right, law (1); **albanagii** of confiscation of property of an alien (2): right of the confiscation of the property of an alien.] **Droit d'aubaine** (q.v.).

jus angariae *n.* [Late L. **jus** right, law (1); **angariae** of angary (2): right of angary.] *International Law.*

In former times, the right of a belligerent to seize neutral ships in its territory and use them for transportation, should the need arise. Also, the right of a belligerent to seize, use, or destroy property of neutral states located temporarily in its territory or that of the enemy.

jus belli *n.* [L. **jus** right, law (1); **belli** of war (2): law of war.] *International Law.* The law applicable to wars, showing the right things to be done by or to belligerent powers and neutral states.

jus bellum dicendi *n.* [L. **jus** right, law (1); **bellum** war (3); **dicendi** of declaring (2): right of declaring war.] The right to declare war.

jus canonicum *n.* [L. **jus** right, law (2); **canonicum** canon (1): canon law.] Church law. Ecclesiastical law. **Jus ecclesiasticum** (q.v.).

jus civile *n.* [L. **jus** right, law (2); **civile** civil (1): civil law.] Civil law. The system of the law peculiar to a particular state, as distinct from international law. *That which any people has established for itself is called jus civile . . .* (Curzon 1979:53). See **jus civile est** etc.

jus civile est quod sibi populus constituit. [L. **jus** right, law (2); **civile** civil (1); **est** is (3); **quod** (that) which, what (4); **sibi** for itself (7); **populus** people, nation (5); **constituit** establishes, decrees (6): Civil law is that which a people establishes for itself.] The civil law is that law which a nation establishes for itself. See **jus civile**.

jus classis immitendae *n.* [L. **jus** right, law (1); **classis** of fleet (2); **immitendae** (of) to be sent in, admitted (3): right of fleet to be sent in.] The right to send a fleet of warships into the territorial waters of another country.

jus cogens *n., pl.* **jura cogentia** [L. **jus** right, law (2); **cogens** compelling, forcing (1): compelling law.] *International Law.* A law which must be followed under all circumstances and cannot be put aside even by mutual agreement.

jus commercii *n.* [L. **jus** right, law (1); **commercii** of commerce (2): right of commerce.] *Roman and Civil Law.* The right to acquire, own, and alienate property, to make contracts, and to have business transactions.

jus commune *n.* [L. **jus** right, law (2); **commune** common (1): common law.] 1. The common law of England. 2. The common or natural law, as distinct from the **jus singulare** (q.v.) set down for special cases. *The government is making every effort not to promulgate any law which may derogate from the jus commune.*

jus communicationis et societatis *n.* [L. **jus** right, law (1); **communicationis** of common ownership (2); **et** and (3); **societatis** of association, fellowship (4): right of common ownership and association.] The right of shared ownership and social connection. . . . *elsewhere*

he had justified, in the name of jus communicationis et societatis, the right of the Spaniards to take possession (Suret-Canale 1971:357).

jus constitui oportet in his quae ut plurimum accidunt, non quae ex inopinato. [L. **jus** right, law (1); **constitui** to be made, established (3); **oportet** ought, is proper (2); **in** in, on (4); **his** these (things) (5); **quae** which (6); **ut plurimum** as much as possible (8); **accidunt** happen (7); **non** not (9); **quae** (those things) which (10); **ex** out of, from, directly after, away from (11); **inopinato** the unexpected (12): Law ought to be made in these things which happen as much as possible, not those things which happen from the unexpected.] Laws should be made to cover those cases which occur frequently, and not those which occur contrary to normal expectations.

jus conubii or **jus connubii** *n.* [L. **jus** right, law (1); **conubii** of marriage (2): right of marriage.] 1. The right of marriage or intermarriage. 2. The collection of rules governing intermarriage.

jus coronae *n.* [L. **jus** right, law (1); **coronae** of crown; diadem (2): right of the crown.] The right to the crown. The right of succeeding to the throne.

jus deliberandi *n.* [L. **jus** right, law (1); **deliberandi** of deliberating (2): right of deliberating.] *Roman and Civil Law.* The right given to an heir to deliberate and decide within a fixed period whether to accept an inheritance or not. Cf. **jus abstinendi**.

jus dicere, et non jus dare. [L. **jus** right, law (2); **dicere** to say, declare, mention (1); **et** and (3); **non** not (4); **jus** right, law (6); **dare** to give (5): to say law, and not to give law.] *Law.* To declare, and not to make, law; i.e., the function of a judge.

jus disponendi *n.* [L. **jus** right, law (1); **disponendi** of disposing (2): the right of disposing.] *Law.* The right or power to dispose of or alienate property. *The owner of self-acquired property has jus disponendi.*

jus distrahendi *n.* [L. **jus** right, law (1); **distrahendi** of alienating, removing (2): right of alienating/removing.] *Law.* The right to sell pledged goods in the event of non-payment.

jus dividendi *n.* [L. **jus** right, law (1); **dividendi** of dividing, distributing (2): right of dividing.] *Law.* The right to dispose of real estate by will.

jus dominationis *n.* [L. **jus** right, law (1); **dominationis** of supremacy, despotism (2): right of supremacy.] *Law.* The right of supremacy. Overriding power.

jus duplicatum *n.* [L. **jus** right, law (2); **duplicatum** double, doubled (1): double right.] *Law.* The right of possession combined with the right of property.

jus ecclesiasticum *n.* [L. **jus** right, law (2); **ecclesiasticum** ecclesiastical (1): ecclesiastical law.] Church law. **Jus canonicum** (q.v.).

jus edicendi *n.* [L. **jus** right, law (1); **edicendi** of decreeing (2): right of decreeing.] *Roman Law.* The right enjoyed by curule magistrates (i.e., aediles, praetors, quaestors and governors of provinces) to make edicts respecting their spheres of jurisdiction. See **jus edicere.** Cf. **jus honorarium.**

jus edicere *n.* [L. **jus** right, law (1); **edicere** to decree (2): right to decree.] Right of decreeing. The right to decree. **Jus edicendi** (q.v.). Cf. **jus honorarium.**

jus emphyteuticarium *n.* [L. **jus** right, law (1); **emphyteuticarium** emphyteutic, pertaining to an inheritable and alienable leasehold (2): emphyteutic right.] The right of inheritable and alienable leasehold. See **emphyteusis.**

jus emphyteuticum *n.* [**jus** right, law (1); **emphyteuticum** emphyteutic, pertaining to an inheritable and alienable leasehold (2): emphyteutic right.] **Jus emphyteuticarium** (q.v.). See **emphyteusis.**

jus est norma recti; et quicquid est contra normam recti est injuria. [L. **jus** right, law (1); **est** is (2); **norma** rule (3); **recti** of right, uprightness (4); **et** and (5); **quicquid** whatever, whatsoever (6); **est** is (7); **contra** against, opposite (8); **normam** rule (9); **recti** of right, uprightness (10); **est** is (11); **injuria** injury (12): Law is a rule of right and whatever is against the rule of right is injury.] *Law.* Law is a rule of right and anything which is against the rule of right is an offense or injury to the law. See **fraus et jus** etc.; **jus et fraus** etc.; and **lex est norma recti.**

jus et fraus numquam cohabitant. [L. **jus** right, law (1); **et** and (2); **fraus** fraud (3); **numquam** never (4); **cohabitant** live/dwell together (5): Right and fraud never live together.] *Law.* Justice and deceit never coexist. See **fraus et jus** etc. and **jus est norma** etc.

jus ex injuria non oritur. [L. **jus** right, law (1); **ex** out of (4); **injuria** injury (5); **non** not (2); **oritur** arises, comes forth (3): Right does not rise out of injury.] *Law.* A right does not come from a wrong. See **ex turpi causa** etc.

jus fruendi *n.* [L. **jus** right, law (1); **fruendi** of enjoying (2): right of enjoying.] *Roman and Civil Law.* The right to enjoy the property of another without damaging it substantially.

jus gentium *n.* [L. **jus** right, law (1); **gentium** of nations, peoples (2): law of nations.] 1. The law of nations. International law; i.e., the law ordained by natural reason and observed by all nations. " . . . *that law which natural reason establishes among all mankind, is observed by all peoples, and is for that reason called jus gentium"* (Gaius in Curzon 1979:53). 2. *Roman Law.* The body of laws regulating the affairs of Rome's subject aliens, and relations between foreigners, or between Roman citizens and foreigners. See **jure gentium; jus inter gentes;** and **quod naturalis ratio** etc.

jus gladii *n.* [L. **jus** right, law (1); **gladii** of sword (2): right of the sword.] *Law.* The right of the sword. The law's power of execution. The right or power derived from control of the forces of coercion, i.e., the

armed forces, the police, etc. The right or power to punish criminals.

jus habendi *n.* [L. **jus** right, law (1); **habendi** of having, holding, regarding (2): right of having.] The right to have real possession of property.

jus habendi et retinendi *n.* [L. **jus** right, law (1); **habendi** of having, holding, regarding (2); **et** and (3); **retinendi** of retaining (4): right of having and retaining.] *Law.* The right to have and retain.

jus hereditatis *n.* [L. **jus** right, law (1); **hereditatis** of inheritance (2): right of inheritance.] The right to inherit.

jus honorarium *n.* [L. **jus** right, law (1); **honorarium** of a magistrate (2) law of a magistrate.] Magisterial law. *Roman Law.* The law laid down by the edicts of the curule magistrates, such as the praetors and the aediles. Cf. **jus edicendi** and **jus edicere.**

jus immunitatis *n.* [L. **jus** right, law (1); **immunitatis** of immunity, exemption from burdens (2): right of immunity.] *Civil Law.* The right to immunity. The law of immunity. The right to be exempted from public obligations.

jus in personam *n.* [L. **jus** right, law (1); **in** against (2); **personam** person (3): right against a person.] *Law.* A right against a person. The right to take legal action against a particular person or persons forming a group, or the right to enforce a legal obligation on them. Cf. **actio in rem.**

jus in re *n.* [L. **jus** right, law (1); **in** in, on (2); **re** matter, thing, property, business, affair (3): right in a thing.] *Law.* A right in a thing. A right which implies complete ownership and possession and can be enforced against anybody in the world. See **actio in rem.**

jus in re aliena *n.* [L. **jus** right, law (1); **in** in, on (2); **re** matter, thing, property, business, affair (3); **aliena** of another (4): right in the thing of another.] *Law.* A right to or based upon the property of another. An easement in another's property.

jus in rem *n.* [L. **jus** right, law (1); **in** into, to, against, for (2); **rem** matter, thing, property, business, affair (3): right against a thing.] *Law.* A right against a thing. It is the right which can be enforced against anybody anywhere in the world who interferes with a legally protected right, such as enjoyment of property or freedom from slander. See **actio in rem.**

jus in re propria *n.* [L. **jus** right, law (1); **in** in, on (2); **re** matter, thing, property, business, affair (4); **propria** one's own (3): right in one's own property.] *Law.* Full ownership as distinguished from jus in re aliena or an easement in another's property.

jus inter gentes *n.* [L. **jus** right, law (1); **inter** among (2); **gentes** nations (3): law among nations.] International law. See **jus gentium.**

jus intrandi *n.* [L. **jus** right, law (1); **intrandi** of entering (2): right of entering.] *Law.* The legal right to enter, i.e., land.

jus mariti *n.* [L. **jus** right, law (1); **mariti** of husband (2): right of a husband.] *Law.* The legal right of a husband, especially his right to his wife's movable property. See **jure mariti**.

jus mercatorum *n.* [L. **jus** right, law (1); **mercatorum** of merchants, traders (2): law of merchants.] Mercantile law. See **lex mercatoria**. Cf. **consuetudo mercatorum**.

jus militare *n.* [L. **jus** right, law (2); **militare** military, martial (1): military law.] The law of the military. Cf. **jus civile**.

jus naturae or **jus naturale** *n.* [L. **jus** right, law (1); **naturae** of nature (2): law of nature.] Natural law. Law based on nature. The law which, supposedly, governed all human beings before the advent of civilization. The law observed by all nations. Jus naturae or jus naturale is essentially the jus gentium, i.e., the law observed by all humankind. See **lex naturalis** Cf. **jus naturale est** etc.

jus naturale est quod apud homines eandem habet potentiam. [L. **jus** right, law (2); **naturale** natural (1); **est** is (3); **quod** (that) which (4); **apud** among (8); **homines** human beings, persons (9); **eandem** the same (6); **habet** has, holds, regards (5); **potentiam** force, power (7): Natural right is that which has the same force among human beings.] Natural right is the kind of right which enjoys recognition throughout the world.

jus non habenti tute non paretur. [L. **jus** right, law (6); **non** not (4); **habenti** (to) the one having, holding, regarding (5); **tute** safely (3); **non** not (1); **paretur** it is obeyed, there is obeying (2): There is no obeying safely the one not having a right.] *Law.* One can disobey with impunity a person who does not have the right. See **extra territorium jus** etc.

jus non patitur ut idem bis solvatur. [L. **jus** right, law (1); **non** not (2); **patitur** allows, permits (3); **ut** that (4); **idem** the same (5); **bis** twice (7); **solvatur** be paid (6): The law does not allow that the same thing be paid twice.] *Law.* The law forbids double payment on the same object. Cf. **bona fides non patitur** etc.

jus non scriptum *n., pl.* **jura non scripta** [L. **jus** right, law (1); **non** not (2); **scriptum** written (3): law not written.] The unwritten law; i.e., custom and similar usages. See **leges non scriptae** and **lex non scripta**. Cf. **lex publica** and **lex scripta**.

jus oneris ferendi *n.* [L. **jus** right, law (1); **oneris** of burden (2); **ferendi** (of) to be carried (3): right of burden to be carried.] *Roman Law.* The right of carrying a burden or load. The right to support and build upon the wall of the house of a neighbor.

jus pecoris pascendi *n.* [L. **jus** right, law (1); **pecoris** of cattle (2); **pascendi** (of) to be pastured, fed (3): right of cattle to be pastured.] *Law.* The right of pasturing cattle. Cf. **servitus pascendi**.

jus personarum *n.* [L. **jus** right, law (1); **personarum** of persons (2): law of persons.] *Law.* Right of persons. The law respecting persons who enjoy special interrelationship such as husband and wife, parent and child, masters and servants. The right of persons who have minimal rights such as foreigners, lunatics, and slaves.

jus possessionis *n.* [L. **jus** right, law (1); **possessionis** of possession (2): right of possession.] *Law.* The right of possession; i.e., ordinary possession which may not include ownership.

jus possidendi *n.* [L. **jus** right, law (1); **possidendi** of possessing (2): right of possessing.] *Law.* The right of possessing i.e., of both ownership and possession.

jus postliminii *n.* [L. **jus** right, law (1); **postliminii** of postliminy, recovery/restoration of rank and privileges (2): right of recovery of rank and privileges.] 1. *Roman and Civil Law.* The right of postliminy; i.e., the right of a person who has been restored to his/her previous condition to be treated as though there had never been a change of status. 2. *International Law.* The right of the owner to recover property captured by the enemy but recaptured by a fellow-citizen, a fellow-subject, or an ally.

jus primae noctis *n.* [L. **jus** right, law (1); **primae** of first (2); **noctis** (of) night (3): right of the first night.] The right of somebody who was not the bridegroom (e.g., a feudal lord) to deflower the bride. *Jus primae noctis is a major point of contention between the English and the Scots in the film "Braveheart."*

jus privatum *n.* [L. **jus** right, law (2); **privatum** private (1): private law.] 1. Private law, i.e., the law governing the conduct, rights, and obligations of individuals. 2. Private right or ownership; i.e., a private person's right or title to property. Cf. **jus publicum**.

jus prohibendi *n.* [L. **jus** right, law (1); **prohibendi** of preventing (2): right of preventing.] *Law.* The right of preventing. The right or power of veto.

jus proprietatis *n.* [L. **jus** right, law (1); **proprietatis** of property (2): right of property.] *Law.* The right of property or ownership. Applicable to right of ownership, regardless of actual possession.

jus publicum *n.* [L. **jus** right, law (2); **publicum** public (1): public law.] 1. Public law; i.e., the law as it relates to government, its functionaries, the constitution, and criminal jurisdiction. 2. Public right/ownership. Cf. **jus privatum**.

jus publicum privatorum pactis mutari non potest. [L. **jus** right, law (2); **publicum** public (1); **privatorum** of private (persons) (7); **pactis** by agreements, contracts (6); **mutari** to be changed (5); **non** not (4); **potest** can, is able (3): Public right cannot be changed by agreements of private persons.] *Law.* Agreements made by private persons cannot change or modify public law or right. See **conventio privatorum** etc.

jus quaesitum *n.* [L. **jus** right, law (1); **quaesitum** to ask for, beg, request (2): right to request.] *Law.* 1. A right to recover. Applicable to the obligee in an obligation. 2. A special or select law.

jus quaesitum tertio *n.* [L. **jus** right, law (1); **quaesitum** to ask for, beg, request (2); **tertio** to/for a third (party) (3): right to request for a third party.] *Law.* Rights to recover on behalf of a third party. *There is no jus quaesitum tertio by way of benefit in a contract.*

jus recuperandi *n.* [L. **jus** right, law (1); **recuperandi** of recovering (2): right of recovering.] *Law.* The right of recovering, e.g., land.

jus relictae *n.* [L. **jus** right, law (1); **relictae** of the woman left behind (2): right of the woman left behind.] The right of the widow. *Scots Law.* The right of a widow to a third of the free movable estate of her deceased husband if they have issue or half of the estate if there are no children. Cf. **jus relicti.**

jus relicti *n.* [L. **jus** right, law (1); **relicti** of the person left behind (2): right of the person left behind.] The right of the widower. *Scots Law.* The right of a widower to a third of his deceased wife's free movable estate if they have issue or half of the estate if there are no children. Cf. **jus relictae.**

jus respicit aequitatem. [L. **jus** right, law (1); **respicit** considers, respects (2); **aequitatem** equity (3): Law considers equity.] *Law.* Law respects fairness. See **lex respicit aequitatem.**

jus respondendi *n.* [L. **jus** right, law (1); **respondendi** of responding (2): right of responding.] *Roman Law.* The right of giving an opinion on or interpreting legal matters. The **jus respondendi** was the right given to some eminent jurists in ancient Rome to interpret the law. If a number of jurists agreed in their interpretation, the advice thus given was apparently binding on the judge.

jus retentionis *n.* [L. **jus** right, law (1); **retentionis** of keeping back, retaining (2): right of keeping back.] *Law.* The right of keeping back or retaining. The right of lien.

jus retractus *n.* [L. **jus** right, law (1); **retractus** of retraction, withdrawal, recantation, revocation (2): right of retraction.] *Law.* The right of retraction or withdrawal. *The maker of a will has jus retractus as long as he/she is alive and compos mentis.*

jus sanguinis *n.* [L. **jus** right, law (1); **sanguinis** of blood (2): right of blood.] *Law.* The right of blood. Blood right. A legal principle that a child's citizenship is determined by the parent's citizenship. *The court adopted the jus sanguinis principle to determine the citizenship of the child.* Cf. **jus soli.**

jus scriptum *n., pl.* **jura scripta** [L. **jus** right, law (2); **scriptum** written (1): written law.] *Law.* Written law, as opposed to **jus non scriptum** (q.v.). Statute law. Cf. **droit écrit.**

jus singulare *n.* [L. **jus** right, law (2); **singulare** unique, individual, particular (1): particular right.] *Roman and Civil Law.* A peculiar/individual rule; i.e., a right or law designed for special cases. Cf. **jus commune** and **lex generalis.**

jus soli *n.* [L. **jus** right, law (1); **soli** of soil (2): right of soil.] *Law.* The law of the place of a person's birth. A legal principle that a child's citizenship or allegiance is determined by the place of birth. Thus, a child of Nigerian parentage born in the U.S.A. can claim American citizenship. Cf. **jus sanguinis.**

jus spatiandi et manendi *n.* [L. **jus** right, law (1); **spatiandi** of walking about (2); **et** and (3); **manendi** of remaining, tarrying (4): right of walking about.] The public's right to walk across an open space or to use it for recreational purposes.

jus strictum or **strictum jus** *n.* [L. **jus** right, law (2); **strictum** tight, strict (1): strict law.] Strict law; i.e., strict and rigorous application of the law. Cf. **aequitas.**

jus suffragii *n., pl.* **jura suffragii** [L. **jus** right, law (1); **suffragii** of vote (2): right of vote.] *Roman Law.* The right to vote. Suffrage. *Democracy thrives best in a situation where citizens exercise their jus suffragii without interference.*

jus suum cuique [L. **jus** right, law (2); **suum** one's own, his/her/its own (1); **cuique** to each (3): one's own law to each.] *Law.* To each individual (is owed) one's own rights.

justa causa *n.* [L. **justa** just (1); **causa** cause, case, reason (2): just cause.] *Law.* A just cause or ground. *The court ruled that the eviction of the tenant by the landlord was based purely on justa causa.*

juste-milieu *n., pl.* **juste-milieux** [Fr. **juste** fair, right (1); **milieu** mean, middle (2): fair mean.] The golden mean, happy medium, or middle course, especially a policy of government marked by moderation as well as give-and-take. See **aurea mediocritas.**

jus tertii *n.* [L. **jus** right, law (1); **tertii** of third (party) (2): right of a third party.] *Law.* The right of a third party. a) *In an action by the plaintiff for the recovery of possession of the premises from the defendant, the court rejected the latter's argument based on jus tertii.* b) . . . *it is no defence for a person who has interfered with goods in the possession of the plaintiff to plead jus tertii, i.e., that some third party has a better title to the goods than the plaintiff* (Rogers 1975:347).

justicies *n., pl.* **justicies** [Late L. You may bring to trial. You may do justice.] *Former English Law.* A writ ordering a sheriff to try a case such as trespass **vi et armis** (q.v.) which ordinarily is beyond his competence. *One way in which the king dealt with these pleas was to issue a writ of justicies which constituted the sheriff as a royal judge and directed him to hear the issue* (Newton 1983:9).

justificandum *n., pl.* **justificanda** [L. that which must be justified.] Something which must be justified.

justificans *n., pl.* **justificantia** [L. justifying.] Something (e.g., a principle) that serves the purpose of justifying.

justitia debet esse libera, quia nihil iniquius venali justitia; plena, quia justitia non debet claudicare;

et celeris, quia dilatio est quaedam negatio. [L. justitia justice (1); debet ought, should (2); esse to be (3); libera free (4); quia because (5); nihil nothing (6); iniquius more unjust/unfair than (7); venali for sale, corrupt, venal, bribe-bought (8); justitia justice (9); plena full (10); quia because (11); justitia justice (12); non not (14); debet ought, should (13); claudicare to limp, to be defective, to be lame (15); et and (16); celeris quick, fast (17); quia because (18); dilatio delay; postponement (19); est is (20); quaedam a certain, a kind of, as one might say (21); negatio denial (22): Justice ought to be free, because nothing (is) more unjust than bribe-bought justice; full, because justice should not be lame; and fast, because delay is a kind of denial.] Law. Justice should be: free, because there is nothing more unjust than justice for sale; complete, because justice should not be faulty or flawed; and quick, because delay is a form of denial.

justitia est constans et perpetua voluntas jus suum cuique tribuendi. Justinian (4883–565). [L. justitia justice (1); est is (2); constans unchangeable, uniform (3); et and (4); perpetua continuous, uninterrupted (5); voluntas inclination, desire (6); jus right, law (10); suum his/her own (thing) (9); cuique to each, each one (8); tribuendi of/for granting, giving (7): Justice is an unchangeable and continous desire for giving to each his/her own.] Justinian. Law. Justice is a uniform and continuous inclination to give (or of giving) to each one his/her right (or what is due).

justitia est duplex, viz., severe puniens et vere praeveniens. [L. justitia justice (1); est is (2); duplex twofold, double (3); viz. abbr. for videlicet namely, that is to say (4); severe severely (6); puniens punishing (5); et and (7); vere truly (8); praeveniens preventing, anticipating (9): Justice is twofold, namely, punishing severely and truly preventing.] Law. Justice plays a twofold role, namely, punishing the guilty severely and truly preventing offenses. Cf. melior est justitia etc.

justitia firmatur solium. [L. justitia by justice (3); firmatur is strengthened, reinforced (2); solium throne (1): The throne is strengthened by justice.] Justice strengthens the power of the monarch or of the government.

justitia nemini neganda est. [L. justitia justice (1); nemini to no one, nobody (4); neganda to be denied (3); est is (2): Justice is to be denied to nobody.] Law. Nobody should be denied justice; i.e., there should be no discrimination in the dispensation of justice. See ad officium etc.; justitia non est etc.; justitia non novit etc.; lex deficere non etc.; lex non debet deficere etc.; lex non deficit etc.; lex non novit etc.; lex uno ore etc.; and nec curia etc.

justitia non est neganda, non differenda. [L. justitia justice (1); non not (3); est is (2); neganda to be denied (4); non not (5); differenda to be deferred,

delayed, protracted (6): Justice is not to be denied, it is not to be delayed.] Law. Justice must be neither denied nor delayed. See justitia nemini etc.

justitia non novit patrem nec matrem; solam veritatem spectat justitia. [L. justitia justice (1); non not (2); novit knows (3); patrem father (4); nec and not, nor (5); matrem mother (6); solam alone (10); veritatem truth (9); spectat looks at, considers (8); justitia justice (7): Justice does not know father nor mother; justice considers truth alone.] Law. Justice knows neither father nor mother; i.e., it ignores blood-ties and aims exclusively at the truth. See justitia nemini etc.

justitia omnibus [L. justitia justice (1); omnibus to/for all (2): justice to all.] Justice for all. Motto of the District of Columbia. It has always been the wish of all people that governments adopt the principle of justitia omnibus.

justitium n. [L. a suspension of the courts, judicial vacation, holiday.] Civil Law. A suspension of judicial proceedings. Judicial vacation.

jus tollendi n. [L. jus right, law (1); tollendi of taking away, removing (2): right of taking away.] Law. The right of removing, i.e., the right to take away what one has added to property if one, being a bona fide possessor, is obliged to surrender the property.

justus titulus n., pl. justi tituli [L. justus just (1); titulus inscription, heading, title, label (2): just title.] Law. Just title.

jus ubique docendi n. [L. jus right, law (1); ubique everywhere (3); docendi of teaching, instructing (2): right of teaching everywhere.] The right to teach anywhere. An eminent scholar enjoys both in theory and in practice jus ubique docendi and may be invited to teach/lecture anywhere in the world.

jus utendi n. [L. jus right, law (1); utendi of using (2): right of using.] Law. The right to use, and derive profit from, property without destroying it substantially. Cf. jus abutendi.

jus utendi, fruendi, abutendi n. [L. jus right, law (1); utendi of using (2); fruendi of enjoying (3); abutendi of abusing (4): right of using, enjoying, and abusing.] Law. The right to use, to enjoy, and to abuse. Applicable to ownership.

jus vagum aut incertum n. [L. jus right, law (4); vagum vague, unsettled (1); aut or (2); incertum uncertain (3): vague or uncertain right.] Law. A law which is vague or uncertain. Bad laws can be borne; but the jus vagum aut incertum . . . is as sore an evil and as heavy a curse as any people can suffer; . . . (Hole v. Rittenhouse, 25Pa.491 [1855], quoted by Megarry 1973:141). Cf. misera est servitus, ubi etc.

jus venandi et piscandi n. [L. jus right, law (1); venandi of hunting (2); et and (3); piscandi of fishing (4): right of hunting and fishing.] Law. The right to hunt and fish.

jus vitae necisque *n.* [L. **jus** right, law (1); **vitae** of life (2); **necisque** and of killing (3): right of life and killing.] The right of life and death. *Roman Law.* Applicable to **patria potestas** (q.v.) or the absolute power of a father over his children, by virtue of which he could banish, enslave, or put a child to death. Indeed, on the birth of a child, this power was given concrete expression during a ceremony, when the father had to decide whether to accept the child or not. See **familia**.

juvenilia *pl. n.* [L. youthful or juvenile things.] Used as either *sing.* or *pl.* 1. Literary or artistic work done when the author was a youth and thus characterized by immaturity. *On his deathbed, the writer requested that his juvenilia be destroyed.* 2. Literary or artistic work done or designed for young people.

juxta conventionem *adv.* [L. **juxta** in accordance with, according to (1); **conventionem** covenant, agreement, compact (2): in accordance with the covenant.] According to the agreement.

juxta donatoris voluntatem [L. **juxta** in accordance with, according to (1); **donatoris** of giver, donor (3); **voluntatem** wish, desire (2): in accordance with the desire of the giver.] According to the wish of the donor.

K

Kaaba *n.* [Ar. **ka'bah** square building.] The holiest shrine of Islam, located in **Mecca** (q.v.), Saudi Arabia. The shrine to which Muslims face in daily prayer.

kabala or **kabbala** See **cabala**.

kabuki or **Kabuki** *n.* [Japan. from **ka** song (1); **bu** dance (2); **ki** art, artist (3): song (and) dance art.] A form of Japanese drama characterized by the elaborate costumes and stylized movements of the actors who both sing and dance.

Kaddish *n.* [Aram. **qaddīs** holy.] *Judaism.* A prayer used in daily praise of God and in mourning for the dead.

kaffee-klatch or **kaffeeklatch** *n., pl.* **kaffee-klatches** or **kaffeeklatches** [Ger. **Kaffeeklatsch: Kaffee** coffee (1); **Klatsch** gossip (2): coffee gossip.] Conversation over coffee or the gathering at which such conversation takes place. Cf. klatch.

Kafir or **Kaffir** or **Cafir** or **Caffir** *n., pl.* **Kafir** or **Kafirs** or **Kaffir** or **Kaffirs** or **Cafirs** or **Caffirs** [Ar. one **kāfir** who denies, infidel.] 1. A member of the Bante family in South Africa. 2. An offensive name for a Xhosa. 3. *Southern Africa.* An offensive term for a Black person. 4. A leguminous tree native to South Africa. —*pl. South Africa.* Mine shares. —also **kaffir** An unbeliever. A person who is not a Muslim.

kahuna *n., pl.* **kahunas** [Haw.] A priest. A holy or wise person. A person with supernatural powers.

kairos *n.* [Gk. right time.] The appropriate time. The moment of opportunity. The critical point. *The student had an instinct for recognizing kairos, for approaching his parents for money at just the right time.*

Kaiser *n., pl.* **Kaisers** [Ger. Caesar, ruler, king, emperor.] The emperor of Germany and Austria. Cf. **Caesar** and **czar**.

kai su teknon? *interj.* Julius Caesar (100–44 B.C.). [Gk. **kai** and, also, even (2); **su** you (1); **teknon** child (3): You, also, child?] You, too, son? The words uttered by Julius Caesar on the Ides of March (March 15) 44 B.C., when he saw Brutus among his assassins. Cf. **et tu, Brute?**

kai ta loipa *abbr.* **K.T.L.** or **k.t.l.** [Gk. **kai** and (1); **ta** the (2); **loipa** remaining (things), rest (3): and the remaining things.] And the rest. And so forth. **Et cetera** (q.v.).

kakemono *n., pl.* **kakemonos** [Japan. from **kake** hanging (1); **mono** object (2): hanging object.] A vertical form of Japanese scroll painting. Cf. **makimono**.

kakidrosis *n., pl.* **kakidroses** [Neo-Gk. from Gk. **kak(os)** evil, bad (1); **(h)idrosis** sweating (2): evil or bad sweating.] Secretion of foul sweat. Secretion of sweat with unpleasant scent.

kamaaina *n.* [Haw. **kama'aina: kama** child (2); **'aina** land (1): land child.] Someone who has lived in Hawaii for an extended period of time.

Kama Sutra *n.* [Skt. **kāma** love (1); **sūtra** thread, rule (2): love rule.] *The Art of Love.* The title of a sex manual in ancient Sanskrit.

kamikaze *n., pl.* **kamikazes** [Japan. **kami** divine (1); **kaze** wind (2): divine wind.] 1. *World War II.* A Japanese pilot who deliberately crashed on a target, usually a ship, often destroying it and, in the process, committing suicide. *The mystique of the kamikaze lives on (Time Int. 1980).* 2. An airplane loaded with explosives and used for the exercise.

kana *n., pl.* **kana** or **kanas** [Japan. from **ka** false (1); **na** name (2): false name, character.] A form of Japanese writing based upon syllabic characters and used especially for transliteration of foreign words. Cf. **hiragana; kanji;** and **katakana**.

kanji *n., pl.* **kanji** or **kanjis** [Japan. from Chin. **han** Chinese (1); **zi** characters (2): Chinese characters.] A Japanese writing system based upon Chinese characters. Cf. **hiragana; kana;** and **katakana**.

Kapelle or **Capelle** *n., pl.* **Kapellen** or **Capellen** [Ger. chapel, band, orchestra.] 1. The orchestra or choir of a papal or royal chapel. 2. An orchestra. A musical group.

Kapellmeister or **capellmeister** *abbr.* **Kpmtr.** *n., pl.* **Kapellmeister** or **capellmeister** [Ger. **Kapel(le)** chapel (1); **Meister** master (2): chapel master, band-master, conductor.] *Music.* Conductor of an orchestra or choir. *Now, in the tradition of European Kapellmeister, Zukerman will both conduct and play with the Saint Paul Chamber Orchestra, . . .* (*Newsweek Int.* Oct. 20, 1980:61). Cf. **maestro di cappella.**

kaput or **kuputt** *adj.* [Ger. tired, exhausted.] 1. Done for. Ruined. Completely destroyed. Finished. 2. Rendered useless or incapable of functioning. 3. Terribly outmoded.

karaoke *n.* [Jap. **kara** empty (1); **ōke(sutora)** orchestra (2): empty orchestra.] *Music.* Pre-recorded background music to accompany live singing.

karate *n.* [Japan. **kara** empty (1); **te** hand (2): empty hand.] A Japanese system of self-defense without the use of weapons, which involves injuring the opponent by using the edge of the open hand, foot, elbow or head to strike the opponent's vital nerve-centers.

karma *n.* [Skt. **karman** deed, fate.] 1. Fate. Destiny. 2. *Hinduism and Buddhism.* The cumulative effect which one's actions in various stages of existence have on an individual's destiny. 3. A special aura or atmosphere.

kasbah See **casbah.**

Kashrut or **kashrut** or **Kashruth** or **kashruth** *n.* [Heb. **kashrut** fitting.] Jewish dietary law.

katabasis or **catabasis** *n., pl.* **katabases** or **catabases** [Gk. **kata** down, from, according to (2); **basis** going (1): going down, the way down, descent.] 1. Marching back. Retreat, particularly in war. 2. *Meteorology.* The flow of cold or cool air in a downward direction.

katakana *n.* [Japan. from **kata** one (1); **kana** character (2): one character.] An angular form of Japanese writing used especially for foreign words and documents.

Katzenjammer *n.* [Ger. **Katz** cat (1); **Jammer** wail, cry (2): cat-wailing, hangover, morning-after feeling, moral qualms, hesitation.] 1. A loud, harsh sound. 2. Hangover. The headache, nausea, and physical weakness which one experiences in the morning following a night of excessive drinking. *Abel woke up in the morning with his wallet almost depleted and a distressing katzenjammer.* 3. Distress, headache, disorganization, and depression resembling a hangover after a night of heavy drinking, but caused by something else. *"The Katzenjammer Kids," an American comic strip popular in the early twentieth century, was about children who caused such distress and headache.*

kayak or **kaiak** *n.* [Inuit.] A light canoe made out of skins with one or two circular openings for paddlers. —*v.* To travel by such vehicle.

kendo *n.* [Japan.] The art of fencing with bamboo sticks.

kenosis *n.* [Gk. **kenōsis** emptying.] *Christianity.* The theological concept that Jesus emptied himself of his divinity when he became human; that is, he put aside

his divine powers and lived on earth with all the physical limitations of a human being. Based upon Philippians 2:7.

kibbutz *n., pl.* **kibbutzim** or **kibbutzes** [Heb. **qibbūs** gathering.] An Israeli collective farm or settlement which is owned and managed by the members of the cooperative. *Thousands of German youngsters flock to Israel every year to work in the kibbutzes* (*Newsweek Int.* May 18, 1981: 21). Cf. **kolkhoz** and **sovkhoz.**

Kiblah or **kiblah** or **qibla(h)** or **kibla** *n.* [Ar. **kibla** that which is opposite.] *Islam.* 1. The direction of the **Kaaba** (q.v.) in **Mecca** (q.v.) towards which praying Muslims face. 2. A niche in the wall of a building facing Mecca. Cf. **mihrab.**

kindergarten or **kindergarden** *abbr.* **kind.** *n., pl.* **kindergartens** or **kindergardens** [Ger. **Kindergarten**: **Kinder** children (1); **Garten** garden (2): children-garden, garden of children, infant-school, nursery-school.] Nursery-school. School for infants. A pre-primary school for children of 4 to 6 years of age, where the pupils play interesting games, sing songs, go through physical exercises, etc., the program being designed to foster the natural and social development of the pupils. —*adj.* Relating to education at the pre-primary school level. *He is a man whose intellectual development does not seem to have advanced beyond the kindergarten stage.*

Kinder, Kirche, Küche [Ger. **Kinder** children (1); **Kirche** church (2); **Küche** cooking, kitchen (3): children, church, and cooking.] Motherhood, religious devotion, and domesticity, the pillars of traditional German womanhood.

kiosk *n.* [Fr. **kiosque** from Turk. **kiushk** pavilion.] A small open booth for selling merchandise or posting advertisements.

kismet *n.* [Turk. from Arab. **kisma(t)** fate.] 1. Destiny. Fortune. 2. The title of a musical by Jerome Kern (1885–1945).

klatch *n., pl.* **klatches** [Ger. **Klatsch** gossip.] A gathering for light conversation and gossip.

Kleinkrieg *n., pl.* **Kleinkriege** [Ger. **klein** small (1); **Krieg** war (2): small war.] Guerrilla warfare.

kleptomania or **cleptomania** *n.* [Neo-Gk. from Gk. **klept(es)** thief (2); **mania** madness (1): madness of a thief, theft-related madness.] *Psychology.* A mental disorder manifested by a compulsive desire to steal, especially, things of minor economic value. *Mrs. Soab's marriage is seriously threatened by her kleptomania, for her behavior at supermarkets causes her husband considerable embarrassment.*

klutz *n., pl.* **klutzes** [Yid. **klots** a blockhead.] A wooden-headed person. A stupid or clumsy person.

koan *n.* [Japan. from **ko** public (1); **an** matter (2): public matter.] *Zen Buddhism.* A paradoxical riddle used for meditation and for the acquisition of innate knowledge.

kobald or **kobold** *n., pl.* **kobalds** or **kobolds** [Ger. **Kobald** goblin in a silver mine.] A mischievous elf or gnome believed to haunt houses and underground places, especially mines and caves. Cf. **leprechaun** and **ogre**.

koine *n., pl.* **koines** [Gk. **koinē** common, the common language.] 1. A form of Greek widely used during the Hellenistic Age and the period of the Roman Empire. 2. A language or dialect which is widely used. Cf. **lingua franca**.

koinonia *n.* [Gk. **koinōnia** fellowship, communion.] *Christianity*. Fellowship among Christians.

kolkhoz *n., pl.* **kolkhozy** or **kolkhozes** *short form* of **kollektivnoe khozyaistvo** [Russ. **koll(ektivnoe) khoz(yaistvo)** economy, farm (2): collective farm.] 1. A collective farm in Russia. 2. A system of collective farming based on the Russian model. Cf. **kibbutz** and **sovkhoz**.

Kol Nidre *n.* [Aram. **kol** all (1); **nidhrē** vows (2): all vows.] *Judaism*. 1. The first words of a prayer recited at the beginning of **Yom Kippur** (q.v.). 2. The prayer itself.

kore *n., pl.* **korai** [Gk. **korē** maiden.] *Art*. A Greek statue, usually in stone, representing a fully-clothed young woman. Cf. **kouros**.

kosher or **kasher** or **koscher** or **coshar** or **cosher** *adj.* [Yid. from Heb. **kāshēr** right.] 1. *Judaism*. Clean. Proper. Ritually pure. Adhering to Jewish dietary regulations. *A kosher meal*. 2. Legitimate. Real. Authentic. *A kosher business deal*.

kouros *n., pl.* **kouroi** [Gk. young man, boy.] *Art*. A Greek statue, usually in stone, representing a naked young man. Cf. **kore**.

kowtow or **kotow** *n.* [Chin. **kou** to knock (1); **tou** head (2): knocking or striking the head.] 1. Chinese custom of kneeling and touching the ground with the forehead as a mark of respect, homage, worship, or submission to a superior person. 2. A display or an act of obsequiousness, servility, or total submission. —*v. intr.* 1. To kneel and touch the ground with the forehead as a mark of respect, homage, worship or total submission. *Like a Chinese, the teacher kowtowed to the headmaster and left the office.* 2. To display obsequious deference to the desires of a superior official, etc. To act obsequiously or with abject servility. To cringe or fawn. *The employee made it unequivocally clear to the arrogant and power-obsessed supervisor that he believed in working industriously, not in kowtowing.*

Kpmtr. *abbr.* for **Kapellmeister** (q.v.).

Kriminalroman *n.* [Ger. **Kriminal** criminal (1); **Roman** novel (2): criminal novel.] A novel about crime. A thriller.

ktema es aei *n.* Thucydides. [Gk. **ktēma** possession (1); **es** into (2); **aei** always (3): a possession into always.] A possession for ever. *The writer hoped that his work would be a ktema es aei and, indeed, he has not been disappointed.* Cf. **monumentum aere perennius**.

K.T.L. or **k.t.l.** *abbr.* for **kai ta loipa** (q.v.).

kudos *n.* [Gk. **kudos** glory, praise.] 1. Glory. Renown. Prestige. Fame emanating from achievement. Credit. *Martha's charitable activities in the town won for her considerable kudos.* 2. Praise bestowed. a) *Navon responded by delivering two highly acclaimed speeches . . . and won kudos even from the hostile Egyptian press (Newsweek Int.* Jan. 10, 1983:15). b) *His daredeviltry earned kudos from his companions, but left him with a cracked vertebra, torn back muscles and a corset for the pain (Time Int.* 1980). Cf. **accolade** 3 and **izzat**.

Kultur *n.* [Ger. culture.] 1. Culture. The body of customary practices and beliefs, societal forms and material features characteristic of a people, religious group, social class, etc. 2. German culture, particularly that of the Nazi period, which was regarded as the best and emphasized the superiority of German civilization to that of other nations.

Kulturgeschichte *n.* [Ger. **Kultur** culture (1); **Geschichte** history (2): culture history.] The history of a culture or civilization. Cf. **Kunstsgeschichte**.

Kulturkampf *n., pl.* **Kulturkämpfe** [Ger. **Kultur** culture (1); **Kampf** struggle (2): cultural struggle.] Conflict or struggle between State and Church (or religious authorities), especially over which side should control education and the appointment of religious officials.

Kulturkreis *n., pl.* **Kulturkreise** [Ger. **Kultur** culture (1); **Kreise** circle (2): culture circle.] Culture or area of culture. A culture complex which originates in one area and spreads over extensive areas.

Kunstsgeschichte *n.* [Ger. **Kunst** art (1); **Geschichte** history (2): art history.] The history of the art of a people, culture, or civilization. Cf. **Kulturgeschichte**.

Kwanza *n.* [Swahili? **kwanzaa** harvest of first fruit.] African-American holiday of cultural solidarity and cooperation celebrated Dec. 26 to Jan. 1.

kyrie eleison. [Gk. **kurie** O lord (1); **eleēson** have mercy, have pity (2): O Lord, have mercy.] 1. The first words of a Christian prayer of petition. Also known as the "Kyrie." 2. A musical composition based on this prayer.

L

l. *abbr.* for 1. **lex** (q.v.). 2. **liaison** (q.v.). 3. **locus** (q.v.).

la *fem. definite article* [Fr. and It. the.] The (followed by the family name of a woman.) Used either in admiration (i.e., "the famous") or in contempt (i.e., "the notorious"). a) *la Pompadour;* b) *la Du Barry;* c) *la Pickford;* d) *la Callas;* e) *la Midler.*

la belle dame sans merci John Keats (1795–1821). [Fr. **la** the (1); **belle** pretty, beautiful, lovely, fine (2); **dame** lady (3); **sans** without (4); **merci** pity, mercy (5): the beautiful lady without pity.] The lady beautiful but without mercy. The title of a poem written by Keats in 1819.

La Belle Époque *n.* [Fr. **la** the (1); **belle** pretty, beautiful, lovely, fine (2); **époque** epoch, period, age (3): the lovely epoch.] The fine age or period; i.e., the Edwardian era or the era of Edward VII of England, an age of opulence and a feeling of material security, spanning the period from c.1890 to 1914, whose civilization was brought to an end by the First World War. *"As a reactionary, I, of course, look back longingly on La Belle Époque," said William F. Buckley* (*Newsweek Int.* Dec. 20, 1982:18). See **belle époque.**

la belle France *n.* [Fr. **la** the (1); **belle** beautiful (2); **France** France (3): the beautiful France.] The beautiful, attractive or pleasant spots, resorts or areas of France. *Some of the best of la belle France is within convenient reach of Paris* (*Time Int.* 1979).

labium majus *n., pl.* **labia majora** [L. **labium** lip (2); **majora** larger, greater (1): larger lip.] An external fatty fold which bounds the vulva. Cf. **labium minus.**

labium minus *n., pl.* **labia minora** [L. **labium** lip (2); **minora** smaller (1): smaller lip.] An internal fold which bounds the vulva. Cf. **labium majus.**

La Bohème *n.* [It. **la** the (1); **Bohème** Bohemia (2): the Bohemia.] "Bohemia, " an 1896 opera by Giacomo Puccini (1858–1924) about a pair of Bohemian lovers in Paris.

la bonne vie *n.* [Fr. **la** the (1); **bonne** good, happy (2); **vie** life (3): the good life.] The happy, comfortable life. Good living. *. . . while there the couple took advantage of la bonne vie by dropping some tanker profits in shops along the chic Avenue Montaigne* (*Time Int.* 1979). Cf. **la dolce vita.**

laborare est orare. [L. **laborare** to work (1); **est** is (2); **orare** to pray (3): To work is to pray.] Working is praying; i.e., menial labor is a form of prayer. For a fuller form, see **orare est** etc.

labor vincit omnia. [L. **labor** work, labor (1); **vincit** conquers (2); **omnia** all things, everything (3): Work conquers all things.] Work conquers everything. Motto of the State of Oklahoma. Cf. **amor omnia vincit.**

L'absence est à l'amour ce qu'est au feu le vent; il éteint le petit, il allume le grand. Comte de Bussy-Rabutin (1681–1693). *Histoire Amoureuse des Gaules: Maximes d'Amour* II. [Fr. **l'** the (1); **absence** absence (2); **est** is (3); **à** to, toward, in, by, with, until (4); **l'** the (5); **amour** love (6); **ce** that (7); **qu'** which (8); **est** is (11); **au** to the, toward the, in the, by the, with the, until the (12); **feu** fire; heat (13); **le** the (9); **vent** wind (10); **il** it (14); **éteint** extinguishes, puts out (15); **le** the (16); **petit** small, little (17); **il** it (18); **allume** lights, sets alight (19); **le** the (20); **grand** great; big (21): Absence is to love that which wind is to fire; it extinguishes the little, it lights the big.] Absence does to love what wind does to fire; it extinguishes the weak, but inflames the strong.

lachryma Christi *n.* [L. **lachryma** or **lacrima** tears (1); **Christi** of Christ (2): tears of Christ.] Christ's tears. A sweet red wine popular in southern Italy.

la ciudad del oro [Sp. **la** the (1); **ciudad** city (2); **del** of the (3); **oro** gold (4): the city of gold.] A place of great wealth and prosperity. El Dorado. *Many young men who flock to Lagos, thinking that it is la ciudad del oro, get frustrated eventually and take to criminal activities.*

La Comédie Humaine *n.* [Fr. **la** the (1); **comédie** comedy (3); **humaine** human (2): the human comedy.]

The Human Comedy, a collection of fiction by Honoré de Balzac (1799–1850), first published in 1842 and published posthumously in 47 volumes, depicting 19th-century society in its broadest and frankest scope. Includes works like **La Cousine Bette** (q.v.) and **La Peau de Chagrin** (q.v.).

La Commedia Divina *n.* [It. **la** the (1); **commedia** comedy (3); **divina** divine (2): the divine comedy.] *The Divine Comedy*, the religious and philosophical Italian epic by Dante Alighieri (1265–1321).

La commedia è finita. Ruggiero Leoncavallo (1858–1919). *I Pagliacci* II, end. [It. **la** the (1); **commedia** comedy (2); **è** is (3); **finita** finished, ended (4): The comedy is finished.] The comedy is over. See **La farce est jouée**.

La Coupe et les Lèvres [Fr. **la** the (1); **coupe** cup (2); **et** and (3); **les** the (4); **lèvres** lips (5): the cup and the lips.] "The Cup and the Lips," a poem by Alfred de Musset (1810–1857).

La Cousine Bette [Fr. **la** the (1); **cousine** (female) cousin (2); **Bette** Bette (3): the cousin Bette.] *Cousin Bette*, an 1847 novel by Honoré de Balzac (1799–1850) and part of **La Comédie Humaine** (q.v.).

la crème de la crème *n.* [Fr. **la** the (1); **crème** cream (2); **de** of (3); **la** the (4); **crème** cream (5): the cream of the cream.] The best of the best. The most distinguished. The most eminent among the elite *At the opening of "La Belle Epoque, 1890–1914," . . . la crème de la crème contributed $500 each to the Met to dine . . .* (*Newsweek Int.* Dec. 20, 1982:18). See **crème de la crème**. Cf. **canaille**; **hoi polloi**; **sansculottes**; and **vulgus**.

lacrimae rerum Vergil (70–19 B.C.). *Aeneid* I,462. [L. **lacrimae** tears (1); **rerum** of matters, things, property, business, affairs (2): tears of things.] The inherent unhappiness of human life. The tragedy of fate, predestination, or human destiny. *The anticlimatic end of our good friend's career is a clear manifestation of lacrimae rerum.* See **hinc illae lacrimae** and **sunt lacrimae rerum**.

lacuna *n., pl.* **lacunae** or **lacunas** [L. ditch, pit, hole, gap, defect.] A gap. A defect. A flaw. A missing part. *He seems to be a highly educated person, but there are some lacunae in his educational background which become glaring during discussions of a sublime nature.* Cf. **lacune**.

lacune *n., pl.* **lacunes** [Fr. from L. **lacuna**.] A gap, flaw, defect, deficiency, missing portion, or vacant space. Cf. **lacuna**.

la dolce vita *n.* [It. **la** the (1); **dolce** sweet, pleasant (2); **vita** life (3): the sweet life.] The life of luxury or happiness. Luxurious living. *After many years of unappreciated and unrewarding hard work in his country, Okoro decided to go elsewhere in pursuit of la dolce vita.* See **dolce vita** and **la bonne vie**.

La donna è mobile. [It. **la** the (1); **donna** woman (2); **è** is (3); **mobile** changeable, fickle (4): The woman

is changeable.] Woman is fickle. From an aria in act 3 of *Rigoletto*, an opera by Giuseppe Verdi (1813–1901). A phrase used to suggest the fickleness of woman. Cf. **varium et mutabile** etc.

laesa majestas *n.* [L. **laesa** injured, wounded (1); **majestas** majesty (2): injured majesty.] High treason. A crime or an offense against sovereign power or a ruler who represents sovereign power. See **crimen laesae majestatis** and **lèse-majesté**.

laesio enormis *n.* [L. **laesio** injury (2); **enormis** enormous, extraordinary (1): enormous injury.] *Roman and Civil Law.* The loss incurred by a vendor who sells something at a loss of 50% or more, or by a purchaser who buys something at double (or more) its price.

laesio ultra dimidium *n.* [L. **laesio** injury (1); **ultra** beyond, over (2); **dimidium** half (3): injury beyond half.] **Laesio enormis** (q.v.).

laesio ultra duplum *n.* [L. **laesio** injury (1); **ultra** beyond, over (2); **duplum** double (3): injury beyond double.] **Laesio enormis** (q.v.).

Laetare *v.* [L. rejoice.] Rejoice. The first word of an ancient Christian prayer. —*n.* The fourth Sunday in Lent, when this prayer has traditionally been recited.

La farce est jouée. François Rabelais (c.1494–c.1553) at the point of death. [Fr. **la** the (1); **farce** farce, comedy (2); **est** is (3); **jouée** played, performed; acted (4): The farce (or comedy) is played.] The farce or comedy of life is over. The farce or comedy has come to an end. See **La commedia è finita**.

l'affaire *n., pl.* **les affaires** [Fr. **l'** the (1); **affaire** affair, matter (2): the affair.] The affair. The incident. Scandal. Invariably followed by the name of the person concerned. *The Chief Executive's image was considerably dented by his handling of l'affaire Cecilia.* See **affaire** —*pl.* Business. Commerce.

La foi consiste à croire ce que la raison ne croit pas. Voltaire (1694–1778). [Fr. **la** the (1); **foi** faith, trust (2); **consiste** consists, is composed of (3); **à** to, toward, in, by, with, until (4); **croire** to believe, believing (5); **ce** that (6); **que** which (7); **la** the (8); **raison** good sense, reason, judgment (9); **ne . . . pas** not (11); **croit** believes (10): Faith consists in believing that which reason does not believe.] Faith consists in believing what cannot be rationally proven. Cf. **Fe que no duda** etc.

la forza del destino [It. **la** the (1); **forza** force (2); **del** of the (3); **destino** destiny, fate (4): the force of the destiny.] The force of destiny or fate. *My grandfather believes that every human act is attributable to la forza del destino.* —**La Forza del Destino** "The Power of Destiny," an 1862 opera by Giuseppe Verdi (1813–1901).

la France profonde *n.* [Fr. **la** the (1); **France** France (3); **profonde** deep, great, profound (2): deep France.] Serious-minded, high-society French people. The lifestyle of such people. *As a former . . . organiser of*

Gaullist rallies, Mr. Pasqua has a close, if far from neutral, feel for la France profonde (*The Economist* 1987).

La gloire et le repos sont choses qui ne peuvent loger en même gîte. Montaigne (1533–1592). *Essais* I,39. [Fr. **la** the (1); **gloire** fame, glory (2); **et** and (3); **le** the (4); **repos** rest, repose (5); **sont** are (6); **choses** things (7); **qui** which (8); **ne** not (10); **peuvent** can, are able (9); **loger** to live, lodge (11); **en** in (12); **même** same (13); **gîte** home, bed (14): Fame and rest are things which cannot live in the same home.] Fame and rest cannot be bedfellows (or dwell together).

laissez-aller or **laisser-aller** *n.* [Fr. **laissez** allow; **aller** to go: allow to go.] Carelessness. Lack of constraint or self-restraint. **Abandon** (q.v.). Carefree or easygoing attitude. *Oil wealth is too often squandered through a general laisser-aller and the conspicuous consumption of imported luxury goods* (Howard Schissel in *West Africa* 1982).

laissez-faire *n.* [Fr. **laissez** allow; **faire** to do: allow to do, non-interference, non-intervention, inaction, passiveness.] 1. The motto of eighteenth-century French economists who disapproved of excessive regulation of industry by the state. 2. A doctrine which opposes state interference in the affairs, especially economic affairs, of individuals. 3. A policy, practice, or philosophy characterized by non-interference with the rights of the individual. A policy of inaction or drift. a) *In general, however, their attitude was one of laissez-faire . . .* (Robinson 1974:100). b) *The government is pursuing a policy of laissez-faire.* —*adj.* Of, relating to, or in accordance with the doctrine, philosophy, or practice of non-interference, or one which advocates the restriction of such interference to measures required for maintaining peace and protecting the rights of property. a) *laissez-faire attitude*; b) *laissez-faire policy*; c) *laissez-faire spirit.*

laissez-passer *n., pl.* **laissez-passers** [Fr. **laissez** allow; **passer** to pass: allow to pass.] Pass. Permit. *The country insists that any foreigner who wishes to enter its territory should obtain a laissez-passer.*

la Jacquerie See **jacquerie.**

La ley favor la vie d'un home. [Obs. Fr. **la** the (1); **ley** law (2); **favor** favors (3); **la** the (4); **vie** life, existence (5); **d'** of (6); **un** a (7); **home** person, human being (8): Law favors the life of a person.] The law favors a human being's life. See **de morte hominis** etc.

La Marseillaise *n.* [Fr. **la** the (1); **Marseillaise** (song) of Marseilles (2): the song of Marseilles.] "The Marseillaise." The French National anthem. The words were written in 1792 by Rouget de l'Isle. The song got its name because it was sung by Marseilles revolutionaries as they entered Paris in 1792.

La mejor salsa del mundo es el hambre. Miguel de Cervantes (1547–1616). *Don Quixote* II,5. [Sp. **la** the (1); **mejor** best (2); **salsa** sauce (3); **del** of the (4); **mundo** world (5); **es** is (6); **el** the (7); **hambre** hunger (8): The best sauce in the world is the hunger.] Hunger is the best sauce in the world. Hunger gives the best taste to food.

la même chose *adj.* [Fr. **la** the (1); **même** same, very (2); **chose** thing (3): the same thing.] The same thing. Unchanged. Unaltered. Constant. *Yet if much remains la même chose at the fabled luxury hotel in Paris, much has also changed* (*Newsweek Int.* April 2, 1979:39). Cf. **Plus ça** etc.

Landwehr *n.* [Ger. **Land** land (1); **Wehr** weapon, defense (2): land defense, militia.] **Militia** (q.v.). Reserve forces. The section of the national armed forces which has completed active military service and constitutes the reserve forces or second line of defense.

la nostalgie de la boue Émile Augier (1820–1889). *Le Mariage d'Olympe* I,1. [Fr. **la** the (1); **nostalgie** nostalgia, homesickness (2); **de** of, for (3); **la** the (4); **boue** mud, mire, filth, dirt (5): the nostalgia for the gutter.] Homesickness for the gutter.

Laocoon *n., pl.* **Laocoons** [Gk. **Laokoōn.**] 1. *Greek and Roman Mythology.* A Trojan who protested against bringing the wooden horse into Troy. As divine punishment, he and his two sons were killed by two huge serpents. A sculpture of the first century B.C., now in the Vatican, shows his heroic struggles against the serpents. 2. A person who struggles bravely with intolerable and perplexing problems. *Dan, though a very controversial man, is generally admired as a Laocoon in the face of crushing difficulties.* —*adj.* Struggling bravely with intolerable and perplexing problems. *A Laocoon attitude.*

La Peau de Chagrin *n.* [Fr. **la** the (1); **peau** skin (2); **de** of, by (3); **chagrin** grief, sorrow (4): the skin of sorrow.] *The Skin of Sorrow,* a novel by Honoré de Balzac (1799–1850) and part of **La Comédie Humaine** (q.v.). See **chagrin.**

lapsus *n., pl.* **lapsus** [L. falling, slip, fall.] A trivial or small fault. An error. A slip. *It is a good well-written book with a few lapsus which, however, do not detract from its quality.*

lapsus calami *n.* [L. **lapsus** slipping, error (1); **calami** of a reed (used as a pen) (2): slipping or error of the reed.] A slip of the pen. An inadvertent or accidental mistake in writing. *The grammatical mistake in the letter is obviously a lapsus calami.*

lapsus linguae *n.* [L. **lapsus** slipping, error (1); **linguae** of tongue (2): slipping or error of the tongue.] A slip of the tongue. An accidental or inadvertent mistake in speech. *The explanation of the witness indicates that the mentioning of Bola's name was no more than a lapsus linguae.*

lapsus memoriae *n.* [L. **lapsus** slipping, error (1); **memoriae** of memory (2): slip of the memory.] A memory lapse. A slip of memory. *When the clarity of a matter is obscured by length of time, the courts* usually make allowance for lapsus memoriae, particularly in the case of the unlettered.

La raison du plus fort est toujours la meilleure. Jean de la Fontaine (1621–1695). *Fables* I,10. [Fr. **la** the (1); **raison** reason, motive (2); **du** of the (3); **plus fort** strongest (person) (4); **est** is (5); **toujours** always, ever (6); **la meilleure** the best (7): The reason of the strongest is always the best.] The reason given by the strongest is always the best. Might makes right.

La reconnaissance de la plupart des hommes n'est qu'une secrète envie de recevoir de plus grands bienfaits. François, Duc de La Rochefoucauld (1613–1680). *Maximes* 298. [Fr. **la** the (6); **reconnaissance** gratitude, thankfulness (7); **de** in, with (1); **la** the (2); **plupart** greatest part, majority (3); **des** of the (4); **hommes** human beings, persons, men (5); **n'** ... **qu'** only, merely (9); **est** is (8); **une** a (10); **secrète** secret (11); **envie** desire, longing (12); **de** of (13); **recevoir** to receive, get (14); **de** of (15); **plus grands** greater, bigger (16); **bienfaits** benefits, favors (17): With the majority of human beings, gratitude is merely a secret desire to receive bigger favors.] With most human beings, gratitude is merely a secret desire to receive even bigger favors.

lares et penates *pl. n.* [L. **lares** protecting deities (1); **et** and (2); **penates** household gods (3): protecting deities and household gods.] 1. *Ancient Rome.* The deities which protect the household and family. 2. A person's most precious personal effects and household goods. *Sue dashed out of the burning house, carrying her lares et penates.*

largesse or **largess** *n.* [Fr. generosity.] 1. The giving of a generous gift or the gift itself. 2. A generous nature.

larghetto *adv./adj.* [It. a little largo.] *Music.* In a somewhat slow manner, faster than **largo** (q.v.) but slower than **adagio** (q.v.). —*n., pl.* **larghettos** A composition or passage played in such a tempo.

largo *adv./adj.* [It. broad, generous.] *Music.* In a slow, dignified tempo, slower than **adagio** (q.v.). —*n., pl.* **largos** A composition or passage played in such a tempo.

L'Arlésienne *n.* [Fr. **l'** the (1); **Arlésienne** woman from Arles (2): the woman from Arles.] "The Woman from Arles," a 1872 play by Alphonse Daudet (1840–1897) for which George Bizet (1838–1875) composed some more well-known background music.

l'art pour l'art Victor Cousin (1792–1867). [Fr. **l'** the (1); **art** art (2); **pour** for (3); **l'** the (4); **art** art (5): the art for the art.] Art for the sake of art. Art for art's sake. The view that art should be given free rein and not subjected to social, political, or moral restrictions; nor should it be produced for economic reasons. See **ars gratia artis.**

La Scala *n.* [It. **la** the (1); **scala** stairs (2): the stairs.] The famous opera house of Milan, Italy.

Lasciate ogni speranza voi ch'entrate! Dante Alighieri (1265–1321). *Inferno* III,9,4. [It. **lasciate** leave, abandon (1); **ogni** each, every (2); **speranza** hope (3); **voi** you (4); **ch'** who (5); **entrate** enter (6): Abandon every hope, you who enter.] Abandon all hope, all you who enter here, i.e., the gates of hell.

lata culpa See **culpa lata.**

lata culpa dolo aequiparatur. [L. **lata** gross, copious (1); **culpa** fault, error, blame, guilt, failure (2); **dolo** to fraud, guile (4); **aequiparatur** is compared, likened (3): Gross negligence is likened to fraud.] *Law.* Serious negligence is equivalent to fraud.

latens ambiguitas *n.* [L. **latens** hidden, concealed, secret, latent (1); **ambiguitas** ambiguity, equivocalness (2): a latent ambiguity.] A hidden ambiguity.

latet anguis in herba. Vergil (70–19 B.C.). *Eclogue* III,93. [L. **latet** lurks, lies hidden (2); **anguis** snake (1); **in** in, on (3); **herba** grass (4): A snake lurks in the grass.] A snake is hiding in the grass. There is a defect, hindrance, or drawback in the matter.... *when Lord Kenyon wished "to illustrate in a strong manner the conclusiveness of some fact, (he) thus addressed the Jury, 'Why, Gentlemen of the Jury, it is as plain as the noses upon your faces! Latet anguis in herba!'"* (Megarry 1973:153). Cf. **anguis in herba.**

latifundio *n., pl.* **latifundios** [Sp. from L.] A large landed estate. **Latifundium** (q.v.).

latifundium *n., pl.* **latifundia** [L. from **latus** broad (1) and **fundus** farm (2): broad farm.] A large landed estate or farm, usually belonging to an absentee owner who uses the services of slave or semi-servile labor in tilling it. It was prevalent in ancient Rome and in eastern Europe in the period before the First World War.

La trahison des clercs Julien Benda. [Fr. **la** the (1); **trahison** treachery, treason (2); **des** of the (3); **clercs** clerks, ecclesiastics, learned people (4): the treason of the learned people.] *The Treachery of the educated classes,* a 1927 philosophical work by Julien Benda (1867–1956).

La Traviata *n.* [It. **la** the (1); **traviata** corrupted woman, prostitute (2): the corrupted woman.] "The Prostitute," an 1853 opera by Giuseppe Verdi (1813–1901).

laudator *n., pl.* **laudators** [L. praiser, eulogizer or panegyrist.] A person who eulogizes or praises. A person who testifies to another's character.

laudator temporis acti *n.* Horace (65–8 B.C.). *Ars Poetica* 173. [L. **laudator** praiser, eulogizer, panegyrist (1); **temporis** (of) time (3); **acti** of passed, spent (2): praiser of passed time.] A person who eulogizes/ praises the past. *Frank is a well-known laudator temporis acti who sees nothing commendable about current fashions which attract the fancy of the youth.*

laus Deo *abbr.* **L.D.** *interj.* [L. **laus** praise (1); **Deo** to God (2): praise to God.] Praise be to God. Cf. **in sha Allah.**

laus Deo et Gloria *abbr.* **L.D.E.G.** *interj.* [L. **laus** praise (1); **Deo** to God (4); **et** and (2); **gloria** glory (3): praise and glory to God.] Praise and Glory be to God.

laus Deo semper *abbr.* **L.D.S.** *interj.* [L. **laus** praise (1); **Deo** to God (2); **semper** always (3): praise to God always.] Praise be to God always.

laus tibi [L. **laus** praise (1); **tibi** to you (2): praise to you.] Praise be to you.

Lavabo *v.* [L. I will wash.] *Christianity*. The first word of a prayer recited by the celebrant while washing his/her hands in preparation for celebrating the Eucharist. —*n.* 1. The prayer itself. 2. The washing of the hands at the Eucharist. —**lavabo** *n., pl.* **lavaboes** A basin used for hand-washing.

La vida es duda, y la fe sin la duda es sólo muerte. Miguel de Unamuno (1864–1937). *Poesías* "Salmo II." [Sp. **la** the (1); **vida** life (2); **es** is (3); **duda** doubt (4); **y** and (5); **la** the (6); **fe** faith (7); **sin** without (8); **la** the (9); **duda** doubt (10); **es** is (11); **sólo** only (12); **muerte** death (13): The life is doubt and the faith without the doubt is only death.] To be alive is to have doubts and a faith without doubts is only the equivalent of death. Cf. **Fe que no duda** etc.

La vida es sueño. [Sp. **la** the (1); **vida** life (2); **es** is (3); **sueño** dream, sleep (4): Life is a dream.] *Life is a Dream*, a play by Pedro Calderón de la Barca (1600–1681). f. **La vie est** etc.

La vie en rose [Fr. **la** the (1); **vie** life (2); **en** in (3); **rose** rose (4): the life in rose.] Life seen through rose-colored glasses. Life seen optimistically. The title of a song made popular by the French chanteuse Edith Piaf (1915–1963).

La vie est un songe. . . . nous veillons dormants et veillants dormons. Montaigne. *Essais* II,12. [Fr. **la** the (1); **vie** life, existence (2); **est** is (3); **un** a (4); **songe** dream (5); **nous** we (6); **veillons** we are awake (8); **dormants** sleeping (7); **et** and (9); **veillants** awake (10); **dormons** we sleep (11): Life is a dream. . . . Sleeping we are awake and awake we sleep.] Life is a dream. We are awake while sleeping and we sleep while awake. Cf. **La vida es sueño.**

La vie parisienne *n.* [Fr. **la** the (1); **vie** life (3); **parisienne** Parisian (2): the Parisian life.] "Parisian Life," an 1866 comic opera by Jacques Offenbach (1819–1880).

La vita nuova *n.* [It. **la** the (1); **vita** life (3); **nuova** new (2): the new life.] *The New Life*, the title of a collection of 31 love poems and prose commentary by Dante Alighieri (1265–1321) written in **dolce stil nuovo** (q.v.) and describing his love for Beatrice and his personal spiritual journey.

layette *n., pl.* **layettes** [Fr. baby-linen.] A full set of clothing, bedding and equipment for a new-born baby.

lb. *abbr.* for **libra** (q.v.).

L.C. or **l.c.** *abbr.* for **loco citato** (q.v.).

L.Ch. *abbr.* for **Licentiatus Chirurgiae** (q.v.).

L.D. *abbr.* for **Laus Deo** (q.v.).

L.D.E.G. *abbr.* for **Laus Deo et Gloria** (q.v.).

L.d'H. *abbr.* for **Légion d'Honneur** (q.v.).

L.D.S. *abbr.* for **laus Deo semper** (q.v.).

Lebensform *n.* [Ger. **Lebens** of/for life (2); **Form** form, shape (1): form of life.] The social and moral aspects of human life.

Lebenslust *n.* [Ger. **Lebens** of/for life (2); **Lust** desire, zest (1): desire for life.] A passion for life. **Joie de vivre** (q.v.).

Lebensraum *n.* [Ger. from **Leben** life (1); **Raum** room, space (2): living space.] A concept popularized by Germany's Nationalist Socialist Party. 1. Territory believed to be necessary for a state's existence and economic growth. *Hitler's Germany coveted vast portions of Europe, regarding them as her Lebensraum.* 2. Land believed to be necessary for the existence, activities and development of an individual, institution, community, etc. *The institution is in dire need of more lebensraum.*

Lebenswelt *n.* [Ger. **Lebens** of life (2); **Welt** world (1): world of life.] A person's immediate environment and experiences. The people, places, and things which make up the world of an individual person.

Le Bourgeois Gentilhomme *n.* [Fr. **le** the (1); **bourgeois** bourgeois (2); **gentil** kind, gentle (3); **homme** man, person (4): the bourgeois gentleman.] *The Bourgeois Gentleman*, a 1670 comedy by Molière (1622–1673).

Le coeur a ses raisons que la raison ne connaît pas. Blaise Pascal (1623–1662). *Pensées* IV,277. [Fr. **le** the (1); **coeur** (2); **a** has (3); **ses** its (4); **raisons** reasons (5); **que** which (6); **la** the (7); **raison,** reason, reasoning (8); **ne . . . pas** not (9); **connaît** know (10): The heart has its reasons which (the) Reason does not know.] Emotions and intellect make decisions on different bases.

le commencement de la fin *n.* Talleyrand (1754–1838). [Fr. **le** the (1); **commencement** beginning, commencement (2); **de** of (3); **la** the (4); **fin** end (5): commencement of the end.] The beginning of the end. For a fuller form of the quotation, see **Voilà le commencement** etc.

le congrès *n.* [Fr. congress.] 1. Legislative congress. 2. *French Law*. A way of disproving a charge of impotence which involved having sexual intercourse before witnesses. It was abolished in 1677. Cf. **coitus coram testibus**.

Le contrat fait la loi. [Fr. **le** the (1); **contrat** contract (2); **fait** makes (3); **la** the (4); **loi** law, rule (5): The contract makes the law.] *Law*. The contract makes the law; i.e., the agreement of the parties to a contract constitutes its law. See **consensus facit legem**.

le contrat social *n.* [Fr. **le** the (1); **contrat** contract, agreement (3); **social** social (2): the social contract.] The ideal social order and relationship between human beings as developed in **Du contrat social** (q.v.), a 1762 political and philosophical treatise by Jean-Jacques Rousseau (1712–1778).

Le crime fait la honte et non pas l'échafaud. [Fr. **le** the (1); **crime** crime (2); **fait** makes (3); **la** the (4); **honte** shame, disgrace (5); **et** and (6); **non pas** not (7); **l'** the (8); **échafaud** scaffold, gallows (9): The crime makes the disgrace and not the scaffold.] *Law*.

What causes disgrace is the crime, not the punishment. See **C'est le crime** etc. and **ex delicto non** etc.

lectio difficilior See **difficilior lectio**.

lector benevole *n.* [L. **lector** reader (2); **benevole** benevolent, kind (1): kind reader.] An address to the kind reader. A writer's plea for understanding from his/her readers.

le droit de talion *n.* [Fr. **le** the (1); **droit** right, law (2); **de** of (3); **talion** retaliation (4): right of retaliation.] The right to retaliate. **Lex talionis** (q.v.). *When asked if retaliatory measures against the families of the suspects—le droit de talion . . .—were excluded, Laclé retorted that . . .* (Achim Rende in *West Africa* 1985).

legalis homo See **homo legalis**.

legato *adv./adj.* [It. bound together.] *Music.* In a bound fashion. With the notes connected or bound together. —*n., pl.* **legatos** A passage played in a bound fashion.

legatos violare contra jus gentium est. [L. **legatos** envoys, ambassadors (6); **violare** to injure (5); **contra** against, opposite (2); **jus** right, law (3); **gentium** of nations (4); **est** it is (1): It is against the law of nations to injure ambassadors.] Injuring ambassadors is forbidden by international law or the law of nations.

legatum *n., pl.* **legata** [L. that which is bequeathed, a bequest, legacy.] *Civil Law.* Bequest or a legacy.

legatum morte testatoris tantum confirmatur sicut donatio inter vivos traditione sola. [L. **legatum** legacy, bequest (l); **morte** by death (4); **testatoris** of testator (5); **tantum** only, alone (3); **confirmatur** is confirmed, established (2); **sicut** just as (6); **donatio** gift, donation (7); **inter** among, between (8); **vivos** living (persons) (9); **traditione** by transfer, surrender (10); **solo** (by) alone, only (11): A legacy is confirmed only by the death of the testator, just as a gift among living persons is confirmed by transfer alone.] *Law.* A bequest is established only by the death of the testator just as among living people a gift becomes a gift only when it is transferred to the recipient. An heir is not entitled to a bequest until the testator dies just as a person does not receive a gift until the giver gives it. See **ambulatoria est** etc.; **nemo est heres** etc.; **nemo heres** etc.; **omne testamentum** etc.; **testamentum omne** etc.; and **voluntas testatoris est** etc.

legatum optionis *n.* [L. **legatum** legacy (1); **optionis** of choice, option (2): legacy of choice.] *Roman and Civil Law.* A legacy in which the testator directs the beneficiary to choose anything from his property.

legatum partitionis *n.* [L. **legatum** legacy, bequest (1); **partitionis** of partition, division, distribution (2): legacy of partition.] *Civil Law.* A legacy of division. Applicable to a situation where a legatee divides the legacy with the heir.

légende des siècles *n.* [Fr. **légende** legend, story (1); **des** of the (2); **siècles** ages, centuries (3): legend of the ages.] 1. The title of a verse history of the French people by Victor Hugo. 2. A comprehensive history

of a people or a nation. *. . . its sixth book summarized the history of man in a légende des siècles, wherein the idea of continuous progress first found clear expression* (Cary 1970:464).

legerdemain *n., pl.* **legerdemains** [Fr. **léger** light, swift (1); **de** of (2); **main** hand (3): light/swift of hand.] Sleight of hand. Conjuring. Magic/trickery performed with the hands. A clever trick/deception. A deceitful, crafty or artful argument. *This is a very big diplomatic problem, and not even the Foreign Minister's well-known legerdemain is likely to solve it.*

leges humanae nascuntur, vivunt, et moriuntur. [L. **leges** laws (2); **humanae** human (1); **nascuntur** are born (3); **vivunt** they live (4); **et** and (5); **moriuntur** they die (6): Human laws are born, they live and they die.] Human laws are made; they have binding force; and they become obsolete.

leges non scriptae *n.* [L. **leges** laws (1); **non** not (2); **scriptae** written (3): laws not written.] Unwritten laws; i.e., customary laws. See **jus non scriptum**.

leges posteriores priores contrarias abrogant. [L. **leges** laws (2); **posteriores** later (1); **priores** former (ones) (4); **contrarias** contrary, conflicting (5); **abrogant** annul, abrogate (3): Later laws annul conflicting former ones.] Later laws negate earlier laws that conflict with them. Where two acts are irreconcilable, the former act is replaced with the latter. Also a later act repeals a former one either expressly or by implication. See **lex posterior** etc.

leges suum ligent latorem. [L. **leges** laws (1); **suum** their own (3); **ligent** should bind (2); **latorem** mover, proposer (4): Laws should bind their own proposer.] The one who proposes a law should be bound by it.

leges vigilantibus, non dormientibus, subveniunt. [L. **leges** laws (1); **vigilantibus** the watchful, vigilant (3); **non** not (4); **dormientibus** the sleeping (5); **subveniunt** come to help, aid (2): Laws come to help the watchful, not the sleeping.] Laws come to the aid of those who are vigilant, not those who are asleep; i.e., laws give relief to those who are conscious of, not those who do not care about, their rights. See **lex vigilantibus** etc.; **vigilantibus, et non** etc.; and **vigilantibus lex succurrit.** Cf. **vigilantibus non dormientibus** etc.

legibus sumptis desinentibus, lege naturae utendum. [L. **legibus** with laws (1); **sumptis** (with) which have been taken up, assumed (2); **desinentibus** (with) ceasing (3); **lege** law (5); **naturae** of nature (6); **utendum** there must be a using of (4): With laws which have been assumed ceasing, there must be a using of the law of nature.] When laws which are ordained by the state fail, we must resort to the law of nature.

Légion d'Honneur *abbr.* **L.d'H.** *n.* [Fr. **légion** legion (1); **d'** of (2); **honneur** honor (3): Legion of Honor.] The Legion of Honor. An Order founded in 1802 by Napoleon, whose membership is conferred for meritorious civil or military service. *Joining French intelligence . . ., Richard gathered information on German U-boat operations for which she received the Légion d'Honneur award* (*Newsweek Int.* Feb. 22, 1982:50). See **cordon rouge** 1.

legionnaire *n., pl.* **legionnaires** [Fr. **légionnaire** legionary.] A member of a legion, particularly the French Foreign Legion. *Mobutu's regime* [was] *saved by the grace of French legionnaires* (*New African* 1980).

legis interpretatio legis vim obtinet. [L. **legis** of law (2); **interpretatio** interpretation (1); **legis** of law (5); **vim** force (4); **obtinet** obtains, acquires (3): Interpretation of the law acquires the force of law.] Interpretations of law are the equivalent of law. Cf. **omnis interpretatio** etc. and **sententia facit jus** etc.

legis nexus *n.* Tacitus (c.55 –c.117 A.D.). *Annals* III,28. [L. **legis** of law (2); **nexus** binding, linking, interweaving, combination (1): binding of law.] The knot of law. The complexity of law.

legitima portio See **portio legitima**.

legitime *n.* [L. according to law, lawfully, legitimately.] *Civil and Scots Law*. A portion of the patrimony of which children cannot be disinherited except with lawful reason. See **pars legitima**; **pars rationabilis**; and **portio legitima**.

legitime imperanti parere necesse est. [L. **legitime** lawfully, legitimately (5); **imperanti** a person commanding (4); **parere** to obey (3); **necesse** necessary (2); **est** it is (1): It is necessary to obey a person commanding lawfully.] *Law*. We must obey a person who exercises lawful authority. See **qui jussu** etc.

Legum Baccalaureus *abbr.* **LL.B.** *n.* [L. **legum** of laws (2); **baccalaureus** bachelor (1): Bachelor of Laws.] A first professional degree in law.

Legum Doctor *abbr.* **LL.D.** *n.* [L. **legum** of laws (2); **doctor** teacher (1): teacher of laws.] Doctor of Laws. An academic degree, usually honorary, for work in the law.

Legum Magister *abbr.* **LL.M.** *n.* [L. **legum** of laws (2); **magister** master (1): Master of Laws.] A predoctoral graduate degree in law.

lei *n., pl.* **leis** [Haw.] A wreath or garland of flowers and other things placed around a person's neck in Hawaii as a mark of love and esteem.

leitmotiv *n., pl.* **leitmotive** [Ger. **Leitmotiv**: **leiten** to lead, guide (1); **Motiv** motive, subject, theme (2): guide theme, key-note.] 1. *Music*. A distinctive theme or phrase, especially one in opera associated with a particular person, idea, or situation and recurring whenever he/she/it reappears. 2. A dominant theme, word, phrase, idea, emotion, or motif that keeps recurring. *The leit-motiv of Hassan's novels is the rejected lover.* Cf. **motif** 1.

Le Malade imaginaire *n.* [Fr. **le** the (1); **malade** ill, sick, diseased (person) (3); **imaginaire** imaginary (2): the imaginary sick person.] *The Hypochondriac,* a 1673 comedy by Molière (1622–1673).

l'embarras des richesses [Fr. **l'** the (1); **embarras** encumbrance, difficulty, embarrassment (2); **des** of the (3); **richesses** riches (4): the difficulty of the riches.] 1. *An Embarassment of Riches,* a 1726 comedy by Abbé D'Allainval (1770–1753). 2. An excess of good choices.

Le Médecin malgré lui *n.* [Fr. **le** the (1); **médecin** doctor, physician (2); **malgré** despite (3); **lui** himself (4): the doctor despite himself.] *The Doctor Despite Himself,* a 1666 comedy by Molière (1622–1673).

Le Misanthrope *n.* [Fr. **le** the (1); **misanthrope** misanthrope, people-hater (2): the people-hater.] *The Misanthrope,* a 1666 comedy by Molière (1622–1673).

lemma *n., pl.* **lemmata** or **lemmas** [Gk. **lēmma** something received, receipt, statement, assumption, theme.] 1. *Logic*. A secondary proposition the validity of which is used to prove a primary proposition. 2. A statement. An assumption. A theme. 3. The word or phrase appearing in a glossary or dictionary entry.

Le Neveu de Rameau *n.* [Fr. **le** the (1); **neveu** nephew (2); **de** of (3); **Rameau** Rameau (4): the nephew of Rameau.] *Rameau's Nephew,* a novel by Denis Diderot (1713–1784), published posthumously.

Le Nozze di Figaro *n.* [It. **le** the (1); **nozze** marriage (2); **di** of (3); **Figaro** Figaro (4): the marriage of Figaro.] "The Marriage of Figaro," an Italian opera (1786) by Wolfgang Amadeus Mozart (1756–1791).

lento *adv./adj.* [It. slowly.] *Music*. In a slow tempo. —*n., pl.* **lentos** A passage played slowly.

Leo *n.* [L. lion.] 1. *Astronomy*. A lion-shaped constellation located near Cancer and Virgo. 2. *Astrology*. The fifth sign of the zodiac dominant from July 23 through August 22. 3. A person born under this sign.

leonina societas See **societas leonina**.

Le Petit Prince *n.* [Fr. **le** the (1); **petit** little (2); **prince** prince (3): the little prince.] *The Little Prince,* a novel by the French aviator and writer Antoine de Saint Exupéry (1900–1944).

leprechaun *n., pl.* **leprechauns** [Ir. **luprachan** from **lu** small (1); **chorp** body (2): small body.] A small supernatural creature usually dressed in green and wearing a hat with a broad rim and buckle. This creature is said to know the location of buried treasure and pots of gold. Cf. **kobald**.

Les absents ont toujours tort. Philippe Néricault dit Destouches (1680–1754). *L'Obstacle imprévu* I,6. [Fr. **les** the (1); **absents** absent (2); **ont** have (3); **toujours** always (5); **tort** wrong, fault (4): The absent have fault always.] The absent are always in the wrong.

Le Sacre du Printemps *n.* [Fr. **le** the (1); **sacre** rite (2); **du** of the (3); **printemps** spring (4): the rite of the spring.] "The Rite of Spring," a 1913 ballet by Igor Stravinsky (1882–1971).

Le salut du peuple est la suprême loi. [Fr. **le** the (1); **salut** safety, salvation (2); **du** of the (3); **peuple**

people, nation (4); **est** is (5); **la** the (6); **suprême** supreme, paramount (7); **loi** law (8): The safety of the people is the supreme law.] *Law.* The most important law is public safety. See **in casu extremae** etc.

Les Contes d'Hoffmann *pl. n.* [Fr. **les** the (1); **contes** tales, stories (2); **d'** of (3); **Hoffmann** Hoffmann (4): the stories of Hoffman.] "The Tales of Hoffmann," the last opera (1880) of Jacques Offenbach (1819–1880) and his only serious one.

lèse-majesté or **lese majesty** or **leze majesty** *n., pl.* **lèse-majestés** or **lese majesties** or **leze majesties** [Fr. **lèse** injured, wounded (1); **majesté** majesty (2): injured or wounded majesty.] *Law.* High treason. A crime against sovereign power. An offense which violates the dignity of a ruler or detracts from the majesty of a sovereign, constituted authority, or a nation. *The commission ... looked severely on their habit of drawing administrators out on wildgoose chases as almost lese-majeste* (*West Africa* 1986). See **crimen laesae majestatis** and **laesa majestas**.

Les Femmes Savantes *pl. n.* [Fr. **les** the (1); **femmes** women (3); **savantes** learned (2): the learned women.] *The Learned Women*, a 1672 comedy by Molière (1622–1673). Cf. **femme savante**.

Les Fleurs du Mal *pl. n.* [Fr. **les** the (1); **fleurs** flowers (2); **du** of the (3); **Mal** evil (4): the flowers of the evil.] *The Flowers of Evil*, a 1857 collection of poems by the French symbolist Charles Baudelaire (1821–1867). Cf. **fleur du mal**.

Les Fourberies de Scapin *pl. n.* [Fr. **les** the (1); **fourberies** knavery, cheating, deceit (2); **de** of (3); **Scapin** Scapin (4): the knavery of Scapin.] *The Knavery of Scapin*, a 1671 comedy by Molière (1622–1673).

Les Guêpes *pl. n.* [Fr. **les** the (1); **guêpes** wasps (2): the wasps.] *The Wasps*, a satirical review by Alphonse Karr (1808–1890).

Les lois ne se chargent de punir que les actions extérieures. [Fr. **les** the (1); **lois** laws (2); **ne ... que** only (6); **se chargent** undertake (3); **de** of (4); **punir** to punish (5); **les** the (7); **actions** actions (9); **extérieures** external, outward (8): The laws undertake to punish only the outward actions.] *Law.* Laws undertake to punish only outward actions. Cf. **actus non facit**.

Les Misérables *pl. n.* [Fr. **les** the (1); **misérables** wretched, miserable (ones) (2): the wretched ones.] 1. *The Miserable Ones*, an 1862 epic novel by Victor Hugo (1802–1885). 2. *short form* **Les Mis** A 1980 musical adaptation of Hugo's novel by Alain Boublil, Claude-Michel Schönberg, and Herbert Kretzmer.

Les Pêcheurs de perles *pl. n.* [Fr. **les** the (1); **pêcheurs** fishers (2); **de** of (3); **perles** pearls (4): the fishers of pearls.] "The Pearl Fishers," an 1863 opera by Georges Bizet (1838–1875).

Les Plaideurs *pl. n.* [Fr. **les** the (1); **plaideurs** litigants, suitors (2): the suitors.] *The Suitors*, a tragedy by Racine (1639-1699).

Les Poètes maudits *pl. n.* [Fr. **les** the (1); **poètes** poets (3); **maudits** cursed (2): the cursed poets.] *The Cursed Poets*, an 1884 literary study, by Paul Verlaine (1844–1886), of several literary artists who were not sufficiently recognized and esteemed in their unhappy lifetimes.

les sans-culottes See **sans-culottes**.

Les Trois Mousquetiares *pl. n.* [Fr. **les** the (1); **trois** three (2); **mousquetiares** musketeers (3): the three musketeers.] *The Three Musketeers*, an 1844 novel by Alexandre Dumas (1803–1870).

Les Troyens *pl. n.* [Fr. **les** the (1); **Troyens** Trojans (2): the Trojans.] "The Trojans," an opera by Hector Berlioz (1803–1869).

Le style, c'est l'homme. [Fr. **le** the (1); **style** style (2); **c'** it (3); **est** is (4); **l'** the (5); **homme** person, human being, man, male (6): The style, it is the person.] A variant of **Le style est l'homme même** (q.v.). *Le style c'est l'homme, and Hoving's style reflects the character he showed when he was in power at the museum—windy, lapel-grabbing and insincerely populist* (*Time Int.* 1981). Cf. **stilus virum arguit**.

Le style est l'homme même. G. De Buffon (1707–1788). [Fr. **le** the (1); **style** style (2); **est** is (3); **l'** the (4); **homme** person, human being, man, male (5); **même** himself/herself (6): The style is the person himself.] The style is the person himself; i.e., the personality of an author is reflected in his/her style. See **L'homme même**.

Le superflu, chose très nécessaire. Voltaire (1694–1778). *Le Mondain* 22. [Fr. **le** the (1); **superflu** superfluous, needless, unnecessary (2); **chose** thing (5); **très** very (3); **nécessaire** necessary (4): The superfluous, a very necessary thing.] The unnecessary is a very necessary thing.

L'état, c'est moi. Louis XIV (1638–1715). [Fr. **l'** the (1); **état** state (2); **c'** it (3); **est** is (4); **moi** me, I (5): The state, it is I.] I am the State; i.e., every power is vested in me. *The leader of the military junta continued to behave as though the country were his patrimony and, like Louis XIV, he might as well have kept on saying, "L'état, c'est moi."*

l'éternel retour *n.* [Fr. **l'** the (1); **éternel** eternal (2); **retour** return (3): the eternal return.] 1. The unceasing or unending return. The view that ideas keep coming back. 2. The belief that souls are continually returning. Transmigration of souls. **Metempsychosis** (q.v.).

Lethe *n.* [Gk. **lēthē** forgetting, forgetfulness.] 1. *Greek and Roman Mythology.* A river in the Lower World whose water, on being drunk, produces forgetfulness of whatever one has done in the past. 2. Oblivion or forgetfulness of the past.

l'étoile du nord. [Fr. **l'** the (1); **étoile** star (2); **du** of (3); **nord** north (4): the star of the north.] The Star of the North. Motto of the State of Minnesota.

le tout Paris *n.* [Fr. **le** the (2); **tout** all (1); **Paris** Paris (3): all (the) Paris.] All Paris. People who set the pace in Parisian fashion. Fashionable Parisians. The socialites or smart set of Paris. *The 500 guests come from the worlds of show business, food, high fashion and that mysterious constellation of trend setters known as le tout Paris* (*Newsweek Int.* Oct. 18, 1982:18). Cf. **tout Paris**.

L'Être et le Néant [Fr. **l'** the (1); **être** to be, being (2); **et** and (3); **le** the (4), **néant** nothingness (4): the being and nothingness.] *Being and Nothingness*, a philosophical treatise by the French existentialist Jean-Paul Sartre (1905–1980). Cf. **en-soi** and **pour-soi**.

lettera liberatoria *n.* [It. **lettera** letter (2); **liberatoria** liberatory (1): a liberatory letter.] A letter which exonerates, exempts, frees, etc.... *Marcinkus produced a lettera liberatoria signed by Calvi that purported to free the Vatican bank from financial responsibility* (*Newsweek Int.* July 19, 1982: 19).

lettre de cachet *n., pl.* **lettres de cachet** [Fr. **lettre** letter (1); **de** of (2); **cachet** seal, stamp (3): letter of seal.] Sealed letter. Arbitrary warrant of arrest, detention, or imprisonment. Letter, usually, from a king or despot, bearing the official seal and ordering the arrest and imprisonment, without the benefit of a trial, of a person named in it. Originally used in France for punishing political opponents and personal enemies, it was abolished during the 1789 revolution. *Galba . . . had but recently saved his life by intercepting a lettre de cachet from Nero . . .* (Cary 1970:595).

lettre de marque *n., pl.* **lettres de marque** [Fr. **lettre** letter (1); **de** of (2); **marque** mark, retaliation, reprisal (3): letter of mark.] A letter of retaliation or reprisal. Letter of marque. A written authority given by a government to a citizen to attack and plunder the goods of citizens of another country in retaliation. A license granted to a citizen by a government, empowering him to fit out a ship and use it for plundering the enemy or for piracy. Officially, the practice was abolished in 1856 by the Congress of Paris. Cf. **marque**.

Lettres Persanes *pl. n.* [Fr. **lettres** letters (2); **persanes** Persian (1): Persian letters.] *Persian Letters*, a satire (1721) by Montesquieu (1689-1755) in which the letters of two Persians traveling in Europe are used to criticize both Persian and French society.

Lettres Portugaises *pl. n.* [Fr. **lettres** letters (2); **portugaises** Portugese (1): Portugese letters.] *Portugese Letters*, an epistolary novel by Gabriel-Joseph de Guilleragues (1628-1685).

levant *adj.* [Fr. rising up.] *Law.* Applicable to trespassing animals. See **couchant** 1 and **levant et couchant**.
—**Levant.** 1. The countries of the eastern Mediterranean, i.e., where the sun rises. 2. A kind of leather. —*adj.* Eastern. *A levant sea.* —*v. British.* To rise up and disappear without paying one's debts.

levant et couchant *adj.* [Fr. **levant** rising up (1); **et** and (2); **couchant** lying down (3): rising up and lying down.] *Law.* Applicable to trespassing animals and meaning that they have remained on the land long enough to lie down, to rest and rise up to feed, the estimated minimum period for such activities being a night and a day, which is adequate to sustain legal distraint. See **couchant** 1 and **levant**.

levari facias *n.* [L. **levari** to be taken, taken away (2); **facias** you should/may cause (1): You should/may cause to be taken away.] *Law.* A writ of execution ordering the sheriff to seize and sell the lands and goods of a judgment debtor for the settlement of the debt, or to use the rents and profits of the judgment debtor's land for the purpose. See **fieri facias**.

levée en masse or **levy en masse** *n., pl.* **levées en masse** or **levies en masse** [Fr. **levée** rising (1); **en** in (2); **masse** bulk, mass (3): rising in mass.] Rising as one body. A mass military uprising. The taking up of arms by citizens to resist external aggression. Mobilization of all able-bodied adult men of military age.

lex *n., pl.* **leges** [L. law.] A law. A statute.

lex actus See **lex loci actus**.

lex aequitate gaudet; appetit perfectum; est norma recti. [L. **lex** law (1); **aequitate** in equity (3); **gaudet** rejoices, delights (2); **appetit** strives for, desires (4); **perfectum** the perfect (5); **est** it is (6); **norma** rule (7); **recti** of right, uprightness (8): The law delights in equity; it strives for the perfect; it is a rule of right.] The law takes delight in equity; it aims at perfection; it is a rule of right.

lex aeterna *n.* [L. **lex** law (2); **aeterna** eternal, everlasting (1): eternal law.] The eternal law established by God. *In its role as guardian of lex aeterna (God's eternal law) the Church had to exercise total sovereignty over the state* (Curzon 1979:55).

lex aliquando sequitur aequitatem. [L. **lex** law (2); **aliquando** sometimes (1); **sequitur** follows (3); **aequitatem** equity (4): Sometimes law follows equity.] Sometimes the law follows fairness. Cf. **aequitas sequitur legem**.

lex celebrationis See **lex loci celebrationis**.

lex citius tolerare vult privatum damnum quam publicum malum. [L. **lex** law (1); **citius** more quickly, rapidly (4); **tolerare** to tolerate, endure (3); **vult** wishes, is minded (2); **privatum** private (5); **damnum** loss, damage (6); **quam** than (7); **publicum** public (8); **malum** evil (9): The law is minded to tolerate more quickly a private loss than a public evil.] *Law.* The law is inclined to tolerate a private loss more readily than a public evil. Thus, when a superior officer, commenting on a subordinate officer in an official report, defames him, the latter has no remedy by way of action against the former. Similarly, no action lies against an advocate or a witness for defamation made in the course of judicial proceedings or inquiry. See **in casu extremae** etc.

lex commercii *n.* [L. **lex** law (1); **commercii** of commerce (2): law of commerce.] *Law.* The law governing business transactions. Commercial law.

lex communis *n.* [L. **lex** law (2); **communis** common, universal (1): common law.] *Law.* The common law. Cf. **droit common** and **droit coutumier**.

lex contractus See **lex loci contractus**.

lex contra id quod praesumit probationem non recipit. [L. **lex** law (1); **contra** against, opposite (5); **id** that (6); **quod** which (7); **praesumit** it presumes (8); **probationem** proof (4); **non** not (2); **recipit** admits, welcomes, entertains (3): The law does not admit proof against that which it presumes.] *Law.* The law does not entertain/welcome proof against what it presumes.

lex deficere non potest in justitia exhibenda. [L. **lex** law (1); **deficere** to fail, be wanting (4); **non** not (3); **potest** can, is able (2); **in** in, on (5); **justitia** justice (6); **exhibenda** that must be delivered, exhibited (7): The law cannot fail in the justice that must be delivered.] *Law.* The law should not fail in its delivery of justice. See **justitia nemini** etc.

lex de futuro, judex de praeterito. [L. **lex** law (1); **de** of, from, about, for (2); **futuro** future (3); **judex** judge (4); **de** of, from, about, for (5); **praeterito** past (6): The law is about the future, the judge about the past.] *Law.* The law concerns itself with the future, the judge with the past.

lex delicti See **lex loci delicti**.

lex dilationes semper exhorret. [L. **lex** law (1); **dilationes** delays (4); **semper** always (2); **exhorret** shudders at, dreads (3): The law always shudders at delays.] *Law.* The law does not like delays. See **infinitum in** etc.

lex domicilii or **lex loci domicilii** *n.* [L. **lex** law (1); **domicilii** of domicile, home, dwelling-place (2): the law of the domicile.] *Law.* The law of the place of a person's domicile. Usually applied in cases respecting marriage, separation, divorce, contracts, etc.

lex est dictamen rationis. [L. **lex** law (1); **est** is (2); **dictamen** dictate, saying (3); **rationis** of reason (4): Law is the dictate of reason.] *Law.* The law is the decree of reason.

lex est exercitus judicum tutissimus ductor. [L. **lex** law (1); **est** is (2); **exercitus** of army (5); **judicum** of judges (6); **tutissimus** safest (3); **ductor** leader, commander, general (4): The law is the safest general of the army of judges.] *Law.* The law is the most reliable guide of the fraternity of judges.

lex est norma recti. [L. **lex** law (1); **est** is (2); **norma** rule, norm (3); **recti** of right, uprightness (4): Law is a rule of right.] *Law.* Law is the standard of uprightness. See **jus est norma recti** etc.

lex est ratio summa quae jubet quae sunt utilia et necessaria et contraria prohibet. [L. **lex** law (1); **est** is (2); **ratio** system, science (4); **summa** greatest, supreme, best (3); **quae** which (5); **jubet** orders, commands (6); **quae** (those things) which, what (7);

sunt are (8); **utilia** useful (9); **et** and (10); **necessaria** necessary (11); **et** and (12); **contraria** contrary (things) (14); **prohibet** forbids (13): Law is the greatest system which orders those things which are useful and necessary and (which) forbids the contrary.] *Law.* Law is the supreme rule/system which commands what is useful and necessary and prohibits the opposite. Cf. **lex est sanctio sancta** etc.

lex est sanctio sancta, jubens honesta et prohibens contraria. [L. **lex** law (1); **est** is (2); **sanctio** sanction (4); **sancta** sacred, inviolable (3); **jubens** ordering (5); **honesta** decent, proper (things) (6); **et** and (7); **prohibens** forbidding, prohibiting (8); **contraria** opposite, contrary, reverse (things) (9): Law is a sacred sanction, ordering decent things and forbidding contrary things.] *Law.* Law is an inviolable sanction, which orders decent conduct and forbids the opposite. Cf. **lex est ratio summa** etc.

lex est tutissima cassis; sub clipeo legis nemo decipitur. [L. **lex** law (1); **est** is (2); **tutissima** very safe, safest (3); **cassis** helmet (4); **sub** under (5); **clipeo** shield (6); **legis** of law (7); **nemo** no one, nobody (8); **decipitur** is deceived (9): Law is the safest helmet; under the shield of law no one is deceived.] *Law.* Law is a very safe helmet; under the shield of law nobody is misled.

lex et consuetudo parliamenti *n.* [L. **lex** law (1); **et** and (2); **consuetudo** custom, usage, tradition (3); **parliamenti** of parliament (4): the law and custom of parliament.] *Law.* The law and custom followed by parliament. *Lex et consuetudo parliamenti permit punishment of contempt committed in its face.*

lex fori *n.* [L. **lex** law (1); **fori** of court (2): law of the court.] *Law.* The law of the court where proceedings are being held or where a case is tried. The law of the court deals with matters of remedy or procedure in the court where a suit is brought, and it is an integral part of the law of the state.

lex generalis *n.* [L. **lex** law (2); **generalis** general (1): general law.] *Law.* A general law; i.e., a law to be applied generally as distinct from a law to be applied to a particular person/situation. Cf. **jus singulare**.

lexicon *n., pl.* **lexica** or **lexicons** [Gk. **lexikon** of or for words.] 1. A dictionary. A wordbook. A book of words, arranged alphabetically, and their meanings. *It is not easy to learn a language for which there is no lexicon.* 2. The vocabulary or stock of words of a language, a particular speaker, a subject, a group of documents, an occupation, etc. *According to his medical lexicon, pregnancy should be terminated only if it jeopardizes the mother's life.* 3. Record. Account. *The man declared that, in his search through the entire lexicon of human endeavors, he has yet to find a single instance of such behavior.* Cf. **lexis**.

lex injusta non est lex. [L. **lex** law (2); **injusta** unjust (1); **non** not (4); **est** is (3); **lex** law (5): An unjust law is not law.] *Law.* An unjust law is not a law at all.

lex intendit vicinum vicini facta scire. [L. **lex** law (1); **intendit** maintains, asserts (2); **vicinum** neighbor (3); **vicini** of neighbor (6); **facta** deeds, acts, facts (5); **scire** to know (4): The law maintains a neighbor knows the deeds of a neighbor.] *Law.* The law asserts that a neighbor is aware of the actions of his/her neighbor. Cf. **vicini viciniora** etc.

lexis *n., pl.* **lexes** [Gk. speech, diction, a word, a phrase, text of an author.] Stock of words. Vocabulary. *The celebrated lexicographer is compiling a lexis of law.* Cf. **lexicon.**

lex loci See **lex loci contractus.**

lex loci actus or **lex actus** *n.* [L. **lex** law (1); **loci** of place (2); **actus** of act (3): law of the place of the act.] *Law.* The law of the place where the deed was done or a transaction took place.

lex loci celebrationis or **lex celebrationis** *n.* [L. **lex** law (1); **loci** of place (2); **celebrationis** of celebration, ceremony (3): law of the place of celebration.] *Law.* The law of the place where a contract or a marriage is celebrated. In case of conflict, the court in deciding the validity of a marriage or a contract, applies the law of the place where the couple were married or the contract was concluded.

lex loci contractus or **lex contractus** or **lex loci.** *n.* [L. **lex** law (1); **loci** of place (2); **contractus** of drawing together, shrinking, contract, agreement (3): law of the place of the contract.] *Law.* The law of the place where a contract was made or is to be performed. a) *Lex loci contractus normally permits the parties to incorporate local customary practices into the agreement.* b) *. . . though the lex loci contractus must regulate and interpret the contract, yet the lex fori must govern the remedy* (Megrah and Ryder 1972:310). See **locus contractus.**

lex loci delicti or **lex loci delicti commissi** or **lex delicti** *n.* [L. **lex** law (1); **loci** of place (2); **delicti** of wrong, offense, crime (3): law of the place of the offense.] *Law.* The law of the place where a wrong or tort is committed. *The courts are permitted by the lex loci delicti to inspect the scene of the action.* See **locus delicti.**

lex loci delicti commissi See **lex loci delicti.**

lex loci domicilii See **lex domicilii.**

lex loci rei sitae or **lex rei sitae** (an inaccurate form) or **lex situs** *n.* [L. **lex** law (1); **loci** of place (2); **rei** (of) matter, thing, property, business, affair (4); **sitae** of situated (3): law of the place of the situated thing/property.] *Law.* The law of the place where a property/thing is located. Applicable to lands and other immovable things which are governed by the law of the country where they are situated. *When Andrew consulted his lawyer about his intention to recover landed properties situated in five countries, he was advised that the lex loci rei sitae would be applied in each case.* See **locus rei sitae.**

lex loci solutionis or **lex solutionis** *n.* [L. **lex** law (1); **loci** of place (2); **solutionis** of payment, performance, solution (3): law of the place of payment.] *Law.* The law of the place of solution; i.e., of the place where payment or performance will take place.

lex lux gentium. [L. **lex** law (1); **lux** light (2); **gentium** of nations, races (3): Law (is) the light of nations.] *Law.* The law is the light which guides nations.

lex mercatoria or **lex mercatorum** *n.* [L. **lex** law (2); **mercatoria** mercantile (1): law of merchants.] *Law.* Mercantile law. Commercial law. The law-merchant. The system of laws adopted and observed by commercial nations. See **jus mercatorum.** Cf. **consuetudo mercatorum.**

lex naturalis *n.* [L. **lex** law (2); **naturalis** natural (1): natural law.] *Law.* The law of nature. The law applicable to all human beings. The law established by natural principles and morality. *Lex naturalis is . . . the result of man's participation in the cosmic law* (Curzon 1979:57). See **jus naturae.**

lex necessitatis est lex temporis scilicet instantis. [L. **lex** law (1); **necessitatis** of compulsion, urgency, necessity (2); **est** is (3); **lex** law (4); **temporis** of time (5); **scilicet** certainly, that is (6); **instantis** of present, immediate (7): The law of compulsion is the law of time, that is, of the present.] *Law.* The law of necessity is the law of the actual time; i.e., of the immediate present. See **in casu extremae** etc.

lex neminem cogit ad vana seu inutilia peragenda. [L. **lex** law (1); **neminem** no one, nobody (3); **cogit** compels, forces (2); **ad** to, at, for, according to (4); **vana** fruitless, vain (things) (5); **seu** or (6); **inutilia** useless (things) (7); **peragenda** to be done, carried out (8): The law compels no one to fruitless or useless things to be done.] *Law.* The law compels no one to the doing of fruitless or useless things. When an obligation, which initially was possible, is rendered impossible by an unforeseen circumstance such as an act of God or an act of law or an act of the obligee, the obligor is released from the obligation. See **impotentia excusat legem.**

lex neminem cogit ostendere quod nescire praesumitur. [L. **lex** law (1); **neminem** no one, nobody (3); **cogit** compels, forces (2); **ostendere** to show (4); **quod** (that) which, what (5); **nescire** not to know (7); **praesumitur** he/she is presumed (6): The law forces no one to show that which he/she is presumed not to know.] *Law.* The law does not force anybody to show/declare what he/she is presumed not to know.

lex nemini facit injuriam. [L. **lex** law (1); **nemini** to no one; nobody (4); **facit** makes, does (2); **injuriam** injury, wrong (3): The law does wrong/injury to no one.] *Law.* The law does not harm anybody. See **actus curiae neminem gravabit.**

lex nemini operatur iniquum. [L. **lex** law (1); **nemini** to no one, nobody (4); **operatur** does, offers (2); **iniquum** unjust, unfair (thing) (3): The law does an unjust thing to no one.] *Law.* The law does injustice to no one. See **actus curiae neminem gravabit.**

lex nil facit frustra. [L. lex law (1); nil nothing (3); facit does, makes (2); frustra in vain, to no purpose (4): The law does nothing to no purpose.] *Law*. The law does not attempt either to do, or to force one to do, what would be futile. See **impotentia excusat legem.**

lex nil facit frustra, nil jubet frustra. [L. lex law (1); nil nothing (3); facit does, makes (2); frustra in vain, to no purpose (4); nil nothing (6); jubet orders, commands (5); frustra in vain, to no purpose (7): The law does nothing in vain; it orders nothing in vain.] *Law*. The law neither does nor orders anything in vain. See **impotentia excusat legem.**

lex nil frustra jubet. [L. lex law (1); nil nothing (3); frustra in vain, to no purpose (4); jubet orders (2): The law orders nothing to no purpose.] *Law*. The law does not order anything in vain. See **impotentia excusat legem.**

lex non a rege est violanda. [L. lex law (1); non not (3); a by (5); rege king (6); est is (2); violanda to be broken, violated (4): The law is not to be broken by the king.] *Law*. The king must not break the law.

lex non cogit ad impossibilia. [L. lex law (1); non not (2); cogit forces, compels (3); ad to, at, for, according to (4); impossibilia impossible (things) (5): The law does not compel to impossible things.] *Law*. The law does not compel one to do the impossible. See **impotentia excusat legem.**

lex non curat de minimis. See **de minimis non curat lex.**

lex non debet deficere conquerentibus in justitia exhibenda. [L. lex law (1); non not (3); debet ought, should (2); deficere to fail, be deficient (4); conquerentibus to those complaining (8); in in, on (5); justitia justice (6); exhibenda to be shown, delivered (7): Law ought not to fail in justice to be delivered to those complaining.] *Law*. The law should not fail to dispense justice to those who bring their complaints. See **justitia nemini** etc.

lex non deficit in justitia exhibenda. [L. lex law (1); non not (2); deficit fails, is deficient (3); in in, on (4); justitia justice (5); exhibenda to be shown, delivered (6): Law does not fail in justice to be delivered.] *Law*. The law does not fail in its dispensation of justice. The law does not fail in the rendering of justice. See **justitia nemini** etc.

lex non exacte definit; sed arbitrio boni viri permittit. [L. lex law (1); non not (2); exacte precisely, exactly (4); definit defines (3); sed but (5); arbitrio to judgment, decision (7); boni of good (8); viri (of) man (9); permittit leaves, entrusts (6): Law does not define precisely, but leaves it to the judgment of a good man.] *Law*. The law does not give exact definitions, but relies on the judgment of a good man. Cf. **judex bonus nihil** etc. and **optima est lex** etc.

lex non intendit aliquid impossibile. [L. lex law (1); non not (2); intendit aims at, gives attention to (3);

aliquid something (4); impossibile impossible (5): Law does not aim at something impossible.] *Law*. The law does not aim at the impossible. See **impotentia excusat legem.**

lex non novit patrem, nec matrem; solam veritatem. [L. lex law (1); non not (2); novit knows (3); patrem father (4); nec nor (5); matrem mother (6); solam alone, only (8); veritatem truth (7): Law knows not father nor mother; the truth alone.] *Law*. The law pays no attention to father or mother, but only the truth. See **justitia nemini** etc.

lex non oritur ex injuria. [L. lex law (1); non not (2); oritur arises (3); ex out of, from, directly after, away from (4); injuria injury (5): Law does not arise from injury.] *Law*. The law does not arise from injury.

lex non praecipit inutilia, quia inutilis labor stultus. [L. lex law (1); non not (2); praecipit orders, bids (3); inutilia useless (things) (4); quia because (5); inutilis useless (6); labor labor, work (7); stultus foolish, silly (8): Law does not order useless things because useless labor is foolish.] *Law*. The law does not order useless things to be done because useless work is foolish. See **impotentia excusat legem.**

lex non requirit verificari quod apparet curiae. [L. lex law (1); non not (2); requirit asks, demands (3); verificari to be proved, verified (4); quod (that) which, what (5); apparet is apparent, evident (6); curiae to court (7): Law does not demand to be proved what is apparent to the court.] *Law*. The law does not demand proof of what is apparent to the court. See **manifesta probatione** etc.

lex non scripta *n*. [lex law (1); non not (2); scripta written (3): law not written.] *Law*. Unwritten law (e.g., custom or common law), as distinct from statutory law. See **jus non scriptum.**

lex patriae *n*. [lex law (1); patriae of fatherland, country (2): law of one's fatherland/country.] *Law*. National law. The law of one's country. *In some cases, an expatriate may enjoy the privilege of being treated in accordance with his/her lex patriae.*

lex plus laudatur quando ratione probatur. [L. lex law (1); plus more (3); laudatur is praised (2); quando when (4); ratione by reason (6); probatur it is approved (5): Law is more praised when it is approved by reason.] *Law*. A commendable law is one which conforms to reason. See **cessante ratione** etc.; **lex semper intendit** etc.; **ratio est legis anima** etc.; **ratio legis est** etc.; and **ubi eadem ratio, ibi eadem** etc. Cf. **sensus verborum est anima legis.**

lex posterior derogat priori. [L. lex law (2); posterior later (1); derogat repeals in part, modifies (3); priori former (4): A later law modifies a former one.] *Law*. A later law overrules one which precedes it. See **constitutiones tempore** etc.; **leges posteriores** etc.; and **priores leges** etc.

lex privata *n*. [lex law (2); privata private (1): private law.] *Roman Law*. A stipulation of a private contract.

lex prospicit, non respicit. [L. lex law (1); prospicit looks forward (2); non not (3); respicit looks backward (4): The law looks forward; it does not look backward.] *Law.* The law looks forward, not backward; i.e., makes provisions for the future, not the past. See nova constitutio etc. and omnis nova constitutio etc.

lex publica n. [lex law (2); publica public (1): public law.] *Roman Law.* A written law or a law passed by one of the popular assemblies. Cf. jus non scriptum.

lex punit mendacium. [L. lex law (1); punit punishes (2); mendacium falsehood, untruth (3): The law punishes falsehood.] *Law.* The law punishes the telling of lies.

lex rei sitae See lex loci rei sitae.

lex rejicit superflua, pugnantia, incongrua. [L. lex law (1); rejicit rejects, disdains (2); superflua superfluous (things) (3); pugnantia fighting (things) (4); incongrua incongruous (things) (5): Law rejects superfluous, fighting, and incongruous things.] *Law.* The law rejects the superfluous, the inconsistent, and the incongruous.

lex reprobat moram. [L. lex law (1); reprobat disapproves of, dislikes (2); moram delay, procrastination (3): Law disapproves of delay.] *Law.* The law dislikes delay or postponement. See infinitum in etc.

lex respicit aequitatem. [L. lex law (1); respicit respects, regards (2); aequitatem equity (3): Law respects equity.] *Law.* The law has regard for fairness. See jus respicit aequitatem.

lex scripta n. [lex law (2); scripta written (1): written law.] *Law.* Statute or an act of parliament. Cf. jus non scriptum.

lex semper dabit remedium. [L. lex law (1); semper always (3); dabit will give (2); remedium remedy, cure, relief (4): Law will always give a remedy.] *Law.* The law will always offer relief. Cf. actio non datur etc.

lex semper intendit quod convenit rationi. [L. lex law (1); semper always (3); intendit aims at (3); quod (that) which, what (4); convenit agrees with (5); rationi reason (6): Law always aims at what agrees with reason.] *Law.* The law always aims at what is consistent with reason. See lex plus laudatur etc.

lex situs n. [lex law (1); situs of location, situation (2): law of location/situation.] *Law.* The law of the location. lex loci rei sitae (q.v.). a) *Litigations affecting immovable properties are usually governed by the lex situs.* b) *. . . in the last resort the land can only be dealt with in a manner permitted by the lex situs* (Morris 1973:61).

lex solutionis See lex loci solutionis.

lex specialis derogat generali. [L. lex law (2); specialis special (1); derogat repeals in part, modifies (3); generali general (4): A special law repeals in part a general one.] *Law.* A special law modifies a general one.

lex spectat naturae ordinem. [L. lex law (1); spectat regards, considers (2); naturae of nature (4); ordinem order (3): Law considers the order of nature.] *Law.* The law takes into consideration the natural order of things.

lex successionis n. [L. lex law (1); successionis of succession, inheritance (2): law of succession.] *Law.* The law of inheritance.

lex succurrit ignoranti. [L. lex law (1); succurrit helps, assists (2); ignoranti ignorant (person) (3): Law helps the ignorant.] *Law.* The law provides assistance to the ignorant person. Cf. ignorantia facti excusat, ignorantia etc.

lex succurrit minoribus. [L. lex law (1); succurrit helps, assists (2); minoribus minors (3): Law helps minors.] *Law.* The law provides assistance to those under age. Cf. succurritur minori etc.

lex talionis n. [L. lex law (1); talionis of retaliation (2): law of retaliation.] *Law.* The law of revenge. The principle of retributive justice which goes back to remote antiquity and whose best known exponents are Hammurabi and Moses ("an eye for an eye; a tooth for a tooth"). See le droit de talion; retorsio facti; and retorsion de droit.

lex terrae n. [L. lex law (1); terrae of land, earth, country (2): law of the land.] *Law.* The common law of the land.

lex uno ore omnes alloquitur. [L. lex law (1); uno with one (4); ore (with) mouth (5); omnes all (3); alloquitur speaks to, addresses (2): Law addresses all people with one mouth.] *Law.* The law speaks to everybody with one mouth; i.e., the law does not discriminate. See justitia nemini etc.

lex validitatis n. [L. lex law (1); validitatis of validity (2): law of validity.] *Law.* The law of validity or legal force. Applicable to presumptions of validity in such matters as contracts, marriages, etc.

lex vigilantibus, non dormientibus subvenit. [L. lex law (1); vigilantibus the awake (3); non not (4); dormientibus the sleeping (5); subvenit helps (2): Law helps those who are awake, not those who are asleep.] *Law.* The law assists those who pay attention, not those who do not. See leges vigilantibus etc.

L'homme est, je vous l'avoue, un méchant animal. Molière (1622–1673). *Tartuffe* V,6. [Fr. l' the (1); homme person, human being, man, male (2); est is (3); je I (4); vous you (7); l' it (6); avoue I admit, admit to (5); un a (8); méchant vicious, wicked (9); animal animal (10): The human being is, I admit to you, a vicious animal.] A human being, I confess to you, is a vicious animal.

L'homme est né libre, et partout il est dans les fers. Jean-Jacques Rousseau (1712–1778). *Le Contrat Social* 1. [Fr. l' the (1); homme person, human being, man, male (2); est is, was (3); né born (4); libre free (5); et and (6); partout everywhere (7); il he (8); est is (9); dans in (10); les the (11); fers chains, fetters

(12): The human being was born free, but everywhere he is in chains.] Human beings are born free but are everywhere enchained.

l'homme même [Fr. **l'** the (1); **homme** person, human being, man, male (2); **même** himself (3): the human being himself.] An author's personality as discerned or reflected in his style. See **Le style** etc.

L'homme n'est qu'un roseau, l'être le plus faible de la nature, mais c'est un roseau pensant. Blaise Pascal (1623–1662). *Pensées* VI,347. [Fr. **l'** the (1); **homme** person, human being, man, male (2); **n'** not (3); **est** is (4); **qu'** but, only (5); **un** a (6); **roseau** reed (7); **l'** the (8); **être** being (9); **le** the (10); **plus** more, most (11); **faible** weak, feeble (12); **de** of (13); **la** the (14); **nature** nature (15); **mais** but (16); **c'** he/she/it (17); **est** is (18); **un** a (19); **roseau** reed (21); **pensant** thinking (20): The human being not is but a reed, the being the most feeble of (the) nature, but it is a thinking reed.] Humankind is only a reed, the weakest being in nature, but it is a thinking reed. Rebecca West's book title *The Thinking Reed* is based upon this statement.

L'hypocrisie est un hommage que le vice rend à la vertu. Duc de la Rochefoucauld. (1613–1680). *Maximes* 298. [Fr. **l'** the (1); **hypocrisie** hypocrisy (2); **est** is (3); **un** a (4); **hommage** homage, praise (5); **que** which (6); **le** the (7); **vice** vice (8); **rend** pays (9); **à** to, toward, in, by, with, until (10); **la** the (11); **vertu** virtue (12): The hypocrisy is a praise which the vice pays to the virtue.] Hypocrisy is praise which vice pays to virtue.

liaison *abbr.* **l.** *n., pl.* **liaisons** [Fr. joining, linking, bond, connection, intimacy, love affair.] 1. Close contact, connection, or bond between independent bodies, entities, etc. Interrelationship. *"We are always in liaison with the Nigerians and have been trying to find ways to facilitate exchanges."* (Gnolera quoted in *West Africa* 1981). 2. An illicit affair between a man and a woman. *. . . there were many notorious examples of incest such as . . . Woodsworth's much-rumored liaison with his sister* (*Newsweek Int.* July 2, 1979:41). 3. Intercommunication between different arms of an organization, such as an army, for effective maintenance of mutual understanding, cooperation, and promptitude of action. *Liaison between the army, navy and air force . . . is handled at the top by a royal military staff* (*Time Int.* 1978). 4. *Linguistics.* The pronunciation of the last consonant of a word which is usually silent when the first letter of the next word is a vowel or silent "h"; e.g., *les affaires.*

Liaisons dangereuses *pl. n.* [Fr. **liaisons** joinings, linkings, bonds, connections, intimacies, love affairs (2); **dangereuses** dangerous (1): dangerous connections.] *Dangerous Liaisons*, a 1792 novel by the French soldier and writer Pierre Ambroise François Choderlos de Laclos (1741–1803).

lib. *abbr.* for **libretto** (q.v.).

libellus famosus See **famosus libellus.**

libera me Domine [L. **libera** free (1); **me** me (2); **Domine** lord (3): Free me, Lord.] "Free me, O Lord." The first words in a traditional Christian prayer for the dead. —*n.* 1. The prayer itself. 2. A musical composition based upon this prayer.

liberavi animam meam. Bernard of Clairvaux (1092–1153). *Epistles* 371. [L. **liberavi** I have freed, liberated (1); **animam** soul, mind (3); **meam** my (2): I have freed my soul.] I have liberated my soul.

libertad *n.* [Sp. freedom.] Freedom. Liberty. a) *Upon arrival many broke into cheers of "libertad!" (Time Int.* 1980). b) *After their first euphoric shouts of "libertad!" many refugees began grumbling about life in their new world (Newsweek Int.* Jan. 5, 1981:42).

libertas est naturalis facultas ejus quod cuique facere libet, nisi quod de jure aut vi prohibetur. [L. **libertas** liberty, freedom (1); **est** is (2); **naturalis** natural (3); **facultas** power, opportunity (4); **ejus** of that (5); **quod** which (6); **cuique** to each (8); **facere** to do (9); **libet** it pleases, is agreeable (7); **nisi** unless, except (10); **quod** (that) which (11); **de** of, from, about, for (13); **jure** right, law (14); **aut** or (15); **vi** by force (16); **prohibetur** is forbidden, prohibited (12): Freedom is the natural power of that which pleases each one to do except that which is forbidden by right or by force.] Freedom is the right bestowed by nature on each one to do as one pleases, provided that one does not do what is forbidden by law or by force.

libertas inaestimabilis res est. [L. **libertas** freedom, liberty (1); **inaestimabilis** invaluable (3); **res** matter, thing, property, business, affair (4); **est** is (2): Liberty is an invaluable thing.] Liberty is priceless. See **libertas non** etc.

libertas non recipit aestimationem. [L. **libertas** freedom, liberty (1); **non** not (2); **recipit** admits, allows (3); **aestimationem** valuation, determination of value (4): Freedom does not allow valuation.] Freedom is beyond price. See **libertas inaestimabilis res est.**

Liberté, Égalité, Fraternité! [Fr. **liberté** liberty, freedom (1); **égalité** equality (2); **fraternité** fraternity, brotherhood (3): Liberty, Equality, Fraternity!] Freedom, Equality, and Brotherhood. A French revolutionary slogan.

liberum arbitrium *n.* [L. **liberum** free (1); **arbitrium** judgment, decision, power (2): free judgment.] Free will.

liberum veto *n.* [L. **liberum** free (1) and Eng. from L. **veto** I forbid, veto (2): free veto. The word **"veto"** is used here in its English sense.] Veto exercised by a member of a body in a situation where unanimous approval is required for acceptance of a proposal. *Though the council is ostensibly a democratic body, the chairman tacitly enjoys the power of liberum veto so that he can overrule the wishes of all other members.*

229   lis mota

libido sexualis *n.* [L. **libido** desire, eagerness (2); **sexualis** sexual (1): sexual desire.] Desire for sexual intercourse. . . . *the nipples, the tongue, the lips, the neck, indeed almost the entire body may be judiciously utilized to maintain and increase the libido sexualis (Newsweek Int.* July 18, 1983:39).

libra *n., pl.* **librae** [L. scales, balance, unit of measure.] *Ancient Rome.* A unit of measure equal to about 12 ounces.—*abbr.* **lb.** An abbreviation for one pound, a unit of weight equal to 16 oz. (453.592 grams) or 12 apothecary ounces. **£** An abbreviation for the pound (equivalent to 100 pence), the monetary unit of Great Britain. —**Libra** 1. *Astronomy.* A scales-shaped constellation located near Scorpio and Virgo. 2. *Astrology.* The seventh sign of the zodiac dominant from September 23 through October 23. 3. A person born under this sign.

libretto *abbr.* **lib.** *n., pl.* **librettos** or **libretti** [It. little book.] 1. The words or text of an opera or a musical play. *The story takes on a tragic intensity, and the words of the libretto come through sharp and clear (Newsweek Int.* Jan. 18, 1982:50). 2. A book which contains such words or text.

licentia loquendi *n.* [L. **licentia** license, leave (1); **loquendi** of/for speaking (2): license for speaking.] *Law of Former Times.* Permission to speak. Leave to imparl. Leave to confer with the plaintiff with a view to settling the dispute. Cf. **congé d'emparler.**

Licentiatus Chirurgiae *abbr.* **L.Ch.** *n.* [L. **licentiatus** licentiate (1); **chirurgiae** of surgery (2): Licentiate of Surgery.] Licentiate in Surgery. An academic degree conferred by a European university for completion of an advanced curriculum in surgery.

licet *v.* [L. It is permitted.] It is allowed.

Liebestod *n., pl.* **Liebestods** [Ger. **Liebes** of love (2); **Tod** death (1): death of love.] *Music.* A song sung by one or two lovers as they prepare, especially in an opera, to commit suicide.

Lied or lied *n., pl.* **Lieder** [Ger. song.] *Music.* An art song sung by a soloist with piano accompaniment.

Lieder ohne Wörter *n.* [Ger. **Lieder** songs (1); **ohne** without (2); **Wörter** words (3): songs without words.] *Songs Without Words,* eight books of short tone poems for piano by Felix Mendelssohn (1809–1847).

lien *abbr.* **ln** *n., pl.* **liens** [Fr. bond, tie, band, chain, fetter.] A charge, encumbrance upon, or right to keep property, personal or real, until the payment of debt or satisfaction of an obligation. It may be acquired either by operation of law or through a contract. *The company was merely exercising its lien on the goods, pending payment.*

lieu *n.* [Fr. place. spot, position, stead.] —**in lieu** *adv.* Instead. *Unlike other mercenaries who received gold and silver as remuneration, mercenaries from the Balearic islands received women in lieu.* —**in lieu of** *prep.* In the place of. Instead of. As a substitute for. *While statute labour in lieu of taxes was legal,*

the requisitioning of manpower had no explicit basis in legislation (Suret-Canale 1971:253).

Limbo *n.* [L. **Limbō** from **in limbō: in** in, on (1); **limbō** border (2): on the border.] *Theology, especially Christianity.* On the border of hell. A place where the souls of the innocent, especially the unbaptized, are kept away from all punishment except separation from God. —**limbo** *n., pl.* **limbos** 1. A place of oblivion, neglect or confinement. A state of oblivion, neglect or confinement. A condition or state of being forgotten, neglected, unwanted or confined. a) *American diplomats in Taipei were working in limbo (Newsweek Int.* March 26, 1979: 37). b) *Travelers who arrived at the closed border found themselves in limbo.* 2. A transitional place, state or situation. *Chiedu is 18 years old, an age which is a limbo between boyhood and adulthood.* 3. An intermediate or uncertain stage. *The decision is still in limbo.*

limes *n., pl.* **limites** [L. boundary, limit, landmark.] *Ancient Rome.* A fortified boundary line, particularly the Empire's system of frontier defense which consisted of the construction of forts, camps, and signal towers which, in conjunction with natural barriers, ditches, or trenches served the purpose of keeping the enemy in check until the arrival of troops from the interior of a province.

lingua *n., pl.* **linguae** [L. tongue, language.] 1. Language. Speech. *The lingua which these students acquired at school still serves them as the medium through which they express themselves when together* (Thomas Cooke in *West Africa* 1985). 2. Tongue. An organ, such as hypopharynx, which structurally and functionally resembles a tongue.

lingua franca *n., pl.* **linguae francae** or **lingua francas** [It. **lingua** language (2); **franca** Frankish (1): Frankish language.] 1. A common language comprising Italian, Spanish, Greek, French, and Arabic which is spoken in Mediterranean ports. 2. A language used for communication over an extensive area by various peoples. a) *Today . . . English is the closest thing to a lingua franca around the globe (Newsweek Int.* Nov. 15, 1982:42). b) *. . . blind nationalism, foolish pride . . . and economic short-sightedness will prevent sub-Saharan Africa from adopting an indigenous lingua franca* (Anyetei Ako-nai in *West Africa* 1986). Cf. **koine.**

liquet *n., pl.* **liquets** [L. it is clear, apparent, evident.] The matter is clear. Used to indicate certainty about the facts or truth of a matter. Cf. **non liquet.**

lis alibi pendens *n.* [L. **lis** suit (1); **alibi** elsewhere (3); **pendens** hanging, pending (2): a suit pending elsewhere.] *Law.* A suit pending elsewhere. Where proceedings in a case between a plaintiff and a defendant are pending in a court, the plaintiff can be prevented from taking the case to another court. Cf. **lis pendens.**

lis mota *n.* [L. **lis** suit, controversy (1); **mota** moved (2): suit moved.] *Law.* Commencement of a suit or controversy. Used with reference to statements or declarations made in connection with a point which subsequently features in legal proceedings. For instance, if a pedigree is made by a member of a family, it is admissible as evidence, if it was made before contemplation of litigation; but if made after, it would be inadmissible.

lis pendens *n.* [L. **lis** suit (2); **pendens** hanging, pending (1): hanging suit.] *Law.* A pending lawsuit. When there is a pending lawsuit, the court trying the case acquires control over the subject matter until judgment is finally delivered. Also, a written notice of the pending suit is recorded in the registry, and it shows the parties, the court handling the case, and the disputed property. The effect of the notice is to warn those who have an interest in the disputed property that they will be bound by whatever judicial decision is taken. See **lite pendente** and **pendente lite** etc. Cf. **lis alibi pendens.**

lite pendente or **pendente lite** *adv.* [L. **lite** with suit (1); **pendente** (with) hanging, pending (2): with the suit hanging.] Pending the suit/litigation. While the litigation or the case is pending. While litigation continues. During litigation. a) *The judge ruled that, lite pendente, the defendant should not leave the country and ordered him to surrender his passport.* b) *Counsel asked for an injunction to restrain the defendant from disposing of the property, pendente lite, and it was granted.* See **lis pendens.**

literatim *var.* of **litteratim** (q.v.).

litotes *n., pl.* **litotes** [Gk. **litotēs** plainness, simplicity, assertion by means of understatement.] *Rhetoric.* A figure of speech in which an assertion is understated by expressing the opposite of the assertion in the negative; e.g., "'How are you?' John asked. 'Not bad,' answered Moses." See **meiosis.** Cf. **hyperbole.**

Litt. B. *abbr.* for **Litterarum Baccalaureus** (q.v.).

litterae or **literae** *pl. n.* [L. letters, literature, documents, records.] Written or literary works. Books. *Instead of personal travel and investigation we find now a pilgrimage over other men's books. This is a literature which is wholly based on litterae* (Lesky 1966:330).

litterae humaniores *pl. n.* [L. **litterae** letters, literature, documents, records (2); **humaniores** more human, humane, refined (1): more humane letters.] The humanities, especially study of Greek and Roman classics. Cf. **humanitas.**

litterae patentes *pl. n.* [L. **litterae** letters, literature, documents, records (2); **patentes** open, evident (1): open/evident letters.] Letters patent.

litterae recognitionis *pl. n.* [L. **litterae** letters, literature, documents, records (1); **recognitionis** of examination, recognition (2): letters of examination.] *Maritime Law.* Bill of lading.

litterae scriptae manent. *abbr.* **L.S.M.** or **l.s.m.** [L. **litterae** letters, literature, documents, records (2); **scriptae** written (1); **manent** remain (3): Written

documents remain.] Written words endure/last. What is written down is a safe record of the past.

littera legis *n.* [L. **littera** letter of the alphabet (1); **legis** of law (2): the letter of the alphabet of the law.] The letter of the law.

Litterarum Baccalaureus *abbr.* **Litt.B.** *n.* [L. **litterarum** of letters, literature, documents, records (2); **baccalaureus** bachelor (1): Bachelor of Letters.] Bachelor of Literature. An undergraduate degree in literature.

Litterarum Magister *abbr.* **Litt.M.** *n.* [L. **litterarum** of letters, literature, documents, records (2); **magister** master (1): Master of Letters.] Master of Literature. A predoctoral graduate degree in literature.

littérateur or **litterateur** *n., pl.* **littérateurs** or **litterateurs** [Fr. a person of letters.] A writer by profession. A literary person. One engaged in literary pursuits.

litterati or **literati** *pl. n.* [L. the lettered, learned, liberally educated.] The educated class. People of letters/learning. The **intelligentsia** (q.v.). Learned people. *The litterati of the country tend to assume that they have not only a monopoly of knowledge but also answers to all the problems of the nation.*

litteratim or **literatim** *adv./adj.* [L. letter for letter.] Literal. Literally. See **au pied de la lettre.**

Litt.M. *abbr.* for **Litterarum Magister** (q.v.).

L.L. or **l.l.** *abbr.* for **loco laudato** (q.v.).

LL.B. *abbr.* for **Legum Baccalaureus** (q.v.).

LL.D. *abbr.* for **Legum Doctor** (q.v.).

LL.M. *abbr.* for **Legum Magister** (q.v.).

ln *abbr.* for **lien** (q.v.).

L'obligation sans cause, ou sur une fausse cause, ou sur cause illicite, ne peut avoir aucun effet. [Fr. l' the (1); **obligation** obligation (2); **sans** without (3); **cause** cause, consideration (4); **ou** or (5); **sur** on, upon (6); **une** a, one (7); **fausse** false, inaccurate (8); **cause** cause, consideration (9); **ou** or (10); **sur** on, upon (11); **cause** cause, consideration (13); **illicite** unlawful, illicit (12); **ne** not (15); **peut** can, is able (14); **avoir** to have (16); **aucun** any (17); **effet** effect (18): The obligation without cause, or based on a false cause, or on an unlawful cause, cannot have any effect.] *Law.* An obligation without consideration, or based upon a false consideration, or based upon an unlawful consideration, cannot have any effect. See **ex turpi causa** etc.

L'Obstacle imprévu *n.* [Fr. l' the (1); **obstacle** obstacle (3); **imprévu** unforeseen, unexpected (2): the unexpected obstacle.] *The Unexpected Obstacle*, a play by Philippe Néricault dit Destouches (1680–1754).

locatio *n., pl.* **locatios** [L. letting out.] *Roman, Scots, and Civil Law.* Letting or leasing.

loco citato *abbr.* **L.C.**, **l.c.** or **loc. cit.** *adv.* [L. **loco** in place (1); **citato** (in) cited, quoted, mentioned (2): in the place cited.] In the passage cited or quoted.

Used in bibliographical references to passages previously cited. See **loco primo citato** and **loco supra citato.**

loco laudato *abbr.* **L.L.** or **l.l.** or **loc. laud.** *adv.* [L. **loco** in place (1); **laudato** (in) praised (2): in the place praised.] In the place cited or quoted with approval.

loco primo citato *abbr.* **loc. primo cit.** *adv.* [L. **loco** in place (1); **primo** first, at first (2); **citato** (in) cited, quoted (3): in the place first cited.] In the passage first quoted or cited. See **loco citato** and **loco supra citato.**

loco supra citato *abbr.* **L.S.C.** or **l.s.c.** *adv.* [L. **loco** in place (1); **supra** above (3); **citato** (in) cited, quoted (2): in the place cited above.] In the passage quoted or cited above. See **loco citato** and **loco primo citato.**

locum tenens *abbr.* **locum, L.T.** or **l.t.** *n., pl.* **locum tenentes** [L. **locum** place (2); **tenens** holding (1): holding a place.] One holding a place or position. A person who holds an office temporarily as a substitute or deputy, especially a clergyman or doctor. A substitute or deputy. *In the absence of the Chief Medical Officer, Dr. Hanson served as locum tenens.*

locus *n., pl.* **loci** or **loca** [L. place, spot, locality.] A place. A place associated with an event of legal significance, or where something happens.

locus celebrationis *n.* [L. **locus** place (1); **celebrationis** of celebration (2): place of celebration.] *Law.* The place of celebration, i.e., of marriage.

locus classicus *n., pl.* **loci classici** [L. **locus** passage, subject (2); **classicus** high-class, classic (1): a high-class passage or subject.] The best known or classic example. A standard passage which is usually used to explain a subject or word. *On the need for the prosecution to prove their case beyond reasonable doubt, the presiding judge referred to* Woolmington v. DPP *(1935) AC 462, a locus classicus.*

locus communis *n., pl.* **loci communes** [L. **locus** place (2); **communis** common (1): common place.] A commonplace. A passage usually quoted in a particular context.

locus contractus *n.* [L. **locus** place (1); **contractus** of drawing together, shrinking, contract, agreement (2): place of the contract.] *Law.* The place where a contract is made. *The locus contractus, needless to say, is the proper forum for the institution of a legal action for damages in case of a breach.* See **lex loci contractus.**

locus contractus regit actum. [L. **locus** place (1); **contractus** of drawing together, shrinking, contract, agreement (2); **regit** rules, governs (3); **actum** act (4): The place of contract rules the act.] *Law.* The law of the place where the contract was made governs it.

locus criminis *n.* [L. **locus** place (1); **criminis** of crime (2): place of the crime.] *Law.* The locality where the crime was perpetrated. *The magistrate moved the court to the locus criminis.*

locus delicti *n.* [L. **locus** place (1); **delicti** of offense (2): place of the offense.] *Law.* The locality where an offense was committed. See **lex loci delicti.**

locus in quo *n.* [L. **locus** place (1); **in** in, on (2); **quo** which (3): place in which.] *Law.* The place where an offense, especially an offense of trespass on another's land, is alleged to have been committed.

locus paenitentiae *n., pl.* **loci paenitentiae** [L. **locus** place (1); **paenitentiae** of repentance (2): place of repentance.] *Law.* An opportunity to withdraw from an incomplete contract before it is legally confirmed. An opportunity to have a change of heart or refrain from an intended crime.

locus regit actum. [L. **locus** place (1); **regit,** rules, governs (2); **actum** act (3): The place rules the act.] *Law.* The place governs the act. A rule in private international law that, if a matter is transacted in one country to be effective in another, it must primarily comply with the laws of the place where the matter is transacted.

locus rei sitae *n.* [L. **locus** place (1); **rei** of matter, thing, property, business, affair (2); **sitae** (of) situated (3): place of a thing situated.] *Law.* The place where a thing is situated. *Ordinarily, proceedings in rem are held at the locus rei sitae.* See **lex loci rei sitae.**

locus sigilli *abbr.* **L.S.** or **l.s.** *n., pl.* **loci sigilli** [L. **locus** place (1); **sigilli** of seal (2): place of the seal.] The place for the seal. *Documents bearing the locus sigilli are deemed to be authenticated.* Cf. **locus signi.**

locus signi *abbr.* **L.S.** or **l.s.** *n.* [L. **locus** place (1); **signi** of seal, signet (2): place of the seal.] The place for the seal. Cf. **locus sigilli.**

locus standi *n., pl.* **loci standi** [L. **locus** place (1); **standi** of standing (2): place of standing.] *Law.* 1. An acknowledged or recognized position. 2. Legal capacity to prosecute or defend an action. Standing. A right to be heard. A right to appear before a court or anybody to answer a particular question. *The landlord's son, who instituted an action against the tenant for ejection, was advised to obtain power of attorney from his father since he had no locus standi.*

Logos *n.* [Gk. word, speech, account.] 1. *Christianity.* The word of God, especially in the second person of the Trinity, as described in John 1:1. 2. The rational, organizing spirit of the world.

longa patientia trahitur ad consensum. [L. **longa** long (1); **patientia** patience, forbearance (2); **trahitur** is dragged (3); **ad** to, at, for, according to (4); **consensum** consent (5): Long patience is dragged to consent.] *Law.* Long forbearance is tantamount to consent. Cf. **qui non improbat, approbat.**

longa possessio jus parit. [L. **longa** long (1); **possessio** possession (2); **jus** right, law (4); **parit** gives birth to, produces, creates (3): Long possession gives birth to right.] *Law.* A long period of possession confers or produces a right to possession.

longa possessio parit jus possidendi; et tollit actionem vero domino. [L. **longa** long (1); **possessio**

possession (2); **parit** gives birth to, produces, creates (3); **jus** right, law (4); **possidendi** of possessing (5); **et** and (6); **tollit** takes away, removes (7); **actionem** action (8); **vero** from true, real, actual (9); **domino** owner (10): Long possession produces right of possessing and takes away action from the true owner.] *Law*. A long or continued possession confers right of possession and takes away right of legal action from the real owner.

longo intervallo *adv*. [L. **longo** by long (1); **intervallo** (by) interval (2): by a long interval.] By a long interval of time.

longum tempus et longus usus, qui excedit memoriam hominum, sufficit pro jure. [L. **longum** long (1); **tempus** time (2); **et** and (3); **longus** long (4); **usus** use (5); **qui** who, which (6); **excedit** exceeds (7); **memoriam** memory (8); **hominum** of humans, people, (9); **sufficit** suffices (10); **pro** for, as (11); **jure** right, law (12): Long time and long use which exceed the memory of people suffices as a right.] *Law*. Length of time and use which extend beyond human memory are sufficient for the purposes of a right.

loquitur *v*. [L. He says.] He speaks.

Los Angeles *pl. n*. [Sp. **los** the (1); **angeles** angels (2): the angels.] City of Our Lady of the Angels. A city in southern California founded by the Spanish in 1781.

lotus or **lotos** *n., pl*. **lotuses** [Gk. **lōtos**.] *Greek Mythology*. A fruit eaten by the Lotophagi or Lotus-eaters which makes a person forget one's home and friends and instead desire to live, in dreamy satisfaction or forgetfulness, in the Lotus-land for ever. —**lotus-eater** An indolent person who indulges in daydreaming. One who lives the life of lazy leisurely enjoyment. *After ten continuous years of strenuous and highly rewarding work, Sam has gone to a holiday resort, where he intends to live the life of a lotus-eater for three months.*

L.S. or **l.s.** *abbr*. for 1. **locus sigilli** (q.v.). 2. **locus signi** (q.v.).

L.S.C. or **l.s.c.** *abbr*. for **loco supra citato** (q.v.).

L.S.M. or **l.s.m.** *abbr*. for **litterae scriptae manent** (q.v.).

L.T. or **l.t.** *abbr*. for **locum tenens** (q.v.).

lubricum linguae non facile trahendum est in poenam. [L. **lubricum** a slipping (1); **linguae** of tongue (2); **non** not (4); **facile** easily, readily (5); **trahendum** to be dragged (6); **est** is (3); **in** into, to, against, for (7); **poenam** punishment, penalty (8): A slipping of the tongue is not easily to be dragged into punishment.] *Law*. A slip of the tongue should not easily be subjected to punishment.

lucri causa *adj./adv*. [L. **lucri** of gain, profit (2); **causa** for the sake of (1): for the sake of gain.] For the purpose of gain. For the purpose of making money.

Law. Used to describe the intent with which larceny is committed.

lucrum cessans *n*. [L. **lucrum** profit, gain (2); **cessans** ceasing (1): ceasing profit.] *Law*. Damages/interest awarded for loss of profit which may be reasonably expected. *. . . the loss may be in the nature of a damnum emergens, not merely a lucrum cessans* (Hanbury 1962:522). See **damnum infectum**. Cf. **damnum emergens**.

lucrum interceptum *n*. [L. **lucrum** profit, gain (2); **interceptum** intercepted (1): intercepted profit.] **Lucrum cessans** (q.v.).

luctuosa hereditas or **luctuosa haereditas** See **hereditas luctuosa**.

lucus a non lucendo *n*. [L. **lucus** clearing, grove (1); **a** from (2); **non** not (3); **lucendo** being light, clear (4): a clearing from not being clear.] *Logic*. An absurd derivation. An illogical explanation. Something whose qualities are at variance with what is suggested by its name. a) *The lecturer spoke at length on political developments, drawing parallels between Nigeria and Ghana, but it was abundantly clear that his conclusion was a lucus a non lucendo.* b) *But though legally immune, he may be liable in equity for equitable waste. This phrase is of the lucus a non lucendo type; it means not waste which is equitable, but, on the contrary, waste which is so inequitable that equity will restrain it, as being a clear abuse of any licence to commit waste* (Hanbury 1962:49). See **non sequitur**.

lues *n., pl*. **lues** [L. plague, pestilence, infection.] *Medicine*. Syphilis.

luftmensch *n., pl*. **luftmenschen** [Yid. from Ger. **Luft** air (1) and **Mensch** person (2): an air person, a dreamer, an airhead.] A person with no definite occupation who indulges in speculation and daydreaming. *But to many of the young in the '60s, the laidback luftmenschen of the counterculture, manners were as superfluous as flatware at McDonald's . . . (Time Int.* 1978).

Luftwaffe *n*. [Ger. **Luft** air (1); **Waffe** weapon (2): air weapon, air force.] The German air force from 1935 to 1945.

lumen naturale *n*. [L. **lumen** light (2); **naturale** natural (1): natural light.] Natural light. Innate understanding. *The child seemed to grasp the concept by lumen naturale.*

lumen siccum *n*. [L. **lumen** light (2); **siccum** dry (1): dry light.] Dry light. Dry understanding. Unadorned wisdom. Rational knowledge of objectivity as described by Francis Bacon (1561–1626).

lumpen *adj*. [Ger. **Lumpen** rags, tatters.] Of, belonging to, relating to, being a member of the indigent, uneducated, inferior subclass of the populace. *In those early books, he spoke with the voice of the outsider, the lumpen-man of the cities, the bum who wasn't* *part of the system of society* (*Newsweek Int.* June 23, 1980:31).

Lumpenproletariat *n.* Karl Marx (1818–1883). [Ger. **Lumpen** rags, tatters (1); Fr. **prolétariat** poor working class (2): the ragged, poor, working class.] The indigent populace. The poor, uneducated masses.

lupanar *n., pl.* **lupanars** [L. house of a she-wolf or prostitute, brothel.] A house of ill repute. A brothel. Cf. **bordello**.

lupus in fabula *n.* [L. **lupus** wolf (1); **in** in, on (2); **fabula** story (3): wolf in the story.] 1. The fabled wolf, especially in the traditional animal fables of Aesop and Phaedrus. 2. The villain in the story. 3. A person who appears just at the time when something is being said about him/her.

lustrum *n., pl.* **lustra** or **lustrums** [L. a purification ceremony, a five-year period.] 1. *Ancient Rome.* The purification of all Romans which was held after the census, i.e., after every five years. 2. *Ancient Rome.* The **census** (q.v.). 3. A period of five years. A **quinquennium** (q.v.). *The regime had a lustrum of good and purposeful administration before plunging into a reign of terror and atrocities.*

lusus naturae *n.* [L. **lusus** game, sport (1); **naturae** of nature (2): a sport of nature.] A game of nature. An unusual product of nature.

lux mundi *n.* [L. **lux** light (1); **mundi** of the world (2): light of the world.] 1. The light of the World. Jesus' description of himself at John 8:12. 2. *Art.* A representation of Jesus holding a light and in search of human souls.

luxe *n., pl.* **luxes** [Fr. luxury.] Elegance. See **de luxe**.

lycée *n., pl.* **lycées** [Fr. from Gk. **Lukeion** a school established by Aristotle in Athens.] A secondary or high school, particularly one established by the state. A **lyceum**. Cf. **baccalauréat**.

Lyceum *n., pl.* **Lyceums** [L. from Gk. **Lukeion** an epithet of the God Apollo.] 1. *Ancient Athens.* A grove sacred to the god Apollo Lykeios where Aristotle held his discourses or taught his pupils. 2. A lecture hall. A place where lectures or public discussions are held. 3. An institution or association which promotes education by organizing public lectures, entertainment, concerts, etc. 4. A **lycée** (q.v.). A secondary school, especially one in continental Europe.

M

M. *abbr.* for **Monsieur** (q.v.).

M.A. *abbr.* for **Magister Artium** (q.v.).

macabre *adj.* [Fr. grim, gruesome, deathly, ghastly.] 1. Dealing with, or treating, death. 2. Designed to produce a horrible effect. Emphasizing the gruesome. In this sense, it may be used as a noun. *Her novels usually dwell on macabre scenes or the macabre.* 3. Ghastly. Distressing. Horrible. Unpleasant. Dreadful. *The sights were macabre to me. Mutilated bodies, mortally injured passengers, . . . (The Guardian* 1986).

machismo *n.* [Sp. masculinity.] Exaggerated masculinity, virility or manly pride. Compulsive desire to show one's virility. Toughness. *Perhaps because of the notorious Argentine machismo, the junta has misjudged Thatcher (Newsweek Int.* April 26, 1982:4).

macho *adj.* [Sp. masculine.] Virile. Extraordinarily masculine, forceful, or energetic. Tough. *He should have known that no American president, particularly a president as macho as Kennedy, could tolerate that (Newsweek Int* Nov. 28, 1983:42).

Machtpolitik *n.* [Ger. **Macht** power, might (1); **Politik** politics (2): power politics.] A political doctrine which emphasizes the use of power, especially physical power, for achieving the objectives of a nation.

Machtübernahme *n.* [Ger. **Macht** power, might (3); **über** over (2); **nehmen** take (1): taking-over power.] Taking over, seizure, coming into, or assumption of power, particularly political power, through violent means. Cf. **coup d'état** and **putsch.**

Madame *abbr.* **Mme** or **Mdme** *n., pl.* **Mesdames** or **Madames** *abbr.* **Mds** or **Mmes** [Fr. **ma** my (1) and **dame** lady (2): my lady, a married or mature woman.] 1. Mistress, Mrs. or Madam. Prefixed to the name of a married French woman as a title of courtesy. 2. Proprietress of a house of prostitution. Cf. **Frau; Fräulein; Mademoiselle; Senhora; Senhorita; Señora; Señorita; Signora;** and **Signorina.**

Mademoiselle *abbr.* **Mlle** *n., pl.* **Mesdemoiselles** or **Mademoiselles** [Fr. **ma** my (1) and **demoiselle** young lady (2): my young lady, a young unmarried woman.] 1. Miss. Prefixed to the name of an unmarried French woman or girl as a title of courtesy. 2. A French woman who is unmarried. 3. A French nurse or governess. Cf. **Frau; Fräulein; Madame; Senhora; Senhorita; Señora; Señorita; Signora;** and **Signorina.**

Madonna *n., pl.* **Madonnas** [It. from **ma** my (1) and **donna** lady (2): my lady.] *Christianity.* A picture or statue of the Virgin Mary, i.e., the mother of Jesus.

madrasah or **medresseh** *n.* [Ar. **madrasa** a place to study.] *Islam.* An advanced school for Islamic studies.

madrigal *n., pl.* **madrigals** [It. simple, original, an unaccompanied song.] *Music.* A musical composition for two or three voices with no instrumental accompaniment.

Maecenas *n., pl.* **Maecenases** [L. Gaius Maecenas (c.70–8 B.C.).] 1. A friend and counselor of the Roman emperor, Augustus. He was a generous patron of literature who sponsored Horace and Vergil. 2. A generous patron or benefactor, particularly a generous patron of art and literature.

maelstrom *n., pl.* **maelstroms** [Obs. Dutch for **maalstroom: malen** whirling (1) and **stroom** stream (2): whirling stream.] 1. A great whirlpool or eddy. Water which moves with great rapidity in a circular direction, producing in the center a cavity into which floating objects in the vicinity are sucked. 2. Something which, like a whirlpool, draws people and things irresistibly and destroys them. A force which is violent and destructive. *He is essentially an innocent boy from the countryside who was attracted to, and destroyed by, the maelstrom of urban life.* Cf. **vortex.**

maestoso *adv./adj.* [It. majestic, majestically.] *Music.* In a majestic manner.

maestro *n., pl.* **maestri** or **maestros** [It. master, great artist.] A person who is accomplished in, or a teacher of, a field such as music or art. An eminent musician, composer, artist, etc. . . . *Jones boasted that he himself was "the maestro of revolutionary sex," able* to copulate "fifteen times a day." (Newsweek Int. June 1, 1981:52). See **Il Maestro**.

maestro di cappella n. [It. **maestro** master (1); **di** of (2); **cappella** chapel (3): master of chapel.] Choirmaster of a church. The director or leader of a church choir. Cf. **Kappellmeister**.

mafia or **maffia** n., pl. **mafias** or **maffias** [It. boldness, a Sicilian criminal society which operates secretly.] 1. A secret organization which engages in political terrorism. *The recent terrorist activities have been attributed to the operations of a mafia from a neighboring country.* 2. A secret criminal international organization which controls such illicit commercial activities as gambling, prostitution, peddling of hard drugs, etc. *The mafia is in such firm control of the city that nobody can engage in certain commercial activities without prior negotiation with it.* Cf. **dacoit**, **petit truand**, and **yakuza**.

mafioso n., pl **mafiosi** or **mafiosos** [It. one connected with the mafia.] A member of the **mafia**. *The man who was assassinated under mysterious circumstances yesterday seems to have been a mafioso.*

Magen David or **Mogen David** n. [Heb. **māgēn** shield (1); **dāwid** of David (2): shield of David.] The six-pointed star of Judaism.

Magister Artium abbr. **M.A.** n. [L. **magister** master (1); **artium** of arts (2): Master of Arts.] A predoctoral graduate degree in the liberal arts. See **Artium Magister**.

Magister Chirurgiae abbr. **M.C.** or **M.Ch.** or **M.Chir.** n. [L. **magister** master (1); **chirurgiae** of surgery (2): Master of Surgery.] A predoctoral graduate degree in surgery. Cf. **Chirurgiae Magister**.

Magister Chirurgiae Dentalis abbr. **M.Ch.D.** n. [L. **magister** master (1); **chirurgiae** (of) surgery (3); **dentalis** of dental (2): Master of Dental Surgery.] A predoctoral graduate degree in dental surgery.

Magister Chirurgiae Orthopaedicae abbr. **M.Ch.Orth.** n. [L. **magister** master (1); **chirurgiae** (of) surgery (3); **orthopaedicae** of orthopaedic (2): Master of Orthopaedic Surgery.] A predoctoral graduate degree in orthopedic or corrective surgery.

magister dixit n. [L. **magister** master, teacher (1); **dixit** said, spoke (2): The master said.] An assertion by an authority, often the founder of a school of thought, though not necessarily proved. **Ipse dixit** (q.v.). . . . *both Marx and Engels mistrusted the use of the word "Marxism" because they sensed in it the odour of dogma and of magister dixit* ('Niyi Alabi in *West Africa* 1983).

magistra vitae n. [L. **magistra** mistress, instructress (1); **vitae** of life (2): mistress of life.] Guide to life. Giver of instructions on life. Something which serves a didactic purpose. *Polybius took history literally as the magistra vitae, trusting that its mastery would lead to an understanding of political situations . . .* (Lesky 1966:776). See **historia vitae magistra**.

magna charta or **magna carta** n., pl. **magna chartas** or **magna cartas** [L. **magna** great (1); **charta** writing, paper, charter (2): great charter.] 1. The charter of rights given by England's King John at Runnymede on June 15, 1215. 2. A statement of principles embodied in a document, usually guaranteeing rights and establishing procedures. *Initially, many Nigerians regarded the constitution of the Second Republic as the nation's magna carta, but their expectations were soon disappointed.*

magna componere parvis adv. [L. **magna** great (things) (2); **componere** to compare (1); **parvis** with little, small (things) (3): to compare great with small.] To compare great with little things. Cf. **si parva licet** etc.

magna cum laude adv./adj. [L. **magna** great (2); **cum** with (1); **laude** praise (3): with great praise.] With great distinction. Used to indicate a high degree of academic performance. *John Mensah graduated from college magna cum laude.* See **cum laude**; **maxima cum laude**; and **summa cum laude**.

Magna Mater n. [L. **magna** great, large (1); **mater** mother (2): great mother.] The Great Mother. The mother goddess. Applied to a number of female fertility deities, especially the Egyptian Isis and the Phrygian Cybele.

magnas inter opes inops adj. Horace (65–8 B.C.). *Odes* III,16,28. [L. **magnas** great (3); **inter** in the midst of, among, surrounded by (2); **opes** wealth, riches (4); **inops** destitute, indigent (1): destitute in the midst of great wealth.] Destitute in the midst of affluence.

Magnificat n., pl. **Magnificats** [L. He/she/it magnifies, extols, or esteems highly.] 1. *Christianity.* The first word of the prayer said by Mary the mother of Jesus at the Annunciation. 2. The hymn or canticle of the Virgin Mary, based on this prayer. See **magnificat anima mea Dominum**. —**magnificat** n., pl. **magnificats** A song of praise.

magnificat anima mea Dominum [L. **magnificat** he/she/it magnifies, extols, or esteems highly (3); **anima** soul, mind (2); **mea** my (1); **Dominum** Lord (4): My soul magnifies the Lord.] My soul glorifies the Lord. The first words of the canticle of Mary at Luke 1:46–55, when she learns from the angel Gabriel that she is to be the mother of Jesus. Cf. **Magnificat**.

magnifico n., pl. **magnificos** or **magnificoes** [It. gorgeous, magnificent.] 1. An eminent person. A person holding a high office. A person of distinguished or attractive appearance. *The ceremony was a grand affair and it attracted all the magnificoes of the town.* 2. Something exceptionally good or outstanding. Something which is superlative or supreme. *Mrs. Toss went Christmas shopping, looking for a gift, a magnifico, for her husband.*

magnifique adj. [Fr. magnificent, great.] Wonderful. Great. Used especially as an exclamation in English. *That was magnifique!*

magno intervallo *adv.* [L. **magno** by big, great (1); **intervallo** (by) interval, distance (2): by a big interval.] By a big interval of time or distance.

magnum bonum *n.* [L. **magnum** great, large (1); **bonum** good (thing) (2): great good (thing).] A great good.

magnum opus *n.* [L. **magnum** great (1); **opus** work (2): great work.] An important literary or artistic work. An artist's or author's greatest work. *Chinua Achebe's* Things Fall Apart *is easily his magnum opus.*

Magus *n., pl.* **Magi** [L. from Gk. **magos** from Old Pers. **magus.**] 1. A priest of Zoroastrianism. One of a class of Median and Persian priests who were also astrologers. 2. One of the wise men who, according to Matthew (2:1–12), came from the East to pay homage to the newborn Jesus. 3. An astrologer, magician, sorcerer, or wise man.

maharajah or **maharaja** *n., pl.* **maharajahs** or **maharajas** [Hindi **mahārājā: mahā** great (1); **rājā** king (2): great king.] An Indian ruler ranked above a **rajah** (q.v.).

maharani or **maharanee** *n., pl.* **maharanis** or **maharanees** [Hindi **mahārājnī: mahā** great (1); **rājnī** queen (2): great queen.] The wife of a **maharajah** (q.v.).

maharishi *n., pl.* **maharishis** [Hindi **mahārshih: mahā** great (1); **rshih** seer, saint (2): great seer.] An Indian teacher of mysticism and spiritualism.

mahatma *n., pl.* **mahatmas** [Hindi **mahātmā: mahā** great (1); **ātmā** soul, spirit, life (2): great life.] *India and Tibet.* An individual honored for wisdom and humanitarianism. —**Mahatma** *Hinduism.* An honorific title applied to someone of deep spirituality and magnanimity. *Mahatma Gandhi.*

Mahdi *n., pl.* **Mahdis** [Ar. **mahdī** one led rightly.] *Islam.* The **messiah** (q.v.) or savior who will come at the end of the world and establish a new order based upon justice and peace.

mahjong or **mahjongg** *n.* [Chin. **má** spotted (1); **jiàng** game piece (2): spotted game piece.] A Chinese game which uses rectangular game pieces or tiles of varied design.

mahzor or **machzor** *n., pl.* **machzorim** or **mahzors** [Heb. cycle.] *Judaism.* The book of prayers used for the Holy days.

mais non [Fr. **mais** but (1); **non** not (2): but not.] Not at all! No, indeed! Indeed, not! No, of course! Certainly not! Oh no! *It may look as if Brigitte Bardot . . . is rehearsing for a fido farce, mais non* (*Newsweek Int.* Nov. 8, 1982:33).

Maison du Parti *n.* [Fr. **maison** premises, home (1); **du** of the (2); **parti** party (3): premises of the party.] Office or headquarters of the Party. *Addressing the National Council of the party at the Maison du Parti in Lome last November, President Eyadema denounced . . .* (*New African* 1979).

maitre *n., pl.* **maitres** [Fr. **maître** master.] Principal. Instructor. Tutor. Teacher. Director. One who is an expert in, or master of, an artistic or scholarly field. *. . . a quiet effort by some 180 dissidents among the school's 600 members to break the maitre's autocratic rule and conduct their own research* (*Newsweek Int.* June 16, 1980:63).

maitre d' *abbr.* for **maître d'hôtel** (q.v.).

maître de ballet or *fem.* **maîtresse de ballet** *n., pl.* **maîtres de ballet** or *fem.* **maîtresses de ballet** [Fr. **maître** master (1); **de** of (2); **ballet** ballet (3): master of ballet.] *Ballet.* Ballet master. A person who organizes and trains a company of dancers.

maître d'hôtel or **maitre d'hôtel** *abbr.* **maître d'** *n., pl.* **maîtres d'hôtel** or **maitres d'hôtel** *abbr.* **maître d's** or **maitre d's** [Fr. **maître** master (1); **d'** of (2); **hôtel** mansion, hotel (3): master of hotel/mansion.] Head cook, chief steward, or head waiter, i.e., of a mansion, restaurant, or hotel. Butler. Manager of a hotel. Cf. **majordomo.**

majestas *n.* [L. dignity, greatness, grandeur, sovereignty.] *Roman Law.* Sovereignty. Majesty.

major *n., pl.* **majors** [L. greater, bigger, larger.] 1. A person who has reached full age and can, therefore, not only manage his/her own affairs but also enjoy civic rights. *Tom told his parents that he is now a major and intends to marry Nancy, whether they give their consent or not.* 2. A subject in which a student specializes. *His major is English, while History is his minor.* 3. Bigger league. *His team plays in the majors.* 4. A military officer who ranks below a lieutenant colonel but above a captain. —*adj.* 1. Superior. Greater in dignity, importance, rank, number, extent, or quantity. Serious. a) *A driver who is on a major road enjoys right of way, but that does not mean that he should not be careful at intersections.* b) *a major sickness.* 2. Having reached full legal age. *Major children may enter liquor stores to buy drinks, though parents do not encourage that practice.*

major annus *n.* [L. **major** greater (1); **annus** year (2): greater year.] Leap year. Bissextile year. A year of 366 days (e.g., 1988).

majordomo *n., pl.* **majordomos** [Obs. It. **maggiordomo** from L. **major** chief (1) and **dom(us)** house (2): chief of the house.] A man entrusted with the care of a great household, such as a royal or princely household. Head/chief steward.

major numerus in se continet minorem. [L. **major** greater (1); **numerus** number (2); **in** in, on (4); **se** itself (5); **continet** contains, comprises (3); **minorem** smaller, less (6): A greater number contains in itself a smaller number.] A larger number includes in itself a smaller number. See **majus continet minus.**

majus continet minus. [L. **majus** greater (1); **continet** contains, comprises (2); **minus** less (3): The greater contains the less.] The larger includes the smaller.

See **cui licet** etc.; **in eo, quod** etc.; **in majore summa** etc.; **in praesentia majoris cessat** etc.; **in praesentia majoris potestatis** etc.; **in toto et** etc.; **major numerus** etc.; **omne majus continet** etc.; **omne majus minus** etc.; **quando licet** etc.; **quando plus fit** etc.; and **ubi major** etc.

majus est delictum seipsum occidere quam alium. [L. **majus** greater, bigger (2); **est** it is (1); **delictum** crime, offense (3); **seipsum** oneself (5); **occidere** to kill (4); **quam** than (6); **alium** another (7): It is a greater crime to kill oneself than another.] *Law.* Suicide is a more serious crime than homicide.

makimono *n., pl.* **makimonos** [Japan. from **maki** rolled (1); **mono** object (2): rolled object.] A horizontal form of Japanese scroll painting. Cf. **kakemono.**

malade imaginaire *n., pl.* **malades imaginaires** [Fr. **malade** invalid, sick person (2); **imaginaire** imaginary (1): an imaginary invalid.] *Medicine.* A hypochondriac. A person who fantasizes that he/she is sick. Cf. **hypochondria.** and **Le Malade imaginaire.**

maladroit *adj.* [Fr. from **mal** bad, badly (1); **adroit** skilled (2): badly skilled.] Clumsy. Poorly coordinated. Cf. **adroit.**

mala fide *adv./adj.* [L. **mala** in bad (1); **fide** (in) faith (2): in bad faith.] *adv.* In/with bad faith. Fraudulently. Deceptively and maliciously. *It is quite clear that the firing of the clerk was done mala fide, since he owed his fate solely to the animosity of his immediate boss.* —*adj.* 1. Fraudulent. Acting, operating, etc. with the intention of cheating or deceiving. *The mala fide agent defrauded many businessmen before he was arrested.* 2. Occupying, holding, etc. by a title which is not sanctioned by law. a) *a mala fide owner*; b) *a mala fide occupant.* 3. Lacking sincerity. Specious. Insincere or dishonest. *A mala fide suggestion.* See **dolus malus.**

mala fides *n.* [L. **mala** bad (1); **fides** faith (2): bad faith.] Intention to defraud or deceive. a) *The prosecutor kept harping upon the mala fides of the accused, though he adduced no evidence to prove it.* b) *Gross negligence may be evidence of mala fides but it is not the same thing* (Megrah and Ryder 1972:200). See **dolus malus.**

mala grammatica non vitiat chartam. sed in expositione instrumentorum mala grammatica quoad fieri possit evitanda est. [L. **mala** bad (1); **grammatica** grammar (2); **non** not (3); **vitiat** vitiates (4); **chartam** paper, document (5); **sed** but (6); **in** in, on (7); **expositione** exposition (8); **instrumentorum** of instruments (9); **mala** bad (10); **grammatica** grammar (11); **quoad** as far as (14); **fieri** to be done (16); **possit** it can, is able (15); **evitanda** to be avoided (13); **est** is (12): Bad grammar does not vitiate a document. But in the exposition of instruments, bad grammar is to be avoided as far as it can be done.] *Law.* Incorrect grammar does

not invalidate a document. But in the composition of legal documents, incorrect grammar should be avoided as far as possible. See **falsa demonstratio** etc.

malaise *n., pl.* **malaises** [Fr. **mal** bad (1); **aise** ease, comfort (2): bad comfort, discomfort, indisposition, uneasiness, faintness.] 1. An uncertain feeling of general debility which often marks the beginning of a sickness. 2. An uncertain feeling of moral, mental, spiritual, etc. uneasiness. a) *economic malaise*; b) *psychological malaise*; c) *spiritual malaise*; d) *Trade experts also point out that foreign competition is not the sole cause of this country's industrial malaise* (*Newsweek Int.* May 30, 1983:19).

mala praxis *n.* [Neo-L. and Gk. from L. **mala** bad (1); Gk. **praxis** practice (2): bad practice.] Malpractice. Used particularly for medical practitioners. *Relatives of the late Mr. Ekwem sued Dr. Effiong for mala praxis in connection with his demise.*

malapropos or **mal à propos** *adv.* [Fr. **mal** badly, at variance (1); **à** to, toward, in, by, with, until (2); **propos** purpose (3): badly to the purpose.] At variance with the purpose. Inappropriately. Unseasonably. Inopportunely. In an inappropriate manner. *The teacher realized that the student was not paying attention when the latter answered the question malapropos.* —*adj.* Inappropriate. Unreasonable. Inopportune. Out of place.

mal de mer *n., pl.* **mals de mer** [Fr. **mal** malady (1); **de** of (2); **mer** sea (3): malady of sea.] Seasickness.

mal du siècle *n.* [Fr. **mal** dislike, repugnance (1); **du** of the (2); **siècle** age, century (3): dislike of the century.] World weariness. Disgust with the present state of affairs in the world. Weariness of life. Cf. **taedium vitae** and **Weltschmerz.**

maleficia non debent remanere impunita; et impunitas continuum affectum tribuit delinquenti. [L. **maleficia** evil deeds, offenses, crimes (1); **non** not (3); **debent** ought, should (2); **remanere** to remain (4); **impunita** unpunished (5); **et** and (6); **impunitas** impunity (7); **continuum** continuous, unbroken (9); **affectum** disposition (10); **tribuit** gives (8); **delinquenti** to one doing wrong, offending (11): Evil deeds should not remain unpunished; and impunity gives continuous disposition to one doing wrong.] *Law.* Evil deeds should not go unpunished, for impunity provides continuous disposition to the criminal. See **impunitas semper** etc.

malgré *prep.* [Fr. despite, in spite of.] Notwithstanding. Despite. *He is a happy and successful man, malgré the persecutions and the campaign of character assassination mounted by detractors.*

malgré lui *adv.* [Fr. **malgré** despite, in spite of (1); **lui** him (self) (2): despite himself.] Despite himself. In spite of himself. Against his will. *Though Francis had moved out of the house, he had to pay the rent malgré lui, since he had not given notice that he was leaving.*

malgré moi *adv.* [Fr. **malgré** despite, in spite of (1); **moi** me (2): despite me.] Despite myself. In spite of myself. Against my will. *Friends came to my aid, malgré moi.*

malgré tout *adv.* [**malgré** despite, in spite of (1); **tout** everything (2): despite everything.] In spite of everything. For all that. Nevertheless. *Malgré tout, the politician remains popular throughout his constituency.*

malis animus *n.* [L. **malis** for evils, offenses, wrongs (2); **animus** mind, intention, inclination (1): a mind for evils.] Evil design or intention. *It is evident from his remarks and actions that Joe has malis animus towards Amos.*

malitia praecogitata *n.* [L. **malitia** malice (2); **praecogitata** premeditated (1): premeditated malice.] *Law.* Premeditated malice. Malice aforethought.

malo animo *adv.* [L. **malo** with bad, evil (1); **animo** (with) mind, intent (2): with bad intent.] *Law.* With an evil mind, intention, or purpose. *The judge had no difficulty in deducing from the testimony of the defendant that he had acted malo animo.*

malum *n., pl.* **mala** [L. a bad, evil thing.] *Law.* An evil. A wrong. An offense against law or right.

malum in se *n., pl.* **mala in se** [L. **malum** offense, wrong, evil (1); **in** in, on (2); **se** itself (3): wrong in itself.] *Law.* A wrong in itself. An offense such as murder which is evil, viewed either from its own nature or by natural law. *The old division of crimes into mala in se . . . and mala prohibita . . . epitomises a division of society's attitudes towards "technical breaches of the law" and those of offences touching deep-rooted moral attitudes* (Curzon 1979:40). Cf. **malum prohibitum.**

malum non praesumitur. [L. **malum** evil (1); **non** not (3); **praesumitur** is presumed (2): Evil is not presumed.] *Law.* Evil is not taken for granted.

malum prohibitum *n., pl.* **mala prohibita** [L. **malum** evil, wrong, offense (2); **prohibitum** prohibited, forbidden (1): a prohibited offense/wrong.] *Law.* A wrong prohibited. An offense prohibited by statute, though it may not be inherently wrong. *Smuggling is a malum prohibitum.* Cf. **malum in se.**

malus usus abolendus est. [L. **malus** bad (1); **usus** usage, custom, practice (2); **abolendus** to be abolished, annihilated (4); **est** is (3): A bad custom is to be abolished.] A bad custom must be done away with.

m. à. m. *abbr.* for **mot à mot** (q.v.).

mama-san *n., pl.* **mama-sans** [Japan. **mama** mother (2); **-san** honorable (1): honorable mother.] *Japan.* A title of honor and respect for a woman in a position of power and authority, especially the female owner of a bar or head of a geisha-house. Cf. **-san.**

mañana *n., pl.* **mañanas** [Sp. tomorrow.] Tomorrow. An unspecified time in the future. . . . *for many countries in Latin America mañana once again looks promising* (*Newsweek Int.* July 6, 1981:38). —*adv.*

In the future. At an unspecified time in the future. **Domani** (q.v.). *The carpenter keeps promising that he will complete the job mañana, but has yet to fulfill his promise.*

mancipatio *n.* [L. from **man(us)** hand (2); **capi(o)** to take, seize (1): taking the hand, purchase, sale.] *Roman Law.* A ceremony in which property is formally transferred from seller to buyer. See **mancipium** and **res mancipi.**

mancipi res See **res mancipi.**

mancipium *n., pl.* **mancipia** [L. from **man(us)** hand (2); **capi(o)** to take, seize (1): taking the hand, purchase, sale.] *Roman Law.* A formal purchase, especially the legal sale of a son by his father as part of the process of emancipation from paternal potestas.

mandala *n., pl.* **mandalas** [Skt. **mandalam** circle.] *Hinduism and Buddhism.* A geometric figure or design, usually circular, which represents the universe and enables a meditator to pass from one level of contemplation to another.

mandamus *abbr.* **mand.** *n., pl.* **mandamuses** [L. We command, enjoin, order.] *Law.* An extraordinary writ which, in the absence of any other legal remedy, is issued by a superior court, commanding an inferior court, tribunal, a corporation, or any person to perform a public duty which is imposed by law.

mandatarius terminos sibi positos transgredi non potest. [L. **mandatarius** mandatary (1); **terminos** bounds, limits (5); **sibi** for himself/herself (7); **positos** fixed, set down (6); **transgredi** to step over/across (4); **non** not (3); **potest** can, is able (2): A mandatary is not able to step over the bounds set for him/her.] *Law.* The recipient of a mandate cannot step over (or exceed) the limits set down for him/her in the mandate.

mandatum *n., pl.* **mandata** [L. command, order, injunction.] *Law.* 1. A mandate; i.e., a command or order issued by a court. 2. A contract of mandate; i.e., a contract whereby one gives a lawful business to another who agrees to perform it gratis.

mandatum nisi gratuitum nullum est. [L. **mandatum** mandate (1); **nisi** unless (2); **gratuitum** done without pay; gratuitous (3); **nullum** no (5); **est** is (4): A mandate, unless done without pay, is no mandate.] *Law.* A mandate is no mandate, if not gratuitous.

mandatum sine clausula *abbr.* **M.S.C.** or **m.s.c.** *n.* [L. **mandatum** mandate, authority (1); **sine** without (2); **clausula** end (3): a mandate without an end.] A mandate or authority with no restriction.

manent *v.* [L. They remain.] Remain or stay on stage. Used as a direction for dramatic performances to indicate that some specified characters are not leaving the stage. Cf. **manet.**

manes *pl. n.* [L. departed spirit, shade, ghost.] 1. *Ancient Rome.* The spirits of departed ancestors, believed to be either protecting their descendants or expecting them to avenge their deaths. 2. Gods of the Lower World. 3. Deified ancestral spirits.

manet v. [L. He/she remains.] Remains or stays on stage. Used as direction for dramatic performances to indicate that a particular character is not leaving the stage.

mania n., pl. manias [Gk. madness, enthusiasm, inspired frenzy.] 1. Psychology. Psychotic excitement characterized by excessive activity, disordered behavior, and elevated mood. 2. A passion, craze, uncontrollable desire, or excessive enthusiasm. a) Ironically, his mania for power is not matched by his ability. b) Henry has a mania for pretty girls, good food, and flashy cars. 3. The object of passion, craze, or uncontrollable desire. Soccer is such a national mania in that country that aliens who make indiscreet remarks whenever the national team loses a match are mercilessly molested. —suf. A passion, craze, uncontrollable desire, or excessive enthusiasm for something. a) discomania; b) squandermania (The habit, practice, propensity, etc. of spending money extravagantly.) But as long as there is one such politician free to enjoy his wealth from the era of "squandermania" Nigerians will never forget . . . that the Second Republic was synonymous with institutionalised pilfering of public funds (West Africa 1986).

manifesta probatione non indigent. [L. manifesta evident, clear, manifest (things) (1); probatione proof (4); non not (2); indigent need, require, demand (3): Manifest things do not need proof.] Clear things do not require proof. See lex non requirit etc.; perspicua vera etc.; quod constat clare etc.; and quod constat curiae etc.

manifesto n., pl. manifestos or manifestoes [It. a manifest, a declaration.] A formal or public statement or declaration of opinion, intention, principles, motives, views, or policy. a) The PMDB manifesto calls for a unilateral debt moratorium . . . (South, 1984). b) Since 1967, the President has moved far from the election-winning APC manifesto (New African 1983). c) The Communist Manifesto.

manna n. [Gk. from Aram. mannâ.] 1. The miraculous food God provided the Israelites in the desert during their flight from Egypt. 2. Nourishment of the soul by God. 3. An unexpected gift. The tax refund was manna from heaven.

mannequin n., pl. mannequins [Fr. dummy, figurine.] 1. A life-size dummy. A dress-maker's, tailor's, or artist's dummy used for displaying clothes, especially in shop-windows and shops. A dress stand. 2. A model. A woman who models or displays clothing.

mano a mano adj. [Sp. mano hand (1); a to (2); mano hand (3): hand to hand.] One to one. Perpetrated by one man against another. Done by one person to/for another. And, at least once a decade, the level of this mano a mano abuse slides far enough up the brutality scale that it simply can't be ignored any longer (Newsweek Int. Feb. 18, 1980:48).

manqué or fem. manquée adj. [Fr. unsuccessful, missed, miscarried, abortive, would-be.] Unsuccessful.

Having failed to achieve one's objective or desired status. Frustrated in one's aspirations. Used as a postpositive adjective. a) As shells fell on the bunker, the Führer, still an architect manqué, brooded over plans for rebuilding Linz (Newsweek Int. May 9, 1983:22). b) She is, it seems, a romantic manquée, who cannot recoup in sex what she has lost in love (Time Int. 1978).

mansuetae naturae adj. [L. mansuetae of tame (1); naturae (of) nature (2): of a tame nature.] Tamed and domesticated. . . . in the case of scienter liability for animals mansuetae naturae, the keeper was only liable if the animal caused some harm of the kind to be expected from its known vicious characteristics . . . (Rogers 1975:400). See domitae naturae animalia.

manu forti adv. [L. manu (with) hand, band (2); forti with strong (1): with strong hand.] Law. With such force as to constitute the crime of breach of the peace. He was arrested, prosecuted, and convicted for acting manu forti. Cf. vi et armis.

manu militari adv. [L. manu (with) hand, band (2); militari with military (1): with military band.] By force. With military force. The tax was levied manu militari, firearms were seized . . . (Suret-Canale 1971:445).

manus n., pl. manus [L. hand, band.] Roman Law. 1. Ownership of property. 2. The power and rights which a husband exercises over his lawfully wedded wife.

manus manum lavat. [L. manus hand, band (1); manum hand, band (3); lavat washes (2): Hand washes hand.] One hand washes the other. One good turn deserves another. "You scratch my back, I scratch yours." "Hand go, hand come." See quid pro quo.

manus mortua n. [L. manus hand (2); mortua dead (1): a dead hand.] Mortmain. Cf. en mort mayne and in mortua manu.

marabout n., pl. marabouts [Fr. from Ar. murābit.] A Muslim religious leader, hermit, monk, or ascetic. Cf. grand marabout.

marasmus n., pl. marasmuses [L. from Gk. marasmos withering, wasting, dying, or fading away.] Medicine. Continuous emaciation, especially in children, as a result of inadequacy or lack of protein, calories, and other nutrients after they have been weaned from breast feeding.

Marathon n. [Gk. Marathon.] A village on the northeastern coast of Attica where Athens, aided by only 1,000 Plataean soldiers, defeated numerically superior Persian troops in September 490 B.C. Before the battle, the Athenians despatched a very fast runner by name Philippides (or Pheidippides) to Sparta to request military aid. He is said to have covered the distance of about 134 miles in two days. By a late, unreliable tradition, after the battle, a soldier ran to Athens, a distance of about 22 miles 1,470 yards, to report the news of the victory. —*pl.* **marathons** 1. A foot race, usually covering a distance of 26 miles 385 yards (or c.42.3 kilometers). 2. Any other race such as swimming, or skating, which covers a long distance. 3. A contest of stamina or endurance. *The party was climaxed by a beer-drinking marathon, which was won by Festus, who drank 18 bottles.* 4. An activity which puts one's stamina or endurance to the test. a) *Luke recalls the 10-day marathon he and his colleagues put in during investigation of last year's Air Florida crash in the Potomac* (*Newsweek Int.* July 25, 1983:42-3). b) *On arrival at Murtala Airport, the visiting Head of State went through a marathon of shaking the hands of 2,000 dignitaries.* —*adj.* 1. Done over, or marked by, unusually long time or distance. a) *Marathon negotiations with the International Monetary Fund are expected to end in a deal before the end of May* (*South* 1985). b) *... a marathon meeting of the Armed Forces Ruling Council ...* (*Sunday Tribune* 1986). c) *By the end of the marathon speech, half of the audience either had walked out or were dozing.* 2. Requiring or demonstrating power of endurance or stamina. *Jamilla rejected the assignment, describing it as marathon and maintaining that she is an employee, not a slave.*

Märchen *n., pl.* **Märchen** [Ger. story, narrative.] A fairy tale.

Mardi Gras *n.* [Fr. **mardi** Tuesday (2); **gras** fat (1): fat Tuesday.] Shrove Tuesday. The Tuesday which immediately precedes Ash Wednesday. It is the climax of a long period of carnival before Lent, and is celebrated with feasting, merrymaking, and parades in certain places, such as New Orleans, Venice, Rio de Janeiro, and Quebec.

mare clausum *n.* [L. **mare** sea (2); **clausum** closed (1): closed sea.] A sea or any navigable waterway which is under the control of one nation and closed to others. Cf. **mare liberum.**

mare liberum *n.* [L. **mare** sea (2); **liberum** free (1): free sea.] A sea or any navigable waterway which may be used by all nations. Cf. **mare clausum.**

Mare Nostrum *n.* [L. **mare** sea (2); **nostrum** our (1): our sea.] *Ancient Rome.* The Mediterranean Sea, which for much of the history of the Roman Empire, was a Roman sea. —**mare nostrum** A sea or any navigable waterway which belongs to a nation or which two or more nations have agreed to share in common.

margaritas ante porcos Matthew 7:6. [L. **margaritas** pearls (1); **ante** before (2); **porcos** pigs, hogs, swine (3): pearls before hogs.] Pearls before swine. Precious objects before those who cannot appreciate them.

marginalia *pl. n.* [L. marginal things.] Marginal notes. Non-essential things. *She usually pays attention to marginalia, ignoring the important issues.*

mariachi *n., pl.* **mariachis** [Sp. perhaps from Fr. **mariage** marriage.] 1. A Mexican street band. 2. Music for such a band. 3. A musician in such a band.

mariage blanc *n., pl.* **marriages blancs** [Fr. **mariage** marriage (2); **blanc** white (1): white marriage.] A marriage in which there is no sexual relationship. A platonic marriage.

mariage de convenance *n., pl.* **mariages de convenance** [Fr. **mariage** marriage (1); **de** of (2); **convenance** convenience, suitability (3): marriage of convenience.] A marriage arranged for the couple. A marriage motivated by considerations of money or position. *The alliance between the radicals and conservatives, like most mariages de convenance, has collapsed like a house of cards.* Cf. **mariage d'inclination.**

mariage d'inclination *n., pl.* **mariages d'inclination** [Fr. **mariage** marriage (1); **d'** of (2); **inclination** propensity, affection, liking (3): marriage of affection.] Love match. Marriage of love. Marriage motivated exclusively by love or passion. Cf. **mariage de convenance.**

marijuana or **marihuana** [Sp. **mariguana.**] 1. The cannabis plant. 2. Dried leaves and flowers from the cannabis plant which, when smoked or eaten, create a state of mental satisfaction and contentment. Cf. **hashish.**

marimba *n.* [Bantu xylophones.] 1. A percussion instrument made of wood and similar to a xylophone. 2. Music for such an instrument.

marionette *n., pl.* **marionettes** [Fr. **marionnette** puppet.] A puppet operated by hand or strings. *He is a man of no conscience who, like a marionette, is manipulated by his cowardly masters.*

maris et feminae conjunctio est de jure naturae. [L. **maris** of male (2); **et** and (3); **feminae** of woman, female (4); **conjunctio** union, marriage (l); **est** is (5); **de** of, from, about, for (6); **jure** right, law (7); **naturae** of nature (8): The marriage of male and female is from the law of nature.] *Law.* The marriage of man and woman is a matter of natural law. See **conjunctio mariti** etc.

maritagium *n., pl.* **maritagia** [Med. L. from Fr. **mariage.**] *Medieval Europe.* 1. Maritage. The property which, in accordance with feudal custom, a girl on marriage brought to the husband. Cf. **conquêts.** 2. The power of a feudal lord to dispose in marriage of a vassal's widow, heiress, or minor heir. 3. Something paid by a vassal for the lord's waiver of such power.

marque *n., pl.* **marques** [Fr. mark, stamp, brand, make.] 1. Retaliation or reprisal as in "letters of marque." 2. Make or brand of an automobile. Cf. **lettre de marque.**

mashgiah or **mashgiach** *n., pl.* **mashgihim** or **mashgichim** [Heb.] *Judaism.* An inspector of kosher facilities to make sure that the dietary rules and regulations are followed.

Masora or **Masorah** *n.* [Heb. **māsora** bound, handed over.] *Judaism.* Commentary on Jewish sacred writings compiled and handed down by scholars since the 10th century A.D.

massage *n., pl.* **massages** [Fr. a rub down.] A rub down or kneading of the body for therapeutic or pleasurable purposes. —v. 1. To rub down or knead the body for such purposes. 2. To work up, change, or manipulate data and information.

masseur or *fem.* **masseuse** *n., pl.* **masseurs** or *fem.* **masseuses** [Fr. one who massages.] A person who massages or practices physiotherapy.

mastaba *n., pl.* **mastabas** [Ar. **mastabah** stone bench.] A trapezoidal-shaped tomb in ancient Egypt.

Marxophobia *n.* [Ger. **Marx** Karl Marx (2); Gk. **phob(os)** fear (1): fear of Marx.] A fear of Marxism or Communism.

matador *n., pl.* **matadors** [Sp. one who kills.] A bullfighter who plays the principal role and ultimately kills the bull. . . . *an elite coterie of aging and cynical matadors dominates the profession* (*Newsweek Int.* Nov. 27, 1978:5).

Mater Dolorosa *n.* [L. **mater** mother (2); **dolorosa** sorrowful (1): sorrowful mother.] 1. The sorrowful mother. A reference to Mary, grieving after the death of her son Jesus. 2. *Art.* A representation of Mary mourning for her dead son. 3. Any mother grieving for the loss of her dead child. Cf. **Stabat Mater Dolorosa.**

materfamilias *n., pl.* **matresfamilias** [L. matron, mistress of household.] *Civil Law.* A woman who is the head of a household. The mother or mistress of a household or family. See **familia.**

materia medica *n.* [L. **materia** matter, stuff (2); **medica** medical (1): medical matter.] *Medicine.* 1. The study of medicinal drugs and their preparation. 2. The ingredients in a medicinal drug.

materia prima *n.* [L. **materia** matter, stuff (2); **prima** first (1): first matter.] *Philosophy.* A primordial substance which, according to the natural physicists, was the original substance from which the universe with its plurality of unrelated elements was made. *Thales, the Greek philosopher, believed that the materia prima was water, while Anaximenes believed that it was air.*

matériel or **materiel** *n., pl.* **matériels** or **materiels** [Fr. material, equipment, implements, apparatus.] The apparatus, equipment, supplies, etc. of a group or organization, especially an army's arms, ammunitions, etc. *The Vietnamese did begin a massive deployment of men and matériel into the war zone* . . . (*Newsweek Int.* March 26, 1979:36). Cf. **personnel.**

materna maternis *n.* [L. **materna** maternal (things) (1); **maternis** for maternal (persons) (2): maternal things for maternal persons.] *French Law.* A maxim which signifies that goods which a deceased person acquired from/through the mother should be inherited by his/her maternal relatives.

mater rixarum *n.* [L. **mater** mother (1); **rixarum** of disputes, quarrels (2): mother of disputes.] Source of disputes. Cause of disputes. *There can be no doubt that joint ownership is a principal mater rixarum.*

matinée or **matinee** *n.* [Fr. **matinée** morning.] Any event, especially a dramatic or musical performance, which is scheduled during the day rather than the evening. An afternoon performance.

matrimonia debent esse libera. [L. **matrimonia** marriages (1); **debent** ought, should (2); **esse** to be (3); **libera** free (4): Marriages ought to be free.] *Law.* Marriages ought to be entered freely, not by force.

matrimonium subsequens tollit peccatum praecedens. [L. **matrimonium** marriage (2); **subsequens** following, subsequent (1); **tollit** takes away, removes (3); **peccatum** transgression, fault (5); **praecedens** preceding (4): Subsequent marriage takes away preceding transgression.] *Law.* Subsequent marriage removes a preceding fault.

matrix *n., pl.* **matrices** [Late L. a female used for breeding purposes, a womb.] 1. The uterus. 2. A rectangular arrangement in rows and columns. 3. The environment in which something develops and grows.

mausoleum *n., pl.* **mausolea** or **mausoleums** [L. from Gk. **Mausōleion**.] 1. Tomb of Mausolus, king of Caria, at Halicarnassus, which is counted among the Seven Wonders of the ancient world. 2. A monumental, imposing or magnificent tomb. . . . *Mao's body may be cremated and his mausoleum expanded to include a pantheon of Chinese revolutionary heroes* (*Newsweek Int.* Jan. 19, 1981:24). 3. A tomb for several persons, usually belonging to the same family. 4. A big, gloomy, highly decorated room, structure, building, etc.

maxima cum laude *adv.* [L. **maxima** greatest (2); **cum** with (1); **laude** praise, excellence (3): with the greatest praise or excellence.] With highest distinction. Used to indicate a very high academic performance, especially in an examination for graduation from college, particularly where Honors are not awarded. See **magna cum laude.**

maxima debetur puero reverentia. Juvenal (c.60–117 A.D.). *Satires* XIV,47. [L. **maxima** greatest (1); **debetur** is owed (3); **puero** to boy (4); **reverentia** respect, reverence (2): The greatest reverence is owed to a boy.] We owe to a child the greatest respect; i.e., we should behave with the greatest decency or propriety before children so as not to hurt their sensibilities, for they are very impressionable.

maximum *n., pl.* **maxima** or **maximums** [L. the biggest, greatest, largest.] The greatest quality or value that can be attained. The highest point or degree. The upper limit that is possible or permissible. *In any examination 100% is the maximum of marks obtainable.* —*adj.* Highest or greatest in quantity, value, quality or degree. *Whoever does not put in maximum effort is certainly not aiming at outstanding success.* Cf. **minimum.**

maximus in minimis [L. **maximus** a very great, large (person) (1); **in** in, on (2); **minimis** very small (matters) (3): a very great person in very small matters.] A big fish in a small pond.

mayorazgo *n.* [Sp. right of first-born son.] *Spanish Law.* The right to certain collective property which must be passed in its entirety forever and successively to the first-born son.

mazel tov or **mazal tov** *interj.* [Heb. **mazzāltob**: **mazzāl** good (1); **tob** luck (2): good luck.] Used to congratulate or wish someone good fortune. Cf. **salute** and **skoal**.

mazuma *n.* [Yid. **mazume** cash.] Money. Cash. Used only in slang.

mazurka or **mazourka** *n., pl.* **mazurkas** or **mazourkas** [Russ. from Polish dance of Mazovia in Poland.] *Music.* 1. A Polish dance similar to a polka. Often used in ballet. 2. A musical composition in 3/4 or 3/8 time with a heavily-stressed second beat.

M.B. *abbr.* for 1. **Medicinae Baccalaureus** (q.v.). 2. **Musicae Baccalaureus** (q.v.).

M.C. *abbr.* for **Magister Chirurgiae** (q.v.).

M.Ch. *abbr.* for **Magister Chirurgiae** (q.v.).

M.Ch.D. *abbr.* for **Magister Chirurgiae Dentalis** (q.v.).

M.Chir. *abbr.* for **Magister Chirurgiae** (q.v.).

M.Ch.Orth. *abbr.* for **Magister Chirurgiae Orthopaedicae** (q.v.).

M.D. *abbr.* for **Medicinae Doctor** (q.v.).

Mdme *abbr.* for **Madame** (q.v.).

Mds *abbr.* for **Mesdames** (q.v.).

mea culpa [L. **mea** my (1); **culpa** fault, error, blame, guilt, failure (2): my fault.] *interj.* I am to be blamed. It is my fault. I am sorry. From the Christian prayer known as the **confiteor** (q.v.). *I have personally settled every entry in the Index; if any entry irritates, please write me. Mea culpa* (Colinvaux 1979:vii). —*n.* Confession of mistake, error, fault, etc. Tendering of apology. *Calculated or not, his statements were not entirely a mea culpa* (*Newsweek Int.* July 25, 1983:16). Cf. **mea maxima culpa**.

mea maxima culpa [L. **mea** my (1); **maxima** greatest (2); **culpa** fault, error, blame, guilt, failure (3): my greatest fault.] *interj.* It is my greatest fault. From the Christian prayer known as the **confiteor** (q.v.). Used to express a most sincere apology for a mistake or error. *For all that has escaped these percipient eyes, mea culpa maxima* (Megarry 1973:xii). Cf. **mea culpa**.

Mecca *n.* [Ar.] A city in Saudi Arabia which, as the birthplace of Mohammed and the location of the **Kaaba** (q.v.), is the most important pilgrimage site in Islam. —**mecca** *pl.* **meccas** 1. A focus of activity and attention. 2. A popular plan of religious pilgrimage, a major tourist attraction, or a recreational site. *A tourist mecca.* Cf. **hajj**.

meden agan Quotation in Plato's *Protagoras.* [Gk. **mēden** nothing (1); **agan** too much, very much (2): nothing too much.] Nothing should be done in excess. See **aurea mediocritas**. Cf. **ne quid nimis**.

Medicinae Baccalaureus *abbr.* **M.B.** *n.* [L. **medicinae** of medicine (2); **baccalaureus** bachelor (1): Bachelor of Medicine.] A predoctoral graduate degree in medicine.

Medicinae Doctor *abbr.* **M.D.** *n.* [L. **medicinae** of medicine (2); **doctor** teacher (1): teacher of medicine.] Doctor of Medicine. A terminal graduate degree in medicine.

medico *n., pl.* **medicos** [Sp./It. physician.] A medical practitioner or student.

mediocre *adj.* [Fr. **médiocre** from L. **mediocris** ordinary, moderate, second-rate, average, middling.] Not outstanding. Second-rate. Ordinary. a) . . . *the quality of what was written, to judge by what has survived, rarely rose above the mediocre* (Laistner 1966:141). b) *The head of the institution is a man of mediocre ability who secured his position through nebulous means.*

mediocria firma [L. **mediocria** middle, average, ordinary (things) (1); **firma** solid, firm (2): ordinary things (are) solid.] The middle course is safe.

mediocritas aurea *n.* [L. **mediocritas** the middle, the mean (2); **aurea** golden (1): the golden mean.] The golden mean.

medio tutissimus ibis. Ovid (43 B.C.–17 A.D.). *Metamorphoses* II,137. [L. **medio** in the middle (3); **tutissimus** most safe (2); **ibis** you will go (1): You will go most safe in the middle.] The middle path is the safest for you. The golden mean is the safest course of action. See **aurea mediocritas**.

medium *n., pl.* **media** or **mediums** [L. middle thing.] 1. A middle course, degree, or quality. A compromise. Something which occupies an intermediate or middle position. *The old man recommends the golden medium for anybody desirous of success in life.* 2. The average, ordinary or usual amount, quantity, condition, etc. *When the economy improves, the department's personnel will be brought to its medium, which is about 40.* 3. A substance through which some other thing, such as an effect or force, is conveyed or transmitted. *Air serves as the medium for conveying sound.* 4. An intermediary. An agent. An agency. A person or thing used for achieving a purpose. a) . . . *it will be the solicitor who will in the appropriate case retain the services of a barrister through the medium of the barrister's clerk* (Newton 1983:77). b) *Raso is the medium used by those who wish to obtain loans from the notorious moneylender.* 5. A means of communicating to, informing, or entertaining a very large audience. *The U.S. indicated an interest in training personnel for the country's print, radio and television media* (T.M. Azonga in *West Africa* 1986). 6. Means for literary, artistic, or any other expression. a) *But Cato used the medium* [i.e., prose] *in his Latin treatise on farming . . .* (Robinson 1974:113). b) *It is a shame that . . . Africans . . . continue to use foreign languages as the official medium of expression* (Kofi Adusei in *West Africa* 1986). 7. *Art.* A liquid used in mixing pigments to make them suitable for painting. 8. A person through whom people communicate with the world of spirits or the other world. —*adj.* Intermediate. Average. Occupying a position between short and long, small and big, etc., in terms of time, degree, quality, quantity, etc. a) *medium height;* b) *medium income;* c) *medium size;* d) *In the medium term, prospects for demand growth in some developing countries are good, . . .* (*South* 1984).

medius *n., pl.* **medii** [L. middle, central.] The middle or central finger.

Medusa *n.* [Gk.] *Greek and Roman Mythology.* A woman transformed into the only mortal Gorgon, i.e., a monster with snakes in her hair and the ability to petrify at a glance. —**medusa** *n., pl.* **medusas** 1. An extremely ugly woman. A gorgon. 2. A type of jellyfish.

mega biblion mega kakon. Callimachus (fl. 250 B.C.). [Gk. **mega** great, big (1); **biblion** book (2); **mega** great, big (3); **kakon** evil, trouble (4): A big book, a big evil.] A large book is a large evil.

megalomania *n.* [Neo-Gk. from Gk. **mega(s)** great (2); **mania** madness, enthusiasm (1): enthusiasm for great things.] 1. A craze or passion for embarking upon grandiose projects. a) *Between World War I and II, this movement attained such power that Japan overreached itself and yielded to a blind megalomania* (*The Guardian* 1986). b) *The active participation of all African states in this crusade will surely keep Colonel Gaddafi's megalomania under restraint* (B. Yaw Owusu in *West Africa* 1986). 2. Retention in adulthood of the childish feelings that one is omnipotent or that one is the most important person in the world. 3. A form of mental disturbance in which the patient believes that he/she is very important, powerful, etc. See **folie de grandeur**.

megalopolis *n., pl.* **megalopoles** [Gk. **mega(s)** great (1); **polis** city (2): a great city.] A very big city. A heavily populated area with several large cities and many suburbs and towns. *Driving in the megalopolis stretching from Boston to Richmond has become a nightmare.*

Mein Kampf *n.* [Ger. **mein** my (1); **Kampf** battle, war, struggle (2): my struggle.] *My Battle,* the personal political manifesto of Adolf Hitler (1889–1945).

meiosis *n., pl.* **meioses** [Gk. diminution.] *Rhetoric.* A figure of speech in which a thing is represented in such a way that it seems smaller than it actually is. Understatement. See **litotes.** Cf. **hyperbole.**

Meistersinger *n., pl.* **Meistersinger** or **Meistersingers** [Ger. **Meister** master (1); **Singer** singer (2): mastersinger.] A member of a guild of composers and performers in 14th–16th century Germany.

me judice *adv.* [L. **me** with me (1); **judice** (with) being judge (2): with me being judge.] In my opinion or view.

melancholia *n., pl.* **melancholias** or **melancholiae** [Gk. **mela(s)** black (1); **cholē** bile (2): black bile, melancholy.] *Medicine.* A mental disorder in which the patient experiences considerable depression of spirits, delusions, baseless fears, hallucinations, and preoccupation with a particular train of thought.

mélange or **melange** *n., pl.* **mélanges** or **melanges** [Fr. mixture, compound, blend, mingling.] A mixture, conglomeration, or mingling. *The band plays delightful music which is a mélange of high-life, juju and rock and roll.* See **potpourri.**

mêlée or **melee** *n., pl.* **mêlées** or **melees** [Fr. mêlée conflict, scuffle.] 1. A confused fight, struggle, or contest. *The soccer match was brought to an abrupt end by a mêlée involving players and supporters of the two teams.* 2. A confused mixture of heterogeneous or incongruous elements. A mélange (q.v.). *The procession was impeded by a mêlée of spectators, pedestrians, bicycles, and cars.* 3. A cavalry demonstration or exercise involving two teams in which horsemen attempt to cut plumes of paper from the helmets of members of the opposing team.

melior est causa possidentis. [L. **melior** better (4); **est** is (3); **causa** cause, case, reason (1); **possidentis** of one possessing (2): The case of the one possessing is better.] *Law.* The person in possession has a better case of ownership. Possession is nine-tenths of the law. See **in aequali jure melior** etc.

melior est conditio possidentis, et rei quam actoris. [L. **melior** better (4); **est** is (3); **conditio** condition (1); **possidentis** of the one possessing (2); **et** and (5); **rei** of defendant (6); **quam** than (7); **actoris** of plaintiff (8): The condition of the one possessing is better, and of the defendant than of the plaintiff.] *Law.* The condition of the party in possession is better; similarly the condition of the defendant is better than that of the plaintiff. See **in aequali jure melior** etc.

melior est conditio possidentis, ubi neuter jus habet. [L. **melior** better (4); **est** is (3); **conditio** condition (1); **possidentis** of the one possessing (2); **ubi** where (5); **neuter** neither of two (6); **jus** right, law (8); **habet** has, holds, regards (7): The condition of the one possessing is better, where neither of two has right.] *Law.* The condition of the possessor is better, where neither the one nor the other has a right to the disputed property. See **in aequali jure melior** etc.

melior est justitia vere praeveniens quam severe puniens. [L. **melior** better (5); **est** is (4); **justitia** justice (1); **vere** truly, really (2); **praeveniens** preventing (3); **quam** than (6); **severe** severely (7); **puniens** punishing (8): Justice truly preventing is better than severely punishing.] *Law.* A system of justice which truly prevents crime is better than one which severely punishes crime. Cf. **justitia est duplex** etc.

melius est petere fontes quam sectari rivulos. [L. **melius** better (2); **est** it is (1); **petere** to seek, make for, aim at (3); **fontes** sources, fountains (4); **quam** than (5); **sectari** run after, chase (6); **rivulos** rivulets, petty streams (7): It is better to seek the sources than to chase the petty streams.] Finding the main cause or source for a situation is more important than ex-amining secondary ones. See **satius est petere** etc.

membrum virile *n.* [L. **membrum** member (2); **virile** male (1): male member.] The male member. The penis.

memento *abbr.* **mem.** *n., pl.* **mementos** or **memen-toes** [L. Remember.] Reminder. Memorial. Keepsake. *He enjoyed the send-off party so much so that he expressed his gratitude, saying that he would carry away mementos of that occasion.* Cf. **memorabilia** and **souvenir.**

memento mori *v.* [L. **memento** remember (1); **mori** to die (2): Remember to die.] Remember that you will die. A command given to individuals during the administration of the ashes on Ash Wednesday. —*n., pl.* **memento mori** Something that reminds one of death. *The sight of a skeleton or a cemetery is a vivid memento mori.*

memo *short form* for **memorandum** (q.v.).

memorabilia *pl. n.* [L. things that deserve remem-brance.] **Souvenirs** (q.v.). Objects which provoke memories. *The elderly actress's home was filled with memorabilia from her career.* Cf. **memento.**

memorandum *short form* **memo** *n., pl.* **memoranda** or **memorandums** [L. something to be remembered.] 1. An informal record of something to be remembered. 2. Reminder. 3. A brief, informal, interdepartmental communication. 4. Exceptions of a clause in a marine insurance policy exempting the insuring company from liability.

memoriae sacrum *abbr.* **M.S.** *adj.* [L. **memoriae** to memory (2); **sacrum** sacred (1): sacred to the memory of.] A tombstone inscription.

memoria technica *n.* [L. **memoria** memory (2); **technica** artificial (1): artificial memory.] An artificial device for aiding memory. A mnemonic system or aid. Cf. **aide-memoire** 1.

memoriter *adv./adj.* [L. from memory.] From memory. By heart. a) *He learned the national anthem and pledge memoriter.* b) *His intellectual ability is such that he is incapable of doing any job which goes be-yond the application of memoriter knowledge.*

ménage *n., pl.* **ménages** [Fr. housekeeping, household, married couple, management.] 1. A household, par-ticularly a man and woman living together. People residing permanently in a house. a) *. . . the ménage is housed in comfortable splendor high above the Hudson River, in an eleven-room apartment . . . (Newsweek Int. April 14, 1980:41-2).* b) *The Bellos have moved to their new house, and their closest neighbors, the Sawyers, are a respectable ménage.* 2. Quarters. A place maintained like a household or where a person lives. *We held the meeting at the secretary's apartment, a well-furnished ménage of four rooms.* 3. Housekeeping. Housework. Manage-ment of a house. *Mrs. Sackey visits Mrs. Quansah every Sunday to observe her excellent ménage.*

ménage à trois *n.* [Fr. **ménage** housekeeping, house-hold, married couple, management (1); **à** to, toward, in, by, with, until (2); **trois** three (3): household with three.] Domestic or matrimonial triangle. A situation or arrangement in which a married couple (or two lovers) and a third person, who is a lover of one of the couple, live together. a) *. . . there are several nice, quirky moments of domestic comedy involving the protagonist, his grandfather and his live-in lady in an innocent but funny ménage à trois (Time Int.* 1982). b) *Nearby is a scandalous ménage à trois on a Spanish beach: a sultry girl reclines ambivalently at a card game, one arm resting in the lap of her brood-ing boyfriend, her rump tucked under the torso of her girlfriend (Newsweek Int. Oct. 16, 1978:49).* See **à trois.**

menagerie *n., pl.* **menageries** [Fr. **ménagerie** house-hold management, cattle management, cattle building.] 1. A collection of animals kept in cages as pets or to be trained for exhibition in a circus. *. . . Bardot left, presumably to go back to her own menagerie where she keeps, among other pets, fifteen male rabbits (Newsweek Int. Dec. 17, 1979: 21).* 2. A group of people who seem weird, strange, foreign, odd, etc. *Mrs. Bonsu could not disguise her indignation when she saw her husband entering the living room with his menagerie of so-called friends.*

menarche *n.* [Neo-Gk. **mēn** month, moon (1); **archē** beginning (2): month beginning, beginning of menstrua-tion.] *Medicine.* The initial menstrual period of a female.

mendacem memorem esse opportet. Quintilian (born c.35 A.D.). *Institutio Oratoria* IV,2. [L. **mendacem** liar (2); **memorem** mindful, having a good memory (4); **esse** be (3); **opportet** it is fitting (that) (1): It is fitting that a liar be mindful.] It is appropriate for a liar to have a good memory. A liar had better re-member his/her lies.

menhir *n., pl.* **menhirs** [Fr. from Breton **men** stone (2); **hir** long (1): long stone.] A monolith executed by pre-historic people in France, Britain, Africa, and Asia.

menopause *n.* [Fr. from Gk. **mēn** month, moon (1); **pausis** stopping, ceasing, pause (2): month ceasing, cessation of menstruation.] *Medicine.* 1. The period, usually starting from the age of about 50, when a woman ceases to menstruate. 2. The experience and changes which a woman undergoes during this pe-riod. Cf. **menses.**

menorah *n.* [Heb. **menora.**] *Judaism.* A candelabrum used in religious celebrations. A nine-branched menorah is used at Hanukkah while a seven-branched one was used in the ancient temple in Jerusalem.

mens cujusque is est quisque. Cicero (106–43 B.C.). *De Republica* VI,26. [L. **mens** mind (1); **cujusque** of each, each one (2); **is** that (3); **est** is (4); **quisque** each, each one (5): The mind of each one, that is each one.] The mind of each person is the person himself/herself.

menses *n.* Either *pl.* or *sing.* in constr. [L. months.] *Medicine.* Menstruation. A woman's monthly discharge of blood from the uterus. Cf. **menopause.**

mens legis *n.* [L. **mens** mind, purpose, intention (1); **legis** of law (2): mind of the law.] *Law.* The purpose/intention/spirit of the law.

mens rea *n.* [L. **mens** mind, purpose, intention (2); **rea** guilty, answerable (1): guilty mind.] *Law.* Criminal intent/purpose. *An act alone cannot make a person criminally responsible, unless it is accompanied by mens rea.* See **actus non facit** etc.

mens sana in corpore sano. Juvenal (c.60–117 A.D.). *Satires* X,356. [L. **mens** mind, purpose, intention (2); **sana** sound (1); **in** in, on (3); **corpore** body (5); **sano** sound (4): a sound mind in a sound body.] A healthy mind in a healthy body. See **orandum est** etc.

mens testatoris in testamentis spectanda est. [L. **mens** mind, purpose, intention (1); **testatoris** of testator (2); **in** in, on (5); **testamentis** wills (6); **spectanda** to be considered (4); **est** is (3): The intention of the testator is to be considered in wills.] *Law.* The intention of the testator must be considered in the interpretation of wills. See **interest reipublicae suprema** etc.

mentor *n., pl.* **mentors** [Gk. **Mentōr.**] 1. Odysseus' old friend whom the goddess Athena impersonates in order to provide advice to Odysseus' son Telemachus in Homer's *Odyssey.* 2. A teacher or tutor. 3. A close, dependable, wise, and competent guide, helper, or counselor. a) *With Confucian thoroughness he sought to be the mentor of his people in all things great and small (Time Int.* 1982). b) *Whenever the Prime Minister has an important decision to make, he consults his mentor, a septuagenarian uncle who has the wisdom of Solomon.*

merci *n., pl.* **mercis** [Fr. thank you.] Thanks. Cf. **gracias** and **grazie.**

meretrix *n., pl.* **meretrices** [L. she who earns money, prostitute, courtesan.] Prostitute. Courtesan. *In his testimony, he described his wife as a meretrix parading in the garb of a respectable woman.* Cf. **cocotte**; **femme libre**; and **succuba.**

merito beneficium legis amittit, qui legem ipsam subvertere intendit. [L. **merito** deservedly, justly (6); **beneficium** benefit, favor (8); **legis** of law (9); **amittit** loses (7); **qui** the one who, he who (1); **legem** law (4); **ipsam** itself (5); **subvertere** to subvert, undermine (3); **intendit** endeavors, aims (2): The one who endeavors to subvert the law itself justly loses the benefit of law.] *Law.* He who endeavors to undermine the law itself deserves to lose the benefit of law. Applicable to a person who seeks the court's assistance in a fraudulent transaction. See **ex turpi causa** etc.

mesa *n., pl.* **mesas** [Sp. from L. **mensa** table.] A table-like geological formation with flat top and steep sides found in the southwestern United States.

mésalliance *n., pl.* **mésalliances** [Fr. misalliance.] Unsuitable marriage. Bad match. Marriage with a person who belongs to a lower social class.

Mesa Verde *n.* [Sp. **mesa** table (2); **verde** green (1): green table.] The green mesa. A mesa in Colorado. Cf. **mesa.**

Mesdames *pl.* of **Madame** (q.v.).

Mesdemoiselles *pl.* of **Mademoiselle** (q.v.).

meshuga or **meshugga** *adj.* [Yid. **meshuge** from Heb. **mesuggā'** crazy, insane.] *Slang.* Without any intelligence or good sense.

meshugaas or **mishegaas** or **mishegoss** *n.* [Yid. **meshegas** from Heb. **mesuggā'** crazy, insane.] *Slang.* An action without intelligence or good sense.

mesne *adj.* [Obs. Fr. mean, middle.] 1. Happening between two dates. *A mesne duty.* 2. Intermediate. Of, relating to, concerning, a position where one is subordinate to a superior and at the same time superior to a lower person. 3. *Law.* Pertaining to a lord who is tenant to a superior and at the same time a lord to a tenant.

Messiah or **Messias** *n.* [Gk. **Messias** from Aram. from Heb. **māshah** anointed one, savior.] 1. *Judaism.* The savior who is to come. 2. *Christianity.* Jesus Christ. —**messiah** A long-awaited savior, liberator or leader. Cf. **Mahdi.**

Messieurs *pl.* of **Monsieur** (q.v.).

Messrs *abbr.* for **Messieurs** (q.v.).

mestizo or *fem.* **mestiza** *n., pl.* **mestizoes** or **mestizos** or *fem.* **mestizas** [Sp. a person of mixed blood, partly foreign and partly native.] A half-caste, such as one who is partly Portuguese or Spanish and partly American Indian.

metamorphosis *n., pl.* **metamorphoses** [Gk. **meta** pertaining to change (1); **morph(ē)** shape (2): change of shape, transformation.] 1. A change, transformation or alteration of character, form, condition, appearance, circumstance, etc.... *the strongest and scariest element in "The Shining" is the face of Jack Nicholson undergoing a metamorphosis from affectionate father to a murderous demon (Newsweek Int.* June 2, 1980:52). 2. An extraordinary change. A change which seems to have been effected through supernatural means. *The spectators attacked the magician for his failure to fulfill his promise to effect the metamorphosis of a man into a chimpanzee.* —**Metamorphoses** The title of an epic poem on changes of form by Ovid (43 B.C.–17 A.D.) and a novel (also known as *The Golden Ass*) by Apuleius (fl. 155 A.D.). —**"The Metamorphosis"** A short story by Franz Kafka (1883–1924).

metanoia *n., pl.* **metanoias** [Gk. **meta** pertaining to change (1); **nous** mind (2): change of mind or heart, repentance, regret.] A fundamental or radical change of character or mind. A spiritual transformation or conversion.

metathesis *n., pl.* **metatheses** [Gk. a place change.] *Linguistics.* The reversing of the order sound or letters in a word, such as "bird" from Old English "brid."

métayage *n., pl.* **métayages** [Fr. system of farming through the use of sharecroppers.] Sharecropping. Farming through the use of the services of métayers. The system was introduced in French colonial tropical Africa after the abolition of slavery, when the freed slaves cultivated the fields of their former masters, paying exorbitant rents. *In 1935 cultivation was limited to 1,500 hectares . . . all under the métayage system . . .* (Suret-Canale 1971:222). Cf. **métayer.**

métayer *n., pl.* **métayers** [Fr. farmer, sharecropper, laborer, tenant-farmer.] A sharecropper. A farmer who is supplied with implements, stock, seeds, etc. by the landlord and cultivates the land, giving the landlord a fixed share, usually one half of the produce. Places where the system is (or was) practiced include Italy, France, French colonial tropical Africa, and the southern United States. Cf. **métayage.**

metempsychosis *n.* [Gk. **metemphychōsis:** met(a) pertaining to change (1); **en** in (2); **psych(ē)** soul, mind (3): change of souls, transmigration of souls.] A belief held by Pythagoreans and others, namely, that on the death of a person, the body, which is mortal, perishes but the soul, which is immortal, leaves the body and enters the body of another creature, either a human being or an animal. It is for this reason that Pythagoreans resolutely refrained from maltreating animals for, according to their belief, the dog which one is maltreating may be carrying the soul of one's dead ancestor. Cf. **l'éternel retour; metensomatosis;** and **palingenesis.**

metensomatosis *n., pl.* **metensomatoses** [Gk. **metensōmatōsis:** met(a) pertaining to change (1); **en** in (2); **sōma** body (3): change of bodies, transmigration of the soul.] Reincarnation. Cf. **metempsychosis** and **palingenesis.**

methexis *n., pl.* **methexes** [Gk. participation.] *Platonic Philosophy.* The participation of objects of the perceptible world (e.g., a beautiful thing) in the absolute, the universal, or the ideal (e.g., beauty).

Methuselah *n.* [Heb.] 1. A biblical patriarch who is said at Genesis 5:27 to have lived 969 years 2. A man who has reached extreme old age.

métier *n., pl.* **métiers** [Fr. trade, occupation, profession, calling, craft, talent.] 1. Trade, vocation, or profession. *His clothes clearly show his métier, i.e., painting.* 2. **Forte** (q.v.). An activity in which one is competent, successful, or experienced. *Debbie's father is an engineer by profession, but his principal métier is painting.* 3. Method, techniques of a field, discipline or art. *With her excellent grasp of the métier of poetry, her poems have always ranked among the best in the world.*

métro or **metro** *short form* of **réseau métropolitain** [Fr. **réseau** (2) network; **métropolitain** (1): metro-

politan network, a subway train system.] A system of trains and subways, especially in Paris and Washington, D.C.

métropole *n., pl.* **métropoles** [Fr. from Gk. **mēt(ē)r** mother (1); **polis** city (2): mother city.] 1. A principal or chief city. Capital. 2. An archepiscopal see. 3. A mother country. A parent state, i.e., of a colony. See **metropolis.**

metropolis *n., pl.* **metropoles** [Gk. **mēt(ē)r** mother (1); **polis** city (2): mother-state, mother-city, capital city.] 1. Mother-country. Founding state or city of a colony. 2. A capital. A chief city of a country. 3. A city well-known for a particular activity. *Members of the Lagos Butchers Association traveled to Maiduguri, a cattle metropolis, to negotiate for the purchase of cows.* 4. A metropolitan see such as that of an archbishop. Cf. **métropole.**

meubles *pl. n.* [Fr. movable things.] *French Law.* **Bona mobilia** (q.v.). Movables. Personal estate. A thing is movable either because of its own nature (e.g., a chair) or because it is determined to be so by the law (e.g., an obligation). See **biens meubles.**

meum *n.* [L. mine.] My property. Cf. **meum et tuum** and **tuum.**

meum et tuum [L. **meum** mine (1); **et** and (2); **tuum** yours (3): mine and yours.] *Law.* The principle of personal property, i.e., that what is mine is mine and what is yours is yours. Cf. **meum** and **tuum.**

mezuzah or **mezuza** *n., pl.* **mezuzot** or **mezuzahs** or **mezuzas** [Heb. **mezuza** doorpost.] *Judaism.* A marker placed on a door as a sign of faith and compliance with Jewish law. Inside the marker is a copy of the Hebrew text of Deuteronomy 6:4–9 and 11:13–21. On the marker is written "Shaddai," a Hebrew word for God.

mezzanine *n., pl.* **mezzanines** [Fr. mid-story.] *Architecture.* A partial story between the ground floor and first floor, especially in a theater.

mezza voce *adv./adj.* [It. **mezza** middle, half (1); **voce** voice (2): half voice.] *Music.* With half voice. In moderate tone.

mezzo *adv./adj.* [It. middle, half.] *Music.* Moderately. Cf. **mezzo forte, mezzo piano,** and **mezzo relievo.** —*n., pl.* **mezzos** A **mezzo soprano** (q.v.).

mezzo forte *adv./adj.* [It. **mezzo** middle, half (1); **forte** strong (2): half strong.] *Music.* Moderately strong or loud.

mezzo piano *adv./adj.* [It. **mezzo** middle, half (1); **piano** soft (2): half soft.] *Music.* Moderately soft.

mezzo relievo or **mezzo-relievo** *n., pl.* **mezzi relievi** or **mezzo-relievos** [It. **mezzo** middle, half (1); **relievo** relief (2): half relief.] *Art.* Figures sculptured not in the round but only to a small depth on a flat background. Cf. **bas relief** and **relievo.**

mezzo soprano *n., pl.* **mezzi soprani** [It. **mezzo** middle, half (1); **soprano** upper (2): half upper.] *Music.* A mid-range **soprano** (q.v.).

miasma *n., pl.* **miasmata** or **miasmas** [Gk. stain, defilement, pollution.] 1. An exhalation of vapor emanating from marshy ground or rotten matter which, it used to be believed, causes diseases such as malaria. *During yellow fever epidemic at Saint Louis, people were advised to go up on to the terraces at night to avoid the miasmata and breathe pure air* (Suret-Canale 1971:404). 2. A thick vapor-like atmosphere or emanation. *The room, apparently a den of disreputable characters, was pregnant with the miasma of marijuana smoke.* 3. A pervasive, corrupting atmosphere or influence. *It is a disturbing story and it tells us something of the miasma of power, the ease with which people in power can act barbarously in relation to individuals . . .* (Ben Okri in *West Africa* 1982).

migraine *n., pl.* **migraines** [Fr. sick headache.] *Medicine.* A sickness characterized by severe recurrent headache, usually restricted to one side of the head, and nausea. *There are indications that persistent criticism has been giving the Administration severe political migraine.*

mihrab *n.* [Ar. **mihrāb** niche.] *Islam.* 1. A niche indicating the direction of Mecca in a mosque. 2. The undecorated rectangular area located in the center of a prayer rug and oriented toward **Mecca** (q.v.). Cf. **Kiblah.**

mikado *n., pl.* **mikados** [Japan. **mi-** honorable (1); **kado** gate (2): honorable gate.] The emperor of Japan. —**The Mikado** A light opera (1885) by Sir William S. Gilbert and Sir Arthur Sullivan. Also known as **The Town of Titipu.**

mikvah or **mikvoth** or **mikvot** or **mikvos** *n.* [Heb. **miqwāh** a tub or pool of water.] *Judaism.* 1. A ritual bath performed before the Sabbath, after menstruation, after male ejaculation, and on other occasions. 2. The building or room in which such a bath is performed.

miles gloriosus *n., pl.* **milites gloriosi** [L. **miles** soldier (2); **gloriosus** boastful, bragging (1): bragging/boastful soldier.] A braggard soldier 1. The title of a Roman comedy by Plautus (254–184 B.C.). 2. A stock character in the comedy of ancient Rome and the Renaissance.

milieu *n., pl.* **milieux** or **milieus** [Fr. middle, environment, society.] Social, historical, cultural, intellectual, etc. environment. *. . . a viable approach to the problem should reckon with the sociological milieu inducing banditry in the society* (*The Guardian* 1986).

militat omnis amans. Ovid (43 B.C.–19 A.D.). *Amores* I,9,1. [L. **militat** fights, serves as a soldier (3); **omnis** each, every (1); **amans** lover (2): every lover serves as a soldier.] Every lover is a soldier.

militia *n., pl.* **militias** [L. military service, warfare, the soldiery, the military.] Home reserve. The citizen army. These are not members of the standing army but in times of emergency they can be called for military service. Cf. **Landwehr.**

millennium *n., pl.* **millennia** or **millenniums** [L. from **mille** one thousand (2) and **annus** year (1): a period of one thousand years.] 1. A unit of one thousand years. *Good museums usually have artefacts dating back many millennia.* 2. *Christianity.* A period of 1,000 years during which, according to Revelation 20:5, Jesus Christ will reign on earth and holiness will prevail. 3. A period in the future characterized by very good government, virtue, general happiness, or the absence of human imperfections.

mimesis *n., pl.* **mimeses** [Gk. **mimēsis** imitation.] The act of imitating. Mimicry. *The work can hardly lay claim to originality, for there are ample indications of mimesis in it.*

minatur innocentibus qui parcit nocentibus. [L. **minatur** threatens (4); **innocentibus** innocent (persons) (5); **qui** one who (1); **parcit** spares (2); **nocentibus** guilty (persons) (3): One who spares the guilty threatens the innocent.] *Law.* One who spares guilty people, threatens innocent ones. See **impunitas semper** etc.

minima poena corporalis est major qualibet pecuniaria. [L. **minima** least, smallest (1); **poena** punishment (3); **corporalis** corporal, bodily (2); **est** is (4); **major** greater, bigger (5); **qualibet** than any (6); **pecuniaria** monetary, pecuniary (7): The smallest corporal punishment is greater than any monetary punishment.] *Law.* The smallest corporal punishment is more severe than a fine.

minime mutanda sunt quae certam habent interpretationem. [L. **minime** least, not at all, by no means (7); **mutanda** to be changed (6); **sunt** are (5); **quae** (those things) which (1); **certam** fixed, settled (3); **habent** have, hold, regard (2); **interpretationem** interpretation (4): Things which have a fixed interpretation are not to be changed at all.] *Law.* Those things which have a definite interpretation must not be changed.

minimum *n., pl.* **minima** or **minimums** [L. the least, smallest.] The least or smallest point or degree. *Ben would accept the appointment only if he could work with a minimum of interference. —adj.* Least or smallest in quantity, value, quality or degree. *He is such a genius that with minimum effort he can achieve what most people achieve only with maximum effort.* Cf. **maximum.**

minor *adj.* [L. smaller, younger, inferior.] 1. Inferior. Relatively unimportant. Lower in position or reputation. Not serious. a) *A driver entering a major road from a minor road should stop and watch carefully.* b) *A minor sickness;* c) *a minor subject or course.* 2. Not having reached the age of majority. *Minor children are not allowed to watch certain films. —n., pl.* **minors** 1. A person who has not attained the age at which one can enjoy full civic rights. *In some countries, minors are not allowed to enter liquor stores.* 2. Subsidiary subject or course. *He obtained a B.A. in English with a minor in History.* 3. Smaller league. *His team plays in the minors.*

minor minorem custodire non debet; alios enim praesumitur male regere qui seipsum regere nescit. [L. **minor** minor (1); **minorem** minor (5); **custodire** to guard, protect (4); **non** not (3); **debet** ought, should (2); **alios** others (13); **enim** for (6); **praesumitur** is presumed (11); **male** badly, poorly (14); **regere** to control, govern, guide (12); **qui** one who (7); **seipsum** oneself, himself/herself (10); **regere** to control, govern, guide (9); **nescit** does not know (8): A minor ought not to guard a minor, for one who does not know how to guide oneself is presumed to guard others badly.] *Law.* A minor should not serve as guardian of a minor, for one who does not know how to control onself is, presumably, not qualified to control others.

minus *prep.* [L. less.] 1. Diminished by. Less. Without. a) *Eleven minus six equals five.* b) *He emerged from the scuffle minus three teeth.* 2. *Law.* Not at all. See **minus solutum.**

minuscule *adj.* [Fr. tiny, minute.] Diminutive. Minute. Tiny. Insignificant. Very small. a) . . . *a pert mystery model wearing . . . a minuscule bikini* (*Newsweek Int.* Sept. 21, 1981:33). b) *Ama rejected the amorous proposals of many affluent suitors and married Ato, a threadbare pauper who receives a minuscule monthly salary.* —*n.* A cursive script used in medieval manuscripts.

minus solutum *adj.* [L. **minus** less, not at all (1); **solutum** paid (2): not at all paid.] *Law.* Not paid.

minus solvit, qui tardius solvit. [L. **minus** less, not at all (5); **solvit** pays (4); **qui** one who, he who (1); **tardius** rather/too late, slowly, tardily (3); **solvit** pays (2): One who pays too slowly pays not at all.] He who pays (a debt) too late or tardily does not pay at all.

minutia *n., pl.* **minutiae** [L. smallness.] Minute or trivial detail. Petty matter. Small thing. *His novels are notable for descriptions of the minutiae of everyday life.*

minyan *n., pl.* **minyanim** or **minyans** [Heb. **minyān** count, number.] *Judaism.* The number of Jews needed to hold a religious service. Cf. **quorum.**

mir *n., pl.* **mirs** [Russ. community, world, peace.] A group of peasant farmers living together in a village in pre-revolutionary Russia. —**Mir** A Russian space station.

mirabile dictu *interj.* [L. **mirabile** wonderful (1); **dictu** in the saying (2): wonderful in the saying.] Amazing to say! a) *In his infancy he was suspected to be a mentally retarded child but he has, mirabile dictu, grown to be one of the greatest intellectual giants of the age.* b) *Within three years of its coming into force, mirabile dictu, it went through sixteen amendments* (Adewoye 1977:235).

mirabile visu *interj.* [L. **mirabile** wonderful (1); **visu** in the seeing (2): wonderful in the seeing.] Amazing to see! *Mr. Adams entered his residence and, mirabile visu, the accused was in his bedroom opening his suitcases.*

mirabilia *pl. n.* [L. wonderful things.] Astonishing, amazing, or strange things.

mirage *n., pl.* **mirages** [Fr. illusion.] 1. An optical illusion or false appearance of water; a pool, lake, or tree observable in a hot desert or on a pavement and caused by heated and rarefied air. 2. Hope, illusion, apprehension, etc. of something which is unattainable. a) *The elder statesman warned the audience that, if people do not change their attitudes, national unity would continue to be a mirage.* b) *We want them to understand that their fears are mirages* (*Newsweek Int.* Feb. 4, 1980:52).

mis. *abbr.* for **misere** (q.v.).

miscellanea *pl. n.* [L. mixed things.] 1. A collection or compendium of various writings, notes, articles, etc. *The book is essentially a compilation of miscellanea comprising contributions from various sources.* 2. A collection of various things. *He is a very complex person, his character being a product of miscellanea of various influences.* See **smorgasbord.**

misce stultitiam consiliis brevem; / dulce est desipere in loco. Horace (65–8 B.C.). *Odes* IV,12,27. [L. **misce** mix, blend (1); **stultitiam** folly, silliness (3); **consiliis** with judgments, wisdom (4); **brevem** little, small (2); **dulce** sweet (6); **est** it is (5); **desipere** to be foolish, silly (7); **in** in, on (8); **loco** place (9): Mix a little folly with wisdom; / it is sweet to be foolish in place.] Blend a little bit of folly with wisdom; it is sweet to be frivolous at the right time and place. For a shorter form of the quotation, see **dulce est desipere** etc.

Mischsprache *n., pl.* **Mischsprachen** [Ger. **misch(en)** mix (1); **Sprache** speech, language (2): mixed or hybrid language.] A language believed to be the product of the mixture of several languages.

mise en abyme *n.* [Fr. **mise** putting, setting (1); **en** in (2); **abyme** abyss (3): putting in an abyss, a reflection in a pool of water, an image reflected into infinity.] 1. *Medieval Europe.* A coat of arms which depicts a coat of arms depicting a coat of arms. 2. An infinite replication of objects, images or concepts, such as Chinese boxes. 3. *Art.* A work of art which depicts the act of creating the artwork; e.g, a painter painting a painter, a sculptor sculpting a sculptor, a writer writing about writing, or a film-maker filming a film about film-making.

mise-en-scène or **mise en scène** *n., pl.* **mise-en-scènes** or **mis en scènes** [Fr. **mise** putting, setting (1); **en** into (2); **scène** stage, scene (3): putting in scene.] 1. Production. Staging. The process of arranging the scenery and actors for a dramatic performance. 2. The setting, background, or environment of an action, event, occurrence, etc. *The three scenarios . . . provide us with a mise en scène from which pertinent issues concerning the state of the Ghanaian nation can be raised, cogitated upon and discussed* (Thomas Cooke in *West Africa* 1985).

misera est servitus. [L. **misera** wretched, miserable (3); **est** is (2); **servitus** slavery, servitude (1): Slavery is wretched.] Being a slave is wretched.

misera est servitus, ubi jus est vagum aut incertum.
[L. **misera** wretched, miserable (2); **est** it is (1); **servitus** slavery, servitude (3); **ubi** where (4); **jus** right, law (5); **est** is (6); **vagum** vague, doubtful (7); **aut** or (8); **incertum** uncertain (9): It is a wretched slavery where the law is vague or uncertain.] *Law.* A situation in which the law is vague and uncertain is tantamount to wretched slavery. Cf. **jus vagum aut incertum.**

Miserere [L. Feel pity. Have mercy. Be merciful.] 1. The title and first word of Psalm 51, a penitential psalm. 2. A musical setting of the Psalm. *The Passion of Jesus was read aloud in eight languages, followed by the singing of the "Miserere"* . . . *(Newsweek Int.* May 18, 1981:52). —**miserere** *abbr.* **mis.** *n., pl.* **misereres** A speech, prayer, or exclamation requesting mercy. *The condemned criminal's miserere made no impression on the judge.*

misericordia *n., pl.* **misericordias** [L. pity, mercy, compassion, sympathy.] *Law.* A penalty inflicted at the court's discretion. Amercement. *The court's misericordia saved the accused from prison.*

misopedia *n.* [Neo-Gk. from Gk. **miso(s)** hate (1); **pais** child (2): hatred of a child.] *Psychology.* Hatred of children. *Right from the beginning it was apparent that the husband's misopedia did not augur well for the success of the marriage.*

mission civilisatrice *n., pl.* **missions civilisatrices** [Fr. **mission** mission (2); **civilisatrice** civilizing (1): civilizing mission.] An expedition for the purpose of spreading civilization, especially the self-imposed mission of European colonialists in their colonies. *What European nations called mission civilisatrice was essentially a selfish plan to exploit the colonies economically.* Cf. **oeuvre civilisatrice.**

Mit der Dummheit kämpfen Götter selbst vergebens. Friedrich von Schiller (1759–1805). *Jungfrau von Orleans* III,6. [Ger. **mit** with (1); **der** the (2); **Dummheit** stupidity, foolishness (3); **kämpfen** fight, struggle, wrestle (6); **Götter** gods (4); **selbst** themselves (5); **vergebens** in vain, to no purpose (7): With stupidity, the gods themselves wrestle to no purpose.] Even the gods fight hopelessly against stupidity.

mitius imperanti melius paretur. [L. **mitius** more mildly (4); **imperanti** (to) one commanding (3); **melius** better (2); **paretur** it is obeyed, there is obeying (1): There is better obeying one commanding more mildly.] One who commands rather mildly receives better obedience. You catch more flies with honey than you do with vinegar.

Mittel-Afrika *n.* [Ger. **mittel** middle, central (1); **Afrika** Africa (2): central Africa.] The central part of Africa. *German imperialist circles worked out projects for a German Mittel-Afrika which would link Kamerun and German East Africa* [Tanganyika.] . . . (Suret-Canale 1971:119).

Mitteleuropa *n.* [Ger. **mittel** middle, central (1); **Europa** Europe (2): central Europe.] Central Europe.

mittimus *n., pl.* **mittimuses** [L. We send.] 1. *Law.* A warrant committing a person to prison. 2. *Law.* A writ authorizing the removal of records from one court to another. 3. Dismissal. Discharge.

mitzvah *n., pl.* **mitzvoth** or **mitzvahs** [Heb. **mishwa** command.] 1. A commandment in the Jewish law. 2. A good deed.

Mlle *abbr.* for **Mademoiselle** (q.v.).

M.M. or **m.m.** *abbr.* for **mutatis mutandis** (q.v.).

Mme *abbr.* for **Madame** (q.v.).

Mmes *abbr.* for **Mesdames** (q.v.).

m.o. *abbr.* for **modus operandi** (q.v.).

mobilia *pl. n.* [L. things which are movable.] Movable things. Movables.

mobilia non habent situm. [L. **mobilia** movable (things) (1); **non** not (2); **habent** have, hold, regard (3); **situm** location, site (4): Movable things do not have location.] *Law.* Movable things do not have fixed positions.

mobilia sequuntur personam. [L. **mobilia** movable (things) (1); **sequuntur** follow (2); **personam** person (3): Movable things follow the person.] *Law.* Movable things or porperty follows the owner wherever he/she lives and may, therefore, be disposed of in accordance with the law of the domicile.

modicum *n., pl.* **modicums** [L. a moderate or small amount.] A small portion or quantity. *Mr. Bailey described his rival as a shameless, worthless, and disreputable man without even a modicum of any redeeming quality.*

modo liceat vivere, est spes. Terence (c.190–159 B.C.). *Heauton Timoroumenos,* 981. [L. **modo** merely, simply (1); **liceat** let it be permitted (2); **vivere** to live (3); **est** (there) is, has been (4); **spes** hope (5): Simply let it be permitted to live, there is hope.] Where there's life, there's hope.

modus *n., pl.* **modi** [L. way, manner, method, mode.] A way, mode, or procedure. *This is a novel problem and there is no known modus of solving it.*

modus adquirendi *n.* [L. **modus** way, manner, method, mode (1); **adquirendi** of acquiring, obtaining (2): way of acquiring.] Manner of acquiring. Manner of acquisition.

modus agendi *n.* [L. **modus** way, manner, method, style, mode (1); **agendi** of doing (2): way of doing.] Standard procedure. The normal routine. *The committee was reluctant to deviate from their modus agendi.*

modus et conventio vincunt legem. See **conventio et modus vincunt legem.**

modus operandi *abbr.* **m.o.** *n., pl.* **modi operandi** [L. **modus** way, manner, method, mode (1); **operandi** of working, operating (2): way of working.] Method of doing things. *Law.* Usually used with reference to criminals' pattern of activity. *The modus operandi of pickpockets is to move about in groups and pass on their booty from one person to another in a chain.*

modus ponens *n., pl.* **modi ponentes** [L. **modus** way, manner, method, mode (2); **ponens** proposing, positing (1): proposing or positing method.] *Logic.* A way of arguing based on a hypothetical proposition, whereby the truth of the consequent is inferred from that of the antecedent. Example: "A" implies "B;" since "A" is true, "B" is true. Cf. **modus tollens**.

modus tenendi *n., pl.* **modi tenendi** [L. **modus** way, manner, method, mode (1); **tenendi** of holding (2): way of holding.] The manner in which the tenure of an estate is held.

modus tollens *n., pl.* **modi tollentes** [L. **modus** way, manner, method, style, mode (2); **tollens** removing, taking away (1): removing or taking away method.] *Logic.* A way of arguing based on a hypothetical, whereby the denial of the consequent implies the denial of the antecedent. Example: "A" implies "B;" since "B" is untrue, "A" is untrue. Cf. **modus ponens**.

modus transferrendi *n.* [L. **modus** way, manner, method, style, mode (1); **transferrendi** of transferring (2): way of transferring.] Manner of transference.

modus vivendi *n., pl.* **modi vivendi** [L. **modus** way, manner, method, mode (1); **vivendi** of living (2): way of living.] A manner of living. A way of life. There is usually the implication that the "way of life" is a truce or compromise satisfactory to contending parties or forces. a) *The two nations have many conflicting interests, but they have managed to set up a modus vivendi.* b) *After many setbacks and psychological problems, Adetunji worked out a respectable modus vivendi.*

moi *pron.* [Fr. I, me.] I. Me. **Ego** (q.v.). Used especially in response to questions. *"Who did it?" "Moi!"*

moira or **moera** *n., pl.* **moirai** or **moerae** [Gk. fate.] One's destiny or lot in life.

molimen *n., pl.* **molimina** [L. great exertion or effort.] *Medicine.* Menstrual discomfort or tension.

moment de vérité *n., pl.* **moments de vérité** [Fr. **moment** moment (1); **de** of (2); **vérité** truth (3): moment of truth.] The moment or occasion when one is confronted with stark reality.

momentum *n., pl.* **momenta** or **momentums** [L. movement, motion, exertion, moment, instant, importance, influence.] Impetus. The force generated by a body's continuous motion. a) *Life is a long-distance journey and we need to apportion our energy in such a way that we do not lose our momentum in the middle of the course.* b) *With the demise of the ringleader, the conspiracy lost its momentum.*

momentum rerum *n., pl.* **momenta rerum** [L. **momentum** cause, that which turns the scales (1); **rerum** of matters, things, property, business, affairs (2): that which turns the scales of things.] Immediate or decisive cause. *No explanation of the Decline* [i.e., of the Roman empire] *can be considered fully adequate unless it singles out some factor which came into play not long before 250 and acted as the momentum rerum* (Cary 1970:773).

momus *n., pl.* **momi** or **momuses** [L. from Gk. **mōmos** blame.] 1. Blame. Reproach. Faultfinding. 2. A person who deliberately looks for faults. A faultfinder. A carping or faultfinding critic. *Jerry is increasingly becoming a momus and getting on the nerves of his family.* See **Zoilus**.

mondaine *n., pl.* **mondaines** [Fr. worldly, fashionable.] A fashionable woman. A society woman. A woman of the world. —*adj.* Fashionable. Worldly. Sophisticated. *Victor had a date yesterday with his mondaine girlfriend.*

monde renversé *n.* [Fr. **monde** world (2); **renversé** reversed (1): reversed world.] 1. The world turned upsidedown. 2. *Theater.* The reversal of social convention which takes place in comedy.

monologue *n., pl.* **monologues** [Fr. from Gk. **mono(s)** one, alone (2) and **log(os)** speaking (1): speaking alone, soliloquy.] 1. A scene in a drama in which only one person talks. 2. A drama performed by a single actor. 3. Soliloquy. 4. A long speech uttered by a person who is holding a conversation or discussion with others. *An otherwise lively evening ended in an anticlimax when Mr. Porter entered the room and dominated the discussions with his boring monologues.*

Monsieur *abbr.* **M.** *n., pl.* **Messieurs** *abbr.* **Messrs.** [Fr. **mon** my (1) and **sieur** lord (2): my lord, sir.] 1. A high-ranking Frenchman. 2. Mister or Mr. Prefixed to a name as a title of courtesy. See **babu**; **Herr**; **san**; **Senhor**; **Señor**; and **Signor**.

Monseigneur *n., pl.* **Messeigneurs** [Fr. my lord.] *Roman Catholic Church.* The French equivalent of **Monsignor** (q.v.).

Monsignor or **monsignor** *n.* [It. my lord.] *Roman Catholic Church.* An honorific title conferred upon a priest or a prelate by the pope. Cf. **Monseigneur**.

mons pietatis *n., pl.* **montes pietatis** [L. **mons** mountain, heap, mass (1); **pietatis** of piety, affection, love (2): mass of affection.] A mistranslation of the Italian **monte di pietà** (q.v.) "loan of pity." *Some European Countries.* A public pawnbroker's office. These establishments are set up by government and authorized to lend small sums of money at reasonable rates with personal property given as security. Cf. **mont-de-piété**.

mons veneris *n.* [L. **mons** mountain, heap, mass (1); **veneris** of Venus, love (2): mountain of Venus.] The female mons pubis. **Pudendum** (q.v.).

montage *n., pl.* **montages** [Fr. set-up, assembly, cutting.] 1. *Art.* A collection of images cut from a variety of sources and grouped to form a single composition. 2. *Film-making.* The editing of a film or a series of rapid scene changes. 3. A disparate group of objects joined together. *A montage of ideas.*

montani semper liberi. [L. **montani** mountaineers (1); **semper** always (2); **liberi** free (3): Mountaineers (are) always free.] Mountaineers are always free. Motto of the State of West Virginia.

mont-de-piété *n., pl.* **monts-de-piété** [Fr. **mont** mountain, mass (1); **de** of (2); **piété** piety, affection, love (3): mass of affection.] A mistranslation of the Italian **monte di pietà** (q.v.) "loan of pity." A licensed pawn-broker's office or shop where small sums of money are loaned at reasonable rates. Cf. **mons pietatis**.

monte di pietà *n.* [It. **monte** mountain, mass (1); **di** of (2); **pietà** pity, mercy, piety (3): mountain of pity, a pawnbroking establishment.] A licensed pawn-shop. See **mons pietatis** and **mont-de-piété**.

monumentum aere perennius *n.* Horace (65–8 B.C.). *Odes* III,30,1. [L. **monumentum** monument (1); **aere** than bronze (3); **perennius** more enduring, lasting (2): monument more enduring than bronze.] A memorial more lasting than bronze. *The celebrated author's book has been described as a* monumentum aere perennius. For a fuller form of the quotation, see **exegi monumentum** etc. Cf. **ktema es aei**.

Mon verre n'est pas grand mais je bois dans mon verre. Alfred de Musset (1810–1857). *La Coup et les Lèvres.* [Fr. **mon** my (1); **verre** glass (2); **n'**... **pas** not (4); **est** is (3); **grand** big, large (5); **mais** but (6); **je** I (7); **bois** I drink (8); **dans** in (9); **mon** my (10); **verre** glass (11): My glass is not big, but I drink in my glass.] My glass is not that big, but at least I drink from my own glass; i.e., I am content with my lot and proud of my self-sufficiency.

mon vieux *n.* [Fr. **mon** my (1); **vieux** old man (2): my old man.] Old buddy! *Well, I understand, mon vieux!*

mora debitoris non debet esse creditori damnosa. [L. **mora** delay (1); **debitoris** of debtor (2); **non** not (4); **debet** ought, should (3); **esse** to be (5); **creditori** to creditor (7); **damnosa** injurious (6): Delay of a debtor should not be injurious to the creditor.] *Law.* Delay on the part of the debtor should not be damaging to the creditor. Thus, when goods, which are to be delivered, are destroyed through the fault of the purchaser or the seller, the party whose fault it is bears the loss. See **periculum rei** etc.

Moralia *pl. n.* [L. moral things.] *Moral Writings*, a collection of sixty miscellaneous essays by the Greek biographer Plutarch (46?–?120 A.D.).

mora reprobatur in lege. [L. **mora** delay, procrastination (1); **reprobatur** is condemned, disapproved of (2); **in** in, on (3); **lege** law (4): Delay is condemned in law.] Delay in legal proceeding is deemed reprehensible. See **infinitum in** etc.

moratorium *n., pl.* **moratoria** or **moratoriums** [L. a thing causing delay.] An authorized period of delay in the fulfillment of a legal obligation, such as the payment of debt. *The World Bank, taking into consideration the change of government, has given the country five years' moratorium on the liquidation of its debts.*

mordant *adj.* [Fr. biting, caustic, sharp, scathing.] 1. Biting. Sarcastic. *The speech was generously spiced with mordant criticisms and wit.* 2. Burning. Acute. Pungent. *The patient's facial expressions clearly show that he is experiencing mordant pains.* 3. Inclined to bite. *The house is securely guarded by four vicious and mordant dogs.*

more geometrico *adv.* [L. **more** (in) manner, way, custom (2); **geometrico** in geometric (1): in a geometric manner.] In geometric fashion. . . . *he assumes four continents distributed more geometrico over the surface of the earth* (Lesky 1966:789).

more majorum *adv.* [L. **more** in/by manner, way, custom (1); **majorum** of ancestors (2): by the custom of the ancestors.] After the manner of our/their ancestors. *The chief urged his people to solve the problem more majorum.*

mores *pl. n.* [L. customs, conduct, manners, morals, character, habits.] 1. The established customs of a society or specific group of people. 2. Morals. 3. Manners. *A great majority of the laws promulgated by the state reflect the mores of the community.*

mores antiqui *n., sing.* **mos antiquus** [L. **mores** customs, conduct, manners, morals, character, habits (2); **antiqui** ancient (1): ancient customs.] The ancient way of life. The customs of the ancestors. . . . *the contrast between the solid excellence of the early centuries, with their mos maiorum and mores antiqui, and the degeneration of later times, . . .* (Laistner 1966:92). Cf. **mos maiorum**.

more Socratico *adv.* [L. **more** in manner, way, custom (1); **Socratico** of Socrates, Socratic (2):) in the manner of Socrates.] In the Socratic manner. Following Socrates' style of teaching through questions and answers.

mors dicitur ultimum supplicium. [L. **mors** death (1); **dicitur** is said, called, named (2); **ultimum** last, extreme (3); **supplicium** punishment (4): Death is called the extreme punishment.] *Law.* The death penalty is the extreme form of punishment. See **ultimum supplicium esse** etc.

morgue *n., pl.* **morgues** [Fr. pride, arrogance, mortuary.] 1. A place where corpses are stored until claimed and buried. 2. A file of clippings in a newspaper or magazine office. —**La Morgue** A building in Paris used for the storage of corpses.

mors omnia solvit. [L. **mors** death (1); **omnia** all (things), everything (3); **solvit** dissolves, cancels, removes (2): Death dissolves all things.] Death cancels everything. Applicable to the death of one of the parties to a suit. See **in restitutionem** etc.

mors sola fatetur / quantula sint hominum corpuscula. Juvenal (c.60–117 A.D.). *Satires* X,172. [L. **mors** death (1); **sola** only, alone (2); **fatetur** proclaims (3); **quantula** how small, little, insignificant (4); **sint** are (5); **hominum** of human beings, people (7); **corpuscula** puny bodies (6): Death alone proclaims / how small are the puny bodies of humans.] Only death acknowledges how very insignificant are the little bodies of human beings.

mort civile *n*. [Fr. mort death (2); civile civil, civic (1): civil death.] Loss of civil rights. *French Law.* Applicable to the status of a person convicted for felony. In theory, it was abolished in 1854, but some aspects of it still remain. Thus, the felon's heirs can still inherit his extant property at the time of the conviction, but the state, by the exercise of its right of prerogative, may seize subsequently acquired property. Cf. droit de déshérence and mortuus civiliter.

mortis causa or causa mortis *adv*. [L. mortis of death (2); causa by reason (1): by reason of death.] Because of death. In contemplation of impending death. *Sam distributed his properties among his children causa mortis.* —*adj.* Made/done in contemplation or anticipation of death. *When Frank consulted his attorney a week ago, nobody suspected that he went to make a mortis causa will.* See causa mortis donatio.

mortis causa donatio See causa mortis donatio.

mortui non mordent. Erasmus (1466?–1536). *Adages* III,6. [L. mortui the dead (1); non not (2); mordent bite (3): The dead do not bite.] The dead cannot attack the living.

mortuum vadium See vadium mortuum.

mortuus civiliter or civiliter mortuus *adj., pl.* mortui civiliter or civiliter mortui [L. mortuus dead (2); civiliter civilly (1): civilly dead.] Deprived of civil rights. Cf. mort civile.

mortuus exitus non est exitus. [L. mortuus dead (1); exitus issue, event (2); non not (4); est is (3); exitus issue, event (5): A dead issue is not an issue.] A dead issue is no issue; i.e., a stillborn child is not an offspring. See non nasci etc.

mortuus sine prole *abbr.* M.S.P. *adj.* [L. mortuus dead (1); sine without (2); prole offspring (3): dead without offspring.] Died without children. Usually used in family trees or genealogical tables. See defunctus sine prole and sine prole.

moshav *n., pl.* moshavim [Heb. mōsāb dwelling.] A group of small, individual farms in a collective Israeli settlement.

mos maiorum or mos majorum *n., pl.* mores maiorum or mores majorum [L. mos custom (1); maiorum of ancestors (2): custom of the ancestors.] Ancestral custom. *These innovations in Roman private life naturally drew protests from those who had a meticulous regard for the mos maiorum* (Cary 1970:264). Cf. mores antiqui.

mos retinendus est fidelissimae vetustatis. [L. mos custom (1); retinendus to be retained (5); est is (4); fidelissimae of truest, most reliable (2); vetustatis (of) antiquity (3): A custom of the most reliable antiquity is to be retained.] A custom of authentic antiquity must be retained.

mot *n., pl.* mots [Fr. word, saying.] A witty saying. A joke. *Her speeches are usually pregnant with mots.* Cf. bon mot.

mot à mot *abbr.* m. à m. *adj./adv.* [Fr. mot word, saying (1); à to, toward, in, by, with, until (2); mot word, saying (3): word by word.] Word for word. Cf. verbatim.

motif *n., pl.* motifs [Fr. purpose, motive, pattern, design.] 1. A recurring theme or idea. A central theme. *Television networks turned the question of Israel's military censorship into one of the central motifs of their early war coverage* (*Newsweek Int.* Jan 31, 1983:4). Cf. leitmotiv. 2. A design or color, i.e., in textile designing or interior decoration. 3. A motivating or prompting stimulus. *This accumulated anger and resentment against colonial rule was to impel the young Adamafio to the nationalist cause and to be a dominant . . . motif of his early political career* (Dr. M. Anafu in *West Africa* 1983).

motto *n., pl.* mottos [It. word.] A word, phrase, or sentence with which a family, organization, or institution is associated and identified, often in conjunction with a seal or emblem.

motu proprio or proprio motu *adv.* [L. motu by motion, impulse (2); proprio by one's own (1): by one's own impulse/motion.] Of one's own accord. *Adams submitted himself to the jurisdiction of the court motu proprio.* —*n.* A rescript which, on his own initiative and of his own accord, the Pope issues. See ex mero motu.

Moyen Âge *n.* [Fr. moyen middle (1); âge age, period (2): middle age.] The Middle Ages. The Medieval period.

M.S. *abbr.* for memoriae sacrum (q.v.).

M.S.C. or m.s.c. *abbr.* for mandatum sine clausula (q.v.).

Muchos pocos hacen un mucho. Miguel de Cervantes (1547–1616). *Don Quixote* II,7. [Sp. muchos many (1); pocos small things (2); hacen make (3); un a (4); mucho large thing (5): Many small things make a large thing.] Many a mickle makes a muckle.

Mudéjar *n., pl.* Mudéjares [Sp.] A Muslim who legally stayed in Spain after the Christian reconquest. —*adj.* Art. Pertaining to a style of 13th-16th Spanish architecture with both Gothic and Moorish elements.

muezzin or muazzin or mueddin *n., pl.* muezzins or muazzins or mueddins [Ar. proclaimer.] A Muslim public crier who stands at the minaret and summons Muslims for prayers. *Every day at dawn Musa looks forward to the sonorous voice of the muezzin, summoning the faithful for prayer at the mosque.*

mufti *n., pl.* muftis [Ar. muftī legal interpreter.] *Islam.* One who interprets Muslim law or shari'a (q.v.).

muliebria *pl. n.* [L. womanly things.] Female genitals. Cf. pudendum.

mullah or mulla or mollah *n., pl.* mullahs or mullas or mollahs [Urdu mullā, Turk. molla from Arab. mawlā master.] A learned scholar or teacher of Islamic law and theology. . . . *a new group of Iranian and Lebanese mullahs have tried to introduce fundamentalist and revolutionary doctrines to corrupt Nigerian Islamic culture . . .* (*West Africa* 1985).

multa conceduntur per obliquum, quae non conceduntur de directo. [L. **multa** many (things) (1); **conceduntur** are allowed, granted (2); **per** through, by (3); **obliquum** the oblique, slanting (4); **quae** which (5); **non** not (6); **conceduntur** are allowed, granted (7); **de** of, from, about, for (8); **directo** direct (9): Many things are allowed through the oblique which are not allowed from the direct.] Many things which are not directly permissible are permissible indirectly. Cf. **nemo potest facere per obliquum** etc.

multa non vetat lex, quae tamen tacite damnavit. [L. **multa** many (things) (4); **non** not (2); **vetat** forbids (3); **lex** law (1); **quae** which (5); **tamen** nevertheless, however (6); **tacite** tacitly, implicitly (8); **damnavit** it has condemned (7): The law does not forbid many things which, however, it has condemned tacitly.] *Law.* There are many offenses which the law does not forbid explicitly, though it implicitly condemns them. Cf. **est aliquid quod** etc. and **non omne quod** etc.

multigravida *n., pl.* **multigravidas** or **multigravidae** [Neo-L. from **mult(us)** much, many (2); **gravida** heavy, big with child (1): heavy with child many (times).] A woman who has been pregnant a number of times. See **gravida**.

multipara *n., pl.* **multiparas** or **multiparae** [Neo-L. from **mult(us)** much, many (2); **pario** give birth (1): giving birth many times.] A woman who has given birth to children a number of times. Cf. **nullipara**; **primipara**; **secundipara**; **sextipara**; **tripara**; and **unipara**.

multiplicata transgressione, crescat poenae inflictio. [L. **multiplicata** (with) having been increased (2); **transgressione** with transgression (1); **crescat** should increase (5); **poenae** of punishment, penalty (4); **inflictio** infliction (3): With transgression having been increased, infliction of punishment should increase.] *Law.* As transgression increases, the infliction of punishment should increase. See **crescente malitia** etc.; **ex frequenti** etc.; and **transgressione multiplicata** etc. Cf. **poenae potius** etc.

multo tutius est stare in subjectione quam in praelatura. Thomas à Kempis (1380–1471). *Imitatio Christi* I,9,1. [L. **multo** much (2); **tutius** safer (3); **est** it is (1); **stare** to stand (4); **in** in, on (5); **subjectione** subjection (6); **quam** than (7); **in** in, on (8); **praelatura** authority (9): It is much safer to stand in subjection than in authority.] It is much safer to be a subject than a ruler.

multum in parvo [L. **multum** much (1); **in** in, on (2); **parvo** little (thing) (3): much in a little thing.] Much in little. Something small in size but large in importance.

Mus.B. *abbr.* for **Musicae Baccalaureus** (q.v.).

Mus.Bac. *abbr.* for **Musicae Baccalaureus** (q.v.).

Mus.D. *abbr.* for **Musicae Doctor** (q.v.).

Mus.Doc. *abbr.* for **Musicae Doctor** (q.v.).

Musicae Baccalaureus *abbr.* **M.B.** or **Mus.B.** or **Mus.Bac.** *n.* [L. **musicae** of music (2); **baccalaureus** bachelor (1): Bachelor of Music.] An undergraduate degree in music.

Musicae Doctor *abbr.* **Mus.D.** or **Mus.Doc.** *n.* [L. **musicae** of music (2); **doctor** teacher (1): teacher of music.] Doctor of Music. The highest academic degree for completion of a graduate curriculum in music.

Musicae Magister *abbr.* **Mus.M.** *n.* [L. **musicae** of music (2); **magister** master (1): Master of Music.] An academic degree for completion of a pre-doctoral graduate curriculum in music.

Muslim or **Moslem** *n.* [Ar. one who surrenders.] 1. A believer in **Islam** (q.v.). —*adj.* Pertaining to Islam.

musique concrète *n.* [Fr. **musique** music (2); **concrète** solid, concrete (1): concrete music.] *Music.* A form of electronic music in which instrumental and natural sounds are combined and transformed during the recording process.

Mus.M. *abbr.* for **Musicae Magister** (q.v.).

muta persona or **persona muta** *n., pl.* **mutae personae** or **personae mutae** [L. **muta** silent, speechless (1); **persona** person, character (2): silent or speechless character.] *Theater.* A mute character. A character who has no speaking parts. *It enables the opening scene to be staged with only two actors (Bia being a muta persona)* . . . (Lesky 1966:255).

mutatis mutandis *abbr.* **M.M.** or **m.m.** *adv.* [L. **mutatis** (with) having been changed (2); **mutandis** with things that must be changed (1): with the things that must be changed having been changed.] The necessary changes being made. After consideration of the respective differences. *The divorce laws of that country may, mutatis mutandis, apply to this country.* Cf. **exceptis excipiendis**.

mutato nomine *adv.* Horace (65–8 B.C.). *Satires* I,1,69. [L. **mutato** with changed (1); **nomine** (with) name (2): with name changed.] Under a different name.

myopia *n., pl.* **myopias** [Late-Gk. from **mu(ō)** shut, blink (1); **ōpē** sight (2): blinked sight.] 1. Shortsightedness. Nearsightedness. 2. Lack of foresight, vision or discernment.

mysophilia *n.* [Neo-Gk. from Gk. **muso(s)** uncleanness, defilement (2); **philia** fondness (1): fondness of uncleanness or defilement.] Extraordinary fondness of filth or dirt.

mysophobia *n.* [Neo-Gk. from Gk. **muso(s)** uncleanness, defilement (2); **phob(os)** fear (1): fear of uncleanness or defilement.] Extraordinary fear or dislike of filth or dirt.

mysterium tremendum *n., pl.* **mysteria tremenda** [L. **mysterium** mystery (2); **tremendum** fearful, dreadful (1): dreadful mystery.] An overpowering mystery. Used especially in reference to human contemplation of divinity and the mystery of life.

mystique *n., pl.* **mystiques** [Fr. mystic system, science, or doctrine.] A complex of mystical or inexplicable beliefs associated with a person, idea, institution, pursuit, or activity, and enhancing its importance, significance, or value. . . . *Alice Lakwena . . . has also created a mystique around herself since she emerged from obscurity in northern Uganda to lead her army of believers, mostly peasants* (*The Guardian* 1987).

mythomania *n.* [Neo-Gk. from Gk. **mutho(s)** tale, story (2); **mania** fondness, enthusiasm (1): enthusiasm for tales or stories.] Abnormal inclination to tell lies or indulge in exaggeration.

mythos *n., pl.* **mythoi** [Gk. **muthos** story, myth.] A traditional story or the collection of traditional stories shared by a particular society or community.

N

n.a. *abbr.* for **non allocatur** (q.v.).

nabi *n., pl.* **nabis** [Heb. **nābī** prophet.] 1. *Theology.* A Hebrew prophet, i.e., someone who speaks to the people on behalf of God. 2. *Art.* A follower of Paul Gauguin (1848–1903) and his style of impressionism.

nabob *n.* [Hindi **nabāb.**] 1. An Indian governor in the period of the Mogul Empire. 2. An individual of great wealth and importance.

Nachlass *n., pl.* **Nachlasse** or **Nachlässe** [Ger. **nach** after (2); **lass(en)** left (1): left after.] The unpublished work of a deceased writer.

nada *n.* [Sp. nothing.] Nothing.

nada *n.* [Skt. **nāda** sound.] *Hinduism.* The primitive sound from which all other sound and creation itself is derived.

nadir *abbr.* **nad.** *n., pl.* **nadirs** [Ar. **nazīr** opposite to.] 1. *Astronomy.* The point of the heavens which is opposite the zenith and thus directly beneath an observer. 2. The lowest point or the bottom. *Sarah was at the nadir of her hope.*

naïf *masc. n.* [Fr. an innocent, gullible male.] An innocent. An easily-deceived male. *Rosco is a naïf who trusts everyone he meets on sight.*

naïve or **naive** *fem. adj.* (but used as masc. or fem. in English) [Fr. innocent, gullible.] Simple. Guileless. Innocent. Unsuspecting. **Ingénue** (q.v.). *The naïve rustic who has just arrived at the city is likely to fall into the trap of urban tricksters.*

naïveté or **naiveté** *n., pl.* **naïvetés** or **naivetés** [Fr. innocence, gullibility.] Simplicity. Innocence. Credulousness. *And there is the naiveté of many well-meaning parents who, during the drug scare of recent years, have pushed alcohol as a safer alternative to other substances* (*Newsweek Int.* Jan. 8, 1979:46).

nam homo proponit, sed Deus disponit. Thomas à Kempis (1380–1471). *Imitatio Christi* I,19,2. [L. **nam** for (1); **homo** person, human being (2); **proponit** proposes, conceives (3); **sed** but (4); **Deus** God (5); **disponit** disposes, arranges (6): For a human being proposes, but God disposes.] Humanity suggests but God arranges. Man proposes, God disposes.

nam risu inepto res ineptior nulla est. Catullus (87–54 B.C.). *Carmina* XXXIX. [L. **nam** for (1); **risu** laughter (7); **inepto** than silly, foolish (6); **res** matter, thing, property, business, affair (4); **ineptior** more foolish, sillier (5); **nulla** no (3); **est** there is (2): For there is nothing sillier than silly laughter.] For there is nothing sillier than a silly joke.

nam tua res agitur, paries cum proximus ardet. Horace (65–8 B.C.). *Epistles* I,18,84. [L. **nam** for (1); **tua** your (2); **res** affair, matter (3); **agitur** is in question, is at stake (4); **paries** wall (7); **cum** when (5); **proximus** next (6); **ardet** is on fire (8): For your affair is at stake, when the next wall is on fire.] When the wall of your immediate neighbor is on fire, your own interest is at stake. Cf. **quod omnes** etc.

N.A.N. *abbr.* for **nisi aliter notetur** (q.v.).

narcoanalysis *n.* [Neo-Gk. from Gk. **nark(ē)** numbness (2); **analysis** solution of a problem (1): solution of a problem through numbness.] *Psychotherapy.* A process of interrogation whereby a person is injected with a chemical substance and while under sedation made to remember repressed experiences.

narcomania *n.* [Neo-Gk. from Gk. **nark(ē)** numbness (2); **mania** fondness, enthusiasm (1): fondness or enthusiasm for numbness.] *Psychology.* Abnormal desire for hard drugs or narcotics.

narcosis *n., pl.* **narcoses** [Gk. **narkōsis** benumbing.] Stupor (q.v.) or unconsciousness induced by drugs.

natale solum *n.* [L. **natale** natal, birth (1); **solum** soil, land (2): native soil.] Birth land.

nati et nascituri *pl. n.* [L. **nati** born (1); **et** and (2); **nascituri** about to be born (3): born and about to be born.] Children, both those already born and those to be born. *Law.* Applicable to heirs.

natura abhorret ab vacuo. [L. **natura** nature (1); **abhorret** shrinks back, differs (2); **ab** from (3); **vacuo**

(something) empty, free, vacant (4): Nature shrinks back from something empty.] Nature abhors a vacuum. Cf. **natura non facit vacuum**; and **natura vacuum abhorret** etc.

natura appetit perfectum; ita et lex. [L. **natura** nature (1); **appetit** desires, longs for (2); **perfectum** perfect, excellent (thing) (3); **ita** so (4); **et** and, also (5); **lex** law (6): Nature desires the perfect thing; so also the law.] *Law*. Nature desires perfection; so also does the law.

naturae enim non imperatur nisi parendo. Francis Bacon (1561–1626). *Novum Organon* I,129. [L. **naturae** (to) nature (4); **enim** for (1); **non** not (2); **imperatur** there is commanding, ordering (3); **nisi** unless, except (5); **parendo** by obeying (6): For there is no commanding nature unless by obeying.] We can only command nature by obeying her.

naturale est quidlibet dissolvi eo modo quo ligatur. [L. **naturale** natural (2); **est** it is (1); **quidlibet** anything (3); **dissolvi** to be dissolved (4); **eo** in that (5); **modo** (in) way (6); **quo** in which (7); **ligatur** it is bound (8): It is natural (that) anything be dissolved in that way in which it is bound.] *Law*. Naturally, anything can be dissolved in the same way in which it was bound; e.g., a record is nullified by a record, a deed by a deed, a decree by a decree, an act by an act, etc. See **eodem modo quo quid constituitur, dissolvitur**.

naturali jure *adv*. [L. **naturali** by natural (1); **jure** (by) right, law (2): by natural law.] *Law*. By the law of nature. *Offenses such as theft and murder are forbidden naturali jure*.

naturalis et interna *adj*. [L. **naturalis** natural (1); **et** and (2); **interna** internal, inward (3): natural and internal.] Cf. **civilis et politica**.

natura naturans *n*. [L. **natura** nature (2); **naturans** creating (1): creating nature.] *Philosophy*. Nature as a creative or procreative force. Cf. **natura naturata**.

natura naturata *n*. [L. **natura** nature (2); **naturata** created (1): created nature.] *Philosophy*. Nature as the result of creation. Cf. **natura naturans**.

natura non facit saltum; ita nec lex. [L. **natura** nature (1); **non** not (2); **facit** makes (3); **saltum** leap (4); **ita** so (5); **nec** and not, also not (6); **lex** law (7): Nature does not make a leap; so also does not the law.] *Law*. Just as nature does not leap, so also doesn't the law. Like nature, the law progresses gradually. See **sicut natura** etc.

natura non facit vacuum, nec lex supervacuum. [L. **natura** nature (1); **non** not (2); **facit** makes, does (3); **vacuum** empty space, vacuum (4); **nec** and not, also not (6); **lex** law (5); **supervacuum** unnecessary, superfluous (7): Nature does not make a vacuum; the law also does not make the superfluous.] *Law*. Just as nature abhors a vacuum, so does the law abhor the superfluous.

natura vacuum abhorret. François Rabelais (c.1494–c.1553). *Gargantua* I,5. [L. **natura** nature (1); **vacuum** vacuum (3); **abhorret** abhors, hates (2): Nature abhors a vacuum.] Nature does not like a vacuum. The tendency of nature is to fill empty space. Cf. **natura abhorret ab vacuo**; and **natura non facit vacuum** etc.

nature morte *n., pl.* **natures mortes** [Fr. **nature** nature (2); **morte** dead (1): dead nature.] *Art*. A still life composition.

Naturphilosophie *n*. [Ger. **Natur** nature (1); **Philosophie** philosophy (2): nature philosophy.] *Philosophy*. Natural philosophy. A philosophical system proposed by Friedrich Wilhelm Schelling (1775–1854) in which absolute natural laws are thought to determine and guide all other aspects of existence.

nausea *n., pl.* **nauseas** [L. from Gk. **nausiē** sea-sickness.] 1. A feeling of discomfort which often results in vomiting. 2. Extreme disgust. Loathing. *The desire for change of government is generally prompted by nausea with prevailing socioeconomic and political conditions*.

Nausée *n*. [Fr. nausea.] *Nausea*, an existentialist novel (1938) by Jean-Paul Sartre (1905–1980).

nautica pecunia *n*. [L. **nautica** naval, nautical (1); **pecunia** money (2): naval money.] A loan given to a shipowner to be repaid only after the ship has successfully reached its destination. The interest on the loan is accordingly extraordinary. Cf. **nauticum faenus** and **respondentia**.

nauticum faenus or **nauticum fenus** *n*. [L. **nauticum** naval, nautical (1); **faenus** interest, usury (2): naval interest.] Interest paid on **nautica pecunia** (q.v.). It corresponds in modern times to interest on contracts of **respondentia** (q.v.) or bottomry.

navette *n*. [Fr. shuttle.] Sending bills back and forth between two legislative houses until a compromise is reached.

N.B. or **n.b.** *abbr*. for 1. **nota bene** (q.v.). 2. **nulla bona** (q.v.).

N.C.D. *abbr*. for **nemine contradicente** (q.v.).

nec curia deficeret in justitia exhibenda. [L. **nec** and not, nor (1); **curia** court (2); **deficeret** should fail, fall short, be wanting (3); **in** in, on (4); **justitia** justice (5); **exhibenda** to be shown, delivered (6): And the court should not fail in justice to be delivered.] *Law*. And the court should not fail to deliver/show justice. See **justitia nemini** etc.

necessitas culpabilis *n*. [L. **necessitas** compulsion, urgency, necessity (2); **culpabilis** blameworthy, culpable (1): culpable compulsion.] *Law*. A necessity which, though excusing an act done under its influence, does not completely exonerate the doer. Cf. **necessitas quod** etc.

necessitas dat legem, non ipsa accipit. Publilius Syrus (c.85–43 B.C.). *Sententiae* 444. [L. **necessitas**

compulsion, urgency, necessity (1); **dat** gives (2); **legem** law (3); **non** not (6); **ipsa** itself (4); **accipit** receives (5): Compulsion gives the law; itself receives it not.] *Law.* Necessity gives the law, but does not itself receive it. See **necessitas quod** etc.

necessitas est lex temporis et loci. [L. **necessitas** compulsion, urgency, necessity (1); **est** is (2); **lex** law (3); **temporis** of time (4); **et** and (5); **loci** of place (6): Compulsion is the law of time and place.] *Law.* Necessity is based upon the limitations of time and location. See **in casu extremae** etc.

necessitas excusat aut extenuat delictum in capitalibus, quod non operatur idem in civilibus. [L. **necessitas** compulsion, urgency, necessity (1); **excusat** excuses (2); **aut** or (3); **extenuat** diminishes, extenuates (4); **delictum** wrong, offense (5); **in** in, on (6); **capitalibus** capital (cases) (7); **quod** which (8); **non** not (10); **operatur** works (9); **idem** the same (11); **in** in, on (12); **civilibus** civil (cases) (13): Compulsion excuses or diminishes an offense in capital cases, which does not work the same in civil cases.] *Law.* A necessity which excuses or extenuates an offense in a capital case does not have the same effect in a civil case.

necessitas facit licitum quod alias non est licitum. [L. **necessitas** compulsion, urgency, necessity (1); **facit** makes (2); **licitum** lawful, permissible (3); **quod** (that) which, what (4); **alias** at other times (5); **non** not (7); **est** is (6); **licitum** lawful, permissible (8): Compulsion makes lawful that which at other times is not lawful.] *Law.* Necessity confers legality on what otherwise is an illegality. See **necessitas quod** etc.

necessitas inducit privilegium quoad jura privata. [L. **necessitas** compulsion, urgency, necessity (1); **inducit** brings, introduces (2); **privilegium** privilege (3); **quoad** as far as, to the extent (4); **jura** rights, laws (6); **privata** private (5): Compulsion introduces a privilege as far as private rights.] *Law.* Necessity confers a privilege in the case of private rights. An act which is usually criminal may be excused by necessity, if it was done for self-preservation, if the person who committed the act acted involuntarily or in obedience, or if the act was the result of an act of God. See **necessitas quod** etc.

necessitas non habet legem. [L. **necessitas** compulsion, urgency, necessity (1); **non** not (2); **habet** has, holds, regards (3); **legem** law (4): Compulsion does not have law.] *Law.* Necessity has no law. See **necessitas quod** etc.

necessitas omnem legem frangit. [L. **necessitas** compulsion, urgency, necessity (1); **omnem** all, every (3); **legem** law (4); **frangit** breaks (2): Compulsion breaks every law.] *Law.* Any law can be broken by necessity. See **necessitas quod** etc.

necessitas publica major est quam privata. [L. **necessitas** compulsion, urgency, necessity (2); **publica** public (1); **major** greater (4); **est** is (3); **quam** than (5); **privata** private (6): Public compulsion is greater than private necessity.] *Law.* Public necessity enjoys precedence over private necessity. See **in casu extremae** etc.

necessitas quod cogit, defendit. [L. **necessitas** compulsion, urgency, necessity (1); **quod** (that) which, what (3); **cogit** it compels (4); **defendit** defends, justifies (2): Compulsion defends that which it compels.] *Law.* Necessity justifies what it compels. See **illud quod alias** etc.; **necessitas dat legem**; **necessitas facit** etc.; **necessitas inducit** etc.; **necessitas non** etc.; **necessitas omnem** etc.; **necessitas sub lege** etc.; **necessitas vincit** etc.; **nihil magis** etc.; **quae propter necessitatem** etc.; **quod alias non fuit** etc.; **quodcunque aliquis** etc.; **quod est necessarium** etc.; **quod necessarium** etc.; and **quod necessitas** etc.

necessitas sub lege non continetur quia quod alias non est licitum necessitas facit licitum. [L. **necessitas** compulsion, urgency, necessity (1); **sub** under (4); **lege** law (5); **non** not (2); **continetur** is restrained (3); **quia** because (6); **quod** (that) which, what (10); **alias** at other times (11); **non** not (13); **est** is (12); **licitum** lawful (14); **necessitas** necessity (7); **facit** makes (8); **licitum** lawful (9): Compulsion is not restrained under the law, because necessity makes lawful that which at other times is not lawful.] *Law.* Necessity is not restrained by the law, because it confers legality on what otherwise is an illegality. See **necessitas quod** etc.

necessitas vincit legem. [L. **necessitas** compulsion, urgency, necessity (1); **vincit** conquers, overcomes, prevails over (2); **legem** law (3): Compulsion conquers the law.] *Law.* Necessity prevails over (or overrules) the law. See **necessitas quod** etc.

necessitas vincit legem; legum vincula irridet. [L. **necessitas** compulsion, urgency, necessity (1); **vincit** conquers, overcomes, prevails over (2); **legem** law (3); **legum** of laws (6); **vincula** fetters, chains, bonds (5); **irridet** it ridicules, laughs at (4): Compulsion conquers law; it ridicules the chains of law.] *Law.* Necessity overcomes the law and laughs at its fetters. See **necessitas quod** etc.

necrophilia *n., pl.* **necrophilias** [Neo-Gk. from Gk. **nekro(s)** corpse, dead (person) (2); **philia** fondness (1): fondness for corpses.] Love for, or tendency to be stimulated by, corpses, usually manifested by sexual intercourse with a dead body.

necrophobia *n.* [Neo-Gk. from Gk. **nekro(s)** corpse, dead (person) (2); **phob(os)** fear (1): fear of dead person.] *Psychology.* Extraordinary or pathological fear of death or corpses.

necropolis *n., pl.* **necropoleis** or **necropoles** or **necropolises** [Gk. **nekro(s)** corpse, dead (person) (1); **polis** city (2): corpse city, city of the dead.] A cemetery, especially a large, elaborate cemetery located in an ancient town. A prehistoric cemetery.

necrosis *n., pl.* **necroses** [Gk. **nekrōsis** state of death.] *Medicine.* A process or condition in which organic material dies or decays as a result of disease or trauma.

nec scire fas est omnia. Horace (65–8 B.C.). *Odes* IV,4,22. [L. **nec** not (1); **scire** to know (4); **fas** permitted (3); **est** it is, has been (2); **omnia** all things, everything (5): It is not permitted to know all things.] It is not possible to know everything.

nectar *n., pl.* **nectars** [Gk. **nektar**.] 1. *Greek and Roman Mythology.* The drink of the gods. 2. A delicious drink. 3. A sweet liquid secreted by plants, collected by bees, and used for making honey. 4. Fruit drinks which combine juice and pureed fruit pulp.

nec veniam, effuso sanguine, casus habet. [L. **nec** nor (1); **veniam** pardon, forgiveness (4); **effuso** (with) having been shed (6); **sanguine** with blood (5); **casus** occasion, event, accident, case (2); **habet** has, holds, regards (3): Nor does the case have pardon, with blood having been shed.] *Law.* When blood is shed, it is an unpardonable case.

nec vi nec clam nec precario *adv.* [L. **nec** neither (1); **vi** by force (2); **nec** nor (3); **clam** secretly (4); **nec** nor (5); **precario** by right granted (6): neither by force nor secretly nor by right granted.] *Law.* Neither forcefully nor secretly nor by permission of owner (or bailer). Applicable in Roman law, inter alia, to conditions requisite for the validity of prescription (or usucapio): Cf. **vi clam** etc.

née or **nee** *adj.* [Fr. born.] 1. Born into a family with the surname. Whose maiden name is. *Mrs. John Peters, née Williams.* 2. Originally or previously called. a) Used for identifying a girl or woman who is using an assumed name. *Singer Mary Fay née Dorothy Simpson.* b) Used for identifying a group, team or organization whose original name has changed. *University of Maiduguri née North East College of Arts and Sciences.* c) Used for identifying a place whose original name has been changed. *Burkina Faso née Upper Volta.*

ne exeat *n.* [L. **ne** not (2); **exeat** let him/her leave, go out (1): Let him/her not leave.] *Law.* A writ issued to restrain a person from leaving the country or a court's jurisdiction, pending a legal action.

ne exeat regno *n.* [L. **ne** not (2); **exeat** let him/her go out of, leave (1); **regno** kingdom (3): Let him/her not leave the kingdom.] *Law.* A writ issued to restrain a person from leaving a kingdom.

ne exeat republica *n.* [L. **ne** not (2); **exeat** let him/her leave, go out of (1); **re publica** the public affair, the state (3): Let him/her not leave the state.] *Law.* A writ issued in civil cases to restrain a person from leaving a state, particularly in the U.S.A., pending a legal action.

nefasti dies [L. **nefasti** unlawful, irreligious, unlucky (1); **dies** days (2): unlucky days.] Days upon which business cannot be conducted. Business holidays.

ne fronte crede [L. **ne** not (1); **fronti** the face (3); **crede** believe, trust (2): Do not trust the face.] Do not rely on appearances.

negatio conclusionis est error in lege. [L. **negatio** denial, negation (1); **conclusionis** of conclusion (2); **est** is (3); **error** error (4); **in** in, on (5); **lege** law (6): Denial of a conclusion is an error in law.] *Law.* Denying a conclusion is a mistake in the law.

negatio duplex est affirmatio. [L. **negatio** denial, negation (2); **duplex** double, twofold (1); **est** is (3); **affirmatio** affirmation (4): A double negation is an affirmation.] A double negative is an affirmative.

negligentia *n.* [L. carelessness, neglect.] *Civil Law.* A significant lack of proper care or forethought, resulting in **culpa** (q.v.) or fault. Cf. **crassa negligentia** and **nimia negligentia**.

negligentia semper habet infortunium comitem. [L. **negligentia** carelessness, neglect (1); **semper** always (2); **habet** has, holds, regards (3); **infortunium** misfortune (4); **comitem** (as a) companion (5): Carelessness always has misfortune as a companion.] Negligence is always accompanied by misfortune.

negotiorum gestio *n.* [L. **negotiorum** of businesses, affairs (2); **gestio** management, performance (1): management of businesses.] *Civil Law.* Management of, or interference with, another's business, particularly without permission. *Must the act of the person who meddled with the property be regarded as an assertion of dominion, however innocent, or can it be regarded as a sort of negotiorum gestio, a means of preserving the property of the true owner?* (Hanbury 1962:458). See **negotiorum gestor.**

negotiorum gestor *n.* [L. **negotiorum** of businesses, affairs (2); **gestor** manager, conductor (1): manager or conductor of businesses.] *Civil Law.* A person who manages, or interferes with, another's business, particularly in the latter's absence, without permission. See **negotiorum gestio.**

négritude *n.* [Fr. Negro life or culture, Negro cultural and spiritual values.] A movement or philosophy among Black Africans, which lays emphasis on pride in the indigenous Negro culture, African personality and identity, the dignity and beauty of the Black race and color, etc., and generally reacts against the assumed superiority of Caucasian culture. One of the leading exponents of the movement is poet and literary theorist Leopold Senghor (1906–), the first President of Senegal.

negrophobia *n.* [Sp. **negro** black (person) (2); Gk. **phob(os)** fear (1): fear of a black (person).] *Psychology.* Intense fear or dislike of black people. *The policies of apartheid South Africa were prompted by negrophobia.*

N.E.I. or **n.e.i.** *abbr.* for **non est inventus** (q.v.).

ne judex ultra petita partium. [L. **ne** let not (1); **judex** judge (2); **ultra** more than, beyond, above (3); **petita** demands, claims (4); **partium** of parties (5): Let not a judge (give) more than the demands of the parties.] *Law.* A judge should not award more than what a plaintiff claims. See **judex non reddit** etc.

nem. con. *abbr.* for **nemine contradicente** (q.v.).

nem. diss. *abbr.* for **nemine dissentiente** (q.v.).

nemesis *n., pl.* **nemeses** [Gk. retribution, righteous anger prompted by injustice, goddess of divine retribution.] 1. Retributive justice. Well deserved punishment for a wrong done. *Nemesis caught up with the rogue the day he was apprehended.* 2. A person who inflicts retribution. A person who punishes or avenges inevitably or relentlessly. 3. A formidable opponent who usually emerges victorious. a) *America's nemesis was, for once, on the receiving end when American naval helicopters attacked an Iranian vessel . . .* (*The Guardian* 1987). b) *China's old nemesis, the Soviet Union* (*Newsweek Int.* Jan. 19, 1981:24). 4. A deed, an act, or a consequence of retributive justice. *Perhaps their confidence is . . . a type of hubris that will now lead to nemesis* (*West Africa* 1981). 5. An unavoidable consequence or result. *His downfall is the nemesis of his own recklessness.*

nemine contradicente *abbr.* **N.C.D.** or **nem. con.** *adv.* [L. **nemine** with no one (1); **contradicente** (with) contradicting, gainsaying (2): with no one contradicting.] No one dissenting or disagreeing. *The proposals were accepted, nemine contradicente.* Cf. **dissentiente**.

nemine dissentiente *abbr.* **nem. diss.** *adv.* [L. **nemine** with no one (1); **dissentiente** (with) dissenting, disagreeing (2): With no one dissenting/disagreeing.] No one dissenting. Without dissent. *The minister had done his homework so thoroughly that his bill was passed nemine dissentiente.* Cf. **dissentiente**.

neminem laedit qui jure suo utitur. [L. **neminem** no one, nobody (6); **laedit** hurts, injures (5); **qui** (one) who (1); **jure** right, law (4); **suo** one's own (3); **utitur** uses, enjoys (2): One who enjoys one's own right hurts no one.] *Law.* One who insists on one's own rights hurts no one else.

neminem oportet esse sapientiorem legibus. [L. **neminem** that no one (2); **oportet** it is necessary, proper (1); **esse** to be (3); **sapientiorem** wiser (4); **legibus** than laws (5): It is necessary that no one should be wiser than the laws.] *Law.* No one should be wiser than the laws. No one should outsmart the law.

nemo admirandus ordinandus est. [L. **nemo** no one, nobody (1); **admirandus** to be admired, wondered at (2); **ordinandus** to be ordained (4); **est** is, has been (3)' No one to be wondered at is to be ordained.] 1. *Christianity.* Someone who attracts attention and notice, for example, for physical deformity, must not be ordained a priest. 2. Individuals who will attract unnecessary attention to themselves should not be placed in the public eye.

nemo agit in seipsum. [L. **nemo** no one, nobody (1); **agit** acts (2); **in** into, to, against, for (3); **seipsum** himself/herself (4): No one acts against himself/herself.] A person cannot be a plaintiff and a defendant at the same time.

nemo alieno nomine lege agere potest. [L. **nemo** no one, nobody (1); **alieno** (in) of another (6); **nomine** in name (5); **lege** by/in law (4); **agere** to act, sue (3); **potest** can, is able (2): No one can act by law in the name of another.] *Law.* No one can bring a suit in the name of another person.

nemo aliquam partem recte intelligere potest antequam totum iterum atque iterum perlegerit. [L. **nemo** no one, nobody (1); **aliquam** any, some (5); **partem** part (6); **recte** properly, correctly (4); **intelligere** to understand, comprehend (3); **potest** can, is able (2); **antequam** until, before (7); **totum** whole, entire (9); **iterum** again (10); **atque** and (11); **iterum** again (12); **perlegerit** he/she has read thoroughly, perused (8): No one is able to understand correctly any part before he/she has read thoroughly the whole again and again.] No one can comprehend correctly part of a document until he/she has thoroughly read the whole of it several times. See the next maxim.

nemo aliquam partem recte intelligere potest antequam totum perlegit. [L. **nemo** no one, nobody (1); **aliquam** some, any (4); **partem** part (5); **recte** correctly, properly (6); **intelligere** to understand (3); **potest** can, is able (2); **antequam** until, before (7); **totum** whole (9); **perlegit** he/she has read thoroughly, perused (8): No one can comprehend correctly any part before he/she has read the whole.] No one can correctly understand part of a document until he/she has read the entire document thoroughly. See the preceding maxim.

nemo allegans suam turpitudinem audiendus est. [L. **nemo** no one, nobody (1); **allegans** alleging (2); **suam** his/her, one's own (3); **turpitudinem** baseness, turpitude (4); **audiendus** to be heard (6); **est** is (5): No one alleging his/her own turpitude is to be heard.] *Law.* No one who alleges his/her own baseness should be heard. No self-incriminating testimony should be heard. See **ex turpi causa** etc.

nemo bis punitur pro eodem delicto. [L. **nemo** no one, nobody (1); **bis** twice (3); **punitur** is punished (2); **pro** for (4); **eodem** the same (5); **delicto** offense, transgression (6): No one is punished twice for the same transgression.] *Law.* A person cannot be punished twice for the same offense. See **infinitum in** etc.

nemo cogitationis poenam patitur. See **cogitationis poenam nemo patitur**.

nemo cogitur rem suam vendere, etiam justo pretio. [L. **nemo** no one, nobody (1); **cogitur** is compelled, forced (2); **rem** matter, thing, property, business, affair (5); **suam** his/her, one's own (4); **vendere** to sell (3); **etiam** even (6); **justo** for just, reasonable, fair (7); **pretio** (for) price (8): No one is forced to sell his/her own property, even for a just price.] *Law.* No one can be forced to sell his/her own property even for a fair price. The maxim, though true in the case of transactions between individuals, is not applicable to transactions between the individual and the state. Thus, the state can compulsorily acquire private property. Cf. **in casu extremae** etc.

nemo contra factum suum venire potest. [L. **nemo** no one, nobody (1); **contra** against, opposite (4); **factum** deed, act, fact (6); **suum** his/her own (5); **venire** to come (3); **potest** can, is able (2): No one can come against his own deed.] *Law.* No one can contravene his/her own deed. The principle of estoppel applicable to deeds or sealed instruments. Thus, a party to a bond cannot deny a fact in it.

nemo damnum facit, nisi qui id fecit quod facere jus non habet. [L. **nemo** no one, nobody (1); **damnum** harm, damage, injury (3); **facit** does (2); **nisi** unless, except (4); **qui** (he) who (5); **id** that (7); **fecit** did (6); **quod** which (8); **facere** to do (12); **jus** right, law (11); **non** not (9); **habet** has, holds, regards (10): No one does harm, except he who did that which he does not have the right to do.] *Law.* A person does not cause injury unless he/she does what he/she does not have the right to do.

nemo dare potest quod non habet. [L. **nemo** no one, nobody (1); **dare** to give (3); **potest** can, is able (2); **quod** (that) which, what (4); **non** not (6); **habet** he/she has, holds, regards (5): No one can give that which he/she does not have.] *Law.* No one is able to give what he/she does not possess. See **nemo dat qui** etc.

nemo dat qui non habet. [L. **nemo** no one, nobody (1); **dat** gives (2); **qui** who (3); **non** not (4); **habet** has, holds, regards (5): No one gives who does not have.] *Law.* A person, who does not have, does not give. See **nemo dare** etc.; **nemo dat quod** etc.; **nemo plus juris** etc.; **nemo potest plus** etc.; **nihil dat** etc.; **non dat** etc.; **non debeo melioris** etc.; **qui non habet, ille** etc.; **qui non habet potestatem** etc.; and **traditio nihil** etc.

nemo dat quod non habet. [L. **nemo** no one, nobody (1); **dat** gives (2); **quod** (that) which, what (3); **non** not (4); **habet** has, holds, regards (5): No one gives that which he/she does not have.] *Law.* No one gives that what he/she does not possess. *A disposition by the tenant for life might therefore present a typical case of the contravention of the maxim nemo dat quod non habet* (James 1982:53). See **nemo dat qui** etc.

nemo debet aliena jactura locupletari. [L. **nemo** no one, nobody (1); **debet** ought, should (2); **aliena** from/at another's (4); **jactura** expense, loss, detriment (5); **locupletari** to be enriched (3): No one ought to be enriched from another's loss.] *Law.* No one should gain at another's expense (or to another's detriment). See **nemo debet ex** etc.

nemo debet bis puniri pro uno delicto. [L. **nemo** no one, nobody (1); **debet** ought, should (2); **bis** twice (4); **puniri** to be punished (3); **pro** for (5); **uno** one (6); **delicto** offense, transgression (7): No one should be punished twice for one offense.] *Law.* No one should be punished more than once for one (or the same) crime. When a court which has competent jurisdiction delivers judgment in a criminal case, the verdict is final and the accused cannot be penalized for the same offense again. See **infinitum in** etc.

nemo debet bis vexari pro eadem causa. [L. **nemo** no one, nobody (1); **debet** ought, should (2); **bis** twice (4); **vexari** to be harassed, worried, disturbed (3); **pro** for (5); **eadem** the same (6); **causa** cause, case, reason (7): No one ought to be harassed twice for the same case.] *Law.* No one should be disturbed more than once for the same reason or legal suit. See **infinitum in** etc.

nemo debet bis vexari si constet curiae quod sit pro una et eadem causa. [L. **nemo** no one, nobody (1); **debet** should, ought (2); **bis** twice (4); **vexari** to be harassed, worried, disturbed (3); **si** if (5); **constet** it be certain, established (6); **curiae** to/by court (7); **quod** (that) which, what (8); **sit** is (9); **pro** for (10); **una** one (11); **et** and (12); **eadem** the same (13); **causa** cause, case, reason (14): No one ought to be harassed twice, if it be established by the court that which is for one and the same case.] *Law.* No one should be twice harassed for what is established by the court to be one and the same case. When a suit is brought and a final judgment delivered after discussion of the merits of a question by the parties, the question is deemed to be settled and cannot be revived in another action. See **infinitum in** etc.

nemo debet esse judex in propria causa. [L. **nemo** no one, nobody (1); **debet** should, ought (2); **esse** to be (3); **judex** judge (4); **in** in, on (5); **propria** his/her own, one's own (6); **causa** cause, case, reason (7): No one should be judge in one's own case.] *Law.* No one should judge one's own case. See **aliquis non** etc.; **iniquum est** etc.; **in propria causa** etc.; **in re propria** etc.; **judex non potest esse** etc.; **judex non potest injuriam** etc.; **nemo potest esse** etc.; **nemo sibi esse** etc.; and **non refert quid notum** etc. Cf. **nemo in propria** etc. and **testis nemo** etc.

nemo debet ex aliena jactura lucrari. [L. **nemo** no one, nobody (1); **debet** should, ought (2); **ex** out of, from, directly after, away from (4); **aliena** of another (6); **jactura** expense, loss (5); **lucrari** to gain, win (3): No one should gain from the loss of another.] *Law.* No one should gain at another person's expense. See **jure naturae** etc.; **nemo debet aliena** etc.; **nemo debet locupletari aliena jactura** etc.; **nemo debet locupletari ex** etc.; **nul ne doit** etc.; and **pro possessore** etc.

nemo debet immiscere se rei ad se nihil pertinenti. [L. **nemo** no one, nobody (1); **debet** should, ought (2); **immiscere se** to take part in, meddle with (3); **rei** matter, thing, property, business, affair (4); **ad** to, at, for, according to (7); **se** himself/herself, oneself (8); **nihil** in nothing (6); **pertinenti** pertaining, relating (5): No one should meddle with a matter pertaining in nothing to himself/herself.] *Law.* No one should meddle in a matter which in no way concerns him/her.

nemo debet in communione invitus teneri. [L. **nemo** no one, nobody (1); **debet** should, ought (2); **in** in, on (4); **communione** fellowship, partnership (5); **invitus** unwilling, against the will (6); **teneri** to be held, kept (3): No one ought to be held in a partnership unwillingly.] *Law.* No one ought to be kept in a partnership against his/her will.

nemo debet locupletari aliena jactura. [L. **nemo** no one, nobody (1); **debet** should, ought (2); **locupletari** to be enriched (3); **aliena** of another (5); **jactura** at/by loss, expense, cost (4): No one should be enriched by the loss of another.] *Law.* No one should be enriched at another's expense. See **nemo debet ex** etc.

nemo debet locupletari ex alterius incommodo. [L. **nemo** no one, nobody (1); **debet** should, ought (2); **locupletari** to be enriched (3); **ex** out of (4); **alterius** another's (5); **incommodo** misfortune, loss, injury (6): No one ought to be enriched out of another's loss.] *Law.* No one should gain from another's loss/ misfortune. See **nemo debet ex** etc.

nemo de domo sua extrahi potest. [L. **nemo** no one, nobody (1); **de** of, from, about, for (4); **domo** home (6); **sua** his/her own (5); **extrahi** to be dragged (3); **potest** can, is able (2): No one is able to be dragged from one's own home.] *Law.* No one can be dragged out of his/her own home; i.e., a person's home is his/ her castle. See **domus sua** etc.

nemo est heres viventis. [L. **nemo** no one, nobody (1); **est** is (2); **heres** heir, successor (3); **viventis** of living (person) (4): No one is heir of a living person.] *Law.* A living person can have no heirs; i.e., a person cannot be heir while the testator is alive.

nemo est supra leges. [L. **nemo** no one, nobody (1); **est** is (2); **supra** above; beyond (3); **leges** laws (4): No one is above the laws.] *Law.* No one is exempted from the law. See **nemo jus** etc.

nemo ex alterius facto praegravari debet. [L. **nemo** no one, nobody (1); **ex** in consequence of, by reason of (4); **alterius** another's (5); **facto** deed, act, fact (6); **praegravari** to be burdened, oppressed (3); **debet** should, ought (2): No one should be burdened in consequence of another's act.] *Law.* Nobody should suffer from the consequences of another's act. See **culpa teneat** etc.; **culpa tenet** etc.; **in quo quis** etc.; and **nemo punitur** etc.

nemo ex consilio obligatur. [L. **nemo** no one, nobody (1); **ex** in consequence of, by reason of (3); **consilio** advice (4); **obligatur** is bound, obliged, put under obligation (2): No one is bound in consequence of advice.] *Law.* No one can be put under obligation in consequence of his/her advice.

nemo ex dolo suo proprio relevetur, aut auxilium capiat. [L. **nemo** no one, nobody (1); **ex** out of, from, directly after, away from (6); **dolo** fraud, guile (9); **suo** his/her own, one's own (7); **proprio** own (8); **relevetur** should be relieved (2); **aut** or (3); **auxilium**

help, aid (5); **capiat** should take (4): No one should be relieved or take help from his/her own fraud.] *Law.* No one should be relieved from, or aided by, his/her own fraud. See **ex turpi causa** etc.

nemo ex proprio dolo consequitur actionem. [L. **nemo** no one, nobody (1); **ex** out of, arising from (4); **proprio** his/her own, one's own (5); **dolo** fraud, wrong (6); **consequitur** pursues (2); **actionem** action (3): No one pursues an action arising from his/her own fraud.] *Law.* Nobody can pursue a legal action which is based on his/her own wrongful act. See **ex turpi causa** etc.

nemo ex suo delicto meliorem suam conditionem facere potest. [L. **nemo** no one, nobody (1); **ex** out of, from, directly after, away from (7); **suo** his/her own, one's (8); **delicto** offense, wrong (9); **meliorem** better (6); **suam** his/her own, one's own (4); **conditionem** condition (5); **facere** to do, make (3); **potest** can, is able (2): No one can make his/her own condition better by his/her own wrong.] *Law.* No one can improve his/her own condition by committing a wrongful act. See **ex turpi causa** etc.

nemo heres est viventis. See **nemo est heres viventis.**

nemo inauditus condemnari debet si non sit contumax. [L. **nemo** no one, nobody (1); **inauditus** unheard (4); **condemnari** to be condemned (3); **debet** should, ought (2); **si** if (5); **non** not (7); **sit** he/she is (6); **contumax** insolent, obstinate (8): No one should be condemned unheard, if he/she is not insolent.] *Law.* No one should be condemned without the benefit of a hearing, unless he/she is insolent. See **audi partem alteram.**

nemo in propria causa testis esse debet. [L. **nemo** no one, nobody (1); **in** in, on (5); **propria** his/her own, one's own (6); **causa** cause, case, reason (7); **testis** witness (4); **esse** to be (3); **debet** should, ought (2): No one should be a witness in one's own case.] *Law.* Nobody should be a witness in his/her own cause. Cf. **nemo debet esse** etc.

nemo jus sibi dicere potest. [L. **nemo** no one, nobody (1); **jus** right, law (4); **sibi** for himself/herself, oneself (5); **dicere** to say, declare, pronounce (3); **potest** can, is able (2): No one can declare the law for his/her self.] *Law.* Nobody should pronounce the law on his/her own behalf; i.e., no one can take the law into his/her own hands. See **nemo est supra leges.**

nemo me impune lacessit. [L. **nemo** no one, nobody (1); **me** me (3); **impune** with impunity, without punishment (4); **lacessit** provokes, irritates, disturbs, attacks (3): No one provokes me with impunity.] Nobody attacks me without punishment. Motto of the Crown of Scotland.

nemo plus juris ad alium transferre potest quam ipse habet. [L. **nemo** no one, nobody (1); **plus** more (4); **juris** of right, law (5); **ad** to, at, for, according to (6); **alium** another (7); **transferre** to transfer (3); **potest** can, is able (2); **quam** than (8); **ipse** himself/herself, oneself (10); **habet** has, holds, regards (9): No one can transfer more right to another than one has oneself.] *Law.* No one can transfer more right to another than the person himself/herself has. See **nemo dat qui** etc.

nemo potest esse simul actor et judex. [L. **nemo** no one, nobody (1); **potest** can, is able (2); **esse** to be (4); **simul** at the same time (3); **actor** plaintiff, prosecutor, complainant (5); **et** and (6); **judex** judge (7): No one can be, at the same time, plaintiff and judge.] *Law.* Nobody can be simultaneously judge and plaintiff, complainant, or prosecutor. See **nemo debet esse** etc.

nemo potest esse tenens et dominus. [L. **nemo** no one, nobody (1); **potest** can, is able (2); **esse** to be (3); **tenens** occupying, holding (4); **et** and (5); **dominus** lord, owner (6): No one can be occupying and owner.] *Law.* No one can be tenant and owner of the same property simultaneously.

nemo potest facere per alium, quod per se non potest. [L. **nemo** no one, nobody (1); **potest** can, is able (2); **facere** to do, make (3); **per** through, by (4); **alium** another (5); **quod** (that) which, what (6); **per** through, by (9); **se** himself/herself, oneself (10); **non** not (8); **potest** can, is able (7): No one can do through another that which he/she cannot do by himself/herself.] *Law.* No one can do through the services of another person what he/she cannot do for himself/herself. Cf. **qui facit per alium** etc.

nemo potest facere per obliquum quod non potest facere per directum. [L. **nemo** no one, nobody (1); **potest** can, is able (2); **facere** to do (3); **per** by, through (4); **obliquum** indirect, oblique (5); **quod** (that) which, what (6); **non** not (8); **potest** he/she can, is able (7); **facere** to do (9); **per** through, by (10); **directum** direct (11): No one can do by the indirect that which he/she cannot do by the direct.] *Law.* No one can do indirectly what he/she cannot do directly. See **quando aliquid prohibetur ex** etc. and **quando aliquid prohibetur fieri** etc. Cf. **multa conceduntur** etc.

nemo potest plus juris ad alium transferre quam ipse habet. [L. **nemo** no one, nobody (1); **potest** can, is able (2); **plus** more (4); **juris** of right, law (5); **ad** to, at, for, according to (6); **alium** another (7); **transferre** to transfer (3); **quam** than (8); **ipse** himself/herself, oneself (10); **habet** he/she has, holds, regards (9): No one can transfer more right to another than he himself (or she herself) has.] *Law.* No one is able to hand over to another person more right than he himself (or she herself) has. See **nemo dat qui** etc.

nemo potest sibi debere. [L. **nemo** no one, nobody (1); **potest** can, is able (2); **sibi** to himself/herself, oneself (4); **debere** to owe (3): No one can owe to himself/herself.] *Law.* No one can be indebted to himself/herself.

nemo praesumitur esse immemor suae aeternae salutis, et maxime in articulo mortis. [L. **nemo** no one, nobody (1); **praesumitur** is presumed (2); **esse** to be (3); **immemor** forgetful, unmindful (4); **suae**

of his/her own, one's own (5); **aeternae** (of) eternal, perpetual (6); **salutis** (of) welfare, safety (7); **et** and (8); **maxime** especially, most particularly (9); **in** in, on (10); **articulo** joint, nick (11); **mortis** of death (12): No one is presumed to be forgetful of his/her own perpetual welfare, and especially in the nick of death.] *Law.* No one is presumed to be forgetful of his/her own eternal welfare, especially at the point of death. See **nemo praesumitur ludere** etc.

nemo praesumitur ludere in extremis. [L. **nemo** no one, nobody (1); **praesumitur** is presumed (2); **ludere** to play, frolic (3); **in** in, on (4); **extremis** utmost (things) (5): No one is presumed to play in utmost things.] *Law.* No one is presumed to indulge in frivolities at the last extremity (or at the point of death). See **nemo praesumitur esse immemor** etc.

nemo praesumitur malus. [L. **nemo** no one, nobody (1); **praesumitur** is presumed (2); **malus** bad, evil (3): No one is presumed bad.] *Law.* Nobody is presumed to be a bad/evil person.

nemo prohibetur pluribus defensionibus uti. [L. **nemo** no one, nobody (1); **prohibetur** is prevented, debarred (2); **pluribus** more, several (4); **defensionibus** defenses (5); **uti** to use (3): No one is prevented from using several defenses.] *Law.* Nobody is debarred from making use of more than one defense. See **facultas probationum** etc.

nemo prudens punit ut praeterita revocentur, sed ut futura praeveniantur. [L. **nemo** no one, nobody (1); **prudens** wise, sagacious, prudent (2); **punit** punishes (3); **ut** in order that (4); **praeterita** past (things) (5); **revocentur** may be recalled, revived (6); **sed** but (7); **ut** in order that (8); **futura** (things) about to be, future (things) (9); **praeveniantur** may be prevented (10): Nobody prudent punishes in order that past things may be recalled but in order that future things may be prevented.] *Law.* A wise person punishes not to recall past wrongs but to prevent future ones. Cf. **lex prospicit** etc.

nemo punitur pro alieno delicto. [L. **nemo** no one, nobody (1); **punitur** is punished (2); **pro** for (3); **alieno** another's, of another (4); **delicto** offense, transgression (5): No one is punished for another's offense.] *Law.* Nobody is punished for someone else's transgression. See **nemo ex alterius** etc.

nemo qui condemnare potest, absolvere non potest. [L. **nemo** no one, nobody (1); **qui** who (2); **condemnare** to condemn (4); **potest** can, is able (3); **absolvere** to acquit, absolve (7); **non** not (6); **potest** can, is able (5): No one who can condemn, cannot acquit.] *Law.* A person who can condemn can also acquit.

nemo repente fuit turpissimus. Juvenal (c.60–117 A.D.). *Satires* II,83. [L. **nemo** no one, nobody (1); **repente** suddenly (3); **fuit** was (2); **turpissimus** most wicked, shameless (4): No one was suddenly most shameless.] No one ever reached the height of shamelessness all of a sudden.

nemo sibi esse judex vel suis jus dicere debet. [L. **nemo** no one, nobody (1); **sibi** for himself/herself (5); **esse** to be (3); **judex** judge (4); **vel** or (6); **suis** to his/her own, one's own (relatives) (9); **jus** right, law (8); **dicere** to declare, pronounce (7); **debet** should, ought (2): No one ought to be a judge for himself/ herself or to pronounce the law to his/her own relatives.] *Law.* No one should be his/her own judge or serve as a judge in cases in which his/her own relatives are involved. See **nemo debet esse** etc.

nemo sui judex [L. **nemo** no one, nobody (1); **sui** of himself/herself (3); **judex** judge (2): no one judge of himself/herself.] *Law.* No one should be his/her own judge. A judge should not sit for a legal process in which he/she has a vested interest.

nemo tenetur ad impossibile. [L. **nemo** no one, nobody (1); **tenetur** is bound (2); **ad** to, at, for, according to (3); **impossibile** impossible (thing) (4): No one is bound to the impossible.] *Law.* No one is under obligation to do the impossible. See **impotentia excusat legem**.

nemo tenetur armare adversarium contra se. [L. **nemo** no one, nobody (1); **tenetur** is bound (2); **armare** to arm, equip, help (3); **adversarium** opponent, enemy (4); **contra** against, opposite (5); **se** himself/herself, oneself (6): No one is bound to arm an opponent against himself/herself.] *Law.* No one is under obligation to arm/help his/her enemy against himself/ herself. See **accusare nemo se** etc.

nemo tenetur divinare. [L. **nemo** no one, nobody (1); **tenetur** is bound (2); **divinare** to foresee, predict (3): No one is bound to foresee/predict.] *Law.* No one is under obligation to foresee the future.

nemo tenetur edere instrumenta contra se. [L. **nemo** no one, nobody (1); **tenetur** is held, bound, obliged (2); **edere** to produce, bring forth (3); **instrumenta** materials, documents (4); **contra** against, opposite (5); **se** himself/herself, oneself (6): No one is bound to produce documents against himself/herself.] *Law.* Nobody is under obligation to produce materials/ documents against himself/herself. This is a rule of Roman law which has survived in criminal cases, but not in civil cases. See **accusare nemo se** etc.

nemo tenetur informare qui nescit, sed quisquis scire quod informat. [L. **nemo** no one, nobody (1); **tenetur** is held, bound, obliged (4); **informare** to inform (5); **qui** who (2); **nescit** does not know; is ignorant of (3); **sed** but (6); **quisquis** everyone, each (7); **scire** to know (8); **quod** (that) which, what (9); **informat** he/she informs (10): No one who does not know is bound to inform, but everyone is bound to know what he/she informs.] *Law.* No one is under obligation to give information about what he/she is ignorant of, but a person is under obligation to know what he/she gives information about.

nemo tenetur prodere seipsum. [L. **nemo** no one, nobody (1); **tenetur** is held, bound, obliged (2); **prodere** to betray (3); **seipsum** himself/herself, oneself (4): No one is bound to betray himself/herself.] *Law.* Nobody is obliged to betray himself/herself, i.e., to testify against himself/herself. See **accusare nemo se** etc.

nemo tenetur seipsum accusare. [L. **nemo** no one, nobody (1); **tenetur** is held, bound, obliged (2); **seipsum** himself/herself, oneself (4); **accusare** to accuse (3): No one is bound to accuse oneself.] *Law.* Nobody is obliged to accuse himself/herself. See **accusare nemo se** etc.

nemo tenetur seipsum infortuniis et periculis exponere. [L. **nemo** no one, nobody (1); **tenetur** is held, bound, obliged (2); **seipsum** himself/herself, oneself (4); **infortuniis** to misfortunes, calamities (5); **et** and (6); **periculis** dangers, hazards (7); **exponere** to expose (3): No one is bound to expose himself/herself to misfortunes and dangers.] *Law.* Nobody is obliged to expose himself/herself to catastrophes and hazards.

nemo tenetur seipsum prodere. See **nemo tenetur prodere seipsum.**

nemo unquam vir magnus fuit, sine aliquo divino afflatu. [L. **nemo** no one, nobody (1); **unquam** ever, at any time (3); **vir** man, male (5); **magnus** great (4); **fuit** was, has been (2); **sine** without (6); **aliquo** any, some (7); **divino** divine (8); **afflatu** inspiration (9): No one was ever a great man without some divine inspiration.] No one ever attained greatness without the aid of some divine inspiration. Cf. **numquam res humanae** etc.

nemo videtur fraudere eos qui sciunt et consentiunt. [L. **nemo** no one, nobody (1); **videtur** seems, is seen, deemed (2); **fraudere** to defraud, cheat (3); **eos** those (4); **qui** who (5); **sciunt** know (6); **et** and (7); **consentiunt** agree, consent (8): No one seems to defraud those who know and agree.] *Law.* No one is deemed to defraud those who are aware of, and agree to, the transactions. See **qui non improbat, approbat.**

ne nimium [L. **ne** not (1); **nimium** too much, excessively (2): not too much.] Nothing in excess. Cf. **meden agan** and **ne quid nimis.**

neophobia *n.* [Neo-Gk. from Gk. **neo(s)** new (2); **phob(os)** fear (1): fear of new things.] Abnormal fear of innovation or novelty.

ne plus ultra *abbr.* **N.P.U.** *n., pl.* **ne plus ultras** [L. **ne** not (1); **plus** more (2); **ultra** farther, beyond (3): not more beyond.] The highest point that can be reached. The apex of achievement. a) *His career at the university reached its ne plus ultra when he was appointed Vice-Chancellor.* b) *The headmaster insulted the teacher in the presence of students, an incident which most observers considered to be a ne plus ultra of humiliation.* Cf. **non plus ultra** and **ultra.**

neque amore et sine odio [L. **neque** neither (1); **amore** with love (2); **et** and (3); **sine** without (4); **odio** hatred, animosity (5): neither with love and without hatred.] Free from love and animosity; i.e., with objectivity. *History is different from fiction and one of its principal* *requirements is that it should be objective, i.e., it should be written neque amore et sine odio.* Cf. **sine ira et studio.**

ne quid nimis [L. **ne** not (1); **quid** anything (2); **nimis** too much, excessively (3): not anything excessively.] Nothing in excess. Translation of Greek **meden agan** (q.v.). Cf. **ne nimium.**

ne repetatur *abbr.* **ne rep.** [L. **ne** not (2); **repetatur** let it be repeated (1): Let it not be repeated.] Do not repeat.

nescit vox missa reverti. Horace (65–8 B.C.). *Ars Poetica* 390. [L. **nescit** does not know how (3); **vox** voice (1); **missa** sent out (2); **reverti** to be turned back, returned (4): A voice sent out does not know how to be turned back.] A spoken word cannot be recalled.

n'est-ce pas? [Fr. **n'**. . . **pas** not (3); **est** is (1); **ce** it (2): is it not?] Isn't it? Sometimes used as an emphatic interrogative tag to English sentences; e.g., "He is dating her, n'est-ce pas?"

Nestor or **nestor** *n., pl.* **Nestors** or **nestors** [Gk. **Nestōr.**] 1. *Greek Mythology.* A Homeric hero famous for his old age and wisdom. 2. A wise elderly adviser or counselor. *Krobitu incurred general displeasure when he insulted Toku, the Nestor of the village.* 3. An old man regarded as an expert in his field. *It is widely rumored that Salisu, the Nestor of African journalism, is being considered for national honors.*

ne sutor supra crepidam judicaret. *short form* **ultra crepidam** Pliny (A.D. 23–79). *Historia Naturalis* II,35,85. [L. **ne** let not (1); **sutor** shoemaker, cobbler (2); **supra** beyond (4); **crepidam** sandal (5); **judicaret** judge (3): Let not a cobbler judge beyond a sandal.] A shoemaker should not make a judgment in matters outside of shoemaking; i.e., individuals should not reach beyond their areas of expertise.

net *adj.* [Fr. neat, clean, clear.] Free of packaging. *The net weight of this is 10 ounces.* —*n.* The clear amount. *His net is $10,000 from a gross of $12,000.* —*v.* To clear. To profit. *He nets $10,000 on a gross of $12,000.*

Neue Sachlichkeit *n.* [Ger. **neue** new (1); **Sachlichkeit** reality, objectivity (2): new objectivity.] *Fine Arts and Literature.* An emphasis upon realism and objectivity instead of idealism and romanticism among German artists, especially in the 1920s.

neuter *adj.* [L. neither.] 1. *Grammar.* Belonging to neither the masculine nor the feminine gender. *"Periculum," the Latin word for "danger," is a neuter noun.* 2. Neutral. Impartial. *He remained neuter during the altercation between his parents.* 3. Sexless. Having neither male nor female reproductive organs. Applicable to plants. 4. Having imperfectly developed, undeveloped, or non-functional reproductive organs. Applicable to insects; e.g., the worker ant or bee. —*n., pl.* **neuters** 1. *Grammar.* A noun, adjective, etc. which belongs to neither the masculine nor the feminine gender. 2. A person or state that is neutral. 3. An insect which has

imperfectly developed, undeveloped, or non-functional reproductive organs, such as a worker ant or bee. 4. A castrated animal, especially a dog or cat. —*v. tr.* To castrate or spay. *The veterinarian neutered three dogs this morning.*

nexum *n., pl.* **nexa** [L. a bond, a pledge.] *Roman Law.* A legal agreement or contract between a lender and a borrower, who usually offered his freedom as his pledge.

nexus *n., pl.* **nexus** or **nexuses** [L. a binding, linking, interweaving, combination.] 1. A binding or connection. 2. A cluster. A group or series of connected ideas, views, images, etc. See **legis nexus.**

nexus *adj., pl.* **nexi** [L. bound.] *Roman Law.* A person bound by a contract of debt, i.e. **nexum** (q.v.), which empowered the creditor to enslave him, if he failed to repay the loan.

Nibelung *n., pl.* **Nibelungen** [Ger. Nibelung.] *Norse Mythology.* A wealthy dwarf. Cf. **Der Ring des Niblungen** and **Nibelungenlied.**

Nibelungenlied *n.* [Ger. **Nibelungen** Nibelung (1); **lied** song, saga (2): Nibelung saga.] A medieval German epic poem about the adventures of the hero Siegfried and the kings of Burgundy.

niche *n., pl.* **niches** [Fr. nook, recess, alcove, retreat.] 1. A recess in a wall used for keeping statues or other ornaments. *Solomon has already secured for himself a niche in the temple of fame.* 2. A place, position, etc. suitable for a person's or thing's capabilities or qualities. *The administrator-cadet or assistant was quickly absorbed into the scene . . . by the colonial environment in which he soon found his niche* (Suret-Canale 1971:318).

nient le fait *n.* [Obs. Fr. **nient** not (1); **le** the (2); **fait** deed, act (3): not the deed.] *Law.* It is not his/her deed. **non est factum** (q.v.).

nihil ad rem *adj.* [L. **nihil** nothing (1); **ad** to, at, for, according to (2); **rem** matter, thing, property, business, affair (3): nothing to the matter.] Nothing to the point. Irrelevant. Cf. **ad rem.**

nihil consensui tam contrarium est quam vis et metus. [L. **nihil** nothing (1); **consensui** to consent, agreement (5); **tam** so (3); **contrarium** opposed, contrary (4); **est** is (2); **quam** as (6); **vis** force (7); **et** and (8); **metus** fear, intimidation (9): Nothing is so contrary to agreement as force and fear.] *Law.* Nothing is so opposed to consent as compulsion and intimidation. For this reason, when money is paid under intimidation, threats of violence, or illegal deprivation of personal freedom, it may be recovered. Similarly, a deed or instrument concluded under such circumstances may be rendered null and void. See **actus me invito** etc. and **non videtur consensum** etc.

nihil dat qui non habet. [L. **nihil** nothing (5); **dat** gives (4); **qui** (he) who (1); **non** not (2); **habet** has, holds, regards (3): He who does not have, gives nothing.]

Law. A person who has nothing gives nothing. See **nemo dat qui** etc.

nihil debet or **nil debet** *n.* [L. **nihil** nothing (2); **debet** he/she owes (1): He/she owes nothing.] *Law.* A plea in a legal action of debt on a simple contract. As a general issue plea, it denies the general complaint rather than introducing special material.

nihil desperandum *var.* of **nil desperandum** (q.v.).

nihil dicit or **nil dicit** *n.* [L. **ni(hi)l** nothing (2); **dicit** he/she says (1): He/she says nothing.] *Law.* A defendant's refusal/failure to answer or plead. A judgment passed against a defendant charged with refusal to answer or plead.

nihil est *n.* [L. **nihil** nothing (2); **est** there is (1): There is nothing.] *Law.* A form of return which a sheriff or an official makes when he cannot serve the writ.

nihil est ab omni / parte beatum. Horace (65–8 B.C.). *Odes* II,16,27–28. [L. **nihil** nothing (1); **est** is (2); **ab** from, by (3); **omni** every, all (4); **parte** part, side (5); **beatum** happy, blessed (6): Nothing is from every / side happy.] No condition is happy in all respects. Every silver lining has its cloud.

nihil est magis rationi consentaneum quam eodem modo quodque dissolvere quo conflatum est. [L. **nihil** nothing (1); **est** is (2); **magis** more (3); **rationi** to/with reason (5); **consentaneum** fitting, consistent (4); **quam** than (6); **eodem** in the same (9); **modo** (in) way (10); **quodque** everything, each thing (8); **dissolvere** to dissolve, disunite (7); **quo** in which (11); **conflatum est** it was produced, composed (12): Nothing is more consistent with reason than to dissolve each thing in the same way in which it was produced.] *Law.* There is nothing more rational than that everything should be dissolved in the same way in which it was produced. See **eodem modo quo quid constituitur dissolvitur**.

nihil facit error nominis cum de corpore constat. [L. **nihil** nothing (4); **facit** makes, does (3); **error** error, mistake (1); **nominis** of name (2); **cum** when (5); **de** of, from, about, for (7); **corpore** body, person, individual (8); **constat** it is certain, established, known (6): An error of name does nothing when it (identity) is established about the person.] *Law.* An error about a name makes no difference as long as the person's identity is established. See **falsa demonstratio** etc.

nihil habet *n.* [L. **nihil** nothing (2); **habet** he has, holds, regards (1): He has nothing.] *Law.* A return which a sheriff makes to a **scire facias** (q.v.) or some other writ, indicating that the defendant has nothing and has accordingly not been served. Cf. **nihil est**.

nihil iniquius quam aequitatem nimis intendere. [L. **nihil** nothing (l); **iniquius** more unjust, unfair (2); **quam** than (3); **aequitatem** equity (5); **nimis** too much (6); **intendere** to extend, stretch (4): Nothing is more unjust than to extend equity too much.] *Law.* Nothing is more unjust than excessive extension of equity.

nihil magis justum est quam quod necessarium est. [L. **nihil** nothing (1); **magis** more (3); **justum** just (4); **est** is (2); **quam** than (5); **quod** (that) which, what (6); **necessarium** necessary (8); **est** is (7): Nothing is more just than that which is necessary.] *Law.* Nothing is more just than what is absolutely essential. See **necessitas quod** etc.

nihil obstat *n.* [L. **nihil** nothing (1); **obstat** hinders, opposes (2): Nothing hinders/opposes.] 1. *Roman Catholic Church.* A censor's certification, indicating that a book conforms with morality and faith. 2. Official approval. Authoritative approval. *He is a celebrated author whose novels have won the nihil obstat of distinguished critics.*

nihil perfectum est dum aliquid restat agendum. [L. **nihil** nothing (l); **perfectum** perfect (3); **est** is (2); **dum** while, as long as (4); **aliquid** something, anything (5); **restat** remains, is left (6); **agendum** to be done (7): Nothing is perfect as long as something remains to be done.] Nothing is perfect as long as something is left which must be done.

nihil possumus contra veritatem. [L. **nihil** nothing (2); **possumus** we can, are able (1); **contra** against, opposite (3); **veritatem** truth (4): We can do nothing against the truth.] We have no power against the truth.

nihil quod est contra rationem est licitum. [L. **nihil** nothing (1); **quod** which (2); **est** is (3); **contra** against, opposite (4); **rationem** reason (5); **est** is (6); **licitum** lawful, permitted (7): Nothing which is against reason is permitted.] *Law.* Nothing which is contrary to reason is lawful. Nothing unreasonable is lawful.

nihil quod inconveniens est licitum est. [L. **nihil** nothing (1); **quod** which (2); **inconveniens** inconvenient (4); **est** is (3); **licitum** lawful, permitted (6); **est** is (5): Nothing which is inconvenient is permitted.] *Law.* Nothing which is not convenient is lawful. A maxim which needs to be qualified. It is a good point against the introduction of a particular precedent or rule which may cause inconvenience. It is, however, not valid in all cases.

nihil tam conveniens est naturali aequitati quam unumquodque dissolvi eo ligamine quo ligatum est. [L. **nihil** nothing (1); **tam** so (3); **conveniens** agreeable, consistent (4); **est** is (2); **naturali** to/with natural (5); **aequitati** equity (6); **quam** as (7); **unumquodque** each (thing) (8); **dissolvi** to be dissolved, unbound (9); **eo** by that (10); **ligamine** (by) band (11); **quo** by which (12); **ligatum est** it was bound (13): Nothing is so agreeable to natural equity as that each thing be unbound by the same band by which it was bound.] *Law.* Nothing is so consistent with natural fairness as the unbinding of a thing by the same means by which it was bound. See **eodem modo quo quid constituitur dissolvitur**.

nihil tam naturale est, quam eo genere quidque dissolvere, quo colligatum est; ideo verborum obligatio verbis tollitur; nudi consensus obligatio

contrario consensu dissolvitur. [L. **nihil** nothing (1); **tam** so (3); **naturale** natural (4); **est** is (2); **quam** as (5); **eo** in that (8); **genere** (in) kind, way (9); **quidque** each thing, everything (7); **dissolvere** to dissolve (6); **quo** in which (10); **colligatum est** it was bound, united (11); **ideo** therefore, for that reason (12); **verborum** of words (14); **obligatio** obligation (13); **verbis** by words (16); **tollitur** is removed, taken away (15); **nudi** of bare, mere (18); **consensus** of consent, agreement (19); **obligatio** obligation (17); **contrario** by contrary, conflicting (21); **consensu** (by) consent, agreement (22); **dissolvitur** is dissolved (20): Nothing is so natural as to dissolve each thing in that way in which it was bound; therefore, the obligation of words is removed by words; the obligation of mere consent is dissolved by contrary agreement.] *Law.* Nothing is more natural than that everything should be dissolved in the same way in which it was bound. Therefore, a verbal obligation is removed by words; an obligation of mere consent is dissolved by contrary consent. See **eodem modo quo quid constituitur dissolvitur.**

nil *n.* [L. contraction of **nihil** nothing.] Not anything. Zero. *The football match ended in three goals to nil in favor of Evergreens United.*

nil admirari Horace (65–8 B.C.). *Epistles* I,6,1. [L. **nil** nothing (1); **admirari** to admire, wonder at (2): nothing to wonder at.] To be amazed at nothing. Reflects an important principle of ancient Epicurean philosophy, which taught that true contentment could be achieved only by a sense of detachment or **ataraxia** (q.v.) from the world.

nil debet See **nihil debet.**

nil desperandum Horace (65–8 B.C.). *Odes* I,7,27. [L. **nil** nothing (1); **desperandum** to be despaired (2): nothing to be despaired.] Never despair. Do not despair.

nil dicit. See **nihil dicit.**

nil facit error nominis cum de corpore vel persona constat. [L. **nil** nothing (4); **facit** makes, does (3); **error** error, mistake (1); **nominis** of name (2); **cum** when (5); **de** of, from, about, for (6); **corpore** body, individual (7); **vel** or (8); **persona** person (9); **constat** it is certain, established, known (10): A mistake of name does nothing when (information) about the individual or person is known.] *Law.* A mistake of name makes no difference as long as the individual person's identity is established. See **falsa demonstratio non nocet.**

nil habet infelix paupertas durius in se / quam quod ridiculos homines facit. Juvenal (c.60–117 A.D.). *Satires* III,152. [L. **nil** nothing (6); **habet** has, holds, regards (3); **infelix** miserable, unfortunate (1); **paupertas** poverty, indigence (2); **durius** harsher, more distressing (7); **in** in, on (4); **se** itself (5); **quam** than (8); **quod** that (9); **ridiculos** ridiculous, laughable (12); **homines** people, human beings (11); **facit** it makes (10): Miserable poverty has in itself nothing harsher / than that it makes human beings ridiculous.] Unfortunate poverty has in itself nothing more distressing than that it makes human beings laughable.

nil mortalibus ardui est. Horace (65–8 B.C.). *Odes* I,3,37. [L. **nil** nothing (1); **mortalibus** for mortals, mankind (4); **ardui** of difficulty (3); **est** is (2): Nothing is of difficulty for mortals.] Nothing is too difficult for humankind.

nil nisi bonum [L. **nil** nothing (1); **nisi** unless, except (2); **bonum** a good thing (3): nothing except a good thing.] *Medicine.* Nothing but good. Do no harm.

nil posse creari / de nilo. Lucretius (c.94–c.55 B.C.). *De Rerum Natura* I,155–156. [L. **nil** nothing (1); **posse** to be able (2); **creari** to be created (3); **de** of, from, about, for (4); **nilo** nothing (5): Nothing to be able to be created / out of nothing.] Nothing can be created out of nothing. Nothing comes from nothing.

nil sine numine [L. **nil** nothing (1); **sine** without (2); **numine** divine power, providence (3): nothing without divine power.] Nothing without Providence. Motto of the State of Colorado.

nil temere novandum *n.* [L. nothing (1); **temere** rashly (3); **novandum** to be changed, altered (2): nothing to be changed rashly.] There should be no rash changes/innovations.

nimbus *n., pl.* **nimbi** or **nimbuses** [L. rainstorm, thundercloud.] 1. *Greek and Roman Mythology.* A bright cloud which surrounds a god or goddess who has appeared on earth. 2. *Art.* A radiant light in the form of a circle, triangle, disc, etc. around the head of a divine person, saint, or king. 3. Halo, cloud, etc. surrounding a person or thing with glory, prestige, authority, etc. *Removing him would cause great shock and damage to the nation; he is surrounded by the nimbus of great authority* (*Newsweek Int.* May 4, 1981:60). 4. A uniformly grey rain cloud which extends throughout the sky during the rainy season.

nimia negligentia *n.* [L. **nimia** excessive, too much (1); **negligentia** negligence (2): excessive negligence.] Extreme negligence. See **culpa.**

nimia subtilitas in jure reprobatur. [L. **nimia** excessive, too much (1); **subtilitas** subtlety (2); **in** in, on (3); **jure** right, law (4); **reprobatur** is condemned, disapproved of (5): Excessive subtlety in law is condemned.] Too much subtlety in the law is reprehensible.

nimium altercando veritas amittitur. [L. **nimium** too much (4); **altercando** by wrangling, disputing (3); **veritas** truth (1); **amittitur** is lost (2): Truth is lost by wrangling too much.] Truth is lost in the midst of excessive altercation.

ninja *n., pl.* **ninja** or **ninjas** [Japan. from **nin** endure (1); **ja** person (2): an enduring person.] One of a special class of highly-trained mercenaries who were used for assassinations and acts of sabotage in 14th-century Japan.

ninjutsu *n.* [Japan. from **nin** invisibility, secrecy (1); **jutsu** art, training (2): invisibility training.] The art of secrecy and espionage which was a traditional part of the training of a **samurai** (q.v.).

nirvana *n., pl.* **nirvanas** [Skt. **nirvāna** extinguished.] 1. *Buddhism.* The state of enlightenment gained by the cleansing of anger, avarice, and other inappropriate tendencies from a human soul. 2. *Buddhism.* The state of liberation achieved after death by an individual who has been cleansed during life.

Nisei *n., pl.* **Nisei** or **Niseis** [Japan. from **ni** second (1); **sei** generation (2): second generation.] A child of a Japanese immigrant to the United States. A second-generation Japanese-American. Cf. **issei** and **Sansei.**

nisi *adj.* [L. unless.] Not absolute. Not final. *Law.* Used to qualify conditional decrees, rules, orders, or judgments. Its use indicates that the decision remains valid unless the affected party challenges it or takes measures to secure its revocation. *In the divorce proceedings, the judge gave the couple a decree nisi to make it possible for them to consider reconciliation.*

nisi aliter notetur *abbr.* **N.A.N.** *adv.* [L. **nisi** unless (1); **aliter** otherwise, differently (3); **notetur** it be noted, signified (2): unless it be noted otherwise.] Unless otherwise noted/signified.

nisi prius *abbr.* **ni. pri.** *n.* [L. **nisi** unless (1); **prius** before (2): unless before.] *Law.* 1. An issue of fact which is to be tried before the assizes or a jury. 2. A writ ordering the sheriff to provide the jury for such a trial. 3. A court of record held for the trial of factual issues before a jury and one judge.

nitchevo *interj.* [Russ. It was nothing.] Never mind. —*n.* The act of saying "never mind." A feeling of hopelessness and resignation.

N.L. or **n.l.** *abbr.* for 1. **non licet** (q.v.). 2. **non liquet** (q.v.).

nobile officium *n.* [L. **nobile** noble (1); **officium** duty, office (2): noble office/duty.] *Law.* The Court of Session's equitable discretion to provide relief in cases where none is provided by the law.

nobiliores et benigniores praesumptiones in dubiis sunt praeferendae. [L. **nobiliores** more splendid, noble (3); **et** and (4); **benigniores** more liberal (5); **praesumptiones** presumptions (6); **in** in, on (1); **dubiis** doubtful (things) (2); **sunt** are (7); **praeferendae** to be preferred (8): In doubtful things, the more noble and liberal presumptions are to be preferred.] *Law.* In case of doubt, we must give preference to the more generous and liberal presumptions. See **in dubio, pars** etc.

noblesse *n., pl.* **noblesses** [Fr. nobility, noble birth, nobleness.] 1. Noble birth. Nobility of birth/rank. Aristocracy. 2. Nobility, particularly French nobility. *. . . the Roman aristocracy lost the rustic character . . . and was becoming as urbanised as the French noblesse of the ancien régime* (Cary 1970:456).

noblesse oblige *n.* [Fr. **noblesse** nobility (1); **oblige** obliges, compels (2): Nobility obliges.] Moral and honorable social behavior required of nobility or high rank. *This rare bird, born in 1819, was a gentleman of means . . . whose leisurely travels to Italy and Switzerland resulted in a vast outpouring of noblesse oblige . . . instructing his countrymen on how to think about art, man and socialism (Time Int. 1982). —adv.* As honorable conduct requires. In accordance with the obligations of aristocratic rank. *The permanent secretary is a very nice man but, noblesse oblige, he does not mix business with pleasure.*

nocturne *n.* [Fr. something pertaining to the night.] 1. *Painting.* Depiction of a night scene. 2. *Music.* An instrumental composition which is meditative and dreamlike.

noema *n., pl.* **noemata** [Gk. **noēma** thought.] *Philosophy.* That which is thought. The result of **noesis** (q.v.).

noesis *n., pl.* **noeses** [Gk. **noēsis** thinking.] *Philosophy.* The act of thinking. The intellectual process.

nol. con. *abbr.* for **nolo contendere** (q.v.).

nolens volens *adj./adv.* [L. **nolens** unwilling (1); **volens** willing (2): unwilling willing.] Whether unwilling or willing. Willy-nilly. *Every Saturday, every inhabitant of the town is required to participate in communal cleaning, nolens volens.*

noli me tangere *n., pl.* **noli me tangeres** [L. **noli** do not wish, do not (1); **me** me (3); **tangere** to touch (2): Do not touch me.] 1. A representation of Jesus Christ when He appeared before Mary Magdalene after His resurrection from the dead (John 20:17). 2. A warning against touching or interfering with something. *Noticing that customers were damaging his displayed goods, the shop-keeper put up a sign of noli me tangere.* 3. A person or something which is not to be touched. *A person who is suffering from smallpox or chickenpox is a noli me tangere.*

nolle prosequi *abbr.* **nolle pros.** or **nol. pros.** or **nolle** *n., pl.* **nolle prosequis** [L. **nolle** to be unwilling, not to wish (1); **prosequi** to prosecute, continue, follow up (2): to be unwilling to continue or follow up.] *Law.* A formal entry on the record of an action, indicating that the plaintiff or prosecutor will no longer continue with the suit or action either wholly or partly. *The judge struck out the case against the accused because the Attorney-General entered a nolle prosequi.* See **non prosequitur; qui semel** etc.; and **retraxit.**

nolo contendere *abbr.* **nol. con.** *n., pl.* **nolo contenderes** [L. **nolo** I do not wish (1); **contendere** to dispute, fight, contend (2): I do not wish to dispute.] *Law.* A plea in a criminal case in which the accused neither admits nor denies the charges. A fine may be imposed on the accused, but the plea cannot be used against him, if a civil action should arise from the case. The plea is usually used in anti-trust actions. See **non vult contendere.**

nom de guerre *n., pl.* **noms de guerre** [Fr. **nom** name (1); **de** of (2); **guerre** war (3): name of war.] An assumed name. A pseudonym. An alias. a) *. . . he was born as Mohammed Ben Brahim Boukharouba . . . but* the world knew him . . . by his nom-de-guerre, Houari Boumedienne (*New African* 1979). b) *Then came a briefing by a dashing officer in sunglasses who had adopted "Commandante Bravo" as his nom de guerre* (*Newsweek Int.* June 25, 1979:23). Cf. **nom de plume** and **nom de théâtre**.

nom de plume *n., pl.* **noms de plume** [Fr. **nom** name (1); **de** of (2); **plume** pen (3): name of (the) pen.] Pen-name. *Jane always uses her nom de plume whenever she writes on controversial issues.* Cf. **nom de guerre** and **nom de théâtre**.

nom de théâtre *n., pl.* **noms de théâtre** [Fr. **nom** name (1); **de** of (2); **théâtre** theater (3): name of (the) theater.] A stage name. A fictitious name used by an actor or some other person in connection with theatrical work. Cf. **nom de guerre** and **nom de plume**.

nomen *n., pl.* **nomina** [L. name.] *Roman Law.* A person's middle name or the name derived from his **gens** or tribe; e.g., Tullius in Marcus Tullius Cicero. Cf. **agnomen**; **cognomen**; and **praenomen**.

nomen dubium *n., pl.* **nomina dubia** [L. **nomen** name (2); **dubium** doubtful, uncertain (1): uncertain name.] *Taxonomy.* An uncertain or doubtful name for a subject under scientific study.

nomenklatura *n. sing.* or *pl.* [Russ. from L. **nomenclatura** from **nomen** name (1); **calo** proclaim (2): proclaiming names.] 1. The system of patronage in Communist countries. 2. A collective term for the privileged bureaucrats in Soviet Russia and in other countries.

nomen nudum *n., pl.* **nomina nuda** [L. **nomen** name (2); **nudum** naked, bare (1): bare name.] *Taxonomy.* A name for a subject which has not yet been published in an appropriate manner.

nominatim *adv.* By name. Expressly. *The informant revealed the identity of the suspects nominatim.*

nominis umbra Lucan (AD 39–65). *Pharsalia* I,135. [Lat **nominis** of a name (2); **umbra** shadow, shade (1): shadow of a name.] Not much more than a name. Without much substance.

nomos *n.* [Gk. law, custom.] The law, especially natural law.

non alio modo puniatur aliquis quam secundum quod se habet condemnatio. [L. **non** not (2); **alio** in another (4); **modo** (in) way, manner (5); **puniatur** should be punished (3); **aliquis** anyone, someone (1); **quam** than (6); **secundum** according to, in accordance with (7); **quod** what (8); **se** itself (11); **habet** has, holds, regards (10); **condemnatio** conviction, condemnation (9): Someone should not be punished in another way than according to what the conviction holds itself.] *Law.* A person should not suffer any other penalty than that prescribed by the sentence.

non allocatur *abbr.* **N.A.** [L. **non** not (2); **allocatur** it is granted (1): It is not granted.] It is not allowed.

non assumpsit *n.* [L. **non** not (2); **assumpsit** he/she undertook (1): He/she did not undertake/promise.] *Law.* A general denial/plea in actions of **assumpsit** (q.v.).

non auditur perire volens. [L. **non** not (4); **auditur** is heard (3); **perire** to perish (2); **volens** wishing, desiring (1): Wishing to perish is not heard.] *Law.* He who wishes to perish is not heard; i.e., a person who confesses guilt of a crime with the intention of being condemned to death is not given a hearing.

non bis in idem *adv.* [L. **non** not (1); **bis** twice (2); **in** into, to, against, for (3); **idem** the same (4): not twice for the same.] *Law.* A person should not be tried or punished twice for the same offense. See **res judicata** as well as **infinitum in** etc.

nonchalance *n., pl.* **nonchalances** [Fr. indifference, unconcern.] A display or attitude of indifference and unconcern. Imperturbability. *The deterioration of cordial relations between Esi and Ama is clearly indicated by the nonchalance with which the latter received the news of the former's misfortune.*

nonchalant *adj.* [Fr. heedless, careless, sluggish, unconcerned.] Showing an attitude of indifference, unconcern, lack of anxiety, enthusiasm, interest or excitement. Imperturbable. Unconcerned. *Bret remained conspicuously nonchalant as everybody appeared visibly shaken by the unbearable tragedy.*

non compos mentis *adj.* [L. **non** not (1); **compos** master, having mastery (2); **mentis** of mind (3): not having mastery of the mind.] *Law.* Not sound of mind. Absolutely devoid of mental ability to understand the nature and implications of a transaction or situation. *The court declared the will of the deceased null and void because he was deemed to have been non compos mentis at the time he had made it.* Cf. **compos mentis**.

non consentit qui errat. [L. **non** not (3); **consentit** consents, agrees (4); **qui** (one) who (1); **errat** mistakes, goes astray (2): One who makes a mistake does not consent.] *Law.* A person cannot consent by mistake. Cf. **qui non improbat approbat**.

non culpabilis *abbr.* **non cul.** *adj.* [L. **non** not (1); **culpabilis** blameworthy, culpable (2): not culpable or blameworthy.] *Legal Pleading.* Not guilty. *The evidence adduced by the prosecution revealed that the accused was non culpabilis.*

non dat qui non habet. [L. **non** not (4); **dat** gives (5); **qui** (one) who (1); **non** not (2); **habet** has, holds, regards (3): One who does not have does not give.] One cannot give what one does not possess. See **nemo dat qui** etc.

non debeo melioris conditionis esse, quam auctor meus a quo jus in me transit. [L. **non** not (2); **debeo** I should, ought (1); **melioris** of better (4); **conditionis** (of) condition (5); **esse** to be (3); **quam** than (6); **auctor** producer, progenitor (8); **meus** my (7); **a** from (9); **quo** whom (10); **jus** right, law (11); **in** into, to, against, for (13); **me** me (14); **transit** passes, crosses (12): I ought not to be of better condition than my progenitor from whom the right passes to me.] *Law.* I should not be in a better condition than the one whose rights I inherited. See **nemo dat qui** etc.

non deberet alii nocere quod inter alios actum esset. [L. **non** not (6); **deberet** should, ought (5); **alii** to someone, another (8); **nocere** to do harm, hurt, injure (7); **quod** (that) which, what (1); **inter** among, between (3); **alios** some, others (4); **actum esset** had been done (2): What had been done among some should not do harm to another.] *Law.* A transaction among other parties should not have a detrimental effect on a third party. See **res inter alios acta alteri** etc.

non debet actori licere quod reo non permittitur. [L. **non** not (6); **debet** should, ought (5); **actori** to plaintiff (8); **licere** to be allowed, permitted (7); **quod** (that) which, what (1); **reo** to accused, defendant (4); **non** not (2); **permittitur** is allowed, permitted (3): What is not allowed to the defendant should not be allowed to the plaintiff.] *Law.* A concession which is not granted to the defendant should not be granted to the plaintiff.

non debet alii nocere, quod inter alios actum est. [L. **non** not (6); **debet** should, ought (5); **alii** to someone, another (8); **nocere** to do harm, hurt, injure (7); **quod** (that) which, what (1); **inter** among, between (3); **alios** some, others (4); **actum est** has been or was done (2): What has been done among some should not do harm to another.] *Law.* A transaction among some parties should not have a detrimental effect on a third party. See **res inter alios acta alteri** etc.

non debet alteri per alterum iniqua conditio inferri. [L. **non** not (4); **debet** should, ought (3); **alteri** to/upon one (person) (6); **per** by, through (7); **alterum** another (8); **iniqua** unfair, unjust (1); **conditio** condition (2); **inferri** to be inflicted (5): An unfair condition should not be inflicted upon one person by another.] *Law.* A person should not impose an unjust condition upon another.

non decipitur qui scit se decipi. [L. **non** not (5); **decipitur** is deceived (6); **qui** (one) who (1); **scit** knows (2); **se** himself, oneself (3); **decipi** to be deceived (4): One who knows onself to be deceived is not deceived.] *Law.* A person who knows that he/she is deceived has not been deceived. See **qui non improbat, approbat.**

non definitur in jure quid sit conatus. See **conatus quid sit, non definitur in jure.**

non est *n.* [L. **non** not (1); **est** he/she/it is, has been (2): He/she/it is not.] Not found. A short form for **non est inventus** (q.v.).

non est certandum de regulis juris. [L. **non** not (2); **est** it is (1); **certandum** to be disputed, challenged (3); **de** of, from, about, for (4); **regulis** rules (5); **juris** of right, law (6): It is not to be disputed about rules of law.] *Law.* Rules of law must not be challenged/disputed.

non est, crede mihi, sapientis dicere "vivam" / **sera nimis vita est crastina. vive hodie.** Martial (c.40–103/4 A.D.). *Epigrammata* I,15. [L. **non** not (2); **est** it is (1); **crede** believe (4); **mihi** me (5); **sapientis** of wise (man) (3); **dicere** to say (6); **vivam** I shall live (7); **sera** late (9); **nimis** too (8); **vita** life (11); **est** is (10); **crastina** of tomorrow, tomorrow's (12); **vive** live (13); **hodie** today (14): It is not of a wise man, believe me, to say "I shall live." / Too late is the life of tomorrow. Live today.] It is not the mark of a wise man, believe me, to say "I shall live." Too late is the life of tomorrow. Live today. For a shorter form, see **sera nimis** etc. Cf. **carpe diem.**

non est disputandum contra principia negantem. [L. **non** not (2); **est** it is (1); **disputandum** to be disputed (3); **contra** against, opposite (4); **principia** principles, elements (6); **negantem** one denying (5): It is not to be disputed against one denying principles.] There is no point in arguing against a person who denies principles.

non est factum *n., pl.* **non est factums** [L. **non** not (2); **est** it is (1); **factum** deed, act, fact (3): It is not a deed.] *Law.* It is not his/her deed. The name of a plea denying the execution of a written instrument on which a suit is brought. *In an action to recover a debt from Loba jointly and severally with Dan, Loba put up a plea of non est factum in respect of the document evidencing the transaction.* See **nient le fait.**

non est inventus or **non inventus** *short form* **non est** *abbr.* **N.E.I.** or **n.e.i.** *n., pl.* **non est inventuses** or **non inventuses** [L. **non** not (2); **est** he/she is, has been (1); **inventus** found (3): He/she has not been found.] *Law.* The return of the sheriff or an official to a writ with mission unaccomplished, i.e., when he/she cannot find in his/her jurisdiction the defendant or the person to be arrested or served.

non est recedendum a communi observantia. See **a communi observantia non est recedendum.**

non est reus nisi mens sit rea. [L. **non** not (2); **est** (one) is (1); **reus** guilty, responsible (3); **nisi** unless (4); **mens** mind, intention (5); **sit** is, may be (6); **rea** guilty, responsible (7): One is not guilty unless the mind is guilty.] *Law.* A person is not guilty unless the intention be guilty. See **actus non facit** etc.

non est vivere, sed valere vita est. Martial (c.40–103/4 A.D.). *Epigrammata* VI,70. [L. **non** not (3); **est** is (2); **vivere** to live, be alive (4); **sed** but (5); **valere** to be in good health (7); **vita** life (1); **est** it is (6): Life is not to live, but it is to be in good health.] Life is not mere living, but living in good health.

non facias malum, ut inde fiat bonum. [L. **non** not (2); **facias** you should do (1); **malum** evil, bad (3); **ut** so that (4); **inde** thence, therefrom (7); **fiat** may come, arise (6); **bonum** good (5): You should not do evil so that good may come thence.] You should not perform evil so that good may come out of it. See **ex turpi causa** etc.

non grata *adj.* [L. **non** not (1); **grata** pleasing, acceptable, agreeable (2): not acceptable/agreeable.] Unwelcome. *At his birthday party, he conspicuously displayed a notice informing anybody who is not a well-wisher that he/she is non grata.* Cf. **persona grata.**

non indiget *adv./adj.* [L. **non** not (2); **indiget** he is poor, he needs (1): He is not poor.] *Law.* As a person who is not poor. *The judgment creditor convincingly argued against the judgment debtor's application to be treated in forma pauperis and submitted that he be considered non indiget.* Cf. **in forma pauperis**.

non licet *abbr.* **N.L.** or **n.l.** [L. **non** not (2); **licet** it is allowed, permitted (1): It is not allowed.] It is not permitted.

non liquet *abbr.* **N.L.** or **n.l.** *n., pl.* **non liquets** [L. **non** not (2); **liquet** it is clear, apparent, evident (1): It is not clear.] 1. *Ancient Rome.* A ruling used by judges when unable to decide on a doubtful case or requesting permission to be excused. 2. Now used to indicate uncertainty about the facts or truth of a matter. *The arbitrator was so baffled by the inconsistencies of the testimonies, the distortions, misrepresentations and collusions that he gave a judgment of non liquet.* Cf. **liquet**.

non nasci, et natum mori, paria sunt. [L. **non** not (1); **nasci** to be born (2); **et** and (3); **natum** having been born (5); **mori** to die (4); **paria** equal (7); **sunt** are (6): Not to be born and to die having been born are equal.] Not to be born and to die immediately after birth are one and the same thing. See **mortuus exitus** etc.

non nobis Domine [L. **non** not (1); **nobis** to us (2); **Domine** lord (3): not to us, lord.] Not to us, Lord. The first words of Psalm 115, often used to show humility in the face of undeserved favor.

non obstante *abbr.* **non obs.** or **non obst.** *adv.* [L. **non** not (1); **obstante** hindering, opposing (2): not hindering/ opposing.] Notwithstanding. —*n. Law.* A license to do something notwithstanding a law or an act of the legislature to the contrary. A dispensation from, or an exception to, a rule.

non obstante veredicto *abbr.* **n.o.v.** *adj.* [L. **non** not (2); **obstante** (with) hindering, opposing (3); **veredicto** with verdict (1): with a verdict not opposing.] *Law.* Notwithstanding a verdict. Pertaining to a judgment for one party, despite a verdict for the other party.

non officit conatus nisi sequatur effectus. [L. **non** not (2); **officit** hurts, is detrimental (3); **conatus** attempt, effort (1); **nisi** unless (4); **sequatur** should follow (6); **effectus** effect, result (5): An attempt does not hurt unless the effect should follow.] *Law.* An effort is not detrimental unless the effect should follow. Cf. **actus non facit** etc.

non olet [L. **non** not (1); **olet** it stinks (2): It does not stink.] Money in any form does not stink.

non omne damnum inducit injuriam. [L. **non** not (1); **omne** every, all (2); **damnum** damage, loss (3); **inducit** brings in, introduces (4); **injuriam** injury, wrong (5): Not every loss brings in injury.] *Law.* It is not every loss that causes injury; i.e., a loss could be such that it is not accompanied by violation of legal rights and is thus not actionable. Such a situation is described as **damnum absque injuria** (q.v.) or **damnum sine injuria** (q.v.). See **actio non datur** etc.

non omne quod licet honestum est. [L. **non** not (1); **omne** every (thing) (2); **quod** which (3); **licet** is lawful, permitted (4); **honestum** honorable, respectable (6); **est** is (5): Not everything which is lawful is honorable.] *Law.* Not everything legal is honorable. Cf. **est aliquid quod** etc. and **multa non vetat** etc.

non omnia possumus omnes. Vergil (70–19 B.C.). *Eclogues* VIII,63. [L. **non** not (2); **omnia** everything (4); **possumus** we are able, can (3); **omnes** all (1): We all are not able (to do) everything.] We all cannot do everything.

nonpareil *adj.* [Fr. **non** not (1); **pareil** equal, like (2): not alike.] Without an equal. Unique. —*n.* Someone or something without an equal.

non placet [L. **non** not (1); **placet** it pleases (2): It does not please.] It is not pleasing. A vote against a proposal or motion.

nonplus *n., pl.* **nonpluses** or **non-plusses** [L. not more.] Perplexity. Bafflement. Dilemma. Quandary. *The problems besetting Usman were so multifarious that he was reduced to a nonplus.* —*v. tr.* Baffle. Perplex. *Though Eric tried to maintain a serene composure, it was easy to discern that he was non-plussed by the unpleasant disclosure.*

non plus ultra [L. **non** not (1); **plus** more (2); **ultra** farther, beyond (3): not more beyond.] **Ne plus ultra** (q.v.). Cf. **ultra**.

non possessori incumbit necessitas probandi possessiones ad se pertinere. [L. **non** not (7); **possessori** possessor (9); **incumbit** weighs upon, burdens (8); **necessitas** compulsion, urgency, necessity (1); **probandi** of proving (2); **possessiones** that possessions (3); **ad** to, at, for, according to (5); **se** himself/herself (6); **pertinere** to belong, relate (4): The compulsion of proving that the possessions belong to himself/ herself does not weigh upon the possessor.] *Law.* The necessity of proving that the possessions belong to him/her does not lie on the one in possession. See **in aequali jure melior** etc.

non potest probari quod probatum non relevat. [L. **non** not (2); **potest** he/she/it can, is able (3); **probari** to be proved (4); **quod** (that) which, what (1); **probatum** proved, having been proved (5); **non** not (6); **relevat** relieves, alleviates (7): That cannot be proved which having been proved does not alleviate.] *Law.* There is no point in proving what does not bring any relief (or what is immaterial).

non potest videri desisse habere qui numquam habuit. [L. **non** not (5); **potest** can, is able (4); **videri** to be regarded, considered (6); **desisse** to have ceased, stopped (7); **habere** to have, hold, regard (8); **qui** (he) who (1); **numquam** never (2); **habuit** had, held, regarded (3): He who never had cannot be considered to have ceased to have.] *Law.* A person who never had something cannot be considered to have ceased to have it. Cf. **non videntur rem** etc.

non prosequitur *abbr.* **non pros.** *n., pl.* **non prosequiturs** [L. **non** not (1); **prosequitur** he prosecutes, pursues (2): He does not prosecute.] *Law.* Applicable to a judgment when the plaintiff/prosecutor fails to prosecute the case within the prescribed time, and the suit is dismissed or the defendant/accused secures a verdict in default. *A plaintiff's case can sometimes be struck out on grounds of non prosequitur.* See **nolle prosequi.**

non quieta movere See **quieta non movere.**

non quod dictum est, sed quod factum est, in jure inspicitur. [L. **non** not (1); **quod** (that) which, what (2); **dictum** said (4); **est** is, has been (3); **sed** but (5); **quod** (that) which, what (6); **factum** done (8); **est** is, has been (7); **in** in, on (10); **jure** right, law (11); **inspicitur** is considered, examined (9): Not what has been said, but what has been done, is considered in law.] *Law.* What matters is not what a person says but what he does. Thus there can be valid delivery even without any word being uttered. See **in traditionibus** etc.

non quod voluit testator, sed quod dixit in testamento inspicitur. [L. **non** not (1); **quod** what (2); **voluit** wished (4); **testator** testator (3); **sed** but (5); **quod** what (6); **dixit** he said (7); **in** in, on (9); **testamento** will (10); **inspicitur** is considered (8): Not what the testator wished but what he said is considered in a will.] *Law.* In construing a will, we need to consider what the testator said, not what he wished.

non refert quid notum sit judici, si notum non sit in forma judicii. [L. **non** not (1); **refert** it matters (2); **quid** what (3); **notum** known (5); **sit** is (4); **judici** to judge (6); **si** if (7); **notum** known (10); **non** not (9); **sit** it is (8); **in** in, on (11); **forma** form (12); **judicii** of judgment (13): It does not matter what is known to a judge, if it is not known in the form of a judgment.] *Law.* What a judge knows makes no difference as long as it is not judicial knowledge. See **nemo debet esse** etc.

non repetatur. *abbr.* **N.R.** or **n.r.** or **non rep.** or **non repetat.** [L. **non** not (1); **repetatur** it should be repeated, renewed (2): It should not be repeated.] Not to be repeated.

non sanae mentis *adj.* [L. **non** not (1); **sanae** of sound, healthy (2); **mentis** (of) mind (3): not of sound mind.] *Law.* Of unsound mind. Devoid of the mental ability to understand the nature and implications of a transaction. Cf. **compos mentis.**

non-sapiens *adj.* [L. **non** not (1); **sapiens** wise (2): not wise.] *Anthropology.* Belonging to, relating to, or being one of the hominids such as the Australopithecus man, Homo Erectus, or Neanderthal man, which preceded Homo Sapiens or modern man in the process of evolution.

non sequitur *abbr.* **non seq** *n., pl.* **non sequiturs** [L. **non** not (1); **sequitur** it follows (2): It does not follow.]

An erroneous inference from premises. a) *Most of the inferences in his thesis are non sequiturs.* b) *But on the hypothesis postulated by the judge, that only the Crown had abandoned the land, counsel's submission became a non sequitur* (James 1982:149). See **lucus a non lucendo.** Cf. **sequitur.**

non sine gloria *adv.* [L. **non** not (1); **sine** without (2); **gloria** glory (3): not without glory.] Gloriously. Not ingloriously. *Georgina emerged from the contest non sine gloria.*

non solent quae abundant vitiare scripturas. [L. **non** not (3); **solent** are accustomed, wont (4); **quae** (those) things) which (1); **abundant** are in excess, superfluous (2); **vitiare** to vitiate, nullify (5); **scripturas** writings (6): Those things which are superfluous are not accustomed to vitiate writings.] *Law.* Ordinarily superfluities do not vitiate documents. Cf. **expressio eorum quae** etc. and **omissio eorum** etc.

non solum quid licet, sed quid est conveniens, est considerandum; quia nihil quod est inconveniens est licitum. [L. **non** not (1); **solum** only (2); **quid** (that) which, what (3); **licet** is lawful, permitted (4); **sed** but (5); **quid** what, (that) which (6); **est** is (7); **conveniens** fitting, proper (8); **est** is (9); **considerandum** to be considered (10); **quia** because (11); **nihil** nothing (12); **quod** which (13); **est** is (14); **inconveniens** not fitting, improper, unsuitable (15); **est** is (16); **licitum** lawful, permitted (17): Not only what is permitted but what is fitting is to be considered; because nothing which is not fitting is permitted.] *Law.* Not only what is lawful but what is proper must be considered, because nothing which is improper is lawful.

non sui juris *adj.* [L. **non** not (1); **sui** of his/her own, one's own (2); **juris** (of) right, law (3): not of one's own right.] *Law.* Not of his/her own right. Dependent. Applicable to minors or mentally unsound persons who are not legally qualified to act for themselves. Cf. **sui juris.**

non sum qualis eram. [L. **non** not (1); **sum** I am (2); **qualis** such as (3); **eram** I was (4): I am not such as I was.] I am not what I used to be.

non temere credere est nervus sapientiae. [L. **non** not (1); **temere** rashly (3); **credere** to believe, believing (2); **est** is (4); **nervus** sinew, nerve (5); **sapientiae** of wisdom (6): Not believing rashly is the sinew/nerve of wisdom.] Incredulity is a mark of wisdom.

non valet donatio nisi subsequatur traditio. [L. **non** not (2); **valet** is valid, effective (3); **donatio** donation, gift (1); **nisi** unless (4); **subsequatur** should follow (6); **traditio** delivery of possession (5): A donation is not valid, unless delivery of possession should follow.] *Law.* A donation is not valid unless followed by delivery of possession.

non videntur qui errant consentire. [L. **non** not (4); **videntur** seem, are considered/deemed (3); **qui** (those) who (1); **errant** make mistake, err (2);

consentire to agree, consent (5): Those who make a mistake are deemed not to consent.] *Law*. Consent arising from a mistake is null and void. In such a case, equity provides relief. Cf. **qui non improbat, approbat.**

non videntur rem amittere quibus propria non fuit. [L. **non** not (5); **videntur** seem, are considered/ deemed (6); **rem** matter, thing, property, business, affair (8); **amittere** to lose (7); **quibus** (those) to whom (1); **propria** their own (4); **non** not (3); **fuit** it was (2): Those to whom it was not their own are not considered to lose the thing.] *Law*. A person is not deemed to lose property which does not belong to him/her. Cf. **non potest videri** etc.

non videtur consensum retinuisse si quis ex praescripto minantis aliquid immutavit. [L. **non** not (8); **videtur** he/she seems, is deemed (9); **consensum** consent, agreement (11); **retinuisse** to have retained (10); **si** if (1); **quis** anyone (2); **ex** out of, from, directly after, away from (3); **praescripto** regulation, direction (4); **minantis** of one threatening (5); **aliquid** something, anything (7); **immutavit** has changed, altered (6): If anyone in consequence of a direction of a person threatening has changed something, he/she is deemed not to have retained consent.] *Law*. A person who makes any alteration when threatened to do so, is deemed not to have consented. See **actus me invito** etc. and **nihil consensui tam** etc.

non videtur perfecte cujusque id esse, quod ex casu auferri potest. [L. **non** not (7); **videtur** seems, is considered/deemed (8); **perfecte** fully, completely (10); **cujusque** of each one (11); **id** that (1); **esse** to be (9); **quod** which (2); **ex** out of, from, directly after, away from (5); **casu** occasion, chance, opportunity (6); **auferri** to be taken away, removed (4); **potest** can, is able (3): That which can be taken away by chance does not seem to be completely of each one.] *Law*. Something which can be taken away from a person by chance does not seem to belong to him/her completely.

non videtur quisquam id capere, quod ei necesse est alii restituere. [L. **non** not (2); **videtur** seems, is deemed (3); **quisquam** anyone, any person (1); **id** that (5); **capere** to take (4); **quod** which (6); **ei** for him (9); **necesse** necessary (8); **est** it is (7); **alii** to another (11); **restituere** to restore (10): Any person is not deemed to take that which it is necessary for him to restore to another.] *Law*. A person is not deemed to take what he should restore to another. Cf. **frustra petis quod mox** etc. and **frustra petis quod statim** etc.

non videtur vim facere, qui jure suo utitur et ordinaria actione experitur. [L. **non** not (9); **videtur** seems, is deemed/considered (10); **vim** force (12); **facere** to make, do (11); **qui** (one) who (1); **jure** right, law (4); **suo** his/her own, one's own (3); **utitur** uses, takes advantage of (2); **et** and (5); **ordinaria** by ordi-

nary, usual (7); **actione** legal action (8); **experitur** tries, attempts (6): One who takes advantage of his/ her own right and tries by usual legal action is not deemed to make force.] *Law*. A person who exercises his/her own right and resorts to ordinary judicial action is not deemed to apply force. See **qui jure suo utitur neminem laedit.**

non vult contendere or **non vult** *n., pl.* **non vult contenderes** or **non vults** [L. **non** not (1); **vult** he wishes (2); **contendere** to contend (3): He/she does not wish to contend.] *Law*. A plea in a criminal case in which the accused neither admits nor denies the charges. See **nolo contendere.**

norma *n., pl.* **normae** [L. rule.] Pattern. Norm. Standard.

Norteamericano or **norteamericano** *adj., fem.* **Norteamericana** or **norteamericana** *pl.* **Norteamericanos** or **norteamericanos** *fem.* **Norteamericanas** or **norteamericanas** [Sp. and Port. **norte** north (1); **americano** American (2): North American.] An inhabitant of America north of Mexico, especially the English-speaking North Americans in the U.S.A. and Canada.

nosce te ipsum. or **Nosce teipsum.** [L. **nosce** know (1); **te** you (2); **ipsum** yourself (3): Know yourself.] Be aware of yourself; i.e., a person should understand his/her own capabilities and deficiencies. See **gnothi seauton.**

noscitur a sociis *n.* [L. **noscitur** it is known, recognized (1); **a** from (2); **sociis** associates, partners (3): It is known/understood from its associates.] *Law*. A doctrine which maintains that the meaning of uncertain words or expressions in a statute may be ascertained by considering the meaning of the words or expressions accompanying them. Also applicable to the view that a person's character can be ascertained by considering the character of his associates; i.e., "Show me your friend and I'll tell you your character." "Birds of a feather flock together." See **noscitur ex socio** etc.

noscitur ex socio, qui non cognoscitur ex se. [L. **noscitur** is known, recognized (6); **ex** out of, from, directly after, away from (7); **socio** companion, associate (8); **qui** (one) who (1); **non** not (2); **cognoscitur** is identified, recognized (3); **ex** out of, from, directly after, away from (4); **se** himself (5): One who is not recognized from himself is known from his companion.] When a person's character is not known, it may be ascertained by considering that of his associate. See **noscitur a sociis.**

nostalgia *n., pl.* **nostalgias** [Neo-Gk. from Gk. **nost(os)** return home, homecoming (2); **alg(eō)** be in pain (1): pain of return home.] 1. Homesickness. 2. Sentimental recollection, or desire for the return, of a real or imaginary experience of the past. a) *Their nostalgia for the good old days is expressed effusively in their praise for the dance bands of the sixties* (Thomas Cooke in *West Africa* 1985). b) *. . . the journey provoked a nostalgia for those days gone by when traveling by* road was both enjoyed and looked forward to (*The Guardian* 1986).

Noster Salvator Iesus Christus *abbr.* **N.S.I.C.** See **Noster Salvator Jesus Christus.**

Noster Salvator Jesus Christus *abbr.* **N.S.J.C.** [L. **noster** our (1); **Salvator** savior (2); **Jesus** Jesus (3); **Christus** Christ (4): Our Savior Jesus Christ.] Jesus Christ, Our Savior.

nostos *n., pl.* **nostoi** [Gk. homecoming.] 1. A journey home, such as Odysseus' ten-year journey back to Ithaca after the Trojan war. 2. A homecoming or return home after a long absence.

nostrum *n., pl.* **nostrums** [L. something ours.] 1. A dubious, secret, or quack medicine or remedy. *Such nostrums as . . . Mrs. Winslow's Soothing Syrup and Wheeler's Nerve Vitalizer, many of which contained cannabis, opiates or alcohol . . . (Newsweek Int.* Nov. 12, 1979:63). 2. A panacea. A questionable device, scheme, plan or remedy. *. . . he opened up to reporters mostly to peddle his right-wing nostrums for restoring America to the greatness he perceived under Calvin Coolidge . . . (Newsweek Int.* April 7, 1980:39).

nota bene. *abbr.* **N.B.** or **n.b.** [L. **nota** note, mark (1); **bene** well (2): Note/mark well.] Note carefully. Used to draw attention to something deemed important. *He came to my office and, nota bene, claimed that he had been authorized to collect the documents from me.* —**nota bene** *n., pl.* **nota benes** A caution. A warning. A piece of advice. *They disregarded his nota benes.*

notabilia *pl. n.* [L. things worthy of note.] Notable things. Items which should be noticed.

notable évolué *n., pl.* **notables évolués** [Fr. **notable** important, worthy (1); **évolué** developed (person) (2): important developed person.] 1. A distinguished person who belonged to the class of enlightened élite, usually the son of a chief, etc. 2. *French Colonial Tropical Africa.* A person belonging to a class of natives who occupied an intermediary position between citizens and subjects. Such natives were exempted from the **indigénat** (q.v.), but did not enjoy French citizenship. *By 1 April, 1943, only eleven persons had been established as notables évolués; . . . by 30 December, 103* (Suret-Canale 1971:477). Cf. **évolué.**

notandum *n., pl.* **notanda** or **notandums** [L. that which must be noted.] **Memorandum** (q.v.). Something which should be noted. A note. *The minister sent to the permanent secretary a notandum on the proposed project.*

note collective *n., pl.* **notes collectives** [Fr. **note** note (2); **collective** joint, collective (1): joint note.] *Diplomacy.* A joint or collective note. A signed formal diplomatic correspondence addressed by the representatives of several states to one state or several states.

note diplomatique *n., pl.* **notes diplomatiques** [Fr. **note** note (2); **diplomatique** diplomatic (1): diplomatic note.] *Diplomacy.* A signed formal diplomatic correspondence, authorized by the state which sends it.

note verbale *n., pl.* **notes verbales** [Fr. **note** note (2); **verbale** verbal, oral (1): a verbal note.] *Diplomacy.* An unsigned diplomatic note, drafted in the third person, which is less formal than a note but more formal than an **aide-mémoire** (q.v.).

Notre Dame *n.* [Fr. **notre** our (1); **dame** lady (2): our lady.] Title given to Mary the mother of Jesus and thus to many churches and institutions dedicated to her. *University of Notre Dame.*

noumenon *n., pl.* **noumena** [Gk. that which is thought.] *Philosophy.* A thing-in-itself. A thing which is conceived exclusively by the intellect and thus cannot be perceived by the senses (e.g., God, soul, etc.). See **Ding an sich.** Cf. **phenomenon.**

nous *n.* [Gk. mind, sense, reason, intellect.] 1. Mind. Reason. Intellect. 2. Common sense.

nouveau *adj.* [Fr. new, fresh, recent.] Fresh. New. Immature. a) *Tayo has bought a house in a nouveau suburb of Lagos.* b) *. . . the nouveau second-tier Foreign Exchange Market . . . (The Guardian* 1986).

nouveau arrivé *n., pl.* **nouveaux arrivés** [Fr. **nouveau** new (1); **arrivé** arrived (2): new arrived.] A new arrival. A person who has recently acquired fame, power, social standing, etc. Cf. **novus homo.**

nouveau riche *n., pl.* **nouveaux riches** [Fr. **nouveau** new, recent (1); **riche** rich, wealthy (person) (2): a new-rich person.] A **parvenu** (q.v.). An upstart. A person of negligible education or sophistication, or of humble birth, who has recently acquired wealth. *The nouveaux riches who joined the side of the landowning nobility were not welcomed* (Jaeger 1970:225). —*attrib.* Characteristic of, relating to, belonging to the newly rich. *For years the Germans . . . spurned Detroit's chromed giants as only suitable for nouveau riche butchers, high-mark call girls and mobsters (Time Int.* 1979).

nouveau roman *n., pl.* **nouveaux romans** [Fr. **nouveau** new (1); **roman** novel (2): new novel.] A post-modern long prose form which rejects the traditional conventions of the novel, including plot, characterization, and consistency of setting; e.g., *Compact* (1966) by Maurice Roche (1925–).

nouvelle *n., pl.* **nouvelles** [Fr. *adj.* new, recent; *n.* news, short story, tale.] A short novel. A work of fiction which in complexity and length is more than a short story but less than a novel. See **novella.**

nouvelle cuisine *short form* **nouvelle** *n.* [Fr. **nouvelle** new, new-fangled (1); **cuisine** cooking, cookery (2): new cooking.] A new or revolutionary method of French cooking which avoids the traditional heavy use of butter and cream and thickens sauces with pureed vegetables and places a special emphasis on the artful presentation of each dish. *Jean Troisgros, . . . talented and influential exponent of the nouvelle cuisine . . . (Newsweek Int.* Aug. 22, 1983:47). See **cuisine.**

nouvelle vague *n.* [Fr. **nouvelle** new, recent (1); **vague** wave (2): new wave.] A new or revolutionary technique of making films which involves a low budget and the utilization of amateur or relatively unknown actors as well as camera-work characteristic of **cinéma vérité** (q.v.). *The pioneer of nouvelle vague prefers to keep the plot a secret . . . (Newsweek Int.* Nov. 12, 1979: 59).

n.o.v. *abbr.* for **non obstante veredicto** (q.v.).

nova *n., pl.* **novas** or **novae** [L. new.] A new star. A star which suddenly, i.e., within a few days, becomes visible and then gradually, over a period of months or a few years, fades away until it eventually becomes as obscure as it originally was.

nova causa interveniens *n.* [L. **nova** new (1); **causa** cause, case, reason (2); **interveniens** intervening (3): new case intervening.] *Law.* A new case which intrudes upon an earlier one. The effect of such a case is to reduce/nullify the responsibility of the previous case for an act or damage. *If the defendant's breach of duty has done no more than provide the occasion for an entirely independent act by a third party and that act is the immediate cause of the plaintiff's damage, then it will amount to a nova causa interveniens and the defendant will not be liable* (Rogers 1975:10). See **novus actus interveniens.**

nova constitutio futuris formam imponere debet non praeteritis. [L. **nova** new (1); **constitutio** constitution, regulation (2); **futuris** future (events) (6); **formam** form, pattern (5); **imponere** to impose on (4); **debet** should, ought (3); **non** not (7); **praeteritis** past (events) (8): A new regulation ought to impose a pattern on future events, not on past events.] *Law.* A new law ought to regulate affairs of the future, not the past; i.e., it should not be retroactive. See **lex prospicit** etc. and **omnis nova constitutio** etc.

novella *n., pl.* **novellas** or **novelle** [It. new, news, short story.] A short story whose plot is pointed and compact. **Nouvelle** (q.v.). *Katherine . . . author of gem-like novellas and short stories that dealt, in her words, with the human propensity for "self-betrayal and self-deception, in all its forms"; . . . (Time Int.* 1980).

Novelle *n.* [Ger. novella.] A novella (q.v.). It is usually based on an unusual event which happened in real life, and one of its principal distinguishing features is the **Wendepunkt** (q.v.), i.e. unexpected turning-point in the narrative.

novena *n., pl.* **novenas** [Med. L. from L. **novem** nine: a period of nine days.] *Roman Catholic Church.* A nine-day period of prayer and devotion to God, especially through the intercession of the Virgin Mary or a saint, usually in hope of or in thanksgiving for a special favor or benefit.

novum judicium non dat jus novum, sed declarat antiquum; quia judicium est juris dictum et per judicium jus est noviter revelatum quod diu fuit velatum. [L. **novum** new (1); **judicium** judgment (2); **non** not (3); **dat** gives (4); **jus** right, law (6); **novum** new (5); **sed** but (7); **declarat** declares, explains (8); **antiquum** old, ancient (9); **quia** because (10); **judicium**

judgment (11); **est** is (12); **juris** of right, law (14); **dictum** assertion utterance (13); **et** and (15); **per** through, by (16); **judicium** judgment (17); **jus** right, law (18); **est** is, has been (23); **noviter** newly (24); **revelatum** unveiled, uncovered (25); **quod** which, that (19); **diu** a long time, long (21); **fuit** was (20); **velatum** veiled, covered (22): A new judgment does not give new law but declares the old (one); because judgment is the utterance of law and through judgment law which was long veiled has been newly unveiled.] *Law.* A new judgment does not make a new law, but states the old law, because a judgment is the expression of the law and by judgment the law which had been covered for a long time is newly uncovered.

Novum Organon *n.* [L. **novum** new (1); Gk. **organon** organ (2): new organ.] *New Organ,* a 1620 philosophical treatise by Francis Bacon (1561–1626).

Novum Testamentum *n.* [L. **novum** new (1); **testamentum** testament (2): new testament.] The Latin New Testament. Cf. **Vetum Testamentum.**

novus actus interveniens or **novus actus** *n.* [L. **novus** new (1); **actus** act, motion (2); **interveniens** intervening (3): a new act intervening.] *Law.* A new action or deed which intrudes upon an earlier one. The effect of such an action is to reduce the responsibility of a previous action, unless it can be proved that the previous act was directly responsible for the act or damage. *After medical treatment, there was a novus actus interveniens when the victim of the motor accident took to native medicinal treatment, resulting in his death.* See **nova causa interveniens.**

novus homo *n., pl.* **novi homines** [L. **novus** new (1); **homo** person, human being (2): a new person.] 1. *Ancient Rome.* A person who is the first in his family to become a Senator. *But the patrician, who regarded the consulship as his birthright, now found himself running against a novus homo who was striving with equal determination to break into the preserves of the aristocracy, M. Tullius Cicero* (Cary 1970:370). 2. An upstart. A self-made man. *Snobbish men from old established families shun Madu's company, since they regard him as a novus homo.* 3. A person pardoned of a crime. A discharged insolvent.

noxa *n., pl.* **noxae** [L. hurt, harm, injury, damage.] *Civil Law.* An injury/damage done by somebody's slave or animal to a person or property, which consequently permits legal action against the offender's owner. See **noxae deditio** and **noxalis actio.**

noxae deditio *n.* [L. **noxae** of hurt, harm, injury, damage (2); **deditio** surrender (1): surrender of harm.] *Ancient Rome.* Noxal surrender. When a slave or an animal caused **noxa** (q.v.), the owner, if he wanted to renounce responsibility, could surrender the slave or animal to the injured person for the satisfaction of the injury. See **noxalis actio.**

noxalis actio *n., pl.* **noxales actiones** [L. **noxalis** of, or relating to, injury/hurt/harm, injurious (1); **actio** action, deed, legal suit (2): injurious legal suit.] *Civil Law.* A legal action relating to harm/injury. Noxal action. Action arising from **noxa** (q.v.). See **noxae deditio.**

noxa sequitur caput. [L. **noxa** hurt, injury, harm, damage (1); **sequitur** follows (2); **caput** head (3): damage follows the head.] *Civil Law.* A person who buys a slave or animal which has caused damage takes over the liability.

noyade *n., pl.* **noyades** [Fr. drowning.] Execution through the process of drowning.

N.P.U. *abbr.* for **ne plus ultra** (q.v.).

N.R. or **n.r.** *abbr.* for **non repetatur** (q.v.).

N.S.I.C. *abbr.* for **Noster Salvator Iesus Christus** (q.v.).

N.S.J.C. *abbr.* for **Noster Salvator Jesus Christus** (q.v.).

nuance *n., pl.* **nuances** [Fr. shade, hue, difference, distinction.] A subtle shade or degree of difference. a) *The reader will look in vain for subtle characterization and sophisticated nuance* (Mark Ralph Bowman in *West Africa* 1982). b) *The difference in any effort between greatness and mediocrity is a nuance . . .* (*Time Int.* 1982).

nubile *adj.* [Fr. from L. **nubilis** marriageable.] Of marriagable age. Physically mature for amorous relationship. Applicable to girls and young women. *The village has an annual festival during which nubile girls are displayed in the most seductive manner.*

nucleus *n., pl.* **nuclei** or **nucleuses** [L. kernel.] 1. A central point or part about which other things gather. *The founding fathers built a hamlet of about ten huts which, as it turned out, became the nucleus of a city.* 2. *Biology.* A cell's kernel. 3. *Physics.* The central part of an atom.

nuda pactio obligationem non parit. [L. **nuda** nude, naked (1); **pactio** agreement, pact (2); **obligationem** obligation (5); **non** not (3); **parit** produces, creates (4): A bare agreement does not produce an obligation.] *Law.* A naked agreement does not create a duty. In order to create a duty, an agreement must be accompanied by a consideration, by the transfer of something of value between one party and the other. Cf. **ex turpi causa** etc.

nuda ratio et nuda pactio non ligant aliquem debitorem. [L. **nuda** naked, bare (1); **ratio** reason, consideration (2); **et** and (3); **nuda** naked, bare (4); **pactio** agreement (5); **non** not (6); **ligant** bind (7); **aliquem** any (8); **debitorem** debtor (9): Bare reason and bare agreement do not bind any debter.] *Law.* Naked reason and naked agreement do not obligate a debtor. In order for such obligation to exist, the reason and the agreement must be accompanied by a consideration, by the transfer of something of value between one party and the other. Cf. **ex turpi causa** etc.

nudi consensus obligatio contrario consensu dissolvitur. [L. **nudi** of naked, nude, bare (2); **consensus** (of) consent, agreement, accord (3); **obligatio** obligation (1); **contrario** by contrary, conflicting (5); **consensu** (by) consent, agreement, accord (6); **dissolvitur** is dissolved (4): The obligation of bare consent is dissolved by contrary consent.] *Law.* The obligation imposed by a naked agreement is broken up by a contrary agreement. See **eodem modo quo quid constituitur dissolvitur.**

nudum pactum *n., pl.* **nuda pacta** [L. **nudum** naked, nude, bare (1); **pactum** pact, agreement (2): a bare agreement.] *Law.* A naked contract. Applicable to a mere promise or informal agreement which cannot be enforced because it lacks a lawful motive or required consideration. *If Joe promises to give Bob $100.00 and subsequently refuses to honor the promise, the payment cannot be enforced, since it is a nudum pactum.*

nudum pactum est ubi nulla subest causa praeter conventionem; sed ubi subest causa, fit obligatio et parit actionem. [L. **nudum** naked, bare, nude (1); **pactum** contract, pact (2); **est** is (3); **ubi** where (4); **nulla** no (5); **subest** is under/underneath (7); **causa** cause, case, reason (6); **praeter** except (8); **conventionem** agreement (9); **sed** but (10); **ubi** where (11); **subest** is under/underneath (13); **causa** cause, case, reason (12); **fit** there is (14); **obligatio** obligation (15); **et** and (16); **parit** produces, creates (17); **actionem** action (18): A bare contract is where no cause is underneath except agreement, but where cause is underneath, there is obligation and it produces action.] *Law.* A naked contract is one which is not supported by any consideration other than an informal agreement, but a contract which is supported by consideration becomes obligatory and actionable.

nudum pactum ex quo non oritur actio. [L. **nudum** naked, bare, nude (1); **pactum** pact, agreement (2); **ex** out of, from, directly after, away from (3); **quo** which (4); **non** not (6); **oritur** arises (7); **actio** action, deed, legal suit (5): A bare pact (is one) from which a legal suit does not arise.] *Law.* A naked pact is one which does not produce a legal action. Cf. **ex turpi causa** etc.

nugae difficiles *pl. n.* [L. **nugae** nuts, trifles (2); **difficiles** difficult (1): difficult trifles.] *Philosophy.* Small or insignificant problems or questions which are so difficult that they consume an inordinate amount of time and attention.

nulla bona *abbr.* **N.B.** or **n.b.** *pl. n.* [L. **nulla** no (1); **bona** goods, property (2): no goods.] *Law.* No goods/property. The return made by a sheriff or any officer to a writ, usually a writ of fieri facias, when he/she finds no leviable goods. See **fieri facias.**

nulla impossibilia aut inhonesta sunt praesumenda; vera autem et honesta et possibilia. [L. **nulla** no (1); **impossibilia** impossible (things) (2); **aut** or (3); **inhonesta** dishonorable, disgraceful (things) (4); **sunt** are (5); **praesumenda** to be presumed (6); **vera** true (things) (8); **autem** but, however (7); **et** and (9); **honesta** honorable (10); **et** and (11); **possibilia** possible (things) (12): No impossible or dishonorable things are to be presumed; but true and honorable and possible things (are).] *Law.* No impossible or dishonorable things must be presumed, but things that are true, honorable, and possible must be. Cf. **odiosa et inhonesta** etc.

nulla pactione effici potest ut dolus praestetur. [L. **nulla** by no (1); **pactione** (by) contract, agreement (2); **effici** to be effected, brought about (4); **potest** it can, is able (3); **ut** that (5); **dolus** fraud (6); **praestetur** be maintained, preserved (7): By no contract can it be effected that fraud be maintained.] *Law.* No contract will succeed in justifying the perpetration of fraud.

nulla poena sine lege [L. **nulla** no (1); **poena** punishment, penalty (2); **sine** without (3); **lege** law (4): no punishment without law.] *Law.* No punishment except in accordance with the law. The state cannot punish a person unless there is a law specifically making the act or behavior an offense. Cf. **nullum crimen sine lege.**

nulla salus extra ecclesiam [L. **nulla** no (1); **salus** safety, salvation (2); **extra** beyond, outside (3); **ecclesiam** church (4): no salvation outside the church.] *Christianity.* No salvation is possible outside the church. Cf. **a cruce salus.**

nulle règle sans faute [Fr. **nulle** no, not (1); **règle** rule (2); **sans** without (3); **faute** fault, offense (4): No rule without offense.] *Law.* There is no rule without a corresponding offense.

nulligravida *n., pl.* **nulligravidae** or **nulligravidas** [Neo-L. **null(us)** no (2); **gravida** pregnant (1): pregnant at no (time).] *Medicine.* A woman who has never had a pregnancy. Cf. **gravida.**

nullipara *n., pl.* **nulliparae** or **nulliparas** [Neo-L. **null(us)** no (2); **pario** give birth (1): giving birth at no time.] *Medicine.* A woman who has yet to give birth to a child. Cf. **multipara.**

nulli secundus or *fem.* **nulli secunda** *adj.* [L. **nulli** to none, nobody (2); **secundus** second, next (1): second to none.] Of first rank. First-class. *He paid tribute to his great friend, describing him as a genius, who was nulli secundus in his field.*

nullius filius or **filius nullius** *n., pl.* **nullius filii** or **filii nullius** [L. **nullius** of no one, nobody (2); **filius** son (1): son of nobody, nobody's son.] An illegitimate son. A bastard. In some communities, a bastard has no rights of inheritance, but in several African societies the word "bastard" is practically irrelevant, and a bastard is recognized as a son in the family, as long as the child enjoys the recognition of the father or mother. See **filius populi.**

nullius in bonis See **in nullius bonis.**

nullius juris *adj.* [L. **nullius** of no (1); **juris** (of) right, law (2): of no right/law.] Of no legal validity or effect. With no legal standing.

nullum crimen sine lege. [L. **nullum** no (1); **crimen** crime, offense, fault (2); **sine** without (3); **lege** law (4): no offense without law.] *Law.* An act is not an offense if there is no law forbidding it. Cf. **nulla poena sine lege; nullum crimen sine poena;** and **ubi non est lex** etc.

nullum crimen sine poena. [L. **nullum** no (1); **crimen** crime, offense, fault (2); **sine** without (3); **poena** punishment (4): no offense without punishment.] *Law.* There is no offense without its corresponding punishment. Cf. **nullum crimen sine lege.**

nullum exemplum est idem omnibus. [L. **nullum** no (1); **exemplum** example (2); **est** is (3); **idem** the same (4); **omnibus** for all (5): No example is the same for all.] *Law.* No example is the same for all cases; i.e., there is no precedent which is applicable to all cases. A maxim applicable to conveyancing.

nullum iniquum est in jure praesumendum. [L. **nullum** no (1); **iniquum** unfair, unjust (thing) (2); **est** is (3); **in** in, on (5); **jure** right, law (6); **praesumendum** to be presumed (4): No unjust thing is to be presumed in law.] No injustice must be presumed in law.

nullum simile est idem. [L. **nullum** no (thing) (1); **simile** similar, like (2); **est** is (3); **idem** the same (4): Nothing similar is the same.] Things that are similar are not the same.

nullum simile est idem nisi quatuor pedibus currit. [L. **nullum** no (thing) (1); **simile** similar, like (2); **est** is (3); **idem** the same (4); **nisi** unless, except (5); **quat(t)uor** on four (7); **pedibus** (on) feet (8); **currit** it runs (6): Nothing similar is the same unless it runs on four feet.] Things that are similar are not the same unless they run on all fours, i.e. unless they are exactly the same in all circumstances and aspects. See **currit quatuor pedibus** and **nullum simile quatuor** etc.

nullum simile quatuor pedibus currit. [L. **nullum** no (thing) (1); **simile** similar, like (2); **quat(t)uor** on four (4); **pedibus** (on) feet (5); **currit** runs (3): Nothing similar runs on four feet.] Things that are similar do not run on all fours; i.e., things which are similar are not exactly the same in all circumstances and aspects. See **currit quatuor pedibus** and **nullum simile est idem nisi** etc.

nullum tempus aut locus occurrit regi. [L. **nullum** no (1); **tempus** time (2); **aut** or (3); **locus** place (4); **occurrit** runs against (5); **regi** the king (6): No time or place runs against the king.] Time and place never run against the king; i.e., the king is not affected by a statute of limitations in regard to time or location.

nullum tempus occurrit regi. [L. **nullum** no (1); **tempus** time (2); **occurrit** runs against (3); **regi** the king (4): No time runs against the king.] Time never runs against the king; i.e., the king is not affected by a statute of limitations in regard to time.

nullum tempus occurrit reipublicae. [L. **nullum** no (1); **tempus** time (2); **occurrit** runs against (3); **rei publicae** the public affair, the state (4): No time runs against the state.] Time never runs against the state; i.e., the state is not affected by a statute of limitations in regard to time.

nullus commodum capere potest de injuria sua propria. [L. **nullus** no (one) (1); **commodum** advantage, gain, profit (4); **capere** to take (3); **potest** can, is able (2); **de** of, from, about, for (5); **injuria** wrong, injury (8); **sua** his/her own, one's (6); **propria** own (7): No one can take advantage from his/her own wrong.] *Law.* No one should derive advantage from his/her own wrong. Thus, if "A" is bound to appear in court on a certain day in connection with an action brought by "B" and the latter gets the former imprisoned before the appointed day, the bond becomes null and void. The maxim is also applicable to fraudulent transactions. See **ex turpi causa** etc.

nullus videtur dolo facere qui suo jure utitur. [L. **nullus** no (one) (1); **videtur** seems, is deemed (6); **dolo** with guile, fraud (8); **facere** to do, act (7); **qui** who (2); **suo** his/her own, one's own (4); **jure** right, law (5); **utitur** uses, takes advantage of (3): No (one) who takes advantage of his/her own right is deemed to act with guile.] *Law.* A person who exercises his/her own right is not deemed to act fraudulently. See **qui jure suo utitur neminem laedit.**

Nul ne doit s'enrichir aux dépens des autres. [Fr. **nul ne** no one, nobody (1); **doit** should, ought (2); **s'** himself/herself (4); **enrichir** to enrich (3); **aux** to the, toward the, in the, by the, with the, until the (5); **dépens** expense, cost (6); **des** of the (7); **autres** others (8): No one should enrich himself/herself at the expense of the others.] *Law.* Nobody should make himself/herself wealthy at other people's expense. See **nemo debet ex** etc.

nul tiel *adj.* [Obs. Fr. **nul** no (1); **tiel** such (2): no such.] *Law.* No such. Not any. Not existant. Used in pleas like *nul tiel corporation* and *nul tiel record* in which the defense denies the existence of a corporation or a record claimed by the plaintiff.

numen *n., pl.* **numina** [L. nod, divine will, divinity.] 1. A spirit which, according to animists, dwells in a natural object. a) *In Italy, . . . the numen of the deity had always been conceived as dwelling in material objects* (Robinson 1974:218). b) *Every Friday the chief priest, accompanied by assistants, comes to the big tree to offer sacrifices to the numen.* 2. A local god. A protective deity. *The clan has a numen to which they offer prayers whenever a clansman is about to embark upon a great project.*

numero uno *n.* [It./Sp. **numero** number (1); **uno** one (2): number one.] The single most important individual. The center of attention.

numerus clausus *n.* [L. **numerus** number (2); **clausus** closed (1): closed number.] A set number, especially a fixed number of members in an organization. *The numerus clausus of the U.S. House of Representations is 435.*

numquam crescit ex post facto praeteriti delicti aestimatio. [L. **numquam** never (4); **crescit** increases (5); **ex** out of, from, directly after, away from (6); **postfacto** (something) done afterwards (8); **praeteriti** of past (2); **delicti** (of) offense, wrong (3); **aestimatio** assessment, valuation (1): The assessment of a past offense never increases from something done afterwards.] *Law.* The assessment of an offense is never increased by any subsequent occurrence.

numquam decurritur ad extraordinarium sed ubi deficit ordinarium. [L. **numquam** never (2); **decurritur** it is hastened (1); **ad** to, at, for, according to (3); **extraordinarium** uncommon (4); **sed** but (5); **ubi** when (6); **deficit** fails (8); **ordinarium** ordinary (7): It is never hastened to the uncommon but when the ordinary fails.] We should never resort to extraordinary measures until the ordinary fails. See **recurrendum est** etc.; **si assuetis mederi** etc. and **ubi cessat** etc.

numquam res humanae prospere succedunt ubi negliguntur divinae. [L. **numquam** never (3); **res** matters, things, property, business, affairs (2); **humanae** human (1); **prospere** prosperously, favorably (5); **succedunt** prosper, succeed (4); **ubi** when (6); **negliguntur** are neglected, ignored (8); **divinae** divine (matters) (7): Human matters never succeed prosperously when divine matters are neglected.] Human affairs never prosper when religion is neglected. Cf. **nemo unquam** etc.

nunc dimittis *n.* [L. **nunc** now (1); **dimittis** you dismiss (2): Now you dismiss.] 1. Luke 2:29 Song of Simeon. You may now dismiss your servant in peace. 2. A declaration of happiness that one is making one's exit from life or an employment.

nunc est bibendum, nunc pede libero / pulsanda tellus Horace (65–8 B.C.). *Odes* I,37,1–2. [L. **nunc** now (1); **est** it is (2); **bibendum** to be drunk (3); **nunc** now (4); **pede** (with) foot (6); **libero** with free (5); **pulsanda** to be beaten (8); **tellus** earth, ground (7): Now it is to be drunk; now with free foot / the ground to be beaten.] Now is the time to drink; now is the time to beat the ground with free step; i.e., it is time for celebration. The shorter form, **nunc est bibendum**, is usually used.

nuncio or **nuntio** *n., pl.* **nuncios** or **nuntios** [It. **nunzio** from Obs. It. **nuntio** from L. **nuntius** messenger.] A diplomatic envoy of the highest rank representing the Pope at the seat of a foreign government. He may be either an ordinary nuncio who deals with general matters or an extraordinary nuncio who is despatched for a special mission. *On Christmas Eve, Monsignor Annibale Bugnini, who represents the Vatican as the papal nuncio in Iran, was allowed to visit the Americans* (*Time Int.* 1981).

nunc pro tunc *n.* [L. **nunc** now (1); **pro** for (2); **tunc** then (3): now for then.] *Law.* Now for then. Used in respect of a judgment, decree, or entry made currently, but applying retroactively to the date when it should have been made.

nunc scio quid sit Amor. Vergil (70–19 B.C.). *Eclogues* VIII,43. [L. **nunc** now (1); **scio** I know (2);

quid what (3); **sit** is (5); **amor** love (4): Now I know what Love is.] Now I know what Love means.

Nun danket alle Gott. Martin Rinckart (1586–1649). [Ger. **nun** now (1); **danket** thank (3); **alle** all (2); **Gott** God (4): Now all thank God.] Now all give thanks to God. The first line of a Christian hymn.

nuptias non concubitus sed consensus facit. [L. **nuptias** marriage (6); **non** not (1); **concubitus** concubinage, cohabitation (2); **sed** but (3); **consensus** consent, agreement (4); **facit** makes (5): Not cohabitation but consent makes marriage.] *Law.* What makes marriage is consent not cohabitation. See **consensus non concubitus** etc.

nymphomania *n.* [Neo-Gk. from Gk. **numph(ē)** bride (2); **mania** madness, inspired frenzy (1): madness, or inspired frenzy, of the bride.] A woman's uncontrollable desire for sexual intercourse. See **andromania**.

O

O.A.M.D.G. *abbr.* for **omnia ad Majorem Dei Gloriam** (q.v.).

ob. *abbr.* for 1. **obiit** (q.v.). 2. **obiter** (q.v.).

obbligato *abbr.* **obb.** or *fem.* **obbligata** *adj.* [It. obligated, obliged.] Obligatory. Applicable, in music, to a sound, usually instrumental, which must accompany, for instance, a solo voice.— *n., pl.* **obbligati** or **obbligatos** 1. *Music.* A prominent instrumental part which must accompany, for instance, a solo voice. 2. An accompaniment. *The activities of the sect, with their uninterrupted obbligato of violence and disturbance of public peace, ultimately attracted the attention of the authorities.*

obedientia est legis essentia. [L. **ob(o)edientia** obedience (1); **est** is (2); **legis** of law (4); **essentia** essence (3): Obedience is the essence of law.] *Law.* Compliance is the most essential part of the law.

obiit *abbr.* **ob.** [L. He/she died.] Died. Followed by the date of the event.

obiit sine prole. or **obit sine prole.** *abbr.* **O.S.P.** or **o.s.p.** or **ob.s.p.** [L. **obiit** he/she died, perished (1); **sine** without (2); **prole** offspring, children (3): He/she died without offspring or issue.] He/she died with no children. See **decessit sine prole**; **decessit sine prole legitima**; **decessit sine prole mascula**; **decessit sine prole mascula superstite**; **decessit sine prole superstite**; and **decessit sine prole virili**.

obiter *adv.* [L. meanwhile, incidentally, on the way.] Incidentally. In passing. By the way.

obiter dictum *n., pl.* **obiter dicta** [L. **obiter** meanwhile, incidentally, on the way (2); **dictum** said (1): said incidentally.] *Law.* Incidental opinion/remark expressed by the judge which is entirely unnecessary for the judgment and is thus not binding. It is also not regarded as a precedent. *In his obiter dictum the judge expressed displeasure that the insurance companies were not joined as parties to the claim for damages.*

objet d'art *n., pl.* **objets d'art** [Fr. **objet** object (1); **d'** of (2); **art** art (3): object of art.] Art object. A work of art. *French customs officials have also been instructed to withhold all export permits on valuable objets d'art . . .* (*Newsweek Int.* Nov. 30, 1981:17).

objet surréaliste *n., pl.* **objets surréalistes** [Fr. **objet** object (2); **surréaliste** surreal, surrealist (1): surreal or surrealist object.] Object of surrealism; i.e., art object characterized by fantastic imagery. *The show of more than 200 works by René Magritte—paintings, drawings and miscellaneous objets surréalistes . . .* (*Time Int.* 1979).

obligatio *n.* [L. an engaging, obligation, pledging.] *Roman Law.* A legal duty to perform something, roughly corresponding to a modern-day contract such as the relationship between a creditor and a debtor.

ob majorem cautelam *adv.* [L. **ob** for, on account of, for the sake of (1); **majorem** greater (2); **cautelam** caution (3): on account of greater caution.] For greater caution. To be on the safe side. See **ad abundantiorem cautelam**.

obscuritas pacti nocet ei qui apertius loqui potuit. [L. **obscuritas** uncertainty, obscurity (1); **pacti** of contract (2); **nocet** does harm, hurts, injures (3); **ei** to him/her, the one (4); **qui** who (5); **apertius** more clearly, plainly (8); **loqui** to speak (7); **potuit** could, was able (6): Obscurity of contract does harm to him/her who could speak more clearly.] *Law.* Obscurity of contract is detrimental to the party who could have explained the terms more clearly. See **quaelibet concessio** etc.

obscurum per obscurius *n.* [L. **obscurum** obscure (thing) (1); **per** through (2); **obscurius** more obscure (thing) (3): obscure thing through the more obscure thing.] *Logic.* The obscure through the more obscure. Attempting to explain what is obscure by making reference to what is even more obscure. *The learned professor's explanation is a classic case of obscurum per obscurius.* Cf. **ignotum per ignotius**.

observandum *n., pl.* **observanda** [L. that which must be observed.] The thing to be observed.

279

ob. s.p. *abbr.* for **obiit sine prole** (q.v.).

obtemperandum est consuetudini rationabili tamquam legi. [L. **obtemperandum** to be obeyed (4); **est** it is (3); **consuetudini** (to) custom, usage, practice (2); **rationabili** to reasonable, rational (1); **tamquam** as much as, just as, as if (5); **legi** (to) law (6): Reasonable custom is to be obeyed just as the law.] *Law.* A reasonable custom must be complied with to the same degree as a law.

ob turpem causam *adv.* [L. **ob** on account of, by reason of (1); **turpem** base, disgraceful (2); **causam** cause, case, reason (3): on account of a base cause.] *Law.* Because of an immoral consideration.

O.C. *abbr.* for **ope consilio** (q.v.).

O.C. or **o.c.** *abbr.* for **opere citato** (q.v.).

occasionem cognosce [L. **occasionem** event, occasion (2); **cognosce** understand, recognize (1): Understand the event.] Observe the circumstances.

occultatio thesauri inventi fraudulosa. [L. **occultatio** concealment (1); **thesauri** (of) treasure (3); **inventi** of found (2); **fraudulosa** fraudulent (4): Concealment of found treasure is fraudulent.] *Law.* Covering up or hiding a found treasure is fraud. In reality, it is not a fraud but a misdemeanor.

occupantis fiunt derelicta. [L. **occupantis** the occupier's, of the occupying (3); **fiunt** become (2); **derelicta.** deserted (things) (1): Deserted things become the occupier's.] *Law.* Deserted things become the property of the person who is the first to occupy them. Squatter's rights. See **res nullius naturaliter** etc.

ochlophobia *n.* [Neo-Gk. from Gk. **ochlo(s)** crowd (2); **phob(os)** fear (1): fear of crowd.] *Psychology.* Abnormal fear of crowds.

odalisque *n., pl.* **odalisques** [Fr. from Turk. **ōdalik** chambermaid.] Odalisk. A female concubine or slave in a harem. *In Ashton's newest work, "Rhapsody," Dowell, who suggests a sultan, and Collier, an odalisque who becomes queen of his harem, spread their passion all over the stage in acrobatic solos and pas de deux . . . (Newsweek Int. July 6, 1981:43).*

odeon or **odeum** *n., pl.* **odeons** or **odea** or **odeums** [L. **odeum** from Gk. **ōideion** a place for song.] 1. *Ancient Greece and Rome.* A building, usually semi-circular, used for performances of song, dance, and other entertainment. 2. A theater or concert hall.

oderint dum metuant. Cicero (106–43 B.C.). *Philippic* I,14. Quoted from Accius (c.170–c.90 B.C.). [L. **oderint** let them hate (1); **dum** provided that, as long as (2); **metuant** they fear (3): Let them hate, provided that they fear.] Let them hate as long as they fear. *The tyrant's insensitivity clearly suggests that he is guided by the principle oderint dum metuant.*

oderint dum probent. [L. **oderint** let them hate (1); **dum** provided that, as long as (2); **probent** they approve (3): Let them hate, provided that they approve.] Let them hate as long as they accept. *He* [i.e., the emperor Tiberius] *brought to his task as emperor a*

stern, not to say defiant, sense of duty—oderint dum probent was his motto . . . (Cary 1970:520).

oderunt peccare boni, virtutis amore; oderunt peccare mali, formidine poenae. [L. **oderunt** hate (2); **peccare** to transgress, offend, sin (3); **boni** good (people) (1); **virtutis** of virtue, moral perfection (5); **amore** through love (4); **oderunt** hate (7); **peccare** to transgress, offend, sin (8); **mali** bad, evil (people) (6); **formidine** through fear, dread (9); **poenae** of punishment (10): Good people hate to transgress through love of virtue; bad people hate to transgress through fear of punishment.] Good people hate to commit an offense because of their love of moral excellence, while evil people do the same because of their fear of punishment.

odeum See **odeon**.

odi et amo; quare id faciam, fortasse requiris. / nescio, sed fieri sentio et excrucior. Catullus (87–54 B.C.). *Carmina* LXXXV. [L. **odi** I hate (1); **et** and (2); **amo** I love (3); **quare** why, wherefore (6); **id** it (8); **faciam** I do (7); **fortasse** perhaps (4); **requiris** you ask, inquire (5); **nescio** I do not know (9); **sed** but (10); **fieri** to happen, occur (12); **sentio** I feel (11); **et** and (13); **excrucior** I am tormented, tortured, crucified (14): I hate and I love; perhaps you ask why I do it. / I do not know, but I feel (it) to happen and I am tormented.] I hate and love; perhaps you ask why I do so. I do not know, but I feel it is happening and I am tortured.

odiosa et inhonesta non sunt in lege praesumenda; et in facto quod in se habet et bonum et malum, magis de bono quam de malo praesumendum est. [L. **odiosa** hateful, odious (things) (1); **et** and (2); **inhonesta** dishonorable, shameful (things) (3); **non** not (5); **sunt** are (4); **in** in, on (7); **lege** law (8); **praesumenda** to be presumed (6); **et** and (9); **in** in, on (10); **facto** deed, act, fact (11); **quod** which, that (12); **in** in, on (14); **se** itself (15); **habet** has, holds, regards (13); **et** both (16); **bonum** good (17); **et** and (18); **malum** bad (19); **magis** more, rather (22); **de** of, from, about, for (23); **bono** good (24); **quam** than (25); **de** of, from, about, for (26); **malo** bad (27); **praesumendum** to be presumed (21); **est** it is (20): Hateful and dishonorable things are not to be presumed in law; and in an act which has in itself both good and bad, it is to be presumed more about good than about bad.] *Law.* Hateful and dishonorable things must not be presumed in law, and in an act which comprises both good and evil, we must make a presumption in favor of good rather than evil. Cf. **nulla impossibilia aut inhonesta** etc.

odiosa non praesumuntur. [L. **odiosa** odious, hateful (things) (1); **non** not (2); **praesumuntur** are presumed (3): Odious things are not presumed.] *Law.* Hateful things are not assumed.

odium *n.* [L. hatred.] Intense hatred. Detestation. An object of intense hatred. *It goes without saying that* *despotic rulers face considerable odium both during and after their reigns.*

odium scholasticum *n.* [L. **odium** hatred (2); **scholasticum** scholarly (1): scholarly hatred.] Bitterness or spitefulness generated during a scholarly discussion or disputation. Cf. **odium theologicum**.

odium theologicum *n.* [L. **odium** hatred (2); **theologicum** theological (1): theological hatred.] Bitterness or spitefulness generated during a religious controversy and usually ending in refusal to continue the discussions. Cf. **odium scholasticum**.

Oedipus or **Oidipous** *n.* [Gk. **Oidipous**.] *Greek Mythology.* A prince of Thebes who unwittingly fulfilled Apollo's warning by killing his father (Laius) and marrying his mother (Jocasta): When the incest was discovered, the queen committed suicide, while Oedipus blinded himself and proceeded into exile. —**Oedipus complex** *Psychology.* The love or even sexual desire which a boy between the age of three and six has for the mother. He may regard the father as a rival for the favors of the mother and accordingly dislike him, though unconsciously. In some extreme cases the feeling continues even when the child has become an adult. *But for a frightening number of teenagers, murdering their parents seems to be a solution to problems as murky as the Oedipus complex . . . (Newsweek Int.* June 27, 1983:38). The female counterpart of the phenomenon is termed Electra complex.

Oedipus Rex *n.* [L. **Oedipus** Oedipus (1); **rex** king (2): Oedipus the king.] *Oedipus Rex.* 1. The Latin title of *Oidipous Tyrannos,* a Greek tragedy (c.431 B.C.) by Sophocles (496?–406 B.C.) about Oedipus' discovery of his true identity. 2. The title of an opera-oratorio in Latin by Igor Stravinsky (1882–1971).

oeuvre *n., pl.* **oeuvres** [Fr. work, product, achievement.] Substantial literary, artistic, or musical work which constitutes the work which a writer, artist or composer did during his lifetime. a) *. . . the* Helen *does claim a special place in Euripides' oeuvre by virtue of the vivaciousness of this fairytale atmosphere . . .* (Lesky 1966:387). b) *Simenon's massive detective oeuvre made Chief Inspector Maigret a household word in 55 languages . . . (Newsweek Int.* Dec. 7, 1981:40).

oeuvre civilisatrice *n.* [Fr. **oeuvre** work (2); **civilisatrice** civilizing (1): civilizing work.] The work of introducing civilization among, or civilizing, people. Cf. **mission civilisatrice**.

officit conatus si effectus sequatur. [L. **officit** harms, is detrimental (2); **conatus** attempt (1); **si** if (3); **effectus** accomplishment, effect (4); **sequatur** should follow (5): An attempt harms if the effect should follow.] An attempt causes harm only if the effect follows. Cf. **actus non facit** etc.

officium nemini debet esse damnosum. [L. **officium** office (1); **nemini** to no one, nobody (5); **debet** ought,

should (2); **esse** to be (3); **damnosum** injurious, hurtful (4): An office should be injurious to no one.] Holding an office should not be harmful to anybody.

ogre *n., pl.* **ogres** [Fr. human-eating giant.] 1. In fables or fairy tales a monster or frightful giant who eats human flesh. 2. A terrifying person or thing. A person or thing which is not easy to cope with. a) *The man is so wicked that even his wife and children regard him as a monstrous ogre.* b) *Third world countries are increasingly shunning the ogre of I.M.F. loans.* Cf. **kobald**.

Ohne Hast, aber ohne Rast. Johann Wolfgang von Goethe (1749–1832) and Friedrich von Schiller (1759–1805). *Zahme Xenien* II,6,281. [Ger. **ohne** without (1); **Hast** haste (2); **aber** but, but yet, still (3); **ohne** without (4); **Rast** rest, repose (5): Without haste, but yet without rest.] Without hurrying yet without resting. **Festina lente** (q.v.). Slow and steady.

o imitatores, servum pecus. Horace (65–8 B.C.). *Epistles* I,19,19. [L. **O** Oh (1); **imitatores** imitators, copyists (2); **servum** slavish, servile (3); **pecus** herd (4): Oh imitators, a servile herd.] Oh imitators, a pack of slaves. Those who imitate are a herd of slaves.

olé *interj.* [Sp. Hurray!] Bravo (q.v.). —*n., pl.* **olés** A shout of cheer or excitement, initially at a bullfight but sometimes extended to other events.

olet lucerna [L. **olet** it smells (1); **lucerna** by/of the lamp (2): It smells of the lamp.] It shows the effects of burning the midnight oil. It is forced or overworked. Used in reference to writing.

olim *adv.* [L. formerly, at one time.] Once upon a time. In times past.

olla podrida *n., pl.* **ollas podridas** [Sp. **olla** pot (2); **podrida** rotten, decayed (1): rotten or decayed pot.] 1. A highly seasoned Spanish stew or soup, made of several kinds of meat and some vegetables, and prepared in an olla. 2. A hodgepodge. A mixture of various things. A collection of various things. A medley. See **potpourri**.

O.M.D.G. *abbr.* for **omnia ad Majorem Dei Gloriam** (q.v.).

omega *n., pl.* **omegas** [Gk. **ōmega**: **ō** the vowel "o" (2); **mega** big (1): big "o," long "o."] 1. The last letter of the Greek alphabet. 2. The end. The last. *From the alpha to the omega of the journey, a distance of about 200 miles, the lady never slept but was reading a novel.* Cf. **alpha**.

omissio eorum quae tacite insunt nihil operatur. [L. **omissio** omission (1); **eorum** of those (things) (2); **quae** which (3); **tacite** tacitly, silently (5); **insunt** are contained within, are in (4); **nihil** nothing (7); **operatur** performs, works (6): The omission of those things which are tacitly contained within works nothing.] *Law.* The omission of those things which are implied does no harm. Cf. **expressio eorum quae** etc. and **non solent quae** etc.

omissis omnibus aliis negotiis *adv.* [L. **omissis** (with) having been laid aside, neglected (4); **omnibus** with all (1); **aliis** (with) other (2); **negotiis** (with) busi-nesses (3): with all other businesses having been laid aside.] With all other businesses neglected. *"The holder of a bill of exchange,"* says Lord Ellenborough, *"is not omissis omnibus aliis negotiis to devote himself to giving notice of its dishonor. . ."* (Megrah and Ryder 1972:139).

omne actum ab intentione agentis est judicandum. [L. **omne** every (1); **actum** deed, act (2); **ab** from, by (5); **intentione** intention (6); **agentis** of the one doing (7); **est** is (3); **judicandum** to be judged, decided (4): Every act is to be judged from the intention of the one doing it.] *Law.* Every act must be judged from the point of view of the intention of the doer. See **actus non facit** etc.

omne crimen ebrietas et incendit et detegit. [L. **omne** every (6); **crimen** crime, offense (7); **ebrietas** drunkenness, intoxication (1); **et** both (2); **incendit** inflames, kindles (3); **et** and (4); **detegit** exposes, betrays (5): Drunkenness both inflames and exposes every crime.] Intoxication not only worsens every crime but also reveals it.

omne ignotum pro magnifico Tacitus (c.55 –c.117 A.D.). *Agricola* XXX. [L. **omne** every (1); **ignotum** unknown, strange (thing) (2); **pro** for, as (3); **magnifico** splendid, great, magnificent (4): every unknown thing as splendid.] What is unknown is usually imagined to be wonderful/splendid.

omne jus aut consensus fecit, aut necessitas constituit aut firmavit consuetudo. [L. **omne** every (1); **jus** right, law (2); **aut** either (3); **consensus** consent (4); **fecit** made (5); **aut** or (6); **necessitas** compulsion, urgency, necessity (7); **constituit** established, con-stituted (8); **aut** or (9); **firmat** confirmed, reinforced (11); **consuetudo** custom, usage, tradition (10): Every right either consent made or compulsion established or custom confirmed.] *Law.* Every right is based on consent or established by necessity or confirmed by custom.

omne majus continet in se minus. [L. **omne** every (1); **majus** bigger, greater (thing) (2); **continet** contains, comprises (3); **in** in, on (4); **se** itself (5); **minus** smaller, lesser (thing) (6): Every greater (thing) contains in itself the lesser (thing).] *Law.* The greater invariably contains the lesser. Thus, in criminal law, if a person is indicted for an offense which comprises other minor offenses of the same category, he/she may be con-victed of the minor offenses also. See **majus continet minus.**

omne majus minus in se complectitur. [L. **omne** every, all (1); **majus** greater, bigger (thing) (2); **minus** smaller, lesser (thing) (6); **in** in, on (4); **se** itself (5); **complectitur** comprises, includes (3): Every greater (thing) includes in itself the lesser (thing).] *Law.* The greater includes the lesser. See **majus continet minus.**

omne principale trahit ad se accessorium. [L. **omne** every (1); **principale** principal, original (thing) (2);

trahit draws, drags (3); **ad** to, at, for, according to (4); **se** itself (5); **accessorium** accessory (thing) (6): Every principal thing draws to itself the accessory thing.] *Law.* Every principal draws to itself the ac-cessory. See **accessorium non ducit** etc.

omne quod solo inaedificatur solo cedit. [L. **omne** everything (1); **quod** which (2); **solo** soil, ground (4); **inaedificatur** is erected on, built on (3); **solo** soil, ground (6); **cedit** accrues, falls to (5): Everything which is erected on the soil accrues to the soil.] *Law.* Every structure erected on the soil belongs to the soil. See **quicquid plantatur** etc.

omne sacramentum debet esse de certa scientia. [L. **omne** every (1); **sacramentum** oath (2); **debet** ought, should (3); **esse** to be (4); **de** of, from, about, for (5); **certa** certain (6); **scientia** knowledge (7): Every oath should be from certain knowledge.] *Law.* All oaths should be based upon clear knowledge. Cf. **juramentum est** etc.

omnes actiones in mundo infra certa tempora habent limitationem. [L. **omnes** all (1); **actiones** actions (2); **in** in, on (3); **mundo** world (4); **infra** below, within (7); **certa** certain, fixed (8); **tempora** times, periods (9); **habent** have, hold, regard (5); **limitationem** limit, limitation (6): All actions in the world have limit within fixed periods.] *Law.* All ac-tions in the world are limited to fixed periods. See **omnis querela** etc.

omne testamentum morte consummatum est. [L. **omne** every (1); **testamentum** will (2); **morte** by death (5); **consummatum** completed, perfected (4); **est** is (3): Every will is perfected by death.] All wills are completed by death. See **legatum morte** etc.

omnia ad Majorem Dei Gloriam *abbr.* **O.A.M.D.G.** or **O.M.D.G.** [L. **omnia** all (things), everything (1); **ad** to, at, for, according to (2); **Majorem** Greater (3); **Dei** of God (5); **Gloriam** Glory (4): All (things) to the greater glory of God.] Everything to God's greater glory. The motto of some orders of St. Francis.

omnia praesumuntur contra spoliatorem. [L. **omnia** all (things), everything (1); **praesumuntur** are pre-sumed (2); **contra** against, opposite (3); **spoliatorem** spoiler, destroyer (4): All (things) are presumed against a destroyer.] *Law.* Everything is assumed against someone who destroys or does wrong. See **in odium** etc.

omnia praesumuntur legitime facta donec probetur in contrarium. [L. **omnia** all (things), everything (1); **praesumuntur** are presumed (2); **legitime** law-fully, legitimately (4); **facta** (to have been) done (3); **donec** until, as long as (5); **probetur** it is proved (6); **in** into, to, against, for (7); **contrarium** the contrary (8): All things are presumed (to have been) done law-fully until it is proved to the contrary.] *Law.* Every act is presumed to be lawful until proved otherwise. Applicable to the acts of public officials. See the next three maxims.

omnia praesumuntur rite esse acta. [L. omnia all (things), everything (1); praesumuntur are presumed (2); rite fitly, rightly (4); esse acta to have been done (3): All (things) are presumed to have been done rightly.] Law. Everything is presumed to have been done in a proper or correct fashion. Applicable to the acts of public officials until the contrary is proved. See the preceding maxim and the two subsequent ones.

omnia praesumuntur rite et solemniter esse acta donec probetur in contrarium. [L. omnia all (things), everything (1); praesumuntur are presumed (2); rite rightly, fitly (4); et and (5); sol(l)emniter solemnly, duly (6); esse acta to have been done (3); donec until, as long as (7); probetur it is proved (8); in into, to, against, for (9); contrarium the contrary (10): All things are presumed to have been done rightly and duly until it is proved to the contrary.] Law. It is presumed that everything has been done rightly and properly until it is proved otherwise. See the two preceding maxims and the subsequent one.

omnia praesumuntur solemniter esse acta. [L. omnia all (things), everything (1); praesumuntur are presumed (2); sol(l)emniter solemnly, duly (4); esse acta to have been done (3): All things are presumed to have been done solemnly.] Law. Everything is presumed to have been done properly. See the three preceding maxims and omnia rite etc.

omnia quae jure contrahuntur contrario jure pereunt. [L. omnia all (things), everything (1); quae which (2); jure by law (4); contrahuntur are contracted (3); contrario by contrary, opposing (6); jure (by) right, law (7); pereunt perish, are undone (5): All things which are contracted by law are undone by contrary law.] Law. Every contract which is lawfully made can be undone by process of law. See eodem modo quo quid constituitur dissolvitur.

omnia quae sunt uxoris sunt ipsius viri. [L. omnia all (things), everything (1); quae which (2); sunt are (3); uxoris of wife (4); sunt are (5); ipsius (of) himself (7); viri of husband (6): All things which are of the wife are of the husband himself.] Law. Everything which belongs to the wife belongs to the husband. An obsolete rule. See vir et uxor censentur etc.; vir et uxor sunt quasi unica persona and vir et uxor sunt quasi unica persona, quia etc.

omnia rite acta praesumuntur. [L. omnia all (things), everything (1); rite fitly, rightly (3); acta (to have been) done (4); praesumuntur are presumed (2): All things are presumed (to have been) done rightly.] Law. Everything is presumed rightly done. See omnia praesumuntur legitime etc.

omnia vincit Amor; et nos cedamus Amori. Vergil (70–19 B.C.). Eclogues X,69. [L. omnia all (things), everything (3); vincit conquers (2); Amor Love (1); et and, also, too (6); nos we, us (5); cedamus let us yield (4); Amori to Love (7): Love conquers all

(things); let us yield also to Love.] Love conquers everything; let us also give in to Love.

omnibus n., short form bus, pl. omnibuses or buses [L. for all (things), everything.] 1. A public means of transportation. 2. A book which contains reprints of several related works. —adj. Relating to many things or items at the same time. a) an omnibus bill; b) an omnibus transport; c) In his farewell speech, he paid omnibus tribute to the organization.

omnis consensus tollit errorem. [L. omnis every (1); consensus consent, agreement (2); tollit removes, destroys (3); errorem error, mistake (4): Every consent removes error.] Law. Every agreement wipes out a mistake. See qui non improbat, approbat.

omnis definitio in lege periculosa. [L. omnis every (1); definitio definition, explanation (2); in in, on (3); lege law (4); periculosa dangerous, hazardous (5): Every definition in law is dangerous.] Law. Definitions in law are hazardous. See in jure omnis etc.

omnis exceptio est ipsa quoque regula. [L. omnis every (1); exceptio exception (2); est is (3); ipsa itself (4); quoque also (5); regula rule (6): Every exception is itself also a rule.] Law. Every exception is by itself also a rule.

omnis indemnatus pro innoxis legibus habetur. [L. omnis every (1); indemnatus uncondemned (person) (2); pro on the side of, for (5); innoxis innocent, blameless (persons) (6); legibus by laws (4); habetur is had, held, regarded (3): Every uncondemned person is regarded by the laws on the side of innocent persons.] Law. Every unconvicted person is considered by the law as innocent.

omnis innovatio plus novitate perturbat quam utilitate prodest. [L. omnis every (1); innovatio innovation (2); plus more (4); novitate by novelty (5); perturbat confuses, disturbs (3); quam than (6); utilitate by usefulness, utility (8); prodest benefits, does good (7): Every innovation disturbs more by novelty than it benefits by utility.] Law. Every innovation introduces more confusion by its novelty than benefit through its utility. Hence, in litigation, a judge should follow precedents and not change established rules of law. See via trita est tutissima.

omnis interpretatio vel declarat, vel extendit, vel restringit. [L. omnis every (1); interpretatio interpretation (2); vel either (3); declarat declares (4); vel or (5); extendit extends (6); vel or (7); restringit restricts (8): Every interpretation declares or extends or restricts.] Law. Each interpretation either defines the law, expands it, or narrows it. Cf. legis interpretatio etc. and sententia facit etc.

omnis nova constitutio futuris temporibus formam imponere debet, non praeteritis. [L. omnis every (1); nova new (2); constitutio constitution, regulation (3); futuris future (7); temporibus times (8); formam form, pattern (6); imponere to impose on (5); debet ought, should (4); non not (9); praeteritis past (10): Every new constitution ought to impose a pattern on future times, not past.] *Law.* Every new constitution should regulate the future, not the past. See **lex prospicit** etc. and **nova constitutio** etc.

omnis querela et omnis actio injuriarum limitata est infra certa tempora. [L. **omnis** every (1); **querela** complaint, accusation (2); **et** and (3); **omnis** every (4); **actio** action, deed, legal suit (5); **injuriarum** of /for injuries, wrongs (6); **limitata** limited (8); **est** is, has been (7); **infra** within, below (9); **certa** fixed, certain (10); **tempora** times, periods (11): Every complaint and every legal suit for injuries has been limited within fixed periods.] *Law.* Complaint and legal actions respecting injuries are limited within fixed periods; i.e., they must take place within a specified period of time after the injury takes place. See **omnes actiones** etc.

omnis ratihabitio retrotrahitur et mandato priori aequiparatur. [Late L. **omnis** every (1); **ratihabitio** ratification (2); **retrotrahitur** is referred/extended backwards (3); **et** and (4); **mandato** (with/to) command, order (7); **priori** with/to previous, former (6); **aequiparatur** is compared, likened (5): Every ratification is referred backwards and is likened to a previous command.] *Law.* Every ratification is retroactive and is comparable to a previous command.

omnis regula suas patitur exceptiones. [L. **omnis** every (1); **regula** rule (2); **suas** its own (4); **patitur** suffers, endures (3); **exceptiones** exceptions (5): Every rule suffers its own exceptions.] *Law.* Every rule has its exceptions.

omnium *n., pl.* **omniums** [L. of all (things).] The totality of the various constituent items in any stock or fund.

omnium-gatherum *n., pl.* **omnium-gatherums** [L. **omnium** of all (2) and Eng. **gather** with L. ending **-um** (1): a gathering of all.] 1. A miscellaneous group or collection of various persons or things. A hodgepodge. *That political party is an omnium-gatherum, comprising members of diverse background and aspirations who are united by one common objective, i.e., personal aggrandizement.* 2. A place where such a miscellaneous group or collection of persons or things can be found. See **potpourri.**

omphalos (Gk.) or **omphalus** (L.) *n., pl.* **omphali** [Gk. umbilical cord, navel, center, middle point.] 1. *Anatomy.* The navel. 2. A focal point. A central portion. *He presented his arguments brilliantly until he reached the omphalos of the issue and then he began to flounder.* Cf. **umbilicus.**

on-dit *n., pl.* **on-dits** [Fr. **on** one, you, we, they (1); **dit** say(s) (2): One says. They say. It is said.] Rumor. Hearsay. *What the author claims to be an historical work should actually be classified as a novel, for it is generously flavored with on-dits.*

On dit que Dieu est toujours pour les gros bataillons. Voltaire (1694–1778). [Fr. **on** one, you, we, they (1); **dit** say(s) (2); **que** that (3); **Dieu** God (4); **est** is (5); **toujours** always, ever (6); **pour** for, in favor of (7); **les** the (8); **gros** great, big, large (9); **bataillons** battalions (10): One says that God is always in favor of the big battalions.] It is said that God is always on the side of the big battalions. Cf. **Aide-toi** etc., **audentis fortuna juvat,** and **fortis fortuna adjuvat.**

On n'est jamais si heureux ni si malheureux qu'on s'imagine. François, Duc de La Rochefoucauld (1613–1680). *Maximes* 49. [Fr. **on** one, you, we, they (1); **n'** . . . **jamais** never (3); **est** is (2); **si** as, so (4); **heureux** happy, blessed (5); **ni** nor, or (6); **si** as, so (7); **malheureux** unhappy, wretched (8); **qu'** as (9); **on** one, we (10); **s'** oneself (12); **imagine** imagines, fancies (11): One is never as happy or unhappy as one imagines.] People are never as happy or unhappy as they think they are.

onomasticon *n., pl.* **onomastica** [Gk. a place for names.] A **lexicon** (q.v.) or vocabulary list.

onomatopoeia *n., pl.* **onomatopoeias** [Gk. **onomatopoiia: onoma** name, word (2); **poieō** make (1): making of a word, the coining of a word in imitation of a sound.] 1. *Linguistics.* Formation of words by imitating the sound associated with a thing or action; e.g., the buzz of a bee. 2. A word formed in such a manner. 3. Using words whose sounds suggest their meanings.

onus *n., pl.* **onuses** [L. a burden, load, duty or responsibility.] A burden. Something objectionable. Blame or stigma. a) *Ayo is an irresponsible father who regards his parental duties as an onus.* b) *He tried to no purpose to shift the onus for the collapse of the marriage upon his wife.* Cf. **commodum.**

onus probandi *n.* [L. **onus** burden (1); **probandi** of proving (2): burden of proving.] *Law.* Burden of proof. *The magistrate reminded the prosecuting team that the onus probandi rested on them.*

op. *abbr.* for l. **opera** (q.v.). 2. **opus** (q.v.).

op. cit. *abbr.* for l. **opere citato** (q.v.). 2. **opus citatum** (q.v.).

ope et consilio or **ope consilio** *abbr.* **O.C.** [L. **ope** by aid, assistance (1); **et** and (2); **consilio** by counsel, deliberation (3): by assistance and counsel.] Aiding and abetting. *Civil Law.* Applicable to accessories.

opera *n., pl.* **operas** [It. work.] 1. Dramatic composition or performance in which music accompanied by orchestra is a principal feature. 2. An organization which engages in the production and performance of such drama.

opéra bouffe *n.* [Fr. **opéra** opera (2); **bouffe** comic (1): comic opera.] A comic opera, usually treating a sentimental subject and marked by parody. —*adj.* Fit or suitable for opéra bouffe. *Veronique is French by birth, a prostitute by profession and the current leading lady in an opéra bouffe scandal that threatens to expose the macho foibles of Italian men* (*Newsweek Int.* March 30, 1981:17). Cf. **opera buffa.**

opera buffa *n.* [It. **opera** opera (2); **buffa** comic (1): comic opera.] An Italian comic opera, especially that of the

18th century, characterized by farce. *Many productions play up the libretto's opera buffa elements—how the fat knight is first tricked by the merry wives of Windsor and then treated, in the magical forest scene at the end, to a beating* (*Newsweek Int.* April 26, 1982:49). Cf. **opéra bouffe.**

opera minora *pl. n.* [L. **opera** works (2); **minora** less important, inferior (1): less important works.] The less important works, especially of a writer.

opera multi sudoris *pl. n.* [L. **opera** works (1); **multi** of much (2); **sudoris** (of) sweat, toil (3): works of much sweat or toil.] Works on which considerable effort or labor has been expended. *. . . none of these opera multi sudoris have survived even in part, . . .* (Laistner 1966:108).

opera omnia *pl. n.* [L. **opera** works (2); **omnia** all (1): all works.] A writer's complete works. *Zeta's recent additions to his library include William Shakespeare's opera omnia.*

opere citato *abbr.* **op. cit.** or **o.c.** *adv.* [L. **opere** in work (1); **citato** (in) cited, quoted (2): in the work cited.] In the previously cited work. Used for bibliographical references. See **opus.**

O povo, unido, jamais sera vencido. [Port. **O** the (1); **povo** people (2); **unido** united (3); **jamais** never (5); **sera** will be (4); **vencido** defeated, vanquished (6): The people, united, will never be vanquished.] A unified people can never be conquered. Cf. **A luta do povo** etc.

opprobrium *n., pl.* **opprobria** or **opprobriums** [L. infamy, disgrace, shame.] Contempt. Distaste. a) *In academic circles opprobrium is attached to dogmatism.* b) *The conviction of the principal for raping one of his female students has cast considerable opprobrium on him.*

opprobrium medicorum *n., pl.* **opprobria medicorum** [L. **opprobrium** reproach, disgrace (1); **medicorum** of physicians (2): the disgrace or shame of physicians.] Medical practitioners' shame or disgrace. *Gout was called opprobrium medicorum . . . because so little could be done to treat it* (*Newsweek Int.* June 30, 1980:51). Cf. **amicus medicorum.**

optima est legis interpres consuetudo. [L. **optima** best (3); **est** is (2); **legis** of law (5); **interpres** interpreter (4); **consuetudo** custom, usage, tradition (1): Custom is the best interpreter of the law.] *Law.* Accepted practice is the best way to interpret the law. See **optima legum** etc.

optima est lex quae minimum relinquit arbitrio judicis; optimus judex qui minimum sibi. [L. **optima** best (1); **est** is (3); **lex** law (2); **quae** (one) which (4); **minimum** least (6); **relinquit** leaves (5); **arbitrio** to pleasure, opinion (7); **judicis** of judge (8); **optimus** best (9); **judex** judge (10); **qui** (one) who (11); **minimum** least (12); **sibi** to himself/herself (13): The best law is one which leaves the least to the pleasure of the judge; the best judge is one who

leaves the least to himself/herself.] *Law.* The best law leaves very little to the discretion of a judge, while the best judge makes very little room for his/her own opinion. See **judex bonus nihil** etc. Cf. **lex non exacte** etc.

optima legum interpres est consuetudo. [L. **optima** best (3); **legum** of laws (5); **interpres** interpreter, expounder (4); **est** is (2); **consuetudo** custom, usage, tradition (1): Custom is the best interpreter of laws.] Accepted practice is the best interpreter of the laws. See **consuetudo est altera lex; consuetudo est optimus** etc.; **optima est legis** etc.; **optimus interpres** etc.; and **optimus legum** etc.

optimis parentibus [L. **optimis** (to) best (1); **parentibus** to parents (2): to the best parents.] For the best parents. A dedicatory inscription.

optimum *adj.* [L. best.] Greatest. Best. *The man has many admirable qualities and he has been putting them to optimum use.*

optimus interpres rerum usus. [L. **optimus** best (2); **interpres** interpreter (3); **rerum** of matters, things, property, business, affairs (4); **usus** use, usage (1): Use is the best interpreter of things.] *Law.* Custom serves the purpose of helping in the interpretation of the intentions of parties, where there is doubt. Also, custom contributes to the interpretation of ambiguous words in an instrument. See **optima legum** etc.

optimus interpretandi modus est sic leges interpretari ut leges legibus concordent. [L. **optimus** best (1); **interpretandi** of interpreting (3); **modus** way (2); **est** is (4); **sic** thus, in such a manner (7); **leges** laws (6); **interpretari** to interpret (5); **ut** that (8); **leges** laws (9); **legibus** with laws (11); **concordent** agree, are consistent, harmonize (10): The best way of interpreting is to interpret laws in such a way that laws agree with laws.] *Law.* The best method of interpretation is to interpret laws in such a way that they are consistent with one another.

optimus legum interpres consuetudo. [L. **optimus** best (2); **legum** of laws (4); **interpres** interpreter (3); **consuetudo** custom, usage, tradition (1): Custom is the best interpreter of laws.] *Law.* Accepted legal practice is the best way to interpret the laws. See **optima legum** etc.

opus *n., pl.* **opera** [L. work, book, deed.] An artistic work or composition, especially musical. Cf. **magnum opus.**

opus citatum *abbr.* **op. cit.** *n., pl.* **opera citata** [L. **opus** work (1); **citatum** cited, quoted (2): the work quoted.] The work quoted from. See **opere citato.**

opusculum *n., pl.* **opuscula** [L. little work.] A minor work, especially one that is literary or musical.

opus Dei *n.* [L. **opus** work (1); **Dei** of God (2): work of God.] God's work. The Divine Office, that is the daily liturgical readings which are a human obligation toward God. —**Opus Dei** *Roman Catholic Church.* An organization of priests and lay people founded in Spain in 1928 in order to reaffirm the place of God and Christianity in the lives of individuals and in society at large.

opus reticulatem *n.* [L. **opus** work (2); **reticulatem** networked (1): networked work.] A masonry pattern in which the bricks set in squares or diamonds create a net-like design.

opus sectile *n.* [L. **opus** work (2); **sectile** cut, divided (1): cut work.] *Art.* A type of floor design in which material of various shapes and sizes is arranged to make a pattern, unlike mosaic work in which material of the same shape and size is used.

ora et labora [L. **ora** pray (1); **et** and (2); **labora** work (3): Pray and work.] Pray and work.

orandum est ut sit mens sana in corpore sano. Juvenal (c.60–117 A.D.). *Satires* X,356. [L. **orandum** to be prayed (2); **est** it is (1); **ut**; that (3); **sit** there should be (4); **mens** mind (6); **sana** sound (5); **in** in, on (7); **corpore** body (9); **sano** sound (8): It is to be prayed that there should be a sound mind in a sound body.] One must pray for a sound mind in a sound body. See **mens sana in corpore sano.**

orans *adj.* [L. praying.] In a position of prayer. —*n.* *Art.* A figure depicted in prayer, e.g., with hands folded or arms extended, kneeling, etc.

ora pro nobis [L. **ora** pray (1); **pro** for, on behalf of, on the side of, for the benefit of, in accordance with, as (2); **nobis** us (3): Pray for us.] Pray for us. Part of a prayer of supplication.

orare est laborare, laborare est orare. [L. **orare** to pray (1); **est** is (2); **laborare** to work (3); **laborare** to work (4); **est** is (5); **orare** to pray (6): To pray is to work; to work is to pray.] Praying is working; working is praying. For a shorter form, see **laborare est orare.**

oratio obliqua *n.* [L. **oratio** speech (2); **obliqua** slanting, indirect (1): slanting speech.] *Rhetoric.* Indirect speech or discourse. Reported speech. A paraphrase instead of an exact quotation. *The great lecture delivered by the distinguished professor is featured in today's newspaper, but it lost some of its flavor, since it is put in oratio obliqua.*

oratio recta *n.* [L. **oratio** speech (2); **recta** straight, direct (1): straight speech.] *Rhetoric.* Speech which is quoted directly.

oratorio *n., pl.* **oratorios** [It. an oratory, a place for prayer.] *Music.* A musical composition combining orchestra and human voices to tell a religious or biblical story without the aid of costumes, scenery, or other dramatic trappings. Named after the Oratory of St. Philip Neri in Rome where many such compositions were performed in the 16th century.

ore tenus *adv.* [L. **ore** mouth (2); **tenus** as far as, unto (1): as far as mouth.] Orally. By spoken word. *At the interview, the candidates were examined ore tenus.* See **viva voce.**

orientalia *pl. n.* [L. eastern or oriental things.] Literary, archaeological, artistic, epigraphical, etc. materials pertaining to the Orient, i.e., the East.

origami *n., pl.* **origamis** [Japan. from **ori** to fold (2); **kami** paper (1): paper folding.] 1. The Japanese art of paper-folding. 2. Paper folded in this fashion.

origo rei inspici debet. [L. **origo** origin (1); **rei** of matter, thing, property, business, affair (2); **inspici** to be considered, examined (4); **debet** ought, should (3): The origin of the thing ought to be considered.] *Law.* The origin of a matter should be taken into consideration. Cf. **satius est petere** etc.

Orlando Furioso [It. **Orlando** Orlando, Roland (2); **furioso** furious, insane (1): furious Orlando.] *Furious Orlando*, a 1516 epic poem by Ludovico Ariosto (1474–1533) about the hero Orlando (Roland), his love for Angelica, and war between the Christians and Moors in the time of Charlemagne (742–814).

Oro y plata [Sp. **oro** gold (1); **y** and (2); **plata** silver (3): gold and silver.] Gold and Silver. Motto of the State of Montana.

o sancta simplicitas! *interj.* John Huss (c.1372–1415). [L. **O** Oh (1); **sancta** holy, sacred (2); **simplicitas** simplicity (3): Oh holy simplicity!] Oh sacred simplicity!

O.S.P. or **o.s.p.** *abbr.* for **obiit sine prole** (q.v.).

ostinato *adj.* [It. obstinate, stubborn.] Appearing again and again. Repeating. —*n., pl.* **ostinatos** A melodic line or passage which is repeated and varied in a composition.

Ostpolitik *n.* [Ger. **Ost** east (1); **Politik** policy, politics (2): east policy.] Eastern policy or politics, especially relations with the former East Germany. a) *Nowhere is the wish to keep détente alive stronger than in West Germany, which adopted its policy of Ostpolitik in 1969 to improve relations with East Germany . . .* (*Time Int.* 1982). b) *Schmidt's efforts to keep his Ostpolitik alive worried Washington even more than Giscard's Gallic histrionics* (*Newsweek Int.* Jan. 5, 1981:33). Cf. **Westpolitik.**

o tempora, o mores! *interj.* Cicero (106–43 B.C.). *In Catilinam* I,1,1. [L. **O** Oh (1); **tempora** times (2); **o** oh (3); **mores** habits, manners (4): Oh the times! Oh the habits!] Oh what times, oh what habits! Used to deplore the degeneracy of an age.

otium cum dignitate *n.* [L. **otium** leisure, rest (1); **cum** with (2); **dignitate** dignity (3): leisure with dignity.] Honorable or dignified retirement.

outrance *n., pl.* **outrances** [Fr. excess.] The last extremity. The bitter end. The utmost. Used with the propositions, at or to. Cf. **à outrance** and **guerre à outrance.**

outré *adj.* [Fr. exaggerated, extravagant, overdone.] Bizarre. Eccentric. Unconventional. Improper. *. . . Graham Greene displayed his outré sense of humor; his contribution to the art of espionage was a proposal to set up a brothel as a listening post* (*Newsweek Int.* June 9, 1980:56).

ouverture *n.* [Fr. opening.] Open-mindedness. Openness. Sincerity. Frankness. Open-door policy. *. . . in his first two or three years Abdou Diouf's policy of* *"ouverture"... tended to estrange him from the party which he had inherited from Senghor (West Africa 1986).*

ovum *n., pl.* **ova** [L. egg.] The female reproductive egg or cell. *The sex of a child is determined by whether the mother's ovum, which always carries a female X chromosome, is fertilized by a sperm carrying another X chromosome or one bearing the male Y chromosome (Newsweek Int. May 30, 1983:74).*

oxyblepsia *n., pl.* **oxyblepsias** [Gk. **oxu(s)** sharp, keen, smart (1); **blep(ō)** see (2): sharp seeing.] Acuteness or sharpness of sight.

oxymoron *n., pl.* **oxymora** [Gk. **oxu(s)** sharp, keen, smart (1); **mōros** fool, idiot (2): something pointedly foolish.] *Rhetoric.* A witty saying or expression which draws its pointed, epigrammatic or incisive effect from its paradoxical, contradictory or seemingly absurd nature; e.g., "splendidly false," "insane wisdom," "mean generosity," "industrious indolence."

oxytocia *n., pl.* **oxytocias** [Neo-Gk. from Gk. **oxu(s)** sharp, keen, smart (1); **tok(os)** childbirth (2): sharp childbirth.] Quick childbirth. See **eutocia.** Cf. **dystokia.**

P

P. or p. *abbr.* for 1. Papa (q.v.); 2. pontifex (q.v.); 3. populus (q.v.).

P. A. or p. a. *abbr.* for 1. par avion (q.v.). 2. per annum (q.v.).

pabulum *n., pl.* pabula or pabulums [L. fodder, food, nourishment.] 1. Food. Nutrient. Especially food for infants. 2. Intellectual nourishment or sustenance. Food for thought. *He is a popular author whose works usually provide mental pabulum.* 3. Insipid or rudimentary ideas. *This newspaper is always churning out emotional pabulum of the worst kind.*

pace *prep.* [L. with/by peace.] With all due respect to. *I do not, pace medical practitioners, lay claim to knowledge of medical science, but I do know that I can recognize a sick man when I see one.*

pace tua *adv.* [L. pace with peace, agreement (2); tua (with) your (1): with your agreement.] With your permission.

pacha See pasha.

pacta dant legem contractui. [L. pacta agreements (1); dant give (2); legem law (3); contractui to drawing together, shrinking, contract, agreement (4): Agreements give the law to a contract.] *Law.* Agreements of parties serve as the law of the contract. See consensus facit legem.

pacta privata juri publico derogare non possunt. [L. pacta agreements, contracts (2); privata private (1); juri right, law (7); publico public (6); derogare to detract from (5); non not (4); possunt can (3): Private agreements cannot detract from public right.] *Law.* Private contracts cannot derogate from public right. See conventio privatorum etc.

pacta quae contra leges constitutionesque vel contra bonos mores fiunt, nullam vim habere, indubitati juris est. [L. pacta agreements, contracts (4); quae which (5); contra against, opposite (7); leges laws (8); constitutionesque and constitutions (9); vel or (10); contra against, opposite (11); bonos good (12); mores morals (13); fiunt are made (6); nullam no (15); vim force (16); habere (to) have, hold, regard (14); indubitati of undoubted (2); juris (of) right, law (3); est it is . . . (that) (1): It is of undoubted law that contracts which are made against laws and constitutions or against good morals have no force.] *Law.* It is an indisputable principle of law that contracts which are contrary to the laws and constitutions or good morals have no binding force. See conventio privatorum etc.

pacta quae turpem causam continent non sunt observanda. [L. pacta agreements, contracts (1); quae which (2); turpem base, disgraceful (4); causam cause, case, reason (5); continent contain (3); non not (7); sunt are (6); observanda to be observed (8): Agreements which contain a base cause are not to be observed.] *Law.* Agreements based on immoral considerations must not be observed. See ex turpi causa etc.

pacta sunt servanda. [L. pacta agreements, contracts (1); sunt are (2); servanda to be observed (3): Agreements are to be observed.] *Law.* Agreements of parties must be observed.

pacta tertiis nec nocent nec prosunt. [L. pacta agreements, contracts (1); tertiis third (persons) (6); nec neither (2); nocent hurt (3); nec nor (4); prosunt benefit, profit (5): Contracts neither hurt nor benefit third persons.] *Law.* Contracts neither hurt nor benefit a third party. See res inter alios acta alteri etc.

pactum or pactio *n., pl.* pacta or pactiones [L. agreement, contract, pact, compact.] 1. *Civil Law.* A pact or agreement, especially one, like nudum pactum (q.v.), without consideration, but one which may entail some legal obligation. 2. *Roman Law.* An agreement involving promises which is usually unenforceable except in certain cases where it is declared enforceable by legal provisions.

pactum constitutae pecuniae *n., pl.* pacta constitutae pecuniae [L. pactum agreement, contract, pact, compact (1); constitutae of appointed, determined (2); pecuniae (of) money (3): agreement of appointed

288

money.] *Civil Law.* An agreement whereby a debtor promises to pay a creditor at a certain time.

pactum de constituenda dote *n., pl.* **pacta de constituenda dote** [L. **pactum** agreement, contract, pact, compact (1); **de** of, from, about, for (2); **constituenda** to be arranged, determined, fixed (4); **dote** dowry (3): agreement about a dowry to be arranged.] *Roman Law.* An informal agreement to offer a dowry.

pactum de constituto *n., pl.* **pacta de constituto** [L. **pactum** agreement, contract, pact, compact (1); **de** of, from, about, for (2); **constituto** compact, settlement (3): agreement about a settlement.] *Roman Law.* A legally enforceable informal agreement in which a person promises to pay another's debt in future or to give security, if the creditor agrees to give the debtor extra time.

pactum de non alienando *n., pl.* **pacta de non alienando** [L. **pactum** agreement, contract, pact, compact (1); **de** of, from, about, for (2); **non** not (3); **alienando** transferring, alienating (4): agreement about not transferring.] *Law.* Agreement forbidding a person to transfer title to property.

pactum de non petendo *n., pl.* **pacta de non petendo** [L. **pactum** agreement, contract, pact, compact (1); **de** of, from, about, for (2); **non** not (3); **petendo** suing, claiming (4): agreement about not suing.] *Civil Law.* Agreement not to bring a suit; i.e., an agreement in which a creditor promises not to sue the debtor or not to demand the due debt.

pactum donationis *n., pl.* **pacta donationis** [L. **pactum** agreement, contract, pact, compact (1); **donationis** of gift, donation (2): agreement of gift.] *Roman Law.* An informal agreement to make a voluntary donation which can be legally enforced against the donor and his heirs.

pactum illicitum *n., pl.* **pacta illicita** [L. **pactum** agreement, contract, pact, compact (2); **illicitum** illegal, illicit (1): an illicit/illegal agreement.] *Civil Law.* An agreement which is unlawful or inimical to public policy.

pactum legitimum *n., pl.* **pacta legitima** [L. **pactum** agreement, contract, pact, compact (2); **legitimum** lawful, legitimate (1): a lawful or legitimate agreement.] *Roman Law.* An informal agreement, rendered enforceable by the emperor's authority.

pactum subjectionis *n., pl.* **pacta subjectionis** [L. **pactum** agreement, contract, pact, compact (1); **subjectionis** of subjection (2): agreement of subjection.] Agreement of subjection to government. *So as to end the insecurity, men entered into a "social contract." It comprised a pactum unionis, whereby men agree "to unite in one political society" and a pactum subjectionis, whereby the majority gives power to a government which will protect the individual* (Curzon 1979:68). Cf. **pactum unionis.**

pactum unionis *n., pl.* **pacta unionis** [L. **pactum** agreement, contract, pact, compact (1); **unionis** of oneness, union, unity (2): agreement of unity.] A pact of unity. Cf. **pactum subjectionis.**

pactum vestitum *n., pl.* **pacta vestita** [L. **pactum** agreement, contract, pact, compact (2); **vestitum** clothed, dressed (1): clothed agreement.] *Roman Law.* An informal agreement rendered enforceable by official act.

padre *n., pl.* **padres** [It./Span./Port. father.] *Christianity.* The title of a priest or the priest himself. Cf. **père.**

padrone *n., pl.* **padroni** [It. patron.] 1. Patron, master, or boss. 2. Landlord. Innkeeper. 3. An employer of labor.

Paedagogiae Baccalaureus *abbr.* **Pd. B.** *n.* [L. **paedagogiae** of pedagogy (2); **baccalaureus** bachelor (1): Bachelor of Pedagogy.] An undergraduate academic degree in education.

Paedagogiae Doctor *abbr.* **Ped. D.** *n.* [L. **paedagogiae** of pedagogy (2); **doctor** teacher (1): teacher of pedagogy.] Doctor of Pedagogy. A terminal graduate degree in education.

Paedagogiae Magister *abbr.* **Pd. M.** *n.* [L. **paedagogiae** of pedagogy (2); **magister** master (1): Master of Pedagogy.] A pre-doctoral undergraduate degree in education.

Paed. D. *abbr.* for **Paedagogiae Doctor** (q.v.).

paideia *n.* [Gk. education, culture, learning.] Physical and mental education which lays emphasis on cultural development and is designed to inculcate an enlightened, liberal, and mature outlook.

pais or **pays** *n.* [Fr. country, district, or region.] *Law.* Used in the expressions in **pais** (q.v.) or in **pays** (Obs. Fr.). In the country, as distinct from in court. Applicable to a transaction that does not go through legal proceedings. Examples: a) *A widow's application for her dower in pais is one made directly to the heir instead of issuing a writ.* b) *A matter in pais is one that is not put in writing, as distinguished from one which is in deed or is of record.* c) *A conveyance in pais is one done by the parties on the land, which is to be transferred.* —per **pais** or per **pays** (Obs. Fr.) By the country. By the jury. Specifically, **trial per pais** or **trial per pays**, i.e., trial by/through the jury.

palaestra or **palaistra** *n., pl.* **palaestrae** or **palaestras** or **palaistras** [Gk. palaistra a place to wrestle.] 1. *Ancient Greece and Rome.* A gymnasium or place for athletic exercises, especially wrestling. 2. A gymnasium. A stadium. 3. The exercise and practice of athletics, especially wrestling.

palam *adv.* [L. openly, publicly, plainly.] In the presence of, or before, many. Openly.

palindromia *n., pl.* **palindromias** [Gk. **palin** back, again (2); **dramein** run (2): running back, relapse.] Repeated occurrence of a disease.

palingenesis or **palingenesia** *n., pl.* **palingeneses** or **palingenesias** [Gk. **palin** back, again (2); **genesis** birth (1): birth again, rebirth, regeneration.] 1. Transmigration or reincarnation of souls. **Metempsychosis**

(q.v.). Cf. **metensomatosis.** 2. *Christianity.* Baptism or regeneration through baptism. 3. *Geology.* The process whereby new rocks are formed deep in the earth by the remelting or refusion of old rocks.

palladium *n., pl.* **palladia** or **palladiums** [L. **Palladium** from Gk. **palladion** a statue of Pallas Athena.] 1. *Greek Mythology.* The statue of Pallas Athena, believed to be Troy's guardian deity. As long as this statue was in the possession of the Trojans, their city was safe. Once it fell into the hands of the Greeks, Troy fell. 2. A safeguard. Something that provides security or protection. *Any constitution which does not provide palladia against violation of civil rights is not acceptable.*

pallida Mors aequo pulsat pede pauperum tabernas / regumque turris. Horace (65–8 B.C.). *Odes* I,4,13–14. [L. **pallida** pale (1); **mors** death (2); **aequo** with impartial, like (3); **pulsat** strikes upon, knocks at (5); **pede** (with) foot (4); **pauperum** of poor (persons) (7); **tabernas** huts, cabins (6); **regum** of kings (10) **que** and (8); **turris** towers (9): Pale Death with impartial foot knocks at the huts of poor persons / and at the towers of kings.] Pale Death with impartial steps knocks at the doors of the huts of the poor and of the palaces of Kings.

pallium *n., pl.* **pallia** or **palliums** [L.] 1. *Ancient Greece and Rome.* An outer cloak. 2. *Christianity.* The vestment worn by the Pope and by archbishops and some bishops as a symbol of their authority from the Pope. 3. *Anatomy.* The mantle over the cortex of the brain. 4. *Zoology.* The covering of some animals, including birds and mollusks.

palmarium *n.* [L. prize, achievement, masterpiece.] *Civil Law.* A conditional professional charge assessed together with the standard legal fees.

panacea *n., pl.* **panaceas** [L. from Gk. **pan** all (2) and **akos** cure (1): cure-all, an herb believed to heal all diseases.] A remedy for every difficulty. Universal remedy. A cure-all. *The President was modest enough to admit that he does not have the panacea for all the problems of the nation.*

panache *n., pl.* **panaches** [Fr. plume, tuft, wreath, show.] 1. A plume or tuft of feathers used to decorate a helmet. 2. Flamboyance. An air of gallantry or confidence. a) . . . *"La Tour" is celebrating its 400th birthday and doing so with all the lavish panache that has long been its hallmark (Newsweek Int.* Oct. 18, 1982:18). b) *Many voters admit that they were impressed by the panache with which the President-elect had conducted his campaign.*

pandemonium or **pandaemonium** *n., pl.* **pandemoniums** or **pandaemoniums** [Neo-Gk. from Gk. **pan** all, entire, whole (1); **daimōn** demon, evil spirit (2): entire evil spirit.] 1.The capital of hell in John Milton's *Paradise Lost.* 2. Hell. The world of the demons. 3. A place of widespread vice. 4. A place of lawless, riotous disorder. A lawless, noisy disorder.

"It was pandemonium, a real wailing and gnashing of teeth," said one Teheran resident (Newsweek Int. Oct. 6, 1980:16).

pandit or **pundit** *n.* [Hindi **pandit** from Skt. **panditás** scholar.] 1. A Brahman scholar. 2. A person of great learning. 3. A title of respect used for such a person in India. Cf. **pundit.**

Pandora *n.* [Gk. **Pandōra.**] *Greek Mythology.* The first woman, created for the punishment of humankind after Prometheus had stolen fire from the gods and given it to human beings. She had a jar which contained every kind of evil and misery. She married Prometheus' brother Epimetheus and, when she opened the jar, all sorts of evils invaded the earth. —**Pandora's box** Something which gives birth to unexpected problems and difficulties. A rich source of unforeseen troubles. *The secretary opened a Pandora's box when she accused her boss of victimization.*

panem et circenses Juvenal (c. 55–130 A.D.). *Satires* X,81. [L. **panem** bread (1); **et** and (2); **circenses** circuses (3): bread and circuses.] Food and entertainment. The only things needed to satisfy the common people.

panophobia *n.* [Neo-Gk. from Gk. **pan** all, whole (2); **phob(os)** fear (1): fear of all.] *Psychology.* A condition in which one has general, vague, or unspecified fears.

panorama *n., pl.* **panoramas** [Neo-Gk. from Gk. **pan** all, whole (1); **horama** spectacle, sight (2): the whole sight or spectacle.] 1. A complete, unbroken view of an area. A thorough presentation of a subject. *Johnson describes the panorama of events in the Caribbean from 1915 to the mid-1920s, which forced the immigration of thousands of West Indians to the U.S. and Europe, . . . (West Africa* 1985). 2. A mental picture of a scene which is continuously before one. A scene which changes continuously. 3. A photograph showing a comprehensive view of a scene, an area or many persons.

panta rhei, ouden menei. Heracleitus (c.540–c.480 B.C.). [Gk. **panta** all (things), everything (1); **(chō)rhei** flows (2); **ouden** nothing (3); **menei** remains (4): Everything flows; nothing remains.] Everything is in a flux; nothing is static.

pantheon *n., pl.* **pantheons** [Gk. **pantheion:** pan all, every (1) and **the(os)** god (2): temple or place consecrated to all gods.] 1. *Rome.* Temple erected by Agrippa (c.64–12 B.C.) during the reign of Augustus and rebuilt by the emperor Hadrian (76–138 A.D.). 2. Temple dedicated to all the national gods. All the officially recognized gods of a nation. 3. *Paris.* Desanctified church where illustrious Frenchmen like Voltaire and Rousseau are buried. 4. Building used as the burial place of distinguished citizens who had passed away. *. . . Mao's body may be cremated and his mausoleum expanded to include a pantheon of Chinese revolutionary heroes (Newsweek Int.* Jan. 19, 1981:24).

pantocrator *n., pl.* **pantocrators** [Gk. **pantokratōp: pant(os)** every, all (1); **krat(eō)** ruler (2): the all-ruler, almighty.] Ruler over all. Applicable to Jesus, especially in the churches of eastern Christianity.

panton chrematon anthropon metron einai. Protagoras (c.490–420 B.C.). [Gk. **pantōn** of all (4); **chrēmatōn** (of) things (5); **anthrōpōn** person, human being (1); **metron** measure (3); **einai** to be, is (2): A human being is the measure of all things.] Man is the rule by which everything is measured. **homo mensura omnium** (q.v.). See **à chacun son goût**.

panzer *n., pl.* **panzers** *short form* of **Panzervidision** [Ger. **Panzer** tank, armor (1); **Division** division, military unit (2): tank division.] Any German armored tank, truck, or van in World War II. —*adj.* Pertaining to a tank or any armored vehicle or military unit.

p.a.p. *abbr.* for **prêt-à-porter** (q.v.).

Papa *abbr.* **P.** *n.* [It. from L. father.] The Holy Father. The Pope.

papabile *adj.* [It. able or likely to be pope.] Pertaining to someone who is widely considered to be a strong candidate in the next papal election.

paparazzo *n., pl.* **paparazzi** [It. from a photographer named Paparazzo in *La Dolce Vita* by filmmaker Federico Fellini (1920–1993).] An independent or freelance photographer who dogs the steps of celebrity subjects in pursuit of marketable candid images.

papier mâché *n.* [Fr. **papier** paper (2); **mâché** chewed (1): chewed paper.] *Art.* Glued layers of paper strips or shreds which are molded and painted or varnished. —*adj.* **papier-mâché** Made of such paper strips or shreds. *A papier-mâché statue.*

par. *abbr.* for **parenthesis** (q.v.).

par *n., pl.* **pars** [L. equal, a match.] 1. Equality. An equality established between the nominal value of the monetary unit of a country, share of stock, etc. and its real selling or purchasing power. 2. The face value of securities or the price at which they are issued. 3. Equality with respect to situation. a) . . . *his comic invention puts him straight away on a par with Selvon,* . . . (K.W. in *West Africa* 1982). b) *His actual accomplishments have never been on a par with his overweening ambitions.* 4. Average, mean, or norm. a) *Jim's health was not up to par.* b) *The audience knew that his scholarly publications were below par.* 5. *Golf.* Each hole's standard score.

parakalo *adv.* [Modern Gk. I ask.] Please. Cf. See **bitte sehr**; **bitte schön**; **per favore**; **por favor**; and **s'il vous plaît**.

paraleipsis *n., pl.* **paraleipses** [Gk. **para** alongside, amiss, wrong (2); **leipsis** leaving, omitting (1): leaving alongside, an omission.] *Rhetoric.* Emphasizing a fact by expressing the intention of ignoring it; e.g., "I will pass over the fact that my opponent is corrupt."

paralysis *n., pl.* **paralyses** [Gk. **paralusis**: **para** alongside, amiss, wrong (1); **lusis** loosening (2): wrong loosening, disability of the nerves.] 1. *Medicine.* Full or partial loss of the ability to feel or move. 2. Inability to move. *He attributed his failure to report for duty*

punctually to paralysis of traffic in the morning. 3. Inactivity. Condition of complete powerlessness. a) . . . *the paralysis of US policy in the region, symbolised by the final withdrawal of US troops from Lebanon in August* (*South* 1984). b) *Lack of raw materials has resulted in industrial paralysis.* Cf. **hemiplegia**; **paraplegia**; and **paresis**.

paramnesia *n.* [Neo-Gk. from Gk. **para** alongside, amiss, wrong (1); **mnēm(ē)** memory, remembrance (2): wrong memory.] 1. A defect of the memory in which one cannot remember the meanings of words. 2. **Déjà vu** 2 (q.v.).

paranoia *n.* [Gk. **para** alongside, amiss, wrong (1); **no(us)** mind (2): wrong mind, insanity.] A chronic psychosis marked by delusions of persecution, baseless suspicion and distrust of others, or delusions of grandeur and megalomania. *Washington has been blinded by anti-Soviet paranoia and as a result has not realized the vast opportunities for cooperation with Moscow* (*Newsweek Int.* Nov 17, 1980:26).

parapherna *pl. n.* [Gk. **para** alongside, amiss, wrong (1) and **phern(ē)** dowry (2): things alongside the dowry.] *Roman and Civil Law.* Goods which a bride brings to her matrimonial home over and above her dowry. Such property belongs to her and cannot be controlled by the husband. Cf. **conquêts**.

paraphernalia *pl. n.* Either *pl.* or *sing.* in constr. [L. from Gk. **para** alongside, amiss, wrong (1) and **phern(ē)** dowry (2): things alongside the dowry.] 1. *Law.* The separate property of a married woman both real and personal, but mostly consisting of clothing and ornaments which she can not only bequeath by her will but also keep after her husband's death. Cf. **conquêts**. 2. Personal effects. 3. Things used as equipment. Tools. a) *As many more have been injured in assassination attempts or so threatened that they have to live ringed by the paraphernalia of security* (*The Economist* 1987). b) The Guardian *was given an exclusive closeup of the various charms and paraphernalia which allegedly helped him sustain his career for so long* (*The Guardian* 1986).

paraphilia *n., pl.* **paraphilias** [Neo-Gk. from Gk. **para** alongside, amiss, wrong (1); **philia** fondness, affection (2): wrong affection.] Preference for abnormal sexual activities. Cf. **pedophilia**.

paraplegia *n., pl.* **paraplegias** [Gk. **para** alongside, amiss, wrong (1); **plēg(ē)** blow, striking (2): wrong blow, paralysis.] *Medicine.* Paralysis of the body's lower part, usually caused by injury to, or disease of, the spinal cord. See **paralysis**.

parataxis *n.* [Gk. from **para** alongside, amiss, wrong (2); **taxis** drawing up, arranging (1): arranging alongside.] *Rhetoric.* The placing together of clauses and phrases without conjunctions. E.g., "They sang, they ate, they slept." Cf. **asyndeton**.

par avion *abbr.* **P.A.** or **p.a.** *adv.* [Fr. **par** by (1); **avion** airplane (2): by airplane.] By air.

parens patriae *n.* [L. **parens** parent (1); **patriae** of country (2): parent of the country.] Father of the country. The state legally regarded as father in the sense that it serves as guardian of those who have no natural guardians, it inherits the property of those who have no natural heirs, and it protects citizens who are incapable of protecting themselves. *"It is in the interest of the sovereign that children should be properly brought up and educated; and according to the principles of our law, the sovereign, as parens patriae, is bound to look to the maintenance and education (as far as it* [sic] *has the means of judging) of all his subjects"* (*Hope v. Hope* [1854] 4 De G.M.&G. 328, 345, quoted by Morris 1973:401). Cf. **pater patriae**.

parenthesis *abbr.* **par.** *n., pl.* **parentheses** [Gk. **par(a)** alongside, amiss, wrong (3); **en** in (2); **thesis** putting, placing (1): placing in alongside, an insertion.] 1. An explanatory word, phrase, clause, etc. inserted in a sentence or passage to which ordinarily it is not related grammatically. 2. A digression. A comment that does not strictly relate to the theme of a narrative, discourse, etc. *One peculiarity of the writer's style is the parentheses which are scattered throughout the work and enliven the narrative.* 3. Interlude. Something incidental. *Mrs. Shore complained about her husband's habit of treating her as though she were a mere parenthesis.* 4. One of two curves, i.e., "( )," used to enclose insertions.

parentum est liberos alere etiam nothos. [L. **parentum** of parents (2); **est** it is (1); **liberos** children (4); **alere** to support, maintain (3); **etiam** even (5); **nothos** the illegitimate (6): It is of parents to maintain children, even the illegitimate.] It is the duty of parents to support their children, even the illegitimate ones.

parergon *n., pl.* **parerga** [Gk. **par(a)** alongside, amiss, wrong (2); **ergon** work (1): work alongside, subordinate or secondary business.] 1. Something which is accessory or subordinate, especially a decorative device. 2. A secondary business or activity. *Pat's father is an accountant who also, as a parergon, drives a taxi at night.*

paresis *n., pl.* **pareses** [Gk. **par(a)** alongside, amiss, wrong (2) and **(h)esis** sending (1): wrong sending, slackening of strength, paralysis.] *Medicine.* Slight or incomplete paralysis which usually occurs in the initial stages of various progressive diseases associated with the nervous system. See **paralysis**.

pareunia *n., pl.* **pareunias** [Neo-Gk. from Gk. **par(a)** alongside, amiss, wrong (2); **eun(ē)** bed (1): bed beside.] Sexual intercourse. See **coitus**.

pareve *adj.* [Yid.] Containing neither meat nor dairy products and therefore edible along with either food type according to Jewish dietary law.

par excellence *adj.* [Fr. **par** by (1); **excellence** excellence (2): by excellence.] Best in a group or of its kind. Being an embodiment. Being an epitome. . . . *both Aristotle and Horace called Homer the epic poet par excellence* (Jaeger 1970:46). —*adv.* Above all others. Particularly. In the highest sense of the word.

par exemple *abbr.* **p.e.** or **p. ex.** *adv.* [Fr. **par** for, through (1); **exemple** example, instance (2): for example.] For instance. By way of an example.

parfait *adj.* [Fr. perfect.] Perfect. Just right. —*interj.* Perfect! Excellent! —*n.* A dessert made of frozen cream, fruit, or ice cream, often layered and served in a tall glass.

pariah *n.* [Tamil **paraiyar** pariah caste.] 1. A person belonging to the lowest social caste of agricultural and household workers in India and Burma. An untouchable. 2. An individual who has been cast out by society.

paribus sententiis reus absolvitur. [L. **paribus** (with) being equal (2); **sententiis** with opinions (1); **reus** the accused, defendant (3); **absolvitur** is acquitted (4): With opinions being equal, the defendant/accused is acquitted.] *Law.* When opinions are equally divided, the accused/defendant is acquitted.

pari causa *adv.* [L. **pari** with equal (1); **causa** (with) cause, case, reason (2): with equal cause.] On an equal footing. With equal right.

pari delicto *adv./adj.* [L. **pari** in equal (1); **delicto** (in) fault, crime (2): in equal fault.] Equally guilty. See **in pari delicto**; **in pari delicto, potior est conditio defendentis**; and **in pari delicto, potior est conditio possidentis**.

pari-mutuel *n.* [Fr. **pari** bet (2); **mutuel** common, mutual (1): mutual bet.] 1. A form of betting, especially on horse races, in which the winnings are shared proportionally according to the amount bet. 2. A machine used for such a betting system.

par in parem imperium non habet. [L. **par** equal (1); **in** into, to, against, for (5); **parem** equal (6); **imperium** authority, control (4); **non** not (2); **habet** has, holds, regards (3): An equal does not have authority against an equal.] *Law.* An equal has no authority/control over an equal. Thus a sovereign country cannot exercise control over another sovereign country, nor can a master exercise control over another master, but only over a subject country or a servant/slave, respectively.

pari passu *adv.* [L. **pari** with equal (1); **passu** (with) pace, stride (2): with equal pace/stride.] At an equal pace or rate. By an equal progress. With no side being given preference. *The rate of national development usually progresses pari passu with the growth of productive manpower and resources.*

pari ratione *adv.* [L. **pari** by equal (1); **ratione** (by) reason, reasoning (2): by equal reasoning.] By a similar method of reasoning. For a similar reason.

Paris vaut bien une messe. Henry IV of France (1553–1610). [Fr. **Paris** Paris (1); **vaut** is worth (3); **bien** well (2); **une** a (4); **messe** mass (5): Paris is well worth a mass.] Becoming king of France is worth becoming Catholic. The reward is worth the sacrifice.

parium eadem est ratio, idem jus. [L. **parium** of equal, like (things) (1); **eadem** the same (2); **est** is (3); **ratio** reason (4); **idem** the same (5); **jus** right, law (6): Of equal things, the same is the reason, the same the law.] *Law.* Where the things (or cases) are identical, the same reason and the same law are applicable. See **eadem est** etc.

parium judicium *n.* [L. **parium** of equals (2); **judicium** judgment (1): judgment of equals.] The judgment of peers. Trial by a jury of a person's equals or peers. Cf. **inter pares** and **per pares.**

parlando or **parlante** *adv.* [It. speaking.] *Music.* In the manner of speech. Used to indicate words to be sung as if they were spoken.

parole *n., pl.* **paroles** [Fr. word, promise.] 1. *Law.* Release of a prisoner from custody on provision of good behavior. 2. *Law.* The length of time for such a provisional release. 3. *Military.* A password. 4. *Linguistics.* Speaking or uttering a word. —*v.* To release a prisoner from custody conditionally.

paronomasia *n., pl.* **paronomasias** [Gk. from **par(a)** alongside, amiss, wrong (2); **onomasis** naming (1): naming alongside.] 1. A play on a word or name. 2. A pun.

parousia *n.* [Gk. **par(a)** alongside, amiss, wrong (2); **on** being, existing (1): being alongside, presence, arrival, visit of a royal personage.] *Christianity.* The second coming or advent of Jesus Christ, the Messiah.

parquet *n., pl.* **parquets** [Fr. enclosure, floor.] 1. A floor made out of wooden inlay. 2. The ground floor of a theater between the orchestra pit and the balcony. 3. *French Law.* The office of the public prosecutor. —*v.* To make a floor of wooden inlay design.

parricidium *n.* [L. **parri-** perhaps related to Gk. **pē(os)** kinsman (1); L. **caedo** kill (2): kin killing.] *Civil Law.* Parricide. Assassination of a parent. Murder of any close relative.

pars legitima *n.* [L. **pars** part, side, party (2); **legitima** legitimate, lawful, legal (1): lawful part.] *Roman, Civil, and Scots Law.* A portion of the estate set aside for the children and, in some cases, other heirs on the death of the father. See **legitime.**

pars pro toto *n.* [L. **pars** part, side, party (1); **pro** for, in the place of (2); **toto** whole (3): part for the whole.] A part representing the whole.

pars rationabilis *n.* [L. **pars** part, side, party (2); **rationabilis** reasonable (1): reasonable part.] *Law.* The portion of a man's property which is lawfully given to his children and widow. See **legitime.**

pars rea *n.* [L. **pars** part, side, party (1); **rea** accused, defendant (2): the party accused.] *Law.* The defendant. The accused.

parte inaudita *adv.* [L. **parte** with a part, side, party (1); **inaudita** (with) having been unheard (2): with a side having been unheard.] *Law.* One side/party being unheard. Used with reference to a legal action taken **ex parte** (q.v.). See **audi partem alteram.**

parte non comparente *adv.* [L. **parte** with a part, side, party (1); **non** not (2); **comparente** (with) appearing (3): with a party not appearing.] *Law.* The party being absent. The party failing to appear.

parte quacumque integrante sublata, tollitur totum. [L. **parte** with a side, part, portion (1); **quacumque** (with) whatsoever, whatever (2); **integrante** (with) making whole (3); **sublata** (with) removed, taken away (4); **tollitur** is removed, taken away (6); **totum** the whole (5): With a part whatsoever making a whole removed, the whole is removed.] *Law.* When any integral part is removed, the whole is removed. Cf. **cuicunque aliquis** etc.

parthenogenesis *n.* [Neo-Gk. from Gk. **partheno(s)** unmarried woman, virgin (2); **genesis** birth, reproduction (2): virgin birth.] Reproduction among some lower plants and invertebrate animals in which the gamete is developed without fertilization or sexual contact.

parti *n., pl.* **partis** [Fr. match, person to be married.] 1. A match. A person eligible for marriage and assessed as a partner with respect to his/her advantages or disadvantages. *After dating Emily for a few days, Kenneth decided that she was a good parti.* 2. A good match. A desirable or suitable match. *Kenneth did not know what a parti Emily was until he had dated her for a few days.*

particeps criminis *n., pl.* **participes criminis** [L. **particeps** participant (1); **criminis** of crime, offense (2): participant of a crime.] *Law.* Participant in a crime. An accessory. An accomplice. See **socius criminis.** Cf. **in pari delicto.**

partie carrée *n.* [Fr. **partie** party (2); **carrée** square (1): square party.] A party of two couples. A party of two men and two women. A foursome. *Being a partie carrée, they ignored the other tables, and went directly to a table for four.*

parti pris *n., pl.* **partis pris** [Fr. **parti** side, decision (1); **pris** taken (2): side or decision taken.] Prejudice. Preconceived or obstinate opinion. Partiality. a) *He is not striving to give victory to one point of view, he is not supporting a parti pris through thick and thin* . . . (Lesky 1966:477). b) *Professor Traus won his reputation for objectivity by writing a history of his own country with hardly any trace of parti pris.*

partita *n., pl.* **partitas** [It. part, party, team.] 1. *Music.* A composition in parts or a group of musical variations, especially for instrumentals. 2. *Music.* One of the parts of such a composition. 3. *Italy.* An athletic contest. A game.

partitio legata *n.* [L. **partitio** partition, division (2); **legata** bequeathed (1): bequeathed partition.] *Civil Law.* A partition authorized by a will. A testamentary partition.

parturient montes, nascetur ridiculus mus. Horace (65–8 B.C.). *Ars Poetica* 139. [L. **parturient** will be in labor, will be pregnant (2); **montes** mountains (l);

nascetur will be born (5); **ridiculus** laughable, ridiculous (3); **mus** mouse (4): Mountains will be in labor, and a laughable mouse will be born.] Mountains will go into labor and give birth to a ridiculous mouse. Applicable to a result or product which, considering the fuss and labor bestowed on the project, is very disappointing.

partus sequitur ventrem. [L. **partus** offspring (1); **sequitur** follows (2); **ventrem** womb, belly (3): The offspring follows the womb.] *Civil Law.* The offspring follows the mother. A rule applied to animals, but not to human beings.

parvenu or *fem.* **parvenue** *n., pl.* **parvenus** or *fem.* **parvenues** [Fr. one who has arrived or succeeded.] An upstart. A self-made person. A person who, by acquiring wealth, position, or power, has moved out of his/her social class, leaving behind his/her former relative poverty or obscurity. A newly rich individual. **Nouveau riche** (q.v.). *The fund-raising ceremony provided a good opportunity for parvenus to make ostentatious donations. —adj.* Having the characteristics of an upstart or parvenu. *A parvenu group within the association is tarnishing its image with its ostentatious display of wealth.*

parvum in magno *n.* [L. **parvum** little, small (thing) (1); **in** in, on (2); **magno** big (thing) (3): a little thing in a big thing.] A microcosm in a macrocosm. *And therefore it was said, that those that had written de fossilibus did observe, that gold hidden in the bowels of the earth, was in respect of the mass of the whole earth, parvum in magno; . . .* (Megarry 1955:305).

pas *n., pl.* **pas** [Fr. step, pace, tread.] 1. Right of precedence. *It is a customary practice in most African societies for youths to yield the pas to their elders.* 2. A step or combination of steps in dancing. A dance.

Paschale Tempore *abbr.* **P.T.** See **Tempore Paschale.**

pas ciseaux Cf. **pas de ciseaux.**

pas d'action *n., pl.* **pas d'action** [Fr. **pas** step (1); **d'** of (2); **action** action, plot (3): step of action.] *Ballet.* A dance which aims at telling a story.

pas de bourrée *short form* **bourrée** *n.* [Fr. **pas** step (1); **de** of (2); **bourrée** packed (twigs) (3): a step of packed twigs.] *Ballet.* A short step performed on **pointe** (q.v.) similar to a step used in a traditional French dance called **bourrée** (q.v.).

pas de charge *n., pl.* **pas de charge** [Fr. **pas** step (1); **de** of (2); **charge** attack, charge (3): step of attack.] *Military.* The quick pace used by foot-soldiers when launching an attack. Charging pace. The double.

pas de chat *n., pl.* **pas de chat** [Fr. **pas** step (1); **de** of (2); **chat** cat (3): step of cat.] *Ballet.* A forward leap like that of a cat.

pas de ciseaux or **pas ciseaux** *n., pl.* **pas de ciseaux** or **pas ciseaux** [Fr. **pas** step (1); **de** of (2); **ciseaux** scissors (3): step of scissors.] *Ballet.* A scissor kick. A leap during which the dancer spreads his/her legs apart in the air.

pas de deux *n., pl.* **pas de deux** [Fr. **pas** step (1); **de** of (2); **deux** two (3): step of two.] 1. *Ballet.* A duet, i.e., a dance for two persons. *. . . the dancers take to the air in jeté after jeté, in dazzling lifts, in fiery pas de deux . . .* (*Newsweek Int.* July 27, 1981:53). 2. A duet, i.e., an action in which two parties participate. *After a less-than-whirlwind courtship, which sees Nureyev pursue her all over town, she agrees to accompany him to Paris. Their pas de deux sours, however, when . . .* (*Newsweek Int.* Jan. 18, 1982:23).

pas de quatre *n., pl.* **pas de quatre** [Fr. **pas** step (1); **de** of, by (2); **quatre** four (3): step by four.] *Ballet.* A dance for four persons.

pas de trois *n., pl.* **pas de trois** [Fr. **pas** step (1); **de** of, by (2); **trois** three (3): step by three.] *Ballet.* A dance for three persons.

pas devant *adv.* [Fr. **pas** not (1); **devant** before, in front of (2): not in front of.] Not in front of the children, the neighbors, or some other inappropriate viewers or listeners.

pas du tout *adv.* [Fr. **pas** not (1); **du** from, of the (2); **tout** all (3): not from the all.] Not at all.

paseo *n., pl.* **paseos** [Sp. stroll.] 1. An unhurried, leisurely outdoor stroll. A **promenade** (q.v.). 2. The path or route for such a walk. 3. The parade of participants into the ring prior to a bullfight.

pasha or **pacha** *n., pl.* **pashas** or **pachas** [Turk. **pasa** from Pahlavi **pati** lord (1); Pers. **shah** king (2): lord king.] A title for military officers or administrative officials in Turkey and North Africa.

paso doble *n.* [Sp. **paso** step, pace (2); **doble** double (1): double step.] 1. A quick dance. 2. Quick dance music played as a march, especially at a bullfight.

pasquinade *n., pl.* **pasquinades** [Fr. from It. **Pasquino,** popular name for a statue in Rome where lampoons were displayed, lampoon.] An anonymous lampoon or satire which is publicly displayed. *The student, who has been posting defamatory pasquinades about lecturers on notice boards, was apprehended yesterday. —v. tr.* To satirize, lampoon or ridicule.

pass. *abbr.* for **passim** (q.v.).

passacaglia *n., pl.* **passacaglias** [It. from Sp. **pasacalle** from **pasar** step (2); **calle** street (1): street step.] *Music.* 1. A slow dance, originally popular in Spain, in 3/4 time with frequent melodic repetition. 2. A court dance based upon the popular dance form.

passade *n.* [Fr. a pass.] 1. A movement in **dressage** (q.v.) in which the horse passes repeatedly over the same spot. 2. A romance. An amorous flirtation.

passé or *fem.* **passée** *adj.* [Fr. past, vanished.] 1. No longer virile or youthfully feminine. Having passed one's prime. *The old man will soon wed a delightful passée woman.* 2. Out of fashion. Outdated. *At first the 50-year-old homemaker . . . thought of hiking across the Himalayas in Nepal. But for Shoening, even that seemed a bit passé* (*Newsweek Int.* June 7, 1982:48).

passepartout *n., pl.* **passepartouts** [Fr. **passe** pass (1); **partout** everywhere (2): pass everywhere.] 1. A master key or something which provides open access across barriers or borders. 2. Matting used to frame a picture or the paper or tape used to make such matting.

passepied *n., pl.* **passepieds** [Fr. **passe** pass (1); **pied** foot (2): pass the foot.] *Music.* 1. A lively court dance popular in 17th- and 18th-century France and England. 2. A musical composition for such a dance or in the style of such a dance.

pas seul *n., pl.* **pas seuls** [Fr. **pas** step (2); **seul** single, sole (1): single or sole step.] *Ballet.* A dance for one person. **Solo** (q.v.).

passim *abbr.* **pass.** *adv.* [L. spread/scattered about.] Here and there. Everywhere. In various places or sections. Used especially in footnotes to indicate that something (e.g., a word or view) is to be found in many places in a book.

pastiche *n., pl.* **pastiches** [Fr. parody, imitation.] 1. A literary, musical, or artistic work which is a close imitation of previous works. *Two key new scenes are the dying Mozart dictating his* Requiem *to Salieri, and the performance . . . of a parody pastiche of Mozart's operas . . . (Newsweek Int.* July 18, 1983:46). 2. A potpourri. A literary or musical work comprising selections from various works. *It is not an original work but a pastiche, with various sections lifted from various sources.* 3. A hodgepodge. An incongruous combination of various styles, materials, etc. . . . *some powerful pastiche has been produced this year: D. M. Thomas's novel* The White Hotel, *which mixed pornography, poetry, psychoanalysis and naturalistic fiction . . . (Newsweek Int.* Jan. 4, 1982:58).

pasticheur *n., pl.* **pasticheurs** [Fr. imitator, parodist.] An author of pastiches. A person who makes pastiches.

pastorale *n., pl.* **pastorali** or **pastorales** [It. shepherd-like, belonging to shepherds.] 1. *Music.* A vocal or instrumental composition using melodies and rhythms suggestive of the tranquil life of a traditional shepherd. 2. A theatrical or operatic performance, popular in 16th- and 17th-century Italy, based upon the setting and themes of the countryside and the amorous lives of shepherds.

p.-à-t. *abbr.* for **pied-à-terre** (q.v.).

patens ambiguitas *n., pl.* **patentes ambiguitates** [L. **patens** evident, manifest (1); **ambiguitas** ambiguity, equivocalness (2): evident ambiguity.] Patent ambiguity.

paterfamilias *n., pl.* **patresfamilias** [L. head of the family, householder.] 1. *Roman Law.* The male head of a family or household. A man who exercises **patria potestas** (q.v.). 2. The father or male head of a family. *The man proudly declared that he is a veritable paterfamilias with five children.* See **familia**.

pater historiae *n.* [L. **pater** father (1); **historiae** of history (2): father of history.] The father of history. Title conferred on Herodotus by Cicero.

pater is est quem nuptiae demonstrant. [L. **pater** father (1); **is** he (3); **est** is (2); **quem** whom (4); **nuptiae** marriage, wedding (5); **demonstrant** show(s), point(s) out (6): The father is he whom the marriage shows.] *Law.* The father is the person whom the marriage points out; i.e., the father of a child is presumed to be the husband of the child's mother. Cf. **heres legitimus** etc.

Pater Noster *n.* [L. **pater** father (2); **noster** our (1): our father.] "Our Father." 1. The first words of the prayer Jesus taught his apostles at Matthew 6:9–13. 2. *pl.* **Pater Nosters** The name of this prayer. 3. A musical composition based upon this prayer. Cf. **fiat voluntas tua**. —**pater noster** *n., pl.* **pater nosters** An elevator consisting of a number of open compartments hung together by a chain and moving slowly enough to allow passengers to enter and leave compartments at will.

pater patriae *abbr.* **P.P.** or **p.p.** *n., pl.* **patres patriae** [L. **pater** father (1); **patriae** of country, fatherland (2): father of the country.] The father of the fatherland. Originally conferred on Cicero after he suppressed the conspiracy of Catiline, the title is applicable to anybody who has rendered remarkable service to his fatherland. Cf. **parens patriae** and **père de la nation**.

pathei mathos Aeschylus (525–456 B.C.) *Agamemnon* 177. [Gk. **pathei** by suffering (2); **mathos** learning (1): learning by suffering.] One learns by suffering. Cf. **quae nocent docent**.

pathétique *adj.* [Fr. moving.] *Music.* Moving. With feeling. Used in the titles of several compositions including the "Pathétique" Sonata of Ludwig Van Beethoven (1770–1827) and the *Symphonie pathétique* of Peter Ilyitch Tchaikovsky (1840–1893).

pathos *n.* [Gk. calamity, misfortune, emotion, passion, emotional style.] 1. A quality in experience, speech, literature, art, or drama which evokes pity, sadness, sympathy, compassion, or tenderness. Ability to evoke such feelings. . . . *a simple speech that was well delivered, without pathos.* (*Time Int.* 1982). 2. A feeling of sympathy, pity, or compassion. *Martin felt a pang of pathos when he heard of the plight of his estranged wife.*

patio *n., pl.* **patios** [Sp. outdoor space.] A outdoor area, usually paved and either adjacent to or within a house, used for entertainment, especially meals.

patisserie *n., pl.* **patisseries** [Fr. **pâtisserie** pastry, bakery.] 1. French pastry. 2. A bakery where French pastries are prepared.

patois *n., pl.* **patois** [Fr. dialect.] 1. A form of speech peculiar to a particular region. 2. A form of speech which is not standard. 3. A special language or vocabulary shared by a small group of people.

patria potestas *n.* [L. **patria** paternal, of the father (1); **potestas** power, authority (2): paternal authority.] The power of the paterfamilias. Originally, in ancient Rome, patria potestas was almost absolute, and a father exercised the power of life and death over his children, slaves, ex-slaves, and even, in some cases, over his wife. See **familia**.

patria potestas in pietate debet, non in atrocitate, consistere. [L. **patria** paternal (1); **potestas** power, authority (2); **in** in, on (5); **pietate** piety, affection, love (6); **debet** ought, should (3); **non** not (7); **in** in, on (8); **atrocitate** atrocity, harshness (9); **consistere** to consist (4): Paternal authority ought to consist in affection, not in atrocity.] Paternal authority should be exercised in love, not in atrocity. See **familia**.

patrimonium *n.* [L. inheritance, paternal estate, patrimony.] *Civil Law.* Something which can be inherited.

paucis verbis *adv.* [L. **paucis** (wtih) few (1); **verbis** with words (2): with a few words.] In a few words. In brief.

pauper *n., pl.* **paupers** [L. poor, of small means.] A very poor person. A destitute person who depends on charity. A criminal defendant who is so poor that the state has to give him defense counsel. A person suing who is so poor that he is exempted from court costs. *He has become fantastically wealthy and has easily forgotten that his father was a threadbare pauper.* See **in forma pauperis**.

pavane or **pavan** *n., pl.* **pavanes** or **pavans** [Fr. from It. **pavana** Paduan, from Padua.] *Music.* 1. A court dance of the 16th and 17th centuries with a slow and majestic tempo. 2. A composition based upon this dance style.

pax *n.* [L. peace, tranquillity, harmony.] 1. *Christianity.* Kiss of peace. 2. *History.* A period of tranquillity, political stability, and general prosperity when there are no major wars, usually due to the predominance of a powerful nation which establishes an empire and whose power is widely respected. 3. *History.* Civilization or culture. —*interj.* Used as an expression of peace. Cf. **shalom**.

pax Americana *n.* [L. **pax** peace (2); **Americana** American (1): American peace.] 1. The American peace. A period of international peace resulting from the power of the United States, especially in the period following World War II. 2. American civilization or culture. *Everywhere in Monrovia, capital of Liberia, there were unmistakable signs of the pax Americana, including cars, denim jeans, the dollar, and restaurants reminiscent of those in America.*

pax Austriaca *n.* [L. **pax** peace (2); **Austriaca** Austrian (1): Austrian peace.] The Austrian peace. A period of international peace consequent upon the power of Austria.

pax Britannica *n.* [L. **pax** peace (2); **Britannica** British (1): British peace.] 1. The British peace. The peace and order established by Britain in her former empire, which supposedly facilitated secure life and property, the development of trade and commerce, and a high standard of life. 2. British civilization and culture. *The pax Britannica of the colonial era is now*

regarded by some nationalists as an instrument of exploitation.

pax Hispanica *n.* [L. **pax** peace (2); **Hispanica** Spanish (1): Spanish peace.] 1. The Spanish peace. A period of international peace resulting from the power of Spain. 2. Spanish civilization or culture.

pax Japonica *n.* [L. **pax** peace (2); **Japonica** Japanese (1): Japanese peace.] 1. The Japanese peace. 2. Japanese civilization or culture. *. . . technology may induce strains in the pax Japonica between management and labor as the economy swings into new sectors that are less labor-intensive (Newsweek Int.* Aug. 9, 1982:28).

pax Romana *n.* [L. **pax** peace (2); **Romana** Roman (1): Roman peace.] 1. The Roman peace; i.e., the peace and prosperity established by ancient Rome in the Mediterranean area. 2. Roman civilization or culture. *Augustus' Principate brought a pax Romana which contributed immensely to the prosperity and happiness of the Roman world.*

pax vobiscum [L. **pax** peace (1); **vobis** you (3); **cum** with (1): peace with you (pl.).] Peace be to you.

pays *var.* of **pais** (q.v.).

P.B. *abbr.* for **Philosophiae Baccalaureus** (q.v.).

P.C. *abbr.* for 1. **per centum** (q.v.). 2. **post cibum** (q.v.).

P.D. *abbr.* for **per diem** (q.v.).

Pd.B. *abbr.* for **Paedagogiae Baccalaureus** (q.v.).

Pd.M. *abbr.* for **Paedagogiae Magister** (q.v.).

p.e. *abbr.* for **par exemple** (q.v.).

peccadillo *n., pl.* **peccadilloes** or **peccadillos** [Sp. **pecadillo** little sin.] A trifling, pardonable, or small offense, fault, or sin. *Mr. Stone is a strict disciplinarian who punishes his children for peccadilloes which would be ignored by the average parent.*

pecca fortiter Martin Luther (1483–1546). [L. **pecca** sin (1); **fortiter** bravely, strongly (2): sin bravely.] Sin boldly.

peccata contra naturam sunt gravissima. [L. **peccata** transgressions, crimes (1); **contra** against, opposite (2); **naturam** nature (3); **sunt** are (4); **gravissima** very/most serious (5): Crimes against nature are very serious.] *Law.* Transgressions committed against natural law are very severe. Applicable to such crimes as patricide and matricide.

peccavi *n., pl.* **peccavis** [L. I have sinned, offended.] A confession. A humble admission of guilt, error, or sin. *The repentant children spontaneously uttered their peccavis.*

peculatus *n.* [L. embezzlement.] *Civil Law.* Embezzlement of public funds.

peculium *n., pl.* **peculia** [L. private property, separate estate.] A property or fund which is exclusively one's own possession. Originally, in ancient Rome, peculium was a private estate which the **paterfamilias** (q.v.) allowed a son, slave, or wife to own.

peculium adventitium *n.* [L. **peculium** property (2); **adventi(c)ium** accidental, imported, foreign (1): foreign/accidental property.] Property acquired through one's own efforts. See **bona adventitia.** Cf. **bona materna.**

pedophilia or **paedophilia** *n., pl.* **pedophilias** or **paedophilias** [Neo-Gk. from Gk. **pai(s)** child (1); **philia** loving, love (2): child-loving, love of children.] Addiction to, or abnormal preference for, sexual intercourse with children. Cf. **paraphilia.**

penates See **lares et penates.**

penchant *n., pl.* **penchants** [Fr. inclining, leaning, tilting, slope.] A strong fondness, propensity, or attraction. a) *. . . the Japanese penchant for pastoral or feminine car names* (*Newsweek Int.* Aug. 8, 1983:45). b) *The authorities with their vast bureaucracies and a distinct penchant for constructing fancy headquarters . . .* (*New African* 1980).

pendente lite See **lite pendente.**

pendente lite nihil innovetur. [L. **pendente** (with) pending, hanging in the air (2); **lite** with suit (1); **nihil** nothing (3); **innovetur** should be renewed, altered (4): With a suit pending, nothing should be altered.] *Law.* During litigation, no change should be introduced. See **lis pendens.**

pendulum *n., pl.* **pendula** or **pendulums** [L. a thing which hangs, an uncertain thing.] 1. A weight suspended on a point in such a way that it swings freely from side to side under the force of gravity, a principle which is used for the construction of clocks and other machines. 2. Something such as public opinion which oscillates between two opposite points. a). *Generally, a politician lives a life of uncertainty, depending, as he is, on the pendulum of capricious public opinion.* b) *Debbie, a victim of unrequited love, hangs on a pendulum which swings from love to hatred and back again.*

penetralia *n., sing.* **penetrale** [L. innermost things.] 1. The innermost/interior/internal parts of a place or thing. 2. Privacy. Hidden things. Secrets. *Bamidele and Aliyu are bosom friends and have admitted each other to the intimate penetralia of their own affairs.*

Pensées *pl. n.* [Fr. thoughts.] *Thoughts,* the collected notes of Blaise Pascal (1623–1662), published posthumously.

pensionnat de jeunes filles *n.* [F. **pensionnat** boarding-school, hostel (1); **de** of, for (2); **jeunes** young (3); **filles** girls, maidens (4): boarding school for girls.] A private, residential school for young women. . . . *she* [i.e., Sappho] *was the principal of a pensionnat de jeunes filles* (Lesky 1966:144–145).

pensum *n., pl.* **pensa** or **pensums** [L. a charge, duty, office, something which is weighed out.] A task, usually punitive, assigned in school. *The loquacious boy was assigned the pensum of cleaning three classrooms.*

pentathlon *n., pl.* **pentathlons** [Gk. **pente** five (1); **athlon** contest (2): five contests, a contest of five exercises.] 1. *Ancient Greece.* An athletic contest in which a contestant had to take part in five distinct events, namely wrestling, footrace (i.e., running), throwing the discus, jumping, and throwing the spear. 2. Any athletic competition in which each contestant

has to participate in five different events. 3. *Modern Olympic Games.* A contest in which each participant has to compete in five events, namely shooting, horseback riding, swimming, fencing, and running.

peon *n., pl.* **peons** [Sp. **peón** laborer, pedestrian.] 1. *Latin American and Southwest U.S.A.* A farmhand or low-skilled laborer. 2. A hireling or lackey.

per *prep.* [L. through, by.] 1. Through. By the agency of. *Please send the parcel per your son.* 2. For each. Throughout. During. *He usually drives at no less than 140 kilometers per hour.* 3. According to. As instructed. *The storekeeper instructed the customer to operate the television set as per the manual of operation.*

per accidens *adv.* [L. **per** through, by (1); **accidens** the happening, chance (2): by chance.] Accidentally. Contingently. *He is not a good mechanic and, if he succeeds in repairing your car, it must have been per accidens.*

per alium *adv.* [L. **per** through, by (1); **alium** another (person) (2): by another person.] Through the agency of another person. *He usually does per alium what he can do by himself.*

per annum *abbr.* **P.A., p.a.** or **per an.** *adv.* [L. **per** through, by (1); **annum** year (2): through the year.] By the year. For each year. For the year. Annually. Every year. *She receives a salary of $20,000 per annum.*

per autre vie *adv.* [Obs. Fr. **per** during, for (1); **autre** other (2); **vie** life, lifetime (3): during other life.] During the lifetime of another person. See **autre vie.**

per aversionem *adj./adv.* [L. **per** through, by (1); **aversionem** turning away (2): by turning away.] *Civil Law.* Through averting. Applicable to a purchase of goods by bulk rather than by piece, weight, or measure, or to the sale of a land tract which is only approximate in size.

per capita *adv./adj.* [L. **per** by (1); **capita** heads (2): by heads.] For/by each person. *The government has imposed a per capita tax of $50.00 per annum.* Cf. **per stirpes.**

per centum *short form* **per cent** or **percent** *abbr.* **P.C.** *adj.* [L. **per** through, by (1); **centum** hundred (2): by hundred.] By the hundred. Percent. In the hundred. Of each hundred. *The candidate obtained sixty-eight per centum in the examination.* —*n., pl.* **percents** A part of a hundred. A percentage.

perceptum *n., pl.* **percepta** [L. perceived or observed thing.] Percept. Perception. Something perceived.

per con. *abbr.* for **per contra** (q.v.).

per contra *abbr.* **per con.** *adv.* [L. **per** through, by (1); **contra** against, opposite (2): by the opposite.] On the contrary. On the other hand. a) *Bisi is not laughing; per contra she is crying.* b) *Paul was expected to give evidence for the prosecution but, per contra, he favored the accused and was accordingly branded a hostile witness.*

per curiam *adv./adj.* [L. **per** through, by (1); **curiam** court (2): by the court.] *Law.* Summarily and by the court's unanimous action. Used with reference to the opinion of the entire court as distinct from the opinion of one judge. Sometimes applicable to a written opinion of the presiding judge or Chief Justice.

per diem *abbr.* **p.d.** *adv.* [L. **per** through, by (1); **diem** day (2): by day.] By the day. Daily. Day by day. *Mrs. Cole has introduced a new domestic budget which makes it possible for her to save $3.00 per diem. —adj.* Daily. Paid daily or every day. *The maidservant receives a per diem remuneration of $5.00. —n., pl.* **per diems** Daily allowance, fee, or rent. *Members of the delegation were given per diems of $100.00.*

perdu or **perdue** *adj.* [Fr. lost, ruined, doomed, wasted.] Unnoticed. Concealed. Remaining unseen. Obscured. Secluded. a) *Immediately after the coup d'etat he made quick his escape to a remote hamlet where he stayed perdu for a week before fleeing across the border.* b) *Jemima's talent remained perdu for years before she was discovered by her agent.*

père *adj.* [Fr. father, senior.] Senior. Older. Used to distinguish a father from a son who bears the same name. *At the moment, Frazier père is selecting his boy's opponents.* (*Newsweek Int.* Nov. 30, 1981:48). Cf. **fils.** —**Père** *n., pl.* **Pères** Christianity. The title of a priest or the priest himself. Cf. **padre.**

père de famille *n., pl.* **pères de famille** [L. **père** father (1); **de** of (2); **famille** family (3): father of family.] The male head of a family. **Paterfamilias** (q.v.).

père de la nation *n., pl.* **pères de la nation** [Fr. **père** father (l); **de** of (2); **la** the (3); **nation** nation (4): father of the nation or country.] Founder of the nation. **Pater patriae** (q.v.). *Leopold Senghor, the first President of Senegal, is regarded by most Senegalese as père de la nation.*

perestroika *n.* [Russ. from **pere** around, again (2); **stroika** construction (1): construction again, reconstruction.] 1. The economic and bureaucratic reorganization of the Soviet Union in the 1980s. 2. A reorganization of an economy or political bureaucracy.

per eundem *adv./adj.* [L. **per** through, by (1); **eundem** the same (2): by the same.] *Law.* By the same judge.

per eundem in eadem *adv./adj.* [L. **per** through, by (1); **eundem** the same (2); **in** in, on (3); **eadem** the same (4): by the same in the same.] *Law.* By the same judge in the same suit/case.

per fas *adv.* [L. **per** through, by (1); **fas** justice, right, that which is lawful (2): through justice or right.] *Law.* By lawful means. Rightfully. *"The arms which an Advocate wields, he ought to use as a warrior, not as an assassin. He ought to uphold the interests of his clients per fas, but not per nefas"* (Cockburn C.J., quoted by Megarry 1955:36). Cf. **per nefas.**

per fas et nefas *adv.* [L. **per** through, by (1); **fas** right, law (2); **et** and (3); **nefas** wrong (4): by right and wrong.] *Law.* Through right and wrong. By lawful and unlawful means.

per favore *adv.* [It. **per** for (1); **favore** favor (2): for a favor.] Please. See **bitte sehr; bitte schön; parakalo; por favor; prego;** and **s'il vous plaît.**

perfecta *n.* [Sp. from **quiniela** game of chance (2); **perfecta** perfect (1): perfect game of chance.] **Exacta** (q.v.).

per fraudem *adv.* [L. **per** through, by (1); **fraudem** fraud, deceit (2): by fraud.] *Law.* By deceit. Used especially with reference to fraudulently obtained discharge in regard to a plea.

pergola *n., pl.* **pergolas** [It.] A structure, often a collonade, with a trellised roof over which vines are often grown.

periculum rei venditae, nondum traditae, est emptoris. [L. **periculum** danger, risk (1); **rei** of matter, thing, property, business, affair (2); **venditae** (of) sold (3); **nondum** not yet (4); **traditae** (of) delivered (5); **est** is (6); **emptoris** of purchaser, buyer (7): The risk of the thing sold (but) not yet delivered is of the purchaser.] *Law.* When something is sold but not yet delivered, it is at the risk of the purchaser. See **damnum sentit dominus; mora debitoris** etc.; and **res perit** etc.

periegesis *n., pl.* **periegeses** [Gk. **periēgēsis: peri** around (2); **(h)ēge(omai)** lead (1): leading around, geographical description, outline.] A geographical description of a place, region, etc.

per impossibile *adv.* [L. **per** through, by (1); **impossibile** impossible (thing) (2): through an impossible thing.] As if not possible. Assuming it were possible, but it is not. *If, per impossibile, I should become a millionaire overnight, I would do wonders.*

per incuriam *adv.* [L. **per** through, by (1); **incuriam** carelessness, negligence (2): through carelessness.] *Law.* By carelessness or negligence. Used in connection with a judge's decision which is clearly attributable to an oversight. *The authority of Oduntan Onisiwo v. Attorney-General was set aside, both the Supreme Court and the full court implying that the judgment in that case was given per incuriam* (Adewoye 1977:259).

per industriam *adv.* [L. **per** through, by (1); **industriam** diligence, industry (2): through industry.] *Law of Former Times.* By diligence. By industry. Applicable, inter alia, to wild animals over which one can have qualified rights of property per industriam, i.e., by reclaiming, taming and bringing them under one's immediate power. See **per industriam hominis.**

per industriam hominis *adv.* [L. **per** through, by (1); **industriam** diligence, industry (2); **hominis** of a person, human being (3): by diligence of a person.] *Law of Former Times.* By human diligence. Applicable to such human efforts as reclamation of land, taming of wild animals, etc., upon which a claim of ownership may be based. See **per industriam.**

per infortunium *adv./adj.* [L. **per** through, by (1); **infortunium** misfortune (2): by misfortune.] Through an unlucky event. Used in criminal cases to describe homicide, i.e., of the kind where a person in the process of performing a lawful act unintentionally and unfortunately causes the death of another. See **homicidium per infortunium**.

peripeteia or **peripetia** *n., pl.* **peripeteias** or **peripetias** [Gk. **peri** around (2); **pipt(ō)** fall (1): falling around, reversal of the normal order, sudden reversal of the plot of a tragedy.] A sudden reversal of circumstances in a literary work or real life. a) *The play ended in a peripeteia which restored confidence in the basic sanity of human nature.* b) *Political, social and economic developments in the country were such that had there not been the peripeteia initiated by the Revolutionary Council, the nation would have collapsed completely.*

periphrasis *n., pl.* **periphrases** [Gk. **peri** around (2); **phrasis** speaking (1): speaking around.] *Rhetoric.* Circumlocution. The use of many words or phrases to express what may be clearly expressed by few words or phrases. A roundabout manner of expression.

periplus *n., pl.* **peripli** [Gk. **periplous**: **peri** around (2) and **plous** sailing, voyage (1): sailing around, circumnavigation, account of a coasting voyage.] 1. Circumnavigation. A voyage around an island, continent, etc. *The Carthaginian general, Hanno, who attempted a periplus of Africa, may have reached the littoral of Cameroon.* 2. Account of a circumnavigation.

per legem terrae *adv.* [L. **per** through, by (1); **legem** law (2); **terrae** of land (3): by the law of the land/country.] *Law.* In accordance with due legal process. *He was brought to trial and found guilty per legem terrae.*

per majorem cautelam *adv.* [L. **per** through, by (1); **majorem** greater (2); **cautelam** caution, precaution (3): through greater caution.] *Law.* For greater caution. See **ad abundantiorem cautelam**.

per mensem *adv.* [L. **per** through, by (1); **mensem** month (2): by the month.] Monthly. Every month. *Most employees in the country are paid per mensem.*

per mille *adv.* [L. **per** through, by (1); **mille** thousand (2): by thousand.] By a thousand. For every thousand. *It is an incontrovertible fact that women outnumber men in that city by a ratio of 1,890 per mille.*

per minas *adv.* [L. **per** through, by (1); **minas** threats (2): by threats.] By means of threats. *Cowards usually act per minas.*

permis de séjour *n., pl.* **permis de séjour** [Fr. **permis** permit, license (1); **de** of (2); **séjour** residence, abode (3): permit of residence.] A residence permit.

permitte divis cetera. Horace (65–8 B.C.). *Odes* I,9,9. [L. **permitte** leave, entrust (1); **divis** to gods, divine beings (3); **cetera** the rest, remaining (2): Leave the rest to the gods.] Entrust everything else to the gods.

per my et per tout [Obs. Fr. **per** through, by (1); **my** half (2); **et** and (3); **per** through, by (4); **tout** whole (5): by half and by whole.] *Property Law.* In part and in whole. Applicable to joint tenancy or ownership which in terms of alienation can be divided into equal parts, but in terms of tenure and survivorship is jointly held as an entire unit. Cf. **per tout** etc.

per nefas *adv.* [L. **per** through, by (1); **nefas** wrong, crime, that which is unlawful (2): through wrong/crime.] *Law.* By unlawful means. Unjustly. Cf. **per fas**.

per pais or **per pays** *adv.* [Obs. Fr. **per** through, by (1); **pais** country (2): through the country.] *Law.* By the country. By jury. See **pais 2**.

per pares *adv.* [L. **per** through, by (1); **pares** equals (2): by equals.] By one's peers or equals. Cf. **inter pares** and **parium judicium**.

per pays See **per pais**.

perpetua lex est nullam legem humanam ac positivam perpetuam esse, et clausula quae abrogationem excludit ab initio non valet. [L. **perpetua** perpetual, permanent, unchangeable, uninterrupted (2); **lex** law (3); **est** it is . . . (that) (1); **nullam** no (4); **legem** law (8); **humanam** human (5); **ac** and (6); **positivam** positive (7); **perpetuam** perpetual, permanent, unchangeable, uninterrupted (10); **esse** to be, is (9); **et** and (11); **clausula** clause (12); **quae** which (13); **abrogationem** repeal (15); **excludit** excludes (14); **ab** from, by (18); **initio** beginning (19); **non** not (16); **valet** is valid (17): It is a perpetual law that no human and positive law can be perpetual, and a clause which excludes repeal is not valid from the beginning.] *Law.* It is a permanent, unchangeable law that no human and positive law can be permanent and unchangeable and that a clause which excludes repeal is null and void right from the beginning.

perpetuum mobile *n.* [L. **perpetuum** perpetual, permanent, unchangeable, uninterrupted (1); **mobile** movable, moving (thing) (2): perpetual moving thing.] 1. Perpetual movement or motion. 2. *Music.* A musical passage or composition in which the rapid notes continue throughout. *To date he has sung exactly 1,582 times . . . Throw in another career as an opera conductor . . . , and you have music's perpetuum mobile in blazing life* (*Newsweek Int.* March 8, 1982:54).

per procurationem *abbr.* **per pro.** or **p.p.** *adv.* [L. **per** through, by (1); **procurationem** agency (2): by agency.] *Law.* By deputy's or agent's authority. By proxy. *He conducts most of his business transactions per procurationem.*

perquisitor *n., pl.* **perquisitors** [L. one who searches thoroughly.] *Law.* The first purchaser or original owner of an estate. A person who searches by warrant.

per quod servitium amisit. [L. **per** through, by (1); **quod** (that) which (2); **servitium** service, servitude (4); **amisit** he lost (3): by (that) which he lost service.] Whereby he lost the service of a servant, daughter, etc. *Law of Former Times.* Used by a master in actions of trespass, where a servant has been beaten or maltreated, or in action brought by a father in connection with the seduction of a daughter. *If a master is wrongfully deprived of his servant's services, he may be able to recover damages from the wrongdoer through one or more of three different actions, the actions of enticement and harbouring, and the action per quod servitium amisit for injury inflicted upon his servant* (Rogers 1975:441).

per rerum naturam factum negantis nulla probatio est. [L. **per** through, by (1); **rerum** of matters, things, property, business, affairs (3); **naturam** nature (2); **factum** deed, act, fact (5); **negantis** of the one denying (4); **nulla** no (7); **probatio** proof (8); **est** there is (6): By the nature of things, of the one denying a fact there is no proof.] By the nature of things, it is not obligatory for the one who denies a fact to prove it. See **actori incumbit** etc.

per saltum *adv./adj.* [L. **per** through, by (1); **saltum** leap, bound, spring (2): by a leap.] At a leap. By a jump. At a single bound. *The lecturer was promoted to the professorship per saltum.*

per se *adv.* [L. **per** through, by (1); **se** itself, oneself, themselves (2): by itself.] 1. In itself. By themselves. As such. *Ancient Spartans believed that stealing per se is not bad, but being caught in the act of stealing is not only bad but also worthy of punishment.* 2. *Law.* The expression, in cases of libel, is used in reference to words which are inherently insulting and thus actionable.

per sempre *adv.* [It. **per** for, by (1); **sempre** ever, always (2): for ever.] For all times. *Fonteyn has been elevated to the title of prima ballerina assoluta (and probably per sempre) (Newsweek Int.* June 6, 1981:43).

persiflage *n., pl.* **persiflages** [Fr. banter, chaff.] Frivolous or lighthearted raillery, teasing, or banter. A frivolous or lighthearted manner of discussing a subject.

persifleur *n., pl.* **persifleurs** [Fr. chaffer, banterer.] A person who engages in persiflage. A person who treats frivolously a matter which normally requires serious consideration.

persona *n., pl.* **personae** or **personas** [L. actor's mask, person.] 1. *Civil Law.* The character by virtue of which a man enjoys certain rights and has certain obligations to discharge. A man can have many characters (e.g., father and son). 2. The role one plays in public. *She took on the persona of a peacemaker in the dispute.* —*pl.* **personae** Characters of a play or novel.

persona designata *n.* [L. **persona** person (1); **designata** pointed out, described (2): the person described.] A person described or pointed out, as distinct from a person vaguely belonging to a group.

persona ficta *n., pl.* **personae fictae** [L. **persona** person (2); **ficta** feigned, fictitious (1): a feigned person.] A fictitious or imaginary person.

persona grata *abbr.* **P.G.** or **p.g.** *n., pl.* **personae gratae** or **persona grata** [L. **persona** person (2); **grata** acceptable, agreeable (1): an acceptable person.] An individual who is acceptable or admissable. Used especially in international law and diplomatic relations. A military attaché in one of the embassies in Moscow was declared to be no longer persona grata. See **persona gratissima**. Cf. **non grata** and **persona non grata**.

persona gratissima *n., pl.* **personae gratissimae** [L. **persona** person (2); **gratissima** very acceptable (1): most acceptable person.] A highly favored person. *In some organizations, appointments and promotions are not given to people on the basis of merit, but strictly to people who are personae gratissimae.* See **persona grata**.

personalia *pl. n.* [L. personal things.] 1. Biographical notes or stories. 2. Personal things or affairs. *Mrs. Brown sued for divorce on the ground that her husband has a nauseating habit of rifling through her personalia, but her action was dismissed by the court.*

personalia personam sequuntur. [L. **personalia** personal (things) (1); **personam** person (3); **sequuntur** follow (2): Personal things follow the person.] *Law.* Personal effects follow the person.

personalis actio *n., pl.* **personales actiones** [L. **personalis** personal, individual (1); **actio** action, deed, legal suit (2): personal legal suit.] *Law.* Personal legal action. An action **in personam**. Cf. **actio in rem**.

persona muta See **muta persona**.

persona non grata *abbr.* **P.N.G.** or **p.n.g.** *n., pl.* **personae non gratae** or **persona non grata** [L. **persona** person (1); **non** not (2); **grata** acceptable; agreeable (3): person not acceptable.] An unacceptable person. The expression is usually used in diplomatic affairs and international law. *An official delivered a note in which the first secretary of the embassy was declared persona non grata.* Cf. **persona grata**.

persona publica *n.* [L. **persona** person (2); **publica** public (1): public person.] A public officer.

persona standi in judicio *n.* [L. **persona** person (1); **standi** of standing (2); **in** in, on (3); **judicio** court (4): person of standing in court.] *Law.* Ability or qualification to appear in court. Capacity or qualification to sue.

personnel *n., pl.* **personnel** or **personnels** [Fr. staff, employees.] 1. The body employed by an organization. Cf. **matériel**. 2. A branch of an establishment which is assigned the responsibility of selecting and training employees as well as formulating employment policies, guidelines, and procedures.—*pl.* **personnel** Persons of a particular professional group, grade or level. a) *police personnel*; b) *medical personnel*; c) *The diamond mining company ... will shortly be laying off a sizeable proportion of its workers including senior personnel* (*West Africa* 1982).

perspicua vera non sunt probanda. [L. **perspicua** clear, manifest, evident (1); **vera** truths, facts (2); **non** not (4); **sunt** are (3); **probanda** to be proved (5): Evident truths are not to be proved.] Evident truths need not be proved. See **manifesta probatione** etc.

per stirpes *adv./adj.* [L. **per** through, by (1); **stirpes** descendants, family stocks (2): by descendants or family stocks.] *Law.* By stocks or branches. Applicable to assigning equal shares of an estate to each descendant family, regardless of how many members it has. *The term "issue" includes not only children but also the children of children who have predeceased the intestate. Division between these is per stirpes, that is to say, the collective share of the children of a deceased child is that which would have belonged to their parent* (Hanbury 1962:471). See **stirps**. Cf. **per capita**.

per subsequens matrimonium *adj.* [L. **per** through, by (1); **subsequens** subsequent (2); **matrimonium** marriage (3): by a subsequent marriage.] By later marriage. By marriage after the fact. Domestic law in Britain recognized legitimation per subsequens matrimonium under certain conditions.

pertinentia *pl. n.* [L. things belonging, relating or pertaining to.] *Law.* Appurtenances of property which, together with the property, belong to the new owner.

per totam curiam *adv./adj.* [L. **per** through, by (1); **totam** whole, entire (2); **curiam** court (3): by the whole court.] *Law.* By the entire court. Unanimous. Unanimously. Applicable to the judgment or decision of the court.

per tout et non per my [Obs. Fr. **per** through, by (1); **tout** whole (2); **et** and (3); **non** not (4); **per** through, by (5); **my** half (6): by whole and not by half.] By the whole and not by a portion (or moiety). *Property Law.* Applicable to concurrent ownership (e.g., property given to husband and wife) which belongs to them as an entire unit and cannot be taken in separate shares.

per universitatem *adv./adj.* [L. **per** through, by (1); **universitatem** the whole, entirety (2): by the whole/ entirety.] *Law.* As a whole. Used to describe the acquisition of an estate in its entirety rather than the acquisition of little portions.

per vaginam *abbr.* **p.v.** *adj./adv.* [L. **per** through, by (1); **vaginam** sheath, vagina (2): through the vagina.] By the vagina. *The essential points required to prove rape are lack of consent by the victim and penetration per vaginam.*

per verba de futuro *adv./adj.* [**per** through, by (1); **verba** words (2); **de** of, from, about, for (3); **futuro** the future (4): by words of the future.] *Law.* By words of the future tense. An expression applicable to marital contracts. Cf. **per verba de praesenti**.

per verba de futuro subsequens copula *n.* [L. **per** through, by (3); **verba** words (4); **de** of, from, about, for (5); **futuro** future (6); **subsequens** subsequent (1); **copula** connection, bond (2): subsequent bond by words of the future.] *Law.* Later marriage by means of words about the future.

per verba de praesenti *adv./adj.* [L. **per** through, by (1); **verba** words (2); **de** of, from, about, for (3); **praesenti** the present (4): through words about the present.]

Law. By words of the present tense. An expression applicable to marital contracts. *If the local law recognises marriage by cohabitation and repute, a union so constituted will be recognised in England. Similarly, if a marriage may be validly constituted per verba de praesenti under the law of the place where it is celebrated, a marriage so constituted will be recognised in England* (Morris 1973:237). Cf. **per verba de futuro**.

pessimum *n., pl.* **pessima** or **pessimums** [L. worst thing.] The environmental condition least favorable for the survival of an organism.

pestis *n., pl.* **pestes** [L. sickness, disease, plague.] An infectious disease. A plague.

petit blanc *n., pl.* **petits blancs** [Fr. **petit** small, little (1); **blanc** white (person) (2): little white person.] A poor white person. A European or Caucasian in a racially heterogeneous community who has no claim to distinction other than the pigmentation of his skin.

petit bourgeois or *fem.* **petite bourgeoise** *n.* [Fr. **petit** small, little (1); **bourgeois** citizen, townsman (2): small townsman or citizen.] A member of the lower middle class or **petite bourgeoisie** (q.v.). A person of limited intellectual outlook. —*attrib.* Characteristic of the lower middle class, petite bourgeoisie, or those who have limited intellectual outlook. *Mostly young and educated, the Mujahedin charge that the ruling clergy's primitivism and "petit bourgeois understanding of Islam" merely pave the way for a return of Western exploitation in Iran (Time Int. 1981).* See **bourgeois**.

petite *adj.* [Fr. small, little.] Little. Small and delicately beautiful. Used to describe a woman. *Kamara's aunt, a petite, loquacious woman, will arrive tomorrow for the festival.*

petite bourgeoisie *n.* [Fr. **petite** small, little (1); **bourgeoisie** middle class (2): small middle class.] The lower middle class, regarded as being of limited intellectual outlook. *Of the former pupils of the Ecole Coloniale who came to make up the majority of the administrative corps, a few came from the upper classes, but most were from the petite bourgeoisie* (Suret-Canale 1971:318). See **bourgeois**.

petite noblesse *n.* [Fr. **petite** small, little (1); **noblesse** nobility, noble birth (2): small nobility.] Nobility of a lower or minor rank, especially French rural landowners of noble descent.

petitio principii *n., pl.* **petitiones principii** [L. **petitio** attack, position, aim, claim, begging (1); **principii** of beginning, foundation, principle (2): postulation of principle.] *Logic.* A fallacy in which a premise is erroneously assumed to be true. Begging the principle. Begging the question; i.e., using the premise itself as proof.

petit mal *n.* [Fr. **petit** small, little (1); **mal** malady, illness (2): small malady/illness.] *Medicine.* A milder form of epilepsy. Cf. **grand mal**.

petit truand *n., pl.* **petits truands** [Fr. **petit** small, petty (1); **truand** crook, swindler (2): petty crook.] Smalltime crook or hoodlum. *Another theory held that the massacre was simply part of a turf war among petits truands* (*Newsweek Int.* Oct. 16, 1978:17). Cf. **dacoit, mafia,** and **yakuza.**

p. ex. *abbr.* for **par exemple** (q.v.).

p.f. *abbr.* for **pro forma** (q.v.).

p. fat. *abbr.* for **praefatus** (q.v.).

P.G. or **p.g.** *abbr.* for **persona grata** (q.v.).

phalanx *n., pl.* **phalanxes** or **phalanges** [Gk. line of battle, heavy infantry in battle order, bone between two joints of the fingers and toes.] 1. *Ancient Greece.* A body of heavily armed footsoldiers formed in close array for fighting. 2. A closely arranged group or body of persons, things, or animals. 3. A body of persons organized for a common objective. *Arriving in Tucson without his usual phalanx of bodyguards, . . .* (*Newsweek Int.* July 25, 1983:29). 4. A bone in the toe or finger.

phallus *n., pl.* **phalli** or **phalluses** [L. from Gk. **phallos** penis, symbol of the penis.] 1. A symbol of the male reproductive organ. *As for the comic actor, the pots and terracottas make it plain that he normally . . . had the phallus* (Lesky 1966:237). 2. Penis. 3. The embryonic precursor of the penis or clitoris.

phantasma *n., pl.* **phantasmata** or **phantasmas** [Gk. apparition, phantom.] Phantasm. A product of phantasy (or fantasy). A spirit or ghost. A plan or thought which is not based on prudent reasoning. *Tim's supposedly great proposal for solving the organization's problems was summarily dismissed as a phantasma, the product of a dream.*

Phar.B. *abbr.* for **Pharmaciae Baccalaureus** (q.v.).

Phar.D. *abbr.* for **Pharmaciae Doctor** (q.v.).

Pharmaciae Baccalaureus *abbr.* **Phar.B.** *n.* [L. **pharmaciae** of pharmacy (2); **baccalaureus** bachelor (1): Bachelor of Pharmacy.] An undergraduate degree in pharmacy.

Pharmaciae Doctor *abbr.* **Phar.D.** or **Pharm.D.** or **Ph.D.** *n.* [L. **pharmaciae** of pharmacy (2); **doctor** teacher (1): teacher of pharmacy.] Doctor of Pharmacy. A terminal graduate degree in pharmacy.

Pharmaciae Magister *abbr.* **Pharm.M.** *n.* [L. **pharmaciae** of pharmacy (2); **magister** master (1): Master of Pharmacy.] A pre-doctoral graduate degree in pharmacy.

pharmacon *n., pl.* **pharmaca** or **pharmacons** [Gk. **pharmakon** drug.] A drug, whether curative or noxious. Medicine. Healing remedy. Poison.

pharmacopedia *n., pl.* **pharmacopedias** [Neo-Gk. from Gk. **pharmako(n)** drug (2); **paideia** education (1): education on drugs.] Information respecting drugs and the preparation of medicines.

pharmacopoeia or **pharmacopeia** *n., pl.* **pharmacopoeias** or **pharmacopeias** [Gk. **pharmakopoiia**: **pharmako(n)** drug (1) and **poieō** make (2): drug making, preparation of drugs.] *Medicine.* An official

or authoritative book, listing drugs, medicines, chemicals, etc., describing them and showing tests for establishing their identity, formula for preparing them, and directions respecting their use.

Pharm.D. *abbr.* for **Pharmaciae Doctor** (q.v.).

Pharm.M. *abbr.* for **Pharmaciae Magister** (q.v.).

pharos *n., pl.* **pharoses** [Gk. **Pharos.**] 1. An island in the bay of Alexandria (Egypt) famous in antiquity for its lighthouse, built by Ptolemy Philadelphus. 2. A lighthouse. 3. A very conspicuous light, particularly the lantern of a ship. 4. A candelabrum, i.e., a large candlestick, usually decorated, with several branches or arms.

Ph.B. *abbr.* for **Philosophiae Baccalaureus** (q.v.).

Ph.D. *abbr.* for 1. **Pharmaciae Doctor** (q.v.). 2. **Philosophiae Doctor** (q.v.).

phenomenon *n., pl.* **phenomena** or **phenomenons** [Gk. **phainomenon** appearing.] 1. A fact or event which can be observed or is observable. A matter of reality or experience. *Despite schisms, heresies and fratricidal wars, world Communism remains a Soviet phenomenon . . .* (*Time Int.* 1982). 2. A fact or event in the changing variety of things as distinct from their permanent or immutable essence. The perceptible as distinct from the true nature of things. *He had . . . met the unending variety of the phenomena of culture and nature with an open mind . . .* (Lesky 1966:680). 3. A rare, odd, or remarkable fact or person. a) *At 32, Zukerman . . . is a phenomenon even in a world of musical prodigies* (*Newsweek Int.* Oct. 20, 1980: 61). b) *Thomas Sankara was a phenomenon in life. In death he looms even larger* (*The Guardian* 1987). Cf. **Ding an sich** and **noumenon.**

Philadelphia *n.* [Gk. from **phil(ia)** love (2); **adelph(os)** brother, sibling (1): brother love.] The city of brotherly love. The largest city in Pennsylvania.

philia *n., pl.* **philias** [Gk. affectionate regard, friendliness, fondness.] Love of one's friends. Love of fellow humans. —*suf.* 1. Inclination or tendency toward. *Hemophilia.* 2. Unusual or excessive fondness or appetite for. a) *Anglophilia*; b) *Francophilia*; c) *necrophilia.*

Philosophiae Baccalaureus *abbr.* **P.B.** or **Ph.B.** *n.* [L. **philosophiae** of philosophy (2); **baccalaureus** bachelor (1): Bachelor of Philosophy.] An undergraduate degree in philosophy, the sciences, the humanities, or any intellectual field.

Philosophiae Doctor *abbr.* **Ph.D.** *n.* [L. **philosophiae** of philosophy (2); **doctor** teacher (1): teacher of philosophy.] Doctor of Philosophy. A terminal graduate degree in philosophy, the sciences, the humanities, or any intellectual field.

Philosophiae Magister *abbr.* **Ph.M.** *n.* [L. **philosophiae** of philosophy (2); **magister** master (1): Master of Philosophy.] A pre-doctoral graduate degree in philosophy.

Ph.M. *abbr.* for **Philosophiae Magister** (q.v.).

phobia [Neo-Gk. from **phob(os)** fear, panic.] *n., pl.* **phobias** An exaggerated, pathological, or morbid fear or dislike. *There is currently a phobia that since the old brigade politicians have been banned, they would stop at nothing to ensure that their stooges assume power* (*The Guardian* 1987). —*suf.* Irrational, pathological, fear or dislike. a) *Marxophobia* (q.v.); b) *Negrophobia*.

phoenix *n., pl.* **phoenixes** [Gk. **Phoinix**.] 1. A mythical bird believed by ancient Egyptians to live for not less than 500 years. When it is about to die, it builds a nest, sets it on fire, is burnt to ashes, and then from the ashes emerges a new phoenix. It is regarded as a symbol of resurrection or immortality. 2. Somebody or something that resembles the phoenix as a model of beauty or excellence. 3. Somebody or something that after destruction undergoes renewal, resurrection, or a sort of rebirth.

phonomania *n.* [Neo-Gk. from Gk. **phono(s)** murder, slaughter (2); **mania** madness, frenzy, passion (1): madness/frenzy for murder.] Excessive inclination to commit homicide.

p. h. v. *abbr.* for **pro hac vice** (q.v.).

physique *n., pl.* **physiques** [Fr. physical constitution, body.] Physical structure, strength, or form; i.e., of the human body, a geographical area, etc. a) *Ivan was mercilessly beaten up by his girlfriend's irate father, a man of magnificent physique.* b) *The physique of the mountain is such that it is easier to climb than descend.*

physis *n., pl.* **physeis** [Gk. **phusis** nature, constitution, the natural form or constitution of a person or thing.] Nature i.e., the source of growth, development, or change. Something which grows or becomes. *The natural philosophers of the sixth century started by inquiring into the origin of the universe, its physis* (Jaeger 1970:155).

pia fraus *n.* [L. **pia** religious, pious (1); **fraus** fraud, deceit (2): religious fraud.] An evasion or disregard of the laws or the truth, prompted by religious considerations and deemed morally justifiable.

pianissimo *abbr.* **pp** [It. very softly.] *adj./adv.* Very soft. Very softly. Used as a musical direction. —*n., pl.* **pianissimi** or **pianissimos** *Music.* A passage sung or played very softly. A very soft sound. *The range of dynamics is remarkable, from assaultive fortissimos to the merest wisps of pianissimos* (*Newsweek Int.* Feb. 1, 1982:46). Cf. **fortissimo**.

piano *abbr.* **p.** *adv./adj.* [It. soft.] *Music.* In a soft manner. Soft. —*n., pl.* **pianos** 1. *Music.* A soft musical passage. Cf. **forte**. 2. Short form of **pianoforte** (q.v.).

pianoforte or **piano** *n., pl.* **pianofortes** or **pianos** [It. **piano** soft (1); **forte** loud (2): soft loud, a keyboard instrument which, unlike a harpsichord, can be played both loud and soft.] A musical instrument in which a keyboard is struck manually in order to operate hammers to strike wire strings; the sound can be softened by hitting the keys more lightly and by the use of a pedal.

piazza *n., pl.* **piazzas** [It.] A large open space, especially a public square in a city or a **veranda** (q.v.) in a home.

picaresque *adj.* [Fr. of a rogue or rascal.] 1. Pertaining to a roguish adventurer. 2. Pertaining to a novel about roguish adventurers, especially a type popular first in Spain and later in France in which the escapades of such a rogue are described with great realism, satire, and humor. 3. Pertaining to novels depicting incidents which follow chronologically but which have little logical connection to each other. —*n.* A roguish adventurer. A **picaro** (q.v.).

picaro *n., pl.* **picaros** [Sp. rogue, scoundrel.] A roguish adventurer. Cf. **picaresque**.

piccolo *adj.* [It. small.] Little. Small. —*n. Music.* A wind instrument smaller than a flute and producing sounds an octave higher.

pictor ignotus *n.* [L. **pictor** painter (1); **ignotus** unknown (2): painter unknown.] By an unknown painter.

pièce de résistance *n., pl.* **pièces de résistance** [Fr. **pièce** piece (1); **de** of (2); **résistance** resistance (3): piece of resistance.] 1. The main dish or course of a meal. 2. The main event or feature. *Their pièce de résistance is a grotesque murder in a shattering, clattering thunder-and-lightning storm that should earn them a special award . . .* (*Newsweek Int.* Oct. 16, 1978:43).

pièce de spectacle *n., pl.* **pièces de spectacle** [Fr. **pièce** piece (1); **de** of (2); **spectacle** spectacle; exhibition (3): a piece of spectacle/exhibition.] A work of art whose merit lies in its conspicuous splendor.

pièce d'occasion *n., pl.* **pièces d'occasion** [Fr. **pièce** piece (1); **d'** of (2); **occasion** occasion (3): a piece of occasion.] A literary work written, or a musical piece composed, for a particular occasion.

pièce justificative *n., pl.* **pièces justificatives** [Fr. **pièce** document (1); **justificative** of vindication, justification (2): document of justification/vindication.] *Law.* A document which aims at justifying an act, conduct, etc. A document cited as supporting or relevant evidence or proof of an assertion. *The works of Sulla and the others, so far as they were pièces justificatives, had as their deliberate aim the defense of the writer's past conduct* (Laistner 1966:36).

pièce noire *n., pl.* **pièces noires** [Fr. **pièce** piece (2); **noire** black, gloomy, dismal (1): a gloomy/dismal piece.] A drama which has a tragic theme and a pessimistic tone. See **film noir**. Cf. **pièce rose**.

pièce rose *n., pl.* **pièces roses** [Fr. **pièce** piece (2); **rose** rosy (1): rosy piece.] A work of art which has a tone of optimism and ends on a happy note. Cf. **pièce noire**.

pied-à-terre *abbr.* **p.-à-t.** *n., pl.* **pieds-à-terre** [Fr. **pied** foot, leg (1); **à** to, toward, in, by, with, until (2); **terre** land, ground (3): foot to ground.] Small flat or occasional residence. A temporary lodging; e.g., one maintained in a city by a person who usually resides in the countryside or a village. *During working days, the company's Director stays at his Ibadan pied-à-terre, but every weekend he goes to Ogbomosho to join his family.*

Pietà *n.* [It. pity.] *Art.* A composition depicting the body of the crucified Jesus in the arms of his sorrowful mother. *Michelangelo's Pietà.*

pietas *n.* [L. piety.] A sense of devotion and duty to one's parents, county, and god.

pinxit *abbr.* **pinx.** or **pnxt** or **pxt.** *v.* [L. He/she painted.] He/she painted it. Used to indicate the author of a painting. Cf. **caelavit.**

piquant *adj.* [Fr. stinging, cutting, stimulating.] 1. Biting or spicy in taste. 2. Charming in wit or character.

pique *n.* [Fr. lance, ill-feeling.] Annoyance or bitterness. A sense of ill-will or wounded pride. —*v.* To annoy or cause ill-will. To incite or provoke.

pirata est hostis humani generis. [L. **pirata** pirate (1); **est** is (2); **hostis** enemy (3); **humani** of human (4); **generis** (of) race (5): A pirate is an enemy of the human race.] *Law.* Piracy is a crime against humanity, and pirates are enemies of all human beings.

pis aller or **pis-aller** *n., pl.* **pis allers** or **pis-allers** [Fr. **pis** worse, worst (2); **aller** to go (1): to go worse.] Last resort. A course of action adopted in the absence of anything better. *The measures introduced by the government for solving the economic problems are no more than pis-allers and have accordingly aroused negligible optimism.*

Pisces *n.* [L. fish.] 1. *Astronomy.* A fish-shaped constellation located near Aries. 2. *Astrology.* The twelfth sign of the zodiac, dominant from February 19 through March 20. 3. A person born under this sign.

pizzicato *adv./adj.* [It. plucking.] *Music.* Plucking a stringed instrument like a violin with the fingers rather than using the bow. —*n., pl.* **pizzicatos** A piece of music played in this manner.

place au soleil *n., pl.* **places au soleil** [Fr. **place** place, seat (1); **au** to the, toward the, in the, by the, with the, until the (2); **soleil** sun (3): a place in the sun.] A chance to enjoy the pleasures of life.

placebo *n., pl.* **placebos** [L. I shall please.] 1. An inactive substance given to a patient to please him/her or for its psychological effect. 2. A thing which tends to please or soothe. *Politicians usually attempt to ingratiate themselves with the electorate by offering the placebo of promises which they do not intend to fulfill.*

placet *n., pl.* **placets** [L. It pleases.] An expression of a vote of approval or assent.

plat du jour *n., pl.* **plats du jour** [Fr. **plat** dish, course (1); **du** of the (2); **jour** day (3): dish of the day.] Today's special dish. A particular day's special dish in a restaurant.

plaudit *n., pl.* **plaudits** [L. He claps, applauds.] Applause. Enthusiastic approval. *His farewell speech received the plaudits of the audience.*

plebiscitum *n., pl.* **plebiscita** [L. from **pleb(s)** the people, the common people (2) and **scitum** decree, resolution (1): resolution of the people.] 1. *Roman Law.* A decree and law made by the plebeian assembly

and binding, originally, on the plebeians, but eventually on all Romans. 2. A vote of the people on a measure brought before them. A plebiscite.

plebs *n.* [L. people, the common people.] 1. *Roman Law.* The ordinary citizens, as distinct from the patricians and knights (or equites). 2. The common people. The plebeians.

plectrum *n., pl.* **plectra** or **plectrums** [L. from Gk. **plektron** that which strikes or plucks.] A small, thin tool used to pluck the strings of some musical instruments. A pick.

plein air *n.* [Fr. **plein** full, open (1); **air** (2): open air.] An area open to the elements. —*adj.* Open to the elements. *While Monet considered himself a plein air painter, much of his work was actually finished in the studio.*

plene administravit *n.* [L. **plene** fully (2); **administravit** he has administered (1): He has administered fully.] *Law.* A plea by an administrator or executor, when sued by an heir, legatee, or creditor, that he/she has completely administered all the assets received, and that there are no more assets for satisfying the claims of the plaintiff. *The representative may avert this calamity* [i.e., when there is a judgment **de bonis testatoris** (q.v.) and the representative is required to pay the creditor from his pocket] *by pleading plene administravit at the time of the action, but this plea must be made at that time; it cannot be advanced in a subsequent action for administration* (Hanbury 1962:506).

plene administravit praeter *n.* [L. **plene** fully (2); **administravit** he has administered (1); **praeter** except (3): He has administered fully except.] *Law.* A plea by an administrator or executor, when sued by an heir, legatee, or creditor, that he has completely administered all the assets received, except some assets which are inadequate for the satisfaction of the plaintiff's claim.

plene computavit *n.* [L. **plene** fully (2); **computavit** he has accounted, computed, reckoned (1): He has accounted fully.] *Law.* A plea that the defendant has completely rendered account.

pleno jure *adv.* [L. **pleno** (with) full (1); **jure** with right, law (2): with full right.] *Law.* With complete authority.

plenum *n., pl.* **plena** or **plenums** [L. full.] 1. The general assembly of an organization or group (e.g., a legislative body). The whole membership of a particular group. 2. A space which is wholly full of matter.

plenum dominium See **dominium plenum.**

pleonexia *n.* [Gk. greed, excess, a larger share.] Greediness.

plethora *n., pl.* **plethoras** [Gk. **plēthōra** fullness, satiety, repletion of blood.] 1. Overabundance. Superabundance. Excess. a) *The FBI will begin to interview witnesses . . . and its slow and secret investigation . . . will sooner or later reduce the plethora of rumors and easy allegations to a sterner version of truth*

(*Newsweek Int.* July 18, 1983:23). *b*) . . . *a plethora of both precolonial and colonial anachronistic legacies reincarnated today in the form of frontier disputes, ethnic rivalries* . . . (Gorkeh G. Nkrumah in *West Africa* 1986). 2. *Medicine.* A condition in which red blood corpuscles are in excess, resulting in florid complexion.

plexus *n., pl.* **plexuses** [L. twining, network.] 1. A network, especially of blood vessels or nerve fibers. 2. An intricate combination of various parts interwoven to form a coherent structure. *The various regions of the country are linked together by a plexus of roads.*

ploce *n., pl.* **ploces** [Gk. **plokē** twisting, twining, web, braid.] *Rhetoric.* Repetition of a word to emphasize its significance; e.g., "A friend in need is a friend indeed."

plurimum juris *n.* [L. **plurimum** most (1); **juris** of right, law (2): most of right.] *Law.* The fullest right. The right of both possession and property. See **droit droit** and **plurimum possessionis**.

plurimum possessionis *n.* [L. **plurimum** most (1); **possessionis** of possession (2): most of possession.] *Law.* The fullest possession. The right of both possession and property. See **droit droit** and **plurimum juris**.

plus *prep.* [L. more.] More. With the addition of. a) *Seven plus three equals ten.* b) *After an absence of six years, he returned home, plus a wife and family.* —*n. pl.* **pluses** or **plusses** 1. The sign indicating addition, i.e., (+). 2. Something which is extra or added. 3. An advantage, asset, or gain. *Joe is an able administrator, whose flair for diplomacy proved to be a definite plus.*

Plus ça change, plus c'est la même chose. Alphonse Karr (1808–1890). *Les Guêpes* 305. [Fr. **plus** more (1); **ça** it, that (2); **change** changes (3); **plus** more (4); **c'** it (5); **est** is (6); **la** the (7); **même** same (8); **chose** thing (9): The more it changes, the more it is the same thing.] The more things change, the more they remain the same. Cf. **la même chose**.

plus quam tolerabile *adj.* [L. **plus** more (1); **quam** than (2); **tolerabile** tolerable, bearable (3): more than tolerable.] Beyond the point of toleration. *Initially, Mr. Phelp exercised considerable self-restraint but, when Mr. Craus' provocation became plus quam tolerabile, he reacted by slapping him.*

plus royaliste que le roi *adj.* [Fr. **plus** more (1); **royaliste** royalist (2); **que** than (3); **le** the (4); **roi** king (5): more royalist than the king.] Applicable to a person who embraces a cause with greater enthusiasm than the one who is most directly affected. *The leader of the sect promptly took to his heels, but Greg, a fanatic, plus royaliste que le roi, fought gallantly until he was arrested.* See **Il ne faut** etc.

plus valet unus oculatus testis quam auriti decem. [L. **plus** more (5); **valet** prevails, avails (4); **unus** one (1); **oculatus** with eyes (3); **testis** witness (2); **quam** than (6); **auriti** with ears (8); **decem** ten (7):

One witness with eyes avails more than ten with ears.] *Law.* One eyewitness carries more weight than ten witnesses whose testimonies are based on hearsay.

plus vident oculi quam oculus. [L. **plus** more (3); **vident** see (2); **oculi** eyes (1); **quam** than (4); **oculus** eye (5): Eyes see more than eye.] *Law.* Many eyes see more than one eye; i.e., the testimonies of two or more eyewitnesses carry more weight than the testimony of one eyewitness.

plutomania *n.* [Neo-Gk. from Gk. **plouto(s)** wealth, riches (2); **mania** madness, passion (1): madness for wealth.] 1. Excessive desire for wealth. 2. A form of insanity characterized by delusions of wealth.

P.M. *abbr.* for **Pontifex Maximus** (q.v.).

P.M. or **p.m.** *abbr.* for 1. **post meridiem** (q.v.). 2. **post mortem** (q.v.).

pneuma *n., pl.* **pneumas** [Gk. wind, breath, spirit of a human being, spiritual/immaterial being.] The soul. The spirit. A life-giving principle in the human being distinct from, and regarded as superior to, the soul (**psyche**) and the body. Cf. **psyche**.

P.N.G. or **p.n.g.** *abbr.* for **persona non grata** (q.v.).

pnxt. *abbr.* for **pinxit** (q.v.).

podium *n., pl.* **podia** or **podiums** [L. elevated place, height, balcony.] 1. *Ancient Rome.* A balcony in a theater equipped with seats for the emperor and other distinguished spectators. 2. A raised platform for the use of a speaker, conductor of an orchestra, lecturer, etc. a) . . . *Zaccagnini smiled wanly as he stepped to the podium* (*Newsweek Int.* March 3, 1980:9). b) *He mounted the podium and delivered a very emotional speech.* c) *The careless driver hit the traffic director's podium.* Cf. **rostrum**.

poena corporalis *n.* [L. **poena** punishment, penalty (2); **corporalis** corporal, of the body (1): corporal punishment.] Physical punishment. *People who belong to the old school of thought believe in the efficacy of poena corporalis.* See **quaelibet poena corporalis** etc.

poenae potius molliendae quam exasperandae. [L. **poenae** punishments, penalties (1); **potius** rather, more (4); **molliendae** to be softened (3); **quam** than (5); **exasperandae** to be roughened (6); **sunt** are (2): Punishments are to be softened rather than roughened.] *Law.* Punishments should be softened rather than intensified. Cf. **multiplicata transgressione** etc.

poena et remedium *n.* [**poena** L. punishment, penalty (1); **et** and (2); **remedium** remedy (3): punishment and remedy.] *Law.* Both penalty and correction. *Incarceration should serve the dual purpose of poena et remedium.*

poena ex delicto defuncti heres teneri non debet. [L. **poena** by punishment, penalty (5); **ex** out of, from, directly after, away from, emanating from (6); **delicto** offense, crime (7); **defuncti** of the dead, deceased (8); **heres** heir, successor (1); **teneri** to be held (4); **non** not (2) **debet** ought, should (3): The heir ought not to be held by a penalty from the offense of the dead.] *Law.* The heir should not be bound by a penalty resulting from a crime of the deceased. See **in restitutionem** etc.

poeta nascitur non fit. [L. **poeta** poet (1); **nascitur** is born (2); **non** not (3); **fit** is made, become (4): A poet is born, not made.] One is born a poet; one does not become a poet. No amount of hard work can make one a poet, if one does not have the poetic instinct.

poète maudit *n., pl.* **poètes maudits** [Fr. **poète** poet (2); **maudit** cursed (1): cursed poet.] A literary artist who is not fully recognized and esteemed during his/her lifetime. See **Les Poètes maudits.**

pogrom *n., pl.* **pogroms** [Russ. destruction, devastation.] An organized persecution or massacre, accompanied by looting, of a people or class of people, especially Jews, usually with official connivance and with the intention of eliminating them.

point d'honneur *n., pl.* **points d'honneur** [Fr. **point** point (1); **d'** of (2); **honneur** honor (3): a point of honor.] A point or issue where one feels that one's honor is at stake.

pointe *n.* [Fr. tiptoe.] *Ballet.* Dancing on tiptoe.

polis *n., pl.* **poleis** [Gk. city, one's city or country.] 1. An ancient Greek city state (e.g., Athens or Corinth). *The Hellenistic age is historically important in that it conclusively overthrew the narrow limits of the polis . . .* (Lesky 1966:695). 2. A state or nation. *. . . it seems, there are elements . . . who prefer playing politics to serving the polis . . .* (*West Africa* 1982).

politburo *n., pl.* **politburos** [Russ. from **polit(icheskoe)** political (1); **byuro** bureau, office (2): political bureau.] The executive committee of a Communist party.

Politeia *n.* [Gk. politics.] *Politics*, a political treatise in eight books by Aristotle (384–322 B.C.).

politesse *n., pl.* **politesses** [Fr. politeness.] Cultivated politeness. Good manners. a) *Her uncle has a charming wife who receives every visitor with politesse.* b) *They shake hands, all politesse* (*Newsweek Int.* Nov. 5, 1979:38).

politiae legibus non leges politiis adaptandae. [L. **politiae** politics (1); **legibus** to laws (3); **non** not (4); **leges** laws (5); **politiis** to politics (6); **adaptandae** to be adapted (2): Politics is to be adapted to the laws, not the laws to politics.] Politics must be adapted to the laws, not the laws to politics.

politico *n., pl.* **politicos** or **politicoes** [It./Sp. political, politician.] A politician, especially one who engages in party politics as a profession or to satisfy his/her personal, or some sectional, interests.

politique *adj.* [Fr. political, prudent, diplomatic.] Shrewd. Tactful. Diplomatic. Impartial. *That remark was not very politique.* —*n.* 1. *French History.* A member of a political group, founded c.1573, which advocated a middle course in the conflict between Catholics and Huguenots for the sake of peace and tranquility. 2. One who prefers the middle ground in a controversy. 3. A political belief or idea.

póliza de cargamento *n.* [Sp. **póliza** policy (1); **de** of (2); **cargamento** cargo, load (3): policy of cargo.] Bill of lading. See **connoissement.**

polizza di carico *n.* [It. **polizza** policy (1); **di** of (2); **carico** cargo, load (3): policy of cargo.] Bill of lading. See **connoissement.**

polka *n., pl.* **polkas** [Czech from Polish **Polka** a Polish woman.] *Music.* 1. A Bohemian dance for couples in a spirited tempo. 2. The music for such a dance.

polonaise *n., pl.* **polonaises** [Fr. *fem.* of Polish.] *Music.* 1. A majestic Polish march danced by couples in **promenade** (q.v.). 2. Music for such a dance.

poltergeist *n., pl.* **poltergeists** [Ger. **Poltergeist**: **poltern** to disturb, to make a noise (2); **Geist** spirit, ghost (1): a ghost making noise.] An invisible ghost or spirit which makes noise and moves objects.

polyandrion or **polyandrium** *n., pl.* **polyandria** or **polyandrions** or **polyandriums** [Gk. **polu(s)** much, many (1); **andr-** man, male (2): many men, common place for men, common burial place.] *Ancient Greece.* A burial ground, especially for those who lost their lives in war.

polycyesis *n.* [Neo-Gk. from **polu(s)** much, many (1); **kyesis** pregnancy (2): many pregnancies, multi-pregnancy, multi-conception.] *Medicine.* Pregnancy in which the uterus has more than one fetus.

polyhistor *n., pl.* **polyhistors** [Gk. **polu(s)** much, many (1); **histor** learned (2): very learned.] A polymath. A person who is learned in many fields.

polyopia *n., pl.* **polyopias** [Neo-Gk. from Gk. **polu(s)** many (1); **ōp(s)** eye (2): many-eyed.] Perception of several images of one object. Multiple sight or vision.

polyphagia *n., pl.* **polyphagias** [Neo-Gk. from **polu(s)** much, many (1); **phag(ein)** to eat (2): much eating, excess in eating.] Ravenous eating. Excessive or abnormal appetite. See **bulimia.**

polypharmacon *n.* [Gk. **polu(s)** much, many (1); **pharmakon** drug (2): something compounded of many drugs.] *Medicine.* A remedy or medicine which is a combination of many ingredients.

polyptoton *n., pl.* **polyptotons** [Gk. **polu(s)** much, many (2); **ptō(sis)** case (1): many cases.] *Rhetoric.* The use of a word in more than one case or part of speech in the same phrase; e.g., **quis custodiet ipsos custodes?** (q.v.) or "Who will guard the guards themselves?"

polysyndeton *n., pl.* **polysyndeta** or **polysyndetons** [Gk. **polusundeton**: **polu(s)** much, many (1); **sun** with, together (3); **de(ō)** bind (2): many bound together, something which uses many conjunctions or connecting particles.] *Rhetoric.* Repetition of identical conjunctions in close sequence; e.g., "When we entered the storeroom, we saw books and envelopes and papers and files and pencils." Cf. **asyndeton.**

ponderantur testes, non numerantur. [L. **ponderantur** are weighed, considered (2); **testes** witnesses (1); **non** not (3); **numerantur** are counted, numbered (4): Witnesses are weighed; they are not counted.] *Law.* The quality of the witnesses' testimony is more important than the number of witnesses. Cf. **testimonia ponderanda** etc.

pons asinorum *n., pl.* **pons asinorums** [L. **pons** bridge (1); **asinorum** of asses, blockheads (2): bridge of asses or blockheads.] 1. Asses' bridge; a humorous term for a very difficult geometry proposition in Euclid. 2. A critical test to determine ability, usually given to the ignorant, inexperienced, or dull-witted. *Candidates who attended the interview were subjected to a pons asinorum, which was unrelated to the requirements of the job.*

pontifex *abbr.* **p.** *n., pl.* **pontifices** [L. priest.] 1. *Ancient Rome.* A member of a body of three (later sixteen) principal religious functionaries, headed by the Pontifex Maximus. 2. High priest. Pontiff.

Pontifex Maximus *abbr.* **P.M.** or **Pont. Max.** *n.* [L. **pontifex** pontiff, priest (2); **maximus** greatest, highest (1): highest priest.] 1. *Ancient Rome.* Chief Priest. 2. *Roman Catholic Church.* The Pope. The Supreme Pontiff.

pontificalia *pl. n.* [L. things related to the pontiff.] The insignia of a pontiff. The vestments, insignia or full attire of a bishop, cardinal, or pope. Pontificals. See **in pontificalibus**.

Pont. Max. *abbr.* for **Pontifex Maximus** (q.v.).

populus *abbr.* **p.** *n.,*[L. people, citizen body.] *Roman Law.* The entire body of Roman citizens, both patricians and plebeians.

populus vult decipi. Cardinal Giovanni Pietro Caraffa, subsequently Pope Paul IV (1476–1559). [L. **populus** people (1); **vult** wishes, wants (2); **decipi** to be deceived (3): The people want to be deceived.] The people do not want to know the truth. Cf. **fere libenter** etc. and **quod enim mavult** etc.

por favor *adv.* [Sp. **por** for (1); **favor** favor (2): for a favor.] Please. See **bitte sehr; bitte schön; parakalo; per favore; prego;** and **s'il vous plaît**.

port de bras *n.* [Fr. **port** carriage (1); **de** of (2); **bras** arms, hands (3): carriage of arms.] *Ballet.* The technique of moving the arms. *Their port de bras is distinctive but never obtrusive, . . . (Newsweek Int.* July 6, 1981:43).

portio legitima or **legitima portio** *n.* [L. **portio** share, portion, part (2); **legitima** lawful, legitimate (1): lawful share or portion.] *Civil Law.* The portion of the inheritance to which a person is entitled by virtue of the relationship between him/her and the testator and which he/she cannot be deprived of except for special reasons. See **legitime**.

portmanteau *n., pl.* **portmanteaus** [Fr. **portemanteau** from **porte(r)** to carry (2); **manteau** coat, cloak (1): coat carrier.] A large suitcase with two compartments attached by a hinge. —*adj.* Attached or joined, especially two words which have been blended or merged, such as "brillig" from "boiling" and "grilling" in the poem "Jabberwocky" by Lewis Carroll (Charles Lutwidge Dodgson; 1832–1889).

poseur or *fem.* **poseuse** *n., pl.* **poseurs** or **poseuses** [Fr. snob, conceited fellow.] A person who assumes a character, attitude, or bearing alien to him/her. A dishonest, insincere, or affected person. *His father is the accomplished poseur who ingratiated himself with the President and was about to be appointed to a sensitive position when his true character was exposed.*

posito uno oppositorum, negatur alterum. [L. **posito** (with) having been asserted, affirmed (3); **uno** with one (1); **oppositorum** of opposite (things) (2); **negatur** is denied (5); **alterum** the other (4): With one of opposite things having been affirmed, the other is denied.] When one of two opposite views has been affirmed, the other is denied. See **designatio unius** etc.

posse *n., pl.* **posses** [L. to be able, to have power.] 1. Potentiality. Possibility. 2. A group of people authorized by the police to search for or arrest a criminal. 3. A crowd of people who share a common interest. See **in posse** and **posse comitatus**.

posse comitatus *n.* [L. **posse** power, force (1); **comitatus** of county (2): power of a county.] The power or force of a county. All able-bodied male inhabitants of a county above the age of fifteen who may be called upon by the sheriff to render assistance in preserving law and order, or enforcing legal orders. *To enlist the armed forces in the war on drugs, the Administration proposes modifying the 100-year-old posse comitatus . . . statutes that bar military involvement in civilian law enforcement (Time Int.* 1981). Cf. **comitatus**.

possessor bona fide See **bona fide possessor**.

possessor mala fide *n.* [L. **possessor** possessor (1); **mala** in bad (2); **fide** (in) faith (3): possessor in bad faith.] A person who owns property and is fully aware that he is not entitled to it. Cf. **bona fide possessor**.

possibile *n., pl.* **possibilia** [L. the possible thing.] Something which is conceivable or possible.

possunt quia posse videntur. Vergil (70–19 B.C.). *Aeneid* V,231. [L. **possunt** they can, are able (1); **quia** because, since (2); **posse** to be able (4); **videntur** they seem, are seen (3): They can because they seem to be able.] They can succeed because they think they can.

post *adv.* [L. after, afterwards, later.] Used in books to refer the reader to a subsequent part. See **infra**. Cf. **supra**.

postbellum *adj.* [L. **post** after (1); **bellum** war (2): after war.] Occurring after war. *The postbellum period saw widespread political consciousness in subject countries.* Cf. **antebellum**.

post cibum *abbr.* **p.c.** *adv.* [L. **post** after (1); **cibum** food (2): after food.] After meals. *The patient was asked to take two tablets three times a day post cibum.*

post coitum [L. **post** after (1); **coitum** intercourse (2): after intercourse.] Following sexual intercourse.

post coitum omne animal triste est [L. **post** after, behind (1); **coitum** sexual intercourse (2); **omne** each, every (3); **animal** animal (4); **triste** sad, unhappy (6);

est is, has been (5): After sexual intercourse every animal is sad.] After sexual intercourse everyone feels unhappy.

post diem *adj./adv.* [L. **post** after (1); **diem** day (2): after the day.] *Law.* After the day or date. Used especially in pleas of payment of money after the due date.

postea *adv.* [L. afterwards.] Afterwards. —*n., pl.* **posteas** The trial judge's entry after verdict in which he/she indicates the issue and summarizes the proceedings. See **ex post facto.** Cf. **ab initio.**

post eventum *adj./adv.* [L. **post** after (1); **eventum** event, occurrence (2): after the event.] After its occurrence. *adj. A post eventum prediction is as good as no prediction.* —*adv. He is a fake soothsayer who lays claim to predictions post eventum.*

post factum *adj.* [L. **post** after (1); **factum** deed, act, fact (2): after the fact.] Retrospective. Happening after the fact.

post hoc *adv.* [L. **post** after (1); **hoc** this (2): after this (time).] After this. Henceforth.

post hoc, ergo propter hoc or **post hoc, propter hoc** [L. **post** after (1); **hoc** this (2); **ergo** therefore, accordingly (3); **propter** on account of, because of (4); **hoc** this (5): after this, therefore, because of this.] *Logic.* A fallacy in which one infers or assumes that something is the cause of something else because the former precedes the latter. *The argument may be formally stated in a way that exposes it as one of the classical examples of the post hoc ergo propter hoc fallacy* (Eysenck 1982:26).

posthumus *adj.* [L. **postumus** late-born or latest born, born after the father's death.] Posthumous. —*n.* A son born after the death of his father. —*neut. pl.* **posthuma** Writings published after the death of the author.

postiche *n., pl.* **postiches** [Fr. false.] 1. Something which is not real. A sham. 2. A hairpiece. A toupee.

postliminium *n., pl.* **postliminia** [L. **post** after (1); **limen** threshold (2): after the threshold, a complete return home, restoration of rank and privileges, postliminy.] 1. *Roman Law.* A doctrine whereby prisoners of war merely had their property and civil rights suspended and so they regained them on their return to Rome. 2. *International Law.* A doctrine whereby persons or things captured in war are, after their return to their country, restored to their original status. See **postliminium fingit** etc.

postliminium fingit eum qui captus est in civitate semper fuisse. [L. **postliminium** postliminy (1); **fingit** pretends (2); **eum** one, him/her (3); **qui** who (4); **captus est** has been captured (5); **in** in, on (8); **civitate** state (9); **semper** always (7); **fuisse** to have been (6): Postliminy pretends (that) one who has been captured has always been in the state.] By the principle of postliminy someone who is a prisoner of war is considered never to have left the state. See **postliminium.**

post litem motam *adv.* [L. **post** after (1); **litem** suit (2); **motam** having been moved, commenced (3): after the suit having been commenced.] *Law.* After the commencement of the suit. Used in former times with respect to depositions on the subject of a suit after the commencement of litigation. Cf. **ante litem motam.**

post meridiem *abbr.* **P.M.** or **p.m.** *adj.* [L. **post** after (1); **meridiem** noon, midday (2): after noon.] In the afternoon. Cf. **ante meridiem.**

post mortem *abbr.* **P.M.** or **p.m.** *adv.* [L. **post** after (1); **mortem** death (2): after death.] After death. *The nature of the disease was determined only when the patients had been examined post mortem.* —**postmortem** *adj.* 1. After death. Associated with the period following death. *The pathologist examined eight postmortem cases.* 2. After the event. Done after the event. *This is essentially a postmortem discussion.* —*n., pl.* **postmortems** 1. An after-death examination. 2. A discussion of an event after its occurrence. An autopsy. *The students indulged in a postmortem after their failure in the examination.* —*v.* To make a postmortem. Cf. **ante mortem.**

post natus or **post-natus** *n., pl.* **post nati** or **post-nati** [L. **post** after (2); **natus** born (1): born after.] 1. A person born after a momentous event and whose legal status is affected by that event. 2. *Britain.* A person born after the union with Scotland. 3. *U.S.A.* A person born after the signing of the Declaration of Independence. Cf. **ante natus.**

post-obit *adj.*, shortened form of **post-obitum** [L. **post** after (1); **obitum** death (2): after death.] Occurring after death. To take effect after death. a) *post-obit bond;* b) *post-obit donation.*

postpartum *adj.* [L. **post** after (1); **partum** birth, delivery (2): after birth.] Relating to the period after birth. a) . . . *a brief respite from the legal battles that have compounded their postpartum pain* (Newsweek Int. Nov 28, 1983:26). b) *Mrs. Groso went to the hospital yesterday for postpartum examination.*

post postscriptum *abbr.* **P.P.S.** or **p.p.s.** [L. **post** after (1); **postscriptum** postscript (2): after the postscript.] Additional postscript.

post rem *adv./adj.* [L. **post** after, behind (1); **rem** matter, thing, property, business, affairs (2): after the thing.] *Philosophy.* Existing after something else, especially a general or universal concept which comes into being only after a particular experience. Cf. **ante rem.**

postscriptum *abbr.* **P.S.** or **p.s.** *n., pl.* **postscripta** [L. **post** after (2); **scriptum** that/what has been written, written (1): written after.] Postscript. A note or notes containing additional information written after the conclusion of a letter, article, book, etc. *Ironically, the most significant information in the letter appeared in a postscriptum.*

postulatum *n., pl.* **postulata** [L. that which is demanded, claimed, requested.] Postulate.

post urbem conditam *abbr.* **p.u.c.** [L. **post** after (1); **urbem** city (2); **conditam** having been founded (3):

after the city having been founded.] After the foundation of the city. *Roman History.* Used for chronology, 753 B.C. being the starting point. See **ab urbe condita** and **anno urbis conditae.**

pot-de-vin *n., pl.* **pots-de-vin** [Fr. **pot** pot (1); **de** of, for (2); **vin** wine (3): pot of wine, bribe, hush-money.] *French Law.* A sum of money, usually more than the amount agreed upon, which is often paid at the time a contract is made. Its effect is to make the contract irrevocable. Cf. **argentum Dei.**

potentia *n., pl.* **potentiae** or **potentias** [L. power.] Power. Potency. Efficacy.

potentia debet sequi justitiam, non antecedere. [L. **potentia** power (1); **debet** ought, should (2); **sequi** to follow (3); **justitiam** justice (4); **non** not (5); **antecedere** to precede, go before (6): Power ought to follow, not to precede, justice.] Justice should take precedence over power, which should be based upon or follow what is just.

potentia non est nisi ad bonum. [L. **potentia** power (1); **non** not (3); **est** is, exists (2); **nisi** unless (4); **ad** to, at, for, according to (5); **bonum** good (thing) (6): Power is not unless for good.] *Law.* Power is conferred only for the public good.

potestas *n., pl.* **potestates** [L. power.] Power such as that of the paterfamilias over his wife, children, and slaves. See **familia** and **paterfamilias.**

potestas abstinendi *n.* [L. **potestas** power (1); **abstinendi** of refraining, abstaining (2): power of refusing.] *Roman Law.* The right given by praetorian law to a necessary heir, i.e., **heres necessarius** (q.v.), to reject the inheritance. See **beneficium abstinendi.** Cf. **tempus deliberandi.**

potestas stricte interpretatur. [L. **potestas** power (1); **stricte** strictly, tightly (3); **interpretatur** is interpreted (2): Power is strictly interpreted.] *Law.* Power is given a strict interpretation.

potior est conditio defendentis. [L. **potior** better, preferable (4); **est** is (3); **conditio** condition (1); **defendentis** of the one defending, of the defender (2): The condition of the defendant is better.] *Law.* The condition of the defendant is preferable to that of the plaintiff. See **in aequali jure melior** etc.

potior est conditio possidentis. [L. **potior** better, preferable (4); **est** is (3); **conditio** condition (1); **possidentis** of the one possessing (2): The condition of the possessor is better.] The condition of the possessor is preferable to that of the person seeking possession. See **in aequali jure melior** etc.

potius sero quam numquam Livy (59 B.C.–17 A.D.). *Ab urbe condita* IV,2. [L. **potius** rather (1); **sero** late (2); **quam** than (3); **numquam** never (4): rather late than never.] Better late than never.

potomania *n.* [Neo-Gk. from Gk. **poto(n)** drink (2); **mania** enthusiasm, mad desire (1): enthusiasm or mad desire for drink.] Alcoholism. An abnormal or uncontrollable desire for alcoholic drinks. See **dipsomania.**

potpourri or **pot-pourri** *n., pl.* **potpourris** or **pot-pourris** [Fr. **pot** pot (2); **pourri** rotten (1): rotten pot or jar, a medley, a hodgepodge.] 1. A collection of highly-scented dried flowers and/or leaves and spices used for sachets or for scenting a room. 2. A medley or series of songs or other artistic productions. *The show was essentially a potpourri of old high-life tunes, juju music, recitation of poems, jokes, etc.* 3. A collection of various literary works. *The book lacks organic unity and is basically a potpourri of extracts from various works.* 4. A collection or mixture of various unrelated persons, things, elements, etc. *. . . to amalgamate the multifarious interest groups and come out with a potpourri of representatives in a cabinet* (*The Guardian* 1986). See **mélange; melée; olla podrida;** and **omnium-gatherum.**

pourboire *n., pl.* **pourboires** [Fr. **pour** for, in order to, to (1); **boire** drink, drinking (2): for drink or drinking, a tip.] A tip to a servant. Gratuity. Cf. **douceur.**

pour encourager les autres *adv.* Voltaire (1694–1778). *Candide* 23. [Fr. **pour** for, in order to, to (1); **encourager** to encourage (2); **les** the (3); **autres** others (4): to encourage others.] To serve as an inducement or a lesson to others. *At the end of every year the company holds a party at which gifts are distributed to industrious and productive employees pour encourager les autres.* See **Dans ce pays-ci** etc.

pour faire rire *adv.* [Fr. **pour** for, in order to, to (1); **faire** to make (2); **rire** to laugh (3): in order to make to laugh.] To cause or raise a laugh. As a joke. Cf. **pour rire.**

pourparler *n., pl.* **pourparlers** [Fr. **pour** for, in order to, to (1); **parler** to talk (2): in order to talk, a parley, negotiation, diplomatic conversation.] *French and International Law.* Negotiations or discussions which precede the conclusion of a contract, treaty, agreement, etc., but do not form part of the actual agreement. Informal discussions or conference preceding diplomatic negotiation.

pour passer le temps *adv.* [Fr. **pour** to, for (1); **passer** to pass (2); **le** the (3); **temps** time, weather (4): to pass the time.] For the sake of amusement. To pass away the time.

pour rire *adj./adv.* [Fr. **pour** for, in order to, to (1); **rire** to laugh, joke (2): in order to laugh or joke.] For fun. For a joke. — *adj.* Used postpositively. a) *The attempt of Elagabalus to merge all other religions in that of the sun-god of Emesa was merely pour rire; . . .* (Cary 1970:762). b) *When high-ranking governmental officials take serious affairs pour rire, then there is cause for alarm.* Cf. **pour faire rire.**

pour-soi *n.* [Fr. **pour** to, for (1); **soi** itself, oneself, himself, herself (2): for itself.] *Philosophy.* The concept of an independent consciousness, as developed by Jean-Paul Sartre (1905–1980) in **L'Être et le néant** (q.v.).

pou sto *n.* [Gk. **pou** where (1); **stō** I am to stand (2): where I am to stand.] A base from which one operates. A standing position. Cf. **dos moi pou sto** etc.

p.p. *abbr.* for **pater patriae** (q.v.), **per procurationem** (q.v.), and **propria persona** (q.v.).

pp *abbr.* for **Papa** 1 and **pianississimo** (q.v.).

P.P.S. or **p.p.s.** *abbr.* for **post postscriptum** (q.v.).

p. r. *abbr.* for **pro rata** (q.v.).

praecipe or **precipe** *n., pl.* **praecipes** or **precipes** [L. order, admonish.] *Law.* 1. A writ asking a defendant to do something or appear and show cause why he/ she should not do it. 2. An order in writing to the clerk of court to issue a specified writ.

praecipuum *n., pl.* **praecipua** [L. something taken before others; something special.] 1. *Roman Law.* A portion of an inheritance taken before the actual distribution. 2. *Scots Law.* An additional portion of an inheritance.

praecognitum *n., pl.* **praecognita** [L. something learned beforehand.] Something that needs to be known before something else can be understood.

praedium dominans *n.* [L. **praedium** estate, farm (2); **dominans** dominant (1): dominant estate.] *Civil Law.* Dominant tenement. An estate which benefits in consequence of an easement exercisable on a servient estate. Cf. **praedium serviens**.

praedium rusticanum *n.* [L. **praedium** estate, farm (2); **rusticanum** rural, rustic, country (1): country estate.] *Roman, Civil, and Scots Law.* Land situated either in the country or town on which no building is constructed.

praedium rusticum *n.* [L. **praedium** estate, farm (2); **rusticum** rural, rustic, country (1): rural estate.] *Roman and Civil Law.* Land set aside and used for pastoral and agricultural activities.

praedium serviens *n.* [L. **praedium** estate, farm (2); **serviens** serving (1): serving estate.] *Civil Law.* Servient estate; i.e., an estate under servitude or easement to another estate. Cf. **praedium dominans**.

praedium servit praedio. [L. **praedium** farm, estate (1); **servit** is under servitude, is subject to an easement (2); **praedio** to farm, estate (3): An estate is under servitude to an estate.] *Law.* An estate (or land) is under servitude to an estate (or land); i.e., a servitude is not a personal right.

praedium urbanum *n., pl.* **praedia urbana** [L. **praedium** estate, farm (2); **urbanum** urban, town (1): urban estate.] *Roman, Civil, and Scots Law.* An estate either in the city or in the country which is meant for human habitation and use, though the adjacent land may be used for other incidental purposes.

praefatus *abbr.* **p. fat.** or **praefat.** *adj.* [L. **prae** before (2); **fatus** having been said (1): having been said before, said beforehand, uttered in advance.] Said previously.

praelegatum *n., pl.* **praelegata** [L. something bequeathed in advance.] *Roman Law.* An advance payment either in whole or in part of an heir's share of the inheritance.

praemium or **premium** *n., pl.* **praemia** or **praemiums**, **premia** or **premiums** [L. a reward, recompense, compensation, prize.] 1. A reward or recompense. *The

school has set aside premiums for academic excellence.* 2. Bonus. Additional remuneration. *The employees of the company receive premiums in addition to their basic salaries.* 3. Something which is given for a loan in addition to the normal interest. *The moneylender expects borrowers to pay a premium before approving their applications for loans.* 4. Payment for a contract of insurance. 5. Payment for instructions in a profession or trade. 6. A value higher than is usually expected of a thing. *Mr. Adetona puts a high premium on accuracy, punctuality, personal integrity, and probity.*

praemium pudicitiae or **premium pudicitiae** [L. **praemium** reward, compensation (1); **pudicitiae** for/ of chastity (2): compensation for chastity.] Compensation for deprivation of chastity. Applicable to compensating a seduced woman.

praemium pudoris or **premium pudoris** [L. **praemium** reward, compensation (1); **pudoris** for/ of shame, modesty (2): compensation for shame.] **Praemium pudicitiae** (q.v.).

praemonitus praemunitus [L. **praemonitus** forewarned (1); **praemunitus** forearmed (2): forewarned, forearmed.] Forewarned is forearmed.

praenomen *n., pl.* **praenomina** or **praenomens** [L. **prae** before (2) **nomen** name (1): name before, first name.] A person's first name or a personal name which distinguishes one from other members of the same family. *Marcus was the praenomen of the Roman Marcus Porcius Cato. James is the praenomen of the Nigerian James Gbadebo Adetunji.* Cf. **nomen**.

praepositus *n.* [L. **prae** before, in front of (2): **positus** having been placed (1): having been placed before, one placed before, in front, or first.] A person from whom descent is traced. *Males in equal degree of relationship to the praepositus were preferred to females* (Parry 1961:142).

praepropera consilia raro sunt prospera. [L. **praepropera** overhasty, precipitate (1); **consilia** counsels (2); **raro** seldom, rarely (4); **sunt** are (3); **prospera** prosperous, favorable (5): Precipitate counsels are seldom favorable.] Hasty advice or plans are rarely good.

praescriptio *n.* [L. from **prae** before (2) and **scriptio** writing (1): writing before, prescription.] *Roman Civil Law.* Acquisition of property by virtue of use and enjoyment over a long period of time. Initially it differed from **usucapio** (q.v.), but the two were merged by Justinian.

praescriptio est titulus ex usu et tempore substantiam capiens ab auctoritate legis. [L. **praescriptio** prescription (1); **est** is (2); **titulus** title (3); **ex** arising from, emanating from (4); **usu** use (5); **et** and (6); **tempore** time (7); **substantiam** substance, validity (9); **capiens** taking, deriving (8); **ab** from, by (10); **auctoritate** authority (11); **legis** of law (12): Prescription is a title arising from use and time and taking substance from the authority of law.] *Law.* Prescription is a title emanating from use and time, and deriving its validity from legal authority. Cf. **sine possessione** etc. and **transferuntur dominia** etc.

praesidium or **presidium** *n., pl.* **praesidia** or **praesidiums, presidia** or **presidiums** [L. a garrison, fortification, defense, protection.] 1. A presiding committee of an organization. 2. *Communism.* A permanent executive committee, selected from a bigger body, supposedly acting for the bigger body but actually exercising full powers.

praestat cautela quam medela. [L. **praestat** is superior, better (2); **cautela** caution, precaution (1); **quam** than (3); **medela** cure, medication (4):) Precaution is better than cure.] Prevention is better than a cure. It is better to avoid a problem than to find a remedy for it.

praesumatur pro justitia sententiae. [L. **praesumatur** it should be presumed (1); **pro** for, on behalf of (2); **justitia** justice (3); **sententiae** of sentence, judgment (4): It should be presumed for the justice of a sentence.] *Law.* The justice of a sentence should be presumed.

praesumptio, ex eo quod plerumque fit. [L. **praesumptio** presumption (1); **ex** arising from (2); **eo** that (3); **quod** which (4); **plerumque** generally, commonly (5); **fit** happens, occurs (6): presumption arising from that which generally happens.] *Law.* Presumption is based on general occurrences.

praesumptio fortior *n.* [L. **praesumptio** presumption (2); **fortior** stronger (1): stronger presumption.] *Law.* Strong presumption; i.e., a presumption based on fact, which must be accorded great credence and thus puts on the opposite party the onus of producing evidence to refute the presumption.

praesumptio hominis *n.* [L. **praesumptio** presumption (1); **hominis** of person, human being (2): presumption of a human being.] *Law.* An individual's natural, spontaneous, or free presumption not bound by any rule.

praesumptio juris *n.* [L. **praesumptio** presumption (1); **juris** of right, law (2): presumption of law.] *Law.* An inconclusive or conditional presumption in which the law assumes that something exists until evidence is adduced to refute it. Cf. **juris et de jure.**

praesumptio juris et de jure *n.* [L. **praesumptio** presumption (1); **juris** of right, law (2); **et** and (3); **de** of, from, about, for (4); **jure** right, law (5): presumption of law and about right.] *Law.* Presumption of law and of right; i.e., a conclusive presumption whose refutation the law will not permit. See **juris et de jure.**

praesumptio violenta plena probatio. [L. **praesumptio** presumption (2); **violenta** forcible, vehement, strong (1); **plena** full (3); **probatio** proof (4): Forcible presumption is full proof.] *Law.* Strong presumption is full proof. See **violenta praesumptio** etc.

praesumptio violenta valet in lege. [L. **praesumptio** presumption (2); **violenta** forcible, vehement (1); **valet** is strong, is valid (3); **in** in, on (4); **lege** law (5):

Forcible presumption is valid in law.] *Law.* Strong presumption carries weight in law. See **violenta praesumptio** etc.

praetor *n., pl.* **praetors** [L. praetor, judge.] *Roman Law.* A magistrate who ranked immediately below the consuls, the highest Roman magistrates, and was entrusted with the duty of administering the law.

praetor peregrinus *n.* [L. **praetor** praetor, judge (2); **peregrinus** foreign (1): foreign praetor.] *Ancient Rome.* The praetor assigned jurisdiction over foreign residents.

praevaricator or **prevaricator** *n., pl.* **praevaricators** or **prevaricators** [L. **prae** before, in front of (2); **varicator** one who straddles (1): one who straddles before, one who walks in a crooked manner, a collusive prosecutor, an unfaithful lawyer.] 1. *Civil Law.* A person who betrays the confidence reposed in him. A lawyer who perfidiously helps the opposite party. 2. A liar.

pratique *n., pl.* **pratiques** [Fr. practice, business, association, intercourse.] Permission given to a ship to transact business in the port(s) of a country after satisfying quarantine requirements or producing a clean bill of health.

praxis *n., pl.* **praxeis** [Gk. doing, exercise, practice, action, act.] 1. Exercise or practice of a skill, art, etc. 2. Habit, custom. Usual manner of doing things.

praxis judicum est interpres legum. [L. from Gk. **praxis** practice (1); **judicum** of judges (2); **est** is (3); **interpres** interpreter (4); **legum** of laws (5): The practice of judges is interpreter of the laws.] *Law.* It is the duty of judges to interpret the laws.

precario *adv.* [L. (by) something obtained by prayer, something which depends on the will of another, something transitory or uncertain.] *Law.* By **precarium** (q.v.). By the right or permission granted by the owner (or bailor) to another (bailee) to use a thing or exercise a right until the former revokes the grant.

precarium *n., pl.* **precaria** [L. something obtained by prayer, something which depends on the will of another, something transitory or uncertain.] *Civil Law.* Something loaned or given to another to be returned whenever the grantor wishes. A contract based on such terms. A precarious or uncertain tenancy.

prece partium *adv.* [L. **prece** at the prayer, request, entreaty (1); **partium** of parties (2): at the prayer of parties.] *Law.* At the request of the parties. Used with reference to the continuation of a suit.

précis *n., pl.* **précis** [Fr. abstract.] A summary or abridgment. A concise abstract. Cf. **epitome.**

prego *adv.* [It. I beg.] Please. See **bitte schön; bitte sehr; parakalo; per favore; por favor;** and **s'il vous plaît.**

Prélude à l'après-midi d'un faune *n.* [Fr. **prélude** prelude (1); **à** to, toward, in, by, with, until (2); **l'** the (3); **après** after (4); **midi** noon (5); **d'** of (6); **un** a (7); **faune** faun (8): prelude to the afternoon of a faun.] "Prelude to the Afternoon of a Faun," the title of a musical composition by Claude Debussy (1862–1918).

premier *adj.* [Fr. first, leading, principal, foremost.] First in rank, importance, position, time, etc. . . . *Nigeria's premier female college, the Queen's College, . . . (The Guardian* 1987). —*n., pl.* **premiers** Prime Minister. Head of state or government.

premier danseur or *fem.* première danseuse *n.* [Fr. **premier** first, principal (1); **danseur** dancer (2): principal dancer.] *Ballet.* The principal dancer of a company. *Porter's Prince was David Wall, indisputably the company's premier danseur (Newsweek Int.* June 30, 1980:480).

première or premiere *n., pl.* **premières** or **premieres** [Fr. **première** first, foremost.] First night, performance, or exhibition of a play, film, etc. *At the première the maestro, reserved but smiling, appeared on-stage at the end and was appropriately showered with flowers (Newsweek Int.* April 26, 1982:49). —*adj.* Principal. First. Chief. Outstanding. *The première item on the evening's program will be a dance by the bride and bridegroom.*

premium See **praemium.**

premium pudicitiae See **praemium pudicitiae.**

premium pudoris See **praemium pudoris.**

prendre or prender *n., pl.* **prendres** or **prenders** [Fr. **prendre** to take, grasp or seize.] *Law.* The right or power to take something instead of waiting for it to be given.

prenomen *var.* of **praenomen** (q.v.).

presidio *n., pl.* **presidios** [Sp. garrison, fortress, protection.] A fort. A military post. A fortified or garrisoned settlement.

presidium *var.* of **praesidium** (q.v.).

Presidium or Presidium *n., pl.* **Praesidia** or **Presidia** or **Praesidiums** or **Presidiums** [Russ. **prezidium** from L. **praesidium** guard, protection, fort.] The chief executive committee of the Communist Party in the former Soviet Union.

presto *adv./adj.* [It. soon, quickly, quick.] 1. Immediately. Quickly. In haste. 2. Fast. At a fast tempo. Used, primarily, as a musical direction. . . . *director Federico Fellini finished "Orchestra Rehearsal" at presto pace: shooting took only seventeen days (Newsweek Int.* March 12, 1979:57). —*n., pl.* **prestos** *Music.* A composition or a portion of a composition played in a fast tempo.

prêt *n., pl.* **prêts** [Fr. loan, lending.] *French Law.* A loan. A contract whereby something is loaned on condition that, after its use, the same article or its equivalent in quality and species should be returned.

prêt-à-porter *abbr.* p.a.p. *adj.* [Fr. **prêt** ready, prepared (1); **à** to, toward, in, by, with, until (2); **porter** to wear, carry (3): ready to wear.] Ready-to-wear. Ready-made. . . . *revolutionary collections of loose-fitting women's clothes, men's designer wear and prêt-à-porter lines (Newsweek Int.* Feb. 28, 1983: 38). —*n.* Ready-made clothing. *In prêt-à-porter, with a billion dollars in worldwide business at stake, young*

Paris designers . . . volleyed back with outré styles of their own . . . (Newsweek Int. Jan. 2, *1984:58).*

prêt à usage *n., pl.* **prêts à usage** [Fr. **prêt** ready, prepared, loan (1); **à** to, toward, in, by, with, until (2); **usage** use (3): loan to use.] *French Law.* Loan to use. Loan for use. A contract whereby one party gives to the other something to be used on condition that the same article should be returned. **Commodatum.** Cf. **commodati actio.**

pretium affectionis *n., pl.* **pretia affectionis** [L. **pretium** price, value (1); **affectionis** of affection, inclination (2): price of affection.] An unrealistic value put on an article by the owner on account of its sentimental associations.

pretium periculi *n.* [L. **pretium** price, value (1); **periculi** of danger, risk, hazard (2): the price of risk.] Premium paid on insurance policies of various kinds.

preux chevalier *n.* [Obs. Fr. **preux** useful, brave, valiant (1); **chevalier** knight (2): valiant knight.] A valiant or chivalrous knight.

prevaricator See **praevaricator.**

Priapus *n., pl.* **Priapi** or **Priapuses** [L. from Gk. **Priapos** god of procreation.] 1. *Greek and Roman Mythology.* A god of sexuality and procreation, and protector of the garden. Usually depicted with an erect phallus. 2. A phallus.

prie-dieu *n., pl.* **prie-dieux** [Fr. **prie** pray (1); **dieu** God (2): pray God.] A prayer-stool with a place to kneel, a railing, and a bookshelf, sometimes with a seat attached.

prima *adj.* [It./L. first.] First. Principal. Leading.

prima ballerina *n., pl.* **prime ballerine** or **prima ballerinas** [It. **prima** principal, leading (1); **ballerina** female dancer (2): leading female dancer.] *Ballet.* The principal or leading female dancer in a company.

prima ballerina assoluta, *short form* **assoluta** *n.* [It. **prima** principal, leading (2); **ballerina** female dancer (3); **assoluta** absolute, complete (1): absolute leading female dancer.] *Ballet.* Principal female dancer. A title of rare honor conferred on a **danseuse** (q.v.). *Fonteyn has been elevated to the title of prima ballerina assoluta . . . (Newsweek Int.* June 6, 1981:43).

prima donna *n., pl.* **prime donne** or **prima donnas** [It. **prima** first (1); **donna** woman, lady (2): first woman/lady.] 1. The leading female singer in an opera or concert group. See **diva.** 2. A person who cannot tolerate criticism or control. A person whose temperament is such that he/she cannot perform satisfactorily when directed or as a member of a group. An arrogant person. a) . . . *political prima donnas like de Gaulle seldom bow out gracefully . . . (Newsweek Int.* March 24, 1980:11). b) *As my deputy after the first year, he disciplined my anarchic tendencies and established coherence in a National Security Council staff of talented prima donnas (Times Int.* 1982).

primae impressionis *adj.* [L. **primae** of first (1); **impressionis** (of) impression (2): of first impression.] *Law.* Of first impression. A case primae impressionis is a case without precedent, which cannot, therefore, be judged by the application of any legal principle but by the application of reason and discretion.

prima facie *adv.* [L. **prima** at/on first (1); **facie** (at/on) view, appearance, sight (2): at first sight.] At first sight or appearance. On the surface. Presumably. *His testimony is prima facie acceptable.* —*adj.* Apparent. Seemingly satisfactory or acceptable, thus warranting judicial proceedings or detailed investigation. *The magistrate decided that the prosecution had failed to make out a prima facie case against the accused and accordingly ordered his release.*

prima materia *n.* [L. **prima** first (1); **materia** material, matter (2): first matter.] *Philosophy.* The first material from which all other creation is derived. Primordial matter.

primigravida *n., pl.* **primigravidae** or **primigravidas** [Neo-L. from L. **prim(us)** first (2); **gravida** pregnant (1): pregnant for the first time.] *Medicine.* A woman who is carrying her first pregnancy. Cf. **gravida**.

primipara *n., pl.* **primiparae** or **primiparas** [Neo-L. from L. **prim(us)** first (2); **par(io)** give birth (1): giving birth for the first time.] *Medicine.* A woman who has given birth to one child or is giving birth to her first child. *Mrs. Rockson, a midwife at the hospital, usually disappears from the maternity ward whenever a primipara is brought in for delivery.* Cf. **multipara**.

primogenitor *n.* [L. from **prim(us)** first (1); **genitor** begetter (2): first begetter.] First ancestor. Ancestor. Forefather. *The Yoruba generally regard Oduduwa as their primogenitor.*

primo venienti [L. **primo** to the first (1); **venienti** coming (2): to the first coming.] *Law.* To the first to come. "First come, first served." Applicable, originally, to the practice in ancient times whereby an executor settled the claims of creditors as they presented them, without considering whether the assets were adequate for all claims or not. See **priori petenti** and **prior petens**.

primum mobile *n., pl.* **primum mobiles** [L. **primum** first (1); **mobile** movable, inconstant (2): the first movable/inconstant.] A primary source of activity or motion. Prime mover. *Over-ambition and the desire to achieve the impracticable seem to be the primum mobile of all his activities.*

primum non nocere [L. **primum** first (thing) (1); **non** not (2); **nocere** to harm, injure (3): The first (thing) (is) not to harm.] *Medicine.* First of all, do no harm. The first rule of the Hippocratic oath.

primus inter pares or *fem.* **prima inter pares** *n., pl.* **primi inter pares** or *fem.* **primae inter pares** [L. **primus** first (1); **inter** among (2); **pares** equals (3): first among equals.] First in a group of equals. *The head of the institution, who by virtue of his position is merely primus inter pares, is so obsessed with power that he acts dictatorially.*

primus non inter pares sed longo intervallo *adj.* [L. **primus** first (1); **non** not (2); **inter** among (3); **pares**

equals (4); **sed** but (5); **longo** by long (6); **intervallo** (by) interval, distance (7): first not among equals but by a long interval.] Not merely first among equals but preeminently first. *In theory, a chief executive of an educational institution is primus inter pares, but, in practice, he/she could be primus non inter pares sed longo intervallo.*

princeps *n., pl.* **principes** [L. the first person, chief, leader.] 1. Somebody or something that is first or foremost. 2. The head of the Roman state/Empire during the imperial period. The Emperor (e.g., Augustus, Tiberius, Nero, etc.). 3. A chieftain or principal official. 4. The first printed edition of a book. **Editio princeps** (q.v.).

principalis debet semper excuti antequam perveniatur ad fideijussores. [L. **principalis** principal (1); **debet** ought, should (2); **semper** always (3); **excuti** to be driven out, removed (4); **antequam** before (5); **perveniatur** it is arrived (6); **ad** to, at, for, according to (7); **fideijussores** guarantors, sureties (8): The principal ought always to be driven out before it is arrived at guarantors.] *Law.* The principal debtor should always exhaust his/her assets before action is taken against the guarantors.

principe *n., pl.* **principes** [It./Sp. /Port. from L. **princeps** the first person, chief, leader.] A prince, especially the eldest son of the king of Spain or Portugal. Cf. **infante** and **infanta**.

principia probant, non probantur. [L. **principia** principles (1); **probant** prove (2); **non** not (3); **probantur** are proved (4): Principles prove; they are not proved.] Fundamental principles are used for proof; they need no proof. See **contra negantem** etc. and **principiorum non** etc.

principiis obsta. [L. **principiis** beginnings, origins (2); **obsta** oppose, thwart (1): Oppose beginnings.] Oppose ills (or diseases) right from their inception. For a fuller form, see **principiis obsta; sero** etc. Cf. **venienti occurrite morbo**.

principiis obsta; sero medicina paratur / cum mala per longas convaluere moras. Ovid (43 B.C.–17 A.D.). *Remedia Amoris* 91. [L. **principiis** beginnings, origins (2); **obsta** oppose, thwart (1); **sero** late, too late (3); **medicina** medicine, remedy (4); **paratur** is prepared (5); **cum** when (6); **mala** ills, evils (7); **per** through, by (9); **longas** long (10); **convaluere** have grown strong, gained strength (8); **moras** delays (11): Oppose beginnings; too late is the remedy prepared / when the ills have grown strong through long delays.] Oppose ills at their inception. It is too late to prepare the medicine when the disease has grown strong through long delay. For shorter form, see **principiis obsta**.

principiorum non est ratio. [L. **principiorum** of principles (4); **non** not (2); **est** there is (1); **ratio** reasoning (3): There is not reasoning of principles.] Fundamental principles need not be proved. Cf. **contra negantem** etc.

principium *n., pl.* **principia** [L. beginning, origin, principle, element.] Basis or fundamental principle.

prior *adj.* [L. former, first, better.] 1. Previous. Antecedent. Preceding in point of time, rank, etc. a) *At the beginning of their conference they reviewed the points covered at their prior meeting.* b) *A prior obligation kept her from attending the performance.* 2. Enjoying precedence in value, importance, etc. *Joseph is a remarkable paterfamilias who regards his responsibility to his family prior to all other considerations.* —*n.* 1. An official in charge of a priory or the member of a religious community ranked immediately below an abbot. 2. A magistrate in the medieval republic of Florence in Italy.

priores leges ad posteriores trahantur. [L. **priores** former, previous (1); **leges** laws (2); **ad** to, at, for, according to (4); **posteriores** later (5); **trahantur** should be drawn (3): Former laws should be drawn to later ones.] *Law.* Earlier laws should be superseded by subsequent ones. See **lex posterior** etc.

priori petenti [L. **priori** to the first (1); **petenti** (to) claiming, demanding, applying (2): to the first applying/claiming.] *Law.* To the first applicant. Applicable to the rule that where several equally qualified persons apply for the grant of administration, the first applicant should get the grant. See **prior petens.**

prior petens *n.* [L. **prior** first (1); **petens** claiming, suing, applying (2): the first applying.] *Law.* The first applicant. See **priori petenti.**

prior tempore potior jure. [L. **prior** first (1); **tempore** in time (2); **potior** better, preferable (3); **jure** in right, law (4): The first in time is preferable in right.] *Law.* He who enjoys priority in time likewise enjoys superiority in right. See **qui prior** etc.

prius *n., pl.* **priora** or **priuses** [L. former, previous, first.] A precondition or prerequisite. Something which takes precedence. Something which precedes.

privatim *adv.* [L. privately.] In a private capacity. Privately. *There is a wide discrepancy between his public and private image for, though he seems strict and austere palam, he is very relaxed and generous privatim.* Cf. **palam.**

privatis pactionibus non dubium est non laedi jus caeterorum. [L. **privatis** by private (8); **pactionibus** (by) agreements, contracts (9); **non** not (2); **dubium** doubtful, uncertain (that) (3); **est** it is (1); **non** not (6); **laedi** to be/is hurt, violated (7); **jus** right, law (4); **c(a)eterorum** of others (5): It is not doubtful that the right of others is not violated by private agreements.] *Law.* There can be no doubt that the rights of others cannot be prejudiced by private agreements. See **res inter alios acta alteri** etc.

privatorum conventio juri publico non derogat. [L. **privatorum** of private (persons) (2); **conventio** agreement, compact (1); **juri** right, law (6); **publico** public (5); **non** not (3); **derogat** impairs, diminishes, detracts from (4): The agreement of private persons does not detract from public right.] *Law.* Agreement by private persons does not impair the public right. See **conventio privatorum** etc.

privatum commodum publico cedit. [L. **privatum** private (1); **commodum** convenience, interest, advantage (2); **publico** to public (4); **cedit** yields (3): Private interest yields to the public.] *Law.* Private interest yields to the public interest. See **in casu extremae** etc.

privatum incommodum publico bono pensatur. [L. **privatum** private (1); **incommodum** inconvenience, misfortune (2); **publico** by public (4); **bono** good (5); **pensatur** is compensated, recompensed (3): Private inconvenience is compensated by the public good.] *Law.* The inconvenience of private individuals is counterbalanced by the public good. See **in casu extremae** etc.

privilegium *n., pl.* **privilegia** [L. law on an individual, a special enactment, privilege.] 1. *Roman Law.* A special legal provision whereby the Roman emperor bestowed on an individual an irregular right, or imposed an irregular obligation or punishment on an individual. 2. *Civil Law.* An extraordinary favor or right conferred by the law. A special claim or lien on property, such as that of seamen on a ship as a guarantee of payment of wages.

privilegium est beneficium personale, et extinguitur cum persona. [L. **privilegium** privilege (1); **est** is (2); **beneficium** benefit, favor (4); **personale** personal (3); **et** and (5); **extinguitur** it is extinguished, annulled (6); **cum** with (7); **persona** person (8): A privilege is a personal favor and it is extinguished with the person.] *Law.* A privilege is a personal favor and its duration ends with the death of the beneficiary.

privilegium est quasi privata lex. [L. **privilegium** privilege (1); **est** is (2); **quasi** just as if, as one might say (3); **privata** private (4); **lex** law (5): Privilege is, so to speak, a private law.] *Law.* Privilege is the equivalent of a private law.

privilegium non valet contra rempublicam. [L. **privilegium** privilege (1); **non** not (2); **valet** is valid/effective (3); **contra** against, opposite (4); **rem publicam** the public affair, the state (5): A privilege is not valid against the state.] *Law.* A privilege loses its validity when it is detrimental to the state. See **in casu extremae** etc.

prix fixe *n.* [Fr. **prix** price (2); **fixe** fixed (1): fixed price.] A fixed-price menu.

P.R.N. or **p.r.n.** *abbr.* for **pro re nata** (q.v.).

pro *prep.* [L. for, on behalf of, in favor of, on the side of, for the benefit of, in accordance with, as.] For. In support of. *Though expected to argue pro the proposal, he was unwittingly arguing con it.* —*n., pl.* **pros** 1. The argument, testimony, or evidence favoring or supporting a position, statement, etc. *The policy was adopted after a careful examination of the pros and cons.* 2. The affirmative side or position. The one maintaining the affirmative side or position. *His conversion from pro to neutral and finally to anti paralleled the erosion of his own standing . . . (Newsweek Int.* Jan 18, 1982: 28). —*adj.* Favoring. Supporting. Relating to the affirmative position. *After a careful examination of the pro and con arguments, the proposal was rejected.* —*adv.* Favorably. In favor. *She argued at length, pro and con, and requested members of the panel to decide on the merits of the case.* —*pref.* 1. Championing. Favoring. Supporting. a) *pro-American;* b) *pro-government;* c) *pro-regime;* d) *pro-Soviet.* 2. Acting for. Taking the place of. a) *pro-Chancellor;* b) *pro-consul;* c) *propraetor.* Cf. **con.**

Pro Archia [L. **pro** for, on behalf of, in accordance with, as (1); **Archia** Archias (2): on behalf of Archias.] *For Archias,* a defense speech for Licinius Archias in 62 B.C. by Marcus Tullius Cicero (106–43 B.C.).

pro aris et focis [L. **pro** for, on behalf of, in favor of, on the side of, for the benefit of, in accordance with, as (1); **aris** altars (2); **et** and (3); **focis** hearths (4): for altars and hearths.] For one's religion and for one's home.

probandi necessitas incumbit illi qui agit. [L. **probandi** of proving (2); **necessitas** compulsion, urgency, necessity (1); **incumbit** falls on, rests on (3); **illi** that (one) (4); **qui** who (5); **agit** sues (6): The compulsion of proving lies on that one who sues.] *Law.* The burden of proof lies upon the person who brings a suit (i.e., the plaintiff or prosecutor). See **actori incumbit** etc.

probatio mortua *n.* [L. **probatio** proof (2); **mortua** dead (1): dead proof.] *Law.* Proving with the aid of inanimate articles such as written evidence.

probationes debent esse evidentes, id est, perspicuae et faciles intelligi. [L. **probationes** proofs (1); **debent** ought, should (2); **esse** to be (3); **evidentes** manifest, clear, evident (4); **id** that (5); **est** is (6) **perspicuae** clear (7); **et** and (8); **faciles** easy (9); **intelligi** to be understood (10): Proofs ought to be evident, that is, clear and easy to be understood.] *Law.* Proofs should be evident, that is, clear and easily understandable.

probatio plena *n.* [L **probatio** proof (2); **plena** full (1): full proof.] *Civil Law.* Full proof; i.e., proof provided by two or more witnesses or an official instrument. See **violenta praesumptio** etc.

probatio semiplena or **semiplena probatio** *n.* [L. **probatio** proof (2); **semiplena** half-full (1): half-full proof.] *Civil Law.* Half or inadequate proof; i.e., proof provided by a single witness or an unofficial instrument.

probatio viva *n.* [L. **probatio** proof (2); **viva** living (1): living proof.] *Law.* Proof provided orally by living witnesses.

probatis extremis, praesumuntur media. See **extremis probatis, praesumuntur media.**

probatum *n., pl.* **probata** [L. something proved.] Something which has been proved.

probitas laudatur et alget. Juvenal (c.60–117 A.D.). *Satires* I,74. [L. **probitas** honesty, probity (1); **laudatur** is praised, commended (2); **et** and (3); **alget** feels cold, is left out in the cold (4): Honesty is praised and left out in the cold.] Honesty is praised but ignored. Cf. **Sans argent l'honneur** etc.

pro bono et malo *adv.* [L. **pro** for, on behalf of, in accordance with, as (1); **bono** good (2); **et** and (3); **malo** evil, bad (4): for good and evil.] For good and ill. *Before a man and a woman contract a conjugal bond, they should have no doubt in their minds that they are prepared to cohabit pro bono et malo.*

pro bono publico *adv./adj.* [L. **pro** for, on behalf of, in accordance with, as (1); **bono** good (3); **publico** public (2): for the public good.] In the interest of the state. For the good of all. *Despite the considerable hardships created by the government's austere economic measures, the populace has accepted them in the belief that they are pro bono publico.*

probus et legalis homo *n., pl.* **probi et legales homines** [L. **probus** good, upright (1); **et** and (2); **legalis** lawful (3); **homo** person, human being (4): a good and lawful person.] *Law.* A good and law-abiding human being. Particularly applicable to a person who is deemed competent both morally and legally to serve on juries or as a witness. Cf. **homo legalis.**

procedendo *n., pl.* **procedendos** [L. by proceeding.] *Law.* 1. Action in which a court of superior jurisdiction orders a lower court to proceed to judgment. 2. A writ issuing from a superior court to an inferior court in which the former directs the latter to take action on certain matters; e.g., a case sent back after it was removed from the inferior court on inadequate grounds.

proceres *pl. n.* [L. noblemen, nobles, the leading men.] Nobles. Lords. Applicable to such bodies as Britain's House of Lords.

processus *n., pl.* **processus** [L. movement, course, process, advance, progress.] Operation. Functioning. Working. *If it were possible to know the processus of another person's mind, perfidy would almost completely be wiped out.*

procès-verbal *n., pl.* **procès-verbaux** [Fr. report, proceedings, minutes, statement of facts.] 1. An official, authenticated written record of proceedings, showing the details of what was said and done. 2. *Law.* A written record of facts presented in a legal action, the procedures adopted, and what the judge did. 3. *International Law.* A written record of negotiations held by representatives of countries. 4. The minutes or written record of the proceedings of an organization.

prochein ami or **prochein amy** or **prochain amy** *n.* [Obs. Fr. **prochein** next (1); **ami** friend (2): next friend.] *Law.* A person who, though not a regularly appointed guardian, brings an action on behalf of a person who is not **sui juris** (q.v.), such as a child or married woman.

pro confesso *adv./adj.* [L. **pro** for, on behalf of, in accordance with, as (1); **confesso** confessed (2): as confessed.] *Law.* Considered as true since it has not been denied. As though admitted. *The defendant was asked to appear in court and answer the allegation, otherwise judgment would be taken pro confesso.*

proconsul *n., pl.* **proconsuls** [L. **pro** on behalf of, for (1); **consul** consul (2): on behalf of the consul.] 1. *Ancient Rome.* An official who, on the expiration of his term of office as a consul, serves as a governor or military commander of a province. 2. *Modern Times.* A governor or extraordinary administrator of a colony, dependency, or occupied territory.

procureur *n., pl.* **procureurs** [Fr. agent, attorney, proxy, procurator.] *French Law.* An attorney, agent, representative, or prosecutor in a lawcourt.

Procureur de la République *n., pl.* **Procureurs de la République** [Fr. **procureur** attorney (1); **de** of (2); **la** the (3); **république** republic (4): Attorney of the Republic.] *French Law.* Public prosecutor who is entrusted with the responsibility of initiating criminal proceedings.

pro def. *abbr.* for **pro defendente** (q.v.).

pro defectu emptorum *adv.* [L. **pro** for, on behalf of, in accordance with, as (1); **defectu** want, lack (2); **emptorum** of buyers (3): for want of buyers.] Due to lack of buyers.

pro defectu exitus *adv.* [L. **pro** for, on behalf of, in accordance with, as (1); **defectu** want, lack (2); **exitus** of issue, result (3): for want of issue.] Due to lack of issue.

pro defectu heredis *adv.* [L. **pro** for, on behalf of, in accordance with, as (1); **defectu** want, lack (2); **heredis** of heir (3): for want of an heir.] Due to lack of an heir.

pro defectu justitiae *adv.* [L. **pro** for, on behalf of, in accordance with, as (1); **defectu** want, lack (2); **justitiae** of justice (3): for want of justice.] Due to lack of justice.

pro defendente *abbr.* **pro def.** *adj.* [L. **pro** for, on behalf of, in accordance with, as (1); **defendente** the one defending (2): for the one defending.] *Law.* For the defendant. *Counsel pro defendente argued with such brilliance, erudition and force that the plaintiff's case was dismissed.* Cf. **pro querente.**

prodigi interdictio *n.* [L. **prodigi** of wasteful, lavish (person) (2); **interdictio** prohibiting, forbidding (1): a prohibiting of a wasteful person.] *Roman Law.* Interdicting a spendthrift, particularly one who wastes property inherited from an intestate, from dealing with his/her own or the inherited property. A feature of Roman law rejected by English law but adopted by some modern systems, especially French law. See **curator prodigi.**

prodigue *n., pl.* **prodigues** [Fr. waster, spendthrift, prodigal.] *French Law.* A spendthrift. A person who wastes his/her property and is consequently deemed

incapable of managing his/her property and should, therefore, be given a **conseil judiciaire** (q.v.) for controlling and administering his/her property. See **curator prodigi.**

prodigus *n., pl.* **prodigi** [L. prodigal, lavish, wasteful.] *Roman Law.* A spendthrift or a prodigal. A person who squanders money to such an extent that he/she cannot manage his/her personal affairs and needs the services of a guardian.

pro domino *adv.* [L. **pro** for, on behalf of, in accordance with, as (1); **domino** master, lord, owner (2): as owner.] In the capacity of an owner.

pro eadem causa *adv.* [L. **pro** for, on behalf of, in accordance with, as (1); **eadem** the same (2); **causa** cause, case, reason (3): for the same reason.] On account of the same cause.

pro emptore *adv.* [L. **pro** for, on behalf of, in accordance with, as (1); **emptore** buyer, purchaser (2): as a buyer.] As the purchaser.

pro et contra *adv.* [L. **pro** for, on behalf of, in favor of, on the side of, for the benefit of, in accordance with, as (1); **et** and (2); **contra** opposite (3): for and against.] On behalf of and in opposition to. *He presented a good paper in which he examined all the issues, pro et contra, and reached an almost irrefutable conclusion.* —**pro et contra** or **pro and contra** *n., pl.* **pros and cons** Argument for and against. *They carefully considered all the pros and cons before making a decision.*

pro facto *adv.* [L. **pro** for, on behalf of, in accordance with, as (1); **facto** deed, act, fact (2): as a fact.] Regarded as a fact. *He has an unscholarly habit of presenting his views, even personal opinions and controversial issues, pro facto.*

profanum vulgus *n.* [L. **profanum** common, ordinary, wicked (1); **vulgus** common people (2): ordinary common people.] The common people. **Hoi polloi** (q.v.).

profecticia dos *n., pl.* **profecticiae dotes** [L. **profecticia** derived from an ancestor (2); **dos** dowry (1): a dowry derived from an ancestor.] *Roman Law.* Profectitious dowry. Dowry derived from an ancestor; i.e., the wife's dowry contributed from the property of her father or paternal grandfather. See **dos.**

proferens *n., pl.* **proferentes** [L. (the one) bringing forth.] *Law.* The initiator of a contract or a term or condition of a contract.

professor emeritus *n., pl.* **professors emeriti** [L. **professor** professor (1); **emeritus** having earned by service (2): professor having earned by service.] A retired professor who still retains his/her position as an honorary title. See **emeritus.**

professor ordinarius *n.* [L. **professor** professor, one who professes (2); **ordinarius** regular, ordinary (1): a regular professor.] A very high-ranking professor in a German university. A professor who occupies a chair, is an authority on his/her subject, and participates in the administration of the university.

profit à prendre or profit a prendre or profit apprendre or profit apprender *n., pl.* profits à prendre or profits a prendre or profits apprendre or profits apprender [Fr. profit profit (1); à to, toward, in, by, with, until (2); prendre to take, seize, grasp (3): profit to take/seize/grasp.] *Law.* The right to take something out of another's land or to take part of the soil. The right includes, inter alia, the right to mine, drill, and log. In the case of mining, the person enjoying the right can enter the land, remove from it whatever is designated, and use as much of the surface as is necessary for taking the product.

pro forma *abbr.* p.f. *adj.* [L. pro for, on behalf of, in accordance with, as (1); forma form (2): in accordance with form.] 1. For the sake of form. As a formality to satisfy legal requirements. *The general principle is that in case of doubt and where words of a contract are in conflict, greater force is to be given to words selected by the parties to express their intent than to general words of a pro forma nature* . . . (Major 1978:11). 2. Relating to or concerning information indicating that goods are ready for shipment. *The businessman received a pro forma invoice on the goods to be shipped by his associates.*

progenitor or *fem.* progenitrix *n., pl.* progenitors or *fem.* progenitrices [L. an ancestor, founder of a family.] 1. A forefather. A lineally direct ancestor. 2. A precursor, predecessor, or originator, i.e., in the academic field, politics, etc.

prognosis *n., pl.* prognoses [Gk. prognōsis: pro before, in front of (2); gnōsis knowing (1): knowing before, foreknowledge, prediction.] 1. Forecast. Prediction. Prognostication. a) . . . *evidence emerges that his prognosis could be mercilessly right* (*The Guardian* 1987). b) *Even that tentative prognosis is welcome news to a once-comfortable little country whose economy has been crumbling for nearly a decade* (*Newsweek Int.* May 4, 1981:28). 2. *Medicine.* Predicting the course of a disease. 3. *Medicine.* The prospect of surviving, or recovering from, a disease based on knowledge of the normal course of the disease or as suggested by peculiar features of that particular case.

pro hac vice *abbr.* p.h.v. *adv.* [L. pro for, on behalf of, in accordance with, as (1); hac this (2); vice part, duty, position (3): for this part or duty.] For this occasion only. *A lawyer who is admitted into a court pro hac vice is allowed to treat only that particular case.* Cf. pro illa vice.

pro herede or pro haerede *adv.* [L. pro for, on behalf of, in accordance with, as (1); herede heir, successor (2): as an heir.] In the capacity of an heir.

prohibetur ne quis faciat in suo quod nocere possit alieno. [L. prohibetur it is forbidden (1); ne that (2); quis one (3); faciat should do (4); in in, on (5); suo one's own, his/her own (6); quod what, (that) which (7); nocere to hurt (9); possit could, may be able (8); alieno another's (10): It is forbidden that

one should do on one's own land what could hurt another's.] *Law.* It is unlawful to do on one's own land what could hurt another's property. See sic utere tuo etc.

pro illa vice *adv.* [L. pro for, on behalf of, in accordance with, as (1); illa that (2); vice part, duty, position (3): for that part or duty.] For that occasion only. For that turn. Cf. pro hac vice.

pro indiviso *adv.* [L. pro for, on behalf of, in accordance with, as (1); indiviso undivided (2): as undivided.] *Law.* As being held in common. *The testator's lands were to be held pro indiviso by his two children.*

pro ipsa rata *adv.* [L. pro for, on behalf of, in accordance with, as (1); ipsa itself (3); rata calculated (2): in accordance with the calculated (part) itself.] In the exact proportion. According to the very calculated factors. *Thus the broker and L/U negotiate the terms of the slip . . . and the slip goes forward to other underwriters as the assured's offer for acceptance pro ipsa rata* (Colinvaux 1979:20).

projet *n., pl.* projets [Fr. scheme, project, design, plan, draft.] 1. *International Law.* The draft of a proposed measure, convention, or treaty. 2. A project or proposed design, especially one which has advanced beyond the stage of a sketch.

pro laesione fidei *adv.* [L. pro for, on behalf of, in accordance with, as (1); laesione injury (2); fidei of faith (3): for injury of faith.] For breach of faith.

pro legato *adv.* [L. pro for, on behalf of, in accordance with, as (1); legato bequest, legacy (2): for a legacy.] As a bequest or legacy.

prolegomenon *n., pl.* prolegomena [Gk. pro before, in front of (2); legomenon that which is spoken (1): that which is spoken before, that foretold.] 1. Introductory remarks or observations, especially an essay or discussion which introduces or explains a work. *The third edition of the book has a very useful and well-written prolegomenon.* 2. Introduction. A reading, lecture, or intellectual discussion preparatory to further knowledge or understanding of a field. *Friedrick August Wolf's Prolegomenon ad Homerum (1795) remains a basic introdution to the Homeric problem.*

prolepsis *n., pl.* prolepses [Gk. prolēpsis: pro before, in front of (2); lēpsis taking hold, seizing (1): seizing before, anticipation.] *Rhetoric.* A not quite appropriate use of a word, especially in expectation of a situation in which the word is appropriate; e.g., "They dug the empty hole."

proletariat *n.* [Fr. prolétariat lowest classes.] The lowest or working-class.

pro majori cautela *adv.* [L. pro for, on behalf of, in accordance with, as (1); majori greater (2); cautela caution (3): for greater caution.] By way of being more cautious. See ad abundantiorem cautelam.

pro memoria *n., pl.* pro memoria [L. pro for, on behalf of, in accordance with, as (1); memoria memory (2): for memory.] *Diplomacy.* A formal note containing a record of diplomatic talks.

promenade *n., pl.* promenades [Fr. a walk, a place to walk.] 1. A walk, usually at a leisurely pace, in a park or other public place. 2. A formal ball or dance. 3. A procession of guests at a formal ball. 4. A counterclockwise, circular movement in a square dance. —*v. intr.* 1. To walk at a leisurely pace in a public place. 2. To make a show as if walking in a public place. *She promenaded around the house clad only in her bathrobe.* Cf. paseo.

Pro Milone *n.* [L. pro for, on behalf of, in favor of, on the side of, for the benefit of, in accordance with, as (1); Milone Milo (2): on behalf of Milo.] *For Milo*, a 52 B.C. speech by Cicero (106–43 B.C.).

promotor fidei *n., pl.* promotores fidei [L. promotor promoter (1); fidei of faith (2): promoter of the faith.] 1. Devil's advocate. 2. *Roman Catholic Church.* An official entrusted with the duty of exposing defects in the evidence adduced in support of the canonization or beatification of a person, or showing that the person is not fit for the honor by reason of his character. See advocatus diaboli. Cf. advocatus dei.

pro non scripto *adv.* [L. pro for, on behalf of, in accordance with, as (1); non not (2); scripto something written (3): as something not written.] As if it had never been written.

pronto *adv.* [Sp./It. prompt, ready, soon.] Promptly. Immediately. At once. Usually used colloquially. *Need we add that the huge debt was paid, pronto?* (*The Guardian* 1988).

pro nunc [L. pro for, on behalf of, in favor of, on the side of, for the benefit of, in accordance with, as (1); nunc now (2): for now.] For the present.

pro-nuncio *n., pl.* pro-nuncios [L. pro for, on behalf of, in favor of, on the side of, for the benefit of, in accordance with, as (1); nuncio nuncio (2): for the nuncio.] A papal representative in a country which does not grant preference or precedence to papal ambassadors. Cf. nuncio.

prooemium *n., pl.* prooemia or prooemiums. [L. from Gk. prooimion: pro before, in front of (2); oim(ē) song (1): song before, an introduction, proem or preface.] A discourse or comment which serves as an introduction to a speech or work.

propaganda *n., pl.* propagandas [L. that which must be spread or propagated.] 1. The Congregatio de propaganda fide, an organization established by Pope Gregory XV and entrusted with the responsibility of supervising missionary activities. 2. Spreading of rumor, ideas, doctrines, etc. with the intention of aiding or hurting a cause, person, organization, etc. *The politician's promise of various amenities was no more than propaganda designed to win the votes of the electorate.* 3. Rumor, allegations, ideas, doctrines, information, facts, etc. deliberately spread to help a person, a cause, etc. or to harm an opponent, the opponent's cause, etc. *Baghdad has also been busy dispensing strident anti-Iranian propaganda in the*

form of radio and TV broadcasts . . . (*Time Int.* 1980). 4. A public action designed to promote one's cause or to damage the cause of an opponent. *Politicians were busy in the villages, distributing worthless gifts, a piece of propaganda which enlightened citizens strongly condemned.* —*attrib.* Characteristic of propaganda. *President Leonid Brezhnev's October speech proclaiming a reduction of Russian forces in East Germany was largely a propaganda ploy* (*Newsweek Int.* Dec. 17, 1979:24).

pro patria [L. pro for, on behalf of, in favor of, on the side of, for the benefit of, in accordance with, as (1); patria country, fatherland (2): for the county.] For one's homeland.

prophylaxis *n., pl.* prophylaxes [Neo-Gk. from Gk. prophulaxis: pro in front, before (2); phulaxis guarding (1): guarding before, advance guard.] *Medicine.* Protective or preventive treatment of disease. Measures designed to promote the preservation of health and prevention of diseases.

propositus *n., pl.* propositi [L. the person proposed, placed before.] 1. The primary person involved in a situation. 2. *Genealogy.* The first person known whose family tree is to be determined.

pro possessore *adv.* [L. pro for, on behalf of, in accordance with, as (1); possessore possessor (2): as a possessor.] As the one in possession.

pro possessore habetur qui dolo injuriave desiit possidere. [L. pro for, on behalf of, in accordance with, as (7); possessore possessor (8); habetur he is had, held, regarded (6); qui (he) who (1); dolo through fraud, guile (4); injuriave or through injury/wrong (5); desiit has ceased, stopped (2); possidere to possess (3): He who has ceased to possess through fraud or injury is regarded as possessor.] *Law.* A person who is deprived of possession through fraud or injury is still deemed to be the possessor. See nemo debet ex etc.

propria persona *abbr.* p.p. *adv.* [L. propria in one's own (1); persona (in) person (2): in one's own person.] *Law.* Personally. Without the assistance of a lawyer or legal representation.

proprio motu See motu proprio.

proprio vigore *adv.* [L. proprio with its own (1); vigore (with) vigor, force (2): with its own force.] By its/their own force. By its/their inherent meaning. *By the lex loci contractus (or celebrationis), every contract is in general to be regulated by the laws of the country in which it is made, which alone are binding proprio vigore on aliens as well as on natural-born citizens or subjects . . .* (Megrah and Ryder 1972:300).

proprium humani ingenii est odisse quem laeseris. Tacitus (c.55 –c.117 A.D.). *Agricola* XLII. [L. proprium characteristic, peculiar (2); humani of human (3); ingenii (of) nature, temperament (4); est it is (1); odisse to hate (5); quem (one) whom (6); laeseris you have hurt (7): It is characteristic of human nature to hate the one whom you have hurt.] It is a special feature of humankind to hate the person whom you have injured.

pro privato commodo adv. [L. **pro** for, on behalf of, in accordance with, as (1); **privato** private (2); **commodo** advantage, convenience (3): for private advantage.] On behalf of personal advantage or gain. *Some politicians behave as though they have the interest of the nation at heart, but anybody with discerning mind and eyes can easily see that in whatever they do, they act pro privato commodo.*

propter aequitatis rationem adv. [L. **propter** on account of, by reason of (1); **aequitatis** of equity, fairness (3); **rationem** consideration, principle (2): on account of consideration of equity.] *Law.* Considering the principles of equity.

propter affectum adv. [L. **propter** on account of, by reason of (1); **affectum** disposition, mood, affection (2): on account of disposition.] On account of partiality or affection. Applicable to a kind of challenge. *His membership in the investigating panel was challenged propter affectum.*

propter defectum adv. [L. **propter** on account of, by reason of (1); **defectum** defect (2): on account of a defect.] Because of a defect. Applicable to a kind of challenge. *His nomination as a juror was challenged propter defectum.*

propter defectum sanguinis adv. [L. **propter** on account of, by reason of (1); **defectum** defect, lack (2); **sanguinis** of blood (3): on account of defect/lack of blood.] For lack of a qualified heir. *The deceased man's estate was taken over by the state propter defectum sanguinis.*

propter delictum adv. [L. **propter** on account of, by reason of (1); **delictum** crime (2): on account of a crime.] Because of conviction for a crime. Applicable to a kind of challenge. *He was nominated as Minister by the President, but he was disqualified because of public scrutiny propter delictum.*

propter honoris respectum adv. [L. **propter** on account of, by reason of (1); **honoris** of rank, office (3); **respectum** respect, consideration (2): on account of respect for rank.] By reason of respect for the office. Applicable to a kind of challenge. *The judge declined the offer to serve as chairman of the "Association of Hoodlums" propter honoris respectum.*

propter odium et atiam adv. [L. **propter** on account of, by reason of (1); **odium** hatred, ill-will (2); **et** and (3); **atiam** hatred, ill-will (4): on account of hatred and ill-will.] Because of animosity and bad feelings. Cf. **de odio et atia**.

propter privilegium adv. [L. **propter** on account of, by reason of (1); **privilegium** privilege (2): on account of privilege.] Because of privilege. Applicable to an exclusive right to hunt and kill wild animals in parks or preserves.

pro querente abbr. **pro quer.** adj. [L. **pro** for, on behalf of, in accordance with, as (1); **querente** the one complaining (2): for the one complaining.] For the plaintiff. *Counsel pro querente contributed not a little to the dismissal of the plaintiff's suit.* Cf. **pro defendente**.

pro rata or **pro rata parte** abbr. **p.r.** adv. [L. **pro** for, on behalf of, in accordance with, as (1); **rata** calculated (2); **parte** part (3): in accordance with the calculated part.] Proportionately. *If "A," "B," "C," and "D" form a company and they are to share a profit of $10,000.00, each of them would receive 25%. But if their respective contributions—investment, duration of participation, etc.—varied, such factors would be taken into consideration in the sharing of the profit. Thus, in a case in 1826, a jury was directed that a clerk employed by the year but apparently paid at intervals within the year could recover salary pro rata down to the time of dismissal if he had been wrongfully dismissed* (Freedland 1976:129). —*adj.* Divided, shared proportionally. Pro rata sharing of profits.

pro re nata abbr. **P.R.N.** or **p.r.n.** adv./adj. [L. **pro** for, on behalf of, in accordance with, as (1); **re** matter, thing, property, business, affair (2); **nata** born (3): according to the matter born.] According to the circumstances of the matter. As and when the occasion arises. *The chief executive of the institution does not operate according to laid down policies, but he takes decisions and implements them pro re nata.*

Pro Roscio n. [L. **pro** for, on behalf of, in favor of, on the side of, for the benefit of, in accordance with, as (1); **Roscio** Roscius (2): on behalf of Roscio.] *For Roscius,* a 80/79 B.C. speech by Cicero (106–43 B.C.).

pro salute animae adv. [L. **pro** for, on behalf of, in accordance with, as (1); **salute** the good, safety (2); **animae** of soul (3): for the safety of the soul.] *Christianity.* For the good/safety of the soul. The purpose of prosecutions in ecclesiastical courts.

prosateur n., pl. **prosateurs** [Fr. prose writer.] A writer of prose.

proscenium n., pl. **proscenia** or **prosceniums** [L. **pro** for, on behalf of, in favor of, on the side of, for the benefit of, in accordance with, as (1); **scenium** scene (2): in front of the scene.] 1. *Greek and Roman Theater.* The area between the orchestra and the backwall of the theater; i.e., the stage. 2. *Modern Theater.* The area between the curtain and the area where the audience is located.

pro se adv. [L. **pro** for, on behalf of, in accordance with, as (1); **se** oneself (2): on behalf of oneself.] In person. For oneself. Personally. *Law.* Applicable to a person who appears in court for himself/herself and does not use the services of a lawyer. See **inops consilii** and **in propria persona**.

prosit adv. [L. **prosit** May it be helpful.] A wish for good health and prosperity, especially in German-speaking areas. Cf. **mazel tov**, **salute**, and **skoal**.

proskunesis or **proskynesis** n. [Gk. **proskunēsis: pros** to, towards, in addition to (2); **kune(ō)** to kiss (1):

kissing towards, prostrating oneself before, adoration, obeisance.] Prostration. Obeisance. Greeting by throwing oneself on the ground. *Among certain ethnic groups in Africa, it is the customary practice for young men to greet elders by performing proskynesis.*

pro socio *adj./adv.* [L. **pro** for, on behalf of, in accordance with, as (1); **socio** partner, associate (2): for an associate.] *Law.* On behalf of a partner. Applicable to an action instituted on behalf of an associate.

pro solido *adv.* [L. **pro** for, on behalf of, in accordance with, as (1); **solido** whole, complete, entire (thing) (2): as a whole/complete thing.] As an entity. As one. Jointly.

prosopopoeia *n., pl.* **prosopopoeias** [Gk. **prosopopoiia**: **prosopon** face, mask, character (1); **poi(eō)** make (2): character making, the putting of speeches into the mouth of characters, the putting of speeches into another's mouth.] 1. *Rhetoric.* A figure of speech in which a person who is absent is portrayed as making a speech or a deceased person is represented as being alive. 2. Personification.

prospectus *n., pl.* **prospectus** [L. **pro** for, on behalf of, in favor of, on the side of, for the benefit of, in accordance with, as (2); **spect(o)** look for, see (1): a looking for, an outlook.] A pamphlet, brochure, or other document describing a proposed or forthcoming project, course of study, etc.

prosthesis *n., pl.* **prostheses** [Gk. **pros** to, towards, in addition to (2); **thesis** placing (1): placing in addition, an addition, application.] 1. *Linguistics.* The addition of a letter, syllable, or sound to a word, especially in the form of a prefix; e.g., "beloved" from "loved." 2. *Medicine.* Inserting an artificial part into the body to replace one that is missing or damaged. The artificial part which is inserted or is to be inserted. *After exposing the ends of Mrs. Thomas's spine, Edwards and his team started to install the prosthesis* (*Newsweek Int.* Sept. 17, 1979:41).

pro tanto *adv.* [L. **pro** for, on behalf of, in accordance with, as (1); **tanto** so much, only so much (2): for so much.] For only so much. Used in respect of partial payment.

protasis *n., pl.* **protases** [Gk. **pro** before, in front of (2); **tasis** stretching, extension (1): stretching before, that which is put forward.] 1. The earlier part of a dramatic or narrative poem. 2. *Logic.* A proposition, especially the premise of a syllogism. 3. *Rhetoric.* The antecedent, subordinate, hypothetical, or "if" clause of a conditional sentence; e.g., "If my father had given me the money, . . ." See **hypothesis** 3. Cf. **apodosis**.

protégé or *fem.* **protégée** *n., pl.* **protégés** or *fem.* **protégées** [Fr. a ward, favorite, protected person, dependent.] 1. A person who is helped or protected in his/her career by an influential person such as a patron, or sponsor. A pupil. a) *Senghor left his post voluntarily and the transfer of power to his protégé*

and successor, Prime Minister Abdou Diouf, was peaceful . . . (Newsweek Int.* Jan 12, 1981:55). b) *While the metropolitan jobs were given to protégés whom it was intended to favor, the colonial jobs were most often granted to protégés of a different kind, namely those whom somebody wished to get out of the way* (Suret-Canale 1971:317). 2. A person living in one country, but protected juridically by another country; e.g., a colonist.

pro tempore *abbr.* **pro tem.** or **p.t.** *adj./adv.* [L. **pro** for, on behalf of, in accordance with, as (1); **tempore** time (2): for a time.] For the time being. Occupying an acting position. *Before his departure for the conference, Seidu appointed Ugo as pro tempore head of the department.*

Proteus *n., pl.* **Proteuses** [L. from Gk.] 1. *Greek and Roman Mythology.* A minor sea-god, who was capable of assuming different shapes, but, if held tenaciously, would revert to his true shape and answer questions. 2. A very versatile person. A person who can undergo endless changes. A person who has a large variety of interests and capabilities. *This comedian is a true Proteus and there is hardly anybody whose mannerisms he cannot imitate.*

prothalamium (L.) or **prothalamion** (Neo-Gk.) *n., pl.* **prothalamia** [L. **pro** before, in front of, in addition to (1); **thalam(os)** chamber, bed chamber, bridal chamber (2): before the bridal chamber, a bridal song.] A song or poem for celebrating a marriage. See **epithalamium**.

pro timore mortis *adv.* [L. **pro** for, on behalf of, in accordance with, as (1); **timore** fear (2); **mortis** of death (3): for fear of death.] Because of fear of death.

pro uno delicto *adv.* [L. **pro** for, on behalf of, in accordance with, as (1); **uno** one (2); **delicto** offense (3): for one offense.] *Law.* For the same offense.

provenance *n., pl.* **provenances** [Fr. origin, source, place of production.] Source. Place of origin. Derivation. *There is hardly a Yoruba state which does not trace its provenance to Ile-Ife.*

proviso *n., pl.* **provisoes** or **provisos** [L. with the precaution taken, with it provided.] *Law.* A clause or article which introduces a limitation or exception in contracts, deeds, leases, mortgages, etc. *The accused person was granted bail with the proviso that he should report to the police charge office every day.*

proxeneta *n., pl.* **proxenetae** [L. from Gk. **proxēnētes**: **pro** for, on behalf of, in accordance with as (1); **xen(os)** stranger (2): on behalf of a stranger, one who acts on behalf of another.] *Civil Law.* A broker. A person who negotiates the terms of a contract on behalf of parties.

proxénète *n., pl.* **proxénètes** [Fr. from Gk. **proxenetēs**.] A pimp. A procurer. A sexual go-between. Cf. **souteneur**.

proximo *abbr.* **prox.** *adj.* [L. in the next (month).] Scheduled for the next month. *The 12th meeting of* the association will be held on the 15th proximo. Cf. **ultimo.**

P. S. *abbr.* for **postscriptum** (q.v.).

pseudepigrapha *pl. n.* [Gk. **pseud(ēs)** false (1), **epi** upon, in addition (3); **graph(ō)** write (2): things written with (something) false written upon (them), things with false title or superscription.] Spurious books, especially those supposedly written by characters of the Bible.

psyche *n., pl.* **psyches** [Gk. **psukhē** ghost, soul, the conscious self or personality, spirit.] 1. The spirit, soul, personality or self. The spiritual or mental element which combines with the body to form a human being or an animal. 2. *Psychology.* The mind or mentality. A combination of the ego, id, and superego, including the conscious aspects of the mind. a) *Having bequeathed to our younger ones this brutalised psyche, we should be getting ready for killers more bestial than Jack the Ripper . . . (The Guardian* 1986). b) *. . . the hobgoblins that lurk somewhere beneath the polished surface of the French psyche (Newsweek Int.* Oct. 20, 1980:11). Cf. **pneuma.**

psychosis *n., pl.* **psychoses** [Gk. **psukhōsis** giving life or soul to somebody/something, animating, quickening.] 1. A serious mental disorganization in which the patient, unable to cope with the demands of his/her environment, loses contact with reality in his/her behavior, feeling, and thinking. 2. A severe mental disorder either of an individual or a group, particularly during situations of momentous significance. *"The government is attempting to create a war psychosis," said a young worker . . . (Newsweek Int.* Jan 4, 1982:10).

psychosoma *n., pl.* **psychosomas** [Gk. **psukhosōma**: **psukh(ē)** soul (1); **sōma** body (2): soul-body.] The mind and body functioning together as a unit.

P. T. *abbr.* for 1. **Paschale Tempore** (q.v.). 2. **pro tempore** (q.v.).

publici juris *adj.* [L. **publici** of public (1); **juris** (of) right, law (2): of public right.] *Law.* Belonging to the public. The expression is used to describe things, such as light, public streets, public water, and air, which are common property, and can thus be used by everybody. It is also used for a copyright which has expired. Cf. **res communes** and **res publicae.**

publicum jus or **jus publicum** *n.* [L. **publicum** public (1); **jus** right, law (2): public law.] *Law.* 1. Public law, i.e., the law relating to government, public functionaries, the constitution, etc. 2. Public right. Common property.

p.u.c. *abbr.* for **post urbem conditam** (q.v.).

pudendum *n., pl.* **pudenda** Used more often in the *pl.* than *sing.* [L. something shameful, disgraceful or abominable.] The external genital organs or private parts of both the male and female, especially the latter. Cf. **mons veneris** and **muliebria.**

puerpera *n., pl.* **puerperae** [L. a woman in labor.] A woman who is in childbirth or has just given birth to a child.

pug *n.* [Hindi **pag**.] A track or trail, especially of footprints or paw prints.

puisne *adj.* [Obs. Fr. **puis** afterwards (2); **né** born (1): born afterwards.] 1. Subordinate. Junior. 2. *Law.* Associate. *The head of the Family Division is the President who is assisted by about 17 puisne judges* (Newton 1983:36). 3. *Law.* Later. Belonging to a later date or time. —*n., pl.* **puisnes** 1. A person who is subordinate or junior. 2. *Law.* A puisne or associate judge.

puissance *n., pl.* **puissances** [Fr. power, strength, authority, force.] Ability to control, influence, or sway. *The electorate should show more awareness of their puissance and not allow themselves to be used by unscrupulous politicians.*

puissant *adj.* [Fr. powerful.] Strong. Influential. *The success of Bayo's career is mainly attributable to the assistance of his puissant uncle.*

pukka or **pucka** *adj.* [Hindi **pakkā** cooked, ripe.] 1. Real. Genuine. 2. First-class.

pulchrum dicitur id quod visum placet. [L. **pulchrum** pretty, beautiful (thing) (6); **dicitur** is said (5); **id** that (1); **quod** which (2); **visum** having been seen (3); **placet** is pleasing (4): That which, having been seen, is pleasing, is said (to be) a beautiful (thing).] Something which is pleasing to look at is said to be a pretty thing.

punctum indifferens *n.* [L. **punctum** point (1); **indifferens** not differing, neither good nor bad (2): a point neither good nor bad.] A neutral or impartial point.

punctum temporis. *n.* [L. **punctum** point (1); **temporis** of time (2): a point of time.] The smallest portion of time. An instant. A moment.

pundit *n.* [Hindi **pandit** from Skt. **panditás** scholar.] 1. A person of great learning or knowledge. 2. An opinionated source, especially in the media. *The pundits were all predicting the resignation of the President.* Cf. **pandit.**

punica fide *adv.* [L. **punica** with Punic, Carthaginian (1); **fide** (with) trust, faith (2): with Punic faith.] With characteristic (or typical) Punic treachery. Romans regarded Carthaginians as very treacherous people. *The friendship between Amos and Noah persisted until the latter, acting punica fide, betrayed the former.*

punica fides *n.* [L. **punica** Punic, Carthaginian (1); **fides** trust, faith (2): Punic trust.] Characteristic (or typical) Punic treachery. See **punica fide.**

pur autre vie *adv./adj.* [Obs. Fr. **pur** for (1); **autre** other, another (2); **vie** life (3): for another life.] *Law.* During the lifetime of another person. Applicable to tenancy of an estate, which depends not on the lifetime of the tenant but of another person. See **autre vie.**

purdah or **pardah** *n., pl.* **purdahs** or **pardahs** [Urdu **pardah** screen, curtain, veil.] A practice prevalent among Muslim and Hindu communities, which involves the seclusion of women by keeping them at the residence behind walls and screens, and by their wearing of clothes, especially veils, which cover almost the entire body. *His colleagues have never met his wife, since she lives in purdah.*

puris omnia pura [L. **puris** for pure, clean (people) (3); **omnia** all things, everything (1); **pura** pure, clean (2): all things pure for pure people.] Everything pure for those who are pure.

purpureus pannus *n., pl.* **purpurei panni** Horace (65–8 B.C.). *Ars Poetica* 14–15. [L. **purpureus** purple, purple-colored (1); **pannus** patch, rag (2): a purple patch or passage.] A literary passage which is conspicuously splendid or brilliant in a work which is generally uninspiring or dull.

pur terme d'autre vie *adj./adv.* [Obs. Fr. **pur** for (1); **terme** term (2); **d'** of (3); **autre** other, another (4); **vie** life (5): for the term of another life.] *Law.* During the lifetime of another person. Until the demise of another person. Applicable to tenancy of an estate, which depends not on the lifetime of the tenant but that of another person. See **autre vie.**

purusha *n.* [Skt. humankind.] 1. *Hindu Mythology.* The sacrificial victim used by the gods in the creation of the world. 2. *Hinduism.* The world soul. The living consciousness of the material world.

putsch or **Putsch** *n., pl.* **Putsche** or **putsches** [Ger. **Putsch** insurrection.] A secretly planned insurrection. Removal, usually secretly planned, sudden or violent, of political opponents, a government, or governmental body. . . . *Suslov was the mind behind the putsch that replaced Nikita Krushchev . . . with the Neo-Stalinist Brezhnev* (*Newsweek Int.* Feb. 8, 1982:53). See **coup d'état** and **Machtübernahme.**

putto *n., pl.* **putti** [It. boy.] *Art.* The figure of a naked or semi-clothed child, sometimes winged, to represent a Greco-Roman cupid or a Christian angel.

p.v. *abbr.* for **per vaginam** (q.v.).

pxt. *abbr.* for **pinxit** (q.v.).

pyromania *n.* [Neo-Gk. from Gk. **pur** fire (2); **mania** madness, enthusiasm (1): madness/enthusiasm for fire.] *Psychology.* Uncontrollable impulse to cause arson.

pyrophobia *n.* [Neo-Gk. from Gk. **pur** fire (2); **phob(os)** fear (1): fear of fire.] *Psychology.* Abnormal fear of fire.

Q

Q. or q. *abbr.* for 1. quaere (q.v.). 2. quasi (q.v.).

Q.C.F. *abbr.* for quare clausum fregit (q.v.).

Q.D. or q.d. *abbr.* for 1. quaque die (q.v.). 2. quasi dicat (q.v.). 3. quasi dictum (q.v.). 4. quater die (q.v.).

Q.E. or q.e. *abbr.* for quod est (q.v.).

Q.E.D. *abbr.* for quod erat demonstrandum (q.v.).

Q.E.F. *abbr.* for quod erat faciendum (q.v.).

Q.E.I. *abbr.* for quod erat inveniendum (q.v.).

Q.E.N. *abbr.* for quare exsecutionem non (q.v.).

Q.H. or q.h. *abbr.* for quaque hora (q.v.).

Q.I.D. or q.i.d. *abbr.* for quater in die (q.v.).

Q.I.P. *abbr.* for quiescat in pace (q.v.).

Q.L. or q.l. *abbr.* for quantum libet (q.v.).

Q.M. or q.m. *abbr.* for quo modo (q.v.).

Q.N. or q.n. *abbr.* for quaque nocte (q.v.).

Q.P. or q.p. *abbr.* for quantum placet (q.v.).

qq.v. *abbr.* for quae vide (q.v.).

Q.S. or q.s. *abbr.* for quantum sufficit (q.v.).

Q.T. *abbr.* for qui tam (q.v.).

qu. *abbr.* for quasi (q.v.).

qua *prep.* [L. by/in which.] In the role or character of. As. a) *Mr. Nwachukwu qua principal of the school ordered that all fees should be paid within a week.* b) *No legal practitioner qua legal practitioner was allowed to appear before a "native" court, although provision was made for the representation of a litigant by a duly authorised relative* (Adewoye 1977:140).

quadrennium or quadriennium *n., pl.* quadrennia or quadrenniums or quadriennia or quadrienniums [L. from quattuor four (1) and annus year (2): a four-year period.] 1. A period of four years. 2. *Civil Law.* A course of four years in legal studies which served as prerequisite for a course on the Code of Imperial Constitutions. Cf. biennium.

quadrivium *n.* [L. quattuor four (1); vi(a) road, way (2): four roads, a place where four roads meet, an intersection.] *Medieval Europe.* The course of study

in the liberal arts following the trivium (q.v.), i.e., arithmetic, geometry, astronomy, and music.

quae ab hostibus capiuntur, statim capientium fiunt. [L. quae (those things) which (1); ab from, by (3); hostibus enemies (4); capiuntur are captured, seized (2); statim immediately (5); capientium of the capturing (persons) (7); fiunt become (6): Those things which are captured from enemies immediately become of the capturing persons.] *International Law.* Things captured from the enemy immediately become the property of the captors.

quae ab initio non valent, ex post facto convalescere non possunt. [L. quae (those things) which (1); ab from, by (4); initio beginning (5); non not (2); valent are valid (3); ex out of, from, directly after, away from (9); postfacto (something) done afterwards (10); convalescere to become valid, grow strong (8); non not (7); possunt can, are able (6): Those things which are not valid from the beginning cannot become valid from something done afterwards.] *Law.* Things which are not valid right from the beginning cannot gain retrospective validity. See quod ab initio etc.

quae accessionum locum obtinent extinguuntur cum principales res peremptae fuerint. [L. quae (those things) which (1); accessionum of additions, accessories (4); locum place (3); obtinent occupy, keep (2); extinguuntur are annulled, extinguished (5); cum when (6); principales original, principal (7); res matters, things, property, business, affairs (8); peremptae fuerint have been extinguished, annihilated (9): Those things which occupy the place of accessories are extinguished when the principal things have been extinguished.] *Law.* Accessories are extinguished when their principals are extinguished. See accessorium non ducit etc.

quae cohaerent personae a persona separari nequeunt. [L. quae (those things) which (1); cohaerent cohere, cling to (2); personae to person

---

323

(3); **a** from (6); **persona** person (7); **separari** to be separated (5); **nequeunt** are unable, cannot (4): Those things which cling to a person are unable to be separated from the person.] *Law.* Things which cohere to the person cannot be separated from that person. Cf. **cuicunque aliquis** etc.

quae contra rationem juris introducta sunt, non debent trahi in consequentiam. [L. **quae** (those things) which (1); **contra** against, opposite (3); **rationem** rule, reason (4); **juris** of right, law (5); **introducta sunt** have been introduced (2); **non** not (7); **debent** ought, should (6); **trahi** to be drawn (8); **in** into, to, against, for (9); **consequentiam** consequence (10): Those things which have been introduced against the rule of law ought not to be drawn to consequence.] *Law.* Decisions which are contrary to a rule of law should not be regarded as valid precedents.

quae dubitationis causa tollendae inseruntur communem legem non laedunt. [L. **quae** (those things) which (1); **dubitationis** of doubt (4); **causa** for the sake of (3); **tollendae** (of) that must be removed (5); **inseruntur** are inserted, introduced (2); **communem** common (8); **legem** law (9); **non** not (6); **laedunt** hurt, violate (7): Those things which are inserted for the sake of doubt that must be removed do not hurt the common law.] *Law.* Insertions that are made to remove doubt do not hurt the common law. See **quae dubitationis tollendae** etc.

quae dubitationis tollendae causa contractibus inseruntur, jus commune non laedunt. [L. **quae** (those things) which (1); **dubitationis** of doubt (5); **tollendae** (of) to be removed (6); **causa** for the sake (4); **contractibus** (in) contracts (3); **inseruntur** are inserted, implanted (2); **jus** right, law (10); **communem** common, general (9); **non** not (7); **laedunt** hurt, harm (8): Those things which are inserted in contracts for the sake of doubt to be removed do not hurt the common law.] *Law.* Clauses inserted in contracts for the avoidance of doubt do not hurt the common law. See **quae dubitationis causa** etc.

quae est eadem [L. **quae** which (1); **est** is (2); **eadem** the same (3): which is the same.] That which is the same. **Que est le mesme** (q.v.).

quae in testamento ita sunt scripta ut intelligi non possint, perinde sunt ac si scripta non essent. [L. **quae** (those things) which (1); **in** in, on (4); **testamento** will (5); **ita** in such a way (6); **sunt** have been (2); **scripta** written (3); **ut** that (7); **intelligi** to be understood (10); **non** not (9); **possint** they can, are able (8); **perinde** just (12); **sunt** are (11); **ac** as (13); **si** if (14); **scripta** written (17); **essent** they had been (16); **non** not (15): Those things which have been written in a will in such a way that they cannot be understood are just as if they had not been written.] *Law.* Things which have been written in a will in such a way that they cannot be understood are considered not to have been written at all.

quaelibet concessio fortissime contra donatorem interpretanda est. [L. **quaelibet** all, any whatsoever (1); **concessio** grant, concession (2); **fortissime** most strongly (5); **contra** against, opposite (6); **donatorem** grantor, donor (7); **interpretanda** to be interpreted (4); **est** is (3): Any grant whatsoever is to be interpreted most strongly against the grantor.] *Law.* Every grant must be interpreted as strongly as possible against the grantor. See **ambigua responsio** etc.; **ambiguum pactum** etc.; **ambiguum placitum** etc.; **benigne faciendae sunt** etc.; **concessio versus** etc.; **contra proferentem**; **contra proferentes**; **in stipulationibus** etc.; and **obscuritas pacti** etc.

quaelibet jurisdictio cancellos suos habet. [L. **quaelibet** any whatsoever, all (1); **jurisdictio** jurisdiction (2); **cancellos** limits, boundaries (5); **suos** its own (4); **habet** has, holds, regards (3): Any jurisdiction whatsoever has its own boundaries.] *Law.* Every jurisdiction has its limits. See **extra territorium jus** etc.

quaelibet poena corporalis, quamvis minima, major est qualibet poena pecuniaria. [L. **quaelibet** any whatsoever, all (1); **poena** punishment (3); **corporalis**; corporal (2); **quamvis** however, however much (4); **minima** least, very small (5); **major** greater, bigger (7); **est** is (6); **qualibet** than any whatsoever, all (8); **poena** punishment (10); **pecuniaria** monetary, pecuniary (9): Any corporal punishment whatsoever, however very small, is greater than any monetary punishment whatsoever.] *Law.* Corporal punishment, no matter how small, is more serious than any fine.

quae mala sunt inchoata in principio vix bono peraguntur exitu. [L. **quae** (those things) which (1); **mala** bad (3); **sunt inchoata** were begun, started (2); **in** in, on (4); **principio** beginning, principle, origin (5); **vix** scarcely, hardly (6); **bono** with good (8); **peraguntur** are carried out, accomplished (7); **exitu** (with) result, end (9): Things which were started bad in the beginning scarcely are accomplished with good result.] *Law.* Things which at the outset were bad scarcely end on a good note. See **quod ab initio** etc.

quae nocent docent. [L. **quae** (those things) which (1); **nocent** harm, hurt (2); **docent** teach (3): Those things which hurt teach.] Harmful things teach. Cf. **pathei mathos**.

quae praeter consuetudinem et morem majorum fiunt neque placent neque recta videntur. [L. **quae** (those things) which (1); **praeter** contrary to, against (3); **consuetudinem** custom, usage (4); **et** and (5); **morem** custom, usage (6); **majorum** of ancestors (7); **fiunt** are done (2); **neque** neither (8); **placent** please, are approved (9); **neque** nor (10); **recta** right, proper (12); **videntur** seem, are deemed (11): Those things which are done contrary to the custom and usage of the ancestors are neither approved nor deemed proper.] Things done contrary to ancestral custom and practice are neither approved nor considered proper.

quae propter necessitatem recepta sunt, non debent in argumentum trahi. [L. **quae** (those things) which (1); **propter** on account of, by reason of (3); **necessitatem** compulsion, urgency, necessity (4); **recepta sunt** were allowed, admitted (2); **non** not (6); **debent** ought, should (5); **in** into, to, against, for (8); **argumentum** argument, reasoning, inference (9); **trahi** to be dragged, drawn (7): Those things which were admitted on account of compulsion ought not to be drawn into reasoning.] *Law.* Things which were allowed on account of necessity should not be questioned. See **necessitas quod** etc.

quaere *n., pl.* **quaeres** [L. ask, seek for.] A query. A question. Used to indicate that what follows or what it refers to is questionable. *Quaere, whether the modern paterfamilias can exercise the absolute powers of his ancient Roman counterpart.*

quaerens See **querens.**

quae rerum natura prohibentur nulla lege confirmata sunt. [L. **quae** (those things) which (1); **rerum** of matters, things, property, business, affairs (4); **natura** by nature (3); **prohibentur** are forbidden, prohibited (2); **nulla** by no (7); **lege** (by) law (8); **confirmata** reinforced, confirmed (6); **sunt** are, have been (5): Those things which are forbidden by the nature of things have been confirmed by no law.] *Law.* Things which are forbidden by the nature of things have not been supported by any law; i.e., human law is consistent with natural law.

quaere verum [L. **quaere** seek (1); **verum** true (thing) (2): Seek the true thing.] Seek the truth.

quaesitum *n., pl.* **quaesita** [L. thing sought for.] An end. A goal. An objective. *There can be no doubt that the quaesitum of most people is a healthy and prosperous life.*

quaestio *n., pl.* **quaestiones** [L. question, inquiry, questioning, investigation.] 1. *Roman Law.* A commission set up to handle the investigation and trial of crimes. Criminal court. 2. *Medieval Law.* Inquisition by torture.

quaestio vexata or **vexata quaestio** *n., pl.* **quaestiones vexatae** or **vexatae quaestiones** [L. **quaestio** question (2); **vexata** vexed, disturbed (1): a vexed question.] A mooted point. A question often discussed but not yet settled. *This is a quaestio vexata and there is no point in discussing it, particularly when no new evidence is available.*

quae vide *pl.* of **quod vide** (q.v.).

quamdiu se bene gesserit *adv.* [L. **quamdiu** as long as (1); **se** himself/herself (3); **bene** well (4); **gesserit** he/she will have behaved, comported (2): as long as he/she will have behaved/comported himself/herself well.] *Law.* During good conduct. A condition attached to letters patent or certain appointments, indicating that they are to continue as long as there is no abuse. Cf. **dum bene** etc. and **durante beneplacito.**

quamvis aliquid per se non sit malum, tamen, si sit mali exempli, non est faciendum. [L. **quamvis**

although (1); **aliquid** something (2); **per** by (3); **se** itself (4); **non** not (6); **sit** may be, is (5); **malum** bad, evil (7); **tamen** nevertheless (8); **si** if (9); **sit** it be, it is (10); **mali** of bad, evil (11); **exempli** (of) example (12); **non** not (14); **est** it is (13); **faciendum** to be done (15): Although something by itself may not be bad, nevertheless, if it is of bad example, it is not to be done.] *Law.* Although something may not be inherently bad, nevertheless, if it sets a bad example, it must not be done. See **quando aliquid per se** etc. and **quod alias bonum** etc.

quando abest provisio partis, adest provisio legis. [L. **quando** when (1); **abest** is absent (4); **provisio** provision (2); **partis** of party (3); **adest** is present (7); **provisio** provision (5); **legis** of law (6): When the provision of a party is absent, provision of law is present.] *Law.* In the absence of any provision by the party, the provision of the law is available.

quando aliquid mandatur, mandatur et omne per quod pervenitur ad illud. [L. **quando** when (1); **aliquid** something, anything (2); **mandatur** is ordered, commanded (3); **mandatur** is ordered, commanded (10); **et** also (11); **omne** everything (4); **per** through, by (5); **quod** which (6); **pervenitur** it is reached, arrived (7); **ad** to, at, for, according to (8); **illud** that (thing) (9): When something is ordered, everything by which it is arrived at that thing is also ordered.] *Law.* When an order is given, every means by which the object is attained is also ordered.

quando aliquid per se non sit malum, tamen si sit mali exempli, non est faciendum. [L. **quando** when (1); **aliquid** something, anything (2); **per** by, through (3); **se** itself (4); **non** not (6); **sit** is (5); **malum** bad, evil (7); **tamen** nevertheless, but yet (8); **si** if (9); **sit** it be (10); **mali** of bad (11); **exempli** (of) example (12); **non** not (13); **est** it is (14); **faciendum** to be done (15): When something by itself is not bad, but yet if it be of bad example, it is not to be done.] *Law.* Even if something by itself is not bad, but it sets a bad example, it should not be done. See **quamvis aliquid per se** etc. and **quod alias bonum** etc.

quando aliquid prohibetur ex directo, prohibetur et per obliquum. [L. **quando** when (1); **aliquid** something, anything (2); **prohibetur** is forbidden, prohibited (3); **ex** out of, from, directly after, away from (4); **directo** the direct (5); **prohibetur** it is forbidden, prohibited (6); **et** also (7); **per** through, by (8); **obliquum** the oblique, indirect (9): When something is forbidden from the direct, it is also forbidden through the indirect.] *Law.* When something is forbidden directly, it is also forbidden indirectly. See **nemo potest facere per obliquum** etc.

quando aliquid prohibetur fieri, prohibetur ex directo et per obliquum. [L. **quando** when (1); **aliquid** something, anything (2); **prohibetur** is forbidden (3); **fieri** to be done (4); **prohibetur** it is forbidden (5); **ex** out of, from, directly after, away from (6); **directo** direct

(7); **et** and (8); **per** through (9); **obliquum** oblique, indirect (10): When something is forbidden to be done, it is forbidden from the direct and through the indirect.] *Law.* When something is forbidden, it is forbidden both directly and indirectly. See **nemo potest facere per obliquum** etc.

quando aliquid prohibetur, prohibetur et omne per quod devenitur ad illud. [L. **quando** when (1); **aliquid** something, anything (2); **prohibetur** is forbidden, prohibited (3); **prohibetur** is forbidden, prohibited (10); **et** also (11); **omne** every (thing) (4); **per** through, by (5); **quod** which (6); **devenitur** there is an arriving (7); **ad** to, at, for, according to (8); **illud** that (thing) (9): When something is forbidden, everything through which there is an arriving at that thing is also forbidden.] *Law.* When something is forbidden, everything by which it is accomplished is also forbidden.

quando charta continet generalem clausulam, posteaque descendit ad verba specialia quae clausulae generali sunt consentanea, interpretanda est charta secundum verba specialia. [L. **quando** when (1); **charta** writing, deed (2); **continet** contains, comprises (3); **generalem** general, generic (4); **clausulam** clause (5); **posteaque** and afterwards (6); **descendit** descends (7); **ad** to, at, for, according to (8); **verba** words (10); **specialia** special (9); **quae** which (11); **clausulae** clause (15); **generali** with general (14); **sunt** are (12); **consentanea** consistent, agreeing (13); **interpretanda** to be interpreted (18); **est** is (17); **charta** writing, deed (16); **secundum** in accordance with, according to (19); **verba** words (21); **specialia** special (20): When a deed contains a generic clause and afterwards descends to special words which agree with the general clause, the deed is to be interpreted according to the special words.] *Law.* When a deed contains generic language and afterwards proceeds to special language which is consistent with the generic language, the deed must be interpreted in accordance with the specialized language. See **generale dictum generaliter est intelligendum.**

quando duo jura concurrunt in una persona, aequum est ac si essent in diversis. [L. **quando** when (1); **duo** two (2); **jura** rights, laws (3); **concurrunt** concur, meet (4); **in** in (5); **una** one (6); **persona** person (7); **aequum** just, like (9); **est** it is (8); **ac** as (10); **si** if (11); **essent** they were (12); **in** in, on (13); **diversis** different, diverse (persons) (14): When two rights meet in one person, it is just as if they were in different (persons).] *Law.* When two rights concur in a single person, it is just as if they were vested in different persons.

quando lex aliquid alicui concedit, concedere videtur et id sine quo res ipsa esse non potest. [L. **quando** when (1); **lex** law (2); **aliquid** something, anything (4); **alicui** to someone, anyone (5); **concedit** gives, grants (3); **concedere** to grant, give (7); **videtur** it

seems (6); **et** also (8); **id** that (9); **sine** without (10); **quo** which (11); **res** matter, thing, property, business, affair (12); **ipsa** itself (13); **esse** to be, exist (16); **non** not (15); **potest** can, is able (14): When the law grants something to anyone, it seems to grant also that without which the thing itself cannot exist.] *Law.* When the law gives something to a person, it is implied that the law also gives whatever is needed for the grant itself to exist. See **cuicunque aliquis** etc.

quando lex est specialis, ratio autem generalis, generaliter lex est intelligenda. [L. **quando** when (1); **lex** law (2); **est** is (3); **specialis** special (4); **ratio** reason, motive (6); **autem** but, however (5); **generalis** general (7); **generaliter** generally (11); **lex** law (8); **est** is (9); **intelligenda** to be understood (10): When a law is special, but its motive general, the law is to be understood generally.] *Law.* When a law is special but its motive is general, the law must be interpreted generally. See **generale dictum generaliter est intelligendum.**

quando licet id quod majus, videtur et licere id quod minus. [L. **quando** when (1); **licet** is allowed, permitted (5); **id** that (2); **quod** which (3); **majus** greater (4); **videtur** seems, is deemed (9); **et** also (10); **licere** to be allowed, permitted (11); **id** that (6); **quod** which (7); **minus** less (8): When that which (is) greater is allowed, that which (is) less is also deemed to be allowed.] *Law.* When the greater is permitted, the less is also deemed to be permitted. See **majus continet minus.**

quando plus fit quam fieri debet, videtur etiam illud fieri quod faciendum est. [L. **quando** when (1); **plus** more (2); **fit** is done (3); **quam** than (4); **fieri** to be done (6); **debet** ought, should (5); **videtur** it seems (9); **etiam** also (8); **illud** that (7); **fieri** to be done (10); **quod** which (11); **faciendum** to be done (13); **est** is (12): When more is done than ought to be done, that also seems to be done which is to be done.] *Law.* When a person does more than he/she should do, he/she is deemed to have done also what he/she must do. In such a case, what the person must do remains valid, but the excess becomes null and void. Thus, if a person who has power to lease property for six years should lease it for twelve years, the lease for six years remains, in equity, valid. See **majus continet minus.**

quando verba et mens congruunt, non est interpretationi locus. [L. **quando** when (1); **verba** words (2); **et** and (3); **mens** mind, intention, purpose (4); **congruunt** agree, coincide (5); **non** not (7); **est** there is (6); **interpretationi** for interpretation (9); **locus** room, place (8): When words and intention agree, there is not room for interpretation.] *Law.* When there is an agreement between words and intention, no interpretation is necessary.

quando verba statuti sunt specialia, ratio autem generalis, generaliter statutum est intelligendum. [L. **quando** when (1); **verba** words (2); **statuti** of statute (3); **sunt** are (4); **specialia** special (5); **ratio** reason, motive (7); **autem** but, however (6); **generalis** general (8); **generaliter** generally (12); **statutum** statute (9); **est** is (10); **intelligendum** to be understood (11): When the words of a statute are special but its reason is general, the statute is to be understood generally.] *Law.* When the words of a statute are special, but its motive general, the statute must be interpreted generally. See **generale dictum generaliter est intelligendum**.

quant. suff. *abbr.* for **quantum sufficit** (q.v.).

quantum *n., pl.* **quanta** [L. how much, how far, as much as.] 1. Amount. Portion. Due share. a) *The headmaster's attitude is guided by his strong conviction that even in the most incorrigible child there is a quantum of goodness.* b) *The court pegged the quantum of damages at $10,000 in favor of the plaintiff.* 2. Aggregate. Bulk. Totality. *The plight of ordinary workers has reached such an alarming point that unless the quantum of the general standard of living is improved, a catastrophe will be inevitable.* —*attrib.* Characteristic of quantum. Rapid, significant, abrupt, etc. a) *quantum evolution*; b) *quantum mechanics*; c) *Though the dispute between the factions has not been settled, there has clearly been a quantum leap towards mutual understanding.*

quantum damnificatus *n.* [L. **quantum** how much/far (1); **damnificatus** wronged, harmed (2): how much wronged/damnified.] *Law.* An issue referred to a court of law by a court of equity with instructions to establish the compensation to be awarded for damages.

quantum libet *abbr.* **Q.L.** or **q.l.** *adv.* [L. **quantum** as much as (1); **libet** it pleases, it is pleasing/agreeable (2): as much as it is pleasing.] As much as you please.

quantum meruit *n.* [L. **quantum** as much as, so much as (1); **meruit** he/she deserved, was entitled to (2): so much as he/she deserved.] *Law.* As much as he/she deserves or is entitled to. A count in a suit brought for **pro rata** (q.v.) remuneration in respect of a contract which, for one reason or another, was not completed. a) *Jidda and Company brought a suit on a quantum meruit in connection with a contract for building a shopping center which was rewarded when the work was almost completed.* b) *If it is the employer who brings the work to an end prematurely, the contractor can sue for damages or on a quantum meruit* (Lewis 1976:62). Cf. **quantum valebant**.

quantum placet *abbr.* **Q.P.** or **q.p.** *adv.* [L. **quantum** as much as, so much as (1); **placet** it pleases (2): as much as it pleases.] As much as you please. At one's discretion. See **quantum vis**.

quantum suff. *abbr.* for **quantum sufficit** (q.v.).

quantum sufficit *abbr.* **Q.S.** or **q.s.** or **quant. suff.** or **quantum suff.** *adv.* [L. **quantum** as much as (1); **sufficit** it suffices (2): as much as suffices.] As much as is needed. *The office attendant was asked to go to the storeroom and take legal stationery, quantum sufficit.*

quantum valebant *n.* [L. **quantum** as much as, so much as (1); **valebant** they were worth (2): so much as they were worth.] *Law.* To the extent of their worth. A count in a legal action brought, for instance, to claim payment for the value of goods delivered, when the supplier did not deliver the actual goods specified in the contract, but different goods, and the purchaser does not reject the goods supplied. Cf. **quantum meruit**.

quantum vis *abbr.* **Q.V.** or **q.v.** *adv.* [L. **quantum** as much as, so much as (1); **vis** you wish, will (2): as much as you wish.] As much as you want. See **quantum placet**.

quaque die *abbr.* **Q.D.** or **q.d.** *adv.* [L. **quaque** in/on every, each (1); **die** (on) day (2): on every day.] Every day. *Medicine.* Each day.

quaque hora *abbr.* **Q.H.** or **q.h.** *adv.* [L. **quaque** in/on every, each (1); **hora** (in) hour (2): in every hour.] *Medicine.* Every hour. Each hour.

quaque nocte *abbr.* **Q.N.** or **q.n.** [L. **quaque** in/on every, each (1); **nocte** (in) night (2): in every night.] *Medicine.* Every night. Each night.

quare clausum fregit *abbr.* **Q.C.F.** *n.* [L. **quare** wherefore (1); **clausum** the enclosure (3); **fregit** he broke (2): wherefore he broke the enclosure.] *Law.* Wherefore he broke the close or property barrier. A writ for the recovery of damages in respect of trespass to lands.

quare executionem non *abbr.* **Q.E.N.** [L. **quare** wherefore, why (1); **executionem** execution (2); **non** not (3): wherefore execution not.] *Law.* Wherefore there should be no execution; i.e., the action should not be carried out.

quasi *abbr.* **qu.** *adv.* [L. just as if, as if, as though, almost.] As if. As it were. Almost. In some sense. a) *A quasi-judicial organization*; b) *quasi-legislative functions.* —*adj.* Resembling. Virtual. Somewhat like. *Law.* Used to indicate that, although two things are inherently different, they resemble each other. a) *quasi corporation*; b) *quasi government*.

quasi dicat *abbr.* **Q.D.** or **q.d.** [L. **quasi** as if (1); **dicat** he/she should say (2): as if one should say.] As if one were to say.

quasi dictum *abbr.* **Q.D.** or **q.d.** [L. **quasi** as if (1); **dictum** said (2): as if said.] As if it were said.

quasi ex contractu *adv./adj.* [L. **quasi** as if (1); **ex** out of, from, directly after, away from (2); **contractu** drawing together, shrinking, contract, agreement (3): as if from a contract.] *Law.* As if it were taken from a contract.

quasi in rem *adv./adj.* [L. **quasi** as if (1); **in** against (2); **rem** matter, thing, property, business, affair (3): as if against the thing.] *Law.* As if it were against a thing.

quasi-traditio *n.* [L. **quasi** as if (1); **traditio** handing over, delivery (2): as if handing over.] *Civil Law.* As if it were delivery. Seeming delivery. Used in a case where a person uses the property of another without objection or a person in possession of property is granted the right to it.

quatenus *adv.* [L. as far as, to the distance that.] In the capacity of. In the quality of. As.

quater die *abbr.* **Q.D.** or **q.d.** *adv.* [L. **quater** four times (1); **die** in a day (2): four times in a day.] Four times a day. See **quater in die**.

quater in die *abbr.* **Q.I.D.** or **q.i.d.** *adv.* [L. **quater** four times (1); **in** in, on (2); **die** a day (3): four times in a day.] Four times a day. See **quater die**.

quatrocento *n.* [It. **quatro** four (1); **cento** hundred (2): the four hundreds.] The 1400s. The 15th century. Used especially in reference to Italian history, literature, and art. Cf. **cinquecento**; **seicento**; and **trecento**.

quatuor pedibus currit. See **currit quatuor pedibus**.

quattuorvir *n., pl.* **quattuorviri** or **quattuorvirs** [L. **quattuor** four (1); **viri** men (2): four men, one of a body of four.] A member of a ruling body of four. Cf. **decemvir**.

Que bello horizonte! *interj.* [Sp. **que** what (1); **bello** beautiful (2); **horizonte** horizon (3): What a beautiful horizon!] How beautiful the horizon is! *Before the service, John Paul squinted into the crowd and then glanced at the mountains that ring the city. "Que bello horizonte," he sighed* (*Newsweek Int.* July 14, 1980:37).

que est le mesme [Obs. Fr. **que** which (1); **est** is (2); **le** the (3); **mesme** same (4): which is the same.] *Law.* That which is the same thing. **Quae est eadem** (q.v.). Used in actions of trespass and others to allege that what is said in the plea and the declaration are the same.

Quel dommage! *interj.* [Fr. **quel** what (1); **dommage** harm, injury, damage (2): What harm!] What a pity! What a shame! Too bad. Often used ironically. *"Poor Hubert," sighs one female acquaintance. "He was always so polite." Quel dommage* (*Newsweek Int.* Aug. 9, 1982:18).

Quelle horreur! *interj.* [Fr. **quelle** what (1); **horreur** horror, shocking or dreadful thing (2): What horror!] Disgusting! How shocking! Often used ironically. *And now highflying Hubert and stony Stefania are locked up in jail. Quelle horreur!* (*Newsweek Int.* Aug. 9, 1982:17).

Quellenforschung *n., pl.* **Quellenforschungen** [Ger. **Quelle** origin, source (1); **Forschung** research (2): origin research, research about origins or sources.] Investigation or examination of sources, i.e., of literary works, etc.

Quellenkritik *n.* [Ger. **Quelle** origin, source (1); **Kritik** criticism (2): origin criticism, criticism about sources or origins.] Source-criticism. Critical examination of sources, i.e., of literary works, etc. *In this age of Quellenkritik, a historian should not only mention the names of his sources but also show awareness of their relative worth.*

quemadmodum ad quaestionem facti non respondent judices, ita ad quaestionem juris non respondent juratores. [L. **quemadmodum** in the way that, just as (1); **ad** to, at, for, according to (5); **quaestionem** question, inquiry (6); **facti** of fact (7); **non** not (3); **respondent** respond, answer (4); **judices** judges (2); **ita** so (8); **ad** to, at, for, according to (12); **quaestionem** question, inquiry (13); **juris** of right, law (14); **non** not (10); **respondent** respond, answer (11); **juratores** jurors (9): In the way that judges do not respond to a question of fact, so jurors do not respond to a question of law.] *Law.* Just as judges do not answer to a question of fact, so jurors do not answer to a question of law. See **ad quaestionem facti** etc.

quem Deus vult perdere, prius dementat. or elliptically **quem Deus vult perdere . . .** [L. **quem** (One) whom (1); **Deus** God (2); **vult** wishes, wants (3); **perdere** to destroy, ruin (4); **prius** first, before (6); **dementat** he makes mad (5): (One) whom God wants to destroy, He first makes mad.] The person God wishes to destroy is first made insane. Cf. **quem Juppiter vult perdere** etc. and **stultum facit fortuna** etc.

quem di diligunt / adulescens moritur. Plautus (254–184 B.C.). *Bacchides* I,817. [L. **quem** (one) whom (1); **di** gods (2); **diligunt** love, esteem (3); **adulescens** a youth, young, youthful (5); **moritur** dies (4): (One) whom the gods love / dies a youth.] The person the gods love dies young.

quem Juppiter vult perdere dementat prius. James Duport (1606–1679). *Homeri Gnomologia* 282. [L. **quem** (one) whom (1); **Juppiter** Jupiter (2); **vult** wishes, wants (3); **perdere** to destroy, ruin (4); **dementat** he makes mad (5); **prius** first, before (6): The one whom Jupiter wants to destroy, he first makes mad.] The person Jupiter wants to destroy he first makes insane. Cf. **quem Deus vult** etc. and **stultum facit Fortuna** etc.

querela *n., pl.* **querelae** [L. accusation, complaint.] *Law.* An action in a court of justice.

querela inofficiosi testamenti *n.* [L. **querela** complaint, action (1); **inofficiosi** of undutiful (2); **testamenti** (of) will (3): complaint of undutiful will.] *Civil Law.* Legal action about a will which violates natural affection; e.g., a suit brought by a disinherited child. Such legal action is based upon the assumption that the testator was not in his/her right mind. See **donatio inofficiosa**.

querens *n.* [L. one complaining/lamenting.] *Law.* A complainant. A plaintiff. Sometimes incorrectly spelled **quaerens**.

questionnaire *n., pl.* **questionnaires** [Fr. a list of questions.] A list of questions asked in a survey, usually in writing, in order to collect statistical data.

qui acquirit sibi acquirit heredibus. [L. **qui** (one) who (1); **acquirit** acquires, gains (2); **sibi** for oneself (3); **acquirit** acquires, gains (4); **heredibus** for heirs, successors (5): (One) who acquires for oneself acquires for heirs.] *Law*. One who gains property for oneself gains it for one's heirs.

qui aliquid statuerit, parte inaudita altera, aequum licet dixerit, haud aequum fecerit. [L. **qui** (one) who (1); **aliquid** something (3); **statuerit** will have decided (2); **parte** (with) side (5); **inaudita** (with) unheard (6); **altera** with one of two (4); **aequum** impartial, fair (thing) (9); **licet** although, notwithstanding (7); **dixerit** he /she spoke, pronounced (8); **haud** not, by no means (11); **aequum** impartial fair (thing) (12); **fecerit** he will have done (10): (One) who will have decided something, with one of two sides unheard, although he/she pronounced an impartial thing, will not have done an impartial thing.] *Law*. Whoever decides on a matter without listening to the two sides, has done injustice, even if his/her decision was just. See **audi partem alteram.**

quia timet *n*. [L. **quia** because (1); **timet** he fears (2): because he is afraid.] *Law*. A bill filed in cases of equity by a party, requesting the assistance of a court because of his/her apprehension of a future possible violation of his/her interests or rights. a) *If no wrong has been committed, but is merely threatened, a quia timet injunction may be asked for, but in these circumstances an injunction will be granted only where there is extreme probability of irreparable injury* (Lewis 1976:118). b) *The existence of the court's power to grant a quia timet injunction is undoubted, but it is not often exercised, for the plaintiff must show both a near certainty that damage will occur and that it is imminent* (Rogers 1975:58–59).

qui cito dat bis dat. [L. **qui** (one) who (1); **cito** quickly, speedily (3); **dat** gives (2); **bis** twice (5); **dat** gives (4): (One) who gives quickly gives twice.] A person who gives hastily gives two times. See **beneficium inopi** etc.

qui concedit aliquid, concedere videtur et id sine quo concessio est irrita, sine quo res ipsa esse non potuit. [L. **qui** (one) who (1); **concedit** grants (2); **aliquid** something (3); **concedere** to grant, concede (5); **videtur** seems, is deemed (4); **et** also (6); **id** that (7); **sine** without (8); **quo** which (9); **concessio** grant, concession (10); **est** is (11); **irrita** useless, invalid (12); **sine** without (13); **quo** which (14); **res** matter, thing, property, business, affair (15); **ipsa** itself (16); **esse** to be, exist (19); **non** not (18); **potuit** could, was able (17): (One) who grants something is deemed to grant also that without which the grant is useless, that without which the thing itself was not able to exist.] *Law*. A person who concedes something is considered also to have conceded that without which the concession is useless, that without which the thing itself could not exist. See **cuicunque aliquis** etc.

qui concedit aliquid concedit omne id sine quo concessio est irrita. [L. **qui** (one) who (1); **concedit** grants (2); **aliquid** something, anything (3); **concedit** grants (4); **omne** all, every (thing) (5); **id** that (6);

sine without (7); **quo** which (8); **concessio** concession, grant (9); **est** is (10); **irrita** useless, invalid (11): (One) who grants something grants all that without which the grant is useless.] *Law*. A person who concedes something concedes everything without which the concession is of no use. See **cuicunque aliquis** etc.

qui contemnit praeceptum contemnit praecipientem. [L. **qui** (one) who (1); **contemnit** despises (2); **praeceptum** order, command (3); **contemnit** despises (4); **praecipientem** the one ordering (5): (One) who despises an order despises the one ordering it.] *Law*. The person who disobeys an order, disobeys the one who ordered it.

quicquid acquiritur servo acquiritur domino. [L. **quicquid** whatsoever, whatever (1); **acquiritur** is acquired (2); **servo** for a servant (3); **acquiritur** is acquired (4); **domino** for a master (5): Whatsoever is acquired for a slave is acquired for a master.] *Law*. Whatever comes into the possession of a slave or an agent becomes the possession of the slave's master or the agent's principal. **accessorium non ducit** etc.

quicquid in excessu actum est, lege prohibetur. [L. **quicquid** whatsoever, whatever (1); **in** in, on (3); **excessu** excess (4); **actum est** has been done (2); **lege** by law (6); **prohibetur** is prohibited, forbidden (5): Whatsoever has been done in excess is prohibited by law.] *Law*. Whatever has been done in excess is forbidden by law. See **aurea mediocritas.**

quicquid judicis auctoritati subjicitur novitati non subjicitur. [L. **quicquid** whatsoever, whatever (1); **judicis** of judge (4); **auctoritati** authority, decision (3); **subjicitur** is placed under, subjected to (2); **novitati** newness, novelty (7); **non** not (5); **subjicitur** is placed under, subjected to (6): Whatever is placed under the authority of a judge, is not subjected to newness.] *Law*. Whatever is brought for a judge's decision is not subjected to innovation. See **pendente lite nihil innovetur.**

quicquid plantatur solo, solo cedit. [L. **quicquid** whatever, whatsoever (1); **plantatur** is planted, affixed (2); **solo** to ground, soil (3); **solo** to ground, soil (5); **cedit** accrues (4): Whatever is affixed to the soil accrues to the soil.] *Law*. Whatever is affixed to the soil belongs to it. Though the rule is generally valid, its severity is reduced by equity. Thus, if a person, sincerely believing that he has absolute title to land, erects a building on it, with the rightful owner not only being aware of the development of the land but also taking no steps to stop the erection of the building, the rightful owner can be compelled by a court of equity to compensate the person for his expenditure on the development of the land. *Equity has followed law, step by step, in relaxing in favor of tenants against landlords the severity of the rule quicquid plantatur solo, solo cedit* (Hanbury 1962:439). See **aedificatum solo** etc.; **aedificia solo cedunt; omne quod** etc.; **quod aedificatur in area** etc.; **quod**

solo inaedificatur etc.; **solo cedit quod solo implantatur; solo cedit quod solo inaedificatur; superficies; and superficies solo cedit.**

qui cum alio contrahit, vel est, vel debet esse, non ignarus conditionis ejus. [L. **qui** (one) who (1); **cum** with (3); **alio** another (4); **contrahit** contracts (2); **vel** either (5); **est** is (6); **vel** or (7); **debet** ought, should (8); **esse** to be (9); **non** not (10); **ignarus** ignorant, unacquainted with (11); **conditionis** of condition (13); **ejus** his/her (12): (One) who contracts with another either is or should be not ignorant of his condition.] *Law.* Someone who makes a contract with another person either is, or should be, aware of the other's condition. Cf. **scire debes cum** etc.

quicumque jussu judicis aliquid fecerit non videtur dolo malo fecisse, quia parere necesse est. [L. **quicumque** whoever, whosoever (1); **jussu** by order (4); **judicis** of judge (5); **aliquid** something (3); **fecerit** will have done (2); **non** not (6); **videtur** seems (7); **dolo** (with) deceit, fraud (10); **malo** with bad (9); **fecisse** to have done (8); **quia** because (11); **parere** to obey (14); **necesse** necessary (13); **est** it is (12): Whoever will have done something by order of a judge does not seem to have done it with bad deceit, because it is necessary to obey.] *Law.* Whoever does something on the order of a judge is not deemed to have acted with evil intent because it is necessary for him/her to obey. See **qui jussu** etc.

quid *n., pl.* **quids** [L. **quid** what.] The quid which is part of the expression **quid pro quo** (q.v.). Something or anything given in reciprocity for, or expectation of, something or anything. *Other noncommunist leaders all over the world are discovering that a Reagan quid does not always require a reciprocal quo* (*Newsweek Int.* Oct. 5, 1981:39).

qui desiderat pacem, praeparet bellum. Vegetius (379–395). *De Rei Militaris* III. [L. **qui** (one) who (1); **desiderat** desires, longs for (2); **pacem** peace (3); **praeparet** let him prepare for (4); **bellum** war (5): (One) who desires peace, let him prepare for war.] Someone who desires peace should prepare for war. See **si vis pacem** etc.

quid non mortalia pectora cogis, / auri sacra fames! Vergil (70–19 B.C.). *Aeneid* III,56–57. [L. **quid** what, in what way (4); **non** not (6); **mortalia** mortal, human (7); **pectora** hearts (8); **cogis** you compel, force (5); **auri** of gold (3); **sacra** accursed, forfeited (1); **fames** hunger, greed (2): Accursed greed of gold, / in what way do you not compel mortal hearts!] Oh accursed greed for gold/money, what compulsion do you not exert on mortal hearts!

quidnunc *n., pl.* **quidnuncs** [L. **quid** what (1); **nunc** now (2): what now?] An inquisitive person, particularly one whose curiosity is centered on petty things. A gossip. A busybody. *Here comes Mr. Knowles, the most notorious quidnunc of the neighborhood.*

qui docet discit. [L. **qui** (one) who (1); **docet** teaches (2); **discit** learns (3): One who teaches learns.] A teacher learns from the act of teaching.

quid pro quo *n., pl.* **quid pro quos** or **quids pro quos** or **quids pro quo** [L. **quid** what (1); **pro** for, on behalf of, in accordance with, as (2); **quo** what (3): what for what.] Something for something. Giving something to receive something else in return. Tit for tat. *Adu is a corrupt official who insists on quid pro quo when transacting business with contractors.* See **do ut des**; **do ut facias; facio ut des; facio ut facias; manus manum lavat; quid;** and **quo.**

quid sit futurum cras fuge quaerere et / quem Fors dierum cumque dabit lucro / appone. Horace (65–8 B.C.). *Odes* I,9,13–15. [L. **quid** what (1); **sit** is (2); **futurum** about to be (3); **cras** tomorrow (4); **fuge** avoid, shun (5); **quaerere** to ask (6); **et** and (7); **quem . . . cumque** whatsoever (8); **Fors** Chance, Luck (10); **dierum** of days (9); **dabit** will give (11); **lucro** for gain (13); **appone** consider, regard, set down as (12): What is about to be tomorrow avoid asking and / whatsoever of days Luck will give set down as gain.] Do not ask what tomorrow will be and count as gain whatever days Fortune will give you.

quid turpi ex causa promissum est non valet. [L. **quid** what (1); **turpi** base, disgraceful (4); **ex** out of, from, directly after, away from (3); **causa** cause, case, reason (5); **promissum est** has been promised, was promised (2); **non** not (6); **valet** is valid (7): What has been promised out of a disgraceful cause is not valid.] *Law.* A promise based on an immoral consideration is not valid. See **ex turpi causa** etc.

quiescat in pace. *abbr.* **Q.I.P.** [L. **quiescat** May he/she rest (1); **in** in, on (2); **pace** peace (3): May he/she rest in peace.] May he/she rest peacefully in death.

quieta non movere *n.* [L. **quieta** calm, undisturbed (things) (3); **non** not (1); **movere** to disturb, move (2): Not to disturb calm things.] Not to disturb a settled/established situation. To leave alone a settled situation. "Let a sleeping dog lie." Let well enough alone. See **res judicata.**

quietus *n., pl.* **quietuses** [L. quiet, undisturbed, acquitted, discharged.] 1. Final and complete discharge from an obligation. *After many years, he has finally obtained a quietus of his debt.* 2. Discharge from life, i.e., death. *Many unfortunate motorists have met their quietus on the Lagos-Ibadan expressway.* 3. Inactivity. *The short quietus of four months has had a telling effect on the boxer.*

qui facit per alium facit per se. [L. **qui** (one) who (1); **facit** does, makes (2); **per** through, by (3); **alium** another (4); **facit** does, makes (5); **per** through, by (6); **se** himself (7): (One) who does something through another does it by himself.] *Law.* Someone who acts through an agent acts by himself. A rule applicable to the rights and liabilities of principals and agents, masters and servants, etc. Thus, if an agent, acting within the scope of his authority, transacts business for his principal, the latter is liable for any damages arising therefrom. *Where . . . the obligation does not involve a personal element, the law permits vicarious performance on the principle that qui facit per alium facit per se . . .* British Waggon Co. v. Lea *(1880)* (Major 1978:179 and 180). See **injuria servi** etc.; **qui mandat** etc.; **qui per alium** etc. and **respondeat superior**. Cf. **in maleficio ratihabitio** etc.; **nemo potest facere per alium** etc.; and **quod per me** etc.

qui in jus dominiumve alterius succedit jure ejus uti debet. [L. **qui** (one) who (1); **in** into, to, against, for (3); **jus** right, law (4); **dominium** ownership, rule, dominion (6); **ve** or domain (5); **alterius** of another (7); **succedit** succeeds (2); **jure** right, law (11); **ejus** his/her (10); **uti** to use, enjoy (9); **debet** ought, should (8): (One) who succeeds to the right or domain of another, ought to enjoy his/her right.] *Law.* A person who inherits the right or property of another should enjoy his/her right; i.e., he/she inherits the assets and liabilities. See **assignatus utitur** etc.

qui in utero est pro jam nato habetur, quoties de ejus commodo quaeritur. [L. **qui** (one) who (1); **in** in, on (3); **utero** belly, womb (4); **est** is (2); **pro** as (6); **jam** already (7); **nato** born (8); **habetur** is had, held, regarded (5); **quoties** as often as (9); **de** of, from, about, for (11); **ejus** his/her (12); **commodo** advantage, benefit (13); **quaeritur** it is asked (10): (One) who is in the belly is regarded as already born as often as it is asked about his advantage.] *Law.* A person who is in the womb is considered as a person already born, whenever a question is raised about his/her benefit. See **en ventre sa mère**.

qui jure suo utitur neminem laedit. [L. **qui** (one) who (1); **jure** right, law (4); **suo** his/her own (3); **utitur** uses, enjoys (2); **neminem** no one, nobody (6); **laedit** hurts, injures, offends (5): (One) who enjoys his/her own right, offends nobody.] *Law.* A person who exercises his/her own right offends nobody. Thus, though "A's" opening of his window disturbs "B's" privacy, "B" cannot sue "A." See **non videtur vim** etc.; **nullus videtur** etc.; and **qui jure suo utitur, nemini** etc.

qui jure suo utitur, nemini facit injuriam. [L. **qui** (one) who (1); **jure** right, law (4); **suo** his/her own (3); **utitur** uses (2); **nemini** nobody, no one (7); **facit** makes, does (5); **injuriam** harm, injury (6): (One) who uses his/her own right, does harm to nobody.] *Law.* Whoever exercises his/her own right, harms no one. See **qui jure suo utitur neminem laedit**.

qui jussu judicis aliquod fecerit non videtur dolo malo fecisse, quia parere necesse est. [L. **qui** (one) who (1); **jussu** by order (4); **judicis** of judge (5); **aliquod** something (3); **fecerit** will have done (2); **non** not (6); **videtur** seems (7); **dolo** (with) contrivance,

guile (10); **malo** with evil (9); **fecisse** to have done (8); **quia** because (11); **parere** to obey (14); **necesse** necessary (13); **est** it is (12): (One) who will have done something by the order of a judge, does not seem to have done it with evil contrivance because it is necessary to obey.] *Law.* Whoever acts in compliance with the order of a judge is deemed not to have acted with wrongful purpose, because it is obligatory for him to obey. The maxim, though valid where a court exercises jurisdiction of a case, is not valid where the court has no jurisdiction. In the latter instance, an officer who executes the order of the court can be sued. See **ejus nulla** etc.; **homicidium ex justitia**; **legitime imperanti** etc.; and **quicumque jussu judicis** etc. Cf. **extra territorium jus** etc.

qui mandat ipse fecisse videtur. [L. **qui** (one) who (1); **mandat** orders, commands (2); **ipse** himself/herself (4); **fecisse** to have done (5); **videtur** seems (3): (One) who orders seems himself/herself to have done it.] *Law.* A person who orders a deed is deemed to have done it himself/herself. See **qui facit per alium** etc.

qui molitur insidias in patriam id facit quod insanus nauta perforans navem in qua vehitur. [L. **qui** (one) who (1); **molitur** undertakes, attempts (2); **insidias** plot (3); **in** against (4); **patriam**; fatherland (5); **id** that (7); **facit** does (6); **quod** which (8); **insanus** mad, insane (9); **nauta** sailor (10); **perforans** perforating (11); **navem** ship (12); **in** in, on (13); **qua** which (14); **vehitur** he/she is carried (15): (One) who undertakes a plot against the fatherland does that which the insane sailor (does), perforating the ship in which he is carried.] A person who plots against his/her fatherland is behaving like the insane sailor who cuts a hole in the ship in which he/she is sailing.

quindecemvir *n., pl.* **quindecemviri** or **quindecemvirs** [L. **quindecem** fifteen (1); **vir** man (2): fifteen man, one of a body of fifteen.] A member of a ruling body of fifteen. Cf. **decemvir**.

qui non habet, ille non dat. [L. **qui** who (2); **non** not (3); **habet** has, holds, regards (4); **ille** that (person) (1); **non** not (5); **dat** gives (6): That person who does not have does not give.] A person does not give what he/she does not have. See **nemo dat qui** etc.

qui non habet in aere, luat in corpore, ne quis peccetur impune. [L. **qui**; (one) who (1); **non** not (2); **habet** has, holds, regards (3); **in** in, on (4); **aere** money, bronze (5); **luat** should pay, suffer (6); **in** in, on (7); **corpore** body (8); **ne** lest, in order that not (9); **quis** anyone (10); **peccetur** offend (11); **impune** with impunity (12): (One) who does not have in money should pay in body, lest anyone offend with impunity.] *Law.* A person who cannot pay a fine should pay the penalty by his/her person so that no one may offend with impunity.

qui non habet potestatem alienandi habet necessitatem retinendi. [L. **qui** (one) who (1); **non** not (2);

habet has, holds, regards (3); **potestatem** power (4); **alienandi** of alienating (5); **habet** has, holds, regards (6); **necessitatem** compulsion, urgency, necessity (7); **retinendi** of retaining (8): (One) who does not have the power of alienating something has the compulsion of retaining it.] *Law.* A person who does not have the power of alienating property is under obligation to retain it. See **nemo dat qui** etc.

qui non improbat, approbat. [L. **qui** (one) who (1); **non** not (2); **improbat** disapproves (3); **approbat** approves (4): (One) who does not disapprove approves.] *Law.* A person who does not disagree agrees. See **agentes et consentientes** etc.; **consensus tollit errorem**; **consentientes et agentes** etc.; **error qui non resistitur** etc.; **fraus est celare fraudem**; **idem est facere** etc.; **in maleficio, ratihabitio** etc.; **longa patientia** etc.; **nemo videtur fraudere** etc.; **non decipitur** etc.; **omnis consensus** etc.; **qui non negat fatetur**; **qui non obstat** etc.; **qui non prohibet** etc.; **qui tacet, consentire videtur**; **qui tacet, consentire videtur, ubi** etc.; **quod quis** etc.; **scienti et volenti** etc.; and **volenti non fit injuria.** Cf. **non consentit** etc.; **culpa caret** etc.; and **non videntur qui** etc.

qui non negat, fatetur. [L. **qui** (one) who (1); **non** not (2); **negat** denies (3); **fatetur** admits, confesses (4): (One) who does not deny admits.] *Law.* A person who does not deny confesses; i.e., failure to deny is equivalent to an admission. See **qui non improbat, approbat.**

qui non obstat quod obstare potest, facere videtur. [L. **qui** (one) who (1); **non** not (2); **obstat** opposes (3); **quod** (that) which (4); **obstare** to oppose, hinder (6); **potest** he can, is able (5); **facere** to do (8); **videtur** seems (7): (One) who does not oppose that which he can oppose seems to do it.] *Law.* A person who does not thwart a deed when it is in his/her power to do so, is deemed to do it. See **qui non improbat, approbat.**

qui non prohibet quod prohibere potest assentire videtur. [L. **qui** (one) who (1); **non** not (2); **prohibet** prevents, forbids (3); **quod** (that) which, what (4); **prohibere** to prevent, forbid (6); **potest** he can, is able (5); **assentire** to assent, approve (8); **videtur** seems (7): (One) who does not prevent that which he can prevent seems to approve.] *Law.* A person who does not prevent what he can prevent is deemed to approve of it. See **qui non improbat approbat.**

quinquennium *n., pl.* **quinquennia** or **quinquenniums** [L. **quinque** five (1); **annus** year (2): a five year period.] Five years. A period of five years. A lustrum. Cf. **biennium**.

quinquevir *n., pl.* **quinqueviri** or **quinquevirs** [L. **quinque** five (1); **vir** man (2): five man, one of a body of five.] A member of ruling body of five. Cf. **decemvir**.

qui parcit nocentibus innocentes punit. [L. **qui** (one) who (1); **parcit** spares (2); **nocentibus** the guilty,

culpable, criminals (3); **innocentes** guiltless, innocent (5); **punit** punishes (4): (One) who spares the guilty punishes the innocent.] *Law.* A person who spares the guilty punishes the guiltless. Cf. **impunitas semper** etc.

qui peccat ebrius, luat sobrius. [L. **qui** (one) who (1); **peccat** offends (2); **ebrius** drunk, intoxicated (3); **luat** should pay, suffer (4); **sobrius** sober, not drunk (5): (One) who offends drunk should pay sober.] *Law.* A person who commits an offense when intoxicated, should pay the penalty when sober.

qui per alium facit, per seipsum facere videtur. [L. **qui** (one) who (1); **per** through, by (3); **alium** another (4); **facit** does, makes (2); **per** by, through (7); **seipsum** himself/herself (8); **facere** to do, make (6); **videtur** seems (5): (One) who does something through another, seems to do it by himself/herself.] *Law.* A person who acts through an agent is deemed to act by himself/herself. See **qui facit per alium** etc.

qui per fraudem agit, frustra agit. [L. **qui** (one) who (1); **per** through, by (3); **fraudem** deceit, guile (4); **agit** acts, performs (2); **frustra** in vain, to no purpose (6); **agit** acts, performs (5): (One) who acts through deceit, acts in vain.] *Law.* A person who acts fraudulently acts in vain. See **ex turpi causa** etc.

qui prior est tempore potior est jure. [L. **qui** (one) who (1); **prior** first (3); **est** is (2); **tempore** in time (4); **potior** superior, preferable (6); **est** is (5); **jure** in right, law (7): (One) who is first in time is superior in right.] *Law.* A person who appears first has a superior claim to a right. See **prior tempore** etc.

qui rationem in omnibus quaerunt rationem subvertunt. [L. **qui** (those) who (1); **rationem** reason (3); **in** in, on (4); **omnibus** all (things) (5); **quaerunt** search for, seek (2); **rationem** reason (7); **subvertunt** subvert (6): (Those) who search for reason in all things subvert reason.] Persons who look for reason in everything subvert reason.

qui sciens solvit indebitum donandi consilio id videtur fecisse. [L. **qui** (one) who (1); **sciens** knowing (2); **solvit** pays (3); **indebitum** not owed, not due (thing) (4); **donandi** of giving, donating (9); **consilio** with the intention (8); **id** that (7); **videtur** seems, is deemed (5); **fecisse** to have done (6): (One) who, knowing, pays a thing not owed seems to have done it with the intention of giving.] *Law.* A person who knowingly pays that which is not owed, is deemed to have done so with the intention of giving a present.

quis custodiet ipsos / custodes? Juvenal (c.60–117 A.D.). *Satires* VI,347. [L. **quis** who (1); **custodiet** will guard (2); **ipsos** themselves (4); **custodes** guards (3): Who will guard / the guards themselves?] Who will watch the guards (to make sure they follow the law)? *In a situation where high-ranking public officers are embezzling huge sums of money, one cannot help but ask "Quis custodiet ipsos custodes?"*

qui semel actionem renuntiaverit amplius repetere non potest. [L. **qui** (one) who (1); **semel** once, at any time (4); **actionem** action (3); **renuntiaverit** will have renounced, given up (2); **amplius** longer (8); **repetere** to sue again (7); **non** not (6); **potest** can, is able (5): (One) who will have given up an action once is not able to sue again longer.] *Law.* A person who renounces an action at any time cannot reintroduce it anymore. See **nolle prosequi.**

qui semel est malus, semper praesumitur esse malus in eodem genere. [L. **qui** (one) who (1); **semel** once, ever, at any time (3); **est** is (2); **malus** criminal, depraved (4); **semper** always (6); **praesumitur** is presumed (5); **esse** to be (7); **malus** criminal, depraved (8); **in** in, on (9); **eodem** the same (10); **genere** kind, class (11): (One) who is once criminal, is always presumed to be criminal in the same class.] *Law.* A person who has ever committed a crime is always presumed to be capable of committing the same kind of crime.

qui sentit commodum sentire debet et onus. [L. **qui** (one) who (1); **sentit** experiences, endures (2); **commodum** advantage (3); **sentire** to experience (5); **debet** ought, should (4); **et** also (7); **onus** burden (6): (One) who experiences advantage should also experience the burden.] *Law.* A person who receives an advantage also ought to receive the burden, responsibility, or cost of this advantage. See **cujus est commodum** etc. and **quod approbo** etc. Cf. **qui sentit onus** etc.; and **secundum naturam est** etc.

qui sentit onus sentire debet et commodum. [L. **qui** (one) who (1); **sentit** experiences (2); **onus** burden (3); **sentire** to experience (5); **debet** ought, should (4); **et** also (7); **commodum** advantage (6): (One) who experiences a burden ought to experience the advantage also.] *Law.* A person who bears the burden also ought to bear the advantage. Cf. **qui sentit commodum** etc.

qui serius solvit, minus solvit. [L. **qui** (one) who (1); **serius** rather late, too late (3); **solvit** pays (2); **minus** less (5); **solvit** pays (4): (One) who pays rather late pays less.] *Law.* A person who pays too late pays less. Cf. **beneficium inopi** etc.

Qui s'excuse s'accuse. [Fr. **qui** (one) who (1); **s'** oneself, himself/herself (3); **excuse** excuses (2); **s'** oneself, himself/herself (5); **accuse** accuses, indicts (4): (One) who excuses oneself accuses oneself.] *Law.* A person who apologizes (or makes excuses) is practically accusing himself/herself. Excuses are a manifestation of a guilty conscience.

quis fallere possit amantem? Vergil (70–19 B.C.). *Aeneid* IV,296. [L. **quis** who (1); **fallere** to deceive (3); **possit** can, is able (2); **amantem** a lover (4): Who is able to deceive a lover?] Who can trick a lover?

quisling *n., pl.* **quislings** [Norw. from Vidkun Quisling (1887–1945), the ruler of Norway under Nazi occupation in World War II.] A traitor who collaborates with an invading enemy and assists in the establishment of a puppet government.

quisquis praesumitur bonus; et semper in dubiis pro reo respondendum. [L. **quisquis** every one, each (1); **praesumitur** is presumed (2); **bonus** good (3); **et** and (4); **semper** always (5); **in** in, on (6); **dubiis** doubts (7); **pro** for, in favor of (9); **reo** the accused, defendant (10); **respondendum** to be decided, answered (8): Every one is presumed good; and always in doubts it is to be decided in favor of the accused.] *Law.* Every one is presumed to be good and, where there is doubt, a decision must always be made in favor of the accused. See **in dubio, pars** etc.

qui tacet, consentire videtur. [L. **qui** (one) who (1); **tacet** is silent, says nothing (2); **consentire** to agree (4); **videtur** seems (3): (One) who says nothing, seems to agree.] *Law.* A person who is silent is deemed to agree; i.e., silence implies consent. See **qui non improbat, approbat.** Cf. **silentio consentum significat.**

qui tacet, consentire videtur, ubi tractatur de ejus commodo. [L. **qui** (one) who (1); **tacet** is silent, says nothing (2); **consentire** to agree (9); **videtur** seems (8); **ubi** when (3); **tractatur** it is being discussed (4); **de** of, from, about, for (5); **ejus** his (6); **commodo** advantage (7): (One) who is silent, when it is being discussed about his advantage, seems to agree.] *Law.* A person who is silent, when his affairs are being discussed, is deemed to agree. See **qui non improbat, approbat.**

qui tacet consentit. [L. **qui** (one) who (1); **tacet** is silent (2); **consentit** consents (3): One who is silent consents.] *Law.* Silence means consent. Cf. **silentio consentum significat.** See **qui non improbat, approbat.**

qui tacet non utique fatetur, sed tamen verum est eum non negare. [L. **qui** (one) who (1); **tacet** is silent, says nothing (2); **non** not (4); **utique** certainly, assuredly (3); **fatetur** confesses, acknowledges (5); **sed** but (6); **tamen** nevertheless, but yet (7); **verum** true (9); **est** it is (8); **eum** that he/she (10); **non** not (12); **negare** denies, to deny (11): (One) who is silent certainly does not confess but nevertheless it is true that he/she does not deny.] *Law.* A person who says nothing certainly does not acknowledge, but nevertheless it is true that he/she does not deny. See **qui non improbat, approbat.**

qui tam *abbr.* **Q.T.** *adj.* [L. **qui** who (1); **tam** as much, as well, in the same degree (2): who as well.] Who as much. —**qui tam action** *Law.* An action which an informer brings as much for himself/herself as for the state. A civil action under statute which provides that part of the penalty should go to the plaintiff, the rest going to the state or an institution.

qui tardius solvit, minus solvit. See **minus solvit, qui tardius solvit.**

qui transtulit sustinet. [L. **qui** (the one) who (1); **transtulit** transferred, transplanted (2); **sustinet** maintains, sustains (3): (The one) who transferred maintains.] He who transferred sustains. Motto of the State of Connecticut.

qui vive *n.* [Fr. **qui** who (1); **vive** lives (2): Who lives? Who goes there?] 1. The challenge of a sentinel. 2. Look-out. Awareness. *It will be difficult to deceive him because he is always on the qui vive.*

quo *n., pl.* **quos** [L. which.] The **quo** which is part of the expression **quid pro quo** (q.v.). Something or anything received in reciprocity for something or anything.

quoad *prep.* [L. as far as, to the extent that.] With respect to. So far as [. . .] in particular is concerned. *The same acts, too, amount to lawful marital intercourse quoad W, but illicit and adulterous copulation quoad H* (Megarry 1973:211).

quoad hoc *adv.* [L. **quoad** as far as, to the extent that (1); **hoc** this (2): as far as this.] As far as concerns this. As to this. *The accused was acquitted of nine of the charges, but with respect to the tenth, he was convicted quoad hoc.*

quoad sacra *adv.* [L. **quoad** as far as, to the extent that (1); **sacra** sacred (things) (2): as far as sacred (things).] As far as sacred things are concerned. For sacred/religious purposes.

quo animo *n.* [L. **quo** with what (1); **animo** (with) mind, intention (2): with what mind/intention.] With what motive. Motive, intention or design. *Members of the investigating committee were urged to consider, first and foremost, the quo animo of the suspect.*

quod ab initio non valet in tractu temporis non convalescit. [L. **quod** (that) which, what (1); **ab** from, by (4); **initio** beginning (5); **non** not (2); **valet** is sound, valid, effective (3); **in** in, on (8); **tractu** course, tract (9); **temporis** of time (10); **non** not (6); **convalescit** gains strength, grows strong (7): That which is not sound from the beginning does not grow strong in the course of time.] *Law.* What is bad from the beginning does not improve in the course of time. For instance, a bad custom will never be acceptable. Also, when a deed is based on an illegal consideration, lapse of time will never remove the illegality. See **quae ab initio** etc.; **quae mala sunt** etc.; and **quod initio** etc.

quod aedificatur in area legata cedit legato. [L. **quod** (that) which, what (1); **aedificatur** is built (2); **in** in, on (3); **area** ground, building-site (4); **legata** bequeathed, left by will (5); **cedit** accrues, belongs (6); **legato** to bequest, legacy (7): What which is built on bequeathed ground belongs to the bequest.] *Law.* What is built on ground bequeathed by will belongs to the legacy. See **quicquid plantatur** etc.

quod alias bonum et justum est, si per vim vel fraudem petatur, malum et injustum efficitur. [L. **quod** (that) which, what (1); **alias** at other times, otherwise (2); **bonum** good (4); **et** and (5); **justum** just (6); **est** is (3); **si** if (7); **per** through, by (9); **vim** force (10); **vel** or (11); **fraudem** fraud, guile (12); **petatur** should be sought (8); **malum** bad (14); **et** and (15); **injustum** unjust (16); **efficitur** is accomplished, made, effected (13): What at other times is good and just, if it should be sought by force or fraud, is made bad and unjust.] *Law.* If what is otherwise good and just should be obtained by force or fraud, it becomes bad and unjust. See **quamvis aliquid per se** etc. and **quando aliquid per se** etc.

quod alias non fuit licitum, necessitas licitum facit. [L. **quod** (that) which, what (1); **alias** otherwise, at other times (4); **non** not (3); **fuit** was (2); **licitum** lawful, permitted (8); **necessitas** compulsion, urgency, necessity (5); **licitum** lawful, permitted (7); **facit** makes (6): (That) which was not lawful at other times compulsion makes lawful.] *Law.* Necessity makes lawful what otherwise was unlawful. See **necessitas quod** etc.

quod approbo non reprobo. [L. **quod** (that) which, what (1); **approbo** I approve (2); **non** not (3); **reprobo** I reject (4): What I approve, I do not reject.] *Law.* I cannot reject what I approve; i.e., you either accept or reject wholly. Thus a legatee cannot accept a will and reject a condition attached to it. See **qui sentit commodum** etc.

quod constat clare non debet verificari. [L. **quod** (that) which, what (1); **constat** is certain, established (2); **clare** clearly (3); **non** not (5); **debet** ought, should (4); **verificari** to be verified (6): (That) which is clearly established ought not to be verified.] *Law.* What is clearly certain does not have to be verified. See **manifesta probatione** etc.

quod constat curiae opere testium non indiget. [L. **quod** (that) which, what (1); **constat** is certain, known (2); **curiae** to court (3); **opere** work (6); **testium** of witnesses (7); **non** not (4); **indiget** needs, requires (5): What is certain to the court does not need the work of witnesses.] *Law.* What is clear to the court does not need the aid of witnesses. See **manifesta probatione** etc.

quod contra legem fit pro infecto habetur. [L. **quod** (that) which, what (1); **contra** against, opposite (3); **legem** law (4); **fit** is done (2); **pro** as (6); **infecto** undone (7); **habetur** is had, held, regarded (5): (That) which is done against the law is held as undone.] Anything done contrary to the law is considered not to have been done.

quodcunque aliquis ob tutelam corporis sui fecerit, jure id fecisse videtur. [L. **quodcunque** whatever (1); **aliquis** anyone (2); **ob** on account of (4); **tutelam** safety (5); **corporis** (of) body (7); **sui** of his/her, one's own (6); **fecerit** will have done (3); **jure** by right, law (11); **id** that, it (10); **fecisse** to have done (9); **videtur** he/she seems (8): Whatever anyone will have done on account of the safety of his/her body, he/she seems to have done it by right.] *Law.* Whatever anyone does to protect himself/herself is deemed to have been done rightly. See **domus sua** etc.

quod di omen avertant. *interj.* Cicero (106–43 B.C.). *Philippic* III,14,35. [L. **quod** which. and this (1); **di**

gods (3); **omen** omen (2); **avertant** may they avert, turn away (4): And this omen may the gods avert.] May God (or the gods) avert this omen! God forbid! See **absit omen**.

quod dubitas, ne feceris. [L. **quod** what (2); **dubitas** you doubt (3); **ne feceris** do not do (1): Do not do what you are in doubt of.] When in doubt, don't do it.

quod enim mavult homo verum esse, id potius credit. Francis Bacon (1561–1626). *Novum Organon* XLIX. [L. **quod** (that) which, what (2); **enim** for (1); **mavult** prefers, chooses (4); **homo** person, human being (3); **verum** true (6); **esse** to be (5); **id** that (7); **potius** rather, more (9); **credit** he/she believes (8): For (that) what a person prefers to be true, that he/she rather believes.] A person rather believes what he/she prefers to be true. Cf. **fere libenter** etc. and **populus vult decipi**.

quod erat demonstrandum *abbr.* **Q.E.D.** [**quod** (that) which (1); **erat** was (2); **demonstrandum** to be proved, demonstrated (3): (that) which was to be proven.] *Geometry* and *Logic*. What had to be demonstrated. Used, especially in abbreviated form, after the point has been proven.

quod erat faciendum *abbr.* **Q.E.F.** *n.* [L. **quod** (that) which, what (1); **erat** was (2); **faciendum** to be done (3): (that) which was to be done.] *Geometry*. What had to be done. Used, especially in abbreviated form after a construction has been demonstrated.

quod erat inveniendum *abbr.* **Q.E.I.** *n.* [L. **quod** which, what (1); **erat** was (2); **inveniendum** to be found out, discovered (3): (that) which was to be found out.] What had to be discovered.

quod est *abbr.* **Q.E.** or **q.e.** [L. **quod** which (1); **est** is (2): which is.] That is.

quod est inconveniens aut contra rationem non permissum est in lege. [L. **quod** (that) which, what (1); **est** is (2); **inconveniens** inconvenient, unsuitable (3); **aut** or (4); **contra** against, opposite (5); **rationem** reason (6); **non** not (7); **permissum** permitted, allowed (9); **est** is, has been (8); **in** in, on (10); **lege** law (11): (That) which is unsuitable or against reason has not been allowed in law.] *Law*. What is inconvenient or unreasonable is not permitted in law.

quod est necessarium est licitum. [L. **quod** (that) which, what (1); **est** is (2); **necessarium** necessary (3); **est** is (4); **licitum** lawful, permitted (5): (That) which is necessary is lawful.] *Law*. What is necessary is permitted. See **necessitas quod** etc.

quod initio vitiosum est non potest tractu temporis convalescere. [L. **quod** (that) which, what (1); **initio** in the beginning (4); **vitiosum** invalid, defective (3); **est** is (2); **non** not (6); **potest** can, is able (5); **tractu** in the course (8); **temporis** of time (9); **convalescere** to recover, become valid, be improved, be remedied (7): (That) which is defective in the beginning is not able to be remedied in the course of time.] *Law*. What is initially invalid cannot become valid over a period of time. See **quod ab initio** etc.

quodlibet *n., pl.* **quodlibets** [L. **quod** what (1); **libet** pleases (2): what pleases.] 1. A topic for theological or philosophical discussion and argument. 2. *Music.* A carefree, humorous composition. A musical joke, especially the playing of several different tunes.

quod meum est sine facto meo vel defectu meo amitti vel in alium transferri non potest. [L. **quod** (that) which, what (1); **meum** mine (3); **est** is (2); **sine** without (11); **facto** deed, act, fact (13); **meo** my (12); **vel** or (14); **defectu** defect (16); **meo** my (15); **amitti** to be lost (6); **vel** or (7); **in** into, to, against, for (9); **alium** another (10); **transferri** to be transferred (8); **non** not (5); **potest** can, is able (4): (That) which is mine cannot be lost or transferred to another without my deed or defect.] *Law*. What is my property cannot be lost or transferred to another without my deed in either alienating or forfeiting it. See **id quod nostrum est** etc.

quod naturalis ratio inter omnes homines constituit, vocatur jus gentium. [L. **quod** (that) which, what (1); **naturalis** natural (2); **ratio** reason, consideration (3); **inter** among, between (5); **omnes** all (6); **homines** people, human beings (7); **constituit** has decreed, established (4); **vocatur** is called (8); **jus** right, law (9); **gentium** of nations, peoples (10): (That) which natural reason has decreed among all human beings is called the law of peoples.] The law which natural reason has established among all people is called the law of nations. See **jus gentium**.

quod necessarium est est licitum. See **quod est necessarium est licitum.**

quod necessitas cogit, defendit. See **necessitas quod cogit, defendit.**

quod non apparet non est. [L. **quod** (that) which, what (1); **non** not (2); **apparet** appears (3); **non** not (5); **est** is, exists (4): (That) which does not appear is not.] What does not appear does not exist. See **de non** etc. and **idem est non esse** etc.

quod non habet principium non habet finem. [L. **quod** (that) which, what (1); **non** not (2); **habet** has, holds, regards (3); **principium** beginning (4); **non** not (5); **habet** has, holds, regards (6); **finem** end (7): (That) which does not have beginning does not have end.] What has no beginning has no end.

quod nullius est, id ratione naturali occupanti conceditur. [L. **quod** (that) which (2); **nullius** of no one (4); **est** is (3); **id** that (1); **ratione** (by) reason (7); **naturali** by natural (6); **occupanti** to the one occupying (8); **conceditur** is granted (5): (That) which is of no one is granted by natural reason to the one occupying.] *Law*. What belongs to no one is by natural reason granted to the first occupant. See **res nullius naturaliter** etc.

quod omnes tangit ab omnibus debet supportari. [L. **quod** (that) which, what (1); **omnes** all (persons) (3); **tangit** touches, affects (2); **ab** from, by (6); **omnibus** all (persons) (7); **debet** ought, should (4);

supportari to be supported (5): (That) which touches all persons ought to be supported by all.] What affects everyone should be supported by everyone. Cf. **nam tua res** etc.

quod per me non possum nec per alium. [L. **quod** (that) which, what (1); **per** through (4); **me** me (5); **non** not (3); **possum** I can (2); **nec** nor, and not (6); **per** through (7); **alium** another (8): (That) which I cannot through me, nor through another.] *Law.* What I cannot do by myself, I cannot also do through the agency of another person. Cf. **qui facit per alium** etc.

quod per recordum probatum, non debet esse negatum. [L. **quod** (that) which, what (1); **per** through, by (3); **recordum** record (4); **probatum** proved (2); **non** not (6); **debet** ought, should (5); **esse** to be (7); **negatum** denied (8): (That) which is proved through record ought not to be denied.] *Law.* What is proved by documentary evidence should not be denied.

quod quis ex culpa sua damnum sentit non intelligitur damnum sentire. [L. **quod** any . . . that, what (1); **quis** anyone (3); **ex** out of (5); **culpa** fault, error, blame, guilt, failure (7); **sua** one's own, his/her own (6); **damnum** harm, injury (2); **sentit** experiences, suffers (4); **non** not (8); **intelligitur** he/she is understood (9); **damnum** harm, injury (11); **sentire** to experience, suffer (10): Any injury that anyone suffers out of his/her own fault, he/she is not understood to suffer injury.] *Law.* When a person suffers injury through his/her own fault, he/she is deemed not to suffer injury. See **qui non improbat, approbat.**

quod solo inaedificatur solo cedit. [L. **quod** (that) which, what (1); **solo** soil, ground, land (3); **inaedificatur** is built on/in (2); **solo** to the soil, ground, land (5); **cedit** accrues (4): (That) which is built on the soil accrues to the soil.] *Law.* What is built on land belongs to the land. See **quicquid plantatur** etc.

quod scripsi scripsi John 19:22. [L. **quod** that which (1); **scripsi** I have written (2); **scripsi** I have written (3): That which I have written I have written.] What is written is written. The words of Pontius Pilate regarding dissatisfaction with the inscription prepared for Jesus' cross, i.e., **Jesus Nazarenus Rex Judaeorum** (q.v.). Sometimes quoted in opposition to changing something which has already been written, published, or decreed.

quod vanum et inutile est, lex non requirit. [L. **quod** (that) which, what (1); **vanum** vain, futile (3); **et** and (4); **inutile** useless (5); **est** is (2); **lex** law (6); **non** not (7); **requirit** demands, requires (8): (That) which is vain and useless the law does not require.] The law does not demand what is futile and useless. See **impotentia excusat legem.**

quod vide *abbr.* **q.v.** *pl.* **quae vide** *abbr.* **qq.v.** [L. **quod** which (1); **vide** see (2): which see.] See this. Used for bibliographical references.

quo jure *adv.* [L. **quo** with what (1); **jure** (with) right, law (2): with what right?] By what title/right/authority?

quo ligatur, eo dissolvitur. [L. **quo** by which (1); **ligatur** it is bound (2); **eo** by that (3); **dissolvitur** it is dissolved, unbound (4): By which it is bound, by that it is unbound.] Something is unbound by the same means by which it is bound. See **eodem modo quo quid constituitur, dissolvitur.**

quo modo *abbr.* **Q.M.** or **q.m.** *n., pl.* **quo modos** [L. **quo** in what (1); **modo** (in) way (2): in what way? how?] Manner. Means. *Jeremiah has been dreaming of a brilliant career in the future, but his principal problem is that he does not know the quo modo for achieving his objective. —adv.* In what way or manner. How. By what means.

quo modo quid constituitur eodem modo dissolvitur. [L. **quo** in what (1); **modo** (in) way (2); **quid** something, anything (3); **constituitur** is made, established (4); **eodem** in the same (5); **modo** (in) way (6); **dissolvitur** it is dissolved (7): In what way something is made, in the same way it is dissolved.] *Law.* A thing is dissolved in the same way in which it is made. See **eodem modo quo quid constituitur dissolvitur.**

quondam *adj.* [L. at one time, at some time, formerly, once.] Former. Who used to be. *Abubakar, a quondam Permanent Secretary of the Ministry of Finance, has established a large farm near his village.*

quorum *n., pl.* **quorums** [L. of which.] A specified minimum number of members required at any meeting of an organization before its deliberations could be valid. *According to the constitution of the club, the quorum for any ordinary meeting is twelve.* Cf. **minyan.**

quota *n., pl.* **quotas** [L. from **quota pars**: **quota** what in number, how many (1); **pars** part, portion (2): what part in number.] 1. The share of something (e.g., benefits, liabilities, etc.) which each member of a group or body is entitled to. a) *Some politicians engage in irrational and destructive criticism instead of contributing their quota to the development of the nation.* b) *Even a successful reclassification as white . . . has its quota of pain* (Newsweek Int. April 19, 1982:35). 2. A restricted percentage or number; e.g., of immigrants. 3. A fixed, assigned or determined goal. a) *export quota*; b) *sales quota*; c) *output quota*; d) *production quota.*

quot homines, tot sententiae. Terence (c.185–159 B.C.). *Phormio*, 454. [L. **quot** as many as (1); **homines** human beings, people (2); **tot** so many (3); **sententiae** opinions (4): As many as human beings, so many the opinions.] There are as many views as there are people.

quot judices, tot sententiae. [L. **quot** as many as (1); **judices** judges (2); **tot** so many (3); **sententiae** opinions (4): As many as judges, so many the opinions.] *Law.* There are as many views as there are judges.

quo vadimus? [L. **quo** to what place, whither (1); **vadimus** are we going (2): To what place are we going?] In which direction are we headed? Cf. **quo vadis?**

quo vadis? John 16:5. [L. **quo** to what place, whither (1); **vadis** are you going (2): To what place are you going?] In which direction are you headed? 1. The question Jesus supposedly asked Peter in a vision as Peter was leaving Rome just before his execution. 2. A question used to introduce a discussion about the future plans of an individual or an organization. —**Quo Vadis?** The title of an 1886 novel by Henryk Sienkiewicz (1846–1916).

quo warranto *n.* [L. **quo** with what (1); **warranto** (with) warrant (2): with what warrant.] *Law.* A writ issued formerly in England on behalf of the king to ask a person to justify a claim to, or usurpation of, office, liberty, franchise, etc. There is still a legal proceeding with similar purpose.

quum de lucro duorum quaeratur, melior est causa possidentis. [L. **quum** when (1); **de** of, from, about, for (3); **lucro** profit, gain (4); **duorum** of two (persons) (5); **quaeratur** there may be asking (2); **melior** better (9); **est** is (8); **causa** cause, case, reason (6); **possidentis** of the one possessing (7): When there may be asking about the gain of two persons, the cause of the one possessing is better.] *Law.* When a question arises as to the advantage of two persons, the cause of the one in possession is better. See **in aequali jure melior** etc.

q.v. *abbr.* for **quod vide** (q.v.).

R

R. or **r.** *abbr.* for 1. **Recht** (q.v.). 2. **recipe** (q.v.). 3. **recto** (q.v.). 4. **rector** (q.v.). 5. **regina** (q.v.). 6. **rex** (q.v.).

R.A. *abbr.* for **Reverendus Admodum** (q.v.).

rabbi *n., pl.* **rabbis** [Heb. **rabbî: rab** master (2); **-î** my (1): my master.] *Judaism.* 1. The head of a Jewish congregation. 2. A scholar trained in Jewish law.

raconteur or *fem.* **raconteuse** *n., pl.* **raconteurs** or *fem.* **raconteuses** [Fr. story-teller.] A narrator. A person accomplished in the art of telling anecdotes.

radix enim omnium malorum est cupiditas. 1 Timothy 6:10. [L. **radix** root (2); **enim** for (1); **omnium** of all (3); **malorum** (of) evils (4); **est** is (5); **cupiditas** greed, desire (6): For the root of all evils is greed.] For the love of money is the root of all evils. Cf. **radix malorum**.

radix malorum *n.* [L. **radix** root (1); **malorum** of evils (2): root of evils.] The root of every evil (or all evils); i.e., money. For fuller form, see **radix enim** etc.

Ragnorok *n.* [Old Norse from **ragna** of the gods (2); **rok** fate (1): fate of the gods.] *Norse Mythology.* The fated end of the gods and of humankind following a cosmic battle with monsters.

raison d'état *n., pl.* **raisons d'état** [Fr. **raison** reason, motive (1); **d'** of (2); **état** state (3): reason of state.] Reason associated with national security; i.e., as justification for an action which is apparently despotic.

raison d'être *n., pl.* **raisons d'être** [Fr. **raison** reason, motive (1); **d'** of (2); **être** to be, existence, being (3): reason of existence.] Justification for, reason for, or purpose of, the existence of a thing. *The primary objective of a South African nuclear option, as indeed the raison d'être of its entire military establishment . . . is to maintain the system of apartheid . . .* (Sammy Kum Buo in *West Africa* 1982).

raj *n.* [Hindi **rāj** rule, kingdom.] Absolute rule, especially British control over India.

rajah or **raja** *n., pl.* **rajahs** or **rajas** [Hindi **rājā** king.] An Indian king or ruler. Cf. **maharaja**.

Rajput or **Rajpoot** *n.* [Hindi **rājpūt** from Skt. **rājaputrah: rājā** king (1); **putrah** son (2): king's son.] A descendant of powerful Hindi landowner or military families in northern and central India.

Ramadan or **Ramadhan** or **Ramazan** *n., pl.* **Ramadans** or **Ramadhans** or **Ramazans** [Ar. **Ramadān** month of dryness.] 1. The ninth month of the Muslim year during which all Muslims, with very few exceptions, should strictly abstain from eating, drinking, smoking, and sexual intercourse from sunrise to sunset. 2. The abstention observed during the month.

ranchero *n., pl.* **rancheros** [Sp. a rancher.] A rancher, herdsman, or small-scale farmer.

rani or **ranee** *n., pl.* **ranis** or **ranees** [Hindi **rānī** queen.] The wife of a **rajah** (q.v.).

rapport *n., pl.* **rapports** [Fr. relation, connection, contact, return.] A relation marked by harmony or accord. Harmonious or sympathetic relationship. a) *The two men developed a personal rapport . . .* (*Time Int.* 1980). b) *The new member of staff has already established a warm rapport with most of his colleagues.*

rapport à succession *n., pl.* **rapports à succession** [Fr. **rapport** relation, connection, contact, return (1); **à** to, toward, in, by, with, until (2); **succession** inheritance, estate (3): return to inheritance.] *French Law.* A hodge-podge. **Collatio bonorum** (q.v.). The practice whereby an heir or legatee restores to the estate or inheritance all advances and gifts received during the lifetime of the decedent so that an equitable distribution may be made.

rapporteur or *fem.* **rapporteuse** *n., pl.* **rapporteurs** or *fem.* **rapporteuses** [Fr. reporter, recorder.] 1. An official entrusted with the duty of recording and presenting reports, especially proceedings of a meeting. 2. An official entrusted with the duty of conducting an investigation and reporting its findings to a body.

rapprochement *n., pl.* **rapprochements** [Fr. bringing together, reconciling, reconciliation.] Reconciliation. Establishment or reestablishment of harmonious relations. Renewal of friendly or cordial relations. a) *Haig foresees a gradual drift by Egypt toward* *rapprochement with the Arab world, . . .* (*Time Int.* 1982). b) *Given the depth of mistrust on both sides, a true rapprochement between Peking and the Vatican seems unlikely in the near future* (*Newsweek Int.* March 9, 1981:31).

raptus *n., pl.* **raptus** or **raptuses** [L. A snatching away.] 1. A condition of spiritual ecstasy characterized by loss of sensation. 2. A condition of deep emotional excitement.

rara avis in terris or (elliptically) **rara avis** *n., pl.* **rarae aves in terris** or **rarae aves** Persius (A.D. 34–62). *Satires* I,46. [L. **rara** rare (1); **avis** bird (2); **in** in, on (3); **terris** the lands (4): rare bird in the lands.] A rare bird in the world. A rarity. A rare person or thing. A person or thing that is remarkable. *Ben described his friend, Pat, as a man of remarkable qualities, indeed, a rara avis.*

rariora *pl. n.* [L. rarer things or items.] A collection of rather rare things. *The Professor emeritus has a library of rariora to which he takes visitors occasionally.*

raro antecedentem scelestum / deseruit pede Poena claudo. Horace (65–8 B.C.). *Odes* III,1,31–32. [L. **raro** rarely, seldom (5); **antecedentem** going in front, preceding (7); **scelestum** miscreant, scoundrel (6); **deseruit** has deserted, abandoned (4); **pede** (with) foot (3); **Poena** Punishment (1); **claudo** with halting, limping (2): Punishment with halting foot has abandoned / rarely the scoundrel going in front.] Rarely has Punishment, though with halting steps, failed to catch up with the scoundrel going before her.

ratihabitio *n.* [L. **ratum** confirmed (1); **habeo** have, hold, regard (2): confirmed holding, approval, sanction.] Confirmation, ratification, ratihabitation; e.g., of a contract.

ratio *n., pl.* **ratios** [L. ground, motive, understanding, computation, calculation, relation, reason, judgment.] 1. Rationale. Reason. *Part of the ratio in that decision was that it was "contrary to custom for the parents to give consent (to marriage) on behalf of the daughter"* (Adewoye 1977:209). 2. Proportion. Rate. The relation between two or several things in terms of number, degree, etc. a) *The ratio between production and consumption.* b) *Girls in the school outnumber boys by a ratio of 2:1.*

ratio cognoscendi *n., pl.* **rationes cognoscendi** [L. **ratio** reason, ground, judgment (l); **cognoscendi** of knowing, understanding (2): reason of knowing.] The ground of knowledge. A thing through which something is known.

ratio decidendi *n., pl.* **rationes decidendi** [L. **ratio** reason, ground, judgment (1); **decidendi** of deciding (2): reason of deciding.] *Law.* Reason for a decision. Ground or reason for making a judicial decision. *Precedents are derived from the ratio decidendi.*

ratio essendi *n., pl.* **rationes essendi** [L. **ratio** reason, ground, judgment (1); **essendi** of being (2): reason of being.] Reason, ground, judgment or cause of a thing's existence. Cf. **raison d'être.**

ratio est legis anima; mutata legis ratione mutatur et lex. [L. **ratio** reason, ground, judgment (1); **est** is (2); **legis** of law (4); **anima** soul (3); **mutata** (with) having been changed (7); **legis** of law (6); **ratione** with reason (5); **mutatur** is changed (10); **et** also (9); **lex** law (8): Reason is the soul of law; with the reason of law having been changed, the law also is changed.] *Law.* Reason is the soul of law. When the reason for a law changes, the law also changes. See **lex plus laudatur** etc.

ratio legis *n.* [L. **ratio** reason, ground, judgment (1); **legis** of law (2): the reason of law.] *Law.* The reason or ground of/for a law.

ratio legis est anima legis. [L. **ratio** reason, ground, judgment (1); **legis** of law (2); **est** is (3); **anima** soul (4); **legis** of law (5): The reason of law is the soul of law.] *Law.* The reason of/for a law constitutes the soul of the law. See **lex plus laudatur** etc.

ratione contractus *adv.* [L. **ratione** by reason, ground, judgment (1); **contractus** of drawing together, shrinking, contract, agreement (2): by reason of contract.] *Law.* On account of a contract.

ratione delicti *adv.* [L. **ratione** by reason, ground, judgment (1); **delicti** of offense, crime, wrong (2): by reason of crime.] *Law.* On account of a crime.

ratione domicilii *adv.* [L. **ratione** by reason, ground, judgment (1); **domicilii** of abode, habitation, domicile (2): by reason of domicile.] *Law.* On account of habitation.

ratione imperii *adv.* [L. **ratione** by reason, ground, judgment (1); **imperii** of order, command (2): by reason of a command.] *Law.* On account of an order.

ratione impotentiae *adv.* [L. **ratione** by reason, ground, judgment (1); **impotentiae** of helplessness, weakness (2): by reason of helplessness.] On account of inability. Applicable to wild animals; e.g., the inability of young ones to run or fly.

ratione personae *adv.* [L. **ratione** by reason, ground, judgment (1); **personae** of person (2): by reason of the person.] On account of the person involved or affected. From the person's character.

ratione rei gestae *adv.* [L. **ratione** by reason, ground, judgment (1); **rei** of matter, thing, property, business, affair (2); **gestae** (of) done, transacted, accomplished (3): by reason of the thing done.] On account of his/her deed/achievement.

ratione rei sitae *adv.* [L. **ratione** by reason, ground, judgment (1); **rei** of matter, thing, property, business, affair (2); **sitae** (of) situated, placed (3): by reason of the thing situated.] By reason of the position or situation of the thing.

ratione soli *adv.* [L. **ratione** by reason, ground, judgment (1); **soli** of soil (2): by reason of the soil.] Because of the soil. On the basis of the soil. *The plaintiff claimed that the building as well as everything on the land belonged to him ratione soli.*

ratio scripta *n., pl.* **rationes scriptae** [L. **ratio** reason, ground, judgment (2); **scripta** written (1): written judgment.] *Law.* A judgment written and delivered.

re *prep.* [L. (in) the thing/affair/matter.] Regarding. Concerning. In the matter of. a) *Re Bukar*, i.e. "in Bukar's case" or "in the matter of Bukar." b) *Re your letter dated January 18th, 1989*, i.e. "with reference to your letter dated January 18th, 1989."

realia *pl. n.* [L. real things.] Tangible objects or facts as opposed to theories or mere descriptions.

Realpolitik or **realpolitik** *n.* [Ger. **Realpolitik**: **real** real, actual (1); **Politik** politics (2): real politics, realist politics.] Practical or realistic politics. Politics motivated by the real needs, circumstances, interests, and power of the nation, as distinct from one based on theory, sentiments, morality, or idealism. Politics considered not as a means to an end but an end in itself. a) . . . *this unlikely alliance, based on realpolitik, has already had wide-ranging repercussions in northwest Africa and beyond* (*South* 1984). b) *Practitioners of realpolitik in the US administration may argue that they can afford to ignore African protests* (*West Africa* 1986).

Realpolitiker *n., pl.* **Realpolitiker** or **Realpolitikers** [Ger. **real** real, actual (1); **Politiker** politician, statesman (2): real politician, realist politician.] A person who believes or engages in **Realpolitik** (q.v.).

rebus *n., pl.* **rebuses** [L. by/with matters, things, property, business, affairs.] Pictures, letter combinations, and other symbols used to suggest a specific word or phrase.

rebus sic stantibus *adv.* [L. **rebus** with matters, things, property, business, affairs (1); **sic** thus (2); **stantibus** (with) standing (3): with things thus standing.] *International Law.* Under these circumstances. As long as the situation has not substantially changed. Usually used to indicate that treaties remain binding as long as conditions remain unchanged.

receptitia dos *n., pl.* **receptitiae dotes** [L. **recepti(c)ia** receptible, recoverable (1); **dos** dowry (2): recoverable dowry.] *Roman Law.* A wife's dowry given with the stipulation that it should be reclaimed on termination of the marital bond. See **dos**.

réchauffé *n., pl.* **réchauffés** [Fr. warmed-up, reheated, stale, warmed-up dish, rehash.] 1. Food which has been warmed up. Warmed-up dish. *He woke up, quickly ate a réchauffé of rice and stew, and drove to the lecture-theater.* 2. A rehash, especially of literary material. *The book is a poor réchauffé of basically worthless material.* —*adj.* 1. Warmed-up. Reheated. *She had a reasonably delicious meal of rice and stew réchauffé this morning.* 2. Rehashed. Restated in another form. *The publication, which comprises almost exclusively réchauffé material, has been receiving uncomplimentary reviews.*

recherché or **recherche** *adj.* [Fr. choice, refined, affected, studied, select.] 1. Sought for or obtained with care. *She gave her boss a gift of recherché perfume.* 2. Rare. Exotic. *An interesting aspect of the author's diction is her recherché expressions.* 3. Refined. Choice. Studied. Exquisite. 4. Farfetched. *The critic*

demolished the writer's thesis, exposing the recherché inferences.

Recht *abbr.* **R.** or **r.** *n., pl.* **Rechte** [Ger. law, right.] *German Law.* 1. Right. Equity. Justice. 2. A privilege, title to. 3. Law. Unwritten law. The entire body of law. Cf. **droit**.

Rechtsstaat *n., pl.* **Rechtsstaats** [Ger. from **Rechts** of the right (2); **Staat** state (1): state of the right.] A lawful state. A state or nation which recognizes the rule of law.

recipe *abbr.* **R.** or **r.** or **rp.** *n., pl.* **recipes** [L. imperative of **recipere** take, accept, receive.] 1. *Medicine.* A prescription. A formula for preparing a drug or medicine. *Though not a certified pharmacist, she finds her recipes highly respected by medical practitioners.* 2. A formula for making something out of several ingredients. A formula for preparing food or drinks. a) *Housewives have been visiting Mrs. Akpan in connection with her recipe for okra soup.* b) . . . *the Show and Talk even has a printer to produce copies of menus and recipes* (*Newsweek Int.* June 22, 1981:3). 3. A procedure, method, or means of achieving a goal, solving a problem, etc. a) *Critics of the government have described the austerity budget as a recipe for economic and political catastrophe.* b) *The best recipe for improving one's knowledge of a language is to read good novels in that language.*

réclame *n., pl.* **réclames** [Fr. publicity, advertisement.] 1. Publicity. Public acclaim or attention which is not necessarily commensurate with, or justified by, achievement. *The journalist's articles, though of questionable quality, have won considerable réclame.* 2. Showmanship. A passion, flair, propensity, or gift for publicity. *His réclame is such that he is recognized wherever he goes.*

recto *abbr.* **R.** or **r.** *n., pl.* **rectos** *short form* of **folio recto** (q.v.). Cf. **verso**.

rector or *fem.* **rectrix** *abbr.* **R.** or **r.** *pl.* **rectors** or *fem.* **rectrices** [L. leader, ruler, director, governor, guide.] 1. The head of an educational institution. 2. The head of any of the seventeen educational departments of France. 3. The head of a secondary or elementary school in Germany. 4. God as ruler of the world. 5. *Roman Catholic Church.* A cleric who is the spiritual head of the parish, religious community, etc. 6. *Anglican Church.* A cleric who has full charge of a parish and has complete right to the tithes of the parish. 7. *Protestant Episcopal Church.* A cleric elected as the head of the parish.

rectum *n., pl.* **recta** or **rectums** [L. the straight, i.e., intestine.] The terminal portion of the large intestine which leads directly to the anus.

recurrendum est ad extraordinarium quando non valet ordinarium. [L. **recurrendum** to be reverted, hastened back (2); **est** it is (1); **ad** to, at, for, according to (3); **extraordinarium** extraordinary (thing) (4); **quando** when (5); **non** not (7); **valet** avails, succeeds

(8); **ordinarium** ordinary (thing) (6): It is to be re-verted to an extraordinary thing when the ordinary thing does not avail.] *Law.* We must take to an extraordinary measure when the ordinary does not succeed. See **numquam decurritur** etc.

Redemptor hominis *n.* [L. **redemptor** redeemer (1); **hominis** of person, human being (2): redeemer of a human being.] *Christianity.* Redeemer of the human race.

redivivus *adj.* [L. renewed, renovated, freshened up.] Reborn. Born again. Resurrected. Restored to life. *Grace has a habit of being taciturn for a long time and then, like a person redivivus, becoming vociferous.*

reductio ad absurdum *n., pl.* **reductiones ad absurdum** [L. **reductio** reduction, reducing (1); **ad** to, at, for, according to (2); **absurdum** absurdity, the absurd (3): reduction or reducing to absurdity.] 1. *Logic.* Reduction or reducing to the point of absurdity. Used with reference to arguing in such a way that the issues are rendered absurd, or to an argument which leads to absurd consequences. *This reductio ad absurdum of the notion of gross negligence depends entirely on the view that negligence is merely a name for a state of mind consisting in the absence of foresight of consequences* (Hart 1978:149). 2. Pushing things to the point of absurdity.

reductio ad impossibile *n.* [L. **reductio** reducing, reduction (1); **ad** to, at, for, according to (2); **impossibile** impossible (3): reducing to the impossible.] Reducing to the point of the impossible. *Logic.* Used in respect of the mode of arguing which disproves a point by showing that it leads to obviously impossible conclusions.

redux *adj.* [L. led back.] Returned. Brought back. Generally used postpositively, as in John Updike's *Rabbit Redux.*

referendum *n., pl.* **referenda** or **referendums** [L. that which must be carried back or referred, something to be submitted for consideration, something to be referred.] 1. A plebiscite. The practice of referring to the electorate for approval a measure proposed or passed by a legislative body. *Parliament decided that a referendum should be held to decide whether or not the austerity measures should be continued.* 2. *International Law.* A note sent by a diplomatic agent to his government asking for instructions on certain matters.

reformado *n., pl.* **reformados** or **reformadoes** [Sp. reformed, reconstructed, or reorganized person.] 1. An officer whose troops have been disbanded or reorganized and has thus lost his command but still retains his rank and receives remuneration either wholly or partly. 2. A volunteer who serves without a commission but has the rank of an officer.

regale *n., pl.* **regalia** [L. kingly thing.] *sing.* Royal power. —*pl.* 1. The paraphernalia or emblems of royalty, such as scepter, crown, attire, and orb. *But the book also describes the rest of the ruler's beaded regalia, including, particularly, the magnificent cloak made for Oba Oyekunle (1916-1934)* (D.W. in *West Africa* 1982). 2. The special costume, ornaments, insignia etc. of an office, order, social group, or fraternity. 3. Costume for a special occasion. *Every Sunday the cobbler, his wife, and children, dressed in their finest regalia, take a taxi and go to church.*

regatta *n., pl.* **regatte** or **regattas** [It. contest, contention.] 1. A boat race organized on the lagoon of Venice, i.e., the Grand Canal. 2. An organized series of races involving rowing-boats, speed-boats, yachts, etc.

reg. gen. *abbr.* for **regula generalis** (q.v.).

régime or **regime** *n., pl.* **régimes** or **regimes** [Fr. system, government, diet.] 1. A method of administration or government. a) *Apartheid régime*; b) *Communist régime*; c) *Marxist régime*; d) *Fascist régime*; e) *democratic régime*; f) *totalitarian régime*; g) *military régime.* 2. The period of a government's rule. Government of. Government headed by. a) *the Castro régime*; b) *Khomeini's régime*; c) *the Obasanjo régime*; d) *the Park régime*; e) *the Shah's régime.* 3. Diet. **Regimen** 1 (q.v.). *He followed a strict régime of black coffee and plain toast every morning.*

régime dotal *n.* [Fr. **régime** system (2); **dotal** dotal (1): dotal system.] *Civil Law.* Dowry system. Regulations governing the administration of the property which the wife brings as her contribution to the assets of the couple. The husband has the right and power to administer the property until the termination of the marriage. With respect to the immovable property, however, neither the husband nor the wife nor the two by their joint decision can alienate or mortgage it. Cf. **conquêts.**

regimen *n., pl.* **regimens** [L. rule, guidance, command, government.] 1. A regulated mode of life, especially one with special diet, exercises, and medication prescribed for medical reasons or as a punitive measure. A treatment or regulation which is expected in due course to be beneficial. *The Kelley program eschews conventional anti-cancer drugs, surgery and radiation in favor of a "holistic" regimen of special diets, nutritional supplements, coffee enemas and infusions of cells from cattle* (Newsweek Int. Oct. 20, 1980:57). 2. Government. Rule. Administration.

regina *abbr.* **R.** or **r.** *n., pl.* **reginae** [L. queen.] A female monarch. Used, inter alia, in the titles of British lawsuits during the reign of a queen. *Regina v. Crayburn*, i.e., the Crown v. Crayburn. Cf. **rex.**

Regius Professor *abbr.* **R.P.** *n.* [L. **regius** kingly, royal (1); **professor** professor (2): royal professor.] *British Universities.* A professor whose chair was established by royal generosity or depends on royal patronage. Such chairs were established by Henry VIII.

règlement de comptes *n., pl.* **règlements de comptes** [Fr. **règlement** settlement (1); **de** of (2); **comptes** accounts (3): settlement of accounts.] Settling of accounts or old scores. *Some cowardly officials tend to* *regard appointment to high office as opportunity for* *règlement de comptes.*

regnat populus. [L. **regnat** rules, reign (2): **populus** people, the citizenry (1): People rule.] The people rule. Motto of the State of Arkansas.

reg. pl. *abbr.* for **regula placitandi** (q.v.).

regula *n., pl.* **regulae** [L. rule.] Regulation.

regula est, juris quidem ignorantiam cuique nocere, facti vero ignorantiam non nocere. [L. **regula** rule (2); **est** it is (1); **juris** of right, law (4); **quidem** certainly, in fact (5); **ignorantiam** that ignorance (3); **cuique** to each one, everybody (7); **nocere** does harm, hurts, injures (6); **facti** of fact (10); **vero** but indeed, however (8); **ignorantiam** ignorance (9); **non** not (11); **nocere** hurts, to hurt (12): It is a rule that ignorance of law certainly does harm to each one, but indeed ignorance of the fact does not harm.] *Law.* It is a legal rule that each one is prejudiced by his ignorance of law, but not by his ignorance of fact. See **ignorantia facti; ignorantia facti excusat; ignorantia facti excusat, ignorantia** etc.; **ignorantia juris haud excusat; ignorantia juris neminem excusat; ignorantia juris non excusat; ignorantia juris quod quisque scire** etc.; **ignorantia juris quod quisque tenetur** etc.; **ignorantia legis neminem excusat; and ignorantia legis non excusat.**

regula generalis *abbr.* **reg. Gen.** or **R.G.** *n.* [L. **regula** rule (2); **generalis** general (1): general rule.] *Law.* A general or standing order. Applicable to a court.

regula placitandi *abbr.* **reg. pl.** *n., pl.* **regulae placitandi** [L. **regula** rule (1); **placitandi** of pleading (2): rule of pleading.] *Law.* A rule or regulation for pleading, especially in a court of law.

regulus *n., pl.* **reguli** or **reguluses** [L. a petty king, a ruler of a small country.] A petty king. A kinglet. A ruler of negligible power.

Reich *n., pl.* **Reiche** [Ger. empire, realm, state, kingdom.] 1. An empire. A state. 2. The German State or Commonwealth. Historically, there are a number of periods: *the First Reich,* i.e., the Holy Roman Empire (9th century to 1806); *the Second Reich* (1871 to 1918); *the Third Reich,* i.e., the period of the Nazis (1933–1945).

rel. *abbr.* for **reliquiae** (q.v.).

relata refero *n.* [L. **relata** reported, related (things) (2); **refero** I report, repeat (1): I repeat reported things.] Repeating (or repetition of) stories or what is reported. *But he is not always content with a relata refero* (Lesky 1966:320).

relator or *fem.* **relatrix** *n., pl.* **relators** or **relatrixes** [L. a reporter, a proposer or mover of motions.] 1. Narrator. A person who relates. *My grandfather is a delightful relator of stories.* 2. An informer. A private person who brings information and on whose behalf a writ quo warranto or mandamus is issued.

relievo *n., pl.* **relievos** [It. relief.] *Art.* Figures partially sculptured on a flat background, i.e., not sculptured in the round. Cf. **bas relief** and **mezzo relievo.**

religieux or *fem.* **religieuse** *adj., pl.* **religieux, religieuses** [Fr. religious.] Pious. Religious. —*n.* *Christianity.* An individual, such as a monk or a nun, who has accepted religious vows and who follows a religious rule.

Religio laici [L. **religio** religion (1); **laeci** of the laity, of the layperson (2): religion of the layperson.] "Religion of a layperson," the title of a poem by John Dryden (1631–1700) in which he describes his personal religious beliefs.

reliquiae *abbr.* **rel.** *pl. n.* [L. relics, remains.] Relics. Remains, especially organic remains or the remains of the dead.

remanent pro defectu emptorum *n.* [L. **remanent** they remain (1); **pro** for (2); **defectu** want, lack (3); **emptorum** of buyers, purchasers (4): They remain for want of buyers.] *Law.* A return made by the sheriff to a writ such as **fieri facias** (q.v.) when the goods have not been bought.

remanet *n., pl.* **remanets** [L. It remains.] Something remaining. A remnant. A case whose hearing is postponed.

Remedia Amoris *n.* [L. **remedia** remedies (1); **amoris** of/for love (2): remedies for love.] *Remedies for Love,* a poem by Ovid (43 B.C.–17 A.D.).

remise en cause *n., pl.* **remises en cause** [Fr. **remise** putting back (1); **en** into (2); **cause** consideration, reason (3): putting back into consideration.] Re-examination. Reconsideration. Self-examination. *We need to discuss, rethink, diverge, disagree, reexamine, break away, to constantly ensure a remise en cause* (*The Guardian* 1987).

remittitur *n., pl.* **remittiturs** [L. It is remitted, abated, sent back.] *Law.* 1. A process whereby a plaintiff either voluntarily or by order of court remits to the defendant a portion of damages considered to be excessive. The court may also order a complete retrial or one restricted to the question of damages. 2. The sending back of a case and record of proceedings from a superior to an inferior court for further action.

renaissance *n., pl.* **renaissances** [Fr. rebirth, revival, renewal.] 1. Rebirth. Renewal. a) *a renaissance in French films* (*Newsweek Int.* Jan 5, 1981:53); b) *The end of military rule is usually followed by a renaissance of party politics with its characteristic acrimony.* 2. A period of considerable improvement or rebirth of cultural, artistic, and literary activity after a period of decay, especially the period of European history from the 14th century to the early 17th century when there was an efflorescence of the arts and letters under the influence of the Classics, and the foundation of modern science was laid. *The Italian Renaissance.*

rencontre *n., pl.* **rencontres** [Fr. meeting, encounter, collision, duel, fight, skirmish.] 1. A combat or duel. A hostile encounter. *By the end of the meeting of the diplomatic representatives of the two sides, it was clear that a rencontre was inevitable.* 2. A debate or contest. *In a lively rencontre between two highly intelligent groups, the group arguing in support of the unpopular cause presented its case so forcefully that it won the day.* 3. A casual or accidental meeting with a person or thing. *Okoro had a very pleasant rencontre with Ifoma at the supermarket yesterday.*

rendezvous *abbr.* **rv.** *n., pl.* **rendezvous** [Fr. meeting-place, appointment, date.] 1. A place and time appointed for meeting or assembly. a) *Reagan ended the talk with "You and I have a rendezvous with destiny"* . . . *(Time Int.* 1981). b) *Khomeini's rendezvous with history began last week at his home-in-exile outside Paris (Newsweek Int.* Feb. 12, 1979:9). 2. A place and time appointed for the assembling of troops, ships, airplanes, etc. in preparation for, or after the completion of, an operation. 3. A date. A meeting at a place and time agreed upon. Agreement to meet. *For weeks she and the prince managed to throw newsmen off the scent by holding secret rendezvous at various royal estates* . . . *(Newsweek Int.* March 9, 1981:13). 4. A place where people usually meet. A popular resort. 5. A meeting place or headquarters of criminals, pirates, etc. —*v. intr.* To assemble, meet or come together at an appointed place and time. *The vehicles would slip one by one into Tehran and rendezvous at a warehouse* . . . *(Time Int.* 1980).

renvoi *n., pl.* **renvois** [Fr. sending back, dismissal, expulsion, reference.] 1. Deportation of an alien. 2. *Private International Law.* A court's reference, in case of conflict of laws, to the rules of foreign law or the law of the forum, i.e., doctrine of renvoi.

reo absente See **absente reo.**

repertoire *n., pl.* **repertoires** [Fr. répertoire repertory, index, list, catalog, collection.] 1. A list of artistic, dramatic, musical, etc. works available or which a person or company can perform. a) . . . *Lord Olivier . . . recently added King Lear to his film repertoire* . . . *(Newsweek Int.* May 9, 1983:17). b) *The music hall is featuring tonight a famous musician with a rich repertoire.* 2. Stock-in-trade. A supply or list of skills, methods, devices, etc. available in a field, or which a person has and uses in his/her, profession, occupation, etc. *The repertoire of that dubious businessman includes treachery, issuing of bouncing checks, cheating, and blackmail.* 3. The dishes or meals available at a restaurant or other places. *The host had a varied repertoire, and the guests really enjoyed the meals.*

repertorium *n., pl.* **repertoria** [L. repertory.] Repository. A storehouse. A collection.

replica *n., pl.* **replicas** [It. repetition.] A duplicate copy or reproduction, especially of a work of art. A **facsimile** (q.v.). a) *Many Argentines are Anglophiles. Buenos Aires has a replica of Big Ben* . . . *(Newsweek Int.* April 26, 1982:4). b) . . . *they touched the feet, the hands and body of the child, admiring its long toes and fingers, straight pointed nose and handsome face, a replica of his father's (The Guardian* 1987).

Répondez s'il vous plaît *abbr.* **R.S.V.P.** [Fr. **répondez** reply, respond (1); **s'** if (2); **il** it (3); **vous** you (5); **plaît** pleases, appeals to (4): Reply, if it pleases you.] Respond, if you please. Please reply.

Répondez vite s'il vous plaît *abbr.* **R.V.S.V.P.** [Fr. **repondez** reply, respond (1); **vite** quickly, soon (2); **s'** if (3); **il** it (4); **vous** you (6); **plaît** pleases, appeals to (5): Reply quickly, if it pleases you.] Respond quickly if you please. Please reply soon.

reprise *n., pl.* **reprises** [Fr. renewal, resumption, revival, repeat.] 1. A repeated event or occurrence. Renewal, resumption or recurrence. a) *If they succeeded . . . , there would almost certainly be a reprise of last August, when the lack of a quorum had cancelled the meeting (West Africa* 1982). b) *The whole episode sounded like a small reprise of the Iranian hostage crisis but without the publicity (Newsweek Int.* Aug. 1, 1983:24). 2. *Music.* Repetition of a theme. 3. Recapitulation.

Requiem *n., pl.* **Requiems** [L. rest, repose.] 1. The first word of the introit of the Latin Requiem Mass. 2. A musical setting of the Mass for the souls of the departed. —**requiem** *pl.* **requiems** 1. A dirge for the repose of the soul(s) of the deceased. 2. Something which resembles or seems to resemble such a dirge. *Now that the dispute has been settled, we may sing its requiem.* —**Requiem Mass** or **requiem mass** A mass sung or said for the repose of the soul of a dead person or the souls of several dead persons, usually at All Souls' Day or funerals. a) *Accompanied by her family, she attended a requiem mass that marked the end of the nation's official mourning period (Newsweek Int.* Oct. 25, 1982:27). b) *At the Requiem Mass that preceded the burial, it rained intermittently (Time Int.* 1978).

requiem aeternam dona eis, Domine. [L. **requiem** rest, repose (4); **aeternam** eternal, everlasting (3); **dona** give, grant (1); **eis** to them (2); **domine** O lord (5): Grant to them eternal rest, O Lord.] Give them eternal rest, Lord. The first words of the introit of the Latin Requiem Mass.

requiescant in pace *abbr.* **R.I.P.** [L. **requiescant** May they rest (1); **in** in, on (2); **pace** peace (3): May they rest in peace.] See **requiescat.** Cf. **requiescat in pace.**

requiescat *n., pl.* **requiescats** [L. May he/she rest.] A prayer for the repose of the soul of a dead person.

requiescat in pace *abbr.* **R.I.P.** [L. **requiescat** May he/she/it rest (1); **in** in, on (2); **pace** peace (3): May he/she/it rest in peace.] See **requiescat.** *The writer's controversial view has been successfully demolished. Requiescat in pace!* Cf. **requiescant in pace.**

Rerum Politicarum Doctor *abbr.* **R.P.D.** *n.* [L. **rerum** (of) matters, things, property, business, affairs (3); **politicarum** of political (2); **doctor** teacher (1): teacher of political matters.] Doctor of Political Science. A terminal graduate degree in political science.

res accessoria *n., pl.* **res accessoriae** [L. **res** matter, thing, property, business, affair (2); **accessoria** accessory (1): accessory thing.] *Civil Law.* An accessory thing, i.e., something connected to a principal thing.

res accessoria sequitur rem principalem. [L. **res** matter, thing, property, business, affair (2); **accessoria** accessory (1); **sequitur** follows (3); **rem** matter, thing, property, business, affair (5); **principalem** principal (4): The accessory thing follows the principal thing.] The accessory follows its principal. See **accessorium non ducit** etc.

res adjudicata See **res judicata**.

res angusta domi Juvenal (c.60 A.D.–c.140 A.D.). *Satires* III,165. [L. **res** matter, thing, property, business, affair (2); **angusta** narrow, difficult (1); **domi** at home (3): difficult matter at home.] A difficult situation at home.

res cogitans *n.* [L. **res** matter, thing, property, business, affair (2); **cogitans** thinking, reflecting (1): a thinking thing.] Something which thinks; i.e., the mind or soul.

res communes *n., sing.* **res communis** [L. **res** matters, things, property, business, affairs (2); **communes** common, public (1): common things.] *Roman and Civil Law.* Common or public things; i.e., things which belong to the public, are used by everyone and cannot be anybody's private property; e.g., air, light, the open sea, etc. Cf. **publici juris** and **res publica**.

res controversa *n., pl.* **res controversae** [L. **res** matter, thing, property, business, affair (2); **controversa** disputed, undecided (1): disputed thing.] *Civil Law.* A disputed or undecided matter. A matter to be determined.

res corporales *n., sing.* **res corporalis** [L. **res** matters, things, property, business, affairs (2); **corporales** corporeal, bodily (1): bodily matters.] *Roman and Civil Law.* Corporeal or tangible things; things that can be perceived by the senses. Cf. **res incorporales**.

rescriptum *n., pl.* **rescripta** [L. something written back, a rescript.] *Roman Law.* A response in writing. The emperor's response to an inquiry on legal matters. Such responses served as precedents and became a source of law.

res derelicta *n., pl.* **res derelictae** [L. **res** matter, thing, property, business, affair (2); **derelicta** deserted (1): a deserted thing.] *Law.* Property which is deserted or abandoned and can thus be acquired by the first occupant or taker. See **res nullius naturaliter** etc.

res divini juris *pl. n.* [L. **res** matters, things, property, business, affairs (1); **divini** of divine (2); **juris** (of) right, law (3): matters of divine right.] *Law.* Matters of divine law. Cf. **res humani juris**.

res dominans *n.* [L. **res** matter, thing, property, business, affair (2); **dominans** dominant (1): a dominant thing.] *Law.* The dominant tenement or property which can enjoy a servitude.

reservoir *n., pl.* **reservoirs** [Fr. tank, container, holder.] 1. A place such as an artificial lake or tank, where water is stored and released for domestic or industrial consumption, as and when the need arises. 2. Anything in which liquid is held. 3. A repository or storehouse, i.e., of facts, ideas, knowledge, data, etc. *The researcher was advised to consult a certain octogenarian who was generally regarded as a veritable reservoir of knowledge on the precolonial history of the area.*

res extra commercium *n., pl.* **res extra commercium** [L. **res** matter, thing, property, business, affair (1); **extra** outside of, beyond (2); **commercium** commerce (3): a thing outside of commerce.] A thing which cannot be owned. A thing which is not subject to private ownership or acquisition. See **extra commercium**.

res fungibiles See **fungibiles res**.

res gestae *pl. n.* [L. **res** matters, things, property, business, affairs (1); **gestae** done, transacted (2): things done.] 1. Things done. Deeds. Exploits. Achievements. Transactions. 2. *Law.* The facts that constitute the environment of a litigation. The circumstances of, and spontaneous utterances relating to, an event or transaction and deemed admissible and useful as illustrations and explanations.

res humani juris *pl. n.* [L. **res** matters, things, property, business, affairs (1); **humani** of human (2); **juris** (of) right, law (3): matters of human right.] *Law.* Matters of human law. Cf. **res divini juris**.

residuum *n., pl.* **residua** or **residuums** [L. the remainder, the rest.] 1. Something which remains after expenses or charges have been paid, or after the completion of a process. Residue. Balance. 2. The remainder of a deceased person's estate after the payment of debts and deduction of legacies.

res immobiles *n., sing.* **res immobilis** [L. **res** matters, things, property, business, affairs (2); **immobiles** immovable, unmoved (1): immovable things.] *Civil Law.* Immovable objects; e.g., land and things connected to it, such as buildings and trees. **Immeubles** (q.v.).

res incorporales *n., sing.* **res incorporalis** [L. **res** matters, things, property, business, affairs (2); **incorporales** incorporeal, intangible (1): intangible things.] *Civil Law.* Incorporeal or intangible things; i.e., things which can be perceived only by the mind. Cf. **res corporales**.

res integra *n., pl.* **res integrae** [L. **res** matter, thing, property, business, affair (1); **integra** untouched, undecided (2): a thing untouched/undecided.] *Law.* A question or case which has not been examined and on which a decision has not been made. See **res nova** and **sub judice**. Cf. **res judicata**.

res inter alios acta *n., pl.* **res inter alios actae** [L. **res** matter, thing, property, business, affair (1); **inter** between, among (3); **alios** others (4); **acta** done (2): a thing done among other persons.] *Law.* A thing done among strangers. Evidence on such acts is not admissible in a court of law, since the accused or defendant is not a party to them. *The defense counsel submitted* *that, since his/her client was not party to the transaction, which was essentially res inter alios acta, he/she was not liable.* See **res inter alios acta alteri** etc.

res inter alios acta alteri nocere non debet. [L. **res** matter, thing, property, business, affair (1); **inter** between (3); **alios** some (persons) (4); **acta** done (2); **alteri** to another (8); **nocere** to do harm, hurt, injure (7); **non** not (6); **debet** ought, should (5): A thing done among some persons ought not to do harm to another.] *Law.* A thing done among strangers ought not to harm a person who is not party to it. Hence, a person cannot be affected by declarations, acts, affidavits, or conduct of other persons. See **debitorum pactionibus** etc.; **inter alios res gestas** etc.; **non deberet alii** etc.; **non debet alii** etc.; **pacta tertiis** etc.; **privatis pactionibus** etc.; and **res inter alios acta**.

res ipsa loquitur. [L. **res** matter, thing, property, business, affair (1); **ipsa** itself (2); **loquitur** speaks (3): The matter itself speaks.] *Law.* The matter speaks for itself. A case in which by merely proving that there was an incident, it could be justifiably inferred that it was the result of the negligence of the accused/defendant, unless the inference is rebutted by convincing explanation.

res judicata or **res adjudicata** *n., pl.* **res judicatae** or **res adjudicatae** [L. **res** matter, thing, property, business, affair (1); **judicata** decided, resolved, concluded (2): a thing/matter decided or concluded.] *Law.* A matter conclusively decided. The rule that, when a case has been finally determined on its merits by a court which has jurisdiction over both the matter and the parties, it cannot be revived. *Res judicata relates to a decision; stare decisis relates to a rule or principle of law involved* (Curzon 1979:241). See **autrefois**; **chose jugée; cosa juzgada; in rem judicatam; non bis in idem; quieta non movere; res judicata pro** etc.; **stare decisis**; and **stare decisis et non** etc. Cf. **res integra; res nova;** and **sub judice**.

res judicata pro veritate accipitur. [L. **res** matter, thing, property, business, affair (1); **judicata** adjudged, decided (2); **pro** as (4); **veritate** truth (5); **accipitur** is accepted (3): A matter adjudged is accepted as the truth.] A final and complete judgment on a matter is accepted as the truth. See **infinitum in** etc. See also **res judicata**.

res litigiosae *n., sing.* **res litigiosa** [L. **res** matters, things, property, business, affairs (2); **litigiosae** disputed, controversial (1): disputed things.] *Roman Law.* Things, rights, or property which are involved in a pending suit.

res mancipi *pl. n.* [L. **res** matters, things, property, business, affairs (1); **mancipi** of legal purchase or **mancipium** (2): things of legal purchase.] *Roman Law.* Things subject to legal purchase or **mancipium**. These were things which could be alienated or transferred only through a formal ceremony of legal purchase called **mancipium** (q.v.) or **mancipatio** (q.v.). Such things included houses, lands, and slaves. Cf. **res nec mancipi**.

res mobiles *n., sing.* **res mobilis** [L. **res** matters, things, property, business, affairs (2); **mobiles** movable, easy to be moved (1): movable things.] Movables. Objects which can be moved. **Meubles** (q.v.).

res nec mancipi *pl. n.* [L. **res** matters, things, property, business, affairs (1); **nec** and not, nor, not (2); **mancipi** of legal purchase (3): things not of legal purchase.] *Roman Law.* Things not subject to legal purchase. All things which could be alienated or transferred without undergoing the formal ceremony of legal purchase. Cf. **res mancipi**.

res non fungibiles *pl. n.* [L. **res** matters, things, property, business, affairs (1); **non** not (2); **fungibiles** fungible (3): things not fungible.] *Civil Law.* Things that are not interchangeable in quality and quantity; e.g., a horse, an antique, etc. Cf. **fungibiles res**.

res non potest peccare. [L. **res** matter, thing, property, business, affair (1); **non** not (3); **potest** can, is able (2); **peccare** to err, offend (4): A thing cannot offend.] *Law.* A thing is not able to err; i.e., only a person can.

res non verba [L. **res** matter, thing, property, business, affair (1); **non** not (2); **verba** words (3): things not words.] Actions not words.

res nova *n.* [L. **res** matter, thing, property, business, affair (2); **nova** new (1): a new thing/matter.] *Law.* A new matter or case. A question which has not been previously decided. See **res integra** and **sub judice**. Cf. **res judicata**.

res nullius *n.* [L. **res** matter, thing, property, business, affair (1); **nullius** of no one (2): a thing of no one.] *Law.* Property which belongs to nobody, whether because it has never been acquired or because its previous owner has completely abandoned it or because, in the case of Roman law, it cannot be privately owned. See **res nullius naturaliter** etc.

res nullius naturaliter fit primi occupantis. [L. **res** matter, thing, property, business, affair (1); **nullius** of no one (2); **naturaliter** naturally (3); **fit** becomes, is (4); **primi** of first (5); **occupantis** (of) occupying, occupant (6): A property of no one naturally becomes that of the first occupant.] *Law.* Property which belongs to no one naturally becomes the property of the first occupant. See **occupantis fiunt derelicta; quod nullius** etc.; **res derelicta; res nullius;** and **terra manens vacua** etc.

res perit suo domino. [L. **res** matter, thing, property, business, affair (1); **perit** perishes, perishes for (2); **suo** to/for its own (3); **domino** for owner (4): The thing perishes for its own owner.] *Law.* The loss is incurred by the owner. When goods in transit are lost, damaged, or delayed through an act of God, any loss arising thereby is incurred by the owner, not the carrier. See **periculum rei** etc.

respice finem [L. **respice** look at (1); **finem** end, limit (2): Look at the end.] Look at the end, especially of life. Cf. **memento mori**.

respondeat superior *n.* [L. **respondeat** let him answer (2); **superior** higher, senior (person) (1): Let the higher person answer.] *Law.* The master is liable for the acts of the servant. The principal is liable for the acts of his/her agent. When an agent commits a wrongful act either with the consent or under the direction of the principal, and the injured party brings a suit, both the principal and the agent are liable. See **qui facit per alium** etc.

respondentia *pl. n.* [L. answering things, things sufficing to meet.] A loan secured on the cargo of a ship to be repaid with maritime interest when the cargo or some of it arrives safely at port. Originally, respondentia and bottomry were two different things, but the former is now used infrequently and the latter is used both in its original sense and for **respondentia**. Cf. **nautica pecunia** and **nauticum faenus**.

respondere non debet. [L. **respondere** to answer (3); **non** not (2); **debet** he/she ought, should (1): He/she should not answer.] *Common Law.* A pleading used by a defendant, who claims immunity or privilege as, for instance, a member of the diplomatic corps, and insists on not responding.

responsa prudentium *n., sing.* **responsum prudentis** [L. **responsa** answers, responses (1); **prudentium** of those experienced (2): responses or answers of those experienced.] *Roman Law.* Opinions of learned jurists on questions or cases referred to them. These opinions were as authoritative as present-day reports and precedents, and they were a very important source of law in early Rome.

res publica or **respublica** *n., pl.* **res publicae** or **respublicae** [L. **res** matter, thing, property, business, affair (2); **publica** public (1): a public affair, state, republic.] A commonwealth, republic or state. —*pl.* Public property or things; i.e., things like the sea, public highways and navigable waters which are regarded as belonging to no individual and are to be used by everybody. Cf. **publici juris**; **res communes**; and **res religiosae**.

res religiosae *n., sing.* **res religiosa** [L. **res** matters, things, property, business, affairs (2); **religiosae** religious (1): religious things.] Religious matters. Things which pertain to religion. Cf. **res communes** and **res publica**.

res serviens *n.* [L. **res** thing, matter, property, business, affair (2); **serviens** serving (1): serving property.] Servient property. A tenement which is subject to a servitude.

restaurant *n.* [Fr. a place for restoration, a place to eat.] An eatery. A restaurant. **Trattoria** (q.v.).

restaurateur or *fem.* **restauratrice** *n., pl.* **restaurateurs** or *fem.* **restauratrices** [Fr. restaurant-keeper.] A person who owns or manages a **restaurant** (q.v.).

restitutio in integrum *n.* [L. **restitutio** restoration, reinstatement (1); **in** into, to, against, for (2); **integrum** the whole, uninjured (3): restoration to the whole or uninjured state.] *Roman and Civil Law.* Restoration to the former condition or the **status quo ante** (q.v.). Restoration of a case to its initial state in order to have a retrial. a) *The general principle underlying the assessment of damages in contract is that of restitutio in integrum* (Freedland 1976:244). b) *When a contract is rescinded, the parties are returned to their original positions; it follows, therefore, that such a return must be possible. If it is not, if there can be no restitutio in integrum, there can be no rescission* (Lewis 1976:65-66).

res transit cum suo onere. [L. **res** matter, thing, property, business, affair (1); **transit** passes, is transferred (2); **cum** with (3); **suo** its (4); **onere** burden (5): A thing is transferred with its burden.] *Law.* Property burdened with a mortgage is transferred with the incumbrance of the mortgage. Cf. **terra transit** etc.

résumé *n., pl.* **résumés** [Fr. summary.] 1. A summary, abstract, or abridged version. a) *However, a brief résumé of the main criticisms of Freudian beliefs may be interpolated here . . .* (Eysenck 1982:10). b) *In résumé, Saho may choose to boldly turn down the offer of office* (Jay Saidy in *West Africa* 1982). 2. A brief account or summary of a person's educational background and career. **Curriculum vitae** (q.v.). a) *. . . he boasts a stellar résumé of corporate and government achievement* (*Newsweek Int.* May 4, 1981:39). b) *Applicants have been asked to appear at the interview with their résumés.* Cf. **epitome** 1.

res universitatis *pl. n.* [L. **res** matters, things, property, business, affairs (1); **universitatis** of the whole, the entirety (2): things of the whole or the entirety.] *Roman and Civil Law.* Things which belong to a community such as a corporation, society, or university, to be used by every member of the community as long as they are used properly, but which no individual can appropriate for his/her exclusive use.

resurgam [L. **resurgam** I will rise again.] I will return.

retorsio facti *n., pl.* **retorsiones facti** [L. **retorsio** returning, retaliation (1); **facti** of act, deed (2): returning of act.] *International Law.* Infliction of injuries by one nation on another in retaliation to the same degree as it has suffered. See **lex talionis**.

retorsion de droit *n., pl.* **retorsions de droit** [Fr. **retorsion** retortion, retaliation (1); **de** of (2); **droit** justice, due (3): retaliation of justice.] *International Law.* Legitimate reprisal or retaliation. See **lex talionis**.

Retournons à nos moutons. Anonymous. *Maistre Pierre Pathelin* 1191. [Fr. **retournons** let us return (1); **à** to (2); **nos** our (3); **moutons** sheep (4): Let us return to our sheep.] Let us get back to our subject.

retraxit *n., pl.* **retraxits** [L. He has withdrawn.] *Law.* A plaintiff's personal renunciation of his/her suit in open court and consequent loss of the right of action. See **nolle prosequi**.

retro me Satana See **vade retro me Satana**.

revanche *n., pl.* **revanches** [Fr. revenge.] Retaliation, especially governmental policy motivated by desire to recover lost territory.

revenant *n., pl.* **revenants** [Fr. one returning; a ghost.] 1. A ghost or specter. 2. A person who, after a long period of absence, returns to his/her former place of residence. 3. A person whose qualities, behavior, views, etc. are reminiscent of a past age. *Our friend, a revenant from the colonial era, believes that we should bring back the colonialists to solve our problems.*

Reverendus Admodum *abbr.* **R.A.** See **Admodum Reverendus.**

Reverendus Pater *abbr.* **R.P.** *n., pl.* **Reverendi Patres** [L. **reverendus** venerable, reverend (1); **pater** father (2): reverend or venerable father.] Reverend Father.

reverie *n., pl.* **reveries** [Fr. **rêverie** dreaming, daydream, musing, idle fancy, fantastic idea.] 1. An impracticable or strange notion, idea, theory, etc. A fanciful or visionary idea. A daydream. *After careful consideration, the committee decided that the proposed scheme was no more than a reverie and rejected it.* 2. A condition of fanciful musing or meditation. Daydreaming. *When Amo entered the room, Abena was so lost in her reverie that she did not notice his presence.*

Rêveries d'un Promeneur Solitaire *n.* [Fr. **rêveries** dreams (1); **d'** of (2); **un** a (3); **promeneur** walker (4); **solitaire** solitary, single (5): dreams of a single walker.] *Dreams of a Solitary Stroller*, reflections on the relationship between nature and humanity by Jean-Jacques Rousseau (1712–1778), published posthumously.

revers or **revere** *n., pl.* **revers** or **reveres** [Fr. back, reverse, wrong side.] A portion of a garment turned inside-out so that the reverse is shown; e.g., a lapel.

revocatur *n.* [L. It is recalled.] *Law.* A term signifying that a judgment has been annulled because of an error of fact.

revue *n., pl.* **revues** [Fr. something seen again, a review, a survey.] 1. A newspaper, magazine, or professional journal. 2. *Theater.* A performance combining acting, singing, and dancing, often with a humorous or satirical tone.

rex *abbr.* **R.** or **r.** *n., pl.* **reges** [L. king.] Male monarch. Used, inter alia, in the titles of British lawsuits during the reign of a king. *Rex v. Crayburn*, i.e., the Crown v. Crayburn. Cf. **regina.**

R.G. *abbr.* for **regula generalis** (q.v.).

rhathymia *n., pl.* **rhathymias** [Gk. **rhathumia** easiness of temper, taking things easily.] The condition of being lighthearted or carefree.

rhombus *n., pl.* **rhombi** [L. from Gk. **rhombos** a magician's circle, a fish.] A parallelogram with two obtuse and two acute angles.

ricochet *v.* [Fr. to rebound.] To bounce back, like a bullet or a ball off a wall. —*n.* The act of bouncing back.

ricksha or **rickshaw** See **jinriksha.**

rictus *n., pl.* **rictus** or **rictuses** [L. the mouth opened wide. The aperture of the mouth.] 1. The orifice of the mouth. 2. A gaping or wide-open grimace. A gaping or broad grin. *He drives an immaculate car*

and at parties his sartorial appearance leaves others betraying a rictus of admiration (Thomas Cooke in *West Africa* 1985).

riens en arrière *n.* [Obs. Fr. **riens** nothing (1); **en** in (2); **arrière** arrears (3): nothing in arrears.] *Law.* With no overdue obligations or unpaid debts. A plea in a suit respecting debt, when it has been alleged that the account is in arrears.

riens per descent *n.* [Obs. Fr. **riens** nothing (1); **per** through, by (2); **descent** descent (3): nothing through descent.] *Law.* The plea of an heir who has been sued for the debt of his/her ancestor, and has no inherited assets for satisfying the claim.

rigor juris *n.* [L. **rigor** stiffness, firmness (1); **juris** of right, law (2): stiffness of the law.] Strictness of the law.

rigor mortis *n.* [L. **rigor** stiffness, firmness (1); **mortis** of death (2): stiffness of death.] *Medicine.* Rigidity of muscles of the body after death, which is used as a test of the time of death.

Rio Grande *n.* [Sp. **rio** river (2); **grande** large, big (2): big river.] The big river. A major river in the southwestern United States.

R.I.P. *abbr.* for 1. **Requiescant in pace** (q.v.). 2. **Requiescat in pace** (q.v.).

riparum usus publicus est jure gentium, sicut ipsius fluminis. [L. **riparum** of banks, river-banks (2); **usus** use (1); **publicus** public (4); **est** is (3); **jure** by right, law (5); **gentium** of nations (6); **sicut** like, just as (7); **ipsius** (of) itself (8); **fluminis** of river (9): Use of river-banks is public by the law of nations just like (the use) of the river itself.] *Law.* The use of river-banks, like that of the river itself, is, by the law of nations, public; i.e., the public has a basic right to make use of the banks of a river as well as the river itself.

riposte *n., pl.* **ripostes** [Fr. parry and thrust, retort, smart reply, counter-stroke.] 1. *Fencing.* A quick return thrust. 2. A retort. A clever retort. *And when Carter attacked his proposal for a 30 per cent tax cut over three years as "irresponsible," Reagan had a deft riposte. "I'll confess to being irresponsible . . . if he'll admit to being responsible"* (*Newsweek Int.* Nov. 3, 1980:27). 3. A counter-attack. A swift retaliation. *The first Libyan riposte was not a close air strike, but high-level bombing from above the range of portable missiles* (*The Economist* 1987). —*v. intr.* 1. *Fencing.* To make a quick return thrust. 2. To retort. To make a quick appropriate response. 3. To retaliate swiftly. To launch a counter-attack.

risorgimento *n., pl.* **risorgimenti** or **risorgimentos** [It. a rising, revival, resurrection.] 1. *Italy.* The historical period in which Italy struggled for independence and unification (1750–1870). 2. *Italy.* The movement for Italian independence and unification. 3. A revival, resurgence, regeneration or renaissance. *The ministry has introduced an extensive program of cultural risorgimento.*

risqué or **risque** *adj.* [Fr. risky, hazardous, daring.] Daring. Somewhat indecent or indelicate. Used to describe a story, remark, comment, etc. *Jones is a perfect gentleman who would never say anything risqué.*

ristourne *n., pl.* **ristournes** [Fr. return or refund of overpaid amount.] *French Colonial Tropical Africa.* The unused revenue after expenditure. It was usually distributed among the territorial governments as subsidy.

risus sardonicus *n.* [L. **risus** laugh, grin (2); **sardonicus** sardonic, devilish (1): devilish grin.] 1. An exaggerated grin or smirk. 2. *Medicine.* A forced grin or smirk caused by a medical condition or disease such as tetanus.

rite *adv./adj.* [L. duly, fitly, in the usual manner.] *British.* With a pass. Used to indicate undistinguished performance in examinations for graduation from school or university.

rite de passage *n., pl.* **rites de passage** [Fr. **rite** rite, ceremony (1); **de** of (2); **passage** passage (3): rite of passage.] A ceremony or ritual to commemorate transition from one stage of life to another.

rococo [Fr. rocklike, highly ornamented and elaborate.] 1. *Art and Architecture.* A highly elaborate style popular in France in the 18th century. 2. *Music.* A highly ornamental musical style which followed the baroque in 18th-century Europe.

rodeo *n., pl.* **rodeos** [Sp. corral.] 1. An enclosure for range cattle. 2. The gathering of range cattle into an enclosure. 3. A show or demonstration of skills used in such a cattle round-up, such as horse-riding, roping, etc.

roi fainéant *n., pl.* **rois fainéants** [Fr. **roi** king (2); **fainéant** do-nothing, idle, lazy (1): a do-nothing king.] A sluggard king. A king who does not perform his royal functions, especially one who has been deprived of, or has delegated, royal power. Cf. **fainéant.**

Roma locuta, causa finita. [L. **Roma** Rome (1); **locuta** (has) spoken (2); **causa** cause, case, reason (3); **finita** (has been) finished, ended: Rome has spoken, the case has been ended.] *Roman Catholic Church.* Rome has spoken, the case is closed. Applicable to decrees or judgments by the Pope or the Vatican bringing controversies to an end. *"This business of Roma locuta, causa finita . . . is a thing of the past," said a clergyman in Sao Paulo* (*Newsweek Int.* July 14, 1980:37). See **Roma locuta est** and **Roma locuta est, causa** etc.

Roma locuta est. Augustine of Hippo (354-430 A.D.). *Sermons* I. [L. **Roma** Rome (1); **locuta est** has spoken, said (2): Rome has spoken.] Rome has spoken; i.e., the imperial power has issued an order bringing the controversy to an end. Applicable to an order, message, instruction, etc. "from above" which arbitrarily brings a controversy or discussion to an abrupt end. See **Roma locuta, causa finita.** For fuller form, see **Roma locuta est, causa** etc.

Roma locuta est, causa finita est. Augustine of Hippo (354-430 A.D.). *Sermons* I. [L. **Roma** Rome (1);

locuta est has spoken (2); **causa** cause, case, reason (3); **finita** finished (5); **est** is (4): Rome has spoken; the case is finished.] Rome has spoken and the case is finished; i.e., concluded. For shorter form, see **Roma locuta est.**

roman à clef or **roman à clé** *n., pl.* **romans à clef** or **roman à clés** [Fr. **roman** novel, romance (1); **à** to, toward, in, by, with, until (2); **clef** or **clé** key, clue (3): novel with a key or clue.] A novel in which real persons or events are disguised under fictitious names. A novel in which the author treats a real event or actual events, using fictitious names to conceal the identity of the persons or the events. a) *So runs the plot of "Samaritan," by Philippe van Rijndt, a roman à clef with a capital R, exploiting the world's fascination with Pope John Paul II* (*Newsweek Int.* Oct. 18, 1982:67). b) *The book is a brilliant roman à clef in which the author cleverly exposes the sordid activities of high-ranking officials, who are more of a liability than an asset to the nation.*

roman à thèse *n., pl.* **romans à thèse** [Fr. **roman** novel, romance (1); **à** to, toward, in, by, with, until (2); **thèse** thesis, argument (3): novel with a thesis.] A didactic novel. A novel which aims at proving a hypothesis or expressing some views, ideas, theories, etc.

roman philosophique *n., pl.* **romans philosophiques** [Fr. **roman** novel, romance (2); **philosophique** philosophical, philosophic (1): a philosophical novel.] A novel which illustrates ideas. *Graham Greene, a British secret agent and novelist, wrote authentic romans philosophiques.*

rondeau *n., pl.* **rondeaux** [Fr. circle, round.] 1. A lyric poem of 13 or 10 lines which repeats its opening as a refrain and uses two sets of rhymes. 2. *Music.* A song popular in medieval France. Cf. **rondel; rondelet;** and **rondo.**

rondel *n., pl.* **rondels** [Fr. circle, round.] A lyric poem of 13 or 14 lines which, like the **rondeau** (q.v.), uses two sets of rhymes and repeats its opening line(s) as a refrain. —**rondel** or **rondelle** *n., pl.* **rondels** or **rondelles** Something round or of circular shape.

rondelet *n., pl.* **rondelets** [Fr. a little circle, a little rondeau.] A seven-line lyric poem which uses two sets of rhymes and repeats the first line as a refrain in lines three and seven. Cf. **rondeau; rondel;** and **rondo.**

rondo *n., pl.* **rondos** [It. circle, round.] *Music.* A work which alternates its main theme three or more times with variations and episodes. Cf. **rondeau; rondel;** and **rondelet.**

rosa sine spina [L. **rosa** rose (1); **sine** without (2); **spina** thorn (3): a rose without a thorn.] A thornless rose. An unmixed joy.

Rosenkavalier *n.* [Ger. **Rosen** rose (1); **Kavalier** knight (2): rose knight.] *The Cavalier of the Rose,* a 1910 opera by Richard Strauss (1864-1949).

rostrum *n., pl.* **rostra** or **rostrums** [L. bird's beak, prow of a ship, stage, orator's platform.] 1. Platform in the Forum of ancient Rome used by public speakers. This platform was decorated with the prows of enemy ships captured in the battle of Antium in 338 B.C. 2. A platform or stage used by a public speaker, conductor, etc. *He mounted the rostrum and delivered a very emotional speech.* 3. A forum or opportunity for communicating with a large audience or readership. . . . *American officials are limited by the Kremlin to one brief appearance on Soviet TV each year on the Fourth of July. Last year Ambassador Thomas Watson lost even that rostrum . . . (Newsweek Int.* March 16, 1981:7). Cf. **podium.**

rotonda *n., pl.* **rotondas** [It. round.] **Rotunda** (q.v.).

rotunda *n., pl.* **rotundas** [L. round, circular, rotund.] 1. A building or hall which is circular and usually has a dome. 2. A large circular room. 3. A big central area in a public building such as a hotel.

roué *n., pl.* **roués** [Fr. a dissolute person.] A profligate. A man who lives a life of excessive sensual pleasures, especially in his amorous affairs. A dissolute elderly man. *Anne's boss is a worthless old roué who spends most of his time in incredible orgies with girls younger than his daughters.* Cf. **vieux marcheur.**

Rouge et Noir *n.* [Fr. **rouge** red (1); **et** and (2); **noir** black (3): red and black.] *The Red and the Black,* an 1831 historical novel by Stendhal (1783–1842).

routine *n., pl.* **routines** [Fr. habitual procedure, sheer habit.] A regular or normal procedure or way of doing things. *It was dawn in Paris, and Gilbert Zemour . . . was going about his usual early-morning routine (Newsweek Int.* Aug. 15, 1983:17). —*adj.* Ordinary or habitual. *Simeon is bored with his routine administrative duties and is looking for an exciting and challenging position.*

rp. *abbr.* for **recipe** (q.v.).

R.P. *abbr.* for 1. **Regius Professor** (q.v.). 2. **Reverendus Pater** (q.v.).

R.P.D. *abbr.* for **Rerum Politicarum Doctor** (q.v.).

R.S.V.P. *abbr.* for **Répondez s'il vous plaît** (q.v.). Cf. **R.V.S.V.P.**

rubato *n., pl.* **rubatos** [It. stolen.] *Music.* Stolen time. A somewhat free use of musical time in which some sections are played slightly slower and others faster in order to create a sense of rhythmic flexibility and emotion.

rubella *n.* [L. reddish.] *Medicine.* German measles.

Rubicon *n., pl.* **Rubicons** [L. **Rubico,** a stream south of Ravenna, Italy.] 1. *Roman History.* The stream which, in the Republican era of ancient Roman history, served as a boundary between Italy and Cisalpine Gaul. Since a Roman general or governor was forbidden to lead his troops in arms across a Roman boundary into Italy, Julius Caesar's crossing of the Rubicon in 49 B.C. meant that he was irrevocably committed to war against Pompey and the senatorial party. 2. A boundary, line or limit whose crossing indicates irrevocable commitment to a decision or a complete break with the past or that the "die is cast." a) *The Prime Minister after considerable deliberation and hesitation, crossed the Rubicon by tendering his letter of resignation.* b) *But in less than 25 years he has crossed an American Rubicon from poor immigrant quarters to the comfortable suites of upper U.S. management as a group vice president . . . (Newsweek Int.* May 4, 1981:37). See **alea jacta est** and **jacta alea est.**

rv. *abbr.* for **rendezvous** (q.v.).

R.V.S.V.P. *abbr.* for **Répondez vite s'il vous plaît** (q.v.). Cf. **R.S.V.P.**

S

S. *abbr.* for 1. **saeculum** (q.v.). 2. **Señor** (q.v.). 3. **Signor** (q.v.). 4. **Signora** (q.v.). 5. **solo** (q.v.).

S.A. *abbr.* for **société anonyme** (q.v.).

S.A. or **s.a.** *abbr.* for 1. **secundum artem** (q.v.). 2. **sine anno** (q.v.). 3. **sub anno** (q.v.).

Sabbath *n.* [Heb. **sabbāt** rest.] 1. Saturday, the seventh day of the week, observed by Jews and other religious groups as a day of rest and religious observance. 2. Sunday, the first day of the week, celebrated by most Christians as a day of rest and religious observance. Cp. **Shabbat**.

sabotage *n., pl.* **sabotages** [Fr. the noise made by sabots, i.e., wooden shoes, planned and organized destruction.] 1. Deliberate and malicious destruction of property with intent to hurt a business enterprise or an institution. Interference with the normal activities of an organization with the same intention. *To prevent future sabotage, the government may call in army units to guard energy installations* (*Newsweek Int.* June 16, 1980:25). 2. Subverting the efforts of a government or a nation, especially during war or a national emergency. —*v. tr.* To destroy or damage.

saboteur *n., pl.* **saboteurs** [Fr. a bungler, a person who engages in or commits sabotage.] Someone involved in the deliberate and malicious destruction of property. a) *Others would stream across into Poland itself to guard railways, roads and bridges against saboteurs* (*Newsweek Int.* Dec. 15, 1980:9). b) *A party commission . . . would decide in due course what sanctions would be applied against the saboteurs* (Achim Remde in *West Africa* 1985).

sachet *n., pl.* **sachets** [Fr. a little sack.] A small cloth sack or envelope filled with pleasantly-scented material and used to perfume closets or other storage areas.

Sacrae Scripturae Baccalaureus *abbr.* **S.S.B.** *n.* [L. **sacrae** of sacred, holy (2); **scripturae** (of) scripture (3); **baccalaureus** bachelor (1): Bachelor of Sacred Scripture.] An undergraduate degree in sacred scripture.

Sacrae Scripturae Doctor *abbr.* **S.S.D.** *n.* [L. **sacrae** of sacred, holy (2); **scripturae** (of) scripture (3); **doctor** teacher (1): teacher of sacred scripture.] Doctor of Sacred Scripture. A terminal graduate degree in sacred scripture.

Sacrae Scripturae Licentiatus *abbr.* **S.S.L.** *n.* [L. **sacrae** of sacred, holy (2); **scripturae** (of) scripture (3); **Licentiatus** Licentiate (1): Licentiate of Sacred Scripture.] An academic degree conferred by European universities and American seminaries for completion of an advanced curriculum in sacred scripture.

Sacrae Theologiae Baccalaureus *abbr.* **S.T.B.** *n.* [L. **sacrae** of sacred (2); **theologiae** (of) theology (3); **baccalaureus** bachelor (1): Bachelor of Sacred Theology.] An undergraduate degree in sacred scripture.

Sacrae Theologiae Doctor *abbr.* **S.T.D.** *n.* [L. **sacrae** of sacred, holy (2); **theologiae** (of) theology (3); **doctor** teacher (1): teacher of sacred theology.] Doctor of Sacred Theology. A terminal graduate degree in sacred theology.

Sacrae Theologiae Licentiatus *abbr.* **S.T.L.** *n.* [L. **sacrae** of sacred, holy (2); **theologiae** (of) theology (3); **licentiatus** licentiate (1): Licentiate of Sacred Theology.] An academic degree conferred by a European university for completion of an advanced curriculum in sacred theology.

Sacrae Theologiae Magister *abbr.* **S.T.M.** *n.* [L. **sacrae** of sacred, holy (2); **theologiae** (of) theology (3); **magister** master (1): Master of Sacred Theology.] A predoctoral graduate degree in sacred theology.

sacramentum *n., pl.* **sacramenta** [L. guarantee, deposit, oath.] *Roman Law.* 1. Oath. Oath of allegiance. 2. A wager of law. In one of the formal legal processes of early Rome, the litigants deposited a sum of money with the court. The successful party took his deposit away, while the losing party lost his deposit, which was then paid into the national treasury.

sacrarium *n., pl.* **sacraria** [L. a holy place.] 1. The sanctuary or sacristy of a church. 2. *Roman Catholic Church.* Piscina. The sink or drain used to dispose of the water with which sacred objects are cleaned.

sacré bleu *interj.* [Fr. **sacré** holy, sacred (1); **bleu** blue (2): holy blue.] A rhyming euphemism for **sacré Dieu** or "holy God." Good Heavens! Good Lord! Damn it! *His unsinkable boat capsized several times in rough seas and sacré bleu! at one point he had to ditch almost 50 liters of good red wine* (*Newsweek Int.* Oct. 6, 1980:57).

sacro egoismo *n.* Antonio Salandra (1853–1931). [It. **sacro** sacred, holy (1); **egoism** egoism (2): holy egoism.] An egoistic emphasis on the interests of one's own country. Excessive nationalism.

sadhu *n., pl.* **sadhus** [Skt. **sādhu** holy, right.] *Hinduism.* A holy man who practices asceticism and has spiritual powers.

saeculum *abbr.* **s.** or **saec.** *n., pl.* **saecula** [L. age, generation, lifetime, hundred years.] A long period of time. Age. Century.

saeva indignatio *n.* Jonathan Swift (1667–1745). [L. **saeva** fierce, ferocious (1); **indignatio** anger, indignation (2): fierce indignation.] Strong or ferocious indignation, especially for human stupidity and foolishness. . . . *his own saeva indignatio at contemporary manners and morals* . . . (Laistner 1966:5).

safari *n., pl.* **safaris** [Ar. **safar** journey.] 1. A land journey, especially in Africa, in search of large game or for purposes of exploration. 2. Any long land journey or trip.

Sagittarius *n.* [L. arrow-shooter, archer.] 1. *Astronomy.* An archer-shaped constellation located near Scorpio and Capricorn. 2. *Astrology.* The ninth sign of the zodiac dominant from November 22 through December 21. 3. A person born under this sign.

sahib *n.* [Hindi **sāhib** master.] *Colonial India.* Used as a term of respect by an Indian for a British employer or master.

saisie *n.* [Fr. seizure, execution, distraint.] *French Law.* Judicial seizure, attachment, or sequestration of property.

saisie-exécution *n.* [Fr. **saisie** seizure, execution, distraint (1); **exécution** execution, carrying out (2): seizure-execution.] *French Law.* A writ whereby the movable property of a debtor is seized, sold, and the proceeds used for satisfying the claims of the creditor. **Fieri facias.** Cf. **fieri facias de bonis propriis.**

saisie-immobilière *n.* [Fr. **saisie** seizure, execution, distraint (1); **immobilière** immovable property: seizure of immovable property.] *French Law.* A writ whereby the immovable property of a debtor is seized, sold, and the proceeds used for satisfying the claims of the creditor. Cf. **fieri facias de bonis propriis.**

S.A.L. or **s.a.l.** *abbr.* for **secundum artis leges** (q.v.).

salaam *n., pl.* **salaams** [Arab. **salām** = Heb. **sālōm** peace.] 1. A greeting of peace. Cf. **pax; shalom;** and

shanti. 2. *India.* A demonstration of submission and obedience in which the greeting is accompanied by a low bow and hand gesture.

salarium *n.* [L. salary, allowance.] 1. *Ancient Rome.* An allowance paid to Roman soldiers so that they could buy salt. Salt-money. 2. Salary. Allowance. An annual remuneration.

sal Atticus *n., pl.* **sales Attici** Pliny the Elder (A.D. 23–79). *Historia Naturalis* XXXI,87. [L. **sal** wit, salt (2); **Atticus** Attic (1): Attic wit.] Poignant or biting, delicate/subtle wit.

saltus *n., pl.* **saltus** or **saltuses** [L. spring, leap, bound.] 1. A break or interruption of continuity. An abrupt transition. 2. *Logic.* Omitting an indispensable step in the process of proof.

salus populi suprema est lex. Cicero (106–43 B.C.). *De Legibus* III,3,8. [L. **salus** safety, welfare (1); **populi** of people (2); **suprema** supreme (3); **est** is (4); **lex** law (5): The safety of the people is the supreme law.] *Law.* Public safety is the supreme law. See **in casu extremae** etc.

salus populi suprema lex esto. [L. **salus** safety, welfare (1); **populi** of the people (2); **suprema** supreme, highest (4); **lex** law (5); **esto** shall be, let it be, be: The safety of the people shall be the highest law.] Let the welfare of the people be the supreme law. Motto of the State of Missouri.

salus publica suprema lex. [L. **salus** safety, welfare (2); **publica** public, state (1); **suprema** supreme, highest (3); **lex** law (4): Public safety is the supreme law.] *Law.* The welfare of the people is the supreme law. See **in casu extremae** etc.

salute *interj.* [It. health, safety.] A toast to good health and prosperity. Cf. **mazel tov** and **skoal.**

salutis gratia *abbr.* **S.G.** *adv.* [L. **salutis** of safety (2); **gratia** for the sake (1): for the sake of safety.] On account of safety.

salva veritate *adv.* [L. **salva** (with being) safe, unharmed (2); **veritate** with truth (1): with truth being safe.] As long as truth remains unimpaired. According to Leibniz's principle that two expressions are deemed to be synonymous if substituting one for the other does not alter the connotation, significance, and truth of the context in which it is used. Cf. **eadem sunt quorum unum** etc.

salve *v., pl.* **salvete** [L. Be well. Hello.] Hello. Greetings. Cf. **ave** and **ciao.**

salvis erroribus et omissis *abbr.* **S.E.e.O.** *adv.* [L. **salvis** (with) safe, unimpaired (4); **erroribus** errors (1); **et** and (2); **omissis** (with) omitted (things), omissions (3): with errors and omissions unimpaired.] Excepting or without prejudice to mistakes and things which have been left out.

salvo *n., pl.* **salvos** *short for* **salvo jure** [L. **salvo** (with/by) safe (1); **jure** right, law (2): by safe law.] 1. *Law.* A saving provision or clause. A reservation or condition.

2. An unexpressed or mental reservation or condition used to evade or avoid a difficulty. 3. An action taken to preserve or salvage one's reputation, dignity, or pride or to ease one's conscience.

sal volatile *n.* [L. **sal** salt (2); **volatile** rapid, swift (1): swift salt.] Ammonium carbonate. Smelling salts.

samizdat *short form* of **samizdatel'stvo** *n.* [Russ. **sam** self (1); **izdat(el'stvo)** publishing house (2): self publishing house.] 1. The publication and circulation of illegal literature in the Soviet Union. 2. Literature circulated illegally in the Soviet Union. 3. An underground publishing house.

samurai *n., pl.* **samurai** or **samurais** [Japan. warrior.] 1. A professional soldier in feudal Japan. 2. The Japanese feudal aristocracy originally based upon military prowess.

san or **-san** *n.* [Japan. honorable.] *Japan.* An honorific title or expression of courtesy. Usually attached as a suffix to a person's name or title; e.g., "Reverend-san," "Captain-san," "Michael-san," and "**Mama-san**" (q.v.). See **babu**; **Herr**; **Monsieur**; **Senhor**; **Señor**; and **Signor**.

sanae mentis et bonae memoriae *adj.* [L. **sanae** of sound (1); **mentis** (of) mind (2); **et** and (3); **bonae** (of) good (4); **memoriae** (of) memory (5): of sound mind and good memory.] *Old English Law.* With a sound mind and a reliable memory. Used to indicate that a testator is mentally fit to make a will. See **compos mentis**.

sanatorium or **sanitorium** or **sanatarium** or **sanitarium** *n., pl.* **sanatoriums** or **sanatoria**, **sanitoriums** or **sanitoria**, **sanatariums** or **sanataria**, **sanitariums** or **sanitaria** [L. a healing/curing place.] 1. An establishment which provides recuperation and rest for patients, especially invalids. *. . . Andropov is still in a special sanitarium for members of the Communist Party Central Committee . . . (Newsweek Int.* Jan. 2, 1984:8). 2. An establishment that provides treatment for diseases requiring protracted attention, such as tuberculosis, mental disorders, or drug addiction.

Sanctae Memoriae *abbr.* **S.M.** *adj.* [L. **sanctae** of holy, sacred (1); **memoriae** (of) memory (2): of holy memory.] Deceased.

sanctorium *n., pl.* **sanctoria** or **sanctoriums** [L. a consecrated/sacred place.] A shrine.

sanctum *n., pl.* **sancta** or **sanctums** [L. something sacred, inviolable, and consecrated.] 1. A sacred or holy place. Something that is hallowed. 2. Office, study, or place of retreat. *He has at his residence a sanctum where he retires whenever he wants to do serious studies.* See **adytum** and **sanctum sanctorum**.

sanctum sanctorum *n.* [L. **sanctum** holy (thing) (1); **sanctorum** of holy (things, matters) (2): holy of holy things.] 1. Holy of Holies. The most holy place. 2. A place of retreat. A place where a person can go to and be free from disturbances. See **adytum** and **sanctum**.

Sanctus *adj.* [L. holy.] *Christianity.* The first word of a prayer of praise at the beginning of the canon of the Catholic Mass. —*n.* 1. The prayer itself. 2. *Music.* A composition based on this prayer.

San Francisco *n.* [Sp. **san** holy, sacred, saint (1); **Francisco** Francis (2): Saint Francis.] A city in northern California, founded as a mission by the Spanish in 1776.

sang-froid or **sangfroid** *n., pl.* **sang-froids** or **sangfroids** [Fr. **sang** blood (2); **froid** cold (1): cold-blood, composure, self-possession.] Cool-headedness. Calmness. Self-control or imperturbability, especially during an emergency or dangerous circumstances. a) *The film . . . caused French critics to abandon their sangfroid; . . . (Newsweek Int.* Feb. 5, 1979:17). b) *There was pandemonium when a snake entered the classroom, but the teacher handled the situation with magnificent sangfroid.*

sannyasi or **sannyasin** *n.* [Hindi **sannyāsī** from Skt. **samnyāsī** renouncer.] *Hinduism.* A wandering begger and ascetic who has renounced all social obligations and material goods for religious reasons.

sans *prep.* [Fr. without.] Devoid of. Deprived of. *She is still a very charming woman, even sans the vivacity of her youthful days.*

Sans argent l'honneur n'est qu'une maladie. Jean Racine (1639–1699). *Les Plaideurs* I,1. [Fr. **sans** without (1); **argent** money (2); **l'** the (3); **honneur** honor (4); **n'. . .qu'** merely, only (6); **est** is (5); **une** a (7); **maladie** malady, disease (8): Without money honor is only a disease.] Honor without money is merely a malady. Cf. **probitas laudatur** etc.

sans cause *adj./adv.* [Fr. **sans** without (1); **cause** cause (2): without cause.] *French Law.* Without cause or reason. **Sine causa** (q.v.). *An obligation sans cause cannot be enforced.*

sans cérémonie *adv.* [Fr. **sans** without (1); **cérémonie** ceremony (2): without ceremony.] Without ceremony. Without any ceremony or formality. Informally. —*adj.* Informal. Unceremonious. Cf. **sans façon**.

sans-culotte *n., pl.* **sans-culottes** [Fr. **sans** without (1) **culotte** pants, breeches (2): without breeches, a rabid or ultra-violent republican.] 1. A member of France's extreme republican party during the Revolution. 2. A radical or extremist politician or political activist, especially one who does not hesitate to resort to violence. An anarchist. A revolutionary. 3. The lowest echelons of society. Cf. **hoi polloi**.

Sansei *n., pl.* **Sansei** or **Sanseis** [Japan. **san** three (1); **sei** generation (2): third generation.] A grandchild of a Japanese immigrant to the United States. A third-generation Japanese-American. Cf. **issei** and **Nisei**.

sans façon *adv.* [Fr. **sans** without (1); **façon** ceremony, fuss (2): without fuss.] Without any ceremony or fuss. Informally. In an offhand manner. —*adj.* Unceremonious. Informal. Cf. **sans cérémonie**.

sans frais *abbr.* **S.F.** or **s.f.** *adv.* [Fr. **sans** without (1); **frais** expenses, cost (2): without expenses.] Without cost. Free of charge.

sans-gêne *n.* [Fr. **sans** without (1); **gêne** shame, restraint (2): without shame, offhandedness, over-familiarity.] 1. Lack of self-restraint or constraint. *Though he helped himself to the spoils of victory with more than the usual sans-gêne of a Roman triumphator, he was by no means ungenerous to his soldiers* (Cary 1970:355). 2. Off-handedness. Failure to observe formality or politeness.

sans jour *adv.* [Fr. **sans** without (1); **jour** day (2): without day.] Indefinitely. Without appointing any future day for a meeting. **Sine die** (q.v.) *The court adjourned at 12:00 noon sans jour.*

sans nombre *adj.* [Fr. **sans** without (1); **nombre** number (2): without number.] Numberless. Countless. **Sine numero** (q.v.).

sans recours *adv./adj.* [Fr. **sans** without (1); **recours** recourse, appeal (2): without recourse.] Without appeal. Applicable to qualified endorsement.

Santa Clara *n.* [Sp. **santa** holy, sacred, saint (1); **Clara** Clare (2): Saint Clare.] 1. A city in Cuba founded in 1689. 2. A city in western California.

Santa Cruz *n.* [Sp. **santa** holy, sacred, saint (1); **cruz** cross (2): holy cross.] 1. A city in Bolivia founded c.1560. 2. A city in western California.

Santa Fe *n.* [Sp. **santa** holy, sacred, saint (1); **fe** faith (2): holy faith.] 1. A city in NE Argentina founded 1573. 2. The capital of New Mexico founded c.1609.

santo *n., pl.* **santos** [Sp. saint.] A saint. A holy person. The image of a saint.

santon *n., pl.* **santons** [Fr. a little saint or holy figure.] **Crêche** (q.v.) figures from Provence.

sapere aude [L. **sapere** to be wise (2); **aude** dare (1): Dare to be wise.] Don't hesitate to use wisdom.

Satan *n.* [Heb. **sātān** adversary, devil.] God's evil adversary. A fallen angel. The devil. Cf. **Shaitan**.

sati See **suttee**.

satis *adv.* [L. enough.] That's enough. **Basta** (q.v.).

satis eloquentiae sapientiae parum [L. **satis** enough (1); **eloquentiae** of eloquence (2); **sapientiae** of wisdom (4); **parum** not enough (3): Enough of eloquence, not enough of wisdom.] Enough good speaking but not enough wisdom.

satis liquet. [L. **satis** adequately, sufficiently (2); **liquet** it is clear, apparent (1): It is adequately clear.] It is sufficiently clear.

satis superque *adj.* [L. **satis** enough (1); **superque** and above (2): enough and above.] Enough and more than enough. *In the opinion of the audience, Angus' explanation of the distinction between ownership and possession was satis superque.*

satis verborum [L. **satis** enough (1); **verborum** of words (2): enough of words.] No more need be said.

satius est petere fontes quam sectari rivulos. [L. **satius** better, preferable (2); **est** it is (1); **petere** to seek, strive after (3); **fontes** sources, fountains (4); **quam** than (5); **sectari** to chase, pursue (6); **rivulos** petty streams, rivulets (7): It is better to seek the sources than to pursue the rivulets.] Looking for the chief source is better than chasing minor paths. See **melius est petere** etc. Cf. **origo rei** etc.

Saturnalia *pl. n.* An English plural ending is sometimes added to this Latin plural, as **Saturnalias**. [L. festival of Saturn.] 1. *Ancient Rome.* A very merry festival of the god Saturn. During the celebration, which began on December 17th, there were tumultuous festivities, slaves were granted temporary freedom, gifts were exchanged and the festival was presided over by a mock king. Elements of the festival were subsequently incorporated into Christmas and New Year's Day celebrations. 2. An orgy. A wild, uncontrolled, tumultuous spectacle, celebration, or festivity. *Members of the football club had a Saturnalia in celebration of their victory in this year's competition.* 3. Excessive emotion or immorality. *The nation was engulfed in such a Saturnalia of moral turpitude that a program of moral reforms became imperative.* 4. The short title for **Conviviorum Saturnaliorum Libri Septem** (q.v.) by Macrobius (late 4th/early 5th century A.D.).

satyriasis *n., pl.* **satyriases** [Gk. **saturiasis** from **satur(os)** satyr, goat-man: condition of a satyr, sexual abnormality characteristic of a lewd, goatish man.] Abnormal desire for sexual pleasure by a male. Cf. **andromania**.

saut du même au même [Fr. **saut** jump, leap (1); **du** from the (2); **même** same (3); **au** to, toward the, in the, by the, with the, until the (4); **même** same (5): jump from the same to the same.] A mistake in copying caused by overlooking words which occur between a word or phrase and its repetition. Cf. **homoioteleuton**.

sauve qui peut *n.* [Fr. **sauve** save oneself, flee, run away (1); **qui** who, whoever (2); **peut** can (3): Flee whoever can.] Anyone who can should save himself/herself. A headlong, disorderly, helter-skelter or precipitate retreat, withdrawal or flight. A total rout. Each one for himself/herself. Panic. Stampede. a) *The flight from office which had already set in during a more prosperous age ended by becoming a general sauve qui peut, . . .* (Cary 1970:741). b) *The result has been an understandable drive toward self-protection in some cases and a less attractive spirit of sauve qui peut in others* (Newsweek Int. June 23, 1980:10).

savant *n., pl.* **savants** [Fr. a learned or well-informed person.] A very learned or erudite person. A scholar.

savoir faire or **savoir-faire** *n.* [Fr. **savoir** to know, know how (1); **faire** to do (2): to know how to do.] Social adroitness or tact. Knowing what is to be done at the right time. *Andrew is a pleasant and versatile man whose savoir faire never fails him.*

savoir vivre *n.* [Fr. **savoir** to know, know how (1); **vivre** to live (2): to know how to live.] Knowing how to live elegantly. Good manners. Etiquette. Tact. *Mrs. Kuntu's lack of savoir vivre has been causing her husband considerable embarrassment.*

sayonara *interj.* [Japan.] Good-bye. Farewell. See **à bientôt.**

sayyid or **saiyid** or **syed** *n.* [Ar. lord, prince.] *Islam.* 1. Title of Husain (62?-669?), the grandson of Muhammad by his daughter Fatima. 2. A descendant of Husain. 3. Title for a Muslim dignitary or holy man.

S.B. *abbr.* for **Scientiae Baccalaureus** (q.v.).

S.C. *abbr.* for 1. **senatus consulto** (q.v.). 2. **senatus consultum** (q.v.).

sc. *abbr.* for 1. **scilicet** (q.v.). 2. **sculpsit** (q.v.).

Scala Caeli *n.* [**scala** stair, ladder (1); **caeli** of sky, heaven (2): the stair of heaven.] *Christianity.* 1. The ladder which leads souls to heaven. Seen in a vision by Jacob in the Old Testament and also by St. Bernard. 2. A church in Tre Fontane, near Rome, where this vision took place. 3. Any religious site where benefits could be gained for the dead souls. 4. Any way to achieve religious salvation.

scala naturae *n.* [L. **scala** stair, ladder (1); **naturae** of nature (2): the stair of nature.] The great chain of being.

scandalum magnatum *abbr.* **scan. mag.** *n., pl.* **scandala magnatum** [L. **scandalum** slander (1); **magnatum** of great (persons) (2): slander of great persons.] *England.* A defamatory publication or speech designed to injure a judge, peer, or other high-ranking officer.

scan. mag. *abbr.* for **scandalum magnatum** (q.v.).

Sc.B. *abbr.* for **Scientiae Baccalaureus** (q.v.).

Sc.D. *abbr.* for **Scientiae Doctor** (q.v.).

scenario *n., pl.* **scenari** or **scenarios** [It. scene.] 1. The outline of a play, film, or opera, including details of the scenes in their sequence. 2. Imagined or projected sequence of events about to take place. a) *Anxious policymakers envisioned a number of frightening scenarios ranging all the way from the inconvenience of an oil-short winter on the Continent to a high-stakes Soviet power play in the Persian Gulf* (*Newsweek Int.* Nov. 10, 1980:13). b) *. . . Europe has little chance of achieving a balance with Japan in the trade arena even under the rosiest scenarios* (*Newsweek Int.* March 23, 1981:10). 3. Plan of a military campaign.

scène à faire *n., pl.* **scènes à faire** [Fr. **scène** scene, episode (1); **à** to, toward, in, by, with, until (2); **faire** make, do (3): a scene to make.] An episode, scene, or event in a novel, play, or other piece of creative writing which is necessary to the plot. *The defense team argued that the scenes in question were not plagiarized but simply scènes à faire which anyone telling this story would have included.*

schadenfreude *n.* [Ger. **Schadenfreude: Schaden** damage, harm, injury (2); **Freude** joy, glee (1): joy about injury.] Enjoyment derived from the misfortune of others. *Contrasting sharply with the general atmosphere of sincere sympathy was the attitude of Eva, the victim's arch-rival, who could not successfully disguise her schadenfreude.*

schema *n., pl.* **schemas** [Gk. **schēma** shape, form.] 1. A diagram. A model. An outline. 2. *Psych.* A model used to organize and understand complex patterns of reality.

scherzando *adv.* [It. joking.] *Music.* In a joking or playful fashion. *The piece was not written to be played scherzando.* —*adj.* Joking or playing. *The pianist played the scherzando passage much too slowly.* — *n., pl.* **scherzandos** A musical composition written in a playful or joking style.

scherzo *n., pl.* **scherzos** [It. joke.] *Music.* A musical movement played in a lively fashion, usually in 3/4 time.

schizophasia *n., pl.* **schizophasias** [Neo-Gk. from Gk. **skhiz(ō)** divide (1); **phasis** utterance (2): divided utterance.] Incoherent speech of the type characteristic of a person suffering from **schizophrenia** (q.v.).

schizophrenia *n., pl.* **schizophrenias** [Neo-Gk. from Gk. **skhiz(ō)** divide (1); **phrēn** diaphragm, mind (2): divided mind.] An abnormal mental condition in which the patient's thoughts are at variance with his/her actions. The patient cannot think logically, experiences paranoia, hallucinations, and delusions, and usually withdraws from the real world and social interaction into a world of fantasy. a) *Miller . . . began slipping into schizophrenia after an older brother committed suicide* (*Newsweek Int.* June 27, 1983:38). b) *These drugs relieved the hearing of voices and delusions typical of schizophrenia . . .* (*Newsweek Int.* Nov. 12, 1979:60). c) *. . . the President's team of economic advisers suffers from a slight case of schizophrenia* (*Newsweek Int.* Sept. 28, 1981:38).

schlemiel or **shlemiel** *n., pl.* **schlemiels** or **shlemiels** [Yid. **shlemiel** from Heb. selumi'ēl.] An unlucky bungler.

schlimazel *n.* [Yid. **shlimazl.**] An unlucky, incompetent person.

schlock or **shlock** *n.* [Yid. **shlak.**] Poor or inferior material or merchandise. —*adj.* Poor. Cheap. Shoddy.

schmaltz or **schmalz** *n., pl.* **schmaltzes** or **schmalzes** [Yid. **shmalts** rendered fat.] Extreme sentimentalism in music, art, etc. Something which is distastefully sentimental. *. . . the group's music, which is a cheerful mishmash of incongruous genres, from reggae and country-Western to torchy American schmaltz and classic Motown* (*Newsweek Int.* Jan. 23, 1984:42).

schmeer or **schmear** or **shmear** *n.* [Yid. **shmir** smear, smudge.] A whole lot or group.

schmooze or **schmoose** *v.* [Yid. **shmues** chat.] To gossip or chat, especially cozily and confidentially. —*n.* A cozy, confidential chat.

schmuck or **shmuck** *n.* [Yid. **shmok** penis, fool.] A person who is clumsy and easily-deceived.

schnook *n., pl.* **schnooks** [Yid. **shnuk** snout.] Someone who is easily tricked or deceived.

schnorrer *n., pl.* **schnorrers** [Yid. **shnorer** begger.] Someone who regularly profits from the generosity of others. A parasite.

sciens *adj., pl.* **scientes** [L. knowing, understanding.] *Law.* Knowing or understanding the implications of an act. *The rule that sciens is not volens has given rise to great difficulty in cases between passengers in cars and drunken or inexperienced drivers* (Rogers 1975:618). Cf. **volens.**

scienter *adv.* [L. knowingly, understandingly.] Knowingly. Deliberately. Willfully. Intentionally. —*n. Law.* 1. A level of knowledge which makes a person legally answerable for his/her act. 2. An allegation, in pleading, that the defendant's degree of knowledge of the circumstances of the cause and his/her conduct make his/her act a crime. —*adj.* Dealing with the level of knowledge which makes a person legally answerable for his/her act. *At common law a person might be liable for damage caused by an animal on one or more of three distinct grounds, namely, ordinary liability in tort, liability under the scienter rule and liability for cattle trespass* (Rogers 1975:392).

scientia. *n., pl.* **scientiae** [L. knowledge.] Knowledge, particularly the type based on collection and analysis of verifiable data. Science.

Scientiae Baccalaureus *abbr.* **S.B.** or **Sc.B.** *n.* [L. **scientiae** of science, knowledge (2); **baccalaureus** bachelor (1): Bachelor of Science.] An academic degree for completion of an undergraduate curriculum in science.

Scientiae Doctor *abbr.* **S.D.** or **Sc.D.** *n.* [L. **scientiae** of science, knowledge (2); **doctor** teacher (1): teacher of science.] Doctor of Science. A terminal graduate degree in science.

Scientiae Juridicae Doctor *abbr.* **S.J.D.** *n.* [L. **scientiae** (of) science, knowledge (3); **juridicae** of juridical (2); **doctor** teacher (1): teacher of juridical science.] Doctor of Juridical Science. A terminal graduate degree in judicial science.

Scientiae Magister *abbr.* **S.M.** or **Sc. M.** *n.* [L. **scientiae** of science, knowledge (2); **magister** master (1): Master of Science.] A predoctoral graduate degree in science.

scientia scientiarum *n.* [L. **scientia** science (1); **scientiarum** of sciences (2): science of sciences.] Philosophy.

scienti et volenti non fit injuria. [L. **scienti** to the one who knows (1); **et** and (2); **volenti** to the one who wishes/wants (3); **non** not (5); **fit** is done (6); **injuria** injury (4): To one who knows and wishes injury is not done.] Injury is not done to a person who knows and wants it. See **qui non improbat, approbat.**

sci. fa. *abbr.* for **scire facias** (q.v.).

scilicet *abbr.* **sc.** or **scil.** or **ss.** *adv.* [L. from **scire** to know (2); **licet** it is permitted (1): It is permitted to know.] Of course. Namely. That is to say. **Videlicet** (q.v.). Used to introduce a more specific statement or detailed list of things already mentioned generally. —*n., pl.* **scilicets** An example of the use of the word.

scintilla *n., pl.* **scintillae** or **scintillas** [L. spark, glimmer, trace, particle.] The slightest trace or particle, especially of light. The smallest or least particle. a) *He has not adduced a scintilla of evidence to support his theory.* b) *There is no scintilla of doubt in my mind that he is immensely qualified for the job.*

scintilla juris *n.* [L. **scintilla** spark, glimmer, trace, particle (1); **juris** of right, law (2): a particle of right.] The smallest amount or piece of right or interest. *The evidence adduced so far clearly indicates that the plaintiff does not have a scintilla juris to the disputed property.*

scintilla temporis *n.* [L. **scintilla** spark, particle (1); **temporis** of time (2): a particle of time.] The smallest amount of time. *Here . . . the mortgagor had had a scintilla temporis of unincumbered ownership . . .* (Hanbury 1962:398).

scire debes cum quo contrahis. [L. **scire** to know (2); **debes** you ought, should (1); **cum** with (3); **quo** whom (4); **contrahis** you are contracting, transacting (5): You ought to know with whom you are contracting.] *Law.* You ought to know the person with whom you are transacting business or making a contract. Cf. **qui cum alio** etc.

scire et scire debere aequiparantur in jure. [L. **scire** to know (1); **et** and (2); **scire** to know (4); **debere** to be bound, under obligation (3); **aequiparantur** are likened, equaled (5); **in** in, on (6); **jure** right, law (7): To know and to be bound to know are likened in law.] *Law.* Knowing and being bound to know are deemed to be the same. See **idem est scire** etc.

scire facias *abbr.* **sci. fa.** *n.* [L. **scire** to know (2); **facias** you should cause, make (1): You should cause/make to know.] *Law.* 1. A judicial writ based upon some matter of record, for instance a judgment, and requiring the person against whom it is issued to show cause why the party at whose instance it is issued should not benefit from the record or, in the case of letters patent, why the record should not be annulled, enforced, or vacated. 2. A legal proceeding prompted by such a writ.

scire feci *n.* [L. **scire** to know (2); **feci** I have caused (1): I have caused to know.] *Law.* The return of a sheriff or an officer to a writ of scire facias that notice has been given to the party or parties concerned.

Sc. M. *abbr.* for **Scientiae Magister** (q.v.).

schola cantorum *n., pl.* **scholae cantorum** [L. **schola** school (1); **cantorum** of singers (2): school of singers.] A singing group.

schottische *n., pl.* **schottisches** [Ger. **Schottische** Scottish.] A Scottish dance. A dance popular in 19th-century England and the United States, especially in the southwest, in which several groups of couples move in a circle at the directions of a caller. Sometimes known as "the German polka."

Scorpio or **Scorpius** *n.* [L. from Gk. **skorpios** scorpion.] 1. *Astronomy.* A scorpion-shaped constellation located near Libra and Sagittarius. 2. *Astrology*. The eighth sign of the zodiac dominant from October 24 through November 21. 3. A person born under this sign.

scotodinia *n., pl.* **scotodinias** [Neo-Gk. from Gk. **skoto(s)** darkness (1); **din(eō)** whirl (2): whirling in darkness, dizziness, vertigo.] *Medicine*. Dizziness, usually accompanied by headache and visual deficiency.

scribere est agere. [L. **scribere** to write (1); **est** is (2); **agere** to act (3): To write is to act.] *Law*. Writing is acting. The writing of treasonable words is equivalent to overt treasonable acts.

scripsit *v.* [L. He/she wrote it.] Used to indicate authorship.

scriptorium *n., pl.* **scriptoria** [L. a place for writing.] A room, especially in a monastery, set aside for writing or copying.

scriptum *n., pl.* **scripta** [L. that which is written.] Something written.

scriptum praedictum non est factum suum. [L. **scriptum** writing (2); **praedictum** previously mentioned (1); **non** not (4); **est** is (3); **factum** deed, act, fact (6); **suum** one's own, his/her own (5): The previously mentioned writing is not his/her deed.] *Law*. The written document in question was not written by this person. Fuller form of **non est factum** (q.v.).

sculpsit *abbr.* **sc.** or **sculp.** or **sculps.** [L. He/she carved it.] He/she carved or engraved it. Used to indicate the author of a piece of sculpture. Cf. **caelavit**.

scutum armorum *n.* [L. **scutum** shield (1); **armorum** of arms (2): shield of arms.] Coat of arms.

Scylla *n., pl.* **Scyllas** [L. from Gk. **Skullē**.] 1. *Greek and Roman Mythology*. A sea-monster believed to inhabit a cave on the headland of the Italian coast opposite Charybdis. She was said to have twelve feet and six heads, each equipped with a triple row of teeth. If a ship sailed near the headland, the monster would seize six sailors at a time and eat them. A sailor who escaped the danger of Charybdis was most likely to fall into the peril of Scylla. 2. A serious danger. A devastating peril. *A good ruler should be adept at the technique of avoiding both the Charybdis of sycophants who resort to abject servility and the Scylla of detractors.* Cf. **Charybdis**.

S.D. *abbr.* for 1. **Scientiae Doctor** (q.v.). 2. **senatus decreto** (q.v.).

S.D. or **s.d.** *abbr.* for 1. **sine dato** (q.v.). 2. **sine die** (q.v.).

sec. *abbr.* for **secundum** (q.v.).

sec. art. *abbr.* for **secundum artem** (q.v.).

sec. leg. *abbr.* for **secundum legem** (q.v.).

sec. nat. *abbr.* for **secundum naturam** (q.v.).

sec. reg. *abbr.* for **secundum regulam** (q.v.).

secretariat *n., pl.* **secretariats** [Fr. **secrétariat** office of secretary.] 1. An administrator, especially governmental, who maintains official records. 2. The office space of such an administrator. 3. The staff or department of such an administrator.

secundigravida *n., pl.* **secundigravidas** [Neo-L. **secund(us)** second (2); **gravida** pregnant (1): pregnant for the second time.] *Medicine*. A woman who is carrying her second pregnancy. A secundigravida woman. Cf. **gravida**.

secundipara *n., pl.* **secundiparas** [Neo-L. **secund(us)** second, for a second time (2); **par(io)** give birth (1): giving birth for the second time.] *Medicine*. A woman who has given birth for the second time. A secundiparous woman. Cf. **multipara**.

secundum *abbr.* **sec.** [L. according to.] According to, in accordance with.

secundum aequum et bonum *adv.* [L. **secundum** according to, in accordance with (1); **aequum** the reasonable, equitable (2); **et** and (3); **bonum** the good (4): according to the reasonable and good.] *Law*. According to what is reasonable and good, i.e., equity. See **aequitas**.

secundum allegata et probata *adv.* [L. **secundum** according to, in accordance with (1); **allegata** charged, alleged (things) (2); **et** and (3); **probata** proved (things) (4): according to alleged and proved things.] *Law*. In accordance with the allegations and proofs. See **allegata et probata**.

secundum artem *abbr.* **S.A.** or **s.a.** or **sec. art.** *adv.* [L. **secundum** according to, in accordance with (1); **artem** art, business, profession (2): according to art.] According to the art, business, trade, or profession.

secundum artis leges *abbr.* **S.A.L.** or **s.a.l.** *adv.* [L. **secundum** according to, in accordance with (1); **artis** of art (3); **leges** rules, laws (2): according to the laws of art.] According to the rules of the art, business, trade, or profession.

secundum bonos mores *adv.* [L. **secundum** according to (1); **bonos** good (2); **mores** customs, usages (3): according to good customs/usages.] *Law*. According to established/accepted customs.

secundum formam chartae *adv.* [L. **secundum** according to (1); **formam** form (2); **chartae** of writing (3): according to the form of the writing.] *Law*. According to the form of the deed or charter.

secundum legem *abbr.* **sec. leg.**, **S.L.** or **s.l.** *adv.* [L. **secundum** according to (1); **legem** law (2): according to the law.] *Law*. In accordance with the law. *Anybody who perpetrates atrocities should be dealt with secundum legem.*

secundum legem communem *adv.* [L. **secundum** according to (1); **legem** law (3); **communem** common (2): according to the common law.] *Law*. In accordance with common law.

secundum naturam *abbr.* **S.n.** or **s.n.** or **sec. nat.** *adv.* [L. **secundum** according to (1); **naturam** nature (2): according to nature.] In accordance with nature. Naturally.

secundum naturam est commoda cujusque rei eum sequi, quem sequuntur incommoda. [L. **secundum** in accordance with (2); **naturam** nature (3); **est** it is (1); **commoda** (that) advantages, profits (4); **cujusque**

of each (5); **rei** (of a) matter, thing, property, business, affair (6); **eum** him (8); **sequi** follow, to follow (7); **quem** whom (9); **sequuntur** follow (11); **incommoda** disadvantages, losses (10): It is in accordance with nature that the advantages of each thing follow him whom the disadvantages follow.] *Law.* It is natural that he who experiences the disadvantages of a thing should experience its advantages. See **qui sentit commodum** etc. and **qui sentit onus** etc.

secundum normam legis *adv.* [L. **secundum** according to (1); **normam** rule, measure (2); **legis** of law (3): according to the rule of law.] *Law.* In accordance with legal rule. *The world would be a better place for the habitation of all humankind if everybody were to behave secundum normam legis.*

secundum regulam *abbr.* **sec. reg.** *adv.* [L. **secundum** according to (1); **regulam** rule (2): according to the rule.] *Law.* In accordance with the rule or standard authority.

secundum tabulas *adv.* [L. **secundum** according to (1); **tabulas** statutes, tables of the law (2): according to the tables of the law.] *Law.* In accordance with the statutes.

securius expediuntur negotia commissa pluribus, et plus vident oculi quam oculus. [L. **securius** more safely, easily, securely (5); **expediuntur** are prepared, settled, arranged, accomplished (4); **negotia** matters, businesses, affairs (1); **commissa** entrusted, assigned (2); **pluribus** to more, several (persons) (3); **et** and (6); **plus** more (9); **vident** see (8); **oculi** eyes (7); **quam** than (10); **oculus** eye (11): Matters entrusted to several persons are settled more easily, and eyes see more than an eye.] Assignments are completed more smoothly by several persons (rather than one), and several eyes can see more than one. Cf. **testis de visu** etc. and **testis oculatus** etc.

secus *adv.* [L. the contrary, otherwise, not so.] *Law.* To the contrary. Otherwise. Used in books to indicate an exception to a stated rule, the rule to be applied in different circumstances and the opposite of a previous proposition.

sedato animo *adv.* [L. **sedato** with settled (1); **animo** (with) mind, intention, purpose (2): with settled intention.] With fixed intention or purpose.

se defendendo *adv.* [L. **se** himself/herself (2); **defendendo** by/in defending (1): by/in defending himself/herself.] *Law.* In self-defense. *The judge ruled that the accused committed homicide se defendendo.* See **homicidium se defendendo** and **vim vi** etc.

sedente curia *adv.* [L. **sedente** (with) sitting (2); **curia** with court (1): with the court sitting.] *Law.* While the court was sitting. During the sitting of the court.

Seder *n., pl.* **Sedarim** or **Seders** [Heb. **sēder** order, arrangement.] *Judaism.* A meal on the first night of Passover, commemorating the exodus of the Jews from Egypt, and consisting of prescribed foods and readings like the **Haggadah** (q.v.).

sederunt *n., pl.* **sederunts** [L. They sat.] 1. A long sitting, for instance, for reading, discussion, and relaxation. *Members of the association organize a sederunt every Saturday evening during which they hold intellectual discussions.* 2. A session of an official body such as an ecclesiastical assembly.

sede vacante *adv.* [L. **sede** with the seat (1); **vacante** being vacant (2): with the seat being vacant.] *Christianity.* While the see of a bishop is vacant.

sed fugit interea, fugit inreparabile tempus. Vergil (70–19 B.C.). *Georgics* III,284. [L. **sed** but (1); **fugit** it flees (3); **interea** meanwhile (2); **fugit** it flees (6); **inreparabile** irreparable, irretrievable (4); **tempus** time (5): But meanwhile it flees, irretrievable time flees.] But, meanwhile, irretrievable time flies. For shorter form, see **tempus fugit.**

sed quaere. [L. **sed** but (1); **quaere** inquire (2): But inquire.] *Law.* Examine this point further. Used to suggest that the correctness of a statement or rule laid down is being questioned.

sed vide [L. **sed** but (1); **vide** see (2): But see.] This remark, followed by a quotation or citation, draws the reader's attention to a conflicting principle or statement.

S.E.e.O. *abbr.* for **salvis erroribus et omissis** (q.v.).

segue *v.* [It. It follows. There follows.] 1. *Music.* To move immediately from one compositional unit or theme to another. 2. To move imperceptibly from one stage, level, or condition to another. *The conversation quickly segued from local gossip to presidential politics.* —*n.* A transition. An introduction. *He adeptly used his political connections as a segue into the organization.*

seicento *n.* [It. **sei** six (1); **cento** hundred (2): the six hundreds.] The 1600s. The 17th century. Used especially in reference to Italian history, literature, and art. Cf. **cinquecento; quatrocento;** and **trecento.**

Seigneur *n., pl.* **Seigneurs** [Fr. lord, squire, nobleman.] A gentleman. A feudal lord. A member of the landed aristocracy. *There was something of the seigneur about him in the ease with which he would walk into the workers' homes, sit, take lunch, . . .* (Chris Dunton in *West Africa* 1986).

semble *adj.* [Fr. It seems. It appears.] *Law.* Apparently. Used, especially in legal judgments and reports, to express an apparent arrangement or a suggestion not confirmed by fact; e.g., a statement made by a reporter or an **obiter dictum** (q.v.). *Semble, the agent must still be employed in his ordinary course of business . . .* (Parry 1961:290).

semel civis semper civis. [L. **semel** once (1); **civis** citizen (2); **semper** always (3); **civis** citizen (4): Once a citizen, always a citizen.] *Law.* Citizenship is permanent.

semel heres, semper heres. [L. **semel** once (1); **heres** heir, successor (2); **semper** always (3); **heres** heir, successor (4): Once an heir, always an heir.] *Law.* The status of heir is permanent.

semi-plena probatio See **probatio semi-plena.**

semper eadem *adj.* [L. **semper** always (1); **eadem** the same (things) (2): always the same (things).] Always the same.

semper fidelis *abbr.* **semper fi** *adj., pl.* **semper fideles** [L. **semper** always, ever (1); **fidelis** faithful, trustworthy (2): Ever faithful.] Always dependable or trustworthy. *During Ronke's moments of tribulation, all her friends and associates deserted her, but Rose, semper fidelis, stood by her side, comforting, encouraging, and assisting her.* The motto of the U.S. Marine Corps.

semper idem *masc.* and *neut. sing.* form of **semper eadem** (q.v.).

semper in dubiis benigniora praeferenda. [L. **semper** always (1); **in** in, on (2); **dubiis** doubtful (things) (3); **benigniora** more favorable, liberal (things) (4); **praeferenda** to be preferred (5): Always in doubtful things more favorable things are to be preferred.] *Law.* In case of doubt, more favorable interpretations must always be given preference. See **in dubio, pars** etc.

semper in stipulationibus et in ceteris contractibus, id sequimur quod actum est. [L. **semper** always (8); **in** in, on (1); **stipulationibus** stipulations, agreements (2); **et** and (3); **in** in, on (4); **ceteris** other, all other (5); **contractibus** contracts (6); **id** that (9); **sequimur** we follow (7); **quod** which (10); **actum est** was done (11): In stipulations and other contracts we always follow that which was done.] *Law.* In stipulations and all other contracts we always consider the actual facts.

semper necessitas probandi incumbit ei qui agit. [L. **semper** always, at all times (1); **necessitas** compulsion, urgency, necessity (2); **probandi** of proving (3); **incumbit** weighs upon, settles on, burdens (4); **ei** him (5); **qui** who (6); **agit** brings a suit, prosecutes (7): At all times the compulsion of proving weighs upon him who brings a suit.] *Law.* At all times the compulsion of proving a case lies on the plaintiff/prosecution. See **actori incumbit** etc.

semper paratus *adj.* [L. **semper** always (1); **paratus** prepared, ready (2): always ready.] Always prepared. Motto of the Boy Scouts of America. —*n. Law.* A plea by which a defendant, particularly in an action of assumpsit, makes an allegation that he has always been ready to comply with what is demanded.

semper praesumitur pro matrimonio. [L. **semper** always (2); **praesumitur** it is presumed (1); **pro** in favor of, on the side of (3); **matrimonio** marriage (4): It is always presumed in favor of marriage.] *Law.* The validity of marriage is always presumed.

semper praesumitur pro negante. [L. **semper** always (1); **praesumitur** it is presumed (2); **pro** in favor of, for (3); **negante** the one denying (4): Always it is presumed in favor of the one denying.] *Law.* The

presumption is always in favor of the person who denies an allegation. A rule applicable when opinion is equally divided. See **actori incumbit** etc.

semper specialia generalibus insunt. [L. **semper** always (3); **specialia** special, particular (things) (1); **generalibus** general (things) (4); **insunt** are contained in, implied in (2): Special things are always implied in general ones.] The particular is implied in the general. See **quando lex est specialis** etc.

semper, ubique, et ab omnibus [L. **semper** always (1); **ubique** everywhere, in every place (2); **et** and (3); **ab** from, by (4); **omnibus** all (5): always, everywhere, and by all.] At all times, in all places, and by everyone. *Human nature is such that there can be no view, doctrine, tenet, etc. accepted semper, ubique, et ab omnibus.*

semplice *adv./adj.* [It. simple, simply.] *Music.* Simply. In a plain way. Without flourish.

sempre *adv.* [It. always.] *Music.* Always in the same way.

senatus academicus or **senatus** *n., pl.* **senatus academici** or **senatus** [L. **senatus** senate (2); **academicus** academic (1): academic senate.] The senate of a university.

senatus consulto *abbr.* **S.C.** *adv.* [L. **senatus** of senate (2); **consulto** by decree, decision (1): by Senate's decree or decision.] By decree or decision of the Senate. See **senatus consultum.**

senatus consultum *abbr.* **S.C.** *n., pl.* **senatus consulta** [L. **senatus** of senate (2); **consultum** decree, decision (1): decree of the Senate.] *Roman Law.* A decree of the Roman Senate. In the early Republic, this decree was initially advice to a magistrate, and did not carry the force of law which it acquired in the imperial period.

senatus decreto *abbr.* **S.D.** *adv.* [L. **senatus** of senate (2); **decreto** by decree (1): by decree of the senate.] By senatorial decision or decree.

Senatus Populusque Romanus *abbr.* **S.P.Q.R.** [L. **senatus** senate (1); **populus** people, citizenry (2); **que** and (3); **Romanus** Roman (4): Senate and Roman People.] *Ancient Rome.* The Senate and the Roman People. A formulaic expression used in decrees and official statements.

S. en C. *abbr.* for **société en commandite** (q.v.).

senex bis puer [L. **senex** old man (1); **bis** twice, a second time (2); **puer** boy (3): An old man (is) a boy a second time.] An old man is twice a boy. Cf. **bis pueri senes.**

Senhor *abbr.* **Snr.** *n., pl.* **Senhors** or **Senhores** [Port. lord or master.] 1. Mister or Mr. Prefixed to the name of a man who is Portuguese or Portuguese-speaking. 2. A Portuguese man or one who speaks Portuguese. See **babu; Herr; Monsieur; san; Señor;** and **Signor.**

Senhora *abbr.* **Snra** *n., pl.* **Senhoras** [Port. mistress.] 1. Mistress or Mrs. Prefixed to the name of a married woman who is Portuguese or Portuguese-speaking. 2. A Portuguese or Portuguese-speaking woman who is married. Cf. **Frau; Fräulein; Madame; Mademoiselle; Senhorita; Señora; Señorita; Signora;** and **Signorina.**

Senhorita *abbr.* **Snrta** *n., pl.* **Senhoritas** [Port. young mistress, young lady.] 1. Miss. Prefixed to the name of an unmarried woman or girl who is Portuguese or Portuguese-speaking. 2. A Portuguese or Portuguese-speaking woman who is unmarried. Cf. **Frau; Fräulein; Madame; Mademoiselle; Senhora; Señora; Señorita; Signora;** and **Signorina.**

S. en N.C. *abbr.* for **société en nom collectif** (q.v.).

Senior *abbr.* **Sr.** *adj.* [L. older.] Older in rank or age. Used as a title in a proper name to indicate the older of two individuals with the same name, especially a father and his son. *John Fitzgerald Kennedy, Sr.* —*n.* **senior** *pl.* **seniors** 1. A person older in rank or age. *A senior citizen.* 2. A fourth-year student in high school or college. Cf. **Junior.**

Se non è vero, è molto ben trovato. Giordano Bruno (1548?–1600). [It. **se** if (1); **non** not (2); **è** it is (3); **vero** true (4); **è** it is (5); **ben** well (6); **trovato** found (7): If it is not true, it is well found.] Even if it is not true, it is a happy discovery. Cf. **ben trovato.**

Señor or **Senor** *abbr.* **S.** or **Sñr.** or **Sr.** *n., pl.* **Señores** or **Senors** [Sp. lord or master.] 1. Mister or Mr. or Sir. A title of courtesy used for, or of, a Spaniard or a Spanish-speaking man. 2. A Spaniard or Spanish-speaking man. See **babu; Herr; Monsieur; san; Senhor;** and **Signor.**

Señora or **Senora** *abbr.* **Sñra** or **SRA** or **Sra** *n., pl.* **Señoras** or **Senoras** [Sp. mistress, lady.] 1. Mistress or Mrs. or Madam. A title of courtesy used for, or of, a married woman who is Spanish or Spanish-speaking. 2. A married woman who is Spanish or Spanish-speaking. Cf. **Frau; Fräulein; Madame; Mademoiselle; Senhora; Senhorita; Señorita; Signora;** and **Signorina.**

Señorita or **Senorita** *abbr.* **Sñrta** or **SRITA** or **Srita** or **SRTA** or **Srta** *n., pl.* **Señoritas** or **Senoritas** [Sp. young mistress, young lady.] 1. Miss. A title of courtesy used for, or of, an unmarried woman or girl who is Spanish or Spanish-speaking. 2. An unmarried woman who is Spanish or Spanish-speaking. Cf. **Frau; Fräulein; Madame; Mademoiselle; Senhora; Senhorita; Señora; Signora;** and **Signorina.**

sensibilia *pl. n.* [L. perceptible things.] Things that can be perceived by the senses.

sensu *prep.* [L. in the sense (of).] With the meaning of.

sensu honesto *adv.* [L. **sensu** (in) sense, meaning (2); **honesto** in honest (1): in an honest sense.] Honestly. Frankly. Used of unprejudiced interpretation of words. *Had he interpreted the words sensu honesto, he would have realized that there is nothing defamatory in the article.*

sensu lato *adv.* [L. **sensu** (in) sense (2); **lato** in broad, wide (1): in a broad sense.] In a wide sense.

sensum *n., pl.* **sensa** [L. something felt or perceived.] Sense-datum. A thing perceived by the senses.

sensus *n.* [L. sense or meaning.] Sense or meaning, especially of words.

sensu stricto or **stricto sensu** *adv.* [L. **sensu** (in) sense (2); **stricto** in strict (1): in the strict sense.] Strictly. In a narrow sense. *Mustapha is, sensu stricto, not my friend, but an acquaintance.*

sensus verborum est anima legis. [L. **sensus** sense, meaning (1); **verborum** of words (2); **est** is (3); **anima** spirit, soul (4); **legis** of law (5): The sense of words is the spirit of law.] The meaning of the words is the soul of the law. Cf. **lex plus laudatur** etc.

sensus verborum est duplex,—mitis et asper; et verba semper accipienda sunt in mitiori sensu. [L. **sensus** meaning (1); **verborum** of words (2); **est** is (3); **duplex** twofold, double (4); **mitis** mild (5); **et** and (6); **asper** harsh, adverse (7); **et** and (8); **verba** words (9); **semper** always (11); **accipienda** to be understood, accepted (12); **sunt** are (10); **in** in, on (13); **mitiori** milder (14); **sensu** sense (15): The meaning of words is twofold, —the mild and the harsh meaning; and words are always to be understood in the milder sense.] *Law.* Words have two possible meanings: mild and harsh; they must always be interpreted in the milder sense.

sententia *n., pl.* **sententiae** [L. opinion, thought, belief, maxim.] A wise saying or opinion. A Maxim. —**Sententiae** *Maxims*, the title of a collection of maxims or proverbs, such as those of Publilius Syrus (first century B.C.).

sententia a non judice lata nemini debet nocere. [L. **sententia** sentence, judgment (1); **a** by (3); **non** not (4); **judice** judge (5); **lata** passed, delivered (2); **nemini** to no one, nobody (8); **debet** ought, should (6); **nocere** to do harm, hurt, injure (7): A sentence passed by not judge should do harm to no one.] *Law.* A sentence passed by a judge who has no jurisdiction over the case ought to hurt no one. See **extra territorium jus** etc.

sententia contra matrimonium numquam transit in rem judicatam. [L. **sententia** sentence, judgment (1); **contra** against, opposite (2); **matrimonium** marriage (3); **numquam** never (4); **transit** passes (5); **in** into, to, against, for (6); **rem** matter (8); **judicatam** decided (7): A judgment against marriage never passes into a decided matter.] *Law.* A judgment against marriage is never a final and complete judgment.

sententia facit jus, et legis interpretatio legis vim obtinet. [L. **sententia** sentence, judgment (1); **facit** makes (2); **jus** right, law (3); **et** and (4); **legis** of law (6); **interpretatio** interpretation (5); **legis** of law (9); **vim** force (8); **obtinet** obtains, acquires, has (7): Judgment makes right and interpretation of law obtains force of law.] *Law.* Judgment gives a right, and interpretation of the law acquires the force of law. Cf. **legis interpretatio** etc. and **omnis interpretatio** etc.

sententia non fertur de rebus non liquidis. [L. **sententia** sentence, judgment (1); **non** not (2); **fertur** is brought, passed (3); **de** of, from, about, for (4);

rebus matters (5); **non** not (6); **liquidis** clear (7): Judgment is not brought about matters not clear.] *Law.* Judgment is not passed on matters which are not clear.

senza sordini *adv.* [It. **senza** without (1); **sordini** mutes (2): without mutes.] *Music.* With string or brass instruments unmuted.

separaliter *adv.* [L. separately.] *Law.* Used in indictments to show that the accused persons are charged separately.

separatim *adv./adj.* [L. separately.] Severally. Apart. Separate.

separatio bonorum *n.* [L. **separatio** separation (1); **bonorum** of goods (2): separation of goods.] *Roman Law.* 1. (a) The separation of the goods of a decedent from those of the heir(s). (b) The right of the creditors of a decedent to insist that his/her goods be kept separate from those of the heir(s). 2. The goods of a decedent, including the original ones and subsequent additions.

seppuku *n.* [Japan. from **seppu** to cut (2); **ku** abdomen (1): abdomen-cutting.] **Hara-kiri** (q.v.).

septemvir *n., pl.* **septemviri** or **septemvirs** [L. **septem** seven (1); **vir** man (2): seven man, one of a body of seven.] A member of a body, group, board, council, association, commission or ruling body of seven. *Meanwhile MacCabe's supporters . . . considered convening the Septemviri, the university court, on the ground that MacCabe's opponents had violated a secrecy rule . . .* (*Newsweek Int.* Feb. 16, 1981:46). Cf. **decemvir.**

Septuaginta *n.* [L. from **sept(em)** seven (1); **-ginta** tens (2): seven tens, seventy.] The 3rd century B.C. translation of the Hebrew Bible into Greek, traditionally said to have been translated by seventy scholars.

seq. *abbr.* for 1. **sequens** (q.v.). 2. **sequitur** (q.v.).

seqq. *abbr.* for 1. **sequentes** (q.v.) or **sequentia.** 2. **sequentibus** (q.v.).

sequamur vestigia patrum nostrorum. [L. **sequamur** let us follow (1); **vestigia** footsteps, tracks (2); **patrum** (of) fathers (4); **nostrorum** of our (3): Let us follow the footsteps of our fathers.] We should follow in the footsteps of our ancestors.

sequens *abbr.* **seq.** *adj./n., pl.* **sequentes** or **sequentia** *abbr.* **seqq.** [L. following.] The following.

sequentes or **sequentia** *pl.* of **sequens** (q.v.).

sequentibus *abbr.* **seqq.** [L. (in) following things.] In the following places.

sequester *n., pl.* **sequesters** [L. trustee, depositary, mediator, go-between.] *Roman and Civil Law.* A person who keeps the property disputed by the litigants, pending the settlement of the suit.

sequestratio *n.* [L. protection under a third party or trustee.] *Roman and Civil Law.* Sequestration. The separation or removal of a disputed property from the person in possession, pending the settlement of the suit in court. It could either be voluntary or ordered by the court.

sequestrator or *fem.* **sequestratrix** *n., pl.* **sequestrators** or *fem.* **sequestratrices** [L. one who receives as a third party or trustee.] *Law.* 1. A person appointed to receive sequestered property. 2. A person appointed to execute a writ of sequestration.

sequi debet potentia justitiam, non praecedere. [L. **sequi** to follow (3); **debet** ought, should (2); **potentia** power, authority (1); **justitiam** justice (4); **non** not (5); **praecedere** to precede, lead (6): Power should follow justice, not precede (it).] *Law.* Power should come after, not before, justice. See **potentia debet sequi** etc.

sequitur *abbr.* **seq.** *n., pl.* **sequiturs** [L. It follows.] *Logic.* A logical inference from a premise. *The article is centered on one premise from which the writer derives many useful sequiturs.* Cf. **non sequitur.**

seraglio *n., pl.* **seraglios** [It. **serraglio** from Turk. **sarayi** enclosure, harem, palace of a sultan.] 1. A **harem** (q.v.). The portion of a Muslim household where the women live, completely secluded from the rest of society. 2. A Turkish palace. A sultan's residence or palace. See **zenana.**

sera nimis vita est crastina; vive hodie. Martial (c.40–103/4 A.D.). *Epigrammata* I,15. [L. **sera** late (2); **nimis** too (1); **vita** life (4); **est** is (3); **crastina** of tomorrow, tomorrow's (5); **vive** live (6); **hodie** today (7): Too late is the life of tomorrow; live today.] Tomorrow it is too late to live; live today. For a fuller form, see **non est, crede** etc.

serenade *n., pl.* **serenades** [Fr. **sérénade** a song in the open air.] 1. A song sung in the open air at night, usually to a beloved. 2. Any song sung in the honor of a particular individual. 3. *Music.* A composition written for a small instrumental group. —*v.* To honor an individual with a song.

seriatim [L. in a series.] *adv.* Serially. One by one. Separately. a) *He received a letter setting forth the terms of his appointment seriatim.* b) *. . . rather than laying down general principles, a number of transactions will be taken seriatim* (James 1982:246). —*adj.* Done, arranged, or set down in a series. *His speech is essentially a seriatim rebuttal of the allegations leveled against him.*

sermo index animi See **index animi sermo.**

servanda est consuetudo loci ubi causa agitur. [L. **servanda** to be observed (7); **est** is (6); **consuetudo** custom, usage, tradition (1); **loci** of place (2); **ubi** where (3); **causa** cause, case, reason (4); **agitur** is brought (5): The custom of the place where the case is brought is to be observed.] *Law.* The custom of the place where the case is being handled must be observed.

servitia personalia sequuntur personam. [L. **servitia** services (2); **personalia** personal (1); **sequuntur** follow (3); **personam** person (4): Personal services follow the person.] *Law.* The the duties and obligations of an individual follow that individual.

servitus *n*. [L. the condition of a servant, slavery, easement, liability.] 1. *Roman and Civil Law*. Slavery. Servitude. 2. *Law of Nations*. Subjection to another's domination, contrary to the principles of natural right.

servitus actus *n*. [L. **servitus** the condition of a servant, slavery, servitude, easement, liability (1); **actus** of the right of way, of the right to drive through a place (2): servitude of the right of way.] *Law*. The right to cross over the land of another.

servitus altius non tollendi *n*. [L. **servitus** the condition of a servant, slavery, servitude, easement, liability (1); **altius** higher (4); **non** not (3); **tollendi** of building, erecting (2): servitude of not building higher.] *Law*. A right attached to a building which empowers the owner to prevent a neighbor from erecting a building higher than his/her own.

servitus aquae ducendae *n*. [L. **servitus** the condition of a servant, slavery, servitude, easement, liability (1); **aquae** of water (2); **ducendae** to be conducted (3): servitude of water to be conducted.] *Law*. The right to conduct water to one's property through another's.

servitus aquae educendae *n*. [L. **servitus** the condition of a servant, slavery, servitude, easement, liability (1); **aquae** of water (2); **educendae** to be drawn out (3): servitude of water to be drawn out.] *Law*. The right to run off water from one's land into another's.

servitus aquae hauriendae *n*. [L. **servitus** the condition of a servant, slavery, servitude, easement, liability (1); **aquae** of water (2); **hauriendae** to be drawn out (3): servitude of water to be drawn out.] *Law*. The right to draw out water to one's property from another's.

servitus itineris *n*. [L. **servitus** the condition of a servant, slavery, servitude, easement, liability (1); **itineris** of passage, way, going (2): servitude of passage.] *Law*. The right to cross over another's property. See **servitus viae**.

servitus ne luminibus officiatur. *n*. [L. **servitus** the condition of a servant, slavery, servitude, easement, liability (1); **ne** in order that not (2); **luminibus** to lights (4); **officiatur** there may be an obstacle (3): servitude in order that there not be an obstacle to lights.] *Law*. The right not to have one's windows' accessibility to light jeopardized by a neighbor's building.

servitus pascendi *n*. [L. **servitus** the condition of a servant, slavery, servitude, easement, liability (1); **pascendi** of pasturing (2): servitude of pasturing.] *Law*. The right to pasture one's cattle on the property of another. Cf. **jus pecoris pascendi**.

servitus viae *n*. [L. **servitus** the condition of a servant, slavery, servitude, easement, liability (1); **viae** of way, road (2): servitude of the road.] *Law*. The right to walk, ride or drive over another's land. See **servitus itineris**.

Servus servorum Dei *n., pl*. **Servi servorum Dei** [L. **servus** servant (1); **servorum** of servants (2); **Dei** of God (3): servant of the servants of God.] One of the Pope's titles.

sesquipedalia *pl*. *n*. [L. from **sesquipes** a distance of one and one half feet: one and one half feet.] Extraordinarily long words. Words of many syllables. *Her lecture was filled with so many sesquipedalia that her audience was unable to discern her main point.*

sextipara *n., pl*. **sextiparas** [Neo-L. from **sext(us)** sixth (2); **par(io)** give birth (1): giving birth for the sixth time.] *Medicine*. A woman who has given birth for the sixth time. Cf. **multipara**.

S.F. or **s.f.** *abbr*. for 1. **sans frais** (q.v.). 2. **sub finem** (q.v.).

S.F.S. *abbr*. for **sine fraude sua** (q.v.).

S.G. *abbr*. for **salutis gratia** (q.v.).

Shabbat *n*. [Heb. **sabbāt** rest.] *Judaism*. Sabbath (q.v.).

shah *n*. [Pers. **shāh** king.] A hereditary monarch in Persia (Iran).

Shaitan *n*. [Ar. **saytān** from Heb. **sātān** adversary, accuser.] *Islam*. The devil. Satan. —**shaitan** *pl*. **shaitans** An evil spirit. Cf. **Satan**.

shalom *interj*. [Heb. **sālom** peace.] Used to greet or say farewell in Jewish and also some Christian communities. Cf. **pax**; **salaam**; and **shanti**.

shaman *n., pl*. **shamans** [Russ. from Tungusian **saman**.] A religious figure, especially in northern Asia, with magical, healing, and seeing powers from the supernatural world.

shanti *n., pl*. **shantis** [Skt. peace.] *Hinduism*. A wish for peace, used as a greeting or as part of the reading of the Upanishads. Cf. **pax**; **salaam**; and **shalom**.

shari'a or **sharia** or **shariat** or **sheria** or **sheriat** *n*. [Ar. **shar'īah** lawfulness.] *Islam*. The body of laws based on the Koran and the **Sunna** (q.v.), governing the religion and almost every aspect of life economic, social, political, ethical, domestic, etc. The established law in every Muslim country. *The law of the land is the harsh Koranic Sharia and is administered by the ulema, . . .* (*Newsweek Int*. March 3, 1980:21).

sharif or **shareef** or **shereef** or **sherif** *n., pl*. **sharifs** or **shareefs** or **shereefs** or **sherifs** [Arab. **sharīf** noble.] A male descendant of Muhammed and his daughter Fatima. —**Sharif** An Arab official or ruler, especially the governor of **Mecca** (q.v.) or the ruler of Morocco.

sharifa *n., pl*. **sharifas** [Arab. feminine form of **sharīf** noble.] The wife of the ruler of Morocco.

shegetz *n., pl*. **shhotzim** [Yid. **sheygets**.] A derogatory term for a non-Jewish boy. Cf. **goy** and **shiksa**.

sheikh or **sheik** or **sheykh** or **shaikh** or **shaykh** *n., pl*. **sheikhs** or **sheiks** or **sheykhs** or **shaikhs** or **shaykhs** [Ar. **shaykh** old man, chief.] 1. The chief or head of an Arab family, clan, tribe, or village. 2. A prince or governor in Arab or Muslim communities. 3. A Muslim scholar or leader.

shekel *n., pl*. **shekels** [Heb. **sheqel**.] 1. Coinage used in ancient and modern Israel. 2. Money, especially coins. Used in slang. Cf. **denarius** and **dinaro**.

shiatsu *n*. [Japan. short for **shiatsuryoho: shi** finger (1); **atsu** pressure (2); **ryoho** treatment (3): finger pressure treatment.] A form of Japanese massage in which finger and palm pressure is used on areas treated in acupuncture.

shibboleth *n., pl.* **shibboleths** [Heb. **shibbōlet** stream, flood, ear of grain.] 1. The word used by Jephthah, when crossing the Jordan, to distinguish the Gileadites, his followers, from the Ephraimites, who pronounced "sh" as "s" (Judges XII:6). 2. A word so difficult for foreigners to pronounce that it is used as an acid test to distinguish foreigners from indigenous inhabitants. 3. A custom or practice which distinguishes one group from another. *Ownership of a Peugeot 504 saloon car is increasingly ceasing to be the shibboleth of the middle class of Nigeria.* 4. A slogan. A catchword. An almost meaningless expression or saying which is usually used by members of a group. Language which is almost exclusively used by members of a particular group. 5. A platitude. A commonplace idea or saying. *All of them are highly individual, all discuss some aspect of that worn shibboleth, the American Dream (Time Int. 1980).*

shikar *n.* [Hindi **shikār** hunt.] 1. The act of hunting. 2. That which is hunted. Game. —*v.* To hunt.

shikari *n., pl.* **shikaris** [Hindi **shikarī** hunter.] 1. A hunter of big game. 2. Someone who guides such a hunter.

shiksa or **shikse** *n.* [Yid. **shikse.**] A derogatory term for a non-Jewish girl. Cf. **goy** and **shegetz.**

shiva or **shivah** or **shibah** *n.* [Heb. **shib'āh** seven.] *Judaism.* A period of mourning for seven days following a funeral.

shlemiel See **schlemiel.**

Shoah *n.* [Heb. destruction.] The Holocaust. The persecution of European Jews by the Nazis.

shogun *n., pl.* **shoguns** [Japan. general.] A Japanese warlord. **Tycoon** 1 (q.v.).

S.H.V. or **s.h.v.** *abbr.* for 1. **sub hac voce** (q.v.). 2. **sub hoc verbo** (q.v.).

si alicujus rei societas sit et finis negotio impositus est, finitur societas. [L. **si** if (1); **alicujus** of any, some (4); **rei** (of) matter, thing, property, business, affair (5); **societas** partnership, association (3); **sit** there should be (2); **et** and (6); **finis** end, termination (7); **negotio** business, affair (10); **impositus** imposed, put on (9); **est** is, has been (8); **finitur** is ended, terminated (12); **societas** partnership, association (11): If there should be a partnership of any affair and an end has been imposed on the business, the association is ended.] *Law.* If there is a partnership for a venture and the business is subsequently terminated, the partnership is similarly terminated. Cf. **solvitur adhuc societas** etc.

si assuetis mederi possis, nova non sunt tentanda. [L. **si** if (1); **assuetis** by usual, familiar (things) (4); **mederi** to heal, cure (3); **possis** you could, should be able (2); **nova** new (things) (5); **non** not (7); **sunt** are (6); **te(mp)tanda** to be attempted, tried (8): If you

could cure by usual things, new things are not to be attempted.] If you can cure a malady by using familiar drugs, you need not try new ones. See **numquam decurritur** etc.

sic *adv.* [L. so, thus, in this way.] 1. In such manner. In this manner. As follows. 2. Intentionally written in this way. Used after a printed word or passage to show that it was deliberately written in that way or that it is an exact reproduction of the original. Used to criticize a writer's language or view without saying so explicitly.

Sic et non *n.* [L. **sic** thus, in this way, yes (1); **et** and (2); **non** not, no (3): yes and no.] *Yes and no,* the title of a theological work by Peter Abelard (1079–1142). —**sic et non** *n., pl.* **sic et nons** A form of medieval argumentation in which scriptural passages were offered in a series of exchanges without commentary.

sic itur ad astra. Vergil (70–19 B.C.). *Aeneid* IX,641. [L. **sic** so, thus, in this way (1); **itur** there is a going (2); **ad** to, at, for, according to (3); **astra** stars (4): In this way there is a going to the stars.] This is the path (or way) to the stars. This is what should be done, if one wants to achieve success, fame, prosperity, etc.

sic passim *adv.* [L. **sic** so, thus, in this way (1); **passim** in different places, scattered about far and wide (2): thus in different places.] So throughout. Usually used to show that an idea, view, word or error, etc. can be found at different places throughout a book or other published source.

sic semper tyrannis [L. **sic** thus, in this way (1); **semper** always (2); **tyrannis** to tyrants, despots (3): Thus always to tyrants.] This is the way tyranny (or despotism) should always end. This should be the fate of all tyrants (or despots). Spoken by John Wilkes Booth (1838–1865) when killing Abraham Lincoln (1809–1865) on April 14, 1865. Motto of the State of Virginia.

sic transit gloria mundi. Thomas à Kempis (1380–1471). *Imitatio Christi* I,3,6. [L. **sic** so, thus, in this way (1); **transit** passes by; passes away (2); **gloria** glory (3); **mundi** of world, universe (4): Thus passes away the glory of the world.] Such is the transitory nature of worldly glory or success. *If we are still here to witness the destruction of our planet some five billion years or more hence, then we will have achieved something so unprecedented in the history of life that we should be willing to sing our swan song with joy. Sic transit gloria mundi (Newsweek Int.* March 29, 1982:44).

sicut alias *n.* [L. **sicut** just as, as (1); **alias** at another time, some other time (2): just as at another time.] *Law.* A second writ sent out when the first could not be executed.

sic utere tuo ut alienum non laedas. [L. **sic** so, thus, in this way, in such a way (3); **utere** use (1); **tuo** yours (2); **ut** that (4); **alienum** another's (7); **non** not (6); **laedas** you may hurt (5): Use yours in such a way that you may not hurt another's.] *Law.* Use your property in such a way that you do not hurt another's. See **aedificare in tuo** etc.; **expedit reipublicae** etc.; **interest reipublicae ne sua** etc.; **interest reipublicae ut quilibet** etc.; **ita utere tuo** etc.; and **prohibetur ne quis** etc.

sicut me Deus adjuvet. [L. **sicut** so (1); **me** me (4); **deus** God (2); **adjuvet** may help (3): So may God help me.] So help me, God.

sicut natura nil facit per saltum, ita nec lex. [L. **sicut** so as, just as (1); **natura** nature (2); **nil** nothing (4); **facit** does (3); **per** by, through (5); **saltum** leap, bound (6); **ita** so, thus, in this way (7); **nec** also not, and not, nor (8); **lex** law (9): Just as nature does nothing by a leap, so also the law does not.] Both nature and the law change slowly. See **natura non facit saltum** etc.

Si Dieu n'existait pas, il faudrait l'inventer. Voltaire (1694–1778). *Épîtres* XCVI. [Fr. **si** if (1); **Dieu** God (2); **n'** . . . **pas** not (4); **existait** existed (3); **il** it (5); **faudrait** would be necessary (6); **l'** him (8); **inventer** to invent, devise (7): If God did not exist, it would be necessary to invent him.] The concept of God would be necessary even if there were no God.

si dis placet *adv.* [L. **si** if (1); **dis** to the gods (3); **placet** it is pleasing (2): if it is pleasing to the gods.] If the gods are willing.

si duo in testamento pugnantia reperientur, ultimum est ratum. [L. **si** if (1); **duo** two (2); **in** in, on (5); **testamento** will (6); **pugnantia** fighting (things) (3); **reperientur** will be found (4); **ultimum** the last (7); **est** is (8); **ratum** valid, confirmed (9): If two fighting things will be found in a will, the last is valid.] *Law.* If two conflicting clauses are found in a will, the last is accepted. See **cum duo inter se** etc. and **testamenta cum duo** etc.

siddur *n., pl.* **siddurim** [Heb. arrangement.] *Judaism.* A book of prayer.

Sieg Heil *interj.* [Ger. **Sieg** victory (2); **heil** hail, long life to (1): Hail, victory.] The Nazi salute. —*n., pl.* **Seig Heils** The shouting of the Nazi salute. *The Sieg Heils of the crowd were enthusiastic and long-lasting.*

sierra *n., pl.* **sierras** [Span. rugged mountains.] A rugged mountain range, i.e., one with many sharp and steep points. Used to identify several ranges in the southwestern United States, including the Sierra Madre and Sierra Nevada.

siesta *n., pl.* **siestas** [Sp. an afternoon nap.] A midday nap. An afternoon rest. A short rest or sleep. *Students of the school have siesta every afternoon from 3:00 to 4:00 P.M.*

si fueris Romae, Romano vivito more; / si fueris alibi, vivito sicut ibi. Jeremy Taylor (1613–1667). [L. **si** if (1); **fueris** you will have been (2); **Romae** at Rome (3); **Romano** in Roman (5); **vivito** live (4); **more** (in) way, manner (6); **si** if (7); **fueris** you will have been (8); **alibi** elsewhere (9); **vivito** live (10); **sicut** just as; as (11); **ibi** there (12): If you will have been

at Rome, live in the Roman way; / if you will have been elsewhere, live just as there.] When in Rome, do as the Romans do. When you are elsewhere, live as they do there.

Sig. *abbr.* for 1. **Signor** (q.v.). 2. **Signora** (q.v.).

Signor or **Signore** *abbr.* **S.** or **Sig.** *n., pl.* **Signors** (for **Signor** only) or **Signori** (for both) [It. lord, master.] 1. Mister or Mr. or Sir. Prefixed to the name of an adult male Italian. 2. A high-ranking adult male Italian. See **babu**; **Herr**; **Monsieur**; **san**; **Senhor**; **Señor**; and **Signor**.

Signora *abbr.* **S.** or **Sig.** *n., pl.* **Signoras** or **Signore** [It. lady, mistress.] l. Mistress or Mrs. or Madam. Prefixed to the name of a married Italian woman. 2. A high-ranking married Italian woman. Cf. **Frau**; **Fräulein**; **Madame**; **Mademoiselle**; **Senhora**; **Senhorita**; **Señora**; **Señorita**; and **Signorina**.

Signorina *n., pl.* **Signorinas** or **Signorine** [It. young lady, young mistress.] 1. Miss. Prefixed to the name of an unmarried Italian woman or girl as a title of courtesy. 2. An Italian woman or girl who is unmarried. Cf. **Frau**; **Fräulein**; **Madame**; **Mademoiselle**; **Senhora**; **Senhorita**; **Señora**; **Señorita**; and **Signora**.

si ingratum dixeris, omnia dixeris. [L. **si** if (1); **ingratum** ungrateful, unthankful (3); **dixeris** you will have said (2); **omnia** all (5); **dixeris** you will have said (4): If you will have said ungrateful, you will have said all.] If you say that a person is ungrateful, you have said it all.

silent enim leges inter arma. Cicero (106–43 B.C.). *Pro Milone* IV,11. [L. **silent** are silent, still (3); **enim** for (1); **leges** laws (2); **inter** among, between (4); **arma** arms, weapons (5): For laws are silent among arms.] During war the laws are silent/inactive; i.e., during war "the law of military necessity" operates. Also **inter arma silent leges**.

silentio consentionem significat. [L. **silentio** silence (1); **consentionem** consent, agreement (3); **significat** means, signifies (2): Silence means consent.] Silence gives consent. Cf. **qui tacit consentit**.

s'il vous plaît *abbr.* **S.V.P.** [Fr. **s'** if (1); **il** it (2); **vous** you (4); **plaît** pleases (3): if it pleases you.] If you please. Please. Cf. **bitte schön**; **bitte sehr**; **per favore**; **prego**; and **por favor**.

simile *n., pl.* **similes** [L. like, similar, resembling.] *Rhetoric.* A figure of speech in which two things are compared. It is usually introduced by words such as "like," "as," and "just as;" e.g., "As busy as a bee."

similia similibus curantur. [L. **similia** like, similar (things) (1); **similibus** with similar, like (things) (3); **curantur** are cured, healed (2): Similar things should be cured with similar things.] Similar remedies are used to cure similar diseases. A principle of homeopathy.

si monumentum requiris circumspice. [L. **si** if (1); **monumentum** monument (3); **requiris** you seek, look for (2); **circumspice** look around (4): If you look for a monument, look around.] If you are looking for my funeral monument, look around you. The tomb inscription of Christopher Wren (1632–1723) in St. Paul's Cathedral in London. Cf. **si quaeris peninsulam amoenam circumspice.**

simpatico *adj.* [It./Span. likeable, agreeable.] Of similar personality and opinion. Agreeable. Attractive.

simplex *adj.* [L. simple.] Having a simple structure. —*n.* A word, sentence, or geometric structure which has a simple form.

simplex commendatio non obligat. [L. **simplex** simple (1); **commendatio** recommendation, praise (2); **non** not (3); **obligat** binds, makes liable (4): Simple recommendation does not bind.] Mere recommendation of something by a vendor is not a guarantee of its quality. See **caveat emptor.**

simplex munditiis Horace (65–8 B.C.). *Odes* I,5,5. [L. *adj.* **simplex** simple (1); **munditiis** in neatnesses, elegances (2): simple in elegances.] Elegant in simplicity. Simple and neat.

simplex obligatio non obligat. [L. **simplex** simple (1); **obligatio** obligation (2); **non** not (3); **obligat** binds (4): Simple obligation does not bind.] An unconditional bond is not binding.

simplicitas est legibus amica. [L. **simplicitas** simplicity (1); **est** is (2); **legibus** to laws (4); **amica** friendly (3): Simplicity is friendly to the laws.] *Law.* A simple or natural interpretation of the laws is the best.

simplicitas est legibus amica; et nimia subtilitas in jure reprobatur. [L. **simplicitas** simplicity (1); **est** is (2); **legibus** to laws (4); **amica** favorable, friendly (3); **et** and (5); **nimia** too much, excessive (6); **subtilitas** subtlety (7); **in** in, on (8); **jure** right, law (9); **reprobatur** is condemned, disapproved (10): Simplicity is favorable to the laws; and excessive subtlety in law is condemned.] *Law.* Simplicity is friendly to the laws while excessive subtlety of meaning is deemed reprehensible.

simpliciter *adv.* [L. simply.] In itself. By itself. Per se. *In the prologue of the lecture, the professor made it clear that he intended to discuss legal ethics, simpliciter, and not ethics generally.*

simulacrum *n., pl.* **simulacra** or **simulacrums** [L. image, portrait, effigy, statue, shadow, semblance, imitation.] 1. Image. Effigy. Representation of somebody or something. *A very beautiful simulacrum of the assassinated patriot has been placed in front of the House of Parliament.* 2. A semblance. A shadowy image. A superficial likeness. *As old age gradually catches up with him, the great scholar has become a mere simulacrum of himself.*

simul cum *prep.* [L. **simul** at the same time, together, simultaneously (1); **cum** with (2): together with.] *Law.* Along with. Accompanied by. Used in actions of tort and prosecution to signify that the wrong in question was perpetrated by some known and unknown

persons. *Musa, Adekunle, Okoro simul cum persons unknown committed the act.*

sine animo revertendi *adv.* [L. **sine** without (1); **animo** mind, intention (2); **revertendi** of returning (3): without the intention of returning.] With no intent of returning. See **animus non revertendi.**

sine animo revocandi *adv.* [L. **sine** without (1); **animo** intention (2); **revocandi** of recalling, revoking (3): without the intention of recalling.] With no intention of revoking. Cf. **animo revocandi** and **animus revocandi.**

sine anno *abbr.* **S.A.** or **s.a.** *adj.* [L. **sine** without (1); **anno** year (2): without a year.] Undated.

sine causa *adv.* [L. **sine** without (1); **causa** cause, case, reason (2): without reason.] For no reason. *The opposition leader was detained sine causa.*

sine dato *abbr.* **S.D.** or **s.d.** *adj.* [L. **sine** without (1); **dato** given (2): without a given (day).] Without date. Undated.

sine decreto *adv.* [L. **sine** without (1); **decreto** resolution, decree, decision (2): without decision/resolution.] *Law.* Without a judge's authority.

sine die *abbr.* **S.D.** or **s.d.** *adv.* [L. **sine** without (1); **die** day (2): without day.] Without any further day being fixed. Indefinitely. *The meeting adjourned sine die.* —*adj.* Indefinite. Made, done, etc, without any future day being fixed. *Under the circumstances, members voted for an adjournment sine die.* Cf. **sans jour.**

sine fraude sua *abbr.* **S.F.S.** *adv.* [L. **sine** without (1); **fraude** fraud (3); **sua** his/her own (2): without his/her own fraud.] *Law.* With no fraud on his/her part.

sine ira et studio *adv.* Tacitus (c.55–c.117 A.D.). *Annales* I,1. [L. **sine** without (1); **ira** anger, indignation (2); **et** and (3); **studio** partisanship (4): without indignation and partisanship.] Without negative emotion and without taking sides. *A serious-minded historian should write sine ira et studio.* Cf. **neque amore et sine odio.**

sine legitima prole or **sine prole legitima** *abbr.* **S.L.P** or **s.l.p.**, or **S.P.L.** or **s.p.l.** *adv./adj.* [L. **sine** without (1); **legitima** legitimate, lawful (2); **prole** offspring, child (3): without legitimate offspring or issue.] With no legitimate children. See **decessit sine prole legitima.**

sine loco *abbr.* **S.L.** or **s.l.** *adv.* [L. **sine** without (1); **loco** place (2): without place.] No place of publication indicated.

sine loco, anno (vel) nomine *abbr.* **S.L.A.N.** or **s.l.a.n.** *adv.* [L. **sine** without (1); **loco** place (2); **anno** year (3); **vel** or (4); **nomine** name (5): without place, year (or) name.] Without the place of publication, year of publication, and name of publisher.

sine loco et anno *abbr.* **s.l. et a.** *adv.* [L. **sine** without (1); **loco** place (2); **et** and (3); **anno** year (4): without place and year.] Without place or year of publication.

sine mascula prole or **sine prole mascula** *abbr.* **S.M.P.** or **s.m.p.**, or **S.P.M.** or **s.p.m.** *adv./adj.* [L. **sine** without (1); **mascula** male, masculine (2); **prole** offspring, child (3): without male offspring or issue.] Without male children. Without sons. See **decessit sine prole mascula.**

sine nomine *abbr.* **S.N.** or **s.n.** *adv.* [L. **sine** without (1); **nomine** name (2): without name.] Anonymously.

sine numero *adj.* [L. **sine** without (1); **numero** number (2): without number.] Without limitation or stint. Sans nombre (q.v.).

sine possessione usucapio procedere non potest. [L. **sine** without (5); **possessione** possession (6); **usucapio** usucaption, prescription (1); **procedere** to proceed (4); **non** not (3); **potest** can, is able (2): Usucaption cannot proceed without possession.] *Law.* Prescription cannot be effected without possession. Cf. **praescriptio est titulus** etc. and **transferuntur dominia** etc.

sine prole *abbr.* **S.P.** or **s.p.** *adv.* [L. **sine** without (1); **prole** offspring, offshoot (2): without offspring/issue.] Without children. *Mr. Jones died sine prole at the age of 68.* See **defunctus sine prole** and **mortuus sine prole.**

sine prole legitima See **sine legitima prole.**

sine prole mascula See **sine mascula prole.**

sine prole superstite *abbr.* **S.P.S.** or **s.p.s.** *adv.* [L. **sine** without (1); **prole** offspring, child (3); **superstite** surviving, remaining alive (2): without surviving offspring.] Without a surviving child. See **decessit sine prole superstite.**

sine qua non *n., pl.* **sine qua nons** [L. **sine** without (1); **qua** which (2); **non** not (3): without which not.] Something considered essential or indispensable. *Air is a sine qua non for human existence.* —*adj.* Essential. Absolutely necessary. Indispensable. *Any official who thinks that he is sine qua non is obviously living in a fool's paradise.*

sine strepitu *adv.* [L. **sine** without (1); **strepitu** confused noise, din (2): without confused noise.] Without acrimony or rancor. Quietly. *Visitatorial panels are expected to settle disputes or solve problems sine strepitu.*

singspiel *n., pl.* **singspiels** [Ger. **Singspiel:** **sing(en)** sing (1); **Spiel** play (2): sing play.] A form of entertainment in 18th-century Germany in which comic dialogue is combined with the singing of folk songs.

singuli in solidum *adj.* [L. **singuli** several, individual (1); **in** into, to, against, for (2); **solidum** the whole, entire (3): several into the whole.] *Law.* Severally for the whole. Severally liable for the entire amount due.

singuli in solidum tenentur. [L. **singuli** several, individual (2); **in** into, to, against, for (3); **solidum** the whole, entire (4); **tenentur** they are held (1): They are held several into the whole.] *Law.* They are liable severally for the entire amount due. Each of them is liable for the whole amount.

Sinon *n., pl.* **Sinons** [Gk. **Sinōn.**] 1. *Greek Mythology.* A Greek who, pretending to have deserted the Greek forces at Troy, told the Trojans false stories about the wooden horse, persuaded them to drag it within the fortifications of Troy, subsequently released the Greek warriors locked up in the "horse" and joined them in sacking Troy. 2. A perfidious person. A traitor who achieves his ends by telling false stories. *A Sinon, who had wormed his way into the organization, was exposed and expelled.*

si non appareat quid actum est, erit consequens ut id sequamur quod in regione in qua actum est frequentatur. [L. **si** if (1); **non** not (2); **appareat** it is evident, apparent (3); **quid** what (4); **actum est** was done (5); **erit** it will be (6); **consequens** fit (7); **ut** that (8); **id** that (10); **sequamur** we follow (9); **quod** which (11); **in** in, on (13); **regione** region, district, place (14); **in** in, on (15); **qua** which (16); **actum est** it was done (17); **frequentatur** is usually done (12): If it is not evident what was done, it will be fit that we follow that which is usually done in the district in which it was done.] *Law.* If the terms of the agreement are not clear, we need to apply the terms usually observed in the place where the agreement was made.

si opus sit *abbr.* **S.O.S.** [L. **si** if (1); **opus** need (3); **sit** there should be (2): if there should be the need.] Should the need arise. Should the occasion demand or require. If necessary.

si parva licet componere magnis Vergil (70–19 B.C.). *Georgics* IV,176. [L. **si** if (1); **parva** small (things) (4); **licet** it is allowed, permitted (2); **componere** to compare, contrast (3); **magnis** with great (things) (5): If it is allowed to compare small things with great things.] If one may compare the small with the great. Cf. **magna componere parvis.**

si plures sint fidejussores, quotquot erunt numero, singuli in solidum tenentur. [L. **si** if (1); **plures** more, several (3); **sint** there should be (2); **fidejussores** guarantors, sureties (4); **quotquot** how many soever (5); **erunt** they shall be (6); **numero** in number (7); **singuli** individual (persons), several (persons) (9); **in** into, to, against, for (10); **solidum** the whole, entire (11); **tenentur** they are held, bound (8): If there should be several guarantors, how many soever they shall be in number, they are bound (as) individual (persons) into the whole.] *Law.* If there should be several guarantors, whatever be their number, they are bound individually for the entire sum.

si quaeris peninsulam amoenam circumspice. [L **si** if (1); **quaeris** you look for, seek (2); **peninsulam** peninsula (4); **amoenam** pleasant, pleasing (3); **circumspice** look around (5): If you look for a pleasing peninsula, look around.] If you seek a pleasant peninsula, look around. Motto of the State of Michigan. Cf. **si monumentum requiris circumspice.**

si quid universitati debetur singulis non debetur, nec quod debet universitas singuli debent. [L. **si** if (1); **quid** anything (2); **universitati** to aggregate, entirety, corporation (4); **debetur** is owed (3); **singulis** to individual (persons) (7); **non** not (5); **debetur** it is owed (6); **nec** nor, and not (8); **quod** (that) which, what (9);

debet owes (11); **universitas** aggregate, corporation (10); **singuli** individual (persons) (12); **debent** owe (13): If anything is owed to a corporation, it is not owed to individuals, and what the corporation owes individuals do not owe.] *Law.* If anything is owed to a corporation, it is not owed to the individual members, nor do the individual members owe what the corporation owes.

si quis praegnantem uxorem reliquit, non videtur sine liberis decessisse. [L. **si** if (1); **quis** any (man) (2); **praegnantem** pregnant (4); **uxorem** wife (5); **reliquit** left (3); **non** not (6); **videtur** he seems (7); **sine** without (9); **liberis** children (10); **decessisse** to have departed (8): If any man left a pregnant wife, he does not seem to have departed without children.] *Law.* If a man dies, leaving behind a pregnant wife, he is deemed not to have died childless.

sirdar *n.* [Hindi **sardār** from Pers. **sar** head (1); **dār** holder (2): head holder.] An individual of great rank.

Siren *n., pl.* **Sirens** [L. from Gk. **Seirēn**.] *Greek Mythology.* A sea creature, often half-female and half-bird, which charms sailors with her song and leads them to death. —**siren** 1. A seductive and dangerous female of great beauty. 2. A device used to emit a loud, warning sound.

sirocco or **sciroccos** *n., pl.* **siroccos** or **sciroccos** [It. **scirocco** wind from the south or south-east.] A warm, humid southern wind, especially one blowing from North Africa across the Mediterranean into southern Europe.

situs *n., pl.* **situs** [L. situation, location, position, site.] The place where something originates, exists, or is considered to belong for purposes of legal jurisdiction or taxation.

situs inversus viscerum *n.* [L. **situs** position (2); **inversus** inverted (1); **viscerum** of the vital organs (3): inverted position of the vital organs.] *Medicine.* A condition in which the position of the internal body organs is reversed.

sit venia verbo *abbr.* **s.v.v.** [L. **sit** let there be (1); **venia** pardon (2); **verbo** for the word (3): Let there be pardon for the word.] Forgive (or pardon) the expression.

Sitzkrieg *n., pl.* **Sitzkriege** or **Sitzkriegs** [Ger. **Sitz** seat (1); **Krieg** war (2): seat war, sedentary or sitting war.] Warfare by avoiding major battles. a) . . . *the mountain war sputtered into something like a sitzkrieg* (*Newsweek Int.* March 12, 1979:22). b) *Quintus Fabius Maximus, acknowledging Hannibal's superior generalship, took to sitzkrieg with the intention of wearing out the enemy.* Cf. **blitzkrieg.**

si vis amari, ama. Seneca (c.4 B.C.–65 A.D.). *Epistles* IX,4. [L. **si** if (1); **vis** you wish, want (2); **amari** to be loved (3); **ama** love (4): If you wish to be loved, love.] If you want to be loved, be loving.

si vis me flere, dolendum est / primum ipsi tibi. Horace (65–8 B.C.). *Ars Poetica* 102–103. [L. **si** if (1); **vis** you wish, want (2); **me** me (3); **flere** to weep (4);

dolendum to be suffered (6); **est** it is (5); **primum** first (7); **ipsi** (by) self (9); **tibi** by you (8): If you want me to weep, it is to be suffered / first by you yourself.] If you want me to shed tears, you yourself must first suffer.

si vis pacem, para bellum. [L. **si** if (1); **vis** you want, wish (2); **pacem** peace (3); **para** prepare for (4); **bellum** war (5): If you want peace, prepare for war.] If you wish for peace, get ready for war. Cf. **qui desiderat** etc.

S.J. or **s.j.** *abbr.* for **sub judice** (q.v.).

S.J.D. *abbr.* for **Scientiae Juridicae Doctor** (q.v.).

skepsis or **scepsis** *n., pl.* **skepses** or **scepses** [Gk. examination, consideration, speculation.] Skepticism. Critical attitude or outlook. Skeptical approach.

skoal *interj.* [Dan. and Norw. from **skaal** cup.] A drinking toast. Cf. **mazel tov** and **Salute.**

S.L. or **s.l.** *abbr.* for 1. **secundum legem** (q.v.). 2. **sine loco** (q.v.).

S.L.A.N. or **s.l.a.n.** *abbr.* for **sine loco, anno (vel) nomine** (q.v.).

s.l. et a. *abbr.* for **sine loco et anno** (q.v.).

S.L.P. or **s.l.p.** *abbr.* for **sine legitima prole** (q.v.).

S.M. *abbr.* for 1. **Sanctae Memoriae** (q.v.). 2. **Scientiae Magister** (q.v.).

smorgasbord *n., pl.* **smorgasbords** [Swed. **smörgåsbord**: **smör** butter (1); **gås** goose (2); **bord** table (3): buttered goose table.] 1. A self-serve meal consisting of a variety of dishes served on a sideboard. 2. A mixture. A collection. **Miscellanea** (q.v.). *The ad-hoc committee met with a smorgasbord of ideas which were suggested to honor the occasion.*

S.M.P. or **s.m.p.** *abbr.* for **sine mascula prole** (q.v.).

S.N. or **s.n.** *abbr.* for 1. **secundum naturam** (q.v.). 2. **sine nomine** (q.v.).

Snr. *abbr.* for **Senhor** (q.v.).

Sñr. *abbr.* for **Señor** (q.v.).

Snra. *abbr.* for **Senhora** (q.v.).

Sñra. *abbr.* for **Señora** (q.v.).

Snrta. *abbr.* for **Senhorita** (q.v.).

Sñrta. *abbr.* for **Señorita** (q.v.).

sobriquet or **soubriquet** *n., pl.* **sobriquets** or **soubriquets** [Fr. **sobriquet** nickname.] A nickname. A fanciful name or epithet. a) *His film-making prowess has earned him the sobriquet "Il Maestro".* . . (*Newsweek Int.* March 12, 1979:57). b) *Jerry Rawlings, Ghana's Head of State, has a number of sobriquets, including "J.J.," "Junior Jesus," "Jerry the Savior" and "Jerry is our Moses."*

societas *n., pl.* **societates** [L. co-partnership, association in business.] *Roman and Civil Law.* Partnership or contract by which two or more persons unite their resources in a common stock to share in the profits.

societas leonina or **leonina societas** *n.* [L. **societas** partnership (1); **leonina** of lions (2): partnership of lions.] *Roman Law.* Applicable to a proposed partnership in which some of the partners take all the profits, while the rest get nothing. Such partnership is void **ab initio** (q.v.). The expression is derived from the story of the lion which formed a hunting partnership with other animals and took all the prey.

societas navalis *n.* [L. **societas** partnership, association (1); **navalis** of ships (2): partnership/association of ships.] An association in which a number of ships sail together to facilitate mutual protection.

societas omnium bonorum *n.* [L. **societas** partnership, association (1); **omnium** of all (2); **bonorum** (of) goods (3): partnership of all goods.] *Roman Law.* A partnership which covers all the goods of the associates or partners. See **societas universorum bonorum**.

Societas Sanctae Crucis *abbr.* **S.S.C.** *n.* [L. **societas** society (1); **sanctae** of holy (2); **crucis** (of) cross (3): Society of the Holy Cross.] *Roman Catholic Church.* A religious society founded in London in 1855 by a small group of Anglo-Catholic priests led by Father Charles Lowder.

societas universorum bonorum *n.* [L. **societas** partnership (1); **universorum** of entire (2); **bonorum** (of) goods (3): partnership of entire goods.] Universal partnership. A partnership which includes all the goods of the partners. See **societas omnium bonorum**.

société *abbr.* **sté** *n., pl.* **sociétés** [Fr. society, association, company, partnership.] *French Law.* An association, society, partnership, or company.

société anonyme *abbr.* **S.A.** *n., pl.* **sociétés anonymes** [Fr. **société** society, association, company, partnership (2); **anonyme** anonymous (1): anonymous society.] 1. *French Law.* Originally, a partnership in which the name of only one member is used for conducting business, all other partners being strictly secret. 2. *Civil Law.* A corporation in which the liability of all the partners is limited to the capital they have invested. Limited liability company. Cf. **commandite**.

société d'acquêts *n., pl.* **sociétés d'acquêts** [Fr. **société** society, association, company, partnership (1); **d'** of (2); **acquêts** acquisitions (3): partnership of acquisitions.] *Law.* A written contract made by a married couple in which they agree to consider as joint property only things acquired during their marriage. Cf. **conquêts**.

société en commandite *abbr.* **S. en C.** *n., pl.* **sociétés en commandite** [Fr. **société** society, association, company, partnership (1); **en** in (2); **commandite** limited partnership, commandite (3): company in limited partnership.] Limited partnership. A partnership in which one party provides capital to the other for business, receiving a portion of the profits and being liable only to the extent of the capital provided. See **commandite**.

société en nom collectif *abbr.* **S. en N.C.** *n., pl.* **sociétés en nom collectif** [Fr. **société** society, association, company, partnership (1); **en** in (2); **nom** name (4); **collectif** joint, collective (3): partnership in joint

name.] *Law.* A partnership in which all the partners are liable jointly and severally.

socii nomine *pl. n.* [L. **socii** comrades, partners (1); **nomine** in name (2): partners in name.] Nominal partners. Partners in name only.

socius criminis *n., pl.* **socii criminis** [L. **socius** associate, partner, accomplice (1); **criminis** of crime (2): associate of crime.] *Law.* Associate/partner/accomplice in crime. Accessory. See **particeps criminis**. Cf. **in pari delicto**.

soi-disant *adj.* [Fr. **soi** oneself (2) **disant** calling (1): calling oneself, so-called, self-styled.] Supposed. Pretended. Would-be. *The police have warned the general public to be on their guard against a soi-disant businessman who has been duping unwary traders.*

soirée or **soiree** *n., pl.* **soirées** or **soirees** [Fr. evening party.] A party, reception or assembly in the evening. *The tragedy was that they . . . were not prevented . . . from relating their exploits with amusement to provide entertainment at colonial soirées* (Suret-Canale 1971:321).

sola ac per se senectus donationem, testamentum aut transactionem non vitiat. [L. **sola** alone (1); **ac** and (2); **per** by, through (3); **se** itself (4); **senectus** old age (5); **donationem** gift (8); **testamentum** will (9); **aut** or (10); **transactionem** transaction (11); **non** not (6); **vitiat** vitiates, nullifies (7): Alone and by itself, old age does not vitiate a gift, will, or transaction.] *Law.* Old age, alone and by itself, does not nullify a gift, will or transaction.

solatium *n., pl.* **solatia** [L. **solacium** comfort, consolation, relief, solace.] Something which compensates for, or alleviates, loss, suffering, or inconvenience. Damages or compensation for injured feelings.

soliste *n., pl.* **solistes** [Fr. soloist.] *Ballet.* A solo dancer.

solitaire *n., pl.* **solitaires** [Fr. solitary.] 1. A hermit. A person who lives alone. 2. *Games.* A card game played by one person or a game for more than one person based upon that game. 3. A piece of jewelry with only one gem in its setting.

solitudinem faciunt pacem appellant. Tacitus (56/57 A.D.–c.118 A.D.). *Agricola* 30. [L. **solitudinem** wasteland (2); **faciunt** they make (1); **pacem** peace (4); **appellant** they call 3): They make a wasteland, they call (it) peace.] They create a wasteland and call it peace.

solo *abbr.* **s.** *n., pl.* **soli** or **solos** [It. alone, lone, sole.] A performance, such as a song, dance, recital, or flight, done by one person. —*adj./adv.* Performed or done alone. Unaccompanied. a) *He is so conceited that he dislikes working with a team and prefers to work solo.* b) *He was not the first solo oarsman to make the Atlantic crossing, but he covered the greatest distance . . . in the shortest time . . .* (*Newsweek Int.* Oct. 6, 1980:57). Cf. **pas seul**.

solo cedit quod solo implantatur. [L. **solo** to soil (5); **cedit** accrues (4); **quod** (that) which, what (1); **solo**

soil (3); **implantatur** is planted on (2): That which is planted on the soil accrues to the soil.] *Law.* Whatever grows on (or is affixed to) the soil belongs to the owner of the soil. See **quicquid plantatur** etc.

solo cedit quod solo inaedificatur. [L. **solo** to soil (5); **cedit** accrues (4); **quod** (that) which, what (1); **solo** soil (3); **inaedificatur** is built on (2): That which is built on the soil accrues to the soil.] *Law.* Any building erected on the soil belongs to the owner of the soil. See **quicquid plantatur** etc.

solutio indebiti *n.* [L. **solutio** payment (1); **indebiti** of what is not due, what is not owed (2): payment of what is not due.] *Civil Law.* Payment of what is not owed. If a person pays what is not owed, performs labor which he/she is not obliged to, or abandons a right when he/she should not, this person may, in any of these cases, demand back what has been done as though it were a loan.

solvit ad diem *n.* [L. **solvit** he paid (1); **ad** to, at, for, according to (2); **diem** day (3): He paid at the day.] *Law.* A plea in legal case concerning a debt that the money was paid on the stipulated day.

solvit ante diem *n.* [L. **solvit** he paid (1); **ante** before (2); **diem** day (3): He paid before the day.] *Law.* A plea in a legal case concerning a debt that the defendant paid the money before the stipulated day.

solvit post diem *n.* [L. **solvit** he paid (1); **post** after (2); **diem** day (3): He paid after the day.] *Law.* A plea in a legal case concerning a debt that the money was paid after the stipulated day, but before the beginning of the suit.

solvitur adhuc societas etiam morte socii. Gaius (fl. c.110–c.180). [L. **solvitur** is dissolved, broken up, solved (3); **adhuc** similarly (1); **societas** partnership (2); **etiam** also (4); **morte** by death (5); **socii** of partner (6): Similarly, a partnership is dissolved also by the death of a partner.] *Law.* In addition, a partnership is broken up by the death of a partner. Cf. **si alicujus rei** etc.

solvitur ambulando [L. **solvitur** it is dissolved, broken up, solved (1); **ambulando** by walking (2): It is solved by walking.] The solution can be found not by thinking but by doing.

solvitur eo ligamine quo ligatur. [L. **solvitur** it is dissolved, broken up, solved (1); **eo** by that (2); **ligamine** (by) bond, tie (3); **quo** by which (4); **ligatur** it is bound, united (5): It is dissolved by that bond by which it is bound.] *Law.* A thing is dissolved in the way in which it is bound. See **eodem modo quo quid constituitur dissolvitur.**

Somnium Scipionis *n.* [L. **somnium** dream, sleep (1); **Scipionis** of Scipio (2): dream of Scipio.] *The Dream of Scipio*, a portion of Cicero's **De re publica** (q.v.) preserved by Macrobius and describing a dream by Scipio Aemilianus in which Scipio is given a vision of the glory of Roman and of eternity by the ghost of his famous ancestor Scipio Africanus.

sonata *n., pl.* **sonatas** [It. that which is sounded, a musical composition.] *Music.* A composition usually written for keyboard and several other instruments and consisting of three or four movements in different tempos.

sonatina *n., pl.* **sonatinas** [It. that which is sounded, a small musical composition.] *Music.* A short **sonata** (q.v.).

sondage *n., pl.* **sondages** [Fr. sounding, boring, probing, borehole.] 1. Sounding of the earth before actual archaeological work. Preliminary archaeological excavation. 2. An opinion poll. *Based upon a recent sondage the politicians decided to include this point in their platform.*

son et lumière *n., pl.* **son et lumières** [Fr. **son** sound (1); **et** and (2); **lumière** light (3): sound and light.] 1. A night show, usually at an historical site, which uses the effect of recorded sound and dramatic lighting to tell a narrative. 2. A flashy kind of writing which seeks the same sort of effect.

sophia *n.* [Gk. wisdom.] Intelligence and understanding.

sophrosyne *n.* [Gk. **sophrosun** moderation, self-restraint, self-control, or temperance.] Self-control. Will-power. Avoidance of extremes. Antonym of **hubris** (q.v.).

soprano *n., pl.* **soprani** or **sopranos** [It. from **sopra** above: an upper range voice.] *Music.* 1. A human voice in the highest singing range, usually that of a woman or a young boy. 2. A person with such a voice. 3. A musical part written for such a voice. 4. An instrument which plays in this range.

sortes Biblicae *n.* [L. **sortes** lots, fates, prophecies (2); **Biblicae** biblical (1): biblical lots.] Randomly selected biblical passages used to tell the future or seek the truth.

sortes Vergilianae *n.* [L. **sortes** lots, fates, prophecies (2); **Vergilianae** Vergilian (1): Vergilian lots.] Random selections from the works of Vergil (70–19 B.C.), especially the *Aeneid*, used to tell the future or seek the truth.

sortie *n., pl.* **sorties** [Fr. going out, coming out, outlet, outburst.] 1. A sally. A sudden attack on the enemy by besieged troops. 2. An attack or combat mission by one plane. 3. The exit of a ship or a fleet of ships from a harbor.

S.O.S. *abbr.* for **si opus sit** (q.v.).

sostenuto *adv./adj.* [It. sustained.] *Music.* With the sound sustained. —*n., pl.* **sostenuti** or **sostenutos** A note, chord, or passage which is sustained.

sotto voce or, simply, **sotto** *adv.* [It. **sotto** under, beneath (1); **voce** voice (2): under voice.] In an undertone or low voice. Privately. a) *Though the notorious gossip was conversing sotto voce, the equally notorious busybody heard everything.* b) *The band's rendition sotto voce won loud applause.* —*adj.* Silent, undisclosed, or unconfirmed. In a low voice. *The rumor, initially sotto voce, burst into the open and spread like wild fire.*

sou *n., pl.* sous [Fr. former French coin worth five centimes, about half a penny.] A penny. A very small sum of money. A trifle. *Though he does not have a sou, he is greatly respected in his community.*

soubrette *n.* [Fr. from Provençal soubreto conceited.] 1. A disrespectful, flirtatious female servant in French comedy and opera. 2. Any young woman who is flighty and flirtatious.

soupçon *n., pl.* soupçons [Fr. suspicion, conjecture, small quantity.] A small amount. A little bit. a) *The erudite lecturer has a delightful way of flavoring his scholarly discourses with soupçons of popular jokes.* b) *No one is so depraved that a soupçon of goodness cannot be found in him.*

sous *adj.* [Fr. under, beneath, below.] Of lower rank. Of subordinate rank. Assistant. Deputy. Usually used in titles.

sous-entendu *adj.* [Fr. sous under, beneath, below (2); entendu heard, understood (1): heard under.] Understood without saying. *Their love affair was sous-entendu to our conversation. —n.* A tacit understanding.

sous seing privé *adj.* [Fr. sous under, beneath, below (1); seing sign, manual, signature (3); privé private (2): under private sign.] *Law.* Under private sign or signature; i.e., signed privately by the parties, but not sealed or witnessed. Such a document does not enjoy the authenticity or validity of one signed before a judge or notary.

souteneur *n., pl.* souteneurs [Fr. protector.] A male who is supported financially by a prostitute or prostitutes under his protection. A pimp. Cf. proxénète.

souvenir *n., pl.* souvenirs [Fr. memory, recollection, keepsake, memento.] Remembrance. Memento (q.v.). Keepsake. Something purchased by, or given to, a person to remind one of an important occasion, place, or person. a) *. . . an ideal gift for intrepid tourists who want souvenirs of some of the world's less photographed wonders . . .* (*Newsweek Int.* Aug. 23, 1982:3). b) *There are many art objects in the living room of Dr. Cobold, souvenirs of his visits to numerous countries.* c) *The scar on the old man's nose is a souvenir of a puerile escapade. —attrib.* For the purpose of a keepsake or remembrance. a) *souvenir items*; b) *souvenir T-shirts*; c) *souvenir cups.* Cf. memorabilia.

soviet *n., pl.* soviets [Russ. sovét council.] Legislative assemblies popularly elected at local, regional, and national levels in the Soviet Union. —Soviet An inhabitant of the Soviet Union. —the Soviets The government of the Soviet Union and its officials. —adj. 1. Pertaining to the Soviet Union. 2. Pertaining to a legislative assembly.

sovkhoz or sovkhos *n., pl.* sovkhozy or sovkhozes *short form* of sovetskoe khozya [Russ. sov(etskoe) soviet (1); khoz(ya) farm(2): Soviet farm.] A farm owned by the state of the U.S.S.R. where people work for wages. Cf. kibbutz and kolkhoz.

S.P. *abbr.* for Summus Pontifex (q.v.).

S.P. or s.p. *abbr.* for sine prole (q.v.).

sparsim *adv.* [L. here and there.] Spread at intervals or widely. *Adegoke sued Awofisan for committing trespass to his property by cutting trees sparsim.*

spécialité de la maison *n.* [Fr. spécialité speciality (1); de of (2); la the (3); maison house (4): speciality of the house.] 1. The house speciality. The particular meal or dish for which a restaurant is known. 2. Any talent or characteristic peculiar to a particular group. *The spécialité de la maison in that family is sarcasm and irony.*

specie *n.* [L. in kind, appearance, resemblance, likeness.] Coined money.

species *n., pl.* species [L. kind, appearance, resemblance, likeness.] 1. A class of individuals with common attributes and bearing a common name. 2. Form, aspect or appearance. 3. *Civil Law.* A shape or appearance given to materials.

specificatio *n.* [L. from species form, species (2); faci(o) make (1): making species.] *Roman Civil Law.* Making a form or species. Something made into a new form or species becomes the property of the maker rather than the owner of the original material. Cf. droit d'accession.

spectatum veniunt, veniunt spectentur ut ipsae. Ovid (43 B.C.–17 A.D.). *Ars Amatoria* I,99. [L. spectatum to see, to watch (2); veniunt they come (1); veniunt they come (3) spectentur they might be seen, watched (6); ut so that, in order that (4); ipsae they (fem.) themselves (5): They come to see; they come in order that they themselves be watched.] Women come to the amphitheater to watch the games; but they also come so that they themselves can be watched.

spectre *n., pl.* spectres [Fr. ghost, apparition.] 1. A ghost, phantom, or apparition. 2. An imaginary, haunting, or perturbing vision. *With the spectre of imminent bankruptcy haunting him, Ziga recovered his sanity and changed his lifestyle.*

spectrum *n., pl.* spectra or spectrums [L. appearance, image, apparition, form.] 1. Apparition. 2. A band or display of colors which is formed when light is refracted and passed through a prism. 3. A continuous (or wide) range/sequence of things. a) *The latter cover a broad political spectrum from ultra-leftists, Communists and radical intellectuals to right-wingers . . .* (*New African* 1979). b) *The spectrum of things that can go wrong at even the most determinedly responsible news organization ranges from premeditated dishonesty . . . to honest misinterpretation* (*Newsweek Int.*, May 4, 1981:47).

spero meliora [L. spero I hope for (1); meliora better (things) (2): I hope for better things.] I hope for the better.

spes accrescendi *n.* [L. spes hope (1); accrescendi of growing up, increasing (2): hope of growing up.] Hope of survival or surviving.

spes impunitatis continuum affectum tribuit delinquendi. [L. spes hope (1); impunitatis of impunity, freedom from punishment (2); continuum continuous, uninterrupted (4); affectum disposition, inclination (5); tribuit gives (3); delinquendi of doing wrong (6): Hope of impunity gives a continuous inclination of doing wrong.] Law. Hope of impunity tends to predispose a man to crime. See impunitas semper etc.

spes recuperandi n. [L. spes hope (1); recuperandi of recovering (2): hope of recovering.] Hope of recovering/recapturing captured goods. Used of goods captured at sea.

spes successionis n. [L. spes hope (1); successionis of succession, inheritance (2): hope of succession.] Hope of succession/inheritance.

Sphinx n. [L. from Gk.] Greek and Roman Mythology. A hybrid creature with the head and upper torso of a woman, the body of a lion, and the wings of a bird, associated with death, and often represented on tombstones. Especially the creature which posed the riddle to the Greek hero Oedipus. —sphinx pl. sphinxes or sphinges 1. Egyptian Mythology and Religion. A creature with a human head and a lion's body. 2. Any individual or object mysterious and difficult to understand.

S.P.L. or s.p.l. abbr. for sine prole legitima (q.v.).

splendide mendax adj. Horace (65–8 B.C.). Odes III,11,35–36. [L. splendide nobly, splendidly (1); mendax untrue, false, deceitful (2): nobly untruthful.] Telling lies in the interest of a noble cause.

S.P.M. or s.p.m. abbr. for sine prole mascula (q.v.).

spolium n., pl. spolia [L. booty, prey, spoil.] Civil and Common Law. Something forcefully and illegally taken away from another.

sponsalia per verba de futuro [L. sponsalia betrothal, engagement (l); per through, by (2); verba words (3); de of, from, about, for (4); futuro future (5): betrothal through words about the future.] Law. Engagement through words about the future; i.e., engagement validated by promise to marry or by references to living in the future as husband and wife.

sponte sua See sua sponte.

sponte virum mulier fugiens et adultera facta, dote sua careat, nisi sponsi sponte retracta. [L. sponte by/of accord, willingly (4); virum man, husband (3); mulier woman, wife (1); fugiens fleeing, running away from (2); et and (5); adultera adulteress (7); facta having been made, having become (6); dote dowry (10); sua her own (9); careat should be deprived of, lose (8); nisi unless (11); sponsi of bridegroom (14); sponte by accord, free will (13); retracta brought back (12): A woman running away from the husband by her own accord and having become an adulteress should be deprived of her own dowry, unless called back by the free will of the bridegroom.] Law. A woman who willingly deserts her husband, particularly after committing adultery, should lose her dowry, unless she is brought back by her husband of his own free will.

S.P.Q.R. abbr. for Senatus Populusque Romanus (q.v.).

S.P.S. or s.p.s. abbr. for sine prole superstite (q.v.).

sputnik n., pl. sputniks short form of sputnik (zemlyi) [Russ. sputnik fellow traveler (1); zemlyi of the earth (2): fellow traveler of the earth.] The first satellite sent into space (by the Soviet Union on October 4, 1957).

Sr. abbr. for Señor (q.v.).

SRA or Sra abbr. for Señora (q.v.).

SRITA or Srita abbr. for Señorita (q.v.).

SRTA or Srta abbr. for Señorita (q.v.).

ss. abbr. for scilicet (q.v.).

S.S. abbr. for supra scriptum (q.v.).

S.S.B. abbr. for Sacrae Scripturae Baccalaureus (q.v.).

S.S.C. abbr. for Societas Sanctae Crucis (q.v.).

S.S.D. abbr. for Sacrae Scripturae Doctor (q.v.).

S.S.L. abbr. for Sacrae Scripturae Licentiatus (q.v.).

st. abbr. for stet (q.v.).

Stabat Mater Dolorosa [L. stabat was standing (3); mater mother (2); dolorosa sorrowful, grieving (1): The grieving mother was standing.] Christianity. The first words of a hymn commemorating the death of Jesus. —n., short form Stabat Mater pl. Stabat Maters 1. The hymn itself. 2. Music. A composition based upon this hymn.

stabit praesumptio donec probetur in contrarium. [L. stabit will stand (2); praesumptio presumption (1); donec until, as long as (3); probetur it be proved (4); in into, to, against, for (5); contrarium the contrary (6): A presumption will stand until it be proved to the contrary.] An assumption will remain valid until proved to the contrary.

staccato abbr. stac. or stacc. adj. [It. detached.] Disconnected. Abrupt. Jerky. a) . . . the corners of his mouth wrenched in a clown's grimace as the voice machine-guns a blast of staccato croaks (Time Int. 1982). b) Whenever Ekechi meets Godwin, she is overwhelmed with love and her heart begins to beat in a frenzied staccato rhythm. —n., pl. staccatos or staccati 1. Music. Releasing one note completely before starting the next one. 2. Something, such as sound or speech, that comes out in short abrupt bursts.

stagnum n., pl. stagna [L. standing water.] Lake, pool or pond which has no outlet.

stante matrimonio adv. [L. stante (with) standing (2); matrimonio with marriage (1): with the marriage standing.] As long as the marriage continues. Stante matrimonio, it is an offense for the husband or the wife to engage in amorous escapades with somebody else.

stare decisis n. [L. stare to stand (1); decisis by decisions, by what has been decided or settled (2): to stand by decisions or what has been decided.] Law. A doctrine which requires judges to follow precedent or established legal principles based on previous judgments unless and until it becomes absolutely necessary to remedy glaring and long continued injustice. *Res judicata relates to a decision; stare decisis relates to a rule or principle of law involved* (Curzon 1979:241). See **res judicata**.

stare decisis et non quieta movere. [L. **stare** to stand (1); **decisis** by decisions (2); **et** and (3); **non** not (4); **quieta** the undisturbed, the quiet (6); **movere** to move, disturb (5): To stand by decisions and not to disturb the undisturbed.] *Law.* To abide by precedents and not to disturb settled matters. *The principle of precedent, whereby a judge is bound generally to apply principles and rules contained in earlier decisions, rests on the doctrine of stare decisis et non quieta movere...* (Curzon 1979:241). See **res judicata**.

stasis *n., pl.* **stases** [Gk. position, state, condition.] 1. Stagnancy. Stagnation. A state of stagnant or stable equilibrium reached by opposing forces or society in its development. a) *His Middle East peace-making process is near stasis, ...* (*Newsweek Int.* Jan. 1, 1979:40). b) *The new regime is making no effort to move the nation out of the economic, social and political stasis bequeathed by its predecessor.* 2. *Medicine.* Stagnation, slowing, or stoppage of the flow of fluid in the body, such as that of blood in the veins or arteries.

stat magni nominis umbra. Lucan (39–65 A.D.). *Pharsalia* I,135. [L. **stat** stands (4); **magni** of great (2); **nominis** (of) name (3); **umbra** shadow, shade (1): The shadow of a great name stands.] There stands the shadow of a great name.

status *n., pl.* **statuses** [L. position, state, condition, rank, situation.] 1. A person's legal condition or position. 2. A political entity's legal condition. 3. Rank or position in a community or society. *My daughter has attained the status of a mother.* 4. A relative rank in a hierarchical system. *Woodrow Wilson used the status of professor as a stepping stone to a political career.* 5. Recognition, high rank or prestige. *Established networks facilitate the search for status.* 6. Situation, condition or state of affairs. *From time to time he gives reports on the status of the negotiations.*

status quo *n.* [L. **status** state, condition, position (1); **quo** in which (2): state/position in which.] The existing state of affairs at any particular time. *The reforms were vigorously opposed by several powerful individuals who had a vested interest in the status quo.*

status quo ante *n., pl.* **status quo ante** [L. **status** state, condition, position (1); **quo** in which (2); **ante** before (3): the state in which before.] The previous state of affairs. The state of affairs prevalent before, i.e., a certain date or the present time. *The new administration, which arrived with copious promises, has done nothing to effect changes in the status quo ante.*

status quo ante bellum *n.* [L. **status** state, condition, position (1); **quo** in which (2); **ante** before (3); **bellum** war (4): the state in which before the war.]

The state of affairs before the war. *The treaty was essentially based on the status quo ante bellum.* Cf. **uti possidetis** 2.

statuta pro publico commodo late interpretantur. [L. **statuta** statutes (1); **pro** for, in favor of (2); **publico** public (3); **commodo** advantage, convenience (4); **late** broadly, widely (6); **interpretantur** are interpreted (5): Statutes for public advantage are interpreted broadly.] *Law.* Statutes made for the public good are given a broad/liberal interpretation.

statutum generaliter est intelligendum quando verba statuti sunt specialia, ratio autem generalis. [L. **statutum** statute (1); **generaliter** generally (4); **est** is (2); **intelligendum** to be understood (3); **quando** when (5); **verba** words (6); **statuti** of statute (7); **sunt** are (8); **specialia** special (9); **ratio** reason (11); **autem** but, however (10); **generalis** general (12): A statute is to be understood generally when the words of the statute are special but the reason (is) general.] *Law.* When the words of a statute are special, but the reason for it is general, the statute must be understood (or interpreted) generally. See **generale dictum generaliter est intelligendum**.

S.T.B. *abbr.* for **Sacrae Theologiae Baccalaureus** (q.v.).

S.T.D. *abbr.* for **Sacrae Theologiae Doctor** (q.v.).

sté. *abbr.* for **société** (q.v.).

stela (L.) or **stele** (Gk.) *n., pl.* **stelae** or **stelai** or **steles** [L. from Gk. **stēlē** a block or slab used as a memorial, an inscribed monument.] 1. A stone or slab bearing an inscription and often used as a gravestone. 2. A monument shaped like a pillar.

stella maris *n.* [L. **stella** star (1); **maris** of the sea (2): star of the sea.] *Roman Catholic Church.* Title given to Mary, the Mother of Jesus, and to many churches dedicated to her.

stemma *n., pl.* **stemmata** or **stemmas** [L. from Gk. wreath, garland.] A genealogical tree showing relationships among family members of manuscripts of a given work. *The book is a collection of short biographies, each with a stemma of the subject.*

Stentor *n., pl.* **Stentors** [Gk. **Stentōr.**] 1. A herald in Homer's *Iliad* whose shout was as loud as those of fifty ordinary men. 2. A person who has a very powerful or loud voice. *The eulogy was delivered by a man who is not only a good orator but also a Stentor.*

stet *abbr.* **st.** [L. Let it stand.] Do not delete. Ignore a previous order to cancel or omit. Used in the corrections of manuscripts or printer's proof.

stet processus *n.* [L. **stet** let stand (1); **processus** process (2): Let the process stop/stand.] *Old English Legal Practice.* An entry in the record of a legal action putting a stop to proceedings.

stigma *n., pl.* **stigmata** or **stigmas** [Gk. tattoo-mark, mark, spot.] 1. Mark of shame, infamy, or discredit. A disgrace, ignominy, or stain. a) *The political history of Africa ... will suffer from the stigma of incompleteness until it ...* (Y.Y. in *West Africa* 1982). b) *The* constituency elected as its senator a man of probity who leaves no stone unturned to avoid the stigma of corruption. 2. An identifying or distinctive mark. *The boy takes great delight in wearing the stigmata of a scout.* —*pl.* **stigmata** Wounds resembling those on the body of the crucified Jesus Christ which mysteriously appear on the bodies of some devout Christians (e.g., St. Francis of Assisi) and are believed to be supernaturally inflicted.

stiletto *n., pl.* **stilettos** [It. dagger.] 1. A dagger, especially one with short, narrow, and tapered blade. 2. A heel shaped like such a dagger. A spike heel. 3. A sewing instrument used to poke holes in fabric. —*v.* 1. To kill with a dagger.

stilus virum arguit [L. **stilus** style (1); **virum** man (3); **arguit** makes clear, proves (2): Style proves the man.] Style proves the person. Cf. **Le style, c'est l'homme même.**

stimulus *n., pl.* **stimuli** [L. prick, goad, incentive, spur.] Incentive. Spur. Something that arouses to activity. *The new management introduced a number of fringe benefits which proved to be a stimulus to productivity.*

stipendium *n., pl.* **stipendia** or **stipendiums** [L. stipend, wages.] Salary or pay.

stirps *n., pl.* **stirpes** [L. stock of a tree, family, lineage, offspring.] Branch of a family. A person who is the ancestor of a branch of a family. See **per stirpes.**

S.T.L. *abbr.* for **Sacrae Theologiae Licentiatus** (q.v.).

S.T.M. *abbr.* for **Sacrae Theologiae Magister** (q.v.).

stratum *n., pl.* **strata** or **stratums** [L. that which is spread out, a covering, bed, couch.] 1. A layer or bed, as of sedimentary rock, earth, atmosphere, tissue, archaeological findings, etc. 2. A socio-economic group or level, comprising people of similar educational background, profession, income, status, cultures etc. *It took care to foment feelings of mistrust and dislike among the various strata of society . . .* (Suret-Canale 1971:440).

stretto *n., pl.* **stretti** or **strettos** [It. narrow, close, constricted.] *Music.* 1. The entrance of voices in close succession in a fugue. 2. An increase in tempo near the end of a composition, especially an oratorio.

stricti juris *adv.* [L. **stricti** of strict (1); **juris** (of) right, law (2): of strict law/right.] According to strict law. Applicable to a license or privilege which a person enjoys not by his/her own right but as an indulgence, and so must be observed strictly. See **strictissimi juris.**

strictissimi juris *adv.* [L. **strictissimi** of strictest (1); **juris** (of) right, law (2): of the strictest law/right.] According to the strictest right. Applicable to licenses and privileges. See **stricti juris.**

stricto jure *adv.* [L. **stricto** in strict (1); **jure** (in) right, law (2): in strict law.] According to strict law.

stricto sensu See **sensu stricto.**

strictum jus See **jus strictum.**

Strukturwandel *n.* [Ger. **Struktur** structure (1); **Wandel** change (2): structure change.] Structural

change. *In West Germany, Strukturwandel . . . is constantly on the lips of industrialists, politicians, economists and union bosses (Time Int.* 1978).

stultum facit Fortuna quem vult perdere. Publilius Syrus (c.85–43 B.C.). *Sententiae* 613. [L. **stultum** foolish, stupid (3); **facit** makes (2); **Fortuna** Fortune, Fate (1); **quem** (one) whom (4); **vult** she wants, wishes (5); **perdere** to destroy (6): Fortune makes stupid one whom she wants to destroy.] One whom Fortune wishes to destroy, she makes stupid. Cf. **quem Deus vult** etc. and **quem Juppiter vult** etc.

stupor *n., pl.* **stupors** [L. senselessness, astonishment, stupidity.] 1. *Medicine.* A condition marked by increased senselessness and diminished awareness, especially caused by the use of drugs. 2. A state of shock and surprise. An inability to think.

stupor mundi *n.* [L. **stupor** senselessness, astonishment, stupidity (1); **mundi** of world (2): the astonishment of the world.] A person of great international power, influence, and reputation, who is respected and feared at the same time. *After the death of Frederick II, the stupor mundi, in 1250, the Roman emperor's sphere of authority was definitely restricted to German soil* (Cary 1970:780).

Sturm und Drang *n.* [Ger. **Sturm** storm (1); **und** and (2); **Drang** stress (3): storm and stress.] 1. A German literary movement of the late 18th century which was a revolt against the Enlightenment. This movement was characterized by native genius, linguistic realism, and emotionalism, and emphasized the revolt of the individual against societal injustice. Cf. **Aufklärung.** 2. A time of storm and stress. Turmoil. Turbulence. a) *Barely two months after his hands-down reelection victory, West German Chancellor Helmut Schmidt faces a gathering economic Sturm und Drang (Newsweek Int.* Dec. 15, 1980:46). b) *In his personality we find a union of all the impulses of the sophistic movement, whose period of Sturm und Drang reached a symbolic end in his dramatic death* (Lesky 1966:357).

sua cuique voluptas Statius (c. 45 A.D.–c.96). *Thebaid* II,2,73. [L. **sua** one's own (1); **cuique** to each (3); **voluptas** pleasure (2): one's own pleasure to each.] Each person has a pleasure of his/her own. To each his/her own pleasure.

suapte natura *adv.* [L. **suapte** in/by its own (1); **natura** (in/by) nature (2): by its own nature.] Intrinsically. In its own nature.

sua sponte or **sponte sua** *adv.* [L. **sua** by his/her/its own (1); **sponte** free will, accord, impulse (2): by his/her/its own accord.] Of one's own accord. Willingly. Freely. *The court accepted the statement of the accused as an exhibit after satisfying itself that it was made sua sponte.* See **ex mero motu.**

suave *adj.* [Fr. pleasant, sweet, nice, mild, soft.] 1. Pleasant, especially to one's senses. 2. Urbane. Agreeably affable, polite, gracious, smooth or easy in manner (though possibly insincere).

suaviter in modo, fortiter in re *adv.* [L. **suaviter** sweetly, pleasantly (1); **in** in, on (2); **modo** manner (3); **fortiter** bravely, strongly (4); **in** in, on (5); **re** matter, thing, property, business, affair (6): sweetly in manner, bravely in the matter.] Gently in manner, resolutely in execution. Applicable to a person (or anything) who, very politely but resolutely, refuses to succumb to pressure and to change his/her mind. *Jim tendered his letter of resignation and, though pressure was exerted on him from all corners, he comported himself suaviter in modo, fortiter in re.*

sub anno *abbr.* **S.A.** or **s.a.** [L. **sub** under, beneath (1); **anno** year (2): under the year.] Invariably followed by a date. Used for reference to entries in a series of annals or in a chronicle.

subauditur *n., pl.* **subauditurs** [L. It is understood.] Something implied or understood.

sub colore juris *adv.* [L. **sub** under (1); **colore** color (2); **juris** of right, law (3): under color of right.] Under the appearance, color, or show of right, power, or law.

sub conditione *adv./adj.* [L. **sub** under, subject to (1); **condi(c)ione** condition (2): under or subject to condition.] *Law.* Conditional. Conditionally. Used for expressing condition in a conveyance and for creating a conditional estate.

sub dio *adv.* [L. **sub** under, beneath (1); **dio** bright, clear (2): under bright (light).] In daylight. In the open air. **Alfresco** (q.v.).

sub finem *abbr.* **S.F.** or **s.f.** [L. **sub** towards (1); **finem** end (2): towards the end.] Near the end.

sub hac voce *abbr.* **S.H.V.** or **s.h.v.** [L. **sub** under (1); **hac** this (2); **voce** word, voice (3): under this word.] Used for references to headwords in dictionaries and other works arranged alphabetically. See **in verbo**.

sub hoc verbo *abbr.* **S.H.V.** or **s.h.v.** [L. **sub** under (1); **hoc** this (2); **verbo** word (3): under this word.] Used for references to headwords in dictionaries and works arranged alphabetically. See **in verbo**.

sub judice *abbr.* **S.J.** or **s.j.** *adj./adv.* [L. **sub** under, before, in the power of (1); **judice** judge (2): before a judge.] *Law.* Under judicial consideration. Undecided. Undetermined. *The police officer said that the matter was sub judice, and so he would not comment on it.* Cf. **res judicata**.

sublata causa, tollitur effectus. [L. **sublata** (with) having been taken away, removed (2); **causa** with cause, case, reason (1); **tollitur** is taken away, removed (4); **effectus** effect (3): With the cause having been taken away, the effect is removed.] *Law.* When the cause is removed, the effect disappears. See **cessante causa** etc. and **ubi aliquid impeditur** etc.

sublata veneratione magistratuum, res publica ruit. [L. **sublata** (with) having been taken away (3); **veneratione** with respect, veneration (1); **magistratuum** of magistrates, public functionaries (2); **res publica** the state, republic (4); **ruit** tumbles down, collapses (5): With respect of magistrates having been

taken away, the state tumbles down.] When magistrates cease to be respected, the state collapses.

sublato fundamento cadit opus. [L. **sublato** (with) having been taken away (2); **fundamento** with foundation, basis (1); **cadit** falls (4); **opus** structure, building (3): With the foundation having been taken away, the structure falls.] A structure collapses when the foundation is removed. See **accessorium non ducit** etc.

sublato principali tollitur adjunctum. [L. **sublato** (with) having been removed, taken away (2); **principali** with principal (1); **tollitur** is taken away, removed (4); **adjunctum** adjunct (3): With the principal having been taken away, the adjunct is taken away.] *Law.* When the principal is removed, the adjunct is similarly removed. See **accessorim non ducit** etc.

sub lite *adv.* [L. **sub** under, beneath (1); **lite** lawsuit, dispute (2): under dispute.] *Law.* Under litigation.

sub modo *adv.* [L. **sub** under (1); **modo** limit, restriction (2): under qualification.] Under qualification, condition, or restriction.

sub nomine *adv.* [L. **sub** under (1); **nomine** name (2): under the name.] In the name of. Under the title or caption of.

sub pede sigilli *adv.* [L. **sub** under (1); **pede** foot (2); **sigilli** of seal (3): under the foot of the seal.] Under seal. See **sub sigillo**.

subpoena *n., pl.* **subpoenas** [L. **sub** under (1); **poena** penalty (2): under penalty.] *Law.* 1. A writ ordering a person named in it to appear in court under penalty for noncompliance. 2. The process whereby a defendant in an action is ordered to appear in court and answer the bill of the plaintiff. —*v.* To serve a subpoena on, or summon with a writ of subpoena. *He was subpoenaed to appear in court.* —*adv.* Under penalty.

subpoena ad testificandum *n., pl.* **subpoenas ad testificandum** [L. **sub** under (1); **poena** penalty (2); **ad** to, at, for, according to (3); **testificandum** testifying (4): under penalty for testifying.] *Law.* Under penalty to testify. A writ ordering a person to appear in court to testify as witness under penalty for noncompliance.

subpoena duces tecum *n., pl.* **subpoenas duces tecum** [L. **sub** under (1); **poena** penalty (2); **duces** you will bring (3); **tecum** with you (4): under penalty you will bring with you.] *Law.* A writ ordering a person to produce at trial documents or evidence deemed pertinent to the case under trial, non-compliance being punishable with a fine or imprisonment.

sub potestate *adj.* [L. **sub** under (1); **potestate** power (2): under power.] *Roman Law.* Applicable to members of the family under the control of the **paterfamilias** (q.v.).

sub rosa *adj.* [L. **sub** under (1); **rosa** rose (2): under the rose.] Secretive. Confidential. *David has enrolled as a member of a sub rosa society.* —*adv.* Without notice or publicity. Confidentially. Privately. *A client's* instruction to a legal practitioner in chambers is expected to be treated *sub rosa*. The meaning of the expression is derived from the oath of secrecy taken in the ancient world when a rose was hung over the council table.

sub sigillo *adv./adj.* [L. **sub** under (1); **sigillo** seal (2): under seal.] In strict confidence.

sub silentio *adv.* [L. **sub** under (1); **silentio** silence (2): under silence.] In silence. Without saying anything. With no notice being taken. *She left her daughter in the care of her neighbor, assuming sub silentio that the daughter would be taken care of gratis.*

sub specie aeternitatis *adv.* [L. **sub** under (1); **specie** aspect, view, appearance, semblance (2); **aeternitatis** of eternity (3): under the aspect of eternity.] From the perspective of eternity. In its essential nature or form.

sub specie perennitatis *adv.* [L. **sub** under (1); **specie** aspect, view, appearance, semblance (2); **perennitatis** of perpetuity, continuance (3): under the aspect of continuance or perpetuity.] As a continuity. As an unbroken (or continuous) span of time. *By considering the past sub specie perennitatis, instead of regarding the various periods as isolated, almost unrelated segments, we get a comprehensive view of the history of humankind.*

sub specie potestatis *adv.* [L. **sub** under (1); **specie** aspect, view, appearance, semblance (2); **potestatis** of power (3): under the semblance of power.] Under the appearance of power.

sub specie temporis *adv.* [L. **sub** under (1); **specie** aspect, view, appearance, semblance (2); **temporis** of time (3): under the view of time.] From the perspective of time as opposed to eternity. Cf. **sub specie aeternitatis**.

sub spe reconciliationis *adv.* [L. **sub** under (1); **spe** hope (2); **reconciliationis** of reconciliation, reconciling (3): under the hope of reconciliation.] In the hope of reconciling. *Mr. Peterson sent a family delegation to his estranged wife sub spe reconciliationis.*

substratum *n., pl.* **substrata** or **substratums** [L. that which is spread under.] 1. A level or layer of a substance, such as earth or rock, beneath another. 2. Foundation. Basis. *After the child's testimony had been subjected to rigorous scrutiny, it was found to contain a substratum of truth.* 3. A substance from which something is produced and which gives it its unique qualities.

sub suo periculo *adv.* [L. **sub** at, under (1); **suo** one's his/her own (2); **periculo** risk, peril, hazard (3): at one's own risk.] At his/her own risk or cost. See **suo periculo**.

sub verbo *abbr.* **S.V.** or **s.v.** [L. **sub** under (1); **verbo** word (2): under the word.] Used for references to headwords in dictionaries and other works arranged alphabetically. See **in verbo**.

sub voce *abbr.* **S.V.** or **s.v.** [L. **sub** under (1); **voce** word, voice (2): under the word.] Used for references to headwords in dictionaries and other alphabetically arranged works. See **hac voce** and **in verbo**.

succès de ridicule *n.* [Fr. **succès** success (1); **de** of (2); **ridicule** ridiculousness, absurdity (3): success of absurdity.] The success, acclaim, or notoriety of a literary or artistic work which is mainly attributable to its absurdity or its ridiculous nature.

succès de scandale *n.* [Fr. **succès** success (1); **de** of (2); **scandale** scandal, disgrace (3): success of scandal or disgrace.] The acclaim or notoriety won by a literary or artistic work (or an artist) by reason of its scandalous contents or associations. a) *The novel's outrageous treatment of cherished traditional customs won for it an instant succès de scandale.* b) *By then, however, the model . . . had become a succès de scandale* (*Newsweek Int.* Sept. 21, 1981:33).

succès de snobisme *n.* [Fr. **succès** success (1); **de** of (2); **snobisme** snobbery (3): success of snobbery.] The success, acclaim or notoriety won by a literary or artistic work by reason of its ability to arouse sympathy among intellectual snobs.

succès d'estime *n.* [Fr. **succès** success (1); **d'** of (2); **estime** esteem, regard (3): success of esteem.] Mild success. Success with a limited public. The critical acclaim which a literary or artistic work wins, though it does not achieve popular or monetary success. a) *His works have consistently won for him succès d'estime, but not the monetary rewards needed to pull him out of his perennial pecuniary embarrassment.* b) *The industry's succès d'estime has received blessings from a series of French governments* (*Newsweek Int.* Nov. 15, 1982:36).

succès fou *n.* [Fr. **succès** success (2); **fou** insane, mad, wild (1): a wild success.] A great or enthusiastic success.

successio ab intestato *n.* [L. **successio** succession, inheritance (1); **ab** from, by (2); **intestato** intestate (3): succession from an intestate.] *Law.* Succession to an intestate. Succession in the event of intestacy. Inheritance of the property of an intestate. Cf. **hereditas ab intestato** and **heres ab intestato**.

succuba or **succubus** *n., pl.* **succubae** or **succubi** or **succubuses** [Medieval Latin from L. **succuba** a person who lies underneath, a prostitute.] 1. A demon who supposedly takes the form of a woman and engages in sexual intercourse with men when they are asleep. 2. A demon, devil, or fiend. 3. A prostitute or whore. Cf **cocotte, femme libre**, and **meretrix**.

succurritur minori; facilis est lapsus juventutis. [L. **succurritur** there is a running to help or aid (1); **minori** (to) young (person) (2); **facilis** easy (6); **est** is (5); **lapsus** slip, error, failing (3); **juventutis** of youth (4): There is a running to help a young person; an error of youth is easy.] *Law.* Minors are helped, for youths easily make mistakes. Cf. **lex succurrit minoribus**.

sudum pactum *n., pl.* **suda pacta** [L. **sudum** clear (1); **pactum** agreement, compact (2): clear agreement.] *Law.* Clear compact or agreement.

suggestio falsi *n., pl.* **suggestiones falsi** [L. **suggestio** suggestion, representation (1); **falsi** of falsehood, untruth (2): suggestion of falsehood.] *Law.* False representation or statement. Suggesting what is false. Deliberately misrepresenting something by either action or speech, even though one does not actually say what is untrue. See **suppressio veri**.

sui generis *adj.* [L. **sui** of its own (1); **generis** (of) kind, class (2): of its own kind/class.] In a class or category of its own. Unique. *A statutory right of occupancy is a right granted to a "native" or "non-native" . . . and though a right of occupancy has many characteristics of a lease, it is sui generis* (James 1982:25).

sui juris *adj.* [L. **sui** of one's own (1); **juris** (of) right, law (2): Of one's own right.] Qualified to enjoy full civil and social rights. Not being a minor any more. Deemed competent, and enjoying full legal rights to take care of or conduct one's own affairs. See **homo sui juris**. Cf. **alieni juris**; **homo alieni juris**; and **non sui juris**.

suite *n., pl.* **suites** [Fr. retinue, attendants, train, continuation, succession, series.] 1. Retinue. A train or company of attendants or followers, especially the private staff of a ruler or high public official, who accompany him/her on a journey for official purposes. 2. A number of rooms in an apartment building, hotel, train, etc. regarded as a set or unit and used by one person or a group of persons. *The Minister and his entourage held discussions with their counterparts in their hotel suite.* 3. A set or group of matched furniture. 4. A number of musical compositions regarded as a set and played one after another.

summa cum laude *adv./adj.* [L. **summa** highest, topmost (2); **cum** with (l); **laude** praise (3): with highest praise.] With highest distinction. Used to indicate the highest performance in school or university. See **magna cum laude**.

summa potestas *n.* [L. **summa** highest, topmost (1); **potestas** power, authority (2): highest power.] Highest power or authority. *A "state" had a different basis from that of other organisations in that it included summa potestas, that is, superior power residing in some individuals* (Curzon 1979:62).

summa ratio *n.* [L. **summa** highest, topmost (1); **ratio** reason, rule (2): the highest reason.] The supreme rule. Applicable to law.

summum bonum *n.* Cicero (106–43 B.C.). *De Officiis* I,2,5. [L. **summum** highest, topmost (1); **bonum** good (2): the highest good.] The supreme good.

summum jus *n.* [L. **summum** highest, topmost (1); **jus** right, law (2): the highest right/law.] *Law.* Extreme right. Strict legal right. Exact or rigorous law. Cf. **aequitas**.

summum jus, summa injuria. [L. **summum** highest, topmost (1); **jus** right, law (2); **summa** highest, topmost (3); **injuria** injury (4): Highest law, highest injury.] *Law.* Extreme right brings extreme injury; i.e., rigorous insistence on a person's strict legal rights could do incalculable harm to others.

summum jus, summa injuria; summa lex, summa crux. [L. **summum** highest, topmost (1); **jus** right, law (2); **summa** highest, topmost (3); **injuria** injury (4); **summa** highest, topmost (5); **lex** law (6); **summa** highest, topmost (7); **crux** torture; misery (8): Highest right, highest injury; highest law, highest misery.] *Law.* Extreme right brings extreme injury; extreme (or strict) law brings extreme misery; i.e., strict insistence on one's legal rights, without regard for equity, could do incalculable harm to others.

Summus Pontifex *abbr.* **S.P.** *n.* [L. **summus** highest (1); **pontifex** pontiff (2): highest pontiff.] Supreme Pontiff. The Pope.

sumo *n.* [Japan.] A Japanese form of wrestling for men.

Sunna or **Sunnah** *n., pl.* **Sunnas** or **Sunnahs** [Ar. **sunnah** established practice, custom.] 1. A body of the traditional practices and customs of Islam based on the sayings and deeds of the Prophet Mohammed. 2. Any practice or custom observed by an individual or a community. A body of such practices and customs. Cf. **Hadith**.

Sunni *n.* [Ar. **sunnĩy** follower of the Sunna.] That part of Islam which considers the legal successors of Mohammed to have been the first four caliphs. —*pl.* **Sunni** or **Sunnis** A Muslim who recognizes this succession. A Sunnite Muslim.

sunt lacrimae rerum. Vergil (70–19 B.C.). *Aeneid* I,462. [L. **sunt** there are (1); **lacrimae** tears (2); **rerum** of matters, things, property, business, affairs (3): There are tears of things.] Human life is inherently (or basically) tragic. See **hinc illae lacrimae** and **lacrimae rerum**.

suo motu *adv.* [L. **suo** by its own (1); **motu** (by) impulse, motion (2): by its own impulse.] By its own impulse or initiative. *The court has power suo motu to order the distribution of the property of the deceased.* See **ex mero motu**.

suo periculo *adv.* [L. **suo** at one's own, his/her own (1); **periculo** risk, hazard (2): at one's own risk.] At his/her own peril. See **sub suo periculo**.

sup. *abbr.* for **supra** (q.v.).

superficies *n., pl.* **superficies** [L. upper side, surface, top, improvements, fixtures, buildings.] 1. The external characteristics of something. Superficial appearance. The surface. *Some people pay more attention to the superficies than the substance of a thing and, not surprisingly, are usually duped.* 2. *Roman and Civil Law.* Things like houses or other structures that are so inextricably connected to a piece of ground as to form part of it. Also an owner's alienation of the surface of the ground in return for a periodic rent. See **quicquid plantatur** etc.

superficies solo cedit. [L. **superficies** structure, building (1); **solo** to ground, soil (3); **cedit** accrues (2): A structure accrues to the ground.] *Law.* Structures constitute a part of the ground. See **quicquid plantatur** etc.

superflua non nocent. [L. **superflua** superfluous (things) (1); **non** not (2); **nocent** do harm, hurt, injure (3): Superfluous things do not do harm.] Superfluities do not hurt.

supersedeas *n., pl.* **supersedeas** [L. You should desist, refrain or forbear.] *Law.* 1. A common law writ ordering a stay of proceedings at law. 2. A writ from a court of appeal prohibiting execution of a writ by reason of an appeal.

Supplices *pl. n.* [L. suppliants.] *The Suppliants.* The Latin title of *Hiketides*, a play by Aeschylus about the myth of the daughters of Danaus, who come as suppliants to Greece in order to avoid marriage with their Egyptian cousins.

suppressio veri *n., pl.* **suppressiones veri** [L. **suppressio** suppression (1); **veri** of truth (2): suppression of the truth.] *Law.* Concealment of the truth. In both law and equity, suppressio veri is equivalent to suggestio falsi and, when proved, is to the advantage of the injured party. See **suggestio falsi**; **suppressio veri, expressio falsi**; and **suppressio veri, suggestio falsi**.

suppressio veri, expressio falsi. [L. **suppressio** suppression (1); **veri** of truth (2); **expressio** expression (3); **falsi** of falsehood (4): Suppression of truth is an expression of falsehood.] *Law.* Suppression of the truth is analogous to expression of falsehood. See **suppressio veri**.

suppressio veri, suggestio falsi. [L. **suppressio** suppression (1); **veri** of truth (2); **suggestio** representation, suggestion (3); **falsi** of falsehood (4): Suppression of the truth is a suggestion of falsehood.] *Law.* Suppression of the truth implies falsehood. See **suppressio veri**.

supra *abbr.* **sup.** *adv.* [L. above, before, previously, formerly.] Above. In the previous or earlier part of this work. Cf. **infra** and **post**.

supra scriptum *abbr.* **S.S.** [L. **supra** above, on the top (2); **scriptum** written (1): written above.] Written earlier in the work.

supremo *n.* [It. supreme person.] 1. Commander-in-chief of an army. 2. The supreme head of a government department, organization, etc. 3. A supreme authority. Cf. **generalissimo**.

sura *n.* [Ar. **sūrah** from Heb. **sura** row, line.] *Islam.* A chapter of the Koran.

Sur le pont d'Avignon [Fr. **sur** on (1); **le** the (2); **pont** bridge (3); **d'** of (4); **Avignon** Avignon (5): on the bridge of Avignon.] The title of a popular French song about a bridge in the city of Avignon.

surrogatum *n., pl.* **surrogata** [L. that which is proposed as a substitute.] Substitute or substitution.

sursum corda [L. **sursum** lift up (1); **corda** hearts (2): Lift up heart.] *Christianity.* "Lift up your hearts." Part of a refrain in the Eucharistic liturgy.

susurrus *n., pl.* **susurruses** [L. whispering or muttering sound.] Mutterings, especially of discontent. Under a tyrannical regime, vociferous popular outbursts make way for the susurruses of the intimidated populace.

sutra *n., pl.* **sutras** [Skt. **sūtra** thread, rule.] 1. A short rule or wise saying, especially one dealing with law, philosophy, or even grammar. 2. *Buddhism.* Sacred scripture. Cf. **Kama Sutra**.

suttee or **sati** *n.* [Hindi **satī** true, virtuous.] *Hinduism.* 1. The practice, now illegal, of self-immolation of a widow upon her husband's funeral pyre as the ultimate act of conjugal devotion. 2. *pl.* **suttees** or **satis** A woman who performs such an act.

suum cuique [L. **suum** one's own, his/her own (2); **cuique** to each (1): to each one's own.] To each according to his/her due. Giving to each one what one deserves. *Social justice demands that people should be treated on the principle of suum cuique.* Cf. **Jeder nach** etc.

suum cuique tribuere [L. **suum** one's own, his/her own (3); **cuique** to each (2); **tribuere** to give; assign (1): To give to each one's own.] **Suum cuique** (q.v.).

suus heres or **suus haeres** See **heres suus**.

S.V. or **s.v.** *abbr.* for 1. **sub verbo** (q.v.). 2. **sub voce** (q.v.).

S.V.P. *abbr.* for **s'il vous plaît** (q.v.).

s.v.v. *abbr.* for **sit venia verbo** (q.v.).

swami *n., pl.* **swamis** [Hindi **svamī** master.] *Hinduism.* 1. A religious instructor. 2. A mystic. A **yogi** (q.v.). 3. A term of honor for such a person.

swastika *n., pl.* **swastikas** [Skt. **svastika** from **su** good (1); **asti** being (2): good being.] 1. A good luck symbol found in ancient India, the Near East, and elsewhere, in which the four arms of a cross are extended with right-angled arms in either a clockwise or counter-clockwise direction. 2. The symbol of the German National Socialist (Nazi) party. 3. A flag with such an emblem.

syce *n.* [Hindi.] A groom or stable worker.

syllepsis *n., pl.* **syllepses** [Gk. **sullēpsis**: **sun** together (2); **lēpsis** taking, seizing (1): taking together, a figure by which a predicate belonging to one subject is attributed to several.] *Rhetoric.* 1. The use of a word, e. g. a verb or an adjective, which governs two or more other words (i.e., noun) but agrees grammatically with only one of them; e.g., the verb in "The boys were happy and likewise the girl." 2. The use of a word grammatically related to two or more other words in such a way that for one the literal sense is applicable, while for the other or others it is the metaphorical sense; e.g., "His argument was so cogent and persuasive that he demolished not only his opponent's thesis but also the opponent himself." Cf. **zeugma**.

sylloge *n., pl.* **sylloges** [Gk. **sullogē** gathering, collecting, summary, collection.] A compendium. A collection.

symbiosis *n., pl.* **symbioses** [Gk. **sumbiosis: sun** with, together (2); **bio(s)** live (1): living with, companionship, good fellowship.] 1. The mutually beneficial living together of organisms of different species. 2. Mutually beneficial cooperation between persons, groups, bodies, etc. a) *Some partners remain bound in awful wedlock by a kind of symbiosis in which mutual dependency may go hand in hand with mutual loathing . . .* (*Newsweek Int.* July 13, 1981:45). b) *. . . publishers and writers need themselves in an intricate symbiosis which must be encouraged by the two groups* (*The Guardian* 1986).

sympatheia *n.* [Gk. **sumpatheia: sun** with, together (2); **path(os)** feeling, suffering (2): feeling with, sympathy.] Fellow-feeling. Sympathy. *The earliest form of tragedy, which was not action but pure passion, used the force of sympatheia, through which the spectators shared the emotions of the chorus . . .* (Jaeger 1970:250).

sympathique *adj.* [Fr. sympathetic, likeable, attractive.] Pertaining to a person, place, or thing which is agreeable and likeable or suitable to one's taste or mood. *That dress is quite sympathique!*

Symphonie fantastique *n.* [Fr. **symphonie** symphony (2); **fantastique** fantastic (1): fantastic symphony.] "The Fantastic Symphony," an 1830 orchestral work by Hector Berlioz (1803–1869).

symposium *n., pl.* **symposia** or **symposiums** [L. from Gk. **symposion: sun** with, together (2); **posi(s)** drinking (1): drinking with, a drinking-party, the room in which a drinking-party is held.] 1. *Ancient Greece.* A drinking-party at which music was played, there was singing and, above all, the guests engaged in conversation. 2. A social gathering or banquet at which people exchange ideas freely. 3. A meeting or conference at which a number of participants speak briefly on some aspects of a topic or on related topics. A discussion. *Ngugi's contribution to the symposium had the quality of a spell* (Ben Okri in *West Africa* 1982). 4. A collection of views on a topic, particularly one published by a journal or periodical. —**Symposium** 1. Title of a philosophical dialogue by Plato (427?–347 B.C.) in which Socrates, Alcibiades, Aristophanes et al. discuss the nature of love at a drinking party. 2. Title of a philosophical dialogue by Xenophon (434?–?355 B.C.) in which Socrates and others discuss their most prized possessions at a drinking party.

synchysis *n., pl.* **synchyses** [Gk. **sugkhusis: sun** with, together (2); **khusis** pouring (1): pouring together, confusion.] *Rhetoric.* A confusing word order, especially one that interlocks words together tightly; e.g., "poor dilapidated John's car" for "poor John's dilapidated car."

syncope *n., pl.* **syncopes** [L. from Gk. **sunkopē: sun** with, together (2); **kopē** cutting (1): cutting with.] 1. *Rhetoric.* The shortening of a word cutting sounds from the middle, as "e'en" for "evening" or "even." 2. *Medicine.* A temporary loss of consciousness caused by inadequate oxygen in the brain.

synecdoche *n., pl.* **synecdoches** [Gk. **sunekdokhē: sun** with, together (3); **ek** out of, from (2); **dekh(omai)** receive, take (1): taking from (someone or something) together with, understanding one thing with another.] *Rhetoric.* The representation of a part for the whole, a whole for the part, the general for the specific, the specific for the general, etc.; e.g, "roof" for "house" or "ship" for "sailors."

synesis *n., pl.* **syneses** [Gk. **sunesis: sun** with, together (2); **(hi)ē(mi)** send (1): sending together, union.] *Linguistics.* The joining of a word according to semantic sense rather than grammatical rule. Occurs commonly in English when a plural pronoun is used to refer to a collective noun; e.g., "If the committee so desires, they may decide the question."

synopsis *abbr.* **synop.** *n., pl.* **synopses** [Gk. **sunopsis: sun** with, together (2); **opsis** seeing (1): seeing together, general view, seeing all together.] A brief outline. An abstract. A summary, abstract or brief outline of a book, treatise, play, film, etc. *The crimes of the Shah are innumerable. Even a synopsis would be too long for me to present in a single session* (*Time Int.* 1980). Cf. **epitome.**

synthesis *n., pl.* **syntheses** [Gk. **sunthesis: sun** with, together (2); **thesis** putting, placing (1): putting together, composition, combination.] 1. The combination of various or diverse elements, factors, parts, ideas, forces, substances, etc. into one consistent or coherent whole. The product of such combination. *Much of Grozier's analysis is plainly derivative: a synthesis of the views of American critics from David Riesman to Milton Friedman* (*Newsweek Int.* Feb. 23, 1981:50). 2. Deducing particular instances from general causes or principles.

Syrinx *n.* [L. from Gk. **Surinx.**] *Greek and Roman Mythology.* A nymph who escaped the amorous advances of the god Pan by transformation into reeds. From these reeds the god made the first pan-pipes, a musical instrument also known as a syrinx. —**syrinx** *pl.* **syrinxes** *Music.* Pan-pipes. A reed instrument in which air is blown through sections of varying lengths of reed to produce sounds.

T

T. or t. *abbr.* for l. tempo (q.v.). 2. tempore (q.v.). 3. tenor (q.v.). 4. tomus (q.v.).

T.A. or t.a. *abbr.* for testantibus actis (q.v.).

tableau *n., pl.* tableaux or tableaus [Fr. picture, description, scene.] Picture. Image. A vivid description. Scene. Artistic grouping. a) *One of the striking features of the book is the author's ability to present admirable tableaux of rural life.* b) *The play opens with an impressive tableau* (Lesky 1966:394). c) *This allows him . . . to make the opera into a series of nightmares and arresting tableaux* (*Time Int.*1979). d) *. . . the report interspersed scenes of mutilations and deaths with tableaus of Argentines at work and at play* (*Newsweek Int.* May 9, 1983:44).

tableau vivant *n., pl.* tableaux vivants [Fr. tableau picture, depiction, scene (2); vivant living (1): living scene.] A skit or performance in which silent, costumed actors reenact a story or scene.

taboo or tabu *adj.* [Polynesian. tabu set aside, restricted, forbidden.] Forbidden or not permitted, especially by religious or social beliefs. —*n., pl.* taboos or tabus An action, word, or thing which is forbidden or not permitted among the members of a particular social or religious group. —*v.* To forbid a particular action, word, or thing.

tabula in naufragio *n.* [L. tabula plank, table, board (1); in in, on (2); naufragio shipwreck (3): plank in a shipwreck.] Law. Used with reference to the power of a third mortgagee, who did not know of the existence of a second mortgagee, to acquire the first incumbrance and get satisfaction even before the second. It has survived in tacking in English law.

tabula rasa *n., pl.* tabulae rasae [L. tabula tablet, slate (2); rasa smoothed, rubbed (1): smoothed or rubbed slate.] Blank slate. Used to describe the state of the mind before it receives external impressions. *Before a man can be really objective and impartial, he must approach an issue with, as it were, a tabula rasa.*

tacenda *pl. n.* [L. things which must be silent.] Items or subjects which must not be discussed because they are embarrassing, controversial, etc.

tacent satis laudant. Terence (died c.159 B.C.). *Eunuch* III,2,23. [L. tacent they are silent (1); satis enough (2); laudant they praise (3): They are silent–enough–they praise.] They are silent enough; they praise enough. Through their silence they praise.

tacet [L. It is silent.] *Music.* Silence. Used to indicate a place in the music where a part is silent.

taedium See tedium.

taedium vitae *n.* [L. taedium weariness, loathing, disgust (1); vitae of life (2): weariness of life.] Disgust with life. Loathing of life. Deep discontent. Cf. mal du siècle and Weltschmerz.

tafsir *n., pl.* tafasir [Ar.] *Islam.* Explanation, understanding and interpretation of the Koran as distinct from mere translation.

talis interpretatio in ambiguis semper fienda est, ut evitetur inconveniens et absurdum. [L. talis such (7); interpretatio interpretation (1); in in, on (2); ambiguis ambiguous, doubtful (things) (3); semper always (5); fienda to be made, done (6); est is (4); ut that (8); evitetur may be avoided (12); inconveniens inconvenient (thing) (9); et and (10); absurdum absurd (thing) (11): Interpretation in ambiguous things is always to be done such that the inconvenient and absurd thing may be avoided.] Law. Whenever there is ambiguity, the passage or clause should be interpreted in such a way that an inconvenient and absurd decision may be avoided. See talis interpretatio semper etc.

talis interpretatio semper fienda est, ut evitetur absurdum et inconveniens, et ne judicium sit illusorium. [L. talis such (5); interpretatio interpretation (1); semper always (3); fienda to be made, done (4); est is (2); ut that (6); evitetur may be avoided (10); absurdum absurd (thing) (7); et and

---

378

(8); **inconveniens** inconvenient (thing) (9); **et** and (11); **ne** in order that not (12); **judicium** judgment (13); **sit** be (14); **illusorium** illusory, worthless (15): Interpretation is always to be done such that the absurd and inconvenient thing may be avoided and in order that judgment not be illusory.] *Law.* Interpretation must always be carried out in such a way that the absurd and the inconvenient may be avoided, and in order that judgment may not be illusory (or worthless). See **talis interpretatio** etc.

tallith or **tallis** *n., pl.* **tallithim** or **talliths** or **tallisim** [Heb. cover.] *Judaism.* A prayer shawl worn by Jews every morning.

tant mieux *interj.* [Fr. **tant** so much (1); **mieux** better (2): so much better.] So much the better! Tough! Cf. **tant pis.**

tant pis *interj.* [Fr. **tant** so much (1); **pis** worse (2): so much worse.] So much the worse! Cf. **tant mieux.**

Tantra or **tantra** *n.* [Skt. loom, doctrine.] *Hinduism, Buddhism, and Jainism.* A secret writing or teaching which uses symbolic, often erotic, language to guide believers to a higher state of reality.

tantum religio potuit suadere malorum. Lucretius (c.94–c.55 B.C.). *De Rerum Natura* I,72. [L. **tantum** so much (1); **religio** religion, religious scruple (4); **potuit** could, was able (3); **suadere** to urge, suggest (5); **malorum** of evils (2): So much of evils could religion urge.] Such a magnitude of evils religion could urge people to commit.

tarantella *n., pl.* **tarantelle** or **tarantellas** [It. dance from Taranto.] 1. *Music.* A traditional Italian dance in a brisk tempo. 2. A composition for this dance or in the style of this dance.

tarde venit *n.* [L. **tarde** late (2); **venit** it came (1): It came late.] *Law.* A writ which was received by the sheriff or any officer too late to be executed before the day of return.

Tartarus *n., pl.* **Tartaruses** [L. from Gk.] 1. *Greek and Roman Mythology.* The infernal regions or the Lower World. 2. Hell. 3. A place which looks like hell. Cf. **Elysium**; **Hades**; and **Valhalla.**

Taurus *n.* [L. bull.] 1. *Astronomy.* A bull-shaped constellation located near Aries. 2. *Astrology.* The second sign of the zodiac, dominant from April 20 through May 20. 3. A person born under this sign.

tchotchke See **chachka.**

tecum vivere amem, tecum obeam libens. Horace (65–8 B.C.). *Odes* III,9,24. [L. **tecum** with you (1); **vivere** to live (3); **amem** I would love (2); **tecum** with you (4); **obeam** I would die (5); **libens** with pleasure, willing (6): With you I would love to live; with you I would die with pleasure.] I would like to live with you and with pleasure I would die with you.

Te Deum *n., pl.* **Te Deums** *short form of* **Te Deum Laudamus** [L. **te** you (2); **Deum** God (3); **laudamus** we praise (1): We praise you, God.] We praise you,

God. *Christianity.* 1. The first words of Latin hymn of praise. 2. A musical composition based upon this prayer. 3. Any hymn of praise.

tedium *n., pl.* **tediums** [L. **taedium** tediousness.] Boredom or monotony. *As a man of action, he soon got disgusted with the tedium of sedentary work.*

tefillin *pl. n.* [Heb. **tepīlin** attachments.] Two small leather boxes containing phrases from the Hebrew bible worn by Jews during morning prayer except on Holy Days.

te judice *adv.* [L. **te** with you (1); **judice** (with being) judge (2): with you being judge.] With you as judge.

telegnosis *n., pl.* **telegnoses** [Neo-Gk. from Gk. **tēle** at a distance, far off (2); **gnosis** knowledge (1): knowledge at a distance.] **Clairvoyance** (q.v.). Knowledge of distant occurrences obtained through mysterious means.

telekinesis *n., pl.* **telekineses** [Neo-Gk. from Gk. **tēle** at a distance, far off (2); **kinesis** movement, motion (1): movement at a distance.] The apparent movement of things at a distance, as though under the influence of spiritual powers, without the application of contact or any physical means.

telos *n., pl.* **teloi** [Gk. end, limit.] Ultimate end or purpose.

temp. *abbr.* for 1. **tempo** (q.v.). 2. **tempore** (q.v.).

tempo *abbr.* **T.** or **t.** or **temp.** *n., pl.* **tempi** or **tempos** [It. time, interval.] 1. *Music.* The rate of rhythmical movement of a passage or piece. . . . *as the tempo of the music quickened, couples launched into a familiar step . . .* (*Newsweek Int.* April 14, 1980:16). 2. Pace. Rate of activity or movement. *The intensity and urgency of these passionate desires become reflected in the quick tempo of the action* (*West Africa* 1987).

tempora mutantur, et nos mutamur in illis. [L. **tempora** times (1); **mutantur** change, are changed (2); **et** and (3); **nos** we (4); **mutamur** we change, are changed (5); **in** in, on (6); **illis** them, those (7): Times change and we change in them.] Times change and we change with them. For fuller form, see **tempora mutantur; nos et** etc. Cf. **Autres temps** etc.

tempora mutantur; nos et mutamur in illis. / quo modo? fit semper tempore pejor homo. John Owen (1560?–1622). *Epigrams.* [L. **tempora** times (1); **mutantur** change, are changed (2); **nos** we (4); **et** and (3); **mutamur** we change, are changed (5); **in** in, on (6); **illis** them, those (7); **quo** in what (8); **modo** (in) way (9); **fit** becomes (13); **semper** always (12); **tempore** with time (10); **pejor** worse (14); **homo** person, human being (11): Times change and we change in them. / In what way? With time, a human being always becomes worse.] Times change and we change with them. How? With time, people always get worse. For shorter form, see **tempora mutantur, et nos** etc. Cf. **Autres temps** etc.

tempore *abbr.* **T.** or **t.** or **temp.** [L. in the time of.] Followed by a name, ordinarily that of a king, queen, or other ruler. Used for approximate chronology when the exact date is unknown. See **Tempore Regis.**

Tempore Paschale or **Paschale Tempore** *abbr.* **T.P.** or: **P.T.** [L. **tempore** at time (1); **Paschale** of Easter, Passover (2): at the time of Easter.] At/during Easter. In Eastertide.

Tempore Regis *abbr.* **T.R.** [**tempore** at time (1); **regis** of king (2): in the time of the king.] During the reign of the king. See **tempore.**

temps perdu *n.* [Fr. **temps** time, weather (2); **perdu** lost (1): lost time.] Past time. The irretrievable past. Cf. **À la Recherche du temps perdu** and **fugit irreparibile tempus.**

tempus deliberandi *n.* [L. **tempus** time (1); **deliberandi** of deliberating (2): time of deliberating.] *Roman, Civil, and Scots Law.* The time which in former times was allowed to an heir to decide whether to accept the inheritance or not. Cf. **beneficium abstinendi** and **potestas abstinendi.**

tempus edax rerum Ovid (43 B.C.–17 A.D.). *Metamorphoses* XV,234. [L. **tempus** time (1); **edax** devouring (2); **rerum** of matters, things, property, business, affairs (3): time, devouring of things.] Time, devourer of things. *Initially, the problems seemed formidable but, thanks to tempus edax rerum, everything has evaporated.* See **tempus est** etc.

tempus est edax rerum. [L. **tempus** time (1); **est** is (2); **edax** devouring, rapacious (3); **rerum** of matters, things, property, business, affairs (4): Time is devouring of things.] Time devours things; i.e., time solves problems. In law, e.g., an **usucapio** (q.v.) which goes unchallenged for a long time becomes a possession. See **tempus edax rerum.**

tempus fugit. [L. **tempus** time (1); **fugit** flies, runs away, flees (2): Time flees.] Time flies. Time passes quickly. For fuller form, see **sed fugit** etc.

tenendum *n., pl.* **tenendums** [L. that which must be be held.] *Law.* Used to introduce a clause which in former times indicated the kind of tenure which was vested in the grantee.

tenet *n., pl.* **tenets** [L. He/she/it holds or maintains.] Opinion, doctrine, or dogma deemed to be true, especially one prevalent among members of a party, organization, profession, or school. *The students refused to sing the national anthem and salute the flag, insisting that such practices are against the tenets of their religion.*

tenor *abbr.* **T.** or **t.** *n., pl.* **tenors** [L. holding on, holding fast, continuance, uninterrupted course.] 1. The general course of thought or literary work. . . . *theories that have radicalised the general tenor of liberation thought in the Third World* . . . (Herbert Ekwe-Ekwe in *West Africa* 1986). 2. Procedure, trend, or direction in an activity or a course. *A man of tenacity of purpose proceeds, like the planets, on the tenor of his course, unperturbed by the criticisms and insubstantial comments of busybodies.* 3. Character, nature, or habit. *This is an authentic work which bears the unmistakable*

tenor of its author. 4. The natural adult male singing voice in its highest range. *"I'm loosening up," says the sensitive singer, who scales down his sugar-coated songs and sweet tenor for his new LP* (*Newsweek Int.* March 26, 1979:35). 5. A person who sings, or an instrument which plays, the kind of note indicated in 4 (above): *"A tenor these days can get $39,000 an evening for appearing at a medium-sized Italian festival,"* . . . (*The Economist* 1987).

teras *n., pl.* **terata** [Gk. wonder, marvel, portent, sign.] Monster. An organism, such as a fetus, which on account of genetic or other causes is grossly amorphous.

ter die sumendum *abbr.* **T.D.S.** or **t.d.s.** [L. **ter** thrice, three times (2); **die** in a day (3); **sumendum** to be taken (1): to be taken thrice in a day.] *Medicine.* To be taken three times daily.

ter in die *abbr.* **T.D.** or **t.d.** *adv.* [L. **ter** thrice, three times (1); **in** in, on (2); **die** day (3): thrice in a day.] *Medicine.* Three times a day.

terminus *n., pl.* **termini** or **terminuses** [L. boundary, end, limit, term.] Finishing point. Starting point. The starting and finishing point of a route. Tip of something.

terminus ad quem *n.* [L. **terminus** boundary, end, limit, term (1); **ad** to, at, for, according to (2); **quem** which (3): the end to which.] Destination. Deadline. Purpose. *In the case of such a contract* [of employment], *there is no natural terminus ad quem short of the retirement date of the employee by reference to which to limit the damages for wrongful dismissal . . .* (Freedland 1976:252). Cf. **dies a quo.**

terminus ante quem *n.* [L. **terminus** boundary, end, limit, term (1); **ante** before (2); **quem** which (3): the end/limit before which.] A date or time firmly established as the latest possible limit of a period. Used by historians to fix the latest possible date of an event. *The age of his parents and his career suggest that the terminus ante quem of his birth is 1940.* Cf. **dies a quo.**

terminus a quo *n.* [L. **terminus** boundary, end, limit, term (1); **a** from (2); **quo** which (3): the end/limit from which.] 1. The starting point of an activity. The point of origin. 2. **Terminus post quem** (q.v.). See **dies a quo.**

terminus post quem *n.* [L. **terminus** boundary, end, limit, term (1); **post** after (2); **quem** which (3): the end/limit after which.] A date or time firmly established as the earliest possible limit of a period. Used by historians to fix the earliest possible date of an event. *Since the terminus post quem of his birth is 1935, while the terminus ante quem is 1940, he is clearly Paul's contemporary.* See **dies a quo.**

terra cognita *n., pl.* **terrae cognitae** [L. **terra** land (2) **cognita** known (1): known land.] A familiar environment or known surroundings.

terra cotta *abbr.* **TC** *n., pl.* **terra cottas** [It. **terra** earth, ground, land (2); **cotta** cooked, baked (1): baked earth.] 1. A hard, fired, usually reddish and unglazed material used for earthenware. 2. An object such as a pot, bowl, or figurine made from such material. 3. A brownish red or orange color. —*adj.* **terra-cotta** A brownish orange color. The color of clay.

terrae filius See **filius terrae.**

terra firma *n.* [L. **terra** earth, ground, land (2); **firma** firm, strong (1): firm ground/earth.] Solid ground. Dry land. A secure foothold.

terra ignota *n., pl.* **terrae ignotae** [L. **terra** land (2) **ignota** unknown (1): unknown land.] An unfamiliar environment or unknown surroundings.

terra incognita *n., pl.* **terrae incognitae** [L. **terra** earth, ground, land (2); **incognita** unknown (1): unknown land.] An unknown territory. An unexplored subject. *Books written by Europeans would make us believe that, before Christopher Columbus' voyage of exploration, America was a terra incognita.*

terra intacta *n.* [L. **terra** earth, ground, land (2); **intacta** untouched (1): untouched land.] Unexplored, untouched land. *Implicit in his discussion . . . is the fact that the Upper Region remains terra intacta as far as excavation is concerned, . . .* (Roger G. Thomas in *West Africa* 1982).

terra manens vacua occupanti conceditur. [L. **terra** earth, ground, land (1); **manens** remaining, staying (2); **vacua** unoccupied, vacant (3); **occupanti** to one occupying (5); **conceditur** is granted, given (4): Land remaining vacant is granted to the one occupying.] *Law.* Land which remains vacant is given to the first person to occupy it. See **res nullius naturaliter** etc.

terra nullius *n.* [L. **terra** earth, ground, land (1); **nullius** of nobody (2): land of nobody.] Land which has not been annexed by any nation. Land which belongs to nobody.

terra transit cum onere. [L. **terra** earth, ground, land (1); **transit** passes, is transferred (2); **cum** with (3); **onere** burden, load (4): Land passes with the burden.] *Law.* Land is transferred with its incumbrance. Cf. **res transit** etc.

terrazzo *n., pl.* **terrazzi** [It.] A marble or stone floor set in mortar and highly polished.

terre-à-terre *adj.* [Fr. **terre** earth, ground, land (1); **à** to, toward, in, by, with, until (2); **terre** earth (3): earth to earth.] 1. Performed on the floor or ground. Performed with hardly any elevation. The dancer is most admirable when he does terre-à-terre dancing. 2. Performing with the feet very close to the floor or ground. *The terre-à-terre dancers in the troupe put up a very outstanding performance.* 3. Commonplace, unimaginative, prosaic or matter-of-fact. Down-to-earth. *The guest of honor almost ruined the occasion with his terre-à-terre speech.*

tertium quid *n.* [L. **tertium** third (1); **quid** what (2): a third what.] 1. Something lying between two mutually exclusive things, but sharing features of both. 2. A third party of uncertain status. *This is a case of a husband, wife, and a tertium quid.*

tertius gaudens *n.* [L. **tertius** third (1); **gaudens** rejoicing (2): a third rejoicing.] *Law.* A third party benefits from a dispute between two other parties.

tertius interveniens *n.* [L. **tertius** third (1); **interveniens** intervening (2): a third intervening.] *Civil Law.* A third person who intervenes. A person who interpleads, i.e., between parties to a suit, usually to protect his/her own interests.

terza rima *n.* [It. **terza** third (1); **rima** rhyme (2): third rhyme.] A type of poetry in which the second line of verse written in triplets rhymes with the first and third verses of the next triplet. This form of rhyme is used in **La Commedia Divina** (q.v.) by Dante Alighieri (1265–1321).

testamenta cum duo inter se pugnantia reperiuntur, ultimum ratum est; sic est, cum duo inter se pugnantia reperiuntur in eodem testamento. [L. **testamenta** wills (3); **cum** when (1); **duo** two (2); **inter** among (6); **se** themselves (7); **pugnantia** fighting (5); **reperiuntur** are found (4); **ultimum** last (8); **ratum** approved (10); **est** is (9); **sic** so (11); **est** it is (12); **cum** when (13); **duo** two (things) (14); **inter** among (17); **se** themselves (18); **pugnantia** fighting (16); **reperiuntur** are found (15); **in** in, on (19); **eodem** the same (20); **testamento** will (21): When two wills are found fighting among themselves, the last is approved; so it is, when two things are found fighting among themselves in the same will.] *Law.* When there are two conflicting wills, the last is accepted. The same rule applies when there are two conflicting provisions in the same will. See **cum duo inter se** etc. and **si duo in testamento** etc.

testamenta latissimam interpretationem habere debent. [L. **testamenta** wills (1); **latissimam** broadest (4); **interpretationem** interpretation (5); **habere** to have, hold, regard (3); **debent** ought, should (2): Wills should have the broadest interpretation.] *Law.* Wills should be interpreted very broadly.

testamenti factio See **factio testamenti.**

testamentum *n., pl.* **testamenta** [L. will, testament.] *Civil Law.* A testament. Will.

testamentum destitutum *n., pl.* **testamenta destituta** [L. **testamentum** will (2); **destitutum** abandoned, deserted (1): an abandoned will.] A deserted will, i.e., an inheritance which no one has entered on. Cf. **hereditas jacens.**

testamentum inofficiosum *n., pl.* **testamenta inofficiosa** [L. **testamentum** will (2); **inofficiosum** undutiful, inofficious (1): an undutiful testament.] *Civil Law.* A will which does not fulfill obligations or duties, i.e., a will that violates natural duty and deprives children and parents of their rightful share in the estate. See **donatio inofficiosa.**

testamentum omne morte consummatur. [L. **testamentum** will (2); **omne** every, all (1); **morte** by death (4); **consummatur** is consummated, perfected (3): Every will is consummated by death.] *Law.* All wills are perfected by the death of the testator. See **legatum morte** etc.

testantibus actis *abbr.* **T.A.** or **t.a.** [L. **testantibus** (with) testifying, bearing witness (2); **actis** with the acts/deeds (1): with the acts testifying.] As the acts show. As the acts indicate. As shown by the acts.

testatoris ultima voluntas est perimplenda secundum veram intentionem suam. [L. **testatoris** of testator (3); **ultima** last (1); **voluntas** will, desire, wish (2); **est** is (4); **perimplenda** to be fully executed (5); **secundum** according to (6); **veram** true (8); **intentionem** intention (9); **suam** his/her (7): The last wish of a testator is to be fully executed according to his/her true intention.] *Law.* A testator's last will must be fully executed according to his/her true intention. See **interest reipublicae suprema** etc.

testatum *n., pl.* **testata** [L. that which has demonstrated, declared, or borne witness to, a writ.] *Law.* 1. The portion of a deed of conveyance which, among other things, states the consideration and contains the operative words. 2. **Testatum capias ad satisfaciendum** (q.v.).

testatum capias ad satisfaciendum or **testatum capias** *n.* [L. **testatum** that which has demonstrated declared, or borne witness to, a writ (2); **capias** you should take (1); **ad** to, at, for, according to (3); **satisfaciendum** satisfying (4): You should take a writ for satisfying.] *Law.* An additional writ issued by a court of one county to a sheriff of another county, if the judgment debtor has moved to the latter county and a writ of **ca. sa.** (q.v.) has been returned, indicating that he/she cannot be found in the county of the issuing court.

testatus *n., pl.* **testati** [L. one who has made a will or testament.] *Civil Law.* A person who has made a will. A testate. A testator.

testes ponderantur, non numerantur. See **ponderantur testes, non numerantur.**

testibus praesentibus [L. **testibus** with witnesses (1); **praesentibus** (with) present (2): with witnesses present.] In the presence of witnesses.

testimonia ponderanda sunt, non numeranda. [L. **testimonia** testimonies, evidences (1); **ponderanda** to be weighed (3); **sunt** are (2); **non** not (4); **numeranda** to be counted (5): Testimonies are to be weighed, not counted.] *Law.* Testimonies must be evaluated by their weight, not their number. See **ponderantur testes** etc.

testimonium *n., pl.* **testimonia** or **testimoniums** [L. evidence, attestation, testimony.] *Law.* The concluding or authenticating clause of a deed or instrument of conveyance, which usually begins with "In witness whereof, the parties to these presents . . ." and contains such information as the date, the parties, and the witnesses.

testis *n., pl.* **testes** [L. witness, a person who attests, testicle.] 1. A witness. A person who gives testimony or witnesses a document. 2. Testicle.

testis de visu praeponderat aliis. [L. **testis** witness (1); **de** of, from, about, for (2); **visu** sight, vision (3); **praeponderat** is regarded as superior to, outweighs (4); **aliis** others (5): A witness from sight outweighs others.] *Law.* An eye-witness outweighs others. See **plus valet unus** etc. and **securius expediuntur** etc.

testis nemo in sua causa esse potest. [L. **testis** witness (4); **nemo** no one (1); **in** in, on (5); **sua** one's own, his/her own (6); **causa** cause, case, reason (7); **esse** to be (3); **potest** can, is able (2): No one can be a witness in his/her own cause.] *Law.* No one can be a witness in a case in which he/she is involved. Cf. **nemo debet esse** etc.

testis oculatus unus plus valet quam auriti decem. See **plus valet oculatus testis quam auriti decem.**

tête-à-tête *n., pl.* **tête-à-têtes** or **têtes-à-têtes** [Fr. **tête** head (1); **à** to, toward, in, by, with, until (2); **tête** head (3): head to head.] A private or confidential conversation or interview, especially between two persons. *. . . the head of France's largest farm union was sitting down for a tête-à-tête with President François Mitterrand (Newsweek Int. Feb. 22, 1982:9). —adj.* 1. Face to face. *As he strolled on the crowded sidewalk, Tony found himself tête-à-tête with the girl he had been avoiding for the past four years.* 2. Private. Done between two persons. *The two lovers had a quiet night, enjoying a tête-à-tête dinner at a secluded villa. —adv.* Privately. Face-to-face. With no third person present. *The lovers had a quiet night, dining, conversing and reading tête-à-tête.* Cf. **vis-à-vis.**

Tetragrammaton *n.* [Gk. **tet(ta)ra** four (1); **gramma** letter (2): four letters.] The four letters (YHWH or JHVH) representing the Hebrew name for God.

textus receptus *n.* [L. **textus** text (2); **receptus** received (1): received text.] The established text in a manuscript tradition, especially that of the Bible.

thanatophidia *pl. n.* [Neo-Gk. from Gk. **thanato(s)** death (2); **ophi(s)** serpent (1): serpent of death.] Poisonous snakes.

thanatophobia *n.* [Neo-Gk. from Gk. **thanato(s)** death (2); **phob(os)** fear (1): fear of death.] An excessive fear of death.

thaumaturgus *n., pl.* **thaumaturgi** [L. from Gk. **thaumaturgos: thaumat(os)** wonder (1); **erg(on)** work (2): wonder-worker.] A person, especially a magician or saint, who performs miracles. Thaumaturge.

Th.B. *abbr.* for **Theologiae Baccalaureus** (q.v.).

Th.D. *abbr.* for **Theologiae Doctor** (q.v.).

theatrum mundi *n.* [L. **theatrum** theater (1); **mundi** of the world (2): theater of the world.] The theater as a mirror of the world.

threnos *n., pl.* **threnoi** [Gk. **thrēnos** lament.] A song of sorrow, especially for the dead. A dirge.

Theologiae Baccalaureus *abbr.* **Th.B.** *n.* [L. **theologiae** of theology (2); **baccalaureus** bachelor (1): Bachelor of Theology.] An undergraduate degree in theology.

Theologiae Doctor *abbr.* **Th.D.** *n.* [L. **theologiae** of theology (2); **doctor** teacher (1): teacher of theology.] Doctor of Theology. A terminal graduate degree in theology.

Theologiae Magister *abbr.* **Th.M.** *n.* [L. **theologiae** of theology (2); **magister** master (1): Master of Theology.] A predoctoral graduate degree in theology.

theophobia *n.* [Neo-Gk. from Gk. **theo(s)** God (2); **phob(os)** fear (1): fear of God.] An excessive fear of God.

thesaurus *n., pl.* **thesauri** or **thesauruses** [L. from Gk. **thesauros** treasure, treasury, store-house.] 1. A collection of information or words, especially one respecting a particular discipline. A dictionary of synonymous expressions. An encyclopedia. *For 130 years Roget's Thesaurus has been the book that writers, students, crossword-puzzle addicts and logophiles turned to when they wondered, "What's another word for . . . ?" (Newsweek Int.* April 26, 1982:34). 2. Storehouse, repository or treasury. *A room in the residence of the Basseys has been converted into a thesaurus of priceless articles.*

thesis *n., pl.* **theses** [Gk. laying down, situation, position assumed and requiring proof.] 1. A statement advanced for discussion and proof. a) *His thesis is simple: the African was the slave because disease selected him for the role* (Kofi Akainyah in *West Africa* 1986). b) *The scholar's thesis, though ably argued, had a fundamental flaw and was with difficulty demolished by the discussants.* 2. A dissertation or essay incorporating the outcome of original research, especially one conducted by a candidate for a high academic degree under competent direction or supervision. Also, an essay written by an undergraduate who is a candidate for an honors degree.

Th.M. *abbr.* for **Theologiae Magister** (q.v.).

thug *n.* [Hindi **thag**.] A hoodlum or ruffian, especially one working in a gang.

tiara *n., pl.* **tiaras** [Gk. crown.] A crown or ceremonial headpiece.

timeo Danaos et dona ferentes. Vergil (70–19 B.C.). *Aeneid* II,49. [L. **timeo** I fear (1); **Danaos** Greeks (2); **et** even (3); **dona** gifts (5); **ferentes** bringing (4): I fear Greeks even bringing gifts.] I fear the Greeks even when they bring gifts; i.e., Be on your guard when dealing with your enemy, even if he/she/they should be nice or should offer gifts. An allusion to the wooden horse given to the Trojans by the Greeks.

tinea pedis *n.* [L. **tinea** worm (1); **pedis** of foot (2): worm of foot.] *Medicine.* Athlete's foot.

tinnitus *n.* [L. ringing.] *Medicine.* A ringing in the ears.

tirade *n., pl.* **tirades** [Fr. diatribe, vituperative speech, string or volley, i.e., of insults.] A vituperative speech. A protracted or prolonged speech, usually full of insulting language. A continuous fire or volley, i.e., of insults, invective, etc. a) *The "pressman" out of the way, it was time for her to release a tirade of insults on her challenger (The Guardian* 1987). b) *Unionist opposition to the Anglo-Irish agreement turned that Stormont experiment into one long tirade of ineffectual protest (The Economist* 1987).

tmesis *n., pl.* **tmeses** [Gk. **tmēsis** cutting, division.] *Linguistics.* Separation of the constituent parts of a compound word by the intrusion of a word or phrase; e.g., "what idea soever" for "whatsoever idea."

toccata *n., pl.* **toccatas** [It. touched.] *Music.* A free-style composition for the keyboard, especially the organ, characterized by big chords and complicated runs.

Tod und Verklärung *n.* [Ger. **Tod** death (1); **und** and (2); **Verklärung** transfiguration, clarification (3): death and transfiguration.] "Death and Transfiguration," an 1889 symphonic poem by Richard Strauss (1864–1949) about a dying man remembering his past and preparing for his death.

toga *n., pl.* **togas** [L. gown, garment.] 1. The loose outer garment normally worn in public by an ancient Roman male citizen. 2. Any similar loose wrapper, like the kente cloth of a Ghanaian, which is draped in such a way that the left arm is covered while the right arm is left uncovered. 3. An official, professional, or academic gown. *An interesting aspect of the convocation ceremony was the colorful procession of graduands and members of the academic staff, each wearing his/her toga.* 4. Authority. An official position. *Clothed with the toga of a chief executive, he assumes omnipotence and omniscience, and in the process makes himself a laughingstock.*

toga virilis *n., pl.* **togae viriles** [L. **toga** gown, garment (1); **virilis** of a man (2): garment of a man.] 1. A man's garment or toga, which the ancient Roman youth started wearing at puberty, i.e., at the age of about fourteen. 2. Maturity. Symbol of maturity, especially intellectual maturity. *A person who holds a responsible position should not behave like one who is yet to wear the toga virilis.*

tolle lege tolle lege Augustine of Hippo (354–430 A.D.). *Confessions* VIII,12,29. [L. **tolle** pick up (1); **lege** read (2); **tolle** pick up (3); **lege** read (4): Pick up, read, pick up, read.] Pick up and read (the book, i.e., the Bible).

tolle voluntatem et erit omnis actus indifferens. [L. **tolle** take way, remove (1); **voluntatem** will, inclination (2); **et** and (3); **erit** will be (6); **omnis** every, all (4); **actus** act, action (5); **indifferens** indifferent, neither good nor bad (7): Remove the will and every action will be indifferent.] *Law.* Take away the will, and every action will be neither good nor bad. See **actus non facit** etc.

tomus *n., pl.* **tomi** *abbr.* **T.** or **t.** [L. from Gk. **tomos** a cutting, volume, book.] A book, especially a serious one or one volume in a series. A tome.

tontine *n., pl.* **tontines** [Fr. from Lorenzo Tonti (1635–1690?).] *Finance.* A scheme in which investors receive shares in a fund and earn annuities for a certain period of time, after which the remaining fund is awarded to the surviving investors.

topos *n., pl.* **topoi** [Gk. place.] A traditional or customary form or theme, especially literature or art.

Torah *n.* [Heb. instruction, teaching.] *Judaism.* 1. The first five books of the Hebrew Bible. The Pentateuch. 2. The scroll containing these books, read at Jewish services. 3. The collection of Jewish religious law and learning, both written and oral.

torso *n., pl.* **torsi** or **torsos** or **torsoes** [It. stock, stem.] 1. The trunk of a human being, i.e., body excluding the head and the limbs. a) *His hands and torso were covered with blood* (*Newsweek Int.* Nov. 12, 1979:15). b) *Seidu wore a shirt which fitted his torso tightly and emphasized his masculinity.* 2. The part of a garment which covers the human trunk. 3. The trunk of the statue of a human being, especially one which is nude or whose head and limbs are mutilated. 4. A thing such as a literary or artistic work which is mutilated or was not completed by the author or artist. 5. Something such as the trunk of a tree which resembles a human being's torso.

totidem verbis *adv.* [L. **totidem** in just so many, just as many (1); **verbis** (in) words (2): in so many words.] In so many words. See **in totidem verbis.**

toties quoties *adv.* [L. **toties** so many times (1); **quoties** as (2): so many times as.] As often as. Repeatedly. Whenever the occasion arises. *The President has been granting indulgence toties quoties.*

totis viribus *adv.* [L. **totis** with the whole (1); **viribus** (with) strength, energy, power (2): with the whole strength/power.] With all one's might. Very vigorously. Energetically. *He is a very industrious man who executes every assignment totis viribus.*

toto caelo *adv.* [L. **toto** by the whole (1); **caelo** (by) sky, heaven (2): by the whole heaven.] In a diametrically opposite way. In an entirely different fashion. *His position differs toto caelo from my own.*

totum tenet et nihil tenet. [L. **totum** the whole (2); **tenet** he holds, has (1); **et** and (3); **nihil** nothing (5); **tenet** he holds, has (4): He has the whole and has nothing.] *Law.* Applicable, **inter alia** (q.v.), to joint tenancy.

touché *interj.* [Fr. touched, a hit, a touch.] A good thrust! A good point! Used to admit a good hit, thrust, point, etc. in fencing, debate, or accusation. *"Touché," said Ben, admitting the validity of a point urged by his opponent. —n., pl.* **touchés** A good hit, thrust, point, etc. in fencing, debate, or accusation.

tour de force *n., pl.* **tours de force** [Fr. **tour** feat, trick (1); **de** of (2); **force** strength, power (3): feat of strength.] A wonderful feat of strength or skill. An extraordinary performance in the literary, artistic, etc. field. a) *One London critic hailed the performance as a tour de force* . . . (*Newsweek Int.* May 30, 1983:64). b) *Donald Erb's Trombone Concerto* . . . *was a half-mad, jazz-inspired tour de force* (*Newsweek Int.* March 3, 1980:44B).

tour d'horizon *n., pl.* **tours d'horizon** [Fr. **tour** course, circuit (1); **d'** of (2); **horizon** horizon (3): circuit of horizon.] A survey. A general survey. *The purpose of the retreat* . . . *was to conduct a thorough tour d'horizon of U.S. foreign policy in the Middle East, Iran and Southwest Asia* (*Newsweek Int.* March 31, 1980:12).

Tous pour un, un pour tous. Alexandre Dumas (1803–1870). *Les Trois Mousquetaires* IX. [Fr. **tous** all (1); **pour** for (2); **un** one (3); **un** one (4); **pour** for (5); **tous** all (6): All for one, one for all.] All for one and one for all. Cf. **Les Trois Mousquetaires.**

tout à fait *adv.* [Fr. **tout** all (1); **à** to, toward, in, by, with, until (2); **fait** deed, act (3): all to deed.] Entirely. Absolutely. Thoroughly.

Tout comprendre, c'est tout pardonner. [Fr. **tout** everything (2); **comprendre** to understand (1); **c'** it (3); **est** is (4); **tout** everything (5); **pardonner** to pardon, forgive (6): To understand everything, it is to pardon everything.] Understanding everything is the same as forgiving everything.

Tout comprendre rend très indulgent. Mme. de Staël (1766–1817). *Corinne* XVIII,5. [Fr. **tout** everything (2); **comprendre** to understand, comprehend (1); **rend** makes (3); **très** very (4); **indulgent** lenient, forbearing (5): To understand everything makes (one) very lenient.] Understanding everything makes a person very tolerant.

tout court *adv.* [Fr. **tout** all (1); **court** short (2): all short, in short.] In brief. *The allegorical equation of Hermes with speech tout court, logos, is reflected in our word hermeneutics* (Burkert 1985:158).

tout de suite *adv.* [Fr. **tout** all, entirely (1); **de** in (2); **suite** succession (3): entirely in succession, immediately.] Right away. Now.

Toute nation a le gouvernement qu'elle mérite. Joseph De Maistre (1753–1821). [Fr. **toute** every (1); **nation** nation (2); **a** has (3); **le** the (4); **gouvernement** government (5); **qu'** which (6); **elle** it, she (7); **mérite** deserves, earns (8): Every nation has the government which it deserves.] Nations get the governments they deserve.

tout ensemble *n.* [Fr. **tout** everything (1); **ensemble** together (2): everything together.] The general effect of something, such as a work of art. Something considered as a whole.

Tout est perdu fors l'honneur. Francis I of France (1494–1547). [Fr. **tout** all (l); **est** is (2); **perdu** lost (3); **fors** except, save (4); **l'** the (5); **honneur** honor (6): All is lost except honor.] Everything is lost except honor.

Tout est pour le mieux dans ce meilleur des mondes possibles Voltaire (1694–1778). *Candide* 30. [Fr. **tout** all (1); **est** is (2); **pour** for (3); **ce** this (4); **mieux** best (5); **dans** in (6); **le** the (7); **meilleur** best (8); **des** of the (9); **mondes** worlds (11); **possibles** possible (10): All is for the best in this best of the possible worlds.] All is for the best in the best of all possible worlds. A reference to the positive philosophy of Gottfried Wilhelm Leibnitz (1646–1716).

tout le haut monde *n.* [Fr. **tout** all (1); **le** the (2); **haut** high, upper (3); **monde** world (4): all the high world.] All the elite of the society. *Yves Saint Laurent toasted his twentieth anniversary as the king of couture last week with a lavish bash for 1,000* . . . , *drawing tout le haut monde and some lesser folks, too* (*Newsweek*

Int. Feb. 8, 1982:50). See **beau monde** and **haut monde.**

tout le monde *n.* [Fr. **tout** all, entirely (1); **le** the (2); **monde** world (3): all the world.] Everybody.

tout Paris *n.* [Fr. **tout** all (1); **Paris** Paris (2): all Paris.] The "beautiful people" of Paris. Affluent fun-loving Parisians. *The ruse works, and Vicky . . . becomes the sensation of tout Paris* (*Newsweek Int.* March 29, 1982:49). Cf. **le tout Paris.**

tout seul *n.* [Fr. **tout** all, entirely (1); **seul** alone (2): all alone.] Completely alone.

tout simple *n.* [Fr. **tout** all, entirely (1); **simple** easy, simple (2): entirely simple.] Altogether simple.

tout un sound [Obs. Fr. **tout** all (1); **un** one (2); **sound** sound (3): all one sound.] Of the same sound. With the same sound. **Idem sonans** (q.v.).

T.P. *abbr.* for **Tempore Paschale** (q.v.).

T.R. *abbr.* for **Tempore regis** (q.v.).

traditio *n.* [L. handing over, delivery, transfer of possession.] *Civil Law.* Delivery of possession, i.e., transference of a corporeal thing by the owner to somebody in return for something.

traditio brevi manu *n.* [L. **traditio** handing over, delivery, transfer of possession (1); **brevi** by short (2); **manu** (by) hand (3): delivery by short hand.] *Law.* An implied delivery in which a person who possesses something in the name of another reaches agreement with the latter to hold possession in his/her own name.

traditio clavium *n.* [L. **traditio** handing over, delivery, transfer of possession (1); **clavium** of keys (2): delivery or transfer of keys.] *Law.* Transfer of ownership of goods in a warehouse by the symbolic act of delivering keys.

traditio longa manu *n.* [L. **traditio** handing over, delivery, transfer of possession (l); **longa** by long (2); **manu** (by) hand (3): delivery or transfer of possession by long hand.] *Law.* A form of delivery in which the owner puts the property in the hands of the receiver or orders the delivery of the property at the receiver's house.

traditio loqui chartam facit. [L. **traditio** handing over, delivery, transfer of possession (1); **loqui** (to) speak (4); **chartam** paper (3); **facit** makes (2): Delivery makes a paper speak.] *Law.* Delivery causes a deed to speak; i.e., a deed becomes effective when there is delivery. Cf. **in traditionibus** etc.

traditio nihil amplius transferre debet vel potest, ad eum qui accipit, quam est apud eum qui tradit. [L. **traditio** handing over, delivery, transfer of possession (1); **nihil** nothing (6); **amplius** more, further (7); **transferre** to transfer (5); **debet** ought, should (2); **vel** or (3); **potest** can, is able (4); **ad** to, at, for, according to (8); **eum** one, him/her (9); **qui** who (10); **accipit** receives, accepts (11); **quam** than (12); **est** is (13); **apud** in the possession of, in the power of (14); **eum** one, him/her (15); **qui** who (16); **tradit** surrenders, delivers (17): Delivery ought, or is able,

to transfer no more to the one who receives than is in the possession of the one who delivers.] *Law.* Delivery should or can transfer to the recipient no more than is possessed by the one who makes the delivery. See **nemo dat qui** etc.

tragédienne or **tragedienne** *n., pl.* **tragédiennes** or **tragediennes** [Fr. an actress in tragedy.] A tragic actress or, by extension, any actress. Cf. **comédienne.**

trahison des clercs *n., pl.* **trahisons des clercs** J. Benda (1873–1956). [Fr. **trahison** treason, perfidy, betrayal (1); **des** of the (2); **clercs** scholars, learned men (3): betrayal of scholars.] 1. The treason of intellectuals who desert academic pursuit and take to politics. 2. The title of a 1927 book by Benda.

trahit sua quemque voluptas. Vergil (70–19 B.C.). *Eclogues* II,65. [L. **trahit** draws, drags (3); **sua** one's own, his/her own (1); **quemque** each one (4); **voluptas** pleasure, delight (2): One's own pleasure draws each one.] Each one is attracted by what interests him/her.

tranche *n., pl.* **tranches** [Fr. slice, installment.] Portion or installment. Portion of bond issue for distribution in another country. *The World Bank has released an initial tranche of 250 million dollars out of a total of 452 million to be granted to Nigeria . . . (Sunday Tribune* 1986).

tranche de vie *n.* [Fr. **tranche** slice, installment (1); **de** of (2); **vie** life (3): slice of life.] A piece of real life, especially in art and literature.

transferuntur dominia sine titulo et traditione, per usucaptionem, scil., per longam continuam et pacificam possessionem. [L. **transferuntur** are transferred (2); **dominia** absolute ownerships (l); **sine** without (3); **titulo** title (4); **et** and (5); **traditione** delivery (6); **per** through, by (7); **usucap(t)ionem** usucaption (8); **scil.(icet)** that is to say, namely (9); **per** through, by (10); **longam** long (11); **continuam** continuous, unbroken (12); **et** and (13); **pacificam** peaceable, peaceful (14); **possessionem** possession (15): Absolute ownerships are transferred without title and delivery through usucaption, namely through long, continuous, and peaceable possession.] *Law.* Absolute ownership may be transferred without title and delivery through usucaption, that is to say, through long, continuous, and uncontested possession. Cf. **praescriptio est titulus** etc. and **sine possessione** etc.

transgressione multiplicata, crescat poenae inflictio. See **multiplicata transgressione, crescat poenae inflictio.**

transire *n., pl.* **transires** [L. to pass, cross over, go through.] A customs document indicating the cargo, the consignor(s), and the consignee(s), and permitting the passage of the vessel.

transitus *n., pl.* **transituses** [L. passage.] Passage of a person or thing from one place to another. Transit.

trattoria *n., pl.* **trattorias** [It. restaurant.] An establishment which sells meals, especially Italian home-style food. A public eating-house. A **restaurant** (q.v.). *A* two course meal with house wine in a nice trattoria has climbed from $10 to $15 . . . (Newsweek Int. May 9, 1983:39).

Trauermusik *n.* [Ger. **Trauer** mourning (1); **Musik** music (2): mourning music.] *Music of Mourning,* a string composition by Paul Hindemuth (1895–1963), written in 1936 on the occasion of the death of King George V of Great Britain.

trauma *n., pl.* **traumata** or **traumas** [Gk. wound, heavy blow.] 1. A physical wound or injury caused by violence, a fall, or a blow. 2. A psychological or emotionally shattering experience. a) *the trauma of divorce*; b) *The Nigerian national trauma is the 1967–70 civil war. The one thing Nigerians do not want to see is a repetition of that conflict* (Odumegwu Ojukwu in *Newsweek Int.* Aug. 8, 1983:14). c) *. . . Japan recovered from the trauma of the war, post 1945, to become the greatest technologically advanced country . . .* (*The Guardian* 1986).

trecento *n.* [It. **tre** three (1); **cento** hundred (2): the three hundreds.] The 1300s. The 14th century. Used especially in reference to Italian history, literature, and art. Cf. **cinquecento**; **quatrocento**; and **seicento**.

très *adv./adj.* [Fr. very.] Very. Too much. *That's très cool.*

très chic *adj.* [Fr. **très** very (1); **chic** stylish (2): very stylish.] Very stylish. Very sophisticated. Cf. **chic**.

tria capita *pl. n.* [L. **tria** three (1); **capita** heads (2): three heads.] *Roman Law.* The three elements of a person's civil status, namely **libertas** "freedom," **civitas** "citizenship" (q.v.), and **familia** "family rights" (q.v.).

trid. *abbr.* for **triduum** (q.v.).

triduo *n., pl.* **tridui** or **triduos** [It./Sp.] A period of three days. **Triduum** 1 (q.v.).

triduum *abbr.* **trid.** *n., pl.* **triduums** [L. three days' time, three days.] 1. A term or period of three days. 2. *Roman Catholic Church.* A period of three days of prayers that usually precedes an important religious occasion such as a feast or first communion.

triennium *n., pl.* **trienniums** or **triennia** [L. **tres** three (1); **annus** year (2): three years, three years' time.] A period or epoch of three years. Cf. **biennium**.

trio *n., pl.* **trios** [It./Sp. three persons.] 1. A musical composition designed for three voices or instruments. A dance performed by three persons. 2. A set or group of three persons, singers, dancers, things, etc. a) *They are the very model of a modern major company, even though two-thirds of the trio has scant experience on the stage* (*Newsweek Int.* June 22, 1981:50). b) *There is a trio of characters: an oil engineer . . . , a secretary . . . and a Bedouin guide . . .* (*West Africa* 1982).

tripara *n., pl.* **triparas** [Neo-L. from **tr(es)** three (2); **par(io)** give birth (1): giving birth for the third time.] *Medicine.* A woman who has given birth for the third time. Cf. **multipara**.

triplex *n., pl.* **triplexes** [L. threefold, triple, a threefold portion.] Something which is threefold. —*adj.*

1. Threefold. Triple. 2. Having three apartments. 3. Having three levels. *A triplex building.* Cf. **duplex**.

triptyque *n., pl.* **triptyques** [Fr. from Gk. **triptukhos** from **tr(es)** three (1); **ptux** fold (2): three folds.] 1. A document issued by departments of customs or motoring associations which permits temporary importation of automobiles and thus facilitates their movement across international boundaries. 2. *Art.* A group of three painted or carved panels which are hinged together.

triskaidekaphobia *n.* [Neo-Gk. from Gk. **triskaideka** three-and-ten, thirteen (2); **phob(os)** fear (1): fear of three-and-ten.] Superstitious fear of the number "13."

triste *adj.* [L./Fr. mournful, sad.] Miserable. Sorrowful. Low-spirited. a) *a triste musical group*; b) *a triste performance.*

tristesse *n.* [Fr. sadness, sorrow.] Unhappiness. Discouragement. Dismay. *She was overcome by tristesse at the bittersweet memory of her lost love.*

tristis successio *n.* [L. **tristis** mournful, sad (1); **successio** succession, inheritance (2): mournful inheritance.] See **hereditas luctuosa.**

triumvir *n., pl.* **triumvirs** or **triumviri** [L. **tr(es)** three (1); **vir** man(2): three man, one of a body of three.] A member of a ruling body of three. *That left Meese, the third and weightiest of the triumvirs . . .* (*Newsweek Int.* Jan 18, 1982:28). Cf. **decemvir.**

trivia *pl. n.* Used as either *sing.* or *pl.* [L. from **trivium** a place where three roads meet, crossroads, intersection, frequented place.] The meaning is influenced by **trivialis** [L. vulgar, commonplace, trivial.] Insignificant or unimportant things or matters. Trifles. Trivialities. a) *. . . a reference to critics who expect the historian to record all kinds of trivia, like the emperor's dinner conversation . . .* (Laistner: 1966:152). b) *Though he holds a very important position, he devotes most of his time to trivia.*

trivium *n.* [L. from **tr(es)** three (1); **vi(a)** road, way (2): three roads, a place where three roads meet, an intersection.] *Medieval Europe.* The initial course of study in the liberal arts, i.e., grammar, rhetoric, and logic. Cf. **quadrivium.**

troika *n., pl.* **troikas** [Russ. group of three.] 1. A Russian carriage or vehicle drawn by a team of three horses abreast. 2. A team or body of three authorities, leaders, rulers, etc. A triumvirate. *The poster is dwarfed by huge red-and-black portraits of Lenin, Marx and Engels. Pictures of the same troika are also available on T-shirts . . .* (*Newsweek Int.,* July 6, 1981:17).

trombone *n., pl.* **trombones** [It. a big trumpet.] *Music.* 1. A brass wind instrument with a bell-shaped mouth and a long tube with a U-shaped slide which moves to create various pitches. 2. A person who plays this instrument in an orchestra or band.

trompe l'oeil *n., pl.* **trompe l'oeils** [Fr. **trompe** deceive, trick (1); **l'** the (2); **oeil** eye (3): deceive the eye, deceptive painting of still life, deception, illusion, camouflage.] Art work, especially painting, which is so realistic that it easily deceives the eye. —*adj.* Characteristic of trompe l'oeil. So realistic that it can be deceptive. a) *From 6000 sq. ft. of marble mosaic floors, up monumental stairways, past trompe l'oeil wall panels, rich brocaded drapes . . .* (*Time Int.* 1982). b) *Barzini concludes that even on its best postwar behavior, Germany is "a trompe l'oeil Protean country," an unpredictable force that continues to mystify and frighten the rest of Europe* (*Newsweek Int.* May 23, 1983:53).

troubadour *n., pl.* **troubadours** [Fr. from Provençal **trobador** composer.] 1. One of a group of lyric poets who flourished in France and northern Italy from the eleventh century to the thirteenth century. 2. An itinerant minstrel. A person who uses the medium of poetry, music, etc. to promote a cause.

troupe *n., pl.* **troupes** [Fr. troop, band.] A company, especially a group of theatrical performers, dancers, etc. or members of a circus. . . . *Joffrey 11, the apprentice touring troupe of the popular New York-based ballet company* (*Newsweek Int.* July 14, 1980:31).

trousseau *n., pl.* **trousseaux** or **trousseaus** [Fr. outfit, bunch, wedding outfit.] A bride's personal outfit, which usually includes clothes, household linen, and accessories.

trouvaille *n., pl.* **trouvailles** [Fr. a find.] A lucky find.

tsaddik or **tzaddik** *n., pl.* **tsaddikim** or **tzaddikim** or **tsaddiks** or **tzaddiks** [Heb. **saddīk** righteous, just.] *Judaism.* An extremely righteous and holy man, especially, for Hasidic Jews, a religious and spiritual guide and authority. *In Chaim Potok's* The Chosen, *Danny's father was a tsaddik who expected his son to follow in his footsteps.*

tsar See **czar**.

tsatske See **chachka**.

tsunami *n., pl.* [Japan. **tsu** port (1); **nami** wave (2): port wave.] A gigantic ocean wave caused by an earthquake or volcanic eruption.

tsuris or **tzuris** *n.* [Yid. **tsores**.] Trouble. Difficulty. Woes.

tu es sacerdos in aeternum. [L. **tu** you (1); **es** you are (2); **sacerdos** priest (3); **in** into, to, against, for (4); **aeternum** perpetuity (5): You are a priest into perpetuity.] *You are a priest for ever. Priesthood is forever. Tu es sacerdos in aeternum . . . we do not return the gift once given* (Pope John Paul II in *Newsweek Int.* Oct. 15, 1979:56).

tu quoque *n., pl.* **tu quoques** [L. **tu** you (1); **quoque** too, also (2): you also.] You too. A retort by a person that the allegations made by another are equally applicable to the one making them. a) *One of the most natural retorts is that of tu quoque* [i.e., in setoff and counterclaims] (Hanbury 1962:42). b) *The arbitration degenerated into a session of tu quoques as the parties kept charging one another with the same offenses.*

turpis causa *n.* [L. **turpis** base, disgraceful (1); **causa** cause, case, reason (2): base cause.] *Law.* A base, immoral or scandalous cause or consideration; i.e., a

cause that is scandalous or base and so deemed inadequate to support a contract or a law suit. See **ex turpi causa** etc.

turpis contractus *n.* [L. **turpis** base, disgraceful (1); **contractus** drawing together, shrinking, contract, agreement (2): base contract.] *Law.* An immoral contract and so unenforceable. See **ex turpi causa** etc.

tutelage *n.* [Fr. guardianship.] *Law.* Care or education under a **tuteur** (q.v.).

tuteur *n., pl.* **tuteurs** [Fr. guardian.] *French Law.* A guardian, trustee, or tutor of a minor.

tuteur officieux or *fem.* **tutrice officieuse** *n.* [Fr. **tuteur** guardian (2); **officieux** unofficial, semi-official, informal (1): unofficial or informal guardian.] *French Law.* A person of not less than fifty years of age who, with the consent of parents or the **conseil de famille** (q.v.), is appointed tutor or guardian of a child who is not less than fifteen years of age and serves **in loco parentis** (q.v.) to him/her.

tuteur subrogé *n., pl.* **tuteurs subrogés** [Fr. **tuteur** guardian (2); **subrogé** surrogate, deputy (1): surrogate guardian.] *French Law.* A surrogate or deputy guardian, i.e., one who performs his/her duties when there is conflict of interests between the substantive guardian and the child.

tutius erratur ex parte mitiore. [L. **tutius** more safely (2); **erratur** it is erred, there is erring (1); **ex** out of, from, directly after, away from (3); **parte** side, part (5); **mitiore** more lenient, mild (4): There is erring more safely from the more lenient side.] *Law.* It is safer to make a mistake on the side of leniency (or mercy). See **in dubio, pars** etc.

tutius semper est errare acquietando quam in puniendo, ex parte misericordiae quam ex parte justitiae. [L. **tutius** safer (3); **semper** always (2); **est** it is (1); **errare** to err (4); **acquietando** in acquitting (5); **quam** than (6); **in** in, on (7); **puniendo** punishing (8); **ex** out of, from, directly after, away from (9); **parte** part, side (10); **misericordiae** of mercy (11); **quam** than (12); **ex** out of, from, directly after, away from (13); **parte** part, side (14); **justitiae** of justice (15): It is always safer to err in acquitting than in punishing, from the side of mercy than the side of justice.] *Law.* It is always safer to make a mistake in acquittal rather than in punishment, on the side of mercy rather than on the side of justice. See **in dubio, pars** etc.

tutti *adj./adv.* [It. all.] *Music.* All perform. Used to direct all performers to participate. —*n., pl.* **tuttis** A section of a composition in which all parts play simultaneously.

tuum *n.* [L. yours.] *Law.* Your property. Cf. **meum et tuum.**

Tyche *n.* [Gk. **tukhē**.] Fortune. Providence. Fate. Chance. Coincidence. Good fortune. *We must therefore kill a cock to Tyche for the great papyrus discovery . . .* (Lesky 1966:202).

tycoon *n., pl.* **tycoons** [Japan. **taikun** great ruler or prince.] 1. Shogun of Imperial Japan. A Japanese military governor in the period before the revolution of the mid-nineteenth century who was more powerful than the emperor. 2. A person of immense power, wealth, and influence, especially one engaged in commerce, or industry. a) *a motor tycoon*; b) *. . . the British soccer-pool tycoon bought seven horses for $13,950,000 . . .* (*Newsweek Int.* Aug. 2, 1982:41). 3. A powerful leader, especially in the political arena.

U

u.a. *abbr.* for **usque ad** (q.v.).

über alles *adv.* [Ger. **über** above, over (1); **alles** everything (2): above everything.] Over everything else. Cf. **Deutschland über alles**.

Übermensch *n., pl.* **Übermenschen** [Ger. **über** over, above (1); **Mensch** human, person (2): the over person.] Superman. A term derived from **Also sprach Zarathustra** (q.v.), an 1883 philosophical treatise by Friedrich Nietzsche (1844–1900). Cf. **Untermensch**.

uberrimae fidei *adj.* [L. **uberrimae** of most abundant, fullest (1); **fidei** (of) faith (2): of the fullest faith.] *Law.* Of the most abundant good faith. Applicable to contracts which require full disclosure of every relevant fact. *In the case of contracts uberrimae fidei, full disclosure of every material fact is required both by law and by equity* (Hanbury 1962:652). See **uberrima fides**.

uberrima fides *n.* [L. **uberrima** most abundant, fullest (1); **fides** faith, confidence, trust (2): the most abundant faith.] The most abundant good faith. Absolute candor and honesty. Perfect good faith. *Contracts of life insurance demand a spirit of uberrima fides.* See **uberrimae fidei**.

ubi aliquid conceditur, conceditur et id sine quo res ipsa esse non potest. [L. **ubi** when, where (1); **aliquid** something (2); **conceditur** is granted (3); **conceditur** is granted (6); **et** also (5); **id** that (4); **sine** without (7); **quo** which (8); **res** matter, thing, property, business, affair (9); **ipsa** itself (10); **esse** to be, exist (13); **non** not (12); **potest** can, is able (11): When something is granted, that also is granted without which the thing itself cannot exist.] *Law.* When something is granted, anything without which the grant cannot exist is also granted. See **cuicunque aliquis** etc.

ubi aliquid impeditur propter unum, eo remoto tollitur impedimentum. [L. **ubi** when, where (1); **aliquid** something (2); **impeditur** is obstructed, prevented (3); **propter** on account of (4); **unum** one (thing) (5); **eo** with that (thing) (6); **remoto** (with)

having been removed (7); **tollitur** is removed (9); **impedimentum** the obstruction, impediment (8): Where something is obstructed on account of one thing, with that thing having been removed, the obstruction is removed.] Where something is obstructed by one factor, the removal of that factor removes the obstruction. See **cessante causa** etc. and **sublata causa**, etc.

ubi bene ibi patria. [L. **ubi** when, where (1); **bene** well (2); **ibi** there (3); **patria** country, home (4): Where well, there country.] One's home (or country) is the place where one is doing well. *Bawa left his fatherland ten years ago when a combination of political turbulence and a shattered economy rendered life intolerable. He now lives happily in a foreign country and his motto is* Ubi bene ibi patria.

ubi caritas et amor, Deus ibi est. [L. **ubi** when, where (1); **caritas** charity, affection (2); **et** and (3); **amor** love (4); **Deus** God (5); **ibi** there (7); **est** is (6): Where there are charity and love, there God is.] Anthem of the ecumenical community of Taize in southeast France. *The Passion of Jesus was read aloud in eight languages, followed by . . . the chanting of "Ubi caritas et amor, Deus ibi est" . . . (Newsweek Int.* May 18, 1981:52).

ubi cessat remedium ordinarium, ibi decurritur ad extraordinarium. [L. **ubi** when, where (1); **cessat** stops, ceases (4); **remedium** cure, remedy (3); **ordinarium** ordinary, usual (2); **ibi** there (5); **decurritur** it is hastened, there is hastening, recourse is had (6); **ad** to, at, for, according to (7); **extraordinarium** extraordinary, uncommon (8): Where the ordinary remedy ceases, there is hastening to the extraordinary.] Where the ordinary remedy is ineffective, we resort to the extraordinary. See **numquam decurritur** etc.

ubicunque est injuria ibi damnum sequitur. [L. **ubicunque** wherever, wheresoever (1); **est** there is (2); **injuria** injury, wrong, insult (3); **ibi** there (4);

damnum damage (5); **sequitur** follows (6): Wherever there is injury damage follows.] *Law.* Wherever there is an injury or a wrong, damage follows. Cf. **actio non datur** etc.

ubi damna dantur victus victori in expensis condemnari debet. [L. **ubi** when, where (1); **damna** damages (2); **dantur** are given (3); **victus** the defeated, vanquished (party) (4); **victori** to the victorious (party) (9); **in** in, on (7); **expensis** payments (8); **condemnari** to be condemned, sentenced (6); **debet** ought, should (5): Where damages are given, the defeated party ought to be condemned in payments to the victorious party.] *Law.* Where damages are given, the losing party should be sentenced to pay the costs of the victorious party.

ubi eadem ratio, ibi eadem lex; et de similibus idem est judicium. [L. **ubi** when, where (1); **eadem** the same (3); **ratio** reason (2); **ibi** there (4); **eadem** the same (6); **lex** law (5); **et** and (7); **de** of, from, about, for (8); **similibus** like, similar (things) (9); **idem** the same (12); **est** is (11); **judicium** judgment (10): Where the reason is the same, there the law is the same; and about similar things the judgment is the same.] *Law.* Where the same reason is operative, the same law operates; and where the cases are similar, the same judgment is passed. See **de similibus idem est judicium**. See also **lex plus laudatur** etc.

ubi eadem ratio, ibi idem jus. [L. **ubi** when, where (1); **eadem** the same (3); **ratio** reason (2); **ibi** there (4); **idem** the same (5); **jus** right, law (6): Where the reason is the same, there the same law.] *Law.* Where the reason is the same, the same law prevails. See **de similibus idem est judicium**.

ubi innocens damnatur pars patriae exsul. [L. **ubi** where, when (1); **innocens** innocent (2); **damnatur** is condemned, convicted (3); **pars** part, piece (4); **patriae** of the country (5); **exsulat** is exiled (6): When an innocent is condemned, a piece of the country is exiled.] *Law.* When an innocent person is convicted unjustly, a piece of the country is lost along with the person.

ubi jus, ibi remedium. [L. **ubi** when, where (1); **jus** right, law (2); **ibi** there (3); **remedium** remedy (4): Where a right, there a remedy.] *Law.* Where there is a right, there is a remedy. Cf. **actio non datur** etc.

ubi jus incertum, ibi jus nullum. [L. **ubi** when, where (1); **jus** right, law (3); **incertum** uncertain (2); **ibi** there (4); **jus** right, law (6); **nullum** no (5): Where uncertain right/law, there no right/law.] *Law.* Where the right/law is uncertain, there is no right/law.

ubi lex aliquem cogit ostendere causam, necesse est quod causa sit justa et legitima. [L. **ubi** when, where (1); **lex** law (2); **aliquem** one, anyone (4); **cogit** compels (3); **ostendere** to show (5); **causam** cause (6); **necesse** necessary (8); **est** it is (7); **quod** that (9); **causa** cause, case, reason (10); **sit** should/may be (11); **justa** just (12); **et** and (13); **legitima** legitimate

(14): Where the law compels anyone to show cause, it is necessary that the cause be just and legitimate.] *Law.* Where the law compels a person to show cause, the cause must be just and lawful.

ubi lex est specialis, et ratio ejus generalis, generaliter accipienda est. [L. **ubi** when, where (1); **lex** law (2); **est** is (3); **specialis** special (4); **et** and (5); **ratio** reason (7); **ejus** its (6); **generalis** general (8); **generaliter** generally (11); **accipienda** to be accepted (10); **est** it is (9): Where a law is special and its reason general, it is to be accepted generally.] *Law.* Where a law is special, but its reason general, it must be applied generally. See **generale dictum generaliter est intelligendum**.

ubi lex non distinguit, nec nos distinguere debemus. [L. **ubi** when, where (1); **lex** law (2); **non** not (3); **distinguit** distinguishes (4); **nec** and not, not also (6); **nos** we (5); **distinguere** to distinguish (8); **debemus** we ought, should (7): Where the law does not distinguish, we also should not distinguish.] *Law.* In a case where the law does not mark a difference, we should not either.

ubi major pars est, ibi totum. [L. **ubi** when, where (1); **major** greater (2); **pars** part (3); **est** is (4); **ibi** there (5); **totum** the whole (6): Where the greater part is, there the whole.] Where the greater part is, there the whole is; e.g., the votes of the majority represent the decision of the whole. See **majus continet minus**.

ubi matrimonium, ibi dos. [L. **ubi** when, where (1); **matrimonium** marriage (2); **ibi** there (3); **dos** dowry (4): Where marriage, there dowry.] Where there is marriage, there is a dowry. Cf. **ubi nullum matrimonium** etc.

ubi non est directa lex, standum est arbitrio judicis, vel procedendum ad similia. [L. **ubi** when, where (1); **non** not (3); **est** there is (2); **directa** direct (4); **lex** law (5); **standum** to be stood (7); **est** it is (6); **arbitrio** by decision, judgment (8); **judicis** of judge (9); **vel** or (10); **procedendum** to be proceeded (11); **ad** to, at, for, according to (12); **similia** similar (things) (13): Where there is not direct law, it must be stood by the decision of the judge or proceeded to similar things.] *Law.* Where there is no direct law, we must abide by the decision of the judge or refer to similar cases.

ubi non est lex, ibi non est transgressio, quoad mundum. [L. **ubi** when, where (1); **non** not (3); **est** there is (2); **lex** law (4); **ibi** there (5); **non** not (7); **est** there is (6); **transgressio** transgression (8); **quoad** as far as (9); **mundum** world (10): Where there is not law, there is not transgression, as far as the world.] *Law.* Where there is no law, there is no transgression, as far as the world is concerned. Cf. **nullum crimen sine lege**.

ubi non est principalis non potest esse accessorius. [L. **ubi** when, where (1); **non** not (3); **est** there is (2);

principalis principal (4); **non** not (6); **potest** there can (5); **esse** to be (7); **accessorius** accessory (8): Where there is not a principal, there cannot be an accessory.] *Law.* Where there is no principal, there can be no accessory. See **accessorium non ducit** etc.

ubi nullum matrimonium ibi nulla dos. [L. **ubi** when, where (1); **nullum** no (2); **matrimonium** marriage (3); **ibi** there (4); **nulla** no (5); **dos** dowry (6): Where no marriage, there no dowry.] Where there is no marriage, there is no dowry. Cf. **ubi matrimonium** etc.

ubi quis delinquit, ibi punietur. [L. **ubi** when, where (1); **quis** anyone (2); **delinquit** does wrong, transgresses (3); **ibi** there (4); **punietur** he/she will be punished (5): Where anyone does wrong, there he/she will be punished.] *Law.* A person who transgresses the law should be brought to trial in the area where the offense was committed.

ubi sunt *n., pl.* **ubi sunts** [L. **ubi** where (1); **sunt** they are (2): Where are they?] A lament for times past and things lost and forgotten, as in the expression "Where are the snows of yesteryear?" *The old timers spent their reunion voicing a series of ubi sunts.*

ubi supra *abbr.* **U.S.** or **u.s.** *adv.* [L. **ubi** when, where (1); **supra** above (2): where above.] Where above mentioned. At the place mentioned above. Used for bibliographical references.

u.d. *abbr.* for **ut dictum** (q.v.).

u.i. *abbr.* for **ut infra** (q.v.).

U.J.D. *abbr.* for **Utriusque Juris Doctor** (q.v.).

ukulele *n., pl.* **ukuleles** *short form* **uke** *pl.* **ukes** [Haw. '**ukulele:** '**uku** flea (1); **lele** jumping (2): flea-jumping.] A small guitar-like instrument with four strings usually strummed with one hand and fingered with the other.

ult. *abbr.* for **ultimo** (q.v.).

ulterior *adj.* [L. farther, on the farther side, more remote, beyond.] 1. Further. *The recommendation was accepted without ulterior discussions.* 2. Remoter. *It was apparent that the administrator had no plans immediate or ulterior.* 3. Situated or located on the further side. *She intends to visit the ulterior region soon.* 4. Latent or intentionally concealed. *Initially, his suggestions seemed altruistic, but it soon became clear that he had ulterior motives.*

ulterior causa *n.* [L. **ulterior** more remote (1); **causa** cause, case, reason (2): more remote cause.] Hidden or latent cause. *Everybody kept emphasizing the immediate cause of the event, and hardly anybody gave a thought to the ulterior causa.*

ultima ratio *n.* [L. **ultima** last, extreme (1); **ratio** consideration, plan, course (2): the last plan.] The last resort or argument. *When all attempts at negotiations with management proved futile, the workers went on strike as the ultima ratio.* Cf. **ultimatum.**

ultima Thule *n.* [L. **ultima** most distant, furthest, extreme (1); **Thule** Thule (2): furthest Thule.] 1. Most northerly inhabitable region known to the ancient Greeks. Often identified with Iceland, Ireland, or Norway. 2. The farthest point of the habitable world. *Many Nigerian civil servants regard a certain town as the ultima Thule of the country and pray fervently not to be transferred there.* 3. A remote goal, objective or end.

ultimatum *n., pl.* **ultimata** or **ultimatums** [L. the final thing.] 1. A final proposition or condition made in the negotiation of treaties or contracts and whose rejection would mark the end of the negotiation and necessitate resort to other measures, usually drastic. *The demand of the workers was tantamount to an ultimatum.* 2. A final end or objective. Cf. **ultima ratio.**

ultima voluntas testatoris est perimplenda secundum veram intentionem suam. [L. **ultima** last (1); **voluntas** will (2); **testatoris** of testator (3); **est** is (4); **perimplenda** to be fulfilled, thoroughly satisfied (5); **secundum** according to (6); **veram** true (8); **intentionem** intention (9); **suam** one's own, his/her own (7): The last will of a testator is to be thoroughly satisfied according to his/her true intention.] *Law.* The last will of a testator must be fulfilled in accordance with his/her true intention. See **interest reipublicae suprema** etc.

ultimo *abbr.* **ult.** *adj.* [L. in the last, i.e., month.] Occurring in the preceding month. Last month. Of the preceding month. *The tenth meeting of the committee was held on the 15th ultimo.* Cf. **proximo.**

ultimum supplicium *n.* [L. **ultimum** extreme, last (1); **supplicium** punishment, penalty (2): the extreme or last punishment.] The death penalty.

ultimum supplicium esse mortem solam interpretamur. [L. **ultimum** last, extreme (2); **supplicium** punishment, penalty (3); **esse** to be (4); **mortem** death (5); **solam** alone (6); **interpretamur** we understand, interpret (1): We interpret the extreme penalty to be death alone.] *Law.* By our interpretation, the extreme punishment is death alone. See **mors dicitur** etc.

ultimus heres or **ultimus haeres** *n.* [L. **ultimus** last, most remote (1); **heres** heir, successor (2): the last or most remote heir.] *Feudal Law.* The sovereign, who is qualified to take property when no capable heirs are available.

ultra *adj.* [L. on the farther side of, beyond, above, exceeding.] Fanatical. Extreme. Going beyond, or doing more than, others or what is considered proper. a) *ultra revolutionaries*; b) *ultra Christians*; c) *ultra fun.* —*n., pl.* **ultras** 1. Fanatic. Extremist. 2. A person belonging to a political group in France of the 19th century, who were mostly returned émigrés and advocated a restoration of the social and political order which prevailed in the period before the 1789 Revolution. —*pref.* Beyond. Beyond the ordinary. Extreme. a) *ultramarine*; b) *ultra-fashionable*; c) *ultra-conservatism.* Cf. **ne plus ultra.**

ultra crepidam *adv.* [L. **ultra** beyond (1); **crepidam** sandal (2): beyond a sandal.] *Short form* for **ne sutor supra crepidam judicaret** (q.v.).

ultra vires *adj./adv.* [L. **ultra** beyond, exceeding (1); **vires** power, strength (2): beyond power/strength.]

Law. Beyond the scope of legal authority. Acting irregularly. Used to describe acts of corporations, legislative bodies, and officials. —*adj.* a) *The contract is ultra vires.* b) *It is obvious that any act ultra vires of a company may not be ratified by its shareholders, whether the purported ratification is by a simple or special majority or, indeed, by the unanimous assent of every member* (Olawoyin 1977:269). —*adv. The police officer acted ultra vires.* See **extra vires**. Cf. **intra vires**.

umbilicus *n., pl.* **umbilici** or **umblicuses** [L. navel, bellybutton.] 1. *Anatomy.* The navel or bellybutton. 2. The center. Cf. **omphalos**.

umbra *n., pl.* **umbrae** or **umbras** [L. shade, shadow.] 1. *Astronomy.* A shadow cast by a heavenly body, usually the moon, during an eclipse. 2. A person who acts like a shadow. Someone who follows another constantly.

Umwelt *n.* [Ger. environment, surroundings.] 1. The natural environment. 2. **Milieu** (q.v.).

una voce *adv.* [L. **una** with one (1); **voce** (with) voice (2): with one voice.] Unanimously. With no dissent. *The proposal was accepted una voce.* Cf. **dissentiente**.

Un ballo in maschera [It. **un** a (1); **ballo** ball (2); **in** in (3); **maschera** mask (4): a ball in mask.] "A Masked Ball," an 1859 opera by Giuseppe Verdi (1813–1901) modeled on the assassination of Gustav III of Sweden.

uncore prist *n.* [Obs. Fr. **uncore** still (1); **prist** ready (2): still ready.] *Law.* A plea by which a party claims that he/she has been, and is, ready to pay or perform what is legitimately required of him/her.

Unding *n.* [Ger. a non-thing, nonsense, absurdity.] An absurdity.

und so weiter *abbr.* **U.S.W.** or **u.s.w.** *adv.* [Ger. **und** and (1); **so** so, thus (2); **weiter** wider, further (3): and so further.] And so on. Et cetera.

Une Saison en Enfer [Fr. **une** one, a (1); **saison** season (2); **en** in (3); **enfer** hell (4): a season in hell.] *A Season in Hell*, a collection of French symbolist prose poetry by Arthur Rimbaud (1854–1891).

unigravida *n., pl.* **unigravidas** [Neo-L. **un(us)** one, single, once (2); **gravida** pregnant (1): pregnant once.] *Medicine.* A woman who is carrying her first pregnancy. Cf. **gravida**.

unipara *n., pl.* **uniparas** [Neo-L. **un(us)** one, single, once (2); **par(io)** give birth (1): giving birth once.] *Medicine.* A woman who has given birth to only one child. A uniparous woman. Cf. **multipara**.

unitas personarum *n.* [L. **unitas** unity (1); **personarum** of persons (2): unity of persons.] *Law.* The bond or unifying factor that subsists among persons such as husband and wife or decedent and heir.

unius omnino testis responsio non audiatur. [L. **unius** of one (2); **omnino** at all (6); **testis** (of) witness (3); **responsio** response, answer (1); **non** not (5); **audiatur** should be heard (4): The response of one witness should not be heard at all.] *Law.* The

testimony of one witness is absolutely inadequate. It is a maxim of the civil and canon law.

universitas *n., pl.* **universitates** [L. the entirety, whole, aggregate.] Something considered by the law as a unit, whether composed of one or more than one element. A corporation.

universitas facti *n.* [L. **universitas** the entirety, whole, aggregate (1); **facti** of deed (2): the aggregate of a deed.] *Civil Law.* A group of corporeal things of the same class considered as a whole; e.g., a flock of sheep.

universitas juris *n.* [L. **universitas** the entirety, whole, aggregate (1); **juris** of right, law (2): the aggregate of right.] *Civil Law.* The aggregate or totality of a person's rights and liabilities. Many things, both corporeal and incorporeal, which are regarded as a unit and belong to a person; e.g., an estate or a legacy. A corporate body of rights.

universitas personarum *n.* [L. **universitas** the entirety, whole, aggregate (1); **personarum** of persons (2): the aggregate of persons.] *Civil Law.* A number of persons in an organization, such as a corporation, institution, or state, operating together as an independent unit.

universitas rerum *n.* [L. **universitas** the entirety, whole, aggregate (1); **rerum** of matters, things, property, business, affairs (2): the entirety of things.] *Civil Law.* A number of objects which, though not really connected to one another, are in law regarded as a whole.

uno absurdo dato, infinita sequuntur. [L. **uno** with one (1); **absurdo** (with) absurd (thing) (2); **dato** (with) having been granted, conceded (3); **infinita** infinite, endless, countless (things) (4); **sequuntur** follow (5): With one absurd thing having been granted, infinite things follow.] When one absurdity is granted, an infinity of absurdities follow suit.

Untergang des Abendlandes *n.* Oswald Spengler (1880–1936). [Ger. **Untergang** setting, decline (1); **des** of the (2); **Abendlandes** occident, west (3): decline of the West.] 1. The German title of Oswald Spengler's *The Decline of the West* (1918, 1922). 2. Spengler's argument that the ascendancy of civilization was moving gradually from Europe and the Americas towards Asia. The decline of Western Civilization.

Untermensch *n., pl.* **Untermenschen** [Ger. **unter** under (1); **Mensch** human, person (2): the under person.] An inferior person. A term derived from **Übermensch** (q.v.) in **Also sprach Zarathustra** (q.v.), an 1883 philosophical treatise by Friedrich Nietzsche (1844–1900) and used in Nazi Germany to refer to a person classified as inferior.

Untersuchungsrichter *n.* [Ger. **Untersuchung** investigation (1); **Richter** judge (2): investigating judge.] *German Law.* Investigating magistrate. **Juge d'instruction** (q.v.).

unum est necessarium Luke 10:42. [L. **unum** one thing (1); **est** is, has been (2); **necessarium** necessary

(3): One thing is necessary.] One thing is needful. Jesus said this to Martha in reference to her complaint that her sister Mary was neglecting domestic chores to sit at the feet of Jesus.

unum est tacere, aliud celare. [L. **unum** one (thing) (2); **est** it is (1); **tacere** to be silent, say nothing (3); **aliud** another (thing) (4); **celare** to hide, conceal (5): It is one thing to say nothing, another to conceal.] *Law.* Thus, though it is not obligatory for a vendor to reveal defects of a commodity, it is a culpable act if he/she attempts to hide them. See **aliud est celare** etc.

unum necessarium Luke 10:42. [L. **unum** one thing (1); **necessarium** necessary (2): one necessary thing.] The single most important thing. Based upon **unum est necessarium** (q.v.).

unumquodque dissolvitur eodem ligamine quo ligatur. [L. **unumquodque** each individual, every (thing) (1); **dissolvitur** is dissolved (2); **eodem** with the same (3); **ligamine** (with) band, tie (4); **quo** with which (5); **ligatur** it is bound, tied (6): Each individual thing is dissolved with the same band with which it is bound.] *Law.* Every obligation is dissolved in the same manner in which it was made. See **eodem modo quo quid constituitur dissolvitur.**

unumquodque eodem modo quo colligatum est, dissolvitur. [L. **unumquodque** every single, each individual (thing) (1); **eodem** in the same (3); **modo** (in) way, manner (4); **quo** in which (5); **colligatum est** it was united, combined (6); **dissolvitur** is dissolved (2): Every single thing is dissolved in the same way in which it was established.] *Law.* See **eodem modo quo quid constituitur, dissolvitur.**

uomo universale *n., pl.* **uomini universali** [It. **uomo** human being, man (2); **universale** universal (1): universal man.] A Renaissance man. Someone who has broad knowledge and skill in a wide number of fields.

Urbi et Orbi [L. **urbi** for city (1); **et** and (2); **orbi** for world (3): for the city and the world.] *Roman Catholic Church.* For Rome and the world. Applicable to a papal proclamation to be observed by all members of the church.

Ursprache *n., pl.* **Ursprachen** [Ger. from **ur-** original (1); **Sprache** speech, language (2): original speech.] 1. The hypothetical earliest human language from which all other languages are derived. 2. The hypothetical origin of a specific language.

Urtext *n., pl.* **Urtexte** [Ger. from **ur-** original (1); **Text** text, written version (2): original text.] The original version of a text, especially the earliest text from which a broad family of manuscript versions is derived.

U.S. or **u.s.** *abbr.* for 1. **ubi supra** (q.v.). 2. **ut supra** (q.v.).

usque ad *abbr.* **u.a.** *adv.* [L. **usque** as far as (1); **ad** to, at, for, according to (2): as far as to.] As far as.

usque ad caelum or **usque ad coelum** *adv.* [L. **usque** as far as, all the way (1); **ad** to, at, for, according to (2); **caelum** sky, heaven (3): as far as the sky.] *Law.* As far as heaven. Up to the heavens. A rule in law

that the landowner's right of air has the sky as its limit. An obsolete rule. See **cujus est solum** etc.

usque ad filum aquae *adv.* [L. **usque** as far as (1); **ad** to, at, for, according to (2); **filum** thread (3); **aquae** of water (4): as far as to the thread of water.] *Law.* As far as the middle or central line of the stream. See **ad filum aquae.**

usque ad filum viae *adv.* [L. **usque** as far as (1); **ad** to, at, for, according to (2); **filum** thread (3); **viae** of road (4): as far as to the thread of the road.] *Law.* As far as the middle or central line of the road. See **ad filum aquae.**

usque ad medium filum aquae *adv.* [L. **usque** as far as (1); **ad** to, at, for, according to (2); **medium** middle (3); **filum** thread (4); **aquae** of water (5): as far as to the middle thread of the water.] *Law.* As far as the middle of the stream. See **ad filum aquae.**

usque ad nauseam [L. **usque** all the way (1); **ad** to, at, for, according to (2); **nauseam** sickness, nausea (3): all the way to nausea.] To the very point of nausea.

usucapio *n.* [L. **usu** by use, enjoyment (2); **capio** seize, capture (1): seizing by use. Acquisition of ownership by use, acquisition by prescription, usucaption.] *Roman Law.* Acquisition of ownership by continuous possession or occupation of property in good faith for the period of one year in the case of movables and two years in the case of immovables.

usura *n., pl.* **usurae** [L. usury.] *Civil Law.* Usury or interest on loan.

usurae usurarum *pl. n.* [L. **usurae** usuries, interests (1); **usurarum** of usuries, interests (2): interests of/on interests.] *Roman Law.* Compound interest.

usura maritima *n.* [L. **usura** usury, interest (2); **maritima** maritime, marine (1): maritime/marine interest.] *Law.* Interest on bottomry, which is proportional to the risk.

usurpatio *n.* [L. a taking into use, making use.] *Civil Law.* Interruption of **usucapio** (q.v.) by the real owner of the property.

usus *n.* [L. use, enjoyment.] *Roman Law.* 1. Use. The act of using something. 2. A personal and inalienable right to use real or personal property with the permission of the owner.

usus et fructus or **usus fructus** or **usufructus** *n.* [L. **usus** use, enjoyment (1); **et** and (2); **fructus** enjoyment (3): use and enjoyment.] *Roman Law.* Usufruct. The right of using and enjoying the profits or fruits of another's property without having full dominion of the property. *Mr. Brown's heir, unaware of the original arrangement between Mr. Brown and Mrs. Whyte, thought that the estate was the former's property, though in fact it was given by the latter in usufructus.*

U.S.W. or **u.s.w.** *abbr.* for **und so weiter** (q.v.).

ut dictum *abbr.* **U.D.** or **ut dict.** [L. **ut** as (1); **dictum** said, having been said (2): as said.] As directed.

uteromania *n.* [Neo-L. from L. **uter(us)** womb (2); Gk. **mania** madness, insanity, passion (1): insanity for the womb.] A woman's excessive desire for sexual pleasure. See **andromania**.

uti *adv.* [L. to use.] *Civil Law.* For necessary use, as opposed to **frui** (q.v.), i.e., for enjoyment.

uti frui *adv.* [L. **uti** to use (1); **frui** to enjoy (2): to use (and) enjoy.] *Civil Law.* The right to use something not only for necessity (**uti** q.v.) but also for enjoyment (**frui** q.v.).

utilitatis gratia *adv.* [L. **utilitatis** of usefulness, expediency (2); **gratia** for the sake of, on account of (1): for the sake of expediency.] On account of expediency.

ut infra *abbr.* **ut inf.** *adv.* [L. **ut** as (1); **infra** below (2): as below.] See subsequent section. Used for bibliographical references. Cf. **ut supra**.

uti possidetis [L. **uti** to use (1); **possidetis** you possess (2): you possess to use.] 1. *Roman and Civil Law.* An interdict for determining the right to the possession of immovable property and for keeping things as they are until the settlement of the suit. 2. *International Law.* A principle in peace treaties to the effect by force of arms. Cf. **status quo ante bellum** and **utrubi**.

Utopia *n.* [Neo-L. from Gk. (**o**)**u** not, no (1); **top(os)** place (2): no place.] Nowhere. The fictional island paradise which gives its name to *Utopia*, a 1516 political treatise about the ideal state by Thomas More (1478–1535).

ut pictura poesis Horace (65–8 B.C.). *Ars Poetica* 361. [L. **ut** as, like (1); **pictura** painting, art of painting (2); **poesis** poetry (3): like painting poetry.] Poetry is like painting.

ut poena ad paucos, metus ad omnes perveniat. [L. **ut** in order that, that (1); **poena** punishment (2); **ad** to, at, for, according to (4); **paucos** few (5); **metus** fear (6); **ad** to, at, for, according to (7); **omnes** all (8); **perveniat** may reach, arrive (3): In order that the punishment may reach to a few, fear may reach to all.] *Law.* That punishment may affect a few, let

fear affect all. A maxim expressing one of the principal reasons for punishing criminals. See **impunitas semper** etc.

ut res magis valeat quam pereat. [L. **ut** in order that, that (1); **res** matter, thing, property, business, affair (2); **magis** more, rather (4); **valeat** may prevail, be strong, be effective (3); **quam** than (5); **pereat** may perish, may be wasted (6): in order that the thing be strong rather than perish.] *Law.* That the thing may be effective rather than be wasted. A maxim which governs, **inter alia** (q.v.), charitable bequest.

Utriusque Juris Doctor *abbr.* **U.J.D.** *n.* [L. **utriusque** of each of two, of both (2); **juris** (of) right, law (3); **doctor** teacher (1): teacher of each of two laws.] Doctor of Both Civil and Canon Law. A terminal graduate degree in civil and canon law.

utrubi *n., pl.* **utrubis** [L. in which of two places.] *Roman and Civil Law.* An interdict for deciding the right to possess movables and keep them **in statu quo** (q.v.) pending the final decision. It serves the same purpose as **uti possidetis** (q.v.) in the case of immovables.

ut supra *abbr.* **U.S.** or **u.s.** or **ut. sup.** *adv.* [L. **ut** as (1); **supra** above (2): as above.] See previous section. Used for bibliographical reference. Cf. **ut infra**.

ux. *abbr.* for **uxor** [L. wife.].

uxor non est sui juris, sed sub potestate viri. [L. **uxor** wife (1); **non** not (3); **est** is (2); **sui** of her own (4); **juris** (of) right, law (5); **sed** but (6); **sub** under (7); **potestate** power (8); **viri** of husband (9): A wife is not of her own right but under the power of her husband.] A wife is not independent, but under the authority of her husband. An obsolete legal maxim.

uxor sequitur domicilium viri. [L. **uxor** wife (1); **sequitur** follows (2); **domicilium** abode, domicile (3); **viri** of husband (4): A wife follows the abode of her husband.] The residence of a wife follows that of her husband.

V

V. or **v.** *abbr.* for 1. **verso** (q.v.). 2. **versus** (q.v.). 3. **verte** (q.v.). 4. **via** (q.v.). 5. **vice** (q.v.). 6. **vide** (q.v.). 7. **virus** (q.v.).

vacantia bona or **vacantia** See **bona vacantia.**

vacatur *n., pl.* **vacaturs** [L. It is vacated.] A court's order vacating a proceeding.

vacua possessio *n.* [L. **vacua** empty, vacant, unoccupied (1); **possessio** possession (2): vacant possession.] *Law.* A possession which is free, without burden, and can be alienated.

vacuum *n., pl.* **vacua** or **vacuums** [L. something empty, vacant.] Empty space. Isolation from external influences. a) *Mr. Adewale's demise has left a profound vacuum in the lives of many relatives and friends.* b) *Aliyu lives in a vacuum and is hardly bothered by activities outside his world. —adj.* Relating to a vacuum. *A vacuum cleaner.*

vade in pace [L. **vade** go (1); **in** in, on (2); **pace** peace (3): Go in peace.] Go in the peace of God.

vade mecum *n., pl.* **vade mecums** [L. **vade** go (1); **mecum** with me (2): Go with me.] 1. A handbook. A manual. *Simi's work has become a standard vade mecum.* 2. Something which a person regularly carries about. *The briefcase is the vade mecum of most businessmen.*

vade retro me Satana. [L. **vade** go (1); **retro** behind (2); **me** me (3); **Satana** Satan (4): Go behind me, Satan.] Get behind me, Satan. The words of Jesus when tempted by the devil at Matthew 16:23, Mark 8:33, and Luke 4:8. These words are also applied to any tempter.

vadium mortuum or **mortuum vadium** *n.* [L. **vadium** pledge (2); **mortuum** dead (1): dead pledge.] A mortgage; i.e., giving an estate as security for a loan on condition that, if the money be not repaid, the mortgagor loses the estate. A pledge in which the rents or profits of the pledged article do not contribute to the payment of the debt. Cf. **vadium vivum.**

vadium vivum or **vivum vadium** *n.* [L. **vadium** pledge (2); **vivum** living (1): living pledge.] Security for a loan which involves giving an estate to the creditor who keeps it until the profits of the estate have paid off the money borrowed. Cf. **vadium mortuum.**

vae victis! Livy (59 B.C.–17 A.D.). *Ab urbe condita* V,49,9. [L. **vae** woe, alas (1); **victis** to the conquered (2): Woe to the conquered!] Woe to the vanquished.

vahanna or **vahan** *n., pl.* **vahannas** or **vahans** [Skt. **vāhana** vehicle.] *Indian Mythology.* The vehicle upon which a god is carried or rides.

vale *v., pl.* **valete** [L. "Be well."] Farewell. Goodbye. Adieu. *—n., pl.* **vales** A greeting. A farewell. *The host wondered why the vales of the guests were so obviously strained.*

valet *n., pl.* **valets** [Fr. footman, manservant.] 1. Male servant employed by a man to perform personal services such as taking care of clothes and running errands. 2. A man employed by a hotel or any public establishment to perform personal services such as taking care of the clothes of guests.

valet de chambre *n., pl.* **valets de chambre** [Fr. **valet** footman, manservant (1); **de** of (2); **chambre** chamber (3): manservant of chamber.] Valet. Man-servant. A man's personal male servant who, among other functions, takes care of his clothes and runs errands. *Though having the same meaning as valet, the valet de chambre usually works in a palace or the household of a noble.*

valet de place *n., pl.* **valets de place** [Fr. **valet** footman, manservant (1); **de** of (2); **place** place (3): manservant of place.] A courier. A person employed by a travel agency to serve as a guide for tourists. Cf. **cicerone.**

Valhalla *n.* [Late L. from Old Norse **Valholl: valr** battle-slain warriors (1); **holl** hall (2): battle-slain warriors' hall.] 1. *Norse Mythology.* The hall where warriors slain on the battlefield spend eternity in feasting with the gods. 2. Heaven. A state of eternal bliss. **Elysium** (q.v.).

Vanitas n. [L. vanity, conceit.] Art. A form of still-life popular in 17th-century Holland into which objects are incorporated which suggest moral lessons and the brevity of life.

vanitas vanitatum! interj. Ecclesiastes 1:2. [L. **vanitas** vanity, conceit (1); **vanitatum** of vanities, conceits (2): vanity of vanities!] Vanity of vanities! Used as a warning about the ultimate futility of human endeavor.

varia lectio n., pl. **variae lectiones** [L. **varia** varied, different (1); **lectio** reading (2): different reading.] A different version of the text, usually based upon another manuscript reading. Cf. **difficilior lectio**.

variatim adv. [L.] In various ways.

variorum [L. of various (persons).] A collection of the various notes and commentaries collected in the complete works of an author.

varium et mutabile semper / femina. Vergil (70–19 B.C.). Aeneid IV,569. [L. **varium** fickle, untrustworthy (thing) (2); **et** and (3); **mutabile** changeable (thing) (4); **semper** always (1); **femina** woman (5): Always a fickle and changeable thing is / woman.] A woman is a fickle and changeable thing. Cf. **Elle flotte** etc.

Vaterland n. [Ger. from **Vater** father (1); **Land** land, country (2): fatherland.] One's native land, especially Germany for Germans.

vates n., pl. **vates** [L. prophet, poet.] A poet with prophetic skill. A prophet-poet.

vaticinatio ex eventu [L. **vaticinatio** prediction, prophecy (1); **ex** after, following (2); **eventu** occurrence, event (3): prediction after the event.] Prediction after the occurrence. Predicting something after its occurrence. Socrates promises in the Apology . . . that others . . . would continue the work of testing people. If we take this sharply as a vaticinatio ex eventu, . . . (Lesky 1966:515). See **ex eventu**.

vaticinium ex eventu var. of **vaticinatio ex eventu** (q.v.).

vaudeville n. [Fr. light comedy.] A light comic performance, especially composed of varied skits and performers. —adj. Pertaining to such a light comic performance.

v.c. abbr. for 1. **verbi causa** (q.v.). 2. **visum cultum** (q.v.).

v. cel. abbr. for **vir celeberrimus** (q.v.).

V.E. abbr. for **venditioni exponas** (q.v.).

vel primus vel cum primis [L. **vel** either (1); **primus** first (person) (2); **vel** or (3); **cum** with (4); **primis** first (persons) (5): either the first or with the first.] Either be first or together with the first. Motto of Adisadel College (Cape Coast, Ghana).

velut inter ignis / luna minores Horace (65–8 B.C.). Odes I,12,47–48. [L. **velut** just as, like (1); **inter** among, in the midst of (3); **ignis** fires (5); **luna** moon (2); **minores** smaller (4): like the moon among the smaller fires.] Like the moon among the stars. Brian towered above his colleagues, to put it in the words of Horace, velut inter ignis luna minores.

vendetta n., pl. **vendettas** [It. revenge, vengeance.] 1. A hereditary feud in which one family seeks to wreak vengeance on another family or a member of that family for an offense done to the family or one of its members. The vendetta between the Abayomi clan and the Falana clan originated from a land dispute many decades ago. 2. A bitter and protracted feud. Alleging an anti-government vendetta, officials refused to renew the work visa of the Australian Broadcasting Company's Jakarta correspondent . . . (Newsweek Int. July 7, 1980:19).

venditio n. [L. a sale or vending.] Civil Law. Sale or contract of sale.

venditioni exponas abbr. **V.E.** n. [L. **venditioni** for sale (2); **exponas** you should expose, exhibit (1): You should expose/exhibit for sale.] A writ ordering any competent official to sell goods, obtained under a fieri facias, or lands seized. See **fieri facias**.

venez-ici adj. [Fr. **venez** come (1); **ici** here (2): Come here.] Seductive, beguiling, or tempting. She appeared without warning on thousands of billboards throughout France—a pert mystery model wearing a venez-ici smile and a minuscule bikini (Newsweek Int. Sept. 21, 1981:33).

venia aetatis n. [L. **venia** favor, indulgence (1); **aetatis** of age (2): favor/indulgence of age.] Roman and Civil Law. Privilege of age. A privilege granted to a minor which permits him/her to enjoy the rights of a person who is of full age or **sui juris** (q.v.).

veni Creator Spiritus [L. **veni** come (1); **Creator** creator (2); **Spiritus** spirit (3): Come, Creator Spirit.] Come Holy Spirit, Creator. The first words of an ancient Christian hymn.

venienti occurrite morbo. Persius (34–62 A.D.). Satires III,64. [L. **venienti** while coming (3); **occurrite** meet (1); **morbo** disease (2): Meet the disease while coming.] Attempt to cure the disease at its early stage. Cf. **principiis obsta**.

venire facias or **venire** n. [L. **venire** to come (2); **facias** you should cause (1): You should cause to come.] 1. A writ for summoning a specific number of qualified persons for jury service at a particular time. 2. An entire list of potenial jurors from which a jury is drawn. 3. English Law. A writ ordering the appearance in court of a person who has been indicted on a penal statute.

venire facias ad respondendum n. [L. **venire** to come (2); **facias** you should cause (1); **ad** to, at, for, according to (3); **respondendum** answering (4): You should cause to come for answering.] Law. A writ summoning a person indicted for misdemeanor to appear in court.

venire facias de novo or **venire de novo** n. [L. **venire** to come (2); **facias** you should cause (1); **de** of, from, about, for (3); **novo** new (4): You should cause to come from new.] Law. You should cause to come anew. A new writ summoning a jury afresh for a retrial because of irregularity or impropriety in the first summons, or unacceptable verdict, or a reversal of judgment.

veni, vidi, vici. *abbr.* **v.v.v.** Julius Caesar (100–44 B.C.). [L. **veni** I came (1); **vidi** I saw (2); **vici** I conquered (3): I came, I saw, I conquered.] Julius Caesar's quasi-telegraphic announcement of his victory over Pharnaces at the battle of Zela in 47 B.C. As quoted by Suetonius (born c. 69 A.D.) at I, 37. *Elated by his spectacular victory in the competition, the victor, quoting Julius Caesar, said "Veni, vidi, vici."*

venter *n., pl.* **venters** [L. belly, womb.] *Law.* Wife or mother. *James was Mr. Bond's son by his first venter.*

ventre à terre *adj.* [Fr. **ventre** stomach, belly (1); **à** to, toward, in, by, with, until (2); **terre** earth, ground (3): belly to the ground.] 1. Belly-flat on the ground. 2. *Art.* Describing an animal in swift movement with legs stretched out parallel to the ground.

venue *n., pl.* **venues** [Fr. coming, arrival, advent.] 1. *Law.* The place where alleged events of an action at law took place. 2. *Law.* The place from which jurors are drawn and where the trial of the case takes place. 3. The scene, real or imaginary, of an event. 4. A place chosen for a proposed meeting, especially a meeting for a sporting event, a political rally, entertainment, lectures, etc.

Venus *n., pl.* **Venuses** [L.] 1. *Roman Mythology.* The goddess of love. 2. A woman believed to bear close resemblance to Venus, goddess of love and beauty. A beautiful, graceful, and charming woman.

vera causa *n., pl.* **verae causae** [L. **vera** true, real (1); **causa** cause, reason, case (2): true cause.] *Philosophy.* The real cause. The true cause for an action or event.

vera copula *n., pl.* **verae copulae** [L. **vera** true, real (1); **copula** union (2): real union.] Full sexual intercourse.

veranda or **verandah** *n.* [Hindi **varandā**.] An extension to a house usually roofed but open at the sides or screened. Cf. **piazza**.

verba accipienda sunt secundum subjectam materiam. [L. **verba** words (1); **accipienda** to be accepted (3); **sunt** are (2); **secundum** according to, in accordance with (4); **subjectam** subject (5); **materiam** matter (6): Words are to be accepted in accordance with the subject matter.] Words must be understood according to the subject matter.

verba generalia generaliter sunt intelligenda. [L. **verba** words (2); **generalia** general (1); **generaliter** generally (5); **sunt** are (3); **intelligenda** to be understood (4): General words are to be understood generally.] General statements must be interpreted generally. Cf. **generale dictum** etc. and **generalia verba** etc.

verba intentioni, non e contra, debent inservire. [L. **verba** words (1); **intentioni** intention (4); **non** not (5); **e** from (6); **contra** against, opposite (7); **debent** should, ought (2); **inservire** to serve (3): Words ought to serve the intention, not from the opposite.] Words should be subservient to the intention, not vice versa. See **falsa demonstratio non nocet**.

verba sunt indices animi. [L. **verba** words (1); **sunt** are (2); **indices** indications, pointers (3); **animi** of mind (4): Words are indications of the mind.] Words indicate thoughts and intentions. See **index animi sermo**.

verbatim *adv.* [L. word for word.] In the exact same words; i.e., of the speaker or document. *Everything you said will appear in the papers verbatim . . . (The Guardian 1986). —adj.* Reported or reproduced word for word. *The prosecutor tendered in evidence a verbatim statement of the accused person's confession recorded at the police station.* Cf. **mot à mot**.

verbatim et litteratim *abbr.* **verb. et lit.** *adv./adj.* [L. **verbatim** word for word (1); **et** and (2); **litteratim** letter for letter (3): word for word and letter for letter.] Exactly as written. *Anybody who reproduces parts of a book, verbatim et litteratim, for sale without obtaining permission from the publishers or the author, may face court action for infringement of a copyright.* See **de verbo in verbum**.

verbi causa *abbr.* **v.c.** [L. **verbi** of word (2); **causa** for the sake (1): for the sake of word.] For example. For instance.

verbi gratia *abbr.* **V.G.** or **v.g.** *adv.* [L. **verbi** of word (2); **gratia** by favor, for the sake (1): for the sake of the word.] For the sake of example. For instance. For example.

verbomania *n.* [Neo-L. from L. **verb(um)** word (2); Gk. **mania** madness, insanity, passion (1): passion for words.] Verbosity. Use of too many words.

verborum obligatio verbis dissolvitur. [L. **verborum** of words (2); **obligatio** obligation (1); **verbis** by words (4); **dissolvitur** is dissolved (3): An obligation of words is dissolved by words.] A verbal obligation can be dissolved by word of mouth. See **eodem modo quo quid constituitur dissolvitur**.

verboten *adj.* [Ger. forbidden.] Forbidden. Prohibited. *Smoking in buses is verboten. —n., pl.* **verbotens** Something forbidden. *An intriguing aspect of that school's philosophy of discipline is that the children, instead of being taught to distinguish right from wrong, are guided by verbotens.*

verbum sapienti *short form* of **verbum satis sapienti** (q.v.).

verbum sapienti sat. See **verbum sapienti sat est**.

verbum sapienti sat est. *abbr.* **verb. sap.** or **verbum sap.** [L. **verbum** word (1); **sapienti** to wise (person) (2); **sat** enough (4); **est** is (3): A word to the wise is enough.] A wise person needs only a word of warning.

verbum satis sapienti. *abbr.* **verb. sap.** or **verb sat.** or **verbum sap.** See **verbum sapienti sat est**.

Veritas [L. truth.] Truth. Motto of Harvard University.

veritas, a quocunque dicitur, a Deo est. [L. **veritas** truth (1); **a** by (2); **quocunque** whomsoever (3); **dicitur** it is said (4); **a** from (6); **Deo** God (7); **est** is (5): Truth, by whomsoever it is said, is from God.] Truth, whatever be its source, is from God.

veritas habenda est in juratore, justitia et judicium in judice. [L. **veritas** truth (1); **habenda** to be had, held, regarded (3); **est** is (2); **in** in, on (4); **juratore** juror (5); **justitia** justice (6); **et** and (7); **judicium** judgment (8); **in** in, on (9); **judice** judge (10): Truth is to be had in the juror, justice and judgment in the judge.] *Law.* The juror must evince truth, the judge justice and judgment. Cf. **ad quaestionem facti** etc.

Veritas et Utilitas [L. **veritas** truth (1); **et** and (2); **utilitas** usefulness (3): Truth and Usefulness.] Truth and Utility. The motto of Howard University.

veritas nihil veretur nisi abscondi. [L. **veritas** truth (1); **nihil** nothing (3); **veretur** fears, is afraid of (2); **nisi** unless, except (4); **abscondi** to be hidden, concealed (5): Truth fears nothing except to be concealed.] Truth fears nothing but its concealment.

veritas nimium altercando amittitur. See **nimium altercando veritas amittitur.**

veritas nominis tollit errorem demonstrationis. [L. **veritas** truth (1); **nominis** of name (2); **tollit** removes, takes away (3); **errorem** error, mistake (4); **demonstrationis** of description, designation (5): The truth of name removes the error of description.] *Law.* Use of the proper name takes away the errors caused by mere description. See **falsa demonstratio non nocet.**

veritas vos liberabit. John 20:15. [L. **veritas** truth (1); **vos** you (3); **liberabit** will free (2): Truth will free you.] The truth will set you free. The motto of The Johns Hopkins University.

veritatem qui non libere pronuntiat proditor est veritatis. [L. **veritatem** truth (4); **qui** (one) who (1); **non** not (2); **libere** freely, openly, frankly (5); **pronuntiat** tells, utters (3); **proditor** traitor, betrayer (7); **est** is (6); **veritatis** of truth (8): He who does not tell the truth freely is a betrayer of truth.] A person who does not tell the truth freely betrays truth.

vers de société *n.* [Fr. **vers** poetry (1); **de** of (2); **société** society (3): poetry of society.] Witty, usually sarcastic, light poetry composed for the amusement of sophisticated readers. *This most versatile of Roman poets* [i.e., Ovid] *composed various kinds of vers de société with unfailing dexterity . . .* (Cary 1970:581).

vers d'occasion *n.* [Fr. **vers** verse (1); **d'** of (2); **occasion** occasion (3): verse of occasion.] Occasional verse. Poetry composed to commemorate a particular anniversary or event. *By assiduous practice in translating the highly finished vers d'occasion of the Hellenistic writers he* [i.e., Catullus] *attained an effortless ease in manipulating the various lyric metres* (Cary 1970:464).

vers libre *n., pl.* **vers libres** [Fr. **vers** verse, poetry (2); **libre** free (1): free verse.] A poetic form which does not use rhyme, meter, and other standard features of poetry.

verso *abbr.* **V.** or **v.** *n., pl.* **versos** short form of **folio verso** (q.v.). Cf. **recto.**

versus *abbr.* **v.** or **vs.** *prep.* [L. turned in the direction of or towards.] 1. Against; i.e., another party or team.

a) *Adagba versus Adegbite*; b) *Unimaid versus Unilag.* 2. As the alternative of. In contrast to. *Freedom versus servitude.*

verte *abbr.* **v.** [L. turn.] Turn over. Turn the page.

vertex *n., pl.* **vertices** [L. top, crown.] The top or crown, as the head of a body, the top of a mountain, the highest point in a geometric figure, or the highest point in the movement of a heavenly body.

vertigo *n., pl.* **vertigines** or **vertigoes** [L. a turning round or whirling, a sensation of dizziness, whirling, or giddiness.] 1. Dizziness. Giddiness. A morbid condition in which things in one's vicinity seem to be turning around one or in which one seems to be turning around in space. 2. Mental dizziness, giddiness, confusion, or bewilderment.

verve *n., pl.* **verves** [Fr. zest, warmth, high spirits.] 1. Vivacity or vigor in the composition or performance of works of literature, music, art, etc. a) *But in haute couture, Yves Saint Laurent . . . showed the verve that has long kept high fashion indisputably French* (*Newsweek Int.* Jan. 2, 1984:58). b) *The author wrote the novel with such verve that every part of it seems to be pregnant with life.* 2. Vitality, energy, enthusiasm. *Felicia's grandfather is an octogenarian who walks with the verve of a teenager.*

vestigium *n., pl.* **vestigia** [L. footprint, sign, trace, token.] *Law of Evidence.* Trace or mark, i.e., left by a person or thing.

Veterinariae Medicinae Doctor *abbr.* **V.M.D.** *n.* [L. **veterinariae** of veterinary (2); **medicinae** (of) medicine (3); **doctor** teacher (1): teacher of veterinary medicine.] Doctor of Veterinary Medicine. A terminal graduate degree in veterinary medicine.

veto *n., pl.* **vetoes** [L. I forbid.] Act of forbidding something such as a plan, proposal, or bill. The right or power to forbid or prevent a plan. a) *There was general criticism of the president's veto of the bill passed by the House of Representatives.* b) *Abimbola resents her parents' veto of her proposed marriage to Aminu.* —*v.* To refuse to approve. *The president vetoed the bill passed by the House of Representatives.*

Vetus Testamentum *n.* [L. **vetus** old, ancient (1); **testamentum** testament (2): old testament.] The Old Testament. The Latin version of the Hebrew bible. Cf. **Novum Testamentum.**

vexata quaestio See **quaestio vexata.**

V.G. or **v.g.** *abbr.* for **verbi gratia** (q.v.).

vi *adj./adv.* [L. by force.] Forcible. Forcibly. By force.

via *n., pl.* **viae** or **vias** [L. path, way, road, street.] Way, road, passage, or right of way. —*prep.* [L. by way, by road.] 1. By way of. *Her goods were shipped from New York via London to Tema.* 2. Through the medium of. By means of. *Some journalists try to attract readers' attention via sensational headlines.*

via affirmativa *n.* [Late L. **via** way, road (2); **affirmativa** affirmative (1): affirmative way.] *Theology.* The use of affirmative or positive statements in describing the nature of God; i.e., stating what God is, not what God is not. Cf. **via negativa.**

via antiqua via est tuta. [L. **via** path, way, road (2); **antiqua** old (1); **via** way, road (5); **est** is (3); **tuta** safe (4): The old way is the safe way.] The safe road or path is the one which has been used in the past. See **via trita est tutissima.**

Via Crucis *n.* [L. **via** path, way, road (1); **crucis** of cross, gallows (2): way/road of the cross.] *Roman Catholic Church and Anglican Church.* The Stations of the Cross. A series of fourteen representations, signifying scenes of the Passion of Christ, before which worshipers meditate and pray. Cf. **Via Dolorosa.**

Via Dolorosa *n.* [L. **via** path, way, road (2); **dolorosa** sorrowful, painful (1): sorrowful/painful road.] The route of Jesus from the judgment hall of Pontius Pilate to Golgotha for crucifixion. Cf. **Via Crucis.** —**via dolorosa** A painfully arduous path or route. A very painful series of experiences. a) *After following her a long way along her via dolorosa we can understand why this weary old woman . . . turns into an avenging demon who gloats over the impotent raging of her victim* (Lesky 1966:374). b) *"To get a license to dig a private well is via dolorosa,"* says Ben-Meir (*Newsweek Int.* Feb. 23, 1981:48).

viae servitus *n.* [L. **viae** of path, way, road (2); **servitus** servitude, service (1): servitude of way.] Right of way; i.e., the right to walk, ride, and drive over the land of another.

via lactea *n.* [L. **via** path, way, road (2); **lactea** milky, milk-white (1): milky way.] 1. The constellation or galaxy in which earth's solar system is located. 2. *Greek and Roman Mythology.* The breast milk which flowed from the goddess Hera when she nursed the infant hero Heracles. This milk became the constellation.

via media *n.* [L. **via** path, way, road (2); **media** middle, mean (1): middle road.] The middle path, road, ground, way, course or conception. A course of action which lies midway between two extremes. *Via media is generally preferable to extremes.* See **aurea mediocritas.**

via negativa *n.* [Late L. **via** way, road (2); **negativa** negative (1): negative way.] *Theology.* The use of negative statements in describing the nature of God; i.e., a belief that one can only state what God is not, not what God is. Cf. **via affirmativa.**

viaticum *n., pl.* **viatica** or **viaticums** [L. traveling money, provision for a journey.] 1. Traveling allowance. *For the conference, each official was given a viaticum of $500.00.* 2. *Christianity.* The communion or Eucharist administered to one who is likely to die soon.

via trita est tutissima. [L. **via** path, way, road (2); **trita** trodden, frequented, familiar (1); **est** is (3); **tutissima** safest (4): The trodden/familiar path is the safest.] Established procedure is preferable to innovation. Thus, a court of law will normally not accept a novel

suggestion which does not enjoy the support of authority or precedent. See **omnis innovatio** etc.; **via antiqua** etc.; and **via trita via tuta.**

via trita via tuta. [L. **via** path, way, road (2); **trita** trodden, frequented, familiar (1); **via** path, way, road (4); **tuta** safe (3): The trodden path is the safe path.] See **via trita est tutissima.**

vi aut clam *adv.* [L. **vi** by force (1); **aut** or (2); **clam** secretly, covertly (3): by force or secretly.] Forcibly or secretly.

vicarius non habet vicarium. [L. **vicarius** substitute, deputy (1); **non** not (2); **habet** has, holds, regards (3); **vicarium** substitute, deputy (4): A deputy does not have a deputy.] *Law.* A delegated power cannot in turn be delegated. See **delegata potestas** etc.

vice *abbr.* V. or v. *prep.* [L. in the position, stead, duty.] In the place of. Succeeding. Taking the place of. *Kwadwo Bonsu has been appointed Chief Accountant vice Peter Kwofie, who has retired.* —*pref.* One who occupies or takes the place of. One who acts or is substitute for. a) *Vice-Chancellor;* b) *Vice-Chairman;* c) *Vice-President;* d) *Vice-consul.*

vice-reine *n., pl.* **vice-reines** [Fr. **vice** in place of (1); **reine** queen (2): in place of the queen.] A viceroy's wife. A woman who is a **viceroy** (q.v.).

viceroy *n., pl.* **viceroys** [Obs. Fr. **vice** in place of (1); **roy** king (2): in place of the king.] The king's representative. The governor of a province, colony, or country. Cf. **vice-reine.**

vice versa *abbr.* v.v. *adv.* [L. **vice** with condition, lot, position (1); **versa** (with) having been changed, altered, reversed (2): with the condition having been reversed.] Conversely. With the reversal of relations. *Mr. Drob is a man who strongly believes that a husband should guide, direct and control his wife rather than vice versa.*

vicini viciniora praesumuntur scire. [L. **vicini** neighbors (1); **viciniora** nearer (places) (4); **praesumuntur** are presumed (2); **scire** to know (3): Neighbors are presumed to know nearer places.] *Law.* Neighbors are presumed to know the neighborhood. Cf. **lex intendit vicinum** etc.

vi clam aut precario *adv.* [L. **vi** by force (1); **clam** secretly (2); **aut** or (3); **precario** by right granted (4): by force, secretly, or by right granted.] *Law.* Forcefully, secretly or by permission of the owner. Cf. **nec vi** etc.

victor ludorum *n., pl.* **victores ludorum** [L. **victor** victor (1); **ludorum** of the games (2): victor of the games.] The winner of a series of athletic competitions. *The New York Yankees are baseball's perennial victor ludorum.*

vide *abbr.* v. or vid. v. [L. See.] See. Refer to. Used for bibliographical references.

vide ante v. [L. **vide** see (1); **ante** before (2): see before.] Used in books to refer the reader to a previous passage or item. See **vide supra** and **vide ut supra.**

vide infra *abbr.* **V.I.** or **v.i.** *v.* [L. **vide** see (1); **infra** below, beneath (2): See below.] Used in books to refer the reader to a subsequent passage or item. See **vide post**.

videlicet *abbr.* **viz.** *adv.* [L. **vide(re)** to see (2); **licet** it is permitted (1): it is permitted to see.] *Law.* Clearly. Of course. Namely. *Expressions such as "namely," "to wit" or "that is to say" are called the "videlicet."*

video meliora, proboque; / deteriora sequor. Ovid (43 B.C.–17 A.D.). *Metamorphoses* VII,7–8. [L. **video** I see (1); **meliora** better (things) (3); **proboque** and I approve of (2); **deteriora** worse (things) (5); **sequor** I follow (4): I see and I approve of better things; / I follow worse things.] I see and approve of the better course, though I follow the worse course. *The legal profession is such that the lawyer has to observe the maxim "Video meliora proboque, deteriora sequor."*

vide post *v.* [L. **vide** see (1); **post** after (2): See after or below.] See **vide infra**.

vide supra *abbr.* **V.S.** or **v.s.** *v.* [L. **vide** see (1); **supra** above (2): See above.] See **vide ante** and **vide ut supra**.

vide ut supra *v.* [L. **vide** see (1); **ut** as (2); **supra** above (3): See as above.] See what is stated above. Used for bibliographical references. See **vide ante** and **vide supra**.

vidimus *n., pl.* **vidimuses** [L. We have seen.] Official inspection of, for instance, a document. A certified copy of a document.

vie de Bohème *n.* [Fr. **vie** life (1); **de** of (2); **Bohème** Bohemian (3): life of a Bohemian.] Bohemian life-style. The unconventional, free, easy-going, life-style adopted by some artists.

vie en rose *n.* [Fr. **vie** life (1); **en** in (2); **rose** rose (3): life in rose.] A naive, unrealistic view of the world, i.e., one seen through rose-colored glasses. Based upon song lyrics made famous by the French chanteuse Edith Piaf (1915–1963).

vi et armis *adv.* [L. **vi** by force (1); **et** and (2); **armis** by arms (3): by force and arms.] By force of arms. Used to qualify trespass and applicable to the common-law action for damages in respect of trespass to property or person. *In its original legal meaning "trespass" signified no more than "wrong" . . . and in course of time the allegation that the trespass was committed vi et armis came to be used as common form in order to preserve the jurisdictional propriety of an action brought in those Courts . . .* (Rogers 1975:31). Cf. **manu forti**.

vieux marcheur *n.* [Fr. **vieux** old (1); **marcheur** walker (2): an old walker.] An elderly profligate. An old lady-killer. An old man who spends most of his time having fun with women. Cf. **roué**.

vigil ales evocat auroram. [L. **vigil** wakeful, awake (1); **ales** bird (2); **evocat** summons, calls forth (3); **auroram** dawn (4): The wakeful bird summons dawn.] The wakeful bird is up early enough to proclaim the arrival of dawn. Motto of the University of Ghana, Legon.

vigilante *n., pl.* **vigilantes** [Sp. guard, policeman.] A member of a group of citizens who have volunteered to maintain law and order. *With the increasing rate of burglary, vigilantes have been patrolling the area every night. —attrib.* Of, belonging to, relating to, characteristic of vigilantes. a) *The government is contemplating setting up vigilante groups to identify troublemakers . . .* (*New African* 1981). b) *. . . some vigilante groups of left-wing whites already are taking matters into their own hands* (*Newsweek Int.* Feb. 23, 1981:11).

vigilantibus, et non dormientibus, jura subveniunt. [L. **vigilantibus** the vigilant (3); **et** and (4); **non** not (5); **dormientibus** the sleeping (6); **jura** rights, laws (1); **subveniunt** aid, assist, help (2): The laws help those who are vigilant, not those who are asleep.] *Law.* The laws assist those who care, not those who do not care, about their rights. See **leges vigilantibus** etc.

vigilantibus lex succurrit. [L. **vigilantibus** the vigilant (3); **lex** law (1); **succurrit** aids, helps, assists (2): The law helps the vigilant.] *Law.* See **leges vigilantibus** etc.

vigilantibus, non dormientibus, aequitas subvenit. [L. **vigilantibus** the vigilant (3); **non** not (4); **dormientibus** the sleeping (5); **aequitas** equity (1); **subvenit** aids, assists, helps (2): Equity helps those who are vigilant, not those who are asleep.] The law helps those who are watchful, not those who are not. *There is an important maxim, "Vigilantibus, non dormientibus, aequitas subvenit," expressed in the vernacular as "delay defeats equities"* (Hanbury 1962:306). Cf. **leges vigilantibus** etc.

vignette *n., pl.* **vignettes** [Fr. small vine, an ornamental border, text illustration.] 1. A border or illustration in a text, especially one which is not marked off by a lined border. Originally, this decoration was often a grape vine. 2. *Architecture.* The use of a grape vine as carved decoration. 3. *Photography.* A depiction of only the upper body, or even the head alone, with a darkened background. 4. A short sketch or description of a person, place, incident, etc. *—v.* 1. *Photography.* To make a photograph of only the upper body or the head alone. 2. To offer a short sketch or description of a person, place, incident, etc.

villa *n., pl.* **villas** or **villae** [L./It. country-house, farm.] A large country residence. A suburban or rural mansion, especially one used as a place of retreat from urban life by an affluent person. *Expatriates live . . . in sprawling villas behind manicured hedges in Nairobi* (*Newsweek Int.* July 19, 1982:23).

vim vi repellere licet, modo fiat moderamine inculpatae tutelae, non ad sumendam vindictam, sed ad propulsandam injuriam. [L. **vim** force (3); **vi** with force (4); **repellere** to repel (2); **licet** it is allowed, lawful (1); **modo** provided only, on condition that (5); **fiat** it is done (6); **moderamine** with/under direction, control (7); **inculpatae** of blameless (8); **tutelae** (of) defense, protection (9); **non** not (10); **ad** to, at, for, according to (11); **sumendam** to be taken (13); **vindictam** vengeance, revenge (12); **sed** but (14); **ad** to, at, for, according to (15); **propulsandam** to be warded off (17); **injuriam** injury (16): It is lawful to repel force with force, on condition that it is done under the direction of blameless defense, not for vengeance to be taken, but for injury to be warded off.] *Law.* It is lawful to repel force with force, provided only that it is prompted by blameless defense, not to take vengeance but to ward off injury. See **homicidium** and **se defendendo**.

vincet amor patriae Vergil (70–19 B.C.). *Aeneid* VI,823. [L. **vincet** will conquer (3); **amor** love (1); **patriae** of country, fatherland (2): Love of country will conquer.] Love of one's country will win out (over personal interests).

vincit qui se vincit. [L. **vincit** conquers (4); **qui** (one) who (1); **se** one's self (3); **vincit** conquers (2): One who conquers oneself conquers.] The person who conquers or controls himself/herself is the victor.

vinciunt leges. [L. **vinciunt** bind (2); **leges** laws (1): The laws bind.] The laws have binding force.

vinculum *n., pl.* **vincula** [L. bond, fetter, chain.] A link. Unifying bond. *There is a strong vinculum between Emmanuel and Jacob which makes them, as it were, inseparable.*

vindicatio rei *n.* [L. **vindicatio** establishment of a right, vindication (1); **rei** of a matter, thing, property, business, affair (2): establishment of a right of a thing.] *Civil Law.* Establishing one's right to a thing.

vindicatio servitutis *n.* [L. **vindicatio** establishment of the right, vindication (1); **servitutis** of servitude (2): establishment of a right of servitude.] *Roman Law.* Establishment of one's right to a servitude. See **actio confessoria**.

vindicatio ususfructus *n.* [L. **vindicatio** establishment of the right; vindication (1); **ususfructus** of usufruct, use and enjoyment (2): establishment of the right of usufruct.] *Roman Law.* Establishment of one's right to use and enjoyment. See **actio confessoria**.

vindicta / nemo magis gaudet quam femina. Juvenal (c.60–117 A.D.). *Satires* XIII,191–192. [L. **vindicta** vengeance, revenge (3); **nemo** no one, nobody (1); **magis** more (4); **gaudet** rejoices in, takes pleasure in (2); **quam** than (5); **femina** woman (6): No one / takes pleasure in revenge more than a woman.] No one takes more delight in revenge than a woman.

violenta praesumptio aliquando est plena probatio. [L. **violenta** forcible, vehement (1); **praesumptio** presumption (2); **aliquando** sometimes (4); **est** is (3); **plena** full (5); **probatio** proof (6): Vehement presumption is sometimes full proof.] *Law.* Occasionally

strong presumption is full proof. See **praesumptio violenta** and **probatio plena** etc.

virago *n., pl.* **viragoes** or **viragos** [L. a manlike woman, heroic maiden, female warrior.] 1. A shrew. A quarrelsome, nagging, overbearing woman. 2. A very strong and courageous woman, especially one who, physically and mentally, has the qualities of a man. See **Amazon** and **Xanthippe**. Cf. **androgynus**.

vir bonus dicendi peritus Cato the Censor. [L. **vir** man, male, husband (2); **bonus** morally good (1); **dicendi** of speaking (4); **peritus** experienced, skilled (3): a morally good man experienced of speaking.] A man of probity accomplished in speaking. *The definition of the ideal orator in ancient Rome was "vir bonus dicendi peritus."*

vir celeberrimus *abbr.* **v. cel.** *n.* [L. **vir** man, male, husband (2); **celeberrimus** most celebrated, distinguished (1): most celebrated man.] A most distinguished man.

virement *n., pl.* **virements** [Fr. transfer, clearing.] Administrative transfer of funds, i.e., in bookkeeping and accounting.

vir et uxor censentur in lege una persona. [L. **vir** man, male, husband (1); **et** and (2); **uxor** wife (3); **censentur** are believed, held, thought (4); **in** in, on (5); **lege** law (6); **una** one (7); **persona** person (8): Husband and wife are in law deemed (to be) one person.] *Law.* A married couple are legally considered to be a single person. A common law rule which is no longer rigidly observed. See **omnia quae sunt** etc.

vir et uxor sunt quasi unica persona. [L. **vir** man, male, husband (1); **et** and (2); **uxor** wife (3); **sunt** are (4); **quasi** just as if, as one might say (5); **unica** sole, single (6); **persona** person (7): Husband and wife are, so to speak, one person.] *Law.* A husband and wife are like one person. See **omnia quae sunt** etc.

vir et uxor sunt quasi unica persona, quia caro et sanguis unus; res licet sit propria uxoris, vir tamen ejus custos, cum sit caput mulieris. [L. **vir** man, male, husband (1); **et** and (2); **uxor** wife (3); **sunt** are (4); **quasi** just as if, as one might say (5); **unica** one (6); **persona** person (7); **quia** because (8); **caro** flesh (10); **et** and (11); **sanguis** blood (12); **unus** one (9); **res** matter, thing, property, business, affair (14); **licet** although, notwithstanding (13); **sit** is; be (15); **propria** belonging to, individual (16); **uxoris** of wife (17); **vir** man, male, husband (19); **tamen** nevertheless, yet (18); **ejus** its (20); **custos** guard, keeper (21); **cum** since (22); **sit** he is (23); **caput** head (24); **mulieris** of woman, wife (25): Husband and wife are just as if one person because they are one flesh and blood; although a thing may be (a) belonging to the wife, nevertheless the husband is its keeper, since he is the head of the wife.] *Law.* Husband and wife are, so to speak, one person because they are one flesh and blood; although property may belong to the wife, nevertheless the husband keeps it, since he is the head of the household. As a rule of civil law, the maxim is no longer quite valid. See **omnia quae sunt** etc

virginibus puerisque *adj.* Horace (65–8 B.C.). *Odes* III,1,4. [L. **virginibus** for maidens (1); **puerisque** and for boys (2): for maidens and boys.] For girls and boys. Applicable, especially, to books considered suitable for youths.

Virgo *n.* [L. virgin, young woman.] 1. *Astronomy.* A constellation shaped like a young woman and located near Leo and Libra. 2. *Astrology.* The sixth sign of the zodiac dominant from August 23 through September 22. 3. A person born under this sign.

virgo intacta *n., pl.* **virgines intactae** [L. **virgo** virgin, young woman (2); **intacta** untouched, intact (1): an untouched virgin.] A woman who has not experienced vaginal intercourse.

virtuoso or *fem.* **virtuosa** *n., pl.* **virtuosi** or **virtuosos** or *fem.* **virtuose** or **virtuosas** [It. learned, virtuous, skilled.] 1. A person interested in pursuing knowledge. A *savant* (q.v.). A person who does research in the sciences or arts. *A group of virtuosi have published the results of their research on sea life in the* Journal of Natural Sciences. 2. A person who is very skilled in the technique of a fine art, for instance a musician. a) *When it comes to singing praises, both gentlemen are virtuosos* (*Newsweek Int.* Feb. 8, 1982:51). b) *Perlman, Prince of the new violin virtuosos* (*Newsweek Int.* April 14, 1980:36). —*adj. Of, characteristic of, relating to, pertaining to, exhibiting the style or ability of a virtuoso.* a) *... Woody Allen, the film-maker, comic and virtuoso jazz clarinetist ...* (*Time Int.* 1979). b) *It was a virtuoso performance* (*Time Int.* 1982).

virtute et armis [L. **virtute** (by/with) courage, valor, strength, virtue (1); **et** and (2); **armis** (by/with) arms (3): by courage and by arms.] By valor and arms. Motto of the State of Mississippi.

virtute officii *adv.* [L. **virtute** by virtue (1); **officii** of office (2): by virtue of office.] Because of one's office. **Ex officio** (q.v.). a) *The sole administrator of the metropolis, acting virtute officii, ordered the demolition of the building.* b) *... the term "legal assets" comprised only what came to the representative virtute officii* (Hanbury 1962:450).

virus *abbr.* **V.** or **v.** *n., pl.* **viruses** [L. a potent juice, venom, poison.] 1. A poisonous element or agent which is the cause of an infectious disease. 2. An infection. Something which has an infectious effect, morally, intellectually, etc. a) *"Emigration is a virus in our society, and it can spread very quickly"* (*Newsweek Int.* Feb. 16, 1981:14). b) *... the seven higher institutions in Anambra had been closed for fear of the solidarity virus spreading into the other campuses* (*The Guardian* 1988).

vis *n.* [L. force, power, strength.] Force or power. —*pl.* **vires** Legal strength or legitimacy. Cf. **extra vires**; **intra vires**; and **ultra vires**.

visa *n., pl.* **visas** [L. things that have been seen.] 1. An endorsement of a document by a superior officer, indicating that it has been examined and found to be satisfactory in form and content. 2. An endorsement on a passport by officials of the country of destination that the bearer is qualified to proceed. —*v.* 1. To give a visa to. *Seth has got his passport visaed and he may soon depart for Italy.* 2. To ratify or approve officially. *Topics of papers to be read at the conference have already been visaed.*

vis a fronte *n.* [L. **vis** force, power (1); **a** from, by (2); **fronte** front (3): force from the front.] A physical force from the front. Cf. **vis a tergo**.

vis armata *n.* [L. **vis** force (2); **armata** armed (1): armed force.] *Civil Law.* Armed force. See **vis cum armis**.

vis a tergo *n., pl.* **vires a tergo** [L. **vis** force (1); **a** from (2); **tergo** back (3): a force from the back.] A force or pressure from behind. *Mr. Mulira approaches every assignment enthusiastically and acts as though propelled by vis a tergo.* See **a tergo**. Cf. **vis a fronte**.

vis-à-vis *prep.* [Fr. **vis** face (1); **à** to, toward, in, by, with, until (2); **vis** face (3): face to face, opposite, in regard to a person opposite.] 1. Opposite. Face to face with. 2. As compared with. *The Syrians are well aware they are in a much inferior position vis-à-vis Israel and that it is not a realistic option to start a war* (*Newsweek Int.* Jan. 4, 1982:17). 3. In relation to. *... taking into account the nation's resources vis-à-vis its population, ...* (*West Africa* 1986): —*n., pl.* **vis-à-vis** 1. A person who is face to face with another, as in an indoor game or dance. One who holds a corresponding or equal position. A person paired with another as a date, an escort, a partner, etc. *Throughout the dinner Mat kept gazing at his vis-à-vis, smiling and admiring her.* 2. A private, intimate conversation. A **tête-à-tête** (q.v.). 3. A carriage in which people sit facing each other. —*adv.* Face to face. In company of each other. *The seats of the bus are such that passengers have to sit vis-à-vis.*

vis consili expers mole ruit sua. Horace (65–8 B.C.). *Odes* III,4,65. [L. **vis** force (1); **consili** of wisdom, sense (3); **expers** devoid of, free from (2); **mole** (with/under) weight (6); **ruit** tumbles down, goes to ruin (4); **sua** with/under its own (5): Force, devoid of wisdom, tumbles down under its own weight.] The use of force which is not based upon wisdom crumbles under its own weight. *The sage concluded his speech on misuse of power with: "vis consili expers mole ruit sua."*

vis cum armis *n.* [L. **vis** force (1); **cum** with (2); **armis** arms, weapons (3): force with arms.] See **vis armata**.

viscus *n., pl.* **viscera** [L. the interior or inner part, the inner parts of the body, the organs.] *Medicine.* An internal organ of the body. *A secret CIA memorandum of 1962 ... details a plan to capture a crocodile in Tanganyika ... and concoct a poison from its viscera ...* (*New African* 1979). —*pl.* Interior or inner contents.

The policemen conducted a thorough search of the house, tearing apart mattresses and sofas to examine their viscera.

vis divina *n.* [L. **vis** force, power (2); **divina** divine (1): divine force.] *Civil Law.* Divine force. An act of God. See **actus Dei nemini est damnosus**.

vis inertiae *n., pl.* **vires inertiae** [L. **vis** force, power (1); **inertiae** of inactivity, idleness (2): force of inactivity.] 1. **Inertia** (q.v.) 1. The physical resistance of matter to a force which tries to change its position or state of movement. 2. A tendency for a person, institution, etc. to prefer the **status quo** (q.v.) to change.

vis legibus est inimica. [L. **vis** force, power (1); **legibus** to laws (4); **est** is (2); **inimica** hostile, inimical (3): Force is hostile to laws.] *Law.* The use of force is hostile to the law.

vis major *n., pl.* **vires majores** [L. **vis** force, power (2); **major** greater, bigger (1): a greater force.] A superior force. A natural force which cannot be prevented by human agency; e.g., a storm, earthquake, or flood. See **actus Dei nemini est damnosus**.

vis medicatrix naturae *n.* [L. **vis** force, power (2); **medicatrix** healing (1); **naturae** of nature (3): the healing force of nature.] The healing power of nature. *In moments of misfortune, tribulation, and despondency, it is advisable to maintain one's presence of mind and submit to vis medicatrix naturae.*

vista *n., pl.* **vistas** [It. sight, view, vision.] 1. A far-reaching or distant view along a corridor or opening. *After the curve, they entered a stretch of the road which showed a beautiful vista of thickly-forested hills interrupted by valleys.* 2. An extensive mental vision or view. *When Sam saw a photograph of Vicky, his former girlfriend, his mind was immediately filled with vistas of the good old days.*

visum cultum *abbr.* **v.c.** [L. **visum** seen (1); **cultum** cultivated (2): seen cultivated.] *Botany.* Seen cultivated.

vis vitae *n.* [L. **vis** force, power (1); **vitae** of life (2): a force/power of life.] Living force.

vis viva *n.* [L. **vis** force, power (2); **viva** living (1): living force.] *Physics.* The principal that the power of an object is equal to its weight or mass multiplied by its speed squared.

vita *n., pl.* **vitae** [L. life.] A short biographical sketch. See **curriculum vitae**.

vita activa *n.* [L. **vita** life (2); **activa** active (1): active life.] Practical life. *A life of action. . . . the ethical necessity which forces the philosopher away from the happiness of the vita contemplativa to the vita activa of political life* (Lesky 1966:530). Cf. **vita contemplativa**.

vita brevis longa ars [L. **vita** art (2); **brevis** short (1); **longa** long (3); **ars** art (4): short life, long art.] Art is long but life is short. Art survives the lifetime of the artist.

vita contemplativa *n.* [L. **vita** life (2); **contemplativa** contemplative (1): contemplative life.] Intellectual or philosophical life. Cf. **vita activa**.

vitae summa brevis spem nos vetat incohare longam. Horace (65–8 B.C.). *Odes* I,4,15. [L. **vitae** of life (3); **summa** sum, total (2); **brevis** short (1); **spem** hope (8); **nos** us (5); **vetat** forbids (4); **incohare** to commence, begin (6); **longam** long (7): The short sum of life forbids us to commence long hope.] Life's short span does not permit us to embark on long-term expectations.

vita nuova *n.* [It. **vita** life (2); **nuova** new (1): a new life.] Changing one's lifestyle for the better. *After maltreating his wife for a decade, Mr. Chuks has realized the senselessness of his attitude and adopted a vita nuova.* See **La vita nuova**.

Viva! *interj.* [It./Sp. Live!] Long live! a) *Viva Federal Republic of Nigeria!* b) *. . . 1,500 supporters briefly blocked her way along the route, banging on the car and shouting "Viva Perón"* (*Newsweek Int.* Dec. 19, 1983:30). See **vivat** and **Vive**.

Viva il Papa! *interj.* [It. **viva** may live (1); **il** the (2); **Papa** Pope (3): May the Pope live!] Long live the Pope! *Arriving that morning for a prayer service at St Patrick's, his face lit up into a benign, contented smile as cries of "Viva il Papa" and applause drowned out the organ music* (*Newsweek Int.* Oct. 15, 1979:48).

vivat! *interj.* [L. Let him/her live. May he/she live.] Long life! Long life and prosperity to . . . ! Hurrah! See **Viva** and **Vive**.

viva voce *abbr.* **v.v.** *adv.* [L. **viva** with living (1); **voce** (with) voice (2): with living voice.] Orally. By word of mouth. *He gave an account of the incident viva voce.* —*adj.* Oral. *We intend to conduct a viva voce examination.* —*n., pl.* **viva voce** Oral examination. See **ore tenus**.

Vive *interj.* [Fr. let live.] Long live! Hail! Up with! *Vive the people of Ghana!* See **Viva** and **vivat**.

Vive la différence! [Fr. **vive** long live (1); **la** the (2); **différence** difference (3): Long live the difference.] Hurray for the difference between the sexes!

Vive le roi! *interj.* [Fr. **vive** let live (1); **le** the (2); **roi** king (3): Let the king live.] Long live the king!

vivum vadium See **vadium vivum**.

vixit *v.* [L. He/she lived.] A tombstone inscription indicating the length of the deceased's life.

vix ulla lex fieri potest quae omnibus commoda sit, sed si majori parti prospiciat, utilis est. [L. **vix** hardly, scarcely (1); **ulla** any (3); **lex** law (4); **fieri** to be made, to become (5); **potest** can, is able (2); **quae** which (6); **omnibus** to all (9); **commoda** favorable, suitable (8); **sit** is, may be (7); **sed** but (10); **si** if (11); **majori** greater (13); **parti** part, side (14); **prospiciat** it should provide for, take care of (12); **utilis** useful (16); **est** it is (15): Hardly can any law be made which is suitable to all, but if it should provide for the greater part, it is useful.] *Law.* There can hardly be any law which is satisfactory to all, but, if a law should take care of the interests of the majority, it is useful.

viz. *abbr.* for **videlicet** (q.v.).

V.M.D. *abbr.* for **Veterinariae Medicinae Doctor** (q.v.).

vocabula artis *pl. n.* [L. **vocabula** expressions, designations (l); **artis** of art (2): expressions of art.] Technical expressions. Technical terms.

vocabula artium explicanda sunt secundum definitiones prudentum. [L. **vocabula** expressions (1); **artium** of arts, skills, professions (2); **explicanda** to be explained, unfolded (4); **sunt** are (3); **secundum** according to, in accordance with (5); **definitiones** definitions, explanations (6); **prudentum** of experienced, skilled (persons) (7): Expressions of arts are to be explained according to the definitions of skilled persons.] *Law.* Technical expressions must be explained in accordance with the definitions of experts.

vocatio in jus *n.* [L. **vocatio** calling, summoning (1); **in** into, to, against, for (2); **jus** right, law (3): a calling into law.] *Early Roman Law.* Summons to court; i.e., the practice of orally calling upon the debtor to follow one to court.

vogue *n., pl.* **vogues** [Fr. fashion.] 1. Popularity. Popular favor, acceptance or use. a) . . . *Paris couturiers tried to bring the '60s miniskirt look back into vogue* (*Newsweek Int.* Jan. 5, 1981:60). b) . . . *the conference will violate the so-called national security law which is still in vogue . . . (Time Int.* 1985). c) . . . *demonstrations against the invasion of an African country by another are not in vogue . . . (New African* 1978). 2. A person or thing that is fashionable or in fashion at a particular time or place. *In the postwar years, when existentialism became an international vogue . . . (Newsweek Int.* April 28, 1980:63).

voilà *interj.* [Fr. There it is.] There!

Voilà le commencement de la fin. Talleyrand (1754–1838). [Fr. **voilà** there is, that is (1); **le** the (2); **commencement** beginning (3); **de** of (4); **la** the (5); **fin** end (6): That is the beginning of the end.] This is where the end begins. In reference to the defeat of Napoleon at Borodino in 1812. See **le commencement** etc. for a shorter form.

voir dire *n.* [Obs. Fr. **voir** truth, true (2); **dire** to say; speak (1): to speak the truth.] *Law.* A preliminary examination which a witness or juror may undergo to ascertain whether he/she is incompetent to serve as witness or juror by reason of his/her interest in the cause. *The witness had to swear on his voir dire.*

volens *adj., pl.* **volentes** [L. willing.] *Law.* Willfully. With purpose. Of choice. A person is volens, if he/she either expressly gives consent or tacitly does not oppose. Cf. **sciens**.

volenti non fit injuria. [L. **volenti** to the willing (4); **non** not (2); **fit** is done (3); **injuria** injury, wrong (1): Injury is not done to the willing.] *Law.* A person who willingly/knowingly exposes himself/herself to

injury is not entitled to damages. Generally, a plaintiff is not entitled to damages for an act for which he/she gave permission. Thus, a man who encourages his wife to commit adultery, or who connives at that adultery, is not entitled to damages. Similarly, a person who receives a defamatory letter and gives it to others to read is the one who is spreading the information contained therein and so cannot sue the writer for defamation. See **qui non improbat, approbat**.

volk *n., pl.* **volks** [Ger. and Dutch **Volk** people, race.] 1. The pure German people, especially during the Nazi era. 2. *South Africa.* The Afrikaners. 3. *South Africa.* Colored employees of whites under **apartheid** (q.v.).

Volksbewegung *n., pl.* **Volksbewegungen** [Ger. **Volks** of people (2); **Bewegung** movement (1): movement of people.] Popular movement, agitation or stir. Spontaneous upsurge of national feeling.

volksgeist *n., pl.* **volksgeists** [Ger. **Volksgeist**: **Volk** people, race (2); **Geist** spirit (1): spirit of people.] The spirit of a people. The distinguishing characteristics of a particular nation or ethnic group.

volkslied *n., pl.* **volkslieds** [Ger. and Dutch **Volkslied**: **Volk** people, race (2); **Lied** song, poem (1): song of people.] 1. A folk-song, especially a German one. 2. *South Africa.* A national anthem.

Völkerwanderung *n., pl.* **Völkerwanderungen** [Ger. **Völker** peoples (2); **Wanderung** wandering, migration (1): wandering of the peoples.] Migration of peoples, especially that of the Teutons, Slavs, and Huns into Europe, beginning in the 2nd century A.D. and ending about the 11th century.

volo ignorari et nihilo reputari. [L. **volo** I wish, want (1); **ignorari** to be ignored, be paid no attention (2); **et** and (3); **nihilo** nothing (5); **reputari** to be reckoned (4): I wish to be ignored and to be reckoned (as) worth nothing.] I wish to be ignored and reckoned to be of no value.

volte-face *n.* [Fr. turning-round.] Reversal. About-face. Total change. *In a dramatic volte-face, Salihu changed from a staunch supporter of the National Popular Party to its most fiery opponent.*

voluit, sed non dixit. [L. **voluit** he wished, willed (1); **sed** but (2); **non** not (3); **dixit** he said (4): He wished, but did not say.] *Law.* He may have so wished, but he did not say so. Used with reference to wills.

voluntas defuncti *n.* [L. **voluntas** will, desire (1); **defuncti** of the dead, deceased (2): desire of the deceased.] *Law.* The will of the deceased.

voluntas donatoris in charta doni sui manifeste expressa observetur. [L. **voluntas** will, desire (1); **donatoris** of donor (2); **in** in, on (5); **charta** paper, deed (6); **doni** (of) gift (8); **sui** of one's own, his/her own (7); **manifeste** clearly, manifestly (3); **expressa** expressed, represented (4); **observetur** should be observed (9): The will of the donor clearly expressed in his/her deed of gift should be observed.] *Law.* The intent of the giver, clearly stated in the deed of gift, should be followed.

voluntas est justa sententia de eo quod quis post mortem suam fieri velit. [L. **voluntas** will, desire (1); **est** is (2); **justa** just, true, reasonable (3); **sententia** decision, opinion (4); **de** of, from, about, for (5); **eo** that (6); **quod** which (7); **quis** any one, some one (8); **post** after (11); **mortem** death (13); **suam** one's/his/her own (12); **fieri** to be done (10); **velit** wishes, wants (9): A will is a true decision about that which someone wishes to be done after his/her own death.] *Law.* A will is a true decision on what a person wants to be done after his/her death.

voluntas et propositum distinguunt maleficia. [L. **voluntas** will, desire (1); **et** and (2); **propositum** aim, purpose (3); **distinguunt** distinguish (4); **maleficia** crimes (5): The will and the aim distinguish crimes.] *Law.* Intention and purpose distinguish crimes. See **actus non facit** etc.

voluntas in delictis, non exitus spectatur. [L. **voluntas** will, desire (3); **in** in, on (1); **delictis** crimes (2); **non** not (4); **exitus** result, end (5); **spectatur** is looked at (6): In crimes the will, not the result, is looked at.] *Law.* In criminal cases, what is considered is the intention, not the result. See **actus non facit** etc.

voluntas reputatur pro facto. [L. **voluntas** will, desire (1); **reputatur** is reckoned, computed (2); **pro** as, for (3); **facto** deed, act, fact (4): The intention is reckoned as the deed.] *Law.* Desire or intention is considered to be the same as the act. See **actus non facit** etc.

voluntas testatoris est ambulatoria usque ad extremum vitae exitum. [L. **voluntas** will, desire (1); **testatoris** of testator (2); **est** is (3); **ambulatoria** ambulatory, alterable (4); **usque** as far as, all the way to (5); **ad** to, at, for, according to (6); **extremum** last, utmost (7); **vitae** of life (9); **exitum** end, termination (8): The will of a testator is alterable as far as to the last end of life.] *Law.* The will of a testator is changeable right up to the final moment of life. See **legatum morte** etc.

voluntas testatoris habet interpretationem latam et benignam. [L. **voluntas** will, desire (1); **testatoris** of testator (2); **habet** has, holds, regards (3); **interpretationem** interpretation (7); **latam** broad (4); **et** and (5); **benignam** liberal, favorable (6): The will of the testator has a broad and liberal interpretation.] *Law.* The will of a testator is interpreted broadly and liberally.

voluntas ultima testatoris est perimplenda secundum veram intentionem suam. See **testatoris ultima voluntas est perimplenda secundum veram intentionem suam.**

vortex *n., pl.* **vortices** or **vortexes** [L. whirl, eddy, whirlpool, whirlwind.] 1. Whirlwind. Tornado. A cyclone's eye. 2. Whirlpool. A powerful, destructive water current which moves very rapidly in a circular manner, sucking down anything that comes within. 3. Anything which resembles a whirlpool or whirlwind. *The secrecy which surrounded the decision naturally aroused a vortex of conjectures and speculations.* 4. A stormy, tempestuous, or turbulent center. *The city, being the capital of the country, became the vortex of every national characteristic, particularly evil influences.* 5. A predicament, force, pursuit, or situation which inexorably draws one. *The religion had such magnetism and popular appeal that within a short time it had sucked large numbers of people into its vortex.* Cf. **maelstrom.**

vox audita perit. [L. **vox** voice, utterance, spoken word (1); **audita** having been heard (2); **perit** perishes (3): The spoken word, having been heard, perishes.] The spoken word disappears as soon as it is heard. Cf. **vox emissa volat** etc.

vox emissa volat, littera scripta manet. [L. **vox** voice, utterance, spoken word (1); **emissa** having been uttered (2); **volat** flies (3); **littera** letter (4); **scripta** having been written (5); **manet** remains (6): The spoken word having been uttered flies, the letter having been written remains.] The spoken word disappears, but the written word remains. Cf. **vox audita perit.**

vox et praeterea nihil [L. **vox** voice (1); **et** and (2); **praeterea** further, besides, hereafter (4); **nihil** nothing (3): voice and nothing further.] Voice and nothing more. Sound but no sense. *He delivered a long speech, but it was clearly vox et praeterea nihil.*

vox nihili *n., pl.* **voces nihili** [L. **vox** voice (1); **nihili** of nothing (2): voice of nothing.] A meaningless word or phrase, especially the result of a scribal or printing error. *The numerical sequence in the margin of the page was apparently no more than a vox nihili.*

vox populi *abbr.* **vox pop.** *n., pl.* **vox populis** [L. **vox** voice (1); **populi** of people (2): the voice of the people.] Popular view or sentiment. a) *Conceivably, Carter could try to persuade electors to switch their allegiances to comply with the vox populi* (*Newsweek Int.*, Nov. 3, 1980:33). b) *The fall of the regime is principally attributable to its stubborn refusal to respect vox populi.*

vox populi vox Dei. [L. **vox** voice (1); **populi** of people (2); **vox** voice (3); **Dei** of God (4): voice of the people, voice of God.] The voice of the people is the voice of God. A saying quoted by Alcuin (c.735–804).

voyage à Cythère *n., pl.* **voyages à Cythere** [Fr. **voyage** journey, voyage, trip (1); **à** to, toward, in, by, with, until (2); **Cythère** Cythera (3): a voyage/trip to Cythera.] A voyage to the island of Aphrodite, goddess of love. A trip to the island of love. A quest for, or pursuit of, amorous pleasure. *Mike's voyage à Cythère ended in ignominy when he was chased away by the girl's boyfriend.*

voyageur *n.* [Fr. traveler.] A worker, boatman or guide hired to transport materials in the Canadian and U.S. Northwest.

voyant or *fem.* **voyante** *n., pl.* **voyants** or *fem.* **voyantes** [Fr. person who can see.] A seer. A Prophet or prophetess. A **clairvoyant** (q.v.). *Arthur Rimbaud's theory of poetry demanded that the poet dismantle his/her senses to become a voyant.*

voyeur *n., pl.* **voyeurs** [Fr. a looker.] 1. A person who derives sexual pleasure from observing the sexual acts of others. A peeping Tom. *The voyeur steals the privacy of another, and part of the pleasure to be found in Hopper is the thrill of the crime* (*Newsweek Int.*, March 2, 1981: 43). 2. A person who pries inordinately, usually searching for scandalous events, acts, or sights. *The sordid domestic fight between Mr. and Mrs. Vandyke attracted the attention of several voyeurs, who came to the residence in the guise of sympathetic neighbors.*

vraisemblance *n.* [Fr. from **vrai** true (1); **semblance** likeness, similarity (2): true likeness.] 1. *Theater.* The principle of verisimilitude, i.e., that theatrical representations should be true to life. 2. A realistic portrait or description of a person or thing.

vs. *abbr.* for **versus** (q.v.).

V.S. or **v.s.** *abbr.* for **vide supra** (q.v.).

vue d'ensemble *n., pl.* **vues d'ensemble** [Fr. **vue** view (1); **d'** of (2); **ensemble** whole, general effect (3): a view of the whole.] A comprehensive view or opinion which takes cognizance of everything that is relevant.

vulgoque veritas jam attributa vino est. [L. **vulgo** generally, commonly (5); **que** and (1); **veritas** truth (3); **jam** now (2); **attributa** attributed, assigned (6); **vino** to wine (7); **est** is (4): And now truth is commonly attributed to wine.] Truth is generally believed to come out of wine. A proverb quoted by Pliny the Elder (A.D. 23–79) in *Historia Naturalis* XIV,141. Cf. **in vino veritas**.

vulgus *n.* [L. the common people.] The populace, rabble or common people. See **canaille**.

v.v. *abbr.* for 1. **vice versa** (q.v.). 2. **viva voce** (q.v.).

v.v.v. *abbr.* for **veni, vidi, vici** (q.v.).

W

Waldsterben *n.* [Ger. **Wald** forest, woods (1); **sterben** to die, be destroyed (2): forest dying.] The destruction of forest and other plant life due to environmental pollution.

Walpurgisnacht *n.* [Ger. **Walpurgis** of St. Walpurga (2); **Nacht** night (1): night of St. Walpurga.] 1. Walpurgisnight. The night of April 30th (the night preceding May Day) when, according to German superstitious belief, witches go out to display their powers. Witches' sabbath. A particular midnight when witches and sorcerers supposedly meet to pay homage to the devil, to celebrate rites, and to take part in orgies. 2. A situation or event which looks like a nightmare or orgy. a) *The marriage, a product of love at first sight, soon became a never-ending Walpurgisnacht.* b) *The ceremony to mark the anniversary of the association was climaxed by a party which proved to be a Walpurgisnacht.*

Wanderjahr *n., pl.* **Wanderjahrs** [Ger. **wander** to wander (1); **Jahr** year (2): wander year.] A period of travel, especially for a young person or a journeyman worker.

Wanderlust *n.* [Ger. **wandern** wander (2); **Lust** desire (1): desire for wandering.] A strong desire for traveling, especially globe-trotting.

Wehmut *n.* [Ger. sadness, melancholy.] A sense of sadness, especially a yearning for the past.

Wein, Weib und Gesang [Ger. **Wein** wine (1); **Weib** woman (2); **und** and (3); **Gesang** song (4): wine, woman, and song.] An expression of a carefree attitude towards life in which the only things that matter are pleasures like drink, sex, and music. Cf. **Wer nicht liebt Wein** etc.

Weltanschauung *n., pl.* **Weltanschauungen** or **Weltanschauungs** [Ger. **Welt** world (1); **Anschauung** view, perception (2): world view.] 1. World view or outlook. A philosophical view respecting the purpose of, and the course of events in, the world. 2. Ideology. Philosophy of life. *The realization that Black elevation was anathema to white Weltanschauung notwithstanding, most blacks remained optimistic* (Tunde Adeleke, unpublished seminar paper, Unimaid, 1987).

Weltbürger *n., pl.* **Weltbürger** [Ger. **Welt** world (1); **Bürger** citizen (2): world citizen.] A cosmopolitan. A citizen of the world.

Weltliteratur *n.* [Ger. **Welt** world (1); **Literatur** literature (2): world literature.] The literature of the world. A literature shared by people around the world.

Weltpolitik *n.* [Ger. **Welt** world (1); **Politik** politics (2): world politics.] International or world politics. Discussion of, and decision on, international affairs.

Weltschmerz *n.* [Ger. **Welt** world (1); **Schmerz** pain (2): world pain.] Distress at, or disgust with, the condition of the world. Pessimism. Sentimental sadness. Cf. **mal du siècle** and **taedium vitae.**

Weltstadt *n., pl.* **Weltstadts** [Ger. **Welt** world (1); **Stadt** city (2): world city.] A city of international standing and significance in the area of commerce, politics, culture, etc. A **cosmopolis** (q.v.).

Wende *n.* [Ger. turning.] Turning-point. Turnabout. Change in direction. *Critics of the Administration have been harping upon the need for a Wende in its policies.*

Wendepunkt *n.* [Ger. **Wende** turning (1); **Punkt** point (2): turning-point.] A moment of decisive change, especially in the events of a **novelle** (q.v.).

Wer nicht liebt Wein, Weib und Gesang, Der bleibt ein Narr sein Leben lang. Martin Luther (1483–1546). [Ger. **Wer** who (2); **nicht** not (3); **liebt** loves, is in love with (4); **Wein** wine (5); **Weib** woman (6); **und** and (7); **Gesang** singing, song (8); **Der** that one (1); **bleibt** remains, stays (9); **ein** a, one (10); **Narr** foolish man, fool (11); **sein** his (12); **Leben** life (13); **lang** long (14): That one who does not love wine, woman, and singing remains a fool his life long.] He who does not love wine, woman, and music, remains a fool throughout his life.

wertfrei *adj.* [Ger. from **Wert** value, worth (1); **frei** free (2): value free.] Without moral bias. Free from value judgment.

Wertfreiheit *n.* [Ger. from **Wert** value, worth (1); **Freiheit** freedom (2): value freedom.] Freedom from moral bias or value judgment.

Westpolitik *n.* [Ger. **west** west (1); **Politik** politics, policy (2): west policy.] The policy of eastern European countries to establish political and economic ties with the countries of western Europe after the fall of Communism.

Wirtschaftswunder *n.* [Ger. **Wirtschaft** economy (2); **Wunder** wonder (1): wonder of the economy.] Economic miracle, specifically West Germany's amazing economic recovery after the Second World War, i.e., the 1950s and 1960s. a) *The firm prospered through the first and second World Wars, and at first shared in the spectacular success of West Germany's Wirtschaftswunder* (*Time Int.* 1979). b) *... the program's moderator pointed out that the days of West Germany's Wirtschaftswunder ... were clearly over* (*Newsweek Int.* Dec. 6, 1982:14).

Wissenschaft *n.* [Ger. knowledge, science, scholarship.] The careful and meticulous use of the scientific method in the pursuit of knowledge. Academic scholarship. See **Geisteswissenschaften.**

Wunderkind *n., pl.* **Wunderkinder** or **Wunderkinds** [Ger. **Wunder** wonder (1); **Kind** child (2): wonder child, infant prodigy.] 1. An infant or child prodigy. 2. A person who shows exceptional ability in a very difficult profession or field at a very early age. *He was playing a role scripted largely by budget director David Stockman, the new wunderkind of Washington* (*Newsweek Int.* Feb. 16, 1981:1).

X

Xanthippe *n., pl.* **Xanthippes** [Gk. **Xanthippē**.] 1. Wife of Socrates, notorious for her bad temper. 2. A woman of bad temper. See **virago**.

xenomania *n.* [Neo-Gk. from Gk. **xeno(s)** foreign, alien (2); **mania** passion, rage (1): passion or rage for foreign things.] Excessive fondness for or attachment to foreign fashions, manners, institutions, customs, etc. *There is widespread xenomania in the country, especially among young men and women.* See **xenophilia**. Cf. **xenophobia**.

xenophilia *n.* [Neo-Gk. from Gk. **xeno(s)** foreign, alien (2); **philia** love, fondness, affectionate regard (1): fondness for foreign things.] Excessive interest in, fondness for, or attraction to foreign things. *Xenophilia breaks out as Teng marches his people toward modernization* (*Time Int.*1978). See **xenomania**. Cf. **xenophobia**.

xenophobia *n.* [Neo-Gk. from Gk. **xeno(s)** foreign, alien (2); **phob(os)** fear (1): fear of foreign things.] Irrational or abnormal fear or hatred of foreigners as well as of foreign fashions, institutions, culture, etc. *France has a long tradition of xenophobia, but sometimes even Frenchmen think it goes a little too far.* (*Newsweek Int.*, Nov. 8, 1982:26). Cf. **xenomania** and **xenophilia**.

Y

yahrzeit *n., pl.* **yahrzeits** [Yid. from German **Jahr** year (1); **Zeit** time (2): year time.] *Judaism.* The anniversary of a person's death, marking the end of the official period of mourning.

yakuza *n., pl.* **yakuza** [Japan. mobster, gangster, racketeer.] 1. The network of Japanese crime organizations. The Japanese mafia. 2. A member of such an organization. A criminal. Cf. **dacoit, mafia,** and **petit truand.**

yang *n.* [Chin. **yáng** sun, light, masculinity.] The cosmic principle of active masculinity in Chinese philosophy. Cf. **yin.**

yantra *n., pl.* **yantras** [Skt. a supporter, fastener.] *Hinduism, Buddhism, and Jainism.* A geometric design used in the **tantra** (q.v.) for meditative purposes.

yarmulke or **yarmelke** *n.* [Yid.] A Jewish prayer cap.

yashmak or **yashmac** *n., pl.* **yashmaks** or **yashmacs** [Turk.] A veil covering the face of Muslim woman in public.

yeshiva or **yeshivah** *n., pl.* **yeshivas** or **yeshivot(h)** [Heb. **yeshībāh**] *Judaism.* A religious school, especially for the study of sacred texts.

yé-yé *adj.* [Fr. from Eng. yeah-yeah.] 1. Describing the popular youth culture of the 1960s. 2. Enthusiastic about this culture. —*n.* 1. A person who is enthusiastic about or connected with this culture. 2. The music of this culture.

yin *n.* [Chin. **yin** moon, darkness, femininity.] The cosmic principle of passive femininity in Chinese philosophy. Cf. **yang.**

yoga *n.* [Skt. **yogah** union, joining.] 1. *Hinduism.* A form of religious discipline in which physical and mental control is used to attain spiritual understanding and peace. 2. Exercises used to achieve such physical and mental control.

yogi *n., pl.* **yogis** [Skt. **yogah** union, joining.] A practioner of **yoga** (q.v.).

Yom Kippur *n.* [Heb. **yom** day (1); **kippur** atonement, propitiation (2): day of atonement.] *Judaism.* The Day of Atonement, a day of fasting and prayer for propitiation of the sins of humankind.

yored *n., pl.* **yordim** [Heb. one who descends.] A person who emigrates from Israel.

Z

zaibatsu *n., pl.* zaibatsu [Japan. from zai wealth (2); batsu powerful individual or family (1): powerful family wealth.] 1. A commercial enterprise controlled by a single powerful family. 2. A conglomerate or cartel (q.v.).

zakat *n.*[Arab. zakā(t) almsgiving.] *Islam.* An annual payment or tax used for the purposes of religious purposes and almsgiving.

zamindar or zemindar *n.* [Hindi zamīndār.] A person charged with collecting land taxes in India.

Zeitgeist *n.* [Ger. Zeit time (1); Geist spirit (2): time spirit, spirit of the age, time, or era.] Moral and intellectual atmosphere, cultural trend, taste, etc. of an age, time, or era. a) *The reforms introduced by the Administration failed dismally mainly because the Zeitgeist of the nation was not taken into consideration.* b) *A single generation, by numbers alone, will have changed the nation's Zeitgeist from young to old* (*Newsweek Int.* March 30, 1981:33).

Zen *n.* [Japan. from Chin. chan meditation.] *Buddhism.* A branch of Buddhism which emphasizes meditation over religious devotion as the means to personal enlightenment.

zenana *n., pl.* zenanas [Hindi zenāna women's quarters.] In India and Persia the section of a house where the women live in seclusion. A harem (q.v.). See seraglio.

zeugma *n., pl.* zeugmata or zeugmas [Gk. yoke, band, bond, joining.] *Rhetoric.* A figure of speech in which a noun, adjective, or verb governs a number of words in such a way that its meaning is strictly applicable to only one of the words, or it applies to each of them in a different sense; e.g., "The boys, dogs, and cats entered the house, shouting." Cf. syllepsis.

ziarat or zearat *n., pl.* ziarats or zearats [Urdu from Pers. ziyārat visit, pilgrimage.] *Islam. A* journey or pilgrimage to a holy shrine.

zither or zithern *n.* [Ger. Zither from L. cithara from Gk. kithara a stringed musical instrument.] A musical instrument with 30–40 strings stretched over a flat sound box. Usually played horizontally either with the fingertips or with a pick. Cf. cithara.

zizith *pl. n.* [Heb. sisīth.] *Judaism.* The religiously-symbolic, knotted fringe on a garment, especially the tallith (q.v.) or prayer shawl.

Zoilus *n., pl.* Zoili or Zoiluses [L. from Gk. Zoilos.] 1. A Greek rhetorician and philosopher of the 4th century B.C., who was notorious for his bitter criticisms of the philosopher Plato, the rhetorician Isocrates, and, above all, the epic poet Homer. 2. An extremely bitter and carping critic. A person who takes delight in unwarranted fault-finding. See momus.

Zollverein *n., pl.* Zollvereins [Ger. Zoll customs, duty (1); Verein union (2): customs union.] A tariff union. An arrangement or system whereby several or many states observe free trade among themselves, while imposing a uniform tariff on states which do not belong to the union.

zut alors! *interj.* [Fr. zut darn, damn (2); alors then, in that case, therefore (1): in that case, darn.] Darn!